ASHE READER SERIES

FOUNDATIONS OF AMERICAN HIGHER EDUCATION

SECOND EDITION

EDITED BY JAMES L. BESS AND DAVID S. WEBSTER

BRUCE ANTHONY JONES, SERIES EDITOR

Pearson
Custom
Publishing

Cover photo: Washington Square Park, New York University Commencement, by Douglas Levere.

Printed in the United States of America

10 9 8 7

Please visit our website at www.sscp.com

ISBN 0–536–01853–7

BA 98601

PEARSON CUSTOM PUBLISHING
75 Arlington Street, Boston, MA 02116
A Pearson Education Company

Contents

Part II: The Participants

Part III: The Conduct of Education and Research

PART IV: THE MANAGEMENT OF THE COLLEGE OR UNIVERSITY

Introduction

JAMES L. BESS

Colleges and universities have played a critical role in the historical transition of American society from an agrarian to industrial to post-industrial social system. They have extended opportunities for higher education to the majority of American youth, and now to many adults, and, by virtue of the production of new knowledge, have fueled technological revolutions in many fields. Higher education aimed at students is defined and put into practice in various ways by different groups and individuals. Depending on the perspective, it can be an essential means of upward job and social mobility, a socializing agency for middle class cultural conditioning, a training ground for work, a locus for learning how to think and express oneself, or a place for personal discovery and growth uninhibited by daily requirements for making a living or caring for a family. In addition to its roles in relation to students, higher education as a center for research has become one source, though certainly not the only source, of new theoretical and often practical knowledge necessary for scientific and economic progress and well-being, as well as a stimulus for new ways of thinking in the arts and humanities.

These multiple purposes have been carried out in an extremely diverse higher education institutional environment, with many colleges and universities opting for different goals for teaching and research and different methods to achieve them. For many students using this book, exposure to the complicated ways and means of higher education will be fresh and new, perhaps astonishing. For others, especially those who have had some practical experience working in institutions of higher education, some of the ideas and controversies will seem familiar. It is hoped that for both groups, this "starter set" of readings covering a wide variety of important topics in the field will provide a useful framework for beginning their own "conceptual organization," of higher education—one that will serve them well as a foundation for their careers in higher education.

As you will quickly see, the field of the career you are pursuing is extremely complex, with many subject matters subsumed under the name of "higher education." The readings chosen here are intentionally introductory and are often descriptive, rather than issue oriented. You may not initially be able to make a great deal of sense of this collection by virtue of reading *just* these selections, but they will give you a significant assist at mapping out the territory, recognizing the key

James L. Bess teaches in the School of Education at New York University. (jim.bess@nyu.edu)

ix

concepts, identifying some of the prominent experts who write about them, and noting some of the still unanswered questions. It remains for the rest of your studies and career to plunge deeper into the meanings and nuances that are here introduced.

The subjects chosen to be included in this reader represent fairly traditional categories, and the selections within them largely "foundational." The Associate Editors worked diligently to find readings that would give you a thorough grounding in what has been and may continue to be viewed as important in the field. In their essays and supplementary bibliographies, however, they have also suggested some gaps in the scope of the selected readings that were necessitated by practical constraints of space. In addition, they sketch out some areas that are in need of further research. Your instructors in the class in which this book is used and your instructors in other, more specialized, classes will elaborate further on the themes introduced herein, as you yourself will, in your own, independent excursions into the literature.

Higher Education Defined

Education has existed since the emergence of higher order animals, as older generations informally and formally inquired into their worlds and passed on their acquired wisdom and skills. Today, the subfield of "higher" education commonly refers to education that is carried out with students who have completed their secondary school studies. Until the late nineteenth century, there were relatively few of these students, representing a quite small percentage of a teenage cohort of the population. There was a great deal of consensus on the subject matters they should be taught, on the methods to be used to teach them, on the character and required expertise of those who should do the teaching, and, finally, on where the teaching should take place. All of these formerly widely accepted models have, in the intervening years, been questioned. Today, more than 40% of high school students in this country at least begin college—though many do not finish—and adults, rather than 18–24 year olds, now constitute the majority of those studying at colleges and universities. But an even more profound change is taking place in the learning settings, as education outside of the formal domain of the college classroom has revolutionized our conception, financial support, and uses of knowledge acquired. With the advent of electronic communication, more and more people are learning college-level subject matters through various forms of computer and world-wide-web assisted methods, both in formal, non-credit courses, and more informally through self-tutorials. While the advent of printed matter centuries ago permitted students the opportunity to learn by themselves from knowledge frozen in a portable medium, electronic media now bring directly to the home or office an enormous variety of contemporary subject matters for vocational, personal growth, and entertainment purposes. In addition, because of these changes in learning settings, teaching modes are shifting. Learning in groups of students with common characteristics has begun be augmented or even replaced by learning in the home or laboratory, where peer emotional support and practical assistance is less available (or at least qualitatively different). Many formal and informal organizations and persons in the society at large, moreover, constitute competing, even unintentionally contradictory, educational forces having important impacts on students studying in colleges and universities.

As you will see, a number of themes permeate virtually all of the readings in this volume. The literature of higher education (and, one would presume, the field itself) is concerned at least with the following ten basic questions about higher education:

1. What is its purpose—e.g., what societal and individual benefits are intended?
2. How can those benefits best be achieved—what combination of activities must be undertaken—e.g., teaching, research, and what else?
3. In what setting(s) should those activities take place—e.g., on a campus or/and elsewhere?
4. Which persons should be educated and for what reasons?
5. What should be investigated and what should be taught?
6. Who possesses the expertise to carry out the activities?

7. What methods should be used?
8. How should the enterprise be organized and administered?
9. Who should pay for it—e.g., the society or/and the individual—and over what time period?
10. How should the efforts at every level be judged?

The issues raised in the readings in this volume will be seen to embrace many or even all of these questions. So, for example, issues of equality of access, general and specialized curricular requirements, the increasing use of adjunct faculty, the possible modification or even abolition of the tenure system, declining leadership quality, and escalating costs all arise out of debates over the answers to these more basic questions.

That there are differences of opinion about the answers is due to the diversity of values that are held by different constituencies. Indeed, deeply held values in different cultures suggest answers that are dramatically different. A society that values inherited hierarchical positions in government and industry, for example, will have answers to the ten questions that are quite different from those found in more egalitarian, achievement oriented societies. In addition, even within cultures, opinions differ because of ambiguities and uncertainties about the facts themselves—for example, what works, what doesn't; who is qualified to learn and to teach; and what does and should it really cost to engage in the required activities. Controversies abound in education. Differences of opinion can also be traced to variations in economic well-being of those with vested interests and to the illegitimate use of power by some who desire to reap or retain excessive benefits from the system at the expense of other participants. And finally, conflicts arise over fundamental philosophical disagreements about the ways in which knowledge is acquired, held, and used, and about the values that are associated with different principles or beliefs.

Overview of the Contents

The book is divided into four parts. The first will introduce you to the scope of higher education in American society and the world. You will read about the historical, philosophical, and sociological foundations of the present system and about the organization of the current array of institutions of higher education. Here are some questions that are likely to arise in reading these selections:

> How has education been conceived historically, and how is it understood today? How can we trace the mainstream origins of higher education in American society? How did higher education arrive at its present national, state and local structure and at the goals and methods that now predominate? What forces in society prevailed at different points in history and operate today to direct and control the shape, purposes, trends, and future of higher education?
>
> What are the qualitative and quantitative natures of the diversity of institutions (universities, four-year colleges, community colleges, corporations, religious organizations, communications media)? What are the differences in goals, students, faculty, impacts? What is the mix of controlling forces? Financial support? Competition? Stratification?
>
> What are higher education's manifest and latent functions? Do they include psychosocial transformation of students? Cognitive development? What models of the "educated" person are assumed. Where does education take place—formally and informally; intentionally, and unintentionally?

Part II is concerned with a consideration of the participants in the system. First, you will become familiar with what being a college student means to the diverse array of students in higher education—from point of entrance to college (and before) to its effects afterwards. Second, you will learn about faculty, the group that delivers much of the intellectual content of the college curriculum and who conduct research that finds its way back to the curriculum and out to the public at large, especially in the economic sector. Among the questions that will arise in this section are:

> How can we better understand the dynamics of changes in students, both those that are biological and psychological, and those that are directly affected by the college environment—e.g., the curriculum or residential environment or out-of-class interactions? Which kinds of students thrive best in

which kinds of environments, and how should our policies of access, aid, and counseling be developed to improve our services to students? How do older adults compare with traditional age students, and what implications do these differences have on educational policy?

What do faculty do? How do they spend their time? What is "tenure," and what is its impact on faculty, and on the institutions in which they work? In the light of the changing society and the changing demographics of students and faculty, what kinds of people should be selected, promoted, and given tenure in colleges and universities? How can the increasingly important roles of adjunct faculty be understood? How can we make sense of the patterns of faculty careers and the concomitant stresses and strains on them and their institutions? What is the impact on faculty of joint loyalties to their institution's goals and their professional associations?

The third section of the book contains readings that look in some detail at the modes by which the activities of the faculty and student affairs staff are carried out—the undergraduate curriculum and its out-of-class counterpart, the "extra-curriculum," both of which constitute the frameworks for the teaching and learning processes. The nature of the research processes in which faculty engage is also included in this section, as are two other chapters describing unique settings that are different from the traditional four-year undergraduate one—graduate, professional, and adult education and community college and proprietary education. Here are some questions you are likely to face as you read these selections.

What are alternative conceptualizations of a "curriculum." What influences the curriculum? How do curricular purposes and learners' goals interact? What should be taught? What is the purpose of "general education," and how is it organized? What is the purpose of the "major," and does it reinforce or detract from general education? "How do students learn? How is the curriculum geared to learning theory and student development theory? How can and do faculty teach "effectively.? How is a curriculum for adults different from the one for 18–22 year olds?

What part does out-of-class activity play in facilitating and/or inhibiting the achievement of the goals of the college or university? Are there different goals for non-classroom activities than for the curriculum? What is the impact of the extracurriculum on different kinds of students—e.g., residential, commuter, or undergraduate-graduate students? How much and which kind of "involvement" in extracurricular activities is useful and how much interrupts the academic enterprise of students?

How do different kinds of students learn? Does the choice of teaching styles make much of a difference on the achievement of students? How about the gender of the faculty member? How can conceptions of teaching and conceptions of learning be matched in terms of aims, criteria for success, and pedagogy?

Who does research in colleges? In universities? What kinds? How is it organized and financed? Who owns and benefits from the results? How is research quality controlled? Are there formal rules and informal norms that guide faculty research behavior? Does scholarship include research for teaching purposes? Do all faculty do research and publish? How often? Should they?

Who are the students at community colleges and proprietary schools and how different are they from traditional four-year college students? Who pays for the education of these students? How much does the "market" for students play a part in the ways in which these institutions are governed? Will proprietary schools increasingly seek degree-granting authority and regional accreditation? Do proprietary schools and community colleges compete for the same students?

How viable are theories of adult student learning? What does it mean to be a "professional?" How do graduate students become socialized to the norms and values of the profession they will enter? Is the organization of graduate education linked too closely to research interests of faculty?

Part IV of the book takes up the support system that allows the faculty and student affairs personnel to conduct their work and considers the nature of the system components outside of the institutions that affect internal policy. In this section, you will look first at the college and university as an aggregation of people, positions, and tasks that are coordinated in many ways like organizations in the corporate sector, but in many other ways uniquely as higher education institutions. Three important spheres of administration and management follow in the next chapter: financing higher education, intercollegiate athletics, and law. Who sets the criteria for judging the quality of what is going on in institutions and how that assessment is carried out comprises the succeeding chapter. The important external influences on the system are next taken up in discussions of federal, state and community relations. And, finally, some issues of policy analysis and formation are introduced. Here are some questions you will encounter in this section:

What are the responsibilities of the various officers of administration in colleges and universities? What is the legal responsibility of a board of trustees? How closely are and should faculty responsibilities be specified? What are the different kinds of authority in use in institutions of higher education, and why do their strengths differ in different kinds of institutions? Are some colleges more "bureaucratic" than others? More "collegial?" More "political?" How does the typical decentralization of decision making affect the procedures for institutional governance? What is the structure and function of an "academic senate?" How is leadership exercised and by whom? How does competition among institutions of higher learning affect the ways that they are organized, administered, and led?

In this litigious society, how does the practice and profession of the law affect the ways that colleges and universities determine their policies? Are incomes of athletic enterprises too influential in policy making? Are alleged surpluses in athletic budgets real? How even-handed is the allocation of funds, especially across gender? If some universities have essentially "professional" student athletes, should the institutions become legally professional? How can we rationally evaluate the quality of colleges and universities? Does the "sticker price" (e.g., tuition rates) mislead? Does student tuition really go toward the education of students or is it redirected to other institutional purposes?

Who sets the standards for evaluating the performance of institutions of higher education? What role should federal and state governments and regional and disciplinary accreditors play in this process? Can assessment be more than a pro forma exercise to which faculty pay little attention because it is conducted to meet the requirements of outside agencies? Should institutions—and especially their students—be evaluated using standardized testing instruments produced externally? Or are locally developed measures more appropriate and effective. Can assessment provide evidence to demonstrate which methods of instruction work best under what circumstances to improve student learning? Will assessment findings be used to provide direction for continuous improvement of institutional programs and services, thus enabling higher education to address its growing competition? And, finally, can we ensure that the benefits of assessment justify its costs?

What are the respective roles of the federal, state, and local governments in the development and execution of policy and performance in colleges and universities? How, if at all, should those roles differ for public versus private institutions? Within the different states, are there discernible patterns of coordination and governance? Where do external policies with respect to higher education originate, and who is involved in their development? How do special interest agencies, especially in Washington, affect policy determination? How do educational policies relate to the values of the American and international communities at large?

What are the tools or models that can be used to understand the nature of higher education as an ever-changing institution? What are the alternative ways in which policies can be written to have positive, innovative impacts on colleges and universities, rather than conservative, deviance-dampening effects? What are the ethical considerations that should be taken into account in the development of policies, particularly with regard to educational opportunity, access and diversity, and equitable cost distribution?

How to Read this Book

By this time, as graduate students you have pretty well figured out how best to access new material and to make it part of your repertory of values and expertise, ready to be used when needed. What is important to remember in encountering so much new material in this book, compacted into just a few readings about many different subjects, is that it may appear daunting. You may feel frustrated at not being able immediately to master it all. It may (or may not) be comforting to know that most of your faculty and teachers, including most of those contributing to this volume, often find themselves similarly baffled. Indeed, the life of the scholar is defined by the never-ending encounter with new material that appears initially as a "buzzing, blooming confusion," to use William James' terms. The difference between us and you is that we have some confidence based on experience that with hard work and continued study, the magic of the meanings emerges. The mastery of new more advanced material takes us as long as it will take you (if we are ambitious and seek truly to expand and deepen our knowledge and understanding), but the persistence pays off in wisdom and understanding.

We all hope that you will succeed in this worthwhile venture, but also that you will find joy in learning, even as you experience doubts in your capacity to make sense of it all. In short, it will come together at some point—at least partially—and you should cherish the journey.

One final thought. There is no "received wisdom" in these readings. As pragmatist philosopher, John Dewey, noted, truth is established in the validity of practice. If it doesn't work, it probably is not true. So, if you have doubts about what you read—and you should, if you read skeptically—do not abandon them too quickly. Challenge the authors with your own ideas and hold fast, though not stubbornly, to your opinions until they are shown to be not workable. Who knows: perhaps your ideas will some day be incorporated in subsequent editions of this book.

James L. Bess

PART I

THE SCOPE OF HIGHER EDUCATION IN AMERICAN SOCIETY

CHAPTER 1

HISTORICAL, PHILOSOPHICAL, AND SOCIOLOGICAL FOUNDATIONS OF HIGHER EDUCATION

ASSOCIATE EDITORS: REBECCA J. MENGHINI AND CLIFTON F. CONRAD

Martin Trow suggests that "American colleges and universities are indeed exceptional, made so by characteristics built deeply into our history and institutions that shape their capacity to respond to unanticipatable events," (p. 10). Certainly, higher education in America has drawn on the lessons of history to build a remarkable system which integrates myriad goals and missions in the effort to educate the people. Just which common goals and foundations lie behind the success of the American system, however, remains a formidable question with many answers proffered, few wholly agreed upon. In this chapter, three authors respectively apply historical, philosophical, and sociological lenses to American higher education. Martin Trow begins with a historical approach, providing a timeline of events critical to the evolution of higher education in the United States. He pays a mindful eye to the value of market forces and explores their influence in the past, present, and future. Howard Bowen philosophizes about some of the shared goals in the field and examines the value of categorizing them. Arthur Levine, concerned that diversity does not always make that list of goals, continues this inquiry with a sociological investigation into the changing demographics of American college and university students and the ramifications of history and change on institutional efforts to address multiculturalism.

In reading and thinking about the foundations presented in these three pieces, we must appreciate that they are not fully inclusive, but are simply representations of time, place, and perspective. Change is happening quickly in American higher education, and while many of our foundations remain, these pieces are offered not as concrete reminders of all that is important, but as beginnings, as bases, in our own timelines of research and inquiry.

Contending that the diversity of the system has allowed American higher education to realize the success and influence it has today, Martin Trow begins our discussion with a historical examination and celebration of the characteristics that make this system unique. He looks not only at how features such as the lay board, the college president, and democratic access to institutions have contributed to forward progress; he also explores how the failure of a proposal for a national university, a Supreme Court decision in 1819 affirming the inviolability of contracts between states and private institutions, and continued lack of central authority have shaped the system over time. Trow nests much of this discussion in a highly affirmative interpretation of the influence of market forces, suggesting that, like business, American higher education responds to the needs of society and the demands of its constituents in a way unparalleled by any other system.

In the next piece, Bowen explores these societal needs and demands and seeks to identify some common goals for higher education. Bringing to the forefront one of the great paradoxes of the field—whether we educate for skill or practicality, for livelihood, or to produce capable human

Rebecca Menghini is a graduate student at the University of Wisconsin-Madison. (rjmenghini@students.wisc.edu) Clifton Conrad teaches in the School of Education at the University of Wisconsin-Madison. (conrad@mail.soemadison.wisc.edu)

beings—Bowen shows how our intended outcomes encompass both sides of the debate and mirror life expectations. He posits that while American higher education leans toward individualism in its direction and is closely related to concepts of democracy, it does not forget about the needs of society. Understanding the limitations and failed consensus in listing desirable outcomes, Bowen closes his piece with a catalogue of goals "meant to be the ingredients of a well-ordered educational system" (p. 66). He is confident that if this catalogue is used carefully, it cannot only help educators set and adopt successful policy, but it can also serve as a guide to judge performance.

Levine, in the final selection of the chapter, engages us in conversation about how societal needs have changed historically in reference to diversity on campus. Showing that the goals of diversity have moved along a continuum from simple representation to pluralism, Levine contends that beyond the poor minority representation numbers and the simple inclusion of those of underrepresented races, genders, religions, and ethnicities, lies the greater problem of an unclear definition and understanding of diversity. In his words: "Academic culture has grown weak and fails to provide colleges and universities with a shared set of beliefs and values that go beyond differences that divide people" (p. 342). Exploring the forces that make diversity a top priority with campus participants, Levine also considers the invisible role of perceptions and how they influence the goals of integration, equity, and symbiosis in the educational arena. He is optimistic that in opening the environment to candid discourse, clearly defining the meaning of diversity, and engaging all the stakeholders on campus, we can "ultimately see diversity as an opportunity and not a problem" (p. 343).

Trow suggests in his closing that American higher education is the key institution in this society, offering many of our most important ideas, values, skills and energies (p. 22). Bowen asks us to consider not only these societal benefits, but to also assume responsibility for our efforts to levitate the individual. Both of these authors recognize that the dedication to both has helped the American system realize its strength and success, and while Levine doesn't seek to take anything from that offer of praise, he does raise for us a significant question of how we are making our system representative of true democracy and encouraging full participation of the diverse American populace. Taken together, these three pieces provide for us a glimpse at the standards and guiding forces of higher education in America, though in much the same way that Levine discusses the missing clarity in defining diversity, the foundations of American higher education remain difficult to pinpoint. Trow, Bowen and Levine do, however, provide for us as readers some touchstones and critical thinking points about which we can further our reading and continue our discourse to foster our understanding of the historical, philosophical and sociological forces that influence the field.

In suggesting these three selections as touchstones, we conclude by gently noting that they are representations more of traditional than of emerging voices. Indeed, the very concept of "foundations" is as much oxymoronic as it is anachronistic to a growing chorus of critics of the traditional representations of the "foundationalists." These critics problematize conventional historical, philosophical, and sociological lenses and, instead, variously advance critical theory, post-structuralist and postmodern, feminist, and multicultural lenses. To illustrate, we invite the reader to conjoin Roger Mourad's evocative new book, *Postmodern Philosophical Critique and the Pursuit of Knowledge in Higher Education*, which is a valuable introduction to one of a growing number of emerging voices.

Suggested Supplementary Readings

Bok, Derek, "What Is Wrong with Our Universities?" In *Harvard Magazine*, May/June, 1990, 77–92.

Brubacher, John S., and Rudy Willis, *Higher Education in Transition: A History of American Colleges and Universities 1636–1976*. 4th edition. New Brunswick, NJ: Transaction Publishers; New Brunswick, NJ., 1976.

Domonkos, Leslie S, "History of Higher Education," *International Encyclopedia of Higher Education*. San Francisco: Jossey-Bass Publishers, 1977, 2017–2040.

Gade, Marian L., "The United States," *International Higher Education, An Encyclopedia*. San Francisco: Jossey-Bass Publishers, 1991, 1081–1095.

Galis, Leon, "Merely Academic Diversity," *The Journal of Higher Education*, January/February, 1993, 64, 1, 93–101.

Geiger, Roger L., *To Advance Knowledge: The Growth of the American Research University, 1900–1940*. New York: Oxford University Press, 1986.

Horowitz, Helen Lefkowitz, *Campus Life: Undergraduate Cultures from the End of the 18th Century to the Present*. New York: Alfred A. Knopf, Inc, 1987.

Jacoby, Russell, *Dogmatic Wisdom: How the Culture Wars Divert Education and Distract America*. New York: Doubleday Press, 1994.

Levine, Lawrence, *The Opening of the American Mind: Canons, Culture, and History*. Boston: Beacon Press, 1996.

Mourad, Roger, *Postmodern Philosophical Critique and the Pursuit of Knowledge in Higher Education*. Westport, CT: Bergin & Garvey, 1997.

Oaldey, Francis, *Community of Learning: The American College and the Liberal Arts Tradition*. Oxford: Oxford University Press, 1992.

Rudolph, Frederick, *The American College and University, A History*. Athens, GA: University of Georgia Press, 1962.

Veysey, Laurence R., *The Emergence of the American University* . Chicago: University of Chicago Press, 1965.

Weinberg, Meyer, "Race in American Education," *A Chance to Learn: The History of Race and Education in the United States*. Cambridge: Cambridge University Press, 1977, 1–7.

American Higher Education—Past, Present and Future

MARTIN TROW

American higher education differs from all others in offering access to some part of the system to almost everyone who wants go to college or university, without their having to show evidence of academic talent or qualification. Private attitudes and public policy—so consensual across the political spectrum that they occasion hardly any comment—affirm that the more people who can be persuaded to enrol in a college or university, the better. The budgets of most American colleges and universities are directly keyed to their enrolments; the private institutions' through tuition payments, the public institutions' through a combination of tuition and funding formulas that link state support to enrolment levels. And this linkage is incentive indeed for almost every institution to seek to encourage applications and enrolments.

Enrolment levels are central to the financial health and social functions of American higher education. I begin this article by reviewing current enrolment trends and forecasts. I then explore the social and historical forces that gave rise to and sustain this unique system and conclude by examining the system's prospects for responding to change, given its peculiar and deeply rooted characteristics.

Enrolment Trends and Forecasts

American higher education is the largest and the most diverse system of postsecondary education in the world. In 1947, just after World War II, 2.3 million students were enrolled in some 1800 American colleges and universities, about half in public and half in private institutions (Andersen, 1968, p. 8009). Although both sectors have grown over the past forty years, the enormous growth of enrolments during the 1960s and 1970s was absorbed largely by public institutions, both four-year and two-year colleges. Thus, by 1986, enrolments in America's roughly 3300 colleges and universities were running at 12.4 million and holding fairly steady, with 77% enrolled in public institutions (see Table 1). No central law or authority governs or coordinates American higher education: the roughly 1800 private institutions are governed by lay boards; the 1500 public institutions (including some 900 public community colleges) are accountable to state or local authorities, but usually have a lay board of trustees as a buffer, preserving a high if variable measure of institutional autonomy.

Forecasts of future growth in higher education are almost uniformly wrong, not only in the United States but also abroad. The efforts of the British to predict the growth of their system after the *Robbins Report* in 1963 were consistently wrong, within a few years and by large amounts (Williams, 1983, p. 13). Clark Kerr has noted that the Carnegie Commission's early estimates of aggregate enrolments in the United States, of the numbers of new institutions, of faculty salaries, and of the proportion of the gross national product spent on higher education were all too high (Kerr, 1980, pp. 6–8). And more recently, nearly everyone concerned with American higher education was predicting a marked decline in enrolments

"American Higher Education—Past, Present and Future," by Martin Trow, reprinted from *Center for Studies in Higher Education*, Vol. 14 (1) 1989, University of California at Berkeley Wellness Letter.

TABLE 1
Higher Education Enrolment, 1947–1985

Year	Total Enrolment in thousands	Percent of Enrolments	
		Public Institutions	Private Institutions
1947	2,338	49 (1,152)*	51 (1,186)
1950	2,297	50	50
1955	2,679	56	44
1960	3,789	59	41
1965	5,921	67	33
1970	8,581	75	25
1975	11,185	79	21
1980	12,097	78	22
1985	12,247	77 (9,479)	23 (2,768)
1986	12,398	77 (9,600)	23 (2,797)

*Numbers in parentheses in thousands.
Sources compiled from: Andersen (1968), Ottinger (1984).
'Fact-file' (1985), 'Mostly Stable' (1987)

starting in 1979, a decline that was inevitable, given the decreased size of the college-age cohorts starting in that year. Indeed, the number of high school graduates did reach a peak of some 3 million in 1979 and did, in fact, decline to about 2.6 million in 1984, a drop of about 13%. The demographic projections (see Figure 1) point to a further decline in the number of high school graduates, down to a four-year trough of about 2.3 million from 1991 to 1994 (McConnell & Kaufman, 1984, p. 29). But the fall in college and university enrolments that was anticipated has simply not occurred; on the contrary, aggregate enrolments grew between 1979 and 1984 by about 6%, and "colleges and universities had close to 1.5 million more students, and $6 billion more revenues than predicted by the gloom and doomers" (Frances, 1984, p. 3).

Although the nation faces a further fall of about 10% in the numbers of high school graduates by 1991, it is unlikely that enrolments in higher education will suffer an equivalent fall. In fact, the Center for Education Statistics projects that college and university enrolments will remain fairly stable through 1991 ("Mostly stable," 1987). Among the reasons for not anticipating any large decline over the next decade are these:

First, there has been a steady growth since the early 1970s in enrolments of older students. During the decade 1972–82, the greatest percentage increase in enrolments was among

people 25 years old and older; those 35-years and older increased by 77%, and the enrolments of 25 to 34-year-old students increased by 70%, as compared with a growth of 35% in total enrolments during that period ("Statistics," 1984).

Second, increasing numbers of students are enrolled part-time. During the decade 1972–82, part-time enrolments increased by two-thirds, while full-time enrolments were growing by less than a fifth.

Third, the past decade has seen very large increases in the enrolments of women and minorities. The number of women in colleges and universities grew by 61% in that decade, and minority enrolments grew by 85%, as compared with 15% for men, and 30% for all white students.

The growing enrolments of older students, of working and part-time students, and of women and minorities are all trends that are not dominated by the changing size of the college-age population. For example, relatively small proportions of Mexican American (Chicano) students in California currently go on to higher education. But the number of Chicanos in California's population, and especially among its youth, is very large. In 1981–82, they were about a quarter of all public school students, and, by the year 2000, will begin to outnumber whites in the under-20 age group (Project PACE, 1984, p. 11). Even small changes in the propensity of Chicanos to grad-

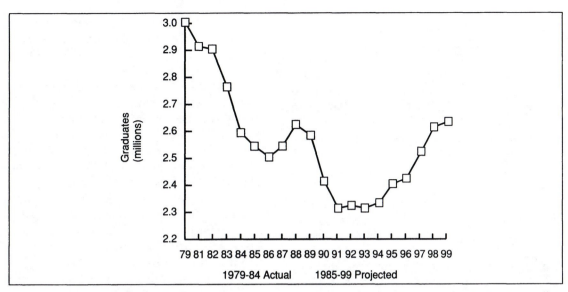

Source: revised from *High School Graduates: projections for the fifty states (1982–2000),* p. 6, by W. R. McConnell & N. Kaufman, 1984, Boulder, Colo., Western Interstate Commission for Higher Education, and unpublished, updated figures from the Western Interstate Commission for Higher Education, June 1985.

Figure 1: United States projections. Total high school graduates 1983–99.

uate from high school and go to college would have a major impact on enrolment levels in California colleges and universities. We would predict a long-term growth in the numbers of Chicanos going on to college, simply on the basis of trends among other ethnic groups throughout American history. Moreover, long-term changes in the occupational structure, such as the growth of the knowledge and information industries, increase the numbers of jobs for college-educated people. And many of our colleges and universities are more than eager to welcome back older people who want to upgrade their skills and equip themselves for jobs in the new industries.

Enrolment levels may yet fall over the next few years. Population movements, changes in the economy, and change in the size of age cohorts will, however, affect various states and regions and their institutions differently. Not only will there be an obvious disparity in the effects for, say, Ohio and Texas, there will also be equally great differences in the effects for each region's public community colleges, minor and elite private four-year colleges, and research universities. Some private colleges will certainly close over the next decade, and perhaps some public institutions will consolidate, though recent figures show an increase in the number of private four-year colleges in

recent years that one would not have predicted (Tsukada, 1986, p. 101, Figure 5.3). But the birth and death of colleges in large numbers throughout our history has been and continues to be a natural outcome of the market's great influence over our diverse and decentralized system of higher education. And although there may be closures, they will be mostly of weaker institutions and may well leave the system as a whole even stronger (Glenny, 1983).

But if it is not prediction in the sense of forecasting, the value of this exercise lies elsewhere. The effort to think about what higher education will look like in 20 or 40 years forces us to think more clearly about the historical forces that have shaped American higher education's unique qualities and character. Eric Ashby has said that we cannot know "what the environments of tomorrow's world will be like," but "we already know what its heredity will be like" (Ashby, 1967). And, as Clark Kerr has observed, heredity in higher education is a particularly strong force. The universities of today can draw a direct line back to Bologna, Paris, Oxford, and Cambridge. Even religious institutions—those vehicles for the eternal verities—have changed more, and political and economic institutions incomparably more, than universities.

The Social and Historical Background[1]

Certain features leap out when one compares American higher education with the systems in other advanced industrial societies. American colleges and universities are indeed exceptional, made so by characteristics built deeply into our history and institutions that shape their capacity to respond to unanticipatable events.

First, the market and market-related forces have a deep, pervasive influence. Second, and related to the first, the structural diversity among institutions is enormous, in their size, functions and curricula, sources of support, configurations of authority, and academic standards, a diversity their student bodies mirror in their age distributions, purposes and motivations, class, ethnic and racial origins, and much else.

Third, the internal differentiation in our comprehensive universities and many of our larger state colleges in academic standards and educational missions gives them great flexibility to respond to the markets for undergraduates, faculty, graduate students, and research support. This internal differentiation among academic departments and professional schools complements the structural differentiation between public and private, large and small, selective and open-access colleges and universities.

Fourth, a cluster of shared characteristics marks our curricula, teaching styles, and patterns of assessment: the unique role of general education as a component of nearly all American first degree courses; the considerable extent of student choice in the selection of courses; and the modular course earning *unit-credits*, an academic currency that makes a system of 3300 separate institutions.

Fifth, our mode of college and university governance is unparalleled. Lay boards and strong presidents, certainly strong by comparison with their counterparts elsewhere, command large administrative staffs located inside the institutions rather than in some central ministry or governmental agency.

The great, unique feature of American higher education is surely its diversity. It is this diversity—both resulting from and making possible the system's phenomenal growth—that has enabled our colleges and universities to appeal to so many, serve so many different functions, and insinuate themselves into so many parts of the national life. And it is through the preservation of diversity that our system will be best prepared to respond to changing demands and opportunities in the years ahead. To see why this is so, review briefly the historical roots of this diversity and the benefits we derive from it today.

America had established nine colleges by the time of the Revolution, when two—Oxford and Cambridge—were enough for the much larger and wealthier mother country. The United States entered the Civil War with about 250 colleges, of which over 180 still survive. Even more striking is the record of failure: Between the Revolution and the Civil War perhaps as many as 700 colleges were started and failed. By 1880, England was doing very well with four universities for a population of 23 million, whereas the state of Ohio, with a population of 3 million, already boasted 37 institutions of higher learning (Rudolph, 1962, pp. 47–48). By 1910, we had nearly a thousand colleges and universities with a third of a million students—at a time when the 16 universities of France enrolled altogether about 40,000 students, a number nearly equaled by the American faculty members at the time.

The extraordinary phenomena of high fertility and high mortality rates among institutions of higher learning are still with us. For example, between 1969 and 1975, some 800 new colleges (many of them community colleges) were created, and roughly 300 others were closed or consolidated, leaving a net gain of nearly 500. This is a phenomenon unique to the United States—one that resembles the pattern of success and failure of small businesses in modern capitalist economies. It is in sharp contrast with the slow, deliberately planned creation of institutions of higher and further education in most advanced industrial societies or their even slower and rarer termination. And this points to the very strong link between higher education in the United States and the mechanisms of the market. This link has been a major factor in the emergence and persistence of large numbers of diverse institutions.

Two important features of markets, as compared with other forms of social action, are (a) that their outcomes are not the result of planning or central purposive decision, and (b) that when producers are relatively numerous, their behaviors are marked by their competition for buyers, which strengthens the buyers' influence over the product's character and quality, indeed, over the producers' very character.

In higher education, we can see this when the buyers are students, and the producers, the colleges and universities, compete for their enrolment. We can see it also when the sellers are graduates competing for job openings. The two together translate opportunities in the job market into the size of academic departments and programs. The key is the considerable autonomy of American colleges and universities, which enables them to move resources between departments in response to changes in student enrolment and demand. Similarly, when research groups compete for scarce funds, funding agencies gain power over the character, direction, and quality of the research they buy. In the United States, apart from the quite unusual period of rapid growth between 1955 and 1975, the supply of places has on the whole outstripped demand; and buyers or potential buyers at both ends, students and the employers of graduates, have had a powerful influence on the behavior of the producers. This influence of buyer over seller is likely to be relatively constant in the decades ahead.

The Influence of Market Forces

We can see the emergence of strong market forces in the early history of American higher education, we can see them today in the very structure and workings of our institutions, and we can compare their strength here with the systems of other societies.

A multiplicity of forces and motives lay behind the establishment of colleges and universities throughout our history: religious motives; fears of relapse into barbarism at the frontier; the need for various kinds of professionals; state pride and local boosterism; philanthropy; idealism; educational reform; speculation in land, among others, and in all

combinations. But the number and diversity of institutions, competing with one another for students, resources, teachers, bringing market considerations and market mechanisms right into the heart of this ancient cultural institution—all also required the absence of any restraining central force or authority. The states could not be that restraining force; under the pressures of competition and emulation they have tended throughout our history to create institutions and programs in the numbers and to the standards of their neighbors. Crucially important has been the absence of a federal ministry of education with the power to charter new institutions, or of a single preeminent university that could influence them in other ways.

The closest we have come as a nation to establishing such a central force was the attempt, first by George Washington, and then by the next five Presidents, to found a University of the United States at the seat of government in Washington, D.C. In fact, Washington made provision for such a university in his will and mentioned it in his first and last messages to Congress. His strongest plea came in his last message to Congress, where he argued that a national university would promote national unity, a matter of deep concern at a time when the primary loyalties of many Americans were to their sovereign states, not the infant nation.

Washington saw also the possibility of creating one first-class university by concentrating money and other resources in it. As he noted in his last message to Congress: "Our Country, much to its honor, contains many Seminaries of learning highly respectable and useful; but the funds upon which they rest, are too narrow, to command the ablest Professors, in the different departments of liberal knowledge, for the Institution contemplated, though they would be excellent auxiliaries" (Hofstadter & Smith, 1961, p. 158). Here, indeed, Washington was right in his diagnosis. The many institutions that sprang up between the Revolution and the Civil War all competed for very scarce resources and all thus suffered to some degree from malnutrition. Malnutrition at the margin is still characteristic of a system of institutions influenced so heavily by market forces.

Defeat of the national university meant that American higher education would develop, to this day, without a single capstone institution. As it was, until after the Civil War, whatever the United States called its institutions of higher learning, it simply did not have a single genuine university—an institution of first-class standing that could bring its students as far or as deep into the various branches of learning as could the institutions of the old world.

A national university would have profoundly affected American higher education. As the preeminent university, it would have had an enormous influence, direct and indirect, on every other college in the country, and through them on the secondary schools as well. Its standards and educational philosophies would have been models for every institution that hoped to send some of its graduates to the university in Washington. It would, in fact, have established national academic standards for the bachelor's degree, for the undergraduate curriculum, for the qualifications for college teachers, even for entrance to college, and thus for the secondary schools. Eventually, it would have surely constrained the growth of graduate education and research universities in the United States.

Similarly, a national university of high standard would surely have inhibited the emergence of the hundreds of small, weak, half-starved state and denominational colleges that sprang up over the next 170 years. They simply could not have offered work to the standard that the University of the United States would have set. The situation would have been familiar to Europeans, for whom the maintenance of high and, so far as possible, common academic standards has been a valued principle, almost unchallenged until recently. In the United States, after the defeat of the University of the United States, no one has challenged the principle of high academic standards across the whole system because no one has proposed it—there have been no common standards, high or otherwise. Indeed, if Europe's slogan for higher education has been "nothing, if not the best." America's has been "something is better than nothing." And in that spirit, we have created a multitude of institutions of every sort, offering academic work of every description and at every level of seriousness and standard. And, by so doing, we have

offered Europeans nearly two centuries of innocent amusement at our expense.

Ironically, however, without any central model or governmental agency able to create one or more national systems, all of our 3300 institutions, public and private, modest and preeminent, religious and secular, are in some way part of a common system bound by membership in a series of markets for students, support, prestige, faculty.

Another event in the early history of the Republic that had powerful effects on the shape and character of American higher education was the 1819 Supreme Court decision in the Dartmouth College case. In 1816, the New Hampshire legislature had passed a bill giving the state government broad powers to "reform" Dartmouth. The rationale for proposed changes in its charter was the plausible argument that, as the college had been estab-lished (though as a private corporation) to benefit the people of New Hampshire, this could best be accomplished by giving the public, through the legislature, a voice in its operation. Chief Justice Marshall, ruling in favor of the college trustees, declared that state legislatures were forbidden, by the Constitution, to pass any law "impairing the obligation of contracts," and that the charter originally granted the college was a contract (Hofstadter & Smith, 1961, p 218). This landmark decision affirmed the principle of the sanctity of contracts between governments and private institutions. In so doing, it gave expression to the Federalist belief that the government should not interfere with private property, even for the purpose of benefiting the public welfare. John Marshall, the then-Chief Justice, had written earlier: "I consider the interference of the legislature in the management of our private affairs, whether those affairs are committed to a company or remain under individual direction as equally dangerous and unwise." He and his colleagues on the Court decided, in the Dartmouth College case, that a private college or university charter was a contract that a state could not retroactively abridge. That decision of 1819 had massive repercussions both for the growth of capitalist enterprises and for the future development of higher education in the United States.

The Dartmouth College decision sustained the older, more modest role of the state in educational affairs against those who looked to the government to take a greater role in the working of society and its institutions. Marshall's decision had the practical effect of safeguarding the founding and proliferation of privately controlled colleges. Thereafter, promoters of private colleges knew that once they had obtained a state charter they were secure in the future control of the institution. By this decision, state university development was slowed or weakened, though, paradoxically, it may be that by making it more difficulty to create them, state universities were ultimately strengthened.

The failure of the University of the United States and the success of Dartmouth College in its appeal to the Supreme Court were victories for local initiative and private entrepreneurship. The first set limits on the federal government's role in shaping the character of the whole of American higher education; the second set even sharper limits on the state's power over private colleges. Together, these two events constituted a kind of license for unrestrained individual and group initiative in the creation of colleges of all sizes, shapes and creeds. As a result, colleges' and universities' behavior came to resemble living organisms' behavior in an ecological system—competitive for resources, highly sensitive to the demands of environment, and inclined, over time, through the ruthless processes of natural selection, to be adaptive to those aspects of their environment that permitted their survival. Their environment also has included other colleges, and later universities. So we see in this frog pond a set of mechanisms that we usually associate with the behavior of small entrepreneurs in a market: the anxious concern for market demands and the readiness to adapt to its apparent preferences; the effort to secure a special place in that market through the marginal differentiation of the product; and a readiness to enter into symbiotic or parasitic relationships with other producers for a portion of that market.

We are employing a language that Europeans tend to find strange and often a bit distasteful when used in connection with institutions of higher learning. But distasteful or not, an American must insist on this as a central and distinguishing characteristic of American higher education—that it has developed as a network of institutions that, in many respects, resembles in its behavior the myriad of small capitalistic enterprises that were springing up everywhere, at the same time and in the same places, and often in response to the same forces.

We are, and have been from the beginning, an acquisitive society, confronted by a continent whose ownership had not been settled by sword and custom since medieval times. In America, as Louis Hartz has noted, the market preceded society, a central and powerful fact whose ramifications can be seen in all of our institutions and throughout our national life (Hartz, 1955). We are, to put it crudely, unembarrassed by the market. By contrast, Europeans and their governments, now, as in the past, dislike market mechanisms and processes in education and do everything they can to reduce their influence. And this difference arises out of our profoundly differing feelings about culture and abut cultural competence. Markets threaten the "cultural integrity" of cultural institutions by increasing the power of consumers as over against producers—that is, as over against the people who are presumably most competent to supply some given kind of cultural entity, whether it be a performance of music or higher studies in philosophy or physics. In colleges and universities, the consumers, ordinarily students or their parents, are by definition incompetent, or at least less competent than the teachers and academic administrators who together provide instruction. Europeans try very hard to reduce the influence of the incompetent mass on high cultural matters and to preserve a realm of elite determination of cultural form and content.

We in the United States, surely the most populist society in the world, accept a larger role for the influence of consumer preference on cultural forms—even in the provision of what and how subjects are taught in colleges and universities. Europeans try to reduce the influence of consumer preference in a number of ways. Most importantly, they try to insulate their financing of institutions of higher education from student fees. By contrast, in the United States, enrolment-driven budgets in all but a few institutions, both public and private, ensure that most institutions are extremely sensitive to student preferences.

Another example of the comparative hospitality of American institutions to market forces in higher education can be seen in the ways Congress has decided to provide major public funding for colleges and universities. After sharp debate in the early 1970s, this country chose to fund colleges and universities chiefly by providing grants and loans to students, rather than through direct support to the institutions themselves; the decision was to subsidize higher education through the consumers, not the producers substantially, without increasing the power of central government over the producers.

The Character and Structure of Our Institutions

We can look at broad patterns of organization and finance of higher education (for example, multiple versus single sources of support) and see the differences between market systems and those dominated by other principles of organization and political decision-making. But we can also see the influence of market mechanisms in the private life of higher education, in the very processes of teaching and learning. Our peculiar system of earned and transferable 'credits,' a kind of academic currency that we all take for granted in American institutions, is one example. The unit-credit system is not found in other countries, where degrees are earned by passing examinations or writing dissertations. But our credits, units that can be accumulated, banked, transferred, and, within limits, automatically accepted as legal academic tender toward an earned degree throughout the country, make possible the extraordinary mobility of our students between fields of study, and between institutions. Moreover, credits that can be accumulated and transferred also allow students to drop out, or 'stop out,' and return to college in ways that are increasingly familiar to us.

An inventory of the unique qualities of American higher education must include a reference to the multiplicity of subjects taught, a product of the extraordinary hospitality of our institutions to almost any subject that might have a claim to be useful or to be rooted in a body of skill and knowledge that can be studied and taught. But this range of studies, often the subject of somewhat derisive comment by Europeans, would not be possible if we had a central agency maintaining 'high standards' and scrutinizing new subjects for their appropriateness as judged by traditional criteria. The openness of our institutions to new subjects is linked to the absence of a central administrative body that certifies institutions and subjects, as well as to our consequent reliance on market forces to sustain our many weak and impoverished institutions.

Or we could point to the intimate links between our colleges and universities and local industry, governments and other institutions and private organizations of all kinds, relationships that are envied and emulated elsewhere but rarely matched in scope (Eurich, 1985).

This inventory leaves us with the question of how these unique characteristics are related, both in their origins and in their current functioning. Let us look, for example, at a cluster of phenomena embedded in American higher education: the lay board, the strong presidency, a weak professoriate, the internal administration, the absence of a central ministry of higher education. The origins of the external nonacademic board of trustees lie in the precedent set at Harvard. The founders of Harvard had intended to "carry on the English tradition of resident-faculty control" (Rudolph, 1962, p. 166). But Harvard had to be founded and not just developed. There simply was not a body of scholars to be brought together to teach and to govern themselves. A *president* could be found to take responsibility for the operation of the institution, and he might find some young men to help him with instruction as tutors. But Harvard had been established for more than 85 years before it had its first professor; Yale for more than 50. "For over a century and a half, American collegiate education relied chiefly on the college president and his young tutors." And for a very long time indeed, well into the 19th century, "The only secure and sustained professional office in American collegiate education was that of the college president himself. He alone had, in the community and before the governing boards, the full stature of a man of learning. To this situation can be traced the singular role and importance of the American college or university president" (Hofstadter & Metzger, 1955, p. 124).

The lay boards that arose to govern America's first college and the great majority of those that followed were created by groups of individuals, not by the state. These boards had to govern; there was no one else. They could appoint a president, and, as busy men themselves, they had to delegate to him the day-to-day running of the institution. He held his office, however, and everywhere in the US still does, wholly at the pleasure of this external board; the president has no security of tenure as president (though he may hold tenure as a professor in the institution). But for a very long time there was no body of learned men making academic life a career and, thus, no challenge to the president's authority, so long as he had the support of his board of trustees.

The near absolute authority of the college president in running an institution was lost over time, especially with the rise of the great research universities and the emergence of a genuine academic profession. In this century, especially in the stronger institutions, a great deal of authority over academic affairs has been delegated to the faculty. But the American college and university president is still more powerful than his counterpart in European institutions, who faces the power held jealously by the professoriate, or by the academic staff more broadly, and by government ministries, trade unions, or student organizations (Trow, 1985a).

The relatively great power and authority of the American college and university president also insured that, when some institutions became very large and needed a big bureaucratic staff to administer them, that staff would be an extension of the president's office, rather than responsible to a faculty body or to state authorities. By keeping the administrative staff within the university, the strong presidency has helped preserve the autonomy of the public university in the face of state authority.

I have mentioned how weak, indeed for a long time nonexistent, the academic profession in America was. When professors did begin to appear, they did not command the enormous prestige and status accorded to the European professor. They were neither part of a prestigious civil service, nor were they recruited from the highest social strata. Indeed, in a society that prized action and worldly success, they were rather looked down on as men who

had stepped aside from the real challenges of life. America, for the most part, has given its honors and respect chiefly to men of action rather than reflection; the very choice of an academic career for a long time suggested that a person was incapable of managing such important matters as the affairs of a university (Hofstadter, 1963, pp. 24–51; Rudolph, 1962, pp. 160–161). This tended to strengthen the hand of the president, who may have been a scholar, but almost certainly was also a man of affairs.

The relatively low status and weakness of the professoriate also meant that, as the academic profession grew, it was not dominated by a handful of prestigious professors. The academic ranks were established during the growth of the research universities after the Civil War, but with almost the whole teaching faculty holding the title of professor of some rank, and with remarkable independence for even young assistant professors. That is partly due to the egalitarian elements in American cultural life, which are still very strong, but partly also to the historic weakness of the senior professor—his lack of real power, social prestige, even scholarly distinction. Academic ambition directed itself not so much to rank—that could be assumed—but to national reputation and to the distinction of the institution or department in which one gained an appointment.

Indeed, many of the most important qualities of American higher education have arisen not from design but from the weakness of its component institutions. For example, as I have suggested, the relatively egalitarian character of American academic life and the independence and authority of its junior members are products not of plan or policy, but of the slow formation of the academic profession and the professoriate and its relative poverty, low status, lack of tenure or civil service rank. But that has meant that we have avoided the bitter struggles between the professors and the other ranks of the academic profession that have marked European systems since World War II. In America, the rank of professor was no great honour and held no great reward; it was, in fact, the rank that every young instructor or assistant professor (and not just the few most talented ones) could expect to achieve in the fullness of time. That ease of access has helped to keep its status relatively low both within the university and outside it—where the title 'professor' still has slightly pejorative or comic overtones.

The connections among a weak academic profession, strong presidents, lay boards, and the power of the market in American higher education lie in the more general lack of other forces that constrain the self-interested actions of individuals and institutions. Most commonly, those constraining forces in other countries are the state authorities allied with the academic professions and its organizations or guilds. In the United States, central state power was initially weak, and in relation to higher education remained weak, in part as a result of the failure of the University of the United States and the Dartmouth College decision which guaranteed an essential role to the private sector. In addition, the weakness of the professoriate greatly reduced its constraint on the market. On the other hand, strong presidents and their administrative staffs could act in pursuit of the self-interest of individual institutions, and lay boards could ensure that those institutions would continue to be responsive to the larger society, and to its markets for students and graduates, rather than to the state or professional guilds. And that certainly has been and will be a source of strength as these institutions face an uncertain future and a changing environment.

Trends in Higher Education Finance

I have been looking backward but now look at the present and near past for trends and developments that might point in the direction of larger changes in the future.

In 1985–86 expenditures of all kinds on American colleges and universities were estimated to be over $102 billion, an increase in current dollars of 32%, and in constant dollars of 17%, over 1981–82. This represents roughly 2.5% of the Gross National Product ('Higher education is,' 1986, p. 3). One important and distinctive characteristic of American higher education is the diversity of its sources of support. The diversity of funding sources has large consequences for the autonomy of American colleges and universities and for their traditions of service to other institutions, both pub-

lic and private, as well as for their finances. Taken in the aggregate, American colleges and universities get support from federal, state and local governments; from private sources such as churches, business firms, foundations, and individuals; from students, in the form of tuition and fees, living expenses in halls of residence, food services, health services, and the like; and from their own endowments, as well as from the sale of their services to others.

Government at all levels together provide nearly half of all current revenues for American higher education, and that excludes federal aid given directly to students, which shows up, for the most part, as tuition and fees from the students. The federal government provides only about 13% of the support for higher education overall, and that includes its support for research and development in the universities, but excludes the aid it provides directly to students. State and local governments (mostly state) provide a third of all support for higher education. Students themselves provide another third, including federal aid they have received. The institutions themselves contribute about 15% from their own endowments and other sources. If we count federal aid to students as federal support to higher education, it increases the federal proportion to about 23% of total support and reduces the student contribution to about the same proportion. Another 6% is provided by individuals, foundations, and private business firms, in the form of gifts, grants, and contracts.

These proportions, of course, differ between public and private colleges and universities, though it must be stressed that all American colleges and universities are supported by a mixture of public and private funds. For example, whereas in 1981–82 public four-year colleges and universities got over 44% of their operating budgets from their state governments, the private institutions got less than 2% from state sources. (But note, private colleges received a slightly larger proportion of their support funds from the federal government than did the public institutions.) The other big difference lies in the importance of students' fees and payments directly to the institution for services: These account for less than a quarter of the revenues to public institutions, but about a half of the support for private institutions (Plisko, 1985, p. 114, Table 2.14).

These proportions differ sharply among even finer categories of colleges and universities; for example, as between public research universities and public four-year colleges.

In 1985–86 student aid from all sources was running at over $21 billion a year, 23% higher than in 1980–81. In real terms, however, student support from all sources had fallen by 3% since 1980–1981, and aid from federally supported programs by 10%, when adjusted for inflation ('Trends in Student Aid,' 1986, p. 2). The Federal Government in fiscal 1985 provided directly and indirectly about $23.7 billion to higher education, of which $10.2 billion was in a complex combination of student grants and loans (derived from 'Higher education funds,' 1986, p. 12). Student aid has widespread support in the Congress as well as in society at large. And although the Reagan administration regularly proposed cuts in that aid, many of its proposals were defeated. In 1985 Congress "blocked virtually all the cuts in aid to college students that the Reagan Administration proposed . . ." and was "drafting legislation to keep grants, loans and work opportunities essentially intact for five years" (Friendly, 1985, p. 15). Although pressures on the federal budget arising out of the large deficits may be reflected in further pressures on federal student aid programs, there is little likelihood of cuts so deep as to endanger the programs. Federal support for students is here to stay.

Increases in student aid at the state and the institution levels (which now comprise 22% of the total student aid reported from all sources) have helped to offset the drop in federal aid. At the federal level, the distribution of student aid has greatly shifted from grants to loans: in 1975–76, 75% of federal student aid was awarded in the form of grants, but by 1984–85 the share of grant aid had dropped to 29%, whereas the share of loans had tripled, from 21% in 1975 to 66% (see Table 2).

Many states did cut their support for public colleges and universities during the severe recession of 1980–82, but thereafter the levels of state support tended to rise about as fast as economic recovery and rising revenues permitted. State tax funds for the operation of higher education (this does not include capital costs) was nearly $31 billion for 1984–1985, up 19% over 1983–1984. "Over the last decade, [1974–1984, state] appro-

TABLE 2
Shift of Federal Student Aid from Grants to Loans

	1975–76	1984–85
Grants	75%	29%
Loans	21%	66%
Work-Study	4%	5%

Source: Frances, (1985).

priations [for higher education] increased 140 per cent nationwide. Adjusted for inflation, the increase was 19 per cent" (Evangelauf, 1985, p. 1ff.).

With regard to federal support for research, also perceived by many as endangered by the Reagan administration, between 1982 and 1985, federal obligations to universities and colleges for research and development increased by 16% in real terms, reaching $6 billion in 1985. Moreover, in that year nearly two-thirds of all federal academic R & D support was committed to basic research projects, compared to about one-half in 1975 (National Science Foundation, 1985, p. 2; see also, 'Higher education funds,' 1986, p. 12).

Other Supports and Benefits of the System[2]

We need not place very great weight on recent trends in enrolments and support. We know, especially from the sad example of British higher education, how rapidly these figures can change when they are built on shallow foundations. In Britain, where the university system has few friends in industry, in the professions, in the trade unions or the political parties, its few friends in the civil service and elsewhere are unable to protect it against economic and political pressures from the Government.

But American higher education has many friends and, more important, many supporters in the society, not just in the Government. The absence of any strong central governing and standardizing authority that can control (and limit) the growth of American higher education and the concomitant responsiveness of our colleges and universities to market forces have allowed and indeed required them to find ways to serve other institutions and groups in their constant search for support. We have not been able to afford the luxury of high academic standards across all our degree-granting institutions. The result is the diversity of standards and functions in our colleges and universities that we find so familiar and that Europeans find so strange. So long as the governing assumption of a system of higher education is that only a minority of students can work at the required standard, that system is constrained both in its size and in the functions it can perform for its students and for the larger society. Such a system may perform the functions of elite selection, preparation, and certification, as most European universities have done and still do. But it cannot penetrate as deeply or broadly into the life of society as American higher education has.

Some of the effects of mass higher education on American society are not, I believe, well recognized. Economists often say that it is best to measure and assess carefully what can be measured, and leave to others—historians, sociologists, educators, politicians—the discussion of higher education's larger effects on society. We cannot measure these very precisely; they are long delayed in their appearance, and 'outcomes' rather than intended effects, and have sources only partly within the system and partly within the society at large (For an economist whose views are similar to those I express below, see Bowen, 1977, pp. 359–387.)

Let me suggest some of those effects here:

(1) Higher education has substantial effects on the attitudes of those exposed to it. A large amount of research supports this assertion—and also that changes in attitudes occurring during the college years persist throughout life (Hyman, Wright, & Reed, 1975; Feldman & Newcomb, 1969). For example, higher education achieves some of what it intends by broadening the perspectives of students, giving them an appreciation of other cultures and groups, making them more tolerant of cultural differences, and weakening the prejudices characteristic of uneducated people. And those changed attitudes in a population, in turn, make possible real changes in social structures, if and when they are accompanied by changes in law and institutional behaviour.

In the United States, the years after World War II saw a steady decline in hostility toward black people and growing readiness on the part of whites to give blacks equal treatment and fair access to education, housing, and jobs. These changes can be seen in studies of attitudes both in the general population as well as among college students during the college years and after (Hyman & Wright, 1979; Stember, 1961; Stouffer, 1955; Clark, Heist, McConnell Trow, & Yonge, 1972). I believe that the considerable progress the United States has made in race relations since World War II has been made possible by the growth of mass higher education and the marked decline in racial prejudice that accompanied it. If that is true, then it represents a very great contribution to the life of the society, one that is almost never acknowledged by economists as a benefit of American higher education.

Higher education has also played a visible role in this revolution by helping to expand and educate black, Hispanic, and Asian middle classes. In 1985, the University of California at Berkeley for the first time admitted a freshman class made up of a majority (52%) of those minority group members. In the next century, those students will be assuming leadership positions in every institution in our society.

(2) People who have been to college or university, on the whole, view public issues in a longer time perspective than do less well-educated people. Such perspectives are important to assessing the significance and recognizing the origins of a problem or issue, yet we do not measure them or give them value, certainly not as outcomes of higher education. Nations and industries cannot plan or develop programs without the help of people who take the long view, who can imagine the outcome of projects that may lie years in the future. And that perspective is very much a benefit of mass higher education.

In an increasingly complex society, it is not enough that a small number of elites have these longer time horizons; the successful development and implementation of plans require such people throughout the society, especially at the middle levels of the civil service in central, regional, and local governments, and in public and private enterprises. Long-range plans require continual adjustments and modifications at the levels where they are implemented; people at those levels must be able to understand the purposes of long-range programs and be able to implement and modify them within planning guidelines.

(3) The capacity of citizens to learn how to learn is another skill that is gained or enhanced by exposure to higher education. So much of what we learn in college or university is obsolescent in 10 years, obsolete in 25, that it is impossible to exaggerate the importance of the ability to continue to learn after finishing formal schooling. Wherever facilities are provided for adult education, they are now quickly filled by people with a degree or some postsecondary education, who already have, as adults, developed a desire to learn (Organization for Economic Co-operation and Development, 1977, p. 27). Modern societies need citizens with that quality of mind, which is also a product, if often a by-product, of higher education. I believe that mass higher education in the United States, especially in its generous provision of education for adults, engenders and distributes more widely the habit of 'life-long learning' than is true in most other countries.

The qualities of mind (they are more than attitudes) that I have mentioned—tolerance of cultural and class differences, a longer time perspective that helps sustain initiative among middle- and lower-level administrators, the ability to learn how to learn—are all created or enhanced by exposure to postsecondary education. As I have suggested, they are usually by-products of that education, but immensely important by-products for the life and progress of any society.

(4) In American political life, higher education has a familiar role as home of the cultural critic of the established political order and the nursery of radical and even revolutionary student movements. But less dramatically and visibly, the expansion and democratization of higher education may also work to legitimate the political and social order by rewarding talent and effort rather than serving merely as a cultural apparatus of the ruling classes by ensuring the passage of power and privilege across generations.

In a time of rising expectations among all social strata around much of the world, nations must provide real opportunities for social mobility to able people from poor and modest origins. They must do so for social and political reasons, as well as for economic growth. In many countries, the armed forces have pro-

vided an avenue of mobility, and they have often gained the support of the poor even when other institutions have lost it. But, for many reasons, higher education is a better instrument for strengthening the legitimacy of a political democracy, and, where it performs that vital function, as it has in the United States, it goes unrecorded on the accounting sheets of the cost/benefits analyst.

A further large benefit of American higher education, yet to be achieved, is the help and guidance extended by colleges and universities to secondary education in other ways than through teacher training and educational research. The many reports and books on public secondary education that have appeared since 1983 (e.g., National Commission on Excellence in Education, 1983; Boyer, 1983: Goodlad, 1983) have led to the creation of a large number of programs by colleges and universities that establish new links between higher and secondary education. Some of those programs are designed to strengthen the academic and college preparatory work of the high schools, not just provide remediation for ill-prepared students after they reach college (Trow, 1985b). It may be that the task is too large and that the structural characteristics of American high schools will defeat all efforts to overcome their "bias against excellence" (Clark, 1985, p. 391). But it will not be for want of trying. Already hundreds of programs that aim to correct or ameliorate deficiencies in the schools have been developed by colleges and universities. Results can already be seen in individual schools, but the larger effects will be long delayed and obscured by many other inputs and forces. My point here is to illustrate the continuing propensity of American higher education to respond to national needs of almost every kind and to try to provide some service, some program, to meet those needs.

Conclusion

I have chosen to look to the past and the present to assess characteristics of our unique system of colleges and universities that may shape the future. It is futile to make specific predictions—they all fail in a few years, even in societies that manage their systems more closely than we do. But my review of the central characteristics of American higher education leads me to believe that it is well equipped to survive major changes in the society and to respond creatively to almost any developments, short of a catastrophe. The strength of our system lies precisely in its diversity, which allows it to respond to different needs and demands on different segments of the system. Over the past forty years, enrolments have grown from about 2.3 million to 12.4 million and, along with this enormous growth, there has been further diversification and democratization of access. By the end of World War II, and perhaps much earlier, we had a system that had the capacity to grow by a factor of five without any fundamental change in its structure or functions, a system able to provide access to a broad spectrum of American society, while still providing education of the highest standard for a small fraction of our youth and research at an equally high standard in the broadest range of scholarly and scientific disciplines.

What besides this massive growth has changed significantly in American higher education over the past forty years? First, the Federal Government has become a major source of support, both for university-based research and through student aid. Yet it still supplies less than a quarter of all support for American higher education. Moreover, the Government's influence on the system has been further muted, precisely because that support has gone to individual scientists and students rather than directly to the institutions. Of course, the Federal Government has become a major actor in shaping the agenda of American science. And yet science still retains a large measure of autonomy to pursue problems and issues that arise internally, rather than at the initiative of the Government.

As the fifty states have increased their support for the public sector of higher education, they have demanded greater accountability from the colleges and universities for the use of these funds. Not long ago these demands by public authorities were seen as the forerunners of a dangerous shift of authority and initiative away from the state colleges and universities to the state houses and governors' office (Trow, 1975). Relations between public universities and state authorities vary too much for any easy generalization, yet my sense is that public authorities and university leaders in many states have been coming to a more reasoned

and mutually acceptable relationship than was seen as possible or likely even ten years ago (Newman, 1987).

Higher education has expanded its relationships with industry in many ways. On the one hand, business firms provide very large and growing amounts of education and training at all levels of skill and sophistication, including degree-granting programs (Eurich, 1985). On the other hand, universities have provided the ideas and professional staffs for new science-based industries and are at the center of their physical clusterings from Boston to Silicon Valley. They also provide an organisational model and style of work for many other institutions, from consulting firms and industrial labs to legislative committees (Muir, 1982). Moreover, community colleges enroll increasing numbers of students who already hold a bachelor's degree but want further training in another specialty—new patterns of continuing education and professional development.

Certainly, the democratisation of the student body has meant more mature, part-time, and working students; these kinds of students in fact have confounded the predictions of enrolment decline after 1979. There seems no limit to this development: American higher education, or at least a large segment of it, seems ready and eager to provide some useful educational service to all nontraditional students. And we have no reason to believe that this will be less true in the future, as more and more of our labor force comes to work in industries whose very survival is predicated on rapid change, new skills, and new ways of thinking.

All of this suggests that American higher education will be an even more important institution in this society in the decades to come: as a supplier of more advanced skills as well as a source of greater social equality, continuing social commentary and criticism, and the transmission of an ever-broadening cultural heritage. Higher education is, today, I believe, the key institution in American society, the source of many of its most important ideas, values, skills, and energies. That will be true, and increasingly true, as far ahead as anyone can see.

Acknowledgements

Revised from *State and Welfare, USA/USSR: Contemporary Policy and Practice*, edited by Gail W. Lapidus and Guy E. Swanson (Berkeley, Calif., Institute of International Studies, University of California, 1988). My thanks to Janet Ruyle for her help with this paper. The Editor thanks the Editor of *Educational Researcher* for permission to reprint this paper which appeared in that journal in April 1988.

Correspondence: Professor Martin Trow, Center for Studies in Higher Education, University of California, Berkeley, California 94720, USA.

Notes

1. This section draws, in part, on my essay "Aspects of Diversity in American Higher Education," 1979.
2. This section draws on my paper, "The State of Higher Education in the United States," 1986.

References

Andersen, C. J. (Comp.). (1968). *A fact book on higher education* (Issue No. 1). Washington, D. C.: American Council on Education.

Ashby, e. (1967, November). Ivory towers in tomorrow's world. *The Journal of Higher Education*, pp. 417–427.

Bowen, H. R. (1977). *Investment in learning. The individual and social value of American higher education.* San Francisco, CA: Jossey-Bass.

Boyer, E. (1983). *High school: A report on secondary education in America.* New York: Harper & Row.

Clark, B. R. (1985, February). The high school and the university: What went wrong in America, Part I. *Phi Delta Kappan*, pp. 391–197.

Clark, B. R., Heist, P., McConnell, T. R., Trow, M. A., & Younge, G. E. (1972). *Students and colleges: Interaction and change.* Berkeley, CA: Center for Research and Development in Higher Education, University of California.

Eurich, N. P. (1985). *Corporate classrooms: The learning business.* Princeton, JY. Carnegie Foundation for the Advancement of Teaching.

Evangelauf, J. (1985, October 30). States' spending on colleges rises 19 pct. in 2 years, nears $31-billion for '85–86. *The Chronicle of Higher Education*, p. 1 ff.

Fact-file fall 1983 enrolment. (1986, October 13). *The Chronicle of Higher Education*, p. 42.

Feldman, K. A., & Newcomb, T. M. (1969). *The impact of college on students (Vol. 2)* San Francisco, CA: Jossey-Bass.

Francis, C. (1984, December) 1983. The economic outlook for higher education. *AAHE Bulletin*, p. 3.

Francis, C. (1985, December) 1986: Major trends shaping the outlook for higher education. *AAHE Bulletin*, p. 5.

Friendly, J. (1983, September 24) Budget as tails to make dent in aid programs for students. *The New York Times*, p. 13.

Glenny, L. A. (1983, July). *Higher education for students: Forecasts of a golden age.* Paper delivered at a seminar sponsored by the Higher Education Steering Committee, University of California, Berkeley, CA.

Goodlad, J. I. (1983). *A place called school. Prospects for the nuture.* New York: McGraw-Hill.

Hartz, L. (1955). *The liberal tradition in America. An interpretation of American political thoughts since the revolution.* New York: Harcourt Brace.

Higher education funds in President Reagan's fiscal 1987 budget. (1986, February 12). *The Chronicle of Higher Education*, p. 12.

Higher education is a U. S. industry, (1986, July 28), *Higher Education of National Affairs*, p. 3.

Hofstadter, R. (1963). *Anti-intellectualism in American life.* New York: Alfred A. Knopf.

Hofstadter, R., & Metzger, W. P. (1955). *The development of academic freedom in the United States.* New York: Columbia University Press.

Hofstadter, R. & Smith, W. (Eds.). (1961) *American higher education: A documentary history* (Vol. 1). Chicago, IL: University of Chicago Press.

Hyman, H. H., & Wright, C. R. (1979). *Education's lasting influence on values.* Chicago, IL. and London: University of Chicago Press.

Hyman, H. H., Wright, C. R., & Reed, J. S. (1975). *The enduring effects of education.* Chicago, IL and London: University of Chicago Press.

Kerr, C. (1980). The Carnegie policy series 1967–1979: Consensus, approaches, reconsiderations, results. In *The Carnegie Council on policy studies in higher education.* San Francisco, CA: Jossey-Bass.

McConnell, W. R., & Kaufman, N. (1984, January). *High school graduates: Projections for the fifty states (1982–2000).* Boulder, CO: Western Interstate Commission for Higher Education.

Mostly stable: College and university enrolments: 1985–1991. (1987, November 25), *The Chronicle of Higher Education*, p. A29.

Muir, W. K. (1982). *Legislature: California's school for politics.* Chicago, IL: University of Chicago Press.

National Commission on Excellence in Education. (1983). *A nation at risk: The imperative for educational reform.* Washington, DC: U. S. Department of Education.

National Science Foundation. (1985, May 9). Federal academic R&D funds continue strong growth through 1983. *Science Resources Studies Highlights* Washington, DC: Author

Newman, F. (1987). *Choosing quality: Reducing conflict between the state and the university.* Denver, CO: Education Commission of the States.

Organization for Economic Co-operation and Development. (1977). *Learning opportunities for adults, general report.* (Vol. 1). Paris: Author

Ottinger, C. A. (Comp.). (1984). *1984–85 fact book.* New York: American Council on Education and Macmillan Publishing Company.]

Project PACE, (1984). *Conditions of education in California, 1984* (No. 84–1). Berkeley, CA: University of California.

Plisko, V. W., & Stern, J. D. (Eds.). (1985). *The condition of education, 1985 edition.* Washington, DC: National Center for Education Statistics.

Rudolph, F. (1962). *The American college and university.* New York: Alfred A. Knopf. Statistics you can use: Growth in nontraditional students, 1972–1982. (1984, June 18). *Higher Education & National Affairs,* p. 3.

Stember, C. H. (1961). *Education and attitude change.* New York: Institute of Human Relations Press.

Stouffer, S. A. (1955). *Communism, conformity and civil liberties.* Garden City, NY: Doubleday.

Trends in student aid: 1980 to 1986. (1986). Washington, DC: The College Board.

Trow, M. (1975, Winter). The public and private lives of higher education. *Daedalus,* 2, 113–127.

Trow, M. (1979). Aspects of diversity in American higher education. In H. Gans (Ed.). *On the making of Americans: Essays in honor of David Riesman* (pp. 271–290). Philadelphia, PA: University of Pennsylvania Press.

Trow, M. (1985a). Comparative reflections on leadership in higher education. *European Journal of Education,* 20, 143–159.

Trow, M. (1985b). Underprepared students and public research universities. In J. H. Bunzel (Ed.). *Challenge to American schools* (pp. 191–215). New York and Oxford: Oxford University Press.

Trow, M. (1986). The state of higher education in the United States. In W. K. Cummings, E. R. Beauchamp, S. Ichikawa, V. N. Kobayashi, & M. Ushiogi (Eds.). *Educational policies in crisis: Japanese and American perspectives* (pp. 171–194). New York: Praeger Publishers.

Tsukada, M. (1986). A factual overview of education in Japan and the United States. In W. K. Cummings, E. R. Beauchamp, S. Ichikawa, V. N. Kabayashi, & M. Ushiogi (Eds.). *Educational policies in crisis: Japanese and American perspectives* (pp. 96–116). New York: Praeger Publishers.]

Williams, G. (1983, November 18). Making sense of statistics. *The Times Higher Education Supplement,* p. 13.

Goals: The Intended Outcomes of Higher Education

HOWARD R. BOWEN

Marx sought to change the world through changing social institutions, Jesus through changing the hearts of men. Higher education tries to do both.[1]

What do educators *hope* will be the results of their efforts? These hopes, though often inconsistent or unrealistic, are the intended outcomes; they are sufficiently esteemed and thought to be sufficiently achievable to qualify as goals (Rivlin, 1973). They are presumably guides to educational decision making and criteria by which actual outcomes can be judged. They are a useful starting point in a study of outcomes because they may be regarded as hypotheses about the consequences of higher education and they give guidance as to what to look for by way of actual outcomes. This starting point also has the advantage of permitting us to begin on familiar terrain. Though surprisingly little is known about outcomes, the goals of higher education have been considered since the time of Plato by philosophers, psychologists, sociologists, literary figures, social critics, and educators. Indeed, if the goals of higher education are defined as a list of desirable objectives, without priorities among them, there is even considerable agreement. As one reviews the literature of educational philosophy, the same goals appear time after time. It is sometimes asserted that higher education is virtually without coherent goals and can be described as "organized anarchy" (Breneman, 1974, pp. 5–6; Coleman in Kaysen, 1973, pp. 368–374; Cohen and March, 1974). In our view this position greatly overstates the case. Higher education does lack hierarchical organization and its goals are not as simple or undimensional as profit maximization, but it nevertheless operates with a quite definite set of goals that command widespread assent.

The literature on the goals of higher education is vast. Some of it is in the great classics, some in the treatises of scholars, some in the writings of critics, and some in fugitive publications such as speeches, tracts, essays, college catalogues, institutional self-studies, and government documents. If, from this literature, a catalogue of widely accepted goals were compiled, it would be a kind of check list for use in the study of actual outcomes. Such a list would doubtless contain some goals that are not in fact achieved, and it might omit some unintended ones—especially negative outcomes. At the very least, however, the list would be a starting point in discovering the outcomes.

This chapter represents a systematic effort to identify widely accepted goals of higher education. Based on a sampling of the extensive literature on goals, it provides general discussion of some of the broader aims of higher education and concludes with a detailed catalogue of specific goals. This catalogue provides a useful taxonomy for considering the possible outcomes of higher education.

The goals included describe the final outputs of higher education, not intermediate or enabling objectives. For example, such objectives as increasing the financial support of higher education, raising the faculty-student ratios, modernizing buildings and equipment, improving curricula—objectives that loom large in the plans of educators—are regarded here not as final outputs but as means (Gross and Grambach, 1974, pp. 43–74). The goals are related to the three main functions of higher education: education, research, and public service.

Goals for Individual Students Through Education

Education, or the teaching-learning function, is defined to embrace not only the formal academic curricula, classes, and laboratories but also all those influences upon students flowing from association with peers and faculty members and from the many and varied experiences of campus life. As we have observed, colleges and universities may be seen as environments exerting influence in many ways and not merely as formal academic programs having only intellectual goals. As Cardinal Newman (1958, p. 123) said: "When a multitude of young persons, keen, open-hearted, sympathetic, and observant, as young persons are, come together and freely mix with each other, they are sure to learn from one another, even if there be no one to teach them; the conversation of all is a series of lectures to each, and they gain for themselves new ideas and views, fresh matters of thought, and distinct principles for judging and acting, day by day."

Woodrow Wilson expressed the same idea when he was trying to change the campus life of Princeton (quoted in Trow, 1975, p. 270): "The real intellectual life of a body of undergraduates, if there be any, manifests itself not in the classroom, but in what they do and talk of and set before themselves as their favorite objects between classes and lectures." The detailed goals for education may be considered in the context of several widely accepted principles.

The whole person

Education should be directed toward the growth of the whole person through the cultivation not only of the intellect and of practical competence but also of the affective dispositions, including the moral, religious, emotional, and esthetic aspects of the personality. No theme runs more consistently through the goal literature. Plato (1974, p. 130) quoted Socrates, "And we shall begin by educating mind and

character, shall we not?" Aristotle, however (Ulich, 1968, p. 65), was less positive on the matter. He said, "There are differences of opinion as to the proper tasks to be set: for all peoples do not agree as to the things that the young ought to learn, either with a view to virtue or with a view to the best life, nor is it clear whether their studies should be regulated more with regard to intellect or with regard to character . . . and it is not at all clear whether the pupils should practise pursuits that are practically useful, or morally edifying, or higher accomplishments." However, Aristotle went on to advocate attention to the intellect, the character, and practical competence.

In his essay "Literature and Science" (1927, p. 62), Matthew Arnold observed that "when we set ourselves to enumerate the powers which go to the building up of human life, and say that they are the power of conduct, the power of intellect and knowledge, the power of beauty, and the power of social life and manners, [we] can hardly deny that this scheme, though drawn in rough and plain lines enough, and not pretending to scientific exactness, does yet give a fairly true representation of the matter. Human nature is built up by these powers; we have the need for them all. When we have rightly met and adjusted the claims of them all, we shall then be in a fair way for getting soberness and righteousness, with wisdom." Nevitt Sanford (1969, p. 76) offers a contemporary restatement of Arnold's theme: "Our goal is to expand both the intellect and the area of motive and feeling, and to bring the two together in a larger whole."

Similarly, Donald Michael (1968, p. 109) argued that: "We must educate for empathy, compassion, trust, non-exploitiveness, non-manipulativeness, for self-growth, and self-esteem, for tolerance of ambiguity, for acknowledgment of error, for patience, for suffering." And Keniston and Gerzon (1972, p. 53) suggested that: "The critical component of education attempts to expose students to multiple and conflicting perspectives on themselves and their society in order to test and challenge their previously unexamined assumptions. It strives to create conditions which stimulate students' intellectual, moral, and emotional growth, so that they may ground their skills in a more mature, humane framework of values. Critical education deliberately tries to stimulate the student to reformulate his goals, his cognitive map of the world, the *way* he thinks, and his view of his role in society. Thus the more successful critical education is, the more difficult that success is to measure, for its aim is the transformation of persons and of the purposes to which they devote their knowledge." This idea is also expressed in such ubiquitous phrases as "intellectual and emotional maturity," "education of the whole person," "full development of personal capabilities," "individual fulfillment," and "education appropriate to the whole of man's nature" (Trent and Medsker, 1968, p. 14). Almost every commentator emphasizes that the goals of instruction transcend intellectual development, though many refer to a close interrelation between the affective side of human personality and academic learning. For example, Spaeth and Greeley (1970, pp. 174–175) concluded: "The cognitive dimension of the personality cannot face critical issues of life in a state of aloof disinterest . . . cognitive development is, in fact, a personality need . . . the late adolescent development process can be helpful in facilitating intellectual development of the student." Similarly, Sanford and Katz stated (1966, p. 400), "We view as one of the chief goals of undergraduate education the application of rationality to the conduct of life. Mere exercise of cognitive skills is not enough." (See also McDaniel, 1976.)

A note of caution about "totalism" in the approach of colleges to students was recently sounded by the Carnegie Commission on Higher Education (1973c). In this matter, the commission struck an almost solitary dissenting chord in a chorus of advocacy for campus concern and responsibility for the "whole person." They wrote (pp. 16–17): "the campus cannot and should not try to take direct responsibility for the 'total' development of the student. That responsibility belongs primarily to the individual student by the time he goes to college . . . the college should particularly devote its attention to what it can do best and to what students cannot obtain anywhere else. The campus is, above all, a place where students can enrich their minds by study. 'Totalism' in the campus approach to students, we believe, is neither wise nor possible." However, the

commission softened its stand by declaring (p. 16) that: "the college years are an important developmental period, and cognitive and affective activities are closely related to each other . . . the college does provide an important environment [for nonintellective personal development]."

Spaeth and Greeley (1970, pp. 172–173) sounded a similar note of caution. They found that the American people "make rather stringent demands on the higher educational enterprise—parent, priest, psychiatrist, master craftsman, confidant, charismatic leader, prophet, social reformer—the college is expected to be all these. It is supposed to *do* something to the people who attend it . . . It seems to us that it would be very desirable if a national consensus could be established that would not make as many demands of the college experience. We are not in agreement with those who argue that all we may expect of higher education is custody and screening, but neither are we willing to agree with those who think that it has failed if it does not produce lots of people with a degree of personal nobility never before seen on a mass basis. Somewhere between screening and ennobling, we suspect, can be found a series of goals for higher education that are both feasible and challenging."

Despite these demurrers, the overwhelming sentiment on the responsibility of higher education in the cognitive and affective domains was summarized by Alexander Heard (1973, p. 15): "Our first concern is the human intellect, but our ultimate concern is the human being . . . The concern for personal development results from the need to be able to cope with those conditions of a technological society that led to the decline in the authority of other institutions. Involved are the development of standards of value, a sense of civic responsibility, the capacity for religious reconciliation, skills, understanding, a sense of purpose, and all the rest required to be a well-integrated person. The institution that can help its student become a better-integrated person, with a sense of command over his own destiny and a sense of how he fits into his complicated and mercurial social environment, will have achieved the most demanding and significant educational objective of our time."

Individuality

A second widely held principle is that education should take into account the uniqueness of individuals. It should help each person develop according to his particular characteristics and potentialities. It should be responsive to the reality that individuals vary in background, abilities, talents, aspirations, and age of readiness, and that a wide range of opportunities and options must be available if all are to be served well. As Cardinal Newman so eloquently remarked (1958, p. 122): "A university is, according to the usual designation, an Alma Mater, knowing her children one by one, not a foundry, or a mint, or a treadmill." A corollary to this principle is that higher education should seek out, develop, and certify talent that is sorely needed in a complex society of vast organizations, advanced technology, and sophisticated culture. Much remains to be learned, however, about the nature of talent.

Accessibility

A third principle is that higher education should be readily and widely accessible to persons of a broad range of abilities, circumstances, and ages. This represents a fairly recent extension of the older idea of equality of opportunity, which was usually based on a somewhat narrow conception of the content and purpose of higher education and on the assumption that only a limited number of persons could benefit from it. Today, most people agree that there should be not only easy access but positive encouragement to attendance through new kinds of institutions, and so on. Husen (1974b, p. 143) has described this concept as the "quest for greater equality of life chances, coping power, and participation." Recently, even openness and equality of access have been declared by some to be obsolete, and demands are heard for equality of *results*, though it is usually acknowledged that equality of results and equality of opportunity are inherently incompatible.

Given basic and perhaps ineradicable individual differences, equality of results appears to be an impossible goal, though disparities in results might be substantially narrowed. John Dewey, who emphasized the implications of education for democracy, proposed equality of

concern as a practicable solution to the equality problem. He used the analogy of a family in which the children are loved and valued equally despite their quite different capacities and interests. The parents in such a family should be concerned for all of the children. But for the best development of each child, the family would not necessarily provide identical or even equal opportunities, and certainly would not expect the results to be equal. As Dewey put it (quoted in Hook, 1973, p. 75), "Moral equality means incommensurability, and inapplicability of common and quantitative standards. It means intrinsic qualities which require *unique* opportunities and differential manifestation." And again Dewey (1974, p. 295) wrote: "What the best and wisest parent wants for his own child, that must the community want for all of its children. Any other ideal for our schools is narrow and unlovely; acted upon, it destroys our democracy." More recently, Nevitt Sanford (1969, pp. 189–190) expressed a similar concept: "As we approach the challenge of universal higher education, we need to keep in mind that the poor, the culturally deprived, even the stupid are our own. In the absence of effective institutions for helping them, a society that cares for its own has no alternative to creating new institutions in which the child or young person who has low intelligence or is 'unmotivated' can be educated up to the level of his potential, which now is usually unknown."

Despite the ascendency of the principle of wide access, some educators express concern that higher education may be expanded only at the cost of educational and cultural excellence (Berman, 1975, pp. 3–11; Craig, 1974, pp. 143–147; Shils, 1975, pp. 1–37). Others, equally concerned, seek ways to reconcile access and excellence (Gardner, 1961; Husen, 1974b). There is a relatively new element in the discussion—the recognition that human talents are relative to social values and are more widely distributed than once had been believed (Cross, 1975; Taubman and Wales, 1972; Levitas, 1974). These matters will be discussed further in later chapters.

The basic principles concerning access were eloquently summarized in the influential report of the 1947 President's Commission on Higher Education (1947, p. 9): "The first goal in education for democracy is the full, rounded, and continuing development of the person . . . [T]o liberate and perfect the intrinsic powers of every citizen is the central purpose of democracy, and its furtherance of individual self-realization is its greatest glory."

Specific goals of education

From these basic principles the specific goals for the education function are derived. This function, which embraces both the formal academic program and the extracurricular life of an academic community, is intended to help students develop as persons in three respects: *cognitive learning*, by expanding their knowledge and intellectual powers; *affective development*, by enhancing their moral, religious, and emotional interests and sensibilities; and *practical competence*, by improving their performance in citizenship, work, family life, consumer choice, health, and other practical affairs.

Insofar as these three goals are achieved, they are the ingredients for the flowering of the total personality. In varying combinations—reflecting individual differences and uniqueness of persons—they define the ideal personalities to which many educators aspire for their students.

Cognitive and affective vs. practical goals

Distinctions among cognitive, affective, and practical goals are blurred, and there is much overlap among them. Moreover, we do not imply that the cognitive and practical outcomes would be derived solely from formal curricula, or that the affective outcomes would be produced solely through extracurricular academic life. All three types of goals may be achieved in part from both formal instruction and extracurricular experience.

The goals relating to the cognitive and affective dimensions of the human personality are of wide applicability. They should enhance the individual's life in all his experiences and endeavors, including his practical activities. The goals relating to practical affairs, on the other hand, tend to be more specific. They are expected to assist the individual in the several practical roles he will be called upon to fill. Recent literature on goals contains many references not only to careers but also to the impor-

tance of preparing individuals to cope with the ordinary affairs of life: preparing for changes in the life cycle as one progresses from adolescence to old age; dealing with interpersonal problems within the family; using the health care system; getting proper legal advice; coping with bureaucracy; managing investments, insurance, and taxes; buying and selling real estate; and so on (Organization for Economic Cooperation and Development, 1973b; Bailey, 1976).

Observers differ sharply about the relative importance of instruction for practical affairs and instruction to develop desirable cognitive and affective personal characteristics. At the one extreme are those who regard higher education primarily as training for practical affairs, particularly work and citizenship, and consider liberal education as secondary or fitted only for an elite. At the other extreme are those who hold that the main task of higher education is to produce good and competent people who possess the desired general cognitive and affective qualities. On this view, liberally educated persons will be able to cope with the practical affairs of life without much special training. John Stuart Mill expressed this second view in a famous passage in his inaugural address as Rector of the University of St. Andrews (1875, pp. 4–335):

> Universities are not intended to teach knowledge required to fit men for some special mode of making their livelihood. Their object is not to make skillful lawyers, or physicians, or engineers, but capable and cultivated human beings. It is very right that there should be public facilities for the study of professions. It is well that there should be Schools of Law and of Medicine. But these things are no part of what every generation owes to the next as that on which its civilization and worth will principally depend . . . Men are men before they are lawyers, or physicians, or merchants, or manufacturers; and if you make them capable and sensible men, they will make themselves capable and sensible lawyers or physicians. What professional men should carry away with them from a University is not professional knowledge, but that which should direct the use of their professional knowledge, and bring the light of a general culture to illuminate the technicalities of a special pursuit. Men

may be competent lawyers without general education, but it depends on general education to make them philosophic lawyers—who demand, and are capable of apprehending principles, instead of merely cramming their memory with details.

Most contemporary opinion lies between the extremes (Martin, 1968; Cheit, 1975). Thoughtful people acknowledge that liberal education designed for development of a whole person is a basic responsibility. They believe that such knowledge and skills as reading, writing, mathematics, science, history, economics, and so on—all associated with liberal education—facilitate the conduct of practical affairs. They also recognize that education in such fields as medicine, law, nursing, architecture, and administration carries with it content of intellectual, moral, and esthetic value and contributes toward development of the whole person. The relative emphasis on liberal and practical education fluctuates. At the moment, the balance seems to be swinging toward the practical side. Yet a preponderance of authority over the centuries gives higher priority to general human development than to the practical training and warns against the persistent tendency to neglect broad human development in favor of training for practical pursuits (compare Bisconti and Solmon, 1976).

Dispositions vs. behaviors

The goals of education are usually expressed as characteristics, skills, abilities, competencies, dispositions, motivations, sensibilities, orientations, commitments, understandings, and so on. To the extent that students achieve these personal qualities by the time of their graduation, it may be assumed that they are headed toward desirable lifetime *behavior patterns*. But *behavior patterns* are the ultimate goals. The basic purpose of instruction is to change lifetime behavior and thus to change lives, not merely to produce abstract dispositions or tendencies toward change that may never materialize.

Each of the specific goals for higher education implies a future behavior pattern. For example, the goal of verbal skill, a subgoal under cognitive learning, implies effective verbal communication as a desired behavior of later life. Similarly, the subgoal of esthetic sen-

sibility implies consistent and sympathetic attention to the arts and to natural beauty. The goals of instruction are in the first instance, to change students with respect to their dispositions and tendencies. But these immediate outcomes reach fruition only as they produce changes in lifetime behavior.

By-products of education as goals

We have referred to the three primary goals of education as the personal development of students with respect to their cognitive abilities, their affective characteristics, and their practical competence. In addition, the additional goals are achieved largely as by-products of instruction: personal self-discovery, career choice and placement, and direct satisfactions and enjoyments.

Personal self-discovery

Closely related to the aim of helping students attain personal development is the goal of helping them discover themselves—their aptitudes, interests, values, commitments, and aspirations. Personal self-discovery is in a sense a by-product of the instructional process, but it is nevertheless one of the most far-reaching purposes of higher education. Colleges and universities are designed to offer students a wide variety of experiences, to introduce them to a broad range of ideas, to put them into contact with peers and role models, to acquaint them with the multiple possibilities that life affords, to allow them to try themselves out in a variety of fields and tasks, to help them discover their limitations, and to motivate them to achieve their ultimate potential as human beings. The goal of self-discovery justifies and makes intelligible the floundering that is characteristic of many college students who are trying to choose courses, major fields, careers, philosophies of life, and even marriage partners.

Career choice and placement

The goal of facilitating appropriate career choice and placement of students is closely related to the goal of personal self-discovery. Both goals together reflect the process by which students will achieve their self-identity and work out their career objectives and style of life.

Colleges and universities assist in career choice and placement through guidance, brokerage, and credentialing. Guidance often occurs through formal counseling and also through the informal influence of peers and professors. Brokerage occurs when colleges and universities serve as middlemen between students or alumni and prospective employers—often through placement offices. Credentialing refers to the issuance of grades, honors and recognitions, letters of recommendation, recommendations by word of mouth, certificates, and degrees signifying academic achievements.

Historically, the practice of credentialing originated as part of the academic incentive system. Grades, degrees, certificates, and so on were designed to motivate students to do good work and encourage them to complete coherent courses of study. While continuing to serve as motivators, they evolved into effective sorting devices for placement in the labor market. In recent years, credentialing has become a subject of sharp controversy. Critics argue that career placement is dominated by paper credentials rather than genuine competency, that educational requirements for many jobs have become excessive, that many competent people without the required paper credentials are unfairly discriminated against, and that the premium earnings received by the college-educated are due largely to their credentials rather than to their superior productivity. On the other hand, the advocates of credentialing argue that it provides a reliable incentive system without which academic standards could not be maintained, that the granting of credentials helps people to find congenial and suitable jobs where they will be productive, that credentialing provides the community with reliable information that would otherwise have to be provided in more costly and less efficient ways, and that credentialing in many cases provides protection for consumers.

Credentialing provides a system of "signals" that alerts prospective employers to worker characteristics that are not easy to observe through ordinary screening for employment. This signal system helps in achieving appropriate placement and avoids costly errors for both employer and employee

(Madden, 1975, pp. 15–16). A degree and other credentials indicate with some reliability that the individual can "speak and write clearly, understand what he reads, reason about matters of some complexity, recognize historical and cultural reference points, feel somewhat at home amidst philosophical and generally abstract ideas" (Harris, 1975, p. 222). A degree or other credential also indicates its holders have "demonstrated the discipline necessary to attend classes, prepare for examinations, [and] bring their minds to bear at least minimally on a certain amount of initially uninteresting material, and an ability to survive in a world focused on intellectual concerns" (Harris, 1975, p. 222).

For the present, we concede that credentialing has both positive and negative results but assert that on balance it is a legitimate and perhaps necessary function of higher education. The granting of credentials motivates students effectively and facilitates efficient allocation of the labor force by taking into account both the interests and competencies of workers and the needs of the economy. We shall have more to say on this subject under the topic, "grading and labeling." (See Chapter Five.)

Direct satisfactions and enjoyments

Many—probably most—students gain pleasure from learning and enjoy being part of an academic community where they may experience the stimulus of interesting people and ideas, sociability, recreation, and agreeable surroundings. Because people spend much of their time in formal education—in some cases as much as a third of their whole lives, and seldom less than a sixth—personal satisfaction and enjoyment is by no means a frivolous goal. And it becomes even more important when one considers that enjoyment of education undoubtedly enhances its effectiveness. Indeed, Jencks (1972, pp. 256–257) has made the radical suggestion (with reference to schools) that, since educators have meager knowledge of the relation between the forms and methods of education and its outcomes, one of the main criteria for deciding on educational method might be the degree of direct satisfaction obtained by students and teachers.

The families and friends of college students also may obtain satisfaction from the college experience. This satisfaction takes many forms: it may be simply vicarious enjoyment from contemplating a rich opportunity available to a loved one; it may be a sense of pleasure in helping open up opportunity to a family member; it may be the introduction of a new source of interest and ideas into a family circle; or it may be sheer relief on the part of parents who are able to shift part of the responsibility for guiding and developing their sons and daughters to an institution. On this point, Adam Smith observed that, in the absence of worthy universities in his time, many families sent their sons abroad for several years. By so doing, he said, "a father delivers himself at least for some time, from so disagreeable an object as that of a son unemployed, neglected, and going to ruin before his eyes." Smith also noted that for a young man of seventeen or eighteen "it is very difficult not to improve a good deal in three or four years" (Smith, 1937). At any rate, anyone who has observed the pride of parents and spouses of graduates on commencement day can hardly deny that the satisfactions to family members are real.

Social Goals of Higher Education

As higher education brings about changes in individuals through its educational function, as it contributes toward the advancement of knowledge and the arts, and as it renders various public services, its work is bound to have broad social consequences. Therefore goals for society, as well as for individuals, must be considered.

Individualism vs. collectivism

There are two opposing extremes on the continuum of educational philosophies in the world today: the individualistic, emphasizing the development of persons as the final end, and the collectivistic, emphasizing the advancement of society as the final end (Emmerij, 1974, pp. 147–151, 170–171, 191–200).

The assumptions underlying the extreme individualistic point of view are (1) that education should be designed to produce autonomous individuals who are civilized and effective in practical affairs; (2) that a society of

such individuals will spontaneously work out a desirable social destiny through the democratic process as a result of their separate and collective decisions and actions; (3) that research and related intellectual and artistic activities of the academic community should be designed to foster learning for its own sake; and (4) that such learning will spontaneously turn out to be useful for both cultural development and practical affairs.

The assumptions underlying the extreme collectivistic point of view are (1) that "society" has goals that may be distinguishable from the interactive summation of individual goals; (2) that education should be designed to shape individuals to serve the purposes of the nation—usually set forth by the government or by a party leadership; and (3) that research and related intellectual and artistic activities should be directed toward the achievement of national goals, including the solution of social problems. The point of view was recently described by Jan Szczepanski, a leading Polish sociologist and educator. He defined higher education (1974, p. 7) as: ". . . a process of intentional formation of the personality according to an established personality idea . . ." He then outlined the goals of higher education as follows (1974, pp. 10–11):

> First is the education of the desired personality type required by the relations of production—to use the Marxian terminology—or, in other words, the type of personality required by the structure of the economy and this type of socialized society.
>
> Next, the most important goal is the vocational and professional education of graduates required by the present state for the expected future development of the economy. . . .
>
> The third goal is preparation for participation in social and cultural life—the development of the cultural values to keep up the cultural identity of the nation. . . .
>
> The final goal is to assure the optimal development of human individuality, to provide the individual with the chance for self-orientation and self-education. This goal is to prepare him fully to function in all contexts of social life, not only in the economic sphere. This is, I might say, an echo of the Humboldtian idea of the fully developed creative personality.

Szczepanski added (1974, pp. 18–19):

> Within every institution of higher education the party organization has to watch that the political line is being respected . . . One of the most important problems is the harmonization of the state and governmental goals and societal goals with the personal goals of the families who send their children to an institution of higher education, and students who want to achieve personal life goals. The traditional images of the role and function of higher education still influence the expectations of students and their families. But the traditional images are irrelevant to contemporary reality.

Each nation must find its place on the continuum between the individualistic and the collectivistic extremes of educational philosophy. American opinion has leaned toward the individualistic view and the concepts of education and democracy have been linked closely, for example, by Thomas Jefferson, Horace Mann, and John Dewey. Education has been regarded as a means of preparing individuals capable of choosing sound goals for society and effective in achieving these goals through the democratic process. Jefferson expressed this idea in his *Notes on the State of Virginia*, recommending a basic law for universal education (1955, p. 148):

> But of all the views of this law none is more important, none more legitimate, than that of rendering the people the safe, as they are the ultimate, guardians of their own liberty. For this purpose the reading in the first stage, where *they* will receive their whole education, is proposed, as has been said, to be chiefly historical. History by apprising them of the past will enable them to judge of the future; it will avail them of the experience of other times and other nations; it will qualify them as judges of the actions and designs of men; it will enable them to know ambition under every disguise it may assume; and knowing it, to defeat its views. In every government on earth is some trace of human weakness, some germ of corruption and degeneracy, which cunning will discover, and wickedness insensibly open, cultivate, and improve. Every government degenerates when trusted to the rulers of the people alone. The people themselves therefore are its only safe depositories. And to render even them safe

> their minds must be improved to a certain degree. This indeed is not all that is necessary, though it be essentially necessary. An amendment of our constitution must here come in aid of the public education.

American thought and practice, however, have never wholly rejected the idea that education should serve national goals. A striking illustration of this idea is found in the title of the first important federal legislation on education after World War II. The National Defense Education Act. Moreover, the American literature on goals is replete with references to the social objectives of earlier education. The contemporary American position is that priorities for education, research, and public service may properly be influenced by broad social goals but not at the cost of unduly warping the personal development of individuals as whole and autonomous persons or of preventing intellectual freedom in the preservation and advancement of knowledge. Americans have traditionally leaned toward the individualistic position and have looked upon the collectivistic position with some suspicion as threatening to basic democratic principles.

Social change vs. social stability

A related issue concerns the seemingly inconsistent functions of higher education as, simultaneously an agent of social change and an agent of social stability goal. A widely acknowledged goal of higher education is to equip students to view their own society with some detachment, to compare it with other societies, to discover discrepancies between its aspirations and its realities, to gain perspective on its social problems and shortcomings, and to acquire the will as well as the political and technical skills needed to work for change. Similarly, a widely accepted goal of research and related intellectual and artistic activities is to induce change through exploring new values and discovering new technologies. Indeed, it is frequently argued that the college or university itself, as a community of learners and researchers, should serve society in the capacity of social critic—as a center from which ideas basic to social change would radiate. The obverse of this theory is that higher education should equip students to understand and appreciate the cultural heritage, to value social continuity, to discover what is right in society as well as what is wrong, to distinguish between the possible and impossible in social reform, and to work toward the preservation of that which is worth preserving. The dual roles of higher education as agent of change and agent of stability, though seemingly incompatible, may not be in conflict. The true goal may be men and women with free minds who can form balanced judgments about change and stability and who can work toward orderly and progressive social development, drawing on both old and new (see Ottoway, 1962; Clark and others, 1972; Ladd and Lipset, 1975).

Conclusions

Regardless of one's views on individualism versus collectivism or on change versus stability as outcomes of higher education, one cannot reasonably avoid the conclusion that higher education has consequences for society. The immediate outcomes of higher education consist primarily of changes in people and changes in ideas. These changes may be in conservative or radical directions, but in either case they inevitably influence the character of social organization, social institutions, and broad social values and attitudes. When millions of college-educated people are inducted into a society, they are bound to affect that society. Similarly, when the ideas derived from the intellectual-artistic pursuits of the academy make their way into a society, these ideas are bound to influence the course of social development. Higher education thus sets in motion a dynamic process leading to changes in society, which in turn will lead to further changes in both individuals and society. This process may extend far into the future and bring about consequences of the most far-reaching import. Though it would be difficult to trace these long-run dynamic influences, it is hard to believe they do not exist (Organization for Economic Cooperation and Development, 1973a, pp. 21, 91–102).

Negative Outcomes

Educators direct their efforts toward outcomes they believe to be beneficial. Despite good intentions, however, actual outcomes may be harmful or may be judged harmful by some

observers. Because it is a potent force, higher education may open up possibilities for bad as well as good outcomes. If it were otherwise and the results always good, higher education would be so unlike real life as to have no practical utility.

In its effect on students, higher education may produce some liars, clients, and con men; it may foster tendencies toward exploitation of other people; it may enhance the capacity of people to employ intellectual jargon for purposes of rationalization and deceit; it may foster indolence in some people; it may cause contempt for the Puritan virtues of thrift and hard work; it may deaden rather than quicken the love of learning; it may offer a shelter that retards maturation; it may produce unfortunate personality traits such as arrogance or superciliousness; it may encourage drug abuse and excessive use of tobacco and alcohol; it may demoralize students who fail or who achieve low social or academic ranking. By enlarging the opportunity and raising the social status of those who are college-educated, college education may correspondingly restrict the opportunity and social status of the less-educated (Solmon and Taubman, 1973).

Some of the results of higher education may be controversial to the extent that some people regard them favorably and others view them adversely. As Hodgkinson (1972, p. 39), speaking to a group of state legislators and other officials, remarked, "Your constituents may not like it if, as a consequence of this greater significance [of higher education] students become aware of the wide range of ways of life, or governmental and economic structures, and more aware and critical of how our society is using its human and natural resources. Is it a benefit to society if the young are exposed to material that will make some of them more critical of that society?"

Higher education may produce religious dissent, political liberalism, or radicalism; conversely, it may harden conservative views. It may lead to espousal of exotic or fundamentalist religion. It may bring about alienation from families. It may widen the generation gap. It may produce pacifist attitudes and thus weaken national military power. It may encourage qualities of independence and autonomy when what is wanted in some jobs is conformity, dependence, and loyalty (Trent and

Medsker, 1968). Further, the direct satisfactions and enjoyments from higher education may be offset wholly or in part by boredom or academic pressure, and some of the most creative students may find regimentation intolerable and drop out (Parnes, 1971). Similarly, in its research and scholarly activities, higher education may discover new forms of nerve gas; it may develop philosophies alien to traditional politics or religion; it may discover psychological techniques for manipulating people (Heard, 1974).

Many controversial outcomes are beset with semantic confusion. For example, if an outcome of higher education is described as helping to induct students into cosmopolitan culture and to emancipate them from provincialism, the result may be considered beneficial; if the same result is described as alienating young people from their families and from the traditions of local communities or ethnic groups, it may be considered harmful. Moreover, some outcomes are viewed differently at times according to the social context. For example, in a time of peace and pacifistic sentiments, the discovery of a new biological weapon may be viewed widely as an outrage; in the midst of a desperate war, the same outcome could be regarded as a justifiable expedient.

Because of such differences of opinion, determination of the operative goals of higher education becomes a major social issue. In the American experience, the goals of higher education have been shaped partly within higher education through the influence of faculties and administrators and partly through external societal influences exerted by governing boards, legislators, donors, students, parents, and others. Though external social control has been ever-present, internal institutional influence on goals has been real in both the public and private sectors. Evolving within a framework of decentralized authority, the goals have been strongly influenced by professional considerations as well as by social dictate. Potential conflict over goals is softened by a dual recognition by many leading members of the public, who believe that it is in the long-run social interest for the academy to maintain substantial control over its own destiny, and by many members of the academy, who believe that their institutions are ultimately responsible to serve society (see Peterson, 1975). Thus,

when we speak of the goals of American higher education, we refer to goals that have evolved through professional discussion and professional practice as tempered by outside influences. The degree of consensus about goals is perhaps greater among the professionals than among members of the general public. Nevertheless, differences of judgment and opinion are real and higher education undoubtedly produces some outcomes that are looked upon by many with askance.

Obviously, differences of opinion about goals complicates the matter of accountability. A report by the Organization for Economic Cooperation and Development (OECD), *Indicators of Performance of Educational Systems* (1973a, p. 31), refers to the multitude of goals for education and the inherent difficulty of translating them into some aggregate criterion of the overall performance of an educational system: "With regard to the multidimensional nature of the goals for the educational system, the weights will be determined by the political decision-making process. There is therefore no such thing as the *productivity* of a specific educational system as long as the idea that education is a multigoal activity is accepted. Different people will give different weights to the different sub-goals, and for a given set of inputs there might be as many productivity measures as there are people." The uncertainties and differences of opinion about goals and outcomes foster that diversity in the higher educational system that it needs serve its varied clienteles, protect it from the colossal errors of monolithic systems that can operate by rigid formulae, and promote a healthy spirit of experimentation and innovation.

A Catalogue of Goals

The goals of higher education are hypotheses about desirable outcomes that can be achieved—or at least approximated—in practice. A useful taxonomy for the study of outcomes, therefore, is a catalogue of widely accepted goals. The catalogue presented in this section forms the outline for all that follows. In subsequent chapters, we try to discover whether and to what extent each goal is actually achieved. The items in the catalogue are meant to be the ingredients of a well-ordered educational system. Taken together, they constitute the model that many educators adopt when setting educational policy, and they provide the criteria by which educators and others ideally try to judge the performance of higher education.

We compiled the catalogue by combing through an extensive literature that includes the writings of noted educational and critics of the past and present, reports of public commissions and faculty committees, and statements of leading educators in speeches, articles, and institutional reports. In going over this literature, we assembled and classified more than 1,500 goal statements from widely varied sources, historical and contemporary. (The sources that were of particular value are marked with an asterisk in the references at the end this book.)

We reviewed a large sampling of the literature to identify goals that important authorities had frequently mentioned. The selection process was simplified by the remarkable agreement among the authorities. It was not, however, a mere polling of the authorities. In the end, the authors' judgment influenced the final selection.

Each of the goals is, to a degree, considered an important responsibility of higher education. But this does not mean that every institution pursues every one of the goals or gives the same emphasis to all of them. There is room for variety among institutions in their goal patterns.

Not all the goals are achieved in practice, and some of them may not even be achievable. Still others may function as ideals—ever to be approached but never to be achieved fully. The catalogue has a utopian quality about it: It appears as a compendium of all possible human virtues and hopes. Higher education has limitations, and educators should not claim so much as to lose credibility. Many are shared goals pursued jointly with the family, the school, the church, the media, governmental agencies, and the workplace (Spaeth and Greeley, 1970). In recent decades, with the weakening of some of these other institutions, more of the load has been shifted to education. The result may be an overloading of the entire educational system, including higher education. In any event, there is need for educators to sort out priorities among the goals, to recognize that there are trade-offs among them, and

to be realistic about what can and cannot be achieved with the resources that are likely to be available. Since each goal in the catalogue is widely accepted as a desirable objective, however, it is hard to avoid the conclusion that the purpose of higher education is to seek all of them to the degree that time, resources, and human improvability permit.

The goals of higher education are concerned with the development of the full potentialities of human beings and of society. The goals correspond closely to the goals of human life. As Alexander Heard (1973, p. 16) has remarked: "Our largest common goal in higher education, indeed in all education, is to create and stimulate the kind of learning that breeds strength and humor and hope within a person, and that helps build a society outside him that stirs his pride and commands his affection." The catalogue of goals for higher education follows.

I. Goals for Individual Students

A. Cognitive Learning

1. *Verbal skills.* Ability to comprehend through reading and listening. Ability to speak and write clearly, correctly, and gracefully. Effectiveness in the organization and presentation of ideas in writing and in discussion. Possibly some acquaintance with a second language.

2. *Quantitative skills.* Ability to understand elementary concepts of mathematics and to handle simple statistical data and statistical reasoning. Possibly some understanding of the rudiments of accounting and the uses of computers.

3. *Substantive knowledge.* Acquaintance with the cultural heritage of the West and some knowledge of other traditions. Awareness of the contemporary world of philosophy, natural science, art, literature, social change, and social issues. Command of vocabulary, facts, and principles in one or more selected fields of knowledge.

4. *Rationality.* Ability and disposition to think logically on the basis of useful assumptions. Capacity to see facts and events objectively—distinguishing the normative, ideological, and emotive from the positive and factual. Disposition to weigh evidence, evaluate facts and ideas critically, and to think independently. Ability to analyze and synthesize.

5. *Intellectual tolerance.* Freedom of the mind. Openness to new ideas. Willingness to question orthodoxy. Intellectual curiosity. Ability to deal with complexity and ambiguity. Appreciation of intellectual and cultural diversity. Historical perspective and cosmopolitan outlook.[2] Understanding of the limitations of knowledge and thought.

6. *Esthetic sensibility.*[3] Knowledge of, interest in, and responsiveness to literature, the fine arts, and natural beauty.

7. *Creativeness.* Imagination and originality in formulating new hypotheses and ideas and in producing new works of art.

8. *Intellectual integrity.* Understanding of the idea of "truth" and of its contingent nature. Disposition to seek and speak the truth. Conscientiousness of inquiry and accuracy in reporting results.

9. *Wisdom.* Balanced perspective, judgment, and prudence.

10. *Lifelong learning.* Love of learning. Sustained intellectual interests. Learning how to learn.

B. Emotional and Moral Development

1. *Personal self-discovery.* Knowledge of one's own talents, interests, values, aspirations, and weaknesses. Discovery of unique personal identity.

2. *Psychological well-being.* Progress toward the ability to "understand and confront with integrity the nature of the human condition" (Perry, 1970, p. 201). Sensitivity to deeper feelings and emotions combined with emotional stability. Ability to express emotions constructively. Appropriate self-assertiveness, sense of security, self-confidence, self-reliance, decisiveness, spontaneity. Acceptance of self and others.

3. *Human understanding.* Humane outlook. Capacity for empathy, thoughtfulness, compassion, respect, tolerance, and cooperation toward others, including persons of different backgrounds. Democratic and nonauthoritarian disposition. Skill in communication with others.

4. *Values and morals.* A valid and internalized but not dogmatic set of values and moral principles. Moral sensitivity and courage. Sense of social consciousness and social responsibility.

5. *Religious interest.* Serious and thoughtful exploration of purpose, value, and meaning.

6. *Refinement of taste, conduct, and manner.*

C. Practical Competence

1. *Traits of value in practical affairs generally.* Virtually all of the goals included under cognitive learning and emotional and moral development apply to practical affairs. In addition, the following traits, which are more specifically related to achievement in practical affairs, may be mentioned:

   a. *Need for achievement.* Motivation toward accomplishment. Initiative, energy, drive, persistence, self-discipline.

   b. *Future orientation.* Ability to plan ahead and to be prudent in risk-taking. A realistic outlook toward the future.

   c. *Adaptability.* Tolerance of new ideas or practices. Willingness to accept change. Versatility and resourcefulness in coping with problems and crises. Capacity to learn from experience. Willingness to negotiate, compromise, and keep options open.

   d. *Leadership.* Capacity to win the confidence of others, willingness to assume responsibility, organizational ability, decisiveness, disposition to take counsel.

2. *Citizenship.* Understanding of and commitment to democracy. Knowledge of governmental institutions and procedures. Awareness of major social issues. Ability to evaluate propaganda and political argumentation. Disposition and ability to participate actively in civic, political, economic, professional, educational, and other voluntary organizations. Orientation toward international understanding and world community. Ability to deal with bureaucracies. Disposition toward law observance.

3. *Economic productivity.* Knowledge and skills needed for first job and for growth in productivity through experience and on-the-job training. Adaptability and mobility. Sound career decisions. Capacity to bring humanistic values to the workplace and to derive meaning from work.

4. *Sound family life.* Personal qualities making for stable families. Knowledge and skill relating to child development.

5. *Consumer efficiency.* Sound choice of values relating to style of life. Skill in stretching consumer dollars. Ability to cope with taxes, credit, insurance, investments, legal issues, and so on. Ability to recognize deceptive sales practices and to withstand high-pressure sales tactics.

6. *Fruitful leisure.* Wisdom in allocation of time among work, leisure, and other pursuits. Development of tastes and skills in literature, the arts, nature, sports, hobbies, and community participation. Lifelong education, formal and informal, as a productive use of leisure. Resourcefulness in overcoming boredom, finding renewal, and discovering satisfying and rewarding uses of leisure time.

7. *Health.* Understanding of the basic principles for cultivating physical and mental health. Knowledge of how and when to use the professional health care system.

D. Direct Satisfactions and Enjoyments from College Education

1. During the college years.
2. In later life.

E. Avoidance of Negative Outcomes for Individual Students

II. Goals for Society

(Note: These goals may be achieved through education, through research and related activities, or through public services.)

A. Advancement of Knowledge

1. Preservation and dissemination of the cultural heritage.
2. Discovery and dissemination of new knowledge and advancement of philosophical and religious thought, literature, and the fine arts—all regarded as valuable in their own right without reference to ulterior ends.
3. Direct satisfactions and enjoyments received by the population from living in a world of advancing knowledge, technology, ideas, and arts.

B. Discovery and Encouragement of Talent

C. Advancement of Social Welfare

1. Economic efficiency and growth.
2. Enhancement of national prestige and power.
3. Process toward the identification and solution of social problems.
4. "Improvement" in the motives, values, aspirations, attitudes, and behavior of members of the general population.
5. Over long periods of time, exerting a significant and favorable influence on the course of history as reflected in the evolution of the basic culture and of the fundamental social institutions. Progress in

human equality, freedom, justice, security, order, religion, health, and so on.

D. Avoidance of Negative Outcomes for Society

Notes

1. This is an adaptation of a quotation for which we are unable to provide the source. It should be noted that Marx's third thesis on Feuerbach reads, "The materialist doctrine that men are products of circumstances and upbringing, and that, therefore, changed men are products of other circumstances and changed upbringing, forgets that it is men that change circumstances and that the educator himself needs educating."

2. Appreciation of the local, provincial, and parochial is commendable. Values such as cosmopolitanism are not undesirable but perhaps they are most valuable when they occur in tension with their opposites, when the person achieves an appreciation of both the cosmopolitan and the provincial and a critical capacity to stress the merits and deficiencies of both.

3. Esthetic sensibility is often classified under affective development rather than cognitive learning. It contains elements of both.

Diversity on Campus

ARTHUR LEVINE

The decade of the 1980s was a time in which the popular press reported a rising level of racism, sexism, antisemitism, and gay bashing in higher education. Commentators said that divisions among diverse groups on campus were growing. A Carnegie Foundation report lamented the decline of campus community.

In this chapter the state of diversity on America's college and university campuses is reported, based on a study of fourteen diverse institutions of higher education. The schools vary geographically—being located in the Northeast, Middle Atlantic, South, Midwest, and West. They differ in control, including public and private institutions as well as sectarian and nonsectarian schools. They vary in size—from about fifteen hundred to over twenty thousand students. And they include four-year colleges and universities.

At each of the schools, interviews were conducted with administrators, faculty, and students. The study examined diversity in academic life—including curriculum, courses, academic organization, the faculty, and scholarships. It also considered diversity in campus life, including orientation, residence, and the co-curriculum. It looked too at the condition of academic freedom and free speech on campus. The history, climate, politics, and recent initiatives carried out in the name of diversity were matters of inquiry as well.

Over the past four decades, diversity has taken on a variety of very different meanings. The earliest conception, a product of the 1960s, is representation in or admission to college. The goal originally was to develop a minority presence on campus. With time, the definition has expanded. The notion of minorities has grown from blacks to include a variety of underrepresented populations ranging across race, religion, gender, and ethnicity. Once thought of largely in terms of students, the focus of diversity has broadened to include faculty, staff, administrators, and trustees. And the idea of presence has shifted from merely increasing the numbers of underrepresented groups to achieving numbers at least comparable to minority percentages in the population.

A second definition of diversity developed in the 1970s is support or retention. The aim is to provide the "new" populations on campus with the sustenance they need to remain in college. This has meant compensatory services, financial aid, diversity support groups and activities, special residential units, and diversity studies departments such as Afro-American and Women's Studies.

A third meaning, a product of the late 1970s and the early 1980s, is integration. The focus is on incorporating historically underrepresented groups, which have become segregated on campuses, into the larger campus population. This has involved the creation of orientation programs for new populations and less frequently for majority students about these populations, the adoption of general education diversity requirements, including scholarship and instruction about diversity within the traditional curriculum, and the addition of a variety of new activities and clubs to the co-curriculum.

"Diversity on Campus," by Arthur Levine, reprinted from *The Higher Learning in America, 1980–2000*, edited by Arthur Levine, 1993, Johns Hopkins University Press.

A fourth and final notion of diversity, emerging today, is pluralism or multiculturalism. Here the aim is to legitimize both the intellectual and the emotional aspects of diverse cultures in academic and campus life in teaching, research, and service. The goal is equity among diverse cultures and a symbiosis among them.

A majority of the schools in the study emphasized the first two definitions of diversity. However, there were schools with programs in all four categories, and recent efforts at several of the institutions focused on the third definition—integration. No institution, with the possible exception of an historically black college, had achieved any of the definitions fully.

Diversity was an issue of concern on at least eleven of the campuses. The level of interest, however, varied dramatically across the schools—from urgency and broad involvement to disinterest and apathy. There were many new initiatives, and three of the schools were in the process of carrying out large-scale projects. In general, however, rhetoric outstripped action.

The most striking feature of the study, however, was the lack of long-range, systematic planning with regard to diversity on the part of at least three-quarters of the schools. Very few were operating with clear definitions of diversity. There was a tendency to think of diversity as a problem, rather than an opportunity to shape an institution's future. The focus was generally on quick fixes.

The Campus Community

What stood out in this study was the small number of campuses, about a third, in which diversity was a priority on the institutional agenda. Three forces seemed to have the power to increase its prominence. The first was a rather rapid and substantial change in a student body, involving large increases in traditionally underrepresented populations. The second was an overt or public act of racism or sexism. Incidents involving physical attacks on minorities, cross burnings, and hate banners were provoking events on three campuses. A third factor was presidential commitment.

Actually, presidential leadership proved to be essential for any effective diversity initiative. The attributes associated with success were a clear vision, resources to support the vision, appropriate and realistic rhetoric to make the vision compelling, the secured commitment of each institutional constituency to embrace the vision, frequent and continuing publicity and communication regarding the initiative to all segments of the college community, and regular monitoring of progress. A few of the efforts on the campuses involved many of these ingredients, but none involved all. Several of the presidents were eloquent, visionary, and even passionately committed. But in no case had a president managed to secure a commitment from his or her faculty. On most campuses, students were unconvinced of presidential commitment as well. In point of fact, on only two of the campuses did the president assume a leadership role in diversity.

The Students

Students were almost universally the driving force behind diversity on the campuses studied. They prodded their colleges to do more and more.

Many of the campuses studied were tense. The minority students interviewed often expressed a feeling of being uncomfortable and feeling illegitimate in traditionally majority institutions. One young black woman said that she felt "like an unwelcome guest on campus" rather than a member of the community.

The topic of diversity evoked a variety of feelings from whites. Students expressed feelings varying from apathy, anger, and fear to calls for action, approbation regarding current conditions, and helplessness. One of the most poignant conversations was with a diverse group of students who could not figure out how to talk to one another; their differences seemed insurmountable, and no one knew how to get past them. There is a lot of anger on many of the campuses studied—some open, much submerged.

In fact, students tended systematically to underestimate the degree of involvement among diverse groups on campus. When black students were asked how many whites had attended a lecture by a renowned black scholar or whites were asked how many blacks had attended a dance, their estimates were always far lower than reality.

Most of the campuses studied were deeply divided perceptually, if not in fact. It is fair to say that their differences appear larger among students, especially members of diversity groups, than do their commonalities. There are centrifugal pressures both within diversity groups and between groups.

Students perceive on campus no culture or commonality broad enough to bring them together. The academic culture that provides a set of shared beliefs and values for faculty is weak and provides little if any cohesion for students. The only institutions at which this pattern did not hold were Catholic schools. The culture of Catholicism was powerful enough to provide at least a vision of shared campus culture.

Students tended to view themselves in smaller and smaller categories. A social mitosis of sorts was occurring on many of the campuses as student groups broke into increasingly smaller subunits. For example, on one campus the gay student society broke by gender into gay and lesbian clubs. And the lesbian group divided by race into white lesbians and lesbians of color. There was talk of dividing further by major. Because of limited resources at several of the schools, each of these subgroups is being pitted against the others in the search for scarce dollars for activities, scarce physical plant for facilities, and scarce time in the curriculum for classes. At these schools, campus life is becoming a Hobbesian world in miniature—a war of each against all.

There is also a growing sense among students of being victims. The language of victimization was heard again and again among majority and minority students, men and women, Christians and non-Christians, every race and ethnic group. The feeling of being "the other"—left out and discriminated against—is powerful.

The Administration

The diversity issue is frightening for the administrators interviewed. It is a tangled and daunting problem with uncertain contours and broad and explosive potential. Administrators fear what would happen if diversity were dealt with directly, what would occur if the genie were allowed out of the bottle. When talked with confidentially and asked candidly what

they would like to see happen with the issue, most senior administrators use the same language. They say they would like it to go away. Diversity tends to be treated by administrators as a series of discrete problems, each arising in isolation. The focus is on quick fixes and Band-Aid approaches.

In general, the administration has delegated the issue of diversity to student affairs. The student affairs people deserve a round of applause for their efforts. No group on campus is doing more to turn the rhetoric of diversity into reality. They have hired staffs that include larger numbers of underrepresented populations than the rest of their campuses, developed staff training programs on diversity issues, established new residence options, added counseling services targeted at underrepresented groups, and created an array of cultural activities for the entire campus community. If student affairs had not filled the void, there is no evidence that any other group on campus would have.

But this is also an area facing huge challenges. Student affairs has an impossible assignment. What makes this task all the more difficult is that student affairs is isolated from much of the rest of the campus community. There is a gulf between student affairs and the faculty, who do not understand the work of student affairs and hold it in low esteem. There is also a gap between student affairs and other senior administrators. As a result, student affairs is being asked to address both the intellectual and the developmental aspects of diversity without the resources and legitimacy to do so.

The Faculty

No group on campus is less involved in the diversity agenda than the professorate. Few teach about or engage in scholarship about diversity. Few seem concerned about diversity. Almost none is engaged in co-curricular activities dealing with diversity.

This is not true of all faculty. There are marvelous examples of engaged professors on almost every campus studied, of faculty, even senior faculty, who are offering classes on diversity issues, integrating new scholarship into their courses, serving key roles on committees, acting as advocates, carrying out research, or working on innovative and exciting ideas for diversity. And on one campus a full fifth of the faculty were regularly attending diversity colloquia. However, it would be accurate to say that the few faculty involved are more likely to be minorities and junior staffers than senior faculty and campus leaders.

There are many reasons for this state of affairs. One is indifference and lack of knowledge about diversity. With this in mind, two of the campuses studied offered voluntary workshops for faculty to enhance their understanding of diversity, with very positive results.

Another rationale is an absence of urgency or pressure. At the moment, the push and pull of this issue is largely between students and administrators. Faculties, because of their atomistic nature, are far more difficult to engage. It is easier for them to opt out. One cynical commentator on a campus studied said that it is almost as if there were an unspoken agreement between administrators and faculty for the faculty to ignore the issue.

Still another cause is the lack of minority faculty on campuses. No institution studied, with the exceptions of a black college and an institution historically committed to diversity, had a faculty even remotely matching the minority population of its region or the nation. And, although several of the institutions were making efforts to gain ground quickly in minority hiring, the result is that nearly all colleges now lack the critical mass of underrepresented peoples to make diversity visible to colleagues, to reduce the level of complacency, to encourage discourse, to provide models for students, and to serve as a catalyst for action. The powerful effect of minority faculty on curriculum diversity could be observed just by walking through any of the campus bookstores.

A fourth consideration is fear. One white faculty member, a historian, said he wanted to teach African-American history, which was not being offered, but he was afraid. Would minority students accept him? Did he have the expertise? Would colleagues, who view ethnic studies as second-class fields, lose respect for him? Would it hurt his chances for promotion? In the end, he found more reasons not to teach the class than to offer it.

One more reality is the lack of incentives for embracing diversity. Programs on the campuses studied offer funds for providing scholarships, developing new courses, remodeling existing courses, encouraging faculty to participate in co-curricular activities, and coaxing departments to hire minorities. Two institutions used mild sticks. On one campus, the chief academic officer asked each department to study the barriers to minorities in its field, discussed the results with the departments individually, and is monitoring progress. On another campus, the departments that did not participate in institutional minority activities were asked to explain why, in person, to the provost. Such efforts are not uncommon but, put simply, the fact is that today there are no systematic incentives for faculty and departments to engage in the diversity agenda.

Programming

The Curriculum

The curriculum at the schools studied remains largely unaffected by concern with diversity. At college after college the programs were described as "Eurocentric." The changes that have occurred in the name of diversity have been largely at the periphery of the curriculum. Several of the institutions have introduced majors and minors in ethnic and gender studies. They have created departments and centers of minority studies. Several schools have added one- or two-semester general education diversity requirements. Two colleges recently sought to adopt such requirements and failed. A least four others are seriously contemplating such a change.

At only one institution, however, had diversity penetrated a significant portion of the course offerings, meaning that classes are being offered on diversity topics; existing courses include diversity scholarship, and reading lists are being expanded with diversity works. At other schools such changes were rare and unusual, occurring only sporadically in the curriculum. Here and there, however, departments in the traditional disciplines embraced diversity in one fashion or another. For example, at a major research university, the English department required all majors to take a course in literature by women or African-American writers, and the history department had established a specialization in African-American history. Perhaps most telling is that, when administrators and faculty were asked what changes had been made in the curriculum to respond to diversity, one of the most common answers was remedial programs.

The Co-Curriculum

Life outside the classroom is a cornucopia, varying dramatically in size from campus to campus, of diversity days, weeks, lectures, meetings, exhibits, films, concerts, workshops, teach-ins, services, theme dormitories, resource centers, counselors, clubs, publications, and meals. Historically, student activities have filled in where the curriculum was weak. That tradition continues.

This broad array of offerings is not without shortcomings. It is immediately apparent that faculty do not participate. In fact, one institution described itself as the Lord of the Flies after five o'clock—no adults anywhere. One consequence is a perceived absence of intellectual leadership. On several campuses, students dismissed the co-curriculum saying, "Sure there is a lot to do, but it isn't serious." The implications is that, if it were serious, it would be part of the curriculum.

Another problem cited on many of the campuses is that groups do not attend each other's events. Minority students regularly complained that white students did not come to their activities and that they felt uncomfortable at majority events. Majority students said they felt unwelcome at minority events. This complaint must be taken with a grain of salt given the student tendency to underestimate participation rates. To some extent, however, the co-curriculum on most campuses seemed to be not a vehicle for encouraging education or interaction among diverse peoples, but rather a mechanism for separating people comfortably according to differences.

Fraternities and sororities deserve special criticism in this regard. They were regularly cited by students and student affairs staff for their deliberate policies of segregation on the basis of individual difference. Stories of objectionable Greek behavior with regard to diversity abounded.

Orientation to college was another much discussed aspect of programming. It suffers from the range of shortcomings associated with the co-curriculum. In recent years, a focus on diversity has been added to the orientation programs at several of the schools studied. It tends to be brief, unconnected to the intellectual life of the campus, and lacking in faculty participation. Minorities were critical of their diversity sessions during orientation, saying that their focus was on "getting minorities ready to deal with the institution." The approach was characterized as one-sided for failing to teach majorities about diversity. However, exceptions to this pattern were found, including an institution with an orientation program several days in length that emphasized diversity and offered sessions for minorities, majorities, and parents, together and separately; in this school the theme of diversity was continued throughout the freshman year in residence hall programs.

Free Speech

Incidents of racism and other attacks on diversity groups were facts of life at many of the institutions we visited. The most frequent victims have been gays, people of color, women, and Jews. Stories were told of ugly public incidents that shook institutions and left long-term scars at a few schools, but far more common were graffiti, name calling, and offensive language. Dormitories were the most common place for such behavior, and classrooms were the least common. It is not clear whether this behavior was occurring more or less often. Some institutions collected numbers; others did not. Some reported increases in hate incidents; others said there were fewer.

Regardless of whether the number of incidents is up or down, campuses have grown increasingly sensitive to the issue. And this situation is encouraging a number of colleges studied, but not by any means a majority, to begin rethinking the standards for free speech which operate on campus. Since the 1960s, most of the institutions embraced the first amendment as their guiding principle. Today, however, several of the schools studied are feeling uneasy about the first amendment approach. Already one has chosen a more limited definition barring offensive talk and acts aimed at individual members of minority groups. Campus conversations lead one to believe that in the next few years debate about the relationship between free speech and diversity will escalate, a number of institutions around the country will consider or adopt standards different from the first amendment, and the courts, as they have already begun to do, will be asked to decide the ground rules.

Conclusions

Several conclusions follow from this study.

- Diversity is poorly defined on campus.
- Goals for diversity are unclear.
- Most colleges and universities lack comprehensive and systematic plans.
- In general, presidents are not providing adequate leadership.
- Students are divided, and tension around diversity is high.
- Faculty for the most part have abdicated.
- Student affairs is being asked inappropriately to assume almost full responsibility for the diversity agenda.
- Diverse populations are highly underrepresented in the student bodies of colleges and universities and on their faculties, senior staffs, and boards of trustees.
- The curriculum has largely peripheralized or neglected diversity.
- The co-curriculum, though rich in diversity programs, lacks intellectual depth, is unconnected with the academic side of higher education, and is largely ignored by the faculty.
- Standards of free speech and academic freedom are being questioned on a number of campuses.
- Academic culture has grown weak and fails to provide colleges and universities with a shared set of beliefs and values that go beyond differences that divide people.

The Future

Conditions on campus with respect to diversity are explosive today. In the 1990s, the pressure will mount.

An exacerbating factor is changing student character. Recent research by Deborah Hirsch and me shows rising optimism, a rebirth of heroes, increasing activism, and growing social involvement among college students (Levine and Hirsch 1990). In the next few years, this constellation of changes is likely to produce a revival among students of political action, more concern with relevance in the curriculum, and a greater emphasis on campus governance. Diversity is likely to be one of the early issues for activism in the 1990s. This has already begun on a number of campuses around the country.

There is no chance that the issue of diversity will go away in the 1990s as was hoped by so many of the senior administrators in the study. Demographics indicate that our campuses will only grow more diverse as the number of eighteen-year-old whites diminishes and the proportions of people of color and older adults increase during the early to mid-1990s (Levine 1989).

The principal difficulty for the academy today is that the meaning of diversity is uncertain. Its implications are unknown. And its consequences are unfathomable.

Diversity is an issue with no intellectual or emotional center in the academy. Higher education is deeply divided about its meaning, its importance, and what should be done. This is why diversity is such a frightening issue and why it is so tempting to try to ignore it or to offer palliatives.

In the 1990s, the twin pressures of student activism and growing diversity will require that the academy directly confront the issue. Thoughtful, creative, and decisive action are possible now. There is time now. However, as pressures mount during the next few years that is not likely to be the case. Colleges will be forced to react rather than act.

The agenda for colleges and universities in the next several years will be

- to open the campus to candid discourse regarding diversity that embraces the entire collegiate community,
- to demand that presidents provide leadership,
- to define clearly the meaning of diversity,

- to engage the faculty and expand the curriculum,
- to develop a comprehensive long-range plan and associated time line for meeting the diversity challenge,
- ultimately to see diversity as an opportunity, not a problem.

References

Levine, A. 1989. *Shaping Higher Education's Future.* San Francisco: Jossey-Bass.

Levine, A., and Deborah Hirsch. 1990. "After the 'Me' Generation: A Portrait of Today's College Students." Paper presented at the annual meeting of the American Educational Research Association, Boston, April.

CHAPTER 2

HIGHER EDUCATION AS A NATIONAL AND INTERNATIONAL SYSTEM

ASSOCIATE EDITOR: WILLIAM VELEZ

The tremendous growth of higher education in the United States during the last four decades has been due in part to a historical pattern of institutional diversity, not just with respect to students, but with respect to institutional type, control, size, purpose, structure, and governance. There are over 3,700 institutions of postsecondary education in the United States, 1655 are public and 2051 are private (Chronicle of Higher Education, 1997). The application of labels such as public or private can be misleading, as some research-oriented private universities receive substantial proportions of their income from the federal government as grants targeted for research and development, and many state universities operate with considerable levels of autonomy from state governments. What is unique about higher education in the United States compared to the rest of the world is the absence of a federal direct control over its affairs. Although the federal government encouraged the creation of public universities in 1862 by providing financial support through the Morrill Act, in this century public subsidies for institutional development has instead come primarily from state legislatures and local government, with the latter playing an important role in the development and expansion of the public two year sector, which includes community colleges. There are over five million students enrolled in the public two year colleges, with these types of colleges offering a virtual universal access for all students living within their geographical boundaries. While over 77% of the 14 million students enrolled in American colleges and universities are found within the public sector, the private sector plays a prominent role in higher education through the impact of several large research universities with substantial endowments and the continued presence of liberal arts colleges.

Aldersley's "Upward Drift is Alive and Well" offers an analysis for the institutional tendency to augment the number of higher-level programs, with a consequent increase in the total number of research and doctoral universities. These are universities which according to the Carnegie Foundation's classification not only offer a full range of baccalaureate programs, but are committed to graduate education through the doctorate, and give high priority to research. The difference between research and doctoral institutions is that those in the first group receive at least $15.5 million or more in federal support and award 50 or more doctoral degrees each year. The increasing importance of research universities is highlighted by the fact that although they make up only 3 percent of all institutions of higher education, they confer 32 percent of all BA degrees. Aldersley suggests upward drift is caused by the desire of ambitious institutions to gain the higher prestige associated with doctorate-level education.

Gilbert's essay, "The Liberal Arts College—Is It Really an Endangered Species?" focuses first on the decline of the liberal arts degree and then on the apparent decline of the liberal arts college

Professor William Velez teaches in the Department of Sociology at the University of Wisconsin-Milwaukee. (velez@csd.uwm.edu)

as reflected in the lower percentage of liberal arts degrees awarded and the decreasing number of institutions that can truly be classified as liberal arts colleges. The Carnegie Foundation's definition of a liberal arts college notes that these are primarily undergraduate colleges with major emphasis on baccalaureate degree programs and that award 40 percent or more of their baccalaureate degrees in liberal arts fields. By making a distinction between Liberal Arts Colleges I, which are very selective, and Liberal Arts Colleges II, many of which do not stand a historical test for classification as liberal arts colleges, Gilbert rejects the notion this type of institution is in the midst of a serious decline. A more recent increase in the number of degrees awarded in Liberal Arts amongst comprehensive universities and colleges and research universities suggests the continued interest in this type of education within higher education.

The last selection by Geiger connects institutional forms and core values in higher education. Geiger argues that although the core value of the university is cognitive rationality (knowing through reason) it also has to incorporate or reconcile its mission with other kinds of knowledge. The uniquely American land grant college establishes the conditions for an equal treatment of the disciplines of engineering and agriculture in the university curriculum. As a result, applied fields such as engineering have flourished alongside the humanities and sciences, in marked contrast to many European countries. However, Geiger warns that universities can never move too far in the direction of an extreme articulation with the workplace, as they would erode their true mission, which is to nurture an intellectual community committed to advancing knowledge in its most basic forms.

As other chapters in this volume suggest, the diversity of American higher education has allowed it to adapt itself to changing conditions in the student marketplace and to new societal needs. New institutional forms such as the research university and the community college are relatively recent examples of this capacity to respond to sometimes conflicting demands from the external environment. With the increasing concentration of the nation's population in metropolitan areas, many universities located in urban areas have begun to redefine their mission under the rubric "metropolitan universities" (Hathaway, Mulholland, and White, 1995). These institutions are characterized by a high enrollment of commuter and minority students, and also by a commitment to establish symbiotic relationships with their metropolitan areas. They offer a wide range of graduate and professional programs but rather than pursue an exclusive attention to attaining eminence as a first rate research university, these institutions commit themselves to respond to the needs of their region through a multidimensional and mutually reinforcing combination of instruction, applied research, and professional outreach. The recently created organization known as the Coalition of Urban and Metropolitan Universities, and the publication of the periodical *Metropolitan Universities Journal: An International Forum* attest to the viability of this new higher education model.

The extensive diversity of higher education in the United States presents a challenge to those who try to construct a typology or classification system to describe it. Widely used classifications such as the one developed by the Carnegie Foundation for the Advancement of Science, with its emphasis on academic mission, simply cannot capture the varied institutional forms hidden from view when one lumps 125 universities as research universities, for example. Pressure from the external environment, whether it is from government or corporate sectors, and continued adjustment to demands from core constituencies will fuel further change on the institutional fabric of the higher education system.

Suggested Supplementary Readings

Fleming, J. *Blacks in College*. San Francisco: Jossey Bass, 1984.

Allen, W., "Black Colleges vs. White Colleges," *Change*, 1987, 19, 3, 28.

Carnegie Foundation for the Advancement of Teaching. *Tribal Colleges*. Princeton, N.J.: Princeton University Press, 1990.

Hathaway. Charles E., Paige E. Mulholland, and Karen A. White, "Metropolitan Universities: Models for the Twenty-First Century," in D. M. Johnson and D. A. Bell (eds.), *Metropolitan Universities: An Emerging Model in American Higher Education*. Denton, TX: University of North Texas Press, 1995, 5–16.

Johnson, David M., and David A. Bell. *Metropolitan Universities: An Emerging Model in American Higher Education*. Denton: TX: University of North Texas Press, 1995.

The Institutional Fabric of the Higher Education System

Roger L. Geiger

Introduction

Higher education is everywhere carried out in formal institutions. The national systems of higher education that were described in the first part of this *Encyclopedia* consist of groupings of different types of institutions, but similar names may conceal quite different realities from one country to another. If the different institutional types are regarded as the warp of the institutional fabric of higher education, then the various functions embedded in those structures can be taken as the woof. This section will examine the constituent elements that comprise the multifarious patterns of individual national systems.

Institutional forms do not in and of themselves determine the processes or outcomes of higher education. Rather, different systems accomplish similar purposes through a variety of institutional means. Institutions nevertheless represent an important and influential dimension. Formal institutions are the means by which governments or organized groups seek to accomplish social purposes; they constitute tangible arrangements for organizing, directing, and financing such purposes. For the people who utilize these institutions, they form part of a matrix of social behavior; for the individuals who inhabit them they become the locus for habits, loyalties, and commitments. For all of these reasons, the institutional fabric of higher education is comparatively rigid. Institutions of higher education yield grudgingly to change, whether instigated from within or imposed from without. Individuals at any given juncture confront a relatively fixed array of institutions, which by their very natures exert powerful effects upon their lives.

Systems and their institutional fabrics nevertheless evolve over time. Indeed, temporal change provides a third dimension that cannot be ignored. Patterns defined by the warp and the woof of the institutional fabric tend to develop without losing their distinctive signatures. Many of the articles that follow convey this inherent dynamism by describing the historical antecedents of their topics. This overview too will endeavor to describe how evolving institutional forms have been related not just to one another, but also to changes in the patterns of the institutional fabric.

Perceiving and interpreting such relationships require some kind of key—a common element discernible in each pattern. That key is the university. Although the university is a Western form of organization, which historically paralleled similar but different traditions in Moslem, Hindu, and Chinese civilizations, it was implanted or imitated throughout the world due to the related forces of European expansion and modern science. Although the term has been borrowed somewhat cheaply on occasion, all national systems contain institutions that in some part of their fundamental nature constitute universities (see *Universities: Since 1900*). Beyond this limited commonality universities can differ widely.

Universities may be regarded as the key to two forms of fundamental differentiation that have shaped systems of higher education. The first is cognitive, and relates to the university's relation to different fields of knowledge (Clark 1983 pp. 53–62). The extent to which different

"The Institutional Fabric of the Higher Education System—Introduction," by Roger L. Geiger, reprinted from *The Encyclopedia of Higher Education*, Vol. 2, edited by Burton R. Clark and Guy R. Neave, 1992, Pergamon U.S.

kinds of knowledge are included in or excluded from universities defines one class of them in the patterns of the institutional fabric. The second form of differentiation concerns instructional tasks—not just the content of instruction, but where students come from in terms of social and educational backgrounds, and where they are destined to fit into the occupational structure. The division of work between universities and other institutions of higher education is an issue that has been forced by the enormous expansion of higher education in the last half of the twentieth century. It has superimposed a different set of motifs on the institutional fabric. This overview offers one way of seeing and sorting the many and variable institutional patterns of national systems of higher education.

1. The Historical Primacy of Universities

Universities are one of the enduring legacies of the medieval world. Although they were by no means the only educational forms of that era, they have persisted by acquiring charters, endowments, and permanent buildings. Clark Kerr has noted how remarkable their achievement was: some 85 Western institutions only can claim a continuous existence since 1520, and 70 of them are universities (Kerr 1982 p. 152). Medieval universities shared a basic institutional form, but were otherwise the results of quite different traditions (see *Universities: 1100–1500*). The university that crystallized in Paris in the late twelfth century was dedicated to approaches to theology and philosophy largely inspired by the Aristotelian tradition. It taught both young students, whom it educated to the level of masters, and students who continued beyond that degree to advanced learning. The University of Bologna, emerging in the thirteenth century, taught law to more mature students. At Salerno, a similar institution that could charitably be called a university was devoted to medicine.

Somewhat anachronistically, the functions of the medieval universities can be likened to professional education, general education, and the pursuit of advanced knowledge. Law was the most clearly drawn profession, and here the study of civil or canon law was closely linked to careers. Medicine was far less orga-

nized, and was still largely taught through apprenticeship. Theology under the dominion of the universal Church was more akin to an intellectual discipline than a profession per se. For aspiring masters, university study in the liberal arts, philosophy, or theology provided a thorough grounding in classical languages as well as an acquaintance with the cultures those writings mirrored (see *Liberal Arts College*). This was the general education of the day. In addition, university students were socialized to associate with the higher orders of medieval society. For the teachers and advanced students of medieval universities, finally, the possibility existed to explore the limits of what was known. They did not presume to increase the stock of knowledge, but they did face a challenging intellectual task in surveying and interpreting the Graeco-Roman heritage and Christian tradition. These three fundamental tasks, inchoate though they were, would define the possibilities for higher education until the nineteenth century.

In the centuries between the Middle Ages and the current era, universities acquired greater definition and many of their characteristic national patterns. Definition came first from their primary responsibility—"the certification of knowledge through the power to award degrees" (see *Universities: 1500–1900*). This power was conferred or withheld by the developing sovereign states. Henceforth, the universities would conform in large measure to the institutional structures of those respective polities. The second defining condition was the elaboration of separate grammar schools, and eventually secondary education. These developments restricted the formerly broad role of universities, causing them to become smaller and more specialized.

Willem Frijhoff identifies three national patterns of universities that formed in this general context (see *Universities: 1500–1900*). At Oxford and Cambridge the universities were purely examining bodies, and teaching was decentralized in resident communities of masters and students. This tutorial or collegiate university was conducive to generalist knowledge. The "professional" university, on the other hand, provided advanced teaching in specialized and highly autonomous faculties. The third model combined college and university in a small, architecturally self-contained institution. This approach, because it lent itself to hierarchy and close state control, was most consistent with the territorialism of Early Modern Europe. Although marginal at first, it adumbrated the modern university by uniting professional training and the study of science.

The notion of general education—what Frijhoff aptly describes as the relation between knowledge and society at large—proved to be surprisingly relative. It varied during the fifteenth to the eighteenth century from letters to theology to law, and even to medicine and natural science. The emphasis of the early modern university nevertheless fell primarily on preparing laymen for careers in civil society, with either the Church or the state. University enrollments boomed during the seventeenth century, for example, while state bureaucracies were expanding. Ultimately, however, it was in the interests of the state and the ruling classes to control and restrain this process. The rigidities of social class were buttressed with explicit legal constraints in order to restrict university attendance.

In the eighteenth century the specialized roles of universities and their purposely narrow constituency made them, for the most part, decadent institutions. In France they were effectively bypassed by special schools, which taught practical subjects eschewed by the faculties and which recruited their students through competitive examinations. It was the founding of a new kind of university in Germany, however, that did most to rejuvenate higher education. The University of Berlin, founded by Wilhelm von Humboldt in 1810, placed the cultivation of learning and the advancement of knowledge at the center of university purpose. Intended for the salvation of Prussia and the German nation, von Humboldt's conception of a university also opened higher education, at least in theory, to individual merit. Through the first half of the nineteenth century this Humboldtian university came to embody the "research imperative"—the commitment to advance knowledge through systematic investigation—within the universities of Prussia and the other German states. By 1900 this model had impressed itself upon much of the rest of the world (see *Universities: Since 1900*).

The German university model derived its compelling power from the institutionalization of systematic investigation. The training of relatively large numbers of advanced students gave breadth and continuity to the German academic community. The widespread adoption of the techniques of scientific research, and their extension to areas outside natural science, like history and languages, brought about a rapid and sustained advancement in all branches of academic knowledge.

As a result of the German model, what Parsons and Platt (1973) later called "cognitive rationality" emerged in the twentieth century as the *sine qua non* of a university. Analyzing the American University in the late twentieth century, they isolated basic categories of activity that the medieval university had foreshadowed more than half a millenium before. The balance, however, was certainly different in the modern university. Cognitive rationality— knowing through reason—was postulated as the core value of the university, embodied in graduate education and research. Indeed, the conventional definition of a university is an educational institution that instructs to the doctoral level. The value of cognitive rationality, in theory, should reign supreme in matters of academic knowledge; but elsewhere it must be reconciled with other kinds of knowledge (cognitive systems, in Parsonian terms). Undergraduate education was seen as providing general knowledge for educated citizenship. Within this overall context of student socialization, however, exposure to cognitive rationality served the specific purpose of cognitive upgrading—enhancing the capacity to deal with more general and theoretical types of knowledge. Although the perspective of Parsons and Platt was peculiarly American, the stress on cognitive upgrading is widely applicable for demarcating mere training from higher education. In professional education, finally, the cognitive rationality of the university must coexist with the imperatives and values of professional praxis. This duality creates an inherent tension that assumes a somewhat different form for each profession. These three Parsonian categories, although they were not intended for such use, may be used to analyze the roles assumed by universities in different national systems of higher education.

2. Inclusion and Exclusion

2.1 GRADUATE EDUCATION AND RESEARCH

The hallmarks of the nineteenth-century German university, the PhD and academic research, were assimilated first and most thoroughly by the great American universities at the end of that century (Slosson 1910, Versey 1965, Geiger 1986a), and then more widely throughout the world. It was the combination of graduate education and research that made universities into engines for the production of new knowledge. Graduate education thus has been the special province of the modern university, but it has nevertheless varied enormously in organization and character from one country to another (see *Graduate Education: Comparative Perspectives*).

In recent years the pattern of the United States has exerted a powerful influence on many other systems. The magnitude of graduate education and its highly structured nature have made it quite effective in providing systematic coverage of a body of knowledge, initiation into the methodology of research, and critical evaluation of results. Graduate education in the United States is clearly demarcated as the stage following a four-year bachelor's degree, but beyond that it has two different faces. Study for the master's degree is largely oriented toward providing limited advanced knowledge of mostly practical fields. Business and education in fact account for half of all degrees. Doctoral study there, as elsewhere, is distinguished by the eventual production of an original piece of scholarship. In such a specialized endeavor, though, it is difficult to achieve the critical mass needed for structured programs. Here the leading American graduate schools excel in being able to offer taught courses and close supervision of progress toward degrees.

Graduate education in other advanced countries lacks one or more of these elements. In the United Kingdom there is a clear demarcation between undergraduate and graduate studies, but graduate programs are small and doctoral students work individually. France has recently unified its several doctoral degrees, but there remains a bewildering variety of pathways at the intermediate advanced level. The German system contains no clear line marking the graduate level of study, a condition that encourages the prolongation of studies. Japan, despite a formal structure much like the American, provides little instruction at the doctoral level, leading students to pursue research almost entirely on their own.

This last condition, which is not unique to Japan, underlines an important point: while universities may monopolize the certification of accomplishments in research by awarding doctorates, the modern university has been less dominant with respect to the advancement of knowledge, even within the pure, academic disciplines. Its role has been greatest in systems that have conformed to the Germanic or American model, but exceptions abound. In the Soviet Union and Eastern Europe universities have emphasized advanced training, and the pursuit of new knowledge has been confided to national academies. Yakov Rabkin has described the soviet academies as a unique phenomenon: "they constitute complex hierarchical structures combining the functions of an honorific society of distinguished scientists and those of a research conglomerate" (see *Academies: Soviet Union*). These special enclaves have been able to harbor a degree of autonomy and freedom which is necessary to science but was not permitted for other institutions in either the Russian Empire or the Soviet Union. These academies also have the authority to confer the highest degrees—*kandidat* and *doktor*.

In France, where university faculties originally served chiefly as examining bodies, research has historically been institutionalized separately from the universities. The *Collège de France* has functioned as a nonteaching center of learning since the sixteenth century. In the twentieth century, the *Conseil nationale de recherche scientifique (cnrs)* has constituted a separately administered research organization, although one that overlaps with the universities through the dual appointments of CNRS directors and university professors (see *Graduate Education: Comparative Perspectives*). The dedicated research focus of German universities has not prevented the emergence of separate institutions for pure research. The *Kaiser Wilhelm Gesellschaft*, a state-supported group of research institutes in the natural sciences, was founded in 1911. Rechristened the Max Planck Society for the Advancement of Science in 1948, it currently includes almost fifty institutes in natural science, medicine, and a few in social science and humanities. More so than in France, appointments to a Max Planck Institute distance top scientists from universities and graduate education.

Edward Shils has identified another phenomenon of this sort—one that draws research outside of even research universities (see *Universities: Since 1900*). The Institute for Advanced Studies in Princeton was perhaps the first modern research institute to provide a cloistered refuge for university-based scholars and scientists. It has been followed by similar institutions, particularly in the social sciences: the Center for Advanced Studies in the Behavioral Sciences in Palo Alto, the Swedish Collegium for Advanced Study in the Social Sciences, and the *Wissenschaftskolleg* in Berlin. Such institutions seem predicated on the idea that scholars need to get away from universities, at least for a time, in order to advance knowledge effectively.

2.2 COLLEGIATE EDUCATION AND THE LIBERAL ARTS

Undergraduate, or first-degree level education has chiefly been comprised of general education in the liberal arts, student socialization, and some degree of contact with the higher learning. These elements, Pfnister points out, have been assembled in different traditions in Europe and North America (see *Liberal Arts College*).

France and Germany represent the European tradition in which a thorough general education is expected to be acquired at the secondary level. The rigorous examinations that certify the successful completion of such studies (*baccalauréat, Abitur*) in fact confer the right to enter the university. In both countries the first university degrees originally represented an advanced level of study in a specialized subject. In the early 1990s, however, the first years of university constitute fairly general studies—*Grundstudium* in Germany; *études universitaires générales* in France. These two countries differ with respect to student socialization, which in France is expected to take place at the secondary level (or in the *grandes écoles*), while German students have traditionally considered their unhurried years at the university

to be socially formative. Despite the large role allotted to secondary schooling, the cognitive upgrading of undergraduates is still an important university function, inherently linked to advanced learning (*Hauptstudium*). This connection may be most evident in university education in the United Kingdom. Although traditionally weak in graduate study, the national tradition has emphasized advanced study in an academic discipline, combined with socialization produced through residency, as the essential elements of a university degree.

Before the last decades of the nineteenth century the United States lacked true universities. Higher education was supplied largely by liberal arts colleges. They provided general knowledge and an intensive socialization, usually in a residential setting. They also offered a pretense of learning through limited study of Latin and Greek. The transformation that took place after 1870 left these colleges in place, but erected universities on the base of the strongest among them. Colleges then existed as both purely undergraduate institutions and as the undergraduate component of universities (see *Liberal Arts College*). Differences of emphasis may be wider within these two types than between them. Liberal arts colleges tend to emphasize the goals of liberal education, but many now award the majority of their degrees in professional subjects. Universities seek to instill liberal learning through a limited number of courses, after which many students finish degrees in professional colleges. Faculty for both freestanding colleges and university colleges are recruited from the same university departments, and curricula reflect the university definition of academic disciplines.

2.3 EDUCATION FOR THE PRIMARY PROFESSIONS

Although the faculties of the principal professions have been considered to be integral parts of the medieval and modern Germanic universities, education in these fields has been located both inside and outside of them. Like any practical skill, professions can be learned directly from practitioners; but they have also sought the intellectual structure and dignification that a place in the university can provide.

Philip Lewis has explicated two major patterns of institutionalization in legal education, as well as a host of intermediate possibilities (see *Legal Education*). In common-law countries, education for the legal profession was traditionally located outside of formal higher education. This education has subsequently moved almost entirely within universities. In the United States, in particular, this movement has been associated with the general movement to enhance the status of the profession. Barriers to entering the profession were gradually raised. Most freestanding law schools were forced out of existence through requirements of accreditation, while in the universities law was progressively converted to a graduate course. This last situation is clearly exceptional in the world; it gives American law schools a narrowly professional curriculum and isolates them from scholarship in other disciplines.

In civil-law countries, legal education has been an undergraduate (or first-degree) program with a fairly broad incidence. It has been the entrée to government employment as well as careers in the legal system per se. In many countries (e.g. Japan and Italy) study of the law constitutes a popular course for a general collegiate education (see *Legal Education*). In these cases the legal curriculum tends to integrate elements of academic disciplines like economics, history, and political science.

Despite the precedent of Salerno, William Rothstein confirms that medical schools, whether connected with universities or not, contributed little to the supply of physicians or to medical knowledge before the nineteenth century (see *Medical Education*). Then, it was the German universities that led the way, establishing university medical education linked with medical research through special institutes. In the United States, university medical schools preceded those of law in raising their instruction to the graduate level and in enhancing the prestige of the profession, but the processes were similar.

The distinguishing features of modern professional education in medicine have been, first, its assimilation of the spirit of university research and, second, its powerful linkages with teaching hospitals. The effects of this situation have been initially to draw medical education into universities, but more recently to distance it from them. The early twentieth-century reform of medical education in the United States, for example, led to the closure of most freestanding and proprietary schools. University medical schools then dominated the field. The huge sums devoted to support for medical research since the mid-1950s made the schools themselves increasingly resemble research institutes, however, while a comparable expansion of the university hospital complex has displaced the center of gravity in that direction. As a result, American medical education has become a separate, virtually autonomous world. Freestanding medical universities, like the University of California, San Francisco, are little different from the medical centers nominally attached to universities. In both cases, the education of physicians has become just one component of their manifold activities. American medical research has exerted great influence throughout the world, but national patterns of medical education, as Rothstein explains, remain diverse.

Theology was once regarded as the queen of the sciences in the Western intellectual tradition, and accordingly schools or faculties of theology have been an important component of universities in many Western countries. Les Goodchild's sweeping survey of advanced education for religious vocations among seven major world religions (see *Religious Vocation (Theological Seminaries)*), however, reveals great variety. In India the education of Hindu leaders has only partially been assimilated with British-style universities. In Buddhism, though, the temple-monasteries have retained control over advanced theological education. Judaism has trained aspiring rabbis largely in *yeshivas*, although these have in some cases been loosely connected with universities. Religious schools in the Muslim world (*madrasahs*) were originally founded to preserve the faith, and in some cases evolved into centers of advanced learning. This tradition stagnated, however, and such institutions have been superseded for advanced instruction by universities, which superficially bear a Western stamp.

The three principal divisions of Christianity—Roman Catholic, Orthodox, and Protestant—incorporate seminaries for educating pastors with varying relations to theological studies in universities. Theology was a central focus of medieval universities, but the Reformation prompted the Catholic Church to develop seminarian education. The Orthodox

Church has relied almost exclusively on seminaries. Where Protestantism became a state religion, faculties of theology generally prevailed; however, among minority denominations some form of seminarian education or denominational college was generally the means for training ministers.

2.4 HIGHER EDUCATION AND PRAXIS

The modern university as it emerged in Europe was closed to fields of study that dealt with the productive economy. Education for engineering, agriculture, and business thus developed under separate institutions in France and Germany, and were only slightly represented in some English universities (Locke 1984). This exclusion was rationalized by the nature of the fields: unlike the primary professions, they were not regarded as subjects that had a theoretical and scientific foundation. This fault supposedly removed them from the cognitive rationality of the university, while also precluding their students from the cognitive upgrading that university study was expected to bring. With the significant exception of France, students were recruited with less secondary schooling and received an education that carried less prestige. In the United States, however, special circumstances brought these fields into the purview of universities.

Engineering provides a paradigm for the development of practical fields in nonuniversity institutions. In Germany, where the province of the university was pure *Wissenschaft*, engineering developed its own parallel (but less prestigious) system of technical *Hochschulen*, which were highly successful in themselves. Although they developed their own traditions of research, they remained separated from university research in the sciences; and their graduates too were denied the aura that association with *Wissenschaft* conferred upon university students (Locke 1984, 1989). This dichotomy has remained a fundamental feature of German higher education, despite contemporary efforts to create institutions that would combine these two realms (Hermanns, Teichler, and Wasser 1982).

In the United Kingdom, engineering was accepted in both the ancient and the civic universities by the early twentieth century. This situation, unlike that in Germany, produced an exceedingly small group of highly educated engineers, and one that was furthermore regarded as lacking in the practical skills required in the workplace. The vast majority of those considered to be engineers in the United Kingdom were trained on the job and in technical night school courses. This disjunction is a perennial issue in engineering education, and indeed in higher education for all the practical fields: an ineluctable gap exists between theoretical knowledge, the province of universities, and the practical skills of the workplace, which are often best taught in narrow technical schools (see *Engineering Education and Institutes of Technology: United States*). This gap was clearly large in the British tradition, but perhaps even more pronounced in France.

Special schools for engineering were originally created by the French state for its own needs (see *Specialized Institutions: Grandes Ecoles*). They differed from engineering schools elsewhere by being highly selective, having a theoretical curriculum, and sending their graduates to prestigious careers, chiefly in government. Largely because of such assured careers, these elite schools became more prestigious than the French universities. This status has encouraged a certain amount of proliferation, so that the *grandes écoles* now occupy well-understood gradations of prestige. Their very success has produced some negative consequences: they largely precluded engineering from developing in universities; their unchallenged status contributed to the isolation and rigidity of some fields; and they have had comparatively little influence on practical engineering in French industry.

Specialized schools for engineers, or monotechnics, formed the pattern adopted in the Soviet Union and throughout Eastern Europe. They resemble *grandes écoles* more than other engineering schools in being highly specialized for particular industries; however they differ in their practical, as opposed to theoretical emphasis. As Valentin Pilipovski explains, these institutions also differ from universities in being vocationally focused and having little involvement with research (see *Technical Institutes: Soviet Union and Eastern Europe*). Their students receive a diploma rather than a degree. Monotechnics thus exemplify the preservation of a separate, applied tradition in engineering education.

In the United States, on the other hand, engineering was most fully assimilated into the university. There too engineering was first taught in a variety of separate institutions, but the Morrill Act of 1862 authorized land grants to the states to establish institutions where engineering and agriculture would be taught alongside arts and sciences (see *Engineering Education and Institutes of Technology: United States*). These "land-grant colleges" soon developed into some of the principal public universities, and they set a pattern for the country by teaching applied fields at the same level as traditional university subjects. Graduate education and research in engineering followed in due course. Periodic evaluations of engineering education have underscored the parallel nature of its curriculum by emphasizing the inclusion of scientific theory and recommending a grounding in the liberal arts.

The American pattern initiated by the Morrill Act is even more distinctive in agricultural education. In most other countries institutions of agricultural education were begun as separate entities (see *Agricultural Universities*). Some began as utilitarian agricultural colleges, offering short courses to farmers, and over time were elevated to postsecondary institutions. Others began as specialized universities with an emphasis placed on agricultural research. American land-grant colleges, on the other hand, brought agriculture into the academy as a component (often quite separate) of comprehensive universities. Additional federal legislation guaranteed that American agricultural schools would integrate teaching, research, and agricultural extension services. These functions are often separated in the freestanding agricultural institutions of other countries.

The development of the study of business within higher education occurred about a generation after that of engineering and in a similar fashion (see *Business Schools: Europe*). The exclusion of business studies from European universities stimulated the founding of separate schools. One of the first was the *Ecole des Hautes Etudes Commerciales* in France (founded in 1881). This school and its less august imitators developed along the lines of *grandes écoles*, even though they had no connection with the state. The results were much the same, too: a small number of managers were given a rigorous, fundamental education and were highly valued by industry, but the schools lacked a tradition of research linked with either academic theory or business praxis. As with engineering, Germany did far better in these respects. Separate "schools of economics" were established in that country (and elsewhere in Northern Europe) from the end of the nineteenth century and soon developed their own tradition of research in business economics. They also educated a relatively large number of students for management positions in German industry.

Since 1960 these earlier patterns have been overlayed by two developments that were influenced significantly by the robust business schools of the United States. In most countries business has been assimilated into the universities. In France, for example, programs in the commercial *grandes écoles* and the university form two distinct traditions. A group of international business schools has also developed, some completely independent and some nominally attached to universities. These schools have adapted with great success to a market that is difficult for universities to address—postexperience business education, either in the form of concentrated MBA programs or short courses for executives.

In the United States, much the same results were achieved through business schools within comprehensive universities. The first such unit, the Wharton School at the University of Pennsylvania (founded in 1881), was established through a gift, but once the precedent was set business schools were established within most major universities. Harvard founded its business school on the graduate level, and other leading schools now restrict themselves to that level of instruction. But business studies as an undergraduate course has been the dominant pattern at most colleges and now constitutes the most popular course of study for the bachelor's degree.

Business schools in the United States are characterized by a functionally focused curriculum and a disciplinary orientation in research (see *Business Schools: United States*). These two facets of business education have produced a persistent tension. The schools themselves tend to be quite insular within universities. Their undergraduate curriculum is shaped by praxis, and this is even more the case for master's degrees (predominantly

MBAs), which are typically earned after some working experience. In addition, requirements for students and teachers are largely determined externally by the accreditation standards of the American Assembly of Collegiate Schools of Business. Academic research nonetheless constitutes an important function: some 90 institutions grant doctorates in business, and the degree is standard for business faculty. The magnitude and vitality of academic research in business in the United States has had a major impact on the subject worldwide. The bipolarity of practical and academic knowledge thus takes an extreme form in American business schools.

The preparation of teachers represents a special case of education for practice. The historical pattern is perhaps more uniform here than in any other field: teachers who were expected to prepare students for university study in academic secondary schools were themselves usually expected to be university graduates; but those who taught at the primary level and in other, nonacademic tracks were generally trained in separate "normal" schools, which were not considered part of higher education for a long time. The upgrading of teacher education occurred at a different pace in different countries. For example, normal schools in the United States were transformed into teachers' colleges for the most part in the 1920s.

The assimilation of education as a discipline into universities has been largely accomplished in most developed countries, but this trend has not been without difficulties. Harry Judge describes how the divergent interests of teacher training, general education, and academic research have been expressed in different settings (see *Teacher Education*). The education schools of the United States have been most affected by academic drift, with a consequent neglect of teacher training. Government policy in the United Kingdom has simultaneously encouraged academic drift within universities while also attempting to stiffen standards of teacher preparation. France has kept most teacher training as a coherent program, which now follows after a university course. The separate, subject-centered preparation of the elite of secondary teachers (*agrégés*) has nevertheless escaped reform. Policy and practice for teacher education have thus reflected

the claims of practice, subject content, and academic research.

3. Growth and Differentiation

Since the Second World War the universal experience of higher education systems throughout the world has been growth. In the classic exposition of this topic, Martin Trow has shown how quantitative expansion from elite to mass higher education ineluctably produces qualitative transformations (Trow 1974). Specifically, when systems of higher education began to serve more than about 15 percent of an age cohort, changes inexorably followed in curricula, student careers, governance, and internal diversification. Such changes almost invariably affected the institutional fabric of higher education. Adaptation became imperative, but the forms that it took produced a variety of patterns. Here too, the university is the most convenient center point for gauging the kind and the degree of differentiation that occurred; but the appearance and roles of nonuniversity institutions also determined the patterns that national systems assumed.

3.1 UNDIFFERENTIATED EXPANSION OF UNIVERSITIES

Countries that combined automatic rights to enter universities for all graduates of academic secondary schools with universities centered upon the traditional professions—the Napoleonic pattern—tended to experience excessive and dysfunctional growth. The more than 100,000 students nominally attending the University of Rome represent one extreme case, but developments have been similar at the National Autonomous University of Mexico, pre-1968 Paris, or the University of Madrid. In such cases the resources available for instruction bear no relation to needs, and the majority of students will not attain the careers in the elite professions for which they are ostensibly preparing.

Two kinds of reactions tend to be provoked by this situation. First, students capable of choice frequently opt for other institutions that offer superior career potential. In France, the selective *grandes écoles* became even more attractive as a result of the massification of the universities; and in Mexico wealthier students sought conservative, private institutions that were better able to place graduates with private industry (see Private Institutions of Higher Education). Second, governments have invariably attempted to achieve better articulation with the labor market by inducing internal differentiation. In France the restructured, post-1968 university system has consistently been pressured in that direction, although progress has been grudging. There and elsewhere, at least in the short run, students long tended to resist practical programs that were inherently less prestigious than the primary professions. Almost a generation after this crisis arose in the late 1960s, student choices show signs of a more realistic acceptance of vocational programs (see *Short-Cycle Higher Education: Europe*).

The universities of Japan and the United States, both of which feature a comparatively unspecialized undergraduate curriculum, have also experienced considerable undifferentiated expansion. The dysfunctional consequences evident in Napoleonic systems have been mitigated, however, for two reasons. Both systems are selective and hierarchical in nature. This feature in itself accomplishes an initial sorting of students. Second, an important part of occupationally determinative training, particularly for the most lucrative fields, takes place after graduation, in American graduate or professional schools and in Japanese firms. Nevertheless, the pressures of graduate un- or underemployment in the 1970s affected these systems too, pushing them in the direction of greater vocationalism. To a large extent this trend has occurred within universities owing to their considerable capacity for internal differentiation.

3.2 INTERNAL DIFFERENTIATION: THE MULTIVERSITY

As depicted by Clark Kerr, the multiversity is both the epitome of internal differentiation in higher education and a peculiarly American institution (Kerr 1982). "A city of infinite variety" (p. 41), Kerr described it, consisting of multiple internal communities which interact to a limited extent with one another as well as with different communities outside of higher education. The multiversity is an entertainment agency for its alumni, a service station to

society, a research institute to the patrons of science, and a means of social ascension for the parents of its undergraduates. Most important for its character, the multiversity is a mechanistic and somewhat arbitrary combination of units and purposes. No two universities contain quite the same elements; virtually any education-related service can be appended as a separate unit, more or less removed from the academic core. Some multiversities consist of multiple campuses (see *Multicampus Universities*). In theory, all the educational functions discussed in this section of the *Encyclopedia* might be combined in a single multiversity. In actuality, a few of the largest American state universities approach that extreme.

More typically, multiversities have been somewhat selective about the commitments they undertake. The tendency has been to emphasize activities that confer prestige, like research, graduate and professional education, and instruction of well-prepared undergraduates. American multiversities have also been willing to perform those tasks that society has demanded and has been willing to pay for, however. They thus easily assimilated those praxis-linked fields that were eschewed by universities in other countries. Furthermore, multiversities have accepted tasks like extension education and research for industry that generate their own income streams. Multiversities, then, may be inherently incoherent, but they have also been highly responsive to the multiple and changeable demands of American society.

3.3 PLANNED DIFFERENTIATION

At the opposite end of the spectrum from the multiversity are found the universities of the United Kingdom and the institutions modeled on them. They have consciously intended to remain consistent with the Oxbridge ideal—relatively small and coherent, focused on high-quality undergraduate education and research. (This, despite the fact that the University of London might be regarded as an early prototype of the multiversity!) Accordingly, the United Kingdom and Australia adapted to the imperative of expansion by implementing a binary policy that protected the established universities from an influx of less well-prepared students and a proliferation of practical studies. As Susan Davies has pointed out, this was a deeply conservative approach to expansion (see *Binary Systems of Higher Education*).

The essence of the binary policy was to establish a second, less academic sector of institutions parallel to the universities. The polytechnics in the United Kingdom and the Colleges of Advanced Education (CAE) in Australia were both intended to be more accessible and more closely linked with occupations, but such an orientation implied a less prestigious role in terms of students, subjects, and functions. Both taught predominately commuting or part-time students. The majority of their students were in technical subjects, teacher education, or studies related to business. They usually offered both degree and nondegree courses, and they were not expected to undertake research. The universities, on the other hand, were able to remain highly selective and single-mindedly academic (Trow 1988). Over time, this combination has proved inherently unstable, largely due to the invidious status differential.

The polytechnics and CAEs have consistently sought to improve themselves by concentrating on activities similar to universities. They have emphasized their degree courses, instead of nondegree programs linked with employment; they have become staffed with teachers boasting university credentials, rather than practical experience; and they have included research where feasible. In 1989 the binary system in Australia was abolished by merging and consolidating all types of institution into larger entities. In 1991, Britain too abandoned the binary system. A government White Paper proposed to unify the funding of both sectors and allow polytechnics to assume the title of universities (*Higher Education* 1991). Distinctions between institutions in both systems will henceforth become more subtle rather than showing the dark contrast implied by the binary concept.

Another influential form of planned differentiation has been the California Master Plan. First elaborated in 1960, the Plan sought to protect the state government from the expansive ambitions of communities and institutions, while also providing all California youth with the opportunity for higher education. The Plan is based upon three strata of institutions. Nine campuses of the University of California recruit undergraduates from the top 12.5 percent of high school graduates and offer programs up to the level of professional and doctoral degrees. The California State University (formerly colleges) is a centrally coordinated system of 19 campuses which recruit their students from the top 33 percent of high-school graduates and offer bachelor's, master's, and professional degrees (except law and medicine). The community colleges are open to all high-school graduates and offer two-year remedial, vocational, and general education, the latter qualifying students to transfer to universities. Under the Master Plan, California has been able to offer the highest quality university education while also providing open access to all aspirants. Some of the same tensions that afflicted binary systems exist within this system, and it has been periodically adjusted; but unlike binary systems it has weathered a full, often turbulent generation and still remains a powerful model (OECD 1989).

The California State University campuses belong to a type of institution that deserves separate mention. In the United States they are classified as "Comprehensive Colleges and Universities"—largely undergraduate institutions that offer master's degrees but not doctorates (Carnegie Foundation for the Advancement of Teaching 1988). Some 45 percent of four-year college students attended such colleges, more than any other type. These institutions nevertheless lack a distinctive identity. Their undergraduate programs resemble those of liberal arts colleges and their master's degree programs are identical with those of universities. In general, the majority of their students enroll in vocationally specific subjects, like education, business, or engineering, and anticipate entering the labor force immediately upon graduation. These institutions are not merely an American phenomenon. Similar institutions in Japan and the Philippines form an important component of those systems.

3.4 UNPLANNED DIFFERENTIATION: PRIVATE HIGHER EDUCATION

Privately controlled institutions contribute disproportionately to the diversity of national systems because, as Daniel Levy has explained, they tend to be more focused in nature (see

Private Institutions of Higher Education). In modern systems of higher education the role of the state has predominated; the nature of private institutions has consequently reflected those tasks that the state would not or could not fulfill adequately. Religion has been the basis for the establishment of a large class of private institutions, although many have become quite secularized over time. Women's colleges too have usually been private foundations. Private institutions are also frequently established to offer specific kinds of professional or vocational instruction.

In secondary education it is common for the elite institutions to be private, but in higher education, which has higher costs that usually require significant subsidization, this situation is less frequent. In some developing countries private colleges and universities serve an elite constituency as a refuge from politicized and massified public universities. In the United States the wealthier private colleges and universities are able to offer high-quality education because of considerably higher per-student expenditures. At the other end of the spectrum, mass private sectors offer access where the government provision is restricted or inadequate. Most of the places thus created are in low-cost, low-quality colleges. Some private universities in such systems grow to enormous size, but most are constrained by economic factors to focus on a limited market niche. By responding to a variety of stimuli, private higher education tends to enhance diversity and adaptability; however, its benefits and drawbacks will depend ultimately on the structural features of national systems (Levy 1986, Geiger 1986b).

3.5 VERTICAL DIFFERENTIATION: SHORT-CYCLE HIGHER EDUCATION

If research and graduate education are the most international component of higher education, short-cycle institutions show the greatest variety from one nation to another. Their reference point is not universal knowledge but rather, local labor markets. Their roles are greatly influenced by the structure of educational systems and, occasionally, cultural factors. Short-cycle higher education would seem to be a necessary accompaniment to mass higher education, or, more accurately, to the

high levels of secondary schooling that make it possible. The essential task of short-cycle higher education is to provide specialized occupational skills needed for transition to the workforce. Beyond this function, however, these institutions can assume a variety of forms.

The movement to develop short-cycle higher education in Western Europe began in the 1960s largely as a result of the preoccupations just described. By the 1980s, however, the institutions created in that era had matured and consolidated into a larger and more valued role (see *Short-Cycle Higher Education: Europe*). Instead of developing along the lines of the community colleges of the United States, as was once envisioned, they have assumed a role more like that of the erstwhile polytechnics in the British binary system. The *Instituts universitaires de technologie* in France, higher vocational institutions in the Netherlands, and regional colleges in Norway have all become selective in student admissions, more autonomous in operations, and linked with desirable careers. They are now considered to be "nonuniversity institutions," and are often in a strong competitive position in relation to universities.

Technical and Further Education (TAFE), as described by Leonard Cantor, includes a heterogeneous collection of short-cycle institutions in the United Kingdom and Australia which are highly vocational in their focus. They are distinguished by offering courses that do not lead to university-level degrees, and thus are completely divorced from the academic portion of higher education. Technical and further education programs generally attract a substantial clientele of adult, part-time students to their vocational programs. In their general incidence, TAFE institutions correspond to some extent with what Dorotea Furth calls the "third sector" (see *Short-Cycle Higher Education: Europe*), and with the tasks fulfilled by proprietary institutions in the United States and elsewhere.

Proprietary higher education operates outside of formal educational systems. It consists of fairly small institutions, operated on a profit-making basis, that concentrate on training students in narrow vocational fields. Such institutions are widespread in most countries, but the area is so ill-defined that precise figures are lacking. Wellford Wilms and Ciu Jiuping estimate that there may be as many as 6,000 of these schools in the United States (see *Proprietary Higher Education*). Their clientele is drawn largely from students who disliked academic schooling; their sole test of success is in securing jobs for their graduates. In general, surveys tend to show that students from these schools do as well as those from similar programs in public institutions.

American community colleges represent the most extensive system of short-cycle higher education, while also encompassing the broadest mission. The associate degree that they confer not only aims to prepare students for the workforce, but also provides the first two years of college for students intending to transfer to four-year institutions. In addition, community colleges offer remedial education to underprepared students, teach occupational skills to those already employed, and conduct cultural and leisure-activities courses to all comers (see *Community Colleges: United States*).

The transfer function distinguishes community colleges in the United States from short-cycle institutions elsewhere. In 1970 most of their graduates in fact prepared to transfer; but since then the balance has shifted decisively toward terminal vocational degrees. In both these activities the community colleges face the difficulty of having to remedy the weaknesses of secondary schooling in the United States (Clark 1985). One consequence is the need to offer remedial or developmental instruction in reading, writing, and mathematics.

Special efforts to assist underprepared students have always been a part of higher education in the United States, and in the 1990s such efforts exist at four-year as well as at community colleges. There is now a much greater sophistication in diagnosing learning disabilities and addressing them effectively. Developmental education is now the preferred designation for these activities, as they seek to overcome many facets of underpreparedness. In doing so, developmental education permits a broadening of access to higher education (see *Developmental Education*). American community colleges, in particular, serve to make higher education open to all who might benefit, not just recent secondary school graduates, but older adults as well. In this respect they fulfill a function that is handled differently in other countries.

Japanese junior colleges would appear to be similar in their role to American community colleges, but appearances in this case mask fundamental differences. The junior colleges of Japan are almost entirely private institutions that exist to meet a specific student demand. Their clientele consists overwhelmingly of 18–20-year old women, straight from secondary school. These women are preparing for limited careers in the workforce, after which they expect to devote themselves to marriage and family. Japanese junior colleges thus occupy a specialized niche in the institutional fabric, and one that may require future adaptation as women adopt less constricted career horizons (see *Junior Colleges: Japan*).

3.6 EXTENDING HIGHER EDUCATION

At least three factors have encouraged the extension of higher education to all segments of the population. The goal of universal access, when taken seriously, has meant adopting whatever means were necessary to bring higher education to students who could not physically attend institutions. The rapid broadening of access also created a generation gap between younger cohorts that benefited and adults who completed schooling under more restrictive conditions. This was a major consideration, for example, in Sweden's decision to extend university admission to adults on special terms (see *Sweden*). In addition, the complex and rapidly evolving knowledge base of modern technological society has required recurrent education to update professional knowledge or change professions.

Adult education began in much of Europe as special classes for workers that were intended to compensate for their lack of formal schooling. Continuing education, on the other hand, was introduced to update the skills of those who had previously received some formal training. Under conditions prevalent in the late twentieth century, a great deal of this activity has been organized as part of higher education. Adult learners are a major constituency of American community colleges, where they take regular classes, often in the evening. Major public universities in the United States commonly contain large extension divisions, although these courses are not generally taught by regular university faculty (see *Adult and Continuing Higher Education*).

Distance education began with correspondence courses, but the advent of television created much more effective possibilities. The British Open University, which was created as an autonomous, degree-granting institution in 1969, has provided the inspiration for similar institutions around the world. Three overlapping purposes are evident in these institutions. The Open University is intended to provide degree courses limited to adult, part-time learners who are not eligible to study in universities or polytechnics. Distance education in Australia, on the other hand, reaches out to a population of university students that is geographically quite dispersed. Perhaps most significant numerically, distance education has provided less developed nations with a means for providing advanced education on a large scale at low cost—an alternative in some cases to low-quality mass private sectors (see *Distance Education at Postsecondary Level*).

4. The Continued Centrality of Universities

Furthering knowledge through cognitive rationality, the cognitive upgrading of developing minds; education for praxis—these three primordial functions of higher education in themselves suggest reasons for the kaleidoscopic complexity and dynamism of the institutional fabric. First, contemporary knowledge-based societies are inherently dependent on the generation of new knowledge, as well as on keeping abreast of knowledge generated elsewhere. Second, the social demand for higher education—which unlike mere training implies a component of cognitive upgrading—has not been misplaced. The occupational structure has increasing need for individuals who can manipulate general knowledge, function independently, and adapt to the rapidly changing knowledge base. Although short-term imbalances have occurred between the supply and demand of educated labor (Dore 1976), there can be no doubt about the general trend. The goals of responsible democratic citizenship and expanded personal fulfillment furthermore imply the need for cognitive upgrading on an ever-increasing scale. Third, the expanding social demand for higher education has never-

theless had to be articulated with occupational structures, and this has been accomplished through education for praxis at all levels of higher education. Finally, praxis itself has increasingly been wed to cognitive rationality. Scientific and technological advancements have affected virtually every field of economic endeavor while also creating entirely new industries such as computer science and biotechnology. Thus the circle is completed: from knowledge to human capital to praxis back to knowledge.

When these three purposes are juxtaposed upon institutional structures, it becomes evident that expansion has resulted in differentiation on each level of higher education. This process is best illustrated by positing, as a broad generalization, that the final phase of higher education at each level tends to be focused on praxis, and thus aimed toward transition to the workplace. The number of years preceding the final phase determines the degree of general and theoretical education—the amount of cognitive upgrading—included in any educational program. Specifically, terminal short-cycle higher education includes a modicum of basic education, but is oriented toward instilling occupational skills. Terminal (or vocation) first-degree programs tend to have about two years of general education, followed by a like amount of occupationally focused study. Undergraduate programs that consist of just academic study—cognitive upgrading without regard to praxis—implicitly assume that graduates will acquire work skills on the job. That traditional pattern in particular, however, has been under pressure since the 1960s. The purely academic first-degree program is not more often followed by further study. Some graduate programs are occupationally focused: for example, master's degrees in business, public administration, teaching, social work, and specialized fields of engineering. The separate professional schools have their own admixture of general and praxis-oriented courses. Finally, the pursuit of theoretical subjects through to the doctoral level becomes, in fact, preparation for intellectual occupations, in tertiary teaching or research.

In the last half of the twentieth century, two successive macro-trends have been evident in many national systems. Initially, the predominant emphasis was on accommodating the widening social demand for undergraduate education—on cognitive upgrading without undue regard for praxis. In research, the agendas of the academic disciplines were ascendant. The drift of change since the 1970s, however, has been predominantly away from such an academic emphasis and toward praxis. The elaboration of short-cycle education, part-time adult education, vocational undergraduate studies, and professional schools have all been predicated on articulation with the workplace. The most rapidly growing areas of research (electronics, engineering, and biotechnology) have been those linked with praxis. What has generally occurred has been a fragmentation of higher education into larger numbers and types of institutions in some systems, or into internally differentiated institutions in others. In the case of specialized institutions with clear and delimited functions, this development has not been problematic. In the case of universities, however, the situation is different.

Edward Shils has enumerated the centrifugal forces acting upon modern universities (see *Universities: Since 1900*). In part, they stem from this macro-shift toward praxis. Certainly the most rapidly growing fields in contemporary universities have been those most closely associated with business and industry. For such fields, both the subject matter and the interested constituency lie outside the academy. But the centrifugal forces are larger and more various.

The university is a central institution for modern knowledge-based societies (Bell 1973). Who attends universities, who teaches there, and what is taught have all become contentious issues. The importance of the university's role in society gives rise to responsibilities to act in a public-spirited manner, and this stance shades imperceptibly into an imperative to assist social change. This externally directed role largely arises from within the university— from factions of committed students and faculty members, and from the highest administrators (Bok 1982). In a similar fashion, the busyness that afflicts universities, regrettable though it may be, is a product of its very importance. When the manifold tasks of the university and its faculty are detailed (Barzun 1968, Rosovsky 1990), there are few that would be voluntarily relinquished. Finally, the scope and scale of modern universities have made

them significant items of public expenditure. This too has brought an external dimension— intrusions from the state in the name of accountability, economy, or efficiency. There is no escaping these fiscal requirements; the appeal to private funders only brings a different form of centrifugal pull.

Against these general tendencies, and to some extent in contradiction to those commentators who have described them, Edward Shils has posited an alternate and more traditional idea of the university (see *Universities: Since 1900*). In his view, the collective self-consciousness of a university is a crucial factor in itself for channeling and realizing the intellectual potentials of dedicated, learned individuals. To achieve this "institutional effect" requires an intellectual community that is both independent and to some degree inward-looking. Universities neither can be nor should be divorced from the world, but an internal coherence and sense of purpose is a prerequisite for the most effective performance of their manifold services to the rest of society.

This conception of a university is at variance with the multiversity described by Kerr (1982). There the intellectual communities are partial and self-contained. The multiversity readily accommodates the inclinations of its faculty to pursue their specialties; it is receptive to the wishes of external constituencies as well, being prepared to provide almost anything for which they will provide support. From Shils's perspective, the multiversity has encouraged those centrifugal tendencies that have sapped it of internal coherence. Faculty communicate more readily with scholars at other institutions who share their esoteric interests and methods. They pursue subdisciplinary specialties with little regard for the unification of knowledge or understanding. The negative effects of rampant academic specialization have been most keenly resented in the United Kingdom and the United States, where it has been blamed for a loss of public confidence in the entire enterprise (Jencks and Riesman 1968, Scott 1984).

The juxtaposition of these two views should make it evident that universities, although central to the institutional fabric of systems of higher education, remain contested and unstable territories. At bottom they are predicated on the assumption "that enlarging and disseminating knowledge are equally important activities and that each is done better when both are done in the same place by the same people" (Rosenzweig 1982 p. 1). Both these tasks, however—enlarging and disseminating knowledge—are too huge in modern industrial societies to be contained within one kind of institution. The result, paradoxically, is likely to be movement in both directions. Some important tasks will in all probability be confided to universities, even as others are hived off. It is possible, for example, to find graduate degrees offered by private institutes or firms even while the ancient universities of the United Kingdom construct graduate schools for returning businesspeople. Similarly, many of the institutions spawned in the great expansion and differentiation of higher education will likely evolve in the direction of universities, particularly in striving to advance knowledge; but unique, highly focused institutions will also be founded, especially where private initiatives are allowed free rein. The interaction of institutions and functions thus shows every likelihood of continuing to produce more intricately patterned institutional fabrics of higher education.

Bibliography

Barzun, J. 1968. *The American University*. Harper & Row, New York

Bell, D. 1973. *The Coming of Post-Industrial Society*. Basic Books, New York

Bok, D. 1982. *Beyond the Ivory Tower: Social Responsibilities of the Modern University*. Harvard University Press, Cambridge, Massachusetts

Carnegie Foundation for the Advancement of Teaching, 1987. *A Classification of Institutions of Higher Education*. Carnegie Foundation, Princeton, New Jersey

Clark, B. R. 1983. *The Higher Education System*. University of California Press, Berkeley, California

Clark, B. R. 1985. *The School and the University: An International Perspective*. University of California Press, Berkeley, California

Dore, R. 1986. *The Diploma Disease: Education, Qualification and Development*. University of California Press, Berkeley, California

Geiger, R. L. 1986a. *To Advance Knowledge: The Growth of American Research Universities, 1900–1940*. Oxford University Press, New York

Geiger, R. L. 1986b. *Private Sectors in Higher Education: Structure, Function and Change in Eight Countries*. University of Michigan Press, Ann Arbor, Michigan

Hermanns, H., Teichler, U., Wasser, H. 1982. *Integrierte Hochschulmodelle: Erfahrungen aus drei Ländern*. Campus, Frankfurt

Higher Education: A New Framework. 1991. Cmnd 1541, HMSO, London

Jencks, C., Riesman, D. 1968. *The Academic Revolution*. University of Chicago Press, Chicago, Illinois

Kerr, C. 1982. *The Uses of the University, 3rd edn*. Harvard University Press, Cambridge, Massachusetts

Levy, D. 1986. *Higher Education and the State in Latin America*. University of Chicago Press, Chicago, Illinois

Locke, R. R. 1984. *The End of Practical Man: Entrepreneurship and Higher Education in Germany, France, and Great Britain, 1880–1940*. JAI Press, New York

Locke, R. R. 1989. *Management and Higher Education since 1940: The Influence of America and Japan on West Germany, Great Britain, and France*. Cambridge University Press, Cambridge

OECD. 1989. *Review of Higher Education Policy in California: Examiners Report and Questions*. Organisation for Economic Co-operation and Development, Paris

Parsons, T., Platt, G. M. 1983. *The American University*. Harvard University Press, Cambridge, Massachusetts

Rosenzweig, R. 1982. *The Research Universities and Their Patrons*. University of California Press, Berkeley, California

Rosovsky, H. 1990. *The University: An Owner's Manual*. Norton, New York

Scott, P. 1984. *The Crisis of the University*. Croom Helm, London

Slosson, E. 1910. *The Great American Universities*. Macmillan, New York

Trow, M. 1974. "Problems in the transition from elite to mass higher education." In: OECD, 1974, *Policies for Higher Education*. Organisation for Economic Co-operation and Development. Paris, pp. 55–101

Trow, M. 1988. Comparative perspectives on higher education policy in the UK and the US. *Oxford Review of Education* 14(1): 81–96

Veysey, L. 1965. *The Emergence of the American University*. University of Chicago Press, Chicago, Illinois

The Liberal Arts College—
Is It Really an Endangered Species?

Joan Gilbert

Education in the liberal arts has received a good deal of attention—concerned attention—in the past few years. Many believe that higher education is rapidly losing sight of its historic mission of offering a broad liberal arts education and that many institutions, including the traditional liberal arts colleges, are moving toward curricula that are focused increasingly on specialized and professional preparation. In this article, I look closely at data from the past and present to determine whether these beliefs reflect reality.

The historical data on the percentage of all bachelor's degrees (BAs) conferred in the liberal arts suggest the belief is correct. The statistics reveal a very long-term decline, beginning at least a century ago. This trend was temporarily interrupted in the 1950s and '60s by atypically high rates of increase in the number of liberal arts degrees awarded by institutions of all types. The decline that followed, between 1970 and 1984, attracted considerable notice, but it generally has been overlooked that this latest dip resulted merely in a close return to the trajectory established over the past century. Since about 1985, moreover, there actually has been renewed interest in the liberal arts, although it has occurred primarily outside liberal arts colleges, in larger institutions with PhD programs.

In considering this history, it is important to recognize the heterogeneity of the subset of institutions ordinarily characterized as "liberal arts colleges." These institutions are not now and never have been uniform in their educational missions. In fact, far fewer of them historically have been as heavily devoted to the liberal arts as has commonly been supposed.

Definitions

The Liberal Arts: I define the liberal arts to include the humanities, life sciences, natural sciences, and the social sciences including psychology.

Professional subjects include engineering, computer science, agriculture, medical sciences, theology, architecture, education, business, communications and librarianship, and social services. These subjects, some of which are aggregates of subfields, are the principal areas found in the CASPAR Database produced by Quantum Research Associates for the National Science Foundation. The Carnegie Foundation for the Advancement of Teaching, in the 1987 edition of *A Classification of Institutions of Higher Education*, distinguishes the following types of institutions:

Research Universities I (R-I) offer BAs and are committed to graduate education through the doctorate degree.

Research Universities II (R-II), Doctorate-Granting Universities I (D-I), and Doctorate-Granting Universities II (D-II) are smaller research universities offering a wide range of BAs through the PhD.

Liberal Arts Colleges I (LA-I) are highly selective institutions that are primarily undergraduate and offer at least 50 percent of their degrees in the liberal arts.

Liberal Arts Colleges II (LA-II) are primarily undergraduate colleges that are less selective but also award at least 50 percent of their degrees in liberal arts. This category also includes a group of colleges that award less than half of their degrees in liberal arts but, because they have fewer than 1,500 students, are considered too small to belong to the category Comprehensive Universities and Colleges II (C-II).

Comprehensive Universities and Colleges I (C-I) offer a range of BAs and graduate education through the master's degree. More than half of their BAs are awarded in two or more occupational or professional disciplines, and they enroll at least 2,500 students.

Comprehensive Universities and Colleges II (C-II) award more than half of their BAs in two or more occupational disciplines and may offer graduate work through the master's degree. Their enrollments range from 1,500 to 2,500 students.

—JG

The Liberal Arts Degree Over The Past Century

Chart 1 displays the relationship between the total number of BAs conferred and the proportion of liberal arts degrees among them for the past century. Four distinct phenomena are observable.

1. The past century has witnessed a steady, and at times explosive, increase in enrollments and degrees granted in higher education. Over that same period, the share of BA degrees awarded in the liberal arts has declined substantially. These trends presumably are due largely to three mutually supporting factors: a) the pre-eminence of business and technology in American life, b) an ever-increasing demand for higher education, and c) a broadened access to the educational system for individuals from a variety of socioeconomic backgrounds. In the process, curricula have become increasingly dominated by vocational and professional preparation.

2. Between 1956 and 1970, a sizeable expansion in the number of degrees granted in general was accompanied by a significant *increase* in the percentage of liberal arts degrees awarded. J. B. Lon Hefferlin's explanation in *Dynamics of Academic Reform* (Jossey-Bass, 1971) is that institutions in the process of transforming themselves from teachers colleges introduced liberal arts curricula as a means of achieving academic respectability. Sarah Turner and William Bowen, in "The Flight From the Arts and Sciences" (*Science*, October 1990), add that favorable labor market conditions and the general mood of optimism that characterized much of the '60s also contributed to this growth in the number of liberal arts majors, as did a movement by women away from majors in education.

3. A substantial decrease in the percentage of liberal arts degrees awarded began in 1970 and terminated in 1984 slightly below the historical trend line. No single explanatory variable accounts for the steep decline in the liberal arts share of BAs during this period. Turner and Bowen attribute it to low growth rates in enrollment (as reflected in the low growth in total BAs), which in turn required institutions to become more competitive and to offer more professional curricula. In addition, they suggest, less favorable labor market conditions and the decision by many women to enter areas (such as business) that were previously closed to them contributed to this decline.

4. Beginning in 1985, however, a modest but continuing increase in the percentage of degrees conferred in the liberal arts has occurred. No one has yet tried to account for this renewed interest in the liberal arts. Perhaps it may reflect growing tendencies by students on one hand to postpone professional education until graduate school and by graduate programs in professional areas on the other to require or to encourage acquisition of an undergraduate liberal arts degree. This explanation is

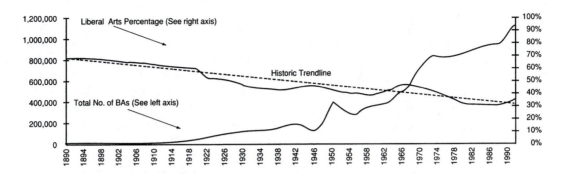

Sources: Data 1890–1961 from Adkins: 1961–1992 IPEDS. All BA degree-granting institutions in the U.S. (N = 1426)

Chart 1 Number of Total BAs Conferred in All BA Degree-Granting Institutions and Percentage of BAs in Liberal Arts (1890–1992)

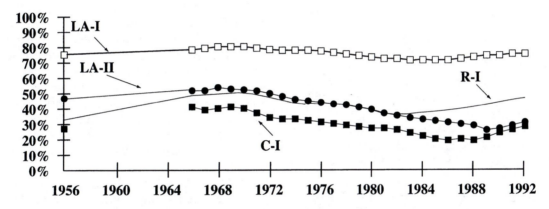

Sources: IPEDS, 1955–56, CASPAR Database, NSF, 1956–1992. The data set for the time-series consists of all LA-I and LA-II institutions reporting in 1956 and a random sample of R-I and C-I universities reporting in 1956.

Chart 2 Average Percentage of Degrees in Liberal Arts in Four Types of Institutions (1956–1992)

tentative, however, and I intend to conduct additional analysis and report it in the future.

Chart 2 shows the decline in shares of liberal arts degrees by type of institution between 1956 and 1992. The year 1956 was chosen because it came well before the expansion in liberal arts education in the '60s and after the expansions caused by the GI Bill in the '40s and early '50s. Several observations about the data depicted in Chart 2 are worth making.

- The growth in the percentage of BA degrees awarded in the liberal arts between 1956 and 1970 was common not only to Liberal Arts Colleges I (LA-I) and Liberal Arts Colleges II (LA-II) but also to Comprehensive Universities and

Colleges I (C-I) and Research Universities I (R-I) [see Definitions box]. Similarly institutions of all these types showed declines in liberal arts shares between 1970 and 1984. Therefore, neither the increase nor the decline of interest in the liberal arts at those institutions can plausibly be attributed to the special circumstances of the LA-I and LA-II colleges. On the other hand, the *magnitude* of this decline in the LA-II colleges and the subsequent failure of LA-II colleges to experience any marked renewal of interest in liberal arts *is* due to the specific features of institutions of this type (which I will identify below).

- The renewal of interest in the liberal arts that began around 1985 was concentrated mainly in the larger institutions (R-I and C-I). In LA-I colleges, the percentage of liberal arts degrees conferred declined from a high of 87 percent in 1970 to a low of 76 percent in 1985 with a slight boost to 78 percent in 1992, 1 percent higher than the 1956 level. In LA-II colleges, interest declined much more substantially—from a high of 56 percent in 1970 to a low of 31 percent in 1985 with no change in 1992, leaving them considerably below their 1956 level of 46 percent. C-I universities reached a level of 43 percent in 1970, declined to 23 percent in 1985, and recovered to 29 percent in 1992. Here, too, interest in the liberal arts in 1992 was slightly above the 28 percent it had been in 1956.

In R-I universities, the liberal arts reached by 1992 a level considerably higher than that of 1956. Interest declined from a high of 54 percent in 1970 to a low of 36 percent in 1985. By 1992 the level of liberal arts degrees conferred was 45 percent—well beyond the level of 34 percent in 1956.

Thus, the most dramatic net changes over the period from 1956 to 1992 occurred at opposite ends of the spectrum: in LA-II and R-I institutions. In light of the anxieties alluded to above concerning the future of the liberal arts and of the liberal arts college, the stability of interest in the liberal arts in LA-I colleges over this period is especially notable.

- Because 1970 was the high point of a bulge that constituted an anomaly in the century-long pattern of decline in the liberal arts, the data for that year do not provide an appropriate standard against which to judge recent experience. If the bulge in the '50s and '60s had not occurred, the levels reached in 1984 would be (as can be seen in Chart 1) close to what would have resulted simply from a smooth continuation of the trend that is observable from the beginning of the century.

The Liberal Arts College

One of the most enduring controversies in the history of higher education has been about the content of the curriculum. A recent resurgence of this controversy may have been stimulated by the work of David Breneman (see *Liberal Arts Colleges: Thriving, Surviving, or Endangered?* Brookings, 1994). Breneman's analysis of the impacts of declining enrollments and increased costs paints a bleak picture for the future of liberal arts colleges. His assessment is particularly compelling because it is supported by quantitative data rather than merely by the rhetoric that so often characterizes discussions of these topics.

In this article, "Are We Losing Our Liberal Arts Colleges?" (*College Board Review*, Summer 1990), Breneman defines "liberal arts college" as an institution in which a minimum of 40 percent of those graduating have majored in liberal arts. This is a generous standard that few would regard as too strict. Breneman uses the 1987 Carnegie Classification to identify the LA-I and LA-II colleges to which his criterion is to be applied. Of the 140 LA-I colleges in the classification, as many as 129 meet his criterion. By contrast, he reports that his criterion is met by only 83 of the 400 LA-II colleges listed. The other 317 LA-II institutions, he writes, "have become small professional colleges with some remnants of a liberal arts tradition." Breneman also points out that the Carnegie Classification include 145 fewer LA-II institutions in 1987 than were listed in 1970.

Breneman attributes this decline in the number of liberal arts colleges to the financial pressures that these institutions have been facing. He argues that the struggle for institutional survival in recent years has driven many of the less prestigious colleges (that is, LA-IIs) to abandon or to scale back sharply their original educational missions in the arts and sciences. They have found it necessary to do this, he suggests, in order to provide more extensive instruction in professional subjects that are in greater demand.

Breneman's views are widely shared. For instance, the author of an article published in the April 1994 issue of *Policy Perspectives* concludes:

TABLE 1
Percentage of Liberal Arts Degrees Conferred in Liberal Arts I and II Colleges (1956 and 1992)

| | LA-I | | | | LA-II | | | |
| | 1956 | | 1992 | | 1956 | | 1992 | |
% LA Degrees Conferred	No.	Share	No.	Share	No.	Share	No.	Share
0–9	0	0%	2	2%	19	8%	27	12%
10–19	0	0%	1	1%	5	2%	31	13%
20–29	2	2%	0	0%	37	16%	58	25%
30–39	1	1%	8	6%	34	15%	50	22%
40–49	11	9%	7	6%	34	15%	34	15%
50–59	10	8%	13	10%	31	13%	14	6%
60–69	21	17%	15	12%	26	11%	11	5%
70–79	14	11%	15	12%	19	8%	2	1%
80–89	21	17%	19	15%	11	5%	2	1%
90–100	44	35%	44	35%	16	7%	3	1%
Total	**124**		**124**		**232**		**232**	

Sources: 1955–56, Hegis-IPEDS Annual Survey of Earned Degrees Conferred: 1992, CASPAR Database, NSF

The most visible and in many ways the most relentless pressure in colleges and universities derives from the changing nature of the American economy and the nearly singular role a college degree has come to play in providing access to good jobs.... Even among the nation's most selective residential institutions, vocationalism is now affecting everything from the choice of an academic major to the demand for student services that focus on job placement.

Similarly, in a June 1994 speech commemorating the 200th anniversary of Bowdoin College, Diane Ravitch, a former assistant secretary of the Department of Education, attributed the decline in the number of liberal arts majors in the '70s and '80s to an escalating careerism among students, which has been helped along by the complicity of many colleges interested in maintaining enrollments:

> Worried about their future, students clamored for courses that would make them marketable when they went for their first job interviews ... and to meet this demand many universities have expanded their offerings in business and vocational programs.... American higher education has remade itself into a vast job-training program in which the liberal arts are no longer central.

Participants in the debate over the alleged loss of the liberal arts college generally neglect the fact that colleges ordinarily identified as such are by no means a homogeneous group, as Table 1 shows. The most selective LA-I colleges have shown a relentlessly consistent devotion to providing a liberal arts education. The missions of the LA-II colleges, however, actually have been quite varied. In particular, many LA-II colleges have not been seriously devoted to a liberal arts curriculum. Indeed, except during the altogether atypical period from 1956 to 1970, many LA-II colleges *never* awarded large percentages of liberal arts degrees. Regardless of the LA-II label, it is simply a mistake to regard them as institutions with "a liberal arts tradition" from which they have recently departed.

No data that examine majors by sector exist for the first half of the 20th century. This article employs 1956 data gathered from 124 LA-I and 232 LA-II colleges to determine whether the full range of liberal arts colleges some 40 years ago were more devoted to the liberal arts than they are now. An effort was made to consider all LA-I and LA-II institutions in 1956. However, many of the institutions existing at that time did not report their data. It seems reasonable to suppose that the data actually collected are biased in favor of academically stronger institutions and that it was mainly the academically weaker schools— some of which were not yet accredited—that did not report the degrees they awarded. Thus, the percentage of LA-II colleges in which liberal arts degrees were less than 40 percent of the total number of degrees awarded—that is, those that would not meet Breneman's criterion for identification as liberal arts colleges— was almost surely higher in 1956 than is shown in Table 1.

In 1956, about 3 percent of the LA-I colleges reporting failed to meet Breneman's criterion, while in 1992 about 9 percent were unable to do so. The net number of LA-I colleges that fell below his benchmark during this period was quite small—8, or about 6 percent of the total. His suggestion that large numbers of institutions have recently ceased to be liberal arts colleges can therefore hold only for institutions in the LA-II category. Even here, however, Breneman's account significantly exaggerates the decline in the emphasis given to the liberal arts.

Of the 232 LA-II colleges that reported degrees conferred in 1956, 41 percent did not grant enough liberal arts degrees to qualify as liberal arts colleges even by Breneman's criterion. It is reasonable to suppose that this percentage is a low estimate for Breneman's larger sample, and hence that more than 41 percent of the 400 LA-IIs that he considers—that is, more than 164 colleges—did not qualify in 1956 as liberal arts colleges by his standard. In order to determine the number that actually changed between 1956 and 1987 from liberal arts to professionalized curricula, these 164 colleges must be subtracted from the 317 institutions that did not meet Breneman's criterion in 1987 and became, as he says, "small professional colleges." They did not *become* professional colleges, because that is what they always were. Thus, no more than 153 colleges, by Breneman's criterion, changed between 1956 and 1987 from liberal arts to professional status.

Once it is recognized that at least 164 of Breneman's 400 LA-IIs had never been liberal arts colleges in the first place, the magnitude of the loss of liberal arts institutions becomes considerably less dramatic than he portrays. Starting from a base not of 400 colleges but of 236 (400 minus 164), we conclude that the number of institutions lost to the liberal arts was not 317 but 153 (236 minus the 83 LA-IIs that met

his criterion). This is still a substantial loss, of course, but it is less than half as severe as the loss Breneman reports.

Table 2 refers to the experience of seven LA-II colleges chosen because they represent a pattern more or less typical of such institutions, but one not normally associated with them— that is, they have over the years steadily declined in the percentage of liberal arts degrees they confer. It is true that this percentage dropped precipitously in each case after 1970. But 1970, in which all seven colleges met Breneman's criterion, was the peak year of an abnormal bulge. None of the seven had met the criterion in 1956 and the decline did no more than to leave them in 1992 near—indeed, with little exception above—their 1956 levels. Except for the temporary increase in percentages of liberal arts degrees awarded between 1956 and 1970, these institutions have always been what they are now—primarily professional.

Table 3 describes the increases and decreases, between 1970 and 1992, in the contributions made by institutions of various types to the national pool of BA degrees in the liberal arts. What is most notable in these data is that the LA-I colleges have increased their share of the national total of liberal arts degrees even though their share of all BA degrees has declined. This pattern also holds for the undergraduate colleges of all PhD-granting institutions (R-I, R-II, D-I, and D-II). Only LA-IIs and C-IIs show decreasing shares of BAs and (even greater) decreasing shares of liberal arts degrees. If one looks at these data in conjunction with the data on SAT scores in Table 4, it would appear that students at schools showing the largest increases in shares of liberal arts majors have the highest SAT scores.

TABLE 2
Percentages of Liberal Arts Degrees in Seven Liberal Arts II Colleges (1956–1992)

Institution	1956	1970	1992
Kansas Newman College	0%	59%	4%
Malone College	7%	43%	10%
Rust College	22%	51%	27%
Manchester College	25%	52%	29%
Briar Cliff College	28%	69%	30%
Curry College	20%	44%	23%
Union College	31%	57%	30%

Source: J. Cass and M. Birnbaum, *Comparative Guide to American Colleges*, 15th edition, N. Y. Harper, 1991

TABLE 3
Percentages of BA and Liberal Arts Degrees in All Four-Year Institutions by Type of Institution
(1970 And 1992)

		Share of BAs (%)			Share of Liberal Arts BAs (%)		
Category	No.	1970	1992	Absolute Change	1970	1992	Absolute Change
C-I	433	35.3	38.4	3.2	33.0	30.7	–2.3
C-II	173	5.1	5.0	–0.1	5.1	4.1	–1.0
D-I	56	9.7	9.2	–0.5	8.8	9.0	0.2
D-II	59	6.6	6.5	–0.1	5.5	5.7	0.2
LA-I	144	4.5	4.4	–0.1	7.7	9.3	1.6
LA-II	434	7.3	6.6	–0.8	8.1	5.2	–2.8
R-I	87	22.4	21.0	–1.3	23.5	26.5	3.0
R-II	40	9.1	8.9	–0.3	8.3	9.4	1.1

Source: CASPAR Database. All BA degree-granting institutions (N = 1426)

TABLE 4
SAT Scores of Entering Freshman Class (1992–93) By Carnegie Type

Quartile	R-I	LA-I	D-I	R-II	D-II	C-II	C-I	LA-II
1st	1320	1252	1203	1190	1157	1078	1068	1047
2nd	1175	1145	1171	1068	1042	1015	970	964
3rd	1087	1092	971	1006	980	943	911	913
4th	1006	999	897	943	903	832	836	822
No.	65	127	42	33	50	—	294	226

Source: ASC data: 1994–1995. SAT score is the mean composite score of the entering freshman class for the institutions within each institutional type (1992–1993).

TABLE 5
Average Percentage of BAs
in Liberal Arts by SAT Quartile

Quartile	LA-I	R-I	LA-II	C-I
1st	89.8	62.1	42.6	36.2
2nd	78.7	59.8	35.1	31.2
3rd	80.4	41.8	26.1	27.6
4th	59.1	40.5	26.4	24.7
No.	127	65	226	294

Source: College Board, ASC, Entering Freshman Class, 1992–1993

Finally, it may be useful to offer possible explanations for the failure of the LA-II colleges to participate in the recent increase in the share of liberal arts degrees conferred.

- When colleges and universities are ranked by the mean combined SAT scores of their entering freshman class (1992–93), and institutions of each type are grouped by SAT quartile, a high correlation exists between the percentage of liberal arts degrees in a group and the average SAT score of the group's incoming freshman class (see Tables 4 and 5). As shown in Table 4, students in almost every quartile of LA-II colleges have lower SAT scores than students in corresponding institutions of other types. Table 5 shows that SAT score is closely associated with the percentage of liberal arts degrees conferred not only among institutions of different types but also among institutions of the same type if they are divided into quartiles by SAT scores. Since SAT scores are lower in LA-II institutions, it is not surprising these institutions award fewer liberal arts degrees.

- The LA-II colleges may be more responsive than larger institutions to changing market demands, and for this reason, they may be more likely to become vocationally oriented. They are probably using adjunct faculty, as are all higher education institutions these days.

However, even small increases in adjunct faculty may make small institutions—which LA-II colleges are—less resistant to curricular change, since there will be fewer full-time and permanent faculty to try to block curricular developments that they perceive as threatening to them.

- LA-II colleges may lack the resources, which are more abundant in larger and more selective institutions, that are needed to sustain a liberal arts curriculum: for example, labs and instrumentation for the sciences, strong library collections, and faculties capable of offering courses in a broad range of subjects.

It is difficult and uneconomical for colleges that grant a high percentage of professional degrees also to support programs leading to small numbers of liberal arts degrees. Harriet Zuckerman, one of my colleagues at the Mellon Foundation, has also suggested that R-I universities may have distinct advantages not only because they are comparatively rich, but also because their investments do double duty—their expenditures on libraries, labs, and specialization serve both undergraduate and graduate education. This helps to explain why the most severe decline in the liberal arts has been among LA-II colleges, which award the lowest percentages of liberal arts degrees.

The Challenge

Although it is true that all of higher education now faces financial pressures from rising costs, competition for students, sluggish growth in enrollments, shrinking sources of student aid, and loss of federal aid for research, these pressures tend to place more severe burdens on the smaller colleges, making it harder for them to compete with larger or wealthier institutions. While the argument that many liberal arts colleges (especially those that are already in financial trouble) will succumb cannot be dismissed, the survival capacity of these institutions should not be underestimated. It is conceivable that pressures similar to those that have forced other industries to consolidate will lead to the elimination of smaller educational institutions and that all but the wealthiest liberal arts colleges will disappear.

The fact that significant numbers of LA-II institutions have become professional colleges does not necessarily bode ill for the liberal arts. The shift away from the liberal arts has been less extreme than Breneman suggested, with relatively few LA-I institutions so far abandoning their commitments to the liberal arts. Moreover, the declining interest in the liberal arts among the smaller and weaker LA-II institutions has been more than offset by an increase from the R-I universities and in other PhD-granting institutions.

The coming challenge will be to find the means to ensure the continued survival of the most viable LA-I colleges as liberal arts institutions and, in larger institutions, to design collegiate environments that can replicate the outcomes that have traditionally been produced within the smaller scale and more intimate settings of the liberal arts colleges.

Joan Gilbert is manager of the Research Office of the Andrew W. Mellon Foundation in Princeton, New Jersey. Special thanks to Fredrick Vars, a Princeton University service, for organizing much of the data reported in this article.

"Upward Drift" Is Alive and Well
Research/Doctoral Model Still Attractive to Institutions

STEPHEN F. ALDERSLEY

Stephen F. Aldersley is associate professor and acting chair of the English department at the National Technical Institute for the Deaf, a college of the Rochester Institute of Technology, Rochester, New York.

In its 1994 edition of *A Classification of Institutions of Higher Education*, the Carnegie Foundation for the Advancement of Teaching notes the continued presence of the phenomenon of "upward drift"—the tendency for institutions to introduce higher-level programs, causing a marked increase in the overall number of research and doctoral institutions. This trend was previously reported in the 1987 edition. At a time when there is much talk on campuses about downsizing and concentrating on the core business of undergraduate teaching, it is interesting that doctoral programs and their accompanying research emphasis apparently are not losing their power as attractive additions to institutional portfolios. In fact, as this article will explore, this latest piece of evidence confirms that traditional indices of institutional prestige are still potent drivers of institutional direction and decision-making.

Four editions of the Carnegie Classification have been published—in 1973, 1976, 1987, and 1994—with the aim of categorizing the majority of postsecondary institutions. Categories range from "Research Universities I" to "Two-Year Community, Junior, and Technical Colleges" (renamed "Associate of Arts Colleges" in the 1994 edition), to "Specialized Institutions." The comparisons described in this article are derived from the 1976, 1987, and 1994 editions and are chiefly concerned with the

four categories of institutions with appreciable doctoral programs: Research Universities I (R-I), Research Universities II (R-II), Doctoral Universities I (D-I), and Doctoral Universities II (D-II). Definitions of these four categories have changed little since 1976. R-I institutions are those that award at least 50 doctoral degrees per year and "give high priority to research," measured by receipt of substantial federal support ($40 million annually in the 1994 edition). R-II institutions also award 50 doctoral degrees each year but enjoy less federal support. D-I institutions award at least 40 doctoral degrees in five or more academic disciplines, while D-II institutions award at least 10 doctoral degrees in three or more disciplines or 20 doctoral degrees in one or more disciplines.

When using the Carnegie Classification, it is important to note the lag between the years in which data were collected and the publication dates of the editions. Data for the 1976 edition were collected in 1973–1975; for the 1987 edition, they were collected in 1983–1984; and for the 1994 edition, they were collected in 1989–1991.

A final introductory note: in his foreword to the 1987 edition, Ernest Boyer emphasizes that "the classification is *not* intended to establish a hierarchy among higher learning institutions." In talking about movement from one category to another, however, it is difficult to avoid use of short-hand terms such as "up," "down," "higher group," and "lower group." These and related terms are used throughout this article, albeit in a non-judgmental manner.

"'Upward Drift' Is Alive and Well: Research/Doctoral Model Still Attractive to Institutions," by Stephen F. Aldersley, reprinted from *Change*, Sept/Oct 1995, Heldref Publications.

TABLE 1
Total Membership in Each of Four Carnegie Doctoral Categories for 1976, 1987, and 1994

		1976	1987	1994
Research I	Publics	29	45	59
	Privates	22	25	29
Research II	Publics	33	26	26
	Privates	14	8	11
Doctoral I	Publics	37	30	28
	Privates	17	20	23
Doctoral II	Publics	19	33	37
	Privates	11	25	22
Total Doctoral	**Publics**	**118**	**134**	**150**
Institutions	**Privates**	**64**	**78**	**85**

Table 1 shows the absolute size of the four doctoral categories as reported in the three editions of the Carnegie Classification. As such, it allows comparison of the rate of expansion of each of the categories over the two periods between the studies, 1976–1987 and 1987–1994. (Comparison required that institutions be categorized in all three editions. This criterion led to exclusion from consideration of just one institution, the University of Central Florida, which was not categorized in the 1976 edition.)

In the R-I category, for example, it is apparent that expansion over the two periods occurred at a fairly stable rate. From 1976 to 1987, the number of public institutions increased by 16, and from 1987 to 1994 it increased by 14. For private institutions, the

number increased by 3 between 1976 and 1987, and by 4 between 1987 and 1994.

Table 1 indicates that absolute growth rates within each of the remaining three doctoral categories varied considerably. However, because much of the change in group size is a function of movement within the four doctoral categories, the data for "Total Doctoral Institutions" provide perhaps the most useful indicator of overall upward drift. Comparison of these data for public and private institutions indicates two different pictures. For public institutions, the growth rate remained the same both during 1976–1987 and during 1987–1994 (increasing by 16 each time), while for private institutions, the growth rate declined over the same period (increasing by only 7 between

TABLE 2
Institutions In Each Doctoral Category in 1994 Compared With Their 1976 Categories

		1994	1976					
			R-I	R-II	D-I	D-II	C-I*	S**
Research I	Publics	59	29	23	5	–	1	1
	Privates	29	22	7	–	–	–	–
Research II	Publics	26	–	9	16	1	–	–
	Privates	11	–	5	6	–	–	–
Doctoral I	Publics	28	–	1	11	11	5	–
	Privates	23	–	2	10	4	3	4
Doctoral II	Publics	37	–	–	5	6	23	3
	Privates	22	–	–	1	7	10	4

* C-I, or "Comprehensive Universities and Colleges I," which became "Master's Colleges and Universities I" in the 1994 edition, refers to those institutions that offer baccalaureate programs, as well as "graduate education through the master's degree."

** S, or "Specialized Institution," refers to institutions with predominantly specialized programs, for example, in the medical, theological, or engineering fields. In the 1994 edition, the name of this category was shortened from its name in earlier editions: "Professional Schools and Other Specialized Institutions."

1987 and 1994 compared to 14 in the earlier period). Thus, expansion in the more recent period was largely a function of new public institutions joining the doctorate-granting ranks, whereas in the earlier period, private institutions were almost equally likely to make the jump as their public counterparts.

In addition to looking at changes in category size and growth rates, it is also of interest to examine the details of inter-group movement. In other words, when institutions changed category, which classifications did they come from? Table 2 gives the 1976 edition origins of institutions that belonged to the four doctoral categories in 1994.

Table 2 indicates that most institutions that changed category from 1976 to 1994 did so in an "upward" direction. Several noteworthy trends are discernible. First, it appears to be quite difficult for an institution that has attained R-I status to drop back down—in fact, no institution that was categorized as R-I in 1976 had fallen from its lofty perch by 1994. Second, public institutions that moved into the R-I category by 1994 were likely to have made bigger "jumps" than their private counterparts. Whereas all 7 new private institutions in 1994 had been classified R-II in 1976, 7 of 30 new public institutions had been classified as "below" R-II in 1976. Interestingly, this relatively greater "upward mobility" applied only to public institutions attaining R-I status. By contrast, 16 of the 17 public institutions newly classified as R-II in 1994 had been classified in the next-lower category—D-I—in 1976, and among new entrants into the D-I category, private institutions were more likely than their public counterparts to have risen from categories below D-II.

Table 2 also shows that a small number of institutions moved down from a higher category in the 1976 listings to a lower one in 1994. This phenomenon occurred most often for public institutions classified as D-I in 1976. Of 37 institutions classified as D-II in 1994, 5 had been D-I institutions in 1976. (The table does not show that a few institutions had moved down by 1987, and then back up again by 1994.)

Overall, and perhaps not surprisingly, Table 2 indicates that the D-II category was the most volatile in the period examined, with only 6 of 37 public institutions and 7 of 22 private

institutions maintaining membership in that category from 1976 to 1994. Indeed, for many institutions, the D-II category appears to be no more than a stopover on the road to greater things. Slightly more than 50 percent of the institutions classified as D-II in 1976 had "moved up" by 1994—leading to the conclusion that once an institution has embarked on doctorate-level education, the chances are better than even that it will not remain satisfied with one or two doctoral programs and a small number of graduates. This finding should be of interest to the 40 institutions moving into D-II from the C-I and S categories between 1976 and 1994.

The most accurate count of institutions that experienced upward drift during the periods 1976–1987 and 1987–1994 can be secured by excluding from the calculation institutions that moved down and stayed down, or those that moved down then back up again. Table 3 provides data on this more limited population and indicates that the total number of institutions experiencing upward drift was virtually identical during the two periods. (It should be noted that though Table 3 shows a total of 145 upward movements for both periods combined, the number of institutions involved is 133—12 of the institutions have been counted twice since they moved up in both periods.)

Tables 4 through 7 identify the institutions included in the composite data provided in Table 3 and provide the previous category of each reclassified institution. The data presented in these tables suggest several general-

TABLE 3
Number of New Institutions in Each Category (Excluding Institutions That Experienced Any Downward Movement) for the Periods 1976–1987 and 1987–1994

		1976–1987	*1987–1994*
Research I	Publics	16	14
	Privates	3	4
Research II	Publics	9	11
	Privates	1	5
Doctoral I	Publics	8	9
	Privates	4	7
Doctoral II	Publics	17	16
	Privates	14	7
Total Doctoral	**Publics**	**50**	**50**
Institutions	**Privates**	**22**	**23**

TABLE 4
New R-I Institutions in 1987 and 1994 (Excluding Institutions That Experienced Any Downward Movement)
With Their Previous Categories

New Members of R-I: 1987	1976 Category	New Members of R-I: 1994	1987 Category
Public Institutions			
Georgia Institute of Technology	R-II	*Arizona State U.	R-II
Indiana U. at Bloomington	R-II	Florida State U.	R-II
Louisiana State U. & Ag./Mech. College	R-II	Iowa State U.	R-II
New Mexico State U.	D-I	SUNY at Buffalo	R-II
Rutgers, State U. at New Brunswick	R-II	Temple U.	R-II
SUNY at Stony Brook	R-II	U. Alabama at Birmingham	D-II
U. California at Irvine	R-II	*U. California at Santa Barbara	R-II
U. California at San Francisco	S	U. Kansas	R-II
U. Cincinnati	R-II	U. Massachusetts at Amherst	R-II
U. Connecticut	R-II	U. Nebraska at Lincoln	R-II
U. Illinois at Chicago	D-I	Utah State U.	R-II
U. Kentucky	R-II	*Virginia Commonwealth U.	R-II
U. New Mexico	R-II	Wayne State U.	R-II
U. Tennessee at Knoxville	R-II	West Virginia U.	R-II
U. Virginia	R-II		
Virginia Poly. Inst. & State U.	R-II		
Total	**16**		**14**
Private Institutions			
Carnegie Mellon U.	R-II	Brown U.	R-II
Howard U.	R-II	Emory U.	R-II
Vanderbilt U.	R-II	Georgetown U.	R-II
		Tufts U.	D-I
Total	**3**		**4**

* = Institutions reclassified as R-II in 1976–1987: see Table 5 (Institutions counted twice in Table 3)

TABLE 5
New R-II Institutions in 1987 and 1994 (Excluding Institutions That Experienced Any Downward Movement)
With Their Previous Categories

New Members of R-II: 1987	1976 Category	New Members of R-II: 1994	1987 Category
Public Institutions			
*Arizona State U.	D-I	Clemson U.	D-I
Southern Illinois U. At Carbondale	D-I	Kent State U.	D-I
SUNY at Albany	D-I	Ohio U.	D-I
*U. California at Santa Barbara	D-I	Texas Technological U.	D-I
U. Delaware	D-I	U. California at Riverside	D-I
U. Rhode Island	D-I	U. California of Santa Cruz	D-I
U. South Carolina at Columbia	D-I	U. Houston	D-I
U. Wyoming	D-I	U. Idaho	D-II
*Virginia Commonwealth U.	D-I	U. Mississippi	D-I
		**U. South Florida	D-I
		U. Wisconsin at Milwaukee	D-I
Total	**9**		**11**
Private Institutions			
Rennselaer Polytechnic Institute	D-I	Brigham Young U.	D-I
		Lehigh U.	D-I
		Northeastern U.	D-II
		Rice U.	D-I
		U. Notre Dame	D-I
Total	**1**		**5**

* = Institutions reclassified as R-I in 1987–1994: see Table 4 (Institutions counted twice in Table 3)

** = Institutions reclassified as D-I in 1976–1987: see Table 6 (Institution counted twice in Table 3)

TABLE 6
New D-I Institutions in 1987 and 1994 (Excluding Institutions That Experienced Any Downward Movement) With Their Previous Categories

New Members of D-I: 1987	1976 Category	New Members of D-I: 1994	1987 Category
Public Institutions			
Bowling Green State U.	D-II	East Texas State U.	D-II
College of William and Mary	D-II	Illinois State U.	D-II
Memphis State U.	D-II	Indiana U. of Pennsylvania	C-I
Miami U.	D-II	*Northern Arizona U.	D-II
Texas Woman's U.	D-II	*Old Dominion U.	D-II
U. Akron	D-II	U. Missouri at Rolla	D-II
**U. South Florida	D-II	U. North Carolina at Greensboro	D-II
Western Michigan U.	D-II	*U. Texas at Arlington	D-II
		*U. Texas at Dallas	D-II
Total	**8**		**9**
Private Institutions			
Nova U.	C-I	Adelphi U.	D-II
Teachers College, Columbia U.	S	*Andrews U.	D-II
Union Institute, Ohio	S	*Clark Atlanta U. (Atlanta U.)	D-II
U. S. International U.	D-II	*Drexel U.	D-II
		*Florida Inst. of Technology	D-II
		Hofstra U.	D-II
		New School for Social Research	D-II
Total	**4**		**7**

* = Institutions reclassified as D-II in 1976–1987: see Table 7 (Institutions counted twice in Table 3)

** = Institution reclassified as R-II in 1987–1994: see Table 5 (Institution counted twice in Table 3)

izations. First, as already noted, there are marked differences in the contribution of public and private institutions to overall upward drift. While 47 public institutions have become R-I or R-II institutions since the 1976 Carnegie Classification (subtract 3 from the total number of R-I and R-II institutions for the 3 institutions that moved up twice—to R-II status by 1987, then to R-I status by 1994), the corresponding number for private institutions is 13. In the two lower categories, D-I and D-II, on the other hand, the picture is rather different—46 new public institutions and 28 new private institutions. It is interesting to speculate whether these newly arrived private institutions will continue their momentum and eventually boost the relative proportion of private institutions in the R-I and R-II classifications.

Interestingly, the success shown over the last 20 years by private institutions in breaking into the D-I and D-II categories may be waning. Table 7 indicates that while 14 private institutions were reclassified as D-II in the 1976–1987 period, this number dropped to 7 in the 1987–1994 period. This rather large differ-

ence would appear to be at least partly a function of the decision by institutions classified as "Specialized" (institutions awarding at least half their degrees in a single discipline) in 1976 to diversify and introduce doctorate-level programs during the 1976–1987 period. Six such institutions were reclassified as D-II in 1987 (three engineering, one theological, one medical, and one "other"); none were reclassified as D-II in the 1987–1994 period.

Finally, one might expect that overall, upward drift would be influenced by geography, more specifically population and economic growth. This expectation is largely borne out by the data. The states with the largest contingents among the 133 institutions that experienced upward drift since the 1976 Carnegie Classification were California (12 institutions), New York (11 institutions), Texas (8 institutions), Ohio (9 institutions), and Pennsylvania (7 institutions), largely mirroring relative population size, and to a lesser extent, population growth.

Examination of the fourth edition of the Carnegie Classification indicates that the phe-

TABLE 7
New D-II Institutions in 1987 and 1994 (Excluding Institutions That Experienced Any Downward Movement) With Their Previous Categories

New Members of D-II: 1987	1976 Category	New Members of D-II: 1994	1987 Category
Public Institutions			
Cleveland State U.	C-I	Florida International U.	C-I
Colorado School of Mines	S	George Mason U.	C-I
Florida Atlantic U.	C-I	Indiana U.–Purdue U. Indianapolis	C-I
Louisiana Technological U.	C-I	Michigan Technological U.	C-I
Middle Tennessee State U.	C-I	New Jersey Inst. of Technology	S
*Northern Arizona U.	C-I	San Diego State U.	C-I
*Old Dominion U.	C-I	Tennessee State U.	C-I
Portland State U.	C-I	Texas Southern U.	C-I
Rutgers, State U. at Newark	C-I	U. Alabama at Huntsville	C-I
SUNY College Env. Science & Forestry	S	U. Alaska at Fairbanks	C-I
Tennessee Technological U.	C-I	U. Colorado at Denver	C-I
U. Alabama at Birmingham	C-I	U. Massachusetts at Lowell	C-I
U. Maryland (Baltimore County)	C-I	U. Puerto Rico at Rio Piedras	C-I
U. Missouri at St. Louis	C-I	U. Southwestern Louisiana	C-I
U. New Orleans	C-I	Wichita State U.	C-I
*U. Texas at Arlington	C-I	Wright State U.	C-I
*U. Texas at Dallas	C-I		
Total	**17**		**16**
Private Institutions			
*Andrews U.	C-I	DePaul U.	C-I
Atlanta U.	S	Pace U.	C-I
Biola U.	C-I	Seton Hall U.	C-I
*Clark Atlanta U. (Atlanta U.)	S	U. LaVerne	C-I
Clarkson U.	S	U. San Diego	C-I
Drake U.	C-I	Wake Forest U.	C-I
*Drexel U.	C-I	Worcester Polytechnic Inst.	C-I
Duquesne U.	C-I		
*Florida Institute of Technology	S		
Hahnemann U.	S		
Mississippi College	C-I		
Pepperdine U.	C-I		
Stevens Institute of Technology	S		
U. San Francisco	C-I		
Total	**14**		**7**

* = Institutions reclassified as D-I in 1987–1994: see Table 6 (Institutions counted twice in Table 3)

nomenon of upward drift continued at least up until 1991, and to approximately the same degree as in the period covered by the third edition. This finding suggests that the graduate/research model that Christopher Jencks and David Riesman identified some 26 years ago as the major characteristic of the postwar "academic revolution" has not lost its power of attraction. Despite pressures to re-emphasize the role of under-graduate education, ambitious institutions are apparently still beguiled by the promise of prestige associated with doctorate-level education. But perhaps this is not such a surprise.

PART II

THE PARTICIPANTS

CHAPTER 3

THE COLLEGE STUDENT

ASSOCIATE EDITORS: ERIC L. DEY AND KENNETH FELDMAN

It is no exaggeration to say that the scholarly and research literature on higher education contains many thousands of books and articles about college students. Yet, in a sense, the concerns of these numerous analyses mostly boil down to an interest in answering three basic questions: What sorts of people go to college, what sorts of experiences do they have there, and, as a consequence, what sorts of people do they become by the end of their matriculation? These questions may seem simple, but answering them is not. In selecting readings for this section, we wanted to provide insight into some of the answers and some of the complexities generated by these questions, while illustrating the wide range of approaches that can be used to address them.

For the question about the sorts of people who go to college, the answer depends in part on the year to which one refers. The first selection, by Dey and Hurtado, provides an overview of a number of important trends in the personal characteristics, attitudes and values, and educational achievements and expectations of students entering college in the United States since 1966. These trends, drawn primarily from national surveys of college students conducted by the Cooperative Institutional Research Program, underscore the profound changes in the nature of students going to college over the past three decades. As an example, the racial and ethnic diversity of students has markedly increased, while the proportion of women has risen to the point where women now represent the majority of students. These and other trends are important in that they force us not only to continuously re-evaluate the answer to the question of who goes to college, but also to consider the practical implications of these trends for higher education. As students change, so do the institutions that intend to serve their needs and promote their development.

The second selection, taken from an article by Attinasi, represents research intended to answer the question of what experiences students have during college. There is also a methodological shift from the approach used in the first selection, based as it is on data derived from surveys completed by millions of students on hundreds of college campuses, to an approach based on open-ended interviews of eighteen Mexican American students and former students, from a single entering class of a large, public southwestern university. What is lost in breadth is gained in depth. The interviews were conducted eight to eleven months following the end of the students' freshman year to obtain their perceptions of their college-going behavior during, and prior to, their freshman year. On the basis of his findings and theoretical interpretations, Attinasi arrives at several interesting proposals about the sociopsychological context of freshman-year persistence.

The third selection, by Weidman, which is excerpted from a longer piece of his, offers a conceptualization of the sorts of experiences students have at college. He sees these experiences as classifiable into such categories as formal academic normative contexts (e.g., institutional and within-institution program quality, the institutional mission, the academic department), informal academic normative contexts (e.g., the "hidden curriculum"), formal social normative contexts (e.g., residential settings), and informal social normative contexts (e.g., peer groups). Weidman

Eric L. Dey is an Associate Professor in the Center for the Study of Higher and Postsecondary Education at the University of Michigan. (dey@umich.edu). Kenneth A. Feldman is Professor of Sociology at the State University of New York at Stony Brook (feldman@ccvm.sunysb.edu)

analyzes the transmission of normative effects through interpersonal interaction, intrapersonal processes (i.e., the student's subjective assessment of his or her experiences), and social and academic integration into campus life. In his analysis, Weidman is careful to point out that the various in-college normative pressures cannot be fully understood or assessed without taking into consideration the student's background characteristics, parental socialization and the student's noncollege reference groups.

The interplay between campus culture and student identity is highlighted in the fourth selection, by Rhoads. Although it is common to think of a general campus culture when considering student experiences, the importance of specific formal and informal subgroupings, which can develop on the basis of any number of factors, has long been recognized in research on college students. The specific issue that Rhoads considers in this selection is the role of identity politics in student organizing and contemporary student activism. The interaction of these factors can play a defining role in the experiences that students have on campuses. The author ends his article with an examination of some educational implications multicultural activism may have to understanding today's diverse students.

The final two selections focus on the outcomes of students' experiences during college. The selection by Feldman is concerned with different orientations that can be used in understanding student outcomes. Organized around a discussion of three major reviews and syntheses of the literature on college students outcomes (Feldman and Newcomb, Bowen, and Pascarella and Terenzini), this selection underscores the different approaches that can be taken in explaining the complexities of student outcomes. The final selection, by Pascarella and Terenzini, provides an accessible overview of the impact that college has upon students. By examining some of the commonly-held "myths" about higher education and its effects on students, the authors effectively extend their extensive review of the college impact literature by calling into question these myths and challenging us to rethink some of our assumptions about higher education.

For those interested in additional analyses of college students, we recommend several readings that supplement the selections made here. The Astin, Parrott, Korn, and Sax monograph provides additional statistical detail on trends among traditional college students, while the articles by Hurtado, Inkeles, Briggs, and Rhee, and St. John, Paulsen, and Starkey extend our first organizing question to who goes to college where (and with what consequence). Most of the other articles and books we recommend (Astin, Baxter-Magolda, Chickering and Reisser, and Kuh) focus in varying degree upon student experiences and how these influence student outcomes. The book by Knox, Lindsay and Kolb is valuable for its concentration on the long-term effects of colleges, while the Pascarella and Terenzini book reflects the most recent effort to provide a comprehensive review of the literature on student outcomes (both short-term and long-term).

Suggested Supplementary Readings

Astin, A. W. *How College Affects Students*. San Francisco: Jossey-Bass, 1991.

Astin, A. W., Parrott, S. A., Korn, W. S., and Sax, L. J. *The American Freshman: Thirty Year Trends*. Los Angeles: Higher Education Research Institute, UCLA, 1997.

Baxter Magolda, M. B. "Cocurricular Influences on College Students' Intellectual Development," *Journal of College Student Development*, 1992, *31*, 203-213.

Chickering, A. W. and Reisser, L. *Education and Identity* (Second edition). San Francisco: Jossey-Bass, 1993.

Hurtado, S., Inkelas, K. K., Briggs, C. L. and Rhee, B. S., "Differences in College Access and Choice Among Racial/Ethnic Groups: Identifying Continuing Barriers," *Research in Higher Education*, 1997, *38*, 1, 43–75.

Kuh, G. D. "The Other Curriculum: Out-of-Class Experiences Associated with Student Learning and Personal Development," *The Journal of Higher Education*, 1995, *66*, 2, 123–155.

Knox, W. E., Lindsay, P, and Kolb, M. N. *Does College Make a Difference? Long-Term Changes in Activities and Attitudes*. Westport, CT: Greenwood Press, 1993.

St. John, E. P., Paulsen, M. B., and Starkey, J. B. "The Nexus Between College Choice and Persistence." *Research in Higher Education*, 1996, *37*, 2, 175–220.

Pascarella, E. T., and Terenzini, P. T. *How College Affects Students*. San Francisco: Jossey-Bass, 1991.

College Impact, Student Impact:
A Reconsideration of the Role of Students Within American Higher Education[1]

Eric L. Dey and Sylvia Hurtado

As the central constituency in American higher education, students have been given a tremendous amount of attention in the popular and scholarly literatures. Traditionally, undergraduates have been viewed by the ways in which their background attributes—such as character, preparation, gender, and race—contribute to and help describe the culture and status of individual campuses and larger systems of higher education institutions. Clark, for example, notes that "students are important to the character of their institution" and that "the student body becomes a major force in defining the institution" (1970, p. 253). Selective admissions policies are often used to select students not only on the basis of academic criteria but on the basis of 'character' and the student's potential to contribute to the college in any number of ways (Klitgaard 1985). In addition, students and their perceived academic quality are often seen as an organizational resource and as a measure of institutional quality (Astin 1985).

More recently, it has become popular to think of undergraduates as the recipient of collegiate influences that produce certain psychological, social, and economic outcomes for individuals as well as the larger society. This perspective has been popularized by the assessment movement and scholarly interest in questions of college impact (Erwin 1991; Pascarella & Terenzini 1991). From such a perspective, high quality programs and institutions are those which bring about the largest growth in student knowledge and personal development (Astin 1985; Jacobi, Astin & Ayala 1987).

In addition to these main perspectives, it is also important to consider the ways in which students influence colleges and universities. This view, which acknowledges students as sources of institutional change, has received much less attention in the research literature (Altbach 1993). The most visible source of student-led change is protest and direct action, which is reinforced by the observation that an "inactive student body is a much more curious phenomenon than one which is involved to some degree in activism" (Lipset 1971, p. 263). Historically, student activists have tended to pursue agendas focused on broad social and political concerns (Altbach 1993), although relatively recent examples of activism include student efforts to institutionalize ethnic studies and multicultural centers, prevent tuition increases, and urge institutions to develop proactive responses to racist and sexist situations on campus (Vellela 1988), It is important to note that not all student-led change comes about as a direct result of student protest or other forms of political action. In fact, a tremendous amount of such change develops as a result of natural institutional responses to changing student needs and preferences.

An Ecological Perspective

Although each of these views is useful in helping us understand different aspects of the role of students within higher education, they can also serve to artificially restrict the ways in which we view students. A more complete view is one in which the relationship between students and the college environment is seen as

"College Impact, Student Impact: A Reconsideration of the Role of Students Within American Higher Education," by Eric L. Dey and Sylvia Hurtado, reprinted from *Higher Education*, Vol. 30, 1995, Kluwer Academic Publishers.

both reciprocal and dynamic. Such an orientation has been described as an ecological perspective (Alwin, Cohen & Newcomb 1991; Bronfenbrenner 1979) and portrays students as actively shaping their interpersonal environments and, by extension, their institutions, with these environments simultaneously providing the potential for transforming the individual.

The ecological perspective is based on Bronfenbrenner's observations about the limitations inherent in the study of human development using traditional perspectives. Of particular concern to Bronfenbrenner was the lack of recognition paid in the research literature to the process of "progressive accommodation between a growing human organism and its immediate environment" (1979, p. 13). Although the importance of the interaction between individuals and environments in fostering human development has long been recognized, psychological research focused almost exclusively on aspects of the individual, to the neglect of the environment and its influence.

Research on students in higher education, in contrast, has long been concerned with environmental influences, yet the conception of the environment is similar to the traditional psychological perspectives described by Bronfenbrenner. In short, the environment is conceptualized as a "static structure that makes no allowance for the evolving processes of interaction" (Bronfenbrenner 1979, p. 17). Such a conception blinds us to the important processes of personal choice and organizational change that have been described as dynamic stability, or "the process by which the individual constructs circumstances which help maintain prior orientations and which in turn feed back on the person so as to maintain stability over time. The person is thus not only the recipient of influences from the environment; she is also an active agent in shaping that environment" (Mortimer et al., cited in Alwin, Cohen & Newcomb 1991, p. 252).

In order to explore an ecological perspective of college students and the dynamic relationship between students and institutions, we will discuss two important social and educational trends that have helped shape American higher education over the past three decades: changes in the demography of higher education, and entering students' educational plans and preferences. We will also consider the changes in the experiences of students *during college* as a third group of data-based observations.

In examining these trends, we hope to show the utility of adopting an ecological perspective by highlighting patterns of institutional change that are related to these student trends. The interplay between students and institutions is both subtle and complex, where direct cause-and-effect relationships are difficult to detect. As such, we hope to illustrate this perspective by linking what we believe to be interrelated trends. Although our preference would be to provide a more definitive analysis, we are unaware of data resources which might allow this sort of analysis. As such is the case, our goal here is to encourage others to see the value of this perspective since it opens up new possibilities for studying students, institutions, and the processes that foster individual and institutional change.

The data on entering college students come primarily from the Cooperative Institutional Research Program (CIRP) coordinated by the Higher Education Research Institute at UCLA. The CIRP data are based on responses from an annual survey of some 250,000 students entering about 600 colleges and universities nationwide (see Astin, Korn & Riggs 1993; Dey, Astin & Korn 1991). Given the large sample sizes we are dealing with, any differences large enough to be interesting are going to be statistically significant. As such, we will refrain from showing formal statistical tests. It should also be recognized that the CIRP focuses primarily on what might be considered "traditional" American students, so the patterns discussed are likely to understate the extent to which changes have occurred in the general college population. Data on the changing pattern of in-college experiences of students is based on various sets of longitudinal surveys of college students who participated in the CIRP freshman surveys and who were followed-up several years later (see Astin & Panos 1969; Green, Astin, Korn & McNamara 1983; Higher Education Research Institute 1992).

The Changing Demography of Higher Education

Despite the many changes that have occurred in access to and enrollment in American higher education over the past several decades, we suspect that the traditional image of college students is surprisingly persistent. One reason that traditional images are common is that we tend to think of specific generations of college students when trying to describe their attributes. Unfortunately, truth and fiction are intertwined in the stereotypes that become attached to each generation.

At the same time, it is important to note that some of these generational stereotypes do come close to describing groups of students at particular institutions. To be sure, some institutions continue to seek and enroll students that fit a "traditional" college student image, while others have taken on more diverse clienteles in order to better serve changing state and local populations. This, then, suggests that there have been changes not only in the type of student now attending college, but there are also related changes in institutional mission and policy that help differentiate institutions across the higher education system. The enrollment patterns associated with the changing demography of higher education have helped to transform the nature of our institutions.

Spurred on by the great social movements of the 1960s, American higher education enrollments have grown considerably and continue to expand (U.S. Department of Education 1992). Despite predictions of a declining number of college-age students, we witnessed a 16 percent increase over the last decade and a record enrollment of 14.4 million students in 1992. Much of the growth over the last three decades has been due to increased access for non-traditional students. Adults over the age of 25 have been the fastest growing group, and currently represent over 40 percent of all students in higher education. There has also been a shift toward part-time enrollment in higher education since 1965, with part-time students now representing about 43 percent of all students.

In addition to the changes wrought by the large numbers of "nontraditional" students, striking changes in the composition of college entrants have also redefined our conception of the "traditional" college student. Table 1 shows the changing demographics of first-time, full-time students entering four-year colleges. A typical American college student in the 1990s is likely to be female: women constituted 53 percent of first year students pursuing a baccalaureate degree in 1991, compared to 44 percent in 1961. As a result of society's changing views of women's roles, coupled with institutional initiatives to enroll more women and an overall increase in the level of educational attainment, today's college student is also more likely to have a mother who has completed a college degree. The proportion of older students attending college for the first time has also steadily increased over time. These changes in the traditional college-going population indicate that child care services, re-entry services, women's centers, women's studies, and incorporating gender-related issues in the classroom will continue to be salient for increasing proportions of campus communities.

Improved access for students of diverse socioeconomic backgrounds is one of the most significant trends of the last three decades that warrants monitoring in the future. The median family income of traditional students attending college in the 1960s was almost twice as high as the national median income. This gap was dramatically reduced by the federal financial aid policies that enabled students of diverse economic backgrounds to pursue a college education. Although national family incomes steadily increased, the trend toward closing the gap between national family income and the families of four-year college students stagnated during the 1980s. This lack of progress toward economic equity may be largely attributable to changes in the federal student aid programs during the Reagan-Bush administrations, rapidly rising college tuition rates, as well as recent economic problems (College Board 1989). The combined effect of these factors during the 1980s suggests that four-year colleges will face the challenge of recruiting and retaining students of diverse economic backgrounds in the years to come.

Table 1 also shows that the proportion of white students has steadily declined, while the representation of all other ethnic minority groups has increased among first-time entrants to four-year colleges. Increased access over the years, coupled with the growing representation of minorities within college-age cohorts, have changed the ethnic composition of many campuses. As a result, campuses will need to continue the restructuring process of becoming multicultural environments. What is not evident from this table, however, is that while all racial and ethnic groups have recorded enrollment gains, some ethnic groups continue to face considerable inequities in access to college. For example, although Hispanics posted gains, they have experienced an actual decline in their college participation rate (Carter & Wilson 1992). Both Native Americans (52 percent) and Hispanics (55 percent) are also more likely to be represented in two-year colleges than either African American or white students (42 and 37 percent respectively) (U.S. Department of Education 1992).

These changing characteristics of America's college students are a direct result of a combination of demographic growth, changing social views, government policies, and institutional initiatives to recruit students from all potential

college populations. Some institutions, for example, have altered their missions and strengthened their commitment to serving special populations. Such changes would have been impossible without the equity reform movements that brought about changes in the nation's collective consciousness as well as tangible federal assistance in the form of financial aid policies. We have witnessed the development of tribal colleges, a strengthened position of many historically black and women's colleges, and now an increasing number of Hispanic-serving institutions.[2] In each of these specific cases, student characteristics have helped give further definition to the institution's mission. Aside from these special types of institutions, we are also witnessing a gradual transformation of "traditional" institutions as they respond to the new student populations by creating new services (Pearson, Shavlik & Touchton 1989; Smith 1989) and incorporating new perspectives in the curriculum and extracurricular programming (Andersen 1988).

TABLE 1
Demographic Characteristics of New Students Entering Four-Year Colleges, 1961–1991

	1961	1971	1981	1991
Percent women	44	46	51	53
Percentage of students with mothers who held a college degree	21	22	30	39
Age distribution				
18 or younger	–	78	76	69
19 or older	–	23	25	31
Socioeconomic background				
Median freshman family income	45,922	41,770	40,289	43,600
National median family income	24,864	33,238	33,346	35,353
Ratio, national to freshman income	.54	.80	.83	.81
Racial/ethnic background				
White/Caucasian	97	91	87	78
African-American/Black	2	7	9	12
American Indian	Z	1	1	2
Asian-American/Oriental	1	1	1	4
Mexican-American/Chicano	–	Z	1	2
Puerto Rican		Z	1	1
Other	Z	1	2	2

Notes: Racial/ethnic labels vary between survey years. Racial ethnic percentages may total more than 100 after 1971 due to multiple responses of students. Family income estimates given in 1990 dollars. Due to differences in response options for mother's education, postsecondary certificate holders are included with high school graduates; those with some graduate school are included with college graduates. Z indicates less than 0.5 percent;—indicates data not available.

Source: 1961 data are from Astin and Panos 1968; 1971 and 1981 data are from Dey, Astin, and Korn 1991; 1991 data are from Dey, Astin, Korn, and Riggs 1992. National median family income estimates are from the Statistical Abstract of the United States, 1992, Table 703, and Current Population Reports (Series P-60), No. 80.

TABLE 2
High School Experience Trends and Expectations for College, Various Years

High school grade point average	1966	1975	1984	1993
A or A+	15	18	20	27
B– to B+	54	60	58	57
C+ or less	31	21	22	16

Estimated chances are very good that they will	1973	1983	1993
Make at least a B average	35	41	47
Graduate with honors	9	12	16
Be elected to an academic honor society	5	7	9
Fail one or more courses	2	1	1
Get tutoring help in specific courses	7[1]	9	16[2]

Student expects to need special tutoring or remedial work during college in	1982	1994	1993
English	11	11	12
Reading	4	5	5
Mathematics	22	27	29
Social studies	2	3	4
Science	9	10	11
Foreign language	7	10	11

Met or exceeded recommended levels of high school preparation in	1984	1988	1992
English (4 years)	93	95	96
Mathematics (3 years)	85	92	93
Foreign language (2 years)	66	79	79
Physical science (2 years)	52	50	47
Biological science (2 years)	34	35	35

Note: Curricular recommendations based on A *Nation at Risk* (National Commission on Excellence on Education, 1982).

[1]Question not asked in 1973; data from 1975 reported.
[2]Question not asked in 1993; data from 1992 reported.

Source: Dey, Astin, & Korn 1991; Astin, Korn, & Riggs 1993.

While these changes may *appear* to have occurred rapidly, change continues to come about slowly for those who confront institutional resistance. A college's historical legacy of exclusion of specific groups may, for example, continue to influence seemingly "neutral" institutional policies (Hurtado 1994). Generating a commitment to institutional transformation among administrators and faculty who refuse to examine their own attitudes and practices that affect students remains one of the greatest challenges (Aiken, Anderson, Dinnerstein, Lensink & MacCorquodale 1988). Thus, ideologies at the institutional and individual level continue to present barriers to recognizing and meeting the needs of the new American college student.

Educational Plans and Preferences

In addition to the changing composition of students, there have been changes in student plans and preferences for college. Some of these patterns appear to be clearly related to student experiences in high school, some are related to larger economic forces, and others seem more closely related to social forces like changing views about the role of women in American society. First, we consider the issue of student academic experiences during high school and how this appears to relate to their expectations for the college experience.

The data in Table 2 show an interesting and complex pattern of changes with regard to student preparation. The top panel of data show that students are now entering college with higher grade point averages than in the past. The percentage of students earning A grades in high school essentially doubled between 1966 and 1993 (from 15 to 27 percent, respectively), while the percentage earning C or worse grades fell by one-half (31 to 16 percent). The relatively high level of student academic success before college appears to have influenced the expectations that students have for college: the CIRP data show strong increases between 1973 and 1993 in the percentage of entering students who expect to earn at least a B average in college, graduate with honors, and be elected to an academic honor society. Over the same period, the percentage of students expecting to fail one or more courses dropped by one-half. In combination, these patterns might suggest that students today are better prepared than those entering college two decades ago.

At the same time, these data also reveal a very different perspective. Despite the high levels of academic success prior to college, students also report that they are in need of additional academic support services. For example, the percentage of students who believe that there is a 'very good chance' that they will get tutoring help in specific courses during college more than doubled between 1975 and 1992, from 7 to 16 percent. Similarly, the percentage of students who expected to get special tutoring or remediation in mathematics, science, and foreign language increased between 1984 and 1993. What makes this interesting is that over the same period, students were more likely to meet recommended levels of preparation in many of these fields. For example, more than 93 percent of students who entered college in 1993 had at least three years of math during high school (up from 85 percent in 1984), while three out of every ten students expected to need special tutoring or remediation in math (up from 22 percent in 1982).

Taken together, these trends suggest that there has been something of a redefinition of the relationship between academic coursework on the high school level and skills related to those courses. This puts tremendous pressure on college and university faculty to work with students who have been very academically successful in high school and met or exceeded recommended levels of high school study, but

who may nevertheless be underprepared for college-level work as traditionally defined.

Next we consider the changing patterns of preferences that students express for various undergraduate majors when they enter college (Table 3). This is an important consideration since beyond all of the educational philosophy that goes into designing a curriculum, a college's ability to maintain its curricular focus is necessarily dependent upon its ability to enroll students in the courses it offers. From a traditional liberal-arts perspective, the past 25 years have not been good ones with regard to interest in liberal arts fields among entering students: interest in majoring in the humanities, the fine and performing arts, and the social sciences has been declining consistently. Interest in majoring in English, for example, dropped by nearly three-quarters between 1967 and 1992. Interest in majoring in biological or physical sciences has remained somewhat stable since the 1960s, while interest in mathematics and statistics has experienced a large decline, dropping from 4 percent in 1967 to 0.6 percent in 1992. Although the relatively new and developing field of computer science may have captured some of the students who otherwise might have majored in mathematics or statistics, the 85 percent decline in the number of students who enter college with an interest in math and statistics is quite alarming. Interest in the engineering fields has been relatively stable over the past several years after peaking in the early 1980s.

Table 3 also shows that the greatest changes in the popularity of different fields is associated with the field of business. After a period of relative stability, the percentage of students interested in business majors increased sharply during the late 1970s and 1980s. During the past few years, however, interest in business has stopped its climb and is currently in steep decline, with student interest now equal to that registered in 1967. The cause for this turnaround is not clear: it may be that competition for jobs has increased in the recent economic slowdown, or that many students are simply disillusioned with the field of business because of scandals such as insider trading, stock fraud, and the savings and loan debacle of the 1980s. While the explanation for these trends may not be clear, one thing is: institutions which rapidly expanded their business

TABLE 3
Undergraduate Major Preferences Among Entering College Students

	Percentage of Entering College Students Expressing an Interest in Various Majors in					
	1967	1972	1977	1982	1987	1992
Biological sciences	4	4	5	4	4	5
Business	16	16	22	24	27	16
Education	11	7	9	6	9	10
Engineering	10	7	9	13	9	9
English	4	2	1	.8	1	1
Health professions (nursing, pre-med, etc.)	5	11	10	9	7	16
History and political science	7	4	3	2	3	3
Humanities	5	4	2	2	3	2
Fine arts (applied and performing)	9	9	6	4	5	5
Mathematics or statistics	4	2	.8	.6	.6	.6
Physical sciences	3	2	2	2	2	2
Social sciences	–	8	5	4	6	6
Undecided	2	5	5	5	7	7

Note: indicates comparable data not available.

Source: Cooperative Institutional Research Program Trends File, Higher Education Research Institute, UCLA.

programs to take advantage of this growth in student interest may soon have to contend with the new problem of having too many highly-paid faculty in the field of business relative to student demand. This problem may be especially troublesome for the many small liberal arts colleges which avoided closure during the 1980s by moving away from a traditional liberal arts program to incorporate business education into the curriculum (see Breneman 1993).

While interest in business is now in steep decline after record-setting increases, interest in majoring in the health professions has been increasing rapidly and is now at an all-time high. This surge of interest may well reflect the students of today who seem to be searching for majors that will lead to profitable and stable careers since business has apparently lost its attraction. It will be more difficult for colleges and universities to respond to this increased interest since education for the health professions, which is largely based in the sciences, is inherently more expensive than that associated with the field of business. Moreover, it is impossible to predict how long this trend will last.

Given the pronounced changes in the major field choices of students entering college, it is not surprising to find that the educational preferences of women have also changed quite dramatically. Table 4, for example, shows trends in aspirations for various postgraduate degrees and interest in different undergraduate majors over the past two decades. This table shows the number of women students interested in certain degrees and fields of study for every 100 men interested in the same option. If men and women were equally likely to aspire to a certain degree we would, for example, see 100 women per 100 men expressing an interest.

These changes clearly show the effectiveness of the women's movement in changing the way that women (and to a lesser extent men) think about certain degrees and careers. For example, with respect to postgraduate degree *aspirations* upon entry into college, Table 4 shows that women have essentially reached a point of parity. Indeed, aspiration for law and medical degrees among women now slightly exceeds that of men. It is important to note, however, that this pattern changes after four years in college: The number of women per 100 men aspiring to law, medical, and doctoral degrees is 91, 51, and 92, respectively (Higher Education Research Institute 1992). The marked drop in aspirations for medical degrees for women relative to that of men underscores the possibility that the undergraduate environment is relatively unsupportive for women aspiring to become physicians.

TABLE 4
Academic Plans of New College Students by Gender

	Number of Women per 100 Men Aspiring to Selected Degrees and Undergraduate Majors in		
	1972	*1982*	*1992*
Postgraduate degree aspiration			
Law	32	81	106
Medical	44	90	103
Doctoral	64	86	99
Undergraduate major field preferences			
Biological sciences	64	103	102
Business	80	115	91
Education	329	375	286
Engineering	3	16	16
English	278	167	167
Health professions (nursing, pre-med, etc.)	550	331	239
History or political science	54	69	83
Humanities	204	163	121
Fine arts (applied and performing)	124	102	60
Mathematics or statistics	100	117	71
Physical sciences	27	38	54
Social sciences	227	275	247

Source: Cooperative Institutional Research Program, Higher Education Research Institute, UCLA.

The bottom panel of Table 4 show how women's preferences for different fields of study have been changing, and reveal a mixture of trends. For example, in the fields where women were most underrepresented in 1972—Engineering, history and political science, biological sciences, and physical sciences—we see a pattern of progress toward parity that varies by field. Engineering, for example, had the smallest representation of women in 1972, and this fact remains true two decades later. Despite a five-fold jump in interest in this field between 1972 and 1982, there has been no real change since that time. There may still be strong institutional barriers—such as heavy mathematical course requirements without a realistic possibility of remediation, and a male-dominated climate that is unwelcoming for women—that are preventing interest levels from moving beyond this plateau. The other science fields with an early underrepresentation of women have fared differently: women's interest in the biological sciences moved quickly to a position of parity, while the physical sciences still have a long way to go despite the doubling of interest that occurred. History and political science have also made progress

in attracting the interest of women, but still remain far below a point of parity.

Other fields have also shown gender differences in patterns of student interest. Education, for example, shows a declining rate of interest among women despite the fact that it remains strongly dominated by women. The health professions which in addition to medicine includes the large, female-dominated field of nursing—now attracts the interest of fewer women relative to men than in the past. In the fields of English, the humanities, and the fine arts we have also seen a lessening of interest among women, with the decline in interest so sharp in the fine arts that women are now underrepresented. Women are now also underrepresented in the field of business, after reaching and exceeding a position of parity in the 1980s.

All of these changes will continue to have an impact on institutions as they attempt to balance their traditional educational missions with the changing interests of students. This is especially true of the changing patterns of interest among women and members of other underrepresented groups as such trends bring with them pressure to remove inequities and achievement barriers for these groups. In addition to influencing institutional policy and practice, these shifts in student interest are also linked to larger social and economic forces (such as the projected job market), and have direct implications for the nation's talent pool. The continued advancement of all fields of practice or inquiry is determined in good part by the pool of student talent in each particular field, and higher education's ability to help meet social and economic needs.

Experiences During College

As one might expect, given the many changes we have described, there have been changes in the nature of the college student experience. Table 5 shows changes in student academic performance, activities, and student satisfac-

tion during college from the late 1960s to the beginning of this decade. Perhaps one of the most striking changes has been the shift toward earning high grades in college and a related drop in the proportion of students who earn less than a 'B–' since the late 1960s. This indicates that performance and academic success in college has been redefined, creating a certain amount of grade inflation relative to earlier eras. This may reflect the fact that students have become more grade conscious over the years and may be more likely to contest their grades. However, it may be that this trend is fueled by external pressure because maintaining good college grades has become more closely linked to such economic considerations as the receipt of financial aid, auto insurance discounts, and access to graduate schools and jobs after college. At the same time that there are more students making high grades, it

TABLE 5
Trends in Student Experiences During College, 1966–70 and 1987–91

	1966–70	1987–91	Percentage difference
Undergraduate grade point average			
A or A+	1	6	5
A– or B+	5	27	22
B	21	36	15
B– or C+	35	24	–11
C	26	7	–19
C– or less	13	2	–11
Activities since entering college			
Joined a fraternity or sorority	20	21	1
Graduated with honors	14	12	–2
Frequent activities during student's last year of college			
Drank wine or liquor	12	22	10
Drank beer	30	38	8
Stayed up all night	8	14	6
Participated in an organized demonstration/ protest*	19	18	–1
Attended a religious service	33	25	–8
Smoked cigarettes	27	12	–15
Percent of students who were satisfied with:			
Overall quality of instruction	92	90	–2
Opportunity to discuss coursework with professors outside of class	84	88	4
Lab facilities	90	88	–2
Library	83	83	0
Overall satisfaction	74	87	13

*Percentage includes those students marking 'frequently' or 'occasionally'.

Source: Unpublished tabulations, Higher Education Research Institute, UCLA.

appears to be more difficult for students to graduate with honors.

Despite the changing political views of students and the persistent (and somewhat contradictory) images of the typical college student as an activist or a member of a fraternity/sorority, we find very little change in the proportion of students who actually participated in either of these activities since the 1960s. This suggests that these two activities are relatively 'generation free' in the sense that a roughly stable proportion of students participate. Despite the apparent constancy in the proportion of students involved in these activities, different generations of students become closely associated with these images due to larger social and political contexts. For example, even though a minority of students participated in demonstrations in the late 1960s, the general perception of this era is somewhat different.

In terms of health and social behavior, students today are less likely to report frequent smoking due in part to increased health awareness and related restrictions on smoking in school, work, and places of entertainment. However, a higher proportion of students reported that they drank wine, liquor or beer in college than in the late 1960s. While most of the students surveyed here would meet drinking-age requirements by their fourth year of college, it is difficult to restrict their associations with other students who are under the age limit. This shift in student behavior makes it extremely problematic for colleges to monitor and comply with legislation that raised the drinking-age in the last decade. Colleges continue to provide opportunities for alcohol-free activities, but providing alternatives for healthy social lives will remain one of the continuing challenges for student affairs staff on campus.

Student satisfaction and retention are aspects of a student's experience that are closely related to college impact and institutional accountability. These data show that student satisfaction with the college experience has remained generally high over time, with only small changes in specific areas of satisfaction. Although students are somewhat less satisfied with lab facilities and the quality of instruction on campus, in the early 1990s they were more satisfied with opportunities to discuss course work with professors outside of class. Overall satisfaction with college has increased from 74 percent in the late 1960s to approximately 87 percent of college students at the beginning of this decade.

It is interesting to note that overall satisfaction remains high, even though student retention has changed over the years. Table 6 shows the proportion of three undergraduate student cohorts who were retained at the college they originally entered using two different retention rates. These data clearly show a decreasing proportion of each cohort that have obtained a degree in four years, while the proportion persisting through four years has remained relatively stable. Taken together, this suggests that students are simply taking longer to graduate than earlier cohorts. There is perhaps no single explanation for why students are taking longer to graduate. Students are now faced with additional financial pressures—financial aid has shifted from grants to loans, and to avoid excessive debt, more students are working and attending college part-time (College Board 1989; Astin, Dey, Korn & Riggs 1991). In addition, the anecdotal evidence suggests that some students are finding it difficult to enroll in required courses at many large institutions, while others may be delaying their completion by taking advantage of study abroad programs or other opportunities that broaden their expe-

TABLE 6
Trends in Undergraduate Retention Rates

Undergraduate cohort	Obtained a Bachelor's degree	Obtained a Bachelor's degree or completed four years
1966–1970	47	59
1978–1982	43	56
1987–1991	40	56

Source: 1966–70 data are from Astin, 1971; 1978–82 data are from Green, Astin, Korn, and McNamara 1983; 1987–91 data are based on unpublished tabulations, Higher Education Research Institute, UCLA.

riences but lengthen the amount of time it takes to earn a degree.

Student retention will remain an important area of institutional accountability and we can expect that more institutions will begin to follow closely the progress of students and make efforts to improve their college experiences. It is clear that trends in student graduation rates have redefined persistence in such a way that we must monitor persistence from year to year and examine degree attainment rates over a longer time span. Six years has become the new guideline established by NCAA Division I institutions that many agree is more accurate that the four-year retention rate. Even so, only 53 percent of 1984 first-time, full-time students graduated in six years from their college (U.S. Department of Education 1992). Administrators, legislators, and the general public are becoming increasingly concerned about institutional retention rates while new federal regulations require that institutions report these rates.

The Complexity of the Student Role

Changes in the composition of the undergraduate student body in American higher education force us to reconceptualize our notions of the typical college student, as well as their influence on institutions and society at large. Our examination of the trends across generations of college students encourages us to adopt a more complex view of the role of students in American higher education. When we think of students and change, we naturally think of the ways institutions influence students: students are supposed to be influenced by the educational programs in which they participate. However, the reverse is also true: many institutions undergo significant change in their recruitment strategies, services, and curricula as the constituencies they serve change.

The value of adopting an ecological perspective is underscored by the changing demography of higher education, trends in student political preferences and academic interests, and significant changes in aspects of the college experience we have reviewed. Service to special populations has become a central mission of some colleges, while changes in the

type of students attending traditional four-year institutions reflect new needs and create new demands for institutional change. In contrast to student protests and political action, a tremendous amount of student-led change arises as the result of natural institutional efforts to serve student needs. Although many of these changes represent responses to recognized problems and come about with pressures from external constituencies (e.g., parents, alumni, taxpayers, legislators, peer institutions), they represent an attempt on the part of institutions to improve aspects of the educational process for students. Concern about student retention offers a prime example. Institutional efforts to improve retention rates have led to the creation of remedial programs in response to shifts in student preparation, the establishment of co-curricular programming to make the social environment more conducive for all students, and the improvement of academic counseling and opportunities for student-faculty contact.

Active attempts by students to change institutions through protest, and other forms of direct action, tend to receive the most attention. As noted above, relatively recent examples of activism include student efforts to institutionalize ethnic studies and multicultural centers, prevent tuition increases, and urge institutions to develop proactive responses to racist/sexist situations on campus (Vellela 1988). Such issues are especially important to the increased numbers of minorities, women, and students of diverse economic backgrounds on college campuses. In many cases, student protest has served as the impetus for institutional self-examination and the adoption of new institutional policy. Given the increasing amount of disaffection with traditional political methods among college students, and the numbers of entering students who report participating in demonstrations, we can expect to see continued protest activity when institutions are slow to respond to student needs or refuse to assume a leadership role in addressing matters of social concern.

Students can also actively resist attempts to be changed by institutions, and administrators may find it particularly problematic to change student social habits at institutions with strong student cultures. The trends in college student experiences show that drinking has increased even though new national policies designed to decrease alcohol use have been implemented. Institutional efforts designed to eliminate hazing, and racist or sexist games in fraternities have also been met with varied success. While the roots of this resistance may be based both in politics and popular youth culture, it is clear that institutional rules and regulations cannot guarantee success in changing student behavior regardless of the amount of input students have in developing such rules and regulations.

Finally, there are many areas that constitute problems for institutions simply because students have their own ideas and preferences. Perhaps the most troubling information we presented has to do with the future talent pool of students in specific fields. How can institutions influence students to pursue careers that will be vital in the future? At some level, students are attuned to job market opportunities, but their goals may not be synchronized with a changing economic future: By the time that students graduate from college with specific training, the availability of jobs in certain fields may have disappeared. The increasing rapidity with which economies have been changing suggests that the extended length of an undergraduate education will plague students seeking careers in fields where there is an unstable pattern of job growth.

Although we have a tendency to think of students in one of several unidimensional ways, a more complete view is one in which the relationship between student and the college environment is seen as both reciprocal and dynamic. Adopting this ecological perspective requires that we rethink the nature of the students' role in relation to institutions and the wider society. Students have proactively and subtly induced institutional and social change throughout history and will continue to do so in the future. These changes, in turn, have altered the nature of the student experience and the impact college has on students. We hope that those interested in higher education will begin to recognize and acknowledge these interconnections, and begin to view the role of college students in different and more complex ways.

Notes

1. Portions of this paper appear as a chapter in Altbach, P.G.. Berdahl, R.O. and Gumport, P.J.

(eds), *Higher education in American society* (3rd edition). Amherst, NY: Promethius.

2. Over the past two decades, 26 tribal colleges have been established and have steadily increased their enrollments (See O'Brien 1992). Women's colleges and historically black institutions have strengthened their position in terms of attaining a relatively stable and increasing student enrollment in the last ten years (Carter & Wilson 1992; see also Touchton & Davis 1991). Hispanic-serving institutions are defined by the Hispanic Association of Colleges and Universities (HACU) as institutions that meet a Hispanic enrollment minimum of 25 percent. An increasing number of institutions are expected to become Hispanic-serving towards the end of this decade (Hispanic Association of Colleges and Universities *Annual Report*, 1990).

References

Aiken, S. H., Anderson, K., Dinnerstein, M., Lensink, J. and MacCorquodale, P. 'Trying transformations: Curriculum integration and the problem of resistance', in Minnich, E., O'Barr, J and Rosenfeld, R. (eds), *Reconstructing the academy: Women's education and women's studies. Chicago:* University of Chicago.

Altbach, P. G. (1993). 'Students: Interests, culture, and activism', in Levine, A. (ed.), *Higher learning in America 1980–2000.* Baltimore, MD: Johns Hopkins University Press.

Alwin, D. F., Cohen, R. L. and Newcomb, T. M. (1991). *Political attitudes over the life span: The Bennington women after fifty years.* Madison, WI: University of Wisconsin Press.

Andersen, M. L. (1988). 'Changing the curriculum in higher education', in Minnich, E., O'Barr, J. and Rosenfeld, R. (eds), *Reconstructing the academy: Women's education and women's studies.* Chicago: University of Chicago.

Astin, A. W. (1985). *Achieving educational excellence.* San Francisco. Jossey-Bass.

Astin, A. W. (1993). *What matters in college: Four critical years revisited.* San Francisco: Jossey-Bass.

Astin, A. W., and Panos, R. J. (1968). *The educational and vocational development of college students.* Washington, DC: American Council on Education.

Astin, A. W., Dey, E. L., Korn, W. S. and Riggs, E. R. (1991). *The American freshman: National norms for Fall 1991.* Los Angeles: Higher Education Research Institute, UCLA.

Astin, A. W., Korn, W. S. and Riggs, E. R. (1993). *The American freshman: National norms for Fall 1993.* Los Angeles: Higher Education Research Institute, UCLA.

Breneman, D. W. (1993). 'Liberal arts colleges: What price survival?', in Levine, A. (ed.), *Higher learn-*

ing in America, 1980–2000. Baltimore, MD: Johns Hopkins University Press.

Bronfenbrenner, U. (1979). *The ecology of human development: Experiments by nature and design.* Cambridge, MA: Harvard University Press.

Carter, D. and Wilson, R. (1992). *Minorities in higher education: Tenth annual status report.* Washington, DC: American Council on Education, Office of Minority Concerns.

Clark, B. R. (1970). *The distinctive college.* Chicago: Aldine.

College Board. (1989). *Trends in student aid: 1980 to 1989.* New York: Author.

Dey, E. L., Astin, A. W. and Korn, W. S. (1991). *The American freshman: Twenty-five year trends.* Los Angeles: Higher Education Research Institute, UCLA.

Dey, E. L., Astin, A. W., Korn, W. S. and Riggs, E. R. (1992). *The American freshman: National norms for Fall 1992.* Los Angeles: Higher Education Research Institute, UCLA.

Erwin, T. D. (1991) *Assessing student learning and development: A guide to the principles, goals, and methods of determining college outcomes.* San Francisco: Jossey-Bass.

Green, K. C., Astin, A. W., Korn, W. S. and McNamara, P. (1983). *The American college student, 1982: National norms for 1978 and 1980 college freshmen.* Los Angeles: Higher Education Research Institute, UCLA.

Higher Education Research Institute. (1992). *The American college student, 1991: National norms for 1987 and 1989 college freshmen.* Los Angeles: Higher Education Research Institute, UCLA.

Hispanic Association of Colleges and Universities. (1990). *Annual report.* San Antonio, TX: Author.

Hurtado, S. (1994). The institutional climate for talented Latino students. *Research in Higher Education, 35*(4).

Jacobi, M. A., Astin, A. W. and Ayala, Jr., F. (1987). *College student outcomes assessment: A talent development perspective* [ASHE-ERIC Higher Education Report no. 7]. Washington, DC: George Washington University.

Klitgaard, R. (1985). *Choosing elites.* New York: Harper & Row.

Lipset, S. M. (1971). *Rebellion in the university.* New York: Little, Brown & Company.

O'Brien, E. M. (1992). *American Indians in higher education* [ACE Research Brief]. Washington, DC: American Council on Education.

Pascarella. E. T. and Terenzini, P. T. (1991). *How college affects students.* San Francisco: Jossey-Bass.

Pearson, C., Shavlik, D.L. and Touchton, J.G. (1989). *Educating the majority: Women challenge tradition in higher education.* New York: ACE/Macmillan.

Smith, D. (1989). *The challenge of diversity: Involvement or alienation in the academy* [ASHE-ERIC Higher Education Report no. 5]. Washington, DC: George Washington University.

Touchton, J. G. and Davis, L. (1991). *Factbook on women in higher education.* New York: ACE/Macmillan.

U.S. Department of Education. (1992). Unpublished tabulations cited in *The Chronicle of Higher Education Almanac* (1993, August 25). Washington, DC: Chronicle of Higher Education.

Vellela, T. (1988). *New voices: Student activism in the '80s and '90s.* Boston: South End Press.

Getting In: Mexican Americans' Perceptions of University Attendance and the Implications for Freshman Year Persistence

LOUIS C. ATTINASI, JR.

In view of its importance for social advancement [11] and its contribution to the improvement of personal well-being [2, 51], it is not surprising that higher education in the United States has become a cynosure for efforts to improve the condition of economically and socially disadvantaged subpopulations. Ironically, the present condition of these subpopulations exists because, in the past, higher education's service as an instrument for social mobility was seldom indiscriminate. America's racial and ethnic minorities have been and continue to be "grossly underrepresented in higher education and in almost all occupational fields that require a college education" [2], and do not, as a consequence, enjoy equitable participation in the larger society's social, economic, and political life.

One racial minority that has been particularly underserved by American higher education, in general, and by the four-year institution, in particular, is the Mexican American. In 1979, according to an estimate by the Bureau of the Census [47], the rate of baccalaureate degree attainment in the general population was more than four times the rate in the Mexican American subpopulation alone. Data presented by Brown [10] tend to confirm the link between social and economic advancement and college graduation. Relative to the total population, Mexican Americans are overrepresented in lower-level, poorer-paying positions, such as those occupied by service workers, artisans, operatives, farm and nonfarm laborers; they are underrepresented in more prestigious, better-paying positions, including those held by professional and technical work-

ers, managers and administrators, and farmers and farm managers.

The low percentage of the Mexican American subpopulation graduating from college is attributable, in part, to high attrition rates at the elementary and secondary school levels, which effectively decrease the number of individuals eligible for college attendance, and to the failure of a substantial number of high school graduates from the subpopulation to enroll in college. Data based on the Bureau of the Census' Current Population Surveys from 1974 through 1978 [2] indicate nationwide a rate of college entry of 23 percent. The corresponding rates for whites are 83 percent and 38 percent, respectively.

The Persistence of Mexican Americans in College

The low percentage of college graduates among Mexican Americans is also due to the failure of many Chicanos, once enrolled in an institution of higher education, to persist to degree completion. Numerous studies involving national [4], regional [11], state [13], and institutional [23, 36, 37] data have shown that Mexican American students graduate from college within a normal time frame—four to five years—at a rate that is from one and a half to two times smaller than the rate for Anglo students. Even if a longer time frame—nine or ten years—is considered, the discrepancy persists. Tracking students who entered college in 1971 until 1980, Astin [2] found that 55 percent of the Anglos but only 40 percent of the Mexican

Americans in his national sample had achieved baccalaureate degrees during the nine-year period.

It is clear that addressing the low percentage of college graduates in the Chicano subpopulation necessitates examinations of Mexican American school-going behavior before, at the point of, and after college entry. The study of Chicano persistence in the elementary and secondary schools [28] has a history of several decades, beginning, most notably, with the U.S. Commission on Civil Rights' Mexican American Education Study in 1971 [48]. Similarly, there has been extensive investigation of the issue of Mexican American access to college [28, 38]. Much less attention, however, has been focused on the persistence of Chicanos at the baccalaureate level.

Of the few attempts to date to isolate factors that influence the persistence of Mexican Americans in college, the most significant is a study by Astin and Burciaga [3] for the Commission on Minorities in Higher Education. Astin and Burciaga analyzed data based on two different longitudinal samples—one covering the first two years of undergraduate work (1975 freshmen followed up in 1977) and the other a nine-year span covering undergraduate and graduate work (1971 freshmen followed up in 1980). For the first sample, persistence was examined as continuous enrollment over the first two years of college; for the second, as attainment of the baccalaureate degree by the ninth year following matriculation. In each case, analysis was by means of a two-stage stepwise linear multiple regression "so that the students' entering characteristics were first controlled before any attempt was made to assess the influence of environmental characteristics" [2, p. 90].

Astin and Burciaga [3] found that the persistence of Chicanos is related statistically to a number of factors including performance and preparation in high school, the education and occupational status of parents, various expectations about the college experience, the nature of financial support, and the institution of initial matriculation. As their analysis was not theory-driven, however, Astin and Burciaga could provide no overarching conceptualization to tie these statistical associations together. Establishing the associations did not lead to a coherent explanation of Chicano persistence in college.

Methods of Studying Persistence in College

Astin and Burciaga's study is not atypical of research on the persistence/attrition of college students. Studies of this subject have either lacked the guidance of a conceptual framework or have uncritically accepted frameworks developed for other sociopsychological phenomena. Investigators not using conceptual frameworks have been content with establishing the correlates of persistence, rather than understanding the phenomenon as a dynamic process.

Since 1967 a number of "models" of persistence/attrition behavior have been developed and tested. These models have been based on selective findings of the correlational research, together with certain sociological and/or psychological constructs adapted from theoretical frameworks for explaining other social phenomena. For example, both Spady [41] and Tinto [45, 46] have proposed conceptualizations of attrition behavior heavily influenced by Durkheim's [15] sociological explanation of suicide. Other prominent models [7, 42] derive their basic theoretical orientations from one or another of the recent conceptualizations of disengagement from work (for example, Price's [34] model of work turnover or Dawis, Lofquist, and Weiss' [12] theory of work adjustment).

Undoubtedly, with the emergence of these conceptual models, the study of student persistence in college has moved in a potentially more fruitful direction. As the preoccupation with the identification of correlates has been replaced by an interest in explaining the processes that lead to persistence and withdrawal behaviors, the models have held out the possibility of reaching an understanding of the underlying dynamics of persistence/attrition phenomena. Still, none of the available models has proved more than very modestly successful in explicating those dynamics [31]. This is the result, in my judgment, of certain conceptual and methodological shortcomings shared by the existing models.

First, as mentioned above, each of the present persistence/attrition theorists has chosen to ground his model in a framework used to explain some other social or sociopsychological phenomenon. But an assumption *at the outset* that dropping out of college is like committing suicide or leaving a job has turned out to be too severe a constraint upon the conceptualizing process [31]. In addition, the models have been developed on the basis of, and tested with, data collected from institutional records and/or by means of fixed-choice questionnaires. These are methods of data collection that effectively strip away the context surrounding the student's decision to persist or not to persist in college and exclude from consideration the student's own perceptions of the process.

Yet, given the present level of our understanding of that decision, it is precisely those characteristics—the context of the decision and the student's perspective on the context—that investigations of student persistence in college must include. What are needed then are naturalistic, descriptive studies guided by research perspectives that emphasize the insider's point of view. [46].[1]

An Exploratory Study

In this article, I report an exploratory study undertaken to collect and analyze qualitative data describing, from the Mexican American student's point of view, the context surrounding his or her decision to persist or not to persist in the university and, on the basis of that description, to develop concepts of the university-going process. The concepts so developed were used to propose hypotheses about the context within which Mexican American students make decisions to persist or not to persist in the university.

In lieu of one of the existing conceptual frameworks of persistence/attrition, the study was guided only by a broad research perspective—the sociology of everyday life [14]. The latter is actually a collection of research perspectives in sociology, all of which focus on everyday social interaction in natural situations and have as their starting points (1) the experience and observation of people interacting in concrete, face-to-face situations, and (2) an analysis of the actors' meanings.

In particular, two of the sociologies of everyday life—symbolic interactionism and ethnomethodology—were used in conducting the inquiry. Symbolic interactionism emphasizes social interaction as a process that forms human conduct: It is from the interaction of the individual with others that the meanings of things arise, and it is on the basis of their meaning that the individual acts toward things. The concern of symbolic interactionists then is shared emergent meanings. Ethnomethodology seeks to understand how actors go about the task of seeing, describing, and explaining the world in which they live, that is, the process of creating shared emergent meanings and using them to account for things in one's everyday world. Two assumptions, following from the research perspective, underlay the study: (1) Persistence behavior is the consequence of a process in which the student is an active participant: He or she takes account of various things in his or her everyday world and acts on the basis of how he or she interprets them. (2) Persistence behavior is related to the manner in which the university becomes and remains, through everyday social interaction, a reality for the student.

Data Collection and Analysis

The conceptualization of Chicano university-going reported here is based on Mexican American university students' perceptions of the own and others' college-going experiences and attitudes, as reported to the author in open-ended interviews. Eighteen students and former students from a single entering class of a large, public southwestern university were interviewed by the author eight to eleven months following the end of their freshman year to obtain their perceptions of their college-going behavior during, and prior to, their freshman year.

Informants for the study were selected from a list provided to the author by the Office of Academic Computing Services at the study university. The list contained the names, addresses, and telephone numbers of individuals who: (1) were new freshman at the university in the fall of 1981, (2) were registered as full-time students (more than eleven credit hours) for that semester, (3) at the time of admission reported their ethnicity to be Hispanic,[2] and (4) at the time of admission were citizens or permanent residents. The list also indicated whether or not and, if so, when each student had withdrawn from the university prior to the twenty-first day of the fall semester of 1982.

The selection of informants from the sampling frame was guided by a single consideration: the sample had to include both persisting and nonpersisting students. In all other respects, the selection process was arbitrary, producing, in essence, a sample of convenience. Individuals who agreed to be interviewed and did, in fact, participate in interviews constituted the sample. Representativeness was not an important consideration in the selection process because the purpose of the study was to discover, rather than to validate, the patterns in a process as it naturally occurs and is understood.

Thirteen of the informants were persisters, that is, they exhibited continuous enrollment through the beginning of their sophomore year; the other five were nonpersisters, having withdrawn at some point between the beginning of the freshman year and the beginning of the sophomore year. A demographic and academic profile of the informants is provided in table I, together with comparable profiles of all new full-time Hispanic freshmen and of all new full-time freshmen matriculating at the study university in fall 1981. Table 2 identifies (pseudonymously) the eighteen informants and provides additional background information on them.

Open-ended interviewing, that is, without an interview schedule, was used in the study so that the author would be free to pursue any area of inquiry suggested by an informant's responses, and the informant would be free to draw upon his or her own experience, rather than prestated alternatives, in responding to the author's questions. The interviews were in-depth modified "life history" interviews; the informants were encouraged to think back over their lives and recount experiences related to their own and others' college-going behavior. For each experience, informants were asked to describe the ways in which other persons were involved in the experience and to recall their own perceptions of it. The interviews were conducted in person at sites of the informants' choosing.

To initiate the analysis, the interviews were open-coded, that is, the contents were coded in as many different ways as possible [9]. A total of one hundred nineteen codes were used in this study. These related to context and setting, informants' definitions of situations, informants' ways of thinking about people and objects, process, activities, events, strategies, and relationships. Some coding categories— like most related to the study's research perspective—were more likely to be used than others. Examples of the former are everyday social interaction and perceptions of the university. Often the coding categories were labeled with the very words (for example, "getting in" and "preparing") used by the informants themselves. Analysis of the data was accomplished by qualitative induction [17]. That is, concepts and hypotheses emerged from an examination of concrete data collected in the field. The induction process was constrained only by the research perspective: any concept or hypothesis that emerged would, perforce, be consistent with the assumptions of the sociology of everyday life.

Coding was followed by a data reduction step in which the number of coding categories was reduced and the analysis became more conceptually oriented. Decisions about the retention, merging, and discarding of codes initially were made on the basis of the saliency of the categories, that is, the number of cases they contained and the extent of their relationships to other categories. Further data reduction was accomplished by "clustering" [44] the remaining coding categories. Connections or linkages between categories were established by identifying higher-order categories under which a number of coding categories fit. Conceptually, the coding categories became subcategories or properties of the higher-order category. For example, the categories "scaling down" and "getting to know" were seen to be linked, because they were both processes that helped students negotiate, or penetrate, the campus geographies. Thus, it was possible to "reduce" these two categories to form the broader category "getting in." "Scaling down" and "getting to know" then became subcategories of "getting in."

TABLE 1
Demographic and Academic Profiles of Various Groups of Fall 1981 Matriculants at the Study University

	All Full-Time, First-Time Freshmen	All Full-Time, First-Time Hispanic Freshmen	The Informants
Number:	3126	147	18
Gender:			
% Male	48.9	50.3	44.4
% Female	51.1	49.7	55.6
Residency status:			
% Resident of state	77.2	81.0	88.9
% Non-resident of state	22.8	19.0	11.1
Average age:	18.4	18.5	18.6
Average rank in high-school graduating class (% from the top):	N/A	24.3	23.1
Average ACT composite score:	N/A	18.5	18.7
Area of major:			
% Agriculture	0.6	0.7	
% Business Administration	23.2	24.5	27.9
% Communication	6.1	2.1	
% Computer Science	6.0	6.8	5.6
% Education	3.3	6.9	
% Engineering	15.2	15.0	16.7
% English	0.5	0.7	
% Fine Arts	5.0	5.5	
% Home Economics	0.7	1.4	11.1
% Mathematics & Natural Science	2.8	2.1	
% Medical Technology	0.6		
% Pre-Professional	13.2	14.4	22.4
% Pre-Architectural	5.2	4.8	5.6
% Pre-Criminal Justice	0.5	0.7	5.6
% Pre-Law	2.5	2.7	5.6
% Pre-Medicine	2.8	3.4	5.6
% Pre-Nursing	1.8	1.4	
% Pre-Social Work	0.4	1.4	
% Psychology	2.0		
% Social Science	2.2	1.4	5.6
% Spanish	0.1	0.7	
% Other foreign language	0.3		
% No Major	18.1	18.4	11.1
Freshman-Year Persistence Status:			
% Persisting	83.5	68.7	72.2
% Non Persisting	16.5	31.3	27.8

This process of "moving out of the data" was facilitated by the writing of research memos [16]. Research memos were notes of varying length that the author wrote to himself in order to capture, on the spot, insights into the data and its analysis. As the analysis proceeded, there was increasing interplay between data reduction and memo writing. Progress in reducing the data and generating conceptual categories expanded the contents of memos and suggested connections between the ideas in separate memos. The latter resulted in

"rememoing," that is, writing memos based on other memos. At the same time, memoing and rememoing facilitated data reduction by suggesting how categories might be collapsed into other categories, and, thus, categories of a higher conceptual level generated.

Getting Ready

Two conceptual schemes for interpreting the college-going behavior of Chicano university students emerged from the study. One of these schemes has reference to behaviors and attitudes of these students prior to college matriculation, the other to behaviors and attitudes after matriculation. Each scheme centers around a major organizing concept. For prematriculation experiences, the concept is "getting ready"; for postmatriculation experiences, it is "getting in."

Among experiences before college attendance reported by the informants were activities that variously engendered a college-going frame of mind; modeled college-going behavior; or simulated, in some way, the experience of going to college. These experiences were seen to constitute five categories, or patterns, of getting-ready behavior: (1) Initial expectation engendering, (2) Fraternal modeling, (3) Mentor modeling, (4) Indirect simulation, and (5) Direct simulation (Table 3).

"Initial expectation engendering" refers to experiences very early in life of an informant that led to a belief or perception, held long before actual college attendance, that the informant would be going to college. Although such an expectation could be encouraged by elementary school teachers and classmates, it was most frequently perceived to be the result of parental exhortation. For example, Julius (all names are pseudonyms) recalled: "That's all [my father] ever preached—college." Rose, after quoting her father's advice: "Go to college. Go to college,'" added, "You know, going to college and getting an education was just everything to my father."

Despite the obvious importance of parents and others in engendering this early college-going expectation, the informants often described the expectation as though it were a conclusion they had reached independently. Some recalled coming to think about college as part of a natural progression. In the words of Anita: "So I thought: 'After high school comes

TABLE 2
Comparative Background Data for Informants

Name	Sex	Age*	Marital Status	Location Of High School(s) Attended	Location of Residence While Attending University	Academic Major*	Persistence Status
Anita	F	18	Single	In-state	On-campus	Bus./Pre-Law	Persister
Barbara	F	18	Single	In-state	Off-campus	Undecided	Persister
Carlos	M	18	Single	In-state	Off-campus	Computer Science	Persister
David	M	18	Single	Out-of-state in-state	Off-campus	Pre-Medicine	Persister
Emmanuel	M	18	Single	In-state	On-campus	Electr. Eng.	Persister
Frances	F	18	Single	In-state	On-campus	Electr. Eng.	Persister
Gregory	M	18	Single	In-state	Off-campus	Bus. Adm.	Persister
Helen	F	17	Single	In-state	Off-campus	Home Ec.	Non-Persister
Isabelle	F	19	Single	In-state	Off-campus	Pre-Architect.	Persister
Jose	M	19	Single	Out-of-state in-state	Off-campus	Management	Persister
Karen	F	18	Single	In-state	On-campus	Crim. Justice	Persister
Linda	F	17	Single	In-state	On-campus	Sociology	Persister
Michael	M	17	Single	In-state	Off-campus	Aerospace Eng.	Non-Persister
Natalie	F	19	Single	Out-of-state	Off-campus on-campus	Marketing	Persister
Thomas	M	19	Single	Out-of-state	On-campus	Pre-Law	Persister
Peter	M	23	Married	In-state	Off-campus	Gen. Construction	Non-Persister
Theresa	F	18	Single	In-state	Off-campus	Home Ec.	Non-Persister
Rose	F	18	Single	In-state	Off-campus	Bus. Adm.	Non-Persister

*At time of matriculation
All names are fictitious

TABLE 3
Dimensions of the "Getting Ready" Categories

Category	Type of Activity	Other Participants	Message Conveyed	Outcome
Initial expectation engendering	Oral communication	Parents Friends Classmates	You are a future college-goer.	Expectation of being a college student.
Fraternal modeling	Observation Oral communication (a description)	Siblings Other relatives	You are a future college-goer. This is what college is like for me, your brother.	Expectation of being a college student. Expectation of what being a college student is like.
Mentor modeling	Oral communication (a description)	High-school teachers (especially mentors)	This is what college was like for me, your teacher.	Expectation of what being a college student is like.
Indirect simulation	Oral communication (a prescription or prediction)	High-school teachers (especially mentors)	This is what you should do in college. This is what college will be like for you.	Expectation of what being a college student is like.
Direct simulation	Participant observation	Campus people	Oh, so this is what college will be like for me, the informant	Expectation/ experience of what being a college student is like.

college, after college comes work'." Other informants linked college-going to future benefits. For example, David recalled this sentiment: "I knew I wanted to go to college anyway because I wanted to be better off." Frances specifically connected the self-realization aspect with the influence-of-others aspect of initial expectation engendering: "Deep down [my sister] doesn't really want to go to school but it's been expected and she knows if she wants to make anything of herself and if she really wants to do something she's going to have to go."

Whatever the particular characteristics of the initial expectation engendering process, the outcome was always perceived to be an expectation that the informant would be a college-goer. Experiences belonging to the remaining categories of getting ready provided substance, in the form of descriptions, prescriptions, and predictions *about* college-going, for the generalized expectation *of* college-going that resulted from initial expectation engendering.

"Fraternal modeling" refers to the informant's having observed, and/or having received information about, the college-going behavior of a relative, usually a sibling. There appear to have been at least two aspects, or features, of this category of getting ready. First, the informant's knowing *that* his or her relative has gone to college often led to a kind of "turn-taking" mind set. Linda provides a description of this feature: "When my brother first went to college, . . . I just assumed at that point, that when I was that age, I would go to college."

The second aspect of fraternal modeling involved the informant's coming to know something *about* the college-going behavior of the relative. Cues given by the relative provided the informant with information about how one went about being a college student, about negotiating the college campus. Oral cues were forthcoming during face-to-face interactions when the relative returned home from college, or, occasionally, over the telephone. Barbara recounted what she learned from her sister: "Well, my sister was in engineering. And she was one of the few girls, which made things worse. She talked about some of her classes and stuff which I knew from then I didn't want to get into anything that I was going to have to be that involved and that so precise and everything." A few informants actually observed, if only in limited contexts, the college-going behavior of a sibling during visits to the campus. Anita reported: "I came and visited my sister a couple of times and . . . I remember going through all the hassles of getting her registered and everything and it was just like uh, it was a big hassle."

Knowing something about the experiences and/or attitudes of the modeler sometimes led to early apprehension about college-going. As a result of experiences like the one described above and of her sister's expressed anxieties, Anita recalled being "scared" about the idea of going to college. This kind of knowledge also resulted in "negative exampling," that is, the modeler's behavior causing the informant to decide to approach college-going differently than the modeler. Barbara's remarks about how her sister's experiences with the engineering major influenced her own choice of major are quoted above. Barbara also made this observation: "I saw the mistake my sister made of thinking she was going to get A's and then she didn't and so I taught myself to be the opposite way around, to know that I wasn't going to."

Modeling behavior which provided the informants with knowledge about college-going behaviors and attitudes also was exhibited by particular high-school instructors. Because the informants reported close relationships with these instructors, they are referred to here as mentors. Invariably, "mentoring modeling" took the form of the mentor relating his or her own experiences in, and attitudes about, college. Anita recalled a high school physics teacher who talked a lot about the subject: "He went [to college] all over but [mentions a university by name] was mostly all he talked about. . . . He is really intelligent and anything he said, we knew it was true." Barbara provided a very specific example of her mentor's influence on her attitude development toward college-going: "One of my high school teachers, probably the best teacher I ever had, flunked out of college two times. He didn't tell his parents when he flunked out. . . . He was real good because all my life everybody's always expecting me to get A's. . . . So

that was the first time I really had a different perspective."

In the case of fraternal or mentor modeling, informants came to have knowledge about college-going as the result of interactions that produced *descriptions* of college-going behaviors and attitudes. Such knowledge could also be the consequence of interactions that led to *prescriptive* or *predictive* statements about college-going. Experiences of the latter kind are examples of "indirect simulation."

Two subcategories of indirect simulation can be differentiated on the basis of the formality of the simulative experience. First, there were the formal, well-planned simulative experiences. These included preparation for college classes. David provided this description of a "college class" that he had taken in high school: "They told us about ACT's and college. It was mainly . . . to prepare us. . . . That's the only class where they really pushed us to go [to college]." Career-day seminars were also simulative experiences of this kind.

Although planned simulations seem to be common to all informants, simulations that were less formal and more spontaneous apparently made a stronger impression. Anita recalled vividly a prediction her high-school chemistry teacher had made about what college-going was going to be like for her and her classmates: "He would expect everybody to go to college, right? And he'd say, 'You think I'm easy now but wait until you get to the university. Those profs are just going to eat you alive if you're like this in class.' He goes, 'I'm very easy compared to some of those profs that you're going to meet'."

While indirect simulations, like modeling experiences, involved the informants in the vicarious acquisition of knowledge about college-going behavior and attitudes, the final category of getting ready—"direct simulation"—includes a whole range of what might be called "quasi-college-going" experiences involving the informants' actual participation. Sorting of these experiences into subcategories of direct simulation (Table 4) was accomplished by evaluating them in the light of six criteria: (1) the intention of the informant, that is, whether his or her purpose was essentially or incidentally related to college-going; (2) the nature of the informant's activity, particularly the kinds of interactions he or she had with campus people; (3) the extent of such interactions; (4) the nature and extent of the informant's use of campus resources; (5) the duration of the experience; and (6) the role the informant occupied during the experience.

"Incidental visiting" refers to experiences that were essentially unrelated to college-going activity, that were typically short in duration and not recurrent, and that involved limited interaction with campus people and limited use of resources. An example is Peter's infrequent visits to the campus to use the gym. Experiences that belong to the subcategory called "related visiting" were related to college-going but indirectly, that is, to the college-going of a person other than the informant. Like incidental visiting, related visiting tended to be characterized by limited interaction with campus people, limited use of campus resources, and a time frame that was short. Informants who participated in visiting experiences often reported that they came away feeling that they had "just barely walked on campus" (Isabel) and had not been "exposed to the real aspect of the university being a university" (Linda).

Experiences that involved extensive use of campus resources, extensive interaction with campus people, and extended or repeated presence on the college campus belong to a subcategory of direct simulation called "attending." One kind of attending (Attending I) refers to

activities that extensively imitated college-going per se. Nevertheless, each experience of this type involved the informant in considerable interaction with campus people, extensive usage of campus resources, and a relatively lengthy or recurrent campus stay. Emmanuel recounted his participation in a summer institute sponsored by the study university: "In the summer of my junior year, between my junior and my senior year, the university, the engineering department, sent me to a summer institute, a seminar for a week. And they try to familiarize you with the campus."

A second level of attending (Attending II) included experiences that, to some degree, constituted college-going, for example, attending college classes as an official enrollee or as the companion of an official enrollee. As an example of the latter, Natalie reported: "My mother was also going to college when I was in high school. So I used to go to classes with her. Sometimes I would just accompany her . . . or if she said that she had a interesting class, I'd listen to it. . . . [I'd go] to classes and the cafeteria." Participation in Attending II experiences blurred the boundary between simulation and the true experience, and it is difficult, on the basis of the available data, to estimate the extent to which such experiences only simulated postmatriculation college-going experiences vis-à-vis actually embodying them. Still, the findings to be presented in the next section

TABLE 4
Subcategories of "Direct Simulation" and Their Dimensions

Subcategory	Intention	Example(s) of Activities	Amount of Interaction	Duration	Use of Resources	Role of Informant
Incidental visiting	Not related to college-going	Taking test Going to gym	None or limited	Short	Very limited	User
Related visiting (I)	Related to college-going (prospectively)	Touring campus	Limited	Short	Very limited	Tourist
Related visiting (II)	Related to college-going (indirectly)	Accompanying sibling	Variable but usually limited	Variable but generally short	Limited	Visitor
Attending (I)	Variable	Participating in summer workshop	Extensive	Relatively long	Relatively extensive	Pseudo-student
Attending (II)	Related to college-going (directly)	Going to college class	Extensive	Long	Extensive	Quasi-student

indicate that having had Attending II experiences did not exempt informants, after official matriculation at the university, from obstacles to their effective negotiation of the university campus.

It should be clear to the reader that each getting-ready experience resulted in either (1) an expectation that the informant would eventually go to college, or (2) an expectation of what it would be like to be college-going. Expectations resulting from experiences belonging to all categories, save direct simulation, were externally prompted, that is, the impetus for the expectation was something said or done by an individual other than the informant. Expectations from direct simulation experiences tended to derive from self-reflexive activity and, hence, were internally prompted.

Each expectation may be understood to be the outcome of an evaluative experience. That is, associated with the prompting of the expectation was a valuation—either positive or negative—of college-going. All of the experiences identified as instances of initial expectation engendering involved only positive valuations. It is hypothesized that experiences of this kind involving negative evaluations do occur, probably to individuals who decide not to attend college. Experiences assigned to the other four categories involved both positive and negative valuations. An interesting case of the latter (an example is described above) is the high-school teacher's use of future college-going as a disciplinary mechanism. However, most experiences in these categories reported by the informants resulted in positive valuations of college-going.

Although experiences belonging to any single category of getting ready were not temporally discrete from those belonging to all others, there was an overall chronological pattern to the occurrence of the experiences relative to their categorical assignments. For example, initial expectation engendering, as is implied by its name, generally took place very early in an informant's life. Fraternal modeling, mentor modeling, and indirect simulation were experienced, more or less simultaneously, some variable length of time after initial expectation engendering. Direct simulation was characteristic of late precollegiate life.

One consequence of this patterning was that experiences belonging to later occurring categories tended to build upon those belonging to earlier ones. As noted above, experiences of the fraternal modeling, mentor modeling, and indirect simulation types provided substance, in the form of descriptions, prescriptions, and predictions about college-going, for the kind of generalized expectation of college-going that resulted from initial expectation engendering. The self-expectation that characterized experiences in the direct simulation category was the result of a valuation of college-going that took into account not only the immediate events but also valuations and expectations resulting from (earlier) experiences belonging to the other categories.

Getting In

Postmatriculation behaviors and attitudes can be understood in terms of a second organizing concept—"getting in." In describing their early impressions of the university, the informants were virtually unanimous in emphasizing a perception of "bigness." The descriptor "big" turned out to be a gloss for articulating the perceived dimensions; namely, mass, distance, and complexity, of three campus geographies: (1) the physical geography, (2) the social geography, and (3) the academic/cognitive geography (Table 5).

For example, mass, distance, and complexity of the physical geography referred to the fact that for some informants the campus was larger in size than their entire hometowns (mass), that from one end of the campus to the other was much longer than the single block their high schools occupied (distance), and that it was not easy to resolve the physical campus into what would be for the informants logical and easily recognizable spaces (complexity). As an aspect of the social geography, mass was often described in terms of the literally hundreds of students with whom the informants attended class, distance as the gap between student and instructor that prevented a close working relationship, and complexity as the total ignorance of one another's lives exhibited by members (including the informants) of the campus population. Mass as an aspect of the academic/cognitive geography exhibited itself in what was perceived to be a seemingly unlimited number of potential fields of study, distance as the giant cognitive step the infor-

TABLE 5
The Perceived Geographies and Their Features

Feature	Physical	Social	Academic/Cognitive
			Geography
Mass	"Is this place large!"	"So many people!"	"So many fields, so many classes one could take."
Distance	"You can't see from one side of the campus to the other."	"I was like in an audience and he had a micro-phone."	"High school to college is a bigger step."
Complexity	"There were all these little signs telling you to go over here, go over there. I got lost."	"You're constantly running into people you don't know."	"They made instruction more complicated than it had to be."

mants had to make in moving from "easy" high-school curricula to "hard" university ones, and complexity as the perceived obtuse-ness of professor talk. The inability to deal with these dimensions led to feelings of "being lost" in one or more of the geographies.[3]

Many of the postmatriculation behaviors reported by the informants may be understood as strategies to fix themselves in the physical, social, and/or academic/cognitive geogra-phies. The behaviors employed in this way, which constitute the categories of getting in, took account, quite naturally, of the perceived dimensions of the geographies. Each represents a potential component of the process by which the informant initiated his or her negotiation of the geographies. Two categories of getting in emerged from an analysis of the date: (1) "get-ting to know" and (2) "scaling down."

A seemingly obvious way for an individual to deal with a milieu that overwhelmed him or her with its size, placed him or her at a distance from important people and things, and posed complexity was to increase his or her familiar-ity with that milieu. The informants reported two different sets of behaviors that led to increased knowledge of the campus geogra-phies. The first set, called "mentoring," in-volved interactive experiences with students, already at the university for some time when the informant matriculated, who functioned as guides or interpreters of the geographies. Frances reported such a person, who had had a profound influence on her early behavior at the university: "She influenced my decision to stay

here [in the dorm]. . . . She told me basically what goes on around here and how to get along around here. . . . Some of the things she said, you know, about the Engineering College and about how band was. I wanted to be in a good band so. And engineering—she told me a lot of things that go on in engineering. She told me what classes to take my first semester because [from] the trouble she had . . . she knew, you know, what you should do first. . . . She just kind of paved the way and guided me through making decisions, you know, as to where to go."

The second set of getting-to-know experi-ences—"peer knowledge sharing"—includes experiences with fellow newcomers in which there was a kind of cooperative exploring of the geographies. Barbara provides a good description of such activity: "It kind of helps if you have somebody to relate to and somebody who's having the same problem. And they find out something you're supposed to do that you didn't know about. So just kind of giving infor-mation back and forth." In Barbara's case, it was with high-school friends, co-matriculants at the university, that she engaged in peer knowledge sharing. In other cases, peer knowl-edge sharing occurred with individuals who were not known to the informants prior to their arrival on campus. Anita reported her strategy of sitting by someone in each class and intro-ducing herself to that person: "That way it makes the class a lot easier. . . . Because, you know, they learn it different, they can explain it in their terms and you can catch on easily and that way you're not so insecure when you go in [-to class]."

Scaling down refers to behaviors and attitudes which resulted in the informant's perception of a more narrowly defined geography, effectively reducing the amount of the geography with which the informant had to be familiar in order to locate himself or herself. In effect, the mass, distance, and complexity dimensions of the geographies were "scaled down." Barbara, for example, explained how she had learned to avoid the "biggest places" on campus. Rather, she ran her "own little circle": "It's not like I'm at [the university]. It's kind of like I'm here in this part of it."

One focus of both the getting-to-know and the scaling-down kinds of experiences was the process of "majoring in." In addition to its manifest function—initiating a focused study of that area of the curriculum that is most closely related to one's life and career goals, selecting an academic major had another, more latent function: it provided a vehicle for locating oneself in the physical, social, and academic geographies; it provided a way of getting in. For the informants, the assumption of an academic major meant that the physical environment was circumscribed, the curriculum was bracketed, an important element of one's self-identity vis-à-vis the campus community was created, and a cynosure for social activities was realized. Hence, the expression,

"I am majoring in——" [a particular academic major is named] or, more simply, "I am in——" [a particular academic major is named], was not merely an idiom but an oral affirmation of the locating function of the academic major. With respect to the role of the major in negotiating the social geography, it is interesting to note that the campus organization most frequently mentioned by the informants—an organization for Hispanic business students—had as its *raison d'être* the sharing of an academic major (Figure 1).

Theoretical Interpretations and Hypotheses

Following Stern [44], who argues that the process of concept development in qualitative research is facilitated by selective sampling of the literature for concepts that can be compared as data, the author looked for available social and/or sociopsychological constructs that could be used to draw out the theoretical significance of the getting ready and getting in concepts.

The construct "significant other," particularly as worked out by Haller and Woelfel [18], is useful for considering the significance of getting ready. In their study of the occupational and educational goals of high-school students,

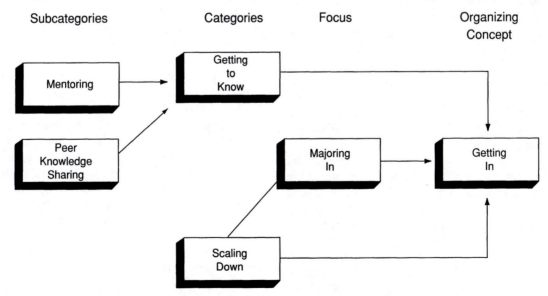

Figure 1: The Categories and Subcategories of "Getting In" and their Relationship to "Majoring In."

Haller and Woelfel [18, pp. 594–95] came to define a "significant other" as:

> A person, known to the focal individual, who either through direct interaction (a definer) or by example (a model) provides information which influences the focal individual's conception of himself in relation to educational or occupational roles or influences his conception of such roles (a conception of an object).

In the present study, parents, high-school teachers and, less frequently, siblings were definers with respect to college-going: These individuals communicated to the informant the fact that he or she belonged to the category of future college-goers and defined for him or her what is meant to be a college-goer. In addition, high-school teachers and siblings created expectations with respect to college-going by modeling college-going behavior. The mere departure of an older sibling for college might have signaled to the informant his or her membership in the category of (future) college-goers. Subsequently, the informant's observations of college-going behavior by siblings and teachers provided insight into the nature of the college-going role.

A second construct that was useful for drawing out the theoretical significance of getting ready was anticipatory socialization.[4] Anticipatory socialization refers to a premature taking on or identification with the behavior and attitudes of an *aspired to* group which "may serve the twin functions of aiding [an individual's] rise into [the aspired to] group and of easing his adjustment after he has become part of it" [24, p. 87]. The concept has been primarily worked out in relation to occupational preparation [33] and the formation of political views [39], but there has been some consideration of it with respect to the role of college student.

Parsons [30], for example, has argued that because, as early as elementary school, high achievers are culled from their classmates so they can be directed toward a college preparatory curriculum, the decision of a high achiever to attend college may be the result of a long period of anticipatory socialization. Silber and his colleagues [40] have reported that some high-school students prepare themselves for college by rehearsing forms of behavior they associate with college students. This role rehearsing may include taking special courses that are viewed as trial college experiences and carrying out assignments the teacher identifies as what one does in college.

Role-rehearsing was clearly an element of getting ready experiences recorded here. It may have been indirect as, for example, the simulation of certain aspects of college-going in the college preparatory classes. A more direct kind of rehearsing occurred when the individual participated in on-campus activities: living in dormitories, going to parties, attending classroom lectures. Another component of anticipatory socialization, the forecasting of future situations, was a feature of getting ready; as, for example, when the informant, upon observing an older sibling depart for college, predicted his or her own matriculation, or when a high-school teacher predicted that college professors would treat the informant and his or her co-students much differently than he or she (the high-school teacher) did.

In drawing out the theoretical significance of the concept "getting in," the author again referred to two existing constructs. The author's consideration of "social integration" as a theoretical datum for comparison with the concept of getting in was initially prompted by his reading of other conceptually oriented investigations of the behavior of undergraduate students. As mentioned above, Spady [41] and later Tinto [45] borrowed the concept from the French sociologist Emile Durkheim as he had elaborated it in his treatise on the causes of suicide [15], in order to conceptualize student withdrawal from college. Durkheim argued that suicide was likely in populations where rates of interaction (collective affiliation) were too low, because this leads to a lack of common sentiments and values (moral consensus) and the precedence of individual interests over social ones. As the individual increasingly frees himself or herself from the social control of the group, he or she removes himself or herself from its prophylactic influence and finds little meaning in life, which comes to appear as an intolerable burden.

Spady (and Tinto after him), in adapting these concepts to an explanation of student withdrawal from college, specified a lack of collective affiliation (friendship) and a lack of moral consensus (cognitive congruence) as having separate effects on dropping out behavior, that is, independently influencing the level of one's social integration. Neither Durkheim nor Spady provides a clear definition of the construct "social integration."

The results of the study reported here suggest that moral consensus is neither the (principal) outcome of collective affiliation (as postulated by Durkheim) nor an independent cause of one's persisting in life or college (as indicated by Spady and Tinto). A student's interaction with others is important for his or her persistence in college not simply or primarily because it leads to the sharing of general values and orientations, but because it assists the student in developing specific strategies for negotiating the physical, social, and cognitive/academic geographies. The getting-to-know category of getting in defines "collective affiliations" with specific individuals—mentors and peers—that "integrate" the student into the physical and academic/cognitive geographies as well as the social geography by providing him or her with knowledge of these geographies and the skills to negotiate them. According to this interpretation, then, students become integrated for distinctly more cognitive, and less moral, reasons.

In theorizing about how exactly students, with the assistance of mentors and peers, come to locate themselves in the perceived geographies, the concept of the "cognitive map" may be important. It is hypothesized [43] that when significant environments (for example, a large university campus) are too large to be apprehended at once, people will form "conceptions" of them. These conceptions, or cognitive maps, are a complex of things learned about the environment, including expectations, stereotypes, and value judgments. In developing cognitive maps of large and complex spaces, individuals make certain simplifications and adjustments in accordance with their own needs and experience. This means, of course, that cognitive maps and mapmaking exhibit considerable interpersonal variation.

The basis of cognitive map formation is the identification of significant objects in the environment, the establishment of the connectedness of the objects to one another and to the observer, and the assignment of meaning, whether emotional or practical, to the objects and their relationships. As the word "map"

implies, the origin and major implication of the cognitive map lie in the spatial domain. But people are thought to organize other phenomena, for example, social interrelations, affective bonds, and temporal relationships, in the same way [22]. Cognitive mapping is similar to the "sense-making activity" of organizational members as described by Weick [49, pp. 148–149]:

> People in organizations try to sort . . . chaos [which is flowing and equivocal] into items, events, and parts which are then connected, threaded into sequences, serially ordered, and related. . . . [Because it is] the individual [who] breaks up chaos so that other forms of order can be created, . . . it stands to reason that what is eventually available for inspection is something very much of the individual's own making.

The student's initial perceptions of the campus geographies may be understood to reflect the absence of cognitive maps. Thus the geographies were perceived to be large-scale environments (mass) in which objects stood separated from one another (distance) and seemed incapable of being resolved into meaningful components (complexity). The student's strategies for getting in are conceptualized to be mechanisms for facilitating the acquisition of these maps. For example, getting-to-know behaviors—knowledge sharing with other neophytes and mentoring relationships with veteran students—are shortcuts to acquiring representations of specific objects within the various geographies and the associations between these representations. Scaling-down behaviors result in more detailed maps of smaller proportions of the geographies—areas of particular concern to the individual.[5, 6]

On the basis of the findings and theoretical interpretations of the research reported here, the following hypotheses regarding the context of the Mexican American's decision to persist in the university are proposed.

(1) For Mexican American freshmen, the effects of so-called "background" variables (for example, high school curriculum, parents' education, parents' occupations) on persistence in college are mediated by significant-other influences. Most of the existing models of college student persistence/withdrawal posit, and are successfully used to test for the influence of prematriculation factors on persistence. The

findings of the present study suggest that where these factors influence the persistence of Mexican Americans in the university it is because they increase these students' exposure to modeling and defining experiences relative to college-going.

(2) For Mexican American freshmen, the extent and nature of anticipatory socialization for college-going has an influence not only on the decision to go to college but, once there, on the decision to stay. Haller and Woelfel [18] have shown that the level of anticipatory socialization for college, in the form of defining and modeling experiences, has a positive impact on an individual's educational goals, that is, the decision to go to college. The results of the present study suggest that these experiences also have an impact on the decision to remain in college. That is, a student's willingness to "stick it out" may reflect early and thorough socializing by family, teachers, and friends for college-going.

(3) For Mexican American freshmen, the extent to which social integration influences persistence is not the extent to which it promotes the individual's moral conformity to the institution but rather the extent to which it endows the individual with the capacity to cognitively manage the university environment, that is, helps him or her to perceive the physical, social, and academic/cognitive geographies as negotiable.

(4) For Mexican American freshmen, persisting at the university is positively related to the development and use of cognitive maps of the physical, social, and academic/cognitive geographies. The persister is more likely to employ strategies (the result of other cognitive maps?) that facilitate the development of such maps.

Implications for Practice

The results of the research reported here suggest a number of strategies that the university might adopt to improve the college-going experience of Mexican Americans and promote their persistence during the freshman year. Consider, for example, early anticipatory socialization for college-going. Parents, teachers, and siblings are generally the key agents for such socialization, and it is not easy to con-

ceive of how the university community could have much direct impact upon it. There are ways, however. An example is an experimental program currently underway at the study university in which members of the staff of the Student Affairs Office are bringing Chicano junior high-school girls and their mothers to the campus in order to introduce them, gradually, to the university and to the college-going process. Each of the girls in the project was selected from a family without any previous college experience. By including mothers, the project directors have acknowledged the important role of parents in socialization for college attendance.

The opportunities for constructive intervention by the university in later anticipatory socialization are many and varied. Indeed, most institutions, including the study university, already play a role in this kind of socialization. For example, universities regularly provide tours of their campuses for high-school students and conduct college day programs. But it is common for host institutions to look upon such events as nothing more than marketing strategies. This is unfortunate, because the results of the present study suggest their potential for significant socialization to college-going; they represent opportunities for orienting the prematriculant to the university experience.

For example, the traditional campus tour might be conducted in such a way that it assists the student to begin to develop a cognitive map of the physical geography. This would involve, for example, the tour director highlighting the importance of places (not just their histories) and indicating their connections with one another. Visual aids might include, in addition to commercial products, sketch maps of the university drawn by veteran students.

Of course, in those situations where the high-school student is on the university campus for an extended period of time, the opportunity for influencing his or her socialization to college-going is maximal. Each case of an extended stay mentioned by the informants in the present study (for example, a yearbook editors' conference and a statewide summer enrichment program) was the result of an effort underwritten by the high school. The university itself should sponsor extended stays, so that students (particularly those being little socialized to college-going at home) can "practice" going to the university.

Still another way for the university to influence later anticipatory socialization would be involvement in the design of curricula for college preparatory classes (for example, writing for college) which are offered by may high schools. Again, the object would be to assist the prematriculant to initiate the processes of developing cognitive maps of the campus geographies.

With respect to getting-in phenomena, the results of the present study have several implications for university intervention to positively influence the process of college-going after matriculation. For example, most institutions, including the study university, introduce new freshmen to their campus by conducting a special program, traditionally called "freshman orientation."[7] The duration of the program varies from institution to institution, being as short as a day and as long as several weeks. Its purpose is to "orient" individuals to a new environment.

The present study should prove useful to the university student affairs office in the conduct of the freshman orientation for Chicano freshmen inasmuch as it provides a conceptualization of how these students "orient" themselves. They build up internal mental representations, or cognitive maps, of the physical, social and academic/cognitive geographies; these maps are mechanisms for finding one's way in a large-scale environment. The map-making process is gradual and apparently exhibits interpersonal variation. For example, students who persist through their freshman year may form maps more quickly than those who do not. This, in turn, may be related to the possession by the persisters of still other cognitive maps—cognitive maps that are, essentially, instructions on how to negotiate new environments. It would behoove university personnel designing orientation sessions to understand the components (for example, knowledge-sharing and mentoring strategies) of such "how to" cognitive maps so that such information can be passed on early to new students. The results of this study also argue for an orientation that continues through the freshman year rather than being limited to one or two weeks at the beginning of the fall semester. This would reflect the gradualness of the process of building cognitive maps and, hence, the importance of monitoring it on a continuous basis.

Future Research

In-depth, nonscheduled interviews of Mexican American university students and former university students conducted from the perspective of the sociology of everyday life proved useful for generating concepts of Chicano university-going. But these concepts need to be refined and verified in subsequent research. This can be accomplished, in the first place, by expanding the qualitative data base on Mexican American university-going initiated by the present study. Although further in-depth interviewing of university sophomores and nonpersisting members of their freshman classes would be useful, interviews of individuals at other points in the life cycle should be conducted as well. The research reported here suggests that the nature of college-going in the freshman year is influenced profoundly by experiences that occur much earlier in life.

Undoubtedly, it would be illuminating to interview individuals on a continuous basis from, say, the time they entered first grade in order to ascertain their immediate perceptions of people and events ultimately influencing their college-going and persistence at the university. To do so would be logistically and financially impractical. More feasible is a research design in which informants are interviewed periodically from the time they enter high school until the time they complete, or fail to complete, their freshman year of college. At minimum, the research design of the present study should be extended so that individuals are interviewed *while* they are in their freshman year.

The findings of the present study suggest specific areas of inquiry for future interviewing. Thus, questioning ought to be focused, for example, on experiences in which college-going is modeled or defined for future college-goers, or on social interactions that contribute to the development and use of cognitive maps of the university. Information on these topics would be collected by means of an interviewing technique that was more structured than that used here so that data obtained from different individuals would be more comparable.

In addition to the question-and-answer format, other procedures for eliciting information would be employed. For example, the notion that there is variation among students in the acquisition and use of cognitive maps might be "tested" by having individuals draw maps of the campus geographies or list categories of objects to be found within them [20].

Qualitative data collection by methods other than interviewing also should be considered in future research. Two of these methods would seem to be particularly useful. Because experiences related to college-going and persistence at the university are extensive in time and occur ubiquitously, the possibility of a researcher's observing and recording even a fraction of these experiences is nil. This problem cannot be circumvented, but comparable kinds of data can be collected by having informants be the observers and recorders of their own experiences. Cooperative and articulate individuals would be trained to record in diaries or logs their experiences and their immediate reactions to their experiences. Periodically, these individuals would be debriefed by the researcher.

The extensiveness of the temporal and spatial contexts of behavior related to college-going and persistence does not mean that direct observation of such behavior is lost to the researcher as a strategy for data collection. The results of the present study (and presumably of interviews in follow-up studies) suggest (or will suggest) places where and times when observation of behavior related to college-going can be conducted most propitiously. For example, on the basis of the present investigation, a researcher wishing to observe various getting-ready experiences might focus on the college preparatory class, the university tour, and/or the high-school career day. Foci for observation of getting-in experiences would include freshman-level classes of varying sizes and extracurricular organizations (such as the Hispanic Business Students' association) that form around the academic major.

In addition to initiating a qualitative database on Mexican American college-going, the present study has hypothesized factors that influence the persistence of Chicanos at the university during the freshman year. Future research should seek to test the relationships specified in these hypotheses. Most likely, this would involve the design of a survey instrument and its administration to a large, random sample of Chicano students stratified on the basis of whether or not they persisted into the sophomore year. Alternatively, first-time university freshmen could be surveyed and their persistence status subsequently ascertained.

Still another way in which the research described here might be followed up would involve examining, with comparable research methods, the college-going and persistence of students from other ethnic backgrounds, of other academic levels, and in other kinds of institutions. One wonders, for example, to what extent the patterns of college-going and persistence described in this study are tied to unique aspects of Mexican American culture. Ramirez and Castañeda [35] have identified four major value clusters within the Mexican American value system, including identification with family, community and ethnic group; personalization of interpersonal relationships; status and role definition in family and community; and Mexican Catholic ideology. Given the centrality of the family to the total socialization of the Chicano child, the importance of parents, siblings, and other relatives for getting-ready behavior is not surprising. Should we expect that for Anglos significant others for socialization to college-going might be drawn more heavily from among elementary and secondary school teachers and counselors? Similarly, in what ways do cultural differences between minority and Anglo students affect how and how effectively cognitive maps of the university environment are "drawn" and utilized?

The present dearth of meaningful studies of Hispanic college students[8] parallels the primitive state of research on Latino education in general [27]. The investigation reported here was undertaken in the spirit of Olivas' [27] call for improvement in both the quality of Hispanic data and theoretical constructs for explaining them. The author hopes it will encourage others to begin to fill the "fertile void in the literature of Hispanic students" [27, p. 136].

The author wishes to thank Elizabeth Fisk Skinner for research advice; John Weidman and others who commented on the version of this article presented at the Annual Meeting of the Association for the Study of Higher Education, San Antonio, Texas, February 1986; and the anonymous referees. The research for this article was supported in part by a Dissertation Research grant from the Arizona State University Graduate Research Council.

Louis C Attinasi, Jr., is assistant professor of education in the Department of Educational Leadership and Cultural Studies at the University of Houston.

Endnotes

1. This approach was adopted by Neumann [25] in a study of the persistence of community college students.
2. Virtually all of the Hispanics who attend the university are Mexican American. For purposes of university reporting, ethnic/racial background is based on the student's response to an item on the university's admission form. Because an unknown number of Hispanics either (along with Anglos) selects the alternative "Other" or declines to respond at all to this item, it is unlikely that the list included *all* new full-time Hispanic freshmen entering in fall 1981. For the purpose of the research reported here, it was not necessary that it do so (see below).
3. Mass, distance and complexity all seem to be related to the sociopsychological concept of alienation, which has been defined as [19, p. 9]: "Different kinds of dissociation, break or rupture between human beings and their objects, whether the latter be other persons or the natural world, or their own creations in art, science and society; and subjectively, the corresponding states of disequilibrium, disturbance, strangeness and anxiety."
4. Other researchers [8, 21, 31] have noted the potential usefulness of this concept for understanding persistence in college.
5. Scaling down behavior may be an example of what Weick [50] calls the "small win" strategy. According to Weick [50, p. 44]: "People with limited rationality have sufficient variety to visualize, manage, and monitor the smaller amount of variety present in scaled-down problem environments. When people initiated small-scale projects there is less play between cause and effect; local regularities can be created, observed, and trusted; and feedback is immediate and can be used to revise theories. Events cohere and can be observed in their entirety when their scale is reduced."
6. The nature of scaling down attitudes and behavior presumably would be of interest to campus ecologists [5] who wish to understand how specific groups and even individual students visualize and use the campus, in order to design environments that better meet these students' needs [6].

7. Pascarella and his colleagues [31] have found participation in freshman orientation to have a significant indirect effect (through social integration) upon the persistence of college students.
8. The recently published *Latino College Students* [28], an edited volume of research studies, is an attempt to address this omission.

References

1. Anderson, K. L. "Student Retention Focused Dialogue: Opening Presentation." paper presented at the annual meeting of the Association for the Study of Higher Education, Chicago, 1985.
2. Astin, A. W. *Minorities in Higher Education: Recent Trends, Current Prospects, and Recommendations.* San Francisco: Jossey-Bass, 1982.
3. Astin, H. S., and C. P. Burciaga. *Chicanos in Higher Education: Progress and Attainment.* ERIC 226–690. Los Angeles: Higher Education Research Institute, 1981.
4. Astin, H. S., and P. H. Cross. *Student Financial Aid and Persistence in College.* ERIC 221–078. Los Angeles: Higher Education Research Institute, 1979.
5. Banning, J. H. "The Campus Ecology Manager Role." In *Student Services: A Handbook for the Profession*, edited by U. Delworth, G. R. Hanson and Associates, pp. 209–27. San Francisco: Jossey-Basey, 1980.
6. Banning, J. H., and L. Kaiser. "An Ecological Perspective and Model for Campus Design." *Personnel and Guidance Journal*, 52 (February 1974), 370–75.
7. Bean, J. P. "The Application of a Model of Turnover in Work Organizations to the Student Attrition Process." *Review of Higher Education*, 6 (Winter 1983), 129–48.
8. _____. "Interaction Effects Based on Class Level in an Explanatory Model of College Student Dropout Syndrome." *American Educational Research Journal*, 22 (Spring 1985), 35–64.
9. Bogdan, R. C., and S. K. Biklen. *Qualitative Research for Education: An Introduction to Theory and Methods.* Boston: Allyn & Bacon, 1982.
10. Brown, G. H. "The Outcomes of Education." In *The Condition of Education for Hispanic Americans*, edited by G. H. Brown et al., pp. 117–215. Washington, D.C.: U.S. Government Printing Office, 1980.
11. Carter, T. P., and R. D. Segura. *Mexican Americans in School: A Decade of Change.* New York: College Entrance Examination Board, 1979.
12. Dawis, R. V., L. H. Lofquist, and D. J. Weiss. *A Theory of Work Adjustment. A Revision.* Minnesota Studies in Vocational Rehabilitation, No. 23. Minneapolis: Center for Industrial Relations, University of Minnesota, 1968.

13. De Los Santos, A. G., Jr., J. Montemayor, and E. Solis. *Chicano Students in Institutions of Higher Education: Access, Attrition, and Achievement.* Research Report Series, Vol. 1, No. 1. ERIC 205–360, Austin: Office for Advanced Research in Hispanic Education, College of Education, University of Texas at Austin, 1980.

14. Douglas, J. D. "Introduction to the Sociologies of Everyday Life." In *Introduction to the Sociologies of Everyday Life,* edited by J. D. Douglas, pp. 1–19. Boston: Allyn & Bacon, 1980.

15. Durkheim, E. *Suicide: A Study in Sociology.* Edited by G. Simpson. Translated by J. A. Spaulding and G. Simpson. Glencoe, Ill.: Free Press, 1951. (Originally published 1897.)

16. Glaser, B. G., and A. L. Strauss. *The Discovery of Grounded Theory: Strategies for Qualitative Research.* New York: Aldine, 1967.

17. Goetz, J. P., and M. D. LeCompte. *Ethnography and Qualitative Design in Educational Research.* Orlando, Fla.: Academic Press, 1984.

18. Haller, A. D., and J. Woelfel. "Significant Others and Their Expectations: Concepts and Instruments to Measure Interpersonal Influence on Status Aspirations." *Rural Sociology,* 37 (December 1972), 591–622.

19. Heinemann, F. H. *Existentialism and the Modern Predicament.* New York: Harper Torchbooks, 1958.

20. Herman, J. F., R. V. Kail, and A. W. Siegel. "Cognitive Maps of a College Campus: A New Look at Freshman Orientation." *Bulletin of the Psychonomic Society,* 13 (March 1979), 183–86.

21. Iverson, B. K., E. T. Pascarella, and P. T. Terenzini. "Informal Faculty-Student Contact and Commuter College Freshmen." *Research in Higher Education,* 21 (1984), 123–36.

22. Kaplan, S., and R. Kaplan. "Introduction to Chapter 3." In *Humanscape: Environments for People,* edited by S. Kaplan and R. Kaplan, pp. 42–43. North Scituate, Mass.: Duxbury Press, 1978.

23. Kissler, G. R. *Retention and Transfer: University of California Undergraduate Enrollment Study.* ERIC 215–597. Berkeley, Calif.: Office of the Academic Vice President, University of California, 1980.

24. Merton, R. K. and A. S. Kitt. "Contributions to the Theory of Reference Group Behavior." In *Continuities in Social Research: Studies in the Scope and Method of 'The American Soldier,'* edited by R. K. Merton and P. F. Lazarsfeld, pp. 40–105. Glencoe, Ill.: Free Press, 1950.

25. Neumann, W. F. "Persistence in the Community College: The Student Perspective." Ph.D. Dissertation, Syracuse University, 1985.

26. Olivas, M. A. *The Dilemma of Access: Minorities in Two-year Colleges.* Washington, D.C.: Howard University Press, 1979.

27. _____. "Research and Theory on Hispanic Education: Students, Finance, and Governance." *Aztlan,* 14 (Spring 1983), 111–46.

28. _____ (ed.) *Latino College Students.* New York: Teachers College Press, 1986.

29. Ortiz, V. "Generational Status, Family Background, and Educational Attainment Among Hispanic Youth and Non-Hispanic White Youth." in *Latino College Students,* edited by M. A. Olivas, pp. 29–46. New York: Teachers College Press, 1986.

30. Parsons, T. "The School Class as a Social System: Some of Its Functions in American Society." *Harvard Educational Review,* 29 (Fall 1959), 297–318.

31. Pascarella, E. T., and D. W. Chapman. "A Multi-institutional, Path Analytic Validation of Tinto's Model of College Withdrawal." *American Education Research Journal,* 20 (Spring 1983), 87–102.

32. Pascarella, E. T., P. T. Terenzini, and L. M. Wolfle. "Orientation to College and Freshman year Persistence/Withdrawal Decisions." *Journal of Higher Education,* 57 (March/April 1986). 155–75.

33. Pavalko, R. M. *Sociology of Occupations and Professions.* Itasca, Ill.: Peacock, 1971.

34. Price, J. L. *The Study of Turnover.* Ames, Iowa: Iowa State University Press, 1977.

35. Ramírez, M., III, and A. Castañeda. *Cultural Democracy, Bicognitive Development, and Education.* New York: Academic Press, 1974.

36. Richardson, R. C., Jr., and L. C. Attinasi, Jr. *Persistence of Undergraduate Students at Arizona State University: A Research Report on in Class Entering the Fall, 1976.* ERIC 223–138. Tempe, Ariz.: College of Education, Arizona State University, 1982.

37. Rosenthal, W. *Summer 1980 report of Persistence-Attrition of Members of Ethnic Groups.* ERIC 191–412. East Lansing, Mich.: Office of Institutional Research, Michigan State University, 1980.

38. Santos, R. "Hispanic High School Graduates: Making Choices." In *Latino College Students,* edited by M. A. Olivas, pp. 104–27. New York: Teachers College Press, 1986.

39. Sheinkopf, K. G. "Family Communication Patterns and Anticipatory Socialization." *Journalism Quarterly,* 50 (Spring 1973), 24–30, 133.

40. Silber, E., et al. "Adaptive Behavior in Competent Adolescents: Coping with the Anticipation of College." *Archives of General Psychiatry,* 5 (October 1961), 354–65.

41. Spady, W. G. "Dropouts from Higher Education: An Interdisciplinary Review and Synthesis." *Interchange,* 1 (April 1970), 109–21.

42. Starr, A., E. L. Betz, and J. Menne. "Differences in College Student Satisfaction: Academic Dropouts, Nonacademic Dropouts, and Nondropouts." *Journal of Counseling Psychology,* 19 (July 1972), 318–22.

43. Stea, D. "The Measurement of Mental Maps: An Experimental Model for Studying Conceptual Spaces." In *Behavioral Problems in Geography: A Symposium* (Northwestern Uni-

versity Studies in Geography, No. 17), edited by K. R. Cox and R. G. Golledge, pp. 228–53. Evanston, Ill.: Department of Geography, Northwestern University, 1969.

44. Stern, P. N. "Grounded Theory Methodology: Its Uses and Processes." *Image*, 12 (February 1980), 20–23.

45. Tinto, V. "Dropout From Higher Education: A Theoretical Synthesis of Recent Research." *Review of Educational Research*, 45 (Winter 1975), 89–125.

46. _____. *Student Leaving: Rethinking the Causes and Cures of Student Attrition.* Chicago: University of Chicago Press, 1987.

47. U. S. Bureau of the Census. *Persons of Spanish Origin in the United States: March 1979.* Current Population Reports, Series P–20, No. 354. Washington, D.C.: U.S. Government Printing Office, 1980.

48. U.S. Commission on Civil Rights. *The Unfinished Education: Outcomes for Minorities in the Five Southwestern States.* Mexican American Educational Series, Report 2. Washington, D.C.: U.S. Government Printing Office, 1971.

49. Weick, K. E. *The Social Psychology of Organizing.* 2nd ed. Reading, Mass.: Addison-Wesley, 1979.

50. _____. "Small Wins: Redefining the Scale of Social Problems." *American Psychologist*, 39 (January 1984), 40–49.

51. Withey, S. B. "Summary and Conclusions." In *A Degree and What Else: Correlates and Consequences of a College Education*, edited by S. B. Withey, pp. 127–32. New York: McGraw-Hill, 1971.

Undergraduate Socialization:
A Conceptual Approach

JOHN C. WEIDMAN

There has been a continuing interest in the study of the ways in which colleges affect the cognitive and affective lives of their students, during the years of enrollment (Pace, 1979; Chickering et al., 1981; Komarovsky, 1985; Katchadourian and Boli, 1985) as well as the years beyond college (Newcomb et al., 1967; Withey, 1971; Solmon and Taubman, 1973; Hyman, Wright, and Reed, 1975; Bowen, 1977; Winter, McClelland, and Stewart, 1981). The primary focus of the bulk of these works has been on identifying individual outcomes, both cognitive and affective, that can be attributed to college attendance. While often comprehensive in their treatment of research on college impact (e.g., Feldman and Newcomb, 1969; Astin, 1977), most of these works tend to focus on description of outcomes and do not deal explicitly with the development of comprehensive theoretical explanations for their occurrence or the building of conceptual frameworks. In part, this is because some of the more influential conceptualizations are fundamentally psychological and emphasize personality rather than social structural constraints (Feldman, 1972).

This pattern has continued into the current decade. In their systematic classification of research on college students during the period from 1969 to 1983, Kuh et al. (1986) found that only 10.8% of the articles published annually had a primary emphasis on theory development (i.e., establishing "causal relationships among sets of variables"). A mere 6.6% of the articles published annually dealt with concept integration (i.e., the production of "new knowledge about college students through analysis and integration of existing ideas"). These authors suggest that researchers have become comfortable with the extant models of student development (e.g., Chickering, 1969) and that the difficulties of building new theoretical models outweigh the efficacy of relying on models that are already widely accepted.

Consequently, the purpose of the present chapter is to extend the body of research and thought on college impact by developing a comprehensive conceptual framework for understanding some salient elements of the socialization process as it occurs in higher education. The framework builds from both psychological and social structural conceptions, drawing upon sociological notions of the socialization process in adolescence and adulthood (e.g., Mortimer and Simmons, 1978; Brim, 1966) as well as more traditional approaches to addressing the importance of social structure in socialization and personality development (Hurrelmann, 1988). The background section traces briefly the pattern of research on college impact historically and identifies important sets of variables appearing in some of the more influential contemporary research on college impact. It is argued that this work, while specifying important variables and testing causal relationships among variables, could be more oriented toward theoretically explicating in a comprehensive fashion the underlying processes of college impact on students focusing particularly on nonintellectual outcomes (e.g., Weidman, 1979, 1984). Because an extensive review of the cognitive dimensions of college impact has already been written (Pascarella, 1985a), this section is concerned primarily with affective dimensions of college impact, especially influences of college on students' values, personal goals, and aspirations. Important conceptual dimensions of the socialization process are discussed, paying particular attention to those characteristics of both individuals and institutions that are likely to enhance the influence of college on students.

A conceptual framework for understanding the undergraduate socialization process is developed in the third section of this chapter. The framework incorporates consideration of socializing influences experienced by undergraduates from a variety of sources, both within and external to the postsecondary educational institution. Particular emphasis is placed on social structural aspects of socialization, rather than on individual processes of dealing with socializing influences, not because the latter are any less important but because they are not under the control of postsecondary educational institutions and, hence, are not as "policy-relevant." More interpretive perspectives that focus more on the individual student's perceptions of the college environment (Huber, 1980) and less on structural aspects of socialization are incorporated, where appropriate, in developing the conceptualization. Attention is also paid to special student populations (e.g., women, minorities, and returning adults). The chapter concludes with a discussion of the implications of this conceptual framework for future research, for the design of collegiate institutions as agencies of socialization, and for students seeking to make informed choices about the types of colleges that are most appropriate for them.

Background

At least one major study of the ways in which college students' lives are influenced during their years of enrollment has been published in each decade since the 1940s. Among the earliest was the study of young women attending Bennington College that was published by Theodore Newcomb (1943). As a social psychologist, Newcomb was interested in learning about the apparently liberalizing influence of attendance at the reputedly avant-garde Bennington College on the values of young women from Brahmin, decidedly conservative

New England families. Interest in collegiate influences on undergraduates continued with research in the 1950s at another eastern women's college, the "Vassar studies," which were directed by another social psychologist, Nevitt Sanford. This work led to the publication of the first volume encompassing a broad spectrum of perspectives, many but not all based upon the Vassar research, on various aspects of the undergraduate experience (Sanford, 1962).

Another group of researchers, this time more sociologically oriented, was also doing related work during the 1950s on changes in undergraduates' orientations during college, the "Cornell Values Study." A major emphasis in this study was the study of changes in career choices and occupational values which built on the seminal work of one of the researchers, Morris Rosenberg (1957). Initially, the reports on this research suggested that the college experience had little, if any, influence on undergraduates' values (Jacob, 1957). The fully elaborated report (Goldsen et al., 1960) did, however, show specific types of college-related value changes.

During the 1960s research on college impact burgeoned, and by the end of the decade, the first systematic review and synthesis of this work was published by another sociologist, Kenneth Feldman, and his mentor, Theodore Newcomb. The Feldman and Newcomb (1969) book provided, for the first time, a sociologically oriented review of the then-extant college-impact literature. Also of great significance was the major theoretical analysis of college student development published by the psychologist Arthur Chickering (1969). More recently, Chickering (1981) has edited a lengthy volume updating such predecessors as Sanford (1962) and Feldman and Newcomb (1969).

Somewhat less well known than the works that have thus far been mentioned is a series of studies that were published in the 1960s by sociologists at the National Opinion Research Center (NORC) of the University of Chicago. Several lines of research are particularly noteworthy. The first involved a large national survey of June 1961 college graduates and focused on various aspects of their collegiate experience. James Davis (1964, 1965) published two volumes that explored the major and career choices of undergraduates along with their aspirations for postcollegiate careers. Not surprisingly, some of the items from the Cornell Values Study appeared on this survey. A second is represented in research on Catholic colleges written by Father Andrew Greeley (1967). A third is a survey study of virtually all of the undergraduates attending a single, small, liberal arts college in the Midwest published by Walter Wallace (1966).

In addition, NORC sponsored the publication of a set of papers dealing with various aspects of peer relationships among college students that was edited by two of the participants in a pair of 1959–1960 conferences at which they were originally presented, Theodore Newcomb and Everett Wilson (1966). Given the sponsorship by a survey research center, it is expectable that several chapters in this volume dealt with methodological issues in the study of college students. There were also, however, several conceptual chapters, among them one by Burton Clark and Martin Trow in which they presented their fourfold typology of college student subcultures (academic, collegiate, nonconformist, and vocational).

Finally, one of the most influential lines of empirical research on college students began with the inauguration in 1966 of a national survey of entering college freshmen by Alexander Astin, then at the American Council on Education. This annual survey has continued to the present and has been used for numerous empirical studies, quite a few of which are incorporated into Astin (1977). Not only did Astin maintain his own survey program, but he also joined forces in 1969 with Martin Trow under funding from the Carnegie Foundation for a follow-up of respondents to his first four freshman surveys, the results of which were published in a volume edited by Trow (1975).

Contemporary research on college impact has tended to draw upon conceptual frameworks (e.g., Chickering, 1969; Tinto, 1975; Astin, 1977; Weidman, 1984; Smart, 1986; Smart and Pascarella, 1986) that include at least four general sets of variables: (1) student background characteristics; (2) college characteristics; (3) measures of students' linkages to the college environment; and (4) indicators of "college effects." The first set of variables, students' background characteristics when they enter college, includes, for example, (a) social status

indicators such as parental income and education, sex, and race; (b) ability and achievement indicators such as test scores and high school class rank; and (c) indicators of personal orientations such as career choices, values, goals, and aspirations prior to matriculation.

Characteristics of the collegiate environment experienced by students can be exemplified by (a) organizational variables such as type of control, size, and quality; (b) indicators of the academic environment such as curricular emphases, the student's major, and expectations held by faculty for student performance in class; and (c) indicators of the extracurricular environment such as residence arrangements, availability of campus organizations, and both formal and informal student activities. The third set, indicators of students' linkages to the organizational, academic, and extracurricular dimensions of the college environment, includes (a) interaction with faculty and peers; (b) amount of time spent studying; (c) involvement in campus life; and (d) both social and academic integration. Finally, "college effect" variables include values, career choices, and personal goals. In longitudinal studies, data on these variables tend to be collected upon entrance to college and then at some later point during the undergraduate years. Studies reflect wide variation in the time interval between college entrance and the subsequent data collection points (ranging from once or twice during college to many times, and sometimes even extending into the postcollege adult years).

When data on the same college effect variables are collected in succeeding years, the most recently collected data become the dependent variables, with previous measures then becoming additional independent variables since current status is generally dependent upon one's previous status on a particular indicator. Appropriately operationalized, these four sets of variables can provide a reasonably accurate portrait of several important aspects of the longitudinal process of college impact.

Research so conceived is especially useful for identifying the types of college effects that occur, the types of students likely to be affected by college attendance, the academic and extracurricular dimensions of colleges that are related to observed effects, and the types of student involvement in campus life that are associated with various dimensions of college impact.

This sort of approach does little, however, to clarify and explain in any systematic fashion the reasons why effects occur. Authors seldom develop and adequately operationalize a conceptual framework to explain the relationships among the variables. Rather, they rely either on intuitive use of *post hoc* conceptual frameworks or on reference to personal experience.

An intuitive approach provides a convenient opportunity for researchers to build an agenda for future research since explanations tend to incorporate unmeasured variables that are posited to be necessary for a fuller understanding of the college effects under investigation. It does not, however, necessarily lead to a systematic understanding of the underlying social processes that bring about college impact. If knowledge of how colleges influence their students is to be extended, researchers on college impact should begin to pay closer attention to identifying and operationalizing the specific social and interpersonal mechanisms that transmit and mediate the influences of the college environment. These conceptual variables can then guide empirical research.

In the next section of the chapter, several conceptual dimensions of the socialization process that are especially important for explaining college impact are discussed. These dimensions are then used to develop a comprehensive framework for understanding undergraduate socialization.

The Socialization Process

Brim (1966) defines socialization as "the process by which persons acquire the knowledge, skills, and dispositions that make them more or less effective members of their society" (p. 3). While society may be viewed as a generalized social structure composed of smaller units (e.g., families, friends, organizations) within which people behave, it can also be thought of as being composed of groups, "each having a distinct subculture" (Clausen, 1968, p. 4). Hence, socialization involves the acquisition and maintenance of membership in salient groups (e.g., familial, occupational, organizational) as well as society at large. Consequently, socialization can always usefully be considered from the perspective of the society (or its constituent groups) as well as the individual. In order to

understand socialization more clearly, it is important to identify social patterns of influence affecting individuals and groups. This is done in the present chapter by focusing on the part played by social relationships in the establishment and maintenance of expectations for appropriate member behavior (i.e., norms) and group integration. Dimensions of general socialization theory are then extended to the specific case of undergraduate socialization.

Norms and Social Integration

From the societal perspective, "socialization efforts are designed to lead the new member to adhere to the norms of the larger society or of the particular group into which he is being incorporated and to commit him to its future" (Clausen, 1968, p. 6). Norms are important for understanding the process of socialization because, according to Hawkes (1975), "a norm may be conceived loosely as a rule, a standard, or a prescription for behavior ... that is in some way enforced ..." (p. 888). Norms provide the basic standards for the regulations of individual behavior in groups as well as in the larger society (Hawkes, 1975, p. 888). Social integration, from this perspective, refers to the extent to which the society or subunit (e.g., institution, organization, group) is characterized by a shared acceptance of common norms that are reflected in solidary, cohesive, and reasonably stable patterns of relationships among its constituent parts (Parsons, Shils, and Olds, 1951, pp. 202–204).

From the perspective of the individual, socialization involves learning the appropriate (i.e., normative) modes of "social behavior and/or role enactment" within the groups in which membership is desired (Mortimer and Simmons, 1978, p. 422). *Role*, in this sense, refers to the "dynamic aspects" (Lipton, 1936, p. 14) of positions or statuses in the group "and may be defined by the expectations (the rights, privileges, and obligations) to which any incumbent of the role must adhere" (Getzels, 1963, p. 311). *Social integration*, from the perspective of the individual, refers to the extent to which an individual's behavior in groups is characterized by willing acceptance of group norms and solidary relationships with other members. In terms of socialization, the more fully integrated an individual is into a group, the greater is that group's capacity for ensuring a reasonably high level of normative compliance among members.

This is not to say, however, that socialization is a completely deterministic process over which the individual being socialized has little or no control. On the contrary, as individuals mature and move toward the assumption of adult roles, there can be considerable flexibility both in the expectations held of new role incumbents and in the variety of ways in which roles may be fulfilled acceptably (Mortimer and Simmons, 1978, p. 424). This suggests the importance of incorporating both objective and subjective dimensions when explaining the socialization process (Hurrelmann, 1988). Furthermore, as individuals move toward adulthood, participation in the settings in which socialization occurs tends to be increasingly voluntary. Hence, individuals who do not find the normative expectations in a setting to their liking or who are not welcomed by members may attempt to seek other settings which are more commensurate with personal orientations.

Reference Groups and Social Relationships

An important step in understanding undergraduate socialization is to identify those sources of influences that are likely to be the most salient for particular students. Reference group theory is especially useful for identifying potentially important sources of socializing influences. According to Kemper (1968, p. 32) a reference group can be a person, group, or collectivity that an individual takes into account when selecting a particular course of action from among several alternatives or "in making a judgement about a problematic issue."

A particularly salient social mechanism for the transmission and processing of socializing influences in reference groups is interpersonal relationships, especially, but not limited to, those which involve close friendships (Shibutani, 1955, p. 568). According to Brim (1966), this process can be described as follows: "the individual learns the behavior appropriate to his position in a group through interaction with others who hold normative beliefs about what his role should be, and who reward or punish him for correct or incorrect actions" (p. 9).

Anticipatory Socialization

General pressures of at least two sorts operate simultaneously during college. First, students frequently have to make choices concerning their activities after completion of college. Second, students need to identify and then to prepare for attaining desirable goals. This process is called *anticipatory socialization*, i.e., "the acquisition of values and orientations found in statuses and groups in which one is not yet engaged but which one is likely to enter" (Merton, 1968, pp. 438–439). Anticipatory socialization prepares individuals for future positions, although much of the preparation is, according to Merton (1968), "implicit, unwitting, and informal" (p. 439).

For many undergraduates, one of the main tasks during college is to make decisions (some certainly more tentative than others) about the type of career or career preparation to pursue upon graduation. Students attempt to determine not only their own suitability for various occupations (both in terms of academic skills and perceived job demands) but also the reactions of significant others to their choices. Colleges, in addition to providing the education and credentials necessary for access to professional, managerial, and upper white-collar occupations, also provide experiences and resources for students to develop more generalized orientations toward work and leisure activities. In this sense, the undergraduate college serves as a context for anticipatory occupational socialization involving the concomitant influences of students' values and occupational aspirations because, according to Rosenberg (1957), "in addition to people choosing an occupation in order to satisfy a value, they may choose a value because they consider it appropriate for the occupational status they expect to fill in the future" (p. 24). The choice of an academic major is a central component of this process.

Temporal Aspects of Socialization

These processes of socialization do not apply only to the late-adolescence/early-adulthood period of life that is characteristic of most undergraduates. Socialization is considered to be a lifelong process that occurs as individuals adapt themselves to a variety of changing circumstances (Bragg, 1976, p. 6), not the least of which are changes in career demands, family responsibilities, and possibly even the employment structure. There are differences, however, in the basic content of socialization (ranging from the regulation of biological drives to specific group norms), the contexts in which socialization occurs (ranging from the dependent status of the child to the organizational settings of adulthood), and the responses of individuals (ranging from the very malleable child to the change-resistant adult) to socializing influences (Mortimer and Simmons, 1978, p. 423). During college, the passage of four years in the life of a late adolescent can result in considerable maturation that may influence receptivity to socialization influences. In fact, going through college as a late adolescent has been shown to have several similarities to a "rite of passage" (Tinto, 1987; Van Gennep, 1960; Kett, 1977). Collegiate institutions are, however, enrolling increasing numbers of undergraduates who are not late adolescents but "nontraditional," adult students who have a very different adaptation to make, including things like juggling family demands or financial exigencies (Bean and Metzner, 1985; Weidman and White, 1985; Metzner and Bean, 1987). They also tend to have much clearer personal and career goals than late adolescent undergraduates. Hence, studies of undergraduate socialization should take into account differences in the age and developmental stages of students.

A second consideration has to do with the duration of influence. Curtis (1974) has shown, for instance, that the socialization potential of an educational institution increases with the amount of time that a student spends enrolled. The sequential nature of certain types of socialization processes is also important. As formulated by Thornton and Nardi (1975), taking on a role can be described as moving through four stages: anticipatory, formal, informal, and personal. In each stage, there is "interaction between individuals and external expectations, including individuals' attempts to influence the expectations of others as well as others' attempts to influence individuals" (Thornton and Nardi, 1975, p. 873).

The first of these stages corresponds to anticipatory socialization. The formal stage occurs when the individual begins to assume the specific demands of the role, meeting the group's official or proclaimed expectations of the role. The informal stage occurs when the individual learns the unofficial or informal expectations for the role and adapts behavior accordingly. In the personal stage, the individual reconciles the formal and informal expectations with personal orientations, assumes full membership in the group, and begins to participate in the group's processes of shaping the expectations that will be held subsequently for new role incumbents.

Summary

Three components of the socialization process are particularly salient for the study of college impact: (1) individual, group, and organizational sources of socializing influences; (2) social processes (both inter- and intrapersonal interaction, social integration) through which these sources of socializing influences are encountered and responded to by students; and (3) resultant socialization outcomes in various college settings. This approach to understanding undergraduate socialization suggests two basic questions about the socialization of individuals in an organizational environment. One pertains to social interaction: What are the interpersonal processes through which individuals are socialized? The other pertains to organizational structure: What are the various characteristics of higher education institutions as socializing organizations that exert influences on students? The importance of considering both individual and organizational characteristics in studying socialization can be explained as follows: "Just as individuals may become differently socialized because of differences in past experience, motivations, and capacities, so may they become differently socialized because of differences in the structure of the social settings in which they interact" (Wheeler, 1966, p. 54).

The essence of this approach as it applies to the relationships among individual and organizational variables in the study of undergraduate socialization can be summarized as follows: Just as students differ in their patterns of interaction and personal orientations upon entrance, colleges differ in their structuring, intentionally or not, of both normative contexts such as student residences and classrooms, and of opportunities for social interaction among college students, faculty, and staff. Furthermore, because socialization occurs over a period of time and is a cumulative process, the relative importance of both settings and significant others may change during the course of the undergraduate years. Hence, it is essential that conceptualizations of undergraduate socialization incorporate the longitudinal aspects of change and stability over four (and often more) years.

The following sections of this chapter elaborate a conceptual framework and apply it to different aspects of undergraduate socialization. Consideration is given to the special problems of women, minorities, and nontraditional students as well as to those aspects of undergraduate socialization that persist through the life course.

Undergraduate Socialization: A Conceptual Framework

Figure 1 shows the conceptual framework developed for this chapter. The framework is intended to contribute to theoretical understanding of collegiate impact and, more gener-

ally, to understanding of socialization in organizations. Underlying this framework, on one level, are concerns for the situational and individual developmental constraints on the choices made by participants in an organizational environment. On another level, the framework explores a set of socialization processes, concentrating largely on the impact of normative contexts and interpersonal relations among an organization's members. It includes consideration of the joint socializing impacts of (1) student background, (2) the normative influences exerted by the academic and social structure of the college through the mechanisms of both inter- and intrapersonal processes, and (3) the mediating impacts of both parental socialization and noncollege reference groups during college despite influences brought to bear upon students by participation in the more immediate campus social structure.

The framework is not, however, intended to be exhaustive. Dimensions and variables other than those which appear could be included, depending upon the particular interests of researchers. The framework is based primarily upon the author's own research (Weidman, 1984, 1989; Weidman and Fried-

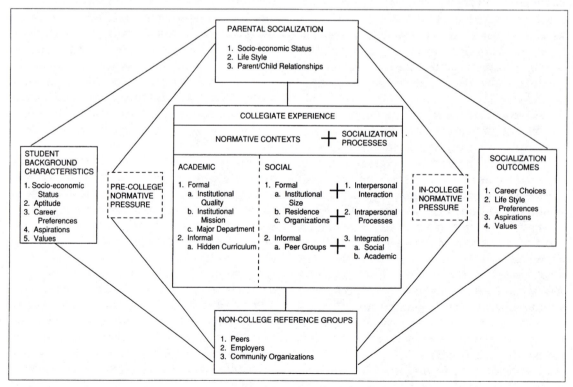

Figure 1: A Conceptual Model of Undergraduate Socialization

mann, 1984; Weidman and White, 1985) as well as the conceptual work of Chickering (1969), Tinto (1975, 1987), and Astin (1977, 1984).

Briefly, the model was designed with several general considerations in mind. As has already been mentioned, it is concerned primarily with noncognitive *Socialization Outcomes*. Of considerable importance among these outcomes is career choice, a process which involves not simply the selection of a career field but also an assessment of the implications of particular occupations for "a style of life and a place in the community status system" (Beardsley and O'Dowd, 1962, pp. 606–607). With respect to *Student Background Characteristics*, the sociological literature on status attainment has demonstrated the necessity of including family socioeconomic status, academic aptitude or ability, and aspirations in studies of occupational attainment because such background characteristics have been shown consistently to be related to outcomes (Alexander and Eckland, 1975; Hauser, Tsai, and Sewell, 1983). Astin (1977) also demonstrates the importance of including student background in studies of college impact.

The selection of conceptions for inclusion in the *Collegiate Experience* box is based largely on the work of Chickering (1969), who identifies six dimensions of college life that influence student development: (1) clarity and consistency of institutional objectives; (2) institutional size; (3) curriculum, teaching, and evaluation; (4) residence hall arrangements; (5) faculty and administration interaction with students; and (6) friends, groups, and student culture. Tinto's (1975, 1987) work suggests the importance of dividing *Normative Contexts* into an "academic" and a "social" component. Further differentiation into a "formal" and an "informal" part is suggested by Sanford (1962, p. 40). The within-in box boundaries do not have solid lines because they are assumed to be rather fluid.

With respect to *Socialization Processes*, the large "pluses" are used to indicate that normative influences can be transmitted to students through several mechanisms. In the conceptual model of dropout from higher education developed by Tinto (1975), goal commitments, aspirations, and values held at entrance to postsecondary education are posited to affect students' academic performances (grades and

intellectual development) and social life (peer-group and faculty interactions) within the institution. Students' decisions to continue or drop out reflect the extent of their "academic integration" and "social integration" within the institution. This integration, in turn, influences subsequent institutional goal commitments as well as assessments of the personal importance of those commitments. Such subjective assessments of experiences in college (e.g., satisfaction, fulfillment of expectations) may be said to reflect "intrapersonal processes" (Weidman and White, 1985).

Because typical educational institutions are not encapsulated environments, it is reasonable to assume that performance in college may be affected by the student's ability to cope with problems at home and other community settings (Weidman and Friedmann, 1984; Weidman and White, 1985; Bean and Metzner, 1985). Atkin's (1982) finding that dropout among first-year college students is related to concern with "family/personal problems" also supports this extension of the framework, as does Tinto's (1982) acknowledgement that his model did not "seek to directly address the impact of financial stress or other forces external to the institution's immediate environment (e.g., external peer groups in an urban environment)" (p. 688). Hence, the present conceptual framework includes consideration of *Noncollege Reference Groups*. In addition, it includes *Parental Socialization* (Weidman, 1984) because it is assumed that such influences are present throughout the college years, even for those students who are independent householders.

In Figure 1, dotted lines appear around the two *Normative Pressure* boxes because they represent influences that tend to be either unmeasured or inaccurately measured in research on undergraduate socialization. Generally, this type of influence is inferred from patterns of joint covariation among variables constituting the college context. That is, inferences about the direction and intensity of normative pressures to which a student is exposed are based on observed relationships among characteristics of their collegiate experience and interpersonal linkages, especially interaction with faculty and peers and other types of participation in formal and informal aspects of college life. The model suggests that, in order to understand "normative pressure" more fully, persisting influences of both "parental social-ization" and "noncollege reference groups" must be taken into consideration.

Finally, the dimensions of the model shown in Figure 1 are assumed to be linked in a bidirectional, as opposed to a unidirectional, causal fashion. It is assumed that there is a reciprocity of influences on undergraduates such that, during the college years, various dimensions can have greater or lesser importance for socialization, depending upon the outcomes considered as well as the particular stage both of students' lives and of their undergraduate experience.

To summarize the general conceptual framework, undergraduate socialization can be conceived of as a series of processes whereby the student: (1) enters college as a freshman with certain values, aspirations, and other personal goals; (2) is exposed to various socializing influences while attending college, including normative pressures exerted via (a) social relationships with college faculty and peers, (b) parental pressures, and (c) involvement with noncollege reference groups; (3) assesses the salience of the various normative pressures encountered for attaining personal goals; and (4) changes or maintains those values, aspirations, and personal goals that were held at college entrance. In the following sections, the dimensions of the framework are described in more detail. Specific attention is also paid to illustrating some of the more important linkages among dimensions.

Parental Socialization

Explicit in this framework is the recognition that the college campus does not, for most undergraduates, constitute a totally encapsulated environment. Parents, for example, influence the career preferences and orientations that students bring with them at college entrance (Winch and Gordon, 1974; Bengston, 1975). Furthermore, since the effects of parental socialization are so very likely to persist during the course of the student's college years, parental pressures and expectations may serve to mediate the impact of college experiences. Consequently, if the susceptibility of students to the socializing influences of the campus environment is to be determined, it is also necessary to assess the importance of parent-child

relationships. Two questions are suggested by this approach: How are various aspects of parental socialization and lifestyles related to the persistence and change of undergraduates' orientations and preferences? How do aspects of the collegiate experience and parental socialization interact with one another in influencing the student during college?

In studies of career development, parental influences have been continuously identified as important contributing factors (Borow, 1966). Sociological research consistently shows that occupational attainment is related to such measures of parental social status as occupational prestige and educational attainment (Blau and Duncan, 1967; Alexander and Eckland, 1975). Other studies indicate that occupational values concerning autonomy in work are associated with a middle-social-class position as measured by educational and occupational status, and that these values are transmitted by parents to their offspring (Kohn, 1977; Morgan, Alwin, and Griffin, 1979; Mortimer, 1974, 1976).

Parental influences appear to be somewhat more important for the precollege socialization of black than white students. For black undergraduates, mothers tend to be very important influences on both college and career choices (Smith, 1981).

While there are strong correlations between such variables as parental lifestyle and career orientations of college freshmen (Weidman, 1984) and parental expectations for freshmen and college persistence (Bank, Slavings, and Biddle, 1986), there is also evidence that parental influences decline in importance during college so that by senior year the correlations between parental characteristics and career choices are no longer significant (Weidman, 1984). This suggests an important temporal dimension to parental influence, with parents decreasing in importance during the college years, especially for those undergraduates who leave their parents' homes to attend college.

It should also be noted, however, that finding no significant parental influences on the career choices of college seniors (Weidman, 1984) may be an artifact of the measures used which were based on students' self-reports of parental characteristics, expectations, and behavior. Studies (Davies and Kandel, 1981; Looker and Pineo, 1983) suggest that adolescents may systematically underestimate the importance of parental influences on aspirations. These authors demonstrate the importance of obtaining information about their attitudes and behavior directly from parents instead of relying solely on reports by adolescents of their parents' influence.

Noncollege Reference Groups

In addition to relationships with parents, undergraduates are likely to maintain ties of various sorts to significant others outside the collegiate environment. In the case of nontraditional students, especially those older than their early twenties, there may be the competing demands of employers and the students' own families at home (i.e., spouses and children) as well (Simpson, 1979; Bean and Metzner, 1985; Weidman and White, 1985). There may also be ties to churches and community organizations that can shape responses to collegiate influences. The support of noncollege significant others, including friends and other relatives (e.g., aunts and uncles, siblings, cousins, in-laws), is also important for older students (Bean, 1985; Weidman and White, 1985) as well as for minority students (Thomas, 1981; Nora, 1987) who have to cope with many competing expectations and, hence, are exposed to potentially conflicting normative pressures.

Student Background Characteristics

Characteristics of individuals that tend to be correlated with specific types of outcomes must be included in any conceptualization of the undergraduate socialization process. The contribution of student background characteristics to understanding college impact is investigated in at least three primary sources of literature: (a) research examining the broad spectrum of college effects on students (Feldman and Newcomb, 1969; Astin, 1977); (b) research on dropouts from higher education (Tinto, 1975; Pantages and Creedon, 1978; Lenning, 1982; Pascarella and Terenzini, 1980; Pascarella and Chapman, 1983); and (c) research on the sociology of status attainment (Sewell, Haller, and Portes, 1969; Sewell, Haller, and Ohlendorf, 1970; Alexander and Eckland, 1975; Jencks, Crouse, and Mueser, 1983; Hauser, et al. 1983). Figure 1 includes five

examples of background characteristics which are not meant to be an exhaustive list, but rather illustrate categories that appear frequently in research. Socioeconomic status generally refers to the parents of the students and is most often measured by some combination of the parents' annual income, educational attainment, and occupational prestige (e.g., Duncan, 1961). Parents' education has been shown to exert a particularly strong influence on the college choices of black students (Litten, 1982).

Aptitude is an indicator of the student's academic ability and is most often measured by standardized test scores (e.g., SAT or ACT). Preferences, aspirations, and values held by students prior to college enrollment form the perspectives and expectations held by students prior to enrollment and shape their encounters with the higher education institution, especially early in the undergraduate years. These orientations also may be shaped by the collegiate experience and subsequently shape post-college attainment. In fact, respondents to a large National Opinion Research Center sample of college graduates stated that their entering plans were a more important influence on ultimate career choice than their in-college grades (Spaeth and Greeley, 1970, pp. 171–172).

Precollege Normative Pressure

Parental socialization, the influence of significant others who are not part of the collegiate environment, and students' background characteristics combine to become crucial determinants of the student's susceptibility to institutional influences early in college. This same combination also influences the patterns of coping that students use to meet the new demands of college. It is assumed that the student entering college as a freshman cannot be considered to be a *tabula rasa*. Rather, prior experiences with family and significant others who are not members of the college community continue to generate normative pressures that shape students' expectations of and responses to their new environment.

Collegiate Experience

Socialization in college may be thought of as a process that "entails a continuing interaction between the individual and those who seek to influence him" (Clausen, 1968, p. 3). Socialization, in this sense, "does imply that the individual is induced in some measure to conform willingly to the ways of ... the particular groups to which he belongs" (ibid. p. 4). Undergraduate socialization can thus be viewed as a process that results from the student's interaction with other members of the college community in groups or other settings characterized by varying degrees of normative pressure.

This portion of the conceptual framework draws heavily from the seminal structural-functional analysis of American universities by Parsons and Platt (1973). Specifically, the framework focuses on two aspects of their argument as it relates to undergraduate socialization. One has to do with what they term the "moral authority of institutions" (Parsons and Platt, 1973, p. 167). This refers to the normative order (including its mission as well as normative expectations of faculty and staff for students) of the college or university as a potent agent of socialization. The various aspects of a collegiate institution's normative order may then be studied by identifying social contexts (e.g., colleges or particular college groups) that are characterized by especially strong expectations for students. In Chickering's (1969) terms, the greater the "clarity and consistency of objectives," the stronger the normative consensus among members of a particular institution, organizational unit, or group within the institution. The second aspect of the Parsons and Platt (1973) discussion has to do with interpersonal relationships among various members of academic settings. According to Parsons and Platt, these interpersonal attachments make an important contribution to the members' social integration within the college.

Furthermore, interpersonal relationships contributing to the social integration of students into the academic system are related not only to the attainment of institutional goals but also to the personal goals of individual students (Tinto, 1975). Close, personal relationships among members of normative contexts contribute materially to the transmission and internalization of normative influences by members (Moore, 1969). Hence, in studying college student socialization, it is important to explore the impacts of normative contexts as well as the ways in which interpersonal relationships among members serve to either reinforce or counteract the normative influences exerted within various specific contexts (Lacy, 1978).

Following Tinto (1975), Figure 1 divides *Normative Contexts* into an *Academic* and a *Social* dimension. The academic dimension refers to those aspects of the collegiate environment that contribute explicitly to the fulfillment of educational objectives (as stated in the institutional mission), including such things as allocation of resources for and organization of instruction, and student selection in the admissions process. The social dimension refers to the ways in which opportunities for interaction among members are organized and clustered within the institution. The academic and social dimensions are further subdivided into "formal" and "informal" components, as suggested by Sanford (1962, p. 49). Formal structures are those designed to achieve the various stated objectives of the organization, generally built around a system of written rules and procedures. Informal structures tend to evolve as individuals adapt their own personal needs and expectations to the demands of the formal structure. Informal structures are characteristically more fluid and organized according to implicit rather than explicit rules and procedures. To understand undergraduate socialization, both the formal and informal aspects of normative contexts need to be investigated along with their relationships to one another.

Normative Contexts: Academic

Institutional and within-institution program quality, though fraught with problems of definition and measurement (Conrad and Blackburn, 1985), continues to be of considerable interest to scholars, policy makers, and consumers of higher education. The "frog-pond effect" (Davis, 1966; Reitz, 1975) suggests that college selectivity decreases students' preferences for seeking educationally high-level careers, largely because the competition between highly able students is greater than in less selective institutions. Other studies (Bassis, 1977; Drew and Astin, 1972), however, found positive effects of selectivity on aspirations and self-evaluations.

More selective institutions tend also to emphasize providing students with a broad liberal education rather than being narrowly job-focused, and thus are more likely to reflect normative pressures that encourage the development of values and aspirations that encompass broader facets of adult life (e.g., use of leisure time, cultural preferences, participation in community affairs) than simply career and income. Solmon and Wachtel (1975) found institutional quality as measured by levels of resource allocation to be positively associated with postcollege career income. Institutional reputation or prestige, often used as the primary measure in studies of quality, has also been shown to be related to both college completion and access to elite careers (Kamens, 1974).

The mission of an institution of higher education provides the statement of institutional purpose that drives resource allocation and establishes educational objectives (Meyer, 1970, 1972). The mission provides a frame of reference both for the student in choosing a particular college and for other external constituencies, especially employers, interested in making judgments about the qualifications of graduates. Institutional mission may also be reflected in affiliation with a religious denomination (Greeley, 1967). The nature of the socializing environment in religiously affiliated institutions can be characterized as follows:

> Studies have indicated that religious-affiliated colleges present the kind of setting that is most conducive to change of any sort. They are small, allowing for more personalized interaction of students and faculty. They have a higher degree of homogeneity in student social background than most colleges. They have a high degree of normative integration, and structural characteristics (residentiality) that support that integration. (Anderson, 1985, p. 323).

A particularly important locus of both faculty and peer influences on students is the academic department (Hearn, 1980; Hearn and Olzak, 1981; Weidman, 1979, 1984). Practically all postfreshman students have some affiliation with an academic department, since it tends to be the organizational unit through which degree requirements are formulated and certification of their successful completion is made. Vreeland and Bidwell (1966) assert that the department "has relatively well-defined goals

and expectations for students, and commands powerful normative and utilitarian sanctions" (p. 238). These authors argue that the socializing impacts of the department are determined by the expressed goals of the faculty for undergraduate education, which, in turn, determine faculty behavior and expectations for students. They identify three areas of faculty emphasis or goals for undergraduate education: providing a broad, liberal education; providing occupational training; and mixed goals, where both are emphasized.

The academic department can be a powerful source of normative influences on student majors, in large part because of the faculty's ability to differentially reward students for their performance in courses, through both the assignment of grades and the encouragement of social interaction (Parsons and Platt, 1973, p. 179). Faculty evaluation of student's performances in class-related activities as well as in other settings can be a significant influence on students' goals and aspirations. In fact, for influences on students' career orientations within the department, major field faculty appear to be more important than major field peers (Phelan, 1979; Weidman, 1984). This may vary, however, by the level of the student. Freshmen, for instance, appear to be more susceptible to peer than faculty influence (Bean, 1985; Bank et al., 1986; Biddle, Bank, and Slavings, 1986). As students pass through the college years faculty may become more salient agents of socialization. It is likely that faculty influence is strengthened by faculty members' increasing contribution to the process of anticipatory socialization for significant adult roles as students concentrate on work in their major fields (Weidman, 1984). There is also evidence that differences in the orientations of students across major fields actually become sharper during the college years, thus suggesting that there are potent socializing influences exerted by major departments (Feldman and Weiler, 1976).

It is also important to remember that the department is part of a larger organization. Consequently, there may be socializing effects of interaction in nondepartmental settings within the college that either add an increment to or even cancel out the department's influences.

On the informal side, the "hidden curriculum" (Snyder, 1971) of higher education can also be a powerful source of influence on students. This term refers to the unspoken and unwritten rules defining faculty expectations for students' academic performance. Do tests, for instance, actually reflect what faculty say is important? Similarly, it could also refer to the unwritten rules of academic behavior as well as to other informal norms about what is acceptable as defined by students (Becker, Geer, and Hughes, 1968).

NORMATIVE CONTEXTS: SOCIAL

Another important dimension here is the formal extracurricular structure of the college. Presumably, those students who participate actively in extracurricular activities may be more likely than their nonparticipant counterparts to look to peers or college staff who supervise the extracurricular activities rather than to departmental faculty as normative referents. It is also possible that the norms held by the extracurricular staff and peers differ from those held by departmental peers and faculty.

The spatial location, especially on- vs. off-campus, of reference groups can also affect their potential for socialization. The importance for socialization of participation in on-campus activities has been described by Vreeland and Bidwell (1965) as contributing to the power of the college to influence students because "the broader the scope of the student's involvement with the college, the more accessible he is to intervention and the more diverse the mechanisms that can be employed (especially mechanisms of indirect manipulation)" (p. 235). Consequently, limited student involvement with on-campus reference groups is likely to reduce the impact of normative pressures exerted by a college. This has clear implications for examining differential socialization in residential and commuter institutions (Chickering, 1974; Pascarella, 1984).

There is also a relationship between the social climate of a living group and members' academic performance (Schrager, 1986). According to Blimling (1988), living in on-campus residence halls tends to increase students' satisfaction with college, increase participation in extracurricular activities, and improve retention.

It is, however, important to differentiate membership groups from reference groups. For instance, it is inappropriate to assume that students from the same residence will necessarily constitute each other's reference group(s). In a classic study of college women, Siegel and Siegel (1957) manipulated choice of residence location by deliberately assigning subjects to nonpreferred locations. The authors discovered that attitude change was greatest when subjects adopted "the imposed, initially nonpreferred membership group as their reference group" (p. 364).

SOCIALIZATION PROCESSES: INTERPERSONAL INTERACTION

An important determinant of the socialization potential of social relationships is the degree of intensity of feelings and other affective attachments between the people involved, namely, their sentiments (Homans, 1950, pp. 37–40). Another critical aspect of interaction is its frequency. The more frequently an individual interacts with specific others, the more he or she is exposed to their attitudes, values, and opinions. Furthermore, as Homans (1961, p. 182) argues, there is often a direct relationship between frequency of interaction with another person and liking that person. Homans (1961, p. 187) does not, however, assert this proposition without a qualification, which is that sentiments exchanged may be so negative that frequent interaction may lead to aversion rather than attraction between those involved. These notions of frequency and sentimental intensity of interaction are basic components underlying this conceptual framework. It is assumed that interaction involving frequent, primary relationships is more likely to have socializing impacts than interaction involving infrequent, impersonal relationships.

An emphasis on norms and social relationships in the academic department has been incorporated into this model for several reasons. First, primary social relationships have already been discussed as contributing to the social integration of, and consequently, to the potential normative pressure exerted on members by groups. Second, as Shibutani (1955) asserted, "socialization is a product of a gradual accumulation of experiences with certain people, particularly those with whom we stand in primary relations" (p. 568). Finally, both students and faculty tend to feel that the most enduring academic impacts of college attendance result from social interaction between faculty and students outside the formal classroom setting (Thielens, 1966; Wilson et al., 1975; Pascarella, 1980; Winteler, 1981). Availability of these opportunities may be a significant enhancer of collegiate influences on students.

SOCIALIZATION PROCESSES: INTRAPERSONAL PROCESSES

Another aspect of the student's collegiate experience included in this framework involves his or her subjective assessment of that experience. As one critic of the structural-functional interpretation of socialization has argued (Wrong, 1961), socialization encompasses both the transmission of norms and the individual processing of normative influences that result in the development of unique personal orientations to social contexts. Not surprisingly, there is a considerable literature dealing with the related phenomenon of "person-environment interaction" at college (Stern, 1970; Walsh, 1973; Moos, 1979). The general question raised by this approach is: How do the individual's perceptions of participation in various segments of the collegiate environment affect the socialization potential of the college? Put in a somewhat different way, the concern is with assessing whether or not favorable student attitudes about various aspects of the collegiate experience enhance the college's impact.

Several dimensions of students' perceptions of their colleges are of interest here. One is student satisfaction with college. In their extensive literature review, Feldman and Newcomb (1969, pp. 94–95) cited four studies of student satisfaction with college that suggest some variability in student satisfaction at different points during college. Sophomores reported the lowest levels (60% satisfied) and seniors reported the highest levels (more than 80% satisfied). This suggests that seniors have accommodated themselves better to the demands and expectations of their college, quite possibly reflecting the socializing influence of the campus over time. Another dimension that enhances the institution's socialization potential is the students' images of college, especially when they encompass subjective assessments of the college's contribution to the attainment of personal goals (Weidman and

Krus, 1979).The student's perceived "fit" or subjective assessment of his or her degree of social integration into the life of the institution is a related dimension of interest in the conceptual framework.

SOCIALIZATION PROCESSES: INTEGRATION

Tinto (1975) described social integration into campus life as being due primarily to interaction with college faculty, administration, and peers as well as participation in extracurricular activities. He suggested that these relationships resulted in varying degrees of affiliation of the student with the college "that modify his educational and institutional commitments" (p. 107). There also continues to be a considerable amount of empirical research using Tinto's model (Ethington and Smart, 1986; Terenzini et al., 1985; Terenzini and Wright, 1986). Perhaps not surprisingly, patterns of results are somewhat different for studies of minority students than they are for studies of white students (Fox, 1986; Nora, 1987).

Social integration, particularly as it relates to primary social relationships with faculty and peers in the transmission of normative influences, has already been discussed. However, there are several other implications of social integration for student socialization. With respect to students' assessments of impersonal treatment on campus, the expectation is that the less favorable the student is in his or her perceptions of the college environment, the less likely that student is to be socialized toward the norms of the college. In addition, students' subjective assessments concerning suitability for careers and their willingness to participate in the formal occupational structure of society are important. There is an expectation that those students who question their ability to develop meaningful careers will also shy away from aspiring to high-status, demanding occupations.

Academic integration refers to the extent to which students accept faculty expectations for their academic performance as legitimate and behave accordingly. Most studies have tended to use grades as a primary indicator of academic integration, but it is certainly not uncommon for those students whose grades are not outstanding to perceive expectations to be appropriate and to embody academic norms.

In-College Normative Pressure

An examination of the socializing effects of normative pressure, expressed as either change or reinforcement of values, and transmitted by departmental members through primary social relationships is of considerable importance. It should also be noted that, while change in student orientations is often an expected outcome, reinforcement of already present student orientations may just as legitimately be expected (Feldman, 1969). Therefore, it is important to pay attention to the absence of observed change as well as significant change during college because both may imply college impact.

This approach parallels the work of Vreeland and Bidwell (1966, pp. 241–242), who posit three conditions that contribute to socialization of students toward departmental norms: faculty interest in undergraduate teaching; student/faculty interaction measured on two dimensions, intimacy and frequency; and faculty and student norms that are "consistent and reinforcing." One way to determine faculty and student norms is to examine the goals of each for attaining such outcomes of a college education as vocational training, development of values, learning an academic discipline, intellectual enlightenment, or general education. The similarity between faculty and student educational goals can provide important information about the potential effect of faculty norms on either maintenance or change in students' incoming orientations.

Vreeland and Bidwell (1966, p. 254) suggest that the departmental faculty's collective conception of goals for undergraduate education conditions the faculty's conception of the instructional task. This, more than specific subject-matter content, determines the social organization of departmental student-faculty interaction. These authors systematize the structure of departmental faculty influence by dividing faculty goals for undergraduate education into two categories: technical and moral. Technical goals concern occupational preparation and the intellectual structure of an academic discipline. Moral goals concern the ethical practice of an occupation and the broadening or humanizing effects of education. According to this formulation, the expressed goals of faculty for undergraduate education determine faculty behavior

and expectations, which, in turn, determine the socializing effects of the department.

Concerning the direction of impact, Vreeland and Bidwell (1966) suggest not only that different patterns of change occur as a function of faculty conceptions of the instructional process, but also that some values are more likely than others to be influenced by either technical or moral goals. Student values concerned with extrinsic rewards of occupational participation (income, status, recognition from colleagues) would be more likely to be influenced positively by technical rather than moral goals. Values concerned with individual creativity or interpersonal relationships, on the other hand, would be more amenable to positive influence by moral rather than technical goals.

Intensity of influence can refer both to the overall importance among faculty of a particular goal and to the consistency of faculty sentiments, i.e., the extent of agreement among faculty on the goals for undergraduate instruction. Consequently, in assessing potential departmental impact, both the general importance of a particular instructional goal and the level of consensus among faculty on the goal's importance should be assessed. Vreeland and Bidwell (1966) classified academic departments at Harvard according to the degree of consensus among faculty on moral and technical goals. Departments having high faculty consensus on technical goals included physics, chemistry, Germanic and Slavic languages, engineering, music, mathematics, astronomy, psychology, and philosophy. Departments having high faculty consensus on moral goals included architectural science, classics, government, economics, history, and fine arts. Departments having low consensus because various faculty members held different goals included romance languages, biology, anthropology, English, geology, and social relations.

A different approach to the analysis of the normative pressures exerted in various academic departments is the Environmental Assessment Technique (EAT) developed by Astin and Holland (1961; Astin, 1963; Holland, 1966). Taking research on the psychology of vocational choice as his basepoint, Holland (1966) developed a scheme classifying occupations in terms of six personality types: realistic, intellectual, social, conventional, enterprising, and artistic. Using these six modal types, Holland (1966, 1985) classified the normative pressures of major field environments according to the vocational preferences and personality orientations of the people in them. Some majors assigned to each of the types include the following: realistic—agriculture, industrial arts, engineering, and forestry; intellectual—mathematics, philosophy, physical science, and anthropology; social—education, nursing, psychology, American civilization, sociology, and social work; conventional—accounting, economics, finance, and business education; enterprising—history, international relations, political science, industrial relations, business administration, and management; and artistic—art and music education, fine and applied arts, English and journalism, and foreign languages and literature.

The usefulness of Holland's classification has also been verified cross-culturally in a study of environments in both British and Canadian universities (Richards, 1974). More recently, Smart (1985) used the Holland typology to study the extent to which major field environments reinforce students' values. He affirms the importance of focusing on organizationally and normatively well-defined units within the larger institution when studying college effects. Again, it should be pointed out that there are racial differences in major choice, especially among males, with whites more likely to choose "intellectual" majors and blacks more likely to choose "enterprising" majors (Braddock, 1981).

In the foregoing discussion of departmental climates, some general patterns appear that are useful in developing an understanding of undergraduate influence processes. Humanities departments tend to be populated by faculty and students who are concerned with intellectual activities, creative endeavors, and the development of values and ethical standards. Occupational value orientations among humanities majors tend to cluster in the area of intrinsic rewards rather than extrinsic rewards, with a moderate "people" orientation. Science and mathematics departments, while also high on members' intellectual orientations, are likely to be high on career orientation and occupational training as well. These areas will probably be relatively high on students' orientations toward both intrinsic and extrinsic

rewards, with relatively low "people" orientations. Compared with other science departments, engineering departments are likely to have students somewhat lower on intrinsic reward orientation, somewhat higher on extrinsic reward orientation, and about the same on "people" orientation. Majors in the social sciences, particularly economics and political science, appear to have the highest extrinsic reward and people orientations, and the lowest intrinsic reward orientations. Faculty tend to be less favorably oriented to the pursuit of extrinsic rewards than students, especially in the humanities and social sciences, where little direct occupational training is provided and large numbers of graduates enter occupations unrelated to their majors.

Socialization Outcomes

The outcomes listed in Figure 1 are a few of the more important ones that have been of continuing concern to higher education scholars, especially as they reflect outcomes that are important both for adult life following college and for their potential contribution to societal well-being (Davis, 1965; Spaeth and Greeley, 1970; Bowen, 1977). While the continuing interest in research on status attainment among sociologists has already been noted, there is also something of a resurgence of interest in the higher education literature that investigates the effects of colleges on occupational attainment (e.g., Smart and Pascarella, 1986; Smart, 1986).

Patterns and Trends

It could be argued that the outcomes of undergraduate socialization during any particular time period are as much a function of the characteristics, values, and aspirations of the students as they are of the socialization processes that occur during college. Certainly, there is considerable documentation of the changes in career orientations over the past few decades, with a general increase in students' interest in obtaining specific occupational skills in college rather than a broad, liberal arts education (Hoge, 1976; Levine, 1980). While this trend holds for both sexes, women have made even greater changes in their career orientations then men, with women now aspiring to combine careers with marriage and family responsibilities (Regan and Roland, 1982). There are also rather different patterns of career socialization for women than for men (Bressler and Wendell, 1980; Perun, 1982; Eisenhart, 1985; Eccles, 1986).

Rather different patterns of college experiences also have been documented for minority students (Willie and Cunnigen, 1981; Thomas, 1981; Astin, 1982; Nettles, Thoeny, and Gosman, 1986). Racial tensions on predominantly white campuses were documented by Peterson et al. (1978) which apparently have surfaced again in the late 1980s. Problems of social and academic integration have also been well documented for minority students (Fox, 1986; Nora, 1987). This suggests that it is necessary to adapt conceptual frameworks to the differing patterns of socialization that may be represented among specific ethnic and gender groups.

PERSISTENCE OVER THE LIFE COURSE

On another level, there is some limited evidence about the persistence of changes in values that occur during college. Interestingly, most of these studies have focused on political values and/or activities (Newcomb et al., 1967; DeMartini, 1983; Wieder and Zimmerman, 1976; Fendrich, 1976). A key factor in the maintenance of political activism after college appears to be the extent to which those views and behavior are supported by significant others, especially husbands of Bennington women (Newcomb, et al., 1967) and employers. A study of students who attended universities in one of the major centers of civil rights protest during the early 1960s posited the following explanation for the persistence of white student activism:

> Those adults who have remained free of the occupational commitments to money, status, and security continue to be political activists. Activists have pursued careers in work environments that either tolerate or encourage commitment to values different from the traditional extrinsic rewards (Fendrich, 1976, p. 96).

DeMartini (1983), in reviewing seven studies of white activists, also concludes that "maintenance of dissident political values is consistent with full integration into adult social roles" (p. 214). Black activists in the Fendrich (1976) study were similar to white activists in that those who valued extrinsic rewards the least were also more active in protest politics. The main racial difference was that black activism tended to focus almost exclusively on "the one-issue politics of advancing the race" (p. 97).

Finally, for those college activists whose fundamental values were learned from parents, the persistence of these values into adulthood can be construed to be an extension of the parental socialization process (DeMartini, 1983). In the case of more extreme behavior such as movement into the student counterculture, students withdraw from participation in major conventional roles, often separating from both parents and college in favor of peer support (Wieder and Zimmerman, 1976).

Discussion and Policy Implications

The emphasis in the foregoing has been on the conceptual aspects of the complex processes of undergraduate socialization. To test empirically the framework that has been developed would require that variables be identified and then operationalized so that they can be measured. While that responsibility lies with the researcher, interested readers can see Lenning (1983) or Endo and Bittner (1985) for long lists of potential variables and Pascarella (1985a) for a discussion of some of the measurement problems involved in operationalizing variables. In addition, appropriate statistical techniques would have to be chosen because the model represents multidirectional processes rather than unidirectional causality.

There is, however, one measurement concern of particular importance. Throughout the discussion, it has been emphasized that the characteristics of specific normative contexts should be related as directly as possible to the student, preferably by identifying a linking mechanism of socialization. One of the best examples of a study that accomplished this linking is the study of undergraduates at a small, midwestern, liberal arts college that was done by Wallace (1966). He used sociometric techniques to quantify each undergraduate's "interpersonal environment," aggregating the questionnaire responses from each individual on campus who was named as being a friend of the student. Large sample survey research is not, however, always amenable to such techniques, especially since confidentiality of responses is often of great concern. It may then be necessary to settle for more general measures of membership group attachments based on friendship or interaction not tied to specific individuals.

The research by Holland (1985) and Smart (1985) suggests very strongly that the distribution of majors within an institution is an important factor in shaping the pattern of influence exerted by the institution. Currently, as colleges jump on the bandwagon and expand majors in business and career-oriented technical fields, there are consequences for the normative pressure on students. When normative pressures gravitate against the liberal arts, the character of an institution can very well change. The framework presented here calls attention to the various normative pressures exerted by different types of majors.

There is also evidence suggesting that first institutional impressions, beginning with freshman orientation, are very important for the anticipatory socialization of undergraduates (Pascarella, Terenzini, and Wolfle, 1986). Consequently, it is in the best interests of colleges to structure orientations in ways that maximize the development of student commitments to the institution, including providing an early opportunity for interaction with faculty.

Finally, the temptation should be resisted to assume that a framework dealing with affective dimensions of undergraduate socialization has no relevance for studies of the "value added" by college to cognitive knowledge and skills. In fact, academic learning can (and should) be reinforced by the sorts of participation in normative contexts that have been discussed. It is unfortunate that much of the current research on student academic learning relies on rather simplistic theories of student learning that tend to exclude the range of variables represented in the framework developed for this chapter.

This is a revised version of a paper presented at the 1987 Annual Meeting of the Association for the Study of Higher Education, Baltimore, Maryland. The author is indebted to John Bean, Kenneth

Feldman, Ludwig Huber, Patrick Terenzini, and Wagner Thielens for helpful comments on the manuscript, and to Charles Bidwell for stimulating consideration of many of the central notions upon which this conceptualization is based.

References

Alexander, K. L., and Eckland, B. K. (1975). Basic attainment processes: a replication and extension. *Sociology of Education* 48: 457–495.

Anderson, K. L. (1985). College characteristics and change in students' occupational values: socialization in American colleges. *Work and Occupations* 12: 307–328.

Astin, A. W. (1963). Further validation of the Environmental Assessment Technique. *Journal of Educational Psychology* 54: 217–226.

Astin, A. W. (1977). *Four Critical Years: Effects of College on Beliefs, Attitudes, and Knowledge*. San Francisco: Jossey-Bass.

Astin, A. W. (1982). *Minorities in American Higher Education*. San Francisco: Jossey-Bass.

Astin, A. W. (1984). Student involvement: a developmental theory for higher education. *Journal of College Student Personnel* 25: 297–308.

Astin, A. W., and Holland, J. L. (1961). The Environmental Assessment Technique: a new way to measure college environments. *Journal of Educational Psychology* 52: 308–316.

Astin, A. W., and Panos, R. J. (1969). *The Educational and Vocational Development of College Students*. Washington, DC: American Council on Education.

Atkins, N. D. (1982). College student performance, satisfaction, and retention. *Journal of Higher Education* 53: 32–50.

Bank, B. J., Slavings, R. L., and Biddle, B. J. (1986). Effects of peer, faculty, and parental influences on student retention. Paper presented at the meeting of the American Educational Research Association, San Francisco, April.

Bassis, M. S. (1977). The campus as a frogpond: a theoretical and empirical reassessment. *American Journal of Sociology* 82: 1318–1326.

Bean, J. P. (1985). Interaction effects based on class level in an explanatory model of college student dropout syndrome. *American Educational Research Journal* 22: 35–64.

Bean, J. P., and Metzner, B. S. (1985). A conceptual model of nontraditional undergraduate student attrition. *Review of Educational Research* 55: 485–540.

Beardsley, D. C., and Dowd, D. D. (1962). Students and the occupational world. in N. Sanford (ed.), *The American College: A Psychological and Social Interpretation of the Higher Learning* (pp. 597–626). New York: Wiley.

Becker, H. S., Geer, B., and Hughes, E. C. (1968). *Making the Grade: The Academic Side of College Life.* New York: Wiley.

Bengston, V. L. (1975). Generation and family effects in value socialization. *American Sociological Review* 40: 358–371.

Biddle, B. J., Bank, B. J., and Slavings, R. L. (1986). Norms, preferences, and retention decisions. Paper presented at the meeting of the American Educational Research Association, San Francisco, April.

Blau, P. M., and Duncan, O. D. (1967). *The American Occupational Structure.* New York: Wiley.

Blimling, G. S. (1988). The influences of college residence halls on students: A meta-analysis of empirical research, 1966–1985. Unpublished doctoral dissertation, Ohio State University.

Borow, H. (1966). The development of occupational motives and roles. In L. W. Hoffman and M. L. Hoffman (eds.), *Review of Child Development Research*, Vol 2 (pp. 373–422). New York: Russell Sage Foundation.

Bowen, H. R. (1977). *Investment in Learning: The Individual and Social Value of American Higher Education.* San Francisco: Jossey-Bass.

Braddock, J. H. (1981). The major field choices and occupational career orientations of black and white college students. In G. E. Thomas (ed.), *Black Students in Higher Education* (pp. 167–183). Westport, CT: Greenwood Press.

Bragg, A. K. (1976). *The Socialization Process in Higher Education.* (ERIC/Higher Education Research Report No. 7). Washington, DC: American Association for Higher Education.

Bressler, M., and Wendell, P. (1980). The sex composition of selective colleges and gender differences in career aspirations. *Journal of Higher Education* 51: 650–663.

Brim, O. G., Jr. (1966). Socialization through the life cycle. In O. G. Brim, Jr., and S. Wheeler, *Socialization After Childhood: Two Essays* (pp. 1–49). New York: Wiley.

Chickering, A. W. (1969). *Education and Identity.* San Francisco: Jossey-Bass.

Chickering, A. W. (1974). *Commuting Versus Residential Students: Overcoming the Educational Inequities of Living Off-Campus.* San Francisco: Jossey-Bass.

Chickering, A. W., et al. (1981). *The Modern American College.* San Francisco: Jossey-Bass.

Clausen, J. A. (1968). Introduction. In J. A. Clausen (ed.), *Socialization and Society* (pp. 1–17). Boston: Little, Brown.

Conrad, C. F., and Blackburn, R. T. (1985). Program quality in higher education: a review and critique of literature and research. In J. C. Smart (ed.), *Higher Education: Handbook of Theory and Research*, Vol. 1 (pp. 283–308). New York: Agathon Press.

Curtis, R. L. (1974). The issue of schools as social systems: socialization effects as inferred from lengths of membership. *Sociological Quarterly*, 15: 277–293.

Davies, M., and Kandel, D. B. (1981). Parental and peer influences on adolescents' educational plans: some further evidence. *American Journal of Sociology* 87: 363–387.

Davis, J. A. (1964). *Great Aspirations.* Chicago: Aldine.

Davis, J. A. (1965). *Undergraduate Career Decisions.* Chicago: Aldine.

Davis, J.A. (1966). The campus as a frogpond: an application of the theory of relative deprivation to career decisions of college men. *American Journal of Sociology* 72: 17–31.

DeMartini, J. R. (1983). Social movement participation: political socialization, generational consciousness, and lasting effects. *Youth and Society* 15: 195–223.

Drew, D. E., and Astin, A. W. (1972). Undergraduate aspirations: a test of several theories. *American Journal of Sociology* 77: 1151–1164.

Duncan, O. D. (1961). A socioeconomic index for all occupations. In A. J. Reiss (ed.), *Occupations and Social Status* (Chap. 6 and Appendix B). New York: Free Press.

Eccles, J. S. (1986). Gender-roles and women's achievement. *Educational Researcher* 15 (June/July): 15–19.

Eisenhart, M. A. (1985). Women choose their careers: a study of natural decision-making. *Review of Higher Education* 8: 247–270.

Endo, J., and Bittner, T. (1985). Developing and using a longitudinal student outcomes data file: the University of Colorado experience. In P. T. Ewell (ed.), *Assessing Educational Outcomes* (pp. 65–80). *New Directions for Institutional Research*, No. 47. San Francisco: Jossey-Bass.

Ethington, C. A., and Smart, J. C. (1986). A path analytic model of the decision to enter graduate school. *Research in Higher Education* 24: 287–303.

Feldman, K. A. (1969). Studying the impacts of college on students. *Sociology of Education* 42: 207–237.

Feldman, K. A. (1972). Some theoretical approaches to the study of change and stability of college students. *Review of Educational Research* 42: 1–26.

Feldman, K. A., and Newcomb, T. N. (1969). *The Impact of College on Students.* San Francisco: Jossey-Bass.

Feldman, K. A. and Weiler, J. (1976). Changes in initial differences among major-field groups: an exploration of the "accentuation effect." In W. H. Sewell, R. M. Hauser, and D. L. Featherman (eds.), *Schooling and Achievement in American Society* (pp. 373–407). New York: Academic Press.

Fendrich, J. M. (1976). Black and white activists ten years later: political socialization and left-wing politics. *Youth and Society* 8: 81–104.

Fox, R. N. (1986). Application of a conceptual model of college withdrawal to disadvantaged students. *American Education Research Journal* 23: 415–424.

Getzels, J. W. (1963). Conflict and role behavior in the educational setting. In W. W. Charters, Jr., and N. L. Gage (eds.), *Readings in the Social Psychology of Education* (pp. 309–318). Boston: Allyn & Bacon.

Goldsen, R. K., Rosenberg, M., Williams, R. M., Jr., and Suchman, E. A. (1960). *What College Students Think*. Princeton, NJ: D. Van Nostrand.

Greeley, A. M. (1967). *The Changing Catholic College*. Chicago: Aldine.

Hauser, R. M., Tsai, S., and Sewell, W. H. (1983). A model of stratification with response error in social and psychological variables. *Sociology of Education* 56: 20–46.

Hawkes, R. K. (1975). Norms, deviance, and social control: a mathematical elaboration of concepts. *American Journal of Sociology* 80: 886–908.

Hearn, J. C. (1980). Major choice and well-being of college men and women: an examination from developmental, organizational, and structural perspectives. *Sociology of Education* 53: 164–178.

Hearn, J. C., and Olzak, S. (1981). The role of college major departments in the reproduction of sexual inequality. *Sociology of Education* 54: 195–205.

Hoge, D. R. (1976). Changes in college students' value patterns in the 1950's, 1960's and 1970's. *Sociology of Education* 49: 155–163.

Holland, J. L. (1966). *The Psychology of Vocational Choice*. Waltham, MA: Blaisdell.

Holland, J. L. (1985). *Making Vocational Choices: A Theory of Vocational Personalities and Work Environments* (2nd ed.) Englewood Cliffs, NJ: Prentice-Hall.

Homans, G. C. (1950). *The Human Group*. New York: Harcourt, Brace & World.

Homans, G. C. (1961). *Social Behavior: Its Elementary Forms*. New York: Harcourt, Brace & World.

Huber, Ludwig (1980). Sozialisation in der Hochschule. In K. Hurrelmann and D. Ulich (eds.), *Handbuch der Sozialisationsforschung*. Weinheim-Basel: Beltz.

Hurrelmann, K. (1988). *Social Structure and Personality Development*. New York: Cambridge University Press.

Hyman, H. H., Wright, C. R., and Reed, J. S. (1975). *The Enduring Effects of Education*. Chicago: University of Chicago Press.

Jacob, R. (1957). *Changing Values in College: An Exploratory Study of the Impact of College Teaching*. New York: Harper & Row.

Jencks, C., Crouse, J., and Mueser, P. (1983). The Wisconsin model of status attainment: a national replication with improved measures of ability and aspiration. *Sociology of Education* 56: 3–19.

Kamens, D. (1974). Colleges and elite formation: the case of prestigious American colleges. *Sociology of Education* 47: 354–378.

Katchadourian, H. A., and Boli, J. (1985). *Careerism and Intellectualism Among College Students*. San Francisco: Jossey-Bass.

Kemper, T. D. (1968). Reference groups as perspectives. *American Sociological Review* 33: 31–45.

Kerckhoff, A. C. (1976). The status attainment process: socialization or allocation? *Social Forces* 55: 368 481.

Kett, J. (1977). *Rites of passage: Adolescence in America, 1790 to the Present*. New York: Basic Books.

Kohn, M. L. (1977). *Class and Conformity: A Study in Values* (2nd ed.). Chicago: University of Chicago Press.

Komarovsky, M. (1985). *Women in College*. New York: Basic Books.

Kuh, G. D., Bean, J. B., Bradley, R. K., Coomes, M. D., and Hunter, D. E. (1986). Changes in research on college students published in selected journals between 1969 and 1983. *Review of Higher Education* 9: 177–192.

Lacy, W. B. (1978). Interpersonal relationships as mediators of structural effects: college student socialization in a traditional and an experimental university environment. *Sociology of Education* 51: 201–211.

Lenning, O. T. (1982). Variable-selection and measurement concerns. In E. T. Pascarella (ed.), *Studying Student Attrition* (pp. 35–53). New Directions for Institutional Research, No. 36. San Francisco: Jossey-Bass.

Levine, A. (1980). *When Dreams and Heroes Died: A Portrait of Today's College Student*. San Francisco: Jossey-Bass.

Linton, R (1936). *The Study of Man*. New York: Appleton-Century-Crofts.

Litten, L. H. (1982). Different strokes in the applicant pool: some refinements in a model of student college choice. *Journal of Higher Education* 53: 383–402.

Looker, E. D., and Pineo, P. D. (1983). Social psychological variables and their relevance to the status attainment of teenagers. *American Journal of Sociology* 88: 1195–1219.

Merton, R K. (1968). *Social Theory and Social Structure*. New York: Free Press.

Metzner, B. S., and Bean, J. P. (1987). The estimation of a conceptual model of nontraditional undergraduate student attrition. *Research in Higher Education* 27: 15–38.

Meyer, J. W. (1970). The charter: conditions of diffuse socialization in schools. in W. R. Scott (ed.), *Social Processes and Social Structures* (pp. 564–578). New York: Holt, Rinehart & Winston.

Meyer, J. W. (1972). The effects of institutionalization of colleges in society. in K. A. Feldman (ed.), *College and Student: Selected Readings in the Social Psychology of Higher Education* (pp. 109–126). New York: Pergamon.

Moore, W. E. (1969). Occupational socialization. in D. A. Goslin (ed.), *Handbook of Socialization Theory and Research* (pp. 861–873). Chicago: Rand McNally.

Moos, R. H. (1979). *Evaluating Educational Environments*. San Francisco: Jossey-Bass.

Morgan, W. R., Alwin, D. F., and Griffin, L. J. (1979). Social origins, parental values, and the transmission of inequality. *American Journal of Sociology* 85: 156–166.

Mortimer, J. T. (1974). Patterns of intergenerational occupational movements: a smallest space analysis. *American Journal of Sociology* 79: 1278–1299.

Mortimer, J. T. (1976). Social class, work and the family: some implications of the father's occupation for familial relationships and sons' career decisions. *Journal of Marriage and the Family* 38: 241–256.

Mortimer, J. T., and Simmons, R. G. (1978). Adult socialization. in R. H. Turner, J. Coleman, ant R. C. Fox (eds.), *Annual Review of Sociology*, Vol. 4 (pp. 421–454). Palo Alto, CA; Annual Reviews.

Nettles, M. T., Thoeny, A. R, and Gosman, E. J. (1986). Comparative and predictive analyses of black and white students' college achievement and experiences. *Journal of Higher Education* 57: 289–318.

Newcomb, T. M. (1943). *Personal and Social Change*. New York: Dryden Press.

Newcomb, T. M., and Wilson, E. K., eds. (1966). *College Peer Groups*. Chicago: Aldine.

Newcomb, T.M., Koenig, K. E., Flack, R., and Warwick, D. P. (1967). *Persistence and Change: Bennington College and its Students After Twenty-Five Years*. New York: Wiley.

Nora, A. (1987). Determinants of retention among Chicano college students: a structural model. *Research in Higher Education* 26: 31–59.

Pace, C. R. (1979). *Measuring Outcomes of College: Fifty Years of Findings and Recommendations for the Future*. San Francisco: Jossey-Bass.

Pantages, T. J., and Creedon, C. F. (1978). Studies of college attrition: 1950–1975. *Review of Educational Research* 48: 49–101.

Parsons, T., and Platt, G. M. (1973). *The American University*. Cambridge: Harvard University Press.

Parsons, T., Shils, E. A., and Olds, L. (1951). Values, motives, and systems of action. In T. Parsons and E. A. Shills (eds.), *Toward a General Theory of Action* (pp. 45–276). New York: Harper Torchbooks (1962).

Pascarella, E. T. (1980). Student-faculty informal contact and college outcomes. *Review of Educational Research* 50: 545–595.

Pascarella, E. T. (1984). Reassessing the effects of living on-campus versus commuting to college: a causal modeling approach. *Review of Higher Education* 7: 247–260.

Pascarella, E. T. (1985a). College environment influences on learning and cognitive development. In J. C. Smart (ed.), *Higher Education: Handbook of Theory and Research*, Vol. 1 (pp. 1–61). New York: Agathon Press.

Pascarella, E. T. (1985b). Students' affective development within the college environment. *Journal of Higher Education* 56: 640–663.

Pascarella, E. T., and Chapman, D. W. (1983). A multiinstitutional, path analytic validation of Tinto's model of college withdrawal. *American Educational Research Journal* 20: 87–102.

Pascarella, E. T., and Terenzini, P. T. (1980). Predicting freshman persistence and voluntary dropout decisions from a theoretical model. *Journal of Higher Education* 51: 60–75.

Pascarella, E. T., Terenzini, P. T., and Wolfle, L. M. (1986). Orientation to college and freshman year persistence/withdrawal decisions. *Journal of Higher Education* 57: 155–175.

Perun, Pamela J., ed. (1982). *The Undergraduate Woman: Issues in Educational Equity*. Lexington, MA: Lexington Books.

Peterson, M. W., Blackburn, R. T., Gamson, Z. F., Arce, C. H., Davenport, R. W., and Mingle, J. R. (1978). *Black Students on White Campuses: The Impacts of Increased Black Enrollments*. Ann Arbor: University of Michigan, Institute for Social Research.

Phelan, W. T. (1979). Undergraduate orientations toward scientific and scholarly careers. *American Educational Research Journal* 16: 411–422.

Regan, M. C., and Roland, H. E. (1982). University students: a change in expectations and aspirations over the decade. *Sociology of Education* 55: 223–228.

Reitz, J. G. (1975). Undergraduate aspirations and career choice. *Sociology of Education* 48:308–323.

Richards, J. M., Jr. (1974). "Environments" of British Commonwealth universities. *Journal of Educational Psychology* 66: 572–579.

Rosenberg, M. (1957). *Occupations and Values*. Glencoe, IL: Free Press.

Sanford, N., ed. (1962). *The American College*. New York: Wiley.

Schrager, R. H. (1986). The impact of living group social climate on student academic performance. *Research in Higher Education* 25: 265–276.

Sewell, W. T., Haller, A. O., and Ohlendorf, G. O. (1970). The educational and early occupational status achievement process: replication and revision. *American Sociological Review* 35: 1014–1027.

Sewell, W. T., Haller, A. O., and Portes, A. (1969). The educational and early occupational attainment process. *American Sociological Review* 34: 82–92.

Shibutani, T. (1955). Reference groups as perspectives. *American Journal of Sociology* 60:562–569.

Siegel, A. E., and Siegel, S. (1957). Reference groups, membership groups and attitude change. *Journal of Abnormal and Social Psychology* 55: 360–364.

Simpson, I. H. (1979). *From Student to Nurse: A Longitudinal Study of Socialization*. New York: Cambridge University Press.

Smart, J. C. (1985). Holland environments as reinforcement systems. *Research in Higher Education* 23: 279–292.

Smart, J. C. (1986). College effects on occupational status attainment. *Research in Higher Education* 24: 47–72.

Smart, J. C., and Pascarella, E. T. (1986). Socioeconomic achievements of former college students. *Journal of Higher Education* 57: 529–549.

Smith, E. J. (1981). The career development of young black females: the forgotten group. *Youth and Society* 12: 277–312.

Snyder, B. R. (1971). *The Hidden Curriculum.* New York: Knopf.

Solmon, L. C., and Taubman, P. J. (1973). *Does College Matter?* New York: Academic Press.

Solmon, L. C., and Wachtel, P. (1975). The effects on income of type of college attended. *Sociology of Education* 48: 75–90.

Spaeth, J. L., and Greeley, A. M. (1970). *Recent Alumni and Higher Education.* New York: McGraw-Hill.

Stern, G. G. (1970). *People in Context: Measuring Person-Environment Congruence in Education and Industry.* New York: Wiley.

Terenzini, P. T., Pascarella, E. T., Theophilides, C., and Lorang, W. (1985). A replication of a path analytic validation of Tinto's theory of college student attrition. *Review of Higher Education* 8: 319–340.

Terenzini, P. T., and Wright, T. M. (1986). Influences on students' academic growth during four years of college. *Research in Higher Education* 26: 161–179.

Thielens, W. W., Jr. (1966). *The Structure of Faculty Influence.* New York: Columbia University, Bureau of Applied Social Research.

Thomas, G. E., ed. (1981). *Black Students in Higher Education: Conditions and Experiences in the 1970's.* Westport, CT: Greenwood Press.

Thornton, R., and Nardi, P. M. (1975). The dynamics of role acquisition. *American Journal of Sociology* 80: 870–885.

Tinto, V. (1975). Dropout from higher education: a theoretical synthesis of recent research. *Review of Educational Research* 45: 89–125.

Tinto, V. (1982). Limits of theory and practice in student attrition. *Journal of Higher Education* 53: 687–700.

Tinto, V. (1987). *Leaving College: Rethinking the Causes and Cures of Student Attrition.* Chicago: University of Chicago Press.

Trow, M., ed. (1975). *Teachers and Students.* New York: McGraw-Hill.

Van Gennep, A. (1960). *The Rites of Passage.* (M. B. Vizedom and G. L. Caffee, trans.). Chicago: University of Chicago Press.

Vreeland, R., and Bidwell, C. E. (1965). Organizational effects on student attitudes: a study of the Harvard houses. *Sociology of Education* 38: 233–250.

Vreeland, R., and Bidwell, C. E. (1966). Classifying university departments: an approach to the analysis of their effects upon undergraduates' values and attitudes. *Sociology of Education* 39: 237–254.

Wallace, W. L. (1966). *Student Culture: Social Structure and continuity in a Liberal Arts College.* Chicago: Aldine.

Walsh, W. B. (1973). *Theories of Person-Environment Interaction: Implications for the College Student.* (ACT Monograph 10). Iowa City: American College Testing Program.

Weidman, J. C. (1979). Nonintellective undergraduate socialization in academic departments. *Journal of Higher Education* 50: 48–62.

Weidman, J. C. (1984). Impacts of campus experiences and parental socialization on undergraduates' career choices. *Research in Higher Education* 20: 445–476.

Weidman, J. C. (1989). The world of higher education: a socialization-theoretical perspective. In K. Hurrelmann and U. Engel (eds.), *The Social World of Adolescents: International Perspectives* (pp. 87–105). Berlin-New York: de Gruyter/Aldine.

Weidman, J. C., and Friedmann, R. R (1984). The school-to-work transition for high school dropouts. *Urban Review* 16: 22–42.

Interpreting Identity Politics: The Educational Challenge of Contemporary Student Activism

Robert A. Rhoads

Although students of the 1990s are concerned with a wide range of social and political issues, clearly the theme of "identity politics" has become a central fiber connecting many of the cases of contemporary student activism. Based on an extensive qualitative study, the author examines some of the educational implications multicultural activism may have for understanding today's diverse students.

Today's colleges and universities are witnessing an upswing in student activism (Levine & Hirsch, 1991; Loeb, 1994). Although the 1930s and 1960s remain the high water marks for student involvement in direct action for social and political change, American higher education may be in the midst of its third great wave of student activism (Altbach & Cohen, 1990). And whereas the 1960s was known for peace demonstrations, the free speech movement, women's liberation, and civil rights initiatives (Carden, 1974; Gitlin, 1987; Heineman, 1993; Lipset, 1976; Lipset & Altbach, 1967; Sampson. 1970; Woodward, 1974), the central theme of contemporary activism tends to revolve around identity politics and reflects in a broad sense a commitment to building a multicultural democracy (Giroux, 1992; Hooks, 1994; Rhoads & Valadez, 1996; Tierney, 1993; West, 1993).

Rationale For Phenomenology

In an effort to make sense of contemporary activism and what I describe as the "multicultural student movement," I employ qualitative case studies rooted in a phenomenological perspective. The general stance of phenomenologists such as Husserl (1970), Merleau-Ponty (1962), and Schutz (1970) is that social science tends to take for granted the experiences of humans acting, doing, or creating, as if the meaning of human activity is self-evident. Instead, a phenomenological approach suggests an interrogation of human behavior and self-reflection; it involves situating human activity not simply as a means to some higher level ends, but as part of a process of creating meaning. For example, Schutz argued that there is much complexity and meaning in the basic elements of social life that need to be rigorously explored. He did not reject traditional social science as a means for understanding human behavior; he simply sought a more phenomenon-oriented approach to research, one focused on the meaning and significance that social experience held for participants. Thus, phenomenologists usually employ qualitative methods to identify the essence of a particular phenomenon and to unravel the meaning such a phenomenon has in people's lives.

Student development research typically has been grounded in the positivist tradition of social science in which the primary focus has been the "effects" of college on the student. The research efforts of Pascarella and Terenzini (1991) and Astin (1993b) are most noteworthy within this dominant tradition. A positivist philosophy of science tends to adopt a linear, causal view of collegiate environments and their interactions with students and the goal has been to identify relevant student "outcomes." Obviously, such methods are best

"Interpreting Identity Politics: The Educational Challenge of Contemporary Student Activism," by Robert A. Rhoads, reprinted from *Journal of College Student Development*, Vol. 38, No. 5, 1997, American Counseling Association.

suited for measuring college impact. However, these methods often portray facets of the collegiate experience as somewhat monolithic. For example, researchers oriented toward positivism might ask: What impact does involvement in a fraternity have on student development? This is a perfectly legitimate and an important question, but certain aspects of the nature (or the *essence*) of the fraternity experience are likely to remain hidden. A phenomenological study on the other hand, would seek to uncover the sense-making processes students employ through their experiences in a fraternity. The benefit of such studies is that the complex and subtle differences in how individuals negotiate the fraternity setting are more likely to be revealed. The findings from such studies provide valuable insights for people who are developing large-scale studies and measuring specific constructs. Phenomenon-oriented studies also provide detailed accounts of human experience and therefore speak directly to officials charged with administering specific collegiate contexts such as Greek life. The latter argument is similar to one Manning (1992) made in her defense of qualitative methods as a general strategy for researching the collegiate experience: "Qualitative research methods that seek to build understanding and discover meaning are immensely practical for student affairs educators" (p. 133).

I do not contend that phenomenological studies are in some way *better* than those studies rooted in the positivist tradition. Instead, I highlight how diverse strategies contribute to different forms of knowledge, all of which are helpful for understanding the complexities of student life. Student affairs professionals and faculty need phenomenon-oriented studies to better understand how students construct meaning around their experiences, and they also need outcomes-oriented research to make sense of the impact of college on students.

In terms of student activism, traditional positivist strategies might explore student activism around questions such as the following: What is the impact of student involvement in activism on grades, cognitive development, affective development, social integration, and other areas? These are important questions to address, and answers to such questions no doubt will prove helpful in understanding contemporary student activism. However, a phe-

nomenological approach suggests removing the black box from the category of "student activism" and pursuing the essence of contemporary activism to uncover what themes exist and, most importantly, how the experience of participation in student activism relates to students' construction of meaning. Presumably, how students envision their lives and the meanings they construct within the context of collegiate life are important to understanding student development; after all, one's perception of reality contributes to how one experiences the environment (Berger & Luckman, 1966; Blumer, 1969; Mead, 1934).

In a phenomenological study, the researcher typically seeks to provide a general overview of the particular phenomenon under study—in this case, contemporary student activism. With this said, in what follows I offer an account of contemporary activism organized around what I have identified as its central theme—identity politics and multiculturalism. How I reached this conclusion is explained in the Methodology section.

Overview of the Phenomenon

In the spring of 1996, thousands of college students joined what was described by organizers as a "National Day of Action." From around the United States, students participated in pickets, rallies, teach-ins, candlelight vigils, and marches in defense of affirmative action, educational access, and immigrants' rights, all the while voicing their opposition to what many student leaders perceived as a "toxic atmosphere" toward students, people of color, and lesbian, gay, and bisexual people. Students were concerned with House legislation (H.R. 2128) that would, in essence, have erased decades of Supreme Court rulings on affirmative action. As evidence of widespread social intolerance, student leaders pointed to anti-immigrant and affirmative action legislation in states such as California, threats to higher education in the form of proposed cuts to the Department of Education and Americorps, and various state initiatives aimed at limiting the rights of lesbian, gay, and bisexual people. Using the Internet to spread the word, the Center for Campus Organizing (in Cambridge,

Massachusetts) played a pivotal role in what turned out to be a highly successful day and a follow-up "Week of Action."

Other events in the Spring of 1996 were also telling. Approximately 300 students from the University of California at San Diego held a demonstration aimed at defeating the anti-affirmative action legislation being pushed through the California legislative process, some of which had already been adopted by the University of California system. Their efforts were part of a statewide plan of action as students took to the offensive in countering hostility directed at minorities, which they saw disguised in the form of the California Civil Rights initiative (Proposition 209). The following day in Corvallis, Oregon, nearly 1,500 students marched on the campus of Oregon State University to demonstrate against a series of racists incidents that had occurred on the campus, including the defacing of Anita Hill posters with racial slurs.

Students from several Washington, D.C., colleges and universities, including Howard University and George Washington University, combined forces to lead a demonstration at House Republican leader Newt Gingrich's D.C. apartment in protest of what they perceived as scapegoating of minorities and immigrants. Students from the Coalition for Economic Justice at the University of North Carolina at Chapel Hill held a speak-out on campus and mini-demonstrations at several places in Chapel Hill, including the office of Senator Jesse Helms. Members of MIT's Committee for Social Justice, Mujeres Latinas, Hunger Action Group, Amnesty International, and South-Asian American Students organized a week of consciousness raising that culminated in a rally aimed at countering racism, homophobia, sexism, and anti-immigration sentiment.

As further evidence of the commitment of students to multiculturalism, about 100 Columbia University students occupied the university's main administration building and demanded that President George Rupp institute an ethnic studies department. Outside the building, another 50 students rallied. The demonstration was a show of support for four students who had entered the 10th day of a hunger strike. After 5 days and after at least a dozen arrests, students walked arm in arm out of Hamilton Hall and chanted "What do we

want? Ethnic studies! When do we want it? Now!" as well as, "The students united will never be defeated!"

The preceding are just a few of the incidents I examined over the past few years in an effort to develop a phenomenological understanding of contemporary student activism. In addition to multicultural initiatives, a variety of other causes have attracted the attention of student activists. For example, students have been drawn to international concerns such as human rights violations in Burma. The Free Burma Coalition (FBC), originating from the work of a graduate student at the University of Wisconsin, now numbers nearly 200 campuses strong. Also, improved working conditions for graduate teaching assistants has attracted a good deal of attention, as revealed by recent events at Yale University. Other issues such as the environment, animal rights, and U.S. intervention in foreign affairs have also inspired student demonstrations.

Although students of the 1990s have been concerned with a wide range of social and political issues, clearly the theme of identity politics has become the central fiber connecting many of the cases of contemporary student movements. And although the phrase *identity politics* is often used negatively by writers such as D'Souza (1991), I suggest that identity politics should be interpreted as a sociocultural phenomenon capable of revealing insights and understandings about the lives and developmental journeys of today's diverse students. Thus, my goal is to provide a research-based analysis of contemporary student activism.

Methodology

In this research study, I sought to advance the knowledge about contemporary student activism. Although questions about the extent and impact of activism in the 1990s are important, I am more concerned in this article with interpreting the nature and context of student activism as seen through the eyes of student participants. Phenomenological analysis generally follows the basic strategies employed in qualitative research. In fact, phenomenology may be understood as a type of qualitative methodology whereby the focus is centered on identifying the essence of a particular phenomenon and developing understandings of how humans construct meaning around their particular experience. The strategy used in this study is not unlike the general goal of qualitative research, although in specifying phenomenology I purposely situated my study within the philosophical tradition of Husserl (1970), Merleau-Ponty (1962), and Schutz (1970), along with symbolic interactionists such as Blumer (1969) and Mead (1934), all of whom have placed the construction of meaning at the center of understanding human experience.

Student activists are difficult to identify outside the context of a particular student struggle. Thus, to examine the phenomenon of student activism, one must identify cases of activism around which to explore the meaning students bring to such struggles. To select specific cases, however, one must first have knowledge of the scope of the phenomenon under study. My first step in selecting a helpful sample of cases was to develop an idea of the terrain of student activism in the 1990s, which I did by analyzing reported cases of student activism as described in regional and national newspapers. Accordingly, I identified over 200 major incidents of student activism and then analyzed them to identify possible themes. The vast majority of campus incidents (nearly 60%) were associated with women's concerns, racial or ethnic struggles, or gay rights activities and represented what some scholars have described, both affectionately and pejoratively, as "culture wars," "campus wars," "multicultural unrest," or "identity politics" (Arthur & Shapiro, 1995; D'Souza, 1991; Hunter, 1991; Rhoads, 1994, 1995; Sidel, 1995). The remaining examples of student activism tended to revolve around funding/governance issues, concerns for world affairs (Burma and Iraq are two countries which drew a great deal of student attention), and environmental concerns.

Once a central theme of contemporary student activism was identified, I purposely selected cases for in-depth study. The goal was to better understand the meaning student activists construct around campus demonstrations tied to identity politics and multiculturalism. Therefore, I selected five cases that covered some of the key identity struggles explained in the broader analysis: (a) the Mills College strike of 1990, (b) the Chicano studies movement at the University of California at Los Angeles (UCLA) in 1993, (c) the gay rights demonstrations at Pennsylvania State University from 1991 to 1993, (d) the African American student movement at Rutgers University in 1995, and (e) the financial aid protests involving Native American students at Michigan State University from 1994 to 1996.

Data collection tools commonly recommended in conducting qualitative investigations were used (Denzin, 1989). Specifically, data collection involved 101 formal and 9 informal interviews with students, alumni, faculty, staff, and community members. Documents such as memos, letters, newspaper articles, and editorials were also obtained and used as sources of qualitative data. Artifacts such as films and audio recordings of campus incidents and student organizing efforts were collected as well. Three of the case studies were retrospective and involved repeat site visits (at least two site visits were conducted at each institution). In some cases, key student leaders had already graduated and were contacted for interviews through alumni offices or through personal contacts. The studies conducted at Pennsylvania State University and Michigan State University were ongoing and concurrent with student demonstrations.

The formal interviews were tape recorded and transcribed verbatim. The interview transcripts, along with documents and field notes from observations, formed the body of data to be examined. In analyzing the data, I employed content analysis as I sought to identify themes helpful in making sense of student organizing efforts (Patton, 1980). The primary concern involved reconstructing an account of various events connected to a specific campus protest movement. Once a general understanding of events emerged, I sought interpretive understandings by coming to terms with the complex meanings campus constituents gave to the various events and student demonstrations. After initial drafts of each case study were completed, students, faculty, and staff were asked to read and comment on the reports. This amounts to what Lincoln and Guba (1985) describe as "member checks" and adds to the trustworthiness of the findings and interpretations.

Findings

In this section I summarize findings from three of the five case studies. I limit my discussion to three cases because of space considerations, as well as the fact that some of the multicultural identity themes are repeated in the case studies.

The Mills College Strike of 1990

When the 1990 Spring semester got under way, the women of Mills College had already heard the rumors that the Board of Trustees might decide to admit men for the first time in the college's 138-year history. For many of the women, such a decision was unfathomable. They had come to treasure the unique environment of Mills. One student explained:

> Mills provides a setting where women are more apt to take risks. They're more apt to speak out in class. They're more apt to take leadership roles. I just think that it really prepares women to go out in the world and do what they want to do. It's a 4-year kind of haven. It's the same argument that you hear for Black colleges. I really believe they're parallel.

As a decision about the future of Mills approached, a sense of urgency fell on the student body. The students increased their efforts to make their position known to the board through a variety of strategies. For example, the week before the decision was to be made, students tied yellow ribbons around campus trees and demonstrated at the campus's front gate. Rallies were held throughout the week, with the largest occurring on Wednesday, April 25. Students spoke about how their efforts represented more than a personal and immediate concern; they highlighted their commitment to future generations of women who ought to have the same opportunity to study in an all-women's environment. Lisa Kremer was a senior and a coeditor of the school's newspaper. She felt strongly about the Mills' tradition:

> The school has a history of commitment to women—a tradition that is older than most of the companies in this country. I think it's important to preserve those traditions. I think it's important to have an alternative education for women. I don't think women have to go to women's colleges, but it

should be an option for them. . . . It really widens your eyes as to how the world works. You really understand better how women work together.

In reflecting on the Spring of 1990, Kremer felt that President Mary Metz and Board Chair Warren Hellman had played down the option of going coed. "At the newspaper we were quite worried about the possibility of coeducation, but they repeatedly told us, 'Oh no, it's not that big of a deal.' They really tried to minimize the possibility of going coed."

Despite strong support from students to remain an all-women's institution, in early May of 1990 college officials announced that Mills College would begin to admit men as early as the Fall of 1991. Within hours of the announcement, Mills women had organized a campuswide meeting to discuss their strategy, and by 7 a.m. the next day the students had blockaded every administrative entrance on the campus. The Mills College strike was under way, and the college was effectively shut down.

The students soon became well schooled in the tactics of civil disobedience as Silja Talvi, an undergraduate at Mills, shared her knowledge of public demonstration and resistance techniques. During the next 2 weeks, the students polished their organizational and communication skills as they developed sophisticated techniques for controlling the extensive media coverage that had converged on the west Oakland campus. Included in their media manipulation was a visit to the *Phil Donohue Show*, which spotlighted Mills College and women's education in general.

Not long into the strike, the students gained the support of the Mills College alumnae. Faxes, e-mail messages, and phone calls poured into the strike headquarters in the student union building as faithful and supportive Mills women from around the country let their voices be heard. Some offered to increase their giving to the college if the board would reverse its decision. Others took a more ominous tone and threatened to have the college cut out of their wills. Faculty also came out in support of the students as pressure on the board to reverse its decision mounted with each day of the strike.

The demonstrations at Mills College in many ways epitomized the power of the student body to influence campus policies and to bring issues into the public's consciousness. One student provided understanding of the depth of emotion and empowerment that many students felt:

> Tuesday's rally filled me with inspiration and a real sense of hope. The turnout was overwhelming. The sound of hundreds of women singing "Remember" [a traditional favorite of Mills students] gave me shivers of exhilaration. You could feel the power in the air, it was sweet and shimmering like champagne. I was intoxicated by the strength of our voice. (Yost, 1990, p. 2)

Through their use of the media, the women of Mills College were able to capture the national spotlight and bring attention to the relevance of a woman-centered education. In the end, the pressure was too much to bear as it became apparent that the board had underestimated the students' commitment to women's education and the importance of institutions such as Mills in fostering a space for women's voices to develop.

The Chicano Studies Movement at UCLA

In May 1993, Marcos Aguilar and five other UCLA students and one faculty member began a hunger strike. Their purpose was to apply pressure on Chancellor Charles Young and the rest of the administration so that Chicano studies would be elevated from program to departmental status. For over 20 years, UCLA had half-heartedly supported a Chicano studies inter-departmental program, only to see its viability called into question almost yearly. Chicana and Chicano students felt the program needed to be strengthened by granting it departmental status with the authority to hire and promote its own faculty.

Two weeks prior to the hunger strike, Aguilar had been among the 90 students and community members arrested for their participation in a sit-in at the UCLA faculty center. The arrests and the treatment they received at the hands of the university and the Los Angeles Police Department only increased their passion to achieve departmental status for Chicano studies. These students saw Chicano studies as a link between an elite institution

and a city comprising the largest Mexican American population in the country. Aguilar commented:

> It was rather obvious to us that we needed to have classes about our own history at the university. We never received such information in high school. . . . It wasn't so obvious to us at first that we needed to have a major. But we started to become aware of the fact that without a department the classes would start to disappear. Our fear was that the social movement that brought about those classes in the first place would eventually be ignored or forgotten. So our goal was not only to preserve those classes but to preserve the spirit of the movement of the '60s and '70s which had institutionalized Chicano studies at UCLA.

The actions by the UCLA Chicana and Chicano students may be seen as part of the larger effort to rebuild their community by asserting the historical and cultural relevance of Mexican heritage. Many of today's Chicana and Chicano students are challenging politicians and university leaders to pay heed to their cultural struggle and their place in a multicultural democracy that, they believe, has for years sought to silence them. The strength of *La Raza* (a manifestation of Chicano racial pride), which first took root in the late 1960s, has been rekindled by a new generation of activists who refuse to stand silently by as their culture fades away from history.

Minnie Ferguson, another student actively involved in the effort to create a Chicana/Chicano studies department saw such a program as intimately tied to the advancement of Mexican American culture and community. She reflected on why she and others supported an autonomous department:

> We saw it as a cultural center where the community could come in with problems. . . . And the center would help the community to do research to solve their problems. . . . We want a place where people can get the kind of service that a university is supposed to provide. What's really important is educating our students. By that I mean not schooling them but truly educating them on their roots, on who they are. They need to graduate from the university and be more than just a doctor for the establishment. They need to go back to their communities and service our people.

It's basically an issue of education versus schooling. What UCLA offers is schooling. They train you. They train you to do things that this society needs in order for the status quo to continue. We wanted a department of Chicana/Chicano studies to be something more than that.

Ferguson's perspective reflected the early motto of the Chicano student movement in Southern California in the late 1960s and early to mid 1970s: "Of the community, for the community" (Gómez-Quiñones, 1978).

One UCLA professor, Leo Estrada, among others, helped to negotiate a compromise as the Cesar Chavez Center for Interdisciplinary Instruction in Chicana and Chicano Studies was created and the 2-week hunger strike was ended. Although the center did not have the status of a "department," it nonetheless had the power to hire and promote its own faculty. Chicana and Chicano students, faculty, and community members hailed the establishment of the César Chávez Center as a victory for "Chicanismo"—a form of racial and ethnic nationalism (Gómez-Quiñones, 1990; San Miguel, 1996)—and a hard-won battle for MEChA *(Movimiento Estudiantil Chicano de Aztlan)* and other Mexican American and Latina/Latino student organizations at the university.

Ferguson and Aguilar, like Mexican American activists of the late 1960s and early 1970s, have embraced the ideals and nationalism of *La Raza* and have identified themselves as Chicanas or Chicanos. They have confronted university officials through demonstrations, sit-ins, hunger strikes, and walk-outs as part of an effort to force the university to be more inclusive in its vision of knowledge and culture. What is perhaps different from their 1960s forerunners is that today's Chicana and Chicano activists no longer hope for university responsiveness—they demand an inclusive community environment and curriculum, in fact so forcefully that some seem ready to die for it.

African American Student Resistance at Rutgers

Over the past three decades, Rutgers University has faced significant challenges to enhance the campus environment for African American students. Part of the institution's commitment was rooted in the Black student protest movement at Rutgers in the late 1960s and the pressure students applied on the administration (McCormick, 1990). By the 1990s, pride in one's racial identity had become critical to many students at Rutgers and tension between African American students and the administration was a strong undercurrent.

Whatever sense of security and freedom of identity exploration African American students felt they had achieved at Rutgers became even more precarious in the Spring of 1995 when three devastating words spoken by President Francis Lawrence became public knowledge. In attempting to explain the university's admission strategy to a group of faculty at the Camden branch campus in November 1994, Lawrence commented that African American students lacked the "genetic, hereditary background" to score well on the Scholastic Aptitude Test (SAT). His point was that the university had to maintain some standards, yet not close its doors to African American students.

Students sought to call national attention to the remarks of President Lawrence at the same time that they demanded his resignation. What they heard was a variety of explanations for a "slip of the tongue," none of which was satisfactory to them. In what seemed a historic moment in the African American resistance movement at Rutgers, the students seized the day. For Clarence Tokley, who was finishing his 2nd year at Rutgers, as well as for other African American students at the university, it was a matter of doing what was right.

It was something seeing all those people pulling together no matter what might happen. We were there because we knew what we had to do. We had that feeling of knowing people and being together.... We were going after what we knew was right. And doing it no matter what—no matter whether President Lawrence apologized or not, or whether the faculty backed us or not. The students were together. When it came down to it, we had to do our work and we did it.

Although students organized numerous marches and rallies, the message they wanted to convey to the American public was not getting across. Finally, in a dramatic form of student demonstration, Jacqueline Williams, a junior at Rutgers, walked onto the basketball court at halftime of the Rutgers versus University of Massachusetts Atlantic 10 basketball game in an effort to ignite a sit-in and ultimately force the game's postponement. Williams had arrived late to the game and had expected to see a student demonstration already in progress. Much to her dismay, she arrived at a relatively calm basketball arena. Sensing the fading opportunity, Williams walked onto the court and sat on the floor. "I had missed my train from Newark, so I got there when half-time was about to start. When I saw there was no demonstration going on, I got kind of frustrated, so I decided to take it upon myself, to just stop the game." University officials gathered around Williams and tried to coax her into leaving. She offered them only one comment: "I will leave when President Lawrence leaves."

Other students, mostly African Americans, soon joined Williams at half-court, and the game eventually was postponed. The event attracted the media's attention and brought Lawrence's comments to a national audience. Other student demonstrations followed the basketball sit-in, but in the end President Lawrence remained at Rutgers, after announcing concessions to boost the university's commitment to students of color.

Identity Politics and Multiculturalism

The experiences of students at Mills College, UCLA, and Rutgers University, and of the 100 or so others who participated in interviews as part of this study revealed one recurring theme of contemporary campus activism: the role that identity plays in student organizing. For example, the Mills College strike was centered around women's issues and a concern that specific institutions were needed where women could develop a clear sense of identity as women. The students felt that an all-women's environment offered the kind of empowering teaching and learning context where they could excel. As one student explained:

> It was like this incredibly protected time to unfold one's true beauty, whatever that may be for each individual. I was so used

to achieving and trying to succeed and do better and better. I was caught in some sort of achievement paradigm. I don't know how I got caught up in that trap in the beginning, but it was there and it's throughout our society. At Mills there was this sort of divine pause. I mean, I just remember having this experience and actually feeling for the first time the sun on my skin. I could feel the heat of the sun . . . and I think it was like this for a lot of the women there.

This student found Mills to be a safe space in which to experiment with her creativity and identity. For her and other students at Mills, the college offered a unique environment where a commitment to the development of women was central. The Mills College students saw such environments as necessary options for women because they still exist in a world largely defined by men and centered around male identity.

Chicana and Chicano students at UCLA saw the nondepartmental status of the Chicano studies program as a direct reflection on their place within the academic community at UCLA and within the larger American culture. Their effort to legitimize Chicano studies was a struggle to assert their rightful place in the broader social fabric. Milo Alvarez, a UCLA student with a long history of involvement in MEChA, noted the connection between Chicana/Chicano studies and larger social concerns:

> Chicana/Chicano studies gives us intellectual space. . . . We're always fighting for our history and culture in an elitist institution such as UCLA. It's about empowering our people. . . . Basically, we are fighting for our own space in one of the most prestigious institutions in the United States.

For the students at Rutgers University, the resistance movement of 1995 was an opportunity to raise the public's consciousness about what it means to be an African American. They saw the comments made by President Lawrence as more than a slip of the tongue, for the words he spoke reflected to them the kind of institutionalized racism they had confronted throughout their educational lives. The protests and demonstrations they organized represented their opportunity to construct African American identity in an empowering way. As Jacqueline Williams explained:

People have to know what Black people are capable of doing. They have seen us over the years, through the 1960s and probably before that. We have the power in our fist. They know we can fight.... But what we have to focus on now is more than an iron fist. We can now win with our intellect. We can use our brains for this.

The two case studies not highlighted in this article—lesbian, gay, and bisexual students at Pennsylvania State University and Native American students at Michigan State University—reveal similar identity struggles (Rhoads, forthcoming). For students at Penn State, the challenge that was played out in campus politics was whether or not lesbian, gay, and bisexual students, faculty, and staff should be included within the university's official statement of nondiscrimination. After several semesters of student direct action, the university in 1992 adopted a sexual orientation clause, and thus, to a degree, officially acknowledged sexual minorities as legitimate members of the academic community. And, at Michigan State University, Native American students battled the Republican governor, John Engler, throughout the academic years 1994–95 and 1995–96 as they sought to preserve the state's Indian Tuition Waiver Program. That their struggle clearly was rooted in cultural identity was made evident by one of the Native American student leaders:

> In college you start thinking more critically about the issues that are affecting your people. You start to realize why things are bad in your community. You start to see maybe a historical basis for it. So then you stop to realize and you start to stand up a little bit more.... I think that a lot of native students our age are getting back more to their roots, as far as like the language and the culture.... You know my parents and grandparents were forbidden to speak their language. Boarding schools were designed to take the Indian out of the Indian—and assimilate and things like that.... Today's generation of Indians is going to reclaim our roots.... We need to push to reclaim our heritage and our identity.

The efforts of women at Mills College, Chicana and Chicano students at UCLA, and African American students at Rutgers are linked to the broad concerns of educational opportunity and social justice for members of groups who typically have been marginalized within academe. Lesbian, gay, and bisexual students at Penn State and Native American students at Michigan State are also part of this larger movement rooted in multiculturalism and grounded in a perception that colleges and universities ought to provide appropriate intellectual space and positive settings for student development. Additionally, other students such as Asian Americans and Arab Americans also have organized around cultural identity and offer their contributions to the multicultural student movement. Scores of progressive-minded Whites have also been demonstrating as part of this movement. All of these "martyrs for multiculturalism," as they were termed in a popular news magazine (Leslie & Murr, 1993), have significant experiences and complex understandings to be shared with the faculty and student affairs professionals charged with guiding their educational endeavors.

Educational Implications of Student Activism

Student affairs professionals and faculty have an educational and developmental obligation to foster student learning in a variety of educational contexts. Clearly, one such context is student activism (Chambers & Phelps, 1993). What can be learned from the multicultural student movement that might be helpful in guiding educational efforts with students?

First and foremost, a variety of developmental stage models have suggested that "identity pride" (often discussed as "immersion") stages are not an end point, but instead represent a lower level of identity development (Atkinson, Morten, & Sue, 1989; Cass, 1979; Cross, 1991). Yet, if racial minorities and lesbian, gay, and bisexual people have significant cultural barriers to overcome throughout society, what good does it do to situate passion toward group identification as a stage to work through on their way to a calmer, more synthesized identity? Who is served by the normalization of a less radicalized identity? Arguably, Afrocentrism, Chicanismo, feminism, and queer politics have much to contribute to social and cultural change, and situating students committed to such agendas as less than fully developed creates a barrier to serious dialogue about cultural differences.

A second implication is that cultural identity is for many students a basic foundation for learning. Time and time again throughout my interviews with students it was apparent that a strong sense of self rooted in one's cultural background (including gender and sexual orientation) was a necessary starting point from which other aspects of the collegiate experience might spring. The relevance of cultural identity and students' sense of self has been addressed by a number of scholars who have explored learning (Bensimon, 1994; Freire, 1970; Hooks, 1994; King & Magolda, 1996; Manning, 1993; Rhoads, 1997). Seen in this light, students engaged in campus identity politics may highlight fundamental institutional weaknesses related to inadequate multicultural structures, policies, and practices.

A third implication concerns the need for students, faculty, and administrators to rethink the notion that students' strong identification with racial, gender, and sexual identity groups contributes to campus divisiveness and harmful self-segregation. Much evidence suggests that students who have a cultural or subcultural base to which they turn for support are able to reach out and engage in serious and ongoing communications with other campus and societal groups (Hurtado, Dey, & Treviño, 1994). Also, whereas critics have pointed to the infusion of multiculturalism into the curriculum as a source of campus tension, empirical studies have suggested the opposite (Astir, 1993a). What I suggest here, as elsewhere (Rhoads & Valadez, 1996), is that identity groups and identity politics should not necessarily be seen as a source of campus fragmentation, as authors such as D'Souza (1991), have contended. Many sources of campus conflict exist (Hurtado, 1992), and pointing a finger at underrepresented students, women, and gays struggling to find their place in academe hardly seems constructive.

In stressing the role of cultural identity as a source of stability and self-knowledge for diverse students and women, we need to rethink traditional views of community that tend to situate difference as a "problem to be solved" (Tierney, 1993). The commitment to multiculturalism evidenced by many of today's student activists reflects a broader movement to build diverse communities in spite of a society strongly rooted in individualism (Bellah, Madsen. Sullivan, Swidler, & Tipton, 1985; Etzioni, 1995). The complex dilemma in working with students is to help them understand that community can be built on diversity and that solidarity is not simply a manifestation of cultural homogeneity.

The struggle of diverse students to instill a broader realization of American democracy brings to mind one of the central obligations embraced by student development and the traditions of liberal learning: Education for citizenship is a key aspect of the college student experience (Barber, 1992; Rhoads & Black, 1995; Rhoads, 1997). Student participation in organizing for social and political change can open the doors to deeper discussions among students, faculty, and student affairs professionals. It is within the philosophical tradition of John Dewey (1916) that faculty and student affairs practitioners approach student efforts to create social and political change as pedagogical moments. The goal, of course, is not to provide answers to some of the complex social and philosophical questions raised by the multicultural student movement but instead to create forums where dialogues across cultural differences are likely to occur. The conflicts often inspired by student activists may in fact offer powerful opportunities to bring campus groups together around common dialogues rooted in advancing our understanding of democracy and multiculturalism.

Correspondence concerning this article should be addressed to Robert A. Rhoads, Department of Educational Administration, Michigan State University; 429 Erickson Hall, East Lansing, MI 48824-1034: telephone 517-353-5979; fax 517-353-6393; rrhoads@pilot.msu.edu

References

Altbach, P. G., & Cohen, R. (1990). American student activism: The post-sixties transformation. *Journal of Higher Education, 61*(1), 32–49.

Arthur, J., & Shapiro, A. (Eds.). (1995). *Campus wars: Multiculturalism and the politics of difference.* Boulder, CO: Westview Press.

Astin, A. W. (1993a). Diversity and multiculturalism on the campus: How are students affected? *Change. 25*(1), 44–49.

Astin, A. W. (1993b). *What matters in college?: Four critical years revisited.* San Francisco: Jossey-Bass.

Atkinson, D. R., Morten, G. & Sue, D. W. (1989). *Counseling American minorities: A cross-cultural perspective* (3rd ed.). Dubuque, IA: Brown.

Barber, B. R. (1992). *An aristocracy of everyone: The politics of education and the future of America.* New York: Oxford University Press.

Bellah, R. N., Madsen, R., Sullivan, W. M., Swidler, A., & Tipton, S. M. (1985). *Habits of the heart.* New York: Harper & Row.

Bensimon, E. M. (Ed.). (1994). *Multicultural teaching and learning: Strategies for change in higher education.* University Park, PA: National Center on Postsecondary Teaching, Learning, & Assessment.

Berger, P. L., & Luckmann, T. (1966). *The social construction of reality: A treatise in the sociology of knowledge.* New York: Anchor Books.

Blumer, H. (1969). *Symbolic interactionism: Perspective and method.* Berkeley: University of California Press.

Carden, M. L. (1974). *The new feminist movement.* New York: Russell Sage Foundation.

Cass, V. C. (1979). Homosexual identity formation: A theoretical model. *Journal of Homosexuality, 4,* 219–235.

Chambers, T., & Phelps, C. E. (1993). Student activism as a form of leadership development. *NASPA Journal, 31*(1), 19–29.

Cross, W. E., Jr. (1991). *Shades of Black: Diversity in African-American identity.* Philadelphia: Temple University Press.

Denzin, N. (1989). *The research act* (3rd ed.). New York: Prentice-Hall.

Dewey, J. (1916). *Democracy and education.* New York: Macmillan Publishing.

D'Souza, D. (1991). *Illiberal education: The politics of race and sex on campus.* New York: The Free Press.

Etzioni, A. (Ed.). (1995). *Rights and the common good: The communitarian perspective.* New York: St. Martin's Press.

Freire, P. (1970). *Pedagogy of the oppressed.* New York: Continuum Books.

Giroux, H. A. (1992). *Border crossings: Cultural workers and the politics of education.* New York: Routledge.

Gitlin, T. (1987). *The sixties: Years of hope, days of rage.* New York: Bantam Books.

Gómez-Quiñones, J. (1978). *Mexican students por La Raza: The Chicano student movement in Southern California.* Santa Barbara, CA: Editorial La Causa.

Gómez-Quiñones, J. (1990). *Chicano politics: Reality and promise, 1940–1990.* Albuquerque: University of New Mexico Press.

Heineman, K. J. (1993). *Campus wars: The peace movement at American state universities in the Vietnam era.* New York: New York University Press.

Hooks, B. (1994). *Teaching to transgress: Education as the practice of freedom.* New York: Routledge.

Hunter, J. D. (1991). *Culture wars: The struggle to define America.* New York: Basic Books.

Hurtado, S. (1992). The campus racial climate: Contexts for conflict. *Journal of Higher Education, 63*(5), 539–569.

Hurtado, S., Dey, E. L., & Treviño, J. G. (1994, April). *Exclusion or self-segregation?: Interaction across racial/ethnic groups on college campuses.* Paper presented at the Annual Meeting of the American Educational Research Association, New Orleans.

Husserl, E. (1970). *The crisis of European sciences and the transcendental phemenology* (D. Carr. Trans.). Evanston, IL: Northwestern University Press.

King, P. M., & Magolda, M. B. B. (1996). A developmental perspective on learning. *Journal of College Student Development, 37,* 163–173.

Leslie, C., & Murr, A. (1993, June 14). Martyrs for multiculturalism: Courses that students at UCLA might die for. *Newsweek, 121*(24), 77.

Levine, A., & Hirsch, D. (1991). Undergraduates in transition: A new wave of activism on American college campuses. *Higher Education, 22,* 119–128.

Lincoln, Y. S., & Guba, E. G. (1985). *Naturalistic inquiry.* Beverly Hills: Sage.

Lipset, S. M. (1976). *Rebellion in the university.* Chicago: University of Chicago Press.

Lipset, S. M., & Altbach, P. (1967). Student politics and higher education in the United States. In S. M. Lipset (Ed.), *Student politics* (pp. 199–252). New York: Basic Books.

Loeb, P. R. (1994). *Generation at the crossroads: Apathy and action on the American campus.* New Brunswick, NJ: Rutgers University Press.

Manning, K. (1992). A rationale for using qualitative research in student affairs. *Journal of College Student Development, 33,* 132–136.

Manning, K. (1993). Liberation theology and student affairs. *Journal of College Student Development, 35,* 94–97.

McCormick, R. P. (1990). *The black student protest movement at Rutgers.* New Brunswick, NJ: Rutgers University Press.

Mead, G. H. (1934). *Mind, self and society* (Charles W. Morris, Ed.). Chicago: University of Chicago Press.

Merleau-Ponty, M. (1962). *Phenomenology of perception* (C. Smith, Trans.). New York: Humanities Press.

Pascarella, E. T., & Terenzini, P. T. (1991). *How college affects students: Findings and insights from twenty years of research.* San Francisco: Jossey-Bass.

Patton, M. Q. (1980). *Qualitative evaluation methods.* Beverly Hills, CA: Sage.

Rhoads, R. A. (1994). *Coming out in college: The struggle for a queer identity.* Westport, CT: Bergin & Garvey.

Rhoads, R. A. (1995). The cultural politics of coming out in college: Experiences of male students. *Review of Higher Education, 19*(1), 1–22.

Rhoads, R. A. (1997). *Community service and higher learning: Explorations of the caring self*. Albany: State University of New York Press.

Rhoads, R. A. (forthcoming). *Freedom's web: Student activism in an age of cultural diversity*. Baltimore: Johns Hopkins University Press.

Rhoads, R. A., & Black, M. A. (1995). Student affairs practitioners as transformative educators: Advancing a critical cultural perspective. *Journal of College Student Development, 36*, 413–421.

Rhoads, R. A., & Valadez, J. R. (1996). *Democracy, multiculturalism. and the community college: A critical perspective*. New York: Garland.

Sampson, E. E. (1970). Student activism and the decade of protest. In E. E. Sampson & H. A. Korn (Eds.), *Student activism and protest: Alternatives for social change* (pp. 1–22). San Francisco: Jossey-Bass.

San Miguel, C. (1996). Actors, not victims: Chicanas/os and the struggle for educational equality. In D. R. Maciel & I. D. Ortiz (Eds.), *Chicanas/os at the Crossroads: Social, economic, and political change* (pp. 159–203). Tucson: University of Arizona Press.

Schutz, A. (1970*). Alfred Schutz on phenomenology and social relations* (H. R. Wagner, Ed.). Chicago: University of Chicago Press.

Sidel, R. (199S). *Battling bias: The struggle for identity and community on college campuses*. New York: Viking.

Tierney, W. G. (1993). *Building communities of difference: Higher education in the 21st century*. Westport. CT: Bergin & Garvey.

West, C. (1993). *Keeping faith: Philosophy and race in America*. New York: Routledge.

Woodward, C. V. (1974). What became of the 1960s? *The New Republic, 171*, 18–25.

Yost, N. (1990, February 16). Inspiration. *Mills College Weekly*, p. 2.

Introduction to the Transaction Edition

Kenneth A. Feldman

I can claim no particular prescience on my and Newcomb's part for writing in the first paragraph of the original preface to this book that "our own attempt at integrating the empirical knowledge and the theoretical propositions generated over the years with respect to the effects of colleges on students... is by no means the first such effort, nor will it be the last." Obviously, research on college students would continue and, just about as obviously, this research would be reviewed, summarized, and synthesized apace. As it turned out, the decades of the seventies and eighties saw "a virtual torrent of studies on the characteristics of collegiate institutions and their students and how students change and benefit during and after their college years from college attendance," as Pascarella and Terenzini (1991, p. xv) have put it in their recent and monumental synthesis. And summaries of this research did follow; citations to them can be found on page 4 of Pascarella and Terenzini's (1991) work.

Of these later reviews and syntheses, those by Bowen (1977) and Pascarella and Terenzini (1991) are the most comprehensive. Within an economics perspective, Bowen (1977) focused on the outcomes of higher education in relation to their costs. A major section of his book concentrates on the consequences of a higher education for individuals. The categories into which he divided pertinent studies are somewhat different from ours; they include most of student attributes discussed in our book, as reconfigured, along with "new" outcome dimensions based on additional research that had been done after our book. Another major section of his book goes beyond ours by concentrating on the consequences of higher learning for society; these consequences include the impacts on society produced by changes in individual students through education, the societal impacts of research and public service connected with colleges and universities, the impact on social equality and inequality, and the monetary returns for the individual and the society for investments in higher education.

Pascarella and Terenzini (1991) deal primarily with effects on individuals. Because the nature of the research in the twenty or so years after our book broadened in content, these scholars were able to cast a wider net than were Newcomb and I in selecting for review the student characteristics affected by the college experience. They considered learning and cognitive developments of students, various of their psychosocial characteristics, their attitudes and values, their moral orientations and behaviors, their educational, occupational, and economic attainments, and the quality of their post-college lives. In doing this, they incorporated important advances in theory, computing technology, and methodology and statistical analysis.

The present book, Bowen's (1977) book, and Pascarella and Terenzini's (1991) book differ in their analytic stance—a difference that is roughly captured by Zelda Gamson's (1991) distinction between a "process" approach and an "effects" approach to the study of what happens to students in college. All three books are concerned with *both* the effects that colleges have on students and the processes that produce these effects, but the "ratio" of emphasis between the two concerns varies among the

"Introduction to the Transaction Edition," by Kenneth A. Feldman, reprinted from *The Impact of College on Students* by K. A. Feldman and Theodore M. Newcomb, 1994. Transaction Publishers.

books. Bowen's book (1977) shows the least interest in processes relative to effects, whereas our book shows the most. Pascarella and Terenzini's book (1991) lies somewhere in between, with a slightly heavier weighting of interest in effects over processes. The differences are signaled in the pattern of titles in each of the books. Thus, in the relevant section in Bowen (1977), chapter titles are "Cognitive Learning," "Emotional and Moral Development," "Practical Competence for Citizenship and Economic Productivity," and so on. Likewise, many of the chapter titles in Pascarella and Terenzini (1991) refer to individual attributes ("Cognitive Skills and Intellectual Growth," "Psychosocial Changes: Identity, Self-Concept, and Self Esteem," "Attitudes and Values," etc.). By contrast, the chapter titles in our book mainly refer to the social structures and social arrangements that presumably influence students ("The Diverse American College," "The Diversity of Major Fields," "Impacts of Residence Groupings," etc.).

To elaborate upon this effects-process distinction, I shall restrict the discussion to a comparison between the present book and that by Pascarella and Terenzini (1991). One way to make clear the difference in analytic stance of these two books is first to contrast two extreme approaches—one psychological and one sociological—to specifying the origin of changes in persons. In an extreme developmental approach, the origin of change is sought *only* in internal or ontogenetic forces that initiate development, whereas in an extreme environmental approach, the origin of change is sought *only* in the external or what have been called "sociogenic" forces (Dannefer, 1984a, 1984b; Featherman and Lerner, 1985) of the prevailing social system and culture. As an example, suppose it is found that a group of young people who *do not* go to college typically change over a four-year period on some outcome measure in exactly the same way as do a group of young people who *do* go to college. Ontogenetic theorists would explain this finding by assuming or postulating internal laws of development that affect the individuals in the two different groups in similar ways, whereas sociogenic theorists would explain the same finding in terms of the impact of societal-wide social and cultural forces on a certain age group (or, perhaps, on the population as a whole).

Let me emphasize at this point that neither Pascarella and Terenzini (1991) nor Newcomb and I opted for either an ontogenetic or sociogenic approach taken to its extreme; nor did they or we use *only* a psychological or *only* a sociological approach, extreme or otherwise. However, a developmental perspective is an important aspect of Pascarella and Terenzini's (1991) view of the interplay between student and college and does underlie a good portion of their analysis of college student change and stability. They are anything but doctrinaire or one-sided in their analysis. They warn of the possibility that what is sometimes referred to as development in college students may in large measure be the results of individuals' responses to the anticipated norms of new social settings or roles, and suggest that "we need to be wary of the tendency to equate the learning of social or cultural norms with development" (p. 364). Any psychological approach they do take in their book is heavily tempered by consideration of the nature of interpersonal settings of colleges, the structural and organizational features of colleges' social environments, and the institutional characteristics of colleges. Newcomb and I essentially took the reverse tack in synthesizing the research on college impacts, by heavily tempering our more sociological approach with psychological considerations. Perhaps the briefest formulation of the difference would be this: We leaned toward *sociological* social psychology, whereas Pascarella and Terenzini (1991) leaned toward *psychological* social psychology. Because this formulation still puts the matter a little too simply, I want to explore further the distinction between the two social psychologies (Stryker, 1977; also see House, 1977), as based on previous analyses I have done (Feldman, 1972, 1991).

The more psychological of the two social psychologies in higher education—particularly when the developmental perspective predominates—is well known, and need not be described in any great detail here. In this approach, student outcome variables are chosen that are direct "growth" or "maturity" variables or are variables more or less directly interpretable in such terms (even if, in some cases, an interpretation within a developmental framework is made somewhat arbitrarily). Although there may be some analysis of the contents and forms of the social structural arrangements and pressures of both the school and the larger society, more systematic concern is typically paid to the psychological dynamics of change rather than to the possible social impetus for such change. Moreover, even when environmental and social structural parameters are systematically analyzed, they tend to be considered only insofar as they are seen as *immediately* impinging on personality development, cognitive development, attitudinal development, or the like.

Compared to psychological social psychologists, social psychologists who are sociologically oriented in their study of higher education tend to focus considerably more on the structure and dynamics of the social pressures impinging on students than on the internal psychological dynamics initiating change or buttressing stability. They are interested in systematically describing and measuring a relatively full range of social structural features of the college environment and subenvironments even though implications for student change and stability may not as yet have been completely or systematically explored in higher education theory and research. Although they may study some of the same outcome variables as do developmentally oriented theorists, the interpretations they make of change or stability of these attributes of students are not necessarily made within a developmental framework. Moreover, they may choose student outcome variables that have little or nothing to do with maturity or growth, or, in some instances, are even incompatible with the developmental approach.

Sociological social psychologists analyze the structural impacts of the environments and subenvironments of colleges in socializing student newcomers into their organization. The term "socialization" is *not* used as a synonym for "development"; rather, it refers to the social pressures on new members of the group to adhere to the prevailing ways of thinking, feeling, and behaving found in the group. This social organizational approach focuses on how college environments and subenvironments vary, from which variation pertinent differential impacts are conceived and predicted. Thus, "impacts" are not necessarily conceived in terms of the "development" or "growth" of the individual.

The more sociological approach also views colleges as organizations that certify their students for certain social and occupational positions in the world of the middle and upper-middle class, channels them in these directions, to some extent ensures them of entrance to such positions, and prepares them for their lives after they leave the organization. One set of interests here resides in analyzing the advantage of graduating from college in terms of future economic, occupational, and status positions; the differential in these advantages due to the kind of certification a student receives (e.g., the kind of college from which the student graduates); and the way in which such future "payoffs" vary by the social, economic, and racial background of the college graduate.

Another set of interests lies in specifying how colleges wittingly or unwittingly prepare students for the new adult roles and positions they will be occupying. One might assume of course that what one learns or becomes in order to move into and function competently in middle-and upper-middle class social and occupational roles automatically entails growth and increases in maturity, thus incorporating these changes into a developmental framework. But this assumption is a restrictive one, and may not always be empirically correct. Some of the changes prompted by new roles in college and by anticipation of future roles may have nothing to do with maturity. Other changes may be seen by some as actually hindering personality growth and development. For instance, if Becker (1964) is right that college students learn "institutional motivation," developmental theorists might well consider this sort of change to be a decrease in maturity, although many sociological social psychologists would not feel compelled to interpret this change within a developmental framework at all.

One way of locating an analysis of college students and their colleges in the landscape of the two social psychologies of higher education is to see how the college environment and subenvironments are brought into play in the analysis. At the outset of their book, for instance, Pascarella and Terenzini (1991) inform the reader that one of their difficult decisions in attempting their synthesis was deciding on an organizing principle for presenting findings; they report that "after a fairly lengthy consideration... [they] decided to organize the evidence in terms of different types of outcomes" (p. 5). This decision, a perfectly reasonable one, is part and parcel of their tilt toward psychological social psychology, I believe. Rather than initially focusing on and describing the features of the college environment in their own right and then asking how such features might or might not affect students regardless of whether or not there are studies about each possible impact, the analysis of the environment essentially has been made dependent upon the student outcomes under investigation and the empirical work that happens to have been done on these outcomes.

The tilt of the present book is in the opposite direction from that of Pascarella and Terenzini (1991). After initially establishing trends in the change and stability of college students during their matriculation, Newcomb and I focused on the college environment and subenvironments, speculating on how they might affect students and then looking at the ways in which, in fact, they do have impacts on students. The two books, of course, are anything but polar opposites; there is a good deal of overlap. Newcomb and I considered psychological development as well as the psychological dynamics of change and stability just as Pascarella and Terenzini (1991) considered socialization and certification as well as social forces that create impacts on individuals. Still, the differences in interpretative frameworks remain—subtle as they may be at some times and not so subtle at others.

References

Becker, H. S., 1964. What do they really learn at college. *Transaction*, 1, 635–647.

Bowen, H R., 1977. *Investment in learning: the individual and social value of American higher education.* San Francisco: Jossey-Bass.

Campbell, D. T., and Stanley, J. C., 1963. Experimental and quasi-experimental designs for research on teaching. In N. L. Gage (Ed.), *Handbook of research in teaching.* Chicago: Rand McNally. Pp. 171–246.

Cooper, H., 1984. *The integrative research review.* Beverly Hills, Calif.: Sage.

Dannefer, D., 1984a. Adult development and social theory: a paradigmatic reappraisal. *American Sociological Review*, 49, 100–116.

Dannefer, D., 1984b. The role of the social in life-span developmental psychology, past and future: rejoinder to Baltes and Nesselroade. *American Sociological Review*, 49, 847–850.

Featherman, D. L, and Learner, R. M. 1985. Ontogenesis and sociogenesis: problematics for theory and research about development and socialization across the life span. *American Sociological Review*, 50, 659–676.

Feldman, K. A., 1971. Using the work of others: some observations on reviewing and integrating. *Sociology of Education*, 44, 86–102.

Feldman, K. A., 1972. Some theoretical approaches to the study of change and stability of college students. *Review of Educational Research*, 42, 1–26.

Feldman, K. A., 1991. "How College Affects Students": what have Pascarella and Terenzini wrought? Keynote address presented at "Assessment of College Teaching and Learning: Implications for Research, Policy, and Practice," a conference held at the Westin Hotel O'Hare in Chicago, Illinois, jointly sponsored by the Public Policy Analysis and Higher Education P.D. programs at the University of Illinois at Chicago and the National Center on Postsecondary Learning, Teaching and Assessment.

Feldman, K. A., and Weiler J., 1976. Changes in initial differences among major-field groups: an exploration of the "accentuation effect." In W. H. Sewell, R Hauser, and D. Featherman (Eds.), *School and achievement in American society.* New York: Academic Press. Pp. 373–407.

Furby, L, 1973. Interpreting regression toward the mean in developmental research. *Developmental Psychology*, 8, 172–179.

Gamson, Z. F., 1991. Why is college so influential? The continuing search for answers. *Change*, 23, 50–54.

Glass, G. V., 1976. Primary, secondary, and meta-analysis of research. *Educational Research*, 5, 3–8.

Glass, G. V., 1977. Integrating findings: the meta-analysis of research. *Review of Research in Education* 5, 351–379.

Glass, G. V., McGaw, B., and Smith, M.L., 1981. *Meta-analysis in social research.* Beverly Hills, Calif.: Sage.

House, J. S., 1977. The three faces of social psychology. *Sociometry*, 40, 161–177.

Kuh, G. D., 1992. What do we do now? Implications for educators of *How College Affects Students. Review of Higher Education*, 15, 349–363.

McNemar, Q. A., 1940. A critical examination of the University of Iowa studies of environmental influence upon the IQ. *Psychological Bulletin*, 18, 47–55.

Moore, W. E., 1973. The accentuation process: some preliminary analyses. Unpublished manuscript, University of Michigan.

Newcomb, T. M., and Feldman, K. A., 1968. The impacts of colleges on students: a report to the Carnegie Foundation for the Advancement of Teaching.

Pascarella, E. G., and Terenzini, P. T., 1991. *How college affects students*. San Francisco: Jossey-Bass.

Stryker, S., 1977. Development in "two social psychologies": toward an appreciation of mutual relevance. *Sociometry*, 40, 145–160.

The Impact of College on Students: Myths, Rational Myths, and Some Other Things That May Not Be True

Ernest T. Pascarella and Patrick T. Terenzini

Academia clings to several myths about higher education and its effect on students. This article outlines 10 of these popular myths—myths about effective teaching styles, indicators of quality education, and the value of faculty research for undergraduate education, to name a few. The authors cite extensive research calling these myths into question and challenge readers to rethink assumptions about higher education.

This paper is about the mythology that surrounds many popular notions of how college influences students. By mythology we are not talking about mystical and often beautifully lyrical notions of the earth suspended on the back of a giant tortoise or of a sun god that daily drove his war chariot from east to west across the sky. Rather, we are talking about what could be called the rational myths of higher education. Rational myths are unsubstantiated notions about college and its impact on students, myths that seem so axiomatic and logical that academics as well as the broader public assume them to be true. We're not going to try to *convince* you that these assertions are myths—we have no naive notions that we can change a great number of minds. After all, the academy has its own culture with its own set of dearly held cultural beliefs and rational mythologies.

No, the most we can hope for is that you might begin to question some of these rational myths in the face of evidence that does not support them. And, possibly, you might see when and how they can be misleading and dysfunctional in terms of how we think about undergraduate education.

Let us turn to a discussion of some of these rational myths.

Myth #1: Changes in test scores during college reflect the impact of college.

Perhaps 90% of all serious assessment efforts in higher education measure changes in students on some variable (e.g., critical thinking, moral development, cognitive development, or abstract reasoning) over a specified period of time (e.g., freshman year to senior year). Unfortunately, things other than college can influence change and development and confound our results (Astin, 1970a, 1970b; Pascarella, 1987). For example, many of the outcomes along which we like to measure the impact of an undergraduate education (e.g., cognitive development, critical thinking, and moral reasoning) are developmentally based. This means students get better simply by getting older, the vintage effect. (A nice thought for those of us who thought aging just meant more fiber in our diets.) It also means that people who don't go to college may also be changing—perhaps just as much as those who go to college. It's almost impossible to tell from simple change scores without a noncollege control group.

The lesson to be learned is that the fact that students mature and change during college doesn't mean that this change is caused by college attendance. And perhaps we should temper our claims from such evidence. Similarly, if people do not change or grow on certain dimensions during college, it doesn't necessarily mean

"The Impact of College on Students: Myths, Rational Myths, and Some Other Things That May Not Be True," by Ernest T. Pascarella and Patrick T. Terenzini, reprinted from *NACADA Journal*, Vol. 15, No. 2, Fall 1995, Edward-Lynne Jones & Associates, Inc.

that college isn't having an impact. Now we know this sounds paradoxical, perhaps even impossible. However, we would remind you that nothing in life is what it seems—with the possible exception of professional wrestling. Consider research on gains in quantitative skills during college. Most evidence suggests that college graduates, in general, leave college with roughly the same level of quantitative skills they had when they left secondary school. However, students whose formal education stopped with high school tend, over the same period of time, to lose many of the quantitative skills they had at high school graduation (Wolfe, 1983, 1987). Thus, on this dimension and perhaps many others, college has an important impact in anchoring development and preventing its retrogression.

Myth #2: College merely socializes adolescents to middle-class status. It has little or no unique impact on student development or maturity.

Since about 1975 there has been a growing concern with estimating the *net* or *unique* influence of college on student development and maturity. The results of this research are unequivocal in suggesting that, over the same period of time, college students make greater changes on a broad range of outcomes than similar individuals whose formal education ends with secondary school. These include (a) verbal and quantitative skills, (b) oral and written communication, (c) critical thinking, (d) reflective judgment, (e) intellectual flexibility, (f) principled reasoning in judging moral issues, (g) value placed on aesthetic and intellectual matters, (h) social and political liberalism, (i) acceptance of nontraditional gender roles, (j) intellectual orientation, (k) internal locus of control, and (l) a series of habits that enhance continued learning (e.g., reading, continuing education, and participation in cultural events).

The bottom line here is that college may indeed function to socialize adolescents into middle-class status, but the evidence clearly suggests that college does considerably more than allocate status with a bachelor's degree. It facilitates a broad range of desirable changes that don't occur to the same extent to similar individuals who don't attend college.

Myth #3: Institutional resources and prestige equal educational quality.

One of the most persistent rational myths in American higher education is that attending a college with all or most of the conventionally accepted earmarks of quality or prestige (e.g., bright student bodies, big libraries, Nobel laureates, lots of educational resources, and large endowments—the kinds of things that lead to high *US. News & World Report* rankings) will lead to greater learning and development during college. In fact, a rather large body of evidence across a wide range of intellectual and developmental outcomes suggests that this is not necessarily true. After taking into account the characteristics, abilities, and backgrounds students bring with them to college, how much students grow and change has only inconsistent, and perhaps trivial, relationships with such popularly accepted measures of institutional quality as educational expenditure per student, student/faculty ratio, faculty salary, faculty research productivity, library size, admissions selectivity, graduation rate, and prestige rankings.

Now let us be very clear about what we are *not* saying here. First, we're not suggesting that graduates of all colleges have reached the same levels of intellectual or psychosocial development. Graduates of some colleges reach a level of achievement or development approximately equal to that of first-year students at other institutions. However, what needs to be remembered is that differences among institutions in various student outcomes are probably attributable substantially more to differences in the kinds of students admitted than to dramatic differences in institutional impact.

Second, we are not saying that all institutions have the same educational impact. It is likely that some institutions stand out as being particularly potent in their impact on student intellectual and personal development. Our point is that it is probably not possible to identify these educationally effective institutions merely by relying on the resource dimensions popularly used to rank institutions on educational quality. These so-called quality indicators may be more appropriately considered as measures of institutional advantage; they may reveal little of substance in terms of educational impact.

There is a corollary to Myth #3: The best measure of the educational quality of a college is the accomplishments of its graduates. We do it all the time. But, in fact, if we simply look at the accomplishments of graduates without taking into account where those individuals were when they entered college, our conclusions will simply reflect what kinds of students enroll at different institutions, not what differences exist in the educational value added by various college environments.

If an institution's stock of human, financial, and educational resources is of questionable value in identifying its educational impact, what does matter? (Note that we are not saying that resources don't matter but that they may often matter considerably less than the programmatic efforts of an institution.) Particularly important are such factors as:

1. the nature and cohesiveness of students' curricular experiences and general education,

2. their course-taking patterns,

3. the quality of the teaching they receive and the extent to which faculty members involve students actively in the teaching-learning process,

4. the frequency, purpose, and quality of students' nonclassroom interactions with faculty members,

5. the nature of students' peer group interactions and extracurricular activities, and

6. the extent to which institutional structures promote cohesive environments that value the life of the mind and facilitate high degrees of student academic and social engagement.

Myth #4: Two-year college attendance penalizes a student.

There has been a widespread belief that somehow two-year, community colleges offer equal access to higher education but don't provide equality of benefits—in short, that they offer a second best educational experience that penalizes a student educationally, occupationally, and economically when compared to those students who attend four-year colleges. Much of this perception probably springs from the often replicated finding that students who start at two-year colleges are about 15% less likely to complete a bachelor's degree in the same period of time as similar students who start at four-year institutions (Dougherty, 1987, 1992). However, there is a growing body of evidence to suggest that two-year colleges may be quite competitive with four-year institutions along a variety of dimensions. For example, in studies of 6 two-year and 7 four-year institutions from 12 U.S. states conducted by the National Center on Postsecondary Teaching, Learning, and Assessment, we found that when controls are made for such factors as initial ability, academic motivation, age, family social origins, work responsibilities, and extent of enrollment, there were only trivial two-year versus four-year college differences in first-year changes on such cognitive skills as reading comprehension, quantitative reasoning, and critical thinking (Bohr et al., 1994; Pascarella, Bohr, Nora, & Terenzini, 1995). Similarly, we also found only trivial two-year/four-year college differences in first-year gains made in such orientations to learning as (a) enjoyment of intellectual challenge and diversity, (b) enjoyment of higher order cognitive tasks, and (c) internal attribution for academic success or failure (Pascarella et al., 1994).

There is also increasing evidence to suggest that any relative disadvantages in bachelor's degree attainment accruing to two-year college students do not necessarily translate into occupational or economic disadvantages. For those two-year college students who can overcome the obstacles of transfer and complete their bachelor's degree, there is essential parity with similar four-year college students in such areas as job prestige, level of employment, job satisfaction, and earnings (Smart & Ethington, 1985; Whitaker & Pascarella, 1994). This set of findings is perhaps more significant when one considers the relatively low costs of community colleges as compared to their four-year counterparts. Thus, community colleges may provide a cost-effective way for students to obtain the first two years of effective postsecondary education without necessarily sacrificing either the intellectual rigor of their college experience or relative competitiveness in the marketplace.

Myth #5: Historically Black colleges do not provide as effective an education for African American students as predominantly White institutions do.

A long-standing critique of historically Black colleges (HBCs) suggests that, as a group, they lack the educational resources (e.g., laboratories, libraries, distinguished faculties, and educational funds) to provide the same intensity of educational experience as predominantly White or non-Black institutions (Bowles & DeCosta, 1971; Jencks & Reisman, 1968; Sowell, 1972). But when we look at the evidence on college impact, we get what is perhaps a different picture. A large body of evidence, for example, suggests not only that African American students attending HBCs perceive lower levels of stress, isolation, and racism on campus than their counterparts at predominantly White institutions but also that the former are more likely than the latter to persist and obtain the bachelor's degree. When student socioeconomic backgrounds, aptitudes, and aspirations are taken into account, the weight of evidence also suggests that attendance at, or graduation from, an HBC does not significantly disadvantage African American students occupationally or economically (Pascarella & Terenzini, 1991) —and African American students at HBCs appear to make about the same level of cognitive and intellectual gains during college as similar African American students at White institutions. In this regard, consider the following recent evidence from the first year of the National Center on Postsecondary Teaching, Learning, and Assessment study. When controls were made for factors such as precollege aptitude, gender, academic motivation, age, socioeconomic status, and on- or off-campus residence, there were only small differences between African American students at HBCs and African American students at predominantly White institutions in first-year gains made in reading comprehension, quantitative reasoning, and critical thinking. The differences that did exist tended to favor African American students at HBCs (Bohr, Pascarella, Nora, & Terenzini, 1995).

Clearly there has been a strong press to increase the student racial and ethnic diversity within American colleges and universities, and recent evidence presented by Alexander Astin (1993) suggests the positive developmental impacts of student body diversity. But perhaps not all African American students benefit equally from racially diverse institutions. The ability of HBCs to create a supportive psychosocial environment for African American students without sacrificing intellectual rigor (along with similar findings about the developmental benefits for women of women's institutions; see Pascarella & Terenzini, 1991) suggests, perhaps, that within the current trend toward increasing institutional diversity, we need to reserve a place in the American postsecondary system for the continued existence and nurturing of those educationally effective homogeneous institutions. In short, even as we seek to increase student body diversity *within* institutions, we need to balance this against preserving the rich diversity *between* American colleges and universities.

Myth #6: Traditional and long-standing methods of instruction provide the most effective ways of teaching undergraduate students.

In the American postsecondary system, lecturing students is still the dominant mode of instruction. Much of the research suggests that teachers in typical undergraduate classes spend 75–80% of their time lecturing or presenting content to students and that, on average, students are attentive to what is being said only about 50% of the time and retain only about 50% of what they actually pay attention to (Pascarella & Terenzini, 1991). When you also consider the often touted finding that in any class of 25 or more 18- to 22-year-olds, no 30-second period passes without at least one of them having a thought about sex, you can see why the lecture method can have its problems.

Now the aforementioned is not to say that lecturing cannot be an effective instructional technique. We probably all remember undergraduate teachers who were exceptional in their ability to motivate, inform, and even inspire with a graceful, lucid, and penetrating presentation of information and ideas. Yet, if you're like us, you probably also remember a far greater number of undergraduate teachers who missed that standard by a considerable margin. Traditional lecturing and lecture-related methods of instruction are often like the little girl with the curl in the middle of her forehead—when she was good, she was very, very good, but when she was bad, she was *horrid!*

The fact is that there are instructional approaches that, under experimental conditions, have been shown repeatedly to be more effective in facilitating subject-matter learning than more traditional approaches. These more effective approaches (e.g., the personalized system of instruction, audiotutorial instruction, computer-based instruction, and cooperative/collaborative learning) differ in some ways, but they seem to stress certain elements:

1. small modular units of instruction,
2. student mastery of one unit before moving on to the next,
3. timely and frequent feedback to students on their progress, and
4. active student involvement in learning rather than passive learning.

The increased cognitive effectiveness of these instructional methods over lecturing and other traditional methods of college teaching probably has multiple sources, but the evidence suggests the following are particularly important.

First, many of these nontraditional instructional methods reverse the time/achievement relationship of lecturing and traditional instruction. In traditional instruction, time in covering content is constant but course learning varies. In the alternative methods, time covering the material varies (i.e., students cover content at their own pace), and attempts are made to make achievement more constant by requiring student mastery of the content. In short, these alternative instructional methods (as opposed to traditional methods) are sensitive to individual student differences in speed of acquiring content.

Second, in contrast to the passive roles students are encouraged to play in most lecture/discussion/recitation classes, individualized and collaborative teaching approaches require active student involvement and participation in the teaching-learning process. Such methods encourage students to take greater responsibility for their own learning; they learn from one another, as well as from the instructor. The weight of evidence indicates that active

learning produces greater gains in course content, and recent evidence clearly supports efforts to employ various forms of collaborative learning.

Please note that we are not suggesting that the kind of alternative individualized and collaborative instructional approaches we have briefly described are any panacea. We only suggest them as potentially effective approaches to undergraduate instruction that are far less frequently employed than more traditional, but perhaps less effective, teaching.

Myth #7: Good teachers have to be good researchers.

One of the most frequent attacks on the quality of contemporary undergraduate education is that faculty members spend so much time on their research and scholarship that it detracts from the time they spend on undergraduate teaching. A major defense against this attack is that faculty members must conduct research or be engaged in scholarship in order to be good teachers. Faculty members actively engaged in research and scholarship, so the argument goes, are more likely to be on the cutting edge in their disciplines; they pass their enthusiasm for learning and the life of the mind on to their students. This fervent belief in the instructional benefits of faculty engagement in research and scholarship is, of course, reflected in our dominant faculty reward structures. Find and reward good scholars and researchers, these structures suggest, and chances are higher that you'll also find and reward good teachers. (We all know first rate scholars who are outstanding teachers—perhaps outstanding at everything they do professionally—though one wonders whether exposure to these exceptional individuals is a common part of an undergraduate's experience in most institutions.)

The systematic evidence, and it is a large and consistent body of research, calls the "good researcher = good teacher" argument sharply into question. Our best estimate from this body of evidence is that the correlation between scholarly productivity and ratings of undergraduate instruction (on those dimensions closely related to student achievement) range from .10 to .16. Put another way, scholarly productivity accounts for between 1 and 2.5% of the differences in undergraduate teaching effectiveness—between 97 and 99% of the differences in teaching effectiveness are due to things other than scholarly productivity (Feldman, 1987). Although such a trend in the research does not support the claim that doing research detracts from being an effective teacher, it certainly calls into question the academic shibboleth that scholarly or research productivity is a required skill for effective undergraduate teaching. Indeed it may well be that effectiveness in these two central dimensions of academic life is largely independent of each other. This being the case, perhaps we need to spend a little more time nurturing and evaluating good teaching (we already are quite good at nurturing and evaluating good research) and not assume that when we tenure, promote, and evaluate good scholars (in the traditional sense), we are probably tenuring, promoting, and evaluating effective undergraduate teachers. This leads to the next myth.

Myth #8: You can't teach people to become good teachers.

In some ways we look at this myth as a logical extension of academic Darwinism: You hire talent—you don't train it. Thus, we've heard many academics dismiss teacher development programs at universities as a waste of resources because good teachers are born (i.e., it's in their genes) not made. Perhaps one reason many faculty members believe this is that American graduate schools have historically done precious little to train Ph.D. students in instructional or teaching methods. If we're lucky, we find a good mentor and perhaps model our teaching after his or hers.

Let us be clear in admitting that there are some natural-born superlative teachers—we've probably all seen them (though, to be realistic, they probably represent a small percentage of our professional ranks). However, the notion that you can't teach people to become more effective teachers simply flies in the face of a rather large and convincing body of evidence to the contrary. In our synthesis of the vast body of evidence on teaching, we found that student learning in a course is unambiguously linked to the ways students themselves describe effective teaching—and we know much about what effective teachers do and

how they behave in the classroom (Pascarella & Terenzini, 1991). Although a number of teacher behaviors are positively linked with student learning (e.g., rapport with students, interpersonal accessibility to students, feedback to students, enthusiasm, and the like), two highly related dimensions stand out as being strongly linked to how much students learn. These are instructor skill (particularly clarity of presentation) and course structure (e.g., class time that is structured and organized efficiently and course goals, objectives, and requirements that are clear). What is perhaps most important is that many of the elements of both of these dimensions of effective teaching can themselves be learned.

Recent evidence from the National Center on Postsecondary Teaching, Learning, and Assessment study of 23 institutions around the country suggests that the positive influence of at least one of these dimensions of teaching effectiveness extends beyond simple course achievement. Using a sample of nearly 2,600 students, we found that the more students reported high levels of course organization in the overall teaching they received at their institution, the more likely they were to make the largest first-year gains in ACT-developed standardized measures of reading comprehension, quantitative reasoning, and critical thinking—and this effect persisted even after controls for the pattern of courses taken and precollege ability on those outcomes (Pascarella, Edison, Nora, Hagedorn, & Braxton, 1995).

Thus, the teachable and learnable elements of effective teaching appear not only to enhance specific course learning; at least one of them also appears to have potential positive impacts on more general dimensions of cognitive and intellectual development during college.

Myth #9: Faculty members' impact on student development and learning resides in the classroom.

Many of us in academia have a rather narrow view of a faculty member's sphere of influence on students. We think that influence, and therefore the faculty obligation to contribute to the education of undergraduates, begins and ends at the classroom or laboratory door. The research evidence on the impact of faculty, however, does not support this narrow view of their influence. What a large body of studies demonstrates is that faculty also exert considerable educational influence in their out-of-class contact and interaction with students.

Consider that as much as 80 to 85% of a student's waking hours are spent outside a classroom, and it has become increasingly clear that a large part of the educational and developmental impact of college can take place during that nonclass time. Obviously, interaction with peers plays a major role in the educational impact of nonclassroom (as well as classroom) experiences. But faculty members also appear to be potentially important agents of nonclassroom socialization on campus. Indeed the literature is compelling that faculty educational potency is significantly enhanced in those campus settings where their contacts with undergraduate students extend beyond the classroom to informal, nonclassroom settings.

Specifically, the evidence is quite clear that even when we control for important student background characteristics, aspirations, and other confounding influences, the extent of students' informal, nonclassroom contact with faculty is positively linked with a broad array of outcomes (Pascarella & Terenzini, 1991). These include:

1. perceptions of intellectual growth during college,
2. increases in intellectual orientation and curiosity,
3. liberalization of social and political values,
4. growth in autonomy and independence,
5. orientation toward scholarly careers,
6. interpersonal skills and sensitivity,
7. educational aspirations,
8. persistence in college and educational degree attainment, and
9. women's interest in, and choice of, sex-atypical (male-dominated) career fields (e.g., law, business, medicine, engineering, and academia).

Interestingly, but not surprisingly, it also appears that the impact of student-faculty informal contact on student development is determined by its content and focus, as well as by its frequency. The most influential forms of interaction appear to be those that focus on ideas or intellectual matters—thereby extending and reinforcing the goals of the academic program.

The fact that faculty members have important educational impact on students beyond the classroom leads to our final myth, although we're not sure whether this is simply a myth or a combination of myth reinforced by bureaucratic expediency. At any rate, we seem to have structured our colleges and universities as though it were true.

Myth #10: Students' academic and nonacademic experiences are separate and unrelated areas of influence on learning and development.

Most theoretical models of learning and student development of which we are aware in no way suggest, much less argue forcefully, that any single experience—or class of experiences—during college will be a crucial determinant of educational impact on students. Rather, our review of a substantial body of evidence suggests that the unique impact of any particular experience during college (e.g., courses, major, residence arrangement, interactions with peers, and so on) tends to be markedly smaller than the overall net effect of attending (vs. not attending) college (Pascarella & Terenzini, 1991). The same evidence also suggests that a majority of the important changes that occur during college are probably the cumulative result of a set of interrelated and mutually supporting experiences, in class and out, sustained over an extended period of time.

For example, students not only become more cognitively and intellectually complex and advanced between the freshman and senior years (e.g., as critical and reflective thinkers), but they also demonstrate *concurrent* changes in values, attitudes, and psychosocial development that are consistent with and probably reciprocally related to cognitive change. Thus, although we can't demonstrate strict causality, it is quite clear that documented change in nearly every outcome area appears to be embedded within an interconnected and perhaps mutually reinforcing network of cognitive, value, attitudinal, and psychosocial changes—all of which develop during the student's college experience. In short, the student changes as a whole, integrated person during college. (All these changes *may* be independent of each other, but we doubt it.)

To further support this notion, we are beginning to see a cumulative body of evidence to suggest the importance of extracurricular involvement and activities in a student's cognitive and intellectual development (Kuh, 1993; Baxter Magolda, 1992). Similarly, other recent work suggests that first-year critical thinking is most affected by the *breadth* of student involvement in the intellectual and social experiences of college and not by any particular type of involvement (Pascarella, 1989). Thus, the greatest college impact on intellectual and cognitive (as well as personal) development may stem from the student's total level of campus engagement, particularly when academic, interpersonal, and extracurricular involvements are mutually supporting and relevant to a particular educational outcome.

The myth that students' academic and nonacademic experiences are separate and independent sources of influence on student learning has been reinforced in most American universities ever since 1870 when Harvard President Charles William Elliot appointed a student dean so he wouldn't have to deal with student discipline. Since then the academic affairs and student affairs functions of most institutions have been running essentially on parallel but separate (and perhaps uneven) tracks: academic affairs tends to cognitive development while student affairs ministers to affective growth.

This bureaucratization of collegiate structures is a creature of administrative convenience and budgetary expedience. It surely has not evolved from any conception of how students learn, nor is it supported by research evidence. Organizationally and operationally, we've lost sight of the forest. Enhancing the effectiveness of undergraduate education may require new forms of collaboration among faculty, academic administrators, and student affairs administrators with the purpose of delivering undergraduate education in a manner that recognizes the comprehensive and integrated ways in which students actually learn. New perspectives from these important constituencies may be needed to capitalize on the interrelatedness of the in- and out-of-class

influences on student learning and the functional interconnectedness of academic and student affairs.

This may start with faculty and academic affairs administrators recognizing the substantial contribution of student affairs to student cognitive and intellectual, as well affective, development. Conversely, as American College Personnel Association President Charles Schroeder (1994) recently pointed out in his perceptive presidential address, it is clearly time for student affairs administrators to recognize their contributions to student learning and focus more of their professional effort and expertise in this arena. They should see themselves as educators whose primary responsibility is to promote student learning and personal development. To this end, it may be well to keep in mind the trenchant proverb that "it takes a whole village to raise a child."

References

Astin, A. (1970a). The methodology of research on college impact (I). *Sociology of Education, 43,* 223–254.

Astin, A. (1970b). The methodology of research on college impact (II). *Sociology of Education, 43,* 437–450.

Astin, A. (1993). *What matters in college: Four critical years revisited.* San Francisco: Jossey-Bass

Baxter Magolda, M. (1992). *Knowing and reasoning in college.* San Francisco: Jossey-Bass.

Bohr, L., et al. (1994). Cognitive effects of two-year and four-year colleges: A preliminary study. *Community College Review, 22,* 4–11.

Bohr, L, Pascarella, E., Nora, A., & Terenzini, P. (1995). Do Black students learn more at historically Black or predominantly White colleges? *Journal of College Student Development, 36,* 75–85.

Bowles, F., & DeCosta, F. (1971). *Between two worlds: A profile of Negro higher education.* New York: McGraw-Hill.

Dougherty, K. (1987). The effects of community colleges: Aid or hindrance to socioeconomic attainment? *Sociology of Education, 60,* 86–103.

Dougherty, K. (1992). Community colleges and baccalaureate attainment. *Journal of Higher Education, 63,* 188–214.

Feldman, K. (1987). Research productivity and scholarly accomplishment of college teachers as related to their instructional effectiveness: A review and explanation. *Research in Higher Education, 26,* 227–298.

Jencks, C., & Reisman, D. (1968). *The academic revolution.* Garden City, NY: Doubleday.

Kuh, G. (1993). In their own words: What students learn outside the classroom. *American Educational Research Journal, 30,* 277–304.

Pascarella, E. (1987). Are value-added analyses valuable? In *Assessing the outcomes of higher education: Proceedings of the 1986 ETS Invitational Conference.* Princeton, NJ: Educational Testing Service.

Pascarella, E. (1989). The development of critical thinking: Does college make a difference? *Journal of College Student Development, 30,* 19–26.

Pascarella, E., Bohr, L., Nora, A., & Terenzini, P. (1995). Cognitive effects of two-year and four-year colleges: *New evidence. Educational Evaluation and Policy Analysis, 17,* 83–96.

Pascarella, E., Edison, M., Nora, A., Hagedorn, L., & Braxton, J. (1995, April). *Effects of teacher organization/preparation and teacher skill/clarity on general cognitive skills in college.* Paper presented at the annual meeting of the American Educational Research Association, San Francisco.

Pascarella, E., et al. (1994). Impacts of 2-year and 4-year colleges on learning orientations: A preliminary study. *Community College Journal of Research and Practice, 18,* 577–589.

Pascarella, E. & Terenzini, P. (1991). *How college affects students: Findings and insights from twenty years of research.* San Francisco: Jossey-Bass.

Schroeder, C. (1994, March). Presidential address. Presentation to the annual meeting of the American College Personnel Association, Indianapolis, IN.

Smart, J., & Ethington, C. (1985). Early career outcomes of baccalaureate recipients: A study of native four-year and transfer two-year college students. *Research in Higher Education, 22,* 185–193.

Sowell, T. (1972). *Black education: Myths and tragedies.* New York: McKay.

Whitaker, D., & Pascarella, E. (1994). Two-year college attendance and socioeconomic attainment: Some additional evidence. *Journal of Higher Education, 65,* 194–210.

Wolfle, L. (1983). Effects of higher education on achievement for Blacks and Whites. *Research in Higher Education, 19,* 3–9.

Wolfle, L. (1987). Enduring cognitive effects of public and private schools. *Educational Researcher, 16,* 5–11.

CHAPTER 4

THE FACULTY

ASSOCIATE EDITOR: JAY CHRONISTER

Faculty on American college and university campuses have become the focus of an increasing amount of attention from a variety of sources in recent years. Included among the questions to which attention has been directed from sources external to the campus are: what is it that faculty do?; how much time do they spend on their jobs?; and are they doing the things we pay them to do? In addition to these questions which are being raised by legislators and tuition-paying students and parents, there are an increasing number of colleagues within the academic community who have been questioning what we do and whether it is the right thing to be doing.

In their 1996 book *American Professors*, Howard Bowen and Jack Schuster presented a status report on the professoriate including a profile of the characteristics of persons fulfilling the faculty role and the tasks inherent in that role. The authors discussed the stress that faculty members face in attempting to balance the demands of their instructional responsibilities with the need to be involved in research and scholarship to meet promotion criteria. In recent years the roles of faculty and how institutions reward the fulfillment of those roles have come under review and discussion by faculty as well as patrons external to the campus. The need to redefine the dimensions of scholarship and the scholarly role of faculty was the thrust of Boyer's challenge to higher education in 1990. In *Scholarship Reconsidered*, he called for a new creative perspective on the meaning of scholarship. Rather than retain only the traditional definition of scholarship with its sole focus on scholarship of discovery, the new perspective would recognize the scholarly dimension of four aspects of the faculty role. In recognition of the multi-faceted faculty role and the mosaic of faculty talent on college and university campuses, Boyer proposed that institutions and professional associations recognize the scholarly dimensions of the discovery of knowledge, the integration of knowledge, the application of knowledge, and the transmission of knowledge (teaching). Through such a redefinition colleges and universities would be able to more effectively fulfill their missions and relate faculty roles and reward systems to institutional missions.

Changes taking place in the academic profession in response to environmental factors and forces have been the focus of a number of studies and reports. Rice stated that a shift in the organizational cultures of colleges and universities from a collegial to a managerial emphasis creates strains for faculty. He views the strain to be a function of the conflict between the collegial tradition of decision-making and the growing use of an administrative authority-based style of management now evident on a growing number of campuses. In addition, he cites the growing emphasis upon an integrative role for faculty as opposed to the highly specialized and polarized academic role that has evolved over the years as another change to which the career academic is being asked to adjust.

Providing a different perspective on the challenges facing the academic profession, Clark views the profession as a multitude of academic tribes and territories that are becoming ever more fragmented and dispersed in responding to the needs and expectations of American society.

Jay Chronister is Professor of Leadership, Foundations and Policy at the University of Virginia. (jlc@virginia.edu)

Among the troubles that he views as challenges to the profession are: problems of "secondarization and remediation," excessive teaching, attenuated professional control, fragmented academic culture, and diminished intrinsic reward and motivation. Clark's attenuated professional control and fragmented academic culture closely align with Rice's issues of change in culture and polarization and the specialization of faculty role. In both cases these issues can be related to the growing influence of external stakeholders in the decisions about the missions and the utilization of faculty as resources in achieving those missions.

In addition to the above challenges to the content and substance of the academic career, the professoriate is undergoing a major structural change. This structural change is reflected in the fact that between 1975 and 1993 the composition of the faculty has changed in at least two ways. In 1975 approximately 70.1 percent of faculty were full-time and 29.9 percent were part-time. By 1993, approximately 58.4 percent of faculty were full-time and 41.6 percent were part-time. The special concerns and issues faced by part-time faculty have been well described in *The Invisible Faculty*.

Another significant change has also taken place within the ranks of the full-time faculty over that same period of time that has implications for the future of the professoriate. If tenure has been the linchpin of faculty careers and the relationship between the individual and the institution, evolving practices are attempting to change that relationship and to substitute alternative contractual ties between institutions and many of their faculty members. In 1975, 52.3 percent of full-time faculty were tenured, 29.1 percent tenure-track, and 18.6 percent non-tenure-track. By 1993, following a 25 percent increase in the overall size of the full-time contingent of faculty, 51.7 percent were tenured, 20.8 percent were tenure track, and 27.3 percent were in non-tenure-track appointments. The increase in the use of full-time non-tenure-track positions with term contracts is evidence of institutional attempts to retain a degree of flexibility in staffing that it is perceived the traditional tenure system does not provide.

As higher education enters the twenty-first century, the American professoriate is faced with the multiple issues of changed expectations of its role and function on campus by external stakeholders and by both external and internal challenges to one of the key characteristics of it as a profession, tenure. Challenges to tenure, managerial decisionmaking rather than traditional collegial governance, and questions about the viability of the pursuit of knowledge for its own sake during times of financial constraint will continue to be aspects of the environment in which the academic profession can expect to function for the foreseeable future.

References

Bowen, H. R. & Schuster, J. H., *American Professors: A National Resource Imperiled*. New York, NY: Oxford University Press, 1996.

Boyer, E. L., *Scholarship Reconsidered: Priorities of the Professoriate*. Lawrenceville, NJ: Princeton University Press, 1990.

Rice, R. E. "The Academic Profession in Transition: Toward a New Social Fiction," *Teaching Sociology*, January, 1985, 12–23.

Clark, B. R. "Small Worlds, Different Worlds: The Uniqueness and Troubles of American Academic Professions". *Daedalus*, Fall, 1997, *126*, 4, 21–42.

Gappa, J. and Leslie, D. W. The *Invisible Faculty*. San Francisco: Jossey-Bass, Publishers, 1993.

Benjamin, E., "Changing Distribution of Faculty by Tenure Status and Gender," Memorandum to the AAUP Executive Committee, January 29, 1997.

Suggested Supplementary Readings

Baldwin, Roger G. "Faculty Career Stages and Implications for Professional Development." In Schuster, Jack H., Daniel W. Wheeler, and Associates, *Enhancing Faculty Careers: Strategies for Development and Renewal*. San Francisco: Jossey-Bass Publishers, 1990.

Blackburn, Robert T. and Janet H. Lawrence. *Faculty at Work: Motivation, Expectation., Satisfaction*. Baltimore: Johns Hopkins University Press, 1995.

Bland, Carole J. and William H. Bergquist. *The Vitality of Senior Faculty Members: Snow on the Roof—Fire in the Furnace*. ASHE-ERIC Higher Education Report Volume 25, No. 7. Washington, D.C.: The George Washington University, Graduate School of Education and Human Development, 1997.

Boyer, Ernest L. *Scholarship Reconsidered: Priorities of the Professoriate*. Princeton, N.J.: Carnegie Foundation for the Advancement of Teaching, 1990.

Boyer, Ernest L., Philip G. Altbach, and Mary Jean Whitelaw. *The Academic Profession: An International Perspective*. Ewing, N.J.: California/Princeton Fulfillment Services, 1994.

Fairweather, James E. *Faculty Work and Public Trust*. Boston. Allyn and Bacon, 1996.

Finkelstein, Martin J., Robert K. Seal, and Jack H. Schuster. *The New Academic Generation: A Profession in Transformation*. Baltimore: The Johns Hopkins University Press, 1998.

Gappa, Judith and David W. Leslie. *The Invisible Faculty*. San Francisco: Jossey-Bass Publishers, 1993.

Glassick, Charles E., Mary T. Huber, and Gene I. Maeroff. *Scholarship Assessed: Evaluation of the Professoriate*. San Francisco: Jossey-Bass Publishers, 1997.

Gumport, Patricia J. "Public Universities as Academic Workplaces," *DAEDALUS*, 1997, *126*, 113–136.

Johnsrud, Linda K., and Christine D. Des Jarlais. "Barriers to Tenure for Women and Minorities," *The Review of Higher Education*, 1994, *17*, 335–353.

Levine, Arthur. "How the Academic Profession is Changing," *DAEDALUS*, 1997, *126*, 1–20.

O'Neil, Robert M. "Academic Freedom: Revolutionary Change or Business as Usual?" *The Review of Higher Education*, 1998, *21*, 257–265.

Tack, Martha W., and Carol L. Patitu. *Faculty Job Satisfaction: Women and Minorities in Peril*. ASHE-ERIC Higher Education Report No. 4. Washington, D.C.: The George Washington University, Graduate School of Education and Human Development, 1992.

Tierney, William G., and Robert A. Rhoads. *Faculty Socialization as a Cultural Process: A Mirror of Institutional Commitment*. ASHE-ERIC Higher Education Report No. 93–6. Washington, D.C.: The George Washington University, College of Education and Human Development, 1993.

Faculty Tasks and Talents

Howard M. Bowen and Jack Schuster

Our purpose in this chapter is to introduce the people who are the subjects of this book. We speak of them individually as "faculty member" or "faculty person" and collectively as "the faculty" or "the professoriate." What we have to say about them is well known to a few academics but is perceived only vaguely in the consciousness of the rank and file of the professoriate and known scarcely at all to the general public. Even when it is known, it is too often left unstated.

The word "faculty" as we use it refers to a corps of professional persons of substantial learning who are employed within American institutions of higher education and are engaged directly in teaching, research, related public service, institutional service, or combinations of these. We include both those who serve full time and those who serve part time. In this connection, the term "institution of higher education" refers to colleges and universities that may be public or private, but are not-for-profit and serve mainly post-secondary students. This definition leaves out a great many learned people who teach or conduct research. It excludes teachers or researchers who serve in institutions other than colleges and universities, for example, in elementary and secondary schools, proprietary schools, the armed forces, government agencies, business corporations, churches, research institutes, and the media. It also leaves out freelance scholars, authors, artists, and others, and excludes unemployed persons who have been or aspire to be members of the professoriate. Associations between faculty members and intellectuals who work outside the academic community are often close, and there is constant movement of persons back and forth between colleges and universities and other institutions or occupations. But only those who are at any given time connected with colleges and universities are considered to be "faculty."

Within higher education, our definition includes only persons who are engaged directly in teaching, research, or public service and hold the rank of instructor or above. It excludes administrators, specialists such as librarians and technicians, graduate assistants, and nonprofessional people employed in clerical or secretarial work, food service, housekeeping, plant maintenance, and the like.[1] The faculty as we define it included in 1982 about 700,000 persons (Table 1), or about a third[2] of the total employees of our colleges and universities.

Frequently it is assumed, given the depressed conditions in higher education since the early 1970s, that the number of faculty members has been declining sharply either because vacancies, as they occurred, have not been filled or because numerous faculty members have been laid off. These assumptions are incorrect. In fact, from 1970–71 on, as shown in Table 1, faculty numbers have increased year after year almost without exception until 1983–84. Since then, however, faculty numbers have leveled off and probably declined slightly.

It is probable that the number of faculty members will decline gradually over the next few years. We expect the downward trend to continue until about 1995–96.

Within the ranks of faculty there is great variety. It is due in part to the individualistic

TABLE 1
Number of Faculty* in Institutions of Higher Education, 1970–71 to 1982–83
(in thousands)

	Total	Full-Time Actual	Part-Time	Full-Time Equivalent
1970–71	474	369	104	402
1971–72	492	379	113	414
1972–73	500	380	120	417
1973–74	527	389	138	433
1974–75	567	406	161	457
1975–76	628	440	188	501
1976–77	633	434	199	501
1977–78	650	447	203	514
1978–79	647	445	202	513
1979–80	657	451	206	520
1980–81	678	466	212	537
1981–82	704	480	224	555
1982–83	713	485	228	561
1983–84	702	477	225	552
1984–85	680	464	216	536
1985–86	663	453	210	523

*Instructor and above

Source: National Center for Education Statistics, *Projections,* 1982, pp. 88–89, and *Digest of Education Statistics,* 1983, p. 103. Figures for 1979–80 to 1985–86 estimated by the National Center for Education Statistics.

personalities of faculty members. It is due also to the wide range of activities that different faculty members are called upon to perform. These vary with the type, size, governance, and affluence of the institutions they serve, and especially with the programs offered and the academic disciplines represented. The variety is also due to differences in gender, age, ethnicity, tenure, rank, and part-time versus full-time status. The professoriate is a mixture of many varied personalities and activities. And as we point out in Chapter 4 the faculty is becoming more diverse. Yet the vast majority of faculty members have much in common. Most have had a similar education culminating in advanced and extended study in perhaps 100 to 150 universities. They share an interest in teaching and learning and, with allowance for differences in disciplines, they conduct their teaching and research in comparable ways. The routines of campus life are remarkably similar over most of the American higher educational system. Faculty members are part of a nationwide communications network consisting of voluntary accreditation, professional associations, public licensing bodies, statewide coordination, multi-campus systems, consortia of institutions, and foundations and governmental granting agencies, and these impose or encourage considerable uniformity. Also there is much communication among institutions because of the mobility of faculty from one college or university to another. Finally, common attitudes and values arise in part because faculties in colleges of lesser prestige tend to emulate those in institutions of greater prestige.

On individual campuses, faculty members from different disciplines are drawn together through committees, senates, and social activities. Further, in the higher educational community there is a somewhat vague but influential conception of what the educated man or woman should be like and of which curricula, degree requirements, and campus extracurricular life are conducive to that ideal. Also the faculties in most colleges and universities engage in the consideration and analysis of values. They are involved in social and artistic criticism. They conduct philosophical systems and ideologies and they appraise existing social policies and recommend new ones. Through all these processes, the academic community creates an ethos. This ethos is not promulgated officially; it is certainly not shared by all the professoriate; it often differs from views prevailing among the general public, and it changes over time. Yet one can say that the weight of academic influence in any given period is directed toward a particular world outlook. Thus, though most faculty members enjoy considerable freedom in their work, and though there are substantial differences among them, it is not wholly outrageous to speak of an academic community as a nationwide (or even worldwide) subculture. And, despite the variety that exists in academe, it is appropriate for many purposes to treat the professoriate as a closely knit social group and not merely as a collection of disparate individuals or unrelated small groups.[3]

The remainder of this chapter and the three next chapters will be devoted to a review of the activities, characteristics, and attitudes of the American professoriate. We want the reader to be slightly skeptical because the available data about faculty are spotty and sometimes out of date. Furthermore, they are difficult to interpret because they are unstandardized. Definitional categories are seldom clearly defined and vary from one source to another.[4]

The Tasks of the Faculty

The faculties in American colleges and universities mostly conduct their work inconspicuously and without much public notice or acclaim. Their work, and its significance, is not widely observed, understood, or appreciated. Faculty members seldom become celebrities. Even Nobel Prize winners, members of the several national academies, or acknowledged great teachers are usually unknown except among members of their own academic fields and among colleagues and students on their own campuses.

There are several explanations of this anonymity. Much of higher learning is specialized and technical and is incomprehensible to the general public. Teaching is usually conducted privately and not as a public event witnessed by many people. The scholarly and research work of faculty goes on in privacy, even solitude. Moreover, knowledge advances through frequent but small accretions. Authentic breakthroughs that command public attention are infrequent. Furthermore, the style of life of most faculty members is quiet and simple. Indeed, they could not afford a notorious style of life even if so inclined. The exceptions to the rule of anonymity are mainly those

faculty members who distinguish themselves in literature and the arts, or become journalists and television personalities, or enter politics, or serve as athletic coaches, or become college presidents. And for this small minority, public fame is achieved by departing from conventional academic endeavors. For most of the professoriate, "fame" consists of the gratitude of students for good teaching and counseling, the respect of immediate colleagues and, above all, national or international recognition of scholarly attainments by members of one's own discipline. The anonymity of most faculty members by no means implies that what they do is unimportant or that it does not demand a high level of talent. Quite the contrary. What they do is extraordinarily important and demanding and should be more widely understood. Therefore, it may be worthwhile to explore what they actually do and what qualifications are required.

The work of college and university faculties may be divided into four overlapping tasks: instruction, research, public service, and institutional governance and operation. Almost all of the work done by academicians may be assigned to one or more of these four categories. Table 2 shows the estimated percentage of time devoted to each of these four tasks.

Instruction

The main function of faculties is instruction, that is, direct teaching of students. All but a few engage at least to some extent in instruction, and the great majority consider it to be their primary responsibility (Warren, 1982, pp. 18–19). Even at universities where research figures very prominently in academic reward systems, faculty on the whole spend most of their time teaching. Instruction involves formal teaching of groups of students in classrooms, laboratories, studios, gymnasia, and field settings. It also involves conferences, tutorials, and laboratory apprenticeships for students individually. In addition, it requires time-consuming backup work. Faculty members must keep up with the literature of their fields, they must prepare for their classroom presentations and discussion, and they must appraise the work of their students.

Instruction also entails advising students on matters pertaining to their current educa-

TABLE 2
Faculty Involvement in Four Tasks, by Type of Institution

	Instruction	Research	Public Service	Institutional Governance and Operation	Total
Private universities	55	25	4	16	100
Public universities	55	22	5	18	100
Elite liberal arts colleges	65	14	3	18	100
Public comprehensive institutions	68	10	5	17	100
Public colleges	68	10	4	18	100
Private liberal arts colleges	68	9	5	18	100
Community colleges	70	5	4	21	100
All institutions	64	14	4	18	100

Source: Baldridge et al., 1978, p. 103.

tional programs, plans for advanced study, choice of career, and sometimes more personal matters. And this advisory work leads naturally to numerous student requests for letters of recommendation and assistance in placement either in advanced study or jobs. When a faculty member is teaching as many as five to eight courses a year, as is common, and is in personal contact in any one term with as many as 50 to 300 students (in some cases more), these tasks become time-consuming and arduous.

Finally, in recounting the instructional duties of faculty, one must include their responsibility to serve as exemplars whom students might emulate (Carnegie Foundation for the Advancement of Teaching, 1977, pp. 82–86). Serving in this capacity is not something that faculty members must consciously work at beyond merely being themselves; but it is a role that many of them occupy—whether they will it or not and whether their influence is positive or negative. In presenting themselves to students they become living representatives of what their particular colleges or universities stand for. Whether intended or not, the character they display represents the values the insti-

tution is setting before its students. As Cardinal Newman observed a century ago:

The general principles of any study you may learn by books at home; but the details, the color, the tone, the air, the life which make it live in us, you must catch all these from those in whom it lives already.

Research[5]

Faculties contribute to the quality and productivity of society not only through their influence on students but also directly through the ramified endeavors we call "research." This term is used as shorthand for all the activities of faculties that advance knowledge and the arts. These include humanistic scholarship, scientific research in the natural and social sciences, philosophical and religious inquiry, social criticism, public-policy analysis, and cultivation of literature and the fine arts. These activities may be classed as "research" if they involve the discovery of new knowledge or the creation of original art and if they result in dissemination usually by means of some form of durable publication.[6] Only through dissemination do they become a significant advancement of knowledge or the arts. A brief comment on each of these activities may be in order.

The work of humanistic scholarship includes the discovery and rediscovery of past human experience, the preservation of texts and artifacts, the constant interpretation and reinterpretation of the knowledge acquired, and transmission of this knowledge from generation to generation. These activities are of inestimable value because they enable each generation to understand itself and its problems in the perspective of human experience.

Scientific research is divided into two overlapping categories: basic research which is intended to discover the laws of nature regardless of practical applicability; and applied research which is intended to discover ways of putting this knowledge to practical use. The distinction between basic and applied is not sharp, but it is important in understanding the role of college and university faculty. They have historically emphasized the pursuit of basic knowledge in quest of "truth" rather than applied knowledge in search of results. Faculty members, on the whole, have been free to choose their research programs in terms of intrinsic scientific interest rather than practical outcome. Experience shows that this freedom of choice often produces outcomes of great though unplanned practical value. For example, penicillin, hybrid seed corn, the computer, polio vaccine, and the "pill" were direct results of basic research conducted in universities.

Higher education has, of course, no monopoly on research. It is conducted also by business, government, private research institutes, labor unions, libraries, museums, performing arts organizations, freelance scholars and writers, and others. Doubtless if colleges and universities should divest themselves of the research function, other organizations could fill the gap. Nevertheless, many members of the higher educational community have for nearly a century engaged in research as an activity complementary to and supportive of their main function, which is instruction. College and university faculties occupy a significant, probably dominant, position in the intellectual and artistic life of the nation.

It is sometimes assumed that academic research is confined largely to major universities. Though they are more heavily committed than other higher educational institutions, all sectors of higher education—even two-year colleges—are involved at least to some degree (see Table 3). The nature of this involvement is shown in Table 4. Also, the research function is shared among faculty members of all disciplines, though the amount in the humanities and fine arts and in professional fields is somewhat less than in the natural and social sciences. Nevertheless substantial research activity occurs in all fields (Ladd & Lipset, 1975, pp. 349–53).

Research as conducted by faculties in higher education is for the most part produced jointly with instruction. The two activities are carried on by the same persons and within the same facilities, and they complement each other so closely that it is difficult, both conceptually and statistically, to identify the relative amounts of faculty time and other resources devoted to each. A few faculty members devote all their time to research and a sizable minority spend most of their time on it; on the other hand, many faculty members are involved in research not at all or only slightly. On the average, it is likely that research as here defined claims not more than a fifth of all faculty time (H. R. Bowen, 1977, pp. 291–94). Nations differ in the degree to which research is carried on within higher education. In the United States the degree of responsibility for research is probably greater than in most other countries.

Many observers ask: Is it necessary for higher education to be so deeply involved in research? Would it be desirable to follow the example of the Soviet Union and some other countries by organizing research in institutes that are separate from the universities? Without trying to answer these questions definitively, we would support an opinion for which there is no proof but which is widely shared in academic circles, namely, that research, and public service as well, contribute to the intellectual aliveness of our universities and colleges by attracting many creative and stimulating faculty members and by encouraging and sustaining their intellectual vitality. It may be added that the success of American science and scholarship, which clearly leads the world (though others are catching up), suggests that it has not been a mistake to entrust the colleges and universities with considerable responsibility for research and public service.

TABLE 3
Faculty Involvement in Research, by Type and Quality of Institution

	Percentage of Faculty Members		
	with Heavy Involvement in Research	with One or More Publications in the Past Two Years	with Teaching Loads of 10 Hours or Less in Class per Week
Universities			
High quality	50	79	91
Medium quality	40	72	85
Low quality	28	57	72
Four-Year Colleges			
High quality	26	54	72
Medium quality	12	37	52
Low quality	10	29	42
Two-Year Colleges	5	14	22
All institutions	24	48	60

Source: Fulton and Trow (in Trow, 1975, pp. 44, 46, 48).

TABLE 4
Median Percentage of Faculty Involved in Research in Various Ways, 1972–73

Primarily committed to research (versus teaching)	24%
Published or edited books (over lifetime to date)	
None	69
1–2	22
3–4	6
5 or more	4
Published writings (in last two years)	
None	53
1–2	24
3–4	12
5 or more	11

Source: Ladd & Lipset, 1975, pp. 349–53.

Moreover, on the much debated question of whether faculty pursuit of research interferes with teaching, our opinion is that it enlivens teaching.[7] There are undoubtedly instances of faculty members who neglect their teaching because of their keen interest in research. But the academic community is surely on the right track when it gives weight to intellectual and artistic achievement when judging faculty members for appointment and promotion. However, they should and generally do also give significant weight to performance in teaching. Fulton and Trow (in Trow, 1975, p. 291) concluded from their detailed study of research in higher education that "only a very small minority of faculty are uninterested in

teaching" and that "the normative climate in the United States, as reflected in academics' personal preferences, is far more favorable to teaching than most observers would have predicted." This view was strongly endorsed by Ladd (1979) who found that three-fourths of faculty respondents agree that their interests lean toward teaching (as contrasted with research) and agree that teaching effectiveness, not publications, should be the primary criterion for promotion of faculty.[8]

Public Service

The public service activities of faculties are perhaps less recognized and less understood than their other functions. Mostly, they are byproducts of instruction and research, but they are far from trivial (Crosson, 1983; Bonner, 1981). If public service is defined narrowly as specifically budgeted activities designed expressly for the benefit of the general public, the percentage of faculty time devoted to public service is quite small. But if public service is defined more broadly, as we think it should be, it looms up as a byproduct of much more than incidental or minor importance.

Some public services are performed by faculty in connection with their teaching and research. The most notable is health care delivered by faculty in university hospitals and clinics. Other examples are the operation by faculties of farms, dairies, hotels, restaurants, and other enterprises related to instruction and research. Similarly, as a byproduct of instruction, some faculty in most colleges and universities are instrumental in providing recreational and cultural activities for persons in surrounding communities. These include dramatic and musical performances, library services, museum exhibits, broadcasting, recreational facilities, and spectator sports.

Faculties are also engaged in activities designed specifically to serve the public, usually in an educational and consulting capacity. The most important example is agricultural extension which combines adult education with consulting services for farmers, agribusiness, and consumers. Some universities offer similar organized consulting services for local government, school districts, public-health organizations, business firms, labor unions, lawyers, and other organizations (Mayville, 1980).

Perhaps the most important public service function of faculties is that they serve as a large pool of diversified and specialized talent available on call for consultation and technical services to meet an infinite variety of needs and problems. The faculty pool of talent would be of value on a standby basis, even if never used, just as hospitals or fire stations or auto repair shops have standby value. But in fact academic faculties are frequently called upon. Sometimes they serve on behalf of their institutions and sometimes on their own as freelance consultants and technical experts. The services may be in the form of technical consulting, public addresses, testimony before legislative committees or courts of law, arbitration, temporary employment on leave of absence, or preparation of studies. For example, if the State Department needs to know some details of Sino-Russian relations, if a physician needs advice about a rare disease, if a museum needs guidance in the restoration of a damaged painting, if a farmer needs assistance in overcoming an infestation of insects, if a community wishes information on land-use planning, faculty members somewhere will be able to help.

Society looks to the academic community not only for information and advice, but also in many cases for actual execution and administration of programs. Faculty members often go on foreign missions, administer governmental laboratories, organize research centers, provide statistical services, etc. Indeed, a new breed of professors has emerged who move easily between the academic world and business or government. Such professors are frequently called upon to serve in the state or federal civil service, they occasionally serve as high-ranking political appointees, they are sometimes elected to public office, they become members of special commissions, they help administer foundations, and they consult with business firms.

In the past decade or two the need for "knowledge transfer" from the discoverers to the users has been increasingly recognized. As Lynton (1982, p. 21) has observed: "The traditional notion of the scholar focusing solely on the discovery of new knowledge and letting its application and dissemination trickle down to the user is simply no longer appropriate."

Institutional Governance and Operation

Faculties, individually and collectively, usually occupy a prominent role in the policies, decisions, and ongoing activities falling within the wide-ranging realm of institutional governance and operation. It is almost inevitable that faculty members would be thus called upon because the work of most colleges and universities is divided among many highly specialized and abstruse disciplines, each of which is well understood only by the faculty members engaged in it. In the largest universities, instruction, research, and public service may be offered in several hundred separate fields or identifiable subfields, and even in small institutions the number of disciplines may range from twenty to fifty or more. Under these conditions, no central authority would be competent to make decisions for all of these fields and subfields as to what should be taught, what research and public service projects should be undertaken, how the teaching and research should be conducted, or what requirements for admission, academic standing, and graduation should be established. Such decisions must be largely delegated to the various specialized faculties, usually organized into departments of professional schools, and within these units the content of particular courses must be decided by individual faculty members. Moreover, no central authority would be qualified to make decisions on the appointment, promotion, tenure, and firing of faculty members, or to decide what kind of building space and equipment each field should have, what books and journals should be in the library, and what kind of secretarial and research support for faculty members should be available. All of these decisions ultimately find their way to the central administration of any institution usually through the budgetary process. Yet in practice, at least among the most reputable institutions, the influence of the departments is substantial and often decisive.

The various specialized departments are interrelated in many ways. They teach each other's students, they compete for enrollment and for budget, they collaborate on research and public service, and they are keenly interested in the success of the whole institution to which they have committed their talents. As a result, there is need for the entire institutional faculty to serve as a deliberative, advisory, and even legislative body. The administration also needs access to faculty opinion and advice and therefore must have lines of communication to faculty. In most institutions there are various senates, committees, councils, task forces, and even kitchen cabinets which create two-way communications between faculty and administration. In a substantial minority of cases, faculty unions figure prominently in faculty-administration communications, and in some of these instances, unions displace the more traditional bodies. Institutions differ in the extent and form of faculty participation in governance, but all must have apparatuses for the delegation of decision-making, for communication and cooperation among the departments,

and for two-way communication between central administrators and faculty. Substantial amounts of faculty time and effort are required for these activities which are not mere busy-work but an essential part of the task of making institutions manageable.

An important feature of faculty participation in the making of institutional policies and decisions is that it has a strong influence on faculty morale. Faculty members are intelligent and highly educated people who feel qualified to have opinions not only on matters affecting them personally and their departments, but also on matters pertaining to the institution as a whole. They also feel entitled to know about events and forces and decisions that are affecting the institutions. Therefore, reasonable involvement of faculty and communication with them are critical in the decision-making process of any college or university. This involvement is of special importance in connection with the appointment of administrative officers. Institutions vary, however, in the extent of faculty participation, and morale tends to vary accordingly.

Faculty members also contribute enormously to institutional success through their efforts to create and sustain a rich cultural, intellectual, and recreational environment on the campus. The list of their contributions to extracurricular life is long but it is worth recounting because it is so impressive and so important. On virtually every campus faculty members contribute their time and effort, and sometimes their money, to enrich the campus environment. They serve as impresarios or committee members in organizing outside lectures, concerts, art exhibits, and plays; they frequently give lectures or performances themselves; they help organize and sustain religious activities for students; they serve as advisers to student housing groups, student clubs, and student newspapers and radio stations; they befriend individual students; they open their homes to students or join students informally or at meals; they organize programs for foreign students; they take students on field trips; they serve on committees related to athletics, student social life, and student discipline; they help carry on an active social life for the faculty itself; they participate in commencement and other events; they keep in touch with alumni; and they perform many other extracurricular services which are often little noticed.

Not all faculty members do all these things but most do some of them some of the time. In doing so, they often express their individual personalities and their special interests, and they help to weld the campus into a meaningful community and to make of it an agreeable and civilized place for both students and faculty.

The role of faculty in the governance and operation of colleges and universities was recognized by the Supreme Court of the United States in the Yeshiva case *(National Labor Relations Board v. Yeshiva University, 444 U.S. 672, 1980)*. In this case the Court ruled that faculty members—at least at some private institutions—are not employees in the ordinary sense but rather are members of "management." On the basis of this finding the Court decided that institutions where these conditions exist are not covered by federal legislation pertaining to collective bargaining. In several recent cases, the National Labor Relations Board has ruled that faculty members are managerial employees and may not bargain collectively under federal labor law (Chronicle of Higher Education, June 6, 1984) unless the employer chooses to permit them to bargain. The Yeshiva case, which is opposed by those faculty who are committed to collective bargaining, clearly recognizes the reality that in many institutions faculty are in effect part of "management." One may add that in institutions where this is not so, changes which will bring about meaningful participation of faculty in governance may be overdue (Strohm, 1983, pp. 10–15). We see no necessary inconsistency, however, between faculty participation and strong presidential leadership (Commission on Strengthening Presidential Leadership, 1984).

Learning

We have identified and described four basic functions of faculties—instruction, research, public service, and institutional service. These are based mostly on a single unifying process, namely, learning. Learning in this sense means bringing about desired changes in the traits of human beings (instruction), discovering and interpreting knowledge (research), applying knowledge to serve the needs of the general public (public service), and creating an envi-

ronment that contributes to and facilitates learning (institutional service). Learning is the chief stock-in-trade of the professoriate. It occurs in all fields, it takes place in diverse settings, and it serves varied clienteles.

Institutions tend to be categorized largely on the basis of their relative emphasis on the four functions. Community colleges and regional four-year institutions focus on instruction and on public service for local or regional constituencies; major universities emphasize research, advanced study, and public service directed toward statewide, national, and international clienteles; liberal arts colleges and smaller universities lie between these extremes by emphasizing instruction and the creation of institutional environments favorable to human development. But most institutions engage in all four functions to some degree. Indeed, these functions are mutually supportive. Instruction may be enriched if it occurs in an environment of discovery, intellectual excitement, and contact with the outside world and its problems. Similarly, research and public service may be enhanced when they are combined with instruction. This does not imply that every community college or liberal arts college should become a great research center. Nor does it deny that the universities can overdo research and service to the neglect of instruction. It implies only that the spirit of inquiry and public service is appropriate in the academic enterprise.

The multifunctional role of a college or university may be illustrated by the work of a typical faculty member. In a given week, in addition to formal teaching, he or she may engage in a variety of activities related to learning. For example, the faculty person may advise several graduate students on their research, counsel with several undergraduates on their academic or personal problems, invite a group of students to a social affair, discuss an intellectual issue with a colleague, write testimony for a legislative committee, give a talk to a local professional society, read one or more professional journals, record data from a laboratory experiment in progress, attend a meeting of the academic senate or of a department, have lunch with a prospective colleague, block out a chapter in a new book, and attend a public lecture.[9]

Qualifications of Faculty

We have defined in a general way the tasks and responsibilities of faculty in American colleges and universities. We turn now to the question: What are the qualifications of persons who undertake these tasks and assume these responsibilities? Faculty members serve in varied institutions ranging from community colleges and small liberal arts colleges to huge universities, they cover a host of disciplines and subdisciplines, and they deal with students of diverse ages, backgrounds, interests, and temperaments. Moreover, the faculty members themselves present a variety of backgrounds, personalities, educational philosophies, interests, and temperaments. Given all this variety, is it possible to say anything useful about the qualifications of people who are to perform successfully the functions of faculty members? We think that to consider this question is possible and worthwhile because it sheds some light on the kinds of people the academic profession needs to recruit and retain, and undergirds the policy recommendations we present in later chapters. We shall begin, by considering the minimal qualifications.

There are no precise formal standards for admission to the professoriate such as exist for physicians, lawyers, or elementary and secondary school teachers. Each institution is free to choose its faculty according to its own best judgment without external regulation. Faculty members, therefore, vary considerably in their formal credentials. The Ph.D. is the most frequent credential for faculty in four-year institutions, and the Master's degree for those in two-year colleges. These two degrees are generally regarded as the basic standard for the two types of institutions. But in both about a quarter of the faculty have other credentials. In such cases, it is usually assumed that the combination of formal education and experience is at least comparable to that of the Ph.D. in four-year institutions, and to the Master's degree in two-year colleges.

How intelligent are faculty members? Leaving aside controversies about the measurement of intelligence, one kind of evidence would be intelligence scores of some sort. Though little such evidence is available, some conception of the caliber of people who earn the Ph.D., and also those who become academics, is provided by the following average IQ scores (Berelson, 1960, p. 139. Cf., Herrnstein, 1973, pp. 111–39; Schwebel, 1968, pp. 207–14; Cole, 1979, pp. 68, 153, 155):

High School students	105
High School graduates	110
College entrants	115
College graduates	121
Graduate students:	
Natural Science	128
Psychology	132
Social Science	124
Humanities	128
Ph.D.s:	
Natural Science	133
Psychology	137
Social Science	124
Humanities	128
Faculty members:	
Physics-Mathematics	143
Sociology	130
Psychology	135
Chemistry	136
Biology	129

These scores suggest that intelligence levels of academic people fall between two and three standard deviations above the mean for the general population.[10]

But the holding of a degree, or its equivalent, is not sufficient qualification for membership in the professoriate. This is particularly true of the Master's degree which often represents little more than eight or ten courses taken beyond the Bachelor's degree. But it is also true of the Ph.D. even though that degree usually involves several years of serious advanced study and the writing of an extended dissertation. But even this endeavor—often extending over a five-to ten-year period—does not guarantee all the competencies required of a faculty member. The characteristics one expects in considerable measure of the faculty member, whether in two-year or four-year institutions, can best be stated in terms of specific qualifications, not merely in terms of earned degrees. In our judgment, these qualifications are as follows (Cf. Levine, 1978, pp. 176–78):

1. Superior general intelligence: in the upper 5 or 10 percent of the population.

2. Sound general education:

a. Ability to communicate correctly and effectively in speaking and writing

b. Intellectual curiosity

c. Open-mindedness and tolerance

d. Breadth: intellectual and cultural interests beyond their special fields and ability to view the special field in a broad context

e. Contemplative disposition.

3. Keen interest in and mastery of the special field:

a. Knowledge of the literature, ability to interpret it, and the energy and motivation to keep up to date

b. Ability to give cogent lectures, to discuss issues, to hold reasoned opinions, to write book reviews, and to prepare essays and memoranda

c. If the special field is practical, the ability and knowledge to be a successful practitioner.

4. Self-motivation:

a. Dedication to teaching as a vocation

b. Capacity for hard work in an environment that provides little direct supervision.

5. Rapport with students: patience, ability to elicit cooperation and respect, and plausibly to serve as exemplar to some.

6. A personage; not a nonentity.

These standards are minimal. They do not include the desirable trait of intellectual or artistic creativity, as evidenced, for example, by the ability to conduct important research, to produce significant works of art, to contribute to the leading journals, or to write learned books. Also these qualifications do not include such useful traits as exceptional entrepreneurial or administrative abilities, or extraordinary skills in the arts of persuasion, including public relations or fund-raising. But even though the above standards are minimal they are not trivial. Only a small minority of the general population can meet them. And surely not all faculty members conform to these criteria.

But the profession should, and in fact does, attract many persons whose talents exceed the minimum requirements. The profession ranges from a few submarginal persons to some of the most brilliant, the most learned, the most dedicated, the most creative, the most versatile people in our society. Many of these persons also have exceptional abilities in entrepreneurship, administration, or the arts of persuasion—talents which are useful within academic communities.

In judging the qualifications of faculty, it should be noted that the great majority of those in four-year colleges have had a rigorous and lengthy education. Though the minimal time for getting the Ph.D. is three years beyond the Bachelor's degree, most doctoral candidates spend much more time than that in formal study, ordinarily six to eight years (see p. 173). Moreover, there is ample evidence that the rank and file of the academic profession are intellectually a superior group (cf., L. Wilson, 1979, p. 22). They may be more contemplative than business executives, less combative than lawyers, and less affluent than doctors, but on the whole they are no less capable.

Whether in the future the professoriate will attract and hold its share of talent, ranging from the marginal to the most gifted, depends on the conditions and remuneration in the profession. If over a period of years these are not competitive, colleges and universities will not attract their share of the best talent and will be forced to operate with faculties of relatively marginal abilities.

Career Options

It is often assumed that members of the professoriate were predestined in youth for academic careers, and that after entering the profession were committed to it for a lifetime. On the contrary, most of the persons who meet the qualifications for the professoriate are versatile and have more than a single career option open to them. The specific characteristics that fit them for faculty positions also qualify them for various non-academic pursuits. Career options are open to them in youth, in mid-career, and even after retirement.

In their youth, before making a commitment to any vocation, most such people may choose among numerous professional careers. In doing so, they can weigh the pluses and minuses of academic life in comparison with other feasible careers.

Even after having prepared for an academic career by earning a Ph.D. or in other ways, various options would still be open to most of them. For example, those prepared for faculty positions in any of the natural sciences, the professional fields, and some of the social sciences might readily become independent practitioners or employees of government, corporations, or private non-profit organizations. Chemists might work for industry and economists for banks, lawyers and physicians might go into independent practice, social workers might be employed by government, and so on. A review of the disciplines included in the curricula of colleges and universities suggests that a large majority of all potential faculty members might, if given time for placement, find employment outside academe if they wished. Those qualified for academic work in all of the following fields would likely have such options:

Health professions: medicine, dentistry, pharmacy, nursing, hospital administration, various allied health professions

Natural sciences and related fields: physical, biological, and earth sciences, engineering, agriculture, home economics, mathematics, statistics, computer science

Social sciences, humanities, and related fields: psychology, economics, law, business administration, public administration, public policy analysis, library science, criminal justice, education, theology.

The only academic fields for which outside opportunities are seriously limited are the humanities such as literature and history and a few social studies such as anthropology. These are important fields educationally, but they do not provide many outside employment opportunities. But even these fields offer increasing options; moreover, some of the people trained in them can if necessary be retooled for employment within or outside academe. Others are more versatile and can adapt rather easily without formal retraining.

Mobility is also possible for faculty persons in mid-career. This is demonstrated by the considerable movement of people into and out of academe year after year, even in times of a depressed economy.[11] The net flow varies from year to year depending on compensation and working conditions in academe relative to that in outside employment. Fulton and Trow (in Trow, 1975, pp. 6–7) reported that 68 percent of all faculty had worked outside the academic profession for at least a year since obtaining their Bachelor's degrees. Freeman (1971, p. 177) found that one in four living Ph.D.s had made a shift from academic to non-academic or the reverse at least once in their careers. Toombs (1979, p. 10) found that 59 percent of a sample of academic people listed in Who's Who had had non-academic work experience, and that 19 percent of a comparable set of people in business or the professions had had an association with the academic world. And several studies (summarized in Chapter 12) reported that half to three-quarters of all faculty earn income for services rendered outside their institutions. Not all of this work is at a high professional level, but much of it is in the form of research, consulting, writing for newspapers and magazines, lecturing, professional practice of various kinds, temporary assignments for government, and other professional work. Even after retirement many professors find remunerative work outside academe.

The facts on mobility and on outside employment tend to verify that many academics are versatile, that their services are of value outside the ivy-covered walls, that they could be mobile if they wished to move, and that their career decisions are responsive to changes in the relative conditions of work and remuneration in higher education. These facts also suggest that colleges and universities must in the long run be able to pay salaries and provide working conditions that render higher education competitive with comparable occupations in government, business, the independent professions, and other occupations.

Concluding Comments

The work of faculty members is extraordinarily important to the economic and cultural development of the nation. To do this work well requires people of considerable talent ranging perhaps from persons in the upper 5 or 10 percent of the population to the most brilliant and gifted persons at the very peak of human abilities. Most of these people have desirable career options. To attract and retain an adequate supply of such persons for our colleges and universities requires compensation and working conditions competitive with those in other occupations end industries for comparable talent. Since about 1970 the competitive position of American higher education has been slipping, and there is danger of continuing deterioration. Under these conditions, the caliber of faculties in our colleges and universities could be on the verge of serious decline with disastrous consequences for the nation. This is a matter we shall consider at length.

The faculties of America are a great national resource which has been subjected to deferred maintenance. Just as deferred maintenance of roads, water systems, dams, and campus buildings may go on for years without causing collapse—or indeed without the damage being noticeable to the casual observer—so the deferred maintenance of faculty may persist over long periods without widely noticeable effects. But eventually, such deferred maintenance of both physical plant and faculty will lead to a day of reckoning and exorbitant costs will be involved in restoration (cf. Lynton, 1982, p. 19). Serious impairment of the nation's academic talent may be closer than is generally realized.

Notes

1. Some of these people may engage part time in instruction and research and if so are counted as part-time faculty.
2. Computed from data in National Center for Education Statistics, *Digest of Education Statistics*, 1983, p. 102.
3. For a concise description of the academic career, see: *Careers, Inc.*, 1984.
4. Frequent problems are that different statistical studies cover different categories of institutions or different categories of faculty, without designating the specific coverage. For example, some include two-year institutions and some do not; some include part-time faculty or assistants or administrators and some do not. Some data are based on full-time equivalent faculty, others on head counts.
5. This section draws substantially upon H. R. Bowen, 1977, chap. 10.
6. Or presentation in the case of sculpture, painting, and the like. It should be noted also that the results of research are sometimes disseminated by word of mouth.
7. Participation by students in faculty-guided research activities constitutes an important mode of student learning, particularly at the graduate level.
8. In a survey directed toward older faculty members, a question was asked as to whether the "growing emphasis on research and publication improved or diminished the quality of instruction." About one-third answered "improved"; one-third, "diminished"; nearly one-fifth answered "no change." AAUP *Academe*, Nov.-Dec. 1983, p. 9. Finkelstein (1984, p. 126) observed: "That good research is both a necessary and sufficient condition for good teaching . . . is not resoundingly supported by the evidence. Resoundingly disconfirmed however, is the notion that research involvement detracts from good teaching by channeling professorial time and effort away from the classroom."
9. For an inventory of 71 activities related to professorial work, see Braxton & Toombs, 1982.
10. In interpreting these figures, it should be noted that not all Ph.D.s become faculty members. Many enter other professions. In our opinion, however, higher education—in the past at least—has been able to compete strongly for intellectual talent.
11. See Chapter 9 and Appendix C.

Small Worlds, Different Worlds: The Uniquenesses and Troubles of American Academic Professions

BURTON R. CLARK

The academic profession is a multitude of academic tribes and territories.[1] As in days of old, it is law, medicine, and theology. It is now also high-energy physics, molecular biology, Renaissance literature, childhood learning, and computer science. Built upon a widening array of disciplines and specialties, it hosts subcultures that speak in the strange tongues of econometrics, biochemistry, ethnomethodology, and deconstructionism. Driven by a research imperative that rewards specialization, its fragmentation is slowed, though not fully arrested, by limited resources to fund all the new and old lines of effort in which academics would like to engage. Already very great, knowledge growth builds in a self-amplifying fashion. Subject differentiation follows in train, not least in a national system of universities and colleges, such as the American, that is both hugely based on research and generously inclusive in adding subjects to the now-endless list of what legitimately can be taught. As subjects fragment, so does the academic profession, turning it evermore into a profession of professions.

No less important in the differentiation of the academic profession in America is the dispersion of faculty among institutions in a system that, when viewed internationally, must be seen as inordinately large, radically decentralized, extremely diversified, uniquely competitive, and uncommonly entrepreneurial. A high degree of institutional dispersion positions American faculty in many varied sectors of a national "system" that totaled 3,600 institutions in the mid-1990s: a hundred-plus "research universities" of high research inten-

sity; another hundred "doctoral-granting" universities that grant only a few doctorates and operate off of a small research base; five hundred and more "master's colleges and universities," a catch-all category of private and public institutions that have graduate as well as undergraduate programs, offering master's degrees but not doctorates; still another six hundred "baccalaureate colleges," heavily private and varying greatly in quality and in degree of concentration on the liberal arts; a huge array of over 1,400 two-year colleges, 95 percent public in enrollment, whose individual comprehensiveness includes college-transfer programs, short-term vocational offerings, and adult education; and finally a leftover miscellany of some seven hundred "specialized institutions" that do not fit into the above basic categories.[2]

These major categories in turn contain much institutional diversity. Buried within them are historically black colleges, Catholic universities, women's colleges, fundamentalist religious universities and colleges, and such distinctive institutions as the Julliard School (of Music), the Bank Street College of Education, and Rockefeller University. The American faculty is distributed institutionally all over the map, located in the educational equivalents of the farm and the big city, the ghetto and the suburbs, the darkened ravine located next to a coal mine and the sunny hill overlooking a lovely valley.

Disciplinary and institutional locations together compose the primary matrix of induced and enforced differences among American academics. These two internal fea-

"Small Worlds, Different Worlds: The Uniquenesses and Troubles of American Academic Professions," by Burton R. Clark, reprinted from *Daedelus*, Vol. 126, No. 4, Fall 1997, American Academy of Arts & Sciences.

tures of the system itself are more important than such background characteristics of academics as class, race, religion, and gender in determining work-centered thought and behavior. These primary dimensions convert simple statements about "the professor" in "the college" or "the university" into stereotypes. We deceive ourselves every time we speak of *the* college professor, a common habit among popular critics of the professoriate who fail to talk to academics in their varied locations and to listen to what they say. Simple summary figures and averages extracted from surveys, e.g., "68 percent of American professors like their mothers" or "On the average, American professors teach eight and a half hours a week," also should be avoided. Understanding begins with a willingness to pursue diversity.

Different Worlds, Small Worlds

The disciplinary creation of different academic worlds becomes more striking with each passing year. In the leading universities, the clinical professor of medicine is as much a part of the basic work force as the professor of English. The medical academic might be found in a cancer ward, interacting intensively with other doctors, nurses, orderlies, laboratory assistants, a few students perhaps, and many patients in a round of tightly scheduled activities that can begin at six in the morning and extend into the evenings and weekends. Such academics are often under considerable pressure to generate income from patient-care revenues; their faculty groups negotiate with third-party medical plans and need a sizeable administrative staff to handle patient billing. Salaries may well depend on group income, which fluctuates from year to year and is directly affected by changes in the health-care industry and the competitive position of a particular medical school-hospital complex. Even in a tenured post, salary may not be guaranteed. Sizeable research grants must be actively and repetitively pursued; those who do not raise funds from research grants will find themselves encumbered with more clinical duties.

The humanities professor in the leading universities operates in a totally different environment. To begin with, teaching "loads" are in the range of four to six hours a week, office hours are at one's discretion, and administrative assignments vary considerably with one's willingness to cooperate. The humanities academic typically interacts with large numbers of beginning students in introductory classes in lecture halls; with small numbers of juniors and seniors in specialized upper-division courses; and with a few graduate students in seminars and dissertation supervision around such highly specialized topics as Elizabethan lyric and Icelandic legend. Much valuable work time can be spent at home, away from the "distractions" of the university office.

About what is the humanities academic thinking and writing? Attention may center on a biography of Eugene O'Neill, an interpretation of what Jane Austen really meant, an effort to trace Lillian Hellman's political passions, or a critique of Derrida and deconstructionism. Professors seek to master a highly specialized segment of literature and maximize individual interpretation. The interests of humanities professors are reflected not only in the many sections and byways of such omnibus associations as the Modern Language Association but also in the specificities of the Shakespeare Association of America, the Dickens Society, the D. H. Lawrence Society of North America, the Speech Association of America, the Thomas Hardy Society of America, and the Vladimir Nabokov Society. Tocqueville's famous comment on the propensity of Americans to form voluntary associations is nowhere more true than in the academic world.

Disciplinary differences are of course not limited to the sharp contrast between life in a medical school and in a department of English. The work of Tony Becher and others on the cultures of individual disciplines has shown that bodies of knowledge variously determine the behavior of individuals and departments.[3] Disciplines exhibit discernible differences in individual behavior and group action, notably between "hard" and "soft" subjects and "pure" and "applied" fields: in a simple fourfold classification, between hard-pure (physics), hard-applied (engineering), soft-pure (history), and soft-applied (social work). Across the many fields of the physical sciences, the biological sciences, the social sciences, the humanities, and the arts, face-to-face research reveals varied work assignments, symbols of identity, modes of authority, career lines, and associational linkages. Great differences in the academic life often appear between letters and science departments and the many professional-school domains in which a concern for the ways and needs of an outside profession must necessarily be combined with the pursuit of science and truth for its own sake. The popular images of Mr. Chips chatting up undergraduates and Einsteinian, white-haired, remote scholars dreaming up esoteric mathematical equations are a far cry from the realities of academic work that helps prepare schoolteachers, librarians, social workers, engineers, computer experts, architects, nurses, pharmacists, business managers, lawyers, and doctors—and, in some academic locales, also morticians, military personnel, auto mechanics, airport technicians, secretaries, lathe operators, and cosmetologists. For over a century, American higher education has been generous to a fault in admitting former outside fields, and new occupations, into the academy—a point made by historians of higher education and of the professions.[4]

Because research is the first priority of leading universities, the disciplinary differentiation of every modern system of higher education is self-amplifying. The American system is currently the extreme case of this phenomenon. Historic decentralization and competitiveness prompted Charles William Eliot at Harvard and others at the old colleges of the last half of the nineteenth century to speed up the nascent evolution from the age of the college to the age of the university. This evolution turned professors loose to pursue specialized research and to teach specialized subjects at the newly created graduate level, even as students were turned loose to pick and choose from an array of undergraduate courses that was to become ever more bewildering. Throughout the twentieth century and especially in the last fifty years, the reward system of promoting academics on the grounds of research and published scholarship has become more deeply rooted in the universities (and would-be universities and leading four-year colleges) with almost every passing decade. The many proliferating specialties of the knowledge-producing disciplines are like tributaries flowing into a mammoth river of the research imperative.

The most serious operational obstacles to this research-driven amplification are the limitations of funding and the institutional need to teach undergraduates and beginning graduate students the codified introductory knowledge of the various fields. There also remains in American higher education the long-standing belief in the importance of liberal or general education—a task, we may note, that Europeans largely assign to secondary schools. The saving remnant of academics who uphold the banner of liberal and general education are able to sally forth in full cry periodically—the 1920s, the late 1940s, the 1990s—to group some specialties into more general courses, narrow the options in distribution requirements from, say, four hundred to one hundred courses, insist that teaching take priority over research, and in general raise a ruckus about the dangers of the specialized mind. Meanwhile, promotion committees on campus continue their steady scrutiny of individual records of research-based scholarship. Central administrators work to build an institutional culture of first-rateness, as it is defined competitively across the nation and the world according to the reputations of noted scholars and departments. Sophisticated general educators and liberal-arts proponents in the universities recognize the primacy of the substantive impulse and learn how to work incrementally within its limits.

Institutional Differentiation

As powerful as self-amplifying disciplinary differences have become in dividing the American professoriate, institutional diversity now plays an even more important role. This axis of differentiation places approximately two-thirds of American academics in settings other than that of doctoral-granting universities. We find about a fourth of the total faculty in the colleges and universities that offer degree work as far as the master's; a small share, about 7 percent, in the liberal-arts colleges; and a major bloc of a third or so (over 250,000) in the nearly 1,500 community colleges.[5] In student numbers in 1994, the universities had just 26 percent of the total enrollment; the master's level institutions, 21 percent; the baccalaureate colleges, 7 percent; the specialized institutions, 4 percent; and the community colleges, 43 percent—by far the largest share.[6] The two-year colleges admit over 50 percent of entering students. There is no secret that academics in this latter section do an enormous amount of the work of the system at large.

These major locales exhibit vast differences in the very basis of academic life, namely, the balance of effort between undergraduate teaching and advanced research and research training. Teaching loads in the leading universities come in at around four to six hours a week, occasionally tapering down to two to three hours—a class a week, a seminar a week—while sometimes, especially in the humanities, rising above six. The flip side is that faculty commonly expect to spend at least half their time in research, alone or in the company of graduate students, other faculty, and research staff. We need not stray very far among the institutional types, however, before we encounter teaching loads that are 50, 100, and 200 percent higher. The "doctoral-granting universities" that are not well supported to do research often exact teaching loads of nine to twelve hours, as do the liberal-arts colleges, especially those outside the top fifty. In master's colleges, loads of twelve hours a week in the classroom are common. In the community colleges, the standard climbs to fifteen hours and loads of eighteen and twenty-one hours are not unknown. Notably, as we move from the research universities through the middle types to the two-year institutions, faculty involvement shifts from advanced students to beginning students; from highly selected students to an open-door clientele; from young students in the traditional college age-group to a mix of students of all ages in short-term vocational programs as well as in course work leading toward a bachelor's degree. In the community colleges, students in the college-transfer track are numerically overshadowed by students in terminal vocational programs, and both are frequently outnumbered by nonmatriculated adults who turn the "college" into a "community center."

The burdens of remedial education are also much heavier as we move from the most to the least prestigious institutions. The open-door approach, standard in two-year colleges and also operational in tuition-dependent four-year colleges that take virtually all comers, means that college teachers are confronted with many underprepared students. Those who work in the less-selective settings also more frequently work part-time. During the last two decades, the ranks of the part-timers have swollen to over 40 percent of the total academic work force,[7] with heavy concentrations in the less prestigious colleges and especially in the community colleges, where over half the faculty operate on a part-time schedule. At the extreme opposite end of the institutional prestige hierarchy from those who serve primarily in graduate schools and graduate-level professional schools in the major universities we find the full-time and, especially, part-time teachers of English and mathematics in downtown community colleges, who teach introductory and subintroductory courses over and over again—the rudiments of English composition, the basic courses in mathematics—to high-school graduates who need remediation and to adults struggling with basic literacy.

With the nature of work varying enormously across the many types of institutions that make up American postsecondary education, other aspects of the academic life run on a parallel course. If we examine the cultures of institutions by discussing with faculty members their basic academic beliefs, we find different worlds. Among the leading research universities, the discipline is front and center, the institution is prized for its reputation of scholarship and research, and peers are the primary reference group. A professor of physics says, "What I value the most is the presence of the large number and diverse collection of scientists who are constantly doing things that I find stimulating." A professor of biology tells us that his university "has a lot of extremely good departments . . . there are a lot of fascinating, interesting people here." A political scientist adds that what he values most "is the intellectual level of the faculty and the graduate students. . . . Good graduate students are very important to me personally and always have been, and having colleagues that are smart is important." And a professor of English states that his institution "is a first-rate university . . . we have a fine library, and we have excellent teachers here, and we have first-rate scholars." Academics in this favored site have much with which to identify. They are proud of the quality they believe surrounds them, experiencing it directly in their own and neighboring departments and inferring it indirectly from institutional reputation. The strong symbolic thrust of the institution incorporates the combined strengths of the departments that in turn represent the disciplines. Thus, for faculty, disciplinary and institutional cultures converge, creating a happy state indeed.

The leading private liberal-arts colleges provide a second favored site. Here, professors often waxed lyrical in interviews about the small-college environment tailored to undergraduate teaching: "It is a very enjoyable setting. The students—the students we get in physics—are a delight to work with," "I can't put it in a word, but I think that it is one of the least constraining environments I know of," "It is a better form of life," or "My colleagues are fantastic. The people in this department are sane, which in an English department is not always the case." These institutions retain the capacity to appear as academic communities, not bureaucracies, in their overall integration and symbolic unity.

But soon we encounter sites where faculty members are troubled by inchoate institutional character and worried about the quality of their environment. In the lesser universities, and especially in the comprehensive colleges that have evolved out of a teachers-college background, at the second, third, and fourth levels of the institutional prestige hierarchy, the setting may be summed up in the words of one professor:

> I think the most difficult thing about being at an institution like [this one] is that it has a difficult time coming to terms with itself. I think the more established institutions with strong academic backgrounds don't have the problem that an institution that pretty much is in the middle range of higher educational institutions around the country does. I'm not saying that [this place] is a bad institution, but it certainly doesn't have the quality students, the quality faculty, the quality programs of the University of Chicago, Harvard, Yale. . . . When it talks about standards, what sort of standards? When it talks about practicality, how practical does it have to be? . . . It doesn't have a strong sense of tradition.

Compared to the research universities, the overall institutional culture is weaker and less satisfying for many faculty members at the same time that disciplinary identifications are weakened as heavy teaching loads suppress research and its rewards.

In these middle-level institutions, professors often spoke of their relationship with students as the thing they value most. Students begin to replace peers as the audience of first resort. That shift is completed in the community colleges, with the identifications of faculty reaching a high point of student-centeredness. In a setting that is distinctly opposed to disciplinary definitions of quality and excellence, pleasures and rewards have to lie in the task of working with poorly prepared students who pour in through the open door. For example: "We are a practical teaching college. We serve our community and we serve . . . the students in our community and give them a good, basic, strong education. . . . We are not sitting here on our high horses looking to publish" and "I really do like to teach, and this place allows me to teach. It doesn't bog me down with having to turn out papers." In the community colleges, the equity values of open door and open access have some payoff as anchoring points in the faculty culture. But in the overall institutional hierarchy, where the dominant values emphasize quality, selection, and advanced work, the community-college ideology can play only a subsidiary role. The limitations cannot be missed: "It would be nice to be able to teach upper-division classes."

As go work and culture, so go authority, careers, and associational life. To sum up the story on authority: in the leading universities faculty influence is relatively strong. Many individuals have personal bargaining power; departments and professional schools are semi-autonomous units; and all-campus faculty bodies such as senates have primacy in personnel and curricular decisions. University presidents speak lovingly of the faculty as the core of the institution and walk gently around entrenched faculty prerogatives. But as we move to other types of institutions, faculty authority weakens and managerialism increases. Top-down command is noticeably stronger in public master's colleges, especially when they have evolved out of a teachers-college background. The two-year colleges, operating under local trustees much like K-12 schools, are quite managerial. Faculty in these places often feel powerless, even severely put upon. Their answer (where possible under state law) has been to band together by means of unionization. The further down the general hierarchy of institutional prestige, the more widespread the unions become, especially among public-sector institutions.

To sum up the associational life of faculty: in the leading universities, faculty interact with one another across institutional boundaries in an extensive network of disciplinary linkages—formal and informal; large and small; visible and invisible; local, regional, national, and international. When university specialists find national "monster meetings" not to their liking, they go anyway to participate in a smaller division or section that best represents their specific interests, or they find kindred souls in small, autonomous meetings of several dozen people. In the other sectors, however, involvement in the mainline disciplinary associations declines; there is less to learn that is relevant to one's everyday life, and travel money is scarce in the institutional budget. Academics then go to national meetings when they are held in their part of the country. They look for special sessions on teaching; they break away to form associations (and journals) appropriate to their sector. Community-college teachers have developed associations in such broad areas as the social sciences and the humanities, e.g., the Community College Humanities Association, and in such special fields as mathematics and biology, e.g., the American Mathematics Association for Two-Year Colleges.[8]

Different worlds, small worlds. Institutional differentiation interacts with disciplinary differentiation in a bewildering fashion that steadily widens and deepens the matrix of differences that separate American academics from each other.

Systemic Problems

When we pursue the different worlds of American professors by emphasizing disciplinary and institutional conditions, deep-rooted problems that are otherwise relegated to the background or only dimly perceived come to the fore. Five systemic concerns may be briefly stated as problems of secondarization, excessive teaching, attenuated professional control, fragmented academic culture, and diminished intrinsic reward and motivation.

Secondarization and Remediation

The long evolution from elite to mass to universal access in American postsecondary education has not been without its costs. One major undesirable effect is a change in the conditions of the academic life that occurs when academics confront poorly educated students who come out of a defective secondary-school system and flow into higher education by means of open access. Academic work then revolves considerably around remedial education. Faced with entering students whose academic achievement is, for example, at the level of ninth-grade English, faculty first have to help the student progress to the twelfth-grade or traditional college-entry level, thereby engaging in the work of the high school. Mathematics instructors may find themselves facing students whose achievements measure at the sixth-grade level and hence need to complete some elementary schoolwork as well as their secondary education. Well known by those who teach in nonselective four-year colleges and especially in community colleges, this situation may seem surprising, even shocking, to others. But like the night and the day, it follows from the structure and orientation of American secondary and postsecondary education. If secondary schools graduate students whose achievement is below the twelfth-grade level, as they commonly do, and if some colleges admit all or virtually all who approach their doors, then college faculties will engage in K-12 work. Remedial education is spread throughout American higher education, from leading universities to community colleges, but it is relatively light when selectivity is high and quite heavy when selection is low or even nonexistent.

The problem of teaching poorly prepared students is compounded in the two-year college by its concentration on the first two years of the four-year undergraduate curriculum and on short-term vocational and semiprofessional programs. This curricular context calls for repetitive teaching of introductory courses. Since community colleges experience much student attrition during and after the first year of study, due to a variety of personal, occupational, and academic reasons, teaching is concentrated in first-year courses. In each department it is usually the general introductory course or two that must be taught over and over again, with little or no surcease. Upper-division courses, let alone graduate courses, are rarely available. While some course diversity can be found at the second-year level, the departmental task is to cover the introductory materials semester by semester, year in and year out. The teaching task is then closer to secondary-school teaching than what is found in selective universities. The task of remedial education adds to the downward thrust, requiring subcollege work on a plane below the regular first-year instruction.

Inherent and widespread in current American education, this teaching context receives relatively little attention in academic and public discussions. It is virtually an institutional secret that academic life is so often reduced to the teaching of secondary-school subjects. With due respect to the difficulties of the work, and the often deep devotion of involved staff to the welfare of underprepared students and immigrant populations, this widely found situation amounts to a dumbing down of the intellectual life of academic staff. Subject content is limited to codified introductory material. Educational euphemisms allow us to blink at this undesired effect of American-style comprehensive secondary schooling and universal higher education, but they do not allow us to escape it. The situation marginalizes faculty. Eroding "the essential intellectual core of faculty work," it deprofessionalizes them.[9]

Excessive Teaching

The complaint that professors do too much research and too little teaching has been prevalent for almost a hundred years. When William James wrote about "the Ph.D. octopus" shortly after the turn of the century, he pointed to the increasing preoccupation of professors in the emerging universities with specialized research, graduate students, and doctoral programs. Since then the protest of too much research has been a perennial battle cry of the American reformer seeking more emphasis on undergraduate programs and on their general or liberal education components in particular.

The 1980s and early 1990s have seen a strong resurgence of this point of view inside and outside the academy. Careful critics beamed their messages at research universities, would-be universities, and even four-year private and public colleges that have opened their faculty reward systems to the research imperative. They understand that professors teach when they supervise students in the preparation of master's and doctoral theses. They are sometimes aware that in the best private liberal-arts colleges professors involve their undergraduate students in research as an effective way to teach and to learn.[10] But the critical comment overall has turned into a generalized charge that "professors" should do less research and more teaching, meaning undergraduate teaching. In the popular press, and even in the academic press, careful targeting is forgone. In the extreme, a minimization of teaching by professors is portrayed as part of a "scam."

But across the dispersed American professoriate, the reality is the reverse: more academics teach too much than teach too little. Fifteen hours of classroom teaching each week is far too much for the maintenance of a scholarly life; even twelve hours is excessive. But as noted earlier, most institutional sectors present such loads, specifying assignments that are two to three times greater than that of professors in research-based institutions. Twelve and fifteen hours a week in the classroom at the college level tend to push professors out of their disciplines. A sense of being a scholar is reduced as the "physicist" becomes entirely a "teacher of physics," the "political scientist" a "teacher of political science"—and then mainly as teachers of introductory courses only. Interest flags in what is going on in the revision of advanced topics; command of the literature weakens. Excessive teaching loads apparently are now becoming a source of academic burnout, importing into higher education the teacher burnout long noted as a problem in the K-12 system. A 1989 Carnegie Foundation faculty survey found that the share of the full-time faculty "intending to retire early" was 25 percent in research universities, 26 percent in liberal-arts colleges, and a huge 49 percent in two-year colleges.[11] A setting characterized by heavy introductory teaching propels academics toward early retirement twice as much—one-half of the total staff!—as settings where professors have light teaching loads, involvement in research, and a more scholarly life as traditionally defined.

Weakened Professional Control

As indicated earlier, command structures are not unheard of in American colleges and universities. Professors in research universities and leading private four-year colleges certainly encounter trustee and administrator influence. Their professional position is also increasingly challenged by the professionalization of administrative occupations clustered around central management; in the words of Gary Rhoades, "faculty are increasingly 'managed' professionals in organizations increasingly run by 'managerial professionals.'"[12] But academics in these favored sites generally have strong countervailing power of a professional kind that is rooted in their personal and collective expertise. Department by department, professional school by professional school, they exercise much internal control. They expect to dominate in choosing who to add to the faculty and what courses should be taught. They expect to be consulted in many matters rather than to receive orders from those in nominally superior positions. But in public and private comprehensive colleges and especially in community colleges, the foundations of authority change. Subject expertise becomes more diffuse, occasionally amounting only to sufficient knowledge in the discipline to teach the introductory course to poorly prepared students, while at the same time the role of trustees and administrators is strengthened, sometimes approaching the top-down supervision found in local school districts. Such managerialism is particularly evident in public-sector institutions, especially when they are exposed to state assertions of accountability.

Adding greatly to the vulnerability of academic professionals to political and administrative dictate is the marginal position of part-time faculty. In all institutional sectors, part-timers have long been with us: witness the traditional use and abuse of faculty spouses in part-time work in foreign language departments of research universities. But the use of part-timers grew greatly during the last two decades as a form of mobile and inexpensive labor. It unfortunately turns out that floating

student "clienteles" require dispensable academic staff, hence the deteriorating situation for staff in community colleges where a majority of faculty now serve part-time. The part-timers themselves have only marginal influence, and their large numbers weaken the influence of full-time faculty vis-à-vis trustees and administrative staff. A relatively powerless proletariat exists in American academic life, centered in employment that is part-time and poorly paid.

Experiments are underway in the two-year colleges, we should note, to create new forms of academic professionalism that are centered on "the disciplines of instruction" rather than on disciplinary affiliation.[13] This approach emphasizes the importance of translating knowledge into more understandable forms by such means as course revision and media preparation. Certain attitudes about teaching, as well as forms of teaching, become the possible basis for professional identity. But while community-college instruction has become a career in its own right, it remains highly unlikely that a strong sense of professionalism can be constructed when disciplinary foundations are weak, part-time work is the main form of employment, and top-down bureaucratic control remains widespread.

Fragmented Academic Culture

All-encompassing academic values are increasingly hard to find in American academic life. The claims frequently made by reformers that academics must somehow find their way back to agreement on core values and assume an overarching common framework become less realistic with each passing year. Different contexts, especially institutional ones, promote different values. Even common terms assume different meanings. "Academic freedom" in one context means mainly the right to do as one pleases in pursuing new ideas; in another, not to have an administrator dictate the teaching syllabus one uses; in another, the right to teach evolution in a college where the local board of trustees is dominated by creationists; in yet another, the right to join an extremist political group. Promotion criteria vary from an all-out emphasis on research productivity to weight put solely on undergraduate instruction, from complicated mixtures of teaching and research and several forms of "service" to heavy weighting of years on the job and seniority rights. As mentioned earlier, professional schools must value their connection to outside professions as well as to other parts of their universities, thereby balancing themselves between two sets of values in a way not required in the letters and science departments. The grounds for advancement then become particularly contentious. All such differences in outlook among academics widen as differentiation of academic work continues.

Diminished Intrinsic Reward and Motivation

Under all the strengths and weaknesses of American academic life, we find the persistent problem of the professional calling. When academic work becomes just a job and a routine career, then such material rewards as salary are placed front and center. Academics stay at their work or leave for other pursuits according to how much they are paid. They come to work "on time" because they must (it is nailed down in the union contract); they leave on time because satisfaction is found after work is concluded. But when academic work is still a calling, it "constitutes a practical ideal of activity and character that makes a person's work morally inseparable from his or her life. It subsumes the self into a community of disciplined practice and sound judgment whose activity has meaning and value in itself, not just in the output or profit that results from it."[14] A calling transmutes narrow self-interest into other-regarding and ideal-regarding interests: one is linked to peers and to a version of a larger common good. The calling has moral content; it contributes to civic virtue.

Professionalization projects seek to provide vehicles by which multitudes of workers are transported to a calling, where they find intrinsic motivation as well as the glories of high status and the trappings of power. The academic profession is lucky in that it has abundant sources of intrinsic motivation in the fascinations of research and the enchantments of teaching. Many academic contexts offer a workaday existence rich in content and consequence. As a confederate gathering, the academic profession's continuing promise lies considerably in the provision of a variety of

contexts that generate "absorbing errands."[15] In that promise lies the best hope in the long term for the recruitment and retention of talent. But when such contexts fade away or become severely weakened, the errands run down and talented people search for other fascinations and enchantments. The systemic problems I have identified—secondarization, excessive teaching, weakened professional control, fragmented academic culture—point to structural and cultural conditions that run down the academic calling.

What, If Anything, Can Be Done?

In a large, decentralized, and competitive system of higher education, apace with great differentiation of institutions and disciplines, student growth and knowledge growth have badly fractured the American academic profession. From a cross-national perspective, the resulting system has had major advantages. More than elsewhere, the system at large has been able to combine academic excellence and scientific preeminence with universal access and weak standards. It has been flexible, even to a fault, with various sectors adjusting to different demands and numerous colleges and universities fashioning individual niches. But a heavy price has been paid, not least in the systemic problems I have identified that seriously weaken the American academic work force. The ever-extending differentiation that is integral to the success of the system produces a host of academic subworlds that downgrade the academic profession overall. They establish conditions hostile to the best features of professionalism.

Can these conditions be reduced, reversing the drift toward secondarization, the weight of excessive teaching, the weakening of professional control, the fragmentation of academic culture, and the diminishing of intrinsic motivation and reward? These weaknesses do not just hurt the professoriate; they also injure universities and colleges. They undermine the hopes of the nation that a well-trained and highly motivated professoriate will continue to staff an academic system second to none.

Four broad ideas can frame future directions of reform. First, *the intellectual core of aca-*

demic work throughout the system should be protected and strengthened. It may be helpful to students in the short run to offer them remedial instruction; it may be helpful to high-turnover clienteles and tight institutional budgets to invest heavily in part-time academics. But such major developments are injurious to the state of the academic profession and hence in the long term to the institutions that depend upon its capability. Higher education has enough to do without including the work of the secondary school. Success in secondary-school reform that instilled serious standards for the high-school diploma would be a major step for those who teach in postsecondary education. Part-timeness needs to be taken seriously, since nothing runs down a profession faster than to shift its work from full-time labor requiring credentialed experts to an operation that can be staffed by casual laborers who must live by their wits as they flit among jobs. Limits on the use of part-timers can be set in institutions: 20 or 25 percent of the total staff is enough; 50 percent is highly excessive and should be seen as institutionally injurious.

Second, *constant attention must be paid to the integration of academic personnel with managerial personnel.* As the gap grows between "faculty" and "administration" inside universities and colleges, faculty seek to promote their special interests more and administrators increasingly see themselves as the only ones who uphold overall institutional concerns. "Shared governance" only works when it is shared to the point where some academics sit in central councils and the rest of the academic staff feel they are appropriately represented, or where decision-making is extensively decentralized to deans and department heads and faculty sit close to these newly strengthened "line managers," or in various other complicated combinations of centralized and decentralized decision-making.

Personal leadership has its place in academe, but the window of opportunity for arbitrary top-down policy generally does not last very long. Anything worth doing in a university or college requires a number of people who want it to happen and will work at it for a number of years. Academic values, as defined by the academic staff, need to be constantly mixed throughout the organizational structure with the influence of the new managerial val-

ues that will be even more necessary in academic institutions in the future than they are now. The linking of academics with overall, long-term institutional interests is central in academic management; with it comes extended professional authority.

Third, *indirect forms of linkage among divergent academic cultures need to be better understood and promoted.* The search for clarified common goals comes up empty-handed. Rhetoric that embraces complex universities and colleges falls back on eternal clichés about research, teaching, and service. Meanwhile, the separate departments and professional schools go on generating their separate cultures. How do these cultures then connect, if at all? Both as modes of reasoning and as knowledge domains, they often have some overlap with neighboring fields. With interdisciplinary fields also helping to bridge the gaps, the many specialties of academics may be seen (in the words of three acute observers) as connected in "chains of overlapping neighborhoods." The connections produce "a continuous texture of narrow specialties," a "collective communication," and "a collective competence and breadth." Academics are partially integrated through "interlocking cultural communities."[16] Then, too, the socialization of graduate students into academic ways still counts for something— an integrating force among university graduates spread out among different types of institutions. Models of behavior also radiate from one type of institution to another. For example, the image of liberal education most strongly embodied in small private liberal-arts colleges clearly serves as a model of what undergraduate education in large public four-year colleges could be if appropriately funded and properly carried out. The many different types of institutions comprising the American system do not operate as value-tight compartments.

Fourth, *the intrinsic rewards of the academic life need to be highlighted and respected.* As earlier reported, academics in diverse settings point to the special joys of teaching, or of doing research, or of combining the two. They speak of the pleasure of shaping the minds of the young, of making discoveries, of carrying forward the intellectual heritage of the nation and the world. They sense that at the end of the day they may have done something worthwhile. They point to such psychic rewards as reasons to be in academic work and as reasons to resist the lure of greater material rewards elsewhere. There is still some devotion to a calling.

Academic fanatics who are fully caught up in this now oddly shaped calling can even feel, as Max Weber put it in a famous essay, that they are in the grip of "a demon who holds the fibers of their very lives."[17] We find the academic demon everywhere: in the professor so intensely interested in her writing that she never checks the clock; in the college teacher who acts way beyond the call of duty as personal mentor and substitute parent for marginal students; in the academic scientist who is in the laboratory instead of at home at two o'clock in the morning; in the lecturer who will not stop talking long after the bell has rung and has to be forced out of the lecture hall or classroom; in the dying academic who works up to the last week, even the last day. George Steiner wrote of the world of "the absolute scholar" as "a haunting and haunted business," a place where "sleep is a puzzle of wasted time, and flesh a piece of torn luggage that the spirit must drag after it . . ."[18]

Even in modest dosages, academic professionalism centered on intrinsic features of the work at hand leads to committed productivity that political and bureaucratic controls cannot generate nor can "market forces" guarantee. Those who seek to replace professional commitment with the nuts and bolts of bureaucratic regulation run down the calling; they take intellectual absorption out of the absorbing errand. Wise academic leaders and sophisticated critics sense that only professional norms and practices are ingrained, person by person, in everyday activity to constructively shape motivation and steer behavior. They then attend to the conditions of professional inspiration and self-regulation. Positioned between state and market, academic professionalism, however fragmented, remains a necessary foundation for performance and progress in higher education.

Endnotes

1. This essay is based largely on two books and two prior articles that report the results of research on academic life in Europe and America: Burton R. Clark, ed., *The Academic Profession: National, Disciplinary and Institu-* *tional Settings* (Berkeley and Los Angeles, Calif.: University of California Press, 1987); Burton R. Clark, *The Academic Life: Small Worlds, Different Worlds* (Princeton, N.J.: Carnegie Foundation for the Advancement of Teaching and Princeton University Press, 1987); Burton R. Clark, "The Academic Life: Small Worlds, Different Worlds," *Educational Researcher* 18 (5) (1989): 4–8; and Burton R. Clark, "Faculty: Differentiation and Dispersion," in Arthur Levine, ed., *Higher Learning in America: 1980–2000* (Baltimore, Md.: Johns Hopkins University Press, 1993), 163–178. For other research-based studies of American academics reported in the 1980s and 1990s, see Martin J. Finkelstein, *The American Academic Profession: A Synthesis of Social Scientific Inquiry Since World War II* (Columbus, Ohio: Ohio State University Press, 1984); Howard R. Bowen and Jack H. Schuster, *American Professors: A National Resource Imperiled* (New York: Oxford University Press, 1986); and Robert T. Blackburn and Janet H. Lawrence, *Faculty at Work: Motivation, Expectation, Satisfaction* (Baltimore, Md.: Johns Hopkins University Press, 1995).

2. Carnegie Foundation for the Advancement of Teaching, *A Classification of Institutions of Higher Education,* 1994 ed. (Princeton, N.J.: Carnegie Foundation for the Advancement of Teaching, 1994), xiv.

3. Tony Becher, *Academic Tribes and Territories: Intellectual Enquiry and the Cultures of Disciplines* (Milton Keynes, England: The Open University Press, 1989).

4. See Walter Metzger, "The Academic Profession in the United States," in Clark, ed., *The Academic Profession: National, Disciplinary, and Institutional Settings,* 123–208; and R. H. Wiebe, *The Search for Order, 1877–1920* (New York: Hill and Wang, 1967).

5. Arthur M. Cohen and Florence B. Brawer, *The American Community College,* 3d ed. (San Francisco, Calif.: Jossey-Bass, 1996), 86.

6. Carnegie Foundation for the Advancement of Teaching, *A Classification of Institutions of Higher Education,* xiv.

7. For tracking the growth of part-time faculty, see David W. Leslie, Samuel E. Kellams, and G. M. Gunne, *Part-Time Faculty in American Higher Education* (New York: Praeger, 1982); Judith M. Gappa, *Part-Time Faculty: Higher Education at a Crossroads,* ASHE-ERIC Higher Education Research Report No. 3 (Washington, D.C.: Association for the Study of Higher Education, 1984); and Judith M. Gappa and David W. Leslie, *The Invisible Faculty: Improving the Status of Part-Timers in Higher Education* (San Francisco, Calif.: Jossey-Bass, 1993).

8. Cohen and Brawer, *The American Community College,* 98.

9. Earl Seidman, *In the Words of the Faculty: Perspectives on Improving Teaching and Education-*

al Quality in Community Colleges (San Francisco, Calif.: Jossey-Bass, 1985), 275.

10. See Robert A. McCaughey, *Scholars and Teachers: The Faculties of Select Liberal Arts Colleges and Their Place in American Higher Learning* (New York: Barnard College, Columbia University, 1994).

11. Carnegie Foundation for the Advancement of Teaching, "Early Faculty Retirees: Who, Why, and with What Impact?," *Change* (July/August 1990): 31–34. On burnout in community colleges, see Cohen and Brawer, *The American Community College*, 90–93.

12. Gary Rhoades, "Reorganizing the Faculty Work Force for Flexibility, *Journal of Higher Education* 67 (6) (November/December 1996): 656.

13. Cohen and Brawer, *The American Community College*, 96–100.

14. Robert N. Bellah, Richard Madsen, William M. Sullivan, Ann Swidler, and Steven M. Tipton, *Habits of the Heart: Individualism and Commitment in American Life* (Berkeley and Los Angeles, Calif.: University of California Press, 1985), 66.

15. A metaphor attributed to Henry James: Exact reference unknown.

16. For a fuller account of these metaphors and perspectives offered respectively by Michael Polanyi, Donald T. Campbell, and Diana Crane, see Clark, *The Academic Life*, 140–142.

17. Max Weber, "Science as a Vocation," in H. H. Gerth and C. Wright Mills, eds., *From Max Weber: Essays in Sociology* (New York: Oxford University Press, 1946), 156.

18. George Steiner, "The Cleric of Treason," in *George Steiner: A Reader* (New York: Penguin Books, 1984), 197–198.

The Academic Profession in Transition: Toward a New Social Fiction

R. EUGENE RICE

In 1837, Ralph Waldo Emerson delivered "The American Scholar," an address that Oliver Wendell Holmes described as "our intellectual Declaration of Independence" (quoted in Jones, Leisy, and Ludwig 1952, p. 424). Using the images and issues of that time and place, Emerson articulated a vision of the scholar in a new democracy, a vision that resonated across nineteenth-century America. He called for the rejection of a past that was alien and debilitating and for the adoption of a new approach to scholarship and a new role for the scholar in society—a role that would be vital and self-confident, or in his words, "blood warm" (Jones, Leisy, and Ludwig 1952, p. 437).

Emerson's address was not so much an assertion of intellectual nationalism as a statement of his own struggle with the problem of vocation, with the nature and meaning of scholarly work in a changing society (Smith 1939). It is this same issue—what it means to be a scholar in an evolving democracy—that confronts us today. Just as Emerson's American scholar was struggling to break away from the cultural tyranny of "the learning of other lands," from patterns of deference that engendered self-doubt and the depreciation of new, adaptive roles, so the academic professional of today is wrestling with the legacy of a social fiction that came to dominate the lives of faculty from the mid-1950s to the mid-1970s, what is all too frequently referred to as the golden age of higher education.

During the past 15 years, most of our academic institutions have experienced monumental changes. The structural contexts in which we work have been transformed, but the normative conceptions by which the majority of faculty measure success in the profession remain unaltered and largely unexamined. The purpose of this paper is to initiate the search for a new conception of the academic professional, one more adaptive for both institutions and ourselves.

The Professionalization of Scholarship

It is significant that Emerson did not use the title "The American Professional," for in the middle of the nineteenth century, the professionalization of scholarship had just begun. Emerson's scholar was "man thinking," whether he was a physician, lawyer, minister, lecturer, writer, or teacher. During the second half of the nineteenth century, the process of professionalization began with a vengeance. The historian Burton J. Bledstein (1976) provides a critical review of the beginning of that process in his important book *The Culture of Professionalism: The Middle Class and the Development of Higher Education in America*. He argues that the self-doubt and status anxieties engendered by a democratic society with little reverence for tradition and no formal class boundaries created a culture of professionalism, which provided middle-class Americans with a basis for authority, an opportunity for mobility, and the standards for judging merit and success. The institution that provided the organizational context and structure for this important cultural development was the American university. Bledstein shows that the

"The Academic Profession in Transition: Toward a New Social Fiction," by Eugene Rice, reprinted from *Teaching Sociology*, Vol. 14, No. 1, January 1986, American Sociological Association.

American university and the culture of professionalism are intrinsically linked, and he traces their development back to the period between 1870 and 1900.

As a part of this critical cultural and structural development, scholarship in America was segmented into professions and disciplines and was institutionalized in newly organized professional associations and a burgeoning system of higher education. The process of professionalization and the institutionalization of scholarship continued during the opening decades of this century. Veysey (1973) contends that the academic revolution Jencks and Riesman (1968) describe actually took place between 1890 and 1910. During those years, the discipline-based departments became the foundation of scholarly allegiance and political power in academic life (Riesman 1980). It was not until after World War II, during the expansionist years in higher education, that this two-edged process, the professionalization of scholarship and its institutionalization in higher education, came to full power in society.

The financial resources and employment opportunities available to the professional scholar in the academic sector were unprecedented. Prestige, status, and influence also accrued to the academic professional. This was consistently demonstrated in the periodic rankings of occupations. For example, between 1953 and 1962, in Gallup poles assessing the suitability or attractiveness of nine leading professions, academic scholars rose from seventh place to third place, a rank they held until 1973 (Metzger 1975). In addition to relatively high status in the eyes of the general public, the faculty member enjoyed considerable influence inside academic institutions.[1]

During the years of incredible growth and expansion in higher education, scholarly activity that had previously been conducted in nonacademic settings was drawn under the extended umbrella of colleges and universities. Prior to this period of educational affluence, scholars—particularly those in such fields as economics and psychology—carried out their work independently of academic institutions. The new sources of funding, the expansion of programs, and the rising prestige in influence of the academic scholar made a college or university appointment not only convenient but almost irresistible. Within a relatively short period of time, being a scholar became virtually synonymous with being an academic professional, and a powerful image of what it meant to be an academic professional took hold.

The Dominant Image of the Academic Professional

Much about life is defined and shaped by socially constructed fictions, by patterns of meaning that cohere in a particular time and place. The great American poet Wallace Stevens said it best:

> The final belief is to believe in a fiction, which you know to be a fiction, there being nothing else. The exquisite truth is to know that it is a fiction and that you believe in it willingly (Stevens 1957, p. 163).

Nowhere in the contemporary world do socially constructed fictions have more power than in the professions. And no profession—with the possible exception of medicine—takes its own professional imagery more seriously than the academic profession. Reference needs only to be made to the years of graduate school socialization and to the power that academic mentors have in the lives of their protégés to make the argument.

The image that dominated the academic profession prior to World War II , particularly in the liberal arts colleges that then played a larger role in higher education, was that of the teacher-scholar. After a two year study of faculty development programs in twenty of the nation's better liberal arts colleges, Nelson (1981) published a book calling for the "renewal of the teacher-scholar." The call for renewal is, itself, testimony to the demise of that occupational ideal. During the earlier decades of this century, however, the teacher-scholar was an image widely shared. Nelson finds the teacher-scholar ideal articulated best in the *Davidson College Faculty Handbook*:

> Ideally the college professor would be a widely respected scholar excited about learning and capable of communicating this excitement to others, a teacher deeply concerned with the welfare of students and eager to have them learn and grow, one who teaches imaginatively both by books and by personal example, a demanding yet

compassionate person who respects the moral worth of students and their potential for growth (Nelson 1981, p. 7.)

Sometime after the mid-1950s, after the impact of the G. I. Bill of Rights and the launching of Sputnik, a major shift took place in the image of what it meant to be an academic professional. The older image of the teacher-scholar was celebrated in the Harbison Awards, sponsored by the Danforth Foundation. These widely publicized awards were given to ten outstanding teacher-scholars each year between 1962 and 1972. The Harbison Award was, however, little more than a nostalgic gesture; the image was dying or already dead, and the award series was established posthumously—in memoriam.

Scholarship became research, and teaching and research became activities that competed for the faculty member's time (Light 1974). The term *scholarship*, if it was used at all, referred to research, not teaching. In the consciousness of the faculty, as they thought about their working lives, the teacher-scholar as a model to be emulated had migrated from the core of the profession to the margins.

The magnitude of the growth and change in higher education that began in the late 1950s is still difficult to comprehend. A few statistics are instructive. Between 1956 and 1966, the proportion of high school graduates that went directly to college went from 32 percent to 53 percent. Between 1960 and 1970, the number of Ph.D.'s granted per year tripled, rising from about 10,000 to about 30,000 (Dressel and Mayhew 1974), and the increase in expenditures in the academic sector outstripped both the increase in enrollments and the rise in cost of living. Much of this early expansion was a direct response to demographic shifts and societal demand. Toward the end of the 1960s, however, growth in higher education had developed a momentum of its own and became what Carter referred to as "a binge of reckless expansion" that lasted well into the 1970s (quoted in Riesman 1980, p. 7).

This period of rapid growth in highest education brought with it a new conception of the academic professional. The constituent parts of this new professional image existed in nascent form throughout the early history of American higher education, but it was only in the heady days of what seemed to be limitless growth, affluence, and societal influence that the component elements fused to form a powerful and dominant conception.

Parsons (1968), in a major essay on the professions, described the "educational revolution" that he saw coming to full fruition in American society after World War II. Fundamental to this revolution was the process of professionalization, a process that he regarded as "the most important single component in the structure of modern societies" (p. 545). According to Parson's influential theory, the keystone in the arch of the professionally oriented society is the modern university, and "the profession *par excellence* is the academic" (p. 545). He also described the impact of professionalization on the role of the typical faculty member:

> The typical professor now resembles the scientist more than the gentleman-scholar of an earlier time. As a result of the process of professionalization, achievement criteria are now given the highest priority, reputations are established in national and international forums rather than locally defined, and the center of gravity has shifted to the graduate faculties and their newly professionalized large-scale research function (Parsons 1968, p. 545).

What is most striking about this statement is that what he describes is not the typical professor. What he articulates is the dominant fiction by which the typical professor measures himself and his colleagues as professionals. The image of the academic professional that emerged during the expansionist days of higher education not only shaped the self-conceptions of faculty but informed institutional policies and determined, in large part, who received promotion, tenure and such amenities as leaves of absence and funding for travel and research.

The Assumptive World of the Academic Professional

In his work on psychosocial transitions, Parkes (1971) demonstrates the significance of what he calls the assumptive world in efforts to cope with change. In periods of stability, a complex of basic assumptions is established. Then in times of transition, this assumptive world is challenged and fundamentally restructured. In the mid-1960s, at the height of affluence and expansion in higher education, a consensus emerged regarding what it meant to be fully professional academically. Clustering around this image were the following basic assumptions:

1. Research is the central professional endeavor and the focus of academic life.

2. Quality in the profession is maintained by peer review and professional autonomy.

3. Knowledge is pursued for its own sake.

4. The pursuit of knowledge is best organized according to discipline (i.e., according to discipline-based departments).

5. Reputations are established through national and international professional associations.

6. The distinctive task of the academic professional is the pursuit of cognitive truth (or cognitive rationality).

7. Professional rewards and mobility accrue to those who persistently accentuate their specializations.

This professional vision and the interrelated complex of assumptions on which it was built contributed to an extraordinary advancement of knowledge. The increased specialization, the new levels of funding for research, and the rigorous exchange and critique of ideas produced undeniable benefits. The several interrelated elements listed above were woven into a fabric of consensus that became the assumptive world into which the large number of new Ph.D.'s from the rapidly expanding graduate schools were initiated. The men and women who were in graduate school during those expansionist days now form the majority of mid-career faculty who are struggling with the problems of steady-state staffing, or worse, retrenchment.

This conception of the academic professional is questioned here not because it is inappropriate but because it has created a one-dimensional view of the academic career, a view that continues to be normative for the majority of faculty regardless of the type of institution in which they work. This conception

has had an especially debilitating effect on higher education; it has been a major stumbling block in efforts to adapt to the profound social, economic, and political changes confronting colleges and universities in these difficult times.

As faculty members look toward what is at best an ambiguous future, they cling tenaciously to that established professional image internalized during graduate school days. Rather than looking for new ways of dealing with the difficult problems confronting higher education or responding to opportunities for renewal or new career options, they accentuate and narrow further the older, established career path. In times of stress, they choose familiar.

New Context, Old Image

John Kenneth Galbraith takes pleasure in reminding us that everyone is a genius in a bull market. The older image of the academic professional could be accommodated without serious dissidence in the area of expansion. New programs and activities could be added on the margins of higher education without challenging the assumptive world at the core. Individuals committed to ideas and practices that moved them toward the margins of the profession (e.g., to the innovations initiated in the experimental colleges during the 1960s) could pursue their dreams with impunity. The context and conditions have changed dramatically in the 1980s but the older professional image continues to exert a debilitating influence on higher education's capacity to proactively shape and adapt to those changes.

The changing context in higher education has been reviewed so frequently that we now have a kind of demographic litany that is recited at the beginnings of most academic conferences. Rather than rehearse what is already too familiar, I focus on a basic organizational shift that is occurring in higher education and relate that shift to the professional self-understanding of faculty.

Shifting Organizational Cultures

American higher education has its deepest roots in the *collegial culture* of the British and Protestant colonial colleges. The collegial culture was also shaped by the German research university, which was based on research specialization and peer review—a pattern first introduced in this country at Johns Hopkins University. The assumptive world of the academic professional identified above was most directly informed by the collegial culture found in the contemporary liberal arts colleges and in research universities, where most faculty in the established disciplines received their graduate education and socialization into the profession.

Much of American higher education is now being profoundly influenced by a competing culture—the *managerial culture*. This culture in higher education can be traced back to the urban colleges and universities that grew out of the Catholic school system. These institutions, which were founded to provide educational opportunities and upward mobility for recent immigrants and the urban poor, were administered by priests and nuns who had strong administrative authority and often previous experience as educational managers. The origin of leadership in the managerial culture was dramatically different from that of the collegial culture, where leaders emerged from the ranks of faculty in the liberal arts colleges or from the successful research scientists in universities. The managerial culture is now being fostered by the increased complexity of the managerial task, by collective bargaining, and by the new professional specialization—educational administration—which has its own training programs, degrees, and associational life. This culture has been adopted by the community colleges and technical schools, and is being rapidly incorporated as the dominant organizational culture in regional state colleges and universities.[2]

The strains between the collegial and managerial cultures are having a major impact on faculty. The self-perceptions of faculty are rooted in the collegial tradition, but the currents of institutional change, including areas of expansion and power, are strengthening the managerial culture. Faculty committed to the peer review process are being evaluated by clients (students), and established liberal arts disciplines have lost ground to burgeoning interdisciplinary programs (business and computer science). Furthermore, knowledge is valued not as an end in itself but because it is economically useful and can be directly applied.

Schuster and Bowen (1985) have shown that these changes are having their most profound effects on liberal arts faculty in mid-career, those individuals who were socialized into the profession during the expansionist days, when the collegial culture was stronger. Professional school faculty and those recently recruited into the new applied, technology programs (i.e., those more attuned to the managerial culture) are not faced with the same decline in real income and deteriorating work environments. Particularly galling to liberal arts faculty is the differential salary structure. The split that is developing between professional school faculty (who are often more recently appointed) and liberal arts faculty (who are generally older and in mid-career) is exacerbated by the tension between the managerial and collegial cultures, a tension that is making the collegial orientation less viable. The professional commitments of liberal arts faculty are anchored in the collegial culture, but the currents of change are strengthening the managerial culture.

The impact of these changing conditions on the lives of faculty can be conceptualized in a variety of ways. Austin and Gamson (1983) have captured the plight of faculty in their discussion of extrinsic and intrinsic rewards in academic careers (see Figure 1).

Austin and Gamson's conclusions coincide with Herzberg, Mausner, and Synderman's (1959) two-factor theory that intrinsic characteristics relate more to satisfaction and commitment and extrinsic factors have more to do with dissatisfaction. Austin and Gamson argue that in the current educational climate, the balance between the extrinsic and intrinsic is delicate indeed. Intrinsic characteristics may help keep satisfaction and commitment fairly high. The conclusion that is especially important for our work here, however, is that intrinsic characteristics may not be able to compensate for serious erosion of the extrinsic rewards. Schuster and Bowen (1985) have reached a similar conclusion.

A key factor in understanding the plight of faculty in the present situation is the professional self-perception of faculty cultivated during the expansionist period of higher education. The present conditions under which faculty labor do not seem particularly bleak when compared to income levels and working conditions prior to 1955. To use 1970 as the

Figure 1: The Impact of Current Conditions on Extrinsic and Intrinsic Rewards

Extrinsic Rewards	Impact of Conditions
Salary	Decreasing
Opportunities	Limited
Workload	Increasing
Supervision	Centralized
Intrinsic Rewards	Impact of Condition
Intellectual challenge	Problematic for midcareer faculty
Interaction with students	Students perceived as unprepared
Autonomy	Limited
Trust	Eroding
Variety/wholeness	Depending upon discipline
Contribution (feedback)	Not as evident

baseline in a comparative assessment of working conditions (as a number of recent studies do) is to make standard for the profession conditions that were, in fact, quite unique.

The problem is made worse by the age distribution of the present faculty. The majority of faculty are in mid-career and were inducted into the profession during that same period of growth. The structural conditions have changed, but the social fiction that defines success in the profession remains intact. I want to take several of the basic assumptions undergirding that dominant conception of what it means to be a professional and examine briefly the ways in which they distort our perception of the new context and conditions.

Research as the Focus of Academic Life

Even in the period of affluence in higher education the model of the academic professional was based upon a distorted view of the working lives of most faculty. Research was never the central professional endeavor or the focus of academic life, as is assumed in the prevailing model. As Ladd (1979) shows, most college and university professors do not think of themselves as researchers; in fact, a clear majority have published little or nothing. Their interests lie primarily in teaching, and they spend most of their time in teaching-related activities. Ladd (1979, p. 5) summarizes the situation forthrightly: "An ascendant model in academe, positing what faculty should be doing, is seriously out of touch with what they actually do and want to do. . . . [it] is also profoundly at odds with the primary goal of promoting the best possible teaching—that is, the best educational experience—in the nation's colleges and universities." The assumptions surrounding

the relationship between teaching, research and the reward structure in most institutions were easy to tolerate in the period of affluence, but the conditions in higher education have changed, and those misleading assumptions must now be challenged.

Wilson (1977) argues that research can no longer be "piggybacked" on teaching, and objects on ethical grounds. Consumer-oriented students have raised the issue in terms of instructional quality, and legislatures and boards of trustees are concerned about cost. The academic professional model assumes an easy, complementary relationship between teaching and research—good teaching will follow from good research. But as Light (1974) has pointed out, the two activities compete for the faculty member's time and for most create a source of severe strain. Good teaching of undergraduates requires the kind of scholarship that does not feed easily into research publication. Thus, the high priority placed on research fosters resentment of the demanding undergraduate and, particularly, of the underprepared student. The academic professional model establishes a normative climate—a professional culture—that fosters a sense of failure and encourages faculty members to withdraw from more difficult (and often more time-consuming) teaching challenges that are a part of the profession today.

The academic professional model is especially pernicious in its effect on tenure and promotion decisions. In the expansionist period, when Ph.D.'s were in demand and faculty were highly mobile, tenure could be taken for granted. But under current conditions, a negative tenure decision can terminate one's academic career. Mauksch (1980) found that the normative pressures to support research are so great that members of faculty promotion committees often vote against their own preferences. He argues that this discrepancy is very similar to the discrepancy between public behavior and private attitudes described by Gunnar Myrdal in *The American Dilemma*. In confidential interviews with members of tenure and promotion committees, Mauksch found that although 75 percent of the committee members wanted to give more weight to teaching in their voting, they did not, because they were certain that their colleagues and the administration had "stacked the cards against such judgments." Ladd (1979, p. 5) supports this conclusion: "When a particular norm is ascendant within a group and is institutionalized in various ways, it is very hard for a member of a group to deny its claim, even if intellectually he is fully convinced of its seriously deficiency." In the current period of retrenchment, when tenure quotas are being imposed and promotions are being limited for fiscal reasons, the publication productivity standard is even more stringent. The older academic professional mode is being used to rationalize very difficult and often arbitrary judgments. In institutions in distress, it is being used as an anesthesia in the management of pain.

Peer Review

Peer review (colleague rather than client evaluation) has long been considered one of the primary characteristics of a profession (Carr-Saunders and Wilson 1928). The medical and legal professions have gone to great lengths to maintain that aspect of professionalism. In the academic world, peer review remains a hallmark of profession, but it is under severe assault. Student evaluation is becoming an established procedure in most institutions, despite occasional protests, particularly among faculty who do not take peer review seriously. A professional prerogative has been challenged, in part, because it was not responsibly maintained. Students also serve on tenure and promotion committees in a number of institutions and have become deeply involved in the appointment process. In years ahead, client evaluation of professionals promises to become even more important in higher education.

Peer review as a professional prerogative is being eroded not only by the encroachments of

the clients (students) but by the increased authority of administrators. This is reflected in the changes taking place in the organizational culture in higher education—i.e., in the shift from a collegial culture to a managerial culture. Supervision, evaluation, and the maintenance of standards are increasingly in the hands of academic managers. Peer review is giving way not only to new demand from below but to more authoritative directives from above.

Even in the arena of scholarly research, where peer review is most appropriate, the process has been redefined. Papers submitted to many journals are subjected to blind review. Thus, no longer is the reputation of the author and his or her mentor, the prestige of the author's institution of affiliation, or the general perception of the author's quality of mind allowed to influence directly the decisions regarding publication. Empirical studies demonstrating the unreliability of nonblind peer review are persuasive (Ceci and Peters 1982). The legitimacy of those older patterns of deference, which at one time passed for standards of excellence, has been eroded.

According to the older academic model, peer review keeps the academic hierarchy open and rational, so that "superiority of competence is the general legitimizing base of superiority of status in the academic system" (Parsons 1978, p. 105). But few would claim that the academic system in America has ever been fully open and rational, that the best always rise to the top. Discrimination based upon ascribed characteristics (e.g., race, religion, and sex) and the incessant press for homogeneity have continued to plague the profession. The changing conditions in higher education, however, are making the system even less open and the legitimizing basis for the superiority of status is losing ground (see Schuster and Bowen 1985, pp. 18–19). In departments that are fully tenured or in departments that have established a tenure quota, temporary faculty with non-tenure-track appointments are frequently as qualified as or better qualified than older, established faculty, and senior faculty often impose standards that even they could not meet. Strains between junior and senior faculty make colleagueship across age cohorts especially difficult. Even the gains that have been made by women and minorities through affirmative action are being threatened as the system contracts (Menges and Exum 1983).

The new conditions in higher education are even making it difficult to identify one's professional peers. Are the temporary non-tenure-track faculty to be regarded as fully enfranchised peers? What about the increasing number of part-time faculty? In community colleges, over half of the teaching faculty are already part-time. The preservation of older notions of peer review could lead to what Wilke (1979, p. xii) refers to as "a dramatic but relatively unnoticed structural transformation of higher education: the emergence of a quasi-closed elite at the top and a permanent under-privileged strata of untouchables at the bottom." To invoke the specter of the caste system is perhaps extreme, but if the one-dimensional academic professional model continues to be accepted as normative, higher education might well develop its own dual labor market.

Peer review is valued because it promotes informed critique, minimizes the abuses of the dilettante, and maintains the autonomy of the disciplines. In so doing, however, peer review keeps the critique inside, limiting contacts with not only other academic disciplines but other sectors in the society. What is needed now is a renewed capacity to reach out to that broader world, not reinforcement of the distance.

Centrality of the Discipline

A key element in the academic professional model is the centrality of the discipline. The commitment to a body of specialized knowledge has become the center point around which the other components turn. In American culture, where professionals already function with narrowly circumscribed work-encapsulated egos, professional identity among academicians is disciplinary: "I am a psychologist," or "I am a physicist." There is a kind of bonding to a disciplinary perspective, a way of thinking (theory) and doing (method). There is a body of literature, a mode of inquiry, and a history. Many faculty can trace their intellectual genealogies back to the founders of their disciplines. Introductory textbooks are often organized in that way and faculty offices are filled with the totems of discipline: books, pictures, and even charts of the lineage.

According to the older academic professional model, there is a distinct ordering of the disciplines, ranging from those that stand at the intellectual core of academic life to those that are obviously on the periphery. Parsons put it bluntly: "It seems quite clear that the faculties of arts and sciences constitute the structural core of the university complex" (1978, p. 103). Within this context, the major task of faculty members in relationships to students is to prepare them for academic careers. The most successful professors are expected to reproduce themselves, a process that is disparagingly referred to as academic cloning. The inappropriateness of this process for most of higher education is obvious.

The strength of the discipline at the center of the profession is institutionally buttressed locally by the discipline-based departmental structure and in more cosmopolitan settings by professional associations (national and international) that honor and reinforce the commitments of the discipline. The intellectual bonding to the discipline, which is nurtured in graduate school, is reinforced at every turn. In this assumptive world, to be a scholar is to be an academic professional within a discipline.

Given the wedding of academic professionalism and the discipline, interdisciplinary studies are by definition marginal. During the expansionist era, interdisciplinary programs were added on at the periphery of institutions without threatening the disciplinary core. During the 1960s, American studies, urban affairs, and various area studies programs flourished. Experimental "cluster" colleges focusing on interdisciplinary themes received much attention. But when budgets tightened in the 1970s, these interdisciplinary programs were the first to be eliminated. The more controversial programs focusing on the study of blacks, Chicanos, and women faced a discipline-based discrimination that was every bit as entrenched as the racism and sexism they were established to confront.

The disciplinary fortress that withstood these earlier assaults is now beginning to crumble in the face of a new interdisciplinary thrust driven by the demands of the market. Enrollment shifts from the arts and sciences to applied interdisciplinary programs in business, communications, and computer sciences are altering the basic character of colleges and universities. Confronted with this major structural tiff, liberal arts faculty argue for the integrity of the discipline and inveigh against the erosion of curricular turf. The legitimate case for the discipline has been tarnished by a contentiousness that is transparently self-serving.

The disciplines—particularly in the humanities and the social sciences, where there is limited consensus in the first place—have been heavily politicized, and the struggle to defend departmental hegemonies has profoundly distorted the educational mission of colleges and universities. Constructive debate over the distinctive intellectual substance separating the disciplines and the contribution each specialization makes to the whole educational enterprise has given way to the development of strategies to maintain FTEs (full-time equivalents) and faculty positions.

This zealous commitment to the discipline—exacerbated by the older academic professional model—has exacted heavy institutional and personal costs. The ideological defense of the discipline and the attendant political posturing have become major stumbling blocks in efforts to reallocate faculty responsibilities to meet changing needs. The adaptive capacity of institutions is being attenuated. For individual faculty, particularly those in mid-career, an inordinately close identification with the discipline limits opportunities for growth and development within the institution and renders the exploration of career options outside higher education virtually unthinkable.

The Pursuit of Knowledge for Its Own Sake

No tenet in the established conception of the academic professional has been more enduring than the commitment to knowledge for the sake of knowledge, to dispassionate reason, to the objective (value-free) study of nature, society, and the individual. Nisbet (1971) lamented the assault upon this ancient belief in his book *The Degradation of the Academic Dogma.* His argument was weakened somewhat when he began to write a regular column for the *Wall Street Journal.* No tenet has been the subject of more rancorous debate or betrayed greater evidence of a "false consciousness" within the profession—a discrepancy between what is said and what is done, between the ideal and the real.

In the early 1960s, scholars, particularly those in the social sciences, claimed to be engaged in the "scholarship of civility," a scholarship that was, if not value-free, certainly "beyond ideology."

During that period, many of these same scholars joined the march to Washington, D. C., and moved into positions of incredible power and influence. In a series of articles published in *Life* magazine in June 1967, Theodore White celebrated the new American action-intellectuals:

> In the past decade this brotherhood of scholars has become the most provocative and propelling influence on all American government and politics. Their ideas are the drivewheels of the Great Society: shaping our defenses, guiding our foreign policy, redesigning our cities, reorganizing our schools, deciding what our dollar is worth.... For such intellectuals now is a Golden Age, and America is the place. Never have ideas been sought more hungrily or tested against reality more quickly. From White House to city hall, scholars stalk the corridors of American Power (quoted in Steinfels 1979, p. 280).

By the late 1960s, it became evident that much of this scholarship, far from transcending biases, was deeply rooted in narrow ideological distortions of class, culture, sex, and race. Knowledge and power were being mixed in ways that became publicly evident. Those who argued for a scholarship of civility, for a scholarship that could rise above ideology, initiated a process that was self-discrediting. The radical caucuses in the professional associations—particularly in the social science associations—forced members to recognize that much of American scholarship had been shaped by and served the interests of rather select groups. The new scholarship produced by women, blacks, and representatives of various Third World groups strengthened the argument. By the end of the decade, the professional commitment to scholarship for its own sake had been severely undermined both within and outside the academy.

The professional arrogance of the early 1960s and the turmoil of the late 1960s produced a demand for a new approach to scholarship. The graduate students and young faculty who formed the new caucuses in the professional associations argued that all knowledge is rooted in a value context, and the radicals among them called for the international politicization of scholarship. Activities within the American History Association are representative. In 1969, the *AHA Newsletter* urged educators to "[broaden] historical abilities and knowledge among the general public . . . [to]demystify the holders of power and serve democracy" (cited in Lightman and Negrin 1981, p. 9). There was a call to reassess the relationship between the roles of scholar and citizen.

By the mid-1970s, scholars were being pressured by more established groups to address immediate public concerns. With the shrinking of available funding for scholarship, public agencies and private foundations became increasingly interested in projects that addressed public-policy issues. In 1976, the congressional reauthorization of the National Endowment for the Humanities mandated support for state councils established to provide public-issue programming for the adult out-of-school population. Participants in a major conference on the "New Scholarship on Women" in 1981 argued that education, itself, is a profoundly political act, that what is taught and learned "controls destinies, gives some persons hope for a particular kind of future, and deprives others even of ordinary expectation for work and achievement" (Howe 1982, p. 28). The commitment to knowledge for its own sake must be fundamentally reconceptualized if it is to make sense to faculty in colleges and universities that are now dominated by applied programs, where the slogan itself has been ideologically tainted by its most vociferous defenders.

Professional Rewards and Mobility Accrue to Those Who Persistently Accentuate Their Specializations

The assumptive world of the academic professional that took full form during the heyday of higher education has implied in it a career development pattern that was assumed to be normative for all. Like other professionals in America, academicians take as a guide for their working lives what Seymour Sarason (1977, p. 123) has called "the one life, one career impera-

tive." Buttressed by the additional commitment to the discipline and to their specialization, academic professionals take this imperative one step further and view their career trajectory as one that continues to narrow and become more firmly focused in the specialization. The reward structure, in both professional associations and local institutions, reinforces this conception of career development. Leaves of absence and research grants are awarded to those who continue to build on and narrow the thrust of their specializatons. Efforts to move in new directions or to develop competencies in other areas are systematically discouraged within the context of that older assumptive world.

My own work with faculty has focused primarily on arts and science faculty in mid-career. It is that large group of mid-career faculty—the majority in most colleges and universities—who are struggling to maintain vitality in their careers and who are having the greatest difficulty accepting the normative conception of what they should be doing with their careers (Rice 1980, 1985).

The literature on adult development and the new research that is being done on careers in other occupational settings indicate that what is needed for continual growth and development in mid-life is not pressure to extend and narrow further our specializations but the opportunity to attend to the development of the other parts of ourselves that has been neglected because of the specialized choices made at an earlier time. Kolb's (1981, 1984) work on adult learning is especially helpful here. He begins with Carl Jung's notion that the age of forty is the noon of life, and believes that "fulfillment in adult development is accomplished through efforts at integration and the cultivation of nondominant modes of dealing with the world" (1981, p. 250).

Kolb argues that what is needed in early career is the opportunity to develop and extend one's specialization; then, in mid-life, the chance to move in new directions, to develop other modes of learning, becomes more important. The movement in mid-life is from specialization to integration. For example, a theoretical physicist should move from an assimilative learning style (combining abstraction and reflection) into a policy-making position combining concrete experience and active experimentation. For Kolb, this is a movement toward wholeness, toward integration, toward the more complete development of the self. He is fond of quoting Yeats: "Nothing can be sole or whole that has not been rent."

The conception of career development that currently dominates the academic professional's self-perception and that informs our staff development policies promotes the perpetual pursuit and narrowing of one's specialization. Professors in their forties, looking ahead to twenty or thirty more years in the same department with the same colleagues teaching the same courses, feel stuck (Kanter 1977). To revitalize our institutions and the individuals within them, we must utilize the talents of this large group of faculty in new and imaginative ways. Again, the assumptive world of the academic professional stands in the way.

Toward a New Fiction

The primary difficulty with the dominant conception of what it means to be professional in the academic world is that it is one-dimensional, that it is applied to an increasingly varied occupational context, and that it is made normative for all. It is a complex of assumptions that developed in a unique period of affluence and expansion. It is probably too soon and would certainly be presumptuous to attempt to construct an alternative conception. Whatever the new professional image, it will emerge in response to the challenges of the new context and will be an elaboration on much of the old. Certainly, the new conception should lend dignity and give support and challenge to faculty where they are—in their everyday working lives—and where they need to be for the good of their students, the society, and the advancement of learning. There are some themes that stand out, however, and might well be included in a more multidimensional approach. I will list those themes and comment briefly.

A key issue is the place of scholarship in the profession. The older professional model takes for granted the bifurcation of the profession into teaching and research and identifies scholarship almost exclusively with the latter. There needs to be a primary focus on scholar-

ship more broadly defined. It may very well lead to publication in highly specialized disciplinary journals, or it may be disseminated in some other, more applied form.

In the older conception, teaching became a secondary activity that, it was assumed, would benefit from scholarly research. The particular kinds of scholarship required for quality teaching were largely neglected; if one was not engaged in substantive research—which is true of the majority of faculty—scholarship could also be deferred. The new conception should make scholarship the central focus of the profession. The demonstration of scholarship should be required, but the form it takes should be allowed to vary broadly, and its ties to teaching and learning should be assessed and honored.

The new image of the profession should also be multifaceted; it should recognize the full legitimacy of a variety of career paths and allow people to build on individual strengths. Heterogeneity should be valued. Despite the pitfalls, there is much to be learned from the corporate sector. Research on managerial careers has demonstrated that organizations benefit from recognizing and rewarding individual differences. The work of Schein (1978) and Driver (1979, 1982), which matches individual career orientations with organizational structure, is helpful here.

This new approach will require deans and department chairpersons to know more about the changing commitments and interests of faculty in their units. They will also need to know about the opportunities available (both within their institutions and without) for enabling faculty to grow and change in ways that benefit both the individual and the organization. Individualized approaches that take into consideration both age and career stage will be necessary.

In the older model, the disciplinary career (research, publication, and associational life) became disassociated from the institutional career (teaching, governance, and program development). A new and more appropriate conception should bridge the two. Autonomy is highly valued by most faculty, and the older academic professional model built upon and extended this concern to the point at which many faculty felt cut-off and isolated from their institutions and even their colleagues. Faculty want their professional lives to be institutionally useful. They want to participate meaningfully in program development and institutional innovation, but they feel de-classed professionally if they become involved in programs perceived to be marginal, programs such as general education or adult learning.

The academic career has three strands: the disciplinary career, the institutional career, and the external career. During the expansionist era, faculty lost connection with the larger society's purposes and tasks. This disconnectedness was caused by the rapid growth and the estrangement of the 1960s and was exacerbated by the high levels of specialization. Faculty are now being called upon to make new connections with what is regrettably called the world of work or, worse, the real world. The descriptions depict the problem. Younger students (aged 18 to 22) are seeking advice on nonacademic careers, and the increasing number of older students are bringing to the classroom a wealth of work experience that needs to be integrated into the process of teaching and learning. Co-op programs and internships abound (Rice 1983). Consulting is now regarded as an asset rather than a liability (Patton 1978, 1980). A number of faculty are having to consider, for the first time, the possibility of nonacademic employment. The disciplinary currency that has been so highly valued in academic settings suffers rapid devaluation in that external market.

The new conception of the academic professional must encompass that external world. The walls between the university and that other world will have to become more permeable to allow for greater movement both ways. At the same time, what is distinctive about the academic profession must be clearly articulated and carefully preserved.

Many of the challenges confronting academic professionals in the years ahead are integrative. They must tie the specialties together and transcend the polarities implied in the older model—i.e., teaching and research, theory and practice, content and process, peer and client. This is not to say that we should return to a simpler, less complex past. The new professional should not be a generalist, the gentleman scholar of an earlier time. Rather, the emerging challenge is to provide new forms of reintegration and build upon the advance-

ments made possible through specialization. During the golden age of higher education, the advances in disciplinary specializations were many and the achievements significant. That effort must be sustained and enhanced. But there is also a need for critical integrative work, which is every bit as legitimate professionally. Relating the parts to the whole and preventing the fragmentation that is always a threat is also of value and must be given priority. Only then will we begin to overcome the culture of separation that pervades society and, especially, higher education (Bellah et al. 1985).

Finally, like Emerson in the 1830s, we must reexamine the place of scholarship in a changing democracy. Much of what we have identified as the dominant conception of the academic professional is rooted in a cultural hegemony that is no longer viable in an open, pluralistic society. Scholars in a democracy have a responsibility not only for what is referred to as scholarly productivity but for what is learned, for how students "make meaning" out of what is written in journals, presented in the classroom, and performed in the laboratory. A developmental approach to the student as learner is required (see Perry 1981). Diversity in background and preparation should be seen as a central vocational challenge rather than a distraction from the real world. Scholarship must be defined in these broader terms to sustain a democracy that is committed to both honoring a plurality of communities and breaking through debilitating ascriptive barriers.

The new conception of the academic profession should take responsibility for learning in the general society, for what has been referred to as the ecology of learning. In the 1960s and 1970s, while the disciplinary specializations were growing and higher education was expanding, the quality of teaching and learning in the schools was seriously eroding (Rice 1984). Whether or not there was a causal connection, the culture of separation evident here can no longer be tolerated.

In his book *The Emergence of Professional Social Science*, Thomas Haskell (1977, p. 67) argues that during the early years of the social science disciplines, the new man of science had to "exchange general citizenship in society for membership in the community of competent." The professional conception discussed above accepted that exchange. The new view needs to reject the choice and affirm the academic professional's responsibility to both the specialized community and the larger society. Bellah et al. (1985) persuasively argue that higher education in our society has become primarily an instrument of individual careerism and that this orientation can provide neither the personal meaning nor the public commitment required to sustain a free society. The American professoriate must restructure its own professional commitments if it is to provide constructive leadership in a changing democracy.

References

Austin, A. E. and Z. F. Gamson, 1983. *Academic Workplace: New Demands, Heightened Tensions.* ASHE-ERIC/Higher Education Research Report No. 10. Washington, D.C.: Association for the Study of Higher Education.

Bellah, R. N., R. Madsen, W. Sullivan, A. Swindler, and S. Tipton. 1985. *Habits of the Heart: Individualism and Commitment in American Life.* Berkeley: University of California Press.

Bergquist, W. H. 1982. "The Future of Professional Development." Keynote address delivered to the Professional and Organizational Development Network in Higher Education, Montebello, Quebec.

Bledstein, B. J. 1976. *The Culture of Professionalism.* New York: Norton.

Carr-Saunders, A. M., and P. A. Wilson. 1928. *Professions: Their Organization and Place in Society.* Oxford: Clarendon.

Ceci, S. J., and D. P. Peters. 1982. "A Naturalistic Study of Peer Review in Psychology: The Fate of Published Articles, Resubmitted." *Behavior and Brain Sciences* 5:187–252.

Dressel, P. L., and L. B. Mayhew. 1974. *Higher Education as a Field of Study.* San Francisco: Jossey-Bass.

Driver, M. J. 1979. "Career Concepts and Career Management in Organizations." Pp. 79–139 in *Behavioral Problems in Organizations*, edited by C. L. Cooper. Engelwood Cliffs, NJ: Prentice-Hall.

———. 1982. "Career Concepts: A New Approach to Career Research." Pp. 38–52 in *Career Issues in Human Resource Management*, edited by R. Katz. Engelwood Cliffs, NJ: Prentice-Hall.

Haskell, T. L. 1977. *The Emergence of Professional Social Sciences: The American Social Science Association and the Nineteenth-Century Crisis of Authority.* Urbana: University of Illinois Press.

Herzberg, F., B. Mausner, and B. Snyderman. 1959. *The Motivation to Work.* New York: Wiley.

Howe, F. 1982. "The New Scholarship on Women: The Extent of the Revolution." *Women's Studies Quarterly* 10:26–29.

Jencks, C., and D. Riesman. 1968. *The Academic Revolution.* Garden City, NY: Doubleday.

Jones, H., E. Leist, and R. Ludwig. 1952. *Major American Writers.* Vol. 1 3rd. ed. New York: Harcourt Brace.

Kanter, R. M. 1977. *Men and Women of the Corporation.* New York: Basic.

Kolb, D. A. 1981. "Learning Styles and Disciplinary Differences." Pp. 232–55 in *The Modern American College: Responding to the New Realities of Diverse Students and a Changing Society*, edited by A. L. Chickering and Associates. San Francisco: Jossey-Bass.

———. 1984. *Experimental Learning: Experience as the Source of Learning and Development.* Engelwood Cliffs, NJ: Prentice-Hall.

Ladd, E. C. 1979. "The Work Experience of American College Professors: Some Data and an Argument." *Current Issues in Higher Education* 22:135–54.

Light, D. 1974. "Introduction: The Structure of the Academic Professions." *Sociology of Education* 47:2–28.

Lightman, M., and H. Negrin. 1981. *Outside Academe: New Ways of Working in the Humanities.* New York: Simon and Schuster.

Mauksch, H. O. 1980. "What Are the Obstacles to Improving Quality Teaching?" *Current Issues in Higher Education* 2:49–56.

Menges, R. J., and W. H. Exum. 1983. "Barriers to the Progress of Women and Minority Faculty." *Journal of Higher Education* 54:123–44.

Metzger. W. P. 1975. "The American Academic Profession in 'Hard Times'." *Daedalus* 104:25–44.

Nelson. W. C. 1981. *Renewal of the Teacher Scholar.* Washington, D.C: Association of American Colleges.

Nisbet, R. 1971. *The Degradation of the Academic Dogma.* New York: Basic.

Parkes, M. C. 1971. "Psycho-social Transitions. A Field of Study." *Social Science and Medicine* 5:101–15.

Parsons. T. 1968. "Professions." *International Encyclopedia of the Social Sciences* 12:536–46.

———. 1978. *Action Theory and the Human Condition.* New York: Free Press.

Patton, C.V. 1978. "Mid-Career Change and Early Retirement." Pp. 69–82 in *New Directions for Institutional Research*, edited by P. Heistaud and J. Warren. Cambridge, MA: ABT Books.

———. 1980. "Consulting by Faculty Members." *Academe* 66:181–85.

Perry, W. C. 1981. "Cognitive and Ethical Growth: The Making of Meaning." Pp. 79–116 in *The Modern American College: Responding to the New Realities of Diverse Students and a Changing Society*, edited by A. L. Chickering and Associates. San Francisco: Jossey-Bass.

Rice, R. E. 1980. "Dreams and Actualities: Danforth Fellows in Mid-Career." *AAHE Bulletin* 32:3–16.

_____. 1983 *Strategies for Relating Career Preparation and Liberal Learning*. St. Paul, MN: Northwest Area Foundation.

_____. 1984. *Toward Reform in Teacher Education: Strategies for Change*. Washington, DC: The Fund for the Improvement of Postsecondary Education.

_____. 1985. *Faculty Lives: Vitality and Change*. St. Paul, MN: Northwest Area Foundation.

Riesman, D. 1980. *On Higher Education*. San Francisco: Jossey-Bass.

Sarason, S. B. 1977. *Work, Aging, and Social Change: Professionals and the One Life-One Career Imperative*. New York: Free Press.

Schein, E. H. 1978. *Career Dynamics: Matching Individual and Organization Needs*. Reading, MA: Addison-Wesley.

_____. 1985. *Organizational Culture and Leadership*. San Francisco: Jossey-Bass.

Schuster, J. H., and H. P. Bowen. 1985. "The Faculty at Risk." *Change* 17:12–21.

Smith, H. N. 1939. "Emerson's Problem of Vocation: A Note on the American Scholar," *New England Quarterly* 12:52–67.

Steinfels, P. 1979. *The New Conservatives: The Men Who Are Changing America's Politics*. New York: Simon and Schuster.

Stevens, W. 1957. *Opus Posthumous*. New York: Knopf.

Veysey. L. 1973. "Stability and Experiment in the American Undergraduate Curriculum." Pp. 1–64 in *Content and Context: Essays on College Education*, edited by C. Kaysen. New York: McGraw-Hill.

Wilke, A. S. 1979. *The Hidden Professorate: Credentialism, Professionalism, and the Tenure Crisis*. Westport, CT: Greenwood Press.

Wilson, E. K. 1977. "Sociology: Scholarly Discipline or Profession?" Paper presented at the annual meeting of the American Sociological Association, Chicago.

Notes

1. Jencks and Riesman's (1968) book describing the increase in faculty domination in colleges and universities was published in the year that faculty domination peaked.
2. This analysis of organizational cultures was first brought to my attention by Bergquist (1982). The most useful book on organizational cultures is Schein (1985).

Part III

The Conduct of Education and Research

CHAPTER 5

THE UNDERGRADUATE CURRICULUM

ASSOCIATE EDITOR: SAMUEL E. KELLAMS

Colleges and universities are places where students come to get an education—that is, to learn. The curriculum and related processes of teaching are the center of formal learning activities in institutions of higher education. It is by no means simple to define curriculum, and the term continues to be used in many different ways. Curriculum is often thought of as a "plan" for student learning. The plan generally has two parts reflected in the following two questions: What is to be learned? That is, what are the purposes and objectives of educational programs? What knowledge, skills, values, attitudes, interests and behaviors should students learn? This is the "content" of the curriculum. The second question is: How is the learning process to be organized? Here, the sequencing of learning experiences in time and space, the calendar, the course requirements and options, the evaluative strategies, etc., are specified. This is the "structure" of the curriculum. The answers to these two questions constitute the plan for learning that we may find in a typical college catalog. But the curriculum is more than a document. It can also be seen as the actual experiences of students as they participate in educational activities (e.g. going to class, doing lab work, reading, discussing assignments with peers, etc.). Moreover, it has become increasingly difficult to distinguish between the formal (academic, curricular) learning processes and the informal (social, co-curricular) learning processes which both theory ("seamless learning environments") and research (Pascarella and Terenzini, 1991) show to be mutually reinforcing. Finally, the term "teaching" usually refers to the particular pedagogic methods and styles used to foster student learning, given a curriculum plan as defined above. Here, too, it is sometimes difficult to see where "curriculum" stops and "instruction" begins, given the widespread autonomy of college faculty to conceive of, plan, conduct and evaluate their courses. All of this is the topic of the first selection here by James Ratcliff (1996). This piece also introduces the reader to the concept of curriculum levels, curriculum models, curriculum influences (the internal and external factors that shape the curriculum), and, finally, the importance of outcomes assessment and evaluation of the curriculum. For an alternative discussion of these conceptual and definitional issues see Stark and Lattuca (1997) who have written the only contemporary textbook on this subject since the early 1970s. Their entire book is based upon the curriculum as a plan which has eight definable elements including: purpose, content, sequence, learners, instructional processes, instructional resources, evaluation and adjustment of the plan.

Historically, a large volume of literature has been produced on the topic of general education, that portion of the curriculum devoted to a broad, sometimes called "liberal," education. General education has often been seen in some kind of battle or tension with specialized education, that portion of the curriculum dealing with greater depth in a more delimited subject, usually a disciplinary, vocational or professional concentration or major.

In the 1980s a new wave of general education came to full flower as the third major general education revival of this century. See Boyer and Levine (1981) and Kellams (1985) for accounts of

Samuel E. Kellams is an Associate Professor in the Curry School of Education, University of Virginia, Charlottesville. (sek@virginia.edu)

these reform cycles. Several landmark reports were issued by study groups convened by the Association of American Colleges during the 1980s and 1990s that, together, reflected the terms of the debate and discussion. These included *Integrity in the College Curriculum* (1985) and its sequel, *A New Vitality in General Education* (1988) from which the second selection is drawn for this Reader. This selection includes many concrete examples of curricular content and structures forming the repertoire of reform proposals across the country. The piece discusses the balance between specific knowledge and modes of thought, the need to identify skills and competencies, the concept of teaching some of these competencies "across the curriculum," the major as general education, concrete processes of inquiry as pedagogy, the encouragement of active and self-directed learning, criteria for core courses and other integrative strategies.

The general education movement has continued into the 1990s and has received new impetus by the student outcomes assessment mandate associated with public accountability, as well as rising college costs and an increasingly consumerist clientele. For focused accounts of particular features of general education and normative trends across institutions, the reader should consult the work of Gaff (1991) and Gaff and Ratcliff (1996). The most recent report, *Reinventing Undergraduate Education: A Blueprint for America's Research Universities*, (1998), sponsored by the Boyer Commission on Educating Undergraduates, promises to continue the debate about the quality of undergraduate education by pointing out how the resources of research universities can be used to enhance undergraduate education rather than to detract from a quality education. To keep up with current trends in general education, and even to participate in the dialog, the reader is referred to the web site of the American Association of Colleges and Universities (http://www.AACU-edu.org).

Before the 1980s the specialized part of the curriculum—the major—was usually considered to be a success story in the curriculum, beyond the criticism directed towards general education. That all changed beginning with the Integrity report of 1985. Since then projects and scholarship have sought to improve the major so that it would reinforce and complement general education goals rather than be seen in opposition to general education (Stark and Lowther, 1989). The Association of American Colleges launched an ongoing project on the major and issued another widely read report, *The Challenge of Connecting Learning* (1990). *Challenge* . . . developed the concepts of the major as: a learning community; a sequence of common courses; a set of connections within, and outside of, the major; and the need for a critical perspective in which one would ultimately transcend the major to view it from multidisciplinary perspectives in order to see the limitations of any one discipline. The best summary of these issues can be found in the work of Carol G. Schneider, Executive Vice President of AAC & U (1996). The final selection in this Reader includes a provocative piece by Carol Schneider (1993) in which she questions the efficacy of the major to produce transferable skills and knowledge in support of general education goals. Her analysis takes on a postmodern tone as she views the major experience as a context bound, enculturation process.

Over the last decade one of the more salient trends in the undergraduate curriculum has been the incorporation of multicultural perspectives. These trends were accompanied by the debate over the canon which received widespread media coverage. For a reasonable and balanced look at this debate the work of spokespersons from many different perspectives is required. See Ravitch (1990) and D'Souza (1991) and, then, Pratt (1992), Graff (1992) and Asante (1991) for views that run the spectrum on this issue. To remind us that canon debates are not new, but have recurred periodically throughout our history and are likely to continue, Lawrence W. Levine (1996) has written a lucid and useful volume for students who want to understand how history shapes this issue.

Suggested Supplementary Readings

Asante, Molefi K. and D. Ravitch, "Multiculturalism: An Exchange: *The American Scholar*, 1991, 60, 267–276.

Association of American Colleges, *Liberal Learning and the Arts and Sciences Major*. Vol. I *The Challenge of Connecting Learning*. Washington, DC: Association of American Colleges, 1990, 1–21.

Boyer, Ernest L. and Arthur Levine, *A Quest for Common Learning*, Princeton: Carnegie Foundation for the Advancement of Teaching, 1981.

D'Souza, Dinesh, "Travels with Rigoberta; Multiculturalism at Stanford," in D. D'Souza, *Illiberal Education*, New York: Vintage Books, 1991.

Gaff, Jerry C., *New Life for the College Curriculum*. San Francisco: Jossey-Bass, Publishers, 1991.

Gaff, Jerry C. and James L. Ratcliff, *Handbook of the Undergraduate Curriculum*. San Francisco: Jossey-Bass, Publishers, 1996.

Graff, Gerald, "The Vanishing Classics and Other Myths: Two Episodes in the Culture War," in Graff, *Beyond the Culture Wars*, New York: Norton, 1992, 16–36.

Kellams, Samuel E., "Current General and Liberal Education Reform Efforts: The Cycle Continues," *Educational Studies*, 1985 16, 2, 117–126.

Levine, Lawrence W., The *Opening of the American Mind*, Boston: Beacon Press, 1996.

Pascarella, Ernest and P. Terenzini, *How College Affects Students*, San Francisco: Jossey-Bass, 1991.

Pratt, Mary L., "Humanities for the Future: Reflections on the Western Culture Debate at Stanford," in Darryl J. Gless and Barbara H. Smith (Eds.), *The Politics of Liberal Education*, Durham, N.C.: Duke University Press, 1992.

Project on Redefining the Meaning and Purpose of Baccalaureate Degrees, *Integrity in the College Curriculum: A Report to the Academic Community*, Washington, DC: Association of American Colleges, 1985.

Ratcliff, James L., "What Is a Curriculum and What Should It Be?", in J.C. Gaff and J.L. Ratcliff et al., *Handbook of the Undergraduate Curriculum*. San Francisco: Jossey-Bass, Publishers, 1996, 5–29.

Ravitch, Diane, "Multiculturalism. E Pluribus Plures," *The American Scholar* 1990, 59, 337–354.

Schneider, Carol G., "The Arts and Sciences Major," in J.C. Gaff and J.L. Ratcliff et al., *Handbook of the Undergraduate Curriculum*. San Francisco: Jossey-Bass, Publishers, 1996, 235–261.

Schneider, Carol G., "Enculturation or Critical Engagement," in Carol G. Schneider (ed.), *Strengthening the College Major*. San Francisco: Jossey-Bass, Publishers, 1993, 43–54.

Stark, Joan S. and Lisa R. Lattuca, *Shaping the College Curriculum*. Boston: Allyn and Bacon, 1997.

Stark, Joan S. and M.A. Lowther, "Exploring Common Ground in Liberal and Professional Education," in R.A. Armour and B. Fuhrmann (eds.), *Integrating Liberal Learning and Professional Education*. San Francisco: Jossey-Bass, Publishers, 1989, 7–10.

Task Group on General Education, "Planning Effective General Education," *A New Vitality in General Education*. Washington, DC: Association of American Colleges, 1988, 3–26.

The Boyer Commission on Educating Undergraduates in the University, *Reinventing Undergraduate Education: A Blueprint for America's Research Universities*, New York: SUNY-Stony Brook, 1998.

What Is a Curriculum and What Should It Be?

JAMES L. RATCLIFF

When a committee, a dean, or a department chair contemplates changing the curriculum, it is dangerously easy to make an assumption that everyone agrees on what a curriculum is. Familiarity *does* breed contempt. Since faculties regularly work with the curriculum, it is deceptively simple to assume that everyone agrees on what it is or should be. Making this leap of faith can lead to unnecessary disputes over nomenclature, and worse, aborted attempts at fundamental change. The committee may fail to recognize that the vision of what is a curriculum is heavily shaped by disciplinary values, educational philosophy, the diversity or homogeneity of students enrolled, and the social and institutional context. Answering what a curriculum is and what it should be is fundamental to understanding and improvement.

Beyond problems of nomenclature, folk wisdom says that reforming undergraduate education is a troublesome, tumultuous, and difficult assignment. Actually, changing the curriculum is easy. The faculty does it every term in thousands of courses. Estimates from research conducted at the National Center on Post-secondary Teaching, Learning, and Assessment indicate that about 5 percent of courses appearing on student transcripts for any one year were not listed in the formal college catalogue or university bulletin for that year (Ratcliff, 1993a). These often are new, experimental courses or one-time offerings. Some become part of next year's catalogue, while many others are dropped. A university of fifteen thousand students might well list more than three thousand courses in its catalogue, from which an undergraduate might choose thirty-five to forty-five to complete a baccalaureate degree. At such a university there would be seventy-five new courses each year (2.5 percent of three thousand, or as many credits as two undergraduates would need to complete their entire program of study! While this represents a substantial amount of curricular innovation, change, and expansion, it is atomistic, course-by-course change. It often involves a single faculty member constructing an innovative outline for a new upper division course or seminar. While such innovation often goes largely unrecognized in the curriculum reform literature, it challenges conventional wisdom that college and university curricula are difficult to change.

What is difficult is getting a group of faculty from many different perspectives and prior institutional and educational experiences to work together to design or change a curriculum to be cogent, coherent, and meaningful to students. A department often finds it difficult to agree on a common core of purposes, a set of required and elective courses, and a sequence of curricular and extracurricular experiences that develop student talents. Even more difficult is revising the general education curriculum, because it involves people from many different disciplines, with differing educational philosophies and diverse prior experiences. It is easy for any individual to design his or her favorite curriculum, but it is hard to get a group to find common ground on what constitutes an effective program of study for a department or institution. That, perhaps, is why academic folklore tells us that it is harder to change the curriculum than it is to move a cemetery.

"What Is a Curriculum and What Should It Be?" by James L. Ratcliff, reprinted from *Handbook of the Undergraduate Curriculum: A Comprehensive Guide to Purpose, Structures, Practices, and Change*, edited by Jerry G. Gaff and James L. Ratcliff and Associates, 1996, Jossey-Bass Publishers, Inc.

In the typical undergraduate curriculum of the 1990s, courses in the catalogue are like so many logs on a stack of firewood from which the students select a few to ignite the flames of intellectual inquiry associated with general, specialized, and liberal learning. Unfortunately, it takes more than logs to build a fire. Certain kindling is necessary and someone needs to light the match. Equally important is the way the logs are arranged. And there are different theories of how best to arrange the logs to produce a quick-starting and heart-warming blaze. Currently there is much debate as to what should be the purpose, content, and structure of the undergraduate curriculum—and often, it all hangs on what people mean by the word *curriculum*.

Curriculum Definition and Change

An *undergraduate curriculum* is the formal academic experience of students' pursuing baccalaureate and less than baccalaureate degrees. Such a curriculum is formalized into courses or programs of study including workshops, seminars, colloquia, lecture series, laboratory work, internships, and field experiences. Here, the term *course* is used generically, to designate a formal unit of undergraduate curriculum. Faculty members most often design and teach these courses singularly. However, there are many instances of team-teaching, teaching in turn, and the use of teaching assistants, student peer tutors, and guest lecturers. Faculty organizing and conducting a course generally control its purpose, process, and content. The role of a course in the curriculum at the inception is largely determined through a review by colleagues, first within the faculty of the home department and division. Subsequent reviews may be conducted at the school, college, or institutional level. The focus of these reviews is often to determine the overlap and duplication of the proposed course with others. The presumption is that if the new course does not substantially duplicate others, it must have merit as a contribution to and representation of the expanding knowledge base. Thus, in contemporary colleges and universities, faculty members individually, independently, and often unilaterally design and conduct the

learning experiences that are referred to collectively and generically as the curriculum. What we call an undergraduate curriculum tends to be a universe of courses, each with its own purpose and environment (Levine, 1978; Ratcliff, 1990; Veysey, 1965).

The term *curriculum* can refer to the educational plan of an institution, school, college, or a department, or to a program or course. At the program level of analysis, undergraduate curricula typically consist of three to four components: general or liberal studies, major specialization, minor specializations, and elective studies (Levine, 1978; Toombs, Fairweather, Amey, and Chen, 1989). The content of general or liberal studies is often set institution-wide by the faculty, while major and minor are prescribed by the department or program offering the particular specialization. The major and minor fields may, in turn, be governed by curricular prescriptions of a professional field represented, by guidelines extended by the disciplinary association, or by state licensure requirements or professional board examinations. While enrollment in elective courses nominally is left to student discretion, a prescribed range of electives may be set by the departmental major or minor.

Prescription or election? A major fulcrum of an undergraduate curriculum is whether the course of study should be determined by the student or by the faculty. The German or Humboldtian philosophy underpinning the research university (described in Chapter Four) presumes that students do not enroll unless they are prepared to take responsibility for their learning, and that they are not admitted unless they have the appropriate prior education to make sound educational choices and to decide upon the direction of their advanced studies. These assumptions support the practice of expecting the student to choose major, minor, and electives and to make sound choices among arrays of options in the general education curriculum. The philosophy of liberal education presumes that students enter undergraduate study for intellectual, personal, and social development; that the faculty have the expertise to and should provide direct guidance to students in that development; and that certain subjects in the curriculum provide essential knowledge, skills, and abilities toward those aims.

The liberal arts assumptions promote the establishment of prescribed core curricula in general and liberal studies, prerequisite courses in the major and minor, and limitations on the range and timing of electives. For example, consider a hypothetical African Dance course at a liberal arts college. Our course bears the department and course number Dance 123, and is offered for two credits. Its 100 series number signifies a first-year course; at this college, its course credits apply to the humanities and fine arts requirements of the general education curriculum. However, Dance 123 is cross-listed with Anthropology 123, signaling that it can qualify toward the social science requirements in general education as well. The general education curriculum committee at this institution regularly debates whether taking Dance 123 or Anthropology 123 should be double counted; that is, should the same credits be applied to both the humanities and social science requirements, or should students be allowed to apply the credits to only one category, and if so, does that render these categorical requirements of the curriculum meaningless? While the faculty struggle to reach an agreement on this matter, the unfortunate students merely trying to navigate the maze may miss the meaningful goals and purposes of the program.

To make matters more complex, general education and major curricula often overlap as well. At our college, there is a three-credit course, Dance 323, African Dance, which is the same as Dance 123 except that it is offered for an additional credit containing a studio component. Dance 323 is numbered as a 300-series course to signify as an upper division or third-year course; its credits may apply to the major requirements in Dance. There is, of course, a corresponding Anthropology 323 with similar expectations. Again, the faculty debate whether a course in the major can also count as a course in general education, and the students scratch their heads in wonder and confusion. The college catalogue grows ever more baroque and bureaucratic. Student decision making about what to study is constrained by a vast array of rules, lists, prerequisites, and course sequences. These too are part of the intentional curriculum. Reform of such curriculum requires questioning who decides when and why the curriculum should be pre-

scribed or elective in nature. How does Dance 123 (or Anthropology 123) help students attain any of the institution's general education goals? Faculty should be asked, in a nonrhetorical manner, "Why should students be required to take these courses?" Answers typically vary according to differing faculty views as to what students should be free to take and what they should be required to take.

External representation. At the macro level, the undergraduate curriculum of a particular college implicitly represents the philosophy and educational aims of that institution. It in effect is its academic policy. The educational program of the institution reflects the norms, values, and behavior of the organizational culture. Those in turn communicate an institutional image to various external constituencies, including prospective students, alumni, and civic and political leaders. Similarly, the curriculum articulates educational content, process, and standards for attainment to state, regional, disciplinary, and programmatic agencies, organizations, and associations. *All* are forms of a prescribed curriculum. *All* implicitly assume the hypothesis that students with different social and educational backgrounds experience different undergraduate curricular experiences and show different resulting rates and types of learning. A presumed primary criterion of the effectiveness of that curriculum is the extent to which it accomplishes its stated aims (Bergquist, Gould, and Greenberg, 1981; Ratcliff, 1990).

Diversity by institutional type. Institutions of higher education are often grouped, coordinated, or controlled according to their curriculum. The institutions that make up the California State College and University System have curricula that reflect the admissions policies prescribed in the California State Master Plan. Two year and community college systems consist of institutions offering a similar array of general and liberal, vocational and career, and adult and continuing education programs (Cohen and Brawer, 1989). Systems of higher education are organized and managed according to these curricular similarities.

Community colleges, historically black colleges and universities, and predominantly white colleges and universities attract different groups of students with different backgrounds, prior learning, and motivation.

Students in their first year at community colleges and historically black colleges and universities showed gains in selected areas of undergraduate learning (writing, critical thinking, science and social science reasoning) equal to or greater than those of students attending four-year colleges and universities and predominantly white institutions. While their gains in learning were similar at each of these institutions, both the entering and exiting knowledge, skills, and abilities of students at these institutions varied significantly (Pascarella and others, 1994). These conclusions do not suggest that all African American students should attend historically black colleges and universities. Instead, it suggests that the curriculum of these institutions is appropriate to some African American students, while others may profit more from attending a predominantly white institution; the key is in the match among prior learning, experience, and abilities and the host institution's curriculum and extracurriculum. Similarly, these findings do not suggest that all students might as well attend community colleges because the first-year learning gains are comparable and the cost is lower. Each institution contains a self-elected population of students, and the key to success is finding the challenging and empowering curriculum appropriate to a given student's prior learning, skills, interests, and abilities.

Different institutions provide different curricula, which produce different types and degrees of learning. While there is variation in curriculum and learning *between* institutions, the variation in student learning is greater *within* institutions than between them (Pascarella and Terenzini, 1991; Ratcliff, 1993a; Pascarella and others, 1994). Thus, the effects of curricula on student learning vary profoundly among students, courses, and programs within individual institutions of higher education. While differences in undergraduate learning clearly do exist from institution to institution, these tend not to be as great as the differential effect of curricula within them, and those institutional differences often are largely attributable to the differences in prior learning of the self-selected population of students who choose them.

Curricular complexity. A curriculum can be seen as a plan for learning an instructional system, a major subsystem of the university, a medium of student development, an analog to the structure of knowledge, and a representation of job skills (Toombs and Tierney, 1991). Also, a curriculum can be viewed from a variety of contexts, including college or university—or program—mission, purpose, or collective expression of what is important for students to learn; a set of experiences that some authorities believe all students should have; the catalogue or schedule of courses offered to students; the set of courses students actually elect from those available to them; the content of a specific discipline; and the time and credit frame in which the college provides education (Stark and Lowther, 1986). The very ambiguity and multiple uses of the term curriculum commend a curriculum committee to begin its work by selecting an operational definition and context for their work. Tyler (1950) has provided a fundamental conception of the basic elements of a curriculum organized around four questions that a committee engaged in design, development, or review activities can use as a guideline:

- What is to be accomplished?
- What learning experiences will help accomplish the purposes?
- How can these learning experiences be effectively organized?
- How can the effectiveness of the learning be evaluated?

These four questions lead the committee not only to consider major attributes of the curriculum, but also to do so in a sequence that reflects a widely adopted curriculum development process (Taba, 1962). *Curriculum development*, in turn, can be viewed as the development of plans for an educational program, including the identification and selection of educational objectives, the selection of learning experiences, the organization of learning experiences, and the evaluation of the educational program (Tyler, 1975).

Curricular theory or curricular model? Discussions of the curriculum may seem loftier if they are guided by theory or advance some model. However, these concepts are often confused as well. Scattered throughout the literature on the undergraduate curriculum are the terms *curricular theory* and *curricular model* (for example, see Brigham, 1982; Weiland, 1989). A *theory* is an explanation of something. A theory of the undergraduate curriculum would describe the relevant theoretical constructs. These constructs might include the major, minor, electives, or some idea of general or liberal learning. Such a theory also would explain how the constructs are related to each other (Borg and Gall, 1983). An interdisciplinary curriculum is defined through the amalgam of two or more disciplines, either concretely or abstractly. *Models* represent theoretical relationships. Curricular models describe observable behaviors. Thus, a curriculum based on demonstrable competencies includes activities to evaluate student attainment of desired skills.

Curricular models take at least two major forms. Dressel and DeLisle (1969); Biglan (1973a); Conrad (1978); Levine (1978); and Bergquist, Gould, and Greenberg (1981) are primarily concerned with describing the formal and informal organizational structures of institutions and their components. These are largely *descriptive* or *prescriptive models* of the way curriculum is or should be. Implicit in these models is the premise that undergraduate curriculum is purposeful beyond the level of the single course. Astin (1970), Pascarella (1985), Ratcliff (1990), the National Center for Research to Improve Post-secondary Teaching and Learning (McKeachie, Pintrich, Lin, and Smith, 1986), and the National Center on Post-secondary Teaching, Learning, and Assessment (Ratcliff and Associates, 1995) have constructed *analytic models* to discover the variables that affect student development and describe the nature of those variable interactions. These analytic models are derived from a differential hypothesis: that students with different educational and social backgrounds undergoing different undergraduate experiences show different rates of learning in different subject areas. Such a hypothesis includes variation in student characteristics, institutional characteristics, and the types of learning outcomes. Thus, two basic types of conceptual curricular models are those concerned with the structure, purpose, and process of undergraduate education and those concerned with assessing its differential effects.

The descriptive and prescriptive curricular models represent the nature and organization of the substantive elements of the curriculum. That is, they present ways to conceptualize and analyze the organizational structure of institutions, colleges, departments, and so on. The institutional-structural models focus on what the university or college prescribes for student study. In contrast, analytic curricular models do not examine curricular structure, organization, and purpose directly. Instead, they describe the relationship and interaction between institutional characteristics (of which the formal curriculum is but one factor) and student social, economic, and educational characteristics as they affect student learning, personal development, and maturation. In short, models for explaining the undergraduate curriculum can also be viewed as describing either the institution's intent or the interaction between student and college environment.

Curriculum designers, reformers, and scholars should not view these two types of models as dichotomous or contradictory; they serve as alternate constructions for framing the knowledge structures that make up the heart of the academic enterprise. A differentiated system of higher education—one that presumes that it is best to have different institutions, programs, and courses of study with different purposes, methods, and measures of attainment—presumes differential effects on student learning. The American undergraduate curriculum is based on a differential structure at the system, institution, and program levels that calls for the examination of those differential effects on students' intellectual, personal, and social growth (Ratcliff, 1996).

Bloom's definition of the curriculum (1981) illustrates both descriptive and analytic qualities of curriculum development. He defines the *manifest curriculum* (or formal curriculum) as the specified subject matter to be studied (such as science, mathematics, social studies, foreign languages, literature, or language arts), plus the behaviors needed for learning the subject matter. The manifest curriculum includes the written goals, objectives, rules, and regulations of an institution. By contrast, Bloom also suggested that there is a *latent curriculum* consisting of the way people value time, order, neatness, promptness, interpersonal relations, and so on. These values are not usually written down and specified, but are evidenced in daily living and interacting in learning environments. Finally, Bloom made a distinction between the terms instruction and curriculum.

Instruction, according to Bloom, is the carrying out of the curricular goals and objectives, while *curriculum* is the stating, structuring, and ordering of them.

The strength of a curricular model like Bloom's rests on its ability to describe and reach meaningful conclusions. Yet models, being simplified or schematic representations, map just part of reality. An effective curricular model is one where the analyst can say with confidence, "Nothing that matters in the real world was left out" (Cronbach, 1983). For Bloom, curriculum is both process and outcome, latent and manifest, substantive and behavioral.

> *A working definition:*
> Curriculum refers to both the process and substance of an educational program. It comprises the purpose, design, conduct, and evaluation of educational experiences. Curricula exist at different levels, ranging from the single course to the educational program to the department or discipline to the college or university. The organization of curricula is defined by educational philosophy, the structure and content of the knowledge imparted, and the institutional context and climate. Effective curricula have coherence and explicit definitions of aims and standards of attainment. They accomplish their aims through sequence and structure of learning experiences to facilitate student learning and development. They provide sufficient content and coverage to exhibit but not exhaust the limits of the subject of study. They include mastery of basic terms, concepts, models, and theories as well as some application of them to situations appropriate to the student, the learning aims, and the institutional context. Good curricula have the hallmarks of effective instruction and the evidence of the enhancement of student learning.

This working definition allows us to identify the curriculum, taking into account the complexity, diversity, and dynamism implicit in it. To determine what a curriculum should be requires us to determine what it is and contrast it with some desired form of purpose, design, conduct, and evaluation (Lindquist, 1978).

It is easy to change the curriculum at the single course level, perhaps because underlying issues of philosophy and purpose, coherence and integration, development and outcomes are not immediately challenged. The inherent complexity and diversity of the curriculum are only marginally addressed. Curriculum change at the program level often begins and ends with discussions about degree requirements, prerequisites, and sequencing—with little careful examination of how the curriculum is defined or what philosophical underpinnings and assumptions have been made relative to the development and attainments of students. Large-scale curriculum reform may be facilitated by careful attention to the different contexts, levels, and meanings associated with the word *curriculum.*

Curricular Influences and Curricular Purposes

The curriculum is purposeful, reflecting the needs of society, the ways of knowing shared within a field, and the students' interests, abilities, and prior learning. Its aims are guided by its educational philosophy—but that philosophy is far from universal. In a single institution and on a single curriculum committee, it is common to find several competing philosophies (Chapter Four). Conflicting and alternate visions of the purposes of undergraduate education frequently also are encountered because curricula exist at multiple levels and across a variety of disciplines and fields. In planning, revising or reforming curricula, it is important to be aware of each of these attributes.

Disciplinary influence. The role of individual disciplines as organizers of the undergraduate curriculum is largely a late nineteenth- and twentieth-century phenomenon. Prior to the rise of research universities, undergraduate education stressed the coherence and unity of knowledge in providing appropriate preparation for the professions (theology, law, medicine) and enlightenment for social, political, and economic leaders of the society (for example, see "The Yale Report of 1828," reprinted in 1961). With the development of new research universities such as Chicago, Stanford, Johns Hopkins, and Cornell, the teaching of research skills and the establishment of academic departments of disciplinary specialization were emphasized. Learned societies and disciplinary associations were established in the late nineteenth century and grew significantly in the twentieth century; through journals and conferences, these organizations provided a common language, discourse, and means of evaluating the merit of scholarship bounded by the discipline. Disciplines defined the means of communication, common methods and modes of inquiry, the exchange of research findings, and the creation of norms and values relative to the conduct of research (Beecher; 1989; Jencks and Riesman, 1968). Disciplinary inquiry often superseded institutional goals in defining the direction and purpose of undergraduate study. Today, colleges and universities often support a hundred or more undergraduate majors, most housed in discipline-defined departments, and all vying for influence over the direction, content, conduct, and evaluation of the undergraduate curriculum.

A *discipline* is literally what the term implies. That is, when one studies a discipline, one subjugates the ways one learns about phenomena to a set of rules, rituals, and routines established by the field of study. One conducts investigations according to these rules, classifying phenomena according to commonly adopted terms, definitions, and concepts. Relationships among phenomena are revealed through the frames provided by the discipline, and the researcher or student arrives at conclusions based on criteria for truth or validity derived from the field.

Disciplines can provide a conceptual framework for understanding what knowledge is and how it is acquired. Disciplinary learning provides a logical structure to relationships between concepts, propositions, common paradigms, and organizing principles. Disciplines develop themes, canons, and grand narratives to join different streams of research in the field and to provide meaningful conceptualizations and frameworks for further analysis (Shulman, 1987). Disciplines impart truth criteria used globally to define differences in the way knowledge is acquired and valued. Disciplines also set parameters on the methods employed in discovering and analyzing knowledge and in the ways they affect the development of students' intellectual skills (Donald, 1986).

Not only are paradigms for inquiry imparted by disciplines (Beecher, 1989; Biglan,

1973a, 1973b; Kuhn, 1962), but so too are values and norms regarding membership and scholarly conduct in the field (Holland, 1963) and preferred modes of learning (Kolb, 1981). Disciplines provide much structure and coherence to learning. It is easy to underestimate their power and importance in the advancement of knowledge and understanding at the undergraduate level. It is not clear whether a student or faculty member can be truly interdisciplinary without first mastering one or more disciplines.

The ascendancy of the disciplines in the late nineteenth century and their continuing dominance throughout the twentieth century have left an indelible imprint on the shape and direction of the academic major, often overwhelming the aims of general and liberal studies. In the late 1980s and 1990s, interdisciplinary studies, multiculturalism, feminist pedagogy, and a renewed concern for the coherence of the undergraduate program have challenged the dominance of academic major and called for cross-disciplinary collaboration.

Discipline-based curricula are a social construction developed by academics. Over time, knowledge has been organized into key terms, concepts, models and modes of inquiry. Academics add to and test these knowledge constructs using their disciplinary associations as means of verbal and written communication. Curricular change is conditioned by the role of the disciplines in conserving and transmitting their organization and representation of what is worth knowing, why, and how. Such a conception of disciplinary knowledge emphasizes the transmission of knowledge from generation to generation, and from academic to novice.

Student influence. Several subjects of study—for example, English literature, the physical sciences, women's studies, and environmental studies—began outside the college curriculum (Brubacher and Rudy, 1976; Rudolph, 1977). There is an inexorable relationship between the curriculum and the extracurriculum. Subjects and topics become areas of student interest and find their way into the curriculum.

Contemporary research suggests that the line between curricular and extracurricular effects on students is blurred and overstated; students' out-of-class experiences are powerful determinants of what, how, and how well they learn (Pascarella and others, 1994). For example, Briar Cliff College (Iowa), a small liberal arts college affiliated with the Catholic Church, underwent significant extracurricular and then curricular change as a result of student unrest, concern, and activism during the 1960s and the early 1970s (Johnson, 1986). Briar Cliff never experienced mass protests on the issues of racism and the Vietnam War like those that occurred at many large American universities. Briar Cliff students and faculty drew their liberal sentiments from the national news depiction of ghetto violence and campus unrest, resistance to the draft, and the protest music of the time. Briar Cliff had a primarily young faculty during the 1970s. This faculty's idealism was further influenced by the college's Franciscan heritage, which emphasized values such as concern for the whole person. More recently there has been a focus on academic activism, which has resulted in the development of a peace curriculum as part of the undergraduate experience. Briar Cliff's experience illustrates how student initiative and interest can migrate from out-of-class activities to take an increasing role in shaping the formal curriculum.

Social criticism, particularly as voiced through historically underrepresented groups such as women, minorities, and gays, provides critical perspectives on the curriculum. These perspectives provide alternate frames for describing the structure of knowledge and the ways of knowing. For example, the ways that women students approach learning have direct implications for the way curriculum is organized and orchestrated, and for the choice of instructional strategy: "It can be argued . . . that students need models of impeccable reasoning, that it is through imitating such models that students learn to reason. But none of the women we interviewed named this sort of learning as a powerful experience in their own lives. . . . Women students need opportunities to watch women professors solve (and fail to solve) problems and male professors fail to solve (and succeed in solving) problems. They need models of thinking as a human, imperfect, and attainable activity" (Belenky and others, 1986).

Critical theorists argue that the conventional canons of inquiry associated with the Western intellectual tradition stress rationalism as the cure for human irrationality (Toombs and Tierney, 1991). Through reason events are planned, societies are organized, and lives are shaped. A logical but extreme end to this process is the so-called iron cage of reason, wherein an individual's freedom and freedom of inquiry are enchained by previously defined reason and rationality dictating every appropriate action. Today the diversity of students and their attendant diverse approaches to learning influence what is taught, how it is taught, and how learning is judged.

Shulman (1987) has argued that the task of teaching is one of reframing disciplinary knowledge in forms that can be understood better by students. Teachers struggle to represent what they know in mental constructs that will render meaning and understanding to their students. The ways of knowing of women and other underrepresented groups challenge academics to represent knowledge, skills, and abilities through new epistemologies and pedagogies that allow for meaningful representations of what is to be learned, how best to learn it, and how to ascertain the extent of learning attained (see Chapters Six and Nine for further discussion of this point). Attendant to the diversification of the student population is the recognition that individuals may possess multiple intelligences, individually or collectively, to which a single pedagogy may be poorly addressed (Gardner, 1985). These, in turn, translate into multiple ways of knowing and learning with profound and practical implications for the undergraduate curriculum (Baxter-Magolda, 1992).

Curriculum reformers, designers, and researchers need to recognize that most colleges and universities are unlikely to find one form of undergraduate curriculum that best serves the learning of all students. This has profound import for general education curricula and some salience for majors and minors as well. Only in the most homogeneous of student groupings may a single curricular approach prove productive for all learners. However, unstructured and incoherent collections of courses are not likely to produce sustained long-term learning, either. Clusters, patterns, and sequences of courses aimed at the needs, interests, and abilities of salient subgroups of students may produce the most resilient reforms (Ratcliff and Associates, 1995).

Social, political, and economic influence. Social conditions exert significant influence on the purpose, organization, and structure of the curriculum. For example, during the nineteenth-century Industrial Revolution, demand for specialization increased and new scientific knowledge and new occupations emerged; in turn, these social trends supported the development and fragmentation of disciplinary knowledge. The Cold War and post-*Sputnik* era saw the rapid expansion of the sciences and technology in many Western and Eastern Bloc countries. The increased subsidization of research, science, and technology fostered disciplinary specialization and the rise of whole new specialties within disciplines. The undergraduate curriculum tilted toward scientific rationalism, specialization, and vocationalism.

While countless other social factors influence the undergraduate curriculum (as discussed in Chapter Six), an important emerging social goal for undergraduate education is the transfer of technological knowledge and skill in an effort to further economic development. The agricultural and mechanical university, pioneered through the Morrill Act of 1862 in the United States, is increasingly sought out to guide the process of technology transfer (Bergsma, 1986). Colleges and universities increasingly are urged to make their undergraduate curriculum more responsive to the needs of business and industry. Rapid growth in higher education enrollment in developed countries has paralleled the demand for college-educated knowledge workers, trained technicians, and specialists in those countries (Ratcliff, 1995). The social, economic, and technological demands for higher education have transformed the forms of knowledge, which in turn have created new stakeholders for the undergraduate curriculum (Walshok, 1995). This jumble of social, economic, and technological factors presents special challenges to curriculum reformers, designers, and scholars, for no one curriculum and no one institution can be entirely responsive to the vast array of new constituents.

Walshok (1995) has proposed a framework for revamping curricula based on this widening array of social demands. She suggests that the curriculum committee begin by sorting the types and dimensions of knowledge needs within a particular area of activity. Some efforts

have been made along these lines. For example, Jones (1994) reviewed the literature on critical thinking, then contacted faculty, local employers of graduates, and relevant policy makers for specific institutions of higher education; these stakeholders were asked to rank and sort those aspects of critical thinking found in the literature that were particularly important or salient to them and their needs. Thus what constituted critical thinking was reshaped in terms meaningful to external constituencies.

After the key areas of knowledge are grouped, sorted, or clustered, the stakeholders advocating curricular reform can be profiled for their level of knowledge and experience relative to the areas of the curriculum to be changed. This process produces a matrix of needs to which curriculum designers, reformers, and analysts can respond (Walshok, 1995). Since no one institution is likely to be able to respond to all the needs identified through this process, such a matrix provides a heuristic for identifying desired changes in the curriculum.

When such an approach is taken to identify needed areas of curricular enhancement or reform, researchers have found that employers, policy makers, and faculty often agree on broad areas of nontechnical knowledge, skills, and abilities to be imparted in undergraduate education (Jones, 1994). Recent surveys and focus groups have suggested that employers and policy makers seek further development of these nontechnical skills among undergraduates. This research is not clear as to whether employers take for granted or value less the specialized education students receive at colleges and universities. However, it is clear that certain knowledge, skills, and abilities associated with general and liberal learning are highly desired among these external constituents (Romer, 1995; Jones, 1994; Walshok, 1995). These include:

- Higher-order applied problem-solving abilities
- Enthusiasm for learning on a continuous basis
- Interpersonal skills, including teamwork and collaboration, and oral and written communication skills
- Sense of responsibility for action (both personal and collective)

- Ability to bridge cultural and linguistic barriers
- Sense of professionalism

What is striking about this list (from Romer, 1995) is how closely it corresponds to many goals set for general education, and how divorced it is from the usual general education course requirements or any particular discipline. External stakeholders and social forces implore curriculum designers, reformers, and analysts to reframe knowledge and pedagogy according to emerging social trends and needs for an educated workforce, but it is remarkable how similar their requests are to the goals of general education and liberal learning (Jones, 1994).

In summary, then, curricular purposes are directed, influenced, and shaped by the academic disciplines and applied fields of study, by student expectations, prior learning and abilities, and by social, political, and economic pressures from the society at large. These forces, internal and external, interact dynamically to define what the curriculum is as well as to create the expectations as to what it should be. Disciplines provide a strong paradigm for coherence and quality in a curriculum; however, those knowledge structures may not be the best representations of how students learn or of what society expects of higher education. Curriculum designers need to provide multiple forms of the curriculum for the diverse needs, interests, and abilities of students. Similarly, the expectations of employers and policy makers need to be carefully, closely, and systematically examined. Faculty, working in committees, must contend with and reconcile these often conflicting forces in formulating, renewing, or transforming the undergraduate curriculum.

Curriculum, Pedagogy, and the Culture At Large

Because curriculum is imported across disciplinary, institutional, and national boundaries, it needs to be adapted to the context and the culture from which the students originate. Curriculum innovations invariably undergo such adaptation—either willfully through the curriculum planners, or as a consequence of

disjunctures with learners, disciplines, or social expectations within the home institution (see Chapter Thirty-One). Such adaptation contributes to variety and uniqueness in the curriculum.

College life, for faculties and students, has traditionally been separate from the values, norms, and behaviors of the larger society. The medieval university strove for independence from church and state. Academic leaders in nineteenth-century America borrowed the German distinction of *akademische Freiheit*, freedom inside and outside the university, to advance the notion of academic freedom (Brubacher and Rudy, 1976). Today, it is part of academic culture to refer to the "real world" outside the college or university to reinforce the notion that values, norms, and behaviors are different in academia. This interaction between the larger society and the academic culture of students and faculty is manifest in the undergraduate curriculum.

In the United States, an uneasy relationship exists between the academic community and the larger society. Since the Bush and Reagan presidencies, a declared cultural war has raged between the intelligentsia (largely housed in colleges and universities) and the social and political conservatives gaining ascendancy to political and public life. The latter accuse universities of harboring ideologically bounded and "politically correct" curricula wherein undergraduates are indoctrinated with radical values, norms, and beliefs.

During the cultural war, Katz (1994, p. 11) argued, the intellectual left sought to distance itself from the status of professional intellectual class, while those on the right sought to separate themselves from any affiliation with the so-called cultural elites. One outcome of these responses was to help redefine the tenuous role of intellectuals in the broader society. Katz writes, "Anti-intellectualism thus creates an environment in which professional intellectuals are apparently pitted against the public." As Hofstadter (1963) put it, "Once the intellectual was gently ridiculed because he was not needed; now he is fiercely resented because he is needed too much" (p. 12). The climate of anti-intellectualism in the United States constrains the potential for debate over so-called political correctness by delimiting the role of the people involved in the debate. The predominant or host culture mediates the undergraduate curriculum. If the larger society does not value a particular line of inquiry, discipline, or field of study, students will come to the college or university with little motivation to include it in their studies. Conversely, if a topic is unresolved in the larger society it may find a transitory place in the curriculum.

The role of themes and troublesome topics. Themes may represent content knowledge to students in a familiar cultural context. Content knowledge in undergraduate classes is often structured so as to illustrate the existence of multiple themes in a written work. As the class reads and reviews several books on a given topic, these themes are intertwined to derive a parallel comprehension of the particular body of literature from which the books were drawn, as well as the history, society and psychology represented in the works. These themes excite and involve the students in ways that speak directly to them. The coherent quality of a theme holds the potential to help them better understand literature in general, history, the world in which they live, and themselves. Such themes are the basis of courses often regarded as fads by some faculty. Yet themes and troublesome topics illustrate an important function of the undergraduate curriculum: it provides a safe haven away from political strife, social conflict, and the pressures of everyday life to examine unresolved social issues. In order to understand the role and life cycle of a troublesome topic in the curriculum, we turn to the example of courses concerning Vietnam.

The Vietnam War has proven to be a difficult topic in the American college classroom. Society at large may very well be unreconciled about the correct interpretation of events leading to, during and concluding American involvement in the Vietnamese civil war. In the 1980s, there was a dramatic increase in American college course offerings about the decade of the 1960s, particularly the period of the American involvement in Vietnam. Collison (1988) found the popularity of the courses to be a result of the demographics and background of the faculty teaching the courses and of the students' curiosity about protest movements. There was a meeting between two generations: younger faculty who had lived through and were unreconciled toward American involvement in Vietnam, and inter-

ested students who had grown up with the war on the evening news every night on TV. Some faculty felt the courses were essential to student understanding of modern life, whereas others believed that more research on the topic was needed. Israel (1985) lamented that the coming generation had little historical memory of the events of the Vietnam War and virtually no emotional investment in the issues discussed. He too felt a special obligation to engage students in an examination of this troublesome topic. The more recent waning of student interest in the topic may modify the instructors' approach to it and may ultimately contribute to its discontinuance from the curriculum.

The field of study imposes discipline and constraint on the passions fueling the interest in troublesome topics like the Vietnam War. Here the discipline renders an order to the examination of an issue otherwise charged with emotion. Pike (1985), for example, urged the use of objectivity in social science inquiry to weigh the conflicting interpretations of the war. He found that there has been a flood of new historical information vastly revising much of what anyone—left, right, or center—knew. Wilcox (1988) advocated the use of primary sources in teaching about the Vietnam War. The approach encouraged student questioning and discussion of issues surrounding the war. He urged the faculty to be certain that students know and understand the reasons for the war and not just repeat rhetoric. The emphasis, again, was on ways of knowing and understanding a troubling period in the collective consciousness of American society. For Wilcox, there appeared to be a belief that there is a correct interpretation of the events to be discovered.

As Kuhn (1962) has pointed out, it is the function of "normal science" to resolve and incorporate new information into the prevailing paradigmatic interpretation of events. It is the role of the political scientist to examine all major competing perceptions of the Vietnam War objectively. Yet it is the intersection between the troublesome topic, the culture at large, and the process and content of the discipline that produces the interest and shapes the inquiry.

Troublesome topics bring excitement, imagination, and motivation to the students who study them and the faculty who teach them. They illustrate the transitional nature of the undergraduate curriculum, as well. Subjects or topics of gripping interest to one generation of students may seem dull to the next. The coursework embodying troublesome topics may enter the curriculum from the extracurriculum, reside in the undergraduate program of study up to a decade or more, and wane or disappear as its salience to society subsides. Ultimately it may be discontinued for lack of student demand or may migrate to the secondary school curriculum as knowledge in the field of study becomes more advanced.

Culture and society affect the undergraduate curriculum. The effect may be indirect and may influence both the content and processes employed with undergraduates. So-called fad courses and new curricular themes should be regarded carefully by those reviewing and revising the curriculum. They may play an important role of mediating between the academy and the society at large. The curriculum becomes not only the way to infuse new knowledge into the college-educated populace, but also the medium to accomplish it. Teaching strategies are modified and new courses are adopted to motivate students, to introduce new subjects, to provide prerequisite concepts or language skills. Thus not only does the new knowledge enter the curriculum as new or adapted courses, but supplemental programs and coursework emerge to prepare and motivate students for the new subjects and fields of study. This tension between society and the academy, and the multiple forms and ways it manifests itself, creates a dynamic that propels curricular change. To miss this dynamic is to understate the role of the curriculum.

Building an Engaging Curriculum: Curricular Evaluation and Assessment

Assessment is the process of defining, selecting, designing, collecting, analyzing, interpreting, and using information to increase students' learning and development. It includes discussions about what should be assessed and how information will be used, not just the hands-on testing of students (Marchese, 1987). The terms *assessment*, *evaluation*, and *measurement* are used in confusing and contradictory ways. In order to be clear in our description, we use Lenning's (1980) differentiation of the terms. *Measurement* is the simple process of gathering and quantifying information. It serves as the basis for assessment and evaluation. *Assessment* occurs when measurements are analyzed. *Evaluation* occurs when judgments are applied to assessment efforts.

Assessment is commonly used in three principal contexts: the assessment of prior learning in preparation for college-level coursework; the assessment of college level learning (of what students learned after one, two, or three years of college); and the assessment of college outcomes relative to college inputs (Sims, 1992, p. 5). Assessment is judged to be most beneficial when it leads to improvement of educational programs and student learning. To be beneficial, it must serve a formative role (Hawthorne, 1989, p. 55). To serve as constructive yardsticks for the success of the curriculum, assessment and evaluation activities need to provide timely feedback to guide improvement. That is, whether feedback goes to students so they can alter their learning strategies, or to the faculty so they can redirect or retarget the curriculum, it must arrive in time to make the necessary adjustments. It must be informative and timely, and must differentiate among those who are benefiting from the curriculum and those who are not.

As noted earlier, there are usually greater differences among students in a single institution than there are differences in students across institutions (Pascarella and Terenzini, 1991). Therefore, colleges and universities need to examine the relationship between coursework chosen by students in various subpopulations and the learning outcomes evidenced in the assessment of general education and general learned abilities. Information about these relationships can be useful in the planning of student advising, course scheduling, curricular change, and faculty instructional development activities, and in the selection of assessment methods and measures (Ratcliff, 1992). In particular, advising can be more effective when tailored to the needs of individual students.

The undergraduate curriculum is typically described in one of two ways. It is profiled either in terms of what is prescribed for students or in terms of what they acquire from their academic experiences. This distinction is represented in the difference between the questions, What does the curriculum intend for students to learn? and What in the curriculum affects student learning? Despite the widespread use of assessment in recent years, the prevalent way to view the college curriculum is still according to its intentions rather than according to its results (Ratcliff, 1990; Warren, 1975; Weiland, 1989). Determining the effect of the undergraduate curriculum on students can be difficult. Most research on undergraduate curricula presumes rather than tests the effect of different patterns of coursework and programs of study on student learning. Therefore, it is important to distinguish at the outset between those patterns of coursework intended to fulfill undergraduate program and degree requirements and those patterns of formal study that students actually choose (Boyer and Ahgren, 1987; Ratcliff, 1990; Warren, 1975; Weiland, 1989). In fact, it is the gap between what was intended and what learning resulted from the curriculum that allows the identification of the discrepancy between curricular aims and educational attainment.

A Few Good Practices in Curricular Design

Coherence in content. A curriculum provides a sequence of learning experiences inside and outside the classroom, resulting in formal coursework to attain specific educational aims. There should be a clear connection between what is to be taught, how it is to be taught, and how learning is evaluated—a topic explored in more depth in Chapter Seven. The coherence between aims, design, and evaluation is premised upon the educational philosophy employed. A heritage-based curriculum refers to the value placed on the reflection and transmission of knowledge and cultural legacies. Its design calls for the identification of essential readings and works to be read, analyzed, and deliberated by students. The Great Books curriculum not only has goals of understanding, comprehension, and analysis of key thinkers and writers, but also bears an implicit design and sequence derived from the rationalist tradition of the Enlightenment. The foundations of inquiry, such as mathematics, language, and logic should precede advanced studies in the arts, humanities, social sciences, and natural sciences.

The curriculum of the medieval university had a design that included sequencing and prerequisites to achieve coherence as well as aims. The subjects of the *quadrivium* (arithmetic, geometry, astronomy, and music) were to follow and build upon study in the *trivium* (logic, grammar and rhetoric). In America, structure and coherence in higher education curricula were reinforced by the ideals of liberal learning as embodied in the writings of John Henry Cardinal Newman. American philosophers and psychologists, principally John Dewey and Henry James, advocated an educational system that could help make social change and socialize individuals to laissez-faire social democracy. Humboldtian ideals fostered the pursuit and advancement of knowledge (associated with German traditions of the research university), but they have helped to break down coherence as scholars seek to teach to their disparate research interests (Ratcliff, 1993b).

Notions of the functional benefits of prescribed development and sequence in coursework now have been largely replaced by the more oblique notion of breadth and depth of study in undergraduate education. Most U.S. institutions of higher education seek coherence and purpose by requiring students to select from lists of courses a certain number of credits to meet degree requirements; these distributional general education requirements are the norm in more than 90 percent of colleges and universities (Toombs, Fairweather, Amey and Chen, 1989). The evidence has shown that students at the same institution do not share a common curricular experience in their pursuit of the bachelor's degree (Boyer and Ahlgren, 1987; Ratcliff, 1990). Curricular coherence never was an expectation of an academic culture in which individual faculty members decide what they wish to teach and individual students decide what lectures and seminars to attend and what they wish to learn. *Lehrfreiheit* (the freedom to teach whatever the individual faculty member thinks is important) and *lernfreiheit* (the freedom of the student to study whatever interests him or her), in an absolute sense, may mitigate against effective and efficient programs and curriculum for mass higher education. A high-stakes environment is needed in which both student and institution share in the responsibility of demonstrating educational results.

Cognitive skill development. Curriculum planners are realizing that speaking, reading, writing, and related linguistic processes are instrumental in all areas of learning. In university departments, teachers of content subjects and language specialists are tending to look at the curriculum as a whole. Faculties in the various disciplines need to be aware of the linguistic process by which students acquire subject-specific information and understanding. English language development is coming to be regarded as the responsibility of all academic staff within and across departments, not just of the individuals charged with teaching English to students. Although the across-the-curriculum approach to reading and writing is often more difficult and complex to implement, it holds promise to assure the successful development of language proficiency (Cheong, 1985). English specialists in non-English speaking countries are also instituting a policy of English language across the curriculum. In the United States, similar curricular reforms have been implemented to encourage and strengthen the development of writing and conceptual skills across the curriculum (Toombs, Fairweather, Amey, and Chen, 1989). Chapters Eighteen and Nineteen discuss this in more detail.

Summary

The undergraduate curriculum at most colleges and universities consists of a wide array of course offerings from which students select a limited number of courses to complete their undergraduate degree program. Student choice of coursework is constrained by institutionally defined degree requirements for general and liberal education, major and minor specializations, and elective studies. Students at a single institution rarely experience a common intellectual experience in the curriculum—no more than 20 percent of coursework—unless the institution specifically prescribes a common core of courses that all students must take. Such prescription is not the norm. Instead, the curriculum expands with the knowledge base, the needs of society and the interests of the students and faculty. The practice of offering an increasing catalogue of courses developed and taught largely by individual faculty members reflects the

implicit assumption that taking different courses produces different types of learning and that such differential learning is a positive attribute of the undergraduate curriculum.

The need for a wider assortment of coursework is a result of differential preparation for college. To the extent that secondary education programs uniformly prepare students for collegiate studies, the need for programs targeted at students with different educational backgrounds is minimized. Similarly, the extent to which higher education is open and assessable to a large proportion of high school graduates will affect the extent to which coursework will need to be crafted to students of differing abilities and interests. Gaps between the prior achievement of entering students and the knowledge, skills, and abilities needed to succeed in college coursework are endemic. Then too, changes are occurring continuously within courses and between courses to reflect shifts in the paradigms of inquiry within the field of study, in the nature of social need and cultural value for the subject of study, in the role a particular course or program may take in the overall curriculum of the college or university or in the interests and inclinations of the students who enroll or the faculty who design the instruction.

The curriculum is described in two ways: by what its intended outcomes are to be or by what its effects are on student learning. Clearly, the prevalent way of portraying curriculum is by its purposes and intentions. Yet, to understand better the role the curriculum plays in higher education, it is incumbent on researchers to uncover its effects. The undergraduate curriculum is the primary educational policy of a college or university. To the extent that an institution develops its own policy, its effectiveness rests with the educational attainment of its students.

Curricular theory is largely descriptive or prescriptive rather than transformational. Curricular models seek to describe and explain how the curriculum functions rather than to direct or guide its effects on students. A prescriptive curriculum explains what students take, what faculty should teach, or what students should learn. A descriptive curriculum portrays how the academic program is organized so that it might be better understood in its entirety by faculty, advisers, and students.

Curricular content, sequence, and process are further constrained by the standards and expectations of associations and organizations representing the fields of study. These groups may accredit academic programs; impose licensure examinations upon graduates; transmit the values, norms, and behavior appropriate to the discipline's faculty; or simply influence the curriculum through the introduction of new knowledge, processes, conceptual frameworks, and modes of inquiry among its members.

The curriculum is strongly mediated by the students and the society that it serves. Faculty members educated and socialized in another culture or country may bring expectations of instructional practices, educational philosophy and purpose, and standards of achievement that may not match student or social interest in the subject area. Disciplinary associations may promote standards of practice not entirely appropriate to the students to be educated.

The curriculum is a powerful tool of academic and social policy in higher education. The prevalent practice has been to assume that the effects of the undergraduate curriculum were what they were intended to be. There is a growing realization that the gap between what is intended in the curriculum and what its effects are must be bridged. We are just beginning to understand the role of coherent curricular design and effective, informative evaluation in narrowing the gap.

References

Astin, A. W. "The Methodology of Research on College Impact. Part I." *Sociology of Education*, 1970, 43, 437–450.

Baxter-Magolda, M. B. *Knowing and Reasoning in College: Gender Related Patterns in Students' Intellectual Development*. San Francisco: Jossey-Bass, 1992.

Beecher, T. *Academic Tribes and Territories: Intellectual Enquiry and the Cultures of Disciplines*. Bristol, Pa.: Open University Press, 1989.

Belenky, M. F., Clinchy, B. M., Goldberger, N. R., and Tarule, J. M. *Women's Ways of Knowing: The Development of Self, Voice, and Mind*. New York: Basic Books, 1986.

Bergquist, W. H., Gould, R. A., and Greenberg, E. M. *Designing Undergraduate Education*. San Francisco: Jossey-Bass, 1981.

Bergsma, H. M. *Technology Transfer through Training: Emerging Roles for the University*. Paper presented at the second annual Regional Conference on University Teaching, Las Cruces, N.M., Jan. 8–10, 1986. (ED 280 336)

Biglan, A. "The Characteristics of Subject Matter in Different Academic Areas." *Journal of Applied Psychology*, 1973a, 57(3), 195–203.

Biglan, A. "Relationships Between Subject Matter Characteristics and the Structure and Output of University Departments." *Journal of Applied Psychology*, 1973b, 57(3), 204–213.

Bloom, B. S. *All Our Children: A Primer for Parents, Teachers, and Other Educators*. New York: McGraw-Hill, 1981.

Borg, W. R., and Gall, M. D. *Educational Research: An Introduction*. (4th ed.) New York: Longman, 1983.

Boyer, C. M., and Ahlgren, A. "Assessing Undergraduates' Patterns of Credit Distribution: Amount and Specialization." *Journal of Higher Education*, 1987, 58, 430–442.

Brigham, T. M. "Social Work Education Patterns in Five Developing Countries: Relevance of U.S. Microsystems." *Journal of Education for Social Work*, 1982, 18(2), 68–75.

Brubacher, J. S., and Rudy, W. *Higher Education in Transition: A History of American Colleges and Universities, 1636–1976*. (2nd ed.) New York: HarperCollins, 1976.

Cheong, L. K. "English Across the University Curriculum." Paper presented at a regional seminar of the SEAMEO Regional Language Centre, Singapore, April 26, 1985. (ED 262 613)

Cohen, A. M., and Brawer, F. B. *The American Community College* (2nd ed.) San Francisco: Jossey-Bass, 1989.

Collison, M. N. K. "Age of Aquarius and Vietnam: Today's Students Flock to Courses about 1960's." *Chronicle of Higher Education*, 1988, 34(37), A33, 34.

Conrad, C. F. *The Undergraduate Curriculum: A Guide to Innovation and Reform*. Boulder, Colo: Westview Press, 1978.

Cronbach, L. J. *Designing Evaluations of Educational and Social Programs*. San Francisco: Jossey-Bass, 1983.

Donald, J. G. "Knowledge and the University Curriculum." *Higher Education*, 1986, 15, 267–282.

Dressel, P. L., and DeLisle, F. H. *Undergraduate Curriculum Trends*. Washington, D.C.: American Council on Education, 1969.

Gardner, H. *Frames of Mind: The Theory of Multiple Intelligences*. New York: Basic Books, 1985.

Hawthorne, E. M. *Evaluating Employee Training Programs: A Research-Based Guide for Human Resource Managers*. New York; Quorum Books, 1989.

Hofstadter, R. *Anti-Intellectualism in American Life*. New York: Vintage Books, 1963.

Holland, J. "Explorations of a Theory of Vocational Choice and Achievement II: A Four Year Predictive Study." *Psychological Reports*, 1963, 12, 547–594.

Israel, J. "Vietnam in the Curriculum." *Teaching Political Science*, 1985, 12(4), 181–186.

Jeneks, C., and Riesman, D. *The Academic Revolution.* New York; Doubleday, 1968.

Johnson, P. *The Activist Decade: Its Influence on Briar Cliff College.* Sioux City,Iowa: Briar Cliff College, 1986. (ED 284 465)

Jones, E. A. *Essential Skills in Writing, Speech, and Listening, and Critical Thinking for College Graduates: Perspectives of Faculty, Employers, and Policy Makers.* University Park, Pa.: National Center on Post-secondary Teaching, Learning, and Assessment, 1994.

Katz, S. N. "The Teacher-Scholar, the University and Society." Paper presented at the Rutgers Conference on the Politics of Research, New Brunswick, NJ., Oct. 21, 1994.

Kolb, D. A. "Learning Styles and Disciplinary Differences." In A. W. Chickering and Associates, *The Modern American College: Responding to the New Realities of Diverse Students and a Changing Society.* San Francisco: Jossey-Bass, 1981.

Kuhn, T. S. *The Structure of Scientific Revolutions.* Chicago: University of Chicago Press, 1962.

Lenning, O. T. "Assessment and Evaluation." In U. Delworth, G. R. Hanson, and Associates, *Student Services: A Handbook for the Profession.* San Francisco: Jossey-Bass, 1980.

Levine, A. *Handbook on Undergraduate Curriculum.* San Francisco: Jossey-Bass, 1978.

Lindquist, J. *Strategies for Change.* Berkeley, Calif: Pacific Soundings Press, 1978.

Marchese, T. J. "Third Down, Ten Years to Go: An Assessment Update." *AAHE Bulletin*, 1987, 40(4), 3–8.

McClelland, J. C. *State, Society and University in Germany, 1700–1914.* Cambridge, England: Cambridge University Press, 1980.

McKeachie, W. J., Pintrich, P. R., Lin, Y. G., and Smith, D. A. F. *Teaching and Learning in the College Classroom: A Review of the Research Literature.* Ann Arbor: National Center for Research and Improvement on Teaching and Learning, University of Michigan, 1986. (ED 314 999)

Pascarella, E. T. "College Environmental Influences on Learning and Cognitive Development: A Critical Review and Synthesis." In J. Smart (ed.), *Higher Education: Handbook of Theory and Research,* Vol. 1. New York: Agathon Press, 1985.

Pascarella, E. T. and Terenzini, P. T. *How College Affects Students: Findings and Insights from Twenty Years of Research.* San Francisco: Jossey-Bass, 1991.

Pascarella, E. T., and others. *What Have We Learned from the First Year of the National Study of Student Learning?* Chicago: National Center on Post-secondary Teaching, Learning and Assessment, University of Illinois, 1994.

Pike, D. "Teaching the Vietnam Experience as a Whole Course." *Teaching Political Science*, 1985, 12(4), pp. 144–151.

Ratcliff, J. L. *Development and Testing of a Cluter-Analytic Model for Identifying Coursework Patterns Associated with General Learned Abilities of College Students: Final Report, May, 1990.* U.S. Department of Education, Office of Educational Research and Improvement, Research Division. Contract No. OERI-R-86-0016. University Park: Center for the Study of Higher Education, Pennsylvania State University, 1990.

Ratcliff, J. L. "Reconceptualizing the College Curriculum." *Perspectives: The Journal of the Association for General and Liberal Studies*, 1992, pp. 122–137.

Ratcliff, J. L. *What We Can Learn from Coursework Patterns About Improving the Undergraduate Curriculum.* University Park, Pa.: National Center on Postsecondary Teaching, Learning and Assessment, 1993a.

Ratcliff, J. L. "Implementing a Quality Assurance Program based on Assessments of Student Learning in a Differentiated System of Higher Education." Paper presented at the first preconference of the International Committee, Association for the Study of Higher Education, State College, Pa., Nov. 1–2, 1993b.

Ratcliff, J. L. "A Rationale for a Differentiated System of Higher Education." *Tertiary Education and Management*, 1996, 2(2), 127–137.

Ratcliff, J. L., and Associates. *Realizing the Potential: Improving Postsecondary Teaching, Learning, and Assessment.* University Park, Pa.: National Center on Postsecondary Teaching, Learning, and Assessment, 1995.

Romer, R. *Making Quality Count in Undergraduate Education. A Report for the ECS Chairman's "Quality Counts" Agenda in Higher Education.* Denver; Education Commission of the States, 1995.

Rudolph, F. *Curriculum: A History of the American Undergraduate Course of Study Since 1636.* San Francisco: Jossey-Bass, 1977.

Shulman, L. S. "Knowledge and Teaching: Foundations of the New Reform." *Harvard Educational Review*, 1987, 57(1), 1–22.

Sims, S. J. *Student Outcomes Assessment: A Historical Review and Guide to Program Development.* Westport, Conn.: Greenwood Press, 1992.

Stark, J. S., and Lowther, M. A. *Designing the Learning Plan: A Review of Research and Theory Related to College Curricula.* Ann Arbor: National Center for Research on Postsecondary Teaching and Learning, University of Michigan, 1986. (ED 287 439)

Taba, H. *Curriculum Development: Theory and Practice.* Orlando, Fla.: Harcourt Brace Jovanovich, 1962.

Toombs, W., Fairweather, J. S., Amey, M., and Chen, A. *Open to View: Practice and Purpose in General Education.* University Park, Pa.: Center for the Study of Higher Education, 1989.

Toombs, W., and Tierney, W. *Meeting the Mandate: Renewing the College and Departmental Curriculum.* ASHE-ERIC Higher Education Report No. 6. Washington, D.C.: School of Education and

Human Development, George Washington University, 1991.

Tyler, R. W. *Basic Principles of Curriculum and Instruction*. Chicago: University of Chicago Press, 1950.

Tyler, R. "Specific Approaches to Curriculum Development." In J. Schaffazick and D. Hampton (eds.), *Strategies for Curriculum Development*. Berkeley, Calif.: McCutchan, 1975.

Veysey, L. *The Emergence of the American University*. Chicago: University of Chicago Press, 1965.

Walshok, M. L. *Knowledge Without Boundaries: What America's Research Universities Can Do for the Economy, the Workplace, and the Community*. San Francisco: Jossey-Bass, 1995.

Warren, J. B. "Alternatives to Degrees." In D. W. Vermilye (ed.), *Learner-Centered Reform: Current Issues in Higher Education*. San Francisco: Jossey-Bass, 1975.

Weiland, J. S. "General Education in the Universities after 1992." *European Journal of Education*, 1989, 24(4), 371–377.

Wilcox, F. A., "Pedagogical Implications of Teaching 'Literature of the Vietnam War.'" *Social Education*, 1988, 52(1), 39–40.

"The Yale Report of 1828." In R. Hofstadter and W. Smith (eds.), *American Higher Education: A Documentary History*. Vol. 1. Chicago: University of Chicago Press, 1961.

Planning Effective General Education

TASK GROUP ON GENERAL EDUCATION

We define general education as the cultivation of the knowledge, skills, and attitudes that all of us use and live by during most of our lives—whether as parents, citizens, lovers, travelers, participants in the arts, leaders, volunteers, or good samaritans.

Ideally one's knowledge, skills, and attitudes should continue developing throughout life. Yet knowledge and skills can stagnate and attitudes be reduced to stereotype, cliché and prejudice. Thus the general education offered by colleges and universities seeks to foster the desire and capacity to keep on learning continuously. Through their general education programs, academic institutions aim to develop habits of and tastes for independent thinking by encouraging active learning and independent investigation, and by helping students assume responsibility for their own intellectual development. These programs exist above all to prevent stagnation of perception and to vivify thought and action through continuing reflection.

Even without attending college, some young adults can lay the foundations for lives continually rich in thought and expressiveness. Literature abounds with illustrations, particularly in the *bildungsroman*, of how young women and men have developed their reflective powers and stature through their own deliberate observation of people, places, and ideas. Their self-education points to ways that educational institutions can aid this process among their students by developing their desire for wide-ranging reading, reflection, and exploration of intellectual connections throughout life. Intellectual power can be acquired if persistently practiced in and out of the classroom, yet it must become a matter of taste. As Aristotle would have it, pleasure must accompany its exercise.

Thus we believe that the chief task of the college years is for students not only to gain the ability to identify perspectives, weigh evidence, and make wise decisions, but also to learn how to think about thinking and to enjoy thinking. Students who have done so have crossed the great divide between merely gaining knowledge in order to return it on examinations and using knowledge by making it their own. Effective general education challenges students to confront both the complexity of knowing and the tentativeness of our knowledge.

This approach to general education requires a different style from that used in most departments for teaching their specialties. The study of specialized subject matter often aims at an increasingly refined investigation of progressively smaller areas of reality. General education is epistemologically different in that it aims at the cultivation of a complex intelligence—the capacity that George Santayana had in mind when he wrote the *Life of Reason*, exploring intelligence in art, religion, science, society, and common sense. Indeed, the vitality of nonspecialist perception probably is an important ingredient in keeping specialist thinking alive. The acquisition of a finely tuned method is no insurance against routine and tepid thought.

Well-conceived general education fosters the ability to formulate questions that point toward new knowledge and new directions for

"Planning Effective General Education," by Task Group on General Education, reprinted from *A New Vitality in General Education: Planning, Teaching, and Supporting Effective Liberal Learning*, 1988, Association of American Colleges.

action. It seeks to provide, in the words of a committee at St. Joseph's University in Philadelphia, "the means for students to exercise control over their lives through thoughtful response to their political, cultural, and natural environments." To work toward this objective calls for sustained imagination and daring on the part of faculty, students, and administrators, since many existing institutional policies and practices are incompatible with them. It requires faculty who are willing to practice fresh approaches to their teaching, students who are unafraid of challenging and even risk-taking experiences, and administrators who measure their institutions' effectiveness by the intellectual habits and intellectual range students acquire as undergraduates and the intellectual pursuits they pursue after they graduate. Most urgently, it requires rethinking educational content and attention to individual competence and skills.

Rethinking the Content

General education involves many tensions: between what to teach and how to teach it, between the great classics of the past and contemporary works, between the classroom and students' out-of-class life, between students' individual objectives and the needs of the community, between what students want and what their institutions think they need, and between its means and ends—that is, between its reality of daily assignments and its goal of fostering the desire and capacity to continue learning. Among these tensions are issues of content. Few faculty are satisfied, even in our more prestigious institutions, with the level of student preparation. In most institutions, discussions of general education center on areas of content and, most often, on the best selection and arrangement of that common knowledge said to define the educated person. As faculty, we repeatedly debate what specific "great" or "important" writings must be studied by students in order for them to be declared generally educated. But what knowledge should we emphasize, and what should we require of all students? Most everyone would agree with the assertion of the National Endowment for the Humanities that "some things are more important to know than others," even though reaching agreement about which things are more important can be frustratingly difficult. In former centuries, the Bible provided for a shared frame of reference that could help communication among students and faculty of many different origins and dispositions. Now, however, the task of building a shared culture and some commonality of intellectual experience within an institution has no similar underpinning. We know from our work with undergraduates that a popular television program such as "General Hospital" or "Hill Street Blues" binds together students across the nation. Cannot then some common intellectual experiences bind together at least the students within an institution?

Some champions of a common core argue that all college students should have a solid grounding in the Western humanist tradition best embodied in a list of books beginning with Homer, Sophocles, Thucydides, and Plato and going forward to Nietzsche, Mann, and T. S. Eliot. At some institutions, the great thinkers of Western civilization have been the *pièce de résistance* of higher education. To others, such a list seems at best limited and at worst an attempt to deny power to ideas emanating from classes that are not upper, races that are not white, cultures that are not Western, and everyone who is not male.

Faculty members in many institutions have sidestepped such seemingly insoluble disputes by establishing general education as a series of distribution requirements, a minimal sampling of disciplines offered more or less willingly by departments. Others have relied on interdisciplinary work to balance disciplinary specialization. And at still others, the "common-body-of-knowledge" approach has been challenged by faculty who emphasize the abilities, skills, competencies, modes of thought, and methods of access to knowledge that students should acquire to pursue investigation independently. Such programs may ask students to write coherent English, to think logically and analytically, to handle information couched in quantitative terms, to acquire historical consciousness, to master a language other than English with proficiency, and to examine or even to acquire values.

In later sections of this publication, we make a case for programs and teaching that focus on specific competencies and abilities that students are expected to develop during their four years in college. But competence in modes of inquiry and in writing does not develop in a vacuum. Thinking is always *about* something, and therefore it is inextricably grounded in content. Thus the question of which content to emphasize must be joined because the choice is inevitable and decisions must be made.

We need, therefore, to deliberate carefully about what college-educated Americans should know and be able to do in the remaining years of the twentieth century and the early decades of the twenty-first. The question is particularly complex because the student body is no longer a homogeneous elite; instead, it varies along virtually all the dimensions on which it is possible for people to differ: age, race, sex, social and economic background, abilities, attitudes, ambitions, and goals.

Despite the diversity in our student bodies—indeed, because of it—we believe that all students can benefit from a common intellectual experience. At a minimum, colleges and universities can select one major text and ask that it be read and intensively discussed both by all students and by all faculty members in an institution. Such a requirement communicates to students and to faculty that they are all members of a community committed both to inquiry and to communication about the results of inquiry. It requires faculty members to consider what issues extend beyond particular fields and are significant for the larger community.

We also believe that colleges and universities can make a commitment to a more ambitious program of common learning. An enduring and adaptable common learning experience is possible when the members of a community make a serious commitment to sustain it. For instance, Columbia University's Contemporary Civilization course has been a part of its curriculum since the First World War.

Programs of common learning should cut across disciplinary or departmental boundaries. General education has too often been defined—or negotiated—in terms of existing departments rather than by an examination of what constitutes good education. Faculty discussions of content have frequently been political in nature, controlled by considerations of departmental turf. Such political debates displace the discussions we ought to be having—

discussions about the intellectual needs of our students and about the kinds of competence most important for them. When we start with departmental turf as our frame of reference, we miss the opportunity to help our students explore potential linkages and complementaries across disciplines and subjects.

One way to approach the development of a general education program is to consider the meaning and value of our common life and our responsibility to and for each other as human beings. Living in a technological revolution, in times of great social transformation, under the threat of nuclear war and diseases with no known cure, and visited daily by graphic images of desperate poverty within plenty, we can decide that issues such as these are as important for our students to understand and act on as are the technical skills for a career. To participate knowledgeably in civic affairs, young adults need mastery of data, theory, commentary, and argument in these problem areas. Well-informed citizens and family members require knowledge about such complex issues as toxic waste disposal, redistribution of income, medical care, and the emotional health of individuals and groups. College students do not learn about these major dilemmas just because they are important. Many students do not even read a daily newspaper or a weekly news magazine. Their information about contemporary issues may be limited to newsbreaks on their music stations.

The great books can find a ready place in a program devoted to such contemporary themes. After all, Plato's *Republic* was a grand attempt to reconstruct Athenian society after the Peloponnesian War, and many of Aristotle's writings were inspired by the desire to make democracy work in the political, legal, and social arenas. We need not set up an opposition between great classics and contemporary relevance. Good education requires continuing inquiry into the relationship between the two. For example, the core curriculum at CUNY-Brooklyn College, filling just over one-quarter of its students' program, deliberately encompasses both the old and the new, the traditional and the contemporary. Students taking it are expected to encounter both the enduring legacies of Western culture and the contemporary perspectives offered by modern science, computer technology, and attention to non-Western studies. If we believe that the great books continue to speak to participants in our own society, then we must help students see the connections between the questions raised in these books and the problems they will confront as persons and as citizens. Too often we neglect such connections, sometimes in the belief that the students will make these links for themselves, sometimes in the belief that it demeans a great work to discuss it out of its originating context. Yet the result of this neglect is that many students see classic works as an imposition to be endured rather than a resource for their own lives. General education programs can and should leave students with effective models for how to draw on the rich resources of our culture in pursuing further learning.

To serve this purpose, we believe attempts to constitute a general education program as a conglomerate of disciplinary courses fall short of the mark. Both students and faculty members benefit when they are challenged to think about the connections among ideas and issues across disciplinary and departmental boundaries.

Similarly, we believe it is unwise to define general education in terms of the traditional division between general learning and specialized learning in a field of concentration. This longstanding distinction between general learning and the major creates a misleading and artificial boundary. For many undergraduates, and especially for those who major in liberal arts disciplines, the fields in which they do their undergraduate work are not directly related to their eventual occupations. Thus their major is often part of their general education rather than preparation for a professional career. Like many graduates of former decades who eventually found themselves in fields that did not exist when they were in college, many of today's students will have careers in occupations that presently do not exist. And unlike students in most other countries, many American students do not enter postsecondary education with a specialty firmly in mind. For many of them, the entire college experience is general education.

For those students who go on to work professionally in the field of their undergraduate concentration, it is equally important that there be broad, integrative dimensions to their study in the major. Whatever their chosen field, study in the major should help students place their particular academic commitments in larger intellectual, historical, and cultural perspectives.

Specialized study of any major can and should be infused with broader meanings and purposes. Too often, however, the traditional dichotomy between liberal or general versus departmental or technical education polarizes virtually all deliberations about the college curriculum. As Elizabeth Coleman has written: *If a course is entitled "Nietzsche, Marx, and Freud," it is for freshmen. If it is "Marx and Freud," it is for sophomores. If it is "Freud," it is for juniors and seniors. And if it is "Freud: The Case Studies," it is a graduate course. I would hope that the assumptions this locks us into regarding the education of freshmen as well as seniors could be examined. I would hope that we could even see that "Freud: The Case Studies" might be a powerful introductory course; just as I hope it is manifestly absurd to deemphasize the activities of integration and synthesis for seniors.* In this spirit, we regard the introductory course in a discipline as an important aspect of general education. The introductory course, whether in a liberal arts subject or in a professional field, ought to become an object of special attention in planning general education. To whom does it introduce what? Many students who select an introductory level course will never take another course in the discipline, so it clearly does not introduce them to further formal work in the field. One special goal of such a course should therefore be some guidance to these students about how they can continue learning in the discipline on their own.

The need to teach one's discipline to students not majoring in it provides a special opportunity for investigating the ways in which that discipline illuminates the problems and questions of our common life. Exploring the role of the course in these students' overall intellectual life need not lead to diluting content. Instead, it can show how the course provides a framework for dealing with intellectually challenging questions that nonspecialists raise or may be induced to raise about the discipline.

In planning introductory courses we might well consider how immersion in a particular discipline shapes one's mind. As faculty members, we have so long been imbued with the thoughtways of our disciplines that we may have lost touch with how we learned to think like scientists or scholars, while first-year students tend to be unaware that academic languages are rather like foreign tongues. Currently, methods courses that are explicit about disciplinary thinking—the "how" of the disciplines—are ordinarily reserved for upper-level majors who are being trained to do research. But aspects of these methods courses should be introduced into the design of many introductory and other courses to teach students to think about thinking and about the differences in the ways in which historians, scientists, or literary critics think about the same issues.

It is a challenging but essential task for faculty members to reflect on what shape they want their introductory course to take, fully acknowledging the fact that for many students this one course will be the only exposure to their discipline. Such reflection is likely to raise basic questions about the nature of the discipline itself, its focus, and its explanatory power. Moreover, by exploring how their course fits in with courses in other subjects, faculty members are likely to find themselves in searching discussions with their colleagues about the connectedness and disconnectedness of subject matters and methods of inquiry. The outcome of such deliberations is not likely to be a unified corpus of scholarship and science. But the discussions themselves are likely to take faculty and students out of disciplinary isolation and toward a spirited inquiry into the foundations, boundaries, and linkages of their disciplines. It may even lead to some reconceptualization of their own disciplines.

Identifying Essential Skills

We propose that when faculty committees rethink general education programs and when instructors plan their own individual courses, they define not only subject matter and readings but also the skills they wish students to practice and develop—specifically, what their students should be able to perceive and do as a result of the program and of the particular courses within it. Skills and competencies cannot be nurtured outside the study of particular contents, but we too often plan contents with insufficient reference to skills beyond those of

memorization and recall. A recent study of liberal arts college faculty showed that while they overwhelmingly aimed at encouraging independent thinking, nearly half of their examination questions involved the regurgitation of course content.

Exploration of the competencies that we as faculty wish our students to achieve is an indispensable prerequisite for planning general education curricula. Defining these competencies helps achieve integration of undergraduate courses and enables students to graduate with an identifiable sense of achievement. By identifying and describing the specific competencies our courses require, we are taking the first steps toward making our ways of thinking, including the thought patterns of our disciplines, explicit to each other and to students. When spelled out in sufficient detail, skills statements expose the inner workings of academic disciplines. As an illustration, consider the skills defined in the Harvard core curriculum statement on literature and arts:

The common aim of courses in this area [Literature and Arts] is to help students develop a critical understanding of how human beings give artistic expression to their experience of the world. Through the examination of selected works, students are expected to enlarge and refine skills of reading, seeing, and hearing; to understand the possibilities and limitations of the artists' chosen medium and the means available for expression; and to appreciate the complex interplay among individual talent, artistic tradition, and historical content.

The value of a statement like this is that it identifies the minimum literary critical skills to be acquired by Harvard students, starting with improving their basic critical capacities, then moving to a consideration of artists' use of their materials, and finally raising complex contextual issues of the individual, tradition, and history. It is. the beginning of a statement about what literary critics and scholars do. It is a very different statement from one scientists or philosophers would make, just as it is a different statement from that of faculty who might add a more personal, experiential dimension to aesthetic understanding.

At the same time, the description just cited uses a vague set of terms—*understand, appreciate, enlarge, refine*. Moreover, terms such as *understand* and *appreciate* imply a student who looks in on the world of literature and the arts, rather than a student who actively engages problems, questions, and issues within these domains. Rather than relying on such terms, we can categorize skills so that they cover a hierarchy of abilities, from *describe* and *summarize* to *analyze, compare, critique, theorize,* and *extend theory.* Once we as faculty agree together on a definition of skills we look for as an outcome of learning in our fields, the clarity of our assignments and exams will improve. Our ability to pinpoint students' intellectual problems will also improve. Too often, when we have been charged to develop courses that will foster students' intellectual abilities, we have simply repackaged old courses—claiming, for example, that "World Music" leads to an understanding of "the possibilities and limitations of the artist's chosen medium."

Faculty at a handful of colleges, however, have become explicit not only about the meaning of each skill statement, but about how each skill or competence can be taught and how it can be documented. They have defined not only broad outcomes of general education, but "how much" and "how well." Most of these colleges tend to serve "new students"—first-generation college students, minority students, low-income students—students for whom the initiation into academic culture is most difficult. But these institutions have something to teach all of us. "New students" clearly benefit from the articulation of criteria and standards for judgment, but all students learn more effectively when agreement about skills replaces "psyching out" the professor.

A look at foreign language instruction illustrates the problems that arise when we give only secondary attention to the achievement of competency, even in a field for whose existence such achievement seems a primary objective. Most everyone would agree that languages are learned best by those who have a use for them. It is also commonly agreed that languages are best retained by those who bring them to some usable level, either for conversation or reading, and that this level can usually be reached only in a minimum of two years and for only a few languages. Yet many institutions do not require students to use a foreign language or even learn it, but merely study it. Often, colleges require only one year's study of a language. If our goal is to have a large num-

ber of students take one year of a language in college and no more, we should design courses accordingly. For instance, it is possible to teach students to read Homer sensitively in a year of ordinary course work without their achieving general proficiency in Greek. But whatever we do, we should define what is to be learned and how—and decide what are realistic objectives and what are not.

Faculty members who want to think about the competencies important to their courses may find studies of intellectual development a useful point of departure. The investigations of Jean Piaget and William Perry in particular have been helpful to many faculty groups interested in understanding intellectual development and its intersection with the development of competence in particular fields or courses. Piaget's distinction between "concrete" and "formal" operations leads us to investigate what sort of practices are necessary to enable students to tell the difference between "fact" and "interpretation." In the words of one student, "a fact is what the teacher says it is." This is true for a learner who has not yet learned to work with abstractions, that is, to operate at a "formal" level with the issues of a field. Such students will find it difficult to grapple with discussions or assignments that presuppose the ability to infer organizing principles from particular data to deal with the relations among the principles.

William Perry's research on the intellectual and ethical development of Harvard students across the four years of college has given us a thoughtful scheme of nine "positions" through which the thinking of college students advances. Perry's scheme begins with an authority-bound phase in which students look for the right answer and want to be told, rather than investigate. When they find out that answers to many problems are tentative and controversial, they move into a position Perry terms "multiplicity," in which one opinion seems as good as the other, their own and the teachers included. Students can be challenged to move beyond this subjectivism through the discovery that there are competent and incompetent ways to gather evidence and develop and test hypotheses. Then they can learn that while there are no final certitudes, there are ways to develop responsible, disciplined, and flexible theories and positions. At the heart of

Perry's work and that of other observers of student intellectual development is a powerful yet simple observation: Students gain intellectual sophistication when they must confront and assess competing and equally well-argued perspectives on an issue or solutions to a problem.

Attention to intellectual skills and competencies puts emphasis on the outcomes of education. Most college transcripts certify that students have passed a required number of courses, but they give little indication of the competencies that students have developed. A focus on competencies is likely to engender lively debate among faculty about the nature of these competencies, which of them are essential, and how they may best be developed. It is also likely to increase student interest in general education. Currently, one of the great virtues of professional education as contrasted to general education is that students carry from it a sense of at least incipient empowerment through their attainment of specific skills. Too many students graduate from college with an uncomfortable sense that the knowledge they have acquired outside their specialty is vague and diffuse. General education that is more deliberately and explicitly geared to the development of competencies defined independently of the passing of individual courses can change their perceptions greatly.

New Content and Competencies

In this section we single out two examples of new approaches to content and competencies: women's studies and general education science courses. Women's studies has a twenty-year history of challenging what were once viewed as accepted ideas and practices, and it is transforming our basic ways of understanding social, psychological, and historical processes. In contrast, general education science courses have long been a traditional part of the higher education curriculum. However, both women's studies and general education science courses illustrate opportunities for engaging students in work that imparts new content, provides new skills, and clarifies values.

Women's studies introduced areas of content—classes of people and their past and present activities—that had been excluded from scholarly inquiry in fields ranging from biology to the history of art. It made the everyday, domestic, emotional, and interpersonal sides of people's lives the subject of intensive exploration and analysis and thus considerably enlarged the comprehensiveness and objectivity of our knowledge. It has pursued the questions raised by the influx of women into the labor force around the world—one of the most profound social changes in recent history—such issues as comparable worth, affirmative action, and distribution of child care responsibilities.

These new questions have provided a powerful stimulus for fresh approaches in the classroom. They are questions of great complexity where student and faculty emotions are strong, where there is no "correct" or traditional approach to problem solving, where unknown content must be uncovered, and where new ways of thinking are required. Faculty have used the intensity of student involvement in the issues as opportunities for having students realize the importance and the power of thinking clearly. The questioning of accepted explanations of topics and problems which has been at the core of the development of women's studies as a field has motivated an emphasis on accurate description, analysis, synthesis, and theory building. The very prolificness of the research emanating from women's studies attests to the power of the questions it is raising and the methods it is employing. Students are exposed to the intellectual excitement of creating a new field of study.

Women's studies programs have often functioned as thorns in the side of traditional departments, pointing out facts—inequities in numbers, salary, and tenure patterns for women faculty—and moving institutions, and the society beyond, to reveal the degree to which they were wedded to maintaining the inequities with which they were confronted. Women's studies has in fresh ways raised the ancient question of the relationship of knowledge to personal and social action.

At this time, there are about five hundred academic programs, some thirty-nine thousand women's studies courses—usually taken as electives or as part of general education—and several refereed journals devoted to scholarship on women. These activities include extensive projects designed to integrate women's studies across the curriculum, a special literature on the philosophy and tactics of curricular change, and an explosion of scholarly work in many disciplines.

The growing literature about women's studies shows that women's studies can be seen as a way of rethinking general education. In a review essay, Margaret Andersen cites five phases of curricular evolution. First, there is the "womanless" curriculum, the curriculum that presents the world as if women were invisible. Second, a few and highly successful women begin to appear; their achievements are added. Third, with the development of extensive scholarship on women's lives and work, women take their place as a group beside men. In phase four, changes in ways of knowing begin to appear. The curriculum reveals a new organization and perspective. It investigates cultural functions, such as affiliation, or understudied aspects of men's lives, such as their emotional lives and nurturant activities. Thinking necessarily becomes more interdisciplinary. Finally, as full transformation is approached, difference and diversity of human experience, sex, race, class, and ethnicity are seen as part of the continuum of human experience, and this introduces a profound shift in world view. While some institutions are still at phase one, others, like Wheaton College in Massachusetts, have undertaken institution-wide curriculum revision.

We turn to the natural sciences as our second example. The task group gave special attention to this domain because the natural sciences comprise an area that is commonly regarded as particularly resistant to general education. Discussions of curricular practices in the sciences and of ways to improve them have often been unsatisfying and evanescent. Yet, the technological society in which we live is faced with challenges and choices ranging from the preservation of plant and animal life to the control of nuclear power, toxic wastes, and devastatingly powerful weaponry. While our current standard of living is largely based on science and technology, the American public, including much of its political leadership, is both ill-educated in science and intimidated by technology.

How can the general lack of scientific understanding in American society be explained? Some insight into our failure can be gleaned from an examination of the paradigms for college science courses and the difficulties that beset them:

- The broad but isolated survey, perhaps entitled "Scientific Ideas of Western Society," that omits experimental experience and emphasizes instead anecdotal history rather than methodological or epistemological issues, and whose scientific content may be minimal.

- The watered-down course, possibly named "Physics for Poets" or "Life Sciences for Nonmajors," that lacks the courage to make the students work on real scientific questions.

- The historical methodology course, possibly called "Methods of Modern Physics" or "Microscopies, Old and New," that seems very "scientific" in its emphasis on the specific, but is devoted to instruments rather than to modes of thought.

- The intensive professional course, such as "Introduction to Physics" or "General Chemistry." These courses may be the appropriate vehicle for getting a great store of technique and knowledge across to future engineers, scientists, and pre-medical students, but they lack continuity with the thinking and the everyday experience of most other students. Indeed, these courses help to convince many students that their negative preconceptions about science were right when the great ideas they have been promised turn out to be a set of formulas designed to tell how fast an elevator falls or which acids ionize weakly.

A properly constructed general education in science allows students to understand the generality, power, and coherence of nature's fundamental principles. To do so, the courses stress methodology, thought patterns, and the nature of those principles themselves. They also stress two other central elements: factual and descriptive knowledge, and an ability to know and use quantitative concepts. The facts remain critical, since conceptualization in the absence of concrete detail risks sterility and vacuousness, just as detail in the absence of concept risks chaos. Such a course in physics can measure acceleration, sound propagation, and magnetic fields. One in chemistry can demonstrate reactions and heat, smells, and solutions. One in geology can dwell on the dynamics and the details of rock formation in the earth's crust.

Science education can equip students to understand reasonable orders of magnitude for physical quantities and to appreciate the process of numerical size estimation and the nature of statistical and probabilistic descriptions. Many of the issues facing our society are clarified immediately if subjected to scrutiny on the basis of reliable estimation. The educated person should be able to criticize the more relevant numerical estimates to which the media constantly subject us, whether they are opinion polls, the chance of winning a lottery, the probability of a catastrophic earthquake, the danger of a meltdown, or risks of cancer from exposure to certain chemicals. Many instances of well-intentioned legislation, regulation, and crying of woe are based on inaccurate estimates. Numbers must be used with knowledge and respect, and measurement must be viewed in the context of theory and of answers to intrinsically important intellectual and socially relevant questions.

In practice, most coursework in science is didactic. Facts and theories are presented, often very well, and ways to derive predictions from these facts and theories are taught. But students need help in reestablishing the contexts out of which scientific questions arise along with the "answers" which at any time constitute the contents of science. One way to provide this help involves the use of paradoxes. Demonstrations that begin with paradoxes challenge students to go beyond their original instincts to gain a deeper and more sophisticated knowledge, and can inspire them to pursue explanatory clues by which they learn the underlying science.

- Why doesn't the water spill out of a glass that is filled above its brim with water? What happens if lighter fluid or mineral oil or alcohol is used instead?
- Why does a sheet of paper spread across the top of a glass of milk keep the milk in when the glass is overturned? Will it still work in a vacuum?

- Why doesn't a tennis ball floating under the spigot in a bathtub float away?
- Why does the size seven shoe lying to the right of the size six look smaller?

These paradoxes help students learn first that initial feeling and empirical guesswork can be very dangerous if incautiously employed, second that measurement or experiment is a proper way to answer a well-posed question, and third that scientific learning and knowledge are not only useful but delightful.

The use of projects can also play an invigorating role in science courses addressed to the general education of students. Through properly chosen and even self-selected projects, students will become more divergent and more independent in their thought, and more aware both of how method can determine action and of how concept development imbues specific facts with meaning and comprehensibility. Classroom presentations can then be organized in concert with these project components so that students perceive the formal presentation of course materials as providing an organized set of constructs with which to order the observations that they themselves have made. For example, after students have observed pollen grains in water, and have noticed that the excursive motions are affected by the temperature of the water and by the size of the grain, the instructors have before them fertile, well-prepared mental ground in which to sow the seminal ideas of viscous drag, random motion, and molecular chaos.

To meet the larger goals of stimulating inquiry and imagination, and to offer opportunities for direct student involvement in scientific reasoning, science courses may be constructed around one or another major theme. For purposes of illustration, consider a possible course entitled "Rates of Change"—a course based on the measurement and understanding of rate phenomena and on linking the concept of equilibrium states to the rate process by which the equilibrium eventuates. Such a course could begin with discussion of the nature of time and of measurements of rates such as the speed of a runner. The teacher would explain why these are important questions and how this type of inquiry is used in scientific research. The teacher could then carry through one simple demonstration, such as measuring the dependence of yeast fermentation rates on sugar concentration, and the students would design and complete their first measurement projects. In analyzing their observations, the students are introduced into the graphical presentation of data, the use of computers, and the treatment or a qualitative concept through quantitative data.

- The next part of the course could be the most challenging, both for the instructor and students. Rather than baldly state such ideas as dynamic equilibrium, the principle of mass action, the differential and integral forms of rate laws, and the idea of limiting behaviors, the teacher can use the students' own lab findings to motivate them as well as illustrate these concepts. For instance, the statistical nature of equilibria and the Boltzmann picture of entropy can be illustrated by the movement of guppies in aquaria. The students can be assigned the analysis of each other's data in terms of rate laws and equilibrium constants.

- In the last part of the course, the simple concepts of rate processes can be tested, both in discussion and in the laboratory, by comparison with more complex phenomena. These can include oscillatory rate processes, first as simple as a marble rolling in a mixing bowl but then proceeding to chemical oscillations, ecological oscillations, and circadian rhythms. Finally, the energetic consequences of rate phenomena can be measured, and catalytic reduction of barriers studied.

To our knowledge, no such course has ever been taught. But each of its parts is currently offered in other courses. By combining them, the course would fulfill almost all of the criteria for a general education course in science, including attention to methodology, thought pattern, actual and descriptive knowledge, and the use of quantitative concepts.

The life sciences offer another opportunity to involve in scientific reasoning students who believe that they dislike or fear science. These students can mobilize natural curiosities about their own bodies and the larger biosphere to form a base for coursework. A one- or two-semester course in biology could be created around any of a number of themes such as the biology of inherited disease. This course could cover classical principles of genetics; molecular aspects of genetics; diseases and malfunctions; and include a laboratory component involving exercises, model experiments, and investigative projects. Several of the most important conceptual bases of science can be examined in this course, among them the mechanism of evolution and of natural selection, or the concept of entropy by considerations of coding and of random as opposed to ordered codes. By evoking students' curiosity about disease with the power of discovery in the laboratory, such a course can provide opportunities for active learning. The instructor can further encourage active learning by making at least some of the formal presentations speculative and suggestive, emphasizing the range of questions still being pursued rather than that which seems presently established.

Such a course can accomplish these objectives:

- The experimental work directly establishes the possible truth or clear falsehood of one or more hypotheses, and students are directly involved in the design and execution of the experiment.

- The procedures are not technique exercises but laboratory studies measuring real properties of real species (eye color of flies, sickling of cells, sterility of offspring).

- The facts are presented in the class room, demonstrated in the preliminary lab work, and discovered in the investigative laboratory. Through observation, students learn important areas of content (osmotic excess can fracture cells, overdense populations can alter behavior), some of which can be directly useful in their lives.

- Numerical estimation enters in a very natural way into some of the key concepts of the course. For instance, if one generation takes twenty-five years for humans but twenty-five hours for some organism, how many generations of each occur in ten thousand years? If a base pair has a mass of four hundred daltons, how many base pairs will fit on a DNA strand of mass three million daltons? By using rather than merely memorizing these concepts, the students acquire an appreciation for what numbers mean and how to manipulate them.

Orienting a general education course in science on such a theme has the virtue of providing a coherent framework without sacrificing knowledge of basic concepts and methods. Different teachers and institutions will naturally want to pick different themes. One physics professor reports that the heat death of the universe as a theme seems to appeal to most students at his college. At another institution, a biology professor is offering a basic biology course organized as the "Biology of Gender," which includes such areas as the evolution of plants and animals, social organization among primates and humans, and genetics. Offered to biology majors and nonmajors alike, she reports that the course helps to demystify science for the nonmajors and that the differing intellectual strengths and perspectives of the students make for richer, mutually instructive discussions.

Science is an intellectual endeavor with many contextual ramifications from and into other modes of thought. Exploring these connections can play a central role in enriching, deepening, and focusing the education of all students. For science majors, general education is crucial since their specialties can be farther from ordinary experience than are the humanities or social sciences. Education that helps science majors place their special interests in larger contexts can make a fundamental difference in the ways these future scientists will think about the larger significance and implications of their work. Both science and scientists will fare best when closely interwoven into the general intellectual life of institutions and society.

Creating New Courses and Programs

We believe that the process through which institutions answer the question of what content and competencies to emphasize can be a major educational experience for students and

other constituencies. The question should be the subject of a visible, ongoing public discussion within institutions, involving faculty, students, administrators, and even alumni and governing boards, with the participation of community leaders, foundation officials, legislators, and other interested laypersons.

Such discussions can be enormously exciting intellectually, particularly if all faculty—whether biochemists, historians, computer scientists, or philosophers—engage the issues both as well-educated professionals and also as parents, spouses, friends, citizens, and neighbors. Equally important, students are seldom drawn into extended discussions of the underlying philosophies that lead us to establish their sequence of courses. They infrequently hear intellectual debate among faculty and even less frequently are given an opportunity to join in. Yet for many students, particularly those who have not previously thought of "ideas" as a source of power or playfulness, such an opportunity can make the difference between regarding education as a static thing to "get" and regarding it as a process of reflection and self-reflection leading to judgment, commitment, and action.

Discussions about general education can draw on the work of a variety of thinkers from varied fields, historical eras, and cultures, including recent reports on American higher education. These reports constitute a good inventory of current claims about the kinds of knowledge graduating college seniors should possess, and these claims can serve as the basis for extensive debate. In *Integrity in the College Curriculum*, the Association of American Colleges identified the following eight areas of experience that, together with "study in depth," are "basic to a coherent undergraduate education":

- Inquiry, abstract logical thinking, critical analysis.
- Literacy: writing, reading, speaking, listening.
- Understanding numerical data.
- Historical consciousness.
- Science.
- Values.
- Art.

- International and multicultural experiences.

But if we look at the sum total of what has been proposed in the many reports, we come to realize that it is vastly greater than can be accomplished within the time that is available for a normal college education. At the same time, there is nothing in such lists that is undesirable, gratuitous, frivolous, or foolish. Every item has its partisans and its opponents. Arguments for adding to or subtracting from the list are deeply in conflict with each other, exhibiting disagreements both about the ends to be achieved and the means thought capable of bringing them about. We disagree about the pedagogic techniques that will bring about such desired results as rigorous thinking. We have difficulties bridging intellectually gaps that are rooted in profound cultural differences. Yet decisions must be made and we can make them at least on the basis of intelligent and thorough discussion. We will say more about ways to support such engagement in the third chapter. But we want to stress at the outset that the discussion of these issues will be less encumbered and the results more easily implemented if institutions seek to safeguard the economic status of professors who are willing to change the contents and structures of their courses.

To bring about new courses and programs, faculty also need help in renewing and expanding their skills. Hamline University illustrates one way of doing so: It has begun rethinking existing courses by initiating a program of faculty renewal. Its English department has pioneered the process by organizing a seminar on new methods of literary criticism that have developed since its current faculty members were in graduate school. The entire department is reading seminal works, discussing key issues among themselves and with consultants, and considering the contents of existing and new courses and course sequences both for majors and nonmajors.

Students also have an important role not only in discussing general education but in planning courses and programs and assisting in monitoring them. To provide settings in which students can take initiative to formulate and test ideas, general education programs should include opportunities for students to experience at least one course in which they are in a special way in charge of the content and methods of learning. An example is furnished by Brown University's Group Independent Study Projects (GISPs), which allow students to choose their own topics for investigation. Subjects of student projects have included environmental pollutants, the effects of a family member's cancer upon the family, and the history and technology of robotics. Students must submit detailed outlines for their project, including a full bibliography, and each project requires committee approval. The students work together and course contents and methods emerge from their mutual collaboration. Faculty members function as consultants, but the ways they are used is determined by the students. At the same time, the students' work is judged by the faculty. The GISPs thus facilitate the achievement of what is essential in general education—the development of the habits of and tastes for independent investigation.

Integrating Content and Inquiry

We believe that efforts to confine general education to the first and second year of college are both chimerical and self-defeating. They assume that freshmen, only starting their exposure to the world of higher learning, can undertake syntheses that few of their instructors could achieve; and they make general education appear to be an isolated activity—requirements to be finished, gotten out of the way, and then forgotten rather than a continuing progress of growing throughout the years. In the opening pages of this report, we defined general education as the cultivation of knowledge, skills, and attitudes important to learning throughout life. If we accept that general education lays a foundation for lifelong learning, then it needs to be structured in such a way that it fosters continuing learning.

The fostering of intellectual habits and tastes as a central objective for general education programs cannot be accomplished in any single course but requires collaborative efforts across courses. A comprehensive plan is necessary if individual competencies are to form part of the student's general intellectual and aesthetic endowment. Yet a persistent comment about faculty is that as a consequence of the domination of the research model, we have specialized to such a degree that we have lost interest in and the capacity for integrating knowledge.

In most instances, students must do their own synthesizing of knowledge. Professors have offered their individual courses, perhaps with some linkage to other courses in mind, and then have relied on students to integrate the new knowledge into larger structures of understanding. The problem is that the logical coherence among subjects is often neither shared nor explicit. It exists in the mind of Professor A, but Professor B constructs it differently, and the students perceive a loose jumble. The students often see little relation between one course and another, and they frequently complain that the rationale for their program eludes them. Integration calls for faculty to collaborate with their colleagues and their students in linking courses toward agreed-upon objectives.

Today, courses in different departments overlap in ways that may be repetitive rather than building on one another, and each of the overlapping courses may be too narrowly focused. Subspecialties of fields have proliferated into hundreds of courses, some so overblown that their substance does not require the amount of time devoted to them, and others so sketchy as to do an injustice to the fields they presume to survey. Equally bothersome is the neglect of emerging new fields and the failure to review critically existing courses whose content and structure have reached canonical status and that are unjustifiably exempt from needing to make a case for themselves.

We should look at courses in their sequences and interrelations to see that they build up to coherent competencies over the four years and to allow students opportunities to practice and demonstrate these competencies. Inadequate attention to the place of individual courses in a student's total program is probably the single most important reason for the student's failure to achieve the competencies we hope for from their undergraduate education.

Leadership in this area has recently come from the writing community. As a consequence of their efforts, more and more institutions have begun to expect students to gain practice in writing in their courses across the disciplines and in a variety of genres in addition to academic research papers. Through these programs in "writing across the curriculum," both students and faculty members can gain insight into the varied ways that different fields frame, approach, and analyze questions. We would hope that ultimately this emphasis on writing as a competence to be practiced throughout the four years will lead not just to skill in articulation but to articulation with style.

Meanwhile, the principle reflected in the "writing across the curriculum" initiatives ought to be extended to many other important areas of student learning, such as critical thinking, problem solving, aesthetic experience, scientific literacy, and historical consciousness. Emphasizing such abilities throughout the undergraduate experience makes use of the psychological phenomenon of reinforcement. Reinforcement is crucial in education; people learn through repetition and encouragement as well as through inspiration and enlightenment.

Given the importance of reinforcement to learning, we can explore ways of using it to develop students' understanding of content as well as their competence in modes of inquiry. For example, faculty might plan to reintroduce certain topics or concepts with differing emphases or applications, at different times and in different contexts, over the four-year undergraduate cycle. We use the concept of entropy as an example.

- The concept of entropy or order, the major quantitative aspect of the second law of thermodynamics, might be introduced as a historical and technological development based on Carnot and the steam engine, and then in the context of a general discussion of equilibrium.

- This can be followed by laboratory experience in which the heat, entropy, and disorder changes that accompany the melting of an ice cube are measured.

- Later, Boltzmann's formal definition of the disorder as exponential entropy might be discussed and used as the basis for determining the order of nature at the low temperatures of the interstellar medium.

- Finally, the entropy changes characteristic of biological processes on the one hand and of economic and other social theory on the other could be calculated and discussed.

By seeing this difficult concept in various guises and at different stages in their careers, students are likely to become more confident both of their ability to comprehend an important central idea in science and of their capacity to deal mathematically with an abstract concept. For students who have completed most of their science and mathematical general education, an upper-level seminar on a concept such as entropy or evolution, combining faculty from several departments, can knit together work in various disciplines. It can also facilitate instructive contacts of students and faculty in different departments.

Many institutions are already linking courses and course content across the curriculum. For example, Colorado College has established a thematic minor: students take at least five courses—from two or more departments outside their major—which relate to one another through a common theme, area of the world, or historical period. Among two-year colleges that have pioneered the development of linked-course curricula, Los Medanos College in California requires students to take a minimum of one course in six major areas of knowledge, ranging from humanistic studies to physical sciences. To be included in the general education program, these courses must give attention to reading and writing, modes of inquiry, aesthetics of knowledge, implications of knowledge, interdisciplinarity, effective thinking, and creativity. These courses are followed by two in-depth courses stressing critical inquiry and self-directed study. The Dallas County Community College district has defined eight competency areas that are not taught in a single course but are reinforced throughout the curriculum and in college degree requirements.

Another successful procedure for using the curriculum to link disciplines and stimulate debate among them has been developed in the Federated Learning Communities program at the State University of New York at Stony Brook. These communities group six courses that are already in the catalogue around a broad theme, such as world hunger, social and ethical issues in the life sciences, or the varied nature of communities. A group of students commit themselves to enroll in the six courses, three in each semester, and the faculty of the six courses meet regularly to discuss their courses and teaching efforts. These faculty jointly conduct a core seminar in which they and the students view the subject matter of the courses from their distinctive disciplinary, epistemological, and individual perspectives. A seventh teacher, called a "master learner," leads a linking seminar that has no independent content but seeks to help students integrate materials from the courses; and this teacher attends the six courses in which the students are enrolled.

There are other approaches we can use to help students explore interconnections across courses and disciplines. We suggest, for example, an expanded use of linking seminars having no independent content but linking two or more courses that students are currently taking and that cluster around related issues or common themes. The function of these seminars is to explore with the students not just interrelations of the subject matters, but the new knowledge that emerges as one looks at the problems on the basis of how they are treated in several disciplines. The introduction of a number of such seminars would reduce the number of traditional courses, but it would be an exciting step of bringing about curricular coherence among these offerings.

At the upper-division level, these seminars could provide students with an opportunity to reflect and analyze experiences and ideas that may not otherwise reach articulate consciousness. At this point in their careers, students are able to approach a wider variety of subject matters with an enlarged capacity for comprehension and for seeing connections and differences. They have been exposed to many subjects, and some have traveled, undertaken field research, or worked at paying jobs in which they have encountered many people, practices, structures, and organizations unrelated to academia. In a linking seminar, students can use this experience to reflect on the methodology and epistemology of their major, what related disciplines attempt to do, how they are doing it, and how well. Unlike traditional capstone courses, which tend to be global in nature and deal with topics of vast comprehensiveness—and may be resented by upper-class students preoccupied with their major—these seminars would focus on issues and themes related to their major.

Teaching linking seminars also brings great intellectual rewards to professors. Working on the connections across fields or topics helps faculty articulate the nature and the purpose of nonspecialized knowledge as well as teach it more effectively. Teaching a linking seminar once every two or three years can provide a freshness of approach to the professor's work while minimizing disruption of other teaching tasks. Although it takes intellectual courage to go beyond the security of a carefully honed disciplinary identity, professors who have taught in such interdisciplinary contexts report not just an enlargement of their scope of thinking but also a fresh impetus in the ways they approach problems in their own discipline.

Enculturation or Critical Engagement?

CAROL GEARY SCHNEIDER

> At its best, liberal learning extends beyond particular subject matter, which inevitably changes over time, to instill qualities of mind.
> —Association of American Colleges (1989)

The discipline and furniture of the mind, mental powers, analytical capacities, reflective judgment—these descriptive phrases have evolved over two centuries of conversation about the purposes and effects of U.S. higher education. Whatever the language used in their rhetoric, faculty have constantly maintained a focus on students' development of usable mental capacities, both as a justification for the importance of higher learning and as an expectation about its lasting effects. As Ernest Pascarella and Patrick Terenzini (1991) observe in their recent synthesis of twenty years of research on the effects of college:

> Abundant evidence suggests that much factual material is forgotten rather soon after it is presented in educational settings.... Thus, beyond postsecondary education's undeniably significant role in the imparting of specific subject matter knowledge, claims for the enduring influence of postsecondary education on learning must be based, to some extent at least, on the fostering of a repertoire of general intellectual or cognitive competencies and skills. These cognitive skills go by a number of different names (reasoning skills, critical thinking, intellectual flexibility, reflective judgment, cognitive complexity, and so on), and they differ somewhat in the types of problems or issues they

address.... These cognitive competencies and skills represent the general intellectual outcomes of college.... [They] are a particularly important resource for the individual in a society and world where factual knowledge is becoming obsolete at an accelerated rate [1991, pp. 114–115].

As we would hope, the research evidence reviewed in Pascarella and Terenzini's important book provides substantial if uneven evidence that college positively affects students' cognitive abilities. Students make "statistically significant gains during the college years on a number of dimensions of general cognitive capabilities and skills," and at least part of these gains can be attributed specifically to college attendance rather than general maturation (Pascarella and Terenzini, 1991, p. 155). Moreover, students' particular choices of majors are not significantly linked to their gains on measures of critical abilities although, unsurprisingly, students do better when a measure of critical ability is similar in structure to problems encountered in their particular major.

Yet a close analysis of some of these reported findings on student learning in college suggests a less positive view than Pascarella and Terenzini report, a view similar in substance to many faculty members' own increasingly unflattering private descriptions of college student's reasoning and communication abilities. Examining reasoning both in the academy and beyond, a number of cognitive researchers argue what common sense would also suggest: that adult life requires the cognitive capacities to make sense of multiplicity, to sort among competing claims and assertions, to

"Enculturation or Critical Engagement?" by Carol Geary Schneider, reprinted from *Strengthening the College Major: New Directions for Higher Education*, No. 84, edited by C. Schneider and W. S. Green, 1993, Jossey-Bass Publishers, Inc.

consider positions in light of both evidence and values, and to construct a grounded analysis that takes into account the varieties of evidence and the strength of opposing positions. In simpler words, in a world where difference is a given and certainty in short supply, adults must develop their own analyses, make their own arguments.

In this context, King and Kitchener's one and one-half decades of findings on students' development of reflective judgment during the college years, usefully summarized in Chapter Two, should give us pause. Though Pascarella and Terenzini cite King and Kitchener's research as evidence of the positive effects of college on cognitive skills, King and Kitchener themselves note that faculty members' normative standards for reasoning in college reveal that faculty expect a level of both skill and intellectual self-awareness well beyond what most students apparently achieve. As King and Kitchener point out, *The Challenge of Connecting Learning*, the Association of American Colleges (AAC) study of the major, argues that students should learn "to state why a question or argument is significant and for whom; what the difference is between developing and justifying a position and merely asserting one; and how to develop and provide warrants for their own interpretations and judgments" (Association of American Colleges, 1991, p. 14). Yet, King and Kitchener (Chapter Two) report, "many seniors are still confused when asked to defend their answers to ill-structured problems, arguing that a solution for such a problem is merely an opinion that cannot be defended as better than any other. . . . As a group, [college seniors] show little evidence of being able to think reflectively, at least as we have defined it." King and Kitchener also report that faculty members assume student's reason at higher stages of the reflective judgment model than they actually do.

If multiplicity is what characterizes the modern world, many college graduates appear inadequately prepared to bring reflective, grounded judgments to bear on that multiplicity. Not recognizing their teachers' working assumption that different domains have their own standards for judgment and evidence, students encounter diversity and label it babel, opinion, or academic games. The acerbic comments from faculty at one public college, for example, illuminate the distance between what standardized tests may report and college faculties' own working standards of judgment. Using a nationally normed test of general college outcomes, this college found that on several measures (for example, communication and research, critical thinking, values clarification, and the like) the college's students both made gains across their four years of study and exceeded national norms. Yet the college's faculty members, when presented with these findings, were unconvinced and unimpressed. Instead they asked, "If this writing is at the 60th percentile, what must it be like to teach in the rest of the country?" (Curry and Hager, 1987, p. 62).

Mental Discipline and Liberal Arts Major

Whatever foundation for acquiring analytical and communication capabilities may be laid in general education courses, students' developed abilities in these areas must be seen as an integral and central responsibility of liberal arts majors. Majors in arts and sciences disciplines emerged as a standard feature of liberal education in the reflected glow of new enthusiasm about disciplinary potential to uncover the essential secrets of nature and human society. Arts and sciences subjects made their initial case for a central place in the college curriculum in the first decades of the twentieth century not simply as a way of bringing order to the confusions of the then-reigning elective system but also because they were expected to help students develop mental discipline. Claims once advanced to defend the study of Greek and Latin as an essential core curriculum that would train mental capacities were successively appropriated by new arts and sciences fields as they contended for legitimacy within the standard curriculum. Each of the emerging disciplinary fields, from chemistry to literature, aspired to some version of systematic or scientific inquiry. The study of literature, for example, entered the research academy as philology, thus making the same claims to become a science advanced by physics, biology, and chemistry. Students' immersion in the methods as well as the findings of a particular scholarly discipline, adherents claimed, would help students develop both methods in inquiry and systematic knowledge. Thus, even as specialized arts and sciences majors displaced the common curricula of the nineteenth-century college, each major also assumed separate responsibility for what early nineteenth-century scholars had described as a college's fundamental commitment to "call into daily and vigorous effort the faculties of the student" (cited in Rudolph, 1977, p.68).

It is educational commitment to foster critical inquiry, analysis, and reflective judgment that is still thought to distinguish study in a liberal arts field from study in a preprofessional subject. Preprofessional studies, so conventional academic wisdom insists, impart technique and know-how rather than insight and judgment. The result is that "in many fields, skills have become ends. . . . We are turning out technicians. But the crisis of our time relates not to technical competence, but to a loss of social and historical perspective, to the disastrous divorce of competence from conscience. . . . Professionals . . . must respond to questions [about] 'why'" (Boyer, 1987, pp. 110-111). Liberal arts fields, by contrast, are supposed to teach students how to question assumptions and push beyond the limits of the given. Hence the conventional equation of liberal arts fields with a cosmopolitan perspective. Assumed to teach students a critical stance and ways of discovering knowledge for themselves, arts and sciences majors are usually defended as forms of study that free students from parochial perspectives and prepare them to deal with complexity, contingency, and the certainty of change.

Disciplinary Enculturation

In recent years, a number of cautionary notes have emerged about this positive picture of the liberating learning and intellectual development supposedly found in liberal arts fields. In 1985, the Association of American Colleges (AAC) sounded a challenge to the traditional justifications of what it called study in depth when it released Integrity in the College Curriculum. In that report, a distinguished group of scholar–teachers and academic administrators had harsh words for the major:

The undergraduate major . . . everywhere dominates, but the nature and degree of that concentration varies widely and irrationally from college to college. Indeed, the major in most colleges is little more than a gathering of courses taken in one department, lacking structure and depth, as is often the case in the humanities and social sciences, or emphasizing content to the neglect of the essential style of inquiry on which the content is based, as is too frequently true in the natural and physical sciences. The absence of a rationale for the major becomes transparent . . . where the essential message embedded in all the [catalogue] prose is: pick eight of the following [Association of American Colleges, 1985, p. 2].

Integrity called particular attention to the political settlements behind the departmental curriculum. Far from offering students systematic and developmental apprenticeships in using the approaches of a field, the AAC panel argued, many majors have allowed "coverage" to take the place of giving students practice in using the disciplines (pp. 27–28). Faculty appointments at the departmental level are made to reflect the major subfields within a discipline; curricular requirements mirror and support this academic division of labor. In place of educational purpose and plan, the liberal arts major too often offers students a cafeteria menu of courses designed to acknowledge the faculty's scholarly interests rather than to provide a coherent and developmental program of study. Such major requirements ensure coverage of disciplinary subfields; their capacity to guide analytical practice and the development of competence in using disciplinary methods is far less certain.

AAC's stringent critique of the state of study in depth might well be construed as no more than a call to honor a long-standing equation of disciplinary method with critical thinking and thereby to restructure majors along principles of guided disciplinary practice as well as content coverage. Study in depth, said Integrity, should provide "a central core of method and theory that serves as an introduction to the explanatory power of the discipline" and provides a framework for subsequent learning (Association of American Colleges, 1985, p. 29). Many of Integrity's readers understood this statement to mean that the liberal arts major should recommit itself to teach disciplinary methods of inquiry and analysis as well as particular knowledge.

But even as AAC seemed to call for studies in depth to redeem the founding claims for disciplinary fields as contexts for mental discipline and reflective judgment, research in fields as various as rhetoric, English composition, linguistics, and cognitive science, and epistemological studies across the disciplines, cast doubt on the founding claims themselves. From many quarters, new studies of disciplinary ethos and practice have raised fundamental questions about both the assumed scientific neutrality of disciplinary method and about the capacity of learning in a discipline to develop general cognitive skills and capabilities. As we will see in the remainder of this chapter, an important vein of scholarly analysis now views disciplines not as combinations of topics and potentially illuminating research methods but as discrete and highly enclosed discourse communities, cut off from one another as well as from nonacademic communities by the barriers of special languages and exclusionary cultural norms. Within these communities, knowledge construction is governed by internal rules, both tacit and explicit, about what is already known, what is assumed, what counts as evidence, and how analysis must be presented. This view calls into question the widespread assumption that college can—and should—teach general models for "good" reasoning and its close ally "good" writing. The standards for both vary with each discipline. What persuades in the psychology department will be received with skepticism in the economics department; arguments out of both these camps will be firmly charged with the crime of egregious writing by the English department.

Jonathan Smith's incisive comments on the disciplines and liberal learning (Chapter One) illustrate a fundamental strand in the emerging view that disciplinary learning involves intellectual enculturation rather than intellectual liberation. In this view, the disciplines do not impart neutral scientific procedures for analysis and investigation. Much less do they teach a general set of cognitive skills that enable discourse across disciplinary lines. What argument within a disciplinary framework requires, growing numbers of scholars contend, is enculturation, socialization into a particular way of looking at the world, a particular set of assumptions that govern argument but that also, because they are widely internalized within the field itself, are rarely opened to searching scrutiny or debate. As Smith and a growing band of scholars suggest, ordinary discourse within a department and its parent field too often excludes second-order reflection on the field itself. Even when a field is riven with profound debates about disciplinary ethos and method—as many of the social sciences and humanities currently are—the major is rarely organized to help students engage those debates directly and consider either their significance or the grounds behind the competing claims. Small wonder, we may well think, that students graduating from college are uncertain about the nature of argument, the existence of standards for evidence, or the possibility of relating findings to context, as King and Kitchener report (Chapter Two). For within the interpretive communities we call disciplines, these matters are seldom open to examination from multiple critical points of view, even though such matters are central to the work of disciplines and to the claims of the academy to free students from parochial frames of reference.

By its general organization, a college or university exposes its students to many disciplinary perspectives. What it does not provide are either methods or venues for thinking about the relations among these perspectives: their complementarity, their dissonance, the bases for their competing claims. In virtually all liberal arts fields, students learn that some points are self-evident; they do not learn that self-evidence is itself a field-specific claim. Mediocre students may spend their entire college careers uncertain how to judge or manage the multiplicity that characterizes the academy; it is these students who show up on developmental studies as multiplists or, in King and Kitchener's term (Chapter Two), "quasi-reflective thinkers," cognizant that diversity marks all intellectual discourse but firmly persuaded that there are no ways to choose among competing claims. The arts and sciences students that faculty consider successful acquire intellectual blinders as well because, to work effectively within a disciplinary framework, these successful students must internalize a set of field-specific assumptions and perspectives that may impede rather than foster critical dialogue and engaged debate across disciplinary boundaries.

English composition studies offer an especially acute analysis of disciplinary enculturation. In an arresting if sobering portrait, David Russell summarizes the emerging view of what actually happens as students learn to make arguments within a particular disciplinary context. If writing and rhetoric are "deeply embedded in the differentiated practices of disciplines," then writing is not "a single elementary skill," and learning to write is actually "a process of socialization or acculturation. . . . The neophyte gradually acquires the community's shared knowledge not only by listening and reading but also by experimenting with verbal formulations, orally . . . and later in writing" (1991, p. 15). Russell stresses that learning to write by "this gradual and often-subtle process of observation, modeling, and intervention requires the neophyte to use the language of the community while participating in its activity not before participating." It is through such participation that a student comes to connect the verbal formulations he or she is learning to the community's meanings and to "learn not only the community's terms and categories but also when and how to apply them: the interactional rules. . . . Eventually, the neophyte so thoroughly internalizes the discourse of the community and, with it, the community's perceptions, assumptions, and behaviors, that she begins to think and act—and write—like a member of the community" (1991, pp. 16–18).

What Russell describes, of course, is the successful neophyte, the student who eventually masters, at least at an intermediate level, the rules of a community's written and verbal discourse. Russell's tale is echoed by research on students' own perceptions of learning to think in academic settings. Belenkey, Clinchy, Goldberger, and Tarule (1986), for example, studying women's experiences of learning in college, capture the voices of women very much aware of following others' prescribed methods for analysis and writing and caught unhappily between the perception that these methods are alien and the recognition that they are what the faculty want. The many students who do not learn the prescribed rules and

methods either fall away or persist on the boundaries of the discipline, paining their instructors with the naïve and awkward quality of their writing and argument. Yet this learning process, as Russell points out, is invisible to or "misinterpreted" by the students' instructors. They themselves have so internalized the strategies of the discipline they teach that they "often cannot see or understand why others, who are writing about the same 'content' do not 'make sense'. Though the students may understand the 'facts', they may not understand the essential rhetorical structures: specialized lines of argument, vocabulary, and organizational conventions, the tacit understandings about what must be stated and what assumed—in short, the culture of the discipline that gives meaning to the 'facts'" (1991, p. 18).

Is the Liberal Arts Major Obsolete?

The emerging view of the enculturative requirements for thinking and writing in the disciplines raises an important challenge to liberal arts majors' traditional claims to foster critical reasoning and reflective judgment. Conventionally, these capacities are seen as transcultural rather than context-bound skills, opening doors beyond local prejudices and viewpoints, making and marking citizens of the world. The major—and especially the liberal arts major—is supposed to provide a passport to all parts of the globe, not incorporation into the student's choice among modern monasteries. In this research on disciplinary socialization, as in so many other intellectual arenas, postmodern scholarship is busily undoing the universalistic assumptions of the Enlightenment, the values that formed the modern university and still provide rationales for many of its espoused goals and educational procedures.

However, it may be that if we had not already invented departmental majors we would discover that something like them is needed in the modern academy. For even as scholarship on rhetoric and composition illuminates the enculturative dimensions of learning in a specific field, research on the development of higher-order reasoning makes a strong case that such enculturation is a necessary and integral dimension of intellectual development. What we find in a large body of research on reasoning and argumentation, usefully summarized by Perkins and Salomon (1989), is persuasive evidence that these highly valued intellectual capacities are, by nature, situated and contextual rather than general and decontextualized. Or, to put it differently, cognitive strategies are least powerful when very general, most effective when linked to context, to well-organized knowledge bases, and to communally negotiated standards for marshalling evidence, analysis, and argument.

Research on novice and expert reasoning forcefully illustrates the importance of well-structured knowledge bases in complex reasoning. When confronted with complex questions, novices address the surface features of the problem (Glaser, 1984). Knowing little of the context from which a particular problem emerges, or of earlier attempts to address the problem, they attempt to solve it at its most superficial level. If they know nothing about a topic, they may resort to conventional wisdom as a source of insight: for example, "We can't do anything about gridlock in Washington because all politicians are greedy." Possessed of a bit more information, they weave it into something superficially resembling an analysis: for example, "the structure of the constitution makes political gridlock inevitable." Experts, by contrast, draw on richly developed knowledge bases to explore the nuances of a problem; they spend much more time than novices developing complex representations of a problem—its dimensions, complexities, and potential ways of viewing and interpreting it. Thus, the expert weaves information into a complex analysis: for example, "One school of thought holds that the ending of the Cold War has fundamentally shifted the relationship between presidential leadership and the members of Congress, leading to greater likelihood that the Congress will reject presidential initiatives. On the other hand, we have seen similar assertions of congressional authority in other transitional periods, such as the period following the Civil War." In each of these examples, the quality of the knowledge base strongly affects the quality of the analysis. Lacking knowledge, the student has nothing out of which to construct an argument.

In a classic piece of research, James Voss and his colleagues at the University of Pittsburgh illustrated the relationship between knowledge and analytical ability in an experiment that challenged social scientists, chemists, and novices to address the problem of agriculture in what was then the Soviet Union (Voss, Greene, Post, and Penner, 1983). Participants were given a brief description of the issue, and Voss then recorded and analyzed the arguments each subject developed to address the problem. He found that the chemists' way of framing the problem was more like that of novices than that of the expert social scientists. Absent a knowledge base relevant to Soviet agricultural difficulties, the chemists' analytical capacities, sophisticated though they were in matters of chemistry, became novice-like in relation to the problem posed. The chemists could not develop complex arguments about the Soviet agricultural problem because they lacked the information to do so.

Sophisticated reasoning requires extensive procedural as well as content knowledge. Beyond information, experts also command well-structured and often routinized analytical structures for organizing, interpreting, and presenting information. Sometimes simply classifying a problem produces a well-established procedure for addressing it: "Oh, that's essentially a supply and demand problem," the economist will say, and present a quick and straightforward analysis. But, often, a problem is open ended, and the expert then has to make a case both as to what information counts and why that information matters. In either case, experts draw on well-developed procedural knowledge about how to make a persuasive argument. The historian of Congress knows, for example, that his fellow historians are not likely to be persuaded by a paper that explains political behavior in terms of the protagonists' childhood experiences. The effective political activist knows that her followers are not likely to be moved to action by a lengthy historical analysis of congressional problems. To be persuasive, and therefore effective, each must use a rhetorical and organizational strategy appropriate to the audience at hand. Here we come back to Russell's portrait of the novice learning to use the language of the community: the historian of Congress can persuade fellow historians—or at least compel a hearing—because he knows, from within, the assumptions, evidentiary standards, and rhetorical strategies used by historians. The effective political activist has learned how activists (and followers) think and learn; she persuades them as she makes an argument in a form they can understand and follow.

These findings on higher-order reasoning reaffirm the importance of work in a focused discourse or interpretive community that provides a context for students' intellectual development. Equally important, they highlight a dual agenda for those who teach in such interpretive communities. Effective study in depth should provide students with opportunities to develop well-structured and integrated knowledge about a designated set of issues, concepts, and topics; it should also provide guided practice in making increasingly complex arguments that use the concepts and analytical methods of the designated field. These two tasks cannot be left to chance, nor is either task alone a satisfactory orientation to the practice of critical inquiry. Student's acquisition of knowledge and of the ability to use that knowledge in making analyses and arguments are both important responsibilities of the liberal arts major.

From Enculturation to Critical Engagement

Does enculturation in a discipline encompass all that we mean by liberal learning? Surely not. The process I have described here teaches a student to work within a community, to speak a restricted language, and to explore the uses of that language and its grammar in framing and examining specific kinds of knowledge. But certainly, as Elaine Maimon suggests in Chapter Six, we want our students to be able to work in multiple communities, to speak more than one language. Given the complexity of the work around us, any individual is hindered if he or she can speak only one language, perform in only one context. Preparation for the modern world requires practice in translating languages, negotiating differences, rethinking one's understandings in light of alternative conceptual frames and points of view.

What this goal suggests is that the work of the major is only half done when students have learned to speak the language of one community well enough to use it in discussion and argument. To engage in critical dialogue, students must encounter more than one community, more than one means of making an argument. They must know something about, for example, how historians work and also how political activists engage colleagues, followers, and opponents. They cannot be expected to develop such knowledge by taking simply one course in history and another in parties and politics. Distributional requirements that lead students to take an array of requirements in different fields, ostensibly to expose the students to disparate ways of knowing, ignore the relational dimension of learning. The history major needs to explore the reasons why history carries less weight than might be hoped with activists; the political activist needs to counter her own analyses with the perspectives and analytical approaches of reflective disciplines. Both of them need to recognize that both history and commitment may have very different meanings in societies other than those they encounter in the United States.

What all of this suggests, then, is that majors, with their structured introduction to a particular field and worldview, are necessary but not sufficient to the kind of liberal learning that we espouse in the academy and require in the wider world. Liberal arts majors can and should provide apprenticeships in particular strategies for thinking, analysis, and argument, but these strategies must be complemented by deliberately countervailing perspectives, strategies, and experiences if students are to recognize the strengths, limitations, and best uses of the points of view they develop in their initial college studies. Genuine critical engagement always involves translation and negotiation as well as argument; students need experiences of taking their arguments and knowledge into disparate contexts and learning to deal with the challenges they will inevitably find there. These experiences of translation and negotiation should extend, moreover, beyond the academic realm. There is a cultural chasm between the world of structured knowledge and the world of practice. If we expect students to use wisely the knowledge and perspective they acquire in the academy, we ought to guide them through experiences in distilling the interrelationships between knowledge acquired through analysis and knowledge developed through practice.

Nor is attention to learning out of school a distraction from the academy's central concerns. Resnick (1987) reports that programs designed to teach critical thinking are most successful when they incorporate the contextual and social features of learning in nonacademic settings.

What then of liberal learning in a disciplinary major? On the one hand, we see that learning in a major is an enculturative process that teaches prescribed and delimited ways of thinking. On the other hand, a well-established tradition of scholarship shows that specific ways of thinking, once acquired, do not readily transfer or generalize to other domains (Perkins and Salomon, 1989). Our successful student, properly socialized, has learned to think like an economist or a philosopher or an accountant. But thinking in particular frames of reference does not, by itself alone, provide students with the capabilities and perspectives they need to traverse the wider world's many knowledge communities and cultures.

Examining these complications in the work of a liberal arts major leads us to a complex view of the responsibilities of liberal learning. There is certainly a case to be made for the major's role in teaching a particular discipline as a foundational apprenticeship in inquiry and analysis. The question is not whether such learning is valuable, but whether, as Integrity argued, the typical organization of the major actually provides guided opportunities for analytical practice and growing sophistication. But there is equally a case to be made for the major's work as integrative and translational or intercultural learning. A student learning the approaches of one field ought to be expected to juxtapose those approaches with the perspectives, values, and contributions of other fields. Students who elect minors and/or double majors should be expected to connect and consider the relations between their disparate studies; students who do neither should be expected to develop minors and/or cognate studies related to their majors that introduce alternative disciplinary perspectives. All students ought to have experiences of learning in nonacademic settings and of reflecting with others on that learning.

When students extend their focused studies beyond departmental and/or disciplinary boundaries, they can begin to perceive both the power and the limits not just of a discipline but of communities themselves as makers and authorizers of knowledge. We cannot escape the local nature of our knowledge. But we can escape the error of believing that knowledge and ways of understanding acquired in a particular community are readily transferable and effortlessly acceptable to all others. By testing the propositions of one community against those of others, students can begin to grapple with one of the most important lessons of liberal learning: the contingency and the provisionality of much that we believe we know.

References

Association of American Colleges. *Integrity in the College Curriculum: A Report to the Academic Community.* Washington, D.C.: Association of American Colleges, 1985.

Association of American Colleges. Mission statement. Washington, D.C.: Association of American Colleges, 1989.

Association of American Colleges. *Liberal Learning and the Arts and Sciences Major.* Vol. 1: *The Challenge of Connecting Learning.* Washington, D.C.: Association of American Colleges, 1991.

Belenkey, M. F., Clinchy, B. M., Goldberger, N. R., and Tarule, J. M. *Women's Ways of Knowing: The Development of Self, Voice, and Mind.* New York: Basic Books, 1986.

Boyer, E. *College: The Undergraduate Experience in America.* New York: HarperCollins, 1987.

Curry, W., and Hager, E. "Assessing General Education: Trenton State College." In D. F. Halpern (ed.), *Student Outcomes Assessment: What Institutions Stand to Gain.* New Directions for Education, no. 59. San Francisco: Jossey-Bass, 1987.

Glaser, R. "Education and Thinking: The Role of Knowledge." *Educational Psychologist.* 1984. 39, 93–104.

Pascarella, E. T., and Terenzini, P. T. *How College Affects Students: Findings and Insights from Twenty Years of Research.* San Francisco: Jossey-Bass, 1991.

Perkins, D. N., and Salomon, G. "Are Cognitive Skills Context-Bound?" *Educational Researcher,* Jan./Feb. 1989, pp. 16–25.

Resnick, L. B. "Learning in School and Out." *Educational Researcher,* Dec. 1987, pp. 13–20.

Rudolph, F. *Curriculum: A History of the American Undergraduate Course of Study Since 1636.* San Francisco: Jossey-Bass, 1977.

Russell, D. R. *Writing in the Academic Disciplines, 1970–1990: A Curriculum History.* Carbondale: Southern Illinois University Press. 1991.

Voss, J. F., Greene, T. R., Post, T. A., and Penner, B. C. "Problem Solving Skill in the Social Sciences." In *The Psychology of Learning and Motivation: Advances in Research and Theory.* Vol. 17. New York: Academic Press, 1983.

CHAPTER 6

STUDENT AFFAIRS IN THE NEXT CENTURY

ASSOCIATE EDITOR: MARVALENE HUGHES

Introduction

The student affairs profession is relatively young when compared to the formal inauguration of higher education in the United States in 1636, the founding year of Harvard University. The exact year when the profession was introduced in higher education institutions remains debated, but the 1937 Student Personnel statement is widely accepted as the document that conceptualized the need to expand the mission of education beyond the traditional focus on intellectual knowledge within academic disciplines (Rentz, 1996). The profession has continued to mature through research and inquiry as well as healthy debates.

The homogeneity of the earliest student body in the United States did not pose the multiple complexities and challenges encountered when women, veterans, ethnic minorities, internationals, older re-entry students, disabled students, and gay/lesbian students entered the university. The student affairs profession gained momentum as diverse populations pursued educational access.

Over time, the areas identified by Sandeen (1996, pp. 437–447) became routine functions in student affairs, although many organizational nuances existed. Presidents have traditionally assigned functions to student affairs as delineated by Sandeen (1996), although if a president's philosophy of an effective organizational structure differs, changes may occur. When presidents perceive that areas in student affairs which are crucial to institutional quality are too peripheral to the academic mission or are marginally managed, some core functions or all of student affairs may be realigned to report to academic administration.

Expected outcomes of services described by Sandeen (1996) varied as the profession matured, but Chickering's (1969) vectors explicated a timeless outcome model: (a) developing competence, (b) managing emotions, (c) developing autonomy, (d) establishing identity, (e) freeing interpersonal relationships, (f) clarifying purpose, and (g) developing integrity.

This section is offered, along with selected reading samples, to highlight some evolving aspects of the profession and to challenge professionals to engage in critical self-examination through research and assessment. Because education is under microscopic scrutiny by numerous public and private sectors, many of which are external to campus, student affairs' pursuit of innovative perspectives to demonstrate its centrality to learning and academic excellence is essential.

Cross-Functional Performance

Today's student affairs administrator will need cross-functional performance skills both within student affairs and in other university areas to create functional synergy and action plans with other vice presidents' units. The ultimate goal is to generate campus partnerships that strengthen

Marvalene Hughes is President of California State University, Stanislaus in Turlock, California. (Hughes_Marvalene@mac-mail.csustan.edu)

services, contribute to academic quality, and create learning opportunities to promote students' success. Academic leaders of the future will defy traditional boundaries, disintegrated functions, and isolated organizational structures to create intra- and inter-campus partnerships. Principles of collaboration and shared governance among colleagues are key to building partnerships. Cross-functional performance can promote a learning-centered environment that is strengthened by operating outside of and across organizational boundaries.

Co-Curricular Versus Classroom Learning

Student affairs professionals must take special measures to keep pace with changes in higher education and to keenly focus on reforming the profession for the 21st century. The tendency to view their roles as facilitators of "co-curricular" or "extra-curricular," learning which occurs outside the classroom may be passé and too restrictive for progressive professionals.

Compartmentalizing learning into "classroom learning" and "co-curricular" or "extra-curricular learning," which ostensibly occurs outside of the classroom, perpetuates a myth about when, where, and how learning occurs. This artificial division reinforces the assumption that when a student enters the classroom a distinct, unique and pedagogically different process is enacted that ends when the class is dismissed. A more functional explanation of learning may be found in the literature on incidental and intentional learning (Krashen, 1993). When students exit the classroom, learning is not a spigot that may be turned off suddenly; likewise, when students participate in intentional learning activities organized by student affairs, learning does not cease because the program or activity ends. Boyer (1987) asserted: "The college of quality remains a place where the curricular and co-curricular are viewed as having a relationship to each other." (p. 195). So much of what students learn and remember is incidental. Both intentional and incidental learning encompass the principles of life-long learning.

The problem with the academic sector is that it devalues incidental learning; the problem with student affairs is that it hesitates to overtly affiliate with intentional learning. The dichotomy prohibits faculty and student affairs from cross-functionally planning learning experiences. Banta and Kuh (1998) asserted:

> Our experience over the past two decades working with scores of campuses has taught us that improving the quality of the undergraduate experience at any institution is so complex and multi-faceted that it demands cooperation by the two groups on campus that spend the most time with students: faculty members and student affairs professionals. (p. 42)

The Intra-Student Affairs Debate Over Theories

Unlike the academic community, research and self-study in student affairs have not been major priorities. This may account for unresolved and lingering debates, such as the continuing dialogue about student development as an undergirding theory. This debate will not propel student affairs to the center of the university's mission since it is internal to the profession. Such discussions may, in fact, deter the development of quality student services. Many new student populations—commuters, re-entries, minorities, disabled, gay/lesbian, and older adults may not have their needs addressed if student affairs professionals cannot generate relevant research and practices to respond to the new student population.

Intra-Student Affairs Proliferation of Organizations

An intra-cultural deterrent to change in student affairs is the splintering of its functions and the proliferation of professional organizations. For nearly every functional area listed by Sandeen (1996), there are national, regional and state organizations, publications and conferences. This creates perceptions of duplications and lack of strategic focus.

The profession has introduced a forward-looking document, The Principles of Good Practices for Student Affairs (1997). These "good practices" represent core values and encourage: promotion of active learning; development of coherent values and ethical standards; elevation of standards and expectations, promotion of systematic inquiry, community building, and creation of partnerships and other effective resource utilization measures.

Cogent assessment of all programs which links learning outcomes to the "good practices" could guide the profession toward greater centrality to the university's mission.

A Theory of Student Involvement

Astin (1985), Kuh (1991), and Boyer (1987) invited the profession to endorse the importance of involving students in campus life as the key factor in their adjustment and success in college. The theory of student involvement offers tools to bring coherence to the diverse literature in the profession which has emerged from "such widely divergent sources as psychoanalysis and classical learning theory" (Astin, 1985, p. 134). The student involvement theory is an especially effective concept that views students and all members of the university community as learners. Astin (1985) defined the student involvement theory as "the amount of physical and psychological energy that the student devotes to the academic experience" (p. 134).

Boyer (1987) measured student involvement by hours spent in selected activities and cautioned students against excessive involvement. Boyer (1987) and Astin (1985) converge in their views that constructive involvement on campus which subjects students to qualitatively sound programs without over-extending themselves will significantly impact their success in college.

Kuh's research (1991) further illuminates the theory of student involvement, using as a backdrop Astin's (1985) and Pascarella, Terezini and Wolf's (1986) documentation that involved students experience positive effects in social integration, satisfaction with college, and institutional commitment.

Creating a Campus Community

Boyer (1990) introduced essential dimensions of a community as: (a) a purposeful place; (b) a communicative place; (c) a just place; (d) a disciplined place; (e) a caring place; and (f) a celebrative place. What is needed in a campus community is a framework for living and learning together in a world that is increasingly diverse. The challenge lies in a university's capacity to institutionalize diversity as the foundation upon which democratic principles are built to encourage the free exchange of ideas. Students may need guidance in managing their emotions when conflict occurs among diverse groups. Respecting differences is essential, but promoting inclusiveness and accepting others ultimately build community. Students need to know they are valued in the community, and they need to feel that they matter.

Jane Fried (1997) offered suggestions on creating an ethical community in a multicultural world. Fried (1997) stated:

> In the present multicultural society of the United States, culture can be rooted not only in ethnicity but also in common life experience and worldview related to race, socioeconomic status, professional identity, gender, sexual orientation, or disability (p. 6).

Clearly ethical judgments and behaviors, virtues, ideals, values, beliefs, assumptions and norms are derived from a cultural context.

Suggested Supplementary Readings

Astin, Alexander W. *Achieving Educational Excellence: A Critical Assessment of Priorities and Practices in Higher Education.* San Francisco: Jossey-Bass Publishers, 1985, 254 pp.

Astin, Alexander. *What Matters in College.* San Francisco: Jossey-Bass, 1993.

Banta, Trudy W. and Kuh, George D. "The Missing Link in Assessment: Collaboration Between Academic and Student Affairs," *Change*, March/April, 1998, 40–46.

Boyer, Ernest L. *The Basic School: A Community for Learning.* Princeton: The Carnegie Foundation for the Advancement of Teaching, 1995.

Boyer, Ernest L. *College: The Undergraduate Experience in America.* New York: Harper & Row, 1987.

Chickering, Arthur. *Education and Identity.* San Francisco: Jossey-Bass, 1969.

Fried, Jane. "Changing Ethical Frameworks for a Multicultural World," in J. Fried (ed.) *Ethical Perspectives in Student Affairs: Educational, Developmental and Institutional.* New Directions in Student Services. San Francisco: Jossey-Bass, 1997.

Fried, Jane & Associates. *Shifting Paradigms in Student Affairs: Culture, Context, Teaching and Learning.* Washington, DC: American College Personnel Association, 1995.

Komives, S. R., Woodard, D. Jr. & Associates. *Student Services: A Handbook for the Profession.* (3rd ed.). San Francisco: Jossey-Bass, 1996.

Komives, S. R. "Increasing Student Involvement Through Civic Leadership Education," in C. C. Schroeder, P. Mable & Associates, *Realizing the Educational Potential of College Residence Halls.* San Francisco: Jossey-Bass, 1994, 218–240.

Komives, S. R. "New Approaches to Leadership," in J. Fried (ed.), *Different Voices: Gender and Perspective in Student Services Administration.* Washington, D.C.: National Association of Student Personnel Administrators, 1994, 46–61.

Komives, S. R. "Advancing Professionally Through Graduate Education," in M. J. Barr & Associates, *The Handbook of Student Affairs Administration.* San Francisco: Jossey-Bass, 1993, 390–411.

Krashen, S. The *Power of Reading: Insights from the Research.* Culver City, CA: Language Education Associates, 1993.

Kuh, George D. *Involving Colleges: Successful Approaches to Fostering Student Learning and Development Outside the Classroom.* San Francisco: Jossey-Bass, 1991.

NASPA. *Principles of Good Practice for Student Affairs.* American College Personnel Association and National Association of Student Personnel Administrators, 1997.

Rentz, Audrey L. *Student Affairs Practice in Higher Education.* 2nd ed. Springfield, IL: Charles C. Thomas, 1996.

Sandeen, Arthur. *Student Services: A Handbook for the Profession.* 3rd ed. San Francisco: Jossey-Bass, 1996.

Organization, Functions, and Standards of Practice

ARTHUR SANDEEN

When LeBaron Russell Briggs was appointed dean at Harvard in 1890, he became a one-person student affairs staff! With no job description, no organizational chart, and no set of professional standards to guide him, he learned to be a dean by listening to the students and helping them with their problems. His colleagues at other institutions, such as Marion Talbot at the University of Chicago and Stanley Coulter at Purdue University, faced similar challenges. When they moved into their offices, they had to create their own organizations!

Although the student affairs profession is still quite young, its organization and functions are now well established, with accepted standards of practice, distinct professional associations, and several professional publications devoted to the field. In 1995, virtually all 3,600 U.S. colleges and universities provided student affairs programs in various forms.

Organization of Higher Education

The internal organization of a college or university is determined by the governing board. The senior executive officer, usually called the president or chancellor, is charged by the governing board with administering the institution in accordance with priorities established by the board. While there is no universal administrative model used by all institutions, most colleges and universities have designated senior officers, appointed by the president, for such major functions as academic affairs, business affairs, institutional advancement, and student affairs. At some institutions, depending upon their complexity and mission, there may also be senior officers for medical affairs and community relations.

The senior officer for student affairs may have the title of vice president, vice provost, associate provost, or dean of students. The responsibilities of the senior officer often vary from one campus to another, depending upon the problems facing the institution, the priorities of the president, the ability of the senior student affairs officer, or the traditions and history of the institution. The senior student affairs officer often reports directly to the president, but in some cases he or she reports to the provost or the senior academic affairs officer. It is rare for all of the student affairs functions described in this chapter to fall under the direct administrative direction of the student affairs division at any given institution; at most institutions, some of the functions are administered by other departments. For example, admissions and registration may be part of academic affairs at some colleges; financial aid may be responsible to the business affairs division; and career and placement services might be part of the development program.

While the organizational chart of a college or university often yields useful information about the institution, the basic functions that provide assistance and support to students often transcend formal organizational lines. It is very important for student affairs staff to understand that to accomplish their goals they must work in collaboration with their colleagues in academic affairs, business, and development. The relationship of the student

"Organization, Functions, and Standards of Practice," by Arthur Sandeen, reprinted from *Student Services: A Handbook for the Profession*, Third Edition, by Susan R. Komives, Dudley B. Woodward, Jr. and Associates, 1996, Jossey-Bass Publishers, Inc.

affairs organization to the institutional organization as a whole is very important but it is not as critical to the success of student affairs as the relationships, coalitions, and cooperative programs that can be developed. Student affairs does not become effective on a campus as a result of the power arrangements described on an organizational chart; it earns its role by successfully accomplishing tasks deemed important to the institution.

The student affairs program and organization should reflect the mission of the institution, its academic goals, and the characteristics and needs of the students. With the great diversity in American higher education in the types and sizes of institutions and in students' academic, economic, and personal backgrounds, there are wide variations in the delivery of student affairs functions (see Chapters Three and Four for detailed information on student and institutional diversity). Moreover, the student affairs functions offered by an institution may reflect the community in which it is located and the financial resources available to it. The National Association of Student Personnel Administrators (NASPA) and the American College Personnel Association (ACPA) have networks and commissions that support many of these functions with newsletters and conferences.

In this chapter, the various functions of student affairs are described, organizational options are presented, standards of practice are reviewed, and trends and issues related to organization are discussed. In addition, examples of organizational arrangements at three different institutions are examined.

Functions of Student Affairs

Despite considerable variations in the style and extent of services, the following student affairs functions are usually found at most U.S. colleges and universities.

Admissions and Recruitment

These services inform prospective students about the institution and its programs and solicit, accept, and screen applicants. Usually students are admitted in accordance with policies established by the faculty, the president, the governing board, or the state legislature. Admissions offices maintain active communications with high schools, community colleges, community agencies, alumni groups, professional testing associations, parents, and others interested in the institution's admissions requirements. In many cases admissions offices target specific groups of students and actively recruit them because of their personal background, academic talents, or other abilities. Admissions offices frequently perform a centralized function for the entire institution, although this service might be decentralized at some institutions (especially large research universities with many graduate programs and professional schools). Establishing equity in admissions practices, determining admissions' relationship to financial aid, and clarifying ethical practices remain key issues in this area.

The National Association of College Admissions Counselors (NACAC) is the major professional association for admissions officers. The *Journal of College Admissions* and the *College Board Review* are the most frequently read professional publications.

Orientation

Orientation (also called new student programs) is the process of helping students learn the history, traditions, educational programs, academic requirements, and student life of the institution.

Programs may last one or two days, or they may extend throughout the first year. Orientation programs used to focus almost exclusively on such matters as registration, finances, and housing, but in recent years they have become much more extensive, involving parents, community leaders, faculty, and student leaders. The emphasis on many campuses is now upon student development, and there is active interest in enhancing the first-year experiences of students. Linking orientation to the academic program and deciding the actual content of orientation programs are major issues that will be addressed in the future.

The National Orientation Directors Association (NODA) is the professional association for this area of student affairs. The *Journal of the Freshman Year Experience* is the major publication.

Registration

In American colleges and universities, the office of the registrar is charged with keeping the official academic records of current and former students. This office also usually conducts the process by which students enroll for their academic courses and publishes the official schedules of courses for the institution. The registrar's office is sometimes linked administratively with admissions and, in some cases, with orientation or student financial aid. Issues that are likely to demand the attention of registrars in the future are how technology can best serve institutions and students and the legal status of student records.

The American Association of Collegiate Registrars and Admissions Officers (AACRAO) is the major professional association for this area. *College and University* is the publication most often read by professionals concerned with registration.

Financial Aid

Most colleges and universities provide a financial aid office to help students with their educational expenses. This student support is composed of grants, loans, scholarships, and student employment. The staff in student financial aid offices work closely with government agencies, banks, loan guarantee agencies, parents, corporate and individual donors, and, of course, student aid recipients. In addition to assessing student financial needs and making decisions about student aid packages, student financial aid staff also assist students with their personal financial planning while in college. On some campuses, the student financial aid office is linked administratively with admissions, retention, and registration. Issues abound in the financial aid arena, including heavy loan dependency of students, linking financial aid to the college's academic goals, and privatization of services.

The National Association of Student Financial Aid Administrators (NASFAA) is the major professional organization in this area. The *NASFAA Newsletter* is the most frequently read publication.

Academic Advising and Support Services

Especially at larger universities, special offices have been established to assist students in making decisions about their course of study. Often, staff specifically trained for this responsibility are hired for tasks that were traditionally assumed by faculty members. At most smaller institutions, the majority of academic advising is still carried out in this manner. The academic advising office often also includes special academic support services to address the needs of students who may need learning assistance, such as in math or writing. This office may be responsible to academic affairs or to student affairs, and it may be administratively linked with the counseling center, the orientation program, or a retention office. Finding adequate resources for advising, coordinating advising with the teaching program, and linking advising to recruitment and retention efforts will remain key issues in this area.

The National Academic Advising Association (NACADA) is the major professional organization for academic advisers. The *NACADA Journal* is the publication with the greatest visibility in this field.

International Student Services

With large numbers of international students in the United States, most colleges and universities have established special offices to meet their needs. These offices help international students with travel, orientation, financial aid, registration, housing, counseling, and (especially) successful adjustment to the campus and community. In many cases international student services offices are responsible for study abroad programs, foreign visitors, and the many international student organizations that exist on most campuses. At some institutions this office may be part of academic affairs or an international programs division; but regardless of where the service is located administratively, student affairs has a major role in its success. Issues likely to be addressed in this area include financial support and tuition, relations with U.S. students, and changing immigration policies.

The National Association of Foreign Student Advisers (NAFSA) is the major professional organization in this area. The *NAFSA Newsletter* is the most frequently read publication.

College Unions and Student Activities Offices

On most U.S. campuses, a college union serves as a center for students, faculty, staff, alumni, student organizations, and their various activities. This office is usually responsible for developing and supervising activities that complement the educational programs and aims of the institution. On some campuses there is a student activities office separate from the college union. Student activities usually advance the political, social, religious, academic, and recreational interests of students, and they are often linked to leadership and community service programs. Depending on the institution, there may be efforts to coordinate parts of the student activities program with the curriculum, especially the general education core curriculum. The student activities office may have responsibility for fraternities and sororities, student publications, and outdoor programming. Funding, user fees, privatization, and the relationship of student activities to the academic program are issues that are likely to be considered in the future.

The major professional organizations in this area are the Association of College Unions International (ACUI) and the National Association of Campus Activities (NACA). The most frequently read publications are the *ACUI Bulletin* and *Campus Activity Programming*.

Counseling Services

American colleges and universities make a substantial effort to help students with their personal development and everyday problems. This is usually accomplished through a counseling service office. Staffed with professionals trained and in some cases licensed to provide assistance to students, this office usually includes mental health and psychological services. Many counseling services now engage in outreach activities with other campus offices, such as residence life and academic departments, and with various community agencies.

The counseling office may also provide services to persons in crisis. It may be part of the student health service, an independent office within student affairs, or attached to a medical center. Issues that will affect the future of counseling centers include privatization, third-party payments from insurance companies, and licensing and accreditation.

The major professional associations serving the interests of counseling centers are the Division of Counseling Psychology of the American Psychological Association (APA), the American Counseling Association (ACA), and the Association of University and College Counseling Center Directors (AUCCCD). The principal publications in this area are the *Journal of Counseling Psychology*, the *Journal of Counseling and Development*, and *Counseling Psychologist*.

Career Development

For many years, this service was known as "the placement office," as its primary function was considered to be to help students obtain jobs after graduation. Now the purposes of this student affairs office include helping students learn about their own interests and skills and developing plans that fit students' career and personal needs. Staff work closely with students, faculty, corporations, and community and government agencies to discover opportunities. The career development program often includes an emphasis on career planning, assessment, cooperative education, internships, placement, and alumni support. The office is sometimes part of academic affairs or the development program, but most frequently it is administratively placed under student affairs. On some large campuses career development services are decentralized into each of the major academic units, especially the professional colleges. Technological developments, privatization, and corporate support represent issues that will demand the attention of career development leaders in the future.

Major professional associations are the College Placement Council (CPC) and the National Career Development Association (NCDA). The most frequently read publications in this area are the *Journal of Career Planning and Employment*, the *CPC Annual*, and the *Career Development Quarterly*.

Residence Life

While not all U.S. colleges and universities provide residential programs for their students, a very substantial number of them do. This office is expected to provide a healthy, clean, safe, and educationally supportive living environment that complements the academic mission of the institution. The office may have responsibility for the financial management and maintenance of residence halls as well as student room assignments, student programming, and support services. Many residential life offices also assume responsibility for residence hall food service operations, whether they are self-operated or contracted out. Planning and supervising new construction may be part of the office's responsibilities as well. Administratively, residence life services may be partly or entirely linked to business affairs or academic affairs, depending on the purposes of the overall program. Most residence life offices, however, are part of the student affairs organization. Facility renovation and enhancement, availability of resources, and privatization are issues that will be actively discussed by residence life professionals in the future.

The major professional association in this area is the Association of College and University Housing Officers—International (ACUHO-I). The leading publications are the *Journal of College and University Student Housing* and the *ACUHO-I Talking Stick*.

Services for Students with Disabilities

Most colleges and universities provide a special service charged with improving the success of students with disabilities and students with special learning problems. This office also works to improve physical conditions and understanding on the campus and in the community. The office often finds itself in an advocacy role, serving as a catalyst in discussions of academic policies and procedures that affect students with disabilities. It may be part of academic affairs, the affirmative action office, or a facilities planning office. Most frequently it is administratively placed within student affairs. Legal clarifications of federal laws, financial support from colleges, and services for learning disabled students are issues that will be debated in the future.

The major professional organization is the Association on Higher Education and Disability (AHEAD). The principal professional publication is the *Journal of Postsecondary Education and Disability*.

Intercollegiate Athletics

Student affairs divisions often have responsibility for directing programs in intercollegiate athletics. These programs provide opportunities for students to participate in athletic competition with students at other institutions in a variety of sports. Intercollegiate athletics programs address issues of sportsmanship, training, nutrition, safety, gender equity, financial support, and institutional representation. Programs at smaller colleges may encourage broad student participation, while programs at some larger institutions may depend upon revenues from one or two sports and thus concentrate on recruiting highly sought after athletes. Establishing gender equity, ensuring financial health, and integrating athletes into mainstream campus life will be issues discussed in the future.

The major professional organizations in this area are the National Collegiate Athletic Association (NCAA) and the National Association of Intercollegiate Athletics (NAIA). The most frequently read publications are the *NCAA Manual* and the *NCAA News*.

Child-Care Services

Many colleges and universities provide child-care services to enable students with young children to pursue an education. These services, often subsidized by student fees, make it possible for students to attend classes and participate in college programs while their children are in child care. Student affairs divisions often initiate child-care programs, and they usually work closely with academic departments and community agencies in conducting them. In some cases the student affairs division contracts this service out to an off-campus agency. In some institutions the child-care program is part of a laboratory school or early childhood education program. Financial support, user fees, equity and safety will continue to be key issues discussed by professionals in this area in the future.

The major professional association in this area is the National Association for the Education of Young Children (NAEYC); its major publication is *Early Childhood News*.

Student Health Services

Most colleges and universities provide some form of health care for their students, whether directly through a service on campus or in conjunction with a community agency or hospital. The purposes of student health services are to provide medical assistance to students who are ill or injured, to encourage good health, and to help prevent illnesses or injuries. Health service staff often extend their work to campus residences, and they usually work closely with community health organizations. An increased emphasis on wellness has effectively linked health centers to many other campus programs, especially fitness centers and recreation programs. On some campuses coverage extends to faculty and staff in addition to students. Where the campus has an academic medical center, the student health service may be linked administratively to the medical school or the research hospital. On some campuses student health services are contracted out to a local health provider. Financial support, extent of services, privatization, and the impact of U.S. health care reform are major issues that will be discussed in the future.

The major professional association in this area is the American College Health Association (ACHA), and the primary publication is the *ACHA Journal*.

Food Services

Whether the campus is residential or commuter in nature, some form of food service program usually exists for students, employees, and visitors. Food service programs vary greatly, with some colleges providing only vending machines and snack bars and others serving full meals daily to thousands of students in many locations. Some institutions also have extensive catering needs for formal and special events. While many colleges and universities operate their own food services, a significant number contract for these services with private companies. Student affairs divisions are often responsible for the food service program and sometimes share this responsibility with another administrative division of the institution. Nutrition, finances, and privatization are issues that will demand the attention of professionals in this area in the future.

The National Association of College and University Food Services (NACUFS) is the professional organization in this area. Their publication is *Newswave*.

Dean of Students

This office, which often has responsibility for several of the functions listed in this section, has traditionally carried with it the expectation of helping to establish and enforce the community standards of the institution. The primary educational role within student affairs is assumed by the dean of students and is expressed most frequently through policy, links with academic departments, and campus leadership. At some colleges the dean of students has assumed the rather undefined but significant role of "conscience of the campus." This office responds to the general concerns of students, faculty, staff, parents, and community members and also organizes and directs the institution's responses to student crises.

The National Association of Student Personnel Administrators (NASPA) and the American College Personnel Association (ACPA) are the major professional associations for deans of students. The major publications are the *NASPA Journal* and the *Journal of College Student Development*.

Community Service and Leadership Programs

While most colleges and universities do not have a formal office dedicated to community service and leadership development, a large number are now conducting such programs, usually from other existing student affairs departments. Students are encouraged to participate in a variety of community service programs or service learning activities connected to their academic course work. Frequent cooperation with community organizations and agencies is necessary in this area. While sometimes organized separately, programs designed to teach and encourage leadership development are often part of such efforts. Future legislation, campus financial support, and integration with academic programs are future issues likely to be debated in this area.

The National Campus Compact and the Campus Outreach Opportunity League are major organizations offering support in this area. Among many publications, the *Compact News* is the most recognized. The Corporation for National Community Service, which includes Americorps, is a federally funded program that supports these efforts. The National Clearinghouse for Leadership Programs and the *Journal of Leadership Studies* are additional resources.

Student Judicial Affairs

To ensure that the academic integrity and behavioral standards of the institution are maintained, colleges and universities have established student judicial affairs offices to develop, interpret, and enforce campus rules and regulations. On many campuses these duties are assumed by the dean of students, but on others a separate office has been created to emphasize the importance of this function. Student judicial offices conduct student hearings, publish rules and regulations that define procedures and student rights, and encourage student learning through direct participation in the judicial system. This office has extensive contact with faculty as well as with police, community service agencies, and attorneys. It is likely that such issues as legal challenges to jurisdiction and increased violence will demand the attention of professionals in this area in the future.

The Association of Student Judicial Affairs (ASJA) is the professional organization in this area, and their publication is the *ASJA Newsletter*. Other publications of interest are *Synthesis*, the *Journal of College and University Law*, and *The College Student and the Courts*.

Student Recreation and Fitness Programs

Student recreation and fitness programs promote good health, teach physical skills, and encourage positive social interaction. This highly popular service has grown rapidly in recent years, leading to the construction of extensive new facilities. In addition to intramural and informal activities, many sports clubs also provide opportunities for students to compete outside the official intercollegiate program. Outdoor adventures and trips are also offered, and they are sometimes linked with teaching programs. On many campuses as many as 90 percent of students are participants in recreation and fitness programs. Funding of facilities, user fees, and privatization represent issues that will be debated in the future.

The National Intramural-Recreational Sports Association (NIRSA) is the professional association in this area. The major publication is the *NIRSA Journal*.

Student Religious Programs

While there is wide variation in the approach colleges and universities take to student religious programs, most campuses provide opportunities for religious groups to interact with their students. At public colleges the religious program may consist of a designated staff liaison and an association of off-campus religious centers; at some private colleges there are full-time staff who plan and develop religious programs and activities for students. Where student religious programs do exist, they are usually part of the student affairs organization. Issues likely to emerge in this area are use of campus facilities and support from activities funds.

Several denominational groups provide professional support for religious advisers. At the current time there is no single national association that represents all student religious advisers.

Special Student Populations

Many campuses have offices to address the special needs of women and minority students. While the major focus may be on the needs of racial and ethnic minorities, these offices might also advise gay, lesbian, and bisexual students; religious minorities; and women. In some cases this office is called the multicultural student services office and may include responsibility for ethnic and cultural centers and events. On campuses where there is not a separate office for these purposes, special efforts are usually made to respond to the educational and social concerns of these student populations. The purpose of such efforts are to help these students become successful at their college and to assist faculty, students, and staff in becoming more knowledgeable about their needs. The future of affirmative action programs; competition among various ethnic, gender, and minority groups for resources; and future funding of federal support programs are issues that will demand the attention of professionals in this area.

There are many professional associations representing the various interests and priorities within minority student programs. Among them are the National Association for Equal Opportunity (NAFEO), the National Association of Student Affairs Professionals (NASAP), and the National Council of Educational Opportunity Associations (NCEOA). Each association has a variety of professional publications.

Commuter Student Services

Commuter students may represent a small percentage of the student body or the majority of students at a college. Recognizing that students who commute to campus may have special needs, many colleges and universities have established offices within student affairs that provide services to them and act as their advocates. Often commuter students are employed off campus and attend classes at times when some services are not in operation. Safety, parking, equal access, recreation, food service, and participation in student life are some of the concerns of commuter student services offices.

The major professional organization in this area is the National Clearinghouse for Commuter Programs (NCCP). Their publication is the *Commuter*.

Program Research and Evaluation

Most student affairs divisions do not have adequate resources to establish a separate office dedicated to research and evaluation of campus programs and services; however, most student affairs divisions do assess their programs, conduct studies of their students, and review student reactions to campus services. These efforts may be undertaken by student affairs staff themselves, in cooperation with state and national testing agencies, or by faculty. Where an institutional research and evaluation office

does exist, student affairs staff may work directly with its personnel to carry out the studies and assessments it needs. The information gained from such studies is considered critical to student affairs staff in planning and improving services and programs. Key issues of concern are likely to be continuing institutional support and establishing effective links with the teaching program.

The American Educational Research Association (AERA) is the leading professional organization in this area. Their publication is the *AERA Journal*.

Additional Functions

Depending on the size and type of institution, such functions as veteran's affairs, outreach programs, testing, speech and hearing clinics, transfer centers, and legal services may be offered. In many cases, of course, these functions are provided in conjunction with other, more general offices on campus.

Organizing Student Affairs Functions

How institutions organize their various student affairs functions depends on such factors as the educational purpose of the programs and services offered, the size of the institution, the nature of the student body, the nature of the external community, and the relationship of student affairs with other institutional functions. These factors are discussed in this section and elaborated on in the following section with examples from the student affairs activities at Lafayette College, Broward Community College, and North Carolina State University.

Educational Purpose

With over 3,500 colleges and universities in the United States, there is a great deal of diversity in their educational goals. These may emphasize liberal arts, vocational preparation, professional education, religious enlightenment, social reconstruction, military training, personal enrichment, or artistic and creative development. Student affairs programs vary along with these educational purposes, of course, since their primary role is to support the academic mission of the institution.

A liberal arts college whose primary focus is on academic scholarship is likely to organize its student affairs functions in ways that closely involve faculty. The boundaries between academic and student affairs are usually less clear at these colleges than at colleges that stress professional or career preparation. Indeed, academic departments at liberal arts colleges may assume some traditional student affairs functions such as academic advising, orientation, and career development. At institutions that view the classroom and laboratory as the exclusive domain of education, there is likely to be a sharper separation between student affairs functions and academic programs. Moreover, the student affairs functions may be organized into relatively independent units themselves, with less participation from faculty in policy making and programming.

Nature of the Student Body

Apart from educational purpose, no other factor is more important in deciding how student affairs functions ought to be organized than the nature of the student body. The student affairs organization should reflect the social, financial, academic, and cultural needs of the students. A college with first-generation students from lower socioeconomic backgrounds will likely place a strong emphasis on recruitment, academic support, financial aid, and career development and will organize these services to maximize their visibility and access. A college that attracts traditional-age, academically talented students from upper-middle-class backgrounds may be more likely to emphasize student activities and leadership programs, service learning, and study abroad programs. A college with older, part-time students who mostly work full time is likely to emphasize such services as child care, financial aid, commuter services, and counseling.

Size of Institution

At smaller colleges, the organizational structure of student affairs divisions may not include separate departments for specialized functions, as staff assume several roles in assisting students. At some community colleges and larger institutions, size alone may dictate that extensive, separate departments, especially in such areas as registration, financial aid, and housing be established. When such large and relatively autonomous departments exist, the distance between student affairs and other campus programs can easily increase.

External Community

A college in an isolated, rural setting may need to offer certain services that colleges in large cities can choose to forego, especially in the areas of student health services, counseling, child care, recreation, and housing. Community colleges, of course, adapt virtually the entire institution to the needs of their surrounding community. Students services at these colleges often emphasize hands-on outreach programs located directly in areas where students live or work.

Relationship to Other Institutional Functions

How a student affairs division is organized also depends on its relationship with academic affairs, business services, development, and the president. At large institutions with academic health programs and professional schools, the structure of student affairs may be affected as well. On some campuses the academic affairs office and business services office assume responsibility for some student affairs functions, and development offices may do so as well. Professional colleges on large campuses may have extensive and sometimes separate student services. All of these arrangements can change with the appointment of a new president, provost, or other administrative officer. No matter how the various student affairs functions are organized, student affairs leaders usually understand that it is beneficial to integrate their efforts with other major units on campus, working to blur administrative boundaries and improve quality of service through cooperation and collaboration.

Three Institutional Examples

Broward Community College

This institution was founded in 1960 and now enrolls more than fifty-five thousand students on its four campuses in Fort Lauderdale, Davie, Coconut Creek, and Pembroke Pines, Florida. Students are enrolled in a large variety of programs, many of which lead to an associate of arts or associate of science degree; about 35 percent of BCC students plan to transfer to a four-year college or university. Each of the four campuses is closely associated with its community, and cooperation with business, government, health, and service agencies is reflected in all its programs.

The vice president for student affairs at Broward Community College has served in this position for twenty-seven years. As the senior student affairs officer, the vice president is responsible for all student affairs functions on the four campuses. There is a principal student affairs officer on each of the four campuses. These officers report to their branch campus provost, and the vice president coordinates overall policy. The vice president has responsibility for all policy matters, staff development, accountability, facilities management, outcomes assessment, and resource development. In addition, the vice president serves as the director of the intercollegiate athletics program.

The student affairs organization at Broward Community College includes six major departments: student financial services, the registrar and enrollment management, student services and evaluation, student life, academic intervention services, and outreach. Each department is led by a director, who reports to the vice president. Among the many program responsibilities assumed by these departments are veterans' affairs, student employment, grant development and administration, disability services, international student programs, transfer evaluation, graduation, intramural sports, entertainment and special events, and precollegiate programs. There is a special emphasis on community service, with large numbers of BCC students participating in local schools and government and community agencies.

Reflecting on the student affairs organization, the vice president indicates that

> we try to put as much responsibility as possible on the people who are the closest to the students in terms of decision making, and while we sometimes get some creative decisions from one campus that are not consistent with another, it generally works better in terms of student outcomes than a more traditional, highly centralized operation. In terms of the future, I think we have to become much more customer service-oriented, less bureaucratic, and more creative. We will need a lot more staff development in order to effectively serve and retain our students. The new students are shoppers and much more conscious of bureaucracies that run them around stumps! (G. Young, personal communication, November 10, 1994)

Lafayette College

Lafayette College, located in Easton, Pennsylvania, and founded in 1826, is a liberal arts and engineering institution with an enrollment of two thousand students. The current dean of students has served as the senior student affairs officer at Lafayette for twenty-eight years. The dean reports to the president of the college and is responsible for intercollegiate athletics, health services, international student services, the food service program, the counseling center, student residences, student activities, the office of the chaplain, and cultural programs, including the art gallery and the theater program. Two other senior officers, the provost and the dean of the college, have responsibility for academic advising admissions, student financial aid, career planning and placement, and the registrar's office. The dean of students also serves as the secretary of the board of trustees committee on athletics and student affairs.

The dean emphasizes that Lafayette's organization depends on who happens to be in a given place at a given time; he has tried to find ways of providing increased opportunities for certain staff to grow and develop, and this has at times influenced the way functions have been aligned. The staff works hard to establish close working relationships with faculty.

Faculty are involved in all student affairs programs and have a significant influence on policy. The dean's daily contact with the provost, the vice president for development, and the vice president for business makes it very important for them to be well informed about student affairs issues and priorities and for the dean to be well informed about their issues and problems as well. The dean has worked for four presidents in his years at Lafayette, and he emphasizes the importance of understanding the president's priorities and of helping presidents achieve their goals. While the organizational structure of Lafayette's student affairs function has not changed greatly in many years, the dean has made adjustments based upon the goals of particular presidents, especially in the areas of athletics, cultural programs, and student behavior. The dean expressed caution that

> personal friendships can sometimes result in awkward problems within the organization, especially at a small college. Relationships with others members of a senior staff become dependent upon so many different variables. The dismissal of a fraternity angers the vice president for development; of course, he is pleased with a league championship and football victory over an arch rival. The vice president for finance really does not want to see students about changes in the meal plan but is pleased when the director of student residence manages to squeeze in a few extra bodies into the residence halls. Ironically, the senior staff seems to come together best when operating under adverse conditions. When all is well and we have the opportunity to run off in our different directions, the glass sometimes breaks. (H. Kissiah, personal communication, November 29, 1994)

North Carolina State University

Located in Raleigh, North Carolina, this institution was founded in 1887 and now enrolls 27,500 students in a great variety of undergraduate, graduate, and professional programs. North Carolina State University is a land grant institution and an active member of the National Association of State Universities and Land Grant Colleges. The current vice chancellor for student affairs has served in this position for the past ten years. The vice chancellor has held a variety of positions within student affairs at the same institution since 1971 and was appointed vice chancellor in 1985. The vice chancellor reports to the university provost and works directly with the vice chancellors for business, academic affairs, and advancement.

The student affairs organization at North Carolina State includes three associate vice chancellors. One has responsibility for honors and scholars programs; one oversees support services such as counseling, financial aid, health services, and registration; and one directs cultural and arts programs for theater, music, dance, crafts, and the visual arts. The student affairs division is also responsible for all Reserve Officer Training Corps (ROTC) programs, university dining services, student development, and student housing. The directors of these four programs report directly to the vice chancellor.

North Carolina State's student affairs organization reflects the institution's large size and also its strong traditional commitment to the performing and creative arts. Holding responsibility for these highly visible programs within student affairs requires close cooperation and collaboration with academic departments and other campus agencies. While the vice chancellor is actively involved in the entire student affairs organization, the decision to have three associate vice chancellors to oversee major components of this large division has resulted in better-quality programs in each of the departments, due to the personal time and attention that the associate vice chancellors can give to their needs. This arrangement has also enabled the vice chancellor to participate more fully in senior management decisions at the university.

The vice chancellor states that

> our student affairs organization obviously includes some components that might seem unusual when compared with some other institutions, such as theater and ROTC. However, part of our mission is to encourage students to develop their leadership skills and their appreciation of the creative and performing arts, and we are very proud to have a major role in these efforts. Two of my biggest challenges within our organization are to make sure that people are communicating effectively with each

other and to bring all these diverse interests we represent into a coherent, unified student affairs division. Our institution has had remarkable stability in its administrative structure; however, when new chancellors have been appointed, we have changed both our organization and some of our focus to meet the priorities of the chancellor. (T. Stafford, personal communication, December 16, 1994)

Standards of Practice

The major professional associations in student affairs (NASPA and the ACPA) have published statements designed to help institutions and their individual members achieve high professional standards. These statements can serve as effective guidelines as institutions develop student affairs organizations and as they consider the ways in which they will deliver various services. NASPAs *Standards of Professional Practice* (1983) addresses seventeen standards, including agreement with institutional goals, conflict of interest, confidentiality of records, hiring practices, performance evaluation, and professional development. The ACPAs *Statement of Ethical Principles and Standards* (1993) emphasizes the ethical obligations of student affairs professionals. Both of these statements are used by institutions and individuals to maximize the effectiveness of student affairs organizations. See Chapter Six for additional information on student affairs standards.

In 1979, in response to the American Council on Education's Advisory Committee on Self-Regulation Initiatives and the encouragement of the Council on Post-secondary Accreditation, twenty-two student affairs professional associations came together to form the Council for the Advancement of Standards for Student Services/Development Programs. (The name was later changed to the Council for Advancement of Standards in Higher Education; the council is generally referred to as simply the CAS.) The council's statement of professional standards and guidelines (Miller, 1986) has had a very significant impact on student affairs organizations on U.S. campuses. The goals of the CAS are to establish professional standards for student affairs, to help institutions and professionals use these standards for program evaluation and accredita-

tion, and to establish a system of regular review of the standards to keep pace with changes in the field (Yerian, 1988). The CAS developed the *Self-Assessment Guide* (Council for the Advancement of Standards for Student Services/Development Programs, 1988), which provides a detailed system of self-evaluation for student affairs programs. This guide has proven very effective in helping institutions upgrade their student affairs organizations and improve the quality of their services and staff.

Trends and Issues Related to Organization

Student affairs organizations have continued to develop new services and programs as the needs of students and institutions have expanded. There are an estimated fifty thousand student affairs staff in higher education today (Bloland, Stamatakos, & Rogers, 1994), and various services are now routinely provided that would not even have been imagined when the field began one hundred years ago. Student affairs leaders face many new challenges in the nineties that will result in new priorities and changes within student affairs organizations. The following issues, while certainly not exhaustive, are presented as major organizational concerns student affairs leaders face.

Diminishing Financial Support

Whether private or public, most institutions of higher education are scrutinizing their entire budget more rigorously than ever before. The emphasis is on creating lean, efficient organizations that stress increased productivity. This drive to cut back on administrative costs is occurring at a time when demands for increased and more rapid services are on the rise. This situation has forced student affairs leaders to become more entrepreneurial in their financial management practices in order to maintain their current level of services or to enhance them. No longer can student affairs leaders simply look to their institution for financial support for needed services. Like most of their academic counterparts on campus, they are expected to create or raise financial resources themselves. As a result, many student affairs organizations have created fund-raising positions in conjunction with their campus development offices for the purpose of supporting specific programs and services. Other approaches include parental fund raising, designated student services fees, student user fees, and direct support from corporations and foundations, especially those that conduct business with the institution.

This diminution of direct, institutional financial support is not specific to student affairs programs and services. It is happening in all areas of higher education, and the trend is likely to continue. It is changing the way student affairs leaders do their jobs, and it will certainly affect the kinds of persons hired by institutions to lead student affairs organizations in the future.

Privatization of Services

As institutions think of ways to conserve their resources and improve the quality of their services, increased attention is being paid to contracting out services to private companies. This practice, common for years in large corporations but relatively new to higher education, is referred to in the public sector and in education as "privatization." Bookstores, food services, housing facilities, and child-care services are now often contracted out by colleges and universities to save money, increase income, and improve the quality of service. There are now companies available to take over financial aid, counseling, placement, and student health operations for institutions. This trend is likely to grow as college leaders and board members look for solutions to increasing costs and ways to satisfy student and parent demands for quality and efficiency. When a private company claims it can provide better services for lower costs, most institutional leaders feel they have an obligation to listen!

The privatization issue has caused some student affairs leaders to look closely at their organization and focus more clearly on matters such as quality, staff effort, and student satisfaction. The best student affairs leaders view privatization not as a threat to their organization, but as healthy competition that can produce better results and higher-quality services. Student affairs leaders are obligated to provide the best student services they can for their

institution. If they can meet this goal most effectively by contracting with private companies, then they should choose this option.

Accountability, Assessment, and Liability

In the 1990s, the emphasis in organizational management is on results. Student affairs leaders are making changes in their organizations that reflect this emphasis. To justify continued support for a service or program, student affairs leaders are now expected to provide assessment and evaluative information to indicate what the actual benefits are. This trend will continue as all institutional programs and services come under greater scrutiny by students, administrators, parents, legislators, and governing board members. Some student affairs organizations have responded by creating a special position responsible for assessing quality, evaluating programs, and measuring student reactions to campus services. Others have made assessment a requirement of each department within the institution. The results of these assessments are used for program planning and budgetary allocations.

With litigation increasing in all areas of American life, colleges and universities now face liability concerns that would have been unimaginable thirty years ago. This has resulted in greatly increased legal costs for institutions, greater caution in sponsoring certain kinds of activities, and much tighter controls over policy-making processes. Student affairs organizations have been influenced significantly by this concern for liability in housing, financial aid, student activities, health service, child care, counseling, and athletics. At some institutions these concerns have caused student affairs leaders to at the same time distance the college or university from student organizations and programs or exert much greater centralized control over their activities.

Technology

Rapid advances in communications, information processing, and computer technology have changed the way colleges and universities conduct their affairs. These advances have also changed the expectations of students and others for efficient, rapid services and around-the-clock access to information. When students and their parents can talk with the college president via electronic mail at any time, and when students have on-line access to data services throughout the world, old-line, top-down, bureaucratic organizational structures are unlikely to be viewed as effective. For student affairs, technological advances have meant greatly improved communication with students, free and easy access to information, improved services, and the blurring of departmental boundaries. Greater contact and cooperation between institutional departments has brought student affairs professionals closer to their colleagues in academic and business affairs. With advances in technology students have more control of their own learning and can participate more fully in the affairs and policy-making decisions of their colleges. This should change the ways colleges relate to their students and make them more open to participation by everyone. Student affairs leaders will benefit by looking beyond their formal organizational structures to the real experiences of their students in cyberspace—the revolution in communications is just beginning!

Community Service and Leadership

Among the most encouraging campus developments in recent years is the surge of interest in community service. With new federal and state initiatives to support such activity, most colleges and universities are encouraging their students to participate in voluntary community service programs or have developed service-related learning activities of their own. Student affairs offices have often taken the lead in developing community service programs on campus, and these programs have brought student affairs organizations into regular contact with academic departments, community agencies, and governmental offices. These efforts are often coordinated with student leadership and multicultural programs, as institutions have found that community service activities offer ideal settings for students to learn to work together. As a result, where community service programs become well established, former departmental barriers begin to disappear, resulting in many cooperative programs between student affairs and academic affairs.

Proliferation of Functions

Ironically, one of student affairs' greatest strengths may reveal one its most serious weaknesses—specialization has produced higher quality but it may have splintered the field. In the past twenty-five years, student affairs functions have become highly professionalized and specialized. As a result, the quality of staff and effectiveness of services have improved substantially. Moreover, each of these specialized areas within student affairs has developed its own national association, complete with conferences and professional publications. But this increased specialization has sometimes led to multiple "fiefdoms" within organizations, poor communication across departments, and confusion among students. With such proliferation, it is difficult to maintain a coherent, unified organization; this balkanization within student affairs is a serious concern of leaders in the field today. As specialized services develop their own accreditation mechanisms, they may become insulated and unresponsive. Adapting services to the actual needs of institutions may become more difficult. The most effective student affairs organizations will find ways to encourage the creativity necessary for specialized services while insisting on a coherent, unified approach to their work with students.

Conclusion

Student affairs organizations are still evolving and will continue to adapt to the changing needs of students and institutions. There is no fixed administrative model that fits every college or university, and an organizational structure that has been in place for many years at one institution may change as well. The principles represented by the professional standards of practice provide excellent guidelines to student affairs leaders who are charged with delivering high-quality programs and services to students. Instead of beginning with a fixed administrative structure, institutions can use the standards as a basis for providing high-quality services to their students. With student affairs staff becoming more specialized and sophisticated, the quality of services and programs will likely increase. As a result, leaders in the profession will be challenged to develop organizational structures that integrate these diverse services and ensure that effective collaboration with other institutional programs occurs. Student affairs is still a young profession; its place within an institution's organizational structure is not set in concrete. The main task for student affairs leaders is to develop and deliver effective services for students that fit the needs of the individual institution.

References

American College Personnel Association. (1993). *Statement of ethical principles and standards.* Alexandria, VA: Author.

Bloland, P. A, Stamatakos, L. C., & Rogers, R. R. (1994). *Reform in student affairs.* Greensboro, NC: ERIC Counseling and Student Services Clearinghouse, 1994.

Council for the Advancement of Standards for Student Services/Development Programs. (1988). *Self-assessment guide.* College Park, MD: Author.

Miller, T. K. (1986). *CAS standards and guidelines for student services/development programs.* College Park, MD: Consortium of Student Affairs Professional Organizations.

National Association of Student Personnel Administrators. (1983). *Standards of professional practice.* Washington, DC: Author.

Rentz, A. L., & Saddlemire, G. L. (1988). *Student affairs functions in higher education.* Springfield, IL: Thomas.

Yerian, J. M. (1988). *Putting the CAS standards to work.* College Park, MD: Council for the Advancement of Standards for Student Services/Development Programs.

Changing Ethical Frameworks for a Multicultural World

Jane Fried

"Seeing is believing" is a truism in the United States. We believe the evidence of our senses. If we see it, it must be real. Reality is so obvious that it needs no definition. Reality is synonymous with common sense. Yet anthropologist Clifford Geertz asserts that "common sense is not what the mind cleared of cant spontaneously apprehends. It is what the mind filled with presuppositions . . . concludes" (1983, p. 84). Common sense is a loosely integrated cultural system that "rests on the same basis that any other system rests on, the conviction by those whose possession it is of its value and validity" (p. 76). A more accurate rendition of the truism might be, "In the view of reality that prevails in the United States, one can trust the evidence of one's senses more than any other kind of evidence." Truisms of that length are rare and probably useless. They do not trip off the tongue at crucial moments or serve as a guide to action in confusing and difficult circumstances.

Ethical beliefs and belief systems are intended to serve as guides to action in confusing and difficult circumstances. The ethical beliefs that have influenced American culture come from a number of sources, chiefly Christianity, scientific empiricism, and a philosophical position called positivism (Fried, 1995). Positivism supports the "correspondence theory of truth," or seeing (measuring, recording, counting) is believing (Lincoln and Cuba, 1985). On a mundane level, "seeing is believing" provides a very comforting approach to evaluation of truth. All the evaluation devices are, literally, in the eyes, ears, and perceptual systems of the beholder. The

premise breaks down, however, when one considers docudramas, photographic manipulation of evidence, or electronic graphics that appear to be "real" but whose reality is virtual, not concrete. When one cannot identify with certainty which black and white segments are clips from history and which are created in black and white for purposes of dramatic emphasis in the films of Oliver Stone, one needs to describe reality in more complex terms than "seeing is believing." Seeing, under what circumstances, in which time frame and context, permits one to believe what, how much, in how much detail, and with what degree of commitment to the truth value of the evidence?

Making ethical judgments has never been easy. In the modern world, developing a reliable ethical perspective has become even more complicated and difficult. In the eighteenth century Benjamin Franklin wrote his ethical precepts in *Poor Richard's Almanac*, and Americans used his truisms as a guide to action for two centuries. In the nineteenth century Davy Crockett lived by a single rule: "Be sure you're right. Then go ahead." He knew what was right. How did he know? Why do we not know now? Or, more accurately, why do so many people have so many different and often conflicting ideas about what is right?

Making ethical decisions has become incredibly difficult and complicated because notions of right and good are embedded in cultural and community consensus about values. In homogeneous societies it is far easier to decide what is right than in societies that include people of many ethnic cultures. In the

"Changing Ethical Frameworks for a Multicultural World," by Jane Fried, reprinted from *Ethics for Today's Campus: New Directions for Student Services*, No. 77, edited by Jane Fried, Spring 1997, Jossey-Bass Publishers, Inc.

present multicultural society of the United States, culture can be rooted not only in ethnicity but also in common life experience and worldview related to race, socioeconomic status, professional identity, gender, sexual orientation, or disability. Most individuals are members of more than one culture, and cultural norms about good and right may vary among them.

This chapter explores the origins of the dominant, *old paradigm* ethical belief system in student affairs, which relies heavily on the application of principles to problems. Challenges to this belief system have emerged from New Paradigm thought, which incorporates ethical beliefs from many cultures and perspectives, "virtue ethics" (discussed at length later in this chapter), and the dynamic interaction between universal principles, particular situations, and individual ways of making meaning. Examples of ethical behavior in professional practice and ethics education for students will be discussed. Finally, a process for examining the ethical implications of decisions will be presented.

Old Paradigm Systems and Ethics

Old paradigm, Eurocentric belief systems are based on assumptions developed by Bacon, Copernicus, Newton, and Descartes during the historical period known as the Enlightenment (Capra, 1982). The most significant Enlightenment beliefs are as follows (Lincoln and Guba, 1985; Harman, 1988): (1) Reality has an objective existence separate and external from the people who perceive it. (2) Objective reality can be described in a value-free manner without reference to the point of view of the observer or describer. (3) Reality can be described accurately without reference to time or context. (4) There are direct causal relationships between events. Every action can be traced to an action that preceded it. (5) Mathematics (in the form of equations) provides the most reliable map of reality, the best picture of relationships between cause and effect. (6) Universal scientific laws govern physical events, and the most satisfactory explanations of phenomena are universal explanations. In addition to these fundamental

assumptions, the Enlightenment perspective also asserted that God was no longer at the center of the human experience, that it was man's (sic) role to master and subdue "nature" through scientific inquiry. Scientific, empirical knowledge was the most, possibly the only, reliable form of knowledge. Authority no longer resided in inspiration, revelation, or tradition but in empirical information (Harman, 1988).

Copernicus, Galileo, Newton, and Descartes established a radically different view of reality than the one that had dominated Christian Europe for the preceding millennium. "In 1600 an educated man (most educated persons were men) *knew* that the Earth was the center of the cosmos—the seat of change, decay, and Christian redemption. . . . A hundred years later this man's equally Christian descendant, say, his great grandson, knew . . . that the Earth was but one of many planets orbiting around one of many stars" (Harman, 1988, p. 8). Harman also points out that the changes in belief about universal authority were also changes in belief about reality in all its aspects. The first man saw the world through a *teleological* belief system that told him that the universe was alive, purposeful, and arranged by God. The second man's view was that the universe was mechanical, knowable and not mysterious, lawful, and not purposeful. God was no longer directly involved, and people were responsible for "husbanding" the earth's resources for human betterment, using science as their tool.

Ethical systems that guide human behavior are always based on fundamental assumptions about reality—the world in which people live, what elements of reality can be considered good for people and the environment, and what issues are of common concern for human welfare. "Every society ever known rests on some set of largely tacit basic assumptions about *who we are, what kind of universe we are in and what is ultimately important to us*" (Harman, 1988, p. 10). During the Enlightenment, all the assumptions that had governed the medieval era in Europe changed. People found themselves in a new world in a new and rudderless era where their former beliefs could not guide them. As Matthew Arnold, lamenting this loss of faith, wrote in "Dover Beach" ([1867] 1962, p. 904)

The Sea of Faith
Was once too at the full and round earth's
    shore . . .
But now I only hear its melancholy, long
    withdrawing roar,
Retreating to the breath of the night wind,
    down the vast edges drear
And naked shingles of the world.

Enlightenment thinking dominated discussions of ethics in student affairs and in most other professions for most of the twentieth century. This means that ethical dilemmas were resolved by referring to universally accepted principles and exploring the implications of acting on those principles in a particular situation (Kitchener, 1985). *Situation Ethics*, written in 1966 by Joseph Fletcher, challenged the Enlightenment position. Fletcher caused an uproar among principle-centered thinkers who had begun to lose faith in traditional principles but were unable to provide a new ethical framework for the post-Holocaust world. Fletcher examined the catastrophic dilemmas of World War II and attempted to focus ethics on a single standard that was so general that it had to be interpreted contextually, or situationally.

The organizing construct for situation ethics was benevolence, an approach to ethical living that treats love and justice as two complementary dimensions of the broader construct. Doing good was equivalent to doing right in situation ethics. If a conflict occurred between a person's ideas about good and right, good was intended to prevail and the notion of right would be adjusted to the situation. Although Fletcher asserted that the use of one principle could guide all ethical decision making, a position that appears to reflect the Enlightenment approach, he can also be seen as the person who began to deconstruct universal-principle approaches to ethics and develop a new constructivist, contextual approach.

Situation ethics states that ethical decisions must be made about particular situations, in particular contexts. Although Fletcher did not specifically discuss the implications of cultural worldviews on ethical decision making, his discussion of a woman who had sex with a concentration camp guard in order to preserve her own life and then loved the child because it symbolized her continuing ability to live and love the rest of her family suggests the dramatic impact of circumstances on ethics. Because different cultures view the world in dramatically different ways and accept a wide range of behavior as good, it is possible to interpret Fletcher as one author who opened the door to taking both culture and context into account in ethics. In student affairs situation ethics is used whenever a conflict between rules and individual needs occurs. For example, many colleges close all residence halls for winter recess, forcing some students to return to their family's home because they have nowhere else to go. Most colleges have students from abusive families. For them, going "home" is harmful. The rules state that all students must leave the residence halls. Using a situation ethics approach, a staff member would be expected to help a student find an alternative place to stay. If the problem were widespread, situation ethics would require the development of alternative housing for students with serious need. The recess dilemma also applies to resident international students who cannot make alternative arrangements as well as students from families living in dangerous neighborhoods who do not want to go home for fear of street violence.

What Is the New Paradigm? Culture, Respect, and Interaction

Whereas the old paradigm embodied universal principles, orderliness, and reversible, linear cause-and-effect relationships, the new paradigm embodies chaos, context, unpredictability and irreversibility of change. The new paradigm emphasizes the power of relationships and information in a context of nonlinear interaction. Robert Shweder, a cultural psychologist, uses the notion of *intentional worlds* to describe the different ways in which human beings from different cultures describe, engage with, and imagine their physical, emotional, and intellectual realities (Stigler, Shweder, and Herdt, 1990). "A principle of intentional worlds is that nothing real 'just is'" (p. 3). Shweder recognizes that people from the same culture tend to interpret the significance of events in roughly equivalent ways, but he does not discount the effect of individual differences on perception, interpretation, or meaning attribution. Shweder characterizes Enlightenment, or old paradigm, thinking via the twin themes of unity and uniformity: "unity in mankind's respect for the sole authority of reason, and evidence . . . ; uniformity in the substantive conclusions about how to live and what to believe . . . (normative uniformity of mankind)" (Shweder, 1984, p. 27). New paradigm thinking, in contrast, asserts that in any given ethical dilemma, multiple ethical belief systems may be operative and interactive. The resultant interpretation of events and the subsequent behavior of those involved might generate ethical chaos, a blend of interpretations in which no particular set of ideas about "the good" would dominate and no resolution or course of behavior would be taken for granted.

Examples of this phenomenon abound. What is the "right" thing for the United States to do in its dealings with countries that use prison or child labor? Is it "right" to impose U.S. standards for childhood freedom and school attendance on impoverished countries where child income is essential to family economic survival? Is it better to put prisoners on chain gangs, as we do in the United States, than to force them to produce goods for the U.S. market, as they do in China? Who is "right" in the Arab/Israeli conflict? Would a single terrorist act change ideas about right and wrong? Was Rabin's murderer right because he justified his action as an act of war and the Talmud permits assassination in time of war?

Closer to home, is it right to designate financial aid for people of color and use different standards for determining qualification or need than one might use for a white person? Can residence halls be justified as "theme houses" if the themes are African American culture or Latin American culture or Wellness? The first two themes imply different meanings than the third because of the history of African Americans and Latinos, as in the United States. Both involve ambiguous situations because an African American theme house houses African American students. The culture cannot be separated from its members. Is a residence hall whose program emphasizes African American culture also a segregated hall, particularly if no white students choose to live in it? What standard should prevail—a student's desire to be comfortable and validated in his or her living

environment or refusal to discriminate on the basis of race?

The ambiguity in these situations reflects a lack of national consensus about what is right and what is good with regard to racial issues. In the absence of consensus, ethical decision making requires extensive dialogue among the concerned groups about the nature of right and good (see Talley, this volume). Ethical and educationally sound practice on most campuses today requires open discussion of the beliefs about right and good that underlie student life policies, because many of these policies were based on the unacknowledged acceptance of principles that have not been made explicit or questioned.

Was it right for the president of a suburban university to permit five white women to move out of a residence suite because the sixth roommate was an African American who had been assigned to live with them? He posed the dilemma to the director of housing as "You can do the right thing [refuse permission to move] and have these and possibly many other white parents down on you and perhaps lose all five students, or you can do the expedient, politically less explosive thing and let them move so that the local civil rights organizations won't be having press conferences on your front lawn." The president and the director were struggling with conflicting ideas about right and good in a fast-moving, emotionally charged situation. If the white students lived in intentional worlds in which black students were seen as either the same as them or different but desirable roommates, the situation would have been framed differently. If the black student were easily frightened or desirous of avoiding conflict, the situation would have been framed differently.

Could principles guide decision making in this situation, or would the situation, with its emotionally chaotic interactions, dominate responses? Principle-oriented ethics assumes linear, cause-and-effect relationships between people and events. Situation ethics more closely resembles New Paradigm assumptions about chaotic interactions, nonlinear relationships, and unpredictable outcomes. Autonomy, faithfulness, institutional reputation, potential for student learning, parental and public oversight, the director's desire to remain employed, and the students' need to confirm their living arrangements immediately were all factors.

Time was a key factor. Students and families wanted a decision in an hour or less. None of the student and family participants were willing to talk to each other. Standing on one principle, such as faithfulness to the institutional policy of nondiscrimination, might have undermined the institution's support for the principle of doing no harm, by forcing people to live together in circumstances so uncomfortable that one or more of them might have withdrawn from school. If the university were perceived as unwilling to support African American students in housing, how could the president retain credibility for his community support programs of tutoring and recreation for local children? The interaction among multiple values and priorities in the situation overpowered the administrative ability to impose a single principle on decision making.

The most effective approach would have involved a matrix in which principles such as faithfulness, justice, and autonomy were balanced against situational factors such as political realities, the intentional worlds of the students, and the ability of the institution to draw students from different racial backgrounds. This type of approach is discussed in the chapters on assessment (Banning) and management (Talley) elsewhere in this volume. It has the capacity to generate consensus about values within a particular campus community and to educate all participants about ethical thinking. Such dialogues are slow and often painful. They cannot occur in the midst of a crisis. Over the long term, however, they can turn crises into opportunities for learning and ethical decision making and to produce effective, widely supported policies that minimize future crises.

Ethical Judgment and Cognitive Complexity

Ethical judgment of the sort required by New Paradigm thinking requires a constructivist approach (Fried, 1993) and a high level of cognitive development (King and Kitchener, 1994). King and Kitchener's Reflective Judgment Model (discussed by Guthrie in this volume) documents changes in cognitive development that permit people to engage in increasingly complex thought about ethical issues and the contexts in which they occur. In the Reflective

Judgment Model cognition develops from pre-reflective thinking in which people "do not acknowledge—or in some cases even perceive—that knowledge is uncertain" (King and Kitchener, 1994, p. 47) through quasi reflective thinking in which "some problems are ill-structured and . . . knowledge claims about them contain an element of uncertainty" (p. 58) to reflective thinking in which "knowledge is not a 'given,' but must be actively constructed and . . . claims of knowledge must be understood in relation to the context in which they were generated" (p. 66). The Reflective Judgment Model describes the cognitive processes by which individuals develop the capacity to take both context, or situation, and principle into account in ethical thinking. In *Developing Reflective Judgment* King and Kitchener describe the processes by which thinkers develop the capacity and skills to manage increasingly complex information within a reasoning system that enables judgments to be made despite the lack of certainty. They provide the conceptual framework within which principle-centered ethics can move toward a more constructivist approach that takes culture into account by describing the ways in which thinking becomes increasingly complex. In developing campus dialogues around ethical issues, the level of cognitive development among students is a key factor in their ability to participate effectively. A significant role for student development educators is assessment of cognitive development and design of appropriate challenge and support mechanisms to enhance students' cognitive development as they participate in the dialogue.

Marcia Baxter Magolda has provided another framework within which the development of increasingly complex thinking can be understood. In *Knowing and Reasoning in College* (1992) she traces cognitive development among college students, taking gender and content into account as well as cognitive structure. Her work provides a map that can be particularly helpful in understanding the cognitions associated with feminist ethics. The works of Baxter Magolda and King and Kitchener are complementary in many ways and provide two frameworks for understanding the processes of ethical development from a psychological perspective.

Principles, Virtues, and Communities

Western ethical thinking has been guided by principles or moral norms presumed to embody universally valued characteristics, such as fidelity, benevolence, nonmalificence, respect for autonomy, veracity, and justice (Meara, Schmidt, and Day, 1996). Sound ethical thinking involves applying relevant principles to a particular problem and deciding which principle takes precedence as a guide to action in that particular case. The dilemma of Heins and the Drug appearing in the work of Kohlbeŕg (1969) is based on this system of assumptions. Although principalist approaches to ethics always involve a dialectic between a person's understanding of a principle and his or her construction of a specific ethical dilemma (Childress, 1994), the universal principal is always presumed to transcend the particulars of the situation and thus to provide a reliable guide to action. Principalism as understood in Eurocentric cultures is grounded in Enlightenment thought. However, it can operate within any cultural context, including contexts defined by gender, sexual orientation, or a corporate environment, because it elevates the principles that guide the culture. In the corporate world the dominant principle is often that of maximizing profits. In a gay or lesbian community, a major principle involves protecting people's privacy in intimate relationships. Principalism becomes difficult to use in situations in which many cultures intersect or cultures are changing so rapidly that no set of principles command universal allegiance or dominate, even within the specific setting.

Principles and the Internet. Extreme examples of the limits of principalism are illustrated by problems on the Internet. The Internet recognizes no national boundaries and has spawned hundreds of "communities of interest" around everything from recreation to politics, science, sexual practices, matters of faith, and help for students with their homework. Freedom of expression is a highly valued principle in the United States. On the Internet Americans are free to produce pornography, express beliefs about ethnic groups, support neo-Nazism, announce rallies for or against anything, and encourage lobbying and other forms of political action. Communities of interest are virtual, usually lacking a geographic or cultural base. Participants usually belong to other political, ethnic, or spiritual communities that may be guided by contradictory values. If the Arab Student Union on a campus in the United States is having a rally to protest Israeli policies or specific actions and wants to announce it on the Internet, sending that message to Arab students in Germany might pose a problem. In Germany freedom of speech and association is limited in cases considered disruptive to domestic tranquillity. If a neo-Nazi group on a U.S. campus posts an announcement to all student organizations on the Internet having "African American" or "Jewish" in their titles, its action might be considered either harassment or freedom of speech. American jurisprudence, generally guided by legal principles, cannot achieve consensus about an approach to hate crimes, including harassment, even though freedom of speech tends to dominate decisions. When communication flows freely between countries having very different legal systems and guiding principles, what is the ethical response of a university's Internet administrator who discovers a "nigger joke" Web site or a site that solicits anti-Semitic essays for worldwide distribution? Once again, this problem is most effectively viewed as an occasion for dialogue rather than one that demands a unilateral decision. Campuses have developed committees whose major purpose is the discussion of these kinds of ethical dilemmas, and the Internet itself is home to numerous discussion sites for exchanging information between campuses.

Principles in Scholarship. In classrooms on campuses in the United States, ethical dilemmas abound when principalism is the dominant approach. A professor of anthropology in a secular university has reported great difficulty in communicating with a Muslim graduate student trained as an undergraduate to interpret all his data through the principles of the Koran (Gailey, in conversation). In the United States, comments from religious texts may be used to support an argument, but they are never used as the sole justification in an academic paper written in a secular college or university. Most Islamic states are theocracies. Separation of church and state is not only unfamiliar to a Muslim student but can easily be seen as a desecration. Which set of principles dominates in this dilemma—the student's faith or the institutional standards for academic work? What status does the principle of freedom of religion hold in this argument? Making decisions about conflicting principles becomes more difficult as authority claims become more absolute.

Universities and colleges have become multicultural organizations because of the many communities in which students, faculty, and staff participate, virtual, ethnic, and other. Each community may have its own set of guiding principles. Each person tends to emerge from several communities, and there is no reliable way to predict which set of principles will dominate at any specific time, in any specific situation. With regard to academic processes and student behavior, a university has the right to pronounce its own principles and to inform students before they matriculate (freedom of information, informed consent), but the administration and faculty cannot predict the relative strength of any specific principle in any specific situation. Two other approaches have recently emerged that can contribute to a matrix that includes context, constructs, principles, and virtues.

Virtue Ethics. Virtue ethics shifts the focus from principles to characteristics of particular people in particular contexts. Virtues or traits are considered to be personal qualities that are deemed meritorious in a particular context. Beauchamp and Childress state that "a virtue is a trait of character that is socially valued and a *moral virtue* is a trait that is morally valued" (Beauchamp and Childress, 1994; cited in Meara, Schmidt, and Day, 1996, p. 24). Virtue ethics provides a more complete picture of the relationship between moral reasoning and moral action. In principle-centered ethics, a person can easily know what he or she ought to do, based on principled reasoning, and still be unable or unwilling to do it. In contrast, "Proponents of virtue ethics believe that motivation, emotion, character, ideals and moral habits situated within the traditions and practices of a culture or other group present a more complete account of the moral life than actions based on prescribed rules" (Meara, Schmidt, and Day, 1996, p. 24).

Virtue ethics is based on ideals of human behavior in particular contexts. Virtue ethics can evolve as new communities evolve. For example, a group of recent graduates of a college student development Master's degree program decided to establish a listserv in order to stay in touch and provide support and consultation for each other. One of the first topics on the list was ethics in the interviewing process. The conversation moved from abstract, "what if" sorts of questions to questions about responses to inappropriate behavior to repetitive complaining with requests for sympathy, but no effort was made to evaluate situations. The next stage in the conversation began when one member raised the issue of conversational content and the ethics of quasi-public professional discussion. The members of this virtual community have begun to set ideals for their listserv community, and their set of virtues will emerge through dialogue.

Meara, Schmidt, and Day (1996) suggest that virtues are community specific and culturally and situationally defined. The virtues they consider most significant in the community of counseling psychologists are *prudence, integrity, respectfulness, and benevolence.* Virtue ethics focuses on ideal behavior and relies on the character and judgment of the agent in addressing particular problems in specific contexts. Every campus is free to construct and publicize its own set of virtues and to use them in setting standards for ethical behavior. Ideas about virtue may vary among campuses because of different campus missions and cultures. Thus a person's virtuous behavior in a particular situation can be more flexible than the behavior of a person who makes principle-centered decisions. Because a great deal of student affairs practice is devoted to helping students, the thinking of counseling psychologists in the domain of ethics transfers well to the student affairs profession.

Student affairs professionals are often faced with dilemmas resulting from the intersection of many value systems in one location. A classic example is the difference in the timing of parties held by African American students and white students. Typically African American student parties begin much later than parties organized by white students and end later as well. If the desired or only available location for a party is in the basement of a residence hall, whose needs and desires prevail—the students who want to party until three in the morning or the students who want to sleep at that time? A student affairs specialist approaching this dilemma from a virtue ethics perspective would be free to discuss the problems with each group, determine the meaning of the activities for each group, and try to create a solution respecting the belief systems, common social behaviors, and values of both groups, with or without an intergroup meeting. Prudence, benevolence, integrity, and respectfulness would all come into play.

A student affairs staff person using principle-centered ethics would be far more constrained in addressing this problem. How does one decide what is fair when both groups want to use the same space to conduct incompatible activities? What is justice when the rules for use of space and time restrictions were decided by an overwhelmingly white administration in ignorance of many social practices of African American students? This is an old problem that has generally been solved by designating nonresidential spaces for late-night parties. When the problem first arose in the 1970s, it was perceived by many white administrators as a case of African American students trying to break the rules. The basis on which the rules had been established, common (white) assumptions about when to sleep and when to socialize, were not easily challenged. They were perceived as common sensical, not to be broken. Many campuses have come a long way since that time, but there are more current problems that illustrate the same "principles versus virtues" dilemma. Two of these dilemmas are acquaintance rape versus rough sex and harassment versus freedom of expression.

Acquaintance Rape or Rough Sex? Campus administrations have tended to address acquaintance rape by attempting to define it and responding to allegations according to rules and principles in a conduct code. Acquaintance rape is said to have happened when two people know each other, one of them does not consent to sexual intercourse with the other, and the other persists to consummation. Any person who has been sexually active or who has seen any X-rated movies understands that rules may be written about acquaintance rape but they do not begin to cover the complexities of sexual interaction. Decisions are made second by second. What would a prudent person do in a sexual encounter? What would a

person of integrity do? A prudent person would probably think far in advance about the level of sexual involvement she or he wants, the dangers involved, the level of trust in the relationship, and personal responsibility. A person of integrity would probably find ways to express in advance what she or he expects or intends. A person who behaves respectfully and benevolently would listen to his or her partner and respect the partner's wishes even if they conflicted with her or his desires. At the moment before intercourse, which is likely to most influence the decision to consummate—principles and rules, or character?

The situation is complex, fast-paced and nonrational even when both persons are from the same culture and are following the same assumptions about sexual behavior. On modern American campuses students often date across racial and ethnic lines. Many students experiment with homosexual as well as heterosexual relationships. A student who is sure about his homosexual identity will tend to have clearer ideas about what will happen on a date than a man who is unsure about his sexual identity. What does consent mean for a young man who is experimenting with sexual behavior if, after the encounter begins, he becomes quite sure that he does not want to continue? He began by consenting, and he changed his mind. Is there any guarantee that the more experienced partner will pay careful attention to the resistance expressed or will respect a request to stop? The same set of circumstances and problems could be raised between a man and woman, either of whom came from a culture that expected virginity before marriage. For a student far from home, excited by the freedom on American campuses and inexperienced, when is a yes a no? When is a no a yes? How does early socialization, particularly for women who are trained to defer to men, work in this situation?

Michael Rion (1989) has suggested a set of questions that individual practitioners can ask about ethically disturbing situations to clarify their thinking and plan action. If a worried student consults a student affairs professional the day after an incident of nonconsensual or upsetting sex, the following questions might be discussed.

Why is this incident bothering the student? Does the student believe that she or he imposed her or his will on somebody else or submitted to an imposition? Did the student violate some previously held beliefs without rethinking the beliefs? Did the behavior seem "right" yesterday and "wrong" today? Did the student do harm to the partner or permit the partner to do harm to him or her? Was the issue alcohol consumption rather than sexual engagement? Is the student upset that she or he did not actually make a decision but just let things happen? Helping students clarify their own thinking and inherent beliefs about non-marital sex begins the action-reflection cycle that leads to increased self-understanding and self-direction.

Who else matters? Does the student need to discuss this with last night's partner, a roommate, a member of the clergy, parents? Is there anyone else who needs to know or has a right to know?

Is it my problem? Does the student have to settle this distress in his or her own mind, apologize to the partner, or discuss her or his drinking patterns with an alcohol counselor? Is the student interested in bringing the problem to the campus judicial officer? Where does the student's responsibility lie in addressing this problem?

What is the ethical concern? This question is the core of the ethical education process in this situation. What are the student's principles, values, and beliefs about good character? The role of a student affairs professional at this point is that of counselor.

What do (significant) others think? After the student has been helped to clarify his or her own thinking, it might be useful or comforting for the student to consider the opinions that significant others hold about nonconsensual or upsetting sex. Would friends advise prosecution, mediation, apology, or counseling? Taking conflicting opinions held by trusted peers into account is an important way of gaining perspective on one's own ideas.

Am I being true to myself? After all the thinking, reflecting, and evaluating, does the student feel as if the resolution "fits" with his or her character? Does she or he believe that they will be able to avoid this type of situation in the future? Is the resolution satisfying, even if last night's behavior was not?

By engaging with a student in a dialogue guided by Rion's questions, the student affairs staff member can support the student without having to decide what "really" happened or if it "really" was a rape. This process leads the student through a thinking/feeling process that brings him or her to increased awareness of his or her ideas about personal ethics, community ethics, principles, and virtues in an atmosphere of respect and acceptance. Although campuses must have rules and opportunities for the redress of injustice in order to ensure fairness and protect student welfare, the rules have limited effectiveness in this situation if the student does not understand his or her own behavior and beliefs. A counselor can focus on virtues, whereas a judicial officer must consider rules and principles. When both approaches are used, the outcome is likely to be more educationally sound than if one were used to the exclusion of the other.

Freedom of Speech or Harassment? A similarly complex problem is that of harassment: racial, sexual, ethnic, electronic, or face-to-face. Freedom of speech is one of the most basic principles in American culture and is absolutely fundamental to campus discourse. Freedom of speech has presented an intractable ethical dilemma for administrators, and, to date, no regulations designed to limit this principle have survived legal challenges. In face-to-face conversation the willingness of most people to be rude and abusive is limited by the potential consequences—receiving equal doses of rudeness and abuse from the other person. Limits on abusive, face-to-face interactions arise from one's reading of nonverbal cues, assessment of potential physical threats, and willingness and ability to respond in kind as well as one's moral upbringing regarding whether fights are virtuous or shameful. In some tribal cultures an insult to one member of the family is considered an insult to the whole family and demands a comparable response in order to maintain family honor. As in a sexual encounter, decisions about advancing toward engagement are made on a second-by-second basis and judgments can change in an instant. Such limits seem not to apply in instances of "flaming" on the Internet, in which the level of verbal abuse, character assassination, and threats to safety have escalated in recent years. Can a principled approach to ethics and student behavior provide an effective guide if an aggressor does not acknowledge the validity of rules and can violate them in anonymity for a long time?

Many cases of harassment fall outside the rules because they involve behavior that was impossible before the development of the Internet. In one case a male student wrote a computer program that automatically kept track of a female student's whereabouts by recording where she logged on (Richardson, personal communication). He could have stalked her, if he wished to do so, through his electronic tracking system. Technically, the student did not violate the judicial code because he had not physically stalked the woman, but he had created an atmosphere of intimidation that was harmful in itself. When an administrator is aware of a potentially harmful situation, there is an ethical obligation to consider taking action. This type of situation raises both ethical and judicial questions for student affairs administrators. Ethical guidelines must be used to address two questions: Should the administrator respond to the situation, and if so, what is the ethical response? Is there an ethical imperative to raise policy questions so that additional instances of this type of behavior will fall within the boundaries of existing policy? Ethical questions tend to precede policy questions in uncharted territory such as this. Policy and judicial codes should be based on clearly stated ethical principles and virtues shared by the community for which they are written. Robert Greenleaf suggests an approach to ethical thinking and action in his work on servant leadership in higher education (1991). Servant leaders are always searching and listening. They are "affirmative builders of a better society" (p. 12) who consistently ask about the effects of their choices on the most privileged and the least privileged members of their community and always ask themselves "What are you trying to do?" (p. 15) before taking action. Servant leadership provides a process model that takes both principles and virtues into account.

Principles and Virtues in the Human Community

On the multicultural campuses of the twenty-first century, no single system of ethical beliefs and practices can or should prevail. The Enlightenment system that has dominated Eurocentric cultures violates or ignores significant elements of ethical systems that dominate in other parts of the world. For example, most Islamic countries are theocracies. Government policies are heavily influenced by Islamic law. Democracies are generally secular and support freedom of religion as well as freedom from religious intrusion in personal life. In a democracy, no person is entitled to political leadership by virtue of his or her ordination or affirmation of faith. People from these two different kinds of cultures have dramatically different ideas about the source or sources of authority in public and private life and about the degree of submission to authority that is expected or can be tolerated. On campuses where Muslims from the Middle East and Christians and Jews from Europe and North America live and study together, the ethical practices of the student affairs staff must take all these variables into account.

There is no single set of principles by which ethical decisions can be made when providing student services to students from a wide range of backgrounds. The virtues suggested by Meara, Schmidt, and Day (1996) provide some guidance—benevolence, respect, prudence and integrity—but these virtues must be used in the context of the principles that govern campus decision making and student conduct. Because every campus can be considered a culture within which several subcultures coexist (Kuh, 1993; Person, 1995), student affairs professionals should address ethical issues as part of all policy discussions. Even operational decisions tend to require a brief examination of ethical implications. A critical element in this process is that of mindfulness, or "mutual co-arising": the notion that everything is connected to everything else and nothing can be taken for granted (Haub, 1987). No single set of principles or beliefs can be assumed to dominate, but all relevant beliefs must be examined for their potential impact on everyone involved. Because of different belief systems and different ways of interpreting events, the consequences of a particular choice can easily move in unanticipated directions because different groups interpret the meaning of events differently and those interpretations may not be known to the decision makers. Student affairs administrators who previously believed that they had a reasonably accurate sense of the ways students would react to decisions, use services, or participate in programs can no longer have the luxury of these beliefs until they have thoroughly reviewed them.

The student affairs profession has evolved in a historical and cultural context that rests on particular assumptions about behavior, values, language, and cognitive categories (Fried, 1995). Student affairs as a profession is practically unique to the United States and is often culturally encapsulated. This profession has been responsible for managing student behavior according to the prevailing codes of the culture and the community. These codes are heavily influenced by the dominant national values. Finally, student affairs operates within the prescribed cognitive categories of U.S. higher education, which tends to separate living from learning, thinking from feeling, spirituality from secular life, teaching from learning, and knowledge from action (Fried, 1995). As a consequence of the cultural encapsulation of student affairs, it might be suggested that this profession has a long road to walk in moving toward a multicultural approach to ethics.

As a profession, we must challenge our own complacency about the ethical principles that have served us in dealing with a more homogeneous student community and begin to examine the multiple value and belief systems on which our current students are basing their lives (Hughes, 1992). Most colleges and universities *in* the United States are no longer completely *of* the United States, as it has been historically represented. Immigrants, refugees. international students, native people, Latinos, African Americans, Asian Americans, gays, lesbians, bisexuals, and people with disabilities populate our campuses and expect their beliefs and behaviors to be respected. Members of each group have slightly different needs, priorities, and expectations about college atten-

dance. Not to attend to this vast range of expectations and priorities is to violate both ethical principles and virtues. To ignore the different beliefs about goodness and virtue held by different groups of students is to ignore the other-regarding virtues of benevolence and integrity and the principles of autonomy justice, fairness, doing good, and doing no harm. This violates the historical belief system of student affairs and fails to honor the historical mission of providing service to students as individuals and members of groups.

Hughes (1992, pp. 210–211) has discovered several universal human values that are interpreted differently from culture to culture but can provide some new and transcendent organizing constructs for the creation of a multicultural ethical process for student affairs. In summary, the values are as follows:

Personal development through spiritual freedom, educational opportunity, and wellness

Human rights and dignity through respect for cultural and individual identity

Collaborative, peaceful approaches to conflict resolution and management

Development of global ethical codes to enhance the quality of human life

Although all people develop their ethical beliefs within a particular cultural milieu, these beliefs do not remain static. They evolve as individuals face situations for which their previous ethical beliefs have not prepared them. These situations arise with increasing frequency as individuals move out into a world where members of different cultural groups interact constantly. Ethical decision making now requires an active inquiry process in which virtues, principles, community expectations, and standards are all examined as choices are made. For student affairs professionals, the dynamic of ethical inquiry suggests two major components: attending to our own ethical assumptions and reexamining them in the light of our student populations, the ways we serve them, and the manner in which we conduct ourselves; and identifying situations in which we can contribute to the ethical education of students who will live their lives in multicultural communities of all sorts—virtual, residential, professional, and spiritual.

Conclusion

Our own professional development and the ethical education of students can be addressed with a combination of Hanh's mindfulness and Hughes's challenge to complacency. Ironically, Aristotle, one of the earliest Western ethicists, provides the framework within which we can move toward these goals. Aristotle believed that the purpose of ethical inquiry was to determine "the good" in both the universal and the particular. He also believed that the public good set the context for individual virtues, intellectual concerns, and practical occupations. In modern terminology, individual welfare had to be examined in the total context of community welfare, and examining one without the other was considered meaningless (McKeon, 1941). In order to challenge complacency and practice mindfulness with students, student affairs professionals can take no outcome for granted and must raise questions when students fail to consider the ethical implications of the choices they make. This approach requires a transcendence of the historical categories of analysis. Asking students what they consider good in a situation slows down the decision-making process, may possibly generate anger or resistance, and forces all participants to examine their basic assumptions before proceeding. Intellect and emotions become involved. Student affairs professionals must be able to reflect student feelings and beliefs and at the same time provide information about ethical decision making and various ethical systems. They must identify issues, challenge and support students, keep the welfare of the individuals and the institution in mind, and reexamine what *good* means in the specific situation. Helping students learn how to think about ethics becomes far more important than helping them make the "right" choice. Notions of right, goodness, and justice vary by culture and need to be understood in the context of campus cultures, national culture, and a variety of other cultures. Guthrie, in this volume, describes the levels of cognitive complexity that are necessary for sound ethical thinking. Her analysis applies to student affairs professionals as well as to students. Taking cultural information, context, virtues, and principles into account is an extremely demanding task. Professional responsibility and competence is the first standard in the "Statement of Ethical Principles and Standards" of the American College Personnel Association (1993). On multicultural campuses, our most demanding professional code of ethics requires that we undertake the task in order to remain competent and responsible.

References

American College Personnel Association, Standing Committee on Ethics. "A Statement of Ethical Principles and Standards." *Journal of College Student Development*. 1993, 34, 89–92.

Arnold, M. "Dover Beach." In M. Abrams (ed.), *The Norton Anthology of English Literature*. Vol 2. New York: W. W. Norton, 1962 (Originally published 1867.)

Baxter Magolda, M. B. *Knowing and Reasoning in College: Gender-Related Patterns in Students' Intellectual Development*. San Francisco: Jossey-Bass, 1992.

Capra, F. *The Turning Point: Science, Society and the Rising of Culture*. New York: Simon and Schuster, 1982.

Childress. J. "Principles Oriented Bioethics." In E. DuBose, R. Hamel, and L. O'Connell (eds). *A Matter of Principles? Ferment in Bioethics*. Valley Forge, Pa.: Trinity International Press, 1994.

Fletcher, J. *Situation Ethics*. Philadelphia, Pa.: Westminster Press, 1966.

Fried, J. *Shifting Paradigms in Student Affairs*. Washington, D.C.: American College Personnel Association, 1995.

Geertz, C. *Local Knowledge*. New York: Basic Books, 1983.

Greenleaf, R. *Servant Leadership*. New York: Paulist Press, 1991.

Hanh, T. N. *Interbeing*. Berkeley, Calif.: Paralax Press, 1987.

Harman, W. *Global Mind Change*. New York: Warner Books, 1988.

Hughes, M. "Global Diversity and Student Development: Educating for World Citizenship." In M. Terrell (ed.), *Diversity, Disunity and Campus Community*. Washington. D.C.: National Association of Student Personnel Administrators, 1992.

King, P. M., and Kitchener, K. S. *Developing Reflective Judgment: Understanding and Promoting Intellectual Growth and Critical Thinking in Adolescents and Adults*. San Francisco: Jossey-Bass, 1994.

Kitchener, K. "Ethical Principles and Ethical Decisions in Student Affairs." In H. J. Canon and R. D. Brown (eds.), *Applied Ethics in Student Services*. New Directions for Student Services, no. 30. San Francisco: Jossey-Bass, 1985.

Kohlberg, L. "Stage and Sequence: The Cognitive Developmental Approach to Socialization." In D. A.

Goslin (ed.). *Handbook of Socialization Theory and Research*. Skokie, Ill.: Rand McNally, 1969.

Kuh, G. (ed.). *Cultural Perspectives in Student Affairs Work*. Washington, D.C.: American College Personnel Association, 1993.

Lincoln, Y., and Guba, E. *Naturalistic Inquiry*. Newbury Park, Calif.: Sage, 1985.

McKeon, R. (ed). *The Basic Works of Aristotle*. New York: Random House, 1941.

Meara, N., Schmidt, L., and Day, J. "Principles and Virtues: A Foundation for Ethical Decisions, Policies and Character." *Counseling Psychologist*, 1996, 24, 4–77.

Person, D. "Students of Color and Student Culture." In J. Fried and Associates (eds.), *Shifting Paradigms in Student Affairs*. Washington, D.C.: American College Personnel Association, 1995.

Rion, M. *The Responsible Manager*. Amherst, Mass.: HRD Press, 1989.

Shweder, R. "Anthropology's Romantic Rebellion Against the Enlightenment, or There's More to Thinking Than Reason and Evidence." In R. Shweder and R. LeVine (eds.), *Culture Theory*. Cambridge, U.K.: Cambridge University Press, 1984.

Stigler, J., Shweder, R., and Herdt, G. *Cultural Psychology*. New York: Cambridge University Press, 1990.

JANE FRIED is associate professor in the Department of Health and Human Services at Central Connecticut State University and is former chair of the Standing Committee on Ethics of the American College Personnel Association.

Life Outside the Classroom

Ernest L. Boyer

The undergraduate college should be held together by something more than plumbing, a common grievance over parking, or football rallies in the fall. What students do in dining halls, on the playing fields, and in the rathskeller late at night all combine to influence the outcome of the college education, and the challenge, in the building of community, is to extend the resources for learning on the campus and to see academic and nonacademic life as interlocked.

The early American college did not doubt its responsibility to educate the whole person—body, mind, and spirit; head, heart, and hands. Faculty members were recruited from men who believed that in serving the cause of truth they were also serving the cause of faith. Student life was tightly regulated. Classroom, chapel, dormitory, playing field—all these areas of college life were thought of as connected.

Not that the relationship between college rules and student conduct was worked out easily or maintained without a struggle. Teenagers then, as now, were inclined to test the limits of tolerance. Throughout the colonial period, and continuing until after the Civil War, there were periodic uprisings in response to oppressive rules and the chronic complaint of "atrocious food." According to Fred and Grace Hechinger, in their important book *Growing Up in America*, Henry Thoreau's grandfather, when a student, confronted a tutor with this demand: "Behold our Butter stinketh and we cannot eat thereof. Now give us we pray thee Butter that stinketh not." In American higher education some things never change.

Religion was a centerpiece of the early college. The historian Dixon Ryan Fox describes how piety marked the beginning of each day at Union College in New York:

> [The] ringing of the Chapel bell called sleepy boys to "repair in a decent and orderly manner" without running violently in the entries or down the stairs, to prayers that were to open the day. We can see the college butler on a cold pitch-black winter morning at his post beside the pulpit stairs, when the officers file in, holding his candle high so that the president may safely mount to read the scripture lesson from the sacred desk, to petition the Almighty on behalf of the little academic group.

Some professors were not happy with the rigidity of nineteenth century campus life and, most especially, with their proctor and detective duties. James McCosh at Princeton confessed: "I abhor the plan of secretly watching students by peeping through windows at night, and listening through keyholes." Still, most academic spokesmen retained faith in the moral uplift generated by the college. "It was a faith undergirded by the notion that mental discipline was provided by a complex of theological, moral, psychological, and behavioral factors whose vagueness was more than offset by the power of popular convictions."

In this climate, chapel was used, not just for morning prayers, but also as the place where reprimands were meted out and confessions made. During the 1870s, little Mount Union College in Alliance, Ohio, had trouble containing student rebelliousness against the rules. The majority of the infractions were

---

"Life Outside the Classroom," by Ernest L. Boyer, reprinted from *College: The Undergraduate Experience in America*, 1987, Harper & Row.

drinking, cursing, gambling, card playing, and leaving campus without a signed excuse. Mount Union's campus historian reports as follows: "Unless the infractions were of an unusually serious nature, most of the major offenders, after a severe reprimand from the faculty, were required to appear publicly in chapel and reaffirm their loyalty to the college and pledge to obey all the rules (taking no mental reservations)."

During the nineteenth century, American higher education grew. The grip of religion was weakened, and scholarship among the professoriate took precedence over piety. In 1869, Harvard decided to break the link between academic status and student conduct. The classroom was the place of learning and social life was viewed as less consequential to the goals of education. Ranking, henceforth would be based on course grades alone. The parallel use of delinquency demerits based on behavior was struck down. Here is how Frederick Rudolph commented on the significance of this development:

> What now mattered was intellectual performance in the classroom, not model behavior in the dormitory or the village tavern. A commitment to the needs of scholarship meant that the universities expressed their purposes no longer in chapel, no longer in the senior year with the president on moral and intellectual philosophy.

Still, the American college did not fully free itself of the vision of educating the whole person. Until well into the twentieth century, chapel attendance was required at many institutions, both public and private. Residence hall living was still monitored by the college. Women, in particular, received heavy doses of regulation. There was ambivalence, to be sure, but in enrolling a student the college clung to the tradition that its responsibility went beyond the classroom. However, since faculty oversight was now limited to scholarly concerns, a cadre of specialists—registrars, chaplains, advisers, house mothers—emerged to guide student life.

The 1960s brought dramatic changes to the American campus. Rules were weakened. Residence halls became coed and often were almost off limits for administrators at the college. Required attendance at chapel services and campus-wide convocations were abolished on most campuses. Students, it was argued, should be treated as adults.

Today, we found on many campuses an uneasy truce. Students still have almost unlimited freedom in personal and social matters. Conduct is generally unguided. And yet, administrators are troubled by the limits of their authority, and there is a growing feeling among students that more structure is required.

There are 168 hours in a week. If the student takes 16 credit hours, and spends 2 hours in study for each credit hour of instruction (a generous estimate!), that means 48 hours of the week are devoted to academics. If 50 hours are assigned to sleep, that leaves 70 hours in the student's life unaccounted for, a block of time greater than either sleep or academics.

How do students spend their time outside the classroom? Here is a partial answer. Our survey of undergraduates revealed that almost all students work. Although researchers have reported that some work can, in fact, be beneficial to the academic and social progress of the student, work can also be excessive. We found, for example, that almost 30 percent of all full-time students and 84 percent of all part-timers work 21 or more hours a week while attending college. And as tuition costs go up, the number of hours students work is likely to increase (Table 1).

What else engages them? Thirty-one percent of the students report devoting more than ten hours a week to informal conversation with other students. Fourteen percent spend more than ten hours a week in front of the television set. (In the student union of one university we visited, the big-screen television set attracts the largest crowd during the noon hour for "All My Children.") The typical student does leisure reading between one and two hours a week. About one fourth say they spend no time studying in the library each week. Organized sports consume the least amount of student time. Almost half devote no time to cultural events, and the same proportion do not participate in any organized student activity (Table 2).

Few students, we found, participate in intercollegiate athletics. Still, they love to cheer. On many campuses sports are the big event,

TABLE 1
Hours Spent Working by Employed Undergraduates in a Normal Week by Enrollment Status
(percentage agreeing)

	Total	Public	Private	Research University	Doctorate- Granting University	Compre- hensive College	Liberal Arts College
			Full-Time Undergraduates				
10 hours or less	29	25	42	31	22	26	41
11–15 hours	20	21	17	26	21	18	12
16–20 hours	22	23	18	21	28	21	15
21–35 hours	21	23	14	16	19	26	14
36+ hours	8	8	9	6	10	9	12
			Part-Time Undergraduates				
10 hours or less	2	2	2	3	4	2	2
11–15 hours	4	5	2	6	2	4	1
16–20 hours	10	10	9	11	7	11	6
21–35 hours	14	16	7	8	18	17	3
36+ hours	70	67	80	72	69	66	88

Source: The Carnegie Foundation for the Advancement of Teaching, National Survey of Undergraduates, 1984.

TABLE 2
Number of Hours Students Spend Each Week on Selected Activities (by percent responding)

Activity	Hours per Week						
	None	1–2	3–4	5–6	7–8	9–10	11 or more
Talking informally to other students	3	19	16	13	9	9	31
Watching television	13	22	18	14	11	8	14
Leisure reading	23	35	17	11	6	4	4
Talking to faculty members	26	56	11	4	1	1	1
Studying in the library	27	24	14	9	5	6	15
Attending campus cultural events	46	36	11	4	1	1	1
Participating in organized student activities (other than athletics)	50	26	10	6	3	2	3
Participating in intramural sports	70	16	8	3	1	1	1
Participating in intercollegiate athletics	93	1	*	*	1	1	4

*= less than 1 percent

Source: The Carnegie Foundation for the Advancement of Teaching, National Survey of Undergraduates, 1984.

and football and basketball games often sell out well in advance.

One large university we visited has an 82,000-seat, multilevel stadium that is visible from virtually all parts of the campus. It was defined by one observer as the "emotional core" of the university. Adjoining this huge edifice are a twenty-five-court tennis center and a student recreation center, complete with basketball courts, volleyball courts, handball courts, weight rooms, and a swimming pool. A coliseum serves as the home of the basketball team as well as the site of other campus activities, including concerts and lectures. Farther

west are track, football practice fields, baseball and rugby fields, and a golf driving range and practice greens.

The athletic center completes the picture. The lobby of this modern shrine is filled with trophy cases for the seventeen intercollegiate sports that are played here. The cases overflow with symbols of success. The walls are lined with photos of star athletes and memorable moments in the university's athletic history. To say that the institution is proud of its athletic teams is an understatement.

On this campus, students don't just get excited about the games, one observer told us, they "go crazy" about their sports programs. Many travel hundreds of miles each Saturday to watch the game and attend pep rallies in massive numbers. They wear university sweat shirts, hats, and shoes and wave pennants and place bumper stickers on their cars and decorate other parts of their autos with memorabilia. Spectator sports seem to be the best way to build a sense of community on most campuses today.

Intercollegiate athletics have been called a "deified monster" on American campuses, going far beyond considerations of health or physical fitness, or just plain fun. Often such programs are the means by which a school acquires a reputation, discretionary funds, and even endowment. "It takes athletics to sell a university" is how one president describes his school's approach to sports. At another university—one that "fields the best teams money can buy," as students and faculty express it—the president expects to raise $6.8 million a year from football alone.

In 1929, The Carnegie Foundation prepared a report entitled *American College Athletics*. It revealed that higher education, almost sixty years ago, was being poisoned by a corrupt and corrupting system. In speaking about the destructive influence of big-time athletics the report said: "More than any other force, [athletics have] tended to distort the values of college life and to increase its emphasis upon the material and the monetary. Indeed, at no point in the educational process has commercialism in college athletics wrought more mischief than in its effect upon the American undergraduate. And the distressing fact is that the college, the Fostering Mother, has permitted and even encouraged it to do these things in the name of education."

The words of this report are as apt today as in 1929. If the situation has changed, it has been for the worse. Several universities we visited have had athletic scandals. At one, the football program went through a major crisis in the late 1970s. Seventy violations of the National Collegiate Athletic Association rules, including the creation of a $35,000 "slush fund" for recruiting, resulted in N.C.A.A. probation and a two-year ban on television appearances and bowl games.

Scandals may be the exception, but even on campuses that live by the rules we found that sports frequently dominate the schedule. Class time, term papers, research in the library— all of these are sacrificed for practice, for travel, and for games. On too many campuses the issue is money, not school spirit. Undergraduate athletes are used as fodder for a competitive machine that pleases the alumni and corporate boosters but violates the integrity of the college and has little, if anything, to do with education.

In the light of the shocking abuses that surround intercollegiate athletics we should reflect on the sentiments of the former president of Stanford, David Starr Jordan, who spoke on the subject over eighty years ago. Jordan said:

> Let the football team become frankly professional. Cast off all the deception. Get the best professional coach. Pay him well and let him have the best men the town and the alumni will pay for.
>
> Let the teams struggle in perfectly honest warfare, known for what it is and with no masquerade of amateurism or academic ideas. The evil in current football rests not in the hired men, but in academic lying and in the falsification of our own standards as associations of scholars and men of honor.

The tragedy is that the cynicism that stems from the abuses in athletics infects the rest of student life, from promoting academic dishonesty to the loss of individual ideals. We find it disturbing that students who admit to cheating often excuse their conduct as being set by college example, such as athletic dishonesty. Again, the 1929 Carnegie report states the issue clearly: "It is the undergraduates who have suffered most and will continue most to suffer from commercialism and its results.... Commercialism motivates the recruiting and subsidizing of players, and the commercial attitude has enabled many young men to acquire college educations at the cost of honesty and sincerity."

Integrity cannot be divided. If high standards of conduct are expected of students, colleges must have impeccable integrity themselves. Otherwise the lessons of the "hidden curriculum" will shape the undergraduate experience.

Colleges teach values to students by the standards they set for themselves. But we believe real reform will come only when a wave of moral indignation sweeps the campuses. Perhaps the time has come for faculty and students at universities engaged in big-time athletics to organize a day of protest, setting aside a time to examine how the purposes of the universities are being subverted and how integrity is lost.

Further, we strongly urge that intercollegiate sports be organized and operated to serve the student athletes, not the institution. Success in class must be the most important objective. At the same time, respect for one's opponents and rules of sportsmanship and fair play must dominate the program.

We also propose that when serious athletic violations are discovered, the accreditation status of the institution should be revoked—along with eligibility status for the National Collegiate Athletic Association. It is ironic that one hears that a university has lost its athletic eligibility but never hears that a college has been on accreditation probation or suspended because of unethical behavior in athletic procedures or in its abuse of students.

We suggest further that presidents of universities and colleges begin to say publicly what they acknowledge privately: that big-time sports are out of control. Campus leaders can meet with each other and agree to a process of cutting back expenditures for recruitment and training, and they can continue to get involved in National Collegiate Athletic Association deliberations. By reaching agreements within various conferences, we can begin scaling back on the commitment to big-time athletics, without individual schools' jeopardizing their public standing.

Further, boards of trustees have an absolutely critical role to play. When a president who wants to fire a coach is told by trustees that his own job is jeopardized if he acts, it seems apparent that the integrity of the institution has been lost.

Against the backdrop of scandals in intercollegiate athletics, intramural sports and recreation are emerging as an encouraging option. Already, 30 percent of the undergraduates participate in such sports and the number appears to be growing. Many students are also keeping fit through jogging, aerobics, lap swimming, weight training, and the like.

At one university we visited, the department of intramurals has a budget of $350,000, drawn from the institution's general fund. Sixty-five percent of the students participate in some program. Over 176,000 students, many of them repeat visitors, were counted in the recreation building during a single academic year. The intramural department offers some forty sports programs, including softball, basketball, volleyball, track, wrestling, and water polo.

According to one student who has played on three intramural teams, "If somebody wanted to, he could play intramurals every afternoon for the whole semester because there are so many teams. Regular exercise is now a way of life for many." We urge every college to develop a comprehensive, well-supported program of intramural sports, one that serves all students, not the select few. We further urge that the intramural program be given top priority when budget decisions about athletics are made and the recreational facility space is assigned.

Most encouraging is the emerging emphasis on wellness. More and more colleges see health and body care as an important educational objective. This, in our opinion, should be a high priority on every campus. The chairman of the intramurals department at one college said the emphasis on wellness is no fad: "Our students are in better shape than they were in the seventies, and there is a new awareness of the importance of caring for the body."

At a large public university on our tour, over two thirds of the students participate in a university-sponsored "wellness program, which includes health education and fitness training. The project also prepares a group of students to be "health promoters" and sends them back to their residences to help others. These "health promoters" study everything from birth control and sexually transmitted diseases to nutrition and how to cope with stress. They not only counsel fellow students, but maintain a first-aid kit and post health information on bulletin boards to keep students abreast of current medical news. We urge that every college consider educating a core of senior students who, in turn, would educate their fellow students through informal seminars about health, nutrition, and first aid.

Health concerns have moved into the cafeteria, too. Menus are now being more closely supervised by dieticians and scrutinized by the students. Health food and vegetarian sections are now standard fare at almost every well-run college in the country. And students are actively involved. Haverford College has a "napkin bulletin board"— a place where students scrawl their reactions to the food on a napkin and tack it up before they leave the cafeteria. Before the day is over, the dietician has posted a reply.

We urge that all students be helped to understand that wellness is a prerequisite to all else. They should be taught about good food, about exercise, and should begin to understand that caring for one's body is a special trust. Further, a professional nutritionist should advise the campus food service and also be available for students as a part of the campus health service. A procedure for students to evaluate the food service also should be available on the campus.

Finally, we suggest that leaders of students' health centers work directly with their counterparts in food service, intramural athletics, residence hall supervision, student government, and even the academic administration to assure that the institution's "wellness" program has the resources and endorsement of the whole campus.

Athletics, health education, and food service are all of direct concern in a college community seriously committed to a quality undergraduate experience.

College life is clearly more than lectures, classes, convocations, and sports events. Wedged in between large group events there must be open spaces—moments when students can spend time alone or relax with one or two close friends. Students need solitude and intimacy as well as togetherness; and they should be able to choose their privacy and their companions without institutional constraint. Open

space is needed for recreation, free expression, and student-initiated activities. Indeed, the most exciting activities we found on campus were informal ones, projects organized by students, whether religious, social, political—center, left, or right. On one mid-sized campus, for example, we found women's rights organizations, a gay and lesbian student group, the Liberty Lobby, the Young Americans for Freedom, Save the Whales, and animal rights advocates. None of these was very large, but they had been organized by loyal advocates who were sufficiently vocal and cohesive to make their mark.

Religious groups are among the fastest-growing organizations on many campuses. At one Midwest state-sponsored college there are religious meetings—revivals, study groups, or songfests sponsored by Christian organizations—almost every night at the student union. These assemblies are very diverse theologically and socially. The Maranathas, Campus Crusade, and the Navigators are evangelical. A middle-of-the-road organization called Ichthus tries to "serve all Christians on the campus." There is the Hillel House for Jewish students and the Newman Club for Catholics. The Ecumenical Campus Ministries, sponsored by the mainstream Protestant denominations, has a rather small following among undergraduates ("If it weren't for their building, you wouldn't know they were here," says one active Christian). Student involvement in religion, which seems to be experiencing a renewal, cuts across all denominations and religious faiths.

In our student survey, we found ambivalence regarding religion and church attendance. It revealed that about three out of four

TABLE 3
Faculty and Undergraduate Appraisal of Their Religious Conviction: 1976 and 1984 (percent agreeing)

		1976	*1984*
I consider myself "deeply religious."	faculty	15	14
	students	15	15
I consider myself "moderately religious."	faculty	45	45
	students	54	63
I am largely "indifferent to religion."	faculty	33	34
	students	26	19
I am basically "opposed to religion."	faculty	7	7
	students	3	3

Source: The Carnegie Foundation for the Advancement of Teaching, National Survey of Undergraduates, 1976 and 1984.

TABLE 4
Political Orientation of College Students, Their Parents, and Faculty: 1976 and 1984

	Left	Liberal	Middle of the Road	Moderately Conservative	Strongly Conservative
Students: How would you characterize yourself politically?					
1984:	2	23	39	31	5
1976:	4	34	39	21	2
Students: How would you characterize your parents?					
1984:	1	10	34	43	12
1976:	*	11	31	46	11
Faculty: How would you characterize yourselves?					
1984:	6	36	27	27	4
1976:	6	38	28	25	3

*= less than 1 percent
Source: The Carnegie Foundation for the Advancement of Teaching, National Survey of Undergraduates, 1976 and 1984.

college students believe there is a God who judges people, but only 42 percent say that most students on their campus are religious. And only 30 percent say that they, personally, are more religious now than when they first came to college.

By comparison, 14 percent of the faculty we surveyed consider themselves "deeply religious" and 45 percent view themselves as "moderately religious." Nearly one third say they are "largely indifferent to religion," and only 7 percent say they are "basically opposed to religion" (Table 3).

As for politics, most students characterize themselves as middle of the road or moderately conservative. They are less likely to characterize themselves as liberals but they consider themselves more liberal than their parents. In contrast, 42 percent of the faculty classify themselves as left of center. Thirty-one percent are either moderately or strongly conservative (Table 4).

We found that on most campuses the conservative viewpoint is getting a better hearing these days. Over the past four years, more than fifty right-wing "alternative" publications have emerged on college campuses. Funded largely by the Institute for Educational Affairs, these publications attack what their supporters see as the "entrenched liberal bias" on the campus.

A striking example is the *Dartmouth Review*, which comments, "We've noticed that women who claim sexual harassment often tend to be low on the pulchritude index," and refers to study programs on women, blacks, and Native Americans as "victims' studies."

The Young Conservative Foundation, Inc., a Washington-based organization, is encouraging students on at least one hundred campuses to protest their schools' investments in companies that do business with the Soviet Union and are, according to the foundation president, "for a few pennies marketing the value of the free world." The group stresses that its effort is not a response to recent anti-apartheid protests, the extent and organization of which they say indicates that the KGB was "without question" involved. A junior at George Washington University who joined the Progressive Student Union and helped form Women's Space, a peace group, says she's been labeled a "radical." The membership of the group is fifteen. "I know that more than fifteen people agree with us," she says, "but because of apathy or fear, they don't show up at meetings."

Despite the drift toward conservatism, today's students still hold a wide spectrum of beliefs. Although only one in three agrees that capital punishment should be abolished, nine out of ten believe more effort should be made

TABLE 5
Attitudes of College Students on Selected Political and Social Issues (percent agreeing)

	1976	1984
More effort should be made to improve relations between the United States and the Soviet Union.	NA	93
Nuclear disarmament should be given high priority by our government.	NA	76
A woman should have the freedom to choose whether or not to have an abortion.	NA	76
I would support stronger environmental legislation even at the expense of economic growth.	84	76
Laws should be enacted to control hand guns.	NA	72
The United States is spending too much on national defense.	56	57
Current unrest in Central America is caused by internal poverty and injustice rather than external political interaction.	NA	54
Our leaders are doing all they can to prevent nuclear war.	NA	52
Capital punishment should be abolished.	40	24

NA: Question not asked in 1976

Source: The Carnegie Foundation for the Advancement of Teaching, National Survey of Undergraduates, 1976 and 1984.

to improve relations between the United States and the Soviet Union. There is also strong support for nuclear disarmament, hand-gun control, environmental protection, and abortion (Table 5).

Thus, the student activities picture in the American college, like the rest of the undergraduate experience, is mixed. On the one hand, the formal structures of student life— student government, convocations and the like— do not seem to be working very well. Only a handful of students are involved, and those who are often seem driven by their own special interests. On the other hand, a lot of informal, less structured activities are flourishing. Students are getting together as private campus citizens, to push their own separate causes.

Self-generated activity adds vitality to the campus, and we could argue that informal student organizations are sufficient. After all, students are adults. They are understandably more committed to organizations that are flexible, responsive, and "cause related," as one student put it.

But even though open time and private space are crucial, a college, we believe, must be something more than a holding company of isolated enclaves. We found it significant that even with athletics and all of the student-sponsored projects, almost two out of five of today's undergraduates still say they do *not* feel a sense of community at their institution. At liberal arts colleges it is only one out of five (Table 6).

We conclude that the effectiveness of the undergraduate experience relates to the quality of campus life. It is directly linked to the time students spend on campus and to the quality of their involvement in activities. In summarizing the research, Alexander Astin reports that participating in almost any type of extracurricular activity, involvement in honors programs, and undergraduate research projects are factors significantly affecting the students' persistence in college. It is not an exaggeration to say that students who get involved stay enrolled.

The campus cannot be satisfied if students separate themselves from one another or, worse, reinforce stereotypes and prejudices. Therefore, even at large complex institutions, with their autonomous units, the goal should be to build alliances between the classroom and campus life, to find group activities, traditions, and common values to be shared. What we seek is a climate in which loyalties can be strengthened. The college cannot be a parent; but neither can faculty and administrators turn their backs on life outside the classroom, where there is so much learning that either enhances

TABLE 6
How Undergraduates Evaluate Community at Their College (percent agreeing)

| | | | By Type of Institution | | | |
	All Institutions	Public	Private	Research University	Doctorate-Granting University	Comprehensive College	Liberal Arts College
I feel a sense of community at this institution.	61	58	74	63	58	57	80

Source: The Carnegie Foundation for the Advancement of Teaching, National Survey of Undergraduates, 1984.

or diminishes the quality of the undergraduate experience.

At an East Coast college we visited, dorms have "living rooms," a fact that pleases students. Students like to sit near the fireplace and socialize. Last December, the director of resident life organized "fireside forums" in the dorms. Forum topics reflected the pressure students feel before exams: "overcoming test anxiety," for example. Forums were also held on social themes. Recently, someone came from Amnesty International to talk about political prisoners and human rights.

Other colleges have suspended classes for a day in order for the entire campus community to discuss a topic of campus-wide concern. Other meetings, of smaller groups, take place in the evenings in various campus settings. At an East Coast public university we visited, students on a December evening could choose among a lecture, "Apartheid in South Africa," sponsored by the women's studies department; a series of one-act plays directed by members of a theater class; and an Egyptian film with English subtitles sponsored by the government department.

Such cultural activities add greatly to the intellectual life of a college community. They have potential for enlarging much of what students are learning in their formal courses. Yet, it was disappointing to observe on most campuses that these kinds of programs receive little support from the faculty. Students are rarely reminded of them, and few efforts are made to connect these out-of-class educational events to ongoing classroom teaching. In a college of quality the faculty will understand the importance of encouraging student participation in campus cultural events. They, too, will be active participants and will attempt to tie their teaching to them whenever possible. In this way, they can contribute to the kind of learning community we wish to support.

Beyond these modest examples, the bringing together of the entire campus community remains the larger vision. Is it possible for the modern campus, with all of its separations and divisions, to find points of common interest? Can students feel both the excitement and responsibility that come from being an active member of a community of learning?

There are all-college convocations. Careful planning can provide such a series on campus that will be a vital force, stirring discussion and controversy, reflection and commitment. For example, Washington University in Saint Louis has such an assembly series every Wednesday morning, featuring poets, artists, political leaders, and others who draw large audiences and help to revitalize the community.

Commencements and alumni weekends can have an equal influence, as can concerts on the campus. And occasionally a college can be brought together to support a worthy cause. Several years ago the State University of New York at Brockport hosted the National Special Olympics. The whole campus came together in a project that stirred inspiration and lifted the vision of both faculty and students.

Carl Schorske, in a brilliant study of creative communities, describes Basel, Switzerland, in the nineteenth century as a place where civic and university creative activities were inextricably interlocked. Professor Schorske said, "The primary function of the university was to foster a civic culture . . . and the city state accordingly assumed, as one of its primary political obligations, the advancement of learning."

If a city can stir a creative, intellectual climate, if merchant families can foster civic culture, what about the intentional community we call a college? While leaving space for privacy and individual interests, we believe there can be celebrations and traditions that tie the institution together and that, through shared experiences, intellectual and social integration on the campus can occur. At such a college all parts of campus life are brought together into what we have called a community of learners.

The college of quality remains a place where the curricular and cocurricular are viewed as having a relationship to each other. At a time when social bonds are tenuous, students, during their collegiate years, should discover the reality of their dependency on each other. They must understand what it means to share and sustain traditions. Community must be built.

Student Involvement:
The Key to Effective Education

ALEXANDER W. ASTIN

How do we go about facilitating talent development in higher education? What are the most effective methods? What theories of student learning seem to be most valid? Even a casual reading of the extensive literature on student development in higher education can be a confusing and perplexing experience. One finds not only that the problems being studied are highly diverse but also that investigators who claim to be studying the same problem frequently do not look at the same variables or employ the same methods. And even when they are looking at the same variables, different investigators may use very different terms in describing and discussing them.

The theory of student involvement presented in this chapter has direct implications for the talent development view of excellence. It has several other virtues as well. First, it can be stated simply: *Students learn by becoming involved.* I have not found it necessary to draw a maze consisting of dozens of boxes interconnected by two-headed arrows in order to explain the basic elements of the theory to others. Second, the theory provides a context for understanding the diverse literature in this field because it seems to explain most of the empirical knowledge gained over the years about environmental influences on student development. Third, the theory embraces principles from such widely divergent sources as psychoanalysis and classical learning theory. Fourth, the involvement concept applies equally to students and to faculty. And finally, the theory of involvement is a useful tool that can be used both by researchers, to guide their investigation of student and faculty develop-

ment, and by college administrators and faculty, as they attempt to design more effective learning environments.

What I mean by involvement is neither mysterious nor esoteric. Quite simply, student involvement refers to the amount of physical and psychological energy that the student devotes to the academic experience. A highly involved student is one who, for example, devotes considerable energy to studying, spends a lot of time on campus, participates actively in student organizations, and interacts frequently with faculty members and other students. Conversely, an uninvolved student may neglect studies, spend little time on campus, abstain from extracurricular activities, and have little contact with faculty members or other students. Let me emphasize that these hypothetical examples are intended to be illustrative only. There are many other possible forms of involvement, which I will discuss in more detail later on.

Although we shall focus our attention here on the student, faculty members too can be characterized in terms of their relative degrees of involvement. A highly involved faculty member would put a lot of time and energy into teaching activities, regularly seek out student advisees to monitor their progress, actively participate in departmental and institutional functions, and make a conscious effort to integrate research and teaching activities.

In some respects the concept of involvement resembles the Freudian concept of cathexis. Freud believed that people invest psychological energy in objects outside themselves. In other words, people can cathect on their friends, families, school-work, jobs, and so on. The involvement concept is also very similar to what learning theorists call "vigilance" or "time-on-task." The concept of "effort," though much narrower than that of involvement, is also relevant here.

To give a better sense of what I have in mind, I want to share with you the results of several hours spent looking into dictionaries and a thesaurus for words or phrases that captured some of the intended meaning. Because involvement is, to me, an active term, the following list uses verb forms:

attach oneself to	plunge into
commit oneself to	show enthusiasm for
devote oneself to	tackle
engage in	take a fancy to
go in for	take an interest in
immerse oneself in	take on
incline toward	take part in
join in	take to
partake of	take up
participate in	undertake

Most of these terms have a behavioral meaning. I could have included words and phrases more interior in nature (value, care for, stress, accentuate, emphasize). But in the sense in which I am using the term, involvement implies a behavioral component. This is not to deny that motivation is an important aspect of involvement but rather to emphasize that the behavioral aspects, in my judgment, are critical. It is not so much what the individual thinks or feels but what he or she does that defines and identifies involvement.

At this stage in its development, the involvement theory comprises five basic postulates:

1. Involvement refers to the investment of physical and psychological energy in various "objects." The objects may be highly generalized (the student experience) or highly specific (preparing for a chemistry examination).

2. Regardless of its object, involvement occurs along a continuum. Different students manifest different degrees of involvement in a given object, and the same student manifests different degrees of involvement in different objects at different times.

3. Involvement has both quantitative and qualitative features. The extent of a student's involvement in, say, academic work can be measured quantitatively (how many hours the student spends studying) and qualitatively (does the student review and comprehend reading assignments, or does the student simply stare at the textbook and daydream?).

4. The amount of student learning and personal development associated with any educational program is directly proportional to the quality and quantity of student involvement in that program.

5. The effectiveness of any educational policy or practice is directly related to the capacity of that policy or practice to increase student involvement.

These last two propositions are, of course, the key educational postulates, since they offer clues about how to design more effective educational programs for students. Strictly speaking, however, they do not qualify as postulates, since they are subject to proof by empirical test. As a matter of fact, much of the recommended research on involvement (discussed later in this chapter) is intended to test these two propositions.

Implicit Pedagogical Theories

The theory of student involvement has important implications for classroom teaching. Whether they admit it or not, all faculty members rely on some sort of pedagogical theory in carrying out their teaching activities (Hunt, 1980). Though these theories are sometimes not clearly stated, they nevertheless govern much of the typical teacher's effort. What is particularly interesting about some of these theories is that they appear to have their roots in traditional conceptions of excellence—in particular, the resources and content views.

In developing the theory of student involvement, I was prompted in part by a dissatisfaction with these implicit ideas about teaching because of their tendency to treat the student as a kind of black box. On the input end of this black box are the various policies and programs of a college or university, and on the output end are various types of achievement measures such as gradepoint average or scores on standardized tests. What seems to be missing is some mediating mechanism that explains how these educational programs and policies are translated into student achievement and development. The inadequacies of these theories are compounded by their implicit, unexamined nature. Even when faculty members and administrators are aware of the theories that guide their actions, they seem to accept them as gospel rather than as testable propositions.

So far I have identified three such implicit pedagogical models: the content, the resources, and the individualized (or eclectic) theories. As I examine them, I shall show how the theory of student involvement can help tie them more directly to talent development.

The Content Theory. This first concept of pedagogy, which might also be called the subject-matter theory, is very popular with college faculties. According to this theory, student learning and development depend primarily on exposure to the right subject matter. Thus, a liberal education consists of an assortment of "worthwhile" courses. Individual courses, in turn, are evaluated in terms of their content, as reflected, for example, in course syllabi. In fact, it is a common practice for most academics to evaluate their colleagues' teaching performance by inspecting course syllabi. Given this strong emphasis on course content, it is not surprising that the practitioners of this theory tend to believe that students learn by attending lectures, doing the reading assignments, and working in the library. Rarely do they use oral presentations by the student as learning tools, and then they generally require that the presentations focus on the content of the reading or the lecture.

Under the content approach to learning, those professors with the greatest specialized knowledge of a particular subject matter have the highest prestige. Thus this approach appears to encourage the fragmentation and specialization of faculty interests and to equate scholarly expertise with pedagogical ability. But perhaps the most serious limitation of the content theory is that it assigns students a passive role in learning. The "knowledgeable" professor lectures to the "ignorant" student so that the student can acquire the same knowledge. Such an approach clearly favors highly motivated students and those who tend to be avid readers and good listeners. Students who read slowly or who have no intrinsic interest in the subject matter of a particular course are not well served by this approach. In fact, recent attempts to expand educational opportunities for under-prepared students have probably been hindered by the continued adherence of most faculty members to the content theory of learning (Astin, 1982).

The Resources Theory. This theory, derives directly from the resources conception of institutional excellence. While most faculty members would support this theory, in principle, it is a particular favorite among administrators and policy makers. The term *resources,* as used here, includes a wide range of things that are thought to enhance students' learning: physical facilities (laboratories, classrooms, libraries, audiovisual aids), human resources (well-trained faculty members, teaching assistants, counselors, and support personnel), and monetary resources (financial aid, endowments, extramural research funds). In effect, proponents say, if adequate resources are brought together in one place, student learning and development will occur. And the more resources there are, the better the learning is. Many college administrators, it should be noted, view the acquisition of resources as their most important function.

One resource measure that is particularly popular with administrators is the student-faculty ratio. It is generally believed that the lower the ratio, the greater the student's learning and personal development. But the resources theory has qualitative as well as quantitative aspects. Thus, the data reported in Chapter Two on undergraduate quality ratings suggest that many faculty members subscribe to the belief that increasing the proportion of high-quality professors on the faculty (quality in this instance being defined primarily in terms of scholarly productivity and national visibility) strengthens the educational environment. As a matter of fact, many research-oriented institutions could probably afford to hire more faculty members if they were less committed to recruiting and retaining faculty members who are highly visible within their disciplines.

In short, such policies involve a trade-off between quantity and quality.

Subscribers to the resources theory of pedagogy also tend to regard high-achieving students as a resource. Thus, many faculty members and administrators believe that having substantial numbers of high-achieving students on the campus enhances the quality of the learning environment for all students. Acting on this belief, some institutions invest a lot of money in recruiting high-achievers.

The resources theory of pedagogy has some of the same limitations as the resources conception of excellence. First, certain resources, such as bright students and prestigious faculty, are finite. As a result, the institutional energies that might otherwise be invested in the teaching-learning process are instead expended in recruiting high-achieving students and prestigious faculty. From a systems perspective, these recruitment activities merely redistribute these finite resources from one institution to another rather than add to the total pool of such resources. In other words, while a successful faculty, or student recruitment program may seem, from a resources standpoint, to benefit a particular institution, such benefit comes at the expense of other institutions. As a consequence, widespread acceptance of the resource theory of pedagogy tends, paradoxically, to reduce the total amount of resources available to the higher education community at large.

The second problem with this pedagogical approach is that it focuses institutional attention on the mere accumulation of resources and shifts attention away from the utilization or deployment of such resources. For instance, having established a multimillion-volume library, the administration may ignore the question of whether students are using it effectively. Similarly, having successfully recruited a faculty "star," the college may pay little attention to whether or not the new faculty member works effectively with students. In fact, when institutions are trying to recruit stars, one of the perks commonly offered is a low (or no) teaching load.

The Individualized (Eclectic) Theory. Since this theory is not derived directly from any of the traditional views of excellence, it is not widely practiced by college faculty members. This theory—a favorite with many develop-

mental and learning psychologists (Chickering and Associates, 1981)—assumes that no single approach to subject matter, teaching techniques, or resource allocation is adequate for all students. Rather, supporters of this approach attempt to identify the curricular content and instructional methods that best meet the needs of the individual student. Given its emphasis on borrowing what is most useful from other pedagogical approaches, this flexible approach might also be termed eclectic.

In contrast to the content approach, which generally results in a fixed set of curricular requirements (courses that all students must take, or "distributional requirements"), the individualized approach emphasizes electives. As a matter of fact, most college curricula represent a mixture of the content and individualized theories, in that students must take certain required courses or satisfy certain distributional requirements but also have the option of taking a certain number of free elective courses.

But the individualized theory goes far beyond the issue of curriculum. Among other things, it emphasizes the importance of advising and counseling and of independent study on the part of the student. It should be noted here that the philosophy underlying most student personnel work (guidance, counseling, selective placement, and student support services) implicitly incorporates the individualized or eclectic theory of student development. It is perhaps no accident that those few institutions that openly advocate an individualized approach to instruction (Empire State College, the Evergreen State College, and Hampshire College, for example) tend to be relatively new (founded since 1960) and therefore are not bound by traditional views of excellence.

The individualized approach is also associated with particular instructional techniques: for instance, self-paced instruction, contract learning, and independent study. In addition, this theory has led some educators to espouse the "competency-based" learning model (Grant and others, 1979; Mentkowski and Doherty 1984), whereby common learning objectives (competencies) are formulated for all students, but the time allowed to reach these objectives is highly variable, and the instructional techniques used are highly individualized.

Although the individualized theory has certain obvious advantages over the content and resources theories, it can be extremely expensive to implement, since each student normally requires a great deal of individualized attention. In addition, because there are virtually no limitations to the possible variations in subject matter and in pedagogical approach, the individualized theory is difficult to define with much precision. Further, given the current state of research on learning, it is impossible at this point to specify which types of educational programs or teaching techniques are most effective with which types of learners. Beyond an "individualization of approach," it is difficult to know just *what* approaches are likely to work best with *what* type of student. In other words, while the theory is appealing in the abstract, it is extremely difficult to put into practice.

The Place of the Theory of Student Involvement

How does the theory of student involvement relate to these traditional pedagogical theories? In my judgment, it can provide a link between the central variables in these theories (subject matter, resources, and individualization of approach) and the learning outcomes of concern to the student and the professor. According to the theory of student involvement, if a particular curriculum or a particular array of resources is to have its intended effects, it must elicit enough student effort and investment of energy to bring about the desired learning and development. Simply exposing the student to a particular set of courses may or may not work. The theory of involvement, in other words, provides a conceptual substitute for the black box that is implicit in the three traditional pedagogical theories.

The content theory, in particular, tends to assign students a passive role—as recipients of information. In contrast, the theory of involvement emphasizes the active participation of the student in the learning process. Recent research at the precollegiate level (Rosenshine, 1982) suggests that learning will be greatest when the learning environment is structured to encourage active participation by the student.

On a more subtle level, the theory of student involvement encourages educators to focus less on what they do and more on what the student does: how motivated the student is, how much time and energy the student devotes to the learning process. It holds that student learning and development will not be very great if educators focus most of their attention on course content, teaching techniques, laboratories, books, and other resources. Under this approach, student involvement—rather than the resources or techniques typically utilized by educators—becomes the focus of concern.

As this discussion suggests, the construct of student involvement in certain respects resembles a much more common construct in psychology, that of motivation. I personally prefer the term *involvement*, however, because it connotes something more than just a psychological state; it connotes the behavioral manifestation of that state. Involvement is more susceptible to direct observation and measurement than is the more abstract psychological construct of motivation. Moreover, involvement seems to be a more useful construct for educational practitioners: "How do you motivate students?" is probably a more difficult question to deal with than "How do you get students involved?"

During the past few years, developmental theories have been receiving a good deal of attention in the higher education literature. These theories are of at least two types: those that postulate a series of hierarchically arranged developmental stages (see, for example, Heath, 1968; Kohlberg, 1971; Loevinger, 1966; Perry, 1970), and those that view student development in multidimensional terms (such as Brown and DeCoster, 1982; Chickering, 1969). (For recent comprehensive summaries of these theories, see Chickering and Associates, 1981, and Hanson, 1982.) The theory of student involvement, however, differs qualitatively from these developmental theories. Whereas they focus primarily on developmental outcomes (the "what" of student development) the theory of student involvement is concerned more with the behavioral mechanisms or processes that facilitate student development (the "how" of student development). Later in this chapter, I discuss how the two types of theories might be studied simultaneously.

Student Time as a Resource

Although higher education administrators are constantly preoccupied with accumulating and allocating fiscal resources, the theory of student involvement suggests that the most precious institutional resource may be student time. According to the theory, the extent to which students are able to develop their talents in college is a direct function of the amount of time and effort they devote to activities designed to produce these gains. To take a specific example: If a greater understanding of history is regarded as an important talent development goal for history majors, the extent to which students reach this goal is a direct function of the time they spend listening to professors talk about history, reading books about history, discussing history with other students, and so forth. Within certain broad limits, the more time students spend in such activities, the more history they learn.

The theory of student involvement explicitly acknowledges that the psychic and physical time and energy of students are finite. Educators are in reality competing with other forces in the student's life for a share of that finite time and energy. The student's investment in matters relating to family, friends, job, and other outside activities represents a reduction in the time and energy the student has to devote to his or her educational development.

In applying the theory of student involvement, administrators and faculty members must recognize that virtually every institutional policy and practice (class schedules; regulations on class attendance, academic probation, and participation in honors courses; policies on office hours for faculty, student orientation, and advising) can affect how students spend their time and how much effort they devote to academic pursuits. Moreover, administrative decisions on many nonacademic issues (the location of new buildings such as dormitories and student unions; rules governing residency; the design of recreational and living facilities; on-campus employment opportunities; the number and type of extracurricular activities and regulations regarding participation; the frequency, type, and cost of cultural events; roommate assignments; financial aid policies; the relative attractiveness of eating facilities on and off campus; parking regulations) also can significantly affect how students spend their time and energy. Ultimately, these allocations of time and effort should have important effects on how well students actually develop their talents.

While this discussion has focused primarily on student involvement, the involvement of faculty and staff members in institutional activities also has potentially important implications for the effectiveness of the institution's educational program. At least two forms of faculty "noninvolvement," for example, would appear to detract from program effectiveness: part-time status and excessive engagement in outside consulting and other professional activities. In both instances the faculty member's time on campus is significantly reduced, and a good deal of professional time and energy is invested in activity unrelated to the institution's educational activities. Clearly, if institutions were to embrace involvement as a critical factor in assessing faculty performance, outside professional and consulting activities would come under much closer scrutiny.

Relevant Research and Its Findings

The theory of student involvement has its roots in a longitudinal study of college dropouts (Astin, 1975) aimed at identifying factors in the college environment that significantly affect the student's persistence in college. As it turned out, virtually every significant effect could be explained in terms of the involvement concept. Every positive factor was one that would be likely to increase student involvement in the undergraduate experience, while every negative factor was one that would be likely to reduce involvement. What were these significant environmental factors? Probably the most important and pervasive was the student's residence. Living in a campus residence was positively related to retention, and this positive effect occurred in all types of institutions and among all types of students regardless of sex, race, ability, or family background. Similar results had been obtained in earlier studies (Astin, 1973a; Chickering, 1974) and have subsequently been replicated on several occasions (Astin, 1977, 1982). It is obvious that students who live in residence halls have more time and more opportunity to get involved in all aspects of campus life. Indeed, simply by virtue of eating, sleeping, and spending their waking hours on the college campus, residential students stand a better chance than do commuter students of developing a strong identification with and attachment to undergraduate life.

These longitudinal studies also showed that students who join social fraternities or sororities or participate in extracurricular activities of almost any type are less likely to drop out. Participation in sports—particularly intercollegiate sports—has an especially pronounced effect on persistence, despite the many stories about college athletes who are exploited and never finish college. Other activities that enhance retention include enrollment in honors programs, involvement in ROTC, and participation in professors' undergraduate research projects.

One of the most interesting environmental factors in retention was holding a part-time job on the campus. Though it might seem that having to work while attending college takes time and energy away from academic pursuits, part-time employment in an on-campus job actually facilitates persistence. It would appear that such work (which also includes the federal College Work-Study program) operates in much the same way as residential living: Because the student spends time on campus, he or she is more likely to come into contact with other students, professors, and college staff. On a more subtle psychological level, reliance on the college as a source of income may serve to develop a greater sense of attachment to it.

Retention suffers, however, if the student works off campus at a full-time job. Clearly in this case the student is spending a lot of time and energy on nonacademic activities that are usually unrelated to student life. Full-time off-campus work thus reduces the investment the student can make in studies and other campus activities.

Findings concerning the effects of different types of colleges are also relevant to the theory of involvement. Thus, the most consistent finding—reported in virtually every longitudinal study of student development—is that the student's chances of dropping out are substantially greater at a two-year college than at a four-year college. The negative effects of attending a community college are observed

even after the effects of the students' entering characteristics and the lack of residence and work are taken into account (Astin, 1975, 1977). Community, colleges are places where the involvement of both faculty members and students appears to be minimal: All students are commuters, and most are part-timers. Thus they presumably manifest less involvement simply because of their part-time status. Similarly, a large proportion of faculty members are employed part-time.

The 1975 study of dropouts also produced some interesting findings regarding the fit between student and college: Students are more likely to persist at religious colleges if their own religious background is similar; blacks are more likely to persist at black colleges than at white colleges (now that white colleges are more fully integrated, however, this finding may no longer hold; see Astin, 1982); and students from small towns are more likely to persist in small colleges. It seems reasonable to suppose that the mechanism for such effects is the student's ability to identify with the institution. One has an easier time becoming involved when the college environment seems comfortable and familiar.

Further support for the involvement theory can be found by examining the reasons that students give for dropping out of college. In the case of men, the most common reason is "boredom with courses." Boredom clearly implies a lack of involvement. In the case of women, the most common reason for dropping out is "marriage, pregnancy, or other family responsibilities." Here we have a set of competing objectives that drain away the time and energy that women might otherwise devote to being students. The persister-dropout phenomenon provides an ideal paradigm for studying student involvement. If we conceive of involvement as occurring along a continuum, the act of dropping out can be viewed as the ultimate form of noninvolvement; it anchors the involvement continuum at the low end.

In view of the apparent usefulness of the involvement theory as it applied to this research on dropping out, I decided to investigate the involvement phenomenon much more intensively in a subsequent study of college impact on a wide range of other outcomes (Astin, 1977). This study, which used longitudinal data on more than 200,000 students and examined more than eight different student outcomes, focused on the effects of several different types of involvement: place of residence, honors programs, undergraduate research participation, social fraternities and sororities, academic involvement, student-faculty interaction, athletic involvement, and involvement in student government. To understand the effects of these various forms of involvement, one should keep in mind the overall results of this study: College attendance in general serves to strengthen students' competence, self-esteem, artistic interests, liberalism, hedonism, and religious apostasy, and to weaken their business interests.

Perhaps the most important general conclusion to emerge from this elaborate analysis was that *nearly all forms of student involvement are associated with greater-than-average changes in the characteristics of entering freshmen.* And for certain student outcomes, *involvement is more strongly associated with change than either entering freshmen's characteristics or institutional characteristics.*

The following is a summary of the results related to specific forms of involvement.

Effect of Place of Residence. Leaving home to attend college makes a substantial impact on most college outcomes. Students who live on campus show greater gains than do commuters in artistic interests, liberalism, and interpersonal self-esteem. And living in a dormitory is positively associated with several other forms of involvement: interaction with faculty members, involvement in student government, and participation in social fraternities or sororities.

Further, living on campus substantially increases the student's chances of persisting and of aspiring to a graduate or professional degree. Residents are more likely than commuters to achieve in such extracurricular areas as leadership and athletics and to express satisfaction with their undergraduate experience, particularly in the areas of student friendships, faculty-student relations, institutional reputation, and social life. Residents are also much more likely to become less religious and more hedonistic (*hedonism* here refers to drinking, smoking, sexual activity, and the like).

Effect of Honors Program Involvement. Students who participate in honors programs gain substantially in interpersonal self-esteem, intellectual self-esteem, and artistic interests.

They are more likely than are those who do not take part to persist in college and to aspire to graduate and professional degrees. Honors participation is also positively related to student satisfaction in three areas—quality of the science program, closeness to faculty, and quality of instruction—and negatively related to satisfaction with friendships and with the institution's academic reputation. These findings suggest that honors participation enhances faculty-student relationships but may isolate students from their peers.

Effect of Academic Involvement. Defined as a complex of self-reported traits and behaviors (such as the extent to which students work hard at their studies, the number of hours they spend studying, their degree of interest in their courses, good study habits), academic involvement produced an unusual pattern of effects. Heavy academic involvement tends to retard those changes in personality and behavior that normally result from college attendance. Thus, students who are heavily involved academically are less likely than are average students to show an increase in liberalism, hedonism, artistic interests, and religious apostasy or a decrease in business interests. The only personality change accentuated by academic involvement is the need for status, which is strengthened. Being academically involved is strongly related to satisfaction with all aspects of college life except friendships with other students.

This pattern reinforces the hypothesis that students who get heavily involved in their college studies tend to become isolated from their peers and consequently to be less susceptible to the peer group influences that seem critical to the development of political liberalism, hedonism, and religious apostasy. On the other hand, they experience considerable satisfaction, perhaps because of the many institutional rewards for good academic performance. Although most research on classroom learning has been carried out at the precollegiate level, the bulk of the evidence from this research provides strong support for the concept of involvement as a critical element in the learning process. "Time-on-task" and "effort," for example, appear frequently in the literature as key determinants of a wide range of cognitive learning outcomes (Bloom, 1974; Fisher and others, 1980).

Effect of Student-Faculty Interaction. Frequent interaction with faculty members is more strongly related to satisfaction with college than any other type of involvement or, indeed, any other student or institutional characteristic. Students who have many contacts with the faculty are more likely than those who do not to express satisfaction with all aspects of their institutional experience, including student friendships, the variety of courses, the intellectual environment, and even the administration of the institution. It would seem that finding ways to encourage greater student involvement with faculty members (and vice versa) might be a highly productive activity on most college campuses.

Effect of Athletic Involvement. Interestingly enough, the pattern of results associated with involvement in athletic activities closely parallels the pattern associated with academic involvement. Students who become heavily involved in athletic activities show smaller-than-average increases in political liberalism, religious apostasy, and artistic interests and a smaller-than average decrease in business interests. Athletic involvement is also associated with satisfaction in four areas: the institution's academic reputation, the intellectual environment, student friendships, and institutional administration. These results suggest that athletic involvement, like academic involvement, tends to isolate students from the peer group effects that normally accompany college attendance. For the studious person, this isolation results from the time and effort devoted to studying. For the athlete, the isolation may result from long practice hours, travel to athletic competitions, and special living quarters.

Effect of Involvement in Student Government. Participating in student government is associated with greater-than-average increases in political liberalism, hedonism, artistic interests, and status needs, as well as with greater-than-average satisfaction with student friendships. This pattern of relationships supports the hypothesis that the changes in attitudes and behavior that usually accompany college attendance are attributable to peer-group effects. That is, students who become heavily involved in student government interact frequently with their peers, and this interaction appears to

accentuate the changes normally resulting from the college experience.

Applications of the Theory by Campus Staff Members

The theory of involvement has a number of interesting implications for practitioners in higher education. Let us briefly consider some of the possible uses that faculty members, administrators, and student personnel workers might make of it.

Faculty Members and Administrators. As already suggested, the content and resources theories of pedagogy tend to favor the well-prepared, assertive student. In contrast, the student involvement theory suggests the need to give greater attention to the passive, reticent, or underprepared student. Of course, not all passive students are uninvolved in their academic work, nor are they necessarily experiencing academic difficulties. But passivity is a warning sign that may denote a lack of involvement. Moreover, devoting more attention to passive students may well serve the interests of greater educational equity, since passivity often characterizes minority and disadvantaged students (H.S. Astin and others, 1971; Astin, 1982).

Perhaps the most important application of the student involvement theory to teaching is that, as I mentioned earlier, the instructor focuses less on content and on teaching techniques and more on what students are actually doing: how motivated they are and how much time and energy they devote to the learning process. Teaching is a complex art. And, like other art forms, it may suffer if the artist focuses too exclusively on technique. Instructors can be more effective if they focus on the intended outcomes of their pedagogical efforts: maximizing student involvement and learning. (Final examinations monitor learning, but they come too late in the learning process to be of much value to the individual student.)

The same point can perhaps be better illustrated with an example from sports. Any professional baseball player will tell you that the best way to develop skill in pitching is to focus not on the mechanics but on the intended result: getting the ball over the plate. If the player overemphasizes such technical matters as the grip, the stance, the windup, and the kick without attending to where the ball goes, he will probably never learn how to pitch well. As a matter of fact, the technique involved in pitching a baseball, shooting a basketball, or hitting a golfball is really unimportant as long as the ball goes where the player wants it to. If the ball fails to behave as intended, *then* the player begins to worry about adjusting his or her technique.

Counselors and Student Personnel Workers. If an institution commits itself to maximizing student involvement, counselors and other student personnel workers will probably occupy a central role in institutional operations. Since student personnel workers usually operate on a one-to-one basis with students, they are uniquely positioned to monitor the involvement of their clients in the academic process and to work with individuals to maximize that involvement. One of the challenges confronting such workers these days is to find a hook that will get students more involved in the college experience: by taking a different array of courses, by changing residential situations, by joining student organizations or participating in various kinds of extracurricular activities, or by associating with new peer groups.

The theory of involvement also provides a potentially useful frame of reference for working with students who experience academic difficulties. Perhaps the first task in working with such students is to understand the principal objects on which the student's energy is focused. It might be helpful, for example, to ask students to keep a detailed time diary, showing when and for how long they study, sleep, socialize, daydream, work at a job, commute to and from college, and so on. From such a diary the counselor can identify the principal activities in which the student is currently involved and the objects on which he or she cathects, and can thereby determine whether the academic difficulties stem from competing involvements, poor study habits, lack of motivation, or some combination of these factors.

In short, the theory of student involvement provides a unifying construct that can help to focus the energies of all institutional personnel on a common objective.

Need for Feedback

A critical consideration in implementing the student involvement theory is to make sure that students, faculty members, and administrators have adequate feedback. In the preceding section I used such phrases as "focus more on what students are actually, doing," "monitor the involvement of their students," and "understand the principal objects on which the student's energy is focused." The importance of feedback may be best illustrated by returning to the art form analogy for a moment.

An essential ingredient in performing artists' development of techniques and skills is the opportunity to view the results of their work. Neophyte painters see what comes out on the canvas, aspiring musicians hear what they play and sing and adjust their behavior accordingly. And artists very often rely on technology to enhance the feedback process: dancers use mirrors, musicians use recording and amplification, and so on. If you have any doubts about the importance of feedback in learning a performing art, consider how it would be to try to learn to paint blindfolded or to play the violin with your ears plugged.

Now if teaching and administration are more like art forms than like mechanistic activities that can be learned by following a how-to manual, then having adequate feedback is essential to learning how to be a good teacher or administrator. And if student involvement is a key ingredient in effective learning, then having regular access to certain information about student involvement would seem to be an essential part of learning and maintaining effective teaching and administration in our colleges.

Feedback on student involvement can be particularly valuable in helping administrators make better use of resources. Ideally, administrators should have regular feedback on the quantity and quality of students' involvement in a wide range of areas: studying, extracurricular activities, faculty members, other students, the library, laboratories, and so on. By monitoring such feedback on a department-by-department basis, administrators should be able to identify potential problem areas and to target resources accordingly (see Chapter Seven for further discussion of these matters).

For the student's part, the importance of feedback in learning is obvious. In the previous chapter I noted that a large body of research (Gagne, 1977) suggests that students learn better when they have a "knowledge of results" (feedback on how well their talent is developing). This sort of feedback occurs, for example, when students have a chance to go over any test they have taken and analyze their errors. And if student involvement is an important ingredient in the learning process, then students would also stand to profit from a better understanding of how they are spending their time and energies and whether they might be able to modify their way of allocating these resources to facilitate their academic progress.

Subjects for Further Research

Applying the theory of student involvement to my research work over the past several years has generated a great many ideas for further study. This research is concerned not only with testing the theory itself but also with exploring educational ideas that grow out of the theory. The following are just a few examples of how institutions might explore the implications of the involvement theory for their own programs and policies.

Different Forms of Involvement. Clearly, one of the most important next steps in developing and testing the involvement theory is to examine ways to evaluate different forms of involvement. As already suggested a time diary might have considerable value in determining what priority the student gives to various objects and activities. From my experience with such time diaries (Astin, 1968a), I know that students spend very different amounts of time on studying, socializing, sleeping, daydreaming, and traveling. How frequently students interact with each other, with faculty members and other institutional personnel, and with people outside the institution is another matter that should be investigated. Finally, the extracurricular activities in which the student participates should be identified, and the time and energy devoted to each activity should be assessed.

Quality Versus Quantity of Involvement. C. Robert Pace, my colleague at UCLA, has developed an extensive battery of devices to assess the quality of effort that students devote to various activities (Pace, 1982). Pace has assembled

an impressive body of evidence showing that talent development may be heavily dependent on both the quality and the quantity of students' involvement. A number of research questions arise in connection with the quality-versus-quantity issue: To what extent can high-quality involvement compensate for lack of quantity? Can students be encouraged to use time more wisely? To what extent does low-quality involvement reflect a lack of motivation, personal problems, and so on?

Involvement and Developmental Outcomes. The research reviewed earlier (Astin, 1977) suggests that different forms of involvement lead to different developmental outcomes. The connection between particular types of involvement and particular outcomes is a problem of obvious significance that should be addressed in future research. For example, do certain kinds of involvement facilitate student development along the various dimensions postulated by theorists such as Chickering (1969), Loevinger (1966), Heath (1968), Perry (1970), and Kohlberg (1971)? It would also be useful to know whether particular student characteristics (such as socioeconomic status, academic preparation, gender) are significantly related to different forms of involvement and whether a given form of involvement produces different outcomes for different types of students.

Role of Peer Groups. A considerable body of research on precollegiate education suggests that the student's commitment of time and energy to academic work is strongly influenced by his or her peers (Coleman, 1961; McDill and Rigsby, 1973). It would be useful to determine whether similar relationships exist at the postsecondary level and, in particular, whether different peer groups can be used consciously to enhance students' involvement in learning.

Locus of Control and Attribution. Learning and developmental theorists in recent years have shown an increasing interest in the concepts of locus of control (Rotter, 1966) and attribution (Weiner, 1979). A considerable body of research, for example, suggests that students' degree of involvement in learning tasks is influenced by whether they see their behavior as controlled by internal or external factors. Weiner argues that even if students view the locus of control as internal, their involvement may be contingent on whether they see these internal factors as controllable (effort, for instance) or as uncontrollable (such as ability). Clearly, the effectiveness of any attempt to increase student involvement may depend heavily on the student's perceived locus of control and attributional inclinations.

Other Topics. Among the other questions that might be explored in future research on the involvement theory are the following: What are the characteristics of the exceptions to the rule—the highly involved students who drop out and the uninvolved students who nonetheless manage to persist in college? Are there particular developmental outcomes for which a high degree of involvement is contraindicated?

Two students may devote the same total amount of time and energy to a task but may distribute their time very differently. For example, in preparing a term paper, one student may work for one hour each night over a period of two weeks, while another may stay up all night to do the paper. What are the developmental consequences of these different patterns?

How do different kinds of involvement interact? Does one form of involvement (in extracurricular activities, for example) enhance or diminish the effects of another form (such as academic work)? What are the ideal combinations for facilitating the maximum learning and personal development?

Although the theory of involvement generally holds that more is better, there are probably limits beyond which increasing involvement ceases to produce desirable results and even becomes counterproductive. Examples of excessive involvement are the "workaholic," the academic "nerd" or "grind," and other personality types who manifest withdrawal and obsessive-compulsive behavior. What are the ideal upper limits for various forms of involvement? Are problems more likely to develop when the student is excessively involved in a single object (academic work, for instance) than they are when he or she focuses on a variety of objects (such as academic work, a part-time job, and extracurricular, social, and political activities)?

And what about the participation of campus educators? Can student involvement be increased if professors interact more with students? Can administrators bring about greater faculty-student interaction by setting an example themselves? Does focusing on student involvement as a common institutional goal tend to break down traditional status barriers between faculty members and student personnel workers?

Summary

In this chapter, I have presented a theory of student development—the student involvement theory—which, in my view, is at once simple and comprehensive, a theory that not only elucidates the mass of findings that have emerged from decades of research on student development but also offers higher education practitioners a tool for designing more effective learning environments.

Student involvement refers to the quantity and quality of the physical and psychological energy the student invests in the college experience. Such involvement takes many forms: absorption in academic work, participation in extracurricular activities, interaction with faculty members and other institutional personnel and so forth. According to the theory, the greater the student's involvement in college, the greater the learning and personal development. From the standpoint of the educator, the theory's most important point is that the effectiveness of any educational policy or practice is directly related to its capacity for increasing student involvement.

The principal advantage of the student involvement theory over traditional pedagogical approaches (including the content, the resources, and the individualized or eclectic theories) is that it directs attention away from subject matter and technique and toward the motivation and behavior of the student. It views student time and energy as institutional resources, albeit finite ones. Given this view, all institutional policies and practices—those relating to nonacademic as well as to academic matters—can be evaluated in terms of the degree to which they increase or reduce student involvement. Similarly, all higher education practitioners—counselors and student personnel workers as well as faculty members and administrators—can assess their own activities in terms of their success in encouraging students to become more involved in the college experience.

CHAPTER 7

TEACHING AND LEARNING

ASSOCIATE EDITOR: AMAURY NORA

There is much that has been published related to teaching and learning in higher education institutions. Many of those articles, books, and chapters have focused exclusively on differential approaches, varying methodologies, and practical advice for practitioners. Most, however, have done so in isolation of the work of other investigators. The results of these disjointed efforts have been a definite lack in establishing a link between theoretically informative pieces and actual practice. Moreover, the quality of those efforts varies because faculty from different fields have often dabbled with the issue. As a consequence, for example, when an economist examines a teaching/learning question, he or she does so by applying the paradigms of the discipline. What has been published has led to some strange results with the state of our knowledge of teaching and learning all over the map. The conclusion is that literature in this area is very diverse, not well-known and not well-integrated. This situation has led to uninformed audiences on both sides. While this situation is found predominantly in the literature, it is hoped that this chapter will provide the reader with a sense of balance between research and practice. The selections included in this chapter encompass a blend of theory/research/practice.

Barr and Tagg's (1995) article on the shift in paradigms from teaching to learning for undergraduate education represents a thoughtful theoretical piece on a learning paradigm. Their work has served as a key piece in getting faculty to think about the learning side of the teaching equation. Parsons' (1959) views on the perception of the school class as a social system provides a similar theoretical emphasis with a focal point on teaching. The intent of the selections was not only to provide differing views on teaching and learning in the classroom but to also point to the shift in paradigms as contrasted by Parsons' classic article (dated 1959) and Barr and Tagg's (1995) more recent publication.

As previously noted, in an attempt to link the theoretical underpinnings of research in the literature with practical interventions and practices in the classroom, articles by Auster and MacRone (1994) and McKeachie (1958) were included in the selections for this chapter. The intent of both articles was to provide a contrast in how faculty, administrators, and practitioners, heretofore, viewed teaching methods (McKeachie, 1958) and a more recent call for a better integration of research and practice (Auster & MacRone, 1994). Auster and MacRone's publication represents a good straightforward study that illustrates the value of research that addresses the really explicit questions on practice. So much higher education research on teaching and learning does not. The article was the first of a group of recent work that focused on the enhancement of learning in the classroom. Concrete instructional behaviors are examined as well as a look at the gender question (e.g., Do women participate less than men in classroom discussion? Does it matter if the faculty member is male or female?).

One area not included in the selection of articles is that of multicultural teaching that stresses the incorporation of multiculturalism in teaching and the curriculum. While there was a period of

Amaury Nora is on the faculty of the College of Education at the University of Houston. (anora@uh.edu)

time in the late 1980s and early 1990s where some literature on multiculturalism in the pedagogical literatures surfaced (e.g., discipline-specific journals, generic journals and journals that regularly publish manuscripts on teaching and learning), it was not widespread and never widely referenced. Currently, there is almost nothing in the literature. One possible reason for the lack of referencing much of that literature was that those empirical works that were found were not prepared by researchers with much connection to the field. What was proposed by those investigators that faculty do, often could not be done very well at all with certain kinds of content (e.g., discussion of difference in math classes, electrical engineering or badminton classes). That situation, coupled with the lack of commitment to diversity on the part of mainstream faculty, extremely limited the pieces that represent the literature on teaching and learning.

The following works are included in this introduction that provide a beginning point for researchers and faculty alike. The first piece is an article by Frederick (1995) titled "Walking on Eggs: The Dreaded Diversity Discussion" published in *College Teaching*. This very practitioner piece by a history professor, while appearing more relevant to those that teach discussible content, provides some very good ideas on the subject. The second reference is a book by Schoem, Frankel, Zuniga, and Lewis (1993) titled *Multicultural Teaching in the University*. The first 71 pages stress the conceptual nature of multicultural teaching and a really strong justification for its importance.

A second area not included in the selection of the articles for this chapter is that of student learning styles or preferences. The literature recognizes that individuals learn in different ways and have different learning styles (Keefe, 1979). The identification and examination of learning styles has become an important area of interest in education primarily because of studies in which achievement has increased by matching students' learning style preferences with corresponding instructional approaches. A great deal of attention has been given to the investigation and application of learning styles of native English speakers over the past thirty years (Carbo, 1985; Dunn, 1985; Dunn, Beaudry, & Klavas, 1989; Reid, 1987). Researchers have developed various theories of learning styles and have pursued their investigations in different ways (Kolb, 1976, 1984, 1985; Dunn, Dunn, & Price, 1979, 1985; Reid, 1987, Dirksen, 1988; Sy, 1991).

Learning style theory has not only investigated individual differences, but also differences among cultural groups. Studies by Cohen (1969), Ramirez III and Castaneda (1974), Shade (1982), and Wiktin (1976) have established the relationship between cultural background and cognitive styles. The investigation of learning styles and learning preferences in relation to teaching styles and student achievement is becoming an important area in education and has implications in areas such as teacher education, curriculum design, classroom instruction, teacher-student relationships, and student achievement.

Suggested Supplementary Readings

Classics:

Bloom, B. S. *The Taxonomy of Educational Objectives*. Longman, Green, 1954, Chapter 1.

Bruner, J. S. *The Process of Education*. Cambridge: Harvard University Press, 1959, Chapter 1.

Cohen, R. "Conceptual Styles, Culture Conflict, and Nonverbal Tests of Intelligence," *American Anthropologist*, 1969, 71, 826–856.

Dressel, P. *The Meaning and Significance of Integration*. National Society for the Study of Education, 57th Yearbook, Integration of Educational Experiences. Chicago: University of Chicago Press, 1958.

Pace, C. R. *Educational Objectives*. National Society for the Study of Education, 57th Yearbook, Part III. Chicago: University of Chicago Press, 1958, Chapter 4.

Tyler, R. W. *Basic Principles of Curriculum Development*. Chicago: University of Chicago Press, 1950.

Contemporary:

Bensimon, E. M. (ed.) *Multicultural Teaching and Learning: Strategies for Change in Higher Education*. State College, PA: National Center on Postsecondary Teaching, Learning, & Assessment, 1994.

Carbo, M. "Research in Learning Styles and Reading: Implications for Instruction," *Theory Into Practice, 23,* 1, 1985, 72–76.

Carby, J. V. "The Multicultural Wars," *Radical History Review, 54,* 7–18, 1992.

Dunn, R. "Learning Style: State of the Science." *Theory Into Practice,* 1985, 23, 1, 10–19.

Dunn, R., Beaudry, J., & Klavas, A. "Survey of Research on Learning Styles," *Educational Leadership,* 1989, 46, 6, 50–58.

Dunn, R., Dunn, K., & Price, G. *Learning Styles Inventory.* Lawrence, KA: Price Systems, 1985.

Dirksen, C. "Learning Styles of Mainland Chinese Studying English," *ELIC Teaching,* 1988, *1,* 1, 9–20.

Frederick, P. "Walking on Eggs: The Dreaded Diversity Discussion," *College Teaching,* 1995.

Keefe, J. W. *Student Learning Styles: Diagnosing and Prescribing Programs.* Reston, VA: National Association of Secondary Principals, 1979.

Kolb, D. A. "Experiential Learning Theory and the Learning Style Inventory: A Reply to Freedman and Stumpf," *Academy of Management Review,* 1981, *6,* 2, 289–296.

Perry, R. P., & J. C. Smart. *Effective Teaching in Higher Education: Research and Practice.* New York: Agathon Press, 1997.

Ramirez III, M., & Castaneda, A. *Cultural Democracy, Cognitive Development and Education.* New York: Academic Press, 1974.

Reid, J. "The Learning Style Preferences of ESL Students," *TESOL Quarterly,* 1987, 21, 1, 87–111.

Shade, B. "Afro-American Cognitive Styles: A Variable in School Success?" *Review of Educational Research,* 1982, 52, 2, 219–244.

Schoem, D., Frankel, L., Zuniga, X., & Lewis, E. A. *Multicultural Teaching in the University.* Westport, CT: Praeger, 1993.

Sy, B. M. "Perceptual Learning Style Preference of English Department Students," *Studies in Foreign Language Teaching,* 1991, *1,* 1, 89–112.

Tierney, W. B. *Building Communities of Difference: Higher Education in the Twenty-first Century.* Westport, CT: Bergin & Garvey, 1993.

Witkin, H. A. "Cognitive Styles in Learning and Teaching," in S. Messick and Associates (eds.), *Individuality in Learning.* San Francisco, CA: Jossey-Bass, Inc., 1976

The Classroom as a Negotiated Social Setting: An Empirical Study of the Effects of Faculty Members' Behavior on Students' Participation

CAROL J. AUSTER AND MINDY MACRONE

In the last two decades, many articles have focused on the role of students' participation in the learning process. While some writers lament that student participation is waning, others point to the importance of engaging students in active learning and offer strategies for increasing their involvement in the classroom (Barnes 1979; Billson 1986; Browne and Litwin 1987; Gimenez 1989; Hamlin and Janssen 1987; Holtz 1989; Rau and Heyl 1990; Wright 1989; Wright and Kane 1991). Despite this extensive literature, however, we have surprisingly little systematically collected empirical data on the impact of faculty members' behavior on students' participation; many of the strategies suggested for increasing students' participation are based only on anecdotal evidence. In this paper we examine empirically the effects of professors' behavior in the classroom on the level of students' participation and also look at similarities and differences between female and male faculty members. We also explore several other factors that may affect the level of student participation, including the student's gender.

Background

Although an increasing number of faculty members believe that participation is very important for students, the definition of student participation is somewhat elusive. For most faculty members, class participation consists of asking and answering questions, and participating in discussions or debate, but it is much more difficult to operationalize the quality of participation and its subsequent value to the student participant. If the predominant goal of participation is to engage students in the intellectual materials—to allow them to meet the ideas on their own terms—then the effect of the participation does not matter for anyone but the student who is participating. Because of the difficulties associated with defining and then measuring the self-reported quality of students' participation, we have limited this study to an examination of the factors that enhance the quantity of participation. Nevertheless, we assume that where the quantity of participation is high, it is more likely that the quality, however it is defined, also might be enhanced as a student asks and responds to questions and tries out new ideas.

One difficulty with a quantitative definition is that students may differ both in their motivations to participate in the classroom and in the strategies they use to communicate. These strategies, in turn, may affect even the quantity of participation. A number of studies, mostly observational, have shown that men are more likely than women to participate in class (French 1984; Graddol and Swann 1989; Hall and Sandler 1982; Karp and Yoels 1976; O'Keefe and Fampel 1987; Spender 1981; Sternglanz and Lyberger-Ficek 1977).

A number of explanations that focus on differences between women's and men's communication styles help to interpret these findings. Some observers describe our educational system as masculine because intellectual

"The Classroom as a Negotiated Social Setting: An Empirical Study of the Effects of Faculty Members' Behavior on Students' Participation," by Carol J. Auster and Mindy MacRone, reprinted from *Teaching Sociology*, Vol. 22, October 1994, American Sociological Association.

exchange occurs as a public display, followed by argument and challenge (Hall and Sandler 1982). Men may be comfortable with this type of environment, but many women would rather not break their classmates' consensus and choose instead to remain silent. This point seems consistent with Tannen's (1990) argument that men and women differ fundamentally in their use of language: men are more likely to use language to gain power, while women are more likely to use it to gain intimacy. Women also offer more positive reinforcement than men to keep the conversation going in mixed-sex groups (DeVault 1990; Fishman 1978; West 1988; West and Zimmerman 1977). Numerous studies also have pointed to women's use of tag questions; such questions may be precisely the cues a student listener needs as encouragement to move from the role of potential participant to that of participant. Tannen (1990) also notes that women provide more listener noise, such as "mm-mm" and "uh-huh". The listener noise provided by a faculty member may encourage the already participating student to elaborate further on his or her ideas.

In short, empirical studies have noted that women's and men's verbal and nonverbal communication typically differ in both content and style. Although women's communication style is often devalued in the public sphere, some studies have found more discussion and participation in classes taught by women (Brooks 1982; Constantinople, Cornelius, and Gray 1988; Crawford and MacLeod 1990). Women's typical communication style, however, may encourage students to participate in the classroom, regardless of the faculty member's gender (Hall and Sandler 1982).

Role theory offers a logical explanation for this possibility. The Lintonian model (Linton 1936:113–15) distinguishes between status and role. Whereas the status of being a teacher or a student in the classroom defines one's position in that particular social system, it is the role—the expected behavior of each party—that brings insight here. By virtue of their status, teachers have more power than students over a variety of aspects of the class, including the syllabus, materials discussed in class, methods of evaluation, and students' grades. Students may feel unimportant in the creation and sharing of knowledge because of the hierarchical relation-

ship and the implied power imbalance; the imbalance often is reinforced by high school experiences. Evidence from case studies of employees' participation shows that they believe most strongly in the importance of their views when they have been accorded a formal place in the governance of the workplace (Zwerdling 1980). Yet the normative expectations about the power imbalance between teachers and students may cause students to believe that their role is to be the passive recipient of the teacher's knowledge; the lecture format only reinforces this expected role.

Despite normative expectations, roles in an actual social relationship are negotiated as each party responds to the role performance of the other (Goffman 1961:85). Karp and Yoels point out that "students and teachers formulate definitions of the classroom as a social setting" (1975:423). Goffman's classic example of the surgeon (1961:115–32) illustrates that the surgical team works most effectively when the surgeon engages in *role distance* by not exploiting his or her full range of power over the other members of the surgical team. Likewise, the teacher who engages in role distance from the traditional definition of powerful and all-knowing scholar and instead assures students of the importance of their questions and ideas creates a social setting that would seem to encourage participation. Several sociologists underscore the importance of teaching so as to create a social structure that emphasizes and enhances the student's role in creating knowledge (Hamlin and Janssen 1987; Karp and Yoels 1976; Wright 1989). Although female students may be disadvantaged by using the women's style of everyday conversation in the classroom, teachers who employ this style may display the role distance that encourages students' efficacy and participation because the style also is associated with groups lacking power (Fishman 1978; Hall and Sandler 1982; Lakoff 1975, 1990). Although Johnson (1994) found that authority predicted conversational patterns more accurately than gender, we believe that the autonomy and flexibility of the college teacher's role allows gender to have a greater effect.

Despite the apparent differences between female and male students' participation, previous survey research on classroom interaction and participation appears problematic because researchers employed one of two different methods. Some researchers asked students to respond to questions in a general sense (for example, see Heller, Puff, and Mills 1985), typically prefacing each question by "In general..." or "In your overall college experience..." We did not want to ask students broad questions about their overall college experience because we were interested in discovering why participation varies from one class to another, not why one student participates more or less than another. Other researchers used a method that was too class-specific in that questions about a specific class were asked while the student was sitting in that class (Boersma et al. 1981; Crawford and MacLeod 1990; Karp and Yoels 1976). Moreover, the students may have been affected by responding while they were in the classroom; students who might have rated the classroom very low on personal interaction might not have been included in the survey because they were less likely to come to class; or perceptions of the class might have been affected unduly by recent feedback from the professor. Still other researchers measured students' satisfaction, grades, networks, or critical thinking skills (Hamlin and Janssen 1987; Rau and Heyl 1990; Shepelak, Curry-Jackson, and Moore 1992; Wilson and Reiser 1982) rather than participation. In short, the methodological shortcomings of previous studies pointed to the need for a new method of questioning students about the effect of faculty behavior on their participation.

Methodology

In the fall of 1992, students in our research methods course constructed a questionnaire on various aspects of social and academic life. In the section on academic life, we included questions allowing us to explore factors that might affect class participation. Because this research was conducted in a research methods class, we made some methodological choices on the basis of their perceived value to learning. For example, we asked students to construct predominantly closed-ended questions for their survey instrument. Although the resulting questionnaire could have been self-administered, the students were required to conduct

face-to-face interviews, using the questionnaire, in order to have that experience. A systematic random sample of 132 students was taken from the approximately 1,800 enrolled at this private liberal arts college. Each of the 22 students in the research methods class then was assigned to interview six respondents.

To overcome the methodological difficulties described earlier, we tried a unique approach. First, we asked respondents to think of the class in which they participated most in the current semester and to answer questions concerning that class. Then we asked respondents to think of the class in which they participated least during the current semester and to answer the same questions. Obviously, the courses chosen by the student are those in which they *perceive* that they are participating the most and the least; we have no independent measures of whether these were actually the courses in which they did so. For example, their perception of themselves may have been influenced by the level of participation by the other students in the class. Thus, our study consists of students' reports on the courses in which *they* believe they participated most and least. Although restricting the questions to the current semester limited the number of courses from which students could choose, we believed that asking only about courses they were taking in that semester would increase the reliability of their responses about faculty members' behavior in those classes.

We used a variety of measures of the interactional aspects of the class. Respondents were asked about the frequency with which the faculty member engaged in such behaviors as calling on the student when he or she volunteered; calling on the student by name; nodding, smiling, and generally communicating interest in what the student said; encouraging the student to elaborate on his or her answers; and giving the student reasonable time to answer a question before going on to another student. These questions were variations on some questions used by Heller et al. (1985), who developed their questions from Hall and Sandler's (1982) list of behaviors that may enhance or inhibit women's participation. For this study, we developed three additional questions about the following behaviors: asking factual questions; asking questions which are analytical, such as applying concepts that the student had learned; and calling on the student when he or she has not volunteered.

All of the questions were asked in the following form: "How often does the professor call on you by name?" or "How often does the professor encourage you to elaborate on answers you have given?" We used *you* (e.g., "call on you by name") to increase the reliability of responses. We thought that respondents would remember more clearly what had happened to them than to other members of the class. The possible responses to these questions about behavior were "often," "sometimes," "rarely," and "never."

Although the chi-squares reported in the data analysis section are calculated on the basis of all four responses, we chose to focus on the percentage of students responding "often." We believed that if faculty members' interactional behavior reflects their perception of the role expected of students, then they send the clearest message when they engage in particular behaviors with noticeable regularity—that is, often. We did not use a measure of central tendency because the mean and the median could have represented quite different arrays of responses.

We recognize that because we have no independent observations of the faculty members' behavior, the reported frequency with which faculty members engaged in these behaviors is based only on the respondents' perception and reporting of such behaviors. The possible discrepancy between students' perception of faculty members' behavior and faculty members' actual behavior also has been acknowledged by those interested in the evaluation of teaching effectiveness (Centra 1979; McKeachie 1979; Scheetz 198; Seldin 1984).

We hypothesized that the presence of each behavior would indicate distance from the traditional role and would result in the creation of the classroom as a social setting, which would encourage students' participation. These behaviors presumably would increase students' efficacy by showing them the importance of their questions ideas, and knowledge. For example, giving a student time to answer before calling on another student and encouraging elaboration would show the student the importance of his or her response, particularly

because the teacher, in the process of doing this, is giving up his or her own time to talk.

We believed that questions about the different behaviors by faculty members would provide insight into the role of the interactional aspects of teaching in shaping students' participation, but we recognized that other factors might also play a role. Because much of the literature on communication addresses gender issues, we will carefully examine the relationship of both the professor's gender and the student's gender to class participation.

Results

Faculty Members' Behavior

With the above hypotheses in mind, we first compared the behavior of professors in classes in which students said they participated the most (hereafter called MOST) with the behavior of professors in classes in which students said they participated the least (hereafter called LEAST). We hoped that we would be able to characterize the behavior of faculty members in the classes in which students participated most. In the three tables provided here, which describe the characteristics of the MOST and the LEAST courses, the findings are based on the approximately 260 courses (130 MOST and 130 LEAST) mentioned by the 130 respondents.

Table 1 shows that for seven of eight measures of faculty behavior, a significantly larger percentage of students reported that faculty members engaged *often* in these behaviors in the MOST class than in the LEAST class. For example, about 85 percent of students reported that the professor called on them often when they volunteered and called on them by name in the MOST course; only about 40 percent reported that the professor engaged often in these behaviors in the LEAST course. The only measure that was not significant was "asking factual questions."

Effects of the professor's gender. We then examined the impact of faculty member's gender on participation. Of the classes mentioned, courses taught by men were somewhat more likely to be mentioned as LEAST (56.9%) than as MOST (43.1%). Conversely, women's courses were much more likely to be mentioned as MOST (65.4%) than as LEAST (34.6%). The differences between courses taught by women and

TABLE 1
Faculty Members' Behavior in the Classes in Which Students Participate Most and Least,
Percentages Reporting "Often"

| Faculty Behavior | Students' Level of Participation | | |
	Most	Least	Significance
Calls On When Student Volunteers	86.7	41.9	.001
Calls On by Name	86.7	36.7	.001
Shows Signs of Approval/Interest	69.3	33.3	.001
Encourages Elaboration	58.7	21.9	.001
Gives Enough Time to Answer	81.3	49.5	.001
Asks Factual Questions	54.7	47.5	ns
Asks Analytic Questions	78.7	36.7	.001
Calls On When Student Does Not Volunteer	14.7	3.1	.001

by men were significant (x^2=11.02, df=1, $p<.001$). Interestingly, the female students' response was nearly identical to the male students' response. What quality in women professors' classes enhances participation? Is it simply their gender, or is it their behavior and interaction with students?

Next we examined the frequency of interactional behaviors in the respondents' MOST class by the gender of the faculty member teaching the class. For seven of the eight measures, we found no significant differences in the reported behavior of male and female professors for the MOST course. The exception was that men (78.7%) were significantly (x^2=12.96, df=3, $p<.005$) more likely than women (52.8%) to be reported as often asking analytic questions. Then we looked at the differences between female and male faculty members for the LEAST course. For six out of eight variables, we found no significant differences between women and men. On the other hand, women (64.3%) were significantly (x^2=9.51, df=3, $p<.03$) more likely than men (36.7%) to be reported as often calling on students by name and encouraging them to elaborate on answers (x^2= 11.95, df=3, $p<.008$), even in the LEAST class. Also, for several other variables such as showing signs of approval, for which the differences were not significant, a larger percentage of respondents reported that women (57.1%) engaged much more often in the behavior than men (33.3%). Thus, although behavior characterizing the class in which students participate MOST appears to be evident, women frequently are described as engaging often in some of these behaviors even in a course in which a student reports that he or she participated least.

We also wanted to test for significant differences between the MOST and the LEAST course for each gender. That is, we wondered whether male faculty members' behavior was reported to be similar or different for the students' reported MOST and LEAST courses; we wondered the same about females. The comparison of the behavior of male professors in the MOST and the LEAST courses shows significant differences for seven of the eight measures (see Table 2). Not surprisingly, a greater percentage of students reported that male professors engaged often in the behaviors thought to encourage participation in the MOST course than in the LEAST course. The only exception was asking factual questions. The comparison of women faculty yielded somewhat different results. As in the case of the men, students were significantly more likely to report that women called on students when they volunteered, gave students enough time to answer, and called on students when they did not volunteer more often in the MOST course than in the LEAST course. Also, as with the men, we found no significant differences between the frequencies with which women faculty asked factual questions in the MOST and the LEAST courses. Unlike the findings for the men, there were some differences on the four remaining measures, but these differences were not significant. For example, the percentages of students reporting that women often encouraged students to elaborate on their answers were nearly equal in the MOST and the LEAST classes.

In summary, the results suggest that the faculty member's gender per se does not matter, but rather that certain behaviors encourage participation, regardless of who is engaging in

TABLE 2
A Comparison of Faculty Behavior in MOST and LEAST Courses, Controlling for Faculty Member's Gender,
Percentages Reporting "Often"

Faculty Behavior	Most	Men Least	Significance	Most	Women Least	Significance
Calls On When Student Volunteers	85.3	41.9	.001	81.1	46.4	.004
Calls On by Name	86.7	36.7	.001	79.2	64.3	ns
Shows Signs of Approval/Interest	69.3	33.3	.001	71.7	57.1	ns
Encourages Elaboration	58.7	21.9	.001	58.5	53.6	ns
Gives Enough Time to Answer	81.3	49.5	.001	92.5	53.8	.001
Asks Factual Questions	54.7	47.5	ns	50.0	67.9	ns
Asks Analytic Questions	78.7	36.7	.001	52.8	51.1	ns
Calls On When Student Does Not Volunteer	14.7	3.1	.001	15.1	3.6	.03

those behaviors. Nevertheless female faculty members are perceived as continuing to engage often, in both the MOST and the LEAST courses, in some of the behaviors that we hypothesized encouraged participation.

Characteristics of Students

Effect of student gender on the level of participation and comfort. Although the above discussion has focused on specific faculty behaviors in the classroom, some variation in students' behavior may be due to characteristics of students, such as gender or year in college. In addition to the eight measures of faculty behavior discussed above, students were asked two questions without regard to a specific class: 1) "On the average, how frequently do you actively participate by asking questions or offering comments in class?" The possible responses were "often," "sometimes," "rarely," and "never." For the purposes of analysis, we combined the three latter responses so that we could focus on "often," the most frequent behavior. Students also were asked, "In general, how do you feel about making contributions in class?" The possible responses were "very comfortable," "somewhat comfortable," "somewhat uncomfortable," and "very uncomfortable." Here, we combined the latter three responses because only eight men responded in the two "uncomfortable" categories. This particular recoding also allowed us to compare

those who were most comfortable with those who were less comfortable.

Male students (58.1%) were significantly (x^2=6.26, df=1, p<.05) more likely than female students (36.3%) to report participating often in class. This pattern persisted when we controlled for college year, even though the differences between women and men were not significant. Although participation generally increased somewhat from the first year to the senior year, the differences for men and for women were not significant.

One factor that may affect participation is the extent to which the student feels comfortable in class. For both men and women, the degree of comfort had a significant impact on the level of participation. Not surprisingly, students who felt *very* comfortable making contributions in class were significantly more likely to participate often than those who were less than very comfortable. We then examined the level of comfort by gender. As with participation, men (46.8%) were significantly (x^2=9.18, df=1, p<.005) more likely than women (21.7%) to feel very comfortable. In addition, the percentages of both men and women reporting that they felt very comfortable making contributions increased with college year. Although differences by college year were not significant for men, they were so for women. For the first three years of college, men were much more likely than women to be very comfortable making contributions in class, but only the difference between junior men and junior women

TABLE 3
Perceptions of Faculty Behavior in MOST and LEAST Courses, Student's Gender, Percentages Reporting "Often"

Faculty Behavior	Most	Men Least	Significance	Most	Women Least	Significance
Calls On When Student Volunteers	85.2	44.8	.001	82.6	41.5	.001
Calls On by Name	78.7	39.0	.001	88.4	44.9	.001
Shows Signs of Approval/ Interest	62.3	37.3	.03	76.8	40.3	.001
Encourages Elaboration	59.0	27.1	.001	58.0	32.8	.001
Gives Enough Time to Answer	86.9	49.2	.001	85.5	53.0	.001
Asks Factual Questions	54.1	50.0	ns	50.0	53.6	ns
Asks Analytic Questions	73.8	45.8	.001	63.8	37.7	.007
Calls On When Student Does Not Volunteer	8.2	3.4	.002	20.3	2.9	.001

was significant. Finally, by the senior year, women and men were nearly equally likely to report feeling very comfortable making contributions in class.

Effect of students' gender on perceptions of faculty members' behavior. In our study, male students reported participating more and feeling more comfortable than female students. As a result of these findings, we wondered whether women and men made similar or different reports of faculty members' behavior in the courses in which they participated most and least. Because much has been written about women's and men's different styles and the classroom climate, we wondered whether the faculty behavior that promotes students' participation would be different for female and male students.

First we examined students' reporting of faculty behavior in their MOST and LEAST courses by student's gender. In the MOST class, we found no significant differences between men and women for seven of eight variables. This result would suggest that female and male students respond similarly to faculty members' interactional attempts to increase participation. Yet, even though the differences were not significant, the women indicated more often than the men that for the MOST course, faculty members called on them by name and showed signs of interest and approval. On the other hand, men reported more often that faculty members

asked analytical questions. These findings, however, could reflect selective perception rather than a difference in reality. Are female students more sensitive to the personal feedback and the cues of professors attempting to increase participation, or did faculty members actually engage in these behaviors more often with women than with men? Likewise, did faculty members ask male students analytical questions more often, or are male students more sharply attuned to such requests for participation? In addition, 20.3 percent of the women (x^2=12.47, df=3, $p<.006$) reported that the faculty members in the MOST course called on them when they had not volunteered; this was true for only 8.2 percent of the men. On the other hand, for the LEAST class, we found no significant differences between the responses of female and male students.

Table 3 shows differences between the MOST and the LEAST class by the student's gender so that within-gender differences could be tested. The frequency with which professors ask factual questions was not significant for either female or male students. On the other hand, for students of both genders, we found significant differences between the MOST and the LEAST class for the other seven variables. In each case, the pattern was the same: The percentage of students reporting that faculty members engaged often in these behaviors was higher for the MOST class. This finding reinforces the notion that with the exception of asking factual questions, the other behaviors promote class participation regardless of the student's gender.

Effect of Class Size on Perceived Behavior by Faculty Members

Crawford and MacLeod (1990) found that smaller classes were more participatory than larger classes. Although our range of class sizes was small (10 or fewer students to 40 or more), MOST classes were significantly ($x2=36.8$, df=4, $p<.001$) more likely than LEAST classes to be small. For example, 87.0 percent of classes with ten or fewer students were designated as the MOST course, in contrast to only 33.3 percent of classes with more than 40 students. If small classes are more likely to be designated as a MOST course, what quality in the larger classes causes some of them also to be named as a MOST course? We then hypothesized that even in larger classes, faculty members engage often in the eight behaviors that appear to increase participation. The differences in reported faculty behavior by the size of the class were not significant for the MOST course. This finding suggests either that professors teaching the large MOST courses were nearly as likely as professors teaching the small MOST courses to engage in these behaviors, or that the range of variation for class size was too small to produce differences. Nevertheless, faculty members teaching the large MOST courses (40 or more students) were more likely than those teaching the small MOST courses to call on students when they had not volunteered. This point suggests that some teachers with large classes use this strategy in an effort to induce students to participate.

Discussion and Conclusion

Faculty members point to the importance of students' participation in class as a way of engaging them in both the subject matter and the intellectual ideas associated with the course. They also believe that the process of learning how to think critically and express ideas has lasting importance for students' intellectual and personal growth. Yet with the exception of the literature on sexual harass-

ment and the "chilly climate" for women, few empirically sound studies have been conducted to examine how specific behaviors by faculty members affect the level of students' participation. The sheer quantity of participation does not guarantee the desired outcomes in the quality of thinking and communicating. As the quantity of participation increases, however, the chances that a student will be comfortable in making additional contributions should increase. In view of the strong link between comfort in making contributions and the level of participation found in this study, greater comfort may increase the student's willingness to try out new ideas and take intellectual risks.

Although many aspects of the communication style typically associated with women (such as listener noise and positive reinforcement to keep a conversation going) have been devalued in the public sphere, classroom behaviors that paralleled these aspects elicited more participation. These behaviors also may show a role distance from the teacher's power; such role distance could create a social setting that enhances student participation. By comparing reported faculty behavior in the MOST classes with that in the LEAST classes, we gained insight into the type of classroom climate that is conducive to participation. Students' participation could be enhanced if faculty members would *often* 1) call on students when they volunteer, and call them by name; 2) provide positive reinforcement in the form of encouragement and approval; 3) ask analytical (not factual) questions and provide students ample time to answer; and 4) ask for students' opinions even when they do not volunteer. In the LEAST course, faculty members reportedly engaged in these behaviors; in the MOST course, however, a much greater percentage of students reported that faculty engaged *often* in these behaviors. This finding reinforces the notion that faculty members must engage in these behaviors regularly, not only on occasion. Regularly engaging in these behaviors helps students understand more clearly their expected role in this negotiated social setting. In addition, because asking factual questions only reinforces the notion of the teacher as all-knowing and is least likely to elicit the critical thinking that faculty members desire, it is not surprising that asking factual questions would be the one measure which did not produce significant differences.

Because so much of the literature on communication has focused on differences between women and men, we wondered whether the professor's gender influenced participation. The literature suggests that women typically engage in many subtle and not-so-subtle behaviors which call for a response by the listener. Possibly these same behaviors also increase students' participation in the classroom. Although female professors' courses were more likely than male professors' courses to be designated as MOST, controlling for the faculty member's gender showed that participation was affected not by gender per se, but rather by how often the faculty member reportedly engaged in the behavior with the respondent. Because women also engaged frequently in some of these behaviors in the LEAST courses, it becomes more difficult to identify the behavior of women faculty members which distinguishes a MOST course from a LEAST course. For male faculty, engaging in behaviors that parallel women's typical communication patterns increases students' participation. Perhaps women faculty not only should continue engaging in "feminine" behaviors, but also should engage more often in interactional behavior typically associated with male faculty, such as asking analytical questions. The suggestions for men and women faculty presume that the students' reporting of the frequency of these behaviors represents real differences, not merely differences in perceptions colored by stereotyped gender expectations of faculty members.

Despite the gender differences between women's and men's communication styles as described in the literature, male and female students apparently respond positively and similarly to these interactional behaviors by faculty members. The only significant difference was that women reported being called on more often when they did not volunteer. Faculty members may be sensitive to women's greater silence in the classroom; suspecting that these silent women have ideas to contribute, faculty members may take the chance of calling on them to encourage their participation.

Although we presumed that the degree of comfort affects participation, we cannot be sure of the direction of the relationship between comfort and participation. It also may be that students become more comfortable making contributions as they participate more. In either case, women students' lower levels of comfort and participation suggest that the classroom climate may be less conducive to women's participation. During lectures or debates, students may be expected to attack readings or refute the opinions of others. If Tannen (1991) is right, this situation may appeal to male students because of their focus on power, but not appeal to female students because of their focus on intimacy and connection. Moreover, students of either gender who are not inclined to assert themselves may not feel comfortable participating. To create a classroom environment that is more conducive to participation by all students, faculty members must work on methods that downplay faculty power and encourage cooperation. This format is popular in many seminar classes, in which learning is a dynamic process whereby students are free to discuss new ideas, receive feedback from one another and the faculty member, and build new ideas together.

Findings by college year showed that both participation and comfort increased with years in college. Possibly these findings reflect the kinds of courses first- and second-year students take, namely larger courses needed to fill distribution requirements. Nevertheless, strategies that enhance comfort and increase participation early in a student's college career may increase comfort further; as a result, students should participate more throughout their college careers. Certainly, instituting a required seminar for first-year students should provide the intensive interactions with faculty members and other students that will encourage future participation outside that particular seminar.

Many educators have pointed to collaborative learning groups as another way to increase students' participation (McKinney and Graham-Buxton 1993; Petonito 1991; Rau and Heyl 1990). Although the student does not necessarily receive individual encouragement and feedback from the faculty member teaching the course, the use of collaborative learning groups may encourage active engagement with the subject matter and intellectual ideas in a particular course. On the other hand, because the students in these groups lack experience as teachers, they may not be providing the encouragement and feedback needed by their peers. Some students believe that their ideas are most valuable when the faculty member hears the ideas directly from the student and encourages elaboration. For such students, sharing ideas in the group may be a good starting place for participation, but they may desire and prefer a direct, immediate response to their ideas from the faculty member.

In general, our findings showed that the smaller the course, the more likely it was to be a course in which students reported participating most rather than least. Our study, however, is limited in two ways. First, we do not know whether the typical format of these classes was lecture, discussion, or some combination. Second, the largest classes at the college typically contain fewer than 50 students, still a relatively small number at many educational institutions. Therefore we know little about the effects of these faculty behaviors on classes of 100 or even 500 students. Nevertheless, our findings suggest that participation is encouraged by the frequency with which the faculty member engages in the behavior with each student. Classes with an enrollment of more than 100 students present a challenge that cannot be overcome without additional efforts by professors. Collaborative learning groups may be one answer; the smaller precepts, recitations, and discussion groups required of undergraduate students and taught by graduate students have the potential to offer some of the most active engagement with course materials. Because graduate students usually lead these smaller sections, they will need formal training in the strategies for increasing both the quantity and the quality of students' participation to be effective.

It would also have been interesting to examine the effect of discipline or subject area. Perhaps the subject matter of some courses lends itself more easily to participation by students. In this study we could not explore disciplinary differences because the 260 courses in the analysis represented nearly 30 departments; thus the number of students mentioning any particular department was too small for analysis. We considered conducting the analysis by division (humanities, social sciences, sciences), but the courses within each division seemed too diverse. Also, we would have had to compare the percentages of students reporting courses as MOST and LEAST to actual course enrollments in each division, and these enrollments were not available to us.

In this study, we have focused predominantly on a few faculty behaviors that we thought might enhance students' participation in the classroom. Future empirical studies might focus on additional behaviors thought to enhance participation as well as on faculty behaviors thought to inhibit participation, to test whether they truly have that effect. Moreover, the impact of the physical setting and the arrangement of the class should be considered. This is the case particularly because they offer clues to students about teachers' expectations of teacher/student roles and interaction, including the extent to which the teachers may wish to embrace or relinquish (as in role distance) the power associated with their position. Other researchers may want to study the effect of student characteristics such as age or race/ethnicity, particularly when such characteristics make students tokens in the classroom. In addition, particular personality traits of students may make them more or less likely to participate regardless of faculty behavior. This study circumvents the need for knowing about such traits by asking about the courses in which the student participated most and least, regardless of the actual level of participation. Also, it would be interesting to examine whether factors such as the reason for taking the course, expected grade in the course, subject area, and previous courses with the faculty member have any effect. Finally we must address the very difficult task of finding a way to measure the impact of faculty members' behavior and these other factors on the *quality* of participation to learn whether the increase in participation is fulfilling the goal of increasing students' critical thinking and communication skills.

In the meantime, we suggest that faculty members familiarize themselves with the existing empirical research on factors which enhance participation and that they be sensitive to the ways in which their behavior can affect students' participation. If they do so, they might be more willing to engage consciously in interactional behaviors that promote students' participation, and might worry less about how many windows there will be in their classroom next semester.

References

Barnes, Patricia W. 1979. "Leading Discussions." Pp. 62–100 in *On College Teaching*, edited by Ohmer Milton. San Francisco: Jossey-Bass.

Billson, Janet M. 1986. "The College Classroom as a Small Group: Some Implications for Teaching and Learning." *Teaching Sociology* 14:143–51.

Boersma, P. Dee, Debora Gay, Ruth A. Jones, Lynn Morrison, and Helen Remick. 1981. "Sex Differences in College Student–Teacher Interaction: Fact or Fantasy?" *Sex Roles* 7:775–84.

Brooks, Virginia R.1982. "Sex Differences in Student Dominance Behavior in Female and Male Professors' Classrooms." *Sex Roles* 8:683–90.

Browne, M. Neil and James L. Litwin. 1987. "Critical Thinking in the College Classroom: Facilitating Movement from Vague Objective to Explicit Achievement. " *Teaching Sociology* 15:384–91

Centra, John A. 1979. *Determining Faculty Effectiveness: Assessing Teaching, Research. and Service for Personnel Decisions and Improvement*. San Francisco: Jossey-Bass.

Constantinople, Anne, Randolph Cornelius, and Janet Gray. 1988. "The Chilly Climate: Fact or Artifact?" *Journal of Higher Education* 59:527–50.

Crawford, Mary and Margo MacLeod. 1990. "Gender in the College Classroom: An Assessment of the 'Chilly Climate' for Women." *Sex Roles* 23:101–22.

DeVault, Marjorie L. 1990. "Talking and Listening from Women's Standpoint: Strategies for Interviewing and Analysis." *Social Problems* 37:96–116.

Fishman, Paula M. 1978. "Interaction: The Work Women Do." *Social Problems* 25:397–406.

French, Jane. 1984. "Gender Imbalance in the Primary Classroom: An Interactional Account." *Educational Research* 26: 127–36.

Gimenez, Martha E. 1989. "Silence in the Classroom: Some Thoughts about Teaching in the 1980s." *Teaching Sociology* 17:184–91.

Goffman, Erving. 1961. *Encounters: Two Studies in the Sociology of Interaction*. Indianapolis: Bobbs-Merrill.

Graddol, David and Joan Swann. 1989. *Gender Voices*. Cambridge, MA: Blackwell.

Hall, Roberta M. and Bernice Sandler. 1982. *The Classroom Climate: A Chilly One for Women*. Washington, DC: Association of American Colleges.

Hamlin, John and Susan Janssen. 1987. "Active Learning in Large Introductory Sociology Courses." *Teaching Sociology* 15:45–54.

Heller, Jack, C. Richard Puff, and Carol J. Mills. 1985. "Assessment of the Chilly College Climate for Women." *Journal of Higher Education* 56:446–61.

Holtz, Harvey. 1989. "Action in Place of Silence: A Response to Gimenez." *Teaching Sociology* 17:192–93

Johnson, Cathryn. 1994. "Gender, Legitimate Authority, and Leader-Subordinate Conversations." *American Sociological Review* 59: 122–35.

Karp, David A. and William C. Yoels. 1976. "The College Classroom: Some Observations on the Meaning of Student Participation." *Sociology and Social Research* 60:421–39.

Lakoff, Robin. 1975. *Language and Women's Place*. New York: Harper and Row.

_____. 1990. *Talking Power: The Politics of Language in Our Lives*. New York: Basic Books.

Linton, Ralph. 1936. *The Study of Man*. New York: Appleton-Century-Crofts.

McKeachie, Wilbert J. 1979. "Student Ratings of Faculty: A Reprise." *Academe* 65:384–97.

McKinney, Kathleen and Mary Graham-Buxton. 1993. "The Use of Collaborative Learning Groups in the Large Class: Is It Possible?" *Teaching Sociology* 21:403–408.

O'Keefe, Tim F. and Charles E. Fampel. 1987. "The Other Face of the Classroom: A Student Ethnography." *Sociological Spectrum* 7:141–55.

Petonito, Gina. 1991. "Fostering Peer Learning in the College Classroom." *Teaching Sociology* 19:498–501.

Rau, William and Barbara Sherman Heyl. 1990. "Humanizing the College Classroom: Collaborative Learning and Social Organization among Students." *Teaching Sociology* 18:141–55.

Scheetz, James P. 1986. "Some Perspectives on the Use of Student Ratings to Evaluate Teaching Effectiveness." *Professions Education Research Notes* 8:4–7.

Seldin, Peter. 1984. *Changing Practices in Faculty Evaluation*. San Francisco: Jossey-Bass.

Shepelak, Norma J., Anita Curry-Jackson, and Vernon L. Moore. 1992. "Critical Thinking in Introductory Sociology Classes: A Program of Implementation and Evaluation." *Teaching Sociology* 20: 18–27.

Spender, Dale. 1981. *Invisible Women: The Schooling Scandal*. London: Writers and Readers Publishing Cooperative.

Sternglanz, Sarah H. and Shirley Lyberger-Ficek. 1977. "Sex Differences in Student-Teacher Interactions in the College Classroom." *Sex Roles* 3:345–52.

Tannen, Deborah. 1990. *You Just Don't Understand: Women and Men in Conversation*. New York: Ballantine.

_____. 1991. "Teacher's Classroom Strategies Should Recognize That Men and Women Use Language Differently." *The Chronicle of Higher Education*. June 19, pp. B1–B3.

West, Candace. 1988. "Conversational Shift Work: A Study of Topical Transitions between Women and Men." *Social Problems* 35:551–75.

West, Candace and Don H. Zimmerman. 1977 "Women's Place in Everyday Talk: Reflections on Parent-Child Interaction." *Social Problems* 24:521–29.

Wilson, Kenneth and Christa Reiser. 1982. "An 'Active' Introduction to Sociology." *Teaching Sociology* 9:273–90.

Wright, Richard A.1989. "Toward a Theoretical Conception of 'Silence in the Classroom': A Response to Gimenez." *Teaching Sociology* 17:194–96.

Wright, Richard A. and Catherine C. Kane. 1991. "'Women Speak This Week': Promoting Gender Equality and Awareness in Class Discussions." *Teaching Sociology* 19:472–76.

Zwerdling, Daniel. 1980. *Workplace Democracy.* New York: Harper and Row.

Carol J. Auster is an associate professor of sociology at Franklin and Marshall College. Her research interests are gender and occupations. She is currently conducting a large-scale, longitudinal study of women and men in engineering funded by the Alfred P. Sloan Foundation. She is also working on a text/reader in work and occupations and an empirical study of ethics in the academic profession. Address correspondence to the author at Department of Sociology, Franklin and Marshall College, Lancaster, PA 17604-3003.

Mindy MacRone graduated cum laude with a B.A. in sociology from Franklin and Marshall College in 1993. She was elected to Phi Beta Kappa and Alpha Kappa Delta. She was also the 1993 recipient of the William M. Kephart Award for excellence in sociology. She is currently pursuing a Master's Degree in occupational therapy at Thomas Jefferson University.

From Teaching to Learning—A New Paradigm for Undergraduate Education

ROBERT B. BARR AND JOHN TAGG

The significant problems we face cannot be solved at the same level of thinking we were at when we created them.

—Albert Einstein

A paradigm shift is taking hold in American higher education. In its briefest form, the paradigm that has governed our colleges is this: A college is an institution that exists *to provide instruction.* Subtly but profoundly we are shifting to a new paradigm: A college is an institution that exists *to produce learning.* This shift changes everything. It is both needed and wanted.

We call the traditional, dominant paradigm the "Instruction Paradigm." Under it, colleges have created complex structures to provide for the activity of teaching conceived primarily as delivering 50-minute lectures—the mission of a college is to deliver instruction.

Now, however, we are beginning to recognize that our dominant paradigm mistakes a means for an end. It takes the means or method—called "instruction" or "teaching"—and makes it the college's end or purpose. To say that the purpose of colleges is to provide instruction is like saying that General Motors' business is to operate assembly lines or that the purpose of medical care is to fill hospital beds. We now see that our mission is not instruction but rather that of producing *learning* with every student by *whatever* means work best.

The shift to a "Learning Paradigm" liberates institutions from a set of difficult constraints. Today it is virtually impossible for them to respond effectively to the challenge of stable or declining budgets while meeting the increasing demand for postsecondary education from increasingly diverse students. Under the logic of the Instruction Paradigm, colleges suffer from a serious design flaw: it is not possible to increase outputs without a corresponding increase in costs, because any attempt to increase outputs without increasing resources is a threat to quality. If a college attempts to increase its productivity by increasing either class sizes or faculty workloads, for example, academics will be quick to assume inexorable negative consequences for educational quality.

Just as importantly, the Instruction Paradigm rests on conceptions of teaching that are increasingly recognized as ineffective. As Alan Guskin pointed out in a September/October 1994 *Change* article premised on the shift from teaching to learning, "the primary learning environment for undergraduate students, the fairly passive lecture-discussion format where faculty talk and most students listen, is contrary to almost every principle of optimal settings for student learning." The Learning Paradigm ends the lecture's privileged position, honoring in its place whatever approaches serve best to prompt learning of particular knowledge by particular students.

The Learning Paradigm also opens up the truly inspiring goal that each graduating class learns more than the previous graduating class. In other words, the Learning Paradigm envisions the institution itself as a learner—over time, it continuously learns how to produce more learning with each graduating class, each entering student.

For many of us, the Learning Paradigm has always lived in our hearts. As teachers, we

"From Teaching to Learning—A New Paradigm for Undergraduate Education," by Robert B. Barr and John Tagg, reprinted from *Change*, Vol. 27, No. 5, November/December 1995, Heldref Publications.

want above all else for our students to learn and succeed. But the heart's feeling has not lived clearly and powerfully in our heads. Now, as the elements of the Learning Paradigm permeate the air, our heads are beginning to understand what our hearts have known. However, none of us has yet put all the elements of the Learning Paradigm together in a conscious, integrated whole.

Lacking such a vision, we've witnessed reformers advocate many of the new paradigm's elements over the years, only to see few of them widely adopted. The reason is that they have been applied piecemeal within the structures of a dominant paradigm that rejects or distorts them. Indeed, for two decades the response to calls for reform from national commissions and task forces generally has been an attempt to address the issues *within the framework of the Instruction Paradigm*. The movements thus generated have most often failed, undone by the contradictions within the traditional paradigm. For example, if students are not learning to solve problems or think critically, the old logic says we must teach a class in thinking and make it a general education requirement. The logic is all too circular: What students are learning in the classroom doesn't address their needs or ours; therefore, we must bring them back into another classroom and instruct them some more. The result is never what we hope for because, as Richard Paul, director of the Center for Critical Thinking observes glumly, "critical thinking is taught in the same way that other courses have traditionally been taught, with an excess of lecture and insufficient time for practice."

To see what the Instruction Paradigm is we need only look at the structures and behaviors of our colleges and infer the governing principles and beliefs they reflect. But it is much more difficult to see the Learning Paradigm, which has yet to find complete expression in the structures and processes of any college. So we must imagine it. This is what we propose to do here. As we outline its principles and elements, we'll suggest some of their implications for colleges—but only some, because the expression of principles in concrete structures depends on circumstances. It will take decades to work out many of the Learning Paradigm's implications. But we hope here that by making it more explicit we will help colleagues to more

fully recognize it and restructure our institutions in its image.

That such a restructuring is needed is beyond question: the gap between what we *say* we want of higher education and what its structures *provide* has never been wider. To use a distinction made by Chris Argyris and Donald Schön, the difference between our espoused theory and our theory-in-use is becoming distressingly noticeable. An "espoused theory," readers will recall, is the set of principles people offer to explain their behavior; the principles we can infer from how people or their organizations actually behave is their "theory-in-use." Right now, the Instruction Paradigm is our theory-in-use, yet the *espoused* theories of most educators more closely resemble components of the Learning Paradigm. The more we discover about how the mind works and how students learn, the greater the disparity between what we say and what we do. Thus so many of us feel increasingly constrained by a system increasingly at variance with what we believe. To build the colleges we need for the 21st century—to put our minds where our hearts are, and rejoin acts with beliefs—we must consciously reject the Instruction Paradigm and restructure what we do on the basis of the Learning Paradigm.

The Paradigms

When comparing alternative paradigms, we must take care: the two will seldom be as neatly parallel as our summary chart suggests (see pages 16 and 17). A paradigm is like the rules of a game: one of the functions of the rules is to define the playing field and domain of possibilities on that field. But a new paradigm may specify a game played on a larger or smaller field with a larger or smaller domain of legitimate possibilities. Indeed, the Learning Paradigm expands the playing field and domain of possibilities and it radically changes various aspects of the game. In the Instruction Paradigm, a specific methodology determines the boundary of what colleges can do; in the Learning Paradigm, student learning and success set the boundary. By the same token, not all elements of the new paradigm are contrary to corresponding elements of the old; the new includes many elements of the old within its larger domain of possibilities. The

Learning Paradigm does not prohibit lecturing, for example. Lecturing becomes one of many possible methods, all evaluated on the basis of their ability to promote appropriate learning.

In describing the shift from an Instruction to a Learning Paradigm, we limit our address in this article to undergraduate education. Research and public service are important functions of colleges and universities but lie outside the scope of the present discussion. Here, as in our summary chart, we'll compare the two paradigms along six dimensions: mission and purposes, criteria for success, teaching/learning structures, learning theory, productivity and funding and nature of roles.

Mission and Purposes

In the Instruction Paradigm, the mission of the college is to provide instruction, to teach. The method and the product are one and the same. The means is the end. In the Learning Paradigm, the mission of the college is to produce learning. The method and the product are separate. The end governs the means.

Some educators may be uncomfortable with the verb "produce." We use it because it so strongly connotes that the college takes *responsibility* for learning. The point of saying that colleges are to *produce* learning—not provide, not support, not encourage—is to say, unmistakably, that they are responsible for the degree to which students learn. The Learning Paradigm shifts what the institution takes responsibility for: from quality instruction (lecturing, talking) to student learning. Students, the co-producers of learning, can and must, of course, take responsibility for their own learning. Hence, responsibility is a win-win game wherein two agents take responsibility for the same outcome even though neither is in complete control of all the variables. When two agents take such responsibility, the resulting synergy produces powerful results.

The idea that colleges cannot be responsible for learning flows from a disempowering notion of responsibility. If we conceive of responsibility as a fixed quantity in a zero-sum game, then students must take responsibility for their own learning, and no one else can. This model generates a concept of responsibility capable of assigning blame but not of empowering the most productive action. The

concept of responsibility as a framework for action is quite different: when one takes responsibility, one sets goals and then acts to achieve them, continuously modifying one's behavior to better achieve the goals. To take responsibility for achieving an outcome is not to guarantee the outcome, nor does it entail the complete control of all relevant variables; it is to make the achievement of the outcome the criterion by which one measures one's own efforts. In this sense, it is no contradiction to say that students, faculty, and the college as an institution can all take responsibility for student learning.

In the Learning Paradigm, colleges take responsibility for learning at two distinct levels. At the organizational level, a college takes responsibility for the aggregate of student learning and success. Did, for example, the graduating class's mastery of certain skills or knowledge meet our high, public standards for the award of the degree? Did the class's knowledge and skills improve over those of prior classes? The college also takes responsibility at the individual level, that is, for each individual student's learning. Did Mary Smith learn the chemistry we deem appropriate for a degree in that field? Thus, the institution takes responsibility for both its institutional outcomes and individual student outcomes.

Turning now to more specific purposes, in the Instruction Paradigm, a college aims to transfer or deliver knowledge from faculty to students; it offers courses and degree programs and seeks to maintain a high quality of instruction within them, mostly by assuring that faculty stay current in their fields. If new knowledge or clients appear, so will new course work. The very purpose of the Instruction Paradigm is to offer courses.

In the Learning Paradigm, on the other hand, a college's purpose is not to transfer knowledge but to create environments and experiences that bring students to discover and construct knowledge for themselves, to make students members of communities of learners that make discoveries and solve problems. The college aims, in fact, to create a series of ever more powerful learning environments. The Learning Paradigm does not limit institutions to a single means for empowering students to learn; within its framework, effective learning technologies are continually identified, developed, tested, implemented, and assessed against one another. The aim in the Learning Paradigm is not so much to improve the quality of instruction—although that is not irrelevant—as it is to improve continuously the quality of learning for students individually and in the aggregate.

Under the older paradigm, colleges aimed to provide access to higher education, especially for historically underrepresented groups such as African-Americans and Hispanics. Too often, mere access hasn't served students well. Under the Learning Paradigm, the goal for under-represented students (and *all* students) becomes not simply access but success. By "success" we mean the achievement of overall student educational objectives such as earning a degree, persisting in school, and learning the "right" things—the skills and knowledge that will help students to achieve their goals in work and life. A Learning Paradigm college, therefore, aims for ever-higher graduation rates while maintaining or even increasing learning standards.

By shifting the intended institutional outcome from teaching to learning, the Learning Paradigm makes possible a continuous improvement in productivity. Whereas under the Instruction Paradigm a primary institutional purpose was to optimize faculty well-being and success—including recognition for research and scholarship—in the Learning Paradigm a primary drive is to produce learning outcomes more efficiently. The philosophy of an Instruction Paradigm college reflects the belief that it cannot increase learning outputs without more resources, but a Learning Paradigm college expects to do so continuously. A Learning Paradigm college is concerned with learning productivity, not teaching productivity.

Criteria for Success

Under the Instruction Paradigm, we judge our colleges by comparing them to one another. The criteria for quality are defined in terms of inputs and process measures. Factors such as selectivity in student admissions, number of PhDs on the faculty, and research reputation are used to rate colleges and universities. Administrators and boards may look to enrollment and revenue growth and the expansion of courses and programs. As Guskin put it, "We

are so wedded to a definition of quality based on resources that we find it extremely difficult to deal with the *results* of our work, namely student learning."

The Learning Paradigm necessarily incorporates the perspectives of the assessment movement. While this movement has been under way for at least a decade, under the dominant Instruction Paradigm it has not penetrated very far into normal organizational practice. Only a few colleges across the country systematically assess student learning outcomes. Educators in California community colleges always seem to be surprised when they hear that 45 percent of first-time fall students do not return in the spring and that it takes an average of six years for a student to earn an associate's (AA) degree. The reason for this lack of outcomes knowledge is profoundly simple: under the Instruction Paradigm, student outcomes are simply irrelevant to the successful functioning and funding of a college.

Our faculty evaluation systems, for example, evaluate the performance of faculty in teaching terms, not learning terms. An instructor is typically evaluated by her peers or dean on the basis of whether her lectures are organized, whether she covers the appropriate material, whether she shows interest in and understanding of her subject matter, whether she is prepared for class, and whether she respects her students' questions and comments. All these factors evaluate the instructor's performance in teaching terms. They do not raise the issue of whether students are learning, let alone demand evidence of learning or provide for its reward.

Many institutions construe teaching almost entirely in terms of lecturing. A true story makes the point. A biology instructor was experimenting with collaborative methods of instruction in his beginning biology classes. One day his dean came for a site visit, slipping into the back of the room. The room was a hubbub of activity. Students were discussing material enthusiastically in small groups spread out across the room; the instructor would observe each group for a few minutes, sometimes making a comment, sometimes just nodding approval. After 15 minutes or so the dean approached the instructor and said, "I came today to do your evaluation. I'll come back another time when you're teaching."

CHART 1
Comparing Educational Paradigms

The Instruction Paradigm	*The Learning Paradigm*

Mission and Purposes

➤ Provide/deliver instruction	➤ Produce learning
➤ Transfer knowledge from faculty to students	➤ Elicit student discovery and construction of knowledge
➤ Offer courses and programs	➤ Create powerful learning environments
➤ Improve the quality of instruction	➤ Improve the quality of learning
➤ Achieve access for diverse students	➤ Achieve success for diverse students

Criteria for Success

➤ Inputs, resources	➤ Learning and student-success outcomes
➤ Quality of entering students	➤ Quality of exiting students
➤ Curriculum development, expansion	➤ Learning technologies development, expansion
➤ Quantity and quality of resources	➤ Quantity and quality of outcomes
➤ Enrollment, revenue growth	➤ Aggregate learning growth, efficiency
➤ Quality of faculty, instruction	➤ Quality of students, learning

Teaching/Learning Structures

➤ Atomistic; parts prior to whole	➤ Holistic; whole prior to parts
➤ Time held constant, learning varies	➤ Learning held constant, time varies
➤ 50-minute lecture, 3-unit course	➤ Learning environments
➤ Classes start/end at same time	➤ Environment ready when student is
➤ One teacher, one classroom	➤ Whatever learning experience works
➤ Independent disciplines, departments	➤ Cross discipline/department collaboration
➤ Covering material	➤ Specified learning results
➤ End-of-course assessment	➤ Pre/during/post assessments
➤ Grading within classes by instructors	➤ External evaluations of learning
➤ Private assessment	➤ Public assessment
➤ Degree equals accumulated credit hours	➤ Degree equals demonstrated knowledge and skills

Learning Theory

➤ Knowledge exists "out there"	➤ Knowledge exists in each person's mind and is shaped by individual experience
➤ Knowledge comes in "chunks" and "bits" delivered by instructors	➤ Knowledge is constructed, created, and "gotten"
➤ Learning is cumulative and linear	➤ Learning is a nesting and interacting of frameworks
➤ Fits the storehouse of knowledge metaphor	➤ Fits learning how to ride a bicycle metaphor
➤ Learning is teacher centered and controlled	➤ Learning is student centered and controlled
➤ "Live" teacher, "live" students required	➤ "Active" learner required, but not "live" teacher
➤ The classroom and learning are competitive and individualistic	➤ Learning environments and learning are cooperative, collaborative, and supportive
➤ Talent and ability are rare	➤ Talent and ability are abundant

Productivity/Funding

➤ Definition of productivity: cost per hour of instruction per student	➤ Definition of productivity: cost per unit of learning per student
➤ Funding for hours of instruction	➤ Funding for learning outcomes

Nature of Roles

➤ Faculty are primarily lecturers	➤ Faculty are primarily designers of learning methods and environments
➤ Faculty and students act independently and in isolation	➤ Faculty and students work in teams with each other and other staff
➤ Teachers classify and sort students	➤ Teachers develop every student's competencies and talents
➤ Staff serve/support faculty and the process of instruction	➤ All staff are educators who produce student learning and success
➤ Any expert can teach	➤ Empowering learning is challenging and complex
➤ Line governance; independent actors	➤ Shared governance; teamwork

In the Instruction Paradigm, teaching is judged on its own terms; in the Learning Paradigm, the power of an environment or approach is judged in terms of its impact on learning. If learning occurs, then the environment has power. If students learn more in environment A than in environment B, then A is more powerful than B. To know this in the Learning Paradigm we would assess student learning routinely and constantly.

Institutional outcomes assessment is analogous to classroom assessment, as described by K. Patricia Cross and Thomas Angelo. In our own experience of classroom-assessment training workshops, teachers share moving stories about how even limited use of these techniques has prompted them to make big changes in their teaching, sometimes despite years of investment in a previous practice. Mimi Steadman, in a recent study of community college teachers using classroom assessment, found that "eighty-eight percent of faculty surveyed reported that they had made changes in their teaching behaviors as a result." This at first was startling to us. How could such small amounts of information produce such large changes in teacher behavior? Upon reflection, it became clear. The information was feedback about learning, about results—something teachers rarely collect. Given information that their students were not learning, it was obvious to these teachers that something had to be done about the methods they had been using. Likewise, we think, feedback on learning results at the institutional level should have a correspondingly large impact on an institution's behavior and on the means it uses to produce learning.

Of course, some will argue, true education simply cannot be measured. You cannot measure, for example, true appreciation of the beauty of a work of art. Certainly some learning is difficult, even impossible to measure. But it does not follow that useful and meaningful assessment is impossible.

If we compare outcomes assessment with the input measures controlling policy in the Instruction Paradigm, we find that measures of outcome provide far more genuine information about learning than do measures of input. Learning outcomes include whatever students do as a result of a learning experience. Any measurement of students' products from an educational experience is a measure of a learning outcome. We could count the number of pages students write, the number of books they read, their number of hours at the computer, or the number of math problems they solve.

Of course, these would be silly methods to determine institutional incentives, and we do not recommend them. Any one of them, however, would produce more useful information on learning than the present method of measuring inputs and ignoring outcomes. It would make more sense to fund a college on the number of math problems students solve, for example, than to fund it on the number of students who sit in math classes. We suspect that *any* system of institutional incentives based on outcomes would lead to greater learning than any system of incentives based on inputs. But we need not settle for a system biased toward the trivial. Right now, today, we can construct a good assessment regime with the tools we have at hand.

The Learning Paradigm requires us to heed the advice of the Wingspread Group: "New forms of assessment should focus on establishing what college and university graduates have learned—the knowledge and skill levels they have achieved and their potential for further independent learning."

Teaching/Learning Structures

By structures we mean those features of an organization that are stable over time and that form the framework within which activities and processes occur and through which the purposes of the organization are achieved. Structure includes the organization chart, role and reward systems, technologies and methods, facilities and equipment, decision-making customs, communication channels, feedback loops, financial arrangements, and funding streams.

Peter Senge, in *The Fifth Discipline*, a book about applying systems theory to organizational learning, observes that institutions and their leaders rarely focus their attention on systemic structures. They seldom think, he says, to alter basic structures in order to improve organizational performance, even though those structures generate the patterns of organizational action and determine which activities and results are possible. Perhaps the recent talk about restructuring, re-engineering, and reinvention in higher education reflects a change in focus and a heightened awareness of both the constraining and liberating power of organizational structures.

There is good reason to attend to structure. First, restructuring offers the greatest hope for increasing organizational efficiency and effectiveness. Structure is leverage. If you change the structure in which people work, you increase or decrease the leverage applied to their efforts. A change in structure can either increase productivity or change the nature of organizational outcomes. Second, structure is the concrete manifestation of the abstract principles of the organization's governing paradigm. Structures reflecting an old paradigm can frustrate the best ideas and innovations of new-paradigm thinkers. As the governing paradigm changes, so likewise must the organization's structures.

In this section, we focus on the main structures related to the teaching and learning process; funding and faculty role structures are discussed later under separate headings.

The teaching and learning structure of the Instruction Paradigm college is atomistic. In its universe, the "atom" is the 50-minute lecture, and the "molecule" is the one-teacher, one-classroom, three-credit-hour course. From these basic units the physical architecture, the administrative structure, and the daily schedules of faculty and students are built. Dennis McGrath and Martin Spear, professors at the Community College of Philadelphia, note that "education proceeds everywhere through the vehicle of the three-credit course. Faculty members [and everyone else, we might add] have so internalized that constraint that they are long past noticing that it is a constraint, thinking it part of the natural order of things."

The resulting structure is powerful and rigid. It is, of course, perfectly suited to the Instruction Paradigm task of offering one-teacher, one-classroom courses. It is antithetical to creating almost any other kind of learning experience. A sense of this can be obtained by observing the effort, struggle, and rule-bending required to schedule even a slightly different kind of learning activity, such as a team-taught course.

In the "educational atomism" of the Instruction Paradigm, the parts of the teaching and learning process are seen as discrete entities. The parts exist prior to and independent of any whole; the whole is no more than the sum of the parts, or even less. The college interacts with students only in discrete, isolated environments, cut off from one another because the parts—the classes—are prior to the whole. A "college education" is the sum of the student's experience of a series of discrete, largely unrelated, three-credit classes.

In the Instruction Paradigm, the teaching and learning process is governed by the further rule that time will be held constant while learning varies. Although addressing public elementary and secondary education, the analysis of the National Commission on Time and Learning nonetheless applies to colleges:

> Time is learning's warden. Our time-bound mentality has fooled us all into believing that schools can educate all of the people all of the time in a school year of 180 six-hour days.... If experience, research, and common sense teach nothing else, they confirm the truism that people learn at different rates, and in different ways with different subjects. But we have put the cart before the horse: our schools ... are captives of clock and calendar. The boundaries of student growth are defined by schedules ... instead of standards for students and learning.

Under the rule of time, all classes start and stop at the same time and take the same number of calendar weeks. The rule of time and the priority of parts affect every instructional act of the college. Thus it is, for example, that if students come into college classes "unprepared," it is not the job of the faculty who teach those classes to "prepare" them. Indeed, the structure of the one-semester, three-credit class makes it all but impossible to do so. The only solution, then, is to create new courses to prepare students for the existing courses; within the Instruction Paradigm, the response to educational problems is always to generate more atomized, discrete instructional units. If business students are lacking a sense of ethics, then offer and require a course in business ethics. If students have poor study skills, then offer a "master student" course to teach such skills.

Instruction Paradigm colleges atomistically organize courses and teachers into departments and programs that rarely communicate with one another. Academic departments, originally associated with coherent disciplines, are the structural home bases for accomplishing the essential work of the college: offering courses. "Departments have a life of their own," notes William D. Schaefer, professor of English and former executive vice chancellor at UCLA. They are "insular, defensive, self-governing, [and] compelled to protect their interests because the faculty positions as well as the courses that justify funding those positions are located therein."

Those globally applicable skills that are the foundation of meaningful engagement with the world—reading, writing, calculating, reasoning—find a true place in this structure only if they have their own independent bases: the English or math or reading departments. If students cannot reason or think well, the college creates a course on reasoning and thinking. This in turn produces pressure to create a corresponding department. "If we are not careful," warns Adam Sweeting, director of the Writing Program at the Massachusetts School of Law at Andover, "the teaching of critical thinking skills will become the responsibility of one university department, a prospect that is at odds with the very idea of a university."

Efforts to extend college-level reading, writing, and reasoning "across the curriculum" have largely failed. The good intentions produced few results because, under the Instruction Paradigm, the teacher's job is to "cover the material" as outlined in the disciplinary syllabus. The instructor charged with implementing writing or reading or critical thinking "across the curriculum" often must choose between doing her job or doing what will help students learn—between doing well, as it were, or doing good.

From the point of view of the Learning Paradigm, these Instruction Paradigm teaching and learning structures present immense barriers to improving student learning and success. They provide no space and support for redesigned learning environments or for experimenting with alternative learning technologies. They don't provide for, warrant, or reward assessing whether student learning has occurred or is improving.

In a Learning Paradigm college, the structure of courses and lectures becomes dispensable and negotiable. Semesters and quarters,

lectures, labs, syllabi—indeed, classes themselves—become options rather than received structures or mandatory activities. The Learning Paradigm prescribes no one "answer" to the question of how to organize learning environments and experiences. It supports any learning method and structure that works, where "works" is defined in terms of learning outcomes, not as the degree of conformity to an ideal classroom archetype. In fact, the Learning Paradigm requires a constant search for new structures and methods that work better for student learning and success, and expects even these to be redesigned continually and to evolve over time.

The transition from Instruction Paradigm to Learning Paradigm will not be instantaneous. It will be a process of gradual modification and experimentation through which we alter many organizational parts in light of a new vision for the whole. Under the Instruction Paradigm, structures are assumed to be fixed and immutable; there is no ready means for achieving the leverage needed to alter them. The first structural task of the Learning Paradigm, then, is to establish such leverage.

The key structure for changing the rest of the system is an institution-wide assessment and information system—an essential structure in the Learning Paradigm, and a key means for getting there. It would provide constant, useful feedback on institutional performance. It would track transfer, graduation, and other completion rates. It would track the flow of students through learning stages (such as the achievement of basic skills) and the development of in-depth knowledge in a discipline. It would measure the knowledge and skills of program completers and graduates. It would assess learning along many dimensions and in many places and stages in each student's college experience.

To be most effective, this assessment system would provide public institutional-level information. We are not talking about making public the status of individual students by name, but about making the year-to-year graduation rate—or the mean score of graduating seniors on a critical thinking assessment, for example—"public" in the sense that they are available to everyone in the college community. Moreover, in the Learning Paradigm college, such data are routinely talked about and acted upon by a community ever dedicated to improving its own performance.

The effectiveness of the assessment system for developing alternative learning environments depends in part upon its being *external* to learning programs and structures. While in the Instruction Paradigm students are assessed and graded within a class by the same instructor responsible for teaching them, in the Learning Paradigm much of the assessment would be independent of the learning experience and its designer, somewhat as football games are independent measures of what is learned in football practice. Course grades alone fail to tell us what students know and can do; average grades assigned by instructors are not reliable measures of whether the institution is improving learning.

Ideally, an institution's assessment program would measure the "value-added" over the course of students' experience at the college. Student knowledge and skills would be measured upon entrance and again upon graduation, and at intermediate stages such as at the beginning and completion of major programs. Students could then be acknowledged and certified for what they have learned; the same data, aggregated, could help shift judgments of institutional quality from inputs and resources to the value-added brought to student learning by the college.

The college devoted to learning first identifies the knowledge and skills it expects its graduates to possess, without regard to any particular curriculum or educational experiences. It then determines how to assess them reliably. It assesses graduating students, and the resulting information is then used to redesign and improve the processes and environments leading to such outcomes. In this manner, enhancing intellectual skills such as writing and problem solving and social skills such as effective team participation become the project of *all* learning programs and structured experiences. The whole would govern the parts.

Information from a sophisticated assessment system will gradually lead to the transformation of the college's learning environments and supporting structures. Such a system seeks out "best practice" benchmarks against which improvements in institutional

performance can be measured in learning terms. It is the foundation for creating an institutional capacity to develop ever more effective and efficient ways of empowering learning. It becomes the basis for generating revenue or funding according to learning results rather than hours of instruction. Most importantly, it is the key to the college's and its staff's taking responsibility for and enjoying the progress of each student's education.

Instead of fixing the means—such as lectures and courses—the Learning Paradigm fixes the ends, the learning results, allowing the means to vary in its constant search for the most effective and efficient paths to student learning. Learning outcomes and standards thus would be identified and held to for all students—or *raised* as learning environments became more powerful—while the time students took to achieve those standards would vary. This would reward skilled and advanced students with speedy progress while enabling less prepared students the time they needed to actually master the material. By "testing out," students could also avoid wasting their time being "taught" what they already know. Students would be given "credit" for degree-relevant knowledge and skills regardless of how or where or when they learned them.

In the Learning Paradigm, then, a college degree would represent not time spent and credit hours dutifully accumulated, but would certify that the student had demonstrably attained specified knowledge and skills. Learning Paradigm institutions would develop and publish explicit exit standards for graduates and grant degrees and certificates only to students who met them. Thus colleges would move away from educational atomism and move toward treating holistically the knowledge and skills required for a degree.

Learning Theory

The Instruction Paradigm frames learning atomistically. In it, knowledge, by definition, consists of matter dispensed or delivered by an instructor. The chief agent in the process is the teacher who delivers knowledge; students are viewed as passive vessels, ingesting knowledge for recall on tests. Hence, any expert can teach. Partly because the teacher knows which chunks of knowledge are most important, the teacher controls the learning activities. Learning is presumed to be cumulative because it amounts to ingesting more and more chunks. A degree is awarded when a student has received a specified amount of instruction.

The Learning Paradigm frames learning holistically, recognizing that the chief agent in the process is the learner. Thus, students must be active discoverers and constructors of their own knowledge. In the Learning Paradigm, knowledge consists of frameworks or wholes that are created or constructed by the learner. Knowledge is not seen as cumulative and linear, like a wall of bricks, but as a nesting and interacting of frameworks. Learning is revealed when those frameworks are used to understand and act. Seeing the whole of something—the forest rather than the trees, the image of the newspaper photo rather than its dots—gives meaning to its elements, and that whole becomes more than a sum of component parts. Wholes and frameworks can come in a moment—a flash of insight—often after much hard work with the pieces, as when one suddenly knows how to ride a bicycle.

In the Learning Paradigm, learning environments and activities are learner-centered and learner-controlled. They may even be "teacherless." While teachers will have designed the learning experiences and environments students use—often through teamwork with each other and other staff—they need not be present for or participate in every structured learning activity.

Many students come away from college with a false notion of what learning is and come to believe falsely that learning—at least for some subjects—is too difficult for them. Many students cruise through schools substituting an ersatz role-playing exercise for learning.

The first time I (Barr) studied calculus as a college freshman, I did well by conventional standards. However, while I could solve enough problems to get A's on exams, I really didn't feel that I understood the Limit Theorem, the derivative, or much else. But 15 years later, after having completed college and graduate school and having taught algebra and geometry in high school, I needed to relearn calculus so that I could tutor a friend. In only two, albeit intense, days, I relearned—or really learned for the first time, so it seemed—two

semesters of calculus. During those days, I wondered how I ever thought calculus was difficult and why I didn't see the Limit Theorem and derivative for the simple, obvious things they are.

What was the difference between my first learning of calculus and the second? It certainly wasn't a higher IQ. And I don't think it was because I learned or remembered much from the first time. I think it was that I brought some very powerful intellectual frameworks to the learning the second time that I didn't have the first time. Having taught algebra and geometry, I had learned their basic structure, that is, the nature of a mathematical system. I had learned the lay of the land, the whole. Through many years of schooling and study, I had also learned a number of other frameworks that were useful for learning calculus. Thus learning calculus the second time within these "advanced" frameworks was easy compared to learning, or trying to learn, calculus without them as I did as a freshman.

So much of this is because the "learning" that goes on in Instruction Paradigm colleges frequently involves only rudimentary, stimulus-response relationships whose cues may be coded into the context of a particular course but are not rooted in the student's everyday, functioning understanding.

The National Council on Vocational Education summarizes the consequences in is 1991 report, *Solutions:* "The result is fractionation, or splitting into pieces: having to learn disconnected sub-routines, items, and sub-skills without an understanding of the larger context into which they fit and which gives them meaning." While such approaches are entirely consistent with educational atomism, they are at odds with the way we think and learn. The same report quotes Sylvia Farnham-Diggory's summary of contemporary research: "Fractionated instruction maximizes forgetting, inattention, and passivity. Both children and adults acquire knowledge from active participation in holistic, complex, meaningful environments organized around long-term goals. Today's school programs could hardly have been better designed to prevent a child's natural learning system from operating."

The result is that when the contextual cues provided by the class disappear at the end of the semester, so does the learning. Howard

Gardner points out that "researchers at Johns Hopkins, MIT, and other well-regarded universities have documented that students who receive honor grades in college-level physics courses are frequently unable to solve basic problems and questions encountered in a form slightly different from that on which they have been formally instructed and tested."

The Learning Paradigm embraces the goal of promoting what Gardner calls "education for understanding"—"a sufficient grasp of concepts, principles, or skills so that one can bring them to bear on new problems and situations, deciding in which ways one's present competencies can suffice and in which ways one may require new skills or knowledge." This involves the mastery of functional, knowledge-based intellectual frameworks rather than the short-term retention of fractionated, contextual cues.

The learning theory of the Instruction Paradigm reflects deeply rooted societal assumptions about talent, relationships, and accomplishment: that which is valuable is scarce; life is a win-lose proposition; and success is an individual achievement. The Learning Paradigm theory of learning reverses these assumptions.

Under the Instruction Paradigm, faculty classify and sort students, in the worst cases into those who are "college material" and those who cannot "cut it," since intelligence and ability are scarce. Under the Learning Paradigm, faculty—and everybody else in the institution—are unambiguously committed to each student's success. The faculty and the institution take an R. Buckminster Fuller view of students: human beings are born geniuses and designed for success. If they fail to display their genius or fail to succeed, it is because their design function is being thwarted. This perspective is founded not in wishful thinking but in the best evidence about the real capabilities of virtually all humans for learning. As the Wingspread Group points out, "There is growing research evidence that all students can learn to much higher standards than we now require." In the Learning Paradigm, faculty find ways to develop every student's vast talents and clear the way for every student's success.

Under the Instruction Paradigm, the classroom is competitive and individualistic, reflecting a view that life is a win-lose proposition. The requirement that the students must achieve individually and solely through their own efforts reflects the belief that success is an individual accomplishment. In the Learning Paradigm, learning environments—while challenging—are win-win environments that are cooperative, collaborative, and supportive. They are designed on the principle that accomplishment and success are the result of teamwork and group efforts, even when it appears one is working alone.

Productivity and Funding

Under the Instruction Paradigm, colleges suffer from a serious design flaw—they are structured in such a way that they cannot increase their productivity without diminishing the quality of their product. In the Instruction Paradigm, productivity is defined as cost per hour of instruction per student. In this view, the very quality of teaching and learning is threatened by any increase in the student-to-faculty ratio.

Under the Learning Paradigm, productivity is redefined as the cost per unit of learning per student. Not surprisingly, there is as yet no standard statistic that corresponds to this notion of productivity. Under this new definition, however, it *is* possible to increase outcomes without increasing costs. An abundance of research shows that alternatives to the traditional semester-length, classroom-based lecture method produce more learning. Some of these alternatives are less expensive; many produce more learning for the same cost. Under the Learning Paradigm, producing more with less becomes possible because the more that is being produced is learning and not hours of instruction. Productivity, in this sense, cannot even be measured in the Instruction Paradigm college. All that exists is a measure of exposure to instruction.

Given the Learning Paradigm's definition, increases in productivity pose no threat to the quality of education. Unlike the current definition, this new definition requires that colleges actually produce learning. Otherwise, there is no "product" to count in the productivity ratio.

But what should be the definition of "unit of learning" and how can it be measured? A single, permanent answer to that question does not and need not exist. We have argued above that learning, or at least the effects of learning, can be measured, certainly well enough to determine what students are learning and whether the institution is getting more effective and efficient at producing it.

The Instruction Paradigm wastes not only institutional resources but the time and energy of students. We waste our students' time with registration lines, bookstore lines, lock-step class scheduling, and redundant courses and requirements. We do not teach them to learn efficiently and effectively. We can do a lot, as D. Bruce Johnstone, former chancellor of SUNY, suggests, to reduce the false starts and aimless "drift" of students that slow their progress toward a degree.

Now let's consider how colleges are funded. One of the absurdities of current funding formulas is that an institution could utterly fail its educational mission and yet its revenue would remain unaffected. For example, attendance at public colleges on the semester system is measured twice, once in the fall and again in the spring. Normally, at California community colleges, for example, about two-thirds of fall students return for the spring term. New students and returning stop-outs make up for the one-third of fall students who leave. Even if only half—or none at all—returned, as long as spring enrollments equal those of the fall, these institutions would suffer no loss of revenue.

There is no more powerful feedback than revenue. Nothing could facilitate a shift to the Learning Paradigm more swiftly than funding learning and learning-related institutional outcomes rather than hours of instruction. The initial response to the idea of outcomes-based funding is likely to be "That's not possible." But, of course, it is. As the new paradigm takes hold, forces and possibilities shift and the impossible becomes the rule.

Nature of Roles

With the shift to the Learning Paradigm comes a change in roles for virtually all college employees.

In the Instruction Paradigm, faculty are conceived primarily as disciplinary experts who impart knowledge by lecturing. They are the essential feature of the "instructional delivery system." The Learning Paradigm, on the other hand, conceives of faculty as primarily the designers of learning environments; they study and apply best methods for producing learning and student success.

If the Instruction Paradigm faculty member is an actor—a sage on a stage—then the Learning Paradigm faculty member is an interactor—a coach interacting with a team. If the model in the Instruction Paradigm is that of delivering a lecture, then the model in the Learning Paradigm is that of designing and then playing a team game. A coach not only instructs football players, for example, but also designs football practices and the game plan; he participates in the game itself by sending in plays and making other decisions. The new faculty role goes a step further, however, in that faculty not only design game plans but also create new and better "games," ones that generate more and better learning.

Roles under the Learning Paradigm, then, begin to blur. Architects of campus buildings and payroll clerks alike will contribute to and shape the environments that empower student learning. As the role structures of colleges begin to loosen up and as accountability for results (learning) tightens up, organizational control and command structures will change. Teamwork and shared governance over time replace the line governance and independent work of the Instruction Paradigm's hierarchical and competitive organization.

In the Learning Paradigm, as colleges specify learning goals and focus on learning technologies, interdisciplinary (or nondisciplinary) task groups and design teams become a major operating mode. For example, faculty may form a design team to develop a learning experience in which students networked via computers learn to write about selected texts or on a particular theme.

After developing and testing its new learning module, the design team may even be able to let students proceed through it without direct faculty contact except at designated points. Design teams might include a variety of staff: disciplinary experts, information technology experts, a graphic designer, and an assessment professional. Likewise, faculty and staff might form functional teams responsible for a body of learning outcomes for a stated number of students. Such teams could have the freedom that no faculty member has in today' s atomized framework, that to organize the learning environment in ways that maximize student learning.

Meeting the Challenge

Changing paradigms is hard. A paradigm gives a system integrity and allows it to function by identifying what counts as information within the infinite ocean of data in its environment. Data that solve problems that the paradigm identifies as important are information; data that are irrelevant to those problems are simply noise, static. Any system will provide both channels for transmitting information relevant to the system and filters to reduce noise.

Those who want to change the paradigm governing an institution are—from the institution's point of view—people who are listening to the noise and ignoring the information. They appear crazy or out of touch. The quartz watch was invented by the Swiss. But the great Swiss watchmakers responded to the idea of gearless timepieces in essentially the same way that the premiere audience responded to Stravinsky's *The Rite of Spring*. They threw tomatoes. They hooted it off the stage.

The principle also operates in the other direction. From the point of view of those who have adopted a new paradigm, the institution comes to sound like a cacophony-generating machine, a complex and refined device for producing more and louder noise. From the perspective of the governing paradigm, the advocates of the insurgent paradigm seem willing to sacrifice the institution itself for pie-in-the-sky nonsense. But from the perspective of the insurgents, the defenders of the present system are perpetuating a system that no longer works.

But paradigms do change. The Church admits Galileo was right. *The Rite of Spring* has become an old warhorse. Paradigms can even change quickly. Look at your watch.

Paradigms change when the ruling paradigm loses its capacity to solve problems and generate a positive vision of the future. This we very much see today. One early sign of a paradigm shift is an attempt to use the tools and ideas of a new paradigm within the framework provided by the old, or to convey information intelligible in the new paradigm through the channels of the old. This, too, is now happening.

In our experience, people will suffer the turbulence and uncertainty of change if it promises a better way to accomplish work they value. The shift to the Learning Paradigm represents such an opportunity.

The Learning Paradigm doesn't answer all the important questions, of course. What it does do is lead us to a set of new questions and a domain of possible responses. What knowledge, talents, and skills do college graduates need in order to live and work fully? What must they do to master such knowledge, talents, and skills? Are they doing those things? Do students find in our colleges a coherent body of experiences that help them to become competent, capable, and interesting people? Do they understand what they've memorized? Can they act on it? Has the experience of college made our students flexible and adaptable learners, able to thrive in a knowledge society?

How do you begin to move to the new paradigm? Ultimately, changing paradigms means doing everything differently. But we can suggest three areas where changes—even small ones—can create leverage for larger change in the future.

First, you begin by speaking. You begin to speak *within* the new paradigm. As we come to understand the Learning Paradigm, we must make our understanding public. Stop talking about the "quality of instruction" or the "instructional program." Instead, talk about what it takes to produce "quality learning" and refer to the college's "learning programs." Instead of speaking of "instructional delivery," speak about "learning outcomes."

The primary reason the Instruction Paradigm is so powerful is that it is invisible. Its incoherencies and deficiencies appear as inherent qualities of the world. If we come to see the Instruction Paradigm as a product of our own assumptions and not a force of nature, then we can change it. Only as you begin to experiment with the new language will you realize just how entrenched and invisible the old paradigm is. But as you and your colleagues begin to speak the new language, you will then also begin to think and act out of the new paradigm.

Second, if we begin to talk about the "learning outcomes" of existing programs, we'll experience frustration at our nearly complete ignorance of what those outcomes are—

the Learning Paradigm's most important category of information is one about which we know very little now. The place to start the assessment of learning outcomes is in the conventional classroom; from there, let the practice grow to the program and institutional levels. In the Learning Paradigm, the key structure that provides the leverage to change the rest is a system for requiring the specification of learning outcomes and their assessment through processes external to instruction. The more we learn about the outcomes of existing programs, the more rapidly they will change.

Third, we should address the legally entrenched state funding mechanisms that fund institutions on the basis of hours of instruction. This powerful external force severely constrains the kinds of changes that an institution can make. It virtually limits them to changes within classrooms, leaving intact the atomistic one-teacher, one-classroom structure. We need to work to have state legislatures change the funding formulas of public colleges and universities to give institutions the latitude and incentives to develop new structures for learning. Persuading legislators and governors should not be hard; indeed, the idea of funding colleges for results rather than seat time has an inherent political attractiveness. It is hard to see why legislators would resist the concept that taxpayers should pay for what they get out of higher education, and get what they pay for.

Try this thought experiment. Take a team of faculty at any college—at your college—and select a group of students on some coherent principle, any group of students as long as they have something in common. Keep the ratio of faculty to students the same as it already is. Tell the faculty team, "We want you to create a program for these students so that they will improve significantly in the following knowledge and cognitive skills by the end of one year. We will assess them at the beginning and assess them at the end, and we will tell you how we are going to do so. Your task is to produce learning with these students. In doing so, you are not constrained by any of the rules or regulations you have grown accustomed to. You are free to organize the environment in any way you like. The only thing you are required to do is to produce the desired result—student learning."

We have suggested this thought experiment to many college faculty and asked them whether, if given this freedom, they could design a learning environment that would get better results than what they are doing now. So far, no one has answered that question in the negative. Why not do it?

The change that is required to address today's challenges is not vast or difficult or expensive. It is a small thing. But it is a small change that changes everything. Simply ask, how would we do things differently if we put learning first? Then do it.

Those who say it can't be done frequently assert that environments that actually produce learning are too expensive. But this is clearly not true. What we are doing now is too expensive by far. Today, learning is prohibitively expensive in higher education; we simply can't afford it for more and more of our students. This high cost of learning is an artifact of the Instruction Paradigm. It is simply false to say that we cannot afford to give our students the education they deserve. We can, but we will not as long as we allow the Instruction Paradigm to dominate our thinking. The problem is not insoluble. However. to paraphrase Albert Einstein, we cannot solve our problem with the same level of thinking that created it.

Buckminster Fuller used to say that you should never try to change the course of a great ship by applying force to the bow. You shouldn't even try it by applying force to the rudder. Rather you should apply force to the trim-tab. A trim-tab is a little rudder attached to the end of the rudder. A very small force will turn it left, thus moving the big rudder to the right, and the huge ship to the left. The shift to the Learning Paradigm is the trim-tab of the great ship of higher education. It is a shift that changes everything.

Robert B. Barr is director of institutional research and planning and John Tagg is associate professor of English at Palomar College, San Marcos, California.

Students, Groups, and Teaching Methods[1]

Wilbert J. McKeachie

One of the most exciting, and frustrating, areas of applied research is research on college teaching—and particularly on the teaching of psychology.

The general psychology course at the University of Michigan is not required, but it is elected by over 90% of the undergraduates. At present the course enrolls approximately 2,700 students a year who are taught in some 55 sections varying in size from 10 to 30. Some of these sections are combined into groups of 50 to 250 for two of the four meetings a week. About 30 graduate students and faculty members are engaged in teaching in the course, and five graduate assistants are employed. This staff meets twice weekly in a seminar and usually develops a strong interest in teaching problems and in experimental treatment of these problems (12).

An excellent research situation is thus available. With a relatively large number of sections and teachers involved, teacher and group differences can be randomized more effectively than in most educational research, and the general interest in research on the part of the teaching staff permits a high degree of control over experimental manipulations. Our research projects have thus involved a number of people. Some of the research has been carried out for doctoral dissertations, while other programs have involved several generations of graduate assistants and teaching fellows, beginning sometimes with a small-scale trial in a single section and developing into a controlled experiment involving several hundred students.

Research on Teaching Methods

In 1946 the best summary of research on the teaching of psychology was that of Wolfle (19). He summarized it by quoting Longstaff's statement of 1932:

> ... the experimental evidence submitted to the present time tends to support the general conclusion that there is little difference in student achievement in large and small classes and, also, that it makes little difference as to what method of presentation of the materials of the course is used (9, p. 33).

Our group of teaching fellows did not accept this conclusion. Strongly influenced by the research of Lewin and his colleagues, we argued a good deal about the merits of discussion teaching. Pressed by our leaders, Harold Guetzkow and Lowell Kelly, we agreed that the only way to settle our arguments was to attempt to devise measures of outcomes by which we could compare the discussion method with other methods of teaching.

Following the model of Lewin, Lippitt, and White's study of authoritarian, democratic, and laissez faire group climates (8), we set up three styles of teaching: recitation, discussion, and group tutorial. As we have previously reported, the results of that experiment did not fit our preconceptions. As compared to discussion and tutorial methods, the more autocratic recitation method proved not only to produce superior performance on the final examination,

"Students, Groups, and Teaching Methods," by Wilbert J. McKeachie, reprinted from *American Psychologist*, Vol. 13, October 1958, American Psychological Association.

but also to produce greater interest in psychology, as measured by the election of advanced courses in psychology (7). Furthermore, students liked it better than the other methods.

During the ensuing years, we were attempting further manipulations of teaching methods, and we continued to be concerned with social psychological variables. We were particularly interested in the *power* of the group to determine its own fate and the degree of interaction between group members. Thus, in our next experiment (1, 2, 11, 13) we compared classes which differed in two major respects. One of these was in the degree of power given to the class in making group decisions about assignments, class activities, etc. The other difference was in the degree to which student-to-student interaction was encouraged. In our experimental classes the group made many group decisions, and the students were encouraged to direct their comments to each other rather than to the teacher. Decisions made by the group in the experimental classes were imposed by the instructor on the control classes. Student participation in class discussion was also encouraged in the control groups, but all interaction was mediated through the instructor. He asked questions, answered student questions, and was the focus of class activities.

As compared with our earlier experiment this experiment was more radical both in the freedom given the experimental groups and in the fact that it involved all of the student's hours in class. However, we tried to do a better job of taking into account students' need for achievement by giving them frequent checks on their progress through summaries and evaluations given in the concluding minutes of class periods.

The results of this experiment were more encouraging for advocates of group-centered methods. This time there was *no* significant difference between the two types of classes on their final examination scores, but one unique bit of qualitative evidence supported our feelings that teaching makes a difference in learning. We recorded class discussions following the showing of the film "Feeling of Rejection." The instructor took no part in these discussions. The transcripts of the discussion were evaluated by two clinical psychologists who knew nothing about the experiment. Both psychologists agreed that the group-centered class showed much more insight into the dynamics of the case and was less frightened and defensive than the instructor-centered class. The instructor-centered class tended to label the behavior of the heroine without apparent understanding of her difficulties (3).

Our conclusion that group-centered teaching tended to promote greater insight was supported by the finding of Gibb and Gibb (5) that their "participative action" method produced greater self-insight and role-flexibility than conventional teaching methods did. Like us, the instructor in the Gibb experiment gave a good deal of initial direction but gradually relinquished control.

What Type of Personality Succeeds in Group-Centered Classes?

Despite these glimmerings of encouragement, it was evident that the conglomeration of variables included under the title group-centered teaching has no great, uniform effect upon student learning. We saw two possible paths of further research. One of these was to attempt to determine more precisely the important group variables involved in group-centered teaching. The second was to investigate what student characteristics made a difference in responses to group-centered teaching. In his doctoral dissertation Joseph Patton, of our group, made a two-pronged attack upon these problems (16).

Patton felt that an important variable in group-centered classes was the students' acceptance of responsibility for learning. In his experiment he compared traditional classes to two classes in which there were no examinations, no lectures, and no assigned readings. Students in the experimental classes decided what reading they would do, what class procedures would be used, what they would hand in, and how they would be graded, so that they had even more power than had our previous experimental groups. At the end of the course, these classes, as compared to the control group, (*a*) felt that the course was more valuable; (*b*) showed greater interest in psychology; and (*c*) tended to give more dynamic, motivational analyses of a problem of behavior.

Patton also obtained individual measures of acceptance of responsibility within the experimental classes and found that the degree to which the student accepted responsibility was positively correlated with gain in psychological knowledge, gain in ability to apply psychology, rating of the value of the course and interest in psychology. Thus the effect of giving students additional responsibility seemed to depend upon the student's readiness to accept responsibility.

But what sort of student will accept responsibility in such a course? Patton's research also investigated this question. He found that the students who liked the experimental class and assumed responsibility were likely to be independent of traditional authority figures and high in need for achievement.

Anxiety and Test Performance

In thinking about student reactions to teaching methods it was inevitable that we should be concerned about the relationship between students and faculty. Perhaps because we were young and inexperienced, we all wanted very much to be liked by our students, and we were well liked—most of the time. I say "most of the time" because all of us dreaded giving and returning tests. No matter how carefully our tests were constructed, they elicited bitter, aggressive reactions from our students. Perhaps the very fact that our students felt accepted by us enabled them to attack our tests more freely than they would have dared to in more authoritarian classes; and, because our tests tried to go beyond straight memory for facts, we probably aroused more anxiety than other examiners did.

One of our teaching fellows, Louis Berman, suggested that some of the aggression might be dissipated by permitting students to write comments on tests. So we tried this experimentally: giving half of the students answer sheets with spaces for comments; and half, standard answer sheets. Our measures of students' feelings about the tests failed to show any difference between the two groups; but, much to our surprise, the students who had the opportunity to write comments made higher scores on the test (18).

We have described elsewhere the series of experiments which followed this finding (14). The important thing was that our results held up in a series of experiments, and these experiments gave us some new ideas about student motivation in a classroom situation.

Up until this point we had thought that our big problem was to increase student motivation. Now it appeared that some of our students were already too highly motivated—at least for performance on tests. We interpreted our findings as indicating that student anxiety during classroom examinations builds up to such a point that it interferes with memory and problem solving. Reducing the stress of the examination by permitting students to write comments thus resulted in improved performance.

Just as our research on teaching methods had directed our attention to the interaction between situational variables and individual differences in motivation, here, too, we became interested in the individual differences in students' reactions to more and less stressful test situations.

In his doctoral dissertation Neil Carrier (4) investigated the manner in which individual differences in four personality variables affected performance in more and less stressful testing situations. In his "low stress" condition students had answer sheets with spaces for comments, and the test was administered in a friendly, relaxed fashion. In the "high stress" condition, the test was taken in a strange room was administered by an austere stranger who announced that he would answer no questions during the test, and students were told that a point would be deducted for every wrong answer but that they must answer every question. In the students' words this was a "real, rugged situation."

The techniques used to increase stress were chosen with an eye on the personality dimensions Carrier intended to study. One of his variables was *need for achievement*, and the announcement of the penalty for wrong answers was specifically aimed at the person whose need for achievement is characterized by a strong fear of failure. Similarly he presumed that the person with a strong *need for affiliation* would be affected by the austere, unfriendly attitude of the proctor. Donald Smith's *permeability* dimension (17) was chosen because it is thought to involve the extent to which an individual is influenced by changes in the external situation, and the highly permeable individual is thought to be dependent upon others in decision making situations. Similarly Smith's *stability* dimension is presumed to indicate the individual's general level of anxiety, and we would expect that highly anxious individuals would be likely to "crack up" under additional stress.

As usual Carrier's results gave us some surprises. The first was that one of the most important variables determining reaction to stress in his experiment was *sex*. Women were hit much harder than men by his stress situation. Once we had Carrier's result, we could think of all sorts of reasons why it should be so—the findings of McClelland, Atkinson, and their associates on sex differences in achievement imagery (10), Guetzkow's findings of sex differences in rigidity (6), and Margaret Mead's descriptions of women's achievement conflicts (15) —but we had just never thought seriously of a sex difference before.

But the tests of the original hypothesis were also interesting. In general, *need for achievement* and *need for affiliation* failed to predict reactions to our stress situation. However, the *permeable* students were detrimentally affected by stress.

Carrier's results encouraged us to investigate other measures of fear of failure and anxiety and their relationship to performance in more and less stressful testing situations. In our next experiment half of a group of 350 students taking a test received conventional IBM answer sheets; half received answer sheets with space for comments. In addition, half of the students had received one of the tranquilizing drugs, meprobamate ("Miltown"), from a physician associated with the Institute of Mental Health Research, while the other half had received a placebo. All of the students had taken a number of tests of anxiety and of need for achievement a week prior to the examination. Thus we were able to investigate a number of relationships. One of the simplest of these was the effect of meprobamate on performance. If most students are too anxious, such a drug should improve test scores. Our results did no confirm this hypothesis. Students who actually had the Miltown reported experiencing less anxiety during the examination than did the placebo group, but they did not make better scores.

The really interesting results of the experiment were the interactions. The sex-drug interaction was significant both in its effect on performance and on anxiety, with women benefiting from the drug more than men. So once again sex turns out to be an important variable.

Discussion

Motivation. At present I begin my consideration of student behavior in terms of motives. Achievement motivation would seem to be a particularly important motive for determining classroom behavior, but our results indicate that it alone is not a good predictor of achievement in our classes. It seems to me now that this is because a lot of motives are directed toward grades. Not that all students are working for *A*s—far from it. But whether a student is trying to maintain a straight *A* average or simply to keep eligible for the football team, grades are such universal student incentives that general motivation measures are not powerful predictors of achievement in a single, typical, college class.

Complicating our problem is the curvilinear effect of motivation on performance. As we saw in our studies of testing situation, it appears that we can push motivation too high. Up to a point, increasing motivation improves performance; but, if we try to scare some of our poorly motivated students into doing better, we may be pushing some of our more anxious students over the brink into disorganization.

Instrumental Behavior. Since motivational measures are not sufficient to give us a complete understanding of student behavior, we must turn to a second intervening variable, which I term instrumental behavior or habit. Our students have been in school for 12 to 15 years. It is not surprising that they have developed rather strong expectations about the instrumental behaviors necessary for them to attain their desired grades. They expect the teacher's behavior and his requirements of them to fit into a particular pattern; and, when this pattern is altered, they are likely to be disturbed unless the instructor clearly indicates the instrumental behaviors now required for them to satisfy their motives.

Situational Factors. In varying our teaching methods we are varying cues to student motives, but more important we are affecting the student's perception of the instrumental behaviors necessary if he is to satisfy his motives. In our initial Lewin-Lippitt-White-type experiment, students did well in the recitation class and liked it because the instrumental behaviors required were ones which almost all students have learned in their earlier schooling.

The importance of the power of the group in our later experiments was that it gave the students some control over the situation. Because the instrumental behaviors were chosen by the group, they were less ambiguous than in a nondirective situation and we would also expect the group to select behaviors which were within the repertoire of most members of the group.

Student-to-student interaction is important, we feel, because of its relation to interpersonal liking. By increasing liking for other group members, we counteract the threat caused by the reduced ability of students to depend upon the teacher. We suspect that this is particularly important for the more dependent students.

Thus, once again we see the importance of situational factors in affecting students' perceptions of the probability that certain instrumental behaviors will be successful.

It is in this area of expectations that differences between colleges are important. For example, students at Brooklyn College rate large classes as favorably as small classes, while students at Grinnell College rate instructors less favorably in classes over 30. I would interpret this as being due to differences in student expectations. Students in different colleges may differ greatly in the degree to which their motivation is bound up in grades, but I suspect that there is even more difference between colleges in student expectations about classroom situations.

It is not surprising that we find that sex is an important variable, since biological and cultural factors interact in differentiating men from women in consistent ways. Like other researchers, we find that women are more highly motivated, achieve more nearly up to their abilities, and are more greatly affected by changes in the classroom situation than are men.

Note

Delivered as the address of the retiring President of the Division on the Teaching of Psychology at the APA Annual Convention, Chicago, Illinois, September 1956. Substantial portions were also included in an address to the Faculty Fall Conference of Stephens College, September 1956.

References

1. Bovard, E. W., Jr. The experimental production of interpersonal affect. *J. abnorm. soc. Psychol.*, 1951, **46**, 521–528.
2. Bovard, E. W., Jr. The psychology of classroom interaction. *J. educ. Res.*, 1951, **45**, 215–224.
3. Bovard, E. W., Jr. Clinical insight as a function of group process. *J. abnorm. soc. Psychol.*, 1952, **47**, 534–539.
4. Carrier, N. A. Stress, personality, and performance on course examinations. Unpublished doctoral thesis, University of Michigan, 1956.
5. Gibb, L. M., & Gibb, J. R. The effects of the use of "participative action" groups in a course in general psychology. *Amer. Psychologist*, 1952, **7**, 247. (Abstract)
6. Guetzkow, H. An analysis of the operation of set in problem-solving behavior. Unpublished doctoral thesis, University of Michigan, 1948.
7. Guetzkow, H., Kelly, E. L., & McKeachie, W. J. An experimental comparison of recitation, discussion, and tutorial methods in college teaching. *J. educ. Psychol.*, 1954, **45**, 193–207.
8. Lippitt, R., & White, R. K. The "social climate" of children's groups. In R. G. Barker, J. S. Kounin, & H. F. Wright, *Child behavior and development*. New York: McGraw-Hill, 1943. Pp. 485–508.
9. Longstaff, H. P. Analysis of some factors conditioning learning in general psychology. Part I. *J. appl. Psychol.*, 1932, **16**, 9–48.
10. McClelland, D. C., Atkinson, J. W., Clark, R. A., and Lowell, E. L. *The achievement motive.* New York: Appleton-Century-Crofts, 1953.
11. McKeachie, W. J. Anxiety in the college classroom. *J. educ. Res.*, 1951, **45**, 153–160.
12. McKeachie, W. J. A program for training teachers of psychology. *Amer. Psychologist*, 1951, **6**, 119–121.
13. McKeachie, W. J. Individual conformity to attitudes of classroom groups. *J. abnorm. soc. Psychol.*, 1954, **49**, 282–289.
14. McKeachie, W. J., Pollie, D., & Speisman, J. Relieving anxiety in classroom examinations. *J. abnorm. soc. Psychol.* 1955, **50**, 93–98.

15. Mead, M. *Male and female*. New York: Mentor, 1955.

16. Patton, J. A. A study of the effects of student acceptance of responsibility and motivation on course behavior. Unpublished doctoral thesis, University of Michigan, 1955.

17. Smith, D. E. P., Wood, R. L., Downer, J. W., & Raygor, A. L. Reading improvement as a function of students' personality and teaching methods. *J. educ. Psychol.*, 1956, **47**, 47–59.

18. Teevan, R., & McKeachie, W. Effects on performance of different instructions in multiple-choice examinations. *Mich. Acad. Sci., Arts, Letters*, 1954, **39**, 467–475.

19. Wolfle, D. L. The first course in psychology. *Psychol. Bull.*, 1942, **39**, 685–712.

The School Class as a Social System: Some of Its Functions in American Society[*]

Talcott Parsons

This essay will attempt to outline, if only sketchily, an analysis of the elementary and secondary school class as a social system, and the relation of its structure to its primary functions in the society as an agency of socialization and allocation. While it is important that the school class is normally part of the larger organization of a school, the class rather than the whole school will be the unit of analysis here, for it is recognized both by the school system and by the individual pupil as the place where the "business" of formal education actually takes place. In elementary schools, pupils of one grade are typically placed in a single "class" under one main teacher, but in the secondary school, and sometimes in the upper elementary grades, the pupil works on different subjects under different teachers; here the complex of classes participated in by the same pupil is the significant unit for our purposes.

The Problem: Socialization and Selection

Our main interest, then, is in a dual problem: first of how the school class functions to internalize in its pupils both the commitments and capacities for successful performance of their future adult roles, and second of how it functions to allocate these human resources within the role-structure of the adult society. The primary ways in which these two problems are interrelated will provide our main points of reference.

First, from the functional point of view the school class can be treated as an agency of socialization. That is to say, it is an agency through which individual personalities are trained to be motivationally and technically adequate to the performance of adult roles. It is not the sole such agency; the family, informal "peer groups," churches, and sundry voluntary organizations all play a part, as does actual on-the-job training. But, in the period extending from entry into first grade until entry into the labor force or marriage, the school class may be regarded as the focal socializing agency.

The socialization function may be summed up as the development in individuals of the commitments and capacities which are essential prerequisites of their future role-performance. Commitments may be broken down in turn into two components: commitment to the implementation of the broad *values* of society, and commitment to the performance of a specific type of role within the *structure* of society. Thus a person in a relatively humble occupation may be a "solid citizen" in the sense of commitment to honest work in that occupation, without an intensive and sophisticated concern with the implementation of society's higher-level values. Or conversely, someone else might object to the anchorage of the feminine role in marriage and the family on the grounds that such anchorage keeps society's total talent resources from being distributed equitably to business, government, and so on. Capacities can also be broken down into two components, the first being competence or the skill to perform the tasks involved in the individual's roles, and the second being "role-responsibility" or the capacity to live up to other people's expectations of the interpersonal behavior appropriate

"The School Class as a Social System: Some of Its Functions in American Society," by Talcott Parsons, reprinted from *Harvard Educational Review*, Vol. 29, No. 4, Fall 1959, Harvard University.

to these roles. Thus a mechanic as well as a doctor needs to have not only the basic "skills of his trade," but also the ability to behave responsibly toward those people with whom he is brought into contact in his work.

While on the one hand, the school class may be regarded as a primary agency by which these different components of commitments and capacities are generated, on the other hand, it is, from the point of view of the society, an agency of "manpower" allocation. It is well known that in American society there is a very high, and probably increasing, correlation between one's status level in the society and one's level of educational attainment. Both social status and educational level are obviously related to the occupational status which is attained. Now, as a result of the general process of both educational and occupational upgrading, completion of high school is increasingly coming to be the norm for minimum satisfactory educational attainment, and the most significant line for future occupational status has come to be drawn between members of an age-cohort who do and do not go to college.

We are interested, then in what it is about the school class in our society that determines the distinction between the contingents of the age-cohort which do and do not go to college. Because of a tradition of localism and a rather pragmatic pluralism, there is apparently considerable variety among school systems of various cities and states. Although the situation in metropolitan Boston probably represents a more highly structured pattern than in many other parts of the country, it is probably not so extreme as to be misleading in its main features. There, though of course actual entry into college does not come until after graduation from high school, the main dividing line is between those who are and are not enrolled in the college preparatory course in high school; there is only a small amount of shifting either way after about the ninth grade when the decision is normally made. Furthermore, the evidence seems to be that by far the most important criterion of selection is the record of school performance in elementary school. These records are evaluated by teachers and principals, and there are few cases of entering the college preparatory course against their advice. It is therefore not stretching the evidence too far to say broadly that the primary selective

process occurs through differential school performance in elementary school, and that the "seal" is put on it in junior high school.[1]

The evidence also is that the selective process is genuinely assortative. As in virtually all comparable processes, ascriptive as well as achieved factors influence the outcome. In this case, the ascriptive factor is the socio-economic status of the child's family, and the factor underlying his opportunity for achievement is his individual ability. In the study of 3,348 Boston high school boys on which these generalizations are based, each of these factors was quite highly correlated with planning college. For example, the percentages planning college, by father's occupation, were: 12 per cent for semi-skilled and unskilled, 19 per cent for skilled, 26 per cent for minor white collar, 52 per cent for middle white collar, and 80 per cent for major white collar. Likewise, intentions varied by ability (as measured by IQ), namely, 11 per cent for the lowest quintile, 17 per cent for the next, 24 per cent for the middle, 30 per cent for the next to the top, and 52 per cent for the highest. It should be noted also that within any ability quintile, the relationship of plans to father's occupation is seen. For example, within the very important top quintile in ability as measure, the range in college intentions was from 29 per cent for sons of laborers to 89 per cent for sons of major white collar persons.[2]

The essential points here seem to be that there is a relatively uniform criterion of selection operating to differentiate between the college and the non-college contingents, and that for a very important part of the cohort the operation of this criterion is not a "put-up job"—it is not simply a way of affirming a previously determined ascriptive status. To be sure, the high-status, high-ability boy is very likely indeed to go to college, and the low-status, low-ability boy is very unlikely to go. But the "cross-pressured" group for whom these two factors do not coincide[3] is of considerable importance.

· Considerations like these lead me to conclude that the main process of differentiation (which from another point of view is selection) that occurs during elementary school takes place on a single main axis of *achievement*. Broadly, moreover, the differentiation leads up through high school to a bifurcation into college-goers and non-college-goers.

To assess the significance of this pattern, let us look at its place in the socialization of the individual. Entering the system of formal education is the child's first major step out of primary involvement in his family of orientation. Within the family certain foundations of his motivational system have been laid down. But the only characteristic fundamental to later roles which has clearly been "determined" and psychologically stamped in by that time is sex role. The postoedipal child enters the system of formal education clearly categorized as boy or girl, but beyond that his *role* is not yet differentiated. The process of selection, by which persons will select and be selected for categories of roles, is yet to take place.

On grounds which cannot be gone into here, it may be said that the most important single predispositional factor with which the child enters the school is his level of *independence*. By this is meant his level of self-sufficiency relative to guidance by adults, his capacity to take responsibility and to make his own decision in coping with new and varying situations. This, like his sex role, he has as a function of his experience in the family.

The family is a collectively within which the basic status-structure is ascribed in terms of biological position, that is, by generation, sex, and age. There are inevitably differences of performance relative to these, and they are rewarded and punished in ways that contribute to differential character formation. But these differences are not given the sanction of institutionalized social status. The school is the first socializing agency in the child's experience which institutionalizes a differentiation of status on nonbiological bases. Moreover, this is not an ascribed but an achieved status; it is the status "earned" by differential performance of the tasks set by the teacher, who is acting as an agent of community's school system. Let us look at the structure of this situation.

The Structure of the Elementary School Class

In accord with the generally wide variability of American institutions, and of course the basically local control of school systems, there is considerable variability of school situations, but broadly they have a single relatively well-marked framework.[4] Particularly in the primary part of the elementary grades, i.e., the first three grades, the basic pattern includes one main teacher for the class, who teaches all subjects and who is in charge of the class generally. Sometimes this early, and frequently in later grades, other teachers are brought in for a few special subjects, particularly gym, music, and art, but this does not alter the central position of the main teacher. This teacher is usually a woman.[5] The class is with this one teacher for the school year, but usually no longer.

The class, then, is composed of about 25 age-peers of both sexes drawn from a relatively small geographical area—the neighborhood. Except for sex in certain respects, there is initially no formal basis for differentiation of status within the school class. The main structural differentiation develops gradually, on the single main axis indicated above as achievement. That the differentiation should occur on a single main axis is insured by four primary features of the situation. The first is the initial equalization of the "contestants'" status by age and by "family background," the neighborhood being typically much more homogeneous than is the whole society. The second circumstance is the imposition of a common set of tasks which is, compared to most other task-areas, strikingly undifferentiated. The school situation is far more like a race in this respect than more role-performance situations. Third, there is the sharp polarization between the pupils in their initial equality and the *single* teacher who is an adult and "represents" the adult world. And fourth, there is a relatively systematic process of evaluation of the pupils' performances. From the point of view of a pupil, this evaluation, particularly (though not exclusively) in the form of report card marks, constitutes reward and/or punishment for past performance; from the viewpoint of the school system acting as an allocating agency, it is a basis of *selection* for future status in society.

Two important sets of qualifications need to be kept in mind in interpreting this structural pattern, but I think these do not destroy the significance of its main outline. The first qualification is for variations in the formal organization and procedures of the school class itself. Here the most important kind of variation is that between relatively "traditional" schools and relatively "progressive" schools.

The more traditional schools put more emphasis on discrete units of subject-matter, whereas the progressive type allows more "indirect" teaching through "projects" and broader topical interests where more than one bird can be killed with a stone. In progressive schools there is more emphasis on groups of pupils working together, compared to the traditional direct relation of the individual pupil to the teacher. This is related to the progressive emphasis on co-operation among the pupils rather than direct competition, to greater permissiveness as opposed to strictness of discipline, and to a de-emphasis on formal marking.[6] In some schools one of these components will be more prominent, and in others, another. That it is, however, an important range of variation is clear. It has to do, I think, very largely with the independence-dependence training which is so important to early socialization in the family. My broad interpretation is that those people who emphasize independence training will tend to be those who favor relatively progressive education. The relation of support for progressive education to relatively high socio-economic status and to "intellectual" interests and the like is well known. There is no contradiction between these emphases both on independence and on co-operation and group solidarity among pupils. In the first instance this is because the main focus of the independence problem at these ages is vis-à-vis adults. However, it can also be said that the peer group, which here is built into the school class, is an indirect field of expression of dependency needs, displaced from adults.

The second set of qualifications concerns the "informal" aspects of the school class, which are always somewhat at variance with the formal expectations. For instance, the formal pattern of nondifferentiation between the sexes may be modified informally, for the very salience of the one-sex peer group at this age period means that there is bound to be considerable implicit recognition of—for example, in the form of teachers' encouraging group competition between boys and girls. Still, the fact of coeducation and the attempt to treat both sexes alike in all the crucial formal respects remain the most important. Another problem raised by informal organization is the question of how far teachers can and do treat pupils particularistically in violation of the universalistic expec-

tations of the school. When compared with other types of formal organizations, however, I think the extent of this discrepancy in elementary schools is seen to be not unusual. The school class is structured so that opportunity for particularistic treatment is severely limited. Because there are so many more children in a school class than in a family and they are concentrated in a much narrower age range, the teacher has much less chance than does a parent to grant particularistic favors.

Bearing in mind these two sets of qualifications, it is still fair, I think, to conclude that the major characteristics of the elementary school class in this country are such as have been outlined. It should be especially emphasized that more or less progressive schools, even with their relative lack of emphasis on formal marking, do not constitute a separate pattern, but rather a variant tendency within the same pattern. A progressive teacher, like any other, will form opinions about the different merits of her pupils relative to the values and goals of the class and will communicate these evaluations to them, informally if not formally. It is my impression that the extreme cases of playing down relative evaluation are confined to those upper-status schools where going to a "good" college is so fully taken for granted that for practical purposes it is an ascribed status. In other words, in interpreting these facts the selective function of the school class should be kept continually in the forefront of attention. Quite clearly its importance has not been decreasing; rather the contrary.

The Nature of School Achievement

What, now, of the content of the "achievement" expected of elementary school children? Perhaps the best broad characterization which can be given is that it involves the types of performance which are, on the one hand, appropriate to the school situation and, on the other hand, are felt by adults to be important in themselves. This vague and somewhat circular characterization may, as was mentioned earlier, be broken down into two main components. One of these is the more purely "cognitive" learning of information, skills, and frames of reference associated with empirical knowledge and technological mastery. The *written* language and the early phases of mathematical thinking are clearly vital; they involve cognitive skills at altogether new levels of generality and abstraction compared to those commanded by the pre-school child. With these basic skills goes assimilation of much factual information about the world.

The second main component is what may broadly be called a "moral" one. In earlier generations of schooling this was known as "deportment." Somewhat more generally it might be called responsible citizenship in the school community. Such things as respect for the teacher, consideration and co-operativeness in relation to fellow-pupils, and good "work-habits" are the fundamentals, leading on to capacity for "leadership" and "initiative."

The striking fact about this achievement content is that in the elementary grades these two primary components are not clearly differentiated from each other. Rather, the pupil is evaluated in diffusely general terms; a *good* pupil is defined in terms of a fusion of the cognitive and the moral components, in which varying weight is given to one or the other. Broadly speaking, then, we may say that the "high achievers" of the elementary school are both the "bright" pupils, who catch on easily to their more strictly intellectual tasks, and the more "responsible" pupils, who "behave well" and on whom the teacher can "count" in her difficult problems of managing the class. One indication that this is the case is the fact that in elementary school the purely intellectual tasks are relatively easy for the pupil of high intellectual ability. In many such cases, it can be presumed that the primary challenge to the pupil is not to his intellectual, but to his "moral," capacities. On the whole, the progressive movement seems to have leaned in the direction of giving enhanced emphasis to this component, suggesting that of the two, it has tended to become the more problematical.[7]

The essential point, then, seems to be that the elementary school, regarded in the light of its socialization function, is an agency which differentiates the school class broadly along a single continuum of achievement, the content of which is relative excellence in living up to the expectations imposed by the teacher as an agent of the adult society. The criteria of this achievement are, generally speaking, undifferentiated into the cognitive or technical component and the moral or "social" component. But with respect to its bearing on societal values, it is broadly a differentiation of *levels* of capacity to act in accord with these values. Though the relation is far from neatly uniform, this differentiation underlies the processes of selection for levels of status and role in the adult society.

Next, a few words should be said about the out-of-school context in which this process goes on. Besides the school class, there are clearly two primary social structures in which the child participates: the family and the child's informal "peer group."

Family and Peer Group in Relation to the School Class

The school age child, of course, continues to live in the parental household and to be highly dependent, emotionally as well as instrumentally, on his parents. But he is now spending several hours a day away from home, subject to a discipline and a reward system which are essentially independent of that administered by the parents. Moreover, the range of this independence gradually increases. As he grows older, he is permitted to range further territorially with neither parental nor school supervision, and to do an increasing range of things. He often gets an allowance for personal spending and begins to earn some money of his own. Generally, however, the emotional problem of dependence-independence continues to be a very salient one through this period, frequently with manifestations by the child of compulsive independence.

Concomitantly with this, the area for association with age-peers without detailed adult supervision expands. These associations are tied to the family, on the one hand, in that the home and yards of children who are neighbors and the adjacent streets serve as locations for their activities; and to the school, on the other hand, in that play periods and going to and from school provide occasions for informal association, even though organized extracurricular activities are introduced only later. Ways of bringing some of this activity under another sort of adult supervision are found in such organizations as the boy and girl scouts.

Two sociological characteristics of peer groups at this age are particularly striking. One is the fluidity of their boundaries, with individual children drifting into and out of associations. This element of "voluntary association" contrasts strikingly with the child's ascribed membership in the family and the school class, over which he has no control. The second characteristic is the peer group's sharp segregation by sex. To a striking degree this is enforced by the children themselves rather than by adults.

The psychological functions of peer association are suggested by these two characteristics. On the one hand, the peer group may be regarded as a field for the exercise of independence from adult control; hence it is not surprising that it is often a focus of behavior which goes beyond independence from adults to the range of adult-*disapproved* behavior; when this happens, it is the seed bed from which the extremists go over into delinquency. But another very important function is to provide the child a source of non-adult approval and acceptance. These depend on "technical" and "moral" criteria as diffuse as those required in the school situation. On the one hand, the peer group is a field for acquiring and displaying various types of "prowess"; for boys this is especially the physical prowess which may later ripen into athletic achievement. On the other hand, it is a matter of gaining acceptance from desirable peers as "belonging" in the group, which later ripens into the conception of the popular teen-ager, the "right guy." Thus the adult parents are augmented by age-peers as a source of rewards for performance and of security in acceptance.

The importance of the peer group for socialization in our type of society should be clear. The motivational foundations of character are inevitably first laid down through identification with parents, who are generation-superiors, and the generation difference is a type example of a hierarchical status difference. But an immense part of the individual's adult role performance will have to be in association with status-equals or near-equals. In this situation it is important to have a reorganization of the motivational structure so that the original dominance of the hierarchical axis is modified to strengthen the egalitarian components. The peer group plays a prominent part in this process.

Sex segregation of latency period peer groups may be regarded as a process of reinforcement of sex-role identification. Through intensive association with sex-peers and involvement in sex-typed activities, they strongly reinforce belongingness with other members of the same sex and contrast with the opposite sex. This is the more important because in the coeducational school a set of forces operates which specially plays down sex-role differentiation.

It is notable that the latency period sex-role pattern, instead of institutionalizing relations to members of the opposite sex, is characterized by an avoidance of such relations, which only in adolescence gives way to dating. This avoidance is clearly associated with the process of reorganization of the erotic components of motivational structure. The pre-oedipal objects of erotic attachment were both intra-familial and generation-superior. In both respects there must be a fundamental shift by the time the child reaches adulthood. I would suggest that one of the main functions of the avoidance pattern is to help cope with the psychological difficulty of overcoming the earlier incestuous attachments, and hence to prepare the child for assuming an attachment to an age-mate of opposite sex later.

Seen in this perspective, the socialization function of the school class assumes a particular significance. The socialization functions of the family by this time are relatively residual, though their importance should not be underestimated. But the school remains adult-controlled and, moreover, induces basically the same kind of identification as was induced by the family in the child's pre-oedipal stage. This is to say that the learning of achievement-motivation is, psychologically speaking, a process of identification with the teacher, of doing well in school in order to please the teacher (often backed by the parents) in the same sense in which a pre-oedipal child learns new skills in order to please his mother.

In this connection I maintain that what is internalized through the process of identification is a reciprocal pattern of role-relationships.[8] Unless there is a drastic failure of internalization altogether, not just one, but both sides of the interaction will be internalized. There will, however, be an emphasis on one or the other, so that some children will more nearly identify with the socializing agent, and others will more nearly identify with the opposite role. Thus, in the pre-oedipal stage, the "independent" child has identified more with the parent, and the "dependent" one with the child-role vis-à-vis the parent.

In school the teacher is institutionally defined as superior to any pupil in knowledge of curriculum subject-matter and in responsibility as a good citizen of the school. In so far as the school class tends to be bifurcated (and of course the dichotomization is far from absolute), it will broadly be on the basis, on the one hand, of identification with the teacher, or acceptance of her role as a model; and, on the other hand, of identification with the pupil peer group. This bifurcation of the class on the basis of identification with teacher or with peer group so strikingly corresponds with bifurcation into college-goers and non-college-goers that it would be hard to avoid the hypothesis that this structural dichotomization in the school system is the primary source of the selective dichotomization. Of course in detail the relationship is blurred, but certainly not more so than in a great many other fields of comparable analytical complexity.

These considerations suggest an interpretation of some features of the elementary teacher role in American society. The first major step in socialization, beyond that in the family, takes place in the elementary school, so it seems reasonable to expect that the teacher-figure should be characterized by a combination of similarities to and differences from parental figures. The teacher, then, is an adult, characterized by the generalized superiority, which a parent also has, of adult status relative to children. She is not, however, ascriptively related to her pupils, but is performing an occupational role—a role, however, in which the recipients of her services are tightly bound in solidarity to her and to each other. Furthermore, compared to a parent's, her responsibility to them is much more universalistic, this being reinforced, as we saw, by the size of the class; it is also much more oriented to performance rather than to solicitude for the emotional "needs" of the children. She is not entitled to suppress the distinction between high and low achievers, just because not being able to be included among the high group would be too hard on little Johnny—however

much tendencies in this direction appear as deviant patterns. A mother, on the other hand, must give *first* priority to the needs of her child, regardless of his capacities to achieve.

It is also significant for the parallel of the elementary school class with the family that the teacher is normally a woman. As background it should be noted that in most European systems until recently, and often today in our private parochial and non-sectarian schools, the sexes have been segregated and each sex group has been taught by teachers of their own sex. Given coeducation, however, the woman teacher represents continuity with the role of the mother. Precisely the lack of differentiation in the elementary school "curriculum" between the components of subject-matter competence and social responsibility fits in with the greater diffuseness of the feminine role.

But at the same time, it is essential that the teacher is not a mother to her pupils, but must insist on universalistic norms and the differential reward of achievement. Above all she must be the agent of bringing about and legitimizing a differentiation of the school class on an achievement axis. This aspect of her role is furthered by the fact that in American society the feminine role is less confined to the familial context than in most other societies, but joins the masculine in occupational and associational concerns, though still with a greater relative emphasis on the family. Through identification with their teacher, children of both sexes learn that the category "woman" is not co-extensive with "mother" (and future wife), but that the feminine role-personality is more complex than that.

In this connection it may well be that there is a relation to the once-controversial issue of the marriage of women teachers. If the differentiation between what may be called the maternal and the occupational components of the feminine role is incomplete and insecure, confusion between them may be avoided by insuring that both are not performed by the same persons. The "old maid" teacher of American tradition may thus be thought of as having renounced the maternal role in favor of the occupational.[9] Recently, however, the highly affective concern over the issue of married women's teaching has conspicuously abated, and their actual participation has greatly increased. It may be suggested that this change is associated with a change in the feminine role, the most conspicuous feature of which is the general social sanctioning of participation of women in the labor force, not only prior to marriage, but also after marriage. This I should interpret as a process of structural differentiation in that the same category of persons is permitted and even expected to engage in a more complex set of role-functions than before.

The process of identification with the teacher which has been postulated here is furthered by the fact that in the elementary grades the child typically has one teacher, just as in the pre-oedipal period he had one parent, the mother, who was the focus of his object-relations. The continuity between the two phases is also favored by the fact that the teacher, like the mother, is a woman. But, if she acted only like a mother, there would be no genuine reorganization of the pupil's personality system. This reorganization is furthered by the features of the teacher role which differentiate it from the maternal. One further point is that while a child has one main teacher in each grade, he will usually have a new teacher when he progresses to the next higher grade. He is thus accustomed to the fact that teachers are, unlike mothers, "interchangeable" in a certain sense. The school year is long enough to form an important relationship to a particular teacher, but not long enough for a highly particularistic attachment to crystallize. More than in the parent-child relationship, in school the child must internalize his relation to the teacher's *role* rather than her particular personality; this is a major step in the internalization of universalistic patterns.

Socialization and Selection in the Elementary School

To conclude this discussion of the elementary school class, something should be said about the fundamental conditions underlying the process which is, as we have seen, simultaneously (1) an emancipation of the child from primary emotional attachment to this family, (2) an internalization of a level of societal values and norms that is a step higher than those he can learn in his family alone, (3) a differentiation of the school class in terms both of actual achievement and of differential *valuation* of achievement, and (4) from society's point of view, a selection and allocation of its human resources relative to the adult role system.[10]

Probably the most fundamental condition underlying this process is the sharing of common values by the two adult agencies involved—the family and the school. In this case the core is the shared valuation of *achievement*. It includes, above all, recognition that it is fair to give differential rewards for different levels of achievement, so long as there has been fair access to opportunity, and fair that these rewards lead on to higher-order opportunities for the successful. There is thus a basic sense in which the elementary school class is an embodiment of the fundamental American value of equality of opportunity, in that it places value *both* on initial equality and on differential achievement.

As a second condition, however, the rigor of this valuational pattern must be tempered by allowance for the difficulties and needs of the young child. Here the quasi-motherliness of the woman teacher plays an important part. Through her the school system, assisted by other agencies, attempts to minimize the insecurity resulting from the pressures to learn, by providing a certain amount of emotional support defined in terms of what is due to a child of a given age level. In this respect, however, the role of the school is relatively small. The underlying foundation of support is given in the home, and as we have seen, an important supplement to it can be provided by the informal peer associations of the child. It may be suggested that the development of extreme patterns of alienation from the school is often related to inadequate support in these respects.

Third, there must be a process of selective rewarding of valued performance. Here the teacher is clearly the primary agent, though the more progressive modes of education attempt to enlist classmates more systematically than in the traditional pattern. This is the direct source of intra-class differentiation along the achievement axis.

The final condition is that this initial differentiation tends to bring about a status system in the class, in which not only the immediate results of school work, but a whole series of influences, converge to consolidate different expectations which may be thought of as the children's "levels of aspiration." Generally some differentiation of friendship groups along this line occurs, though it is important that it is by no means complete, and that children are sensitive to the attitudes not only of their own friends, but of others.

Within this general discussion of processes and conditions, it is important to distinguish, as I have attempted to do all along, the socialization of the individual from the selective allocation of contingents to future roles. For the individual, the old familial identification is broken up (the family of orientation becomes, in Freudian terms, a "lost object") and a new identification is gradually built up, providing the first-order structure of the child's identity apart from his originally ascribed identity as son or daughter of the "Joneses." He both transcends his familial identification in favor of a more independent one and comes to occupy a differentiated status within the new system. His personal status is inevitably a direct function of the position he achieves, primarily in the formal school class and secondarily in the informal peer group structure. In spite of the sense in which achievement-ranking takes place along a continuum, I have put forward reasons to suggest that, with respect to this status, there is an important differentiation into two broad, relatively distinct levels, and that his position on one or the other enters into the individual's definition of his own identity. To an important degree this process of differentiation is independent of the socio-economic status of his family in the community, which to the child is a prior ascribed status.

When we look at the same system as a selective mechanism from the societal point of view, some further considerations become important. First, it may be noted that the valuation of achievement and its sharing by family and school not only provides the appropriate values for internalization by individuals, but also performs a crucial integrative function for the system. Differentiation of the class along the achievement axis is inevitably a source of strain, because it confers higher rewards and privileges on one contingent than on another within the same system. This common valuation helps make possible the acceptance of the crucial differentiation, especially by the losers in the competition. Here it is an essential point that this *common* value on achievement is shared by

units with different statuses in the system. It cuts across the differentiation of families by socio-economic status. It is necessary that there be realistic opportunity and that the teacher can be relied on to implement it by being "fair" and rewarding achievement by whoever shows capacity for it. The fact is crucial that the distribution of abilities, though correlated with family status, clearly does not coincide with it. There can then be a genuine selective process within a set of "rules of the game."

This commitment to common values is not, however, the sole integrative mechanism counteracting the strain imposed by differentiation. Not only does the individual pupil enjoy familial support, but teachers also like and indeed "respect" pupils on bases independent of achievement-status, and peer-group friendship lines, though correlated with position on the achievement scale, again by no means coincide with it, but cross-cut it. Thus there are cross-cutting lines of solidarity which mitigate the strains generated by rewarding achievement differentially.[11]

It is only *within* this framework of institutionalized solidarity that the crucial selective process goes on through selective rewarding and the consolidation of its results into a status-differentiation within the school class. We have called special attention to the impact of the selective process on the children of relatively high ability but low family status. Precisely in this group, but pervading school classes generally, is another parallel to what was found in the studies of voting behavior.[12] In the voting studies it was found that the "shifters"—those voters who were transferring their allegiance from one major party to the other—tended, on the one hand, to be the "cross-pressured" people, who had multiple status characteristics and group allegiances which predisposed them simultaneously to vote in opposite directions. The analogy in the school class is clearly to the children for whom ability and family status do not coincide. On the other hand, it was precisely in this group of cross-pressured voters that political "indifference" was most conspicuous. Non-voting was particularly prevalent in this group, as was a generally cool emotional tone toward a campaign. The suggestion is that some of the pupil "indifference" to school performance may have a similar origin. This is clearly a complex phenomenon and cannot be further analyzed here. But rather than suggesting, as is usual on common sense grounds, that indifference to school work represents an "alienation" from cultural and intellectual values, I would suggest exactly the opposite: that an important component of such indifference, including in extreme cases overt revolt against school discipline, is connected with the fact that the stakes, as in politics, are very high indeed. Those pupils who are exposed to contradictory pressures are likely to be ambivalent; at the same time, the personal stakes for them are higher than for the others, because what happens in school may make much more of a difference for their futures than for the others, in whom ability and family status point to the same expectations for the future. In particular for the upwardly mobile pupils, too much emphasis on school success would pointedly suggest "burning their bridges" of association with their families and status peers. This phenomenon seems to operate even in elementary school, although it grows somewhat more conspicuous later. In general I think that an important part of the anti-intellectualism in American youth culture stems from the *importance* of the selective process through the educational system rather than the opposite.

One further major point should be made in this analysis. As we have noted, the general trend of American society has been toward a rapid upgrading in the educational status of the population. This means that, relative to past expectations, with each generation there is increased pressure to educational achievement, often associated with parents' occupational ambition for their children.[13] To a sociologist this is a more or less classical situation of anomic strain, and the youth-culture ideology which plays down intellectual interests and school performance seems to fit in this context. The orientation of the youth culture is, in the nature of the case, ambivalent, but for the reasons suggested, the anti-intellectual side of the ambivalence tends to be overtly stressed. One of the reasons for the dominance of the anti-school side of the ideology is that it provides a means of protest against adults, who are at the opposite pole in the socialization situation. In certain respects one would expect that the trend toward greater emphasis on independence, which we have associated with progressive education, would accentuate the strain in this area and hence the tendency to decry adult expectations. The whole problem should be subjected to a thorough analysis in the light of what we know about ideologies more generally.

The same general considerations are relevant to the much-discussed problem of juvenile delinquency. Both the general upgrading process and the pressure to enhanced independence should be expected to increase strain on the lower, most marginal groups. The analysis of this paper has been concerned with the line between college and non-college contingents; there is, however, another line between those who achieve solid non-college educational status and those for whom adaptation to educational expectations at *any* level is difficult. As the acceptable minimum of educational qualification rises, person near and below the margin will tend to be pushed into an attitude of repudiation of these expectations. Truancy and delinquency are ways of expressing this repudiation. Thus the very *improvement* of educational standards in the society at large may well be a major factor in the failure of the educational process for a growing number at the lower end of the status and ability distribution. It should therefore not be too easily assumed that delinquency is a symptom of a *general* failure of the educational process.

Differentiation and Selection in the Secondary School

It will not be possible to discuss the secondary school phase of education in nearly as much detail as has been done for the elementary school phase, but it is worthwhile to sketch its main outline in order to place the above analysis in a wider context. Very broadly we may say that the elementary school phase is concerned with the internalization in children of motivation to achievement, and the selection of persons on the basis of differential capacity for achievement. The focus is on the *level* of capacity. In the secondary school phase, on the other hand, the focus is on the differentiation of *qualitative types* of achievement. As in the elementary school, this differentiation cross-cuts sex role. I should also maintain that it cross-cuts the levels of achievement which have been differentiated out in the elementary phase.

In approaching the question of the type of capacity differentiated, it should be kept in mind that secondary school is the principal springboard from which lower-status persons will enter the labor force, whereas those achieving higher status will continue their formal education in college, and some of them beyond. Hence for the lower-status pupils the important line of differentiation should be the one which will lead into broadly different categories of jobs; for the higher-status pupils the differentiation will lead to broadly different roles in college.

My suggestion is that this differentiation separates those two components of achievement which we labeled "cognitive" and "moral" in discussing the elementary phase. Those relatively high in "cognitive" achievement will fit better in specific-function, more or less technical roles; those relatively high in "moral" achievement will tend toward diffuser, more "socially" or "humanly" oriented roles. In jobs not requiring college training, the one category may be thought of as comprising the more impersonal and technical occupations, such as "operatives," mechanics, or clerical workers; the other, as occupations where "human relations" are prominent, such as salesmen and agents of various sorts. At the college level, the differentiation certainly relates to concern, on the one hand, with the specifically intellectual curricular work of college and, on the other hand, with various types of diffuser responsibility in human relations, such as leadership roles in student government and extracurricular activities. Again, candidates for post-graduate professional training will probably be drawn mainly from the first of these two groups.

In the structure of the school, there appears to be a gradual transition from the earliest grades through high school, with the changes timed differently in different school systems. The structure emphasized in the first part of this discussion is most clearly marked in the first three "primary" grades. With progression to the higher grades, there is greater frequency of plural teachers, though very generally still a single main teacher, though uncommon, is by no means unheard of. With junior high school, however, the shift of pattern becomes more marked, and still more in senior high.

By that time the pupil has several different teachers of both sexes[14] teaching him different subjects, which are more or less formally organized into different courses—college preparatory and others. Furthermore, with the choice of "elective" subjects, the members of the class in one subject no longer need be exactly the same as in another, so the pupil is much more systematically exposed to association with different people, both adults and age-peers, in different contexts. Moreover, the school he attends is likely to be substantially larger than was his elementary school, and to draw from a wider geographical area. Hence the child is exposed to a wider range of statuses than before, being thrown in with more age-peers whom he does not encounter in his neighborhood; it is less likely that his parents will know the parents of any given child with whom he associates. It is thus my impression that the transitions to junior high and senior high school are apt to mean a considerable reshuffling of friendships. Another conspicuous difference between the elementary and secondary levels is the great increase in high school of organized extracurricular activities. Now, for the first time, organized athletics become important, as do a variety of clubs and associations which are school-sponsored and supervised to varying degrees.

Two particularly important shifts in the patterning of youth culture occur in this period. One, of course, is the emergence of more positive cross-sex relationships outside the classroom through dances, dating, and the like. The other is the much sharper prestige-stratification of informal peer groupings, with indeed an element of snobbery which often exceeds that of the adult community in which the school exists.[15] Here it is important that though there is a broad correspondence between the prestige of friendship groups and family status of their members, this, like the achievement order of the elementary school, is by no means a simple "mirroring" of the community stratification scale, for a considerable number of lower-status children get accepted into groups including members with higher family status than themselves. This stratified youth system operates as a genuine assortative mechanism; it does not simply reinforce ascribed status.

The prominence of this youth culture in the American secondary school is, in comparison with other societies, one of the hallmarks of the American educational system; it is much less prominent in most European systems. It may be said to constitute a kind of structural fusion between the school class and the peer-group structure of the elementary period. It seems clear that what I have called the "human relations" oriented contingent of the secondary school pupils are more active and prominent in extracurricular activities, and that this is one of the main foci of their differentiation from the more impersonally and technically-oriented contingent. The personal qualities figuring most prominently in the human relations contingent can perhaps be summed up as the qualities that make for "popularity." I suggest that, from the point of view of the secondary school's selective function, the youth culture helps to differentiate between types of personalities which will, by and large, play different kinds of roles as adults.

The stratification of youth groups has, as noted, a selective function; it is a bridge between the achievement order and the adult stratification system of the community. But it also has another function. It is a focus of prestige which exists along side of, and is to a degree independent of, the achievement order focussing on school work as such. The attainment of prestige in the informal youth group is itself a form of valued achievement. Hence, among those individuals destined for higher status in society, one can discern two broad types: those whose school work is more or less outstanding and whose informal prestige is relatively satisfactory; and vice versa, those whose informal prestige is outstanding, and school performance satisfactory. Falling below certain minima in either respect would jeopardize the child's claim to belong in the upper group.[16] It is an important point here that those clearly headed for college belong to peer groups which, while often depreciative of intensive concern with studies, also take for granted and reinforce a level of scholastic attainment which is necessary for admission to a good college. Pressure will be put on the individual who tends to fall below such a standard.

In discussing the elementary school level it will be remembered that we emphasized that the peer group served as an object of emotional

dependency displaced from the family. In relation to the pressure for school achievement, therefore, it served at least partially as an expression of the lower-order motivational system *out* of which the child was in process of being socialized. On its own level, similar things can be said of the adolescent youth culture; it is in part an expression of regressive motivations. This is true of the emphasis on athletics despite its lack of relevance to adult roles, of the "homosexual" undertones of much intensive same-sex friendship, and of a certain "irresponsibility" in attitudes toward the opposite sex—e.g. the exploitative element in the attitudes of boys toward girls. This, however, is by no means the whole story. The youth culture is also a field for practicing the assumption of higher-order responsibilities, for conducting delicate human relations without immediate supervision and learning to accept the consequences. In this connection it is clearly of particular importance to the contingent we have spoken of as specializing in "human relations."

We can, perhaps, distinguish three different levels of crystallization of these youth-culture patterns. The middle one is that which may be considered age-appropriate without clear status-differentiation. The two keynotes here seem to be "being a good fellow" in the sense of general friendliness and being ready to take responsibility in informal social situations where something needs to be done. Above this, we may speak of the higher level of "outstanding" popularity and qualities of "leadership" of the person who is turned to where unusual responsibilities are required. And below the middle level are the youth patterns bordering on delinquency, withdrawal, and generally unacceptable behavior. Only this last level is clearly "regressive" relative to expectations of appropriate behavior for the age-grade. In judging these three levels, however, allowance should be made for a good many nuances. Most adolescents do a certain amount of experimenting with the borderline of the unacceptable patterns; that they should do so is to be expected in view of the pressure toward independence from adults, and of the "collusion" which can be expected in the reciprocal stimulation of age-peers. The question is whether this regressive behavior comes to be confirmed into a major pattern for the personality as a whole. Seen in this perspective, it seems legitimate to maintain that the middle and the higher patterns indicated are the major ones, and that only a minority of adolescents comes to be confirmed in a truly unacceptable pattern of living. This minority may well be a relatively constant proportion of the age cohort, but apart from situations of special social disorganization, the available evidence does not suggest that it has been a progressively growing one in recent years.

The patterning of cross-sex relations in the youth culture clearly foreshadows future marriage and family formation. That it figures so prominently in school is related to the fact that in our society the element of ascription, including direct parental influence, in the choice of a marriage partner is strongly minimized. For the girl, it has the very important significance of reminding her that her adult status is going to be very much concerned with marriage and a family. This basic expectation for the girl stands in a certain tension to the school's curricular coeducation with its relative lack of differentiation by sex. But the extent to which the feminine role in American society continues to be anchored in marriage and the family should not be allowed to obscure the importance of coeducation. In the first place, the contribution of women in various extra-familial occupations and in community affairs has been rapidly increasing, and certainly higher levels of education have served as a prerequisite to this contribution. At the same time, it is highly important that the woman's familial role should not be regarded as drastically segregated from the cultural concerns of the society as a whole. The educated woman has important functions *as wife and mother*, particularly as an influence on her children in backing the schools and impressing on them the importance of education. It is, I think, broadly true that the immediate responsibility of women for family management has been increasing, though I am very skeptical of the alleged "abdication" of the American male. But precisely in the context of women's increased family responsibility, the influence of the mother both as agent of socialization and as role model is a crucial one. This influence should be evaluated in the light of the general upgrading process. It is very doubtful whether, apart from any other considerations, the motivational prerequisites of the general process could be sustained without

sufficiently high education of the women who, as mothers, influence their children.

Conclusion

With the general cultural upgrading process in American society which has been going on for more than a century, the educational system has come to play an increasingly vital role. That this should be the case is, in my opinion, a consequence of the general trend to structural differentiation in the society. Relatively speaking, the school is a specialized agency. That it should increasingly have become the principal channel of selection as well as agency of socialization is in line with what one would expect in an increasingly differentiated and progressively more upgraded society. The legend of the "self-made man" has an element of nostalgic romanticism and is destined to become increasingly mythical, if by it is meant not just mobility from humble origins to high status, which does indeed continue to occur, but that the high status was attained through the "school of hard knocks" without the aid of formal education.

The structure of the public school system and the analysis of the ways in which it contributes both to the socialization of individuals and to their allocation to roles in society is, I feel, of vital concern to all students of American society. Notwithstanding the variegated elements in the situation, I think it has been possible to sketch out a few major structural patterns of the public school system and at least to suggest some ways in which they serve these important functions. What could be presented in this paper is the merest outline of such an analysis. It is, however, hoped that it has been carried far enough to suggest a field of vital mutual interest for social scientists on the one hand and those concerned with the actual operation of the schools on the other.

Notes

* I am indebted to Mrs. Carolyn Cooper for research assistance in the relevant literature and for editorial work on the first draft of this paper.
1. The principal source for these statements is a study of social mobility among boys in ten public high schools in the Boston metropolitan area, conducted by Samuel A. Stouffer,

Florence R. Kluckhohn, and the present author. Unfortunately the material is not available in published form.

2. See table from this study in J. A. Kahl, *The American Class Structure* (New York: Rinehart & Co., 1953), p. 283. Data from a nationwide sample of high school students, published by the Educational Testing Service, show similar patterns of relationships. For example, the ETS study shows variation, by father's occupation, in proportion of high school seniors planning college, of from 35 per cent to 80 per cent for boys and 27 per cent to 79 per cent for girls. (From *Background Factors Related to College Plans and College Enrollment among High School Students* [Princeton, N.J.: Educational Testing Service, 1957]).

3. There seem to be two main reasons why the high-status, low-ability group is not so important as its obverse. The first is that in a society of expanding educational and occupational opportunity the general trend is one of upgrading, and the social pressures to downward mobility are not as great as they would otherwise be. The second is that there are cushioning mechanisms which tend to protect the high status boy who has difficulty "making the grade." He may be sent to a college with low academic standards, he may go to schools where the line between ability levels is not rigorously drawn, etc.

4. This discussion refers to public schools. Only about 13 per cent of all elementary and secondary school pupils attend non-public schools, with this proportion ranging from about 22 per cent in the Northeast to about 6 per cent in the South. U.S. Office of Education, *Biennial Survey of Education in the United States, 1954–56* (Washington: U.S. Government Printing Office, 1959), chap. ii, "Statistics of State School Systems, 1955–56," Table 44, p. 114.

5. In 1955–56, 13 per cent of the public elementary school instructional staff in the United States were men. *Ibid.*, p. 7.

6. This summary of some contrasts between traditional and progressive patterns is derived from general reading in the literature rather than any single authoritative account.

7. This account of the two components of elementary school achievement and their relation summarizes impressions gained from the literature, rather than being based on the opinions of particular authorities. I have the impression that achievement in this sense corresponds closely to what is meant by the term as used by McClelland and his associates. Cf. D. C. McClelland *et al.*, *The Achievement Motive* (New York: Appleton-Century-Crofts, Inc., 1953).

8. On the identification process in the family see my paper, "Social Structure and the Development of Personality," *Psychiatry*, XXI (November, 1958), pp. 321–40.

9. It is worth noting that the Catholic parochial school system is in line with the more general older American tradition, in that the typical teacher is a nun. The only difference in this respect is the sharp religious symbolization of the difference between mother and teacher.

10. The following summary is adapted from T. Parsons, R. F. Bales *et al.*, *Family, Socialization and Interaction Process* (Glencoe, Ill.: The Free Press, 1955), esp. chap. iv.

11. In this, as in several other respects, there is a parallel to other important allocative processes in the society. A striking example is the voting process by which political support is allocated between party candidates. Here, the strain arises from the fact that one candidate and his party will come to enjoy all the perquisites—above all the power—of office, while the other will be excluded for the time being from these. This strain is mitigated, on the one hand, by the common commitment to constitutional procedure, and on the other hand, by the fact that the nonpolitical bases of social solidarity, which figure so prominently as determinants of voting behavior, still cut across party lines. The average person is, in various of his roles, associated with people whose political preference is different from his own; he therefore could not regard the opposite party as composed of unmitigated scoundrels without introducing a rift within the groups to which he is attached. This feature of the electorate's structure is brought out strongly in B. R. Berelson, P. F. Lazarsfeld and W. N. McPhee, *Voting* (Chicago: University of Chicago Press, 1954). The conceptual analysis of it is developed in my own paper, "'Voting' and the Equilibrium of the American Political System" in E. Burdick and A. J. Brodbeck (eds.), *American Voting Behavior* (Glencoe, Ill.: The Free Press, 1959).

12. *Ibid.*

13. J. A. Kahl, "Educational and Occupational Aspirations of 'Common Man' Boys," *Harvard Educational Review*, XXIII (Summer, 1953), pp. 186–203.

14. Men make up about half (49 per cent) of the public secondary school instructional staff. *Biennial Survey of Education in the United States, 1954–56, op. cit.*, chap. ii, p. 7.

15. See, for instance, C. W. Gordon, *The Social System of the High School: A Study in the Sociology of Adolescence* (Glencoe, Ill.: The Free Press, 1957).

16. J. Riley, M. Riley, and M. Moore, "Adolescent Values and the Riesman Typology" in S. M. Lipset and L. Lowenthal (eds.), *The Sociology of Culture and the Analysis of Social Character* (Glencoe, Ill.: The Free Press, to be published in 1960).

CHAPTER 8

KNOWLEDGE CREATION AND DISSEMINATION

ASSOCIATE EDITOR: JOHN M. BRAXTON

Knowledge creation and its dissemination are core functions of higher education. At the level of faculty, knowledge creation and knowledge transmission are the core functions of the academic profession (Parsons and Platt, 1973). The creation of knowledge results from the scholarly activities of college and university faculty members. The scholarly activities of college and university faculty manifest themselves in the form of publications: books, monographs and refereed journal articles (Braxton and Toombs, 1982). As a consequence, the scholarly role of college and university faculty members is considered interchangeable with publication activity.

Publication activity is important for other reasons. First, the doctoral training process stresses preparation for the scholarly role (Jencks and Riesman, 1968; Cole and Cole, 1973; Merton, 1973; Braxton and Toombs, 1982). Second, some scholars such as Donald Light (1974) limit membership in the academic profession to those faculty members who publish. Third, career advancement in an academic discipline depends on publication activity. Light calls this "single channel mobility," (1974). Fourth, the tenure and promotion systems at most colleges and universities use publication activity as a criterion (Fox, 1985). Fifth, faculty salary increments are highly influenced by publication activity (Tuckman and Hagemann, 1976).

As a consequence, several questions emerge: Does the publication activity of faculty vary across different types of colleges and universities? What criteria can be applied to assess the quality of faculty publications? These questions are addressed by the selected readings of this chapter.

The article "Changes in Academic Research Performance Over Time: A Study of Institutional Accumulative Advantage," by Richard Bentley and Robert Blackburn addresses the first questions. In addition to providing evidence that publication activity of faculty varies according to mission of colleges and universities, Figure 3 demonstrates that faculty publication rates are highest in research oriented universities and the lowest in colleges and universities that emphasize teaching more than research (Comprehensive-I institutions). Despite the dominance of research oriented universities, Bentley and Blackburn present evidence that faculty members in other types of colleges and universities have increased their level of publication activity over the past 20 years.

The other two selected readings focus on the assessment of scholarly performance or the assessment of the publication activity of individual college and university faculty members. The piece by Charles E. Glassick, Mary T. Huber and Gene I. Maeroff titled "Standards of Scholarly Work" proposes a set of criteria that can be used to appraise a given publication, whereas John M. Braxton and Alan E. Bayer discuss various types of publications that may be used to evaluate faculty scholarly performance in "Assessing Faculty Scholarly Performance." Glassick, Huber and Maeroff posit that six standards can be used to assess a broad range of publications. These standards are: (1) clear goals, (2) adequate preparation, (3) appropriate methods, (4) significant results, (5) effective presentation, and (6) reflective critique. Each of these criteria or standards is described

John Braxton teaches at Peabody College of Education and Human Development, Vanderbilt University. (braxtojm@ctr-vax.vanderbilt.edu)

in some detail. Glassick, Huber and Maeroff make the important point that these six standards should be used together rather than on a selective basis.

Braxton and Bayer describe the various forms of publications that can be used to appraise faculty scholarly performance: books and journal articles. Numerical counts of books and articles are a frequent approach to assessing the quantity of publications. They discuss the problems the use of each form presents. They argue that weighting systems are needed to make comparisons between numerical counts of articles and books. Braxton and Bayer also describe the different forms journal articles take: full-length articles, research notes, and book reviews. In addition to such quantitative indicators, the use of citations to published works are also discussed as a proxy measure of publication quality. The limitations of the use of citations as a measure of quality are discussed.

Other topics of importance to understanding knowledge creation and publication activity as its public manifestation are as follows: what are the explanations for varying rates of publication activity by college and university faculty members? How can the definition of scholarship be broadened so that the scholarly activities of more faculty can be portrayed? What forms might a more expansive definition of scholarship take? Because of space limitations, selected readings addressing these basic questions could not be provided.

For individuals wishing to become familiar with each of these questions, readers are directed to the selections by Mary Frank Fox, "Publication, performance, and reward in science and scholarship," and by John Creswell, *Faculty Research Performance: Lessons from the Sciences and Social Sciences*. Fox and Creswell offer a set of explanations for varying degrees of publication activity by individual faculty members. A third reading is Ernest L. Boyer's *Scholarship Reconsidered: Priorities of the Professoriate*. Boyer proposes that the definition of scholarship be broadened beyond the scholarship of discovery to include the scholarships of application, integration, and teaching.

Suggested Supplementary Readings

Blackburn, Robert T. & Janet H. Lawrence, *Faculty at Work: Motivation, Expectation, Satisfaction*. Baltimore: Johns Hopkins University Press, 1995.

Braskamp, Larry A. & John C. Ory, *Assessing Faculty Work. Enhancing Individual and Institutional Performance*. San Francisco: Jossey-Bass, 1994.

Braxton, J. M. and Toombs, W. "Faculty Uses of Doctoral Training: Consideration of a Technique for the Differentiation of Scholarly Effort from Research Activity," *Research in Higher Education*, 1982, 16, 265–282.

Boyer, Ernest L., *Scholarship Reconsidered: Priorities of the Professoriate*, Lawrenceville, NJ: Princeton University Press, 1990.

Centra, John A., *Reflective Faculty Evaluation: Enhancing Teaching and Determining Faculty Effectiveness*. San Francisco: Jossey-Bass, 1993.

Cole, Jonathon R. and Steven Cole. *Social Stratification in Science*. Chicago: University of Chicago Press, 1973.

Fox, M. F. "Publication, Performance, and Reward in Science and Scholarship," in J. C. Smart (ed.), *Higher Education: Handbook of Theory and Research*, Volume 1. New York: Agathon Press, 1985, 255–282.

Jencks, C. J. and Riesman, D. The *Academic Revolution*. Garden City, NY: Doubleday Anchor Books, 1969.

Light, D. "The Structure of the Academic Profession," *Sociology of Education*, 1974, 47, 2–28.

Merton, R. K. *The Sociology of Science: Theoretical and Empirical Investigations*. Chicago: University of Chicago Press, 1973.

Parsons, T. and Platt, G. M. *The American University*. Cambridge: Harvard University Press 1973.

Tuckman, H. P. and Hagemann, R. P. "An Analysis of the Reward Structure in Two Disciplines," *Journal of Higher Education*, 1976, 47, 447–64.

Changes in Academic Research Performance Over Time: A Study of Institutional Accumulative Advantage

RICHARD BENTLEY AND ROBERT BLACKBURN

This study examines changes in institutional research performance over time by analyzing data from four national surveys of the American professoriate conducted between 1969 and 1988. To assess whether groups of institutions may be accumulating advantage relative to others, research activities are compared across five Carnegie institution types. Weights are created to adjust for sampling differences and research output measures are standardized to adjust for variation by discipline. Findings show an overall strengthening of research emphasis reflected by a stronger orientation toward research (more faculty holding Ph.D.'s and having a primary interest in research) and higher research output (grant and publication performance). While Research-I universities have retained their initial (1969) advantage, they have not accumulated more. Meanwhile, Doctoral-Granting-I universities have gained strength relative to Research-II institutions. Research at Comprehensive-I was also up, but at a slower rate than the other Carnegie groups.

As research expenditures have risen, some observers of the higher education enterprise worry about a growing stratification in academic science such that only a few elite institutions are capable of conducting high-quality research. Smith and Karlesky (1977) found that less eminent research institutions are more susceptible to declines in external funding sources, reductions in research opportunities for younger scientists, and deterioration of instrumentation. A general decline in faculty working conditions, such as inadequate supplies and insufficient clerical help (Bowen and Schuster, 1986, p. 156), may be especially bur-

densome at comprehensive colleges and universities where faculty balance research interests with higher teaching loads.

Another example of strained competition between the so-called "have" and the "have not" institutions is evidenced by the growing dissatisfaction with federal peer review. A number of universities have circumvented competitive scientific review by hiring outside lobbyists and seeking direct legislative sponsorship (Graves, 1986; McCarthy, 1986). Some groups (e.g., the Association of American Universities that represents the largest research universities) criticize this approach as "pork barrel" and warn that it could harm the peer review process, the hallmark of the scientific community (Graves, 1986). However, others counter saying that peer review unfairly favors a select group of eminent research institutions (Rose, 1986).

Despite concerns about growing stratification, longitudinal studies documenting changes in academic research performance by institutional type are rare. For example, science trend data collected by the National Science Foundation (1987) and the National Research Council (1987) do not differentiate by college type. While a number of national faculty surveys provide comprehensive data on higher education (e.g., see literature reviewed by Blackburn, Lawrence, Ross, Okoloko, Bieber, Meiland, and Street, 1986), attempts to combine these data for longitudinal analysis have been hampered by variations in sampling framework and survey question design (see Drew and Tronvig, 1988).

"Changes in Academic Research Performance Over Time: A Study of Institutional Accumulative Advantage," by Richard Bentley and Robert Blackburn, reprinted from *Research in Higher Education*, Vol. 31, No. 4, 1990, Human Sciences Press, Inc.

The purpose of this study is to examine changes in institutional research performance over time by analyzing data from four national surveys of the American professoriate conducted between 1969 and 1988. To assess whether groups of institutions may be accumulating advantage relative to others, research output is compared across five Carnegie (1973, 1976, and 1987) institution types: Research-I (Res-I), Research-II (Res-II), Doctoral-granting-I (Doc-I), Doctoral-granting-II (Doc-II), and Comprehensive-I (Comp-I) institutions. Weights are created to adjust for sampling differences and research output measures are standardized to adjust for variation by discipline.[1]

Theoretical Framework

Stratification emerges as a central theme in studies on academic research performance (Cole and Cole, 1973; Merton, 1968; Zuckerman, 1977). However most of this research focuses on the hierarchy of individuals rather than institutions (Cole and Cole, 1973; Lazarsfeld and Thielens, 1958; Lotka, 1926; Price, 1963). For example, in 1926 Lotka posited his "inverse square law of scientific productivity" explaining why a few scientists account for most publication productivity.

Accumulative advantage is frequently cited as one reason why some individual researchers achieve eminence over others (Allison and Stewart, 1974; Cole and Cole, 1973; Merton, 1968; Zuckerman, 1977). Put simply, this theory suggests that the rich get richer as they accumulate advantage in terms of resources and recognition. As such, resources and recognition act as feedback loops that contribute to subsequent research support and productivity. A good example of accumulative advantage is Zuckerman's (1977) profile of Nobel laureates who are more likely to attend elite universities, study with prestigious mentors, graduate earlier, and be hired by elite institutions. Accumulative advantage is seen as an important factor in explaining why faculty publication and output varies so markedly (Allison and Stewart, 1974; Cole and Cole, 1973).

However, advantage can accrue to institutions as well as individuals. This situation is illustrated by the lion's share of federal support and super-star researchers (e.g., Nobel laureates) concentrated at top research universities. Institutional prestige can act as a "halo effect," thereby providing an additional edge in the grant and publication peer review process (Cole, Rubin, and Cole, 1978; Rose, 1986). The strong predictive power of institutional type and prestige on publication output indicates the important relationship of institutional affiliation. (See the literature reviews by Finkelstein, 1984 and Creswell, 1985.) For instance, a longitudinal study by Long (1978) found that publication patterns changed when natural scientists moved to new institutions, and they reflected the publication norms of the new institution. That is, if they moved to a university of highly productive faculty, they increased their output.

Methodology

The study explores two aspects of institutional academic research: (1) general research orientation or potential and (2) overall research output. Changes in research orientation or potential are based on (1) the percent of faculty holding Ph.D.'s and (2) the percent of faculty with a primary interest in research (over teaching). Changes in research output include (1) the proportion of faculty receiving sponsored research support (from government, industry, and foundations), (2) the level of faculty publication productivity (two-year publications and total books published), and (3) an aggregate measure of research output combining grants, two-year publications, and books.

Data are drawn from four national surveys of the American professoriate. The first two were sponsored by the Carnegie Commission on Higher Education in 1969 (Bayer, 1970; Trow, 1975) and 1975 (Roizen, Fulton, and Trow, 1978). The 1980 survey was conducted by the University of California at Los Angeles' Higher Education Research Institute (1983). The 1988 survey was conducted by the University of Michigan National Center for Research to Improve Postsecondary Teaching and Learning (Blackburn and Lawrence, 1989).

The Population

Table 1 presents the distributions of institution and faculty subsamples by Carnegie type. The subsamples include all assistant, associate, and full professors with principal teaching appointments in eight departments (biology, chemistry, English, history, psychology, sociology, political science, and mathematics/statistics). These departments represent the humanities, natural sciences, and social sciences.

Despite two revisions of the Carnegie classification since 1973 (in 1976 and 1986), considerable institutional stability was found within Carnegie type across survey years. The most significant fluctuation occurred with the redefinition of Res-I universities in 1987. However, all seven Res-I universities in the 1988 sample were also Res-I universities in 1976.

Much of the variation in institution and faculty sample sizes reflects differences in sampling design. For example, the large percentage of Res-I faculty in 1969 reflects the overrepresentation of high-rated universities in 1969 (Roizen, Fulton, and Trow, 1978, pp. 320–323). Of greatest concern is the potential response bias with the 1980 data that has a relatively low response rate (34%).[2] The concern is illustrated by the differences in faculty distribution between the 1969 and 1980 subsamples (see Table 1). These two distributions should be similar because the 1980 survey replicated the 1969 sampling framework and drew a representative one-third subset of the same institutions that participated in 1969 (HERI, 1983). However, the 1980 distribution suggests a lower response rate for Res-I faculty. (There is evidence that the HERI subsample was not random.)

Weighting

Weights were created to adjust for sampling differences across the four survey subsamples. Table 2 presents both the weighted and unweighted sample N's by Carnegie type, control, and department. The weights are designed to estimate the true distribution of faculty and are based on faculty data reported in the *American Universities and Colleges* directories (1968, 1983, and 1987).[3] Random samples by Carnegie type and control were drawn from three directories that corresponded closest to the 1969, 1980, and 1988 survey years. The 1975 weights were interpolated because the directory had ceased publication between 1972 and 1983.

Variable Definitions and Procedures

Measures of research potential and output are based on six survey questions repeated across survey years (only one variable, faculty preference for research, is missing in 1980). Specific variable definitions include the following:

1. PHD—Percent of faculty holding a Ph.D.

2. RESPREF—Percent of faculty primarily interested in research. Of four possible categorical responses, this variable combines faculty reporting interests either (1) leaning very heavily toward research or (2) both in teaching and research but leaning more toward research.

3. PUB2YR—Number of self-reported professional writings published or accepted for publication in the last two years. This variable was recoded into mean categorical values to estimate the actual number of publications (i.e., a category indicating a range of 5 to 10 publications was recoded 7.5).[4]

4. BKSALL—Number of books and monographs published over a faculty member's career. Like PUB2YR, this variable was recoded into mean categorical values (i.e., a category indicating a range of 3 to 4 publications was recoded 3.5). Lifetime books are included, in addition to two-year publications, because the disciplinary norms in some fields (e.g., political science) place more emphasis on books than articles (Biglan, 1973). At the same time, inclusion of BKSALL will be influenced by the aging of the faculty work force, which has increased since 1969, since lifetime publications are correlated positively with career experience (Bayer and Dutton, 1977).

5. ALLGRT—Percent of faculty receiving any externally sponsored grant support within in the past year. This dichotomous variable (yes or no) was created by computing a new variable that

TABLE 1
Institution and Faculty Subsample Sizes

Carnegie Type	1969 Carnegie — Institution Subsample		1969 Carnegie — Faculty Subsample		1975 Carnegie — Institution Subsample		1975 Carnegie — Faculty Subsample		1980 UCLA-HERI — Institution Subsample		1980 UCLA-HERI — Faculty Subsample		1988 UM-NCRIPTAL — Institution Subsample		1988 UM-NCRIPTAL — Faculty Subsample	
	N	%	N	%	N	%	N	%	N	%	N	%	N	%	N	%
Res-I	30	25.6	1432	45.2	30	21.6	994	28.2	7	19.4	409	27.4	7	15.2	579	24.3
Res-II	15	12.8	479	15.1	20	14.4	602	17.1	6	16.7	264	17.7	3	6.5	241	10.1
Doc-I	28	23.9	639	20.2	16	11.5	287	8.1	7	19.4	321	21.5	5	10.9	296	12.4
Doc-I	10	8.5	178	5.6	19	13.7	389	11.0	4	11.1	150	10.0	6	13.0	311	13.1
Comp-I	34	29.1	438	13.8	54	38.8	1251	35.5	12	33.3	349	23.4	25	54.3	956	40.1
Total	117		3166		139		3523		36		1493		46		2383	
Original Survey N	303		20008[a]		427		25062		96		9351		155		3972	
Original[b] Survey Response %			59.8%				51.5%				33.6%				49.7%	
Subsample %	38.6%		15.8%		32.6%		14.1%		37.5%		16.0%		29.7%		60.0%	

Note: The Carnegie classification was set up in 1973 and revised in 1976 and 1987. The 1969 data use the 1973 classification; the 1975 and 1980 data use the 1976 classification; and the 1988 data use the 1987 classification.

[a] The 1969 data are a one-third random sample of the original N of 60,028.

[b] Bayer, 1970, pp. 2–3; Roizen, Fulton, and Troy, 1978, p. 75; HERI, 1983, p. 6.

[c] The 1988 survey sampled the eight departments that are included in this subsample. This is why the subsample is comparably larger than the other surveys that surveyed faculty from all disciplines and professional schools.

TABLE 2
Comparison Between Unweighted and Weighted Subsamples by Carnegie Type, Department, and Control

	1969 Carnegie				1975 Carnegie				1980 UCLA-HERI				1988 UM-NCRIPTAL			
	Unweighted		Weighted		Unweighted		Weighted		Unweighted		Weighted		Unweighted		Weighted	
Carnegie Type	N	%	N	%	N	%	N	%	N	%	N	%	N	%	N	%
Res-I	1432	45.2%	773	24.4%	994	28.2%	676	19.2%	409	27.4%	266	17.8%	579	24.3%	383	16.1%
Res-II	479	15.1%	381	12.0%	602	17.1%	488	13.8%	264	17.7%	215	14.4%	241	10.1%	267	11.2%
Doc-I	639	20.2%	427	13.5%	287	8.1%	277	7.9%	321	21.5%	181	12.1%	296	12.4%	227	9.5%
Doc-II	178	5.6%	123	3.9%	389	11.0%	367	10.4%	150	10.0%	104	7.0%	311	13.1%	245	10.3%
Comp-I	438	13.8%	1463	46.2%	1251	35.5%	1716	48.7%	349	23.4%	727	48.7%	956	40.1%	1260	52.9%
Total	3166		3167		3523		3524		1493		1493		2383		2382	
Department	N	%	N	%	N	%	N	%	N	%	N	%	N	%	N	%
Chemistry	445	14.1%	384	12.1%	449	12.7%	387	11.0%	187	12.5%	155	10.4%	267	11.2%	237	9.9%
Math/Stats	537	17.0%	482	15.2%	556	15.8%	536	15.2%	242	16.2%	226	15.1%	301	12.6%	392	16.4%
Biology	244	7.7%	382	12.1%	340	9.7%	438	12.4%	152	10.2%	189	12.7%	314	13.2%	304	12.8%
Psychology	435	13.7%	364	11.5%	389	11.0%	449	12.7%	201	13.5%	202	13.5%	332	13.9%	301	12.6%
Sociology	232	7.3%	208	6.6%	283	8.0%	268	7.6%	148	9.9%	123	8.2%	218	9.1%	190	8.0%
Pol. Sci.	283	8.9%	259	8.2%	330	9.4%	289	8.2%	134	9.0%	123	8.2%	223	9.4%	205	8.6%
English	576	18.2%	682	21.5%	693	19.7%	722	20.5%	229	15.3%	296	19.8%	437	18.3%	470	19.7%
History	414	13.1%	405	12.8%	483	13.7%	435	12.3%	200	13.4%	180	12.0%	291	12.2%	285	12.0%
Total	3166		3166		3523		3524		1493		1494		2383		2384	
Control	N	%	N	%	N	%	N	%	N	%	N	%	N	%	N	%
Public	2286	72.2%	2331	73.6%	2261	64.2%	2646	75.1%	1140	76.4%	1074	71.9%	1786	74.9%	1771	74.3%
Private	880	27.8%	836	26.4%	1262	35.8%	879	24.9%	353	23.6%	419	28.1%	597	25.1%	612	25.7%
Total	3166		3167		3523		3525		1493		1493		2383		2383	

Note: Data include all faculty holding academic rank of assistant, associate, or full professor.

summed five possible sources of support: federal, state and local government, industry, foundation, and other sources.[5]

6. TOTPROD—Aggregate grant and publication output was developed by combining standardized scores from three variables: two-year publications (PUB2YR), total books (BKSALL), and sponsored research support within the past year (ALLGRT).[6]

In addition to presenting mean and percent figures, publication and grant output variables are converted into standardized z-scores. Standardized scores avoid potentially overstating performance for those institutions where a disproportionate share of faculty may have been in departments with higher than average publication rates and sponsored research. Standardization also adjusts for publication norms that often vary by discipline (Blackburn, Behymer, and Hall, 1978; Wanner, Lewis, and Gregorio, 1981).

To standardize publications and grants, z-scores were created separately for each of the eight disciplines and then summed across disciplines. A new z-score is then created from the sum of scores across disciplines. Standardized scores for total productivity (TOTPROD) were created by summing the three standardized scores for two-year publications (PUB2YR), lifetime books published (BKSALL), and total grants received within the past year (ALLGRT) and creating a new z-score from the aggregate measure.

Findings are presented both in raw data form and as standardized z-scores in order to provide a more solid context to assess changes over time. ANOVAs were run across Carnegie types and include Scheffe post hoc multiple-range tests to compare differences between groups.

Cautions Affecting Interpretation

In conducting these analyses several assumptions have been made that could potentially affect the measures that have been used. The principle ones are pointed out and their likely consequences are indicated.

1. Summing individual departmental faculty productivity and taking that average as the measure of department faculty output clearly is a change in the level of analysis, from the individual to the organizational. Summing departments across institutions to calculate a productivity measure for an institution type raises the level of analysis one level higher and encompasses the same potential pitfalls. Both of these procedures were used here even though the complications are known (see Young, Blackburn, Conrad, and Cameron, 1989).

Two scenarios illustrate the possible distortions in the construct. Suppose eight faculty in a department have produced 40 articles in the past two years. If all eight published 5 articles (or even 4 or 6) the construct of department productivity as the sum of the individuals seem appropriate. However, if the 40 articles were produced by two faculty and six did nothing (or some similar distribution with a high skewness and standard deviation), one now has a couple of highly productive individuals but not really a productive department. A similar example could be constructed by summing institutions within a type to compare with another type. Whether it makes conceptual sense to add and average institutional productivity units, irrespective of the arithmetic ease of the process, depends on the variance of the sample being summed.

A problem with relying on Carnegie type as the unit of analysis is that research performance can differ significantly across institutions within the same classification type. ANOVAs run on 1988 two-year publications by institution yielded significant differences ($p<.05$) for four of the five Carnegie groups included in the study. Only Doc-I institutions ($p<.05$) did not vary across institutions ($p=.17$). This suggests some caution in assuming similarity in research performance within Carnegie classifications.

On the other hand, research performance levels when compared within departments appear to be more similar. ANOVAs run on 1988 two-year publications by department (for Res-I only) showed no significance at six out of eight departments (e.g., ranging from $p=.36$ for sociology to .70 for political science). However, 1988 mathematics ($p<.05$) and biology ($p<.01$) departments showed significant difference across institutions.

2. The dollar values of the grants that faculty have received are not known, only the number of grants (as self-reported).[7] The dollar amount is no doubt higher in later years, except in 1975, where the National Science Foundation (1981, p. 76) clearly shows a decrease in most funding sources, especially at the federal level, which is the highest contributor. However, the value of succeeding dollars from a 1969 standard is clearly less. Also the real costs of conducting research may be higher today. In short, the quantitative consequences of an increased number of grants (i.e., research support) are most likely overestimated by the data.

3. A subtle but not unimportant consideration is the possible changing value of an article at different points in time. Both the amount of journal space available to publish in and the number of faculty seeking to publish in that space differ at each point in time. That is, article values can change. Bieber and Blackburn (1989) have found that when the ratio of space to potential contributors is determined for 1972 (the base year they used) each article must be deflated by about one-half. Said another way, our reported increased productivity is misleading, at least in this respect.[8]

Despite these limitations to this inquiry, one can still retain a high degree of confidence in the results that indicate different growth rates across institutional types, that is, accumulative advantage, since the potential distorting causes for the most part should be nearly random throughout all institutional types.

Results

Findings are reported in four parts. First, changes in research orientation and potential of campuses to accumulate research advantage are shown (Figures 1 and 2, with Tables A1 and A2). Second, indices of research publication output, including two-year publications and lifetime books published, are presented (Figures 3–6 with Tables A3–A6). Third, grant acquisition is displayed (Figures 7 and 8, with Tables A7 and A8). Fourth, an aggregate measure of research output that combines grants and publications is shown (Figure 9, with Table A9). Last, a summary of Scheffe tests findings

on the grant publication variables is presented in Table 3.

Research Orientation

In general, the data suggest a growing emphasis on research orientation and potential. This observation is supported by the growing number of faculty holding Ph.D.'s as well as the increasing percentage of faculty whose interest in research is greater than in teaching[9] (see Figures 1 and 2). A growth in Ph.D. faculty was most marked at Comp-I institutions between 1969 and 1975 (up from 72.9% to 84.5%), although this rate of growth has since tapered. Doc-II institutions also increased (from 82.9% to 92.9% between 1969 and 1980). This larger growth rate, of course, was made possible because of their lower initial percentage.

Of all five Carnegie groups, Doc-I and Doc-II showed the greatest increase between 1969 and 1975 of the proportion of faculty with primary interest in research. Doc-I's rose from 43.7% to 55.1% during this time, while Doc-II's rose from 23.1 to 41.9%. Comp-I's show little change in research interests despite their growth in percentage of faculty with Ph.D.'s

Publication Performance

Faculty publishing rates have risen at all types of institutions since 1969 (see Figure 3). For example, the mean number of two-year publications at Res-I universities rose from 3.7 to 5.2 between 1969 and 1988 (see Table A3). Doc-I's have expanded two-year publication output considerably, especially between 1969 and 1980 (rising from an average of 2.9 to 3.8 articles), and surpassed Res-II universities for that moment in time.

A similar picture emerges after two-year publication figures are standardized by discipline before summing (see Figure 4). Standardized two-year publication data suggest even a more pronounced gap between Comp-I and other institutions. A Scheffe post hoc test shows a significant difference between Comp-I and Doc-II's ($p<.05$) beginning in 1975 (see Table 3).

Lifetime book publication totals also have risen since 1969. For example, the mean number of books published at Res-I's rose from 1.4 to 2.0 (see Table A5). As with two-year

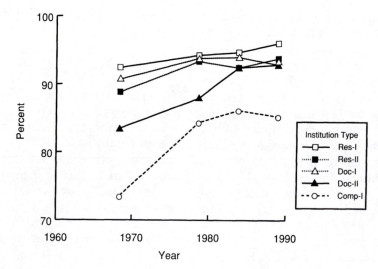

Figure 1: Percent of faculty with Ph.D.'s.

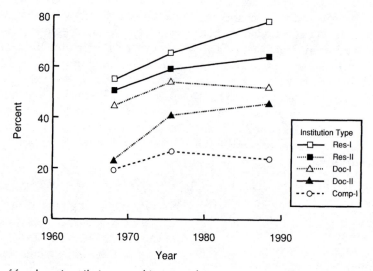

Figure 2: Percent of faculty primarily interested in research.

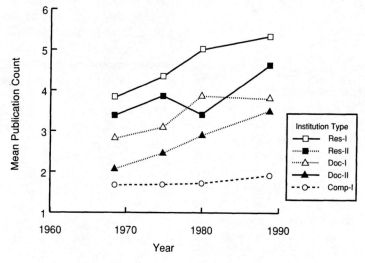

Figure 3: Mean two-year professional publication rate.

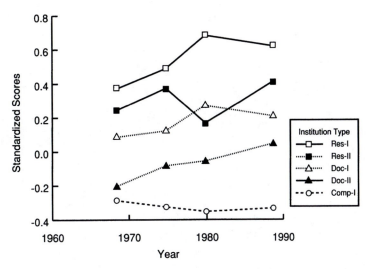

Figure 4: Standardized two-year professional publication rate (adjusted for differences by discipline).

TABLE 3
Scheffe Post Hoc Tests Significant at .05 Comparing Differences by Carnegie Institution Type

	Comp-I	Doc-II	Doc-I	Res-II
Two-Year Publications				
Comp-I				
Doc-II	75 80 88			
Doc-I	69 75 80 88			
Res-II	69 75 80 88	69 75 88		
Res-I	69 75 80 88	69 75 80 88	69 75 80 88	80
Lifetime Books				
Comp-I				
Doc-II				
Doc-I	75 80			
Res-II	75 80	75 80		
Res-I	69 75 80 88	69 75 80 88	69 75 88	75 88
Grants				
Comp-I				
Doc-II	75			
Doc-I	69 75 80 88			
Res-II	69 75 80 88	75		
Res-I	69 75 80 88	75 80 88	75 80	75 80
Total* Performance				
Comp-I				
Doc-II	75 80 88			
Doc-I	69 75 80 88	80		
Res-II	69 75 80 88	69 75 80 88		
Res-I	69 75 80 88	69 75 80 88	69 75 80 88	75 80 88

*Combines grants, two-year publications, and lifetime books.

Note: All ANOVA F-scores significant ($p<.001$). Scheffe test pairs of Carnegie groups different at the .05 level. Significant differences are identified by survey year (e.g., 75 = 1975 survey data).

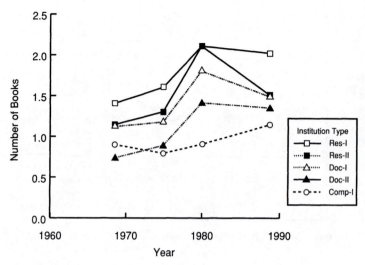

Figure 5: Lifetime books published.

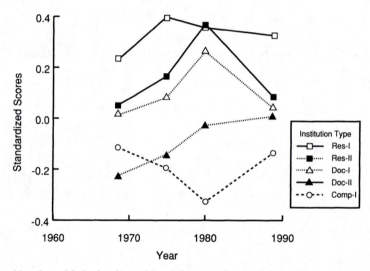

Figure 6: Standardized books published (adjusted for differences by discipline).

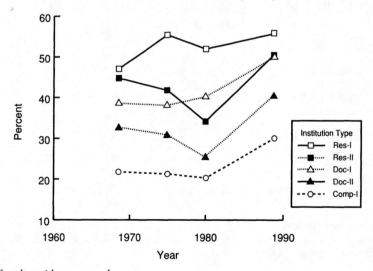

Figure 7: Percent faculty with sponsored grants.

publications, there appears to be a strong parallel in book publication rates between Res-II and Doc-I institutions. Figure 5 shows how both institution types rose between 1975 and 1980 (from 1.3 to 2.1 and from 1.2 to 1.8, respectively) and dropped in 1988 (both to 1.5).

The same trend between Res-II and Doc-I institutions emerges when mean book publication rates are converted into standardized scores to adjust for differences by discipline (see Figure 6 and Table A6). Again a parallel movement is evident. Meanwhile, standardized mean book publications show a steady increase in Doc-II's between 1969 and 1988 compared to the decline at Res-II's and Doc-I's after 1980.

Grant Support

The percent of faculty receiving federal support is slightly higher in 1988 than in 1969. In 1988, for example, 56.3% of the Res-I faculty sampled reported receiving federal support compared to 47.2% in 1969. Similarly, slight increases were reported by faculty in the other institutional groupings. (See Figure 7 and Table A7.) The federal curtailment of the 1970s is shown for all but the Res-II universities.

Once again Doc-I's appear to be an increasingly strong contender with Res-II in the ability of their faculty to compete for grants from government, industry, and foundations. This same trend is not diminished when the grant data

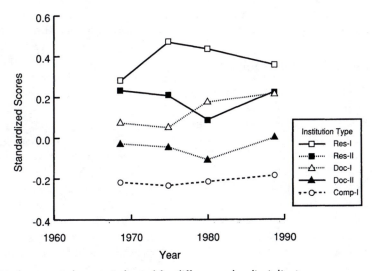

Figure 8: Standardized sponsored grants (adjusted for differences by discipline).

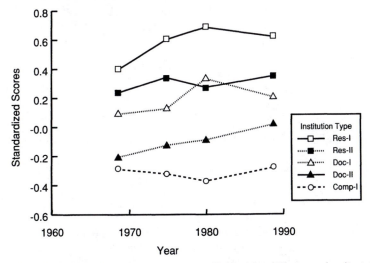

Figure 9: Standardized publication and grant performance (adjusted for differences by discipline).

are standardized. (Compare Figures 7 and 8 and Tables A7 and A8).

Comparing standardized grant support by Carnegie-type shows that Res-I universities have declined steadily since 1975 while Res-II and Doc-I institutions have remained steady. Scheffe tests showed significant differences ($p<.05$) between Res-I and all other Carnegie groups in 1975 and 1980, and in 1988 Scheffe tests showed no significance among Res-I, Res-II, and Doc-I institutions (see Table 3). This erosion of Res-I grants supports the argument that "pork barreling" may be taking grants that used to go to Res-I's in a peer review process and may be giving them to institutions that received less in the past. (As noted before, we do not have dollar amounts and Res-I's may even be gaining in total funding even if number of grants has declined. They can be the recipients of the larger dollar awards.)

Total Publication and Grant Output

As with changes in publications and sponsored grants, Doc-I institutions appear to be in a stronger competitive position with Res-II institutions when publication (PUB2YR and BKSALL) and grants (ALLGRT) output are aggregated (see Figure 9 and Table A9). After surpassing Res-II's in 1980, Doc-II's dropped slightly below the Res-II universities in 1988. Meanwhile, Res-I universities have retained their overall research output superiority since 1969. Scheffe tests showed significant differences between Res-I's and Res-II's in every year except 1969 (see Table 3).

Overall research output has declined somewhat at Comp-I institutions, although there has been a slight upswing since 1980 (see Figure 9).

Discussion

Over the past 20 years the emphasis on research has intensified at all five Carnegie types included in this study. This trend is reflected not only in their orientation toward research (more faculty holding Ph.D.'s and expressing a primary interest in research) but also in actual research output (grant and publication performance). For example, the mean number of lifetime books and publications in the past two years is up, while a greater per-

centage of faculty are receiving externally sponsored grant support.

While Res-I universities retain their dominant position in the hierarchy, other institutions, notably Res-II and Doc-I institutions, have enhanced their competitive position. The initial (1969) advantage of Res-I's has not accumulated. Perhaps the most interesting sign of competition arises from Doc-I institutions that are gaining on Res-II universities in competing for grants and in overall research performance—aggregate grants and publications.

At the same time, faculty at Comp-I institutions also have broadened their research emphasis. They produce more books and are obtaining more grants than in 1969. However, this growth in research output at Comp-I's has not matched that of other institutional types. In fact, Comp-I's have lost ground—in particular, with respect to Doc-II institutions.

Finally, the lack of any clear "winners" and "losers" of accumulated advantage may be due to constraints inherent in the study's unit of analysis that aggregates institutions by Carnegie type. The variation in publications within Carnegie type suggests that such aggregation may be too broad. In fact, it may be masking evidence of some institutions actually enjoying accumulative advantage. Therefore, to test institutional accumulative advantage, it may be more appropriate to track subgroups of institutions by other criteria such as publication output or levels of grant support. The similarity of publication output within departments suggests that departments, rather than institutions, may be a more conceptually sound method of analysis to assess the concept of accumulated advantage.

Notes

1. Carnegie definitions vary somewhat over time (1973, 1976, 1987). Res-I's and Res-II's award at least 50 Ph.D.'s yearly. They are within the top 50 and 100 institutions, respectively, in receiving federal financial support. Doc-I's award a minimum of 40 Ph.D.'s and receive at least $3 million in federal support, while Doc-II's award at least 20 Ph.D.'s yearly. Comp-I's enroll at least 2,000 students (2,500 in 1987) and offer the Masters as the highest degree.
2. The response rates of the 1969, 1975, and 1988 surveys were 60%, 52% and 50% respectively (see Table 1).

3. For each survey year, the number of faculty was estimated based on random samples drawn by Carnegie type, control, and department, yielding 80 separate cells (e.g., 1969, Res-I, public, biology). Furthermore, faculty estimates were compared with a similar sampling conducted by Bieber and Blackburn (1989) and were found to be alike.

4. Mean categorical publication values attenuate data for the highest-producing faculty (e.g., more than 10 publications). However, a comparison between recoded mean categorical values and the actual number of publications reported in 1988, the only survey with true interval publication data available, showed a high correlation (about .80) between the actual publications and recoded mean categorical values.

5. We also examined institutional and departmental support but these grants are excluded from our analysis.

6. Combining lifetime books and two-year publications may inadvertently result in some double counting. However, any such double counting of books published within the past two years is expected to be minimal.

7. All data in these national surveys are self-reported and hence are open to some measure of error. However, studies by Allison and Stewart (1974), Blackburn, Bobert, O'Connell, and Pellino (1980), and Clark and Centra (1982) checking vitae against self-reports of publications find faculty are generally fully honest in providing factual information about themselves.

8. Actually we know this is the case for psychologists and biologists and suspect it will turn out to be true for English faculty as well, the three disciplines used in the study.

9. ANOVA F-scores for all of the comparisons by Carnegie type reported in this paper are significant ($p<.001$).

References

Allison, P. D., and Stewart, J. A. (1974). Productivity differences among scientists: Evidence for accumulative advantage. *American Sociological Review* 39: 596–606.

American Universities and Colleges (1968). Washington, DC: American Council on Education.

American Universities and Colleges (1983). Washington, DC: American Council on Education.

American Universities and Colleges (1987). Washington, DC: American Council on Education.

Bayer A. E. (1970). *College and University Faculty: A Statistical Description* (Vol. 5, No. 5). Washington, DC: American Council on Education.

Bayer, A. E., and Dutton, J. E. (1977, May–June). Career age and research-professional activities of academic scientists. *Journal of Higher Education* 48:259–282.

Bieber, J., and Blackburn, R. T. (1989). Faculty research productivity 1972–1988: Development and application of constant units of measurement. Paper presented at the annual Association for the Study of Higher Education meeting. Atlanta, GA.

Biglan, A. (1973, June). The characteristics of subject matter in different academic areas. *Journal of Applied Psychology* 57(3): 195–203.

Blackburn, R. T., Behymer, C. E., and Hall, D. E. (1978). Correlates of faculty publications. *Sociology Education* 51: 132–141.

Blackburn, R. T., Bobert, A., O'Connell, C., and Pellino, G. R. (1980). *Project for Faculty Development Program Evaluation*. Ann Arbor: Center for the Study of Higher Education, University of Michigan.

Blackburn, R. T., and Lawrence, J. H. (1989). *Faculty at Work: Final Report of the National Survey*. Ann Arbor; National Center for Research to Improve Postsecondary Teaching and Learning.

Blackburn, R. T., Lawrence, J. H., Ross, S., Okoloko, V. P., Bieber, J., Meiland, R., and Street, Terry (1986). *Faculty as a Key Resource*. Ann Arbor: National Center for Research to Improve Postsecondary Teaching and Learning.

Bowen, H. R., and Schuster, J. H. (1986). *American Professors: A National Resource Imperiled*. New York: Oxford University Press.

Carnegie Commission on Higher Education (1973). *A Classification of Institutions of Higher Education*.

Carnegie Council on Policy Studies in Higher Education (1976). *A Classification of Institutions of Higher Education, revised edition*.

Carnegie Foundation for the Advancement of Teaching (1987). Carnegie foundation's classifications of more than 3,300 institutions of higher education. *The Chronicle of Higher Education*. 22–26, 28–30.

Clark, M. J., and Centra, J. A. (1982). *Conditions Influencing the Career Accomplishments of Ph.D.'s* (ETS Research Report 82–18). Princeton: Educational Testing Service.

Cole, J. R., and Cole S. (1973). *Social Stratification in Science*. Chicago: University of Chicago Press.

Cole, S. S., Rubin, L., and Cole, J. R. (1978). *Peer Review in the NSF: Phase I of a Study*. Washington, DC: National Academy of Sciences.

Creswell, J. W. (1985). *Faculty Research Performance* (ASHE-ERIC Higher Education Report No. 4). Washington, DC: Association for the Study of Higher Education.

Drew, E. D., and Tronvig, J. A. (1988). *Assessing the Quality of National Data About Academic Scientists*. Claremont: The Claremont Graduate School, Claremont, CA.

Finkelstein, M. J. (1984). *The American Academic Profession*. Ohio: Ohio State University Press.

Graves, P. (1986, July/August). Hog heaven. *Common Cause Magazine*, pp. 17–23.

Higher Education Research Institute (1983). Technical Report to 1980 National Survey (exact title unknown). Los Angeles: Higher Education Research Institute, University of California, Los Angeles, CA.

Lazarsfeld, P. F., and Thielens, W., Jr. (1958). *The Academic Mind: Social Scientists in a Time of Crisis*. Glencoe, IL: Free Press.

Long, J. S. (December 1978). Productivity and academic position in the scientific career. *American Sociological Review* 43: 889–908.

Lotka, A. J. (1926). The frequency distribution of scientific productivity. *Journal of the Washington Academy of Sciences* 16(12): 317–323.

McCarthy, C. (1986, July 19). Pork with a Ph.D. *The Washington Post*.

Merton, R. K. (1968). The Matthew effect in science. *Science* 159: 56–63.

National Research Council (1987). *Summary Report 1986: Doctorate Recipients from United States Universities*. Washington, DC: National Academy Press.

National Science Foundation (1981). *Science Indicators—1981*. Washington, DC: National Science Board, National Science Foundation.

National Science Foundation (1987). *Science and Engineering Indicators—1987*. Washington, DC: National Science Board, National Science Foundation.

Price, D. (1963). *Little Science, Big Science*. New York: Columbia University Press.

Roizen, J., Fulton, O. and Trow, M. (1978). *Technical Report: 1975 Carnegie Council National Surveys of Higher Education*. Berkeley: Center for Studies in Higher Education, University of California.

Rose, R. M. (1986, October 8). Pork-barrel science vs. peer review. *The Chronicle of Higher Education*, p. 96.

Smith, B. L., and Karlesky, J. J. (1977). *The State of Academic Science: Universities in the Nation's Research Effort*. New York: Change Magazine Press.

Trow, M. A. (1975). Technical report on the 1969 Carnegie Commission survey of faculty and student opinion. *Teachers and Students*. Berkeley: The Carnegie Foundation for the Advancement of Teaching.

Wanner, R. A., Lewis, L. S., and Gregorio, D. I. (1981). Research productivity in academia: A comparative study of the sciences, social sciences, and humanities. *Sociology of Science* 54: 238–253.

Young, D. L., Blackburn, R. T., Conrad, C. F., and Cameron, K. S. (1989). Leadership, student effort, and department program quality: An exploration of quality across levels of analysis. *Review of Higher Education* 12(13): 265–278.

Zuckerman, H. (1977). *Scientific Elite: Nobel Laureates in the United States*. New York: Free Press.

TABLE A1
Percent of Faculty Holding Ph.D.'s

Carnegie Type	1969 (N=3166) %	1975 (N=3523) %	1980 (N=1493) %	1988 (N=2383) %
Res-I	92.8	95.6	96.0	97.9
Res-II	89.7	93.3	93.0	94.7
Doc-I	91.5	94.1	94.7	93.8
Doc-II	82.9	89.5	92.9	93.5
Comp-I	72.9	84.5	87.2	86.7
Average	82.6	89.2	91.0	90.8

Note: Weighted data represent all faculty holding academic rank of assistant, associate, or full professor in eight departments (biology, chemistry, English, mathematics, political science, sociology, mathematics, and psychology).

TABLE A2
Percent of Faculty Primarily Interested in Research*

Carnegie Type	1969 (N=3166) %	1975 (N=3523) %	1980 (N=1493) %	1988 (N=2383) %
Res-I	55.7	66.8	Data	77.2
Res-II	52.1	58.9	not	64.4
Doc-I	43.7	55.1	in	50.9
Doc-II	23.1	41.9	1980	46.1
Comp-I	20.7	27.3	survey	25.1
Average	36.3	42.9		42.3

*Faculty reported interests either "very heavily in research" or "in both (teaching and research) but leaning heavily toward research."

Note: Weighted data represent all faculty holding academic rank of assistant, associate, or full professor in eight departments (biology, chemistry, English, history, mathematics, political science, sociology, and psychology).

TABLE A3
Mean Faculty Two-Year Publication Rates

Carnegie Type	1969			1975			1980			1988		
	Mean	SD	N	Mean	SD	N	Mean	SD	N	Mean	SD	N
Res-I	3.7	3.2	750	4.2	3.3	674	4.9	3.4	260	5.2	3.4	374
Res-II	3.3	3.1	375	3.8	3.3	485	3.4	3.1	212	4.5	3.5	258
Doc-I	2.9	2.9	418	3.1	2.8	277	3.8	3.2	179	3.7	3.2	221
Doc-II	2.1	2.8	120	2.5	2.7	365	2.8	2.8	104	3.3	3.0	237
Comp-I	1.7	2.3	1423	1.7	2.2	1709	1.7	2.4	719	2.0	2.5	1230
Average	2.6	2.9	3086	2.7	2.9	3510	2.9	3.1	1474	3.1	3.2	2320
F-Ratio	72.1			122.9			70.3			111.1		
Probability	0.000			0.000			0.000			0.000		

Note: Weighted data represent all faculty holding academic rank of assistant, associate, or full professor in eight departments (biology, chemistry, English, history, mathematics, political science, sociology, and psychology).

TABLE A4
Standardized Two-Year Publication Rates*

Carnegie Type	1969			1975			1980			1988		
	Mean	SD	N	Mean	SD	N	Mean	SD	N	Mean	SD	N
Res-I	0.38	1.08	750	0.51	1.10	674	0.67	1.09	260	0.64	1.04	374
Res-II	0.24	1.07	375	0.37	1.10	485	0.18	0.96	212	0.43	1.08	258
Doc-I	0.11	1.02	418	0.15	0.97	277	0.30	1.03	179	0.21	1.00	221
Doc-II	−0.18	0.98	120	−0.05	0.94	365	−0.02	0.94	104	0.07	0.95	237
Comp I	−0.28	0.82	1423	−0.32	0.80	1709	−0.37	0.79	719	−0.34	0.82	1230
F-Ratio	68.5			119.4			70.7			105.9		
Probability	0.000			0.000			0.000			0.000		

*Standardized z-scores were created separately for each of the eight departments to account for differences by discipline.

Note: Weighted data represent all faculty holding academic rank of assistant, associate, or full professor in eight departments (biology, chemistry, English, history, mathematics, political science, sociology, and psychology).

TABLE A5
Mean Faculty Total Lifetime Books Published

Carnegie Type	1969			1975			1980			1988		
	Mean	SD	N	Mean	SD	N	Mean	SD	N	Mean	SD	N
Res-I	1.4	1.7	747	1.6	1.7	673	2.1	1.7	262	2.0	1.9	374
Res-II	1.1	1.5	372	1.3	1.6	487	2.1	1.8	214	1.5	1.7	256
Doc-I	1.1	1.6	417	1.2	1.4	277	1.8	1.8	179	1.5	1.7	222
Doc-II	0.8	1.3	120	0.9	1.3	364	1.4	1.6	104	1.3	1.6	237
Comp-I	0.9	1.4	1413	0.8	1.3	1705	0.9	1.4	724	1.1	1.5	1226
Total	1.1	1.5	3069	1.1	1.5	3506	1.4	1.6	1483	1.4	1.7	2315
F-Ratio	13.0			45.3			40.2			18.9		
Probability	0.000			0.000			0.000			0.000		

Note: Weighted data represent all faculty holding academic rank of assistant, associate, or full professor in eight departments (biology, chemistry, English, history, mathematics, political science, sociology, and psychology).

TABLE A6
Standardized Faculty Total Lifetime Books Published*

Carnegie Type	1969			1975			1980			1988		
	Mean	SD	N	Mean	SD	N	Mean	SD	N	Mean	SD	N
Res-I	0.22	1.10	747	0.40	1.19	673	0.37	1.02	262	0.35	1.09	374
Res-II	0.04	0.99	372	0.15	1.07	487	0.38	1.06	214	0.07	0.97	256
Doc-I	0.02	1.02	417	0.09	0.99	277	0.27	1.14	179	0.04	1.00	222
Doc-II	-0.22	0.86	120	-0.13	0.89	364	-0.05	0.95	104	0.01	0.97	237
Comp-I	-0.11	0.93	1413	-0.19	0.86	1705	-0.31	0.83	724	-0.13	0.96	1226
F-Ratio	15.2			48.4			40.9			17.2		
Probability	0.000			0.000			0.000			0.000		

*Standardized z-scores were created separately for each of the eight departments to account for differences by discipline.

Note: Weighted data represent all faculty holding academic rank of assistant, associate, or full professor in eight departments (biology, chemistry, English, history, mathematics, political science, sociology, and psychology).

TABLE A7
Percent of Faculty Receiving Sponsored Grant Support

Carnegie Type	1969 (N=3166) %	1975 (N=3523) %	1980 (N=1493) %	1988 (N=2383) %
Res-I	47.2	58.6	51.5	56.3
Res-II	45.7	46.1	34.4	50.8
Doc-I	38.4	40.3	40.9	50.7
Doc-II	32.5	32.9	24.0	40.9
Comp-I	22.4	23.3	19.3	30.3
Total	34.0	35.7	30.1	40.0

*Self-reported sources of external support include federal and state government, foundations, industry, and other sources received within the past year.

Note: Weighted data represent all faculty holding academic rank of assistant, associate, or full professor in eight departments (biology, chemistry, English, history, mathematics, political science, sociology, and psychology).

TABLE A8
Standardized Faculty-Sponsored Grant Support*

Carnegie Type	1969			1975			1980			1988		
	Mean	SD	N	Mean	SD	N	Mean	SD	N	Mean	SD	N
Res-I	0.26	1.01	758	0.49	1.06	676	0.45	1.06	266	0.34	0.99	374
Res-II	0.22	1.00	374	0.20	1.01	488	0.10	1.05	2125	0.22	1.00	258
Doc-I	0.08	0.99	411	0.07	0.98	277	0.20	1.04	181	0.22	1.02	221
Doc-II	-0.02	0.94	120	-0.04	0.99	367	-0.08	0.98	104	0.02	1.02	237
Comp-I	-0.23	0.95	1400	-0.26	0.89	1716	-0.24	0.88	727	-0.20	0.95	1230
F-Ratio	38.1			78.0			28.3			29.3		
Probability	0.000			0.000			0.000			0.000		

*Standardized z-scores were created separately for each of the eight departments to account for differences by discipline.

Note: Weighted data represent all faculty holding academic rank of assistant, associate, or full professor in eight departments (biology, chemistry, English, history, mathematics, political science, sociology, and psychology).

TABLE A9
Standardized Total Publication and Grant Performance*

Carnegie Type	1969			1975			1980			1988		
	Mean	SD	N	Mean	SD	N	Mean	SD	N	Mean	SD	N
Res-I	0.40	1.02	744	0.63	1.06	674	0.69	0.95	260	0.62	0.96	374
Res-II	0.24	1.06	370	0.32	0.96	485	0.30	0.92	212	0.32	0.91	258
Doc-I	0.10	1.01	407	0.12	0.88	277	0.35	1.06	179	0.24	1.05	221
Doc-II	-0.18	1.10	119	-0.09	0.96	365	-0.06	1.05	104	0.02	0.91	237
Comp-I	-0.29	0.87	1386	-0.35	0.88	1709	-0.41	0.86	719	-0.31	0.95	1230
F-Ratio	72.0			146.8			87.7			81.4		
Probability	0.000			0.000			0.000			0.00		

*Publications include two-year publications and lifetime books. Standardized z-scores were created separately for each of the eight departments to account for differences by discipline.

Note: Weighted data represent all faculty holding academic rank of assistant, associate, or full professor in eight departments (biology, chemistry, English, history, mathematics, political science, sociology, and psychology).

Standards of Scholarly Work

CHARLES E. GLASSICK, MARY TAYLOR HUBER, AND GENE I. MAEROFF

To give the four kinds of scholarly activities the weight that each deserves, they all must be held to the same standards of scholarly performance. The paradox is this: in order to recognize discovery, integration, application, and teaching as legitimate forms of scholarship, the academy must valuate them by a set of standards that capture and acknowledge what they share as scholarly acts.

Faculty handbooks seldom highlight the qualities and characteristics common to the different kinds of scholarship. Rather, current wisdom assumes that research, teaching, and applied scholarship—the kinds of faculty activities recognized for purposes of evaluation on most campuses—each has its own special yardstick.

In judging research, each discipline uses its own criteria, while estimates of teaching abilities tend to ignore strategies specific to subject matter. Service is in a league of its own. The activities that count as professional and/or public service may be identified, but aside from the general expectation of "high quality" in such work, handbooks offer scant guidance as to what quality might mean. Indeed, the University of California is unusual in its thoughtful requirements for practitioners in its professional schools. It singles out "leadership in the field" and "demonstrated progressiveness in the development or utilization of new approaches and techniques for the solution of professional problems."'

Most college and university guidebooks implicitly suggest that different types of standards apply to different kinds of faculty work, leaving the impression that standards for research and creative work come from the various disciplines; standards for teaching are institutionally defined; and standards for professional service vary so greatly by project and profession that hardly any guidance can be offered. This fragmented paradigm reflects the differential respect accorded research, teaching, and applied scholarship at most institutions. It also, we believe, helps to perpetuate the hierarchy that places greatest importance on research. As Lee Shulman observed, "Like it or not, the forms of scholarship that are seen as intellectual work in the disciplines are going to be valued more than forms of scholarship (such as teaching) that are seen as non-disciplinary." One can understand how teaching and applied work often suffer devaluation in this taxonomy of unequals.

In recent years, though, academics have opened discussion about standards for teaching and applied scholarship at both the national and campus levels. The disciplinary associations have begun to address this issue. The American Mathematical Society, for example, has pioneered an ambitious program to improve the teaching of calculus and to define the qualities of good undergraduate teaching in mathematics. Scholars doing applied work in most of the humanities and social sciences are organizing sessions at disciplinary conferences and airing substantive methodological and ethical concerns in newsletters and journals. Even integrative scholarship claims the attention of growing numbers of disciplinary peers; for instance, the *Journal of American History* now regularly reviews museum exhibitions. "Museum exhibits and their related

"Standards of Scholarly Work," by Charles E. Glassick, Mary Taylor Huber, and Gene I. Maeroff, reprinted from *Scholarship Assessed: Evaluation of the Professoriate*, 1997, Jossey-Bass Publishers, Inc.

elements are a distinct medium for identifying, organizing, comparing, analyzing, and communicating historical information and interpretation," the editor of the reviews wrote.

The emerging climate at colleges and universities supports the idea that different types of scholarly work merit formal consideration. In experiments across the country, faculty are assembling a wide variety of evidence to demonstrate their achievements in the four areas of scholarship. Many institutions are also trying to improve how peers are brought into the review of teaching. Shulman captures the mood precisely when he speaks of making teaching "community property," while the aptly titled theme of the 1995 AAHE Conference on Faculty Roles and Rewards was "From 'My Work' to 'Our Work.'"

Reform, however, seldom moves evenly on all fronts, and innovative attempts to broaden definitions of scholarship are likely to remain pilot efforts if institutions do not also change the standards by which they evaluate scholarship for purposes of faculty retention, promotion, and tenure. As Richard Chait noted, recognizing different forms of scholarship involves "less certainty about the qualities and characteristics of scholarship—about what should count." Clearly, evaluation that uses different standards for research, teaching, and professional service has outlived its day. Academia needs a single standard, but it cannot implement that standard simply by applying to other forms of scholarship the traditional criteria that have usually been used for judging research.

What are the common features that enable scholars involved in different fields of study and different types of scholarly work to feel they are engaged in a common task? Wayne Booth observed that the academic world has an evaluative language beyond the disciplinary or professional rhetoric of the cutting edge. Booth said that faculty already can use this common evaluative language to ask if a colleague's "style of presentation . . . accords with standards we recognize," to examine the general quality of someone's reasoning, and to see whether talking with a colleague adds to one's own intellectual life.

Could there lie in this public square some clues that might help us find a vocabulary to define the common dimensions of scholarship? Are there already some general standards available for judging scholarly performance?

In an attempt to answer these essential questions, we accumulated a voluminous file of documents, including guidelines on hiring, tenure, and promotion practices from dozens of colleges and universities. We also got responses from fifty-one granting agencies and from editors and directors of thirty-one scholarly journals and fifty-eight university presses whom we asked about the standards they use to decide the scholarly merit of proposals and manuscripts. In addition, we collected many of the forms that institutions provide to students and occasionally to faculty peers to evaluate college teaching.

Ostensibly, these lists of standards and criteria vary considerably. Some are long, some short. Some are systematic, some jumbled. Many include items tailored to specific needs. The National Science Foundation, for instance, is interested in the effect a proposed project might have on the infrastructure of science and engineering. Before publishing an article, the *Journal of Organic Chemistry* wants to know if the compounds reported are "adequately characterized with regard to identity and purity"; the University of California Press, as many other university publishers, asks hopefully: is a manuscript "likely to be required reading in specific undergraduate or graduate courses?"

The most remarkable feature of these various guidelines, though, is not how much they contain that is unique but the degree to which they share elements. Our survey of standards indicates that the key to these commonalities lies in the *process* of scholarship itself. If this process can be defined with some clarity, it will provide terms by which scholars can discuss almost any project without denying either its uniqueness or its connections to other projects, whatever the discipline or type of scholarship. Indeed, we found it possible to identify in these lists and guidelines a set of six shared themes. All works of scholarship, be they discovery, integration, application, or teaching, involve a common sequence of unfolding stages. We have found that when people praise a work of scholarship, they usually mean that the project in question shows that it has been guided by these qualitative standards:

1. Clear goals
2. Adequate preparation
3. Appropriate methods
4. Significant results
5. Effective presentation
6. Reflective critique

It is important, we believe, to give these familiar standards—already in common use—explicit articulation. Everyone will recognize them one by one, but taken together, they provide a powerful conceptual framework to guide evaluation. Their very obviousness suggests their applicability to a broad range of intellectual projects.

Clear Goals

A scholar must be clear about the aims of his or her work. The first issue that many reviewers are asked to address in their evaluations of manuscripts and grant or fellowship proposals concerns the scholar's goals. The *American Journal of Sociology* asks, "Is an important issue being addressed?" The Johns Hopkins University Press, in its review of a scholarly manuscript, inquires, "What is the author's goal? " The journal *Environmental Science and Technology* wants to know, "Is the basic question to be addressed clearly stated?"

We also found a strong emphasis on goals when it comes to assessing teaching. One evaluation instrument asks, "Did the professor clearly state the objectives of the course?" Another wants to know, "Did the proposed objectives agree with those actually taught?" At the University of Kentucky, professors being reviewed for promotion and tenure are asked to submit a brief, reflective statement that sets forth their philosophy and objectives as teachers. The clarity of goals was considered for works of applied scholarship as well. The National Institute of Justice, which funds projects for the U.S. Department of Justice, wants to know, "Does the proposal address a critical issue or aspect of the problem area?"

These, then, are questions that ought to be asked about all types of scholarly work:

- Does the scholar state the basic purposes of his or her work clearly?

- Does the scholar define objectives that are realistic and achievable?

- Does the scholar identify important questions in the field?

Goals precede all other considerations because to plan, carry out, and present any scholarly project, a scholar must know what questions to ask. A master scholar is a master question-raiser—a designation that fits, almost by definition, anyone who can be called a pathbreaker in scholarly and creative work. The most basic lessons taught to students in their graduate training involve learning how to see and state an intellectual problem. The Council of Graduate Schools noted in describing the nature and purpose of doctoral programs: "A well-prepared doctoral student will have developed the ability . . . to apply appropriate principles and procedures to the recognition, evaluation, interpretation, and understanding of issues and problems at the frontiers of knowledge."

Scholarly work usually has multiple goals, making it crucial that the scholar define each goal clearly within *all* relevant contexts, disciplinary or interdisciplinary, public or professional, and educational as well, For example, a teacher may select an intellectually significant problem for a new course but teach poorly because of ill-defined pedagogical goals. "Bad teaching most often results from a pursuit of the wrong ends, either because the teacher is unclear about his or her purposes or because plausible but harmful purposes get in the way of good ones," Booth observed. Only by stating objectives clearly can the stage be set for conversations about appropriateness of goals.

Having clear goals also means understanding a project's scope. Good guiding questions help the scholar define a project, give it structure, recognize relevant material, identify exceptions, and see new possibilities. Of course, the goals of a project may shift over time. Much of the excitement of scholarly work comes when a particular line of inquiry leads to new questions and these lead to new ones again.

A scholar's goals must also be realistic, taking account of the limitations and the possibilities of the situation. Hopelessly grandiose goals may fade Into irrelevancy. Goals should be practical and defensible. Even clear objectives hold little value if they cannot be reasonably met.

Adequate Preparation

The documents we examined repeatedly identified adequate preparation as one of the most basic aspects of scholarly work. The University of Alabama Press, for example, asks this question of reviewers: "Does the scholarship appear current?" In other words, has the scholar's preparation for the investigation adequately considered the state of the field? The University Press of New England asks, "Is the author in command of both primary sources and the standard secondary literature of the field?" Regarding teaching, one evaluation instrument we looked at asks, "Did the instructor display a clear understanding of the course topics?" and "Was the instructor well prepared for each class?" Agencies that support applied projects agree. The Mott Foundation, for example, wants to know: "Does the applicant have the leadership and staff competence to carry out the project, or the ability to secure those essential resources?"

Any evaluation should consider the following questions when assessing a scholar's achievements:

- Does the scholar show an understanding of existing scholarship in the field?

- Does the scholar bring the necessary skills to his or her work?

- Does the scholar bring together the resources necessary to move the project forward?

The pursuit of scholarly work depends, fundamentally, on the depth and breadth of the scholar's understanding of subject matter. Every scholar bears a responsibility to keep up with the literature in the field in which he or she works. Scholarship is, in essence, a conversation in which one participates and contributes by knowing what is being discussed and what others have said on the subject. Therefore, a project that does not speak to current issues of theory, fact, interpretation, or method is unlikely to contribute to its field, regardless of other virtues.

Artistry necessarily accompanies knowledge in the projects a scholar undertakes. All scholarly work involves practical skills and rules of thumb that one usually learns by doing and by observing the work of others. This is what Shulman called "the wisdom of practice" in teaching, what Donald Schön described as "reflection-in-action" in applied work, and what C. Wright Mills called "the practice of a craft" in research. Such know-how is crucial even in the heartland of basic science, the laboratory itself, where, as Jacob Bronowski observes, "the skill of head and hand go together." Mastery of necessary skills should be taken into account in evaluating a scholarly project.

Professional preparation also requires one to ascertain the availability of the right resources for the project at hand. A scholar, in weighing the human resources, should know who is doing similar work, who is supporting such work, and who is interested in the findings. A particular project might require, for example, such background work as learning a new language or exploring new software. Resources, of course, can determine the success or failure of a project, and questions about resources are pertinent in evaluating adequacy of preparation. Was the scholar imaginative and thorough in finding source material? Were the resources adequate for the project? Did the scholar use the resources as well as possible?

Appropriate Methods

As a third standard, scholars also must use procedures appropriate to the project, choosing methods wisely, applying them effectively, and modifying them judiciously as a project evolves. Virtually all evaluating agencies inquire into the merit of a scholar's methods. The University of Iowa Press, in judging a scholarly manuscript, asks, "Is the scholarship adequate in terms of methodology?" The journal *Physical Review Letters* expresses it this way: "Is the work scientifically sound?" The journal *Child Development* urges reviewers to consider "the formal design of the research," that is, its methodology. Kansas State University judges the quality of projects in terms of the "development and application of effective ways to identify problems and assess needs."

Methods and procedures make a great difference in teaching. This is true from the logic of the syllabus to pedagogical procedures and student assessment. One teacher evaluation instrument asks, "Were the methods of evaluating student work fair and effective?" Another wants to know, "Was the amount of material the instructor attempted to cover appropriate?" Students at Clemson University are asked whether the course was "presented in a logical sequence. The State University of New York College at Old Westbury looks at the professor's "responsiveness to the distinctive and varied needs of our students" and "successful experimentation with varied approaches to teaching."

We suggest, then, that evaluators ask these questions about a scholar's work:

- Does the scholar use methods appropriate to the goals?

- Does the scholar apply effectively the methods selected?

- Does the scholar modify procedures in response to changing circumstances?

At the most basic level, appropriate methodology gives a project integrity and engenders confidence in its findings, products, or results. To gain standing among scholars, a project must use methods recognized in the academic community. Edward Shils said: "The obligations of the academic profession are inherent in the custodianship of the pursuit, acquisition, assessment, and transmission of knowledge through systematic study, in accordance with methodical procedures including observational techniques, rules of evidence, and principles of logical reasoning." Shils's observation is most obvious in scientific research, where reason and experiment have often defined what science is and what it is not. All fields of scholarly inquiry are both theoretical and methodical, although the method may not be the kind of controlled observation that the phrase *scientific method* usually conveys.

The choice of method is critical because upon it depends not only the project's chances for success at discovery, integration, application, or teaching but also the likelihood that colleagues will understand and accept the project. Scholars who favor quantitative studies, for example, may be reluctant to accept findings based on qualitative approaches, whatever the intrinsic merit of the work. Yet all scholars would probably concede the value of approaches other than their own, however incompatible the methodological styles. They might argue for the primacy of one approach or another, but most important is that the method selected be carefully justified and appropriate to the project's goals.

Scholars have an obligation to carry out their projects competently. To expect a project to unfold according to the method, outlined, however, is not to ask a scholar to follow blindly a detailed, preconceived plan. Scholarship does not and should not proceed like that. Flexibility is essential to allow the scholar to respond to change, to pick up a clue and follow it as a project proceeds, and even to redesign the project itself. C. Wright Mills advised the young scholar to "be a good craftsman: Avoid any rigid set of procedures ... let theory and method again become part of the practice of a craft." This admonition holds for the mature scholar as well.

Significant Results

Any act of scholarship must also be judged by the significance of its results. A project should contribute to knowledge or to artistic expression, stimulate learning, or, where appropriate, help solve problems outside the academy. Publishers and journal editors are invariably direct about this standard when they consider manuscripts reporting findings from research. The University of Hawaii Press asks, "What has the author accomplished?" The University of Arizona Press wants to know if the manuscript "makes a significant contribution to the literature." And the *Journal of Physical Chemistry* asks if the manuscript has "extremely important results." The scholarship of application also is judged by outcomes. At the University of Illinois, peers are asked to comment on the extent to which a colleague's service activity has made a substantial contribution that is "recognized by other scholars, public policy makers, or practitioners."

Teaching, too, must in the end be judged not merely by process but by results, however eloquent a teacher's performance. The evaluation forms we studied ask students questions that clearly seek to measure the significance of what they learned: "Was your interest in the subject stimulated by this course?" "Did you improve your competence due to this course?" "Did you learn something you consider valuable?"

The following questions, we believe, help colleagues chart the significance of a scholar's work:

- Does the scholar achieve the goals?
- Does the scholar's work add consequentially to the field?
- Does the scholar's work open additional areas for further exploration?

To ask that the outcome of a scholarly project have significance is to ask, first, that it meet its own goals. Its results, in other words, should have meaning within the parameters that the scholar has set for the project. A course in which students conduct their own research under faculty supervision should show evidence that students gained insights into methods of investigation. A consultation should actually help clients while contributing to the scholar's understanding the general issues involved. Experiments that aim to unearth new findings should in fact do so—even, of course, when the findings simply eliminate a hypothesis by concluding that "no significant difference was found." A book designed to introduce an arcane topic to a nonacademic audience should reach that group of readers with the requisite, integrity, imagination, and style.

A fundamental indication of a project's significance is its contribution to the field. Chemist-philosopher Michael Polanyi once suggested that scientists typically judged scientific research by its plausibility, originality, and scientific value—"a composite," explained science writer Richard Rhodes, "consisting of equal parts accuracy, importance to the entire system of whatever branch of science the idea belonged to, and intrinsic interest." Many scholars use some variant of this scheme in judging a work's contribution. Of course, the language of praise varies among the disciplines. Anthropologist Clifford Geertz observed that mathematicians speak of the differences between "'deep;' 'elegant;' 'beautiful;' 'powerful;' and 'subtle' proofs"; physicists talk of "such peculiar words of praise and blame as 'tact' or 'skimming'"; and literary critics invoke "the relative presence of a mysterious property,

to outsiders anyway, called 'realization.'" Significance in these instances takes on a meaning and appreciation specific to a field, attesting to the need to acknowledge the specialized nature that significance may sometimes assume.

Clearly, teaching, integration, and application can contribute to their own scholarly realms. For example, a new way of teaching undergraduate calculus might serve as a model for colleagues at the same institution or beyond. A diagnostic method developed by a clinician-scholar might influence practitioners. The results of a scholar's integrative efforts might help shape public debate and broaden understanding of the issues at hand. Because the four types of scholarship dynamically interact, their contributions to each other can be traced as well. New developments in research, for instance, can contribute to ideas about teaching or application, while ideas generated in teaching, integration, or application can suggest new lines of research.

Finally, when thinking about significance, one can note works of scholarship that, through some happy combination of freshness and timing, open whole new areas for further expansion. Certainly, originality increases the potential for breaking new ground. As Oliver Sacks, a neurologist, noted, "Creativity in this sense involves the power to originate, to break away from the existing ways of looking at things. . . ." Such a project may have an early and obvious impact when the timing is right, attracting an important audience, compelling assent, or stirring debate. Breakthroughs like these are best known in the scholarship of discovery and the scholarship of application, but why should they not also occur when teaching and integrative scholarship become community property?

Effective Presentation

The contribution made by any form of scholarship relies on its presentation. Scholarship, however brilliant, lacks fulfillment without someone on the receiving end. The discovery should be made known to more than the discoverer; teaching is not teaching without students; integration makes scant contribution unless it is communicated so that people may benefit from it; and application becomes application by addressing others' needs.

The criteria used by scholarly presses and professional journals invariably refer to effective communication. Cambridge University Press simply asks, "Is the manuscript well written? " The University Press of Kansas wants to know, "Is the writing style effective?" The *Journal of the American Mathematical Society* says, "Papers must be written clearly," and then adds this fascinating comment: "At least the referee should be able to understand them without undue difficulty." It also says that the paper must be of interest to an appropriate number of readers—not just to the authors, students, and a few colleagues—suggesting that the intended audience of scholarship should be reasonably broad. In this spirit, Kent State University Press asks, "Would there be interest in this book beyond its specialist field? "

The scholarship of application, too, adheres to this standard. The National Academy Press asks, "Are sensitive policy issues treated with proper care?" The Mott Foundation prefers to fund applied projects that "contain an appropriate plan for . . . reporting and dissemination." And the University of Georgia says in its Guidelines for Faculty Appointment, Promotion, and Tenure that the effectiveness of public service should be judged, at least in part, on "the quality and impact of the written documents produced."

The importance of presentation is readily apparent when it comes to teaching. The evaluation forms for teaching that we studied are full of such questions as "Did the instructor speak with good expression?" "Did the teacher explain course material clearly?" "Did the instructor introduce stimulating ideas?" The scholarship of teaching should lead to communication with colleagues, as well as with students. In this spirit, we agree with those colleges and universities that take as an indicator of excellence in teaching the sharing of innovative instructional materials and concepts through formal publications, conferences, and seminars, as well as through more informal means.

In reviewing a scholar's work, these questions should be asked about presentation:

- Does the scholar use a suitable style and effective organization to present his or her work?

- Does the scholar use appropriate forums for communicating work to its intended audiences?

- Does the scholar present his or her message with clarity and integrity?

Good presentation involves a sense of audience and careful attention to the best ways of reaching each of its members. The presentation of scholarship is a public act, and although some work is highly esoteric, it must ultimately be known and understood by at least the members of that special audience. Quite simply, scholars must communicate well. Teaching, for instance, should use images, metaphors, analogies, and examples that connect the subject matter to who the students are and how students learn. A teacher should also take advantage of special opportunities, what educator Parker Palmer calls "critical moments." The first day of class, the first grades awarded, confusion over a key concept, or a disagreement, all offer occasions "when a learning opportunity will either open up or shut down for your students—depending, in part, on how you respond."

The scholarship of application typically calls for communication with practitioners or even public audiences who bring little specialized knowledge to the table. Effective presentation to such groups may require the scholar to learn the different communicative styles of government officials, corporate officers, for-profit laboratory researchers, documentary filmmakers, or primary and secondary school teachers and principals. This may involve media relations and learning how to present one's views in radio and television interviews or through op-ed columns and magazines of general circulation. Effective presentation under these circumstances may require the scholar to do more listening than speaking, recognizing that what the audience says is part of communication. Physicist Freeman Dyson recalls the lengthy process by which a local community was persuaded to permit its resident university to build a laboratory for recombinant DNA research. A series of hearings enabled questioners and critics to have their say and, perhaps, to influence the final outcome. As Dyson noted: "The first lesson that we learned was the importance of listening. The only effective way to dissipate distrust is for the people who are distrusted to sit down and listen to what their critics have to say."

Teaching and applied scholarship can remain incomplete acts unless presentation at some point reaches beyond students, clients, or the public in order to connect with colleagues. Shulman argues that work that is valued is work that is presented to colleagues. The failure to make this kind of wider connection weakens the sense of community. This happens in scholarly life when such essential functions as professional service or teaching do not get discussed openly or often enough. It also occurs when the standards of scholarly communication are poor.

The printed page remains the most common forum by which scholarly work reaches beyond the library, laboratory, seminar room, or conference hall. Unfortunately, though, standards of writing in many academic circles are low. Jargon and obtuse prose deprive scholars of the benefit of the interplay that could result from more effective presentation. If scholars present their work in language as clear and simple as the subject allows, scholarly communication would be improved not only among colleagues but with the public as well. Patricia Nelson Limerick said:

> The redemption of the university, especially in terms of the public's appraisal of the value of research and publication, requires all the writers who have something they want to publish to ask themselves the question: Does this have to be a closed communication, shutting out all but specialists willing to fight their way through thickets of jargon? Or can this be an open communication, engaging specialists with new information and new thinking, but also offering an invitation to nonspecialists to learn from this study, to grasp its importance and, by extension, to find concrete reasons to see value in the work of the university?

Scholars, as a result of technological advances, can increasingly present their work in nontraditional forms. Scholarly communication now flows through electronic networks, where standards for what to say and how to say it are closer to those for oral communication, Scholarly work is also carried by film and television, in the popular press, and even in Hollywood, where academic specialists consult on the lives and times of historical figures, the habits of dinosaurs, and the lives of scholars themselves—witness the portrayal of Robert Oppenheimer in *Fat Man and Little Boy* and the depiction of C. S. Lewis in *Shadowlands*. Museums and galleries display scholarly and creative work; dramatists and musicians from the academy perform in theaters and concert halls.

Popularization, done well, brings together the right materials creatively and helps the audience, whether they be students, clients, the public, or colleagues, appreciate the complexities and importance of the problems addressed in the particular field. In all scholarly work—including that which passes into the popular domain—evidence, analysis, interpretation, and argument should be handled carefully and honestly.

Reflective Critique

Our final standard involves the scholar thinking about his or her work, seeking the opinions of others, and learning from this process so that scholarship itself can be improved. We found little evidence that this standard figures prominently in the evaluation of scholarship as matters now stand, although it is recognized when funding agencies insist on plans for project evaluation, and by colleges or universities that encourage professional development. Nonetheless, the following questions are important to ask:

- Does the scholar critically evaluate his or her own work?
- Does the scholar bring an appropriate breadth of evidence to his or her critique?
- Does the scholar use evaluation to improve the quality of future work?

Throughout history, the ideal of scholarship has been shadowed by the hazard of pedantry. For many, it is wisdom that makes the difference. For example, Abraham Ibn Ezra, the twelfth-century Jewish polymath, warned that "a scholar of the traditional text, who learns nothing else, is like a camel carrying a load of silk: silk and camel are of no use to each other." In the nineteenth century, Ralph Waldo Emerson saw "thinking" as the scholar's true calling, and in our own century C. Wright Mills referred to the "imagination" of the scholar.

Reflection gives the lie to the common but unflattering characterization of scholars as narrow specialists, unable or unwilling to emerge from the depths of their subspecialties for a breath of fresh air. Biologist Barbara McClintock, for example, always urged harried young scientists, rushing on to the next experiment, to "take the time and look." With proper reflection, a scholar can examine his or her project from multiple perspectives—moving more easily beyond the narrow confines within which work in the academy is sometimes observed. The aim is to summon the muses, give free play to intuition—and then take that intuition and clothe it in thought that leads to the next step in one's scholarly career.

Through reflection comes creativity. This ability to invent, devise, envisage, and improvise, is the key to success in all types of scholarly work. Indeed, in his recent study *Making the Case for Professional Service*, Ernest Lynton sees creativity as the essential, and perhaps even defining, characteristic of scholarship. According to Lynton, scholarship is the "antithesis of rote and routine. . . . Scholarly work is not carrying out a recurring task according to a prescribed protocol, applying standard methodologies. What unifies the activities of a scholar, whether engaged in teaching, research, or professional service, is an approach to each task as a novel situation, a voyage of exploration into the partially unknown."

The work of Donald Schön, in particular, draws attention to the extent to which effective professional practice depends not only on how tasks are approached and problems defined but also on how work proceeds. Effective professionals think about what they are doing while they are carrying out their work. And what is true of professional work generally applies to scholarship as well. Its practice requires reflection as the project unfolds so as to adapt to changing circumstances and come to a successful solution. As Schön writes in his influential book *The Reflective Practitioner*, the professional is "open to the situation's back-talk." Scholars, too, recognize and respond to whatever is unique and unexpected in carrying out their work.

Insightful reflection involves self-awareness that continues after the completion of a project. An appropriate plan of inquiry should allow for evaluation, guiding the scholar's thinking about what went right and what went wrong, what opportunities were taken, and which ones were missed. As part of the evaluation, a scholar should solicit opinions and show the ability to respond positively to criticism. Finally, a scholar might follow through with activities enabling the development of new skills or knowledge: attending a program at the institution's center for the improvement of teaching, participating in a workshop on a new research technique, taking time to familiarize oneself with a new body of literature or to design a new course.

In the end, reflective critique both promises and promotes intellectual engagement. It leads to better scholarship. Careful evaluation and constructive criticism enrich scholarly work by enabling old projects to inform new ones. It is precisely the reflection encouraged by these activities that connects separate projects and makes them integral parts of some larger intellectual quest. As the scholar turns to the next research task, the next article, the next course or consultation, older projects feed ideas to the new ones. While the new ones return the favor and enrich the range of implications of those that came before.

We conclude, then, that there is a common language in which to discuss the standards for scholarly work of all kinds, a language that enables us to see clearly what discovery, integration, application, and teaching share as scholarly activities. We acknowledge that these six standards—clear goals, adequate preparation, appropriate methods, significant results, effective presentation, and reflective critique (see Exhibit 2.1)—define phases of an intellectual process that are in reality not so neatly categorized. Still, we find value in analyzing the qualities that scholars admire in finished work, while conceding the playful, anarchic, and unpredictable aspects of the life of the mind. Confidence in the assessment of scholarship depends on using standards that are appropriate to the full range of scholarly work.

Clear Goals

Does the scholar state the basic purposes of his or her work clearly? Does the scholar define objectives that are realistic and achievable? Does the scholar identify important questions in the field?

Adequate Preparation

Does the scholar show an understanding of existing scholarship in the field? Does the scholar bring the necessary skills to his or her work? Does the scholar bring together the resources necessary to move the project forward?

Appropriate Methods

Does the scholar use methods appropriate to the goals? Does the scholar apply effectively the methods selected? Does the scholar modify procedures in response to changing circumstances?

Significant Results

Does the scholar achieve the goals? Does the scholar's work add consequentially to the field? Does the scholar's work open additional areas for further exploration?

Effective Presentation

Does the scholar use a suitable style and effective organization to present his or her work? Does the scholar use appropriate forums for communicating work to its intended audiences? Does the scholar present his or her message with clarity and integrity?

Reflective Critique

Does the scholar critically evaluate his or her own work? Does the scholar bring an appropriate breadth of evidence to his or her critique? Does the scholar use evaluation to improve the quality of future work?

Assessing Faculty Scholarly Performance

John M. Braxton and Alan E. Bayer

The measurement of research performance is fundamentally important for both organizational and professional assessment in colleges and universities. Research performance is assessed at the organizational level by comparing individual performance to the attainment of organizational goals (Dornbusch and Scott, 1975). Colleges and universities are professionally dominated organizations (Clark, 1963), and academic professionals demand autonomy, not only in the performance of professional tasks but also in the evaluation of the performance of such tasks. Nevertheless, in order to preserve such autonomy, assessment of professional performance by the community of the profession is necessary (Goode, 1957; Clark, 1963). Moreover, institutions need to make distinctions among generally competent faculty in appointment, tenure, and promotion decisions (Centra, 1977). The surplus of new doctoral degree recipients and declining enrollments make such differentiations among faculty and candidates for faculty posts necessary, as the supply of faculty greatly exceeds the number of faculty appointed to positions and awarded tenure and promotion.

Academic administrators, consequently, who evaluate departmental and institutional performance, and institutional researchers who provide information to faculty personnel committees, can profit from a detailed discussion of types of faculty research performance measures. This chapter will present the full array of measures and provide an assessment of each measure. Although individual research performance will be the central focus of this analysis, individual performance can be aggregated to assess departmental, college, and institutional quality or excellence (Hagstrom, 1971; Conrad and Blackburn, 1985).

Importance of Research Assessment According to Institutional Types

Research and scholarly writing play minor roles in the academic life of most faculty. More than one-third of all academics spend no time in research and scholarly writing, more than two-fifths have never published a journal article, and more than three-fifths have never published a book, manual, or monograph (Bayer, 1973). An estimated 10 percent of all scientists produce 90 percent of all published works (Wilson, 1967).

In research universities, in particular, one-fourth have never published a journal article of any kind, and one-half have never published a book or monograph (Bayer, 1973; Bayer and Dutton, 1977). Still, research universities, as compared to other types of institutions, exhibit the strongest orientation toward research output and scholarly writing. A university may have a segment of its faculty, designated as research faculty, who have major time assignments in research and who are evaluated on the basis of research performance. A university may also have standards and criteria for research that vary among departments, disciplines or subject fields, and subspecialities within fields.

"Assessing Faculty Scholarly Performance," by John M. Braxton and Alan E. Bayer, reprinted from *Measuring Faculty Research Performance: New Directions for Institutional Research*, No. 50, edited by John W. Cresswell, 1986, Jossey-Bass Publishers, Inc.

In doctoral-granting universities and comprehensive colleges (where research is less institutionalized), the number and quality of publications are also of increasing importance in evaluating faculty for promotion, tenure, and salary increases. More specifically, Centra (1977) found that department heads at both doctoral-granting universities and comprehensive colleges and universities place some emphasis on both quantity and quality of publications. Moreover, Bowen and Schuster (1986) note an increasingly heavier emphasis on research performance for tenure and promotion at such institutions.

Subjective Assessment

Personnel action, predicated at least in part on the evaluation of one's research and scholarly performance, is ultimately and unavoidably a subjective assessment. Whether the yardsticks used are vague and qualitative or highly replicable and quantifiable, their interpretation is necessarily subjective. Yet it is also the case that existing methods are routinely assessed or altered to ensure greater objectivity, or that new, improved, objective methods are advocated and instituted to supplement or replace existing subjective assessment. Nevertheless, fully objective measurement is illusionary and elusive. A measurement or evaluation tool or procedure may be more or less qualitative or quantitative, but its interpretation or use in personnel decisions or performance assessment remains subjective.

The traditional method of assessing faculty research and scholarly performance—by peers—is particularly subject to the charge of being subjective, or biased. Nevertheless, a peer review system—by an elected committee, the tenured faculty of one's department, or a single pseudopeer (one's dean or department head)—is close to a universal procedural standard in academia. The work of the local peer review group may involve compilation of various quantitative measures of performance, but the result is a qualitative assessment of a faculty member's scholarly products (books and monographs, journal articles, patents, funding proposals, experimental designs, works of an artistic or creative nature, public performances, or whatever may be appropriately defined,

within a discipline or specialty field, as scholarship or research).

One allegation made against the peer system is that peers, because of day-to-day contact, will be unable to apply fully universalistic or merit-based standards. Moreover, local peers are unlikely to be engaged in the same area of subspecialty as the candidate, and so their capability to evaluate the candidate's scholarship is diminished. Thus, for important decisions regarding tenure and promotion, many institutions request outside evaluators' opinions of a candidate's scholarship. Besides being thought to ensure more objective evaluations than might be obtained from local peers, the procedure can be helpful in securing input from those most directly engaged in the same subspecialty as the candidate.

However, the procedure for selecting outside reviewers of scholarly credentials in itself contradicts the notion of objectivity, particularly when the candidate is consulted for names of possible outside reviewers. This carries the connotation that personal contact, rather than universalistic criteria, enters the process even for outside review. The conventional wisdom is that outside reviewers selected by the candidate are more inclined to strongly support the candidate; hence, their input might be partly discounted. Less recognized is the likelihood that unenthusiastic outside evaluations may be submitted by evaluators selected by the candidate. Frequently, candidates contact outside persons for their consent to having their names submitted as evaluators. Under the circumstances of personal contact, it is difficult to decline such a request. This subtle coercion can result in unreliable evaluations. In contrast, when a request comes from an administrator unknown to the potential outside evaluator, it is easier to decline if one cannot offer a positive assessment of the candidate's scholarship.

Because peer review, even when supplemented by the input of outside evaluators, is assumed to be unavoidably subjective to some degree, other assessment tools are also typically employed. Awards, honors, and prizes, for example, may be considered to be objective criteria. Yet Webster (1981) notes that these, too, are conferred largely on the basis of subjective judgments. Indeed, the same can be said of an editorial board's decision to accept a paper for publication, a scientist's decision to cite a piece of work, or a reviewer's appraisal of a book or an artistic creation. In effect, as noted by Cartter (1966), such objective measures are in fact "subjective measures once removed" (p. 4).

In sum, the evaluation of virtually all aspects of one's professional performance is subjective, or "subjective once removed." Hence, while the remainder of this chapter covers performance–assessment measures—some of which are highly quantifiable and independently replicable, and many of which are popularly characterized as objective—it is critical to remember that none of these tools offers a panacea for the problem of subjectivity in the evaluation of faculty scholarship and research performance.

Quantitative Measures

The products or outcomes of research that are in written form provide replicable measures of individual faculty research. Such products can be classified as published (publications) or unpublished and easily lend themselves to the objective process of "straight counting" (Lindsey, 1980). The use of written products of research for assessment of performance fits well with the assertion of Etzioni and Lehman (1967) that assessments tend to be based on the attributes that are the easiest to measure. Both published and unpublished written products of individual research performance will be discussed in subsequent subsections.

Publications. Counts of publications are among the most common measures of research performance (Folger and others, 1970), and books and journal articles are the two major categories utilized (Neumann, 1977). Each of these categories presents its own set of problems, as well as the need for some form of weighting system to make comparisons between journal articles and books.

Books present a problem, since several types of books can be used to measure research performance. Among the types of books are original scholarly books, theoretical or research monographs, edited books, and textbooks. A chapter in a book of readings may also be classified as a book form.

Several weighting systems have been developed to make comparisons among types of books and journal articles. These systems differ not only in the criteria on which the weights are based but also in the methods for obtaining the weights. The weighting systems developed by Glenn and Villemez (1970), Crane (1965), and Braxton and Toombs (1982) utilize specified criteria, while the systems developed by Manis (1951), Knudsen and Vaughan (1969), Lightfield (1971), Wilson (1964), and Cartter (1966) are not based on any specified criteria.

Glenn and Villemez (1970) used importance to the discipline as the criterion in the development of their weighting system. The numerical weights were derived from ratings made by a random sample of sociologists holding appointments in graduate departments of sociology. Respondents were informed that a weight of ten had been assigned to an article published in the *American Sociological Review* (*ASR*) and were asked to assign numerical weights to other types of publications on the basis of their importance to the discipline, with an article in *ASR* as their anchoring point for comparison.

The weighting system developed by Crane (1965) differs from Glenn and Villemez's in two respects. First, the numerical weights applied were not derived from ratings made by disciplinary peers but were arbitrarily assigned by Crane. Second, the index constructed by Crane was predicated on the contribution to scientific knowledge made by a publication through its cumulative effect on such knowledge. Thus, in order for the weights to be applied, this index requires attention to the content of publications, as a single problem or as a set of related problems. Crane made distinctions between major and minor publications, with weights applied only to major publications. Full-length articles, research reports, books, and textbooks were classified as major publications, whereas edited books, laboratory manuals, and translations were classified as minor publications. For major publications, four articles that met the criteria described here were equated with a single book. These weights were developed for application to biology, political science, and psychology.

Like Glenn and Villemez (1970), Braxton and Toombs (1982) employed a more objective method of weight assignment by using a panel of scholars of the academic profession or of graduate education to make the assessments used to develop this weighting system. If however, the criterion Braxton and Toombs used differs from that of both Crane (1965) and Glenn and Villemez (1970), in the degree to which professional knowledge and skill are utilized in the performance of a given activity. The judges were asked to rate the provided activities on a scale of zero to ten. The median ratings obtained were used to construct the weights produced.

The various weighting systems and their corresponding weights for various types of books, as well as for journal articles, are shown in Table 1. Although the weighting systems vary on the criteria employed and the methods for assigning the weights, original scholarly books and monographs receive higher weights than do journal articles. Textbooks are also weighted higher than edited books, while edited books are weighted equally with articles published in high-quality journals but higher than articles published in journals of lower perceived quality.

These observations suggest that the criteria and the methods for assigning weights have little effect on the relative weights of various book forms in comparison to journal articles. A possible explanation is rooted in the academic disciplines or disciplinary orientations of the scholars who developed the weighting systems. Biglan (1973) found that faculty in academic areas that are characterized as having "soft" paradigms tend to publish book- or monograph-length works more often than do faculty in "hard" paradigmatic fields. As these weighting systems were developed by and for "soft" paradigmatic areas, various book forms

received higher weights than journal articles did. In contrast, journal articles might have been weighted higher relative to the various book forms had the weighting systems been constructed by "hard" paradigm scholars. Thus, weighting systems that take differences among academic subjects into account should be developed. More specifically, different weighting systems should be constructed for different academic areas, for use not only by academic departments but also by faculty at the college-wide or university-wide level, in order to ensure more equitable and objective measurements of faculty research performance (Roskens, 1983).

Journal Articles. Like books, journal articles take different forms. Full-length articles, research notes, book reviews, commentaries and debates, and responses to commentaries and debates are pieces published in academic journals. Because forms of articles vary in length, the question of weighting emerges. Knudson and Vaughan (1969) do not count research notes as a form of journal article, whereas Glenn and Villemez (1970) equate research notes with full-length articles. However, Glenn and Villemez (1970) make distinctions between commentaries and debates on the basis of length, with long comments counted as full-length articles and short comments excluded. While neither Knudson and Vaughan nor Glenn and Villemez discuss book reviews, a weight of 8.8 was obtained by Braxton and Toombs, indicating a high degree of professional knowledge and skill is used in the preparation of a book review.

TABLE 1
Weighting System for Comparisons Among Book Types and Journal Articles

Publications	Weighting Systems							
	BT	CT	CR	GV	KV	L	M	W
Book Types								
Book chapter	NA	NA	NA	NA	NA	1	NA	NA
Edited book	4.2	2	NA	10	16	NA	1	NA
Original scholarly book	NA	NA	4		NA	4[a]	18	2
Textbook	9.3	3	4	15	24	NA	NA	N
Theoretical or research monograph	NA	6	NA	30	48	NA	NA	NA
Journal Article	NA	1	1	4–10	8–16	1	1	1

BT Braxton and Toombs (1982)   *CV* Glenn and Villemez (1970)   *M* Manis (1951)
CT Cartter (1966)   *KV* Knudsen and Vaughan (1969)   *W* Wilson (1964)
CR Crane (1965)   *L* Lightfield (1971)

[a] Each 100 pages = 1 journal article

As the literature offers few criteria for making such differentiations, academic administrators and institutional researchers are urged to consider the development of weights that address differentiations among these article forms and the ways they differ across disciplines. Such weights should be developed with a view toward the objective and equitable counting of the various forms of journal articles.

Journal characteristics, such as refereed-nonrefereed, and perceived quality are additional considerations that warrant discussion. Refereed journals are putatively "prestige" journals, characterized by the review of manuscripts by experts in the field (Miller and Serzan, 1984). An article published in a refereed journal is assessed and certified as a contribution to knowledge. Thus, articles published in refereed journals may be assessed higher than articles in nonrefereed journals. Caution in the application of this standard is urged; Miller and Serzan found that most academic and professional journals demonstrate editorial and reviewing procedures of wide variability. Rather than abandoning the use of refereed journals as a yardstick, institutional researchers, academic administrators, and faculty personnel committees should familiarize themselves with pertinent journals to determine the reviewing and editorial procedures that ensure standardized and objective assessment of an article.

Because academic and professional journals also vary in terms of quality, this factor becomes another variable in the measurement of individual research performance. Peer review or ratings of journals provide an objective method for making differentiations among journals. Glenn and Villemez (1970) provide ratings for twenty-two journals that frequently publish articles on sociological topics. These ratings are based on perceptions of a random sample of sociologists working in graduate departments.

Ratings of journals in the social sciences were also developed by Nelson and others (1983) from assessments made by departmental chairpersons in sixty-five United States and eighteen Canadian universities. These ratings used a five-point scale: 5=outstanding and 1=poor. As the various journals of different fields are categorized as having high, moderate,

and low visibility, interdisciplinary comparisons are possible for college and university-wide personnel committees. The mean ratings of these journals provide a readily available set of perceived quality rankings and can serve as weights for comparisons within fields.

Peer ratings of journals, however, have limitations and are not a panacea for the problem of equitable and objective assessment of articles published in academic journals of different levels of quality. Nelson and others (1983) cite several limitations: (1) The quality of the individual article is not being measured in peer reviews. (2) Journals vary in scope of articles published; some journals favor incremental contributions to knowledge, while others may emphasize more creative contributions. (3) Rankings do not take into account possible different rankings by faculty working in disciplinary subspecialties. (4) Peer ratings can change rapidly, since changes in editorial staff and publishing policies may affect the perceived quality of academic journals.

In addition to peer ratings of journals, the impact factor for each journal may also be employed as a means to assess the quality of academic journals (Gordon, 1982; McDonough, 1975; Smart and Elton, 1981). The impact factor for a given journal is the average number of citations received for each article published in that journal (Smart, 1983). Impact factors are displayed in the annual volumes of the *Journal Citation Reports* and in the various citation indexes published by the Institute for Scientific Information. However, the limitations that apply to citations of individual scholarly work, which are discussed elsewhere in this chapter, are pertinent to impact factors.

Unpublished Research Outcomes. Papers presented at professional meetings are probably the most prevalent type of unpublished research. Final reports of funded research are another type of unpublished research, and these also can be used to measure individual research performance.

Several factors emerge for consideration in the use of unpublished reports of research. The eventual publication of unpublished research suggests the possibility of double-counting of research activity. Moreover, distinctions among funding agencies and professional associations indicate that weighting systems are needed for equitable and objective assessment of research performance on the basis of unpublished research. Weights may be needed because of the perceived prestige and funding criteria of granting agencies. For example, a grant from the National Science Foundation is perceived as more prestigious than one received from an institutional research fund. Professional associations also vary in geographical scope. A paper presented at the annual meeting of the American Psychological Association might be weighted higher than a paper presented at a regional meeting of the Eastern Psychological Association.

The counting of published and unpublished research outcomes is greatly limited by failure to take differences in form into account. The various weighting systems discussed here do take these differences into account and do permit equitable and objective measurement based on the individual faculty member's published or unpublished form of research; however, the content and the quality of research are neglected. Because of this, citation analysis—a relatively new tool, widely advocated as a better, more quantifiable, and more objective measure than traditional measures—will be singled out for extensive discussion in this chapter.

Citation Measurement: A Quantifiable Quality Proxy

Acknowledgment by others of scholar's contributions is one of the primary ways by which work in academe is rewarded. In many fields, and especially in science, acknowledgment is manifested particularly through reference and citation. While referencing and citing have been established conventions in scientific writing since the beginning of the twentieth century (Garfield, 1979), they are now acknowledged (Merton, 1973) as principal mechanisms of reward, supporting the critical norms of open publication and free transmission of the ideas and work of scholars.

The founding of the Institute for Scientific Information (ISI) by Eugene Garfield has led to a burgeoning use of citation measures in the last quarter-century. The principal products of the ISI—the establishment of the *Science Citation Index* (in 1961), the *Social Science Citation Index* (in 1973), and the *Arts and Humanities Citation Index* (in 1978)—led to eas-

ily accessible measurement of citations in a wide range of archival sources, including some years before these indexes were introduced. Currently, the ISI covers more than 7,000 source journals (Garfield, 1985).

While the principal utility of the *Citation Indexes* was envisioned to be for literature searching, Garfield (1955) had earlier anticipated the use of citation compilations to assess the impact of scholars' contributions to contemporary research and thinking. Until the advent of the ISI Indexes, only a few scholars—most notably Clark (1957) and Price (1953)—had attempted the use of citation counts to assess scholarship. With the availability of the *Science Citation Index*, two research teams at the National Academy of Sciences (Creager and Harmon, 1966; Bayer and Folger, 1966) quickly began to assess the utility and application of this new tool.

Since that time, citation analysis, based almost exclusively on ISI products, has grown impressively. Since 1980, an annual average of about three hundred articles addresses citation practice (see Table 2). Among those that report quantitative assessments based on ISI materials, many focus on the evaluation of particular research papers or articles, on research teams, on linkages between papers or between scholars, on journal "quality" or "impact," on scientific research organizations or academic institutions and departments, and on different nations' rates of productivity.

Also prevalent in this body of literature is the application of citation measures when the unit of analysis is the individual scholar. Perhaps even more prevalent is the unpublished administrative use of such measures to evaluate the contributions of individual scholars. However, no national-scale survey data are currently available to determine the extent of administrative use (and misuse) of citation data for making personnel decisions in academe. The widespread availability of the ISI products, the growing awareness of their existence and utility, and anecdotal accounts all suggest that citation measures are now being widely incorporated into the administrative evaluation process in academe.

Citing Practice. A scholar establishes a professional contribution and reputation primarily through publication of ideas and findings. The pressure for diffusion of one's work through publication is accompanied by an obligation within the scholarly community for the user of that knowledge to make open reference to the sources that influenced a new idea, finding, or application. As Merton (1973) comments, "Not to do so is to incur sanctions visited upon those judged guilty of stealing another's intellectual property" (p. 48). A publication is property and citing practice is a social device for coping with problems of property rights and priority claims (Kaplan, 1965). Citing is a way of acknowledging property rights, as well as providing an "income" to the original owner of the property (Ravetz, 1971).

Of course, some works are cited for reasons other than their contributions as building blocks for ideas, concepts, findings, method, or instrumentation. Some works are cited for negative purposes, for perfunctory reasons, and because they were earlier works by citing authors or by their colleagues. Some works are cited when the citing author merely lifts the citation from another paper. Conversely, an important and pertinent paper may not be cited because the author was not aware of it, could not obtain it, harbored animosity toward the author, or could not read the language in which it was published. It is also true that not everything read and found useful is cited. Indeed, some key ideas and concepts or even entire publications become so integrated into the literature that they are "obliterated," no longer requiring explicit citation.

Despite the ambiguities of citation practices, considerable evidence exists to suggest that citation counts provide an objective measure of productivity, significance, quality, utility, influence, effectiveness, or impact of a scholar and his or her scholarly products, However, there are a number of allied citation-assessment issues that need to be acknowledged.

Assessment Problems. Three principal problem areas are related to employing citations. The first is in the establishing of baselines, or reference points, from which to evaluate an individual's performance. The second set of issues relates to the particular way in which the resource bases, the ISI *Citation Indexes*, are constructed. Finally, there are problems related to the publication process itself, as well as the allied problems of ascribing meaning to the citations generated by a scholarly product.

Baseline. There are dramatic differences between fields and disciplines in the rates of publication and in the acceptance rates of journals in various fields, disciplines, and subspecialties (Zuckerman and Merton, 1971; Hargens, 1985). Consequently, it is not surprising that there are also substantial differences in citation rates among various fields, disciplines, and subspecialties. However, there are no "benchmark" or "normative" averages available. Nevertheless, it is sufficient to note that administrative comparison for evaluation purposes should

TABLE 2
Number of Published Articles Addressing Citations[a] by Two-Year Periods for the Past Two Decades

Years	Number of Articles[b]
1984–85[c]	708
1982–83	830
1980–81	575
1978–79	415
1976–77	91
1974–75	38
1972–73	37
1970–71	19
1968–69	19
1965–67	12

Source: Subject index of annual issues of ISI's *Social Science Citation Index.*
[a]Subject search term is "citation."
[b]With "citation" in title.
[c]1985 total estimated; actual number of listings for first one-third of year (January–April 1985) multiplied by three.

Note: The growth shown here is partly an artifact of the increasing number of journals covered by ISI over time. Moreover, not all titles referring to citations necessarily deal with citations in the sense that this chapter uses.

not be made between scholars in different disciplines, or even between scholars in different subspecialties within the same discipline.

It should also be noted that the likelihood is low that any single piece of scholarly work will be cited more than once. Of all cited articles published in journals covered in the *Science Citation Index* in 1975, More than one-half were cited only once within the next decade (see Table 3). While there are no data on the number of articles that never garnered subsequent citations, it is clear that the modal number of lifetime citations to a piece of scholarship is either zero or one.

Thus, the general baseline for comparative purposes is extremely low. The average scholar would expect less than one citation per publication over a finite period of time subsequent to publication. Conversely a scholar who has published a number of pieces in a fixed period of time might, on average, expect to generate at least a few citations. In sum, there is no sufficient "baseline" reference for citation counts.

Indexing Practice. The compilation structure of the ISI *Citation Index* poses several problems. Only first authors are indexed, and only surnames and initials are used. Thus, a scholar who is a junior author of a piece would be missed in simple counts. If an author has a common surname, name homographs may appear (including those of others with the same initials), thereby inflating actual citation counts. Moreover, some surnames are subject to common misspellings by citing authors, and these errors are preserved in the *Citation Indexes*. While these problems decrease the reliability of citation counts in many cases, they

are less problematic when careful administrative compilation is made in conjunction with the author's curriculum vitae, including the complete listing of scholarly works. The complete bibliography allows looking up a piece under the cited senior author's name. Cited name homographs can be eliminated by inspecting the source and date of each citation against the curriculum vitae bibliography. Common misspellings (and references with only the first initial) can also be readily checked for inclusion or exclusion in counts.

Another limitation is that not all the world's archival literature is used for compiling citing sources in the ISI *Citation Indexes*. Moreover, books and monographs are not included as citing documents. Nevertheless, the degree of ISI source coverage is sufficiently extensive and inclusive that the coverage problem generally is considered to be a minor one (at least for United States scholars). This is especially true because all cited documents (including books, monographs, patents, unpublished papers, proceedings, review articles, notes, and letters), regardless of source, are listed by ISI if they were cited in any of the 7,000 citing source journals.

Other Caveats. Elsewhere, caution has been urged in comparing citation data across disciplines or specialties, given differences in publication rates and acceptance rates of journals. It also should be noted that there are differences in lag rates of citations (due in large measure to significant disciplinary differences in average lag time between acceptance of manuscripts and their publication) and in citation-frequency decay rates (citation half-lives).

TABLE 3
Citation Frequency for 1975 Articles Cited in SCI[a]

Citation Frequency	Number of Articles
1	521,100
2-4	224,900
5-9	93,200
10-14	40,000
15-24	36,500
25-49	27,400
50-99	10,600
100-199	3,090
200-299	520
300 or more	340

Source: Garfield, 1985, p. 6.
[a] Counts are from date of publication to 1984.

Citation decay rates vary substantially (Line, 1984). Thus, faculty with long career spans have, on average, more publications and more opportunity to be cited than those who are relatively new in their careers. Therefore, citation counting must either restrict compilation to a fixed span of time, not only for the citing sources but also for the cited documents, or otherwise adjust data for the total number of publications available from a scholar that could be cited (and further adjust counts for the declining likelihood of citation as the papers age). In some circumstances, compilations of citation rates for collaboratively authored papers may also be adjusted, with multi-authored contributions receiving only a proportion of the count attributable to a single-authored piece of work. Citation counts are of virtually no utility for assessing people who are just entering their publishing years.

Finally, several critics of citation tools have noted that self-citations may distort measurement. Prolific publishers can inflate their own raw citation counts. Self-citation may be no more than an ego-enhancing mechanism, or one to further one's own self-interest, if a citation count becomes a widely used evaluative criterion. Conversely, self-citation is a legitimate practice when a scholar is building on an idea through a series of papers over time (a practice somewhat distorted by publication of LPU's—least publishable units—whereby a number of short papers are submitted separately in order to maximize the number of bibliographic entries). Therefore, while in the general case the inclusion or exclusion of self-citations is likely to make no difference (Lawani and Bayer, 1983), in specific applications for administrative applications, self-citations should be excluded.

Citations as a Solitary Measure. A citation count, even when carefully compiled and adjusted to compensate for artifactual weaknesses, is not a measure of scholarly performance for use without the other methods discussed here. It is, however, a useful adjunct tool, providing a more quantitative assessment of a qualitative dimension than some of the other measures. It is also a fallible tool; an occasional piece may be frequently cited for its flaws. Conversely, a high-quality piece may go unrecognized for years, uncited until long after its first appearance in the literature.

There is strong evidence that citations alone cannot reliably differentiate among individual scholars or individual scholarly contributions (Lawani and Bayer, 1988). Greater aggregation (at the departmental, program, or research-team levels) may provide more reliable measurement for administrative use, but it increases the risks of grouping scholars with dissimilar citation rates, attributable to dissimilarities of citation profiles in different specializations. Citation measures are not a panacea. They must be accompanied by caveats and acknowledgment of flaws and must be employed judiciously. Nevertheless, they add to the information base for administrative decision making.

The various measures of individual research performance discussed in this chapter fail to capture the day-to-day scholarly activities of many academics, especially academics who have seldom published or received citations to their works. Measures that assess day-to-day activities are needed to evaluate the performance of such individuals. The next section of this chapter presents an array of such measures.

Measures of Day-to-Day Scholarly Performance

Scholarship encompasses a much wider range of performance than that measured through publications (Braxton and Toombs, 1982; Pellino and others, 1984). Although employing different definitions of scholarly work and different methodologies, both Braxton and Toombs and Pellino and others identify measures of scholarly performance that are differentiated from scholarly books, monographs, and journal articles. Pellino and others used faculty perceptions of activities characteristic of their scholarly roles as the operational definition of scholarly work, whereas Braxton and Toombs defined scholarly work as "that form of work which involves the application or use of knowledge and skill acquired through and certified by doctoral research training" (p. 267). While the components of scholarship identified by Pellino and others were obtained through faculty perceptions of their scholarly roles, Braxton and Toombs used a panel of scholars of the academic profession or of graduate education to identify activities that utilize varying degrees of doctoral research training.

The measures identified through these two research efforts cast a broad net over the definition of scholarship. More specifically, community and public service activities, institutions and departmental activities, and various teaching or course activities were identified as categories of measures of scholarly performance by both Braxton and Toombs and Pellino and others. Moreover, public talks and lectures and public disciplinary writings are categories of measures of scholarly performance (Braxton and Toombs, 1982) that focus on the lay public.

Activities identified by Braxton and Toombs and by Pellino and others include day-to-day scholarly activities, which may be appropriate for the assessment of the research performance of individual faculty who have seldom or never published. Furthermore, these measures may be commensurate with the performance patterns of faculty employed in colleges and universities where research has not been well institutionalized. Numerical weights for making distinctions among the various measures of scholarly performance are provided by Braxton and Toombs and are available from the factor analysis in Pellino and others.

Additional Measures

Written but unpublished reports of research funded by various granting agencies were previously discussed. The writing of research proposals and proposals for the development of new academic programs are additional measures of research performance, broadly conceived (Braxton and Toombs, 1982). Although numerical weights for making distinctions among these activities are provided by Braxton and Toombs, the prestige of the granting agency, the amount of money awarded, and whether proposals were accepted for funding are additional considerations. Service as a reviewer of grant proposals is another pertinent measure (Pellino and others, 1984).

The development of computer software programs is another measure of scholarly performance, given the rapid emergence of the use of microcomputers on college and university campuses. Weights need to be developed and distinctions made among types of programs

developed. One such distinction is between programs developed for local use, as contrasted with those developed for external use.

Conclusion

An array of measures of individual faculty research performance has been presented and reviewed in this chapter. From this review, three conclusions are warranted.

1. None of the types of measures presented is without problems; each requires careful consideration in its application. Put differently, none of the measures is simple and straight-forward, and objective and equitable assessment of performance is a salient concern. The problems surrounding each type of measure have been presented and should be addressed before use of the measure by academic administrators, institutional researchers, and faculty personnel committees.

2. Measurement of research performance is multidimensional. The predominant or singular use of any one type of measure results in failure to assess the full range of professional role performance and results in a biased and incomplete assessment. Consequently, all the measures presented should be used, as well as a common weighting system that allows for differentiation among these measures. Weighting systems developed to make distinctions among book forms and forms of journal articles may be on a different metric than citations, computer software, grant proposals, patents, new procedures and instrumentation, or the scholarly activities identified by Pellino and others (1984) and by Braxton and Toombs (1982). A composite weighting system, which places all selected and correspondingly weighted measures on the same weighting scale, may be useful. A first step in the development of such a scale is the selection of a criterion to undergird the numerical weights assigned to the various measures to be used.

3. *Publication, research,* and *scholarship* are terms used in this chapter. Undeveloped distinctions among these terms have been made and are reflected in the assessments of the measures presented. A typology that clarifies the distinctions among these terms and measurable components is needed. Such a typology might be organized around the following distinctions: *Scholarship* may be considered as a process, as well as a product, with the application of professional knowledge and skill as its core determinant. Thus, scholarship may include research activity but may also involve the analysis and synthesis of extant knowledge. *Research*, however, has a more narrow focus than scholarship; it is disciplined inquiry designed to produce original knowledge. *Publication* may be the product of either scholarship or research. With careful differentiation among these terms comes a fuller and more complete assessment of professional behavior.

The focus of this chapter has been on the assessment of individual research performance. Attention should also be given to the assessment of teaching and public service, with consideration to factors that may be problematic to the objective and equitable assessment of these dimensions of the faculty role.

References

Bayer, A. E. "Teaching Faculty in Academe; 1972–73." *ACE Research Reports*, no. 2. Washington, D.C: American Council on Education, 1973.

Bayer, A. E., and Dutton, J. E. "Career Age and Research—Professional Activities of Academic Scientists." *Journal of Higher Education*, 1977, 48, 259–282.

Bayer, A. E., and Folger, J. K. "Some Correlates of a Citation Measure of Productivity in Science." *Sociology of Education*, 1966, 39, 381–390.

Biglan, A. "Relationship Between Subject Matter Characteristics and the Structure and Output of University Departments." *Journal of Applied Psychology*, 1973, 57(3), 204–213.

Bowen, H. R., and Schuster, J. H. *American Professors: A National Resource Imperiled*. New York: Oxford University Press, 1986.

Braxton, J. M., and Toombs, W. "Faculty Uses of Doctoral Training: Consideration of a Technique for the Differentiation of Scholarly Effort from Research Activity." *Research in Higher Education*, 1982, 16(3), 265–286.

Cartter, A. M. *An Assessment of Quality in Graduate Education*. Washington, D.C: American Council on Education, 1966.

Centra, J. A. *How Universities Evaluate Faculty Performance: A Survey of Department Heads*. Princeton, N.J.: Educational Testing Service, Graduate Record Examinations Program, 1977.

Clark, B. R. "Faculty Organization and Authority." In T. Lanoford (Ed.), *The Study of Academic Administration*. Boulder, Colo.: Western Interstate Commission on Higher Education, 1963.

Clark, K. E. *America's Psychologists: A Survey of a Growing Profession*. Washington, D.C.: American Psychological Association, 1957.

Conrad, C. F., and Blackburn, R. T. "Correlates of Departmental Quality in Regional Colleges and Universities." *American Educational Research Journal*, 1985, 22(2), 279–295.

Crane, D. "Scientists at Major and Minor Universities: A Study of Productivity and Recognition." *American Sociological Review*, 1965, 30(5), 699–714.

Creager, J. A., and Harmon, L. R. *On-the-Job Validation of Selected Variables*. Technical Report no. 26. Washington, D.C.: National Academy of Sciences, 1966.

Dornbusch, S. M., and Scott, W. R. *Evaluation and the Exercise of Authority: A Theory of Control Applied to Diverse Organizations*. San Francisco: Jossey-Bass, 1975.

Efzioni, A, and Lehman, E. W. "Some Dangers in 'Valid' Social Measurement." *The Annals*, 1967, 373, 1–15.

Folger, J. K., Astin, H. S., and Bayer, A. E. *Human Resources and Higher Education: Staff Report of the Commission on Human Resources and Advanced Education*. New York: Russell Sage Foundation, 1970.

Garfield, E. "Citation Indexes for Science." *Science*, 1955, 122, 108–111.

Garfield, E. *Citation Indexing: Its Theory and Application in Science Technology, and Humanities*. New York: Wiley, 1979.

Garfield, E. "Current Comments." *Current Contents: Social and Behavioral Sciences*, 1985, 44, 3.

Glenn, N. D., and Villemez, W. "The Productivity of Sociologists at 45 American Universities." *American Sociologist*, 1970, 5 (3), 244–251.

Goode, W. J. "Community Within a Community: The Professions." *American Sociological Review*, 1957, 22, 194–200.

Gordon, M. D. "Citation Rankings Versus Subjective Evaluation in the Determination of Journal Hierarchies in the Social Sciences." *Journal of the American Society for Information Science*, 1982, 33, 55–57.

Hagstrom, W. O. "Inputs, Outputs, and the Prestige of University Science Departments." *Sociology of Education,* 1971, 44, 375–397.

Hargens, L. "Disciplinary Differences in Journal Acceptance Rates." Paper presented at the annual meeting of the Society for Social Studies of Science, Troy, New York, October, 1985.

Kaplan, N. "The Norms of Citation Behavior: Prolegomena to the Footnote." *American Documentation,* 1965, 16, 179–184.

Knudsen, D. D., and Vaughan, T. R. "A Re-evaluation of the Rankings of Sociology Departments in the Cartter Report." *American Sociologist,* 1969, 4(1), 12–19.

Lawani, S. M., and Bayer, A. E. "Validity of Citation Criteria for Assessing the Influence of Scientific Publications: New Evidence with Peer Assessment." *Journal of the American Society for Information Science,* 1983, 34, 59–66.

Lightfield. E. T. "Output and Recognition of Sociologist." *American Sociologist,* 1971, 6(2), 128–133.

Lindsey, D. "Production and Citation Measures in the Sociology of Science: The Problem of Multiple Authorships." *Social Studies of Science,* 1980, 10, 145–162.

Line, M. B. "Citation Decay of Scientific Papers: Variation According to Citations Received." *Journal of Information Science,* 1984, 9, 90–91.

McDonough, C. C. "The Relative Quality of Economics Journals Revisited." *Quarterly Review of Economics and Business,* 1975, 15, 91–97.

Manis, J. G. "Some Academic Influences Upon Publication Productivity." *Social Forces,* 1951, 29(3), 267–272.

Merton. R. K. *The Sociology of Science: Theoretical and Empirical Investigations.* Chicago: University of Chicago Press, 1973.

Miller, A. C., and Serzan, S. "Criterion for Identifying a Referred Journal." *Journal of Higher Education,* 1984, 55(6). 673–699.

Nelson, T. M., Buss, A. R., and Katzko, M. "Rating of Scholarly Journals by Chairpersons in the Social Sciences." *Research in Higher Education,* 1983, 19(4), 469–497.

Neumann, Y. "Standards of Research Publication: Differences Between the Physical Sciences and the Natural Sciences." *Research in Higher Education,* 1977, 7, 355–367.

Pellino, G. R., Blackburn, R. T. and Boberg, A. L. "The Dimensions of Academic Scholarship: Faculty and Administrator Views." *Research in Higher Education,* 1984, 20(1), 103–115.

Price, D. J. *Little Science, Big Science.* New York: Columbia University Press, 1963.

Ravetz, J. R. *Scientific Knowledge and Its Social Problems.* Oxford: Clarendon, 1971.

Roskens, R. W. "Implications of Biglan Model Research for the Process of Faculty Advancement." *Research in Higher Education,* 1983, 18, 285–297.

Smart, J. C. "Stability of Education Journal Characteristics: 1977–1980." *Research in Higher Education,* 1983, 19, 285–293.

Smart, J. C., and Elton, C. F. "Structural Characteristics and Citation Rates of Education Journals." *American Education Research Journal,* 1981, 18, 399–413.

Webster, D. S. "Advantages and Disadvantages of Methods of Assessing Quality." *Change,* 1981, 13(7), 20–24.

Wilson, L. *The Academic Man.* New York: Octagon Press, 1964.

Wilson, L. "The Professor and His Roles." In C. Lee (Ed.), *Improving College Teaching.* Washington, D.C: American Council on Education, 1967.

Zuckerman, H., and Merton, R. K. "Patterns of Evaluation in Science: Institutionalization, Structure, and Functions of the Referee System." *Minerva,* 1971, 9, 66–100.

John M. Braxton is visiting assistant professor of higher education at Loyola University of Chicago. His research interests are the measurement of faculty role performance, faculty publication productivity, and social control in the academic profession.

Alan E. Bayer is professor and head of the department of sociology, Virginia Polytechnic Institute and State University. His research interests include national surveys of the professoriate, assessment of performance in academe, factors associated with professional performance, the nature of collaborative scholarship, and the ethical and normative structure of collaborative enterprises.

CHAPTER 9

COMMUNITY COLLEGES
AND PROPRIETARY SCHOOLS

ASSOCIATE EDITOR: ROSEMARY GILLETT-KARAM

Two inestimable American patriots left an indelible mark on the idea and history of education in America. As republican zealots who were highly conscious of the rising middle class in America, each reacted to education in different ways. For Jefferson, an American aristocracy could emerge via education; his educational scheme recruited from the masses individuals who were exceptionally gifted leaders. Their higher education curriculum retained the best of the European-Oxbridge example, a classical liberal arts education. For all his talk about farming, Jefferson never saw the benefit of agricultural training.

Franklin, not so sanguine, held a different concept of education that emphasized pragmatism and utilitarianism. He claimed he would not educate the young in frivolous arts and graces, the dead tongues or the classics; rather, his purpose was "to train youth to serve the public with honor to themselves, and to their country, and to fit them for successful careers in business" (Curti, 1966, p. 36). Franklin was clearly devoted to experimental science; after all, he reasoned, the practical applications of science promised to make agriculture, commerce, and industry more profitable and everyday life more comfortable. Like Locke, Franklin believed that most people are what they are by virtue of their training and discipline, which they could either receive or provide themselves, i.e., through self-education.

Not surprising, the ideas of these two men form the bases of continuing debate about the purposes of education in modern society. For all the emphasis on the practicality of education, there are those scholars who remain adamant that a quality education is one associated with a liberal arts (read classical) education. Many, for example, would argue that the difference between a four-year and two-year higher educational institution is bound up in this controversy. Still others would argue that all education must respond to the needs of society for work, careers, and the general welfare of a capitalist society. Some have the opinion that higher education is responsible for combining liberal arts education with career orientations.

By turning to trends and emphases in higher education at the end of the twentieth century we can measure this nation's response to the Jefferson-Franklin debate. In large, the occupations that were necessary to maintain the early republic, clergy and statesmen and republican zealots, are no longer the careers of a post-industrial, information oriented, global society, and although Jefferson still stirs our imaginations with the promise of an elite citizenry developed through education, Franklin's emphasis on practicality has influenced the contention. He has been aided along that road by the influence of Dewey and Freire as educational philosophers. The community college and the proprietary school have subscribed to their ideas.

In principle, the first junior colleges evolved out of the four year institutions' need for separation between the first two years of college (practical) and the last two years of college (research).

Rosemary Gillett-Karam is associate professor in the Department of Adult and Higher Education at North Carolina State University. (rgk@poe.coe.ncsu.edu)

The evolution of the junior-community college, as author George Vaughan (1995) discusses, follows at minimum a two-track model, one fulfilling the transfer function and the other oriented toward career training. Given its modern mission, interpreted through the G.I. Bill (1944) and the Zook Commission (1947), the modern community colleges promote open access and emphasize meeting the needs of the business and social community in which they are located. Dubbed the "people's college," the post World War II vision for postsecondary education was to provide educational opportunity for anyone who wanted to attend college.

So strong is the element of egalitarianism tied to community colleges that some envision it associated primarily with the needs of its community and only secondarily with education (Gleazer, 1980). Cited by many as the only uniquely American institution of higher education, the community college historically is tied to European folk schools, American chautauguas and lyceums, and to the land-grant institutions. As a populist reality, community colleges are mirrors reflecting the needs of the nontraditional and the underrepresented learner struggling to become middle class through career training.

Career training has been classified differently from education mainly because of competition between those institutions who offer the training: community colleges and proprietary schools. In a spirited discussion, contributors to the Clowes and Hawthorne (1995) book compare and contrast community colleges and proprietary schools. Arguing that the confusion over differences between the two stem from a national system of funding regulations and accountability, authors claim either conflict or convergence. Whereas authors agree that convergence comes because both institutions offer specialized education and training, they also make claims of conflict when considering mission, governance and cost. In a provocative essay, Cheng and Levin focus on students of community colleges and proprietary schools. Using data from the National Center for Educational Statistics in their work, *High School and Beyond*, the authors distinguish student characteristics among proprietary, not-for-profit private two- and four-year colleges, two-year public colleges, and four-year public and private universities. The issue of transfer is also addressed by the authors who examine educational aspirations of the student cohort groups.

Hittman, writing in *A Handbook on the Community College in America* (Baker, 1993), continues to reference differences between two-year community colleges and proprietary schools. Not only are they different because one emphasizes education (community colleges) and the other emphasizes training, they also are different in terms of accountability. In a notable explanation of stakeholders, Hittman suggests a list of publics including lay and formal boards, faculty, foundation givers, legislators, and students, all of whom have decision-making roles in community colleges. The list of stakeholders in proprietary colleges is shorter; only private owners or the corporate level management are decision makers.

Perhaps the most compelling argument for the proprietary stakeholder is contained in the article, "University of Phoenix, Beat 'em or Join 'em" (Fishetti et al., 1998). This for-profit system is the largest private university in the nation espousing the values of both proprietary schools and community colleges while placing them in a four-year setting. John Sperling, the founder of the Apollo Group, is the main shareholder of the now $2 billion dollar educational business of stripped down curricula, flexible scheduling, and real-world emphases. In April, 1998, University of Phoenix had 98 campuses in 31 states with an enrollment of 55,000 students. Are colleges or proprietary schools concerned?

Perez and Copenhaver say they are. They believe students are reassessing career pathways and questioning course content, sequencing, and delivery of degree programs. The new stage for college examination, they claim, is the global economy. Intransigence in college practice is giving way and declining because of competition from educational systems that can meet student demands of anytime, anywhere, anyplace. Using innovative practices from one community college as evidence of forward thinking, Perez and Copenhaver concur that information technology industries' boom period demands technical skills, not credentials. Certificate programs of 18 to 24 hours couple degree requirements with specialty skills oriented to the latest innovations in industry, especially information technology. The creators of these programs call them inverted. Skills and immediate experience come before a student takes general education classes.

Franklin would have been proud.

Articles

1. Vaughan, G. (1995). *The community college story: A tale of American innovation.* Washington, D.C.: The American Association of Community Colleges. Last page number: 43.
2. Cheng, X. & Levin, B. (1995)."Who are the students at community colleges and proprietary schools?" In D. Clowes, & Hawthorne, E. (Eds.), *Community colleges and proprietary schools: Conflict or convergence?* (pp. 51–60). *New Directions for Community Colleges,* No. 91 (Fall) San Francisco: Jossey-Bass. Last page number: 105.
3. Hittman, J. 1993. "The impact of proprietary schools on the viability of community colleges," In George A. Baker (Ed.), *A handbook on the community college in America: Its history, mission, and management.* (pp. 535–546). Westport, CN: Greenwood Press. Last page number: 681.
4. Fishetti, M., Anderson, J., Watrous, M., Tanz, J. & Gwynne, P. (1998, March-April). *University of Phoenix, Beat 'em or Join 'em.* In *University business: Strategies for today's higher education* (pp. 44–51).
5. Perez, S. & Copenhaver, S. (1998, March). *Certificates on center stage: Occupational education for a working economy.* League for Innovation as Leadership Abstracts, Vol. 11, No 3. Laguna Hills, CA: League for Innovation.

Bibliography (For further reading)

Appling, R., & Aleman, S. (1990). *Proprietary schools.* Congressional Research Service Report for Congress 90-428EPW. Washington, DC: Library of Congress.

Baker, G. (1994). *Handbook on the community college in America.* Westport, CT: Greenwood Press.

Bensimon, E., & Neumann, A. (1993). *Redesigning collegiate leadership.* Baltimore, MD: Johns Hopkins Press.

Bogue, J. *(1950). The community college.* New York: McGraw-Hill.

Brint, S., & Karabel, J. (1989). *The diverted dream: Community colleges and the promise of educational opportunity in America, 1900–1985.* New York. Oxford.

Boone, E. J. (1997). *Community-based programming: An opportunity and imperative for the community college.* Washington, D. C.: Community College Press.

Clowes, D., & Hawthorne, E. (1995). *Community colleges and proprietary schools: Conflict or convergence? New Directions for Community Colleges,* No. 91 (Fall). San Francisco: Jossey-Bass.

Cohen, A., & Brawer, F. (1994). *Managing community colleges: A handbook for effective practice.* San Francisco: Jossey-Bass.

Curti, M. (1966). *The social ideas of American educators.* Totowa, NJ: Littlefield, Adams.

Gleazer, E. (1980). *The community college: Values, vision and vitality.* Washington, DC: American Association of Community and Junior Colleges

Green, M. (1988). *Leaders for a new era: Strategies for higher education.* New York: ACE/Macmillan.

Gutmann, A. (1987). *Democratic education.* Princeton, NJ: Princeton University Press.

Karabel, J., & Halsey, A. (1977). *Power and ideology in education.* New York: Oxford.

Lee, J., & Merisotis, J. (1990). *Propietary schools: Programs, Policies, and Prospects.* ASHE-ERIC Higher Education Report No. 5. Washington, DC: Association for the Study of Higher Education.

McGrath, D., & Spear, M. B. (1991). *The academic crisis of the community college.* NY: State University of New York Press.

Tierney, W. (1991). *Culture and ideology in higher education: Advancing a critical agenda.* New York: Praeger.

Rhoads, R., & Valadez, J. (1996). *Democracy, multiculturalism, and the community college: A critical perspective.* New York. Garland Publishers.

Witt, A., Wattenbarger, J., Gollattscheck, J., & Suppinger, J. (1994). *America's community colleges: The first century.* Washington, DC: Community College Press.

The Impact of Proprietary Schools on the Viability of Community Colleges

JON A. HITTMAN

The effect of proprietary schools on the viability of community college poses an interesting conceptual dilemma. While both are considered postsecondary institutions, tradition suggests that these entities emerged to satisfy two separate and distinct needs.

Proprietary schools are defined as educational institutions (trade and technical, business, cosmetology, and barber schools) "which are privately owned and managed, and which in addition to being service oriented, are profit motivated" (Fulton 1969). Historically these schools have focused on vocational training. Proprietary school owners respond to marketplace demands for trained labor by providing short-term instruction in specific subjects with immediate employment for the graduate as the prime objective (Shoemaker 1973). By contrast, the original function of the junior/community college was to provide liberal arts education. Community colleges structured their curricula in the university image and established the "collegiate function" with transfer to the university as the primary goal (Cohen and Brawer 1984). Given this historic disparity in function, it is not surprising that a 1975 study (Erwin) noted that most proprietary schools do not compete directly with community colleges for students.

Since the publication of the Erwin study, the educational environment has changed significantly. There has been a dramatic shift in the mission of community colleges and a change in the autonomy of proprietary schools. External forces, such as the economy, work-force requirements, and legislation have had a profound effect on the viability of both community colleges and proprietary schools. The change engendered by the shifting environment has, to a certain extent, diminished the clarity of the differentiation between them and has fostered an atmosphere of competition.

The remainder of this chapter will (1) describe the historically dissimilar roles of proprietary schools and community colleges, (2) describe the specific features that have traditionally distinguished community colleges from proprietary schools, (3) explain how these features have been affected by watershed events, and (4) conclude with some of the effects of these events upon community colleges and proprietary schools.

Historical Role of the Community College

The predominantly twentieth-century and purely American phenomenon known as the community college has its roots in the university system. The purpose of higher education has always been debated from various perspectives. There is loose agreement, however, that the first two years of postsecondary education are preparatory. This notion, combined with the effects of population growth and increasing demands on education, created fertile ground for the development of the public junior/community college concept. Rapid growth in information and population in the late nineteenth

"The Impact of Proprietary Schools on the Viability of Community Colleges," by Jon A. Hittman, reprinted from *A Handbook on the Community College in America: Its History, Mission, and Management*, edited by George A. Baker III, 1994, Greenwood Publishing Group.

and early twentieth centuries began to pressure the system of higher education. Between 1870 and 1900, the U.S. population doubled, while university enrollment increased by 450 percent. Universities confined their enrollment to students who had demonstrated the academic skill to prosper in an academic environment committed to scholarship and research. But many students with and without preferred academic skills demanded acceptance.

As a solution, a four-year university education was divided into two levels. The first two years were labeled the "college," and the second two years were called the "university." It was not until 1892 that William Rainey Harper, president of the University of Chicago, made this concept a reality. Harper established the Academic College (the first two years) and the University College (second two years). He later changed the names to Junior College and Senior College, respectively. Harper was instrumental in establishing the first public junior college by convincing the Joliet, Illinois, school board to expand the Joliet High School curriculum to include the 13th and 14th grades. This gave birth to the modern public junior/community college movement.

Harper's purpose in establishing junior colleges was to provide the University of Chicago with a ready supply of academically capable students while reducing the population of students who were academically inadequate. The time, effort, and problems associated with the student selection process were exported to the junior college.

During the early 1900s, legislation in California allowed public, secondary school boards to offer postgraduate courses to "approximate the first two years of university study." Further legislation provided public funds to support the junior college system. The popularity of the two-year, publicly funded, post-secondary community college grew from these beginnings.

Historical Role of the Proprietary School

The documented history of proprietary education in the United States is understandably limited because proprietary schools (1) are organized in various ways making their for-profit status difficult to determine, (2) are operated on a profit motive, which has been spurned by the traditional academic community, (3) have not previously been perceived as a threat to traditional segments of postsecondary education, and (4) have not previously been genuinely recognized and included in planning and policy-making activities (Carr 1980). Despite a dearth of research, there is agreement that correspondence instruction was the first type of proprietary training to be offered in the United States. According to Katz (1963), the *Boston Gazette* carried the following statement regarding the instruction of shorthand in 1728: "Any persons in the country desirous to learn this art may by having the several lessons sent weekly to them, be as perfectly instructed as those that live in Boston." Proprietary resident schools became relatively common in the middle of the eighteenth century. Classes were conducted in places of business, or sometimes at the homes of the proprietors, who also were instructors.

Historically, proprietary schools have been dependent upon the marketplace for income. Rapid industrialization in the United States provided a favorable environment for these schools. Other factors contributing to their growth have been (1) a student and employer market base that has not been traditionally courted or served adequately by public institutions (Carr 1980) and (2) the inefficiency of the American apprenticeship system for business and occupational training (Tonne 1954).

The phenomenon of multiple schools with a single corporate structure began to evolve as early as 1850 with the establishment of Bacon's Mercantile Colleges. These schools, founded by R. C. Bacon, were located in several Midwestern cities, including Madison, Cincinnati, and Cleveland. The Bryant-Stratton chain was organized in 1852 by H. D. Stratton and H. B. Bryant. By the end of the Civil War, the chain had grown to more than fifty schools in almost as many cities. This growth can be attributed to the development and employment of effective advertising campaigns, to the delivery of high-quality training using a uniform system of instruction and textbooks, and to the fact that the schools filled an important need not addressed by public education.

During the late nineteenth and early twentieth centuries, career growth for women was an important but relatively unheralded contribution of proprietary education (Lee and Merisotis 1990). The Civil War forced businesses to employ women as clerks, but they often lacked business training. As a result of the introduction of the key shift typewriter and the Gregg shorthand method, proprietary schools identified women as an untapped student market. Prior to the Civil War, most women who wanted to work were directed into teaching.

In the 1970s and 1980s there was a surge in the growth of proprietary school popularity. Proprietary school success has been attributed to the traditional characteristics of flexibility and specialization of service (Carr 1980) which have been enhanced by the relative autonomy afforded proprietary schools because of their private, for-profit structure.

Summary of Traditional Role Distinctions

Traditionally, community colleges have been considered slow and nonflexible. On the other hand, proprietary education has been considered flexible, providing training for new technologies as soon as they develop (Clark and Sloan 1966). One explanation for this disparity is that community colleges provide education whereas proprietary schools deliver training. Education is a slow, highly individual, lifelong process—but training is not (Wilms 1973). Training can be done quickly and effectively.

Proprietary schools are by definition private, for-profit entities existing in the marketplace and dependent upon tuition for revenue. As such, they traditionally have been more autonomous and subject to less governmental and accrediting body oversight than traditional public postsecondary institutions.

Specific Traditional Differences

Funding

Sources of funding is the most obvious characteristic that distinguishes traditional public junior/community colleges from proprietary schools. Public institutions receive revenue from both public (local taxes, state and federal funding) and market (tuition and fees) sources.

Proprietary schools traditionally have been dependent solely upon the marketplace for revenue. As a result, most proprietary schools have well-developed recruiting and placement functions (Simmons 1975).

Curriculum

Original curricular offerings of public junior/community colleges were primarily collegiate academic studies in preparation for the universities. Early occupational training delivered by the public junior/community college was pre-professional: pre-law, pre-medicine, and pre-engineering. Eells (1931) reported that, in 1929, proportional enrollment in California public junior colleges was 80 to 20 in favor of the collegiate academic studies over the pre-professional education.

Operating from the assumption that the length of a program is directly related to its quality, state departments of education, regional accrediting bodies, and professional groups have a prescribed length and course content (Wilms 1975). This assumption produces rigid scheduling and curricular offerings.

Totally dependent upon the marketplace for income, proprietary schools have aggressively sought to identify and address the unmet needs of business and industry. Therefore, early proprietary programs were truly occupational in nature, and subjects that did not directly contribute to job skills were minimized. Traditionally, successful proprietary schools exploited differences between the offerings at community colleges and at their own institutions. The following distinct characteristics of proprietary school offerings have emerged:

1. Flexible program and course schedules designed to increase accessibility (Belitsky 1969)

2. Flexible curricula designed to make it easy for the student to enter, exit, and reenter, thereby increasing the probability of enrollment and completion (Erickson et al. 1972)

3. Flexible instruction to accommodate special student needs for individual attention, help, and encouragement (Kincaid and Podesta 1966)

4. Sensitivity and responsiveness to changes in level of demand for trained manpower and an emphasis on curriculum objectives (Katz 1973), that reflect current hiring criteria (Simmons 1975)

5. Unique occupational training programs that public colleges are seldom willing or able to offer.

Decision-making Process and Governance

Owners or corporate-level management generally make the critical decisions in proprietary schools. In community colleges, the decision-making authority is more broadly distributed among boards of trustees, administrators, and faculty organizations.

The two sectors also differ in motivations behind the decision-making process. The critical success factor of profitability is a primary consideration that strongly influences private school owners and managers. Decisions regarding equipment and facilities, program offerings, and faculty salaries are made with profitability as a crucial criterion.

While fiscal matters are of a high priority in public junior/community colleges, they are influenced by different circumstances. Lay boards, academic departments, and tenured faculty are all stakeholders in the decision-making structure. Their views must be considered. With the exception of large corporate chain schools, the private, for-profit schools benefit from a more streamlined decision-making process.

Instructor Qualifications and Compensation. The proprietary schools that offer direct training for jobs tend to employ faculty based primarily upon experiences related to the jobs for which the students are to be prepared (Gilli 1976). These instructors establish themselves as trainer models rather than as traditional teachers. In these institutions, educational background is not of primary relevance, and many instructors are hired from industry. In fact, many are also found to be concurrently employed in a field related to the one in which they are teaching (Wolman et al. 1972). The proprietary institutions offering degrees are notable exceptions. In the case of degree-granting institutions, the faculty education

requirements are comparable to those in public colleges.

Regional accreditation is a requirement for public colleges, and these institutions are bound by the standards of the various regional accrediting bodies. As a result of these educational standards, community college faculty are more likely to hold degrees.

It is difficult to draw comparisons regarding compensation for the instructors employed by the two types of institutions. Salaries of proprietary school faculty might not represent their total earnings, and they are more likely to work a standard year instead of a nine-month academic year. However, proprietary school teachers tend to be less well paid, in general, than community college instructors (Belitsky 1969).

Community college faculty are more likely to have salaries set through the collective bargaining process. They also enjoy more job security or contract assurances, such as tenure.

Important Events Altering the Distinguishing Characteristics

The Servicemen's Readjustment Act, commonly known as the GI Bill, was early legislation that affected the role of the community college and the autonomy of the proprietary school (Conrad and Cosand 1976). The GI Bill provided financial support for returning World War II veterans who wished to pursue postsecondary education, and, in all, 7.8 million veterans benefited from this program at a total cost of $14.5 billion (Tiedt 1966). At the end of the Korean War, an additional 2.25 million veterans received financial assistance through the GI Bill (Tiedt 1966).

The GI Bill encouraged the development of the career education function of the community colleges. As the veterans returned from war, they created a greater demand for noncollegiate vocational courses than for traditional transfer courses. The community colleges moved to fill the need for this vocational/technical type of curriculum. The GI Bill set the precedent for future, broad-based federal assistance for postsecondary education institutions, including proprietary schools.

For proprietary schools, eligibility to participate in the veterans program required federal and appropriate state agency approval. The immediate impact of the approval process was minimal because the criteria varied from state to state. The importance of this precedent is that, although eligibility was allowed, it was contingent on the implementation of an approval process.

Legislation at the state level also significantly affected the growth of the vocational function of the community college. As early as the late 1940s, Texas lawmakers enacted legislation requiring that community colleges offer a minimum of 40 percent of their courses in the so-called "terminal" (occupational) fields to qualify for state aid (Bogue 1950). The Vocational Education Act of 1963 and subsequent amendments in 1968 and 1972 greatly increased the federal funds available for career education, thereby encouraging the community colleges to alter their mission to include a greater emphasis on vocational training (Cohen and Brawer 1984).

Further encouragement for vocational education came from state and local governments, which matched these federal funds on a multiple basis. An example is the Illinois system which gave $6 from state and local governments for every federally appropriated dollar to community college districts after 1974, provided that 50 percent of the programs offered were in vocational education (Davenport et al. 1975). As a result, 1,871 of the statewide curricula were vocational in nature (Illinois Community College Board 1976).

The 1972 Higher Education Act Amendments

Amendments to the Higher Education Act in 1972 established the Basic Educational Opportunity Grant (BEOG, later renamed "Pell Grants" for Senator Claiborne Pell) and the Student Loan Marketing Association (Sallie Mae). The amendments were designed to increase middle-income and economically disadvantaged students' accessibility to higher education.

The 1972 amendments included proprietary schools in the definition of "eligible insti-

tutions," making them full partners with traditional higher education in respect to receipt of student aid (Lee and Merisotis 1990). Now proprietary and public postsecondary students are considered equally for federal financial aid based on financial need.

In an effort to ensure delivery of quality education, Congress made access to federal financial aid contingent upon certain fundamental requirements, including (1) state authorization or licensure for the institution, (2) accreditation by an Education Department-recognized entity, and (3) adherence to U.S. Department of Education regulations. These requirements had little impact upon community colleges because they were already subject to mandatory quality assurance scrutiny due to the public financial support (local taxes, state and federal funding) they received.

Though full partnership with traditional higher education in student financial aid matters enabled proprietary school students access to funding, it also brought additional state and federal regulation for proprietary institutions. Increased oversight and regulations have reduced their capacity for flexibility and market responsiveness. As a result, proprietary schools have developed some of the characteristics of public community colleges.

Because proprietary schools are market driven, they have implemented successful recruiting strategies, and their student population is generally considered to be "high risk" (poor, female, and minority) students (Lee and Merisotis 1990). Thus, they receive a disproportionate share of the funding made available by the amendments to the 1972 Higher Education Reauthorization Act. For the same reasons, proprietary school students have a disproportionate share of the guaranteed student loan defaults. Proprietary schools, whether they deserve it or not, have become the lightning rod in the guaranteed student loan default debate. The issue of guaranteed student loan default is too complex to address here, but it should be noted that recently passed legislation (ability-to-benefit and student right-to-know), as well as currently pending legislation designed to reduce loan default, has affected community college programs.

Changes in Role, Mission, and Autonomy

As the "baby boom" generation ages, a dwindling work force, underprepared to function productively in a technology-oriented, fiercely competitive global marketplace, follows. While vocational and technical training have always been a component of the community college mission, this role has taken on greater significance as the colleges respond to a changing economic climate.

As a result, community colleges are becoming more responsive to industry training needs by providing more focused job-specific training. Offering this "training" rather than traditional "education" allows community colleges to be more competitive with proprietary schools. This new focus streamlines the decision-making process and reduces the response time because, in most cases, training courses do not require board of trustees or state higher education board approval.

Since general education is not normally required in training-oriented courses, the length of the course or program can be reduced. Also, the instructor qualifications are less stringent. This enables community colleges to employ part-time instructors who are concurrently employed in the private sector. The advantage of this is that these instructors are familiar with state-of-the-art equipment and techniques used in industry.

Flexibility, job-specific training conducted by instructors from the field, and market responsiveness now being demonstrated by community colleges to support the economic development mission have long been considered proprietary school strengths.

Proprietary school leaders recognize the current work-force dilemma confronting business and industry and most are well positioned to respond. However, eligibility for and utilization of federal financial aid programs have changed their operations.

Proprietary schools have traditionally depended upon student-paid tuition and fees for revenue. While this is still true, proprietary school *students* have become increasingly dependent upon Title IV aid since the passage of the 1972 Higher Education Reauthorization Act. This federal aid, available in grants and loans, finances the eligible student's education. According to a recent study, 78 percent of proprietary school students receive federal assistance of some kind (Merisotis 1991). A U.S. Department of Education study (1989) revealed that proprietary school students accounted for 36.7 percent of all those who borrowed and 36.4 percent of the total dollars borrowed in the guaranteed student loan program during FY '89. As proprietary school students receive greater portions of the federal assistance money, less is available for community college students. The increasing use of federal financial assistance by proprietary school students has resulted in a concomitant escalation in institutional regulation and oversight by governmental agencies. Proprietary schools are more closely scrutinized and must provide greater documentation of accountability than ever before. Now the proprietary sector's traditional competitive advantage is diminished because flexibility and response time to customers is impaired by required compliance with regulations and reporting procedures.

Conclusions

Current trends suggest that proprietary schools can be expected to seek degree-granting authority in increasing numbers (Lee and Merisotis 1990). More schools will pursue and obtain regional accreditation and strive to develop transfer agreements with high schools (two-plus-two programs) and traditional higher education institutions.

The need for a highly trained and productive work force is acute (National Center on Education and the Economy 1990). It is unlikely that this competitive environment will negatively affect the viability of vigorous and healthy community college programs. But as legislators, state agencies, and college administrators respond to demands for accountability for the expenditure of tax dollars, programs with low competition and placement rates will be scrutinized, and some will face closure.

The continued effectiveness of existing community college programs might be enhanced by collaborating with proprietary schools to meet regional educational and training needs. The inherent expense and duplication of service caused by competition can be mitigated through cooperation. Models of cooperation exist in which proprietary schools provide skills training and community colleges provide the general and theoretical education in applied associate degree programs. This strategy is particularly sensible for community colleges when specialized and expensive equipment is required to complete the student's training. State agencies of higher education can encourage and coordinate these collaborative efforts. In an environment where (1) training and retraining of the work force is becoming a critical need, (2) the cost of education is rising, (3) state and federal financial support for education is dwindling, (4) proprietary schools are adopting a more traditional educational model, and (5) community colleges are becoming more entrepreneurial, cooperation seems a prudent alternative to unbridled competition.

References

Belitsky, A. H. 1969. *Private vocational schools and their students: Limited objectives, unlimited opportunities.* Cambridge, Mass.: Schenkman Publishing.

Bogue, J. P. 1950. *The community college.* New York: McGraw-Hill.

Carr, D. 1980. *The impact of accreditation and degree status on proprietary business, trade, and technical schools in New York State.* Ann Arbor, Mich.: University Microfilms.

Clark, H. F., and H. S. Sloan. 1966. *Classrooms on main street.* New York: Teachers College Press.

Cohen, A. M., and F. B. Brawer. 1984. *The American community college.* San Francisco: Jossey-Bass.

Conrad, C., and J. Cosand. 1976. *The implications of federal education policy.* Washington, D.C.: American Association for Higher Education.

Davenport, L. F., et al. 1976. Vocational education in the 1980s. Paper presented at annual meeting of the American Association of Community and Junior Colleges. Washington, D.C. ERIC Document no. ED 124 249.

Eells, W. C. 1931. *The junior college.* Boston: Houghton Mifflin.

Erickson, E. W., et al. 1972. *Proprietary business schools and community colleges: Resource allocation, student needs, and federal policies.* ERIC Document no. ED 134 790.

Erwin, J. M. 1975. *The proprietary school: Assessing its impact on the collegiate sector.* ERIC Document no. ED 145 791.

Fulton, R. A. 1969. Proprietary schools. *Encyclopedia of education research,* 4th ed., ed. R. Ebel. Toronto: Macmillan.

Gilli, A. C. 1976. *Modern organizations of vocational education.* University Park: Pennsylvania State University Press.

Illinois Community College Board. 1976. *Curriculum enrollment summary in the public community colleges of Illinois: 1975–76.* Springfield, Ill.: Illinois Community College Board.

Katz, H. H. 1973. *A state of the art study of the independent private school industry in the state of Illinois.* Springfield: Illinois Advisory Council on Vocational Education.

Kincaid, H. V., and E. A. Podesta. 1966. *An exploratory survey of proprietary vocational schools.* Palo Alto Calif.: Stanford Research Institute.

Lee, J. B., and J. Merisotis. 1990. *Proprietary schools: Programs, policies, and prospects.* ASHE-ERIC Higher Education Report no. 5. Washington, D.C.: George Washington University, School of Education and Human Development.

Merisotis, J. P., ed. 1991. *The changing dimensions of student aid.* New Directions for Higher Education, no. 74. San Francisco: Jossey-Bass.

National Center on Education and the Economy. 1990. *America's choice: High skills or low wages.* Rochester, N.Y.

Shoemaker, E. A. 1973. Community colleges: the challenge of proprietary schools. *Change* 5(6):71–72.

Simmons, H. C. 1975. A descriptive of degree granting proprietary schools and their relationships to the development of community colleges in Pennsylvania. Ph.D. diss., Florida State University.

Tiedt, S. 1966. *The role of the federal government in education.* New York: Oxford University Press.

Tonne, H. A. 1954. *Principles of business education.* 2d ed. New York: McGraw-Hill.

U.S. Department of Education. 1989. *FY 1989 guaranteed student loan programs databook.* Washington, D.C.

Wilms, W. 1973. A new look at proprietary schools. *Change* 5(6):6–7, 80.

_____. 1975. *Public and proprietary vocational training: A study of effectiveness.* London: D. C. Heath and Company.

Wolman, J., V. M. Campbell, S. M. Jung, and J. M. Richards. 1972. *A comparative study of proprietary and non-proprietary vocational training programs.* 2 vols. Palo Alto, Calif.: American Institutes for Research.

University of Phoenix: Beat 'em or Join 'em

Mark Fischetti, John Anderson, Malena Watrous, Jason Tanz, and Peter Gwynne

It's tempting to dismiss the University of Phoenix as McEducation: a chain of quick-serve classrooms shoveling empty calories to a clientele of little interest. So what if the for-profit juggernaut and its surrogate programs already have 98 campuses in 31 states and an enrollment of more than 55,000, making Phoenix the largest private university in the nation? So what if it has aggressively applied savvy business strategies such as convenience, customer service, mass production, and corporate partnerships on its march across the country? These tactics have no place at your institution, do they? Phoenix poses no threat to the purveyors of *serious* education, right? Perhaps. Or perhaps it's time to wake up and sniff the competition. CONSIDER THE FOLLOWING:

A majority of the nation's colleges have adult- or continuing-education programs, now nearly a $100-billion annual market that's expected to grow as the economy generates more demand for knowledge workers and adults quicken their pace of changing jobs. In 2002, 6.4 million adult students (aged 25 and up) will enroll in higher education. Schools of all kinds are becoming more and more dependent on the relatively easy income these courses generate.

Most institutions' continuing-ed programs may be used to competing with those from similar, neighboring schools. But the field will change drastically as Phoenix, with its Wall Street war chest, pursues its plan to push into every state in the union. And though Phoenix has so far stressed job training and a business orientation, there's now talk of the school expanding into adult remedial education and other courses of study.

Phoenix has won the endorsement of some serious people, not the kind who'd be interested in simple McEducation. One of the most impressive is J. Jorge Klor de Alva, a distinguished anthropologist and Guggenheim Fellow who took a leave from his endowed chair at the University of California at Berkeley to head Phoenix's academic cabinet and become a corporate officer. Klor de Alva says he believes that traditional education's mission of generating knowledge and its devotion to intellectual pursuits are still critical. But he is simply more excited by Phoenix's mission. "I have always been interested in producing effects in the empirical world, not just the world of ideas," he says. "We're erasing the moment in life when you either make it as a student or you don't," he told *The New York Times*. "This is a second-chance outfit geared to an expanding world economy."

Phoenix has attracted weighty corporate customers, including Kodak, IBM, and General Electric. "Our relationship has been super," says an official at AT&T, who clearly appreciates the university's business slant, including a special tuition scheme and flexible schedules for the 800 AT&T employees now taking individual courses or pursuing bachelor's degrees and MBAs at various Phoenix campuses. "Basically, we're trading 'Ivy' for practicality."

Join them, beat them, learn from them? Whatever you do, it would be risky to ignore the Phoenix phenomenon. We offer the following tactical information to help formulate counterstrategies.

"University of Phoenix: Beat 'em or Join 'em," by Mark Fischetti, John Anderson, Malena Watrous, Jason Tanz, and Peter Gwynne, reprinted from *University Business*, March/April 1998.

The Man

John Sperling, whom some would call the evil genius behind the University of Phoenix, is a 77-year-old egotist who loves controversy. "You gotta know where I come from," he says. "Out of poverty. Out of the American heartland. I wasn't ever some spoiled son-of-a-bitch who thought I was entitled—*entitled*—to an education at Harvard or Yale or Princeton."

Sperling, the son of Missouri sharecroppers, claims to have been virtually illiterate when he joined the merchant marine in his teens. Despite those humble beginnings, he has spent a lot of time in traditional academe: he learned to read and appreciate books from his fellow sailors, went to San Francisco Junior College, studied liberal arts at Reed College on the GI bill (he was an Air Force pilot during World War II), got a master's degree in history at the University of California at Berkeley, and earned a Ph.D. in economic history at no less than Cambridge University. Sperling was a tenured professor at San Jose State University in the 1960s and early 1970s. There he had an experience that triggered the inspiration for Phoenix.

An activist in those days, Sperling was working in the community with delinquent teenagers, local police officers, and schoolteachers. To his surprise, the police officers and teachers had a keen interest in getting more education. He became convinced that many working adults wanted to earn degrees but couldn't find convenient class times. San Jose State let Sperling set up an evening adult curriculum, but he couldn't get the faculty to deliver the practical programs he felt the students wanted. "My colleagues couldn't stand the heat," says Sperling with disdain. "Those cops were very, very assertive. They'd say, "Show me how what you're teaching applies to my everyday life."

Sperling quit San Jose, set up the Institute for Professional Development, and contracted with the University of San Francisco, the University of Redlands, and St. Mary's College to create classes for firefighters, policemen, and teachers. Students liked his down-to-earth, working-world emphasis. Enrollment in his classes reached 2,500. But some administrators and regular faculty at the three institutions attacked Sperling, calling his institute a diploma mill. The Western Association of Schools threatened to revoke the colleges' accreditations if they didn't drop Sperling's program. In 1974, having tried and failed to work within the existing system, he decided to invent his own. He moved to Phoenix—with a booming economy, and in the jurisdiction of a different accrediting body—and founded the University of Phoenix. He also enlisted the help of consultant Robert Tucker, a psychologist who runs InterEd, an assessment service for higher education. Tucker created an extensive series of assessment tests that in 1976 helped the new university win accreditation from the North Central Association of Colleges and Schools. With that approval Sperling began to expand the University of Phoenix into a national presence.

The recent financial success of the university has made Sperling a wealthy, and therefore powerful, man. It is also strong reinforcement for his central conviction that the practical side of education—training for a promotion or a better job—is what's important to adult students. "Any damned fool can see that an education is a prerequisite to advancement in life," says the self-made academic and millionaire founder of Apollo Group, Inc. "It got me out of the trenches, didn't it?"

The Company

University of Phoenix is the primary subsidiary of Apollo Group, Inc., a for-profit holding company based in Phoenix. Eighty percent of Apollo's revenue comes from the university's 59 campuses; most of the rest is generated by the Institute for Professional Development, which has set up 39 adult education programs at 18 independent colleges that are located for the most part in states where Phoenix has failed to win licenses. In September Apollo bought the College for Financial Planning, a Denver-based school that grants certificates and degrees through self-study correspondence programs; it also picked up the nonprofit institution's 22,000 students. In 1995 it acquired the Western International University, a nonprofit operation in Phoenix and London, most of whose 1,300 adult students are employees of overseas companies.

When Apollo first went public, in December 1994, shares sold for a mere $2.50 each. Today, after splitting four times in less than three years, the price per share has soared beyond $40, giving the company a market capitalization of more than $2 billion. "Wall Street," Sperling quips, "is our endowment."

Sperling (Apollo's president and chairman) and his son Peter (vice president of administration, secretary, and treasurer) each own 10 million shares of the corporation, a combined 42 percent that is valued at nearly $1 billion. They also own 87 percent of the separate voting stock, giving them complete control of Apollo.

Beyond the Sperlings and other officers of the corporation, Boston-based Putnam, a large institutional investor, owns 8.5 percent of the company's shares. The list of other major investors is a veritable who's who of blue-chip mutual funds and financial services firms. And here's a shocker: college administrators and professors also have invested heavily in Phoenix's educational style. TIAA-CREF, the New York State Teachers, and the California Teacher Retirement System are on the list of Phoenix's top 25 institutional investors.

By applying a classic production model to education, Apollo has enjoyed staggering growth. Its revenues have jumped an average of 30 percent every year since 1994; during the last fiscal year the company took in $283 million, added 17 new locations, and increased enrollment at all its schools by 22 percent—to 57,000. The University of Phoenix's newest additions include campuses in Tampa, Seattle, and Portland, Oregon.

"Apollo has shown it can produce predictable cash flow and high returns," says Gerald Odening, an analyst at Salomon Smith Barney who tracks the market in for-profit education. "There's a high barrier to entry for any newcomer—years of designing curriculum and satisfying accreditors. Apollo has a huge lead."

Tactics

Convenience: Stripped-down curricula and flexible schedules allow most students to earn a Phoenix degree in far less time than the national average. Class cycles begin monthly, year round. Classes for a typical three-credit course are held one night a week for four hours; for another four hours per week students are required to work together and share their professional experience in an outside study session. The entire course lasts only six weeks, versus ten to 12 weeks at conventional institutions. The average class has 14 students. Phoenix has no requirement for prerequisites that "don't enhance the careers of working adults," as Sperling puts it.

Phoenix claims to situate its "campuses"—sometimes little more than a few rented floors in a downtown office building—so that students won't have to drive more than 20 minutes from their workplaces.

Phoenix also offers distance education in a variety of styles: 4,700 students all over the world are taking classes and working toward Phoenix degrees while never leaving the comfort of their home computers, fax machines, and telephones.

Real-World Emphasis: Following the model he set up for his fledgling Institute for Professional Development in the early 1970s, Sperling designed a practical approach for the University of Phoenix. For the most part, its undergraduate degrees cover business administration and nursing; master's degrees are given in these subjects as well as education, counseling, and information systems. Typical courses include "Business Geography" and "Critical Thinking and Decision-Making." Phoenix's part-time professors are not academics but professionals with master's degrees or higher and an average of 16 years' work in the fields they teach. So students learn accounting, for example, from a working accountant after business hours. All Phoenix classes encourage students to work in small groups, mimicking the team approach now in vogue in business.

Phoenix's emphasis on the needs of working people means employers often share tuition costs. (At $6,300 to $8,000 for an academic year, it's not cheap, but well below the national average for private schools.) Half the students are reimbursed by their companies for at least half the cost. AT&T covers the entire tuition for its employees.

Low Overhead: Phoenix owns little in the way of land or buildings; most of its classrooms are rented office space. By hiring moonlighters, the university sidesteps high salaries, tenure, and other thorny issues usually connected to faculty. (Professors are paid $1,000 per course.) The study sessions that are required for every course are unsupervised and off campus, thereby costing the university nothing. And the no-frills atmosphere enables Phoenix to forego physical libraries (an electronic one serves all campuses), student unions, and other ivy-covered niceties associated with what Sperling calls youth-centered education.

Mass Production: Replication is the key to the university's exponentially increasing profits. In Phoenix a central body of 26 course designers develops the curriculum for every course. Standardized teaching methods, handouts, texts, and tests are then farmed out to the 4,100 faculty nationwide. It's a simple and relatively inexpensive matter to duplicate the programs as the university expands. "Setting up each new campus is like setting up a franchise," says one Phoenix vice president. "We hire a local manager to run the campus, or move a manager from an established site."

The strategy gives Phoenix a competitive edge in any new market it may care to enter. Likely new academic territories include even K-12 education. As for geographical frontiers, Sperling and Klor de Alva have been scouting the possibilities in Malaysia, Singapore, Taiwan, and Hong Kong.

Customer Service and Quality Control: The University of Phoenix tests students' knowledge and skills before and after courses; it surveys students' satisfaction with teachers and class materials; and it asks teachers to assess students' preparedness and performance. Phoenix asks its alumni whether the program has helped their job progress, and it asks their alumni's employers to rate Phoenix graduates against other employees.

The architect of this fanatical quality-control program is Robert Tucker, the consultant and testing guru who helped Phoenix win its original accreditation. According to Sperling, it is Tucker's battery of tests that continues to convince the North Central Association that the University of Phoenix is actually making students smarter. The same test results give Phoenix a persuasive marketing pitch to corporate clients; how many other universities can show before-and-after assessments of their students' knowledge? Tucker's efforts, coupled with Phoenix's standardized, centralized structure, also enable it to hold faculty accountable and to continually improve its "products." "The big achievement is not designing the surveys," Tucker says, "but institutionalizing the feedback on a university scale."

Lobbying: Apollo campaigns for its vision of a national for-profit university just as any large corporation pushes for what it wants. "We have 24 state lobbyists under contract, plus three national staffers, including one in D.C., and a national lobbyist to head up the effort," explains Sperling. "You put the pressure on the governor, and he puts the pressure on the state ed department, and you'd be surprised how quickly you can get your license." Last summer Apollo's lobbyists convinced Pennsylvania legislators to revoke a ban on for-profit universities; the University of Phoenix is now applying for a license there. Sperling's current targets: Texas, New York, New Jersey, Ontario, and British Columbia. "We have a local lobbyist in every one," he says.

Counterstrategies

"This is not a freak event," says Arthur Levine, president of Teachers College, Columbia University. "Phoenix heralds a potential revolution in higher education." Levine points out that only one in six college students now fits the old stereotype: aged 18 to 22, full-time, and living on campus. The new student he describes chooses a school as a consumer buys a car: for convenience, service, quality, and low cost. No wonder for-profit businesses such as Phoenix are moving in.

If higher education fails to react, Levine believes it could make itself irrelevant. He suggests that traditional schools form partnerships with the for-profits. Indeed this is a path already chosen by the 18 colleges—mostly small religious schools—that have hired the University of Phoenix to set up continuing-education programs on their campuses, sharing revenues with its Institute for Professional Development. Bigger names have entered into partnerships, too: Johns Hopkins University, for example, has teamed with the Caliber Learning Network—a joint venture of MCI Communications and Sylvan Learning

Systems—to offer degrees in the business of medicine.

Yet for most institutions—who are neither ready to marry for-profit giants nor willing (or able) to compete head to head—there is an alternative. The burgeoning field of adult education holds plenty of potential niches, academic officials argue, and is large enough for schools of many different styles.

Arizona State University, with campuses in the University of Phoenix's primary backyard, is a case in point. "I think we compete at the margin, but not at the core," says Provost Milton Glick. Fourteen years ago the university opened ASU West, a commuter campus located in Phoenix and designed to serve largely adult students and transfers from community colleges. Many classes are taught between 6 and 10 p.m. and, at least in its College of Business, professors are also practitioners—clear parallels to the University of Phoenix approach. But ASU West provost Elaine Maimon sees her campus' connection to the larger ASU system as an important distinction for students seeking what one colleague in the business college calls a "nationally ranked product." "We are a 'Research I' environment because we are still part of ASU," says Maimon. "Faculty are still involved with cutting edge discovery."

Glick agrees. He believes the university's primary mission should remain a traditional one, doing research, providing a liberal education, and developing the whole student as a good citizen, in the Jeffersonian model. "Where the University of Phoenix does things well, we can learn from them," says Glick. "We have to test whether the kind of course we teach can be done in that condensed format, the four-week or six-week course. But we don't want to become them."

Another campus in Phoenix that caters to a different slice of the market in adult working students is run by Ottawa University, a school with headquarters in Kansas. Although it is a nonprofit, Baptist-affiliated institution, Ottawa has been following a variation on the Phoenix model since before there was a University of Phoenix. Its programs—in Tempe, Scottsdale, Phoenix, Milwaukee, Ottawa, and Kansas City—concentrate on practical degrees in high demand: education, counseling, business, and management. Like Phoenix, Ottawa schedules classes at night and on weekends, and cre-atively translates students' previous nonstandard education into academic credit.

But Ottawa officials say there is an important difference. "We attract students who are much less certain about what the eventual outcome of their adult education will be," explains John Neal, an Ottawa vice president. Ottawa's students, who tend to be younger—and not as successful professionally as they'd like to be—receive a good deal of personal attention from faculty, even one-on-one counseling. The school is so sure of its niche that, according to Neal, it even refers certain applicants to the University of Phoenix: "especially older students, from their upper 30s on, who want a very streamlined, utilitarian, and narrow education, students who know exactly what they need in terms of business goals."

A more specialized twist on the Phoenix model will be unveiled next year in Claremont, California: the Keck Graduate Institute for Applied Life Sciences, which will become the seventh member of the Claremont Consortium of Colleges, will tailor its offerings to students seeking industrial careers in such areas as biotechnology, pharmaceuticals, and medical devices. At present, explains President Henry Riggs, these students have few opportunities for graduate training because U.S. universities concentrate on producing medical doctors and Ph.D.'s trained for academic research.

Keck is hardly vulnerable to competition from the University of Phoenix, because its specialized focus doesn't fit the company's mass-production model. And though Keck plans to have close links to industry and its courses will likely follow an unconventional calendar, Riggs says Phoenix serves not so much as an example of how to do things but as an example of what can be done: "It points out that there's a huge market in nontraditional students."

Back in Arizona, Linda Thor, president of Rio Salado Community College, says unequivocally that Phoenix is competition. "Like them, we're focused on workplace relevance, convenience, and access," says Thor, "but we have an edge in our dedication to making higher education affordable, and in our commitment to working mothers and fathers." In some areas Thor appears intent on "out-Phoenixing" Phoenix. Rio Salado's distance-learning program now serves 12,000 students, primarily adults. Whereas Phoenix gives its students the flexibility of starting campus-based classes every four weeks, Rio Salado's on-line classes start every two weeks. (Thor sounds serious when she says she'd like eventually to give students the choice of starting a class on any day of the week.) Her college even has its own variation on Phoenix's Institute for Professional Development, though not in the adult market: it runs programs in 20 high schools for ambitious students who would like to earn Rio Salado college credits early.

Rio Salado's total head count is now 24,717, a 17.5-percent increase over last year. That doesn't quite rival Phoenix's numbers, but for the moment at least, business is booming. This suggests that there is more than one way to market adult education successfully—and that, as Thor asserts, the University of Phoenix may be a useful source of inspiration.

"From my office window, I see first the Rio Salado chancellor's home, and then, farther down the road, the University of Phoenix headquarters," says Thor. "My boss and the competition—right in plain sight. I like to call this my wake-up call."

This article was reported and written by **mark fischetti, john anderson, malena watrous, jason tanz,** *and* **peter gwynne.**

Who Are the Students at Community Colleges and Proprietary Schools?

XING DAVID CHENG AND BERNARD H. LEVIN

Researchers remain divided regarding the basic demographic characteristics—gender, race, and socioeconomic status (SES)—of the proprietary school student. While a significant volume of research on proprietary students has been published during the past quarter century, we detect no movement toward consensus. Several factors may be operating, including differences in vintage; accidental and institution-based subject samples (for example, Wilms, 1974, 1980) versus national and stratified random samples (for example, Levin and Clowes, 1987); extreme variations in statistical treatment; and the issues concerning the definition of terms that are referred to above and in the text that follows. The result is a confusing, not very pretty picture.

In some literature, proprietary students are reported as disproportionally female (Levin and Clowes, 1987; Friedlander, 1980; Kincaid and Podesta, 1967). Other literature shows them to be male (Belitsky, 1969; Braden and Paul, 1971). In general, those researchers who agglomerate institution types or who focus on programs such as hair styling, health professions, data processing, and business report a predominantly female student population. Those researchers who focus on barbering, mechanical trades, truck driving, and (occasionally) business schools (for example, Hoyt, 1966–67) report predominantly male populations. The interaction of gender with curriculum is typical (Apling, 1993). Lee and Merisotis (1990) were correct when they claimed, "The tremendous variation in the types of programs

offered at proprietary schools makes generalizations tenuous at best" (p. 19).

Race may also interact with program type (Wolman, Campbell, Jung, and Richards, 1972). Three studies report that approximately 25 percent of their student population was black (Friedlander, 1980; Proprietary Education in Georgia, 1975; Doherty, 1973). The National Postsecondary Student Aid Study (1987) reports that 21 percent of proprietary students are African American, while 14 percent are Hispanic. Wolman, Campbell, Jung, and Richards (1972) claim that minorities would avoid proprietaries on cost grounds, while Wilms (1980) appears to claim that Hispanic and Asian minorities are disproportionally represented in proprietary institutions. While Levin and Clowes (1987) found that proprietary students are disproportionally likely to be white, and Apling (1993) found that proprietary students are disproportionally likely to be minorities, Wagner (1982) found that proprietary students and community college-technical institute students do not differ in race. Morris (1993) found that most of the subjects in his proprietary sample were black or Hispanic. Some care is urged in interpreting these differences. For example, Wilms used only four sites, two of which were in communities with a large Hispanic population. Further, Morris used only three sites; all were located in Hispanic areas.

The literature on the SES of proprietary students is also contradictory. The typical proprietary student has been reported to be from a middle-class family (Levin and Clowes, 1987), or from a blue-collar family (Juhlin, 1976; Morris, 1993), or from a family with below-average income (Apling, 1993; Morris, 1993), or from a lower-income family than the typical community college student (Apling, 1993; Friedlander, 1980; Christian, 1975; Wagner, 1982). The National Postsecondary Student Aid Study (1987) reports an average annual income below $11,000 but throws a new wrinkle into the data—this figure includes both dependent and independent students. Juhlin (1976) does report an anomaly—white proprietary students are disproportionally from high-income families. Finally, in three articles over three years, Wilms himself found conflicting results (1973, 1974, 1975).

Researchers tend to agree that most proprietary students are from less-educated families, at least less educated than those attending community colleges and four-year institutions. Morris (1993) maintains that the parental background of proprietary students is "predominantly uneducated" (p. 25). For 20 percent of proprietary students, neither parent had graduated high school (Apling, 1993). Proprietary students also may be less independent. Korb (1988) reports that about half of proprietary students (and college students) live with their parents. Morris (1993) reports that "Despite a mean age of more than 26, 4 out of 5 subjects were . . . still living with their parents" (p. 25).

It is also commonly believed that proprietary students' academic background is weaker than those attending community colleges and four-year institutions. The National Postsecondary Student Aid Study (1987) reports that the academic ability of proprietary students is lower than that of college students. Nonetheless, Levin and Clowes (1987) found a composite aptitude score to be unrelated to selection of a proprietary or not-for-profit institution as opposed to a two-year institution. Using a self-report measure, Morris's (1993) proprietary students had a high school mean grade point average of slightly less than 3.0. Friedlander's (1980) conclusion is nearly identical.

There are some gray areas in the literature concerning proprietary students' academic credentials. One report, "Proprietary Education in Georgia" (1975), indicates up to 10 percent of proprietary students already have at least a two-year degree. Hanson and Parker (1977) emphasize that most proprietary school students are high school dropouts, and some reports state that most proprietary school students have a high school diploma (Friedlander, 1980; Juhlin, 1976; Morris, 1993). Levin and Clowes (1987) and the National Postsecondary Student Aid Study (1987) found that proprietary students are likely to have been in a vocational-technical program in high school. In addition, students' transfer activities to and from proprietaries certainly add to the complexity of this issue of credentials.

Moore and Kuchinke's (1991) study on private career schools shows that, in Minnesota, fully one third of the proprietary students had tried a community college before attending a proprietary school. In a statewide survey of Virginia private career schools, Moore and Smith (1991) found that nearly half of all proprietary students had attended another institution. Among those who had attended another institution, about half had attended a community college and over one third had attended a four-year institution.

Finally, numerous studies have assessed the educational attainment of students at two- and four-year colleges and universities. However, very little has been done to measure proprietary student educational attainment, nor has much been said about proprietary students' aspirations and dreams for higher education. Morris (1993) says that "more than three fourths of the interview sample anticipated completing at least an associate's degree at some later time" (p. 26). But he also reinforces the suspicion of many researchers and counselors that educational aspirations may lack a reality check—26 percent of his proprietary sample anticipated earning a master's degree or doctorate. Cheng, Clowes, and Muffo (1992) found that the educational attainment of proprietary students was significantly lower than that of community college students, and community college students' attainment was lower than that of four-year students.

Method

Findings reported in this study are based on an extract file from High School and Beyond (HSB), a nationwide longitudinal study of high school students sponsored by the National

Center for Education Statistics (NCES) of the U.S. Department of Education. The data include the base-year survey, which was conducted in 1980, and three follow-up surveys through 1986. The senior cohort data were used in this study, and that sample includes a total of 11,995 students.

An NCES-generated program was used to identify respondents' patterns of attendance in different types of postsecondary institutions. For those who attended more than one school from 1980 to 1986, the first postsecondary institution was used to place the student into one of four types of institutional attendance for purposes of this study. These four types of postsecondary institutions are (1) proprietary schools (PROP); (2) private, not-for-profit schools (NFP), including both two-year and less-than-two-year institutions; (3) two-year public institutions (2YR), mostly community colleges, but also including some less-than-two-year schools; and (4) four-year institutions (4YR), including both public and private colleges and universities.

Since respondents' patterns of postsecondary enrollment are based on self-reported variables, we suspect that at least two factors might contribute to the relatively small sample size for PROPs and NFPs as compared to 2YR and 4YR samples. First, some PROP and NFP programs are so short that respondents did not even count them as part of their postsecondary experience. Second, PROP and NFP schools are not the first choices for most high school graduates, at least not for the first few years after high school graduation. While crossing the PROP and NFP samples with other variables, we suffered further loss of data due to missing cases in one or more variables. We chose not to make any estimation to make up these losses for fear of disturbing the result.

Another limitation of the HSB senior data is that those who dropped out of school prior to the twelfth grade are not included at all. We are not aware of any research on proprietary students that examines separately those who dropped out prior to twelfth grade. Thus, we have no basis for guessing whether our results and conclusions might have been different had the dropouts been included. The remainder of this text should be viewed with these limitations in mind.

Results

Both PROPs and NFPs are twice as likely to be female as male. In contrast, both 2YRs and 4YRs are only 54 percent female. Also, blacks are nearly three times as likely to attend PROPs as NFPs, but more than 57 percent of blacks in postsecondary institutions are in 4YRs. A similar pattern holds for whites in that whites are more than twice as likely to attend a PROP as an NFP, but 58 percent of whites in postsecondary institutions are in a 4YR institution. The pattern of Hispanic attendance is quite different. Hispanics are about fifty times as likely to attend a 2YR school and six times as likely to attend a PROP, compared to an NFP. More than half of Hispanics in postsecondary institutions are in 2YR institutions.

As one ascends SES, the likelihood of attending a 4YR increases and the likelihood of the other three alternatives decreases. Not surprisingly, family income shows a pattern similar to SES. The higher the income, the less likely is attendance at a PROP or NFP or 2YR. Parental education evinces the same sort of relationship as SES and family income. The higher the educational level of the parent, the less likely the student is to attend either a PROP or an NFP or a 2YR. For example, of students whose parents had earned no more than a high school diploma, 7.9 percent attended a PROP. In contrast, of students whose parents had earned at least a masters degree, only 1.9 percent attended a PROP.

Dependency or immaturity does not seem to characterize PROP and NFP students. Those who attended 4YR institutions are the least independent group, while NFP students turned out to be the most independent. In general, from one-half to two-thirds of postsecondary students either still lived with their parents or other guardians or did not have their own home, apartment, or other residence six years after their high school graduation.

A series of cognitive tests was administered to HSB participants in order to measure their verbal and quantitative abilities. The general belief was confirmed that the higher the test quartile, the less likely the student is to attend either a PROP or an NFP or a 2YR. The distribution pattern of the four quartile groups is very similar between NFPs and 2YRs. The striking contrast exists between PROPs and 4YRs: almost five times as many first-quartile students as fourth-quartile students attended PROPs, while more than three times as many fourth-quartile students as first-quartile students attended 4YR institutions.

Although some of the samples are small, it is clear that the pattern of high school grades for the noncollegiate institutions is much different from the four-year patterns. Among PROP, NFP, and 2YR students, the median grade in high school was B. In contrast, the median grade in high school for 4YR students was A.

PROP's appeal to students from different types of high schools is similar to that of 2YRs. On the other hand, 4YRs attracted disproportionally more private and Catholic high school graduates. Students from urban high schools are more likely than rural or suburban students to attend PROPs. Urban students are less likely to attend NFPs. Neither 2YR nor 4YR attendance seems much affected by locus of high school.

Two thirds of 4YR students had been in an academic program while in high school. In contrast, only 20 percent of PROP students, 31 percent of two-year students, and 41 percent of NFP students had been in an academic high school program. The present data show that almost all PROP students are high school graduates. The proportion of high school dropouts in PROPs and NFPs is only trivially different from that in 2YR and 4YR institutions.

Another way to look at PROP and NFP students' academic ability is to see if these students have any postsecondary experience before and after their study in a noncollegiate school. Our data show that about one-third of PROP and NFP students transferred to a 2YR or 4YR institution, and about one-third of 2YR students transferred to 4YR institutions. Reverse transfer is common. Between 5 and 6 percent of 2YR and 4YR students transferred to PROP and NFP schools. Over one-fifth of 4YR students transferred to 2YR institutions. Further, the number of students transferring from 2YR to 4YR is not much different from the number of students transferring from 4YR to 2YR.

A comparison between students' educational aspirations and their attainment reveals interesting results. A first glance at the data shows that PROP students are the ones with the lowest educational aspirations: 16 percent of them never had any postsecondary education aspirations or plans versus only 2 percent of 4YR students; the proportion of PROP students aspiring to a four-year degree is also significantly lower than that of other students. However, PROPs seem to be very effective in bringing vocational and technical education to those who aspired to something other than traditional baccalaureate degrees or higher. While 61 percent of PROP students aspired to (and over one-half of them received) a license, certificate, or two-year vocational degree, fewer than one-half of 2YR students had the same aspirations, and fewer than one-third of them actually reached their goals six years after high school graduation. Not surprisingly, while 23 percent of PROP students aspired to a four-year degree or higher, only 0.7 percent of them reached their goal. However, if we look at the overall educational attainment at different levels, it is clear that NFP students display a pattern very similar to their 2YR counterparts: while 38 percent of NFP students completed a vocational program or degree and 8.7 percent received a four-year degree, 32 percent and 7.8 percent respectively in 2YRs did so.

Discussion

Our results indicate that the often controversial depictions of student demographic characteristics at proprietary schools reflect to a certain extent the complex student body in these schools. However, while comparing the so-called proprietaries (including PROPs and NFPs) and community colleges, the trend of convergence is apparent. For instance, about 60 percent of students at both PROPs and 2YRs were minorities; also, the lower a student's SES, family income level, and parental education level, the more likely that student is to attend a PROP, an NFP, or a 2YR. With respect to academic background, 4YR students were clearly stronger than their counterparts in other types of schools. This relatively disadvantageous position for PROP, NFP, and 2YR students in academic background is further evident when the variables of high school type, high school program, and educational attainment come into play: the proportion of students from private high schools in four-year institutions is much higher than that in the other three types of postsecondary institutions; two-thirds of students in four-year institutions are from an academic high school program, while the other three types of institution have from one-fifth to two-fifths academic high school students; and finally, while nearly two-fifths of students attending four-year institutions received at least a bachelor's degree in a six-year period, less than one-tenth in each of the other three types achieved the same.

The HSB data allow us to look into the two major sectors within the proprietaries—private, for-profit, and private, not-for-profit—and reveal some previously unknown commonalities and differences between the schools generally called "proprietaries" and community colleges.

First, the ethnic composition of PROPs and NFPs for these two groups of schools differs to a certain extent. While approximately 60 percent of students in PROPs and 2YRs are minorities, a majority of students attending NFPs and 4YRs are white. Apparently, in terms of serving minority groups, NFP schools display a pattern similar to four-year institutions. This may be one of the reasons researchers differ in estimating ethnic composition in different types of institutions when PROPs and NFPs are combined. Otherwise, ethnic composition in different types of postsecondary institutions remains complicated. Blacks and whites are equally likely to attend 4YRs (56 and 58 percent, respectively), while considerably fewer (41 percent) Hispanics attend 4YRs. More than half of Hispanics choose 2YRs as their postsecondary option, in contrast with only one-third of blacks and whites. Neither PROPs nor NFPs account for as much as 8 percent of any racial or ethnic group. These attendance patterns require further study.

Second, NFP students' relatively high-SES family background seems to have brought a combined PROP and NFP group level closer to that for community colleges. For instance, NFPs served more high-SES students than PROPs (42 percent versus 31 percent). NFPs attracted more middle-class (with family income between $20,000 and $37,000) background students than PROPs and even slightly more than 2YRs. Also, 11 percent of NFP students' parents have a college degree or higher,

as compared to fewer than 7 percent for PROPs.

Third, NFP students' aptitude test scores are also higher than that of PROPs. NFPs display a pattern similar to 2YRs with respect to student's academic background. Compared to 2YRs, NFPs actually attracted slightly more students in the third test quartile and with mostly A grades in high school. What is even more surprising is that the likelihood of an NFP student coming from an academic high school program is two times higher than that of a PROP student and one quarter higher than a 2YR college student. As a result, the proportion of NFP students who eventually received a baccalaureate degree is also closer to or even slightly higher than that of 2YR students. These findings indicate that NFP students are less "disadvantaged" academically and that they have a higher potential for educational attainment, compared to other proprietary students.

Another difficult issue is how to compare the outcomes and effectiveness of proprietaries and community colleges. Each school is set up to implement its own mission. The common wisdom is that proprietaries were always leaning toward utilitarian purposes, while community colleges were more for general lower-division education. Our study of proprietary students' transfer behavior reveals the possibility that proprietary and especially NFP students in the long run may not be so desperate for "quick, specialized training to gain employment" (Morris, 1993) as they appear to be on matriculation. In fact, one-third of these students transferred to a 2YR or 4YR institution in a six-year period. This at least shows that they aspire to attain higher levels of postsecondary education. When we compare the educational attainment of PROP and NFP students with those in 2YRs, we find that 60 percent of 2YR students had not received anything more than a high school diploma six years after high school, but the comparable figure for PROP students is only 48 percent. Meanwhile, over one half of PROP students received a license, certificate, or associate degree in a six-year period, as compared to fewer than one third of 2YR students. Then why have so few PROP students moved further to successfully receive a baccalaureate degree compared to their NFP and 2YR counterparts? Our data support the assertion by Cheng, Clowes, and Muffo (1992) that the low aptitude and relatively poor academic background of these students hinder their achievement in higher education.

Since the major mission for most PROP and NFP schools is vocational education and job training, our data lead to the conclusion that these schools have done reasonably well in meeting the students' needs. The vocational orientation of PROP and NFP programs appeals to those who neither aspire to nor possess the skills sufficient to earn an academic degree, though the preceding is more true of PROP than of NFP. Proprietary schools have helped raise the educational levels of a great number of young adults to a considerable height, given the relatively low aptitude and low SES of their students. This is another area where proprietaries and community colleges come close to each other.

We conclude that proprietaries and community colleges have not been serving the same students in the past (Levin and Clowes, 1987) though the type of students each is serving has changed a bit. A factor that needs to be taken into account is the private not-for-profit sector. Their students certainly do not fit the overall picture of proprietary students. Whether the characteristics of proprietary students will eventually move closer to those of community college students is speculative. However, if community colleges begin to emphasize noncredit training as a major center for growth and profit (Levin and Perkins, in press), we expect that convergence in student bodies will follow this convergence in mission.

We consider the separate treatment of NFPs a very important factor in any future studies on proprietary schools. On a practical level, we recommend that market researchers carefully examine the strategies used by proprietaries and community colleges, including their effectiveness and efficiency as related to mission. Such examination not only would benefit the daily operations of both types of institutions but also would have the potential to improve their strategic planning and policymaking processes.

References

Apling, R. N. "Proprietary Schools and Their Students." *Journal of Higher Education*, 1993, *64* (4), 379–416.

Belitsky, A. H. *Private Vocational Schools and Their Students: Limited Objectives, Unlimited Opportunities.* Cambridge, Mass.: Schenkman 1969.

Braden, P. V., and Paul, K. K. "Vocational Education and Private Schools." In G. F. Law (ed.), *Contemporary Concepts in Vocational Education.* Washington D.C.: American Vocational Association, 1971, 200–204.

Cheng, X., Clowes, D. A., and Muffo, J. A. "Assessing the Educational Attainment of Proprietary Students from National Data." Unpublished report, 1992. (ED 342 458)

Cheng, X. D., and Levin, B. H. "Demographic Characteristics, Academic Background, and Educational Aspirations of Community College and Proprietary School Students." Unpublished report, 1995. (ERIC data base document; ED number not yet assigned.)

Christian, C. E. "Analysis of a Pilot Survey of Proprietary Schools." Los Angeles: Higher Education Research Institute, 1975.

Doherty, G. P. "Case Study: The Bell and Howell Schools." In D. W. Vermilye (ed.), *The Future in the Making*, San Francisco: Jossey-Bass, 1973.

Friedlander, M. C. *Characteristics of Students Attending Proprietary Schools and Factors Influencing Their Institutional Choice.* Cincinnati, Ohio: South-Western, 1980.

Hanson, G. A., and Parker, E. C. "The Vocational Education Industry." In W. G. Meyer (ed.), *Vocational Education and the Nation's Economy.* Washington, D.C.: American Vocational Association, 1977.

Hoyt, K. B. "The Vanishing American." *Delta Pi Epsilon Journal*, 1966–67, *9* (2), 1–8.

Juhlin, L. A. *Characteristics of Students Enrolled in Resident Proprietary Schools in Illinois.* Carbondale: Southern Illinois University, 1976.

Kincaid, H. V., and Podesta, E. A. "An Exploratory Socio-Economic Study of Private Vocational Schools," 1967.

Korb, R., Shantz, N., Stowe, P., and Zimbler, L. "Undergraduate Financing of Postsecondary Education: A Report of the 1987 National Postsecondary Aid Study." Washington, D.C.: U.S. Department of Education, Office of Educational Research and Improvement, National Center for Education Statistics, 1988.

Lee, J. B., and Merisotis. J. P. *Proprietary Schools: Programs, Policies, and Prospects.* ASHE-ERIC Higher Education Report No. 5. Washington, D.C.: School of Education and Human Development, George Washington University, 1990. (ED 331 337)

Levin, B. H., and Clowes, D. A. "Competition Between Community Colleges and Postsecondary Proprietary Schools: Reality or Myth?" *Journal of Studies in Technical Careers*, 1987, *9* (4), 317–323.

Levin, B. H., and Perkins, J. R. "The Future of Community College Continuing Education." *Catalyst*, in press.

Moore, R. W., and Kuchinke, K. P. "The Role and Quality of Proprietary Schools: Minnesota Students' Perspective." Paper presented at the annual convention of the American Educational Research Association, Chicago, 1991.

Moore, R. W., and Smith, E. J. "Student Perspective on Quality: A Quality Assessment of Virginia Private Career Schools." Research report sponsored by the Virginia Association of Private Career Schools, 1991.

Morris, W. V. "Avoiding Community Colleges: Students Who Attend Proprietary Vocational Schools." *Community College Journal of Research and Practice*, 1993, *17* (1), 21–28.

National Postsecondary Student Aid Study. Washington, D.C.: U.S. Department of Education, Office of Educational Research and Improvement, National Center for Education Statistics, 1987.

"Proprietary Education in Georgia." Atlanta: Georgia State Postsecondary Education Commission, 1975. (ED 138 746)

Wagner, A. P. "Postcompulsory Education and Training: An Inventory of Programs and Sources of Support." *Education and Urban Society*, 1982, *14*, 271–300.

Wilms, W. W. *Proprietary Versus Public Vocational Education*. Berkeley: Center for Research and Development in Higher Education, University of California, 1973.

Wilms, W. W. "Proprietary and Public Vocational Students." *Collegiate and University Bulletin*, 1974, *26* (7), 3–6.

Wilms, W. W. *Public and Proprietary Vocational Training: A Study of Effectiveness*. Lexington, Mass.: D.C. Heath, 1975.

Wilms, W. W. "Vocational Education and Social Mobility: A Study of Public and Proprietary School Dropouts and Graduates." Los Angeles: Graduate School of Education, University of California, Los Angeles, 1980. (ED 183 966)

Wolman, J., Campbell, V. M., Jung, S. M., and Richards, J. M. *A Comparative Study of Proprietary and Non-Proprietary Vocational Training Programs*. Palo Alto, Calif.: American Institutes for Research in the Behavioral Sciences, 1972. (ED 067 523)

Xing David Cheng is coordinator of institutional research at Colorado Community College in Denver.

Bernard H. Levin is professor of psychology at Blue Ridge Community College in Weyers Cave, Virginia.

Certificates on Center Stage: Occupational Education for a Working Economy

STELLA A. PEREZ AND CAROL C. COPENHAVER

Not so long ago, college graduates followed career paths leading from campuses to companies where they worked throughout their 30- to 40-year professional lives. Many of our parents and grandparents climbed a single corporate ladder through a series of promotions to the culmination of their careers and into retirement. During these times, college degrees ensured access and opportunity for professional lifestyles. Degrees also served symbolically and functionally to secure a position for graduates as contributing members of the American middle class.

Several changes in higher education and the work force in recent years have called into question the college degree as the certain ticket to career success. As a result, students are reconsidering their career pathways, and colleges are redesigning the content, sequencing, and delivery of their degree programs to make them more relevant and accessible. This abstract traces the development and implications of the change in status of the college degree and examines how one community college is responding by "reengineering" a number of its Associate of Science degree programs to put certificates on center stage, give students immediate job skills, and answer employer needs for a new kind of educated citizenry.

Changing Higher Education Backdrop

Institutions of higher education are no longer the sole proprietors of knowledge or the exclusive developers of new professionals. Since the founding of this country, the seat of postsecondary educational power has migrated from the church to the state, and now it is "getting down to business." Originally, churches, monasteries, and seminaries controlled higher knowledge and reserved it for the elite classes. Later, state-governed colleges and universities brought advanced educational opportunity to a broader spectrum of class, color, and gender groups. Recently, businesses and corporations—out of self-proclaimed competitive necessity—have moved into postsecondary teaching and professional development activities, bringing a new cast of characters to the story of American occupational preparation.

The backdrop for this new stage of higher education is the colossal macroeconomic factor redefining American corporations and lives—global competition. The magnitude of this change is evident in the everyday corporate language of the 1990s. Downsizing, rightsizing, reduction-in-force, and outsourcing were unheard of in job placement discussions with

"Certificates on Center Stage: Occupational Education for a Working Economy," by Stella A. Perez and Carol C. Copenhaver, reprinted from *Leadership Abstracts*, Vol. 11, No. 3, March 1998, League for Innovation in the Community College.

college graduates of the 1940s, '50s, '60s, or '70s. In these eras, the American Dream endured and the link between college diploma and career security was intact.

Changing Players and Scripts

Today the scene has changed. The factors affecting higher education—new players in the marketplace and the backdrop of global competition—also influence the professional roles that contemporary college graduates expect to play. Workers now expect to change jobs, if not careers, many times during their lives, and they increasingly recognize job skill development as a lifelong endeavor.

A catalytic subplot underlying changes in higher education and the work force over the last two decades is the explosion of information technology, the *Tell-Tale Heart* of the Information Age. Scholars, researchers, and economists agree that these interdependent factors have created the most rapid changes our society has ever experienced. Couple these elements with some of the lowest unemployment rates on record, which normally signal less demand for education and training, and the imminent shortage of technology workers, which cries for highly specific skills training, and a sizzling higher education drama emerges.

The current scene churns these influences. Higher education leaders struggle with less preparation and higher expectations, and industry races to remain competitive in the face of employee skill deficiencies. The news is filled with stories of how the pipeline of information technology workers is running dry. Public institutions are watching their former understudies, the proprietary colleges, take on leading roles. New for-profit institutions, such as University of Phoenix, promising to fulfill *anytime, anywhere, and anyplace* learner demands, are now significant contenders. As public institutions confront increasing competition, they continue to face the higher education reality of the '90s—growing accountability mandates and diminishing fiscal resources.

Old Baccalaureate Props

Community colleges, recognized for their adaptability and responsiveness, generally balk at playing out the script of unraveling public higher education. These institutions do not dispute the educational pathway to success documented by the American Council on Education in 1994, which noted that baccalaureate graduates earn $12,000 to $14,000 more per year than high school graduates. Rather, they take their cues from detonating new facts about how today's technical employee, with two years of technical skills training, often earns as much as a four-year college graduate.

Kenneth Gray, professor of education at Penn State University, studies the relationship between education and career outcomes and dubs the traditional degree pathway to the work force the *baccalaureate myth*. Gray's research reveals that 70 percent of our nation's high school graduates enter college, but one in three does not complete a degree. Of those who graduate, one third take jobs they could have obtained without the expense of a college degree—a cost he estimates at $11,112 per year. Gray argues that beyond the three R's of *reading, 'riting, and 'rithmetic*, America needs to add a fourth R to the higher education curriculum—*reality*.

Adding Reality to the Curriculum

One college taking on the challenge to add reality to its curriculum is St. Petersburg Junior College (SPJC). SPJC is the oldest community college in Florida—a state, like many others, that is experiencing the lowest unemployment rates recorded in 10 years. Information technology industries are exploding, and these companies offer prime wages for technical skills. The currency in this new marketplace is *skills*, not *credentials*. College leaders recognize that the traditional degree pathway may not work for students who come to the community college with an urgency to obtain skills to get a good job or advance in their careers.

Rightsizing the A.S. Degree

In the last year, SPJC has responded to the skill-based marketplace by developing 34 new one-year certificate occupational education programs and revamping 6 existing ones in high-demand program areas such as technology, health management, manufacturing, and public safety. These were developed using a dual process of "looking back"—relying on existing resources—while "thinking forward"—designing programs to meet work force needs and student goals as the first step toward an Associate of Science degree.

Lacking resources to develop entirely new courses and processes, the college relied on extensive market analysis and guidance from local work force development boards and welfare reform advisors to rebundle existing courses with new skill-based offerings. The new certificate programs are 18- to 24-credit-hour programs that couple basic degree requirements with specialty skills oriented to the latest innovation in industry training, with particular attention given to new developments in information technology. Course are closely calibrated to business and industry standards and are offered evenings, weekends, and in other flexible formats. These new skill-based programs allow students to complete a one-year certificate training sequence and get immediate experience in their field of study before taking general education courses.

Inverted Degree Plan

Course sequencing and content are changed in the new program design. Participating students enroll in a technical certificate program and begin taking technical skills courses immediately. They engage in internships or work-related activities while completing their certificate and getting a job. While working in their chosen field, they may return to complete the A.S. degree requirements or transfer to pursue a four-year degree. This "inverted" degree plan creates a direct path for students whose goals are to gain, maintain, or retrain into high-wage, high-demand technical occupations.

Judging Success

The reengineered A.S. degree programs at SPJC are too new to evaluate for long-term effects, but early responses have been strongly positive. Interviews with students and employers suggest both groups appreciate the "reality" built into the new certificates. As one student observed, "I have a bachelor's degree, and I value that, but this program gives me the opportunity to jump in and be productive in my job TODAY." Enrollments in many of these program areas have increased already. In addition, some faculty members involved in program revamping have reported professional development benefits, such as one who described the process as a "shot in the arm for the whole department."

Recasting Programs for Work

Colleges experimenting with rightsizing and inverting technical degree programs may be judged avant-garde or threatening by traditional academics. Some may argue that such programs encourage vocational tracking. Yet, the data beg the question that if over 60 percent of America's high school graduates are not attempting or completing college degree programs, where are they going, if not to work? Most community college students do not have the luxury of staying out of the work force until completing their higher education goals. These students need educational pathways that complement, rather than compete with, their need to work.

If higher education is to keep alive the classic tale of hope and progress for future American workers, it must try out new designs to place alongside traditional programs that no longer "play" to all audiences. Industry-related certificate-first programs that integrate flexible course scheduling, inverted degree design, and high-demand technical skills training may be one answer to meeting powerful work force demands and student needs in a new era of work. These new occupational education program designs may even signal a new era in higher education—the stage call to many encores.

Stella A. Perez and Carol C. Copenhaver are Associate Vice President and Vice President, respectively, for Educational and Student Services at St. Petersburg Junior College (FL). The authors can be contacted at perezs@email.spjc.cc.fl.us or copenhaverc@email.spjc.fl.us.

CHAPTER 10

GRADUATE, PROFESSIONAL, AND ADULT EDUCATION

ASSOCIATE EDITOR: JUDITH GLAZER RAYMO

Graduate, professional and adult education represent three distinct conceptualizations of higher education. Their emergence in the United States can be traced to the rise of the modern university, beginning in the late nineteenth century, a period of great economic, social, and political change. Their diversity has been attributed to a number of factors: the propagation of research as an integral function of the university, the decentralization of higher education institutions into departments, divisions, and schools; and the growth of professional associations to protect and promote the role of the university in preparing practitioners, creating new knowledge, and enhancing the prestige and status of professional fields.

The development of graduate education in arts and science disciplines paralleled the growth of sponsored research supported by private philanthropy and, following World War II, by the federal government. As Patricia Gumport observes in her essay, graduate schools afforded intellectual, economic, and political legitimacy to universities which fostered the proliferation of graduate and professional programs. Between 1969 and 1994, graduate enrollments almost doubled, from 955,000 to 1,721,000 students. By 1994, the number of graduate degree recipients reached an all-time high: 387,070 master's, 75,400 first professional, and 43,185 doctoral degrees (Babco, 1997). Clearly, graduate education represents a significant segment of the academic enterprise. However, as Gumport demonstrates, the interrelationships between graduate education and research which fostered the university's growth now threaten its viability. Major policy issues emerging in the past two decades focus attention on institutional dependence on uncertain sources of funding for doctoral education, the growing presence of industrial R&D, and the shrinking academic labor market for new doctorates, not only in the sciences but in the humanities and the social sciences.

Professional education originated as part of the baccalaureate program of colleges and universities at a time when medicine, law, theology, and architecture constituted the dominant specializations. Spurred on by three groups—professional associations, practitioners, and the state—these programs were gradually elevated and integrated into the university as postbaccalaureate schools of equal status with graduate arts and science faculties. In a society that valued useful knowledge and productive citizens, professional education was readily accepted by employers, legislators, and alumni, spurring external support for autonomous professional schools, professional degree programs, and research faculty in the health sciences, engineering, social work, and business. The university became both an arena of interprofessional competition for fiscal resources and a major ally in building the modern, dominant, American professions (Abbott, 1988).

Implicit in the structure of professional education is the notion of professionalism. In his essay, Eliot Freidson proposes an ideal-typical model of professionalism based on elements of collegiality and egalitarianism and tied to the university which has historically supported intellectuals,

Judith Glazer Raymo teaches in the School of Education at Long Island University's C. W. Post Campus. (raymo@phoenix.liu.edu)

scholars, and scientists in their research and teaching. He draws an analogy between professional education and professional practice in the recruitment, training, and employment of faculty supported economically by the practice of teaching in circumstances that enable them to pursue research and scholarship.Freidson expresses similar concerns to Gumport regarding the vulnerability of the professions to economic and political pressures. He senses weaknesses in the face of the state's power to use economic incentives to advance ideological claims over the work of professional practitioners and to exercise greater bureaucratic control of the professional schools.

Adult education spans undergraduate, graduate, and professional education. Rather than a disciplinary focus, it emphasizes lifelong learning in adult and continuing education programs offered both on and off campus for credit and non-credit and financed mainly by students or their sponsoring organizations. Sharan Merriam provides an overview of adult learning theories derived from several studies focusing on the characteristics of adult learners, their diverse social roles and responsibilities, and their personal and professional development. While adult education as a field of study is relatively new, these theories provide a useful starting point for discussing the design and implementation of adult and continuing education programs which incorporate more reflective models of teaching non-traditional students.

Such programs provide the opportunity for exploring distance learning, self-directed and self-paced instruction, flexible scheduling unfettered by conventional academic requirements, general studies programs for returning adults, experiential education in workplace environments, and the continuing professional development of advanced degree holders. Creative and entrepreneurial program developers have utilized continuing and adult education programs as a means of developing stronger links between the university and the community, for experimenting with innovative teaching and learning strategies and curriculum concepts outside the boundaries of academic regulations and faculty committees, for utilizing campus facilities on a year-round basis, and for designing self-supporting, sustainable, and inventive lifelong learning opportunities.

At the close of the twentieth century, the lines between graduate, professional, and adult and continuing education have begun to blur as the professionalization of master's and doctoral degrees has gained momentum. In a credential society in which degrees are social currency, the National Center for Educational Statistics forecasts continued increase in the number of bachelor's, master's, and doctoral degrees awarded through the year 2005 (Babco, 1997). Continuing education programs are becoming the laboratories for experimenting with flexible scheduling of instruction, home schooling, distance learning, computer-assisted instruction, and campuses without walls. As these innovations are integrated into university libraries and their professional and graduate schools by a new generation of faculty and administrators, new degree structures will evolve to meet the needs of a technological and professionalized society.

Suggested Supplementary Readings

Adult Education

Bright, B.P. (ed.), *Theory and Practice in the Study of Adult Education: The Epistemological Debate*. London: Routledge, Chapman, and Hall, 1989.

Brookfield, Stephen. "Developing Criteria for Formal Theory Building in Adult Education." *Adult Education Quarterly*, Winter, 1992, 42, 2, 79–93.

Brookfield, Stephen. *Training Educators of Adults: The Theory and Practice of Adult Education*. London: Routledge, 1988.

Cassara, Beverly B. (ed.). *Adult Education in a Multicultural Society*. London and New York: Routledge, 1990.

Cross, K. Patricia. *Adults as Learners*. San Francisco: Jossey-Bass, 1981.

Davenport, J. & Davenport, J. "A Chronology and Analysis of the Andragogy Debate." *Adult Education Quarterly*, 1985, 35, 152–159.

Houle, Cyril O. *Patterns of Learning*. San Francisco: Jossey-Bass, 1984.

Jarvis, Peter. *Adult and Continuing Education*. London: Croom Helm, 1995.

Knowles, Malcolm S. *The Modern Practice of Adult Education: From Pedagogy to Andragogy*. (2nd edition). Chicago: Follett, 1980.

Knowles, Malcolm S. *Andragogy in Action: Applying Modern Principles of Adult Learning.* San Francisco: Jossey-Bass, 1984.

Merriam, Sharan (ed.). 1993. *An Update on Adult Learning Theory. New Directions in Adult and Continuing Education,* No. 57. San Francisco: Jossey-Bass, 1993.

Merriam, Sharan & Cunningham, S.B. (eds.). *Handbook of Adult and Continuing Education.* San Francisco: Jossey-Bass, 1989.

Mezirow, Jack & Associates. *Fostering Critical Reflection in Adulthood: A Guide to Transformative and Emancipatory Learning.* San Francisco, CA: Jossey-Bass, 1990.

Peters, John, Jarvis, Peter and Associates. *Adult Education: Evolution and Achievements in a Developing Field of Study.* San Francisco: Jossey-Bass, 1991.

Usher, Robin, Bryant, Ian, and Johnston, Rennie. *Adult Education and the Postmodern Challenge: Learning Beyond the Limits.* London and New York: Routledge, 1997.

Usher, Robin and Bryant, Ian. *Adult Education as Theory, Practice, and Research: The Captive Triangle.* London: Routledge, 1989.

Graduate Education

Baird, Leonard L. (ed.). *Increasing Graduate Student Retention and Degree Attainment. New Directions for Institutional Research,* No. 80. San Francisco: Jossey-Bass, 1993.

Baird, Leonard L. "The Melancholy of Anatomy: The Personal Development of Graduate and Professional School Students." In *Higher Education: Handbook of Theory and Research.* Vol. 6. New York: Agathon Press, 1990.

Berelson, Bernard. *Graduate Education in the United States.* New York: McGraw Hill, 1960.

Bowen, William G. and Rudenstine, Neil L. *In Pursuit of the Ph.D.* Princeton, NJ: Princeton University Press, 1992.

Breneman, David and Youn, Ted. (eds.) *Academic Labor Markets and Careers.* Philadelphia: the Falmer Press, 1988.

Clark, Burton R. (ed.). *The Research Foundations of Graduate Education: Germany, Britain, France, and the United States.* Berkeley: University of California Press, 1993.

Conrad, Clifton, Haworth, Jennifer G., and Millar, Susan. *A Silent Success: Master's Education in the United States.* Baltimore, MD: Johns Hopkins University Press, 1993.

Cole, Jonathan. *Fair Science: Women in the Scientific Community.* New York: The Free Press, 1979.

Glazer, Judith S. *The Master's Degree: Tradition, Diversity, Innovation.* ASHE-ERIC Research Report No. 6. Washington, DC: Association for the Study of Higher Education 1986.

Glazer, Judith S. *A Teaching Doctorate? The Doctor of Arts, Then and Now.* Washington, D.C.: American Association for Higher Education, 1993.

Haworth, Jennifer G. (ed.). *Assessing Graduate and Professional Education: Current Realities, Future Prospects. New Directions for Institutional Research,* No. 62. San Francisco: Jossey-Bass, 1996.

Jones, L., Gardner, L. and Coggeshall, P. (eds.). *An Assessment of Research Doctorate Programs in the US: Social and Behavioral Sciences.* Washington, D.C.: National Academy Press, 1982.

Kernan, Alvin (ed.) *What's Happened to the Humanities?* Princeton: Princeton University Press, 1997.

Malaney, G.D. "Graduate Education as an Area of Research in Higher Education." in J. C. Smart (ed.), *Higher Education: Handbook of Theory and Research,* Vol. 4. New York: Agathon Press, 1988.

National Research Council. *Survey of Earned Doctorates: Summary Report.* Washington, D.C.: National Academy Press, 1997.

Pelikan, Jaroslav. *Scholarship and Its Survival: Questions on the Idea of Graduate Education.* Princeton: Carnegie Foundation for the Advancement of Teaching, 1983.

Professional Education

Abbott, Andrew. *The System of Professions: An Essay on the Division of Expert Labor.* Chicago: University of Chicago Press, 1988.

Burrage, Michael and Torstendahl, Rolf. (Eds.). *Professions in Theory and History: Rethinking the Study of the Professions.* London: Sage, 1990.

Clark, Burton R. (ed.). *The Academic Profession: National, Disciplinary, and Institutional Settings.* Berkeley: University of California Press, 1987.

Curry, Lynn, Wergin, John and Associates (eds.). *Educating Professionals: Responding to New Expectations for Competence and Accountability.* San Francisco: Jossey-Bass, 1993.

Dinham, Sara M. & Stritter, F.T. "Research on Professional Education," in M.D. Wittrock (ed.), *Handbook of Research on Teaching* (3rd edition). New York: Macmillan, 1986.

Freidson, Eliot. *Professionalism Reborn: Theory, Prophecy and Policy.* Oxford: Polity Press, Blackwell Publishers, 1994.

Freidson, Eliot. "The Theory of Professions: State of the Art," in *The Sociology of the Professions: Doctors, Lawyers, and Others.* London: Macmillan, 1983.

Geison, Gerald L. (ed.). *Professions and Professional Ideologies in America.* Chapel Hill: University of North Carolina Press, 1983.

Glazer, Judith S. "Feminism and Professionalism in Teaching and Educational Administration," *Educational Administration Quarterly,* 1991, 27, 3, 321–342.

Haug, Marie R. "The Deprofessionalization of Everyone?" *Sociological Focus,* 1973, 6, 197–213.

Kennedy, M. "Inexact Sciences: Professional Education and the Development of Expertise." *Review of Research in Education,* 1987, 14, 133–167.

Larson, Margali S. *The Rise of Professionalism.* Berkeley: University of California Press, 1977.

Rhode, Deborah. "Gender and Professional Roles," *Fordham Law Review,* 63, 1994, 39–72.

Schön, Donald. *Educating the Reflective Practitioner: Toward a New Design for Teaching and Learning in the Professions.* San Francisco: Jossey-Bass, 1987.

Schön, Donald. *The Reflective Practitioner: How Professionals Think in Action.* New York: Basic Books, 1983.

Stark, Joan S., Lowther, Malcolm A. & Hagerty, Bonnie M. *Responsive Professional Education: Balancing Outcomes and Opportunities.* ASHE-ERIC Report No. 3. Washington, DC: Association for the Study of Higher Education, 1986.

Wilensky, Harold. "The Professionalization of Everyone?" *American Journal of Sociology,* 1964, 70, 137–58.

Witz, Anne. *Professions and Patriarchy.* London and New York: Routledge, 1992.

Graduate Education and Organized Research in the United States

Patricia J. Gumport

National systems of higher education exhibit different histories of efforts to integrate organized research and advanced education. They also reflect different beliefs about the desirability of that ambition and to what extent it has been achieved. At one end of the international continuum, the American arrangements for doctoral education and academic science have become organizationally, politically, and economically so tightly linked that American participants and observers alike have difficulty conceiving of one without the other. As one prominent observer notes, "In American universities the two are done together, in the same places and by the same people."[1]

The American system of graduate education extends beyond the most visible top tier of one hundred doctoral-granting universities into a vast enterprise. Compared to other countries, the scale of operations is awesome, spanning some 800 of the country's 3,400 American higher education institutions, enrolling almost 1.5 million graduate students, and awarding annually about 300,000 master's degrees, 75,000 professional degrees, and 33,000 doctorates.[2] Graduate education programs are embedded within universities as a distinct layer resting atop undergraduate arts and sciences programs, usually drawing on the same faculties and relying on resources derived from an institution's teaching as well as research missions. Reflecting strong local organization, the structural and normative underpinnings of graduate programs reside in academic departments characterized by decentralized faculty authority.

In contrast to the more gradual progression that occurs in the German system, entry to this level of the American higher education system for an advanced degree comes about after a sharp break upon completion of undergraduate education. The majority of incoming graduate students in the letters and science departments have attended comprehensive public schools for their secondary education, usually earning a high school diploma at age seventeen or eighteen, followed by a bachelor's degree from a range of selective institutions, where coursework was a mix of general education and a disciplinary major. Fewer were chosen from the less selective four-year colleges (and the two-year colleges that may lead to them); courses taken here instead often lead to terminal degrees. Selectivity is the key ingredient reinforcing the pivotal role of the graduate school as a site for professional socialization and disciplinary reproduction. As Diana Crane describes the rationale: "The best students are selected by the top scientists, and from this highly selected group come the next generation's most productive scientists."[3]

Retaining the initial Humboldtian imprint from over a century ago, graduate programs reflect a widespread belief, internalized by faculty, administrators, and research sponsors alike, that linking graduate education and organized research produces excellence in both. Accordingly, the basic model for doctoral

"Graduate Education and Organized Research in the United States," by Patricia J. Gumport, reprinted from *The Research Foundations of Graduate Education: Germany, Britain, France, United States, Japan,* edited by Burton R. Clark, 1993, University of California Press.

education has been distinctive: a few years of prescribed course work, followed by examinations for advancement to candidacy, culminating in a dissertation that reflects original research done by the student under the guidance of a faculty committee. Common across fields is an apprenticeship experience intended to integrate teaching and research training.

The linkage of this pattern of doctoral training with sponsored research has historical roots in a national context that has valued these activities for their instrumental contributions to two crucial national tasks—the production of research and the preparation of trained research personnel. To establish and reinforce the research-training fabric, an elaborate, decentralized, competitive funding system has allocated the bulk of basic research resources in individual project grants to university researchers who, as principal investigators, employ graduate student research assistants in campus laboratories. With the exception of a small number of competitive fellowship programs, funding allocations have corresponded to short-term and long-range national priorities, such as economic competitiveness, defense, and health care. Thus, financial support for the integration of graduate education and research has been achieved, for the most part, indirectly and more for its instrumental value rather than for its inherent legitimacy as an ideal. And as research and research training have been transformed into more capital-intensive endeavors, especially in the leading one hundred universities, the stakes have become high for all concerned.

This chapter begins with a historical overview of the development of the American research university. The second and third sections describe the contemporary systems of graduate education and organized research, focusing on policy issues of organization and sponsorship that have prevailed during the last two decades.

Historical Development

Modern research universities have become the principal home of graduate education and research in the United States. Although scholars have documented separately the rise of modern American science, the emergence of the American research university, and the

emergence of graduate education, little scholarly work has been done at their intersection to examine the factors that account for their interrelationship and for their persistence.[4]

As is true of most social institutions in the United States, the development of research universities has occurred neither linearly nor with centralized planning. Rather, the university research system emerged incrementally through a series of initiatives on the part of universities and a plurality of funding sources, within an economic and political context that increasingly encouraged scientific research.

In contrast to other countries, institutional initiative has been a prominent driving force. Over the past century the expansion of the modern university research system was fueled first and foremost by the ambitions of universities to establish themselves as modern research complexes, either by transforming smaller classical colleges or by establishing new, larger universities. Such ambitions were spurred on by an emerging national system of science that crystallized in the late nineteenth century and a funding system that did not develop formally on a national scale until the mid-twentieth.

The Emergence of Graduate Education

Graduate education achieved a stable American presence during the last two decades of the nineteenth century, when awarding the Ph.D. became a laudable academic goal. The earliest signs of doctoral education in the United States were the granting of the first Ph.D. in 1861 by Yale's Sheffield Scientific School, the second Ph.D. by the University of Pennsylvania in 1871, and the third by Harvard a year later.[5] More significant was the explicit organizational mission of graduate education in the founding of Johns Hopkins University in 1876 and Clark University in 1889. Hopkins especially became known as the "prototype and propagator" of research as a major university function. Coupled with its commitments to scientific research, Hopkins offered merit-based graduate fellowships for full-time study that included state-of-the-art research training.[6]

Both within and immediately surrounding higher education, interest in science had been burgeoning since the mid-nineteenth century, when science was still the individual pursuit of amateurs. Scientists and those seeking advanced study often traveled to Germany for the requisite exposure; work in chemistry even into the 1870s required a trip to Germany.[7] On the American front, after initial resistance to the German idea of studying science for its own sake and after conflicts between self-identified pure and applied scientists, scientific research gradually gained more acceptance, although it took on a distinctive meaning in the American context: American science, Dael Wolfle wrote, would be "a collective enterprise like those in business. Modern science needed labor, capital and management."[8]

Between the founding of Hopkins in 1876 and Clark in 1889, the conceptualization of scientific research had shifted from a personal dream to an exalted vocation. Proclamations at Hopkins reflect this change from what Laurence Veysey called "a rare and peculiar opportunity for study and research, eagerly seized by men who had been hungering and thirsting for such a possibility," to an increasingly more prestigious endeavor, proclaimed by Clark's president as "the very highest vocation of man—research."[9] Science became an increasingly specialized activity that professors could pursue autonomously yet with the security of support, personal advancement, and even prominence, within (and extending beyond the local loyalty to) an academic institution.[10]

Hopkins and Clark were not long to remain isolated experiments dominated by ideals of scientific research and graduate education. Other graduate schools emerged in the 1890s as parts of larger universities whose undergraduate missions and size offered a broad and stable base of support in endowment funds and tuition. Some were established by the founding of a new university soon to offer both undergraduate and graduate instruction, as in Stanford (1891) and Chicago (1892). Others added the graduate school onto an older established private college, as in Harvard and Columbia. Some existing state universities—Wisconsin, Michigan, and Illinois—evolved further from their origins as land grant colleges established with government funds for agriculture and mechanical arts through the Morrill Acts of 1862 and 1890 and the funding of experimental agricultural stations through the Hatch Act of 1887.[11] By 1900 the number of Ph.D.-granting institutions had

grown to fourteen, awarding a total of three hundred Ph.D.'s.[12]

In addition to taking on scientific research commitments, Ph.D. programs came to be seen as an attractive feature for expansion and for advancing an institution's competitive position in the growing higher education system. Based on a desire to heighten prestige in their institutions, an increasing number of institutions sought to hire faculty with research interests and to obtain sponsored research funds to build laboratories that would attract eminent scientists. Since faculty increasingly wanted to pursue basic research and to train selectively chosen graduate students, institutions were propelled to provide them with opportunities for research and advanced training, and hence graduate programs, across the disciplines.

The widespread adoption of graduate programs within higher education institutions was enhanced by the development of departmental organization that occurred in the last quarter of the nineteenth century. Departments provided a flexible organizational structure for decentralizing and compartmentalizing graduate instruction. If Ph.D. programs were integrated organizationally as a separate level from the liberal education of undergraduate colleges, they also were made parts of departments responsible for undergraduate instruction in a discipline, a linking arrangement that has been remarkably stable and uniform over time and across campuses. The drive to conform to this structure was so strong that Hopkins and Clark expanded their organizational structures to offer undergraduate as well as graduate programs.

This organizational arrangement permitted control of undergraduate and graduate programs to reside within the same group of faculty.[13] Course work as well as research training could be designed which was appropriate to each discipline and coordinated by each department's faculty. One functional by-product of this arrangement was that graduate programs maintained both faculty and institutional continuity: they allowed faculty to reproduce themselves by training their professional successors, and they promoted cohesion of the university, since the responsibility for graduate students kept faculty attentive to their departments. Graduate programs kept the research and teaching activities interlocked and the institution functionally integrated in spite of increased disciplinary specialization.

Corresponding to established areas of knowledge at the time, departments were able to design different kinds of research apprenticeships that were appropriate to the specialized training in each of the disciplines. The specialization of disciplines mirrored by departments represented professors' vocational aspirations, which were especially apparent in the newly established natural and social science departments whose very existence was justified on the basis of specialized research. Beyond the campus level, as disciplines crystallized into national professional associations, they came to serve as visible external reference groups that would give a semblance of standardization across graduate programs.[14] "Disciplines and departments had powerful reciprocal effects upon one another," Roger Geiger has noted, in reinforcing the authority of departments on campus and the professional judgments of faculty nationally.[15] Thus, the emergence of disciplinary associations further facilitated the development of Ph.D. programs.

Especially during the 1890s, the growing size and complexity of the graduate education and research enterprise encouraged academic management, coordination, and control, which were reflected in the emergent bureaucratic administration on campuses. Even though departments served faculty interests for autonomy over research and instruction, the hierarchies of rank within departments and competition across departments served administrative interests for "productive work" as measured by research output. One observer notes, "Clearly it had become a necessity, from the administrator's point of view, to foster the prestigeful evidences of original inquiry."[16]

The dual tasks of graduate education and research were institutionalized most easily in those institutions that had greater resources, both financial and reputational. Thus at the systemwide level, those who succeeded in the competitive drive for advancement became a leading peer group of institutions. The prominence of this tier in the U.S. system was reflected in their founding of the Association of American Universities in 1900, which marked the culmination of nineteenth-century efforts to establish graduate education and research activities.. Ostensibly the AAU was founded to establish uniformity of standards, yet it simultaneously functioned as an exclusive club.[17] The establishment of the AAU signified an implicit systemwide division of labor: a group of institutions differentiated themselves as a sector at the top of a hierarchy of prestige on the basis of their engagement in graduate education and research.[18] Although institutions continued to compete with one another for faculty, graduate students, and philanthropic support, a persistent concentration of fiscal and status resources in this sector became an enduring distinctive feature of the American system, one that amounted to an institutional version of the Matthew effect in which cumulative advantage helps the rich to become richer.[19]

Characterized as "a new epoch of institutional empire-building,"[20] this period of American higher education reflects the surfacing of university concerns for status in an increasingly stratified system. Such concerns were evident in dynamics of academic rivalry such as bidding for faculty and emulating academic programs. Even if the American system is not unique in its inclination toward stratification, the institutional drive for competitive advancement within the research university sector has reflected, according to one American scholar, "almost an obsession."[21]

Thus, the end of the nineteenth century marks the creation of the research university as a new kind of social institution devoted to scientific research as well as to graduate training. The extent of institutional ambition was so pervasive that the developing universities imitated one another in the programs and faculties they sought to develop. On campuses across the country, the homogeneity in the proliferation of graduate programs and faculty positions suggests that universities sought to acquire not only intellectual legitimacy but a new kind of economic and political legitimacy as well.[22]

The Rise of Sponsorship for University Research

The emergence of graduate education in the modern university developed hand in hand with the expansion of a national system of sponsored research. Initially, external resources for academic science were amassed principally from philanthropic foundations, while industry played a minimal role. Not until after World War II were foundations and industry eclipsed by the surge of federal government involvement.

The earliest sources of research sponsorship were wealthy benefactors and their philanthropic foundations. In the 1870s philanthropic contributions to higher education averaged $6 million per year—mainly to individual scientists.[23] By 1890 philanthropic support reflected a more widespread and instrumental orientation, directing funds to the emerging universities for their potential contributions to industrial growth, employment, and commercial endeavors.[24] Philanthropic funds supported a wide array of institutional activities, especially in the applied sciences, including funds for equipment, overall plant expansion, and new professional schools. In some cases the support provided a considerable amount of money, for example, John D. Rockefeller's $35 million endowment to the University of Chicago.

On a national scale John D. Rockefeller and Andrew Carnegie established the principle of systematic philanthropy. The two largest foundations involved in research were the Rockefeller Foundation, established in 1913 with $182 million, and the Carnegie Corporation, created in 1911 with $125 million. In the early 1920s these foundations favored donations to separate research institutes, such as the Rockefeller Institute of Medicine and the Carnegie Institute of Washington. Universities were uncertain whether foundations would be stable sponsors for academic science.[25] By the 1930s foundations reoriented their giving to become an integral funding base for university research. They allocated project grants and postdoctoral fellowships (the latter preeminently by the Guggenheim Foundation), especially in medical research and the natural sciences, somewhat less so the social sciences. In 1934, for example, the Rockefeller Foundation, which alone provided 35 percent of all foundation giving, gave 64 percent of all foundation funds to social science support and 72 percent of funds made available to the natural sciences.[26]

Although philanthropists may indeed have been "a hidden presence on every American campus,"[27] as put by Frederick Rudolph, their voluntary contributions enabled universities to have essential resources required to institutionalize graduate education and scientific research. Universities and their faculties built their own rationales and adapted organization structures to expand the scope of their research activities, while training the next generation of knowledge producers. Much of this adaptation to undertake applied research became incorporated into the ideal of service, especially for public universities.

Upholding university autonomy and academic freedom became not only institutional concerns but also issues for individual faculty. Consequently, faculty claimed expert authority in order to establish some distance from the agendas of campus governing boards and the increasingly prominent philanthropists.[28] Professionalization efforts of faculty in this era, were, in part, due to the huge presence of external mandates for research, and not merely, as commonly cited, an outgrowth of the explosion of knowledge.

While philanthropic support continued until World War II, private industry had entered the academic scene during the interwar years as an unpredictable supplement.[29] As industry R&D expenditures rose in the 1920s, corporations conducted both applied and basic research in their own industrial labs in the technological areas of electricity, communications, and chemicals. Since industry could also benefit from academic science, corporations needed to demonstrate that business interests were compatible with the university ideal of disinterested inquiry. The success of industrial sponsorship for university research in this era was exemplified by ventures with two prestigious research universities: Massachusetts Institute of Technology (MIT) and the California Institute of Technology (Cal Tech). Nevertheless, corporate R&D funds generally remained in industrial laboratories through the 1930s and thereby continued as a marginal contributor to the support of academic science.

By the late 1930s university research was genuinely flourishing, although it did so primarily in the nation's most visible universities. Evidence for this concentration of research activity is also documented by a similar concentration of research training activity: in 1937 sixteen universities accounted for half of the expenditures on university research and granted 58 percent of the Ph.D.'s.[30] The consolidation of research resources has become linked with doctoral-granting activity, a pattern developed under philanthropic support, which would prove durable and capable of great expansion.

The Surge of Federal Involvement

The national government's sponsorship of research and research training developed incrementally rather than through a coordinating policy on science or on graduate education. Until World War II the federal government played only a minimal role in advancing either scientific research or higher education. The principal exception, noted earlier, was the successful effort in the nineteenth century, with much practical utility in mind, to sponsor agricultural research. But it was many decades later, after two world wars, that the government came to consider universities as a national resource for basic research and training that could assist in economic growth, national security, and health care.

Early signs of federal involvement in academic science began with efforts to designate advisory boards for scientific research. Signifying both the value placed upon modern science and a perceived need to oversee the country's research intentions, the first national organization was the National Academy of Sciences. Founded in 1863 by a congressional charter as "a private, non-profit, self-governing membership corporation of distinguished scholars in science and engineering research," NAS was to "advise the government on scientific and technical matters to further science and technology and their use for the general welfare." Over the next decade, NAS became the site of severe conflicts over membership (limited to fifty) and mission as American scientists from different fields vied for control of the scientific community. It did not develop a powerful relationship to the national government. Instead, Robert V. Bruce has noted that "the federal government remained disinclined to seek the Academy's counsel or even receive it when offered, thus negating the Academy's official reason for being."[31]

A half-century passed before the federal government mandated additional organizational arrangements that were to be more influential in the advancement of scientific research as a national enterprise. In 1919 the National Research Council was established by NAS, essentially to carry out the earlier congressional mandate. As the principal operating agency of both the National Academy of Science and (after 1964) the National Academy of Engineering, the NRC was intended to serve as a bridge between the federal government, the public, and the community of scientists and engineers. Over time the NRC has become a principal organizational base for overseeing national research efforts, including manpower training, and for monitoring how federal funds are channeled into university research.

Rather than actually advising the government, however, the NRC, along with the American Council of Learned Societies (founded in 1919) and the Social Sciences Research Council (founded in 1923), depended upon the resources of philanthropic foundations to assume a prominent role in the promotion of university research. As channels for foundation funds, these organizations provided interested sponsors with access to scientists and scholars as well as administrative assistance in selecting recipients of small research grants and postdoctoral fellowships in the areas of mathematics, physics, and chemistry. By the 1920s, in Geiger's formulation, American science was mobilized under "the guidance of the private elites" who "came together for the purpose of furthering science." The memberships of the National Research Council and the National Academy of Sciences were constituted by "the same group of individuals [who] encountered one another, in slightly different combinations."[32]

The national government's expansion of a large-scale, multiagency funding system to support academic science developed incrementally during and after each world war, culminating in the post-World War II era. In the late 1930s annual federal expenditures for science were estimated at $100 million; most of these funds went to applied research in federal bureaus, especially agriculture, meteorology, geology, and conservation.[33] Some drift in interest toward academia occurred when the expertise of academic researchers became a valued commodity, notably as the federal government called on them to assist in wartime.[34] For example, during World War I, the federal government financed psychologists to construct intelligence tests and encouraged other scientists to follow up on diagnostic physical examinations of close to four million people who were drafted. For such work, universities granted leaves to physical scientists and life scientists as well as to social scientists and historians. The government also began to allocate funds for researchers to work on their home campuses. By 1940 federal funds for university research totaled $31 million. During the 1940s the Office of Naval Research contracted with over two hundred universities to do about twelve hundred research projects involving some 3,000 scientists and 2,500 graduate students.[35] This pattern of mission-agency contracting became the precedent for arrangements made later for the support of relevant research by such agencies as the Atomic Energy Commission (AEC), created in 1946, and the National Aeronautics and Space Administration (NASA), established in 1958. During the war years, 1941–1945, the United States spent $3 billion on research and development (R&D), mostly funded by the federal government, of which one third was for university research aimed at winning the war and devising "new instruments of destruction and defense."[36]

The expansion of sponsored research in universities was coupled with the expansion of research training. Between 1920 and 1940 institutions awarding doctoral degrees increased from fifty to one hundred. In those two decades doctorates awarded annually increased from 620 to 3,300, a fivefold increase.[37] The caliber of doctoral students also improved significantly. As late as the 1920s the majority of graduate students had been "undistinguished," reflecting "uneven preparation, uncertain motivation and unproven ability."[38] In the 1930s stiffened graduate admissions began seriously to bar unfit students and to seek and aid outstanding ones. To give departments another means of assessing student ability, on a national scale, leading Eastern private universities cooperated in the late 1930s in the development of the Graduate Record Examination (GRE), a durable device used ever more widely during the following half-century.

By the 1950s the federal government had come to look upon research universities as a precious public resource for research and

research training, a set of institutions worthy of a "partnership," even during peacetime. The establishment of the National Science Foundation (NSF) in 1952 reflected a growing federal belief that universities were, as Vannevar Bush's 1945 report to President Roosevelt had proclaimed, ideal settings for research that offered "an endless frontier." As the federal research budget grew, the academic research enterprise was solidified in the top tier of institutions. In 1953–1954 the top twenty universities spent 66 percent of federal-sponsored research funds for academic science and awarded 52 percent of the doctorates, mainly in the life sciences, physical sciences, and engineering, the same fields that were receiving most of the federal research funds.[39]

Spurred on by the Russian launching of *Sputnik I* in 1957, the national government provided even more funds for basic research. Federal sponsorship of research increased every year from 1958 to 1968.[40] In that decade alone annual federal contributions to academic research increased fivefold from $1 billion to $5 billion (in 1988 constant dollars). As the federal investment increased, so did the universities' share of basic research, from one-third to one-half in that decade.[41] As a result the basic research expenditures of research universities tripled from $433 million in 1960 to $1.64 billion in 1968.

Thus, the post–World War II period clearly established that research was a separate function and operation largely paid for by the federal government, and that universities could perform a large share of the nation's research effort.[42] At the same time as higher education was perceived as having an increasingly legitimate research role, higher education enrollment rose from 3 million to 7 million students, doubling within doctoral granting universities, from 1.24 million to 2.5 million, for undergraduate levels combined. Annual Ph.D. production in science and engineering grew dramatically, from near 6,000 in 1958 to over 14,000 a decade later.[43]

The allocation of research funds by the national government has consistently exhibited two characteristic features: multiagency support and field-initiated competitive research grants. Federal sponsorship has entailed a clear presidential directive (Executive Order #10521 in 1954) that no single agency within the government should be given sole responsibility for distributing research funds. Rather, each federal agency should sponsor research related to its mission, be it health, defense, or energy. In 1959, 96 percent of federal sponsorship came from five agencies: Department of Defense; Department of Health, Education, and Welfare (largely the national Institutes of Health [NIH]), Atomic Energy Commission, National Science Foundation, and Department of Agriculture. Over 96 percent of the $1.4 billion spent that year went for research in the life sciences, physical sciences, and engineering, leaving the social sciences and, particularly, the humanities neglected.[44]

Although such expansion in research funds lacked a unified policy specifying purposes, funding has been indirectly and loosely coordinated by peer review. The mechanism for reviewing research proposals and awarding research grants on a competitive basis became the primary vehicle through which the national government thought it would insure support and encouragement of the best research.[45] For the most part, although some effort was made to disperse resources across geographic locations and to smaller institutions, the federal agencies' priorities were to nurture excellence. The resulting pattern of funding reinforced the leading tier of research universities, which presently constitute only about 3 percent of all U.S. institutions of higher education, and gave support primarily to the sciences, with life sciences and physical sciences accounting for over one half of the basic research budget.[46] In 1958 the top one hundred universities spent 95 percent of all federal university R&D funds; a decade later their share had fallen somewhat but it was still a hefty 86 percent.[47]

Similar to the expansion of federal basic research funding, the federal support for doctoral education intensified, mostly for training science and engineering personnel. Aside from short-term interests to advance science and technology, the national government was mindful of improving the country's research capacity and developing a longer-term pipeline of trained scientists and engineers. The National Cancer Act of 1937, which called for grants-in-aid to nongovernment scientists and direct student aid in the form of fellowships, set a precedent for this twofold agenda. In the 1950s the National Science Foundation offered over five hundred prestigious portable fellowships each year. A variety of mechanisms were employed to attract and keep talented students in the pipeline: direct student aid (fellowships), student aid channeled through institutions (traineeships), and individual project grants to individual faculty that included salary for graduate student research assistants.[48]

Congressional response to the Soviet launching of *Sputnik* in 1957 reflected another surge in federal commitment to the improvement of research training. The National Defense Education Act of 1958 conveyed a commitment to rebuild the nation's research capability and specifically to support science education through a host of fellowship and traineeship programs to be launched by a variety of federal agencies (NIH, NSF, NASA). National Research Service awards, administered through three federal agencies in the 1960s, constituted a second major initiative. These training programs were deliberate efforts to attract talented students with stipends for predoctoral and postdoctoral support as well as to improve the training environment on campuses with institutional allowances. In the decade between 1961 and 1972 these programs assisted over 30,000 graduate students and 27,000 postdoctoral scholars.[49]

With direct support of doctoral education through fellowships and traineeships provided on a competitive basis, talent and support continued to concentrate at the leading research universities where federally sponsored research was centered. The resulting consolidation of resources for both research and doctoral education gave these institutions a double competitive edge in attracting high-quality students and faculty. Thus, federal initiatives were instrumental in cementing the legitimacy of the interdependence between sponsored university research for its short-term R&D value and graduate education for its manpower training.

A New Era of Expansion for Graduate Education

Within the context of expanded, sponsored research opportunities and a shifting funding base, the graduate education system became dispersed into a wide range of doctoral and master's programs, both growing at a constant rate each decade. Doctorates increased from

6,000 in 1950 to 10,000 in 1960: more doctorates were granted in the decade of the 1950s than in all the years prior.[50] A dramatic threefold increase during the 1960s then brought the total up to nearly 30,000.[51] The expansion of master's degrees followed a similar pattern. From a base of about 25,000 granted in 1940, master's degrees dramatically increased to about 60,000 in 1950, 75,000 in 1960, and close to 300,000 two decades later.[52] Thus, while the concentration of Ph.D.'s in the top tier of universities has been most visible, a larger penumbra of institutions account for graduate education at the master's level.[53]

Both doctoral and master's degrees reflect an overall increase in degrees awarded across all fields of study, especially in the sciences and professional fields. In 1965 the physical sciences, the life sciences, and engineering accounted for close to one half of the doctorates; two decades later they still dominated, although the life sciences edged out the other two fields. The social sciences (including psychology) remained fairly constant at about 20 percent, humanities dropped from 20 percent to 10 percent, and education increased from about 15 percent to 25 percent, reflecting an increased professional orientation of graduate study.[54] The fields in which doctoral degrees are awarded have diversified tremendously. An already large number of about 150 at the end of the first World War grew to over 550 fields in 1960. In addition, forty-seven types of doctoral degrees besides the Ph.D. developed: e.g., doctor of education, doctor of social work, doctor of business administration, doctor of theology, doctor of arts.[55] A similar orientation to the demands of the marketplace is evident in master's degrees. Revealing a marked shift since 1965, roughly 85 percent of master's degrees reflect practitioner-oriented programs such as education (down from 40 percent to 30 percent), business (up from 7 percent to 23 percent), engineering (10 percent), and the health professions (about 6 percent), while only 16 percent were in research-oriented master's programs.[56]

The early 1970s brought an economic crisis that threatened even the strong research-training link of the sciences and the solid resource base of the most prominent research universities. An era of retrenchment, roughly between 1969 and 1975, began with a tightening academic labor market and inflation in the wider economy. Most important, the national government reduced funds to support the research infrastructure it had dramatically expanded in the postwar era. Between 1968 and 1971 the basic research budget fell over 10 percent in real terms.[57] Academic research expenditures contributed annually by the federal government declined from $5 billion in 1968 to $4.7 billion in 1974. The government's attention turned to short-term research, which would make scientific knowledge technologically relevant. As a result, cutbacks in funds meant that physical resources, such as equipment and campus buildings, were neglected.

As funds for academic science declined, so did support for graduate students; thus both became "victims of federal benign neglect."[58] Although doctoral degrees peaked in 1973 at 33,000, the government abruptly withdrew the bulk of its direct fellowship support to graduate students, especially in some of the larger programs of the National Institutes of Health. In the space of a few years, from 1968 to 1970, 57,000 fellowships and traineeships fell to 41,000.[59] As graduate fellowships were "cut back too fast and too far," a series of national reports conducted on the finance of graduate education cited the destabilizing effects of "stop-and-go" federal funds and the disadvantages of smaller-scale fellowships.[60] In place of the wider base of support, the government compelled the bulk of doctoral students to get direct support from loans and indirect support from short-term R&D assistantships.

Institutions responded with their own initiatives, with teaching assistantships and research assistantships drawing on institutional funds from endowments and tuition; public institutions drew from state revenues. Institutions also used their own funds to support research activities, including facilities and equipment improvement and stepped-up efforts to collaborate with industry. In seeking a broader base of funding in specialized areas of interdisciplinary and applied research, American universities have elaborated their organizational structures in the form of extradepartmental research units, with an increasing number of nonfaculty research personnel, who vary as to the extent of their involvement in graduate education.

Contemporary System of Graduate Education

Since the mid-1970s graduate education in the United States has grown to be an even larger and more diverse system. With an enterprise so vast, as the following chapter makes clear, there is a tremendous variation in the actual educational experiences of graduate students in the same fields at different institutions as well as across departments within the same institution. But that variation occurs within a larger framework of system sponsorship that is subject to the impact of shifts in primary funding sources.

The historical patterns that crystallized in the quarter-century immediately after World War II have remained prominent in the past two decades: the production of doctorates and the production of research are concentrated at the leading universities in the American system, although some decentralization of doctoral production has occurred at the base. Graduate education and postdoctoral work continued to be supported more heavily in the sciences than in other fields.

Master's degree programs have grown enormously since the mid-1970s, with education and business alone accounting for one half of the total annual degrees conferred.[61] Although the majority of Ph.D. recipients (over 80 percent) hold master's degrees, increasingly the latter is taken as a terminal degree earned. Master's degrees in the professions account for 85 percent; the other 15 percent are in liberal arts.[62] Many of these master's programs, which are the highest degrees given in certain fields, do not fit into a linear sequence with undergraduate or doctoral programs. Some are in problem-centered areas, such as urban planning, social work, or counseling. Others are more directly linked to the demands of the marketplace, such as technically oriented computer science or nursing sciences. Unlike doctoral programs, the explicit focus of these programs is on training the student for practice rather than for theory or knowledge development. Consistent efforts have been made by the Council of Graduate Schools, which represents four hundred higher education institutions, urging standardization of masters' degree programs.[63]

Overall enrollment in master's and doctoral programs totaled over 1.5 million students by the end of the 1980s, accounting for about 10 percent all higher education enrollments in the United States. Roughly one third of all science and engineering students are not U.S. citizens and hold only temporary visas; in some fields such as mathematics, engineering, and computer science, foreign students were over 40 percent of the graduate enrollment and about two thirds of postdoctoral appointments in engineering.[64]

The distinctive American model for doctoral education has remained the same. Students begin with a few years of prescribed course work, classes, and seminars led by a faculty member. Passing examinations marks advancement to candidacy, when students undertake a dissertation that reflects original research under the guidance of a faculty committee. In the past decade, across the disciplines, doctoral students are taking longer to complete their programs, averaging 6.8 registered years, with humanities taking about eight years and engineering less than six years.[65]

During the Ph.D. program, across all fields, students and faculty establish some kind of apprenticeship relationship that is often formalized and tied to a form of financial support. Teaching assistantships are standard. Research assistantships, largely tied to federally sponsored research projects, are most prominent in the sciences. More than one position may be held at a time, although the convention is not to exceed half-time employment in order not to interfere with progress toward the degree. As we shall see in greater detail in chapter 8, in the sciences, where research is laboratory-intensive, a graduate student may work alongside or be closely supervised by a faculty advisor; the dissertation may arise as one piece of a faculty research project. In the humanities, where research is library-intensive, a student is more likely to work independently with infrequent contact with faculty supervisors or even graduate student peers.

Changes in the funding of graduate education and research during the 1970s and 1980s appear to have altered significantly the nature of the research-training experience. When the national government eliminated the bulk of its fellowship programs, it reduced support of graduate education as an intrinsically worthwhile activity and instead linked it more directly to the production of research. The funding base became centered more on research assistantships embedded in short-term academic research projects, supplemented by a variety of loan programs. The impact of changes in the funding mechanisms has been most evident in the research training experiences of Ph.D. students in the sciences.

One set of concerns focuses on the lengthening of time to completion. Students acquire more loan indebtedness the longer they defer employment and become discouraged from the loss of momentum. In an effort to speed up the process, several programs across the country are reducing requirements for course work so that students begin working on their dissertations earlier. The University of Chicago, for example, instituted a reduced course work policy in 1982 in order, a university report said, to encourage students "to engage in their doctoral research as quickly, as clearly, and as self-consciously as possible," which will lead to a "healthier emphasis on the research stage of graduate student work."[66] The need for such a change is especially apt for the humanities, where the prior tendency has always been to handle knowledge changes cumulatively, with increasing amounts of material incorporated into graduate course work; in the sciences (for example, physics and biological sciences) the faculty revamp the curricula every few years instead. Along similar lines, the expectations for the dissertation are being revised, especially in the sciences, including economics, where shorter publishable articles are more important than a long treatise.[67]

Such changes may also reflect the recognition that many Ph.D.'s do not end up in research settings, or, if on an academic path, they tend to teach in a nonresearch university, thus rendered "forgotten scientists."[68] Even though those institutions offer the master's as the highest degree, they employ research-oriented faculty who earned doctorates from the country's leading research universities. As a case in point, San Diego State University is now encouraging research activity of its faculty through several mechanisms, including release time from teaching, summer funding, travel funds, graduate student assistantships, and so on.[69] Although it is not chartered as a research university nor is it doctoral granting, that institution is attempting to raise its research profile.

A second set of concerns focuses on the nature of student-faculty relationships during research training, especially for students in the sciences. The historical ideal envisioned a student working "at the bench" with a mentor. Since sponsored research has become the medium for supervision and potential collaboration, there is some critical concern that faculty have become more like project managers and administrators rather than mentor-professors, and that students are being supervised in a more directive manner, treated like employees and technicians rather than as apprentices. As a sociologist of science suggests, "the roles of faculty member (mentor) and principal investigator (employer) are becoming inconsistent, straining the incumbents. Principles and practices that the *mentor* would prefer are inconsistent with the needs of the scientist as *employer*."[70]

Graduate student research assistants face the exigencies of an increasingly competitive arena of research support: time schedules of short-term project grants mean less leeway for mistakes; less available grant money means more competition and pressure to produce better results; sharing capital-intensive instrumentation means long hours of work, often in other cities; increased size of research teams entails perfecting a technique on one part of a project rather than completing an entire project from beginning to end; and time spent in research is valued over time spent in the "burden" of teaching younger graduate students or undergraduates. The arrangements emphasize efficiency and productivity, which promote an organizational climate of a factory floor, or a "quasi-firm," rather than a learning arena.[71]

In the context of efforts to reduce the federal deficit, the Tax Reform Act in 1986 included a provision to tax stipends associated with research and teaching assistantships that had previously been excluded from income tax. In addition to requiring technical changes in the administration of financial assistance, this change has been cited by concerned scholars and practitioners as another sign that graduate students are increasingly conceived of as workers producing short-term R&D rather than as longer-term national investments whose advanced study and training is inherently worthy of support. Although universities and their representatives lobbied on behalf of themselves and their graduate students to have this legislation amended, the outcome was to deem as taxable income the assistantship stipends but not fellowships and tuition awards.

Other signs that graduate students have become more like academic laborers are evident in campus controversies that surface for public discussion, especially on campuses where graduate students have unionized. In some cases students perceive and faculty admit that advanced students are kept on in laboratories longer than is necessary for their training because of their productive contributions. In other cases disputes over academic authorship and ownership of intellectual property appear. The tensions are heightened with the blurring of boundaries in university-industry collaboration: if the exploitation of students for a faculty member's academic advancement is historically grounded in the university research system, it is another matter for a professor to profit financially from a student's work on a commercial venture.[72]

One organizational arrangement to mitigate these tensions is to expand the structure of research training. Moving away from a short-term, product-oriented conception of graduate training, the longer-term professional development of the student can be made explicit, as in science fields where postdoctoral positions have become the norm. In fact, it is now a necessary one-to-three-year component of research training after the doctorate in such fields as physics and biological sciences. The "postdoc" position is generally seen as an attractive opportunity to begin publishing and to refine research skills in a market that is increasingly competitive for both industrial and academic positions. Across the country in 1986 there were an estimated 24,000 postdocs, 90 percent of whom are located in the top one hundred universities and 30 percent in the top ten. One year later the number rose to 25,300, a 5 percent increase.[73] Even if the expansion of postdoctoral training has been praised mainly as a way of enabling young scientists to enhance their expertise and to gain a competitive edge, it may also have a hidden value for the graduate education and research system by providing a

rationale for graduate students to patiently climb a longer ladder.

Another feature of the university research system that mitigates these tensions is widespread loan assistance programs. In compensating for the reduction in fellowship support, loans increased substantially in one decade alone, from 15 percent in 1974 to 44 percent in 1984 of all students enrolled in graduate programs.[74] In the latter year over 500,000 students working on graduate degrees borrowed $2 billion from the federal government in guaranteed student loans.[75] Graduate students also contributed more self-support, especially in the nonscience fields.

Indeed, the finance of graduate education entails major policy issues, with the quality of education and training at stake. Strains have been severe in the humanities and social sciences, where there has been little or no federal support. They have also increased in the sciences and engineering over the past fifteen years with the decline in federal funding of various types of studentships. Graduate education continues to be federally supported in an ad hoc and largely indirect fashion. The largest potential funding base, that of the national government, is essentially unstable. Professors are under pressure to develop lean research budgets, while at the same time including salaries for students. The trends in government financing during the 1970s and 1980s suggest a need to examine more closely what material conditions are required to sustain effective research training in universities as well as to consider what arrangements can safeguard the autonomy and creativity of institutions, faculty, and students alike.

Contemporary System of Organized Research

Research in the United States is performed in a variety of organizational settings: intramural government laboratories, industrial laboratories, nonprofit research institutes, and universities. Shifting patterns of research sponsors and research performers over the past two decades point to two themes. First, the involvement of government and, increasingly, industrial sponsors has resulted in a blurring of boundaries, if not purposes, between academic researchers and external sponsors. Second, the proportion of basic research done in university settings may decline, unless industrial sponsorship replaces the federal involvement. Such contemporary trends in the organization of research have implications for the research training component of graduate education.

Of the total $130 billion national R&D effort in 1986, about one half ($55 billion) was provided by the federal government and about one half ($60 billion) by industry.[76] Most R&D funds go toward development. Federal funds of $14.5 billion went for basic research, making the national government the largest sponsor, at about two thirds, in this category; industry was second largest sponsor at about $3 billion; and higher education institutions themselves were third at $1.5 billion.

The national government itself also performs about 10 percent of the country's R&D effort and employs 8 percent of the scientists and engineers.[77] Located in government laboratories, the amount of basic research conducted by the federal government ranks second to universities. Although generally perceived to be less effective than university labs in generating high-quality basic research, a few labs stand out as first rate, such as the National Institutes of Health (NIH), which allocates 15 percent of its research funds to intramural researchers on its own "campus."[78]

In contrast to government laboratories, industry performs about three quarters of the total national R&D effort and employs 75 percent of all engineers and 50 percent of all scientists.[79] But as performers of basic research, industry ranks third behind university and government labs. Compared to other countries, industry's share of basic research in the United States is greater than industry's share in France but less than in Japan. Especially in American biotechnology research, small firms play a big role.

Nonprofit research institutes now perform about 3 percent of the total national R&D effort.[80] Several kinds of institutes fall into this classification, including applied research institutes (Stanford Research Institute), operating foundations (Institute for Advanced Study), endowed institutes (Brookings Institution, Sloan Kettering), and project institutes (Institute for Cancer Research, Bureau of Social Science Research).[81] Some institutes have merged with or converted into universities; others have acquired the right to award degrees: the Mellon Institute merged with the Carnegie Institute of Technology to form Carnegie Mellon University; the Woods Hole Oceanographic Institute in Massachusetts became a doctoral-granting enterprise.[82] Some institutes managed by universities that have been deeply involved in research sponsored by the Department of Defense have had to sever their university connections: SRI from Stanford, Electronics Research Laboratories from Columbia, and Draper Laboratory from Massachusetts Institute of Technology.[83] A closely related setting consists of federally funded R&D centers that together perform about 3 percent of national R&D.[84] Funded directly to meet the particular needs of a federal agency, such as the Department of Energy or the Air Force, many of these centers are administered, or hosted, by universities or nonprofit institutions.

Universities perform about one half of all basic research. Sponsored research resources are concentrated: the top one hundred institutions account for over 80 percent of all academic R&D funds, the top fifty over 60 percent, the top ten over 20 percent. The distribution of academic R&D across fields has remained essentially the same over the past two decades, with the life sciences consistently receiving the largest share ($4.5 billion in 1987) of federal obligations for basic research and the physical sciences receiving the next largest share ($2 billion). The behavioral and social sciences have seen a decline from $1 billion in 1972 to $.78 billion in 1987.[85]

Whether basic research is done in academic or nonacademic settings makes a difference in programmatic autonomy. Usually, basic research is ideologically grounded in the norms of academic science, where professionals have autonomy to choose and conduct research projects, to communicate extensively with domestic and international colleagues, and to compete in a system of peer review. Universities ostensibly do research with a greater degree of independence than government or industry, which have more explicit political and commercial interests.

The organization of research in university settings has historically been anchored in the departmental structure, where departmental faculty work as both individual investigators and mentors to their advanced graduate students in the department's degree programs. The major persistent exception to this mode of organization in the contemporary period is the organized research unit (ORU).

ORUs are academic units outside departments and lacking degree-granting status. Prior to the twentieth century, ORUs were primarily observatories and museums, but in the post-World War II expansion of academic research, ORUs proliferated to meet new societal demands for research that did not correspond to instructional areas outlined by departments or that was disproportionate to departments in magnitude and expense. Funded by the national government, state governments, industry, and foundations, ORUs have extended university research into interdisciplinary, applied, and capital-intensive endeavors.[86] By the end of the 1980s, there were over two thousand of them on American campuses: they continued to emerge in new fields of biotechnology, microelectronics, material sciences, and artificial intelligence.

While the presence of external funds from a sponsor is often the impetus for a proposed ORU, other criteria include the presence of a critical mass of faculty and the availability of administrative support. Some ORUs even have explicit commitments to graduate education, such as graduate fellowships offered by the Stanford Humanities Center. ORUs can offer important advantages for graduate education. Intellectually, they can mediate between the world of disciplinary training and real world needs and problems.[87] Practically, they can provide dissertation support and stipends for graduate students. They may make available more and better research equipment. Finally, as an indirect benefit to graduate students, they employ specialists (postdoctoral or nonfaculty researchers) in a temporary home, akin to the departmental home, in which graduate students can participate.

The administration of research and training in ORUs evokes a new set of challenges, as it is increasingly incompatible with departmental organization. Full-time nonfaculty research personnel may supervise graduate student research assistants but do not have faculty status.[88] Generally, students and younger faculty want the opportunity to work in ORU settings,

with trained researchers and up-to-date equipment. Older department-based faculty and administrators may feel threatened that these centers draw intellectual, organizational, and economic vitality away from departmental graduate programs and thereby jeopardize the continued viability of various departments. Not only do faculty loyalties become divided between organizational units, but budgets for research are overseen by different managers than those who handle departmental instructional budgets. Thus, a significant component of research training ends up staffed and financed by complex administrative arrangements in which faculty allocations and budget allocations may no longer be congruent with the actual practice of department-based graduate education. In short, the actual research training activity of graduate education may become organizationally less visible as it increasingly falls between the lines of departmental organization.

In recent years ORUs have become a highly visible and controversial receptacle for forthcoming industrial funds, especially as federal initiatives have been launched to encourage industrial contributions for larger-scale operations on campuses. Beginning with the mid-1970s, the NSF established the Industry-University Cooperative Research Projects; again in the late 1980s, NSF promoted proposals for engineering Research Centers as well as Science and Technology Centers at universities. These programs were to be funded initially by congressional appropriations and to be gradually weaned from NSF funds through industrial contributions. Generating controversy across these programs was an explicit orientation for universities to aid in the nation's economic competitiveness.

Graduate education and research are affected in mixed ways by these kind of initiatives that combine—or seek to replace—federal support with industrial sponsorships. Resources become not only more concentrated but less flexible, for once a center is established it has to be fed. Moreover, industrial sponsorship, whether formally arranged in these kinds of ORUs or as informal collaboration, carries some potential constraints in terms of the research process (for example, secrecy) and the product (for example, agreements on patents). However, by favoring new interdisciplinary and applied sciences and by bringing to the campus research personnel to staff those facilities, industrial sponsors provide graduate students with exposure to timely problems, to state-of-the-art research and technique, and to internships that are job placement opportunities in industry, and they provide faculty with supplemental income.[89]

Attracting some university administrators and researchers to industrial collaboration or sponsorship is the recognition of a formidable problem: how will universities sustain the material conditions required for first-class, capital-intensive science? Direct appeals by universities to the federal government have brought limited results. With much lobbying on the part of university representatives, the federal government has reluctantly agreed to sponsor some of the rebuilding and replacement of campus research facilities and equipment that was neglected throughout the 1970s and insufficient as science became more capital-intensive in the 1980s. Both the NIH and the NSF participated in this revitalization through regular research grants and center grants.[90]

Another strategy for universities to recover the enormous costs incurred in campus research has been to renegotiate the indirect cost rate for overhead on research grants, although university administrators, campus-based researchers, and the federal agencies have been struggling to reconcile their conflicting interests. The indirect cost rate is a mechanism for distributing among sponsors and research projects the indirect costs the institution incurs through lighting, heat, libraries, and general maintenance of the campus. Since a university wants to recoup the maximum possible and the researcher wants as much as possible for the research process itself, administrators and researchers disagree. Universities vary considerably in their indirect cost rates, from Stanford University at over 75 percent to leading state universities at around 50 percent. The government wants more adequate justification of university expenses.[91] Underlying these discussions is a widespread perception that instrumentation in university labs compares poorly to government or commercial labs and the conviction that a decline in quality of instrumentation in research universities may cause a decline in research productivity of aca-

demic scientists as well as in the first-rate training opportunities for graduate students.

Overall, the concern is whether universities will be able to respond to interdisciplinary research and research training without reducing the strength of traditional, disciplinary graduate education. The fear is that if universities do not make, as put by Kenneth Hoving, "some realistic accommodation . . . an increasingly large portion of basic research and academic activity which is necessary to the quality of (graduate) education . . . will move outside the university structure."[92] In spite of universities' current role as the site of over one half of American basic research, an increase in proportional shares may occur in industry, especially as industry decides whether to collaborate with universities or to keep funds for its own laboratories. Ultimately, the concern is that academic departments would no longer be on the frontiers of research and that the best researchers would be moved away from graduate students, thereby jeopardizing the premise of the whole system—that "the best and the brightest" produce the best science and scientists at centers of excellence.[93]

Conclusion

Over the past century graduate education and organized research have become so interwoven in American higher education that graduate education and research have emerged as the foremost explicit raison d'etre for universities in the top tier, as an increasingly noble aim for lower tiers to emulate, and as an implicit professional imperative for faculty devoted to the production of new knowledge and the preparation of new generations of knowledge producers. This distinctive linkage between graduate education and research has occurred fundamentally in the most visible top layer of doctoral training, which has helped raise the country to international eminence in science and scholarship but at the same time has overshadowed the vitality of a wide array of thriving master's degree programs.

As with the evolution of other social institutions, the forces establishing this arrangement differ from those that sustain it. Historical evidence on the organization and sponsorship of graduate education and organized research reveals that the linkage of doctoral education and research in the leading modern universities was created out of opportunities from major societal changes: the use of scientific research for national defense and economic priorities, the rise in the research budget of the federal government for R&D allocations and for basic research funds, the plurality of funding agencies to help stabilize university autonomy, and a system of peer review to insure distribution of resources for the best science. Universities became the main performers of basic research, with an abundance of funds unconnected to their instructional budgets, and the federal government became the dominant external source for funds.

As historical circumstances changed, sustaining this linkage between government and universities proved to be a fundamental challenge for research universities. Although still in a system without centralized planning, an array of factors have enhanced the structural partnership. First, public and private universities alike have become heavily dependent on research funds from the federal government and other patrons, given the capital-intensive requirements for university expansion. Second, protecting the legacy of excellence in doctoral education, universities have an incentive to retain a dominant role in the country's basic research enterprise, for otherwise they would be unable to attract talented faculty and students for doctoral study. Third, the many federal funding agencies maintain their instrumental course, ever vigilant that universities keep their end of the bargain by contributing to the production of knowledge and the preparation of trained science and engineering personnel.

At the same time, however, a changing social and economic climate has strained the university-government linkage. During the 1970s and 1980s, shifts in organization and sponsorship of university research produced a context of greater uncertainty, as funding sources and amounts reflected changing perceptions of the appropriate role of the federal government in sponsoring research and research training. Despite the immense post-World War II surge of funds, the government has become an unstable base of economic and political support for university research and graduate education.

There may be powerful negative consequences in sustaining what now seems to be a problematic partnership. Two sets of policy concerns have been most prominent in this regard. The first characterizes a federal fiscal presence less as one of support and more as one of regulation. Most obvious for university researchers and their doctoral students are the ways in which rhythms of federal research funding have come to dominate not only the conduct of university research and research training but its content. The second set focuses on the patterns of distribution of research funds across institutions as well as fields of study. Although concentration of funds enhances more concentrated activity and ultimately knowledge advancement, the perennial concern is that the dispersion of funds required for maintaining a broader base of activity across campuses and disciplines does not appear to enhance the current science and technology agenda.

At both levels of campus and national policy discussions, much of the discourse centers on strategies for sustaining the linkage while simultaneously protecting the autonomy of higher education institutions and the professionals who work within them. From the university perspective, the drive for competitive advancement makes the leading one hundred institutions most vocal. As research performers and trainers of scientific personnel, universities have competed to sustain a share of basic research funds. This is the modern research imperative, the vehicle whereby universities protect if not advance their institutional mobility, for the institution which is not steadily advancing is certainly falling behind.[94] These institutions have consistently and aggressively competed for talented faculty and graduate students, while simultaneously seeking to preserve their autonomy through stabilizing a base of support from a plurality of sources in external sponsors and internal revenues. Through their own initiatives, they have created increasingly complex organizational structures in order to minimize the skewing of institutional priorities toward the economic incentives of short-term R&D sponsors.

Somewhat less vocal and certainly less visible internationally, the vast majority (seven hundred) of institutions engaged in graduate education at master's and doctoral levels emulate the model of the leading tier of research universities. If, at the leading institutions, all fields could be covered within the aim of undertaking more sponsored research and expanding Ph.D. production, the less elite institutions have a lower resource base in facilities, departmental funds, and critical masses of faculty and students and can invest their resources only in selected fields. Not until the 1970s did asserting a distinctive institutional mission become a strategy for gaining a competitive edge in specialized areas. These campuses have indeed become more research oriented, as they encourage and reward faculty to seek sponsored projects. Given the insufficient magnitude of scale, though, as the next chapter will reveal, these campuses are also vulnerable to the agendas of short-term R&D sponsors, in that fiscal support for applied research projects from government or industry provides a relatively larger boost to a smaller base, and thus more visibly may draw faculty away from their basic instructional missions.

Thus, throughout the American system, the contemporary era reveals an increasing disjuncture between nineteenth-century ideals and the exigencies of transforming campuses into modern research complexes. Universities have been continually challenged by an inherently unstable federal funding base that left direct support to doctoral education concentrated in the physical and life sciences, weak in the social sciences, and virtually nonexistent in the humanities. Particularly in the past two decades, the tension has become heightened as the national government has replaced many fellowships and traineeships with loans that are incurred by individual students, leaving the bulk of support as indirect, through research assistantships on R&D projects that strain the ideal mentor-apprentice research training relationships.

Substantial changes in the volume and nature of academic research as well as in the economic and political role of universities obscure the more significant issue: whether the support of graduate education is motivated by a desire to purchase short-term R&D labor or to make a long-term investment in the nation's research capability. During the 1970s and 1980s, the short-term view has been much in evidence among external sponsors, necessitating compensatory action by universities traditionally devoted to the production of knowledge for its own sake and to the effective training of future generations of scientists and scholars.

Notes

The author gratefully acknowledges research resources from the Spencer Foundation, editorial suggestions from Burton R. Clark, and research assistance from Ronald Opp.

1. Rosenzweig, "Rationale for a Federal Role," p. 11.
2. American Council on Education, *1986–87 Factbook on Higher Education*; Glazer, *Master's Degree*; Hauptman, *Students in Graduate and Professional Education*.
3. Crane, "Scientists at Major and Minor Universities," p. 713.
4. For the rise of modern American science, see Bruce, *Launching of Modern American Science*. For the emergence of the research university, see Geiger, *To Advance Knowledge*, and Veysey, *Emergence of the American University*. For graduate education, see Storr, *Beginnings of Graduate Education in America*, and Berelson, *Graduate Education in the United States*. For an analysis of their interdependence, see Ben-David, *Centers of Learning*.

The strategy for this analysis finds its conceptual underpinnings in the social theories of Durkheim and Weber. Specifically, there are four conceptual anchors: a Durkheimian notion of the division of labor process; a Weberian notion that beliefs and structures together determine change; a Weberian view on the causes and consequences of social stratification; and an institutional view that the establishment of a new classification of social institutions is a social and political process of acquiring legitimacy.
5. Bruce, *Launching of Modern American Science*, p. 335.
6. Ibid., p. 337.
7. Ibid., p. 335.
8. Wolfle, *Home of Science*, p. 4.
9. Veysey, *Emergence of the American University*, pp. 149, 168.
10. Ibid., pp. 318–319.
11. Hofstadter and Hardy, *Development and Scope of Higher Education in the United States*, pp. 44–45.
12. Berelson, *Graduate Education in the United States*, p. 33.
13. Mayhew, *Reform in Graduate Education*, p. 6; Ben-David, *Centers of Learning*, p. 61.
14. Ben-David, *Centers of Learning*, p. 102.
15. Geiger, *To Advance Knowledge*, p. 37.
16. Veysey, *Emergence of the American University*, p. 177.
17. Geiger, *To Advance Knowledge*, p. 19. The original AAU institutions were: California, Catholic, Chicago, Clark, Columbia, Cornell, Harvard, Johns Hopkins, Michigan, Pennsyl-

vania, Princeton, Stanford, Wisconsin, and Yale; they were joined by Illinois and Minnesota in 1907, and California Institute of Technology and Massachusetts Institute of Technology after World War I.

18. According to the Carnegie Classification (1987), the U.S. system may be differentiated vertically by sectors; roughly 800 institutions offer graduate programs of which the top 213 are distinguished for doing both doctoral education and federally sponsored research. The next sector consists of 595 comprehensive colleges and universities in which the master's degree is the highest level offered. NSF (1989) data for science and engineering doctorates in 1985–1986 show that the top sector of 213 universities produced 95 percent of the doctorates and 72 percent of the master's degrees. Within that sector the leading 104 produced 83 percent of the doctorates and 53 percent of the master's. The comprehensive sector awarded 1.2 percent of the doctorates and 23 percent of the master's.

19. Merton, "Matthew Effect in Science." The Matthew effect of the rich getting richer, as hypothesized by Merton, signifies a cumulative advantage in the allocation of rewards and resources, thereby enhancing one's already eminent position in the social system of science.

20. Veysey, *Emergence of the American University*, p. 312.

21. Trow, "Analysis of Status," p. 134.

22. DiMaggio and Powell, "Iron Cage Revisited." In this macrosocial theory of organizational change, institutional isomorphism is posited as part of a modernization in which the state and the professions come to replace bureaucratization as forces for rationalization.

23. Bruce, *Launching of Modern American Science*, pp. 329–334.

24. Rudolph, *American College and University*, pp. 425–427.

25. Berelson, *Graduate Education in the United States*; Geiger, *To Advance Knowledge*, especially pp. 140–173 for a thorough discussion of foundation giving and university-foundation relations in the interwar years.

26. Geiger, *To Advance Knowledge*, p. 166.

27. Rudolph, *American College and University*, p. 430.

As philanthropists became more prominent, some observers were uncomfortable, warning that these benefactors used their wealth to transform and redirect higher education through the funding of selected institutions. See Fosdick, *Adventure in Giving*. As a case in point, this was the procedure by which medical education, with its attention to basic biological and chemical science research, was established in its modern form. See Flexner, *Medical Education in the United States and Canada*; Brown, "Public Health in Impe-

rialism," Sacks, *Caring by the Hour*, and Starr, *Social Transformation of American Medicine*, p. 120. Other observers were uncomfortable with philanthropic support, for its potential compromise of the ideals of scholarship toward business interests, including Veblen (1918) in his famous treatise, *Higher Learning in America*.

28. Rudolph, *American College and University*, p. 427.

29. See Geiger, *To Advance Knowledge*, especially p. 175 and p. 192. For a description of the role of private industrial support in the interwar years, see pp. 174–245.

30. Ibid., p. 262.

31. Bruce, *Launching of Modern American Science*, pp. 301–305 and 315–317. Quotation is on p. 315.

32. Geiger, *To Advance Knowledge*, pp. 13, 100, 165, 256. Geiger states that these elites met in committees of the NRC, on the boards of the Carnegie and Rockefeller philanthropies, and as trustees of recipient [universities]. . . . Such gatherings brought together the elite of American science, the heads of the philanthropic world, research directors and corporate leaders of the major research-based firms of the day . . . [with] the enduring effect of bringing industry, foundations, and universities into closer cooperation and of consecrating the direction of science policy to a private elite that represented the leadership of those institutions. The federal government, which the NRC had originally been meant to advise, was pushed into the background during the 1920s. (p. 100).

33. Ibid., p. 255.

34. All historical data here are from Starr, *Social Transformation of American Medicine*, especially p. 193.

35. Wolfle, *Home of Science*, p. 110, and Dickson, *The New Politics of Science*.

36. Rivlin, *Role of the Federal Government in Financing Higher Education*, p. 31.

37. Finkelstein, *American Academic Profession*, p. 24.

38. Geiger, *To Advance Knowledge*, p. 220.

39. Rivlin, *Role of the Federal Government in Financing Higher Education*, p. 47.

40. Dickson, *The New Politics of Science*.

41. Government-University-Industry Research Roundtable, "Science and Technology in the Academic Enterprise."

42. Ben-David, *Centers of Learning*, p. 119.

43. Government-University-Industry Research Roundtable, "Science and Technology in the Academic Enterprise."

44. Knight, et al. *Federal Government and Higher Education*, pp. 135–137.

45. The peer review system places responsibility for allocating funds with the science community. The criteria used for judging scientific merit are: research performance competence,

intrinsic merit of research, utility or relevance of research, effect of research on the infrastructure of science and engineering, including research education and the manpower base. The latter two criteria are often brought in with a dual system of peer review, where the first stage entails technical review by a panel of experts and a second stage in which both scientists and lay representatives from government or industry evaluate the research in terms of broader priorities, such as geographic distribution. NIH uses the dual review system as does the NSF's Engineering Research Center program. For critical analysis of peer review and the conduct of science, see Chubin and Hackett, *Peerless Science*.

46. National Science Foundation, *Science and Technology Data Book*, p. 17.

47. Wolfle, *Home of Science*, pp. 118–120.

48. The national government has also shown a preference for supporting individuals rather than institutions, as the history of financial assistance reflects.

49. Coggeshall and Brown, *Career Achievements of NIH Postdoctoral Trainees and Fellows*; National Academy of Sciences, *Personnel Needs and Training for Biomedical and Behavioral Research*.

50. Berelson, *Graduate Education in the United States*; p. 30.

51. Berelson, *Graduate Education in the United States*; National Research Council, *Summary Report 1986*.

52. Department of Education and National Center for Education Statistics, *Digest of Educational Statistics 1989*; Glazer, *Master's Degree*.

53. National Research Council, *Century of Doctorates*, p. 4; Berelson, *Graduate Education in the United States*, p. 93; Ben-David, *Centers of Learning*, p. 110; National Science Foundation, unpublished data 1989.

54. National Research Council, *Summary Report 1986*.

55. Berelson, *Graduate Education in the United States*; p. 35; National Research Council, *Summary Report 1986*.

56. Glazer, *Master's Degree*.

57. Government-University-Industry Research Roundtable, "Science and Technology in the Academic Enterprise."

58. Kidd, "Graduate Education," p. 43.

59. Wolfle, *Home of Science*, p. 256.

One estimate is that funds for federal fellowships and traineeships alone were cut by one-third. The National Research Service Awards were cut dramatically, so that by 1983 there were 11,500 positions and by 1985 the awards were under $200 million, which was down 17 percent in constant dollars from 1971. Given inflation and the substantial increase overall in national research expenditures, these cutbacks were devastating (National Academy of Sciences, *Personnel Needs and Training for Biomedical and Behavioral Research*, p. 8).

In the past, humanities fellowships have come from foundations, the leader being the Andrew W. Mellon Foundation. However, some major privately funded programs have been eliminated, including the Ford Foundation (which had 600 graduate fellowships), the Woodrow Wilson Foundation (which over twenty years supported 18,000 graduate students in humanities and social sciences), and the Danforth Foundation (which over twenty-eight years supported 3,500 students in the same fields). (See Bowen, "Graduate Education".)

60. See Kidd, "Graduate Education."

The major national reports exploring the federal role in graduate education were by the Carnegie Commission in 1968 and again in 1973, the National Science Board in 1969, President's Task Force on Higher Education in 1970 and in 1973, and the National Board on Graduate Education in 1973.

One of the earlier reports, by Alice Rivlin (1969), noted problems in the dependence on federal support, quoted in Kidd, "Graduate Education" (p. 46):

The project system has many advantages and should be retained, but it has also generated some imbalances: a) decreases in professors' loyalty to institutions; b) inadequate attention to teaching; c) relatively weak support of humanities and social sciences; d) overconcentration of federal support in relatively few institutions.

61. Glazer, *Master's Degree*.

62. Ibid.

63. Mayhew, *Reform in Graduate Education*, pp. 81–82.

64. National Science Board, *Science and Engineering Indicators*, p. 44; National Research Council, *Foreign and Foreign-Born Engineers*. In 1987 foreign citizens constituted 43 percent of the science/engineering postdocs, 41 percent of those in the sciences, and 65 percent of those in engineering, as well as about 45 percent of all full-time graduate student enrollments, which is up from 36 percent in 1977 (National Science Foundation, 1989).

65. National Research Council, *Summary Report 1986*.

66. University of Chicago, "Report of the Commission on Graduate Education," p. 126.

67. Berger, "Slowing Pace to Doctorates Spurs Worry on Filling Jobs," *New York Times* (May 3, 1989): A-1.

68. Drew, *Strengthening Academic Science*; and Drew, "Finest Science Not Always Found in Fanciest American Universities."

69. Wanberg, "Encouraging Research and Scholarship," pp. 1–2.

70. Hackett, "Science as a Vocation in the 1990s," p. 267.
71. Etzkowitz, "Entrepreneurial Scientists and Entrepreneurial Universities in American Academic Science."
72. Kenney, *Biotechnology*.
73. National Science Foundation, *Academic Science/Engineering Graduate Enrollment and Support*, p. e-21; National Science Foundation, unpublished data, 1989.
74. Hauptman, *Students in Graduate and Professional Education*.
75. Ibid., p. 57.
76. National Science Board, *Science and Engineering Indicators*; National Science Foundation, *National Patterns of Science and Technology Resources*.
77. National Science Foundation, *National Patterns of Science and Technology Resources*, p. 1.
78. Newman, *Higher Education and the American Resurgence*.
79. National Science Foundation, *National Patterns of Science and Technology Resources*, p. 1.
80. Ibid.
81. Orlans, *The Non Profit Research Institute*, pp. 3–4.
82. Ibid., pp. 152–157.
83. Ibid., pp. 148–149.
84. National Science Foundation, *National Patterns of Science and Technology Resources*, p. 1.
85. National Science Foundation, *Science and Technology Data Book*; Gerstein et al., *The Behavioral and Social Sciences*, p. 251.
86. Geiger, "Organized Research Units." Research units can also be established by federal agencies where ordered to do so by Congress, bypassing peer review procedures. This type of "pork barrel" funding is criticized because it is not based on scientific merit. The White House has generated a "hit list" questioning the worthiness of apparently trivial projects, ridiculing some campus-based operations, such as the Berry Research Center at Rutgers University, a poultry laboratory at the University of Arkansas, and a center for wildflower research at New Mexico State University. See Cordes, "Berry Research Center at Rutgers, Ridiculed by Reagan, Will Get Funds After All."
87. Friedman and Friedman, "Organized Research Units in Academe Revisited."
88. The term "unfaculty" or "non-faculty" has been applied to academic researchers to signify their marginal status. See Kerr's *Uses of the University*. Estimates of the number of nonfaculty researchers now employed in universities range from 5,000 (National Science Board, *Science and Engineering Indicators—1987*) to over 30,000 (Kidd, "New Academic Positions"; Teich, "Research Centers and Non-Faculty Researchers," Government-University-Industry Research Roundtable, "Science and Technology in the Academic Enterprise").

Several issues concerning their rights and responsibilities have surfaced: Should they be permitted to participate in campus governance? Should they be granted tenure or its equivalent? Should they have principal investigator status? Should they permitted to chair dissertation committees or even to be a committee member at all? See Kruytbosch, *Organization of Research*; Kidd, "New Academic Positions"; Teich, "Research Centers"; Smith and Karlesky, *State of Academic Science*, p. 237.
89. National Science Board, University-Industry Research Relationships; Irwin Feller, "University-Industry Research and Development Relationships."
90. Smith, *State of Graduate Education*; National Science Board, *Science and Engineering Indicators*, p. 84.
91. Association of American Universities, *Report on Instrumentation Needs*, p. 20.

  The perception by government and researchers is that administrative expenses were inadequately justified (Donchin and Wilson, "Negotiating the Indirect Cost of Research). The role of indirect cost in peer review is a matter of controversy. There is currently a dual system. At NIH the proposal review panels see only the direct cost; whereas at NSF the total amount is shown. If a university's ICR increases, and a multiyear award has a fixed total, the NSF grant would remove funds from the researcher's project operating budget, while the NIH grant puts pressure on the federal agencies to make up the difference. It is not surprising that the federal government prefers the NSF approach because it puts pressure on the researchers and universities to keep the indirect cost rate down (White House Science Council, *Renewed Partnership*, p. 220).
92. Hoving, "Interdisciplinary Programs, Centers and Institutes," p. 2.
93. Kruytbosch, "Future Flow of Graduate Students into Scientific Research"; Smith, *State of Graduate Education*, pp. 29–30.
94. Rudolph, *American College and University*, p. 329, quoting James Angell, president of the University of Michigan in 1871. On the possible negative consequences of embracing research, see Gumport, "Research Imperative."

Bibliography

American Association for the Advancement of Science. *Research and Development FY 1990, Report XIV*. Washington, D.C., 1989.

American Council on Education. *1986–87 Factbook on Higher Education*. New York: Macmillan, 1987.

Association of American Universities. *Report on Instrumentation Needs*. Washington, D.C., 1980.

Ben-David, Joseph. *Centers of Learning: Britain, France, Germany, United States.* New York: McGraw-Hill, 1977.

Berelson, Bernard. *Graduate Education in the United States.* New York: McGraw-Hill, 1960.

Bowen, William G. "Graduate Education: Prospects for the Future," *Educational Record* (Fall 1981): 20–30.

Brademus, John. "Graduate Education: Signs of Trouble and Erosion," *Change* 16, no. 2 (March 1984): 8–11.

Brown, E. Richard. "Public Health in Imperialism: Early Rockefeller Programs at Home and Abroad," *American Journal of Public Health* 66, no. 9 (1976): 897–903.

Bruce, Robert V. *The Launching of Modern American Science: 1846–1876.* New York: Alfred A. Knopf, 1987.

Carnegie Foundation for the Advancement of Teaching. *A Classification of Institutions of Higher Education.* Princeton, N.J.: Princeton University Press, 1987.

Chubin, Daryl, and Edward Hackett. *Peerless Science.* New York: SUNY Press, 1990.

Clark, Burton R. *The Higher Education System: Academic Organization in Cross-National Perspective.* Berkeley, Los Angeles, London: University of California Press, 1983.

Coggeshall, Porter, and Prudence Brown. *The Career Achievements of NIH Postdoctoral Trainees and Fellows.* NIH Program Evaluation Report by Commission on National Needs for Biomedical and Behavioral Research Personnel and Institute of Medicine. Washington, D.C.: National Academy Press, 1984.

Cordes, Colleen. "Berry Research Center at Rutgers, Ridiculed by Reagan, Will Get Funds After All." *Chronicle of Higher Education* (July 20, 1988): A17–A19.

Crane, Diana. "Scientists at Major and Minor Universities: A Study of Productivity and Recognition." *American Sociological Review* 30 (1966): 699–714.

Department of Education and National Center for Education Statistics. *Digest of Education Statistics 1989.* Washington, D.C.: U.S. Government Printing Office, 1989.

Dickson, David. *The New Politics of Science.* Chicago: University of Chicago Press, 1984.

DiMaggio, Paul, and Walter Powell, "The Iron Cage Revisited: Institutional Isomorphism and Collective Rationality in Organizational Fields." *American Sociological Review* 48 (April 1983): 147–160.

Donchin, Emanuel, and Linda Wilson. "Negotiating the Indirect Cost of Research." *American Psychology* 40, no. 7 (July 1985): 836–848.

Drew, David Eli. "Finest Science Not Always Found in Fanciest American Universities." *Los Angeles Times* (October 18, 1987): 3, 6.

_____. *Strengthening Academic Science.* New York: Praeger, 1985.

England, J. Merton. *A Patron for Pure Science: The National Science Foundation's Formative Years, 1945–1957.* Washington, D.C.: National Science Foundation, 1982.

Etzkowitz, Henry. "Entrepreneurial Scientists and Entrepreneurial Universities in American Academic Science." *Minerva* XXI, no. 2/3 (1983): 198–233.

Feller, Irwin. "University-Industry Research and Development Relationships." Paper prepared for the Woodlands Center for Growth Studies for Conference on Growth Policy in the Age of High Technology: The Role of Regions and States, 1988.

Finkelstein, Martin. *The American Academic Profession.* Columbus: Ohio State University Press, 1984.

Flexner, Abraham. *Medical Education in the United States and Canada.* New York: Carnegie Foundation, 1910.

Fosdick, Raymond. *Adventure in Giving: The Story of the General Education Board, a Foundation Established by John D. Rockefeller.* New York: Harper & Row, 1962.

Frances, Carol. "1984: The Outlook for Higher Education," *AAHE Bulletin* 37, no. 6 (February 1985): 3–7.

Friedman, Robert S., and Renee C. Friedman. "Organized Research Units in Academe Revisited." In *Managing High Technology: An Interdisciplinary Perspective,* ed. B. Mar, W. Newell, and B. Saxburg. North Holland: Elsevier Science Publishers, 1985. Pp. 75–91.

Geiger, Roger L. *To Advance Knowledge: The Growth of American Research Universities in the Twentieth Century, 1900–1940.* New York: Oxford University Press, 1986.

_____. "Organized Research Units: Their Role in the Development of University Research." *Journal of Higher Education* 61, no. 1 (January/February 1990): 1–19.

Gerstein, Dean, R. Duncan Luce, Neil Smelser, and Sonja Sperlich, eds. *The Behavioral and Social Sciences: Achievements.* Washington, D.C.: National Academy Press, 1988.

Glazer, Judith S. *The Master's Degree: Tradition, Diversity, Innovation.* ASHE-ERIC Higher Education Report No. 6. Washington, D.C.: Association for the Study of Higher Education, 1986.

Government-University-Industry Research Roundtable. "Science and Technology in the Academic Enterprise." Washington, D.C.: National Academy Press, 1989.

Gumport, Patricia J., "The Research Imperative." In *Culture and Ideology in Higher Education: Advancing a Critical Agenda,* ed. William Tierney. New York: Praeger, 1990. Pp. 87–105.

Hackett, Edward J. "Science as a Vocation in the 1990s." *Journal of Higher Education* 61, no. 3 (May/June 19909): 241–279.

Hauptman, Arthur M. *Students in Graduate and Professional Education: What We Know and Need to Know.* Washington, D.C.: Association of American Universities, 1986.

Hofstadter, Richard, and C. Hardy. *The Development and Scope of Higher Education in the United States.* New York: Columbia University Press, for the Commission on Financing Higher Education, 1952.

Hoving, Kenneth. "Interdisciplinary Programs, Centers and Institutes: Academic and Administrative Issues." Paper presented at the annual meeting of the Council of Graduate Schools. Washington, D.C., December, 1987.

Kenney, Martin. *Biotechnology: The University-Industrial Complex.* New Haven, Conn.: Yale University Press, 1986.

Kerr, Clark. *The Uses of the University.* New York: Harper & Row, 1963.

Kidd, Charles V. "Graduate Education: The New Debate." *Change* (May 1974): 43–50.

_____. "New Academic Positions: The Outlook in Europe and North America." In *The Research System in the 1980s: Public Policy Issues,* ed. John M. Logsdon. Philadelphia: Franklin Institute Press, 1982. Pp. 83–96.

Knight, Douglas, et al. *The Federal Government and Higher Education.* Englewood Cliffs, N.J.: Prentice-Hall, 1960.

Kruytbosch, Carlos. "The Future Flow of Graduate Students into Scientific Research: a Federal Policy Issue?" Paper presented at annual meeting of Council of Graduate Schools, Orlando, Florida, December 5–7, 1979.

_____. *The Organization of Research in the University: The Case of Research Personnel.* Ph.D. Dissertation. University of California, Berkeley, 1970.

Mayhew, Lewis B. *Reform in Graduate Education.* SREB Research Monograph No. 18. Atlanta: Southern Regional Education Board, 1972.

Merton, Robert K. "The Matthew Effect in Science." *Science* 159, no. 3810 (January 1968): 56–63.

Metzger, Walter P. "The Academic Profession in the United States." In *The Academic Profession: National, Disciplinary, and Institutional Contexts,* ed. Burton R. Clark. Berkeley, Los Angeles, London: University of California Press, 1987. Pp. 120–208.

National Academy of Sciences. *Personnel Needs and Training for Biomedical and Behavioral Research.* The 1985 Report of the Committee on National Needs for Biomedical and Behavioral Research Personnel and the Institute of Medicine. Washington, D.C.: National Academy Press, 1985.

_____. Panel on Science and Technology Centers. *Science and Technology Centers: Principles and Guidelines.* Washington, D.C. 1987.

National Research Council. *A Century of Doctorates: Data Analyses of Growth and Change.* Washington, D.C.: National Academy of Sciences, 1978.

_____. *Outlook for Science and Technology: The Next Five Years.* San Francisco: W. H. Freeman & Co. 1982.

_____. *Humanities Doctorates in the United States: 1985 Profile.* Washington, D.C.: National Academy Press, 1986.

_____. *The New Engineering Research Centers: Purposes, Goals and Expectations.* Report of Cross-Disciplinary Research Committee and Commission on Energy and Technical Systems. Washington, D.C.: National Academy Press, 1986.

_____. *Summary Report 1986: Doctorate Recipients from United States Universities.* Washington, D.C.: National Academy Press, 1987.

_____. *Foreign and Foreign-Born Engineers in the United States: Infusing Talent, Raising Issues.* Washington, D.C.: National Academy Press, 1988.

National Science Board. *University-Industry Research Relationships: Myths, Realities and Potentials.* Washington, D.C.: U.S. Government Printing Office, 1982.

_____. *Science and Engineering Indicators—1987.* Washington, D.C.: U.S. Government Printing Office, 1987.

National Science Foundation. *Federal Support to Universities, Colleges and Selected Nonprofit Institutions, FY 1985, Detailed Statistical Tables.* Washington, D.C.: January, 1987a.

_____. *Science and Technology Data Book, 1988.* No. NSF 87–317. Washington, D.C.: 1987b.

_____. *Academic Science/Engineering Graduate Enrollment and Support: Fall 1986, Detailed Statistical Tables.* Report No. 88–307. Washington, D.C., 1988a.

_____. *Proposal Review at NSF: Perceptions of Principal Investigators.* Report No. 88–4. Washington, D.C., February, 1988b.

_____. *Science/Engineering Degrees Awarded by Carnegie Category and Degree Level, 1985–86.* Unpublished data. Washington, D.C., 1989.

_____. Division of Science Resource Studies. *National Patterns of Science and Technology Resources, 1986.* Report No. 86–309. Washington, D.C., March 1986.

Newman, Frank. *Higher Education and the American Resurgence.* Princeton, N.J.: Carnegie Foundation for the Advancement of Teaching, 1985.

Office of Science and Technology Policy. White House Science Panel on the Health of the U.S. Colleges and Universities. *A Renewed Partnership.* Washington, D.C., February, 1986.

Orlans, Harold. *The Non Profit Research Institute.* New York: McGraw-Hill, 1972.

Queval, Francoise Alice. *The Evolution Toward Research Orientation and Capability in Comprehensive Universities. A Case Study: The California State University System.* Ph.D. Dissertation, University of California at Los Angeles, 1990.

Rivlin, Alice. *The Role of the Federal Government in Financing Higher Education.* Washington, D.C.: Brookings Institution, 1961.

Rosenzweig, Robert M. "The Rationale for a Federal Role in Graduate Education." *Change* 16, no. 2 (March 1984) 11–13.

Rudolph, Frederick. *The American College and University: A History*. New York: Vintage/Random House, 1962.

Sacks, Karen B. *Caring by the Hour: Women, Work and Organizing at Duke Medical Center*. Urbana and Chicago: University of Illinois Press, 1988.

Smith, Bruce L. R., ed. *The State of Graduate Education*. Washington, D.C.: Brookings Institution, 1985.

Smith, Bruce L. R., and Joseph Karlesky. *The State of Academic Science: The Universities in the Nation's Research Effort*. Vol. I. New York: Change Magazine Press, 1977.

Starr, Paul. *The Social Transformation of American Medicine*. New York: Basic Books, 1982.

Storr, Richard. *The Beginnings of Graduate Education in America*. Chicago: University of Chicago Press, 1953.

Teich, Albert H. "Research Centers and Non-Faculty Researchers: A New Academic Role." In *Research in the Age of the Steady-State University*, ed. Don Phillips and Benjamin Shen. AAAS Selected Symposium Series, no. 60. Washington, D.C.: American Association for the Advancement of Science, 1982. Pp. 91–108.

Trow, Martin A. "The Analysis of Status." In *Perspectives on Higher Education: Eight Disciplinary and Comparative Views*. ed. Burton R. Clark. Berkeley, Los Angeles, London: University of California Press, 1984. Pp. 132–164.

U.S. General Accounting Office. *University Funding: Assessing Federal Mechanism for University Research*. RCED 86–75. Washington, D.C., 1986.

University of Chicago. "Report of the Commission on Graduate Education," *University of Chicago Record* 16 (May 3, 1982): 2.

Veblen, Thorstein. *The Higher Learning in America: A Memorandum on the Conduct of Universities by Business Men*. New York: Sentry Press, 1918.

Veysey, Laurence. *The Emergence of the American University*. Chicago and London: University of Chicago Press, 1965.

Wangberg, Elaine. "Encouraging Research and Scholarship in Master's Only Institutions." Paper presented at the annual meeting of the Council of Graduate Schools, Washington, D.C., December 4, 1987.

Weber, Max. "Science as a Vocation." In *From Max Weber: Essays in Sociology*, ed. H. H. Gerth and C. Wright Mills. New York: Oxford University Press, 1958. Pp. 129–156.

Webster, David. "America's Highest Ranked Graduate Schools 1925–1982." *Change* 15, no. 4 (May/June 1983): 14–24.

_____. *Academic Quality Rankings of American Colleges and Universities*. Springfield, Ill.: Charles Thomas, 1986.

White House Science Council. *Renewed Partnership*. A Report of the White House Science Council on the Health of U.S. Colleges and Universities to the Office of Science and Technology Policy. Washington, D.C., 1986.

Wolfle, Dael. *The Home of Science: The Role of the University*. New York: McGraw-Hill, 1972.

Professionalism as Model and Ideology

ELIOT FREIDSON

Professionalism is under attack today. In the case of law, both radicals and liberals accuse the profession of elitism, discriminating against minorities in recruitment, training, and employment, and failing to protect the interests of the poor and the underprivileged. Its members are charged by, for example, Auerbach (1976) with being hired guns who protect the interests only of those able to pay them handsomely—namely, the rich and the powerful. Others, far more politically influential over the past decade or so, argue from the point of view of both the consumer movement and that of neoclassical economics that law is a business like any other and should be subjected to free competition in the market-place, unprotected by any special privileges. When the leaders of the profession invoke ethics and the values of professionalism, critics declare it a self-serving ideology that masks the reality of naked self-interest. At their most charitable, they consider professionalism to be an antiquated survival of an earlier day that has no relevance to the work of those called professionals today. Does the idea of professionalism have any relevance to us?[1] Is it at all defensible in light of the patent deficiencies of its institutions? What are the central issues of professionalism?

These questions cannot be answered easily because much of the debate about professionalism is clouded by unstated assumptions and inconsistent and incomplete usages. Most important, it is not informed by a systematic method of thinking. In this paper I hope to be able to clarify the issues by first distinguishing the characteristic limitations of the most common usages employed in the debate and noting the absence of a systematic analytic or ideal model of professionalism. I will then sketch such a model and discuss its relationship to the alternatives that underlie most attacks on the professions. Finally, I will discuss how the professions can be defended by the use of an analytic model and the implications an effective defense would have for the regulation of the professions.

Versions of Professionalism

The idea of profession or professionalism is developed in a number of distinctly different ways. First of all, it is a naturally created social label applied by lay people to a limited number of occupations that are considered to be in some way superior to ordinary occupations. This is the lay or folk idea (Becker, 1970, p. 92). It is a very loosely organized construct including within it criteria of relatively high prestige, extended, specialized training, and being paid for one's work. It might be useful to call it the *commonsense* idea of professionalism.

The commonsense idea of professionalism is developed passively: it is not elaborated, systematized or refined self-consciously so much as it grows out of everyday, social usage. Among professionals themselves, as Nelson and Trubek (1992) rightly argue, its substance varies with the arenas in which they work and their perspectives on them. When it is expanded and articulated by those who think about it self-consciously, it changes. In English-speaking nations, where professions have often been self-organized rather than created by the state, the idea of profession is elaborated by

"Professionalism as Model and Ideology," by Eliot Freidson, reprinted from *Professionalism Reborn: Theory, Prophecy, and Policy*, 1994, Polity Press.

their leaders in the course of making a claim to professional standing and used as a political tool for dealing with legislatures, the media, and the public at large. It is this larger policy arena that concerns me here. In that arena it is used to represent the profession not only to outsiders, but also to its own members. Commonsense usage is expanded to emphasize those characteristics of an occupation that justify special standing and privilege: it becomes a *profession's* portrayal of profession. Its content is determined largely by the political and ceremonial needs of the profession, and it is used primarily to advance and defend its position. While many versions emphasize the same things—for example, probity and public service—its ideological character, particularly in those substantive areas where the profession's internal politics of self-interest is threatened, precludes its development into a systematic and consistent whole.

Most of the debate that surrounds professions compares the actual performance of their members with either the ideological claims made by those supporting them or the commonsense expectations of the public and the commentators. Comparison between promise and performance reveals discrepancies that lead some critics, for example, Roth (1974), to reject the relevance of the idea of profession for understanding occupations with professional standing and others to attack professional standing itself. But what is rejected is professionalism either as a commonsense idea or as the professions' ideology, neither of which is developed as a model or analytic concept.

The needs of analysis are different from the needs of either commonsense thinking or ideology, for neither of the latter is impelled to create a systematic, logically coherent model of all essential characteristics based on a stated rationale or principle. Commonsense thinking need not concern itself with contradictions between various usages so long as it can segregate them from each other by invoking them in different contexts. Ideological and ceremonial conceptions of professionalism are shaped primarily by convenience and necessity and need include only those elements that defend threatened interests by denying accusations of damning characteristics and claiming laudable characteristics. This variation in emphasis on the part of those who speak for professions is clearly

shown by Solomon's analysis (1992) of the responses of leaders of the Bar to the crises they perceived over a thirty-year period.

By contrast, an analytic model attempts to seek out and resolve contradictions in order that it be logically consistent, and to include within its framework all that is necessary to create a systematic whole. It can be a model only when it does not attempt to describe reality and instead attempts to create a conceptual yardstick against which the empirical world can be compared. It attempts to create a systematic way of thinking about reality by picking out what is most consequential or important about it. It is most satisfying when its terms explain what they address, but if not, nonetheless shows plausibly how they hang together, how the model works.

Models of Professionalism

An important but often overlooked characteristic of analytic models in the social sciences is that, while they can be used in a purely neutral fashion, they can also be used prescriptively to represent what should exist and to guide practical efforts to realize them. They too can be ideologies employed to focus and organize political activity. Indeed, the most effective ideologies are those based on models that are sufficiently abstract to allow their application to a wide range of issues and circumstances. They are the sources both of systematic explanation of what is wrong with the world and of the guidelines by which wrong can be righted. The most persuasive attacks on professions come from those who themselves, explicitly or implicitly, are advancing an ideology based on an analytic model. For them, professions are attacked not merely for deficiencies in their performance but because their existence stands in the way of realizing another model.

The basic policy question underlying discussions of professionalism is *how the work of those we now call professionals should be organized and controlled.* Two quite different models for organizing work can be fairly easily recognized as the foundation for the most powerful criticism of professionalism today. One is advanced by neoclassical economists who attack professionalism as a barrier to what *should* exist— namely, individual freedom of workers in the market-place to offer whatever goods and services they desire and of consumers to decide to buy whatever they wish. The implicit and often explicit analytic model, which is wholly logical and utopian in character, is that of the perfectly free market. A quite different model is implicit in critiques of professionalism that stress order, efficiency, and comprehensive service: many conservative and some radical critics attack professionalism as a barrier to the attainment of a planned system of efficient services that would exist if it were subject to the centralized, monocratic control of either private corporate capital firms or (representing the people) agencies of the state. The underlying model is that of rational-legal bureaucracy.

There is in theory a third model implied by the critical position of some of those who criticize the professions for elitism and who advance an egalitarian ideal whereby all workers collectively, rather than managers or experts, determine what work is to be done, who is to do it, and how.[2] However, a plausible model for the exercise of collective or egalitarian control over work seems to presuppose a very simple division of labor in which all work is sufficiently unskilled to be easily learned, performed, or understood by all workers. There is no provision for the elaborate forms of specialized work that are characteristic of large, complex societies with an advanced standard of living.[3] Perhaps this theoretical difficulty is responsible for the paradox that much of the criticism of professionalism by radicals seems to advance the implicit alternative of the individualistic free market that underlies capitalism (e.g., Collins, 1979, pp. 197–204). Without presenting a plausible alternative model of their own, egalitarian and populist critics sustain their position solely by rhetoric.

There are, then, two clear alternative models for envisioning how professional services can be organized after eliminating professional privileges—Adam Smith's free market and Max Weber's monocratic, rational-legal bureaucracy. But no analogous model of professionalism figures in policy debates in the same way and on the same level of abstraction. Nonetheless, as Gordon and Simon (1992) note, professionalism can be conceived of as a distinct alternative to the free market and bureaucracy. Let me sketch out the essentials of such a model and then discuss its relevance to the debate.

An Ideal-Typical Model of Professionalism

Professionalism, like the free market and bureaucracy, represents a method of organizing the performance of work. It differs from the free market and from bureaucracy in that it revolves around *the central principle that the members of a specialized occupation control their own work*. By control, I mean that the members of the occupation determine the content of the work they do. Absolute control presupposes controlling the goals, terms, and conditions of work as well as the criteria by which it can be legitimately evaluated. By contrast, in the free market, consumer demand and the free competition of workers for consumer choice determine what work will be done, who shall do what work, how, and for how much pay. In bureaucracy, the market for labor and its products is institutionalized by rational-legal methods: the executives of organizations decide what product will be made or service offered, who shall make it, by what methods, and how it shall be offered to consumers.

Given this fundamental criterion of occupational control over work, one can build a model around the circumstances and characteristics that are necessary for occupations to gain and maintain such control. This requires attention to methods of controlling recruitment and training, entrance into the labor market under conditions that allow gaining a living from performing the work, and the procedures and criteria by which performance is organized and evaluated at work. In the professional model, both individual consumers and executives or managers (who are corporate or organizational consumers of labor) are excluded from such control. But since specialized knowledge and skill have no intrinsic connection with material (as opposed to cultural) capital or power, an occupation can fend off control by individual or corporate consumers of their work only by having power delegated to it by the state. An essential element of an analytic model of professionalism must therefore be to specify the activities and institutions that obtain the delegation of state power and subsequently maintain the conditions that assure its continuation.

In order to have power delegated to it, an occupation must be organized as an identifiable group: it cannot be a mere aggregation of individuals who claim to have the same set of skills. Only if it is an organized group, or if someone speaking for it manages to establish a corporate identity for its members, can it be dealt with collectively as a defined social category. The profession becomes an organized, corporate body either by the action of its own members independently of the state, as has commonly been the case in English-speaking nations, or by the actions of the state in creating specialized civil servants, as was more common in countries on the European continent. However the occupation becomes organized, those holding power must be persuaded that the body of knowledge and skill ascribed to the occupation is of such a special character as to warrant privilege. A number of claims have provided the ground for privilege—the functional importance of the body of knowledge and skill for the well-being of some significant segment of society, its intrinsic cultural importance, its unusually complex and esoteric character, and its superiority over the knowledge and skills claimed by competing occupations. Perhaps the most powerful claim is that there would be grave danger to the public if there were no control over those who offer their services—that the work provides access to "guilty knowledge" (Hughes, 1971, p. 288) that only those who can be trusted should have, and that serious consequences to the individual or the public at large can result from poor work. Central to effective claims is the idea that the profession's skills are so complex and esoteric that lay people are not well enough informed to be able to choose the competent over the incompetent, or to judge the quality of the work and even its outcome.

Beyond being persuaded that the occupation's body of knowledge and skill is worthy of special protection, the state must also be persuaded that the occupation as a corporate body is organized in such a way as to be able to control itself without abusing its privilege. The occupation must display institutional arrangements that make self-regulation plausible. Such arrangements include methods of recruiting new members selectively and restrictively by using screening criteria of ability or probity, and the maintenance of training institutions that are sufficiently standardized to permit assuming that all who complete their training successfully

will be of at least minimally acceptable competence. Additional assurance can be provided by requiring examinations of those who have completed their training before allowing them to work. Not only competence but also trustworthiness must be assured. The claim may be that recruits are selected who have "good character" in addition to potential competence. Codes of ethics may be created both to display concern for the issue and to provide members with guides to proper performance at work. Peer or collegial review to assure adequate performance at work may be established, as may regulatory institutions such as disciplinary committees. Floating above all such claims and activities, of course, is the ceremonial rhetoric of the leadership.

With their material interests secured by their control over their work and their protected position in the market-place, members of professions are able to develop a deep life-long commitment to and identification with their work: it becomes a "central life-interest" (Dubin et al., 1976). Concerned with advancing the discipline to which they have become committed, some will experiment, innovate and do research to expand their body of knowledge and skill both for its own sake and to find new practical applications for it. And to protect the integrity of their profession and its work, they will monitor and correct each other's work and discipline or even expel deviants when necessary.

Collegiality is a central element of the professional model (Waters, 1989), distinguishing professionalism from both the unfettered individualistic competition among workers in a free market and the formal hierarchies of rational-legal bureaucracy. Protection from competition by other workers aids in the development and maintenance of such collegiality, of course, but bitter competition between members themselves and between various specialties within the profession is always possible. In order to promote a professional community professions attempt to limit potentially divisive economic competition among their members by promulgating rules designed both to temper the spirit and substance of intra-professional competition and to establish a basic income floor for all its members. Established within the profession is an egalitarian, collegial atmosphere in which the greatest rewards are symbolic. As Parsons (1939) pointed out some time ago, professionals are not distinguished from people in business by being altruistic rather than self-interested. They, too, are self-interested, but their goal hinges more on gaining the symbolic rewards offered by their colleagues than on gaining a high income. Professional honors are accorded to those who advance the discipline by unusual achievements in its daily practice, in innovation, and in employing it to make an important contribution to the public good.

The Virtues of Professionalism

All this should sound familiar, for it is composed of bits and pieces freely borrowed from the major writers on the professions. But here those bits and pieces are brought together in a systematic way, and are not advanced as empirical facts. They are advanced as a model of the elements that together allow people to control their own highly specialized work in the spirit of service to others and the advancement of their discipline. The model specifies the conditions for professionalism, just as those of the free market and rational-legal bureaucracy specify the conditions for "universal opulence" (in Adam Smith's words) and formal rationality respectively. None of those models faithfully describes the way professions, markets, and bureaucracies actually perform. All are both ideological and analytic in character, advancing a desired ideal as well as an analytic construct.

Both economists and planners for state and corporate enterprises are well aware of the way empirical versions of the professional model obstruct their aims. Understandably, they have not dwelt on its virtues. Rather, they dwell on the virtues of what they claim will be gained by their own alternatives once the obstruction of professionalism is removed—more goods and services at lower prices and greater variety, more innovation, more predictability and reliability, greater efficiency, and the like. In contrast, those speaking for the professions today have employed a purely reactive, mostly commonsense and ceremonial defense.[4] But once one conceives of professionalism as a model, one can identify potential virtues that commonsense thinking alone overlooks.

The professional model is based on the democratic notion that people are capable of controlling themselves by cooperative, collective means and that, in the case of complex work, those who perform it are in the best position to make sure that it gets done well. It contains within it the assumption that when people can control their own work, and when their work, while specialized, is complex and challenging, they will be committed to it rather than alienated from it. According to the terms of the model, people find intrinsic value and interest in the work itself, which leads them to want to do it well. Furthermore, they constitute a kind of community in that they interact on grounds of strongly held common interests both in maintaining their professional position and in performing the work they do (Goode, 1957). Thus, they are alienated neither from their work nor from each other, nor, insofar as they believe they advance the good of others through their work, are they alienated from society. In short, as Gordon and Simon observe (1992), the ideal of professionalism provides many of the conditions that neutralize those specified in Marx's analysis of alienation from work under capitalism.

There is an additional activity of some importance that is encouraged by professionalism. It provides a milieu which encourages intellectual innovation—the development of new knowledge, skills, and ideas. But that innovation is not restricted merely to developing new modes of satisfying the perceived needs or demands of consumers in a marketplace, nor of those who control organizations. More important, because it is insulated from the need to be immediately responsive to the demands of others, it can go beyond the status quo and so depart from received opinion as to be revolutionary. The amount and kind of innovation that is possible are richer and more varied than would otherwise be the case. Research and theorizing that threaten the foundation of the practical work of normal science become possible, as does questioning the legitimacy of conventional practices and policies.

It may seem inappropriate to impute to professionalism the function of critical thinking and the creation of new ideas and knowledge. The former function is usually assigned to those whom social scientists call intellectuals, while the latter is assigned to scholars and scientists. To many, the professional is someone who merely applies available knowledge to the solution of practical problems—the practicing doctor and lawyer being prominent exemplars.[5] Intellectuals, scholars, and scientists, in turn, are not considered to be professionals. How one chooses to use a word is, of course, a somewhat arbitrary matter, but if we wish to take into account the institutions that make such activities as the "disinterested" pursuit of knowledge for its own sake possible on a regular and predictable basis by a large number of people, then we must include scholars and scientists among professionals. They could not exist without such institutions. Neither could most intellectuals.

Ever since the nineteenth century and the decline of the gentlemanly amateur scholar/scientists who relied on personal or patronage resources for their living, the institutions of professionalism, tied to universities, have been responsible for creating the shelters within which modern intellectuals, scholars, and scientists can do their work. Like the practicing professions, they control the recruitment, training, and employment of their members. Furthermore, most cannot make a living by scholarship or research any more than most intellectuals can do so by their writing. The university teaching jobs that they control provide them with their living. Those jobs require daily concern with the issues of scholarship and research and provide the free time in which to pursue rather than merely teach them. Following Parsons (1969), then, I would include scholars and scientists among those occupations today that resemble the ideal model of professionalism.

There is more to it than including scholars and scientists among the professions, however. It must also be recognized that the conventional practicing professions also produce new knowledge and techniques by exploring their own concepts and theories rather than merely serving others' demands passively. The traditional professions have been graced by individual practitioners in the past who made new discoveries or who have raised their voices against the accepted practices of their time, and there remain some who do so today. But the closer reality comes to the model of professionalism, the more such activity becomes possible on a routine, institutionalized basis primarily by members of the profession who serve in the special role of teaching.

Practitioners of course, are heavily involved in the day-to-day activity of serving others, so one cannot expect most of them to be routinely engaged in scholarship, research, or the like. But professions control the recruitment, training, and certification of their own members, and insofar as the process is institutionalized so as to assure some standardization of the outcome, formal schools will perform those functions, with special members of the profession serving as faculty. Insofar as they are full-time faculty, those in professional schools are in the same position as conventional scientists and scholars in universities—supported economically by the practice of teaching in circumstances that leave them a fair amount of free time to theorize and do research. They, too, are insulated from the practical demands and needs of the outside world and in a position to develop ideas and make discoveries independently of it. Like scholars and scientists in universities, concerned with the development and practice of their specialized body of knowledge and skill, committed to the goals or purposes of their craft, they may pursue the unexamined logical implications of what is known and extend them well past immediate practical necessity.

While these institutional grounds for independent thought and research that professionalism provides are much too important to ignore, it is obviously dangerous to exaggerate the degree of independence that is possible. Quite apart from the impossibility of ever being entirely free of the perspectives and prejudices of one's historical time and place, a practical limit on independence is posed by the impotence of knowledge and the dependence of its bearers on the dominant powers for their protection. What they do collectively, therefore, cannot deviate so far from the interests of those powers as to threaten them overtly. But the collectivity provides a general shelter within which highly critical modes of thought can develop well past what is conventionally accepted.

These innovative cognitive activities characteristic of professionalism provide a source of growth and enrichment in knowledge, values, and technique that could not be produced by workers who are wholly dependent on satisfying the demands that others formulate, and who are concerned primarily with serving their own material interests. While the extension of old ideas and the conception of new may lead to the creation of new demands that increase the number and value of professional jobs, it is only the most vulgar view that implies deliberate intention to do so. In any case, without meaning to imply that professions have a corner on the market for Truth, their capacity to pursue new knowledge, techniques, values, and ideas from a relatively independent point of view is a valuable virtue. It can make an important contribution to the possibility of developing a more humane, richer, and effectively functioning society.

The Inadequacy of the Present Defense

This conceptual construct, professionalism, advances a kind of blueprint for organizing work in a manner that can be argued to be more desirable than the others. It sketches a coherent alternative, shows how and why it deviates from the free competition and rational order advanced by the others, and justifies its deviation by its virtues. It shows the interrelationship between various attitudes, activities, and institutions and given ends. Thus it provides the resources not only for a defensive ideology employed merely to fend off criticism, but also for an aggressive or offensive ideology directed at extending and strengthening professionalism in the real world so as to get closer to the ideal model and its benefits.

In current debate, few if any from outside the professions have defended them. Indeed, most who are not members of conventionally recognized professions have joined in the attack even though a great many of them are academics whose position is sheltered by professional institutions. Among academics, most sociologists attack professions for exclusionary practices that contribute to inequality, often sounding like advocates of a free market. Political scientists (e.g., Gilb, 1966) attack them as private governments unresponsive to public needs. Historians (e.g., Auerbach, 1976) attack the elitist and exclusionary nature of their past activities. And economists understandably attack them as monopolists who interfere with

the free operation of the market. Among those prominent in practical policy affairs—planners and heads of state agencies in the public sector, and executives, managers, and investors in the private sector—professions are more often than not seen as obstructions to their goals.

Most of those who attempt to reply to such criticism have been members of the conventionally recognized professions—some in their capacity as officials of professional associations, and some especially prominent in other ways. This has made for a focus on individual professions rather than on the principle of professionalism, and encouraged reactive and defensive rather than assertive tactics. Those who defend their own profession do not defend other professions and even join others in attacking them—representatives of medicine and law, for example, often attack one another publicly. They have shown little awareness that all professions share a common interest that is threatened by exponents of the alternative models. Furthermore, because the defenders are usually official or quasi-official representatives of their professions, they cannot escape being prisoners of the conflicting interests to be found in the politics of their own associations. They can neither openly concede patently indefensible abuses as anything other than anomalous or rare, nor propose or agree to corrective actions that are unacceptable to some important segment of their profession. The consequence is that their defense has been weak, partial, inconsistent, and in some cases even misleading.

Because all professions in the United States today can count on a fair degree of respect and trust, albeit ambivalent and varying in degree from one to another, many of their claims are likely to be accepted by the public and the politicians who sanction their privileges. But when the position of the professions seriously interferes with the economic and political interests of capital or the state, capital and the state have the power to change public opinion and reduce support for professional institutions. Like all workers, intellectual or no, professionals have no tangible power of their own. They possess only their knowledge and skill, the essence of their labor. Therefore, the professions are highly vulnerable to political and economic pressures. Medicine, the most prestigious and wealthy of them all, provides an instructive example of ultimate weakness in the face of the power of the state and of capital. It is being forced to change in ways that were inconceivable twenty years ago, and it is possible (though not probable) that law will share its fate in the future. While I certainly do not believe that the professions are on the way to settling into the position of a true industrial proletariat—indeed, not even industrial workers in the United States may be said to be in such a position—it is quite possible that the conditions of professional work will move further away from those specified by the ideal-typical model I have sketched here. A decline in relative income is likely, but that has little relevance to professionalism as such so long as it does not drop to truly penurious levels.

Present defenses, I believe, can do little to prevent the changes going on in the United States today. I have already noted that the leaders of the professions are the intellectual prisoners of a purely reactive ideology as well as the political prisoners of the conflicting interests that characterize their associations. As Schneyer's analysis (1992) of the process of creating the 1983 American Bar Association Model Rules of Professional Conduct shows, the official reforms that are pressed are limited mostly to what is acceptable to a heterogeneous membership. They are also limited by an ideology that is insufficiently systematic to provide adequate intellectual guidance, and seriously distorted by reliance on elaborations of traditional, commonsense conceptions of professionalism. The ideology they employ is an intellectual patchwork created from selected fragments of idealized history, moral precepts, pious exhortations, optimistic interpretations of the profession's members' capacity and inclination to serve the public good generously, and obsession with symbolic matters of tradition, convention, and propriety such as advertising, unionization, and the like. The worn thread that holds the patchwork together is almost always spun from a naive, commonsense conception of human action in which the knowledge, values, and attitudes of individuals provide the major source of motivation and direction for their behavior. And so their main emphasis is on reforming the way recruits are selected and trained while paying little attention to changing the institutional and economic structures within which their members do their work. As

the model of professionalism specifies, the two are interdependent: the latter provides the resources that either corrupt or reinforce the consequences of the former.

I wish to suggest that an aggressive ideology advancing the terms of the analytic model of professionalism can perform far more effective service for the professions' defense than a commonsense version. It can do so, first of all, because it is better equipped to argue the greater desirability of professionalism than the alternatives implied or asserted by exponents of the free market or of rationalized corporate or state authority. It is able to acknowledge monopoly without apology, for monopoly in and of itself is a vice only if one assumes that a free market is a virtue, and that a monopoly exercised by an independent body of specialized workers cannot serve the public interest better than a monopoly of authority exercised by functionaries of capital or the state. It can observe that there is no reasonable basis for expecting people to serve the public good if they cannot be assured of a reasonably secure (but by no means necessarily luxurious) income for themselves and their families. And it can argue that a monopoly held by an occupation whose members are committed to maintaining the integrity of a craft that is of value to others is a more desirable and less destructive solution to an important social problem than is the free play of unbridled material interest or the reduction of all work to formally specified procedure proposed by its critics. The practical issue then becomes regulating the conduct of those who possess the monopoly so as to assure adequate performance, and not eliminating monopoly itself.

Following the model, however, a truly consistent and principled ideologue will go on to specify what must be done by the professions in order to come close to realizing the virtues claimed for the ideal model. A principled ideologue for the free market cannot serve as an apologist for concentrations of economic power that prevent the free play of individual choices to produce, offer, and buy services and goods on the basis of material interest. A principled ideologue of rational-legal bureaucracy cannot condone the use of anything other than competence to decide who shall hold a position or any exception to the rule-governed exercise of authority employed to gain the ends specified by the ultimate authorities. By the same token, a principled ideologue of professionalism cannot condone a monopoly that serves primarily to protect rather than seek out and control the incompetent, the venal, and the negligent among its members, any more than condone a monopoly in which all are free to maximize their incomes at the expense of a public which has nowhere else to turn.

A principled defense of the professions, in short, is offensive as well as defensive. In contrasting its ideal-typical model with those of its critics, it asserts it as no more or less utopian than theirs, and argues that the characteristic pathologies to be found in empirical forms of the other models are even less desirable than those to be found in professionalism. It is aggressive in joining the attack on the pathologies that stem from material self-interest in the market-place, and from the reduction of work and its products to formal procedure in bureaucracy. But it can be no less aggressive in joining the attack on the practices of professionals that compromise the integrity of the model. Only by maintaining its own integrity can it succeed in leaving no doubt of its superiority over the atomistic play of individual self-interest or the iron cage of formal rationality.

Notes

1. Another question of some intrinsic value is why all this criticism of professionalism arose when it did. For a lively chronicle of the rise of such criticism among sociologists and historians, and a tentative explanation of it, see Metzger (1987).

2. See, for example, Gordon (1977). In Wright's considerably more sophisticated analysis, expertise is recognized as a source of exploitation, but it is not considered *intrinsically* exploitative so long as "ownership rights in skiffs have been equalized . . . [when] differential incomes and control over the social surplus cease to be linked to differential skills" (Wright, 1985, p. 85). This position is extremely rare among left-oriented critics, who tend to be hostile to specialized skill.

3. Rothschild and Russell's review of studies of democratic participatory productive organizations (1986) finds that they all tend to have a simple division of labor. My guess is that the primary source of difficulty for exponents of egalitarianism lies in their inability to recognize that functional differentiation need not represent inequality, and in their conflation of two quite different things—the authority of political, economic, and administrative power with the authority of expertise. While many, Foucault (e.g., 1980, pp. 146–65) being the most prominent, would impute "power" to expertise, they refer to the influence of discourse or persuasion and semantically conflate it with the power of material sanctions, which they recognize as quite different.

4. For a discussion of the ideal of professionalism in law in light of the approach of economists, see Simon (1985).

5. They too, however, are in a position in which they exercise judgment that is independent of their clients', balancing the interest of the client against that of other clients and the public at large. For a sophisticated and sensitive analysis of the independence of practicing lawyers, see Gordon (1988).

Adult Learning and Theory Building: A Review

SHARAN B. MERRIAM

Sharan B. Merriam is Professor of Adult Education, the University of Georgia. The writing of this paper was funded in part by the Office of Higher Education and Adult Learning of the Office of Educational Research and Improvement (Contract No. OERI-P-86-3016).

The one factor that all adult education agencies, programs, and professionals have in common is that all deal with adults in learning situations. Perhaps that is why there has been more theory building in adult learning than in other areas of adult education. It is the adult learner, after all, which distinguishes this field from other areas of education. This article assesses the state-of-the-art of theory building efforts in adult learning. The theories have been divided into three categories: (a) those based on adult learner characteristics, (b) those emphasizing the adult's life situation, and (c) those focusing upon changes in consciousness. Components common to most of the theories are identified, and it is concluded that, taken as a whole, theory building efforts in adult learning contribute to our understanding of the phenomenon.

Since its inception as a field of practice, adult education with its mystifying array of programs, philosophical orientations, clienteles, and delivery systems has challenged its professionals to evolve some theory or principles or coherent structures that capture and explain the phenomenon. Research and some theory building have occurred in the areas of program planning, instruction, history, philosophy, and policy analysis. The area that has received the most attention, however, has been

adult learning. There are at least two reasons for this: first, the one and perhaps only factor that all agencies, programs and professionals have in common is that all deal with adults in learning situations; second, it is the adult learner which distinguishes adult education from other areas of education.

Research and theory building in adult learning have taken many directions. Some researchers have investigated why adults participate in learning activities, or what adults learn on their own, or how they structure learning, or how learning ability changes with age. Others have sought to explain how adult learners are different from children. The purpose of this article is to assess the state-of-the-art with regard to theory building efforts in adult learning.

The Need for Theory

Before reviewing adult learning theories one might ask whether the field "needs" adult learning theory, and if so, whether it is an obtainable goal. Courtney (1986) argues that because "adult education is principally a species of moral and social intervention rather than a science, it cannot be expected to generate theory" (p. 162). But because adult education is not a science does not mean that research and theory building should be shunned. Whatever the nature of the field, there are good reasons for investigating and conceptualizing practice. "The systematic accumulation of knowledge is essential for progress in any profession" (Cross, 1981, p. 110). It also

"Adult Learning and Theory Building: A Review," by Sharan B. Merriam, reprinted from *Adult Education Quarterly*, Vol. 37, No. 4, Summer 1987, American Association for Adult & Continuing Education.

stimulates thinking about practice, and brings understanding and insight to the field. Kidd (1973) observes that a theory of adult learning would "(1) provide a guide for developing curricula and selecting methods and teaching styles; (2) offer hypotheses for research; and (3) establish criteria for evaluation" (p. 188).

Unfortunately, there has been little theory building in adult education overall. Courtney (1986) sees the reasons being related to the field's non-scientific nature as well as the ways adult educators are trained. Several other reasons for the lack of theory include the enormous diversity of adult learning situations, its multidisciplinary nature, the marketplace orientation, the lack of researchers compared to practitioners, and "the lack of desire or perceived need for theory" (Cross, 1981, p. 221).

Lack of clarity as to *what* is needed with regard to theory results in individuals pursuing their own idiosyncratic interests. Systematic lines of inquiry with one study building on another thus fail to develop. In adult learning itself, questions can be raised as to what should be studied—motivation, participation, adult development, instruction, or adult versus child learning (Cross, 1981). Most writers in adult education recognize the difficulty, if not the futility, in trying to devise a theory of adult learning. Kidd (1973) says that "no such magical or scientific theory is likely to arise or be formulated soon" (p. 188), although he welcomes "attempts at greater coherence" (Kidd, 1977, p. 19). Brookfield (1986) writes that "there can be few intellectual quests that . . . assume so much significance and yet contain so little promise of successful completion as the search for a general theory of adult learning" (p. 25). Cross agrees, suggesting that "there will be many theories useful in improving our understanding of adults as learners" (1981, p. 112).

Part of the task in reviewing and evaluating what theory building has been done involves delineating what a theory of adult learning might look like, and what criteria might be used for judging its significance. To begin with, there are many definitions of "theory," a fact which led Knowles to conclude that "a theory is what a given author says it is" (Knowles & Associates, 1984, p. 5). Nearly all definitions, however, incorporate the notion that there is a set of interrelated ideas, principles, or concepts that explain some phenomena. Confusion occurs when the terms "model," "framework," "conceptual scheme," or "system" are used interchangeably with theory. While distinctions can be made, if what is being referred to is a set of interrelated concepts or principles that attempt to explain the phenomenon of adult learning, it will be included in this review.

Several writers have thought about what a theory of adult learning should include. Hartree (1984) notes that such a theory should be three dimensional, including how adults learn, what they learn when it is distinctive, and why they learn. Jensen (1957), in an early but still relevant work, says that educators should keep several principles in mind when building a theory of adult learning: that it should be applicable to the problems of practice, be able to be internalized by the practitioner, be based on empirical findings, and be revised from time to time. He also suggests four content areas: (a) the structure and dynamics of groups, (b) processes, structures and activities found in formal social systems: (c) personality organization including cognitive, emotional and motor aspects; and (d) community institutions and ideologies. Houle (1974) who sees the learning process of adults and children as "fundamentally the same," notes that all theories or "systems" address four basic concerns: the nature of the learner, the goals sought, the social and physical milieu of instruction, and the techniques of learning or teaching (p. 5). Various theories develop as a result of the infinite number of ways these components can be arranged.

These thoughts on theory building provide a backdrop against which the adult learning theories can be assessed. In addition, three recently proposed criteria for evaluating the importance of research questions (Rachal, 1986) reflect the concerns and themes that have emerged from this discussion of theory building in adult learning. The first criterion suggested is that of practical application. A second criterion asks to what extent the research (or the theory) contributes to a deeper understanding of the field. Finally, universality is a criterion that needs to be judiciously considered. Rachal (1986) observes that "questions of universality are addressed through theory building which can permeate the thinking and influence the practice of those throughout the field" (p. 158). Practicality, understanding, and universality appear to be relevant criteria for the field of adult education and will be considered in the closing discussion of theory building in adult learning.

A theory of adult learning, then, would be a set of interrelated principles that enable us to understand how adults learn. Carried a step further, if we understand how adults learn we should be able to predict when and how learning will take place, and, as practitioners, arrange for its occurrence.

Theory building in adult learning is in its infancy. We have attempts, tentative formulations, rather than fully developed theory. No theory has been universally acclaimed as *the* explanation of adult learning. Most fall short of achieving widespread acceptance on one of two points: the theory is not unique to adults, or it fails to account for all types of learning. Of course such a theory may never evolve. It is more likely that we will have many explanations, each of which contributes something to our understanding of adult learning. It is from this perspective that theory building attempts in adult learning will be examined. These attempts at theory are grouped into three categories: (a) those that are based on adult learner characteristics, (b) those that emphasize the adult's life situation, and (c) those that focus upon changes in consciousness. None of the theories reviewed define learning in the traditional sense of behavioral change or cognitive functioning, although these dimensions may be present. Rather, the theories reviewed within each of the three categories explicitly or implicitly define learning in conjunction with adult social roles and life situations. To do otherwise would lose what is most important, perhaps unique, to learning in adulthood.

Theories Based on Adult Characteristics

The best known "theory" of adult learning is andragogy, defined by Knowles (1980) as "the art and science of helping adults learn" (p. 43). It is based upon four assumptions, all of which are characteristics of adult learners:

1. As a person matures his or her self-concept moves from one of a dependent personality toward one of a self-directing human being;

2. An adult accumulates a growing reservoir of experience, a rich resource for learning;

3. The readiness of an adult to learn is closely related to the developmental tasks of his or her social role; and

4. There is a change in time perspective as individuals mature, from one of future application of knowledge to immediacy of application; thus an adult is more problem-centered than subject-centered in learning. (pp. 44–45).

From each of these assumptions Knowles draws numerous implications for the design, implementation, and evaluation of learning activities with adults.

This theory, or "model of assumptions" as Knowles also calls it (1980, p. 43), has given adult educators "a badge of identity" which distinguishes the field from other areas of education, especially childhood schooling (Brookfield, 1986, p. 90). Many would agree with Bard, that andragogy "probably more than any other force has changed the role of the learner in adult education and in human resource development" (Bard, 1984, p. xi).

It has also caused more controversy, philosophical debate, and critical analysis than any other concept/theory/model proposed thus far. One of the early points of criticism was Knowles' original inference that andragogy, with all its technological implications for instruction, characterized adult learning, and that pedagogy, with another set of implications, characterized childhood learning. He later clarified his position stating in essence that andragogy-pedagogy represent a continuum and that the use of both techniques was appropriate at different times in different situations regardless of the age of the learner (Knowles, 1980). Since he no longer claims andragogy to be unique to adults, its status as a theory of adult learning is, in Cross's words, "up in the air" (1981, p. 225).

As a theory of adult learning andragogy has been challenged on other grounds. Hartree (1984) observes that it is not clear whether Knowles has presented a theory of learning or a theory of teaching, whether adult learning is different from child learning, and whether there is a theory at all versus principles of good practice. The assumptions, she notes, "can be read as descriptions of the adult learner . . . or as prescriptive statements about what the adult learner *should* be like" (p. 205). Because the assumptions are "unclear and shaky" on several counts. Hartree (1984) concludes that:

> Whilst many adult educators might accept that the principles of adult teaching and conditions of learning which he evolves have much to offer, and are in a sense descriptive of what is already recognized as good practice by those in the field, conceptually Knowles has not presented a good case for the validity of such practice . . . Although he appears to approach his model of teaching from the point of view of a theory of adult learning, he does not establish a unified theory of learning in a systematic way. (pp. 206–207).

Brookfield (1986), who raises the question of whether andragogy is a "proven theory," takes the tack of assessing to what extent a "set of well-grounded principles of good practice" can be derived from andragogy (p. 98). Application to practice, it will be recalled, is one of the three criteria, along with contributions to understanding and universality, that can be used for judging research and theory (Rachal, 1986). Brookfield argues that three of the assumptions are problematic when drawing inferences for practice: self-direction is more of a desired outcome than a given condition, and being problem-centered and desiring immediate application can lead to a narrow reductionist view of learning. Brookfield finds only the experience assumption to be "well grounded" (1986, p. 98).

Davenport and Davenport (1985) review the use of the term "andragogy" and chronicle the history of the debate as to whether it is a theory. They note that andragogy has been classified "as a theory of adult education, theory of adult learning, theory of technology of adult learning, method of adult education, technique of adult education, and a set of assumptions" (p. 157). They feel that the debate will be resolved through the accumulations of empirical studies and that if research confirms the underlying assumptions, "andragogy may

well possess the explanatory and predictive functions generally associated with a fully developed theory" (p. 158).

A second attempt at theory building that rests upon characteristics of adults is Cross's Characteristics of Adults As Learners (CAL) model. Cross (1981) offers it as "a tentative framework to accommodate current knowledge about what we know about adults as learners" (p. 234). It is based upon differences between children and adults and consists of two classes of variables: personal characteristics and situational characteristics. Personal characteristics include physical, psychological, and sociocultural dimensions. These are continua and reflect growth and development from childhood into adult life. Situational characteristics focus on variables unique to adult participants—for example, part-time versus full-time learning, and voluntary versus compulsory participation.

Cross feels that her model incorporates completed research on aging, stage and phase developmental studies, participation, learning projects, motivation, and so on. The model also can be used to stimulate research by thinking across and between categories. It might be asked, for example, if there is a "relationship between stage of ego development and voluntary participation in learning" or if "transition points" in development "generate extra amounts of volunteer learning" (p. 248). Rather than providing implications for practice, as Knowles' theory does, the model offers a "framework for thinking about *what* and *how* adults learn" (p. 248). And this she sees as the real need in terms of theory building—that is, models are needed that can incorporate new knowledge as it is produced and at the same time stimulate new questions to be investigated.

While the CAL model appears comprehensive, as was its intent, it is perhaps so broad as to make operationalizing it difficult. In other words, it can incorporate knowledge about adult learning, but how does a practitioner use it to explain or better understand the specifics of an adult learning situation? Cross's CAL model has yet to be critically evaluated or empirically tested.

Theories Based on an Adult's Life Situation

The two theories just discussed, andragogy and CAL, emanate from the characteristics of adult learners. The two theories to be reviewed in this section—McClusky's Theory of Margin, and Knox's Proficiency Theory—are anchored in an adult's life situation with its attendant roles and responsibilities. Both theories are also built on the notion of a discrepancy—between current and desired proficiencies (Knox, 1980), or between power and load (McClusky, 1970).

McClusky presented his Theory of Margin in a 1963 publication followed by discussions of application in 1970 and 1971. Adulthood is a time of growth, change, and integration in which one constantly seeks balance between the amount of energy needed and the amount available. This balance was conceptualized as a ratio between the "load" of life, which dissipates energy, and the "power" of life which allows one to deal with the load. The energy left over when one subtracts load from power. McClusky called "margin in life." He describes how the theory works:

> Margin may be increased by reducing Load or increasing Power, or it may be decreased by increasing Load and/or reducing Power. We can control both by modifying either Power or Load. When Load continually matches or exceeds Power and if both are fixed and/or out of control, or irreversible, the situation becomes highly vulnerable and susceptible to breakdown. If, however, Load and Power can be controlled, and better yet, if a person is able to lay hold of a reserve (Margin) of Power, he is better equipped to meet unforeseen emergencies, is better positioned to take risks, can engage in exploratory, creative activities, is more likely to learn, etc., i.e. do those things that enable him to live above a plateau of mere self-subsistence. (1970, p. 83).

This theory, he felt, helped explain the dynamics of adult learning. A learning situation requires the expenditure of resources, that is, "a necessary condition for learning is access to and/or the activation of a Margin of Power that may be available for application to the processes which the learning situation requires" (1970, p. 84). The particular adult life situation

focus of this theory is reflected in his recognition that "adjustments of Load to Power become matters of overarching concern as a person accumulates and later relinquishes adult responsibilities and modifies the varying roles which the successive stages of the life cycle require" (1970, p. 84).

There have been a few studies of adult learning and teaching using the theory of margin as a conceptual framework (Main, 1979). Its greatest application, however, has been with middle-aged and older adults. Using an instrument developed to measure margin in life, Stevenson (1980) compared the load, power, and margin patterns of independent older adults, nursing home residents, and young and middle-aged adults. Baum (1980) tested the theory using a randomized sample of 100 widows. McClusky felt that older persons could enhance their self esteem through learning and education relevant to their life situation. "The preeminent" need of the aging, he wrote, "is the need for the kind of education that will assist them in creating margins of power for the attainment and maintenance of well-being and continuing growth toward self-fulfillment" (1971, p. 2).

Knox's (1980) Proficiency Theory also speaks to an adult's life situation. Adult learning, he writes, is distinctive on at least two counts—"the centrality of concurrent adult role performance," (p. 383) and the "close correspondence between learning and action beyond the educational program" (p. 384).

Proficiency, as defined by Knox, is "the capability to perform satisfactorily if given the opportunity" and this performance involves some combination of attitude, knowledge and skill (1980, p. 378). At the core of his theory is the notion of a discrepancy between the current and the desired level of proficiency. This concept of proficiency helps explain "adult motivation and achievement in both learning activities and life roles. Adults and society," Knox (1985) writes, "expect that individual adults will be proficient in major life roles and as persons generally" (p. 252).

His theory is based upon assumptions that adult learning is both developmental and transactional. It is developmental in that learning is integral to the changes adults undergo as they age, changes which are internally and externally precipitated. Learning is also transactional in that (a) learners are motivated to learn through interaction with their social context, and (b) they interact with people and resources within the learning situation. The model that represents the theory contains the following interactive components: General Environment. Past and Current Characteristics, Performance, Aspiration, Self, Discrepancies, Specific Environments, Learning Activity, and Teacher Role.

The Proficiency Theory presents a set of interrelated concepts that hinge upon what Knox (1980) defines as being the purpose of adult learning (whether self-directed or in organized programs): "to enhance proficiency to improve performance" (p. 399). The theory can help explain why adults engage in learning, and it also offers numerous research possibilities related to the total teaching-learning transaction. For example, how do adults delineate desired proficiencies which lead them to learning? Is it through generalized images, role models, or formal standards of performance? What teaching style or procedures are most effective in acquiring different proficiencies? What contextual factors are important in teaching and learning? For other suggestions as to how the Proficiency Theory might be useful in structuring research studies, see Knox (1980, 1985).

Theories Based on Changes in Consciousness

The theories so far discussed attempt to explain the phenomenon of adult learning from the perspective of adult characteristics, adult social roles and responsibilities, and adult growth and development. The theoretical formulations to be discussed in this section have a stronger cognitive focus in that they deal with the mental construction of experience and inner meaning, and with the changes that occur therein. Reflection upon the content of one's environment and one's experiences is a common component of the theories in this section. Reflective thought, some propose, may even be *the* thought structure to emerge in adulthood and "a necessary prerequisite to asking questions, discovering problems and to contradiction becoming a basis for thought" (Allman, 1983, p. 114).

The most developed "theory" in this group is Mezirow's Perspective Transformation. Drawing from the writings of German philosopher Habermas, Mezirow defines three areas of cognitive interest: technical, which is task related and focuses upon work; practical, which involves interaction and interpersonal understanding; and emancipatory, which is characterized by interest in self-knowledge and insights gained through self-reflection. This third domain is what Mezirow (1981) equates with perspective transformation:

> Perspective transformation is the emancipatory process of becoming critically aware of how and why the structure of psychocultural assumptions has come to constrain the way we see ourselves and our relationships, reconstituting this structure to permit a more inclusive and discriminating integration of experience and acting upon these new understandings. It is the learning process by which adults come to recognize their culturally induced dependency roles and relationships and the reasons for them and take action to overcome them. (pp. 6–7)

Critically reflecting upon our lives, becoming aware of "*why* we attach the meaning we do to reality, especially to our roles and relationships . . . may be the most significant distinguishing characteristic of adult learning" (p. 11). Learning in adulthood is not just adding to what we already know. Rather, new learning transforms existing knowledge into a new perspective and in so doing "emancipates" the learner. The ultimate result of this type of learning is to become aware of the "cultural assumptions governing the rules, roles, conventions and social expectations which dictate the way we see, think, feel and act" (1981, p. 13).

The process of perspective transformation begins with a "disorienting dilemma" to which one's old patterns of response are ineffective. This situation precipitates a self-examination and assessment of assumptions and beliefs. A movement begins whereby one revises "specific assumptions about oneself and others until the very structure of assumptions becomes transformed" (1981, p. 8). Perspective transformation results in a new agenda for action. Action out of one's new perspective is an integral part of the theory. Mezirow feels that adult educators have a responsibility which "gives adult education its distinctive mission and even its meaning" (1985, p. 148). It is not enough to help learners "perform, achieve and produce." The one significant commitment of adult education is "to help learners make explicit, elaborate and act upon the assumptions and premises . . . upon which their performance, achievement and productivity is based" (1985, p. 148).

The praxis (reflection and action) component of Mezirow's theory and the notion of a change in perspective are central concepts in Freire's "theory" of conscientization. Freire is a Brazilian educator whose theory of adult education is set within a larger framework of radical social change. Education for Freire is never neutral; it either oppresses or liberates. Conscientization, "the process in which men, not as recipients, but as knowing subjects, achieve a deepening awareness both of the socio-cultural reality which shapes their lives and of their capacity to transform that reality" is what takes place in an authentic educational encounter (1970a, p. 27). Increasing awareness of one's situation involves moving from the lowest level of consciousness where there is no comprehension of how forces shape one's life, to the highest level of critical consciousness. Similar to Mezirow's "critical reflectivity" (1981), critical consciousness is marked by an in-depth analysis of problems, self awareness, and self reflection.

Within Freire's theory of education for social change are components relevant to adult learning situations. He distinguishes between "banking" and "problem-posing" education. In traditional banking education, deposits of knowledge are made into student receptacles; in problem-posing, teachers and students cooperate in a dialogue which seeks to humanize and liberate. Central to the learning is a changed relationship between teacher and student. They are co-investigators into their common reality, the socio-cultural situation in which they live. Dialogue is the method by which this sharing takes place and by which consciousness is raised. Generative themes, concerns which are posed by the learners themselves, become the content of a learning situation. The end goal is liberation, or praxis, "the action and reflection of men upon their world in order to transform it" (1970b, p. 66).

Freire has operationalized his theory of education into techniques that have had demonstrated success in combating illiteracy, especially in the Third World. Its application in North America has been limited, perhaps due to the necessary corollary of social change. Others have suggested that conscientization is not comprehensive enough to explain various types of learning that an adult might experience, or that the emphasis upon active involvement, experiential learning, and dialogue are not new. If taken out of its political context, conscientization shares with perspective transformation the idea that *adult* learning is the process of becoming aware of one's assumptions, beliefs and values, of transforming those assumptions into a new perspective or level of consciousness. This "awakening . . . proceeds to action, which in turn provides the basis for new perception, new reflection" (Lloyd, 1972, p. 5).

Several other conceptualizations of adult learning share an emphasis upon the reconstruction of inner meaning. Candy (1982), drawing upon the personal construct theory of psychologist Kelly, proposes the concept "personal paradigm transition" as characteristic of adult learning. "We all seek to make sense out of the world around us," according to Candy (1980), "and to do so, construct more or less elaborate, multi-dimensional models of reality inside our heads." When something happens "we try to fit it into our system of constructs," or if it doesn't fit, "we either develop a new . . . construct, or we modify our perceptions of the experience" (p. 9). Comparing these construct changes to Kuhn's notion of paradigm shifts, Candy writes that "transformation may be traumatic, and accompanied by the same anxiety and uncertainty we characterize paradigm shifts in science, but many of them occur stealthily; they may be unrecognized by the person as part of a developmental sequence" (1982, p. 62). Candy feels that Kelly's theory has many implications for adult learning, a major one being that it makes it possible "to distinguish between learning by construction—which we might call *forming* meanings, values, skills, and strategies—and reconstruction—which means *transforming* meanings, values, shifts, and strategies" (1982, p. 64). Also drawing upon Kelly's ideas in the formulation of a theory of "self-organized" learning,

Thomas and Harri-Augstein (1985) see real personal learning as the construction of internal referents, and "the ability to monitor the construction and reconstruction of personal meaning over time" (p. xxix).

Finally, while not proposing a "theory" of learning, Brookfield's characterization of adult learning as "transactional encounter" seems to share the orientation of theorists presented in this section. "The particular function of the facilitator," he writes, "is to challenge learners with alternative ways of interpreting their experience and to present to them ideas and behaviors that cause them to examine critically their values, ways of acting, and the assumptions by which they live" (1986, p. 23).

In summary, the approaches to adult learning covered in this section emphasize the importance of inner meaning and mental constructs in defining the nature of learning in adult life. More so than the theories based on learner characteristics or adult life position, the theories or formulations in this section give rise to philosophical and ethical issues. For example, what right do adult educators have to "tamper" with the world view (mental set, perspective, paradigm or state of consciousness) of the learner? How is the end goal of educational intervention to be determined? What responsibility does the educator have for the action component of praxis? There is little consensus among the writers of this orientation as to the answers to these and other questions that this perspective raises.

Concluding Observations

There is a substantial amount of literature on the topic of adult learning. Much of it is descriptive and much of it draws from disciplines outside adult education. Nevertheless, adults as learners are getting attention and are the focus of a growing number of empirically-based investigations, especially in the areas of learning ability and characteristics of adult learners including participation, motivation, and adult development. Certainly, description of a phenomenon is a necessary preliminary to theory building.

And, as evidenced by this review, we do have several theoretical formulations that attempt to explain adult learning. Houle (1984)

complains that current theories are too concerned with "how the longitudinal aspect" (meaning age) "influences learning from birth to death" (p. xi). "Learning," he says, "has depth and breadth as well as length. At any given time in one's life, a person is likely to be engaged in several different kinds of learning." He proposes a "sequential patterns of learning" approach to life span education. Some of the theories do claim to take into account the totality of the adult learning experience— Knox's Proficiency Theory and Cross's CAL in particular. Houle, as noted earlier, however, works from the assumption that child and adult learning are fundamentally the same.

One might also evaluate the theories from the assumption that a theory of adult learning should be based on that which is *unique* to adult learning. The third set of theories discussed—those that emphasize the restructuring of meaning or transformation of perspective, attempt to capture that which is unique about adult learning.

When evaluating the theories using the criteria of practical application, understanding, and universality (Rachal, 1986), some further generalizations can be made. No theory fares well when all three criteria are applied. This is perhaps due to the very newness of theory building in adult learning. Few of those reviewed have been empirically tested at all, and none is supported by a substantial body of research. Until there is more empirical support, the criterion of universality, or how well the findings based on a theory are generalizable, is a moot question. While all at least allude to practical implications, only Knowles' andragogy has been widely applied in practice (Knowles & Associates 1984). Finally, the extent to which a particular theory helps us to better understand the phenomenon of adult learning depends somewhat upon elegance of expression and the sophistication of the consumer. Mezirow's perspective transformation and Freire's conscientization require familiarity with philosophical and psychological concepts. Understanding the interaction of ten different components in Knox's theory requires some concentrated effort.

Taken as a whole, however, theory building efforts in adult learning do contribute to our growing understanding of adult learning. Most of the theories reviewed identify components of adult learning relative to: (a) self-direction/autonomy as a characteristic or as a goal of adult learning; (b) the relationship of experiences, especially those of adult life, to learning; (c) the importance of reflection upon one's own learning, and (d) action as some sort of necessary expression of the learning that has occurred. While one theory to explain all of adult learning may never emerge, the process does stimulate inquiry, reflection, and research, all of which will eventually provide us with some of the answers to our questions about adult learning.

References

Allman, P. (1983). The nature and process of adult development. In M. Tight (Ed.), *Adult learning and education*. London: Croom Helm.

Bard, R. (1984). Forward. In M. S. Knowles and Associates (Eds.), *Andragogy in action*. San Francisco: Jossey-Bass.

Baum, J. (1980). Testing the theory of margin using a population of widows. *Proceedings of the 21st Adult Education Research Conference*, May 7–9, Vancouver, Canada.

Brookfield, S. (1986). *Understanding and facilitating adult learning*. San Francisco: Jossey-Bass.

Candy, P. C. (1980). A personal construct approach to adult learning. (Paper available from Adelaide College of Arts and Education, Holbrook Road, Underdale, South Australia.)

Candy, P. (1982). Personal constructs and personal paradigms: Elaboration, modification, and transformation. *Interchange on Educational Policy*. 13(4), 56–69.

Courtney, S. (1986). On derivation of the research question. *Adult Education Quarterly, 36*, 160–165.

Cross, K. P. (1981). *Adults as learners*. San Francisco: Jossey-Bass.

Davenport, J., & Davenport, J. (1985). A chronology and analysis of the andragogy debate. *Adult Education Quarterly, 35*, 152–159.

Freire, P. (1970a). *Cultural action for freedom, Harvard Educational Review*. Monograph series No. 1.

Freire, P. (1970b). *Pedagogy of the oppressed*. New York: Herder and Herder.

Hartree, A. (1984). Malcolm Knowles' theory of andragogy: A critique. *International Journal of Lifelong Education, 3*, 203–210.

Houle, C. O. (1974). *The design of education*. San Francisco: Jossey-Bass.

Houle, C. O. (1984). *Patterns of learning*. San Francisco: Jossey-Bass.

Jensen, G. (1957). Principles and content for developing a theory of learning. *Adult education, 8*, 131–134.

Kidd, R. J. (1973). *How adults learn*. New York: Association Press.

Kidd, J. R. (1977). Adult learning in the 1970's. In R. M. Smith (Ed.). *Adult learning: Issues and innovations*. (Information Series No. 8.) DeKalb: Information Program in Career Education. Northern Illinois University.

Knowles, M. S. (1980). *The modern practice of adult education: From pedagogy to andragogy* (2nd ed.). Chicago: Follett.

Knowles, M. S. and Associates. (1984). *Andragogy in action*. San Francisco: Jossey-Bass Publishers.

Knox, A. B. (1980). Proficiency theory of adult learning. *Contemporary Educational Psychology, 5*, 378–404.

Knox, A. B. (1985). Adult learning and proficiency. In Kleiber, D. and Maehr, M. (Eds.) *Advances in motivation and achievement: Vol. 4. Motivation in adulthood*. Greenwood, Conn: JAI Press, Inc.

Lloyd, A. S. (1972). Freire, conscientization, and adult education. *Adult Education, 23*, 3–20.

McClusky, H. Y. (1963). The course of the adult life span. In W. C. Hallenbeck (Ed.). *Psychology of adults*. Washington D.C.: Adult Education Association of the USA.

McClusky, H. Y. (1970). An approach to a differential psychology of the adult potential. In S. M. Grabowski (Ed.). *Adult learning and instruction*. Syracuse, NY: ERIC Clearinghouse on Adult Education. (Reported in *The adult learner: A neglected species*, by Malcolm Knowles. Houston: Gulf Publishing Company, 1984. [3rd Edition].)

McClusky, H. Y. (1971). *Education: Background*. Report prepared for the 1971 White House Conference on Aging. Washington, DC.

Main, K. (1979). The power-load-margin formula of Howard Y. McClusky as the basis for a model of teaching. *Adult Education, 30*, 19–33.

Mezirow, J. (1981). A critical theory of adult learning and education. *Adult Education, 32*, 3–27.

Mezirow, J. (1985). Concept and action in adult education. *Adult Education Quarterly, 35*, 142–151.

Rachal, J. (1986). Assessing adult education research questions: Some preliminary criteria. *Adult Education Quarterly, 36*, 157–159.

Stevenson, J. J. (1980). Load, power and margin in older adults. *Geriatric Nursing, 1*(2), 50–55.

Thomas, L. F. and Harri-Augstein, E. S. (1985). *Self-organized learning*. Boston: Routledge and Kegan Paul.

Part IV

The Management of the College or University

CHAPTER 11

ORGANIZATIONAL BEHAVIOR, DECISION MAKING, AND LEADERSHIP

ASSOCIATE EDITOR: MARVIN W. PETERSON

The study of colleges and universities as complex organizations has been a central focus of scholarship on higher education for the past five decades. It has produced an extensive literature which is not easily summarized in a few brief articles in an introductory volume. The serious student is encouraged to consult the *ASHE Reader on Organization and Governance in Higher Education*, Vol. IV for a more complete review of the topic.

Colleges and universities as complex organizations can be examined at three distinctive levels: first, the interorganizational patterns that describe the relationships among colleges or universities—their ecology, the types of institutions, their character as an industry, patterns of collaboration and/or competition; second, the organizational level that treats the entire institution as an organization and attempts to understand its structure, function, and major dynamics; and third, the interorganizational patterns among units and the processes by which the organization functions. The selections in this section of the Foundation's Reader cannot do justice to these three levels. So in addition to the reprinted readings, a section of suggested additional references is included.

An Evolutionary Perspective

As complex organizations, colleges and universities have been viewed from a variety of theoretical or conceptual perspectives. Following World War II, as higher education grew from a system or industry of traditional institutions to a mass higher education system with new four year and university institutions and an explosion of community colleges designed to serve large segments of high school graduates, the literature on their organizational nature began to emerge. These perspectives and those that follow which have for the most part been drawn from other academic disciplines and fields, reflect the growing complexity of our understanding of them, and largely emerge as higher education grew or faced new challenges.

In the 1950s and 1960s as higher education and its institutions both grew rapidly in size and complexity and struggled with the problems of growth, they were viewed either as collegial community (Millett, 1962; Goodman, 1964) or formal rational organizations (Stroup, 1966). In the later 1960s and early 1970s as we struggled with social and political upheaval on campuses and the advent of collective bargaining, they came to be viewed as organizations composed of political interest groups (Baldridge, 1971).

In the 1970s, confronted with an economic recession, slowed enrollment growth, and the governmental enforcement of a student oriented financial aid system, higher education became a postsecondary system or industry including proprietary institutions. Our organizational perspective

Marvin W. Peterson is Professor of Higher Education at the Center for the Study of Higher and Postsecondary Education at the University of Michigan.

shifted to a more managerial (Lawrence & Service, 1977) or marketing oriented perspective (Kotler, 1975). As institutions continued to expand in size and complexity, our understanding of the autonomous patterns of subunits in large institutions became clear. We began to view colleges and universities as organized anarchies (Cohen & March, 1974) or loosely couple systems (Weick, 1976).

In the early 1980s, as enrollment and financial constraints increased, the importance of the external environment became clear, and issue of effectiveness became dominant. We began to think of colleges and universities as strategic organizations (Chaffee, 1985; Keller, 1983; Peterson, 1981), entrepreneurial organizations, or even matrix organizations (Albert, 1985). By the late 1980s borrowing from our concerns about excellence in the business arena and reflecting the growing public interest in focus on academic quality, we revived an earlier theme (Clark, 1970) and began to reexamine colleges and universities as organizational cultures (Masland, 1985; Tierney, 1988). We even attempted to understand them as cognitive processing or learning organizations (Birnbaum, 1988) which encompassed many of the earlier conceptual perspectives.

During the early 1990s, the focus on institutional quality and academic quality has been accentuated but in the context of growing revenue limitations, cost constraints and increased competition for students. These have introduced new management approaches (TQM, assessment, performance indicators, resource centered management and the like) but new organizational perspectives have been slow to emerge. As we face the 21st Century and the advent of the information age, postsecondary education is faced with numerous societal forces—the telematics revolution, expanding concerns for diversity, growing emphasis on quality of learning, pressures for economic development, increased demand for adult postsecondary learning and relearning experiences, globalization of knowledge based institutions, growth of complex interdisciplinary research agendas. These appear to be reordering our postsecondary system or industry into a postsecondary knowledge industry that includes non-educational as well as postsecondary organizations focuses on a broader array of postsecondary learning and learning experiences. New organizational modes—conglomerate, network, entrepreneurial, and virtual organizations are now being discussed. New interorganizational joint ventures, alliances, subsidiaries, incubator units etc. are emerging among business, government and postsecondary institutions to serve educational, research, service and economic development functions. The literature to describe and capture this evolving industry, the new organizational models and their decision making and leadership patterns has yet to develop.

The articles reproduced in this section of the reader are intended to provide an overview and an underpinning for understanding how postsecondary education is organized, governed, and led. The focus is on conceptual and theoretical patterns and does not include works that describe various organizational types or attempt to address specific governance issues, management processes or leadership techniques. The articles included cover both interorganizational and organizational levels of behavior.

At the organizational level the reprinted article by J. Victor Baldridge et al, "Alternative Models of Governance In Higher Education," captures both the nature of colleges and universities as organizations and systematically contrasts three early models of organization and governance or decision making—bureaucratic, community and political. Among the suggested additional readings, one by Marvin Peterson and Lisa Mets, "An Evolutionary Perspective on Academic Governance, Management and Leadership," offers a good overview of the literature through the mid 1980s. Unfortunately the only comparison that updates this with the development through the 1980s is book-length. Robert Birnbaum's, *How Colleges Work*, weaves in the interests in organizational culture and organizational learning or cybernetics that emerged in the 1980s. Other recommended readings that capture key conceptions of organization and governance from the 1970s through the 1990s are: 1) on bureaucracy or formal-rational organization: Stroup's, *Bureaucracy in Higher Education* and Henry Mintzberg's "The Professional Bureaucracy"; 2) on community: Burton Clark's "The Organizational Saga"; John Millett's *The Academic Community*, and Paul Goodman's *The Community of Scholars* 3) on political organization and governance: J. Victor Baldridge's *Power and Conflict in the Universe*; 4) on complexity: Daniel Alpert's "Performance and Paralysis" describing a matrix view of organization, Karl Weick's "Educational Organizations as Loosely Coupled

Systems" and Michael Cohen and James March's "The Process of Choice" which describes the ambiguous nature of an organized anarchy; and 5) on culture: Andrew Masland's "Organizational Culture In Higher Education" and William Tierney's "Organizational Culture In Higher Education."

On leadership, the reprinted chapter by Estella Bensimon, Anna Neumann, and Robert Birnbaum, "Higher Education and Leadership Theory," provides a comprehensive overview of the theoretical and conceptual perspectives on this complex topic. While the literature on leadership is extensive, several suggested additional readings capture some of the essential features of this process in higher education. Jeffrey Pfeffer's "The Ambiguity of Leadership," captured early on some of the dilemmas for leadership in higher education. Michael Cohen and James March elaborate on the ambiguous nature of leadership in discussing "Leadership in an Organized Anarchy." It is difficult to discuss leadership in higher education without focusing on the president and Clark Kerr and Marion Gade provide both experiential and research insight in *The Many Lives of Academic Presidents*. In a more focused treatment of the topic of leadership, David Dill's "The Nature of Administrative Behavior" and David Whetten and Kim Cameron's treatment of "Administrative Effectiveness In Higher Education" provide perspectives useful below the presidential level.

The interorganizational patterns of the structure of our higher education system are seldom discussed in the literature—"we don't have a national system of higher education"—or are addressed by literature specifically focused—on state level organization, institutional associations, accreditation, consortia or other specific forms of postsecondary interorganizational arrangements. The reprinted, Marvin Peterson and David Dill's chapter "Understanding the Competitive Environment of the Postsecondary Knowledge Industry," offers an examination of the changing nature of our industry (a set of interrelated organizations), the forces currently reshaping it and some of its possible institutional implications that suggest emerging new organizational and decision making models and leadership challenges. In two suggested additional readings Kim Cameron's "Organizational Adaptation in Higher Education" provides a framework for examining organization-environment interaction and Ellen Chaffee's "Strategy and Effectiveness in Systems of Higher Education" focuses on the dynamics of complex systems.

The reality, of course, is that none of these models is sufficient alone. As our view of colleges and universities has become more sophisticated, our perspective on the processes of organization, governance or decision making and leadership has reflected the complexity of multiple models of organization and differing levels of analysis. Once again the student interested in a more in depth treatment is referred to the most recent edition of the *ASHE Reader on Organization and Governance in Higher Education*.

Suggested Supplementary Readings

Alpert, D. "Performance and Paralysis: The Organizational Context of the American Research University." *Journal of Higher Education*, 1985, *56*, 3.

Baldridge, J. V. *Power and Conflict in the University*. New York: Wiley, 1971.

Baldridge, J. V. et al. "Alternative Models of Governance in Higher Education," in J. V. Baldridge and G. Riley (eds.) *Governing Academic Organization*. McCutchan Publishing Corporation, 1977.

Bensimon, E. M., Neumann, A. and Birnbaum, R. "Higher Education and Leadership Theory," in *Making Sense of Administrative Leadership: The "L" Word in Higher Education*. Report No. 1. ASHE-ERIC Higher Education Research Reports. George Washington University, 1989.

Birnbaum, R. *How Colleges Work*. San Francisco: Jossey-Bass, 1988.

Chaffee, E. E. "Strategy and Effectiveness in Systems of Higher Education," in J. C. Smart (ed.). *Higher Education: Handbook of Theory and Research*. Vol. V. New York: Agathon Press, 1989, 1–30.

Clark, B. *The Distinctive College*. New York: McGraw-Hill, 1970.

Clark, B. R. "The Organizational SAGA in Higher Education," *Administrative Science Quarterly*, 1972, *17*, 2.

Cohen, Michael D. and March, James G. "The Processes of Choice," in M. D. Cohen and J. G. March, *Leadership and Ambiguity*. New York: McGraw-Hill, 1974.

Cohen, Michael D. and March, James G., "Leadership in Organized Anarchy," in *Leadership and Ambiguity: The American College President*. New York: McGraw-Hill, 1974.

Dill, David D. "The Nature of Administrative Behavior in Higher Education," *Educational Administration Quarterly*, 1984, *20*, 3.

Kerr, Clark & Marian L. Gade, *The Many Lives of Academic Presidents/Time, Place and Character*. Washington: Association of Governing Boards, 1986, 125–157.

Masland, A. "Organizational Culture in the Study of Higher Education," *Review of Higher Education*, 1985, *88*, 1.

Millett, John. *The Academic Community*. New York: McGraw-Hill, 1962.

Mintzberg, Henry. "The Professional Bureaucracy," in *The Structuring of Organizations*, Englewood Cliffs, New Jersey: Prentice-Hall, 1979.

Peterson. Marvin W. and Dill, David. "Understanding the Competitive Environment of the Postsecondary Knowledge Industry," in M. Peterson, D. Dill, and L. Metz, *Planning and Management for a Changing Environment*. San Francisco: Jossey-Bass, 1997.

Peterson, Marvin W. and Mets L. "An Evolutionary Perspective on Academic Governance, Management and Leadership," in M. Peterson and L. Mets (eds.). *Key Resources in Higher Education. Governance, Management, and Leadership*. San Francisco: Jossey-Bass, 1987.

Peterson, Marvin W. "Analyzing Alternative Approaches to Planning" in P. Jedamus and M. W. Peterson, *Improving Academic Management*. San Francisco: Jossey-Bass, 1981.

Peterson, Marvin W., Chaffee, Ellen, and White, T. (eds.). *ASHE Reader on Organization and Governance in Higher Education*. Vol. 4, Lexington, Mass: Ginn Press, 1991.

Pfeffer, Jeffrey. "The Ambiguity of Leadership". *The Academy of Management Review*, 1977, *12*, 1.

Stroup, Herbert. *Bureaucracy In Higher Education*. New York: Free Press, 1966.

Tierney, William G. "Organizational Culture in Higher Education," *The Journal of Higher Education*, 1988, *59*, 1.

Weick, Karl "Educational Organizations as Loosely Coupled Systems," *Administrative Science Quarterly*. Vol. 21, Issue 1, 1976.

Whetten, D.A. and Cameron, K. S. "Administrative Effectiveness in Higher Education," *Review of Higher Education*, 1985, *9*, 1.

Alternative Models of Governance in Higher Education

J. Victor Baldridge, David V. Curtis, George P. Ecker, and Gary L. Riley

Organizations vary in a number of important ways: they have different types of clients, they work with different technologies, they employ workers with different skills, they develop different structures and coordinating styles, and they have different relationships to their external environments. Of course, there are elements common to the operation of colleges and universities, hospitals, prisons, business firms, government bureaus, and so on, but no two organizations are the same. Any adequate model of decision making and governance in an organization must take its distinctive characteristics into account.

This chapter deals with the organizational characteristics and decision processes of colleges and universities. Colleges and universities are unique organizations, differing in major respects from industrial organizations, government bureaus, and business firms.

Distinguishing Characteristics of Academic Organizations

Colleges and universities are complex organizations. Like other organizations they have goals, hierarchical systems and structures, officials who carry out specified duties, decision-making processes that set institutional policy, and a bureaucratic administration that handles routine business. But they also exhibit some critical distinguishing characteristics that affect their decision processes.

Goal Ambiguity

Most organizations are goal-oriented, and as a consequence they can build decision structures to reach their objectives. Business firms want to make a profit, government bureaus have tasks specified by law, hospitals are trying to cure sick people, prisons are in the business of "rehabilitation."

By contrast, colleges and universities have vague, ambiguous goals and they must build decision processes to grapple with a higher degree of uncertainty and conflict. What is the goal of a university? This is a difficult question, for the list of possible answers is long: teaching, research, service to the local community, administration of scientific installations, support of the arts, solutions to social problems. In their book *Leadership and Ambiguity*, Cohen and March comment:

> Almost any educated person could deliver a lecture entitled "The Goals of the University." Almost no one will listen to the lecture voluntarily. For the most part, such lectures and their companion essays are well-intentioned exercises in social rhetoric, with little operational content. Efforts to generate normative statements of the goals of the university tend to produce goals that are either meaningless or dubious [Cohen and March, 1974, page 195].

Goal ambiguity, then, is one of the chief characteristics of academic organizations. They rarely have a single mission. On the contrary, they often try to be all things to all people. Because

"Alternative Models of Governance in Higher Education," by J. Victor Baldridge, David V. Curtis, George P. Ecker, and Gary L. Riley, reprinted from *Governing Academic Organizations: New Problems, New Perspectives*, edited by Gary L. Riley and J. Victor Baldridge, 1977, McCutchan Publishing Group.

their existing goals are unclear, they also find it hard to reject new goals. Edward Gross (1968) analyzed the goals of faculty and administrators in a large number of American universities and obtained some remarkable results. To be sure, some goals were ranked higher than others, with academic freedom consistently near the top. But both administrators and faculty marked as important almost every one of forty-seven goals listed by Gross!

Not only are academic goals unclear, they are also highly contested. As long as goals are left ambiguous and abstract, they are readily agreed on. As soon as they are concretely specified and put into operation, conflict erupts. The link between clarity and conflict may help explain the prevalence of meaningless rhetoric in academic policy statements and speeches. It is tempting to resort to rhetoric when serious content produces conflict.

Client Service

Like schools, hospitals, and welfare agencies, academic organizations are "people-processing" institutions. Clients with specific needs are fed into the institution from the environment, the institution acts upon them, and the clients are returned to the larger society. This is an extremely important characteristic, for the clients demand and often obtain significant input into institutional decision-making processes. Even powerless clients such as schoolchildren usually have protectors, such as parents, who demand a voice in the operation of the organization. In higher education, of course, the clients are quite capable of speaking for themselves—and they often do.

Problematic Technology

Because they serve clients with disparate, complicated needs, client-serving organizations frequently have problematic technologies. A manufacturing organization develops a specific technology that can be segmented and routinized. Unskilled, semiskilled, and white collar workers can be productively used without relying heavily on professional expertise. But it is hard to construct a simple technology for an organization dealing with people. Serving clients is difficult to accomplish, and the results are difficult to evaluate, especially on a short-term basis. The entire person must be considered; people cannot be separated easily into small, routine, and technical segments. If at times colleges and universities do not know clearly *what* they are trying to do, they often do not know *how* to do it either.

Professionalism

How does an organization work when its goals are unclear, its service is directed to clients, and its technology is problematic? Most organizations attempt to deal with these problems by hiring expertly trained professionals. Hospitals require doctors and nurses, social welfare agencies hire social workers, public schools hire teachers, and colleges and universities hire faculty members. These professionals use a broad repertoire of skills to deal with the complex and often unpredictable problems of clients. Instead of subdividing a complicated task into a routine set of procedures, professional work requires that a broad range of tasks be performed by a single employee.

Sociologists have made a number of important general observations about professional employees, wherever they may work:

1. Professionals demand *autonomy* in their work. Having acquired considerable skill and expertise in their field, they demand freedom from supervision in applying them.

2. Professionals have *divided loyalties*. They have "cosmopolitan" tendencies and loyalty to their peers at the national level may sometimes interfere with loyalty to their local organization.

3. There are strong tensions between *professional values* and *bureaucratic expectations* in an organization. This can intensify conflict between professional employees and organizational managers.

4. Professionals demand *peer evaluation* of their work. They believe that only their colleagues can judge their performance, and they reject the evaluations of others, even those who are technically their superiors in the organizational hierarchy.

All of these characteristics undercut the traditional norms of a bureaucracy, rejecting its hierarchy, control structure, and management procedures. As a consequence, we can expect a distinct management style in a professional organization.

Finally, colleges and universities tend to have *fragmented* professional staffs. In some organizations there is one dominant professional group. For example, doctors are the dominant group in hospitals. In other organizations the professional staff is fragmented into subgroups, none of which predominates. The faculty in a university provides a clear example. Burton R. Clark comments on the fragmented professionalism in academic organizations:

> The internal controls of the medical profession are strong and are substituted for those of the organization. But in the college or university this situation does not obtain; there are twelve, twenty-five, or fifty clusters of experts. The experts are prone to identify with their own disciplines, and the "academic profession" overall comes off a poor second. We have wheels within wheels, many professions within a profession. No one of the disciplines on a campus is likely to dominate the others. . . . The campus is not a closely knit group of professionals who see the world from one perspective. As a collection of professionals, it is decentralized, loose, and flabby.
>
> The principle is this: where professional influence is high and there is one dominant professional group, the organization will be integrated by the imposition of professional standards. Where professional influence is high and there are a number of professional groups, the organization will be split by professionalism. The university and the large college are fractured by expertness, not unified by it. The sheer variety supports the tendency for authority to diffuse toward quasi-autonomous clusters [Clark, 1963, pages 37, 51].

Environmental Vulnerability

Another characteristic that sets colleges and universities apart from many other complex organizations is environmental vulnerability. Almost all organizations interact with their social environment to some extent. But though no organization is completely autonomous, some have considerably greater freedom of action than others. The degree of autonomy an organization has vis-à-vis its environment is one of the critical determinants of how it will be managed.

For example, in a free market economy, business firms and industries have a substantial degree of autonomy. Although they are regulated by countless government agencies and constrained by their customers, essentially they are free agents responsive to market demands rather than to government control. At the other extreme, a number of organizations are virtually "captured" by their environments. Public school districts, for example, are constantly scrutinized and pressured by the communities they serve.

Colleges and universities are somewhere in the middle on a continuum from "independent" to "captured." In many respects they are insulated from their environment. Recently, however, powerful external forces have been applied to academic institutions. Interest groups holding conflicting values have made their wishes, demands, and threats well known to the administrations and faculties of academic organizations in the 1970s.

What impact does environmental pressure have on the governance of colleges and universities? When professional organizations are well insulated from the pressures of the outside environment, then professional values, norms, and work definitions play a dominant role in shaping the character of the organization. On the other hand, when strong external pressure is applied to colleges and universities, the operating autonomy of the academic professionals is seriously reduced. The faculty and administrators lose some control over the curriculum, the goals, and the daily operation of the institution. Under these circumstances, the academic professionals are frequently reduced to the role of hired employees doing the bidding of bureaucratic managers.

Although colleges and universities are not entirely captured by their environments, they are steadily losing ground. As their vulnerability increases, their governance patterns change significantly.

"Organized Anarchy"

To summarize, academic organizations have several unique organizational characteristics.

They have *ambiguous goals* that are often strongly contested. They serve *clients* who demand a voice in the decision-making process. They have a *problematic technology,* for in order to serve clients their technology must be holistic and adaptable to individual needs. They are *professionalized organizations* in which employees demand a large measure of control over institutional decision processes. Finally, they are becoming more and more *vulnerable to their environments.*

The character of such a complex organizational system is not satisfactorily conveyed by the standard term "bureaucracy." Bureaucracy carries the connotation of stability or even rigidity; academic organizations seem more fluid. Bureaucracy implies distinct lines of authority and strict hierarchical command; academic organizations have blurred lines of authority and professional employees who demand autonomy in their work. Bureaucracy suggests a cohesive organization with clear goals; academic organizations are characteristically fragmented with ambiguous and contested goals. Bureaucracy does adequately describe certain aspects of colleges and universities, such as business administration, plant management, capital outlay, and auxiliary services. But the processes at the heart of an academic organization—academic policy making, professional teaching, and research—do not resemble the processes one finds in a bureaucracy. Table 1 summarizes the differences between the two types of organizations.

Perhaps a better term for academic organizations has been suggested by Cohen and March. They describe the academic organization as an "organized anarchy"—a system with little central coordination or control:

> In a university anarchy each individual in the university is seen as making autonomous decisions. Teachers decide if, when, and what to teach. Students decide if, when, and what to learn. Legislators and donors decide if, when, and what to support. Neither coordination . . . nor control [is] practiced. Resources are allocated by whatever process emerges but without explicit accommodation and without explicit reference to some superordinate goal. The "decisions" of the system are a consequence produced by the system but intended by no one and decisively con-

trolled by no one [Cohen and March, 1974, pages 33–34].

The organized anarchy differs radically from the well-organized bureaucracy or the consensus-bound collegium. It is an organization in which generous resources allow people to go in different directions without coordination by a central authority. Leaders are relatively weak and decisions are made by individual action. Since the organization's goals are ambiguous, decisions are often by-products of unintended and unplanned activity. In such fluid circumstances, presidents and other institutional leaders serve primarily as catalysts or facilitators of an ongoing process. They do not so much lead the institution as channel its activities in subtle ways. They do not command, but negotiate. They do not plan comprehensively, but try to apply preexisting solutions to problems.

Decisions are not so much "made" as they "happen." Problems, choices, and decision makers happen to come together in temporary solutions. Cohen and March have described decision processes in an organized anarchy as

> sets of procedures through which organizational participants arrive at an interpretation of what they are doing and what they have done while they are doing it. From this point of view an organization is a collection of choices looking for problems, issues and feelings looking for decision situations in which they might be aired, solutions looking for issues for which they might be the answer, and decision makers looking for work [Cohen and March, 1974, page 81].

The imagery of organized anarchy helps capture the spirit of the confused organizational dynamics in academic institutions: unclear goals, unclear technologies, and environmental vulnerability.

Some may regard "organized anarchy" as an exaggerated term, suggesting more confusion and conflict than really exist in academic organizations. This is probably a legitimate criticism. The term may also carry negative connotations to those unaware that it applies to specific organizational characteristics rather than to the entire campus community. Nevertheless, "organized anarchy" has some strong points in its favor. It breaks through the traditional for-

TABLE 1
Organizational Characteristics of Academic Organizations and More Traditional Bureaucracies

	Academic organizations (colleges and universities)	Traditional bureaucracies (government agency, industry)
Goals	Ambiguous, contested, inconsistent	Clearer goals, less disagreement
Client service	Client-serving	Material-processing, commercial
Technology	Unclear, nonroutine, holistic	Clearer, routinized, segmented
Staffing	Predominantly professional	Predominantly nonprofessional
Environmental relations	Very vulnerable	Less vulnerable
Summary image	"Organized anarchy"	"Bureaucracy"

mality that often surrounds discussions of decision making, challenges our existing conceptions, and suggests a looser, more fluid kind of organization. For these reasons we will join Cohen and March in using "organized anarchy" to summarize some of the unique organizational characteristics of colleges and universities: (1) unclear goals, (2) client service, (3) unclear technology, (4) professionalism, and (5) environmental vulnerability.[1]

Models of Academic Governance

Administrators and organization theorists concerned with academic governance have often developed images to summarize the complex decision process: collegial system, bureaucratic network, political activity, or participatory democracy. Such models organize the way we perceive the process, determine how we analyze it, and help determine our actions. For example, if we regard a system as political, then we form coalitions to pressure decision makers. If we regard it as collegial, then we seek to persuade people by appealing to reason. If we regard it as bureaucratic, then we use legalistic maneuvers to gain our ends.

In the past few years, as research on higher education has increased, models for academic governance have also proliferated. Three models have received widespread attention, more or less dominating the thinking of people who study academic governance. We will examine briefly each of these models in turn: (1) the bureaucracy, (2) the collegium, and (3) the political system. Each of these models has certain points in its favor. They can be used jointly to examine different aspects of the governance process.

The Academic Bureaucracy

One of the most influential descriptions of complex organizations is Max Weber's (1947) monumental work on bureaucracies. Weber discussed the characteristics of bureaucracies that distinguish them from less formal work organizations. In skeleton form he suggested that bureaucracies are networks of social groups dedicated to limited goals and organized for maximum efficiency. Moreover, the regulation of a bureaucratic system is based on the principle of "legal rationality," as contrasted with informal regulation based on friendship, loyalty to family, or personal allegiance to a charismatic leader. The hierarchical structure is held together by formal chains of command and systems of communication. The bureaucracy as Weber described it includes such elements as tenure, appointment to office, salaries as a rational form of payment, and competency as the basis of promotion.

Bureaucratic characteristics of colleges and universities. Several authors have suggested that university governance may be more fully understood by applying the bureaucratic model. For example, Herbert Stroup (1966) has pointed out some characteristics of colleges and universities that fit Weber's original description of a bureaucracy.

They include the following:

1. Competence is the criterion used for appointment.

2. Officials are appointed, not elected.

3. Salaries are fixed and paid directly by the organization, rather than determined in "free-fee" style.

4. Rank is recognized and respected.

5. The career is exclusive; no other work is done.

6. The style of life of the organization's members centers on the organization.

7. Security is present in a tenure system.

8. Personal and organizational property are separated.

Stroup is undoubtedly correct in believing that Weber's paradigm can be applied to universities, and most observers are well aware of the bureaucratic factors involved in university administration. Among the more prominent are the following.

1. The university is a complex organization under *state charter*, like most other bureaucracies. This seemingly innocent fact, has major consequences, especially as states increasingly seek to exercise control.

2. The university has a *formal hierarchy*, with offices and a set of bylaws that specify the relations between those offices. Professors, instructors, and research assistants may be considered bureaucratic officers in the same sense as deans, chancellors, and presidents.

3. There are *formal channels of communication* that must be respected.

4. There are definite *bureaucratic authority relations*, with certain officials exercising authority over others. In a university the authority relations are often vague and shifting, but no one would deny that they exist.

5. There are *formal policies and rules* that govern much of the institution's work, such as library regulations, budgetary guidelines, and procedures of the university senate.

6. The bureaucratic elements of the university are most vividly apparent in its *"people-processing" aspects*: record keeping, registration, graduation requirements, and a multitude of other routine, day-to-day activities designed to help the modern university handle its masses of students.

7. *Bureaucratic decision-making processes* are used, most often by officials assigned the responsibility for making routine decisions by the formal administrative structure. Examples are admissions pro-

cedures, handled by the dean of admissions; procedures for graduation, routinely administered by designated officials; research policies, supervised by specified officials; and financial matters, usually handled in a bureaucratic manner by the finance office.

Weaknesses in the bureaucratic model. In many ways the bureaucratic model falls short of encompassing university governance, especially if one is primarily concerned with decision-making processes. First, the bureaucratic model tells us much about authority—that is, legitimate, formalized power—but not much about informal types of power and influence, which may take the form of mass movements or appeals to emotion and sentiment. Second, it explains much about the organization's formal *structure* but little about the dynamic *processes* that characterize the organization in action. Third, it describes the formal structure at one particular time, but it does not explain changes over time. Fourth, it explains how policies may be carried out most efficiently, but it says little about the critical process by which policy is established in the first place. Finally, it also ignores political issues, such as the struggles of various interest groups within the university.

The University Collegium

Many writers have rejected the bureaucratic model of the university. They seek to replace it with the model of the "collegium" or "community of scholars." When this literature is closely examined, there seem to be at least three different threads running through it.

A description of collegial decision making. This approach argues that academic decision making should not be like the hierarchical process in a bureaucracy. Instead there should be full participation of the academic community, especially the faculty. Under this concept the community of scholars would administer its own affairs, and bureaucratic officials would have little influence (see Goodman, 1962). John Millett, one of the foremost proponents of this model, has succinctly stated his view:

> I do not believe that the concept of hierarchy is a realistic representation of the interpersonal relationships which exist within a college or university. Nor do I believe that a

structure of hierarchy is a desirable prescription for the organization of a college or university. . . .

I would argue that there is another concept of organization just as valuable as a tool of analysis and even more useful as a generalized observation of group and interpersonal behavior. This is the concept of community. . . .

The concept of community presupposes an organization in which functions are differentiated and in which specialization must be brought together, or coordination, if you will, is achieved not through a structure of superordination and subordination of persons and groups but through a *dynamic of consensus* [Millett, 1962, pages 234–235].

A discussion of the faculty's professional authority. Talcott Parsons (1947) was one of the first to call attention to the difference between "official competence," derived from one's office in a bureaucracy, and "technical competence," derived from one's ability to perform a given task. Parsons concentrated on the technical competence of the physician but others have extended this logic to other professionals whose authority is based on what they *know* and can *do*, rather than on their official position. Some examples are the scientist in industry, the military adviser, the expert in government, the physician in the hospital, and the professor in the university.

The literature on professionalism strongly supports the argument for collegial organization. It emphasizes the professional's ability to make his own decisions and his need for freedom from organizational restraints. Consequently, the collegium is seen as the most reasonable method of organizing the university. Parsons, for example, notes (page 60) that when professionals are organized in a bureaucracy, "there are strong tendencies for them to develop a different sort of structure from that characteristic of the administrative hierarchy . . . of bureaucracy. Instead of a rigid hierarchy of status and authority there tends to be what is roughly, in formal status, a company of equals."

A utopian prescription for operating the educational system. There is a third strand in the collegial image. In recent years there has been a growing discontent with our impersonal contemporary society. The multiversity, with its thousands of students and its huge bureau-

cracy, is a case in point. The student revolts of the 1960s and perhaps even the widespread apathy of the 1970s are symptoms of deeply felt alienation between students and massive educational establishments. The discontent and anxiety this alienation has produced are aptly expressed in the now-famous sign worn by a Berkeley student: "I am a human being—do not fold, spindle, or mutilate."

As an alternative to this impersonal, bureaucratized educational system, many critics are calling for a return to the "academic community." In their conception such a community would offer personal attention, humane education, and "relevant confrontation with life." Paul Goodman's *The Community of Scholars* (1962) still appeals to many who seek to reform the university. Goodman cites the need for more personal interaction between faculty and students, for more relevant courses, and for educational innovations to bring the student into existential dialogue with the subject matter of his discipline. The number of articles on this subject, in both the mass media and the professional journals, is astonishingly large. Indeed, this concept of the collegial academic community is now widely proposed as one answer to the impersonality and meaninglessness of today's large multiversity. Thus conceived, the collegial model functions more as a revolutionary ideology and a utopian projection than a description of actual governance processes at any university.

Weaknesses in the collegial model. Three themes are incorporated in the collegial model: (1) decision making by consensus, (2) the professional authority of faculty members, and (3) the call for more humane education. These are all legitimate and appealing. Few would deny that our universities would be better centers of learning if we could somehow implement these objectives. There is a misleading simplicity about the collegial model, however, that glosses over many realities.

For one thing, the *descriptive* and *normative* visions are often confused. In the literature dealing with the collegial model it is often difficult to tell whether a writer is saying that the university is a collegium or that it ought to be a collegium. Discussions of the collegium are frequently more a lament for paradise lost than a description of reality. Indeed, the collegial image of round-table decision making is not an accurate description of the processes in most institutions.

Although at the department level there are many examples of collegial decision making, at higher levels it usually exists only in some aspects of the committee system. Of course, the proponents may be advocating a collegial model as a desirable goal or reform strategy. This is helpful, but it does not allow us to understand the actual workings of universities.

In addition, the collegial model fails to deal adequately with the problem of *conflict*. When Millett emphasizes the "dynamic of consensus," he neglects the prolonged battles that precede consensus, as well as decisions that actually represent the victory of one group over another. Proponents of the collegial model are correct in declaring that simple bureaucratic rule making is not the essence of decision making. But in making this point they take the equally indefensible position that major decisions are reached primarily by consensus. Neither extreme is correct, for decisions are rarely made by either bureaucratic fiat or simple consensus.

The University as a Political System

In *Power and Conflict in the University* (1971), Baldridge proposed a "political" model of university governance. Although the other major models of governance—the collegial and the bureaucratic—have valuable insights to offer, we believe that further insights can be gained from this model. It grapples with the power plays, conflicts, and rough-and-tumble politics to be found in many academic institutions.

Basic assumptions of a political model. The political model assumes that complex organizations can be studied as miniature political systems. There are interest group dynamics and conflicts similar to those in cities, states, or other political entities. The political model focuses on policy-forming processes, because major policies commit an organization to definite goals and set the strategies for reaching those goals. Policy decisions are critical decisions. They have a major impact on an organization's future. Of course, in any practical situation it may be difficult to separate the routine from the critical for issues that seem minor at one point may later be decisive, or vice versa.

In general, however, policy decisions bind an organization to important courses of action.

Since policies are so important, people throughout an organization try to influence them to reflect their own interests and values. Policy making becomes a vital target of interest group activity that permeates the organization. Owing to its central importance, then, the organization theorist may select policy formation as the key for studying organizational conflict and change, just as the political scientist often selects legislative acts as the focal point for his analysis of a state's political processes. With policy formation as its key issue, the political model operates on a series of assumptions about the political process.

1. To say that policy making is a political process is not to say that everyone is involved. On the contrary, *inactivity* prevails. Most people most of the time find the policy-making process an uninteresting, unrewarding activity. Policy making is therefore left to the administrators. This is characteristic not only of policy making in universities but of political processes in society at large. Voters do not vote; citizens do not attend city council meetings; parents often permit school boards to do what they please. By and large, decisions that may have a profound effect on our society are made by small groups of elites.

2. Even people who are active engage in *fluid participation*. They move in and out of the decision-making process. Rarely do people spend much time on any given issue. Decisions, therefore, are usually made by those who persist. This normally means that small groups of political elites govern most major decisions, for they invest the necessary time in the process.

3. Colleges and universities, like most other social organizations, are characterized by fragmentation into *interest groups* with different goals and values. When resources are plentiful and the organization is prospering, these interest groups engage in only minimal conflict. But they are likely to mobilize and try to influence decisions when resources are

tight, outside pressure groups attack, or internal groups try to assume command.

4. In a fragmented, dynamic social system *conflict* is natural. It is not necessarily a symptom of breakdown in the academic community. In fact, conflict is a significant factor in promoting healthy organizational change.

5. The pressure that groups can exert places severe *limitations on formal authority* in the bureaucratic sense. Decisions are not simply bureaucratic orders but are often negotiated compromises between competing groups. Officials are not free simply to issue a decision. Instead they must attempt to find a viable course acceptable to several powerful blocs.

6. *External interest groups* exert a strong influence over the policy-making process. External pressures and formal control by outside agencies—especially in public institutions—are powerful shapers of internal governance processes.

The political decision model versus the rational decision model. The bureaucratic model of organizational structure is accompanied by a rational model of decision making. It is usually assumed that in a bureaucracy the structure is hierarchical and well organized, and that decisions are made through clear-cut, predetermined steps. Moreover, a definite, rational approach is expected to lead to the optimal decision. Graham T. Allison has summarized the rational decision-making process as follows:

1. *Goals and objectives.* The goals and objectives of the agent are translated into a "payoff" or "utility" or "preference" function, which represents the "value" or "utility" of alternative sets of consequences. At the outset of the decision problem the agent has a payoff function which ranks all possible sets of consequences in terms of his values and objectives. Each bundle of consequences will contain a number of side effects. Nevertheless, at a minimum, the agent must be able to rank in order of preference each possible set of consequences

that might result from a particular action.

2. *Alternatives.* The rational agent must choose among a set of alternatives displayed before him in a particular situation. In decision theory these alternatives are represented as a decision tree. The alternative courses of action may include more than a simple act, but the specification of a course of action must be sufficiently precise to differentiate it from other alternatives.

3. *Consequences.* To each alternative is attached a set of consequences or outcomes of choice that will ensue if that particular alternative is chosen. Variations are generated at this point by making different assumptions about the accuracy of the decision maker's knowledge of the consequences that follow from the choice of each alternative.

4. *Choice.* Rational choice consists simply of selecting that alternative whose consequences rank highest in the decision maker's payoff function [Allison, 1971, pages 29–30].

The rational model appeals to those who regard their actions as essentially goal-directed and rational. Realistically, however, we should realize that the rational model is more an ideal than an actual description of how people act. In fact, in the confused organizational setting of the university, political constraints often undermine the force of rationality. A political model of decision making requires us to answer some new questions about the decision process:

The first new question posed by the political model is *why* a given decision is made at all. The formalists have already indicated that "recognition of the problem" is one element in the process, but too little attention has been paid to the activities that bring a particular issue to the forefront. Why is *this* decision being considered at *this* particular time? The political model insists that interest groups, powerful individuals, and bureaucratic processes are critical in drawing attention to some decisions rather than to others. A study of "attention cues" by which issues are called to the community's attention is a vital part of any analysis.

Second, a question must be raised about the right of any person or group to make the decisions. Previously the *who* question was seldom raised, chiefly because the decision literature was developed for hierarchical organizations in which the focus of authority could be easily defined. In a more loosely coordinated system however, we must ask a prior question: Why was the legitimacy to make the decision vested in a particular person or group? Why is Dean Smith making the decision instead of Dean Jones or why is the University Senate dealing with the problem instead of the central administration? Establishing the right of authority over a decision is a political question, subject to conflict, power manipulation, and struggles between interest groups. Thus the political model always asks tough questions: Who has the right to make the decision? What are the conflict-ridden processes by which the decision was located at this point rather than at another? The crucial point is that often the issue of *who* makes the decision has already limited, structured, and pre-formed *how* it will be made.

The third new issue raised by a political interpretation concerns the development of complex decision networks. As a result of the fragmentation of the university, decision making is rarely located in one official; instead it is dependent on the advice and authority of numerous people. Again the importance of the committee system is evident. It is necessary to understand that the committee network is the legitimate reflection of the need for professional influence to intermingle with bureaucratic influence. The decision process, then, is taken out of the hands of individuals (although there are still many who are powerful) and placed into a network that allows a *cumulative buildup* of expertise and advice. When the very life of the organization clusters around expertise, *decision making is likely to be diffused, segmentalized, and decentralized.* A complex network of committees, councils, and advisory bodies grows to handle the task of assembling the expertise necessary for reasonable decisions. Decision making by the individual bureaucrat is replaced with decision making by committee, council, and cabinet. Centralized decision making is replaced with diffuse decision making. The process becomes a far-flung network for gathering expertise from every

corner of the organization and translating it into policy [Baldridge, 1971, page 190].

The fourth new question raised by the political model concerns alternative solutions to the problem at hand. The rational decision model suggests that all possible options are open and within easy reach of the decision maker. A realistic appraisal of decision dynamics in most organizations, however, suggests that by no means are all options open. The political dynamics of interest groups, the force of external power blocs, and the opposition of powerful professional constituencies may leave only a handful of viable options. The range of alternatives is often sharply limited by political considerations. Just as important, there is often little time and energy available for seeking new solutions. Although all possible solutions should be identified under the rational model, in the real world administrators have little time to grope for solutions before their deadlines.

In *Power and Conflict in the University,* Baldridge summed up the political model of decision making as follows:

First, powerful political forces—interest groups, bureaucratic officials, influential individuals, organizational subunits—cause a given issue to emerge from the limbo of on-going problems and certain "attention cues" force the political community to consider the problem. Second, there is a struggle over locating the decision with a particular person or group, for the location of the right to make the decision often determines the outcome. Third, decisions are usually "preformed" to a great extent by the time one person or group is given the legitimacy to make the decision; not all options are open and the choices have been severely limited by the previous conflicts. Fourth, such political struggles are more likely to occur in reference to "critical" decisions than to "routine" decisions. Fifth, a complex decision network is developed to gather the necessary information and supply the critical expertise. Sixth, during the process of making the decision political controversy is likely to continue and compromises, deals, and plain head cracking are often necessary to get any decision made. Finally, the controversy is not likely to end easily. In fact, it is difficult even to know when a decision *is* made, for the political processes have a habit of unmaking, confusing, and muddling whatever agreements are hammered out.

This may be a better way of grappling with the complexity that surrounds decision processes within a loosely coordinated, fragmented political system. The formal decision models seem to have been asking very limited questions about the decision process and more insight can be gained by asking a new set of political questions. Thus the decision model that emerges from the university's political dynamics is more open, more dependent on conflict and political action. It is not so systematic or formalistic as most decision theory, but it is probably closer to the truth. Decision making, then, is not an isolated technique but another critical process that must be integrated into a larger political image [Baldridge, 1971, pages 191–192].

It is clear that a political analysis emphasizes certain factors over others. First, it is concerned primarily with problems of goal setting and conflicts over values, rather than with efficiency in achieving goals. Second, analysis of the organization's change processes and adaptation to its environment is critically important. The political dynamics of a university are constantly changing, pressuring the university in many directions, and forcing change throughout the academic system. Third, the analysis of conflict is an essential component. Fourth, there is the role of interest groups in pressuring decision makers to formulate policy. Finally, much attention is given to the legislative and decision-making phases—the processes by which pressures and power are transformed into policy. Taken together these points constitute the bare outline for a political analysis of academic governance.

The revised political model: an environmental and structuralist approach. Since the political model of academic governance originally appeared in *Power and Conflict in the University*, we have become aware that it has several shortcomings. For this reason we offer a few observations about some changes in emphasis, a few corrections in focus.

First, the original political model probably underestimated the impact of routine bureaucratic processes. Many, perhaps most, decisions are made not in the heat of political controversy but according to standard operating procedures. The political description in *Power and Conflict in the University* was based on a study of New York University. The research occurred at a time of extremely high conflict when the university was confronted with two crises, a student revolution and a financial disaster. The political model developed from that study probably overstresses the role of conflict and negotiation as elements in standard decision making, since those were the processes apparent at the time. Now we would stress that it is important to consider routine procedures of the governance process.

Second, the original political model, based on a single case study, did not do justice to the broad range of political activity that occurs in different kinds of institutions. For example, NYU is quite different from Oberlin College, and both are distinctive institutions compared to local community colleges. Many of the intense political dynamics observed in the NYU study may have been exaggerated in a troubled institution such as NYU, particularly during the heated conflicts of the late 1960s.

Third, we want to stress even more strongly the central role of environmental factors. The NYU analysis showed that conflict and political processes within the university were linked to environmental factors. But even more stress on the environmental context is needed.

Finally, as developed in *Power and Conflict in the University*, the political model suffered from an "episodic" character. That is, the model did not give enough emphasis to long-term decision-making patterns, and it failed to consider the way institutional structure may shape and channel political efforts. Centralization of power, the development of decision councils, long-term patterns of professional autonomy, the dynamics of departmental power, and the growth of unionization were all slighted by the original model. There are other important questions concerning long-term patterns: What groups tend to dominate decision making over long periods of time? Do some groups seem to be systematically excluded from the decision-making process? Do different kinds of institutions have different political patterns? Do institutional characteristics affect the morale of participants in such a way that they engage in particular decision-influencing activities? Do different kinds of institutions have systematic patterns of faculty participation in decision making? Are decision processes highly centralized in certain kinds of institutions?

Finally, we are not substituting the political model for the bureaucratic or collegial model of academic decision making. In a sense, they each address a separate set of problems and, taken together, they often yield complementary interpretations. We believe, however, that the political model has many strengths, and we offer it as a useful tool for understanding academic governance. See Table 2 for a comparison of the three decision-making models.

Images of Leadership and Management Strategies

Thus far we have made two basic arguments: (1) colleges and universities are unique in many of their organizational characteristics and, as a consequence, it is necessary to create new models to help explain organizational structure, governance, and decision making; and (2) a political model of academic governance offers useful insights in addition to those offered by the bureaucratic and collegial models. In this section we will suggest that some alternative images of leadership and management style are needed to accommodate the unique characteristics of academic organizations.

Leadership Under the Bureaucratic Model

Under the bureaucratic model the leader is seen as a hero who stands at the top of a complex pyramid of power. The hero's job is to assess problems, propose alternatives, and make rational choices. Much of the organization's power is held by the hero. Great expectations are raised because people trust the hero to solve their problems and to fend off threats from the environment. The image of the authoritarian hero is deeply ingrained in most societies and in the philosophy of most organization theorists.

We expect leaders to possess a unique set of skills with emphasis on problem-solving ability and technical knowledge about the organization. The principles of "scientific management," such as Planning, Programming, Budgeting

Systems (PPBS) and Management by Objectives, are often proposed as the methods for rational problem solving. Generally, schools of management, business, and educational administration teach such courses to develop the technical skills that the hero-planner will need in leading the organization.

The hero image is deeply imbedded in our cultural beliefs about leadership. But in organizations such as colleges and universities it is out of place. Power is more diffuse in these organizations; it is lodged with professional experts and fragmented into many departments and subdivisions. Under these circumstances, high expectations about leadership performance often cannot be met. The leader has neither the power nor the information necessary to consistently make heroic decisions. Moreover, the scientific management procedures prescribed for organizational leaders quickly break down under conditions of goal ambiguity, professional dominance, and environmental vulnerability—precisely the organizational characteristics of colleges and universities. Scientific management theories make several basic assumptions: (1) the organization's goals are clear; (2) the organization is a closed system insulated from environmental penetration; and (3) the planners have the power to execute their decisions. These assumptions seem unrealistic in the confused and fluid world of the organized anarchy.

Leadership Under the Collegial Model

The collegial leader presents a stark contrast to the heroic bureaucratic leader. The collegial leader is above all the "first among equals" in an organization run by professional experts. Essentially, the collegial model proposes what John Millett calls the "dynamic of consensus in a community of scholars." The basic role of the collegial leader is not so much to command as to listen, not so much to lead as to gather expert judgments, not so much to manage as to facilitate, not so much to order but to persuade and negotiate.

Obviously, the skills of a collegial leader differ from those required by the scientific management principles employed by the heroic bureaucrat. Instead of technical problem-solving skills, the collegial leader needs professional expertise to ensure that he is held

TABLE 2
Three Models of Decision Making and Governance

	Bureaucratic	Collegial	Political
Assumptions about structure	Hierarchical bureaucracy	Community of peers	Fragmented, complex professional federation
Social	Unitary: integrated by formal system	Unitary: integrated by peer consensus	Pluralistic: encompasses different interest groups with divergent values
Basic theoretical foundations	Weberian bureaucracy, classic studies of formal systems	Professionalism literature, human-relations approach to organization	Conflict analysis, interest group theory, community power literature
View of decision-making process	"Rational" decision making; standard operating procedures	Shared collegial decision: consensus, community participation	Negotiation, bargaining, political influence, political brokerage, external influence
Cycle of decision making	Problem definition; search for alternatives; evaluation of alternatives; calculus; choice; implementation	As in bureaucratic model, but in addition stresses the involvement of professional peers in the process	Emergence of issue out of social context; interest articulation; conflict; legislative process; implementation of policy; feedback

in high esteem by his colleagues. Talent in interpersonal dynamics is also needed to achieve consensus in organizational decision making. The collegial leader's role is more modest and more realistic. He does not stand alone, since other professionals share the burden of decision making with him. Negotiation and compromise are the bywords of the collegial leader; authoritarian strategies are clearly inappropriate.

Leadership Under the Political Model

Under the political model the leader is a mediator or negotiator between power blocs. Unlike the autocratic academic president of the past, who ruled with an iron hand, the contemporary president must play a political role by pulling coalitions together to fight for desired changes. The academic monarch of yesteryear has almost vanished. In his place is not the academic hero but the academic statesman. Robert Dahl has painted an amusing picture of the political maneuvers of Mayor Richard Lee of New Haven, and the same description applies to academic political leaders:

> The mayor was not at the peak of a pyramid but rather at the center of intersecting circles. He rarely commanded. He negotiated, cajoled, exhorted, beguiled, charmed, pressed, appealed, reasoned, promised, insisted, demanded, even threatened, but he most needed support and acquiescence from other leaders who simply could not be commanded. Because the mayor could not command, he had to bargain [Dahl, 1961, page 204].

The political interpretation of leadership can be pressed even further, for the governance of the university more and more comes to look like a "cabinet" form of administration. The key figure today is not the president, the solitary giant, but the political leader surrounded by his staff, the prime minister who gathers the information and expertise to construct policy. It is the "staff," the network of key administrators, that makes most of the critical decisions. The university has become much too complicated for any one man, regardless of his stature. Cadres of vice-presidents, research men, budget officials, public relations men, and experts of various stripes surround the president, sit on the cabinet, and help reach collec-

tive decisions. Expertise becomes more critical than ever and leadership becomes even more the ability to assemble, lead, and facilitate the activities of knowledgeable experts.

Therefore, the president must be seen as a "statesman" as well as a "hero-bureaucrat." The bureaucratic image might be appropriate for the man who assembles data to churn out routine decisions with a computer's help. In fact, this image is fitting for many middle-echelon officials in the university. The statesman's image is much more accurate for the top administrators, for here the influx of data and information gives real power and possibilities for creative action. The statesman is the innovative actor who uses information, expertise, and the combined wisdom of the cabinet to plan the institution's future; the bureaucrat may only be a number manipulator, a user of routine information for routine ends. The use of the cabinet, the assembly of expertise, and the exercise of political judgment in the service of institutional goals—all this is part of the new image of the statesman leader which must complement both the hero leader and the collegial leader.

Table 3 presents a summary and comparison of the three basic images of leadership and management we have just described.

Summary

Colleges and universities are different from most other kinds of complex organizations. Their goals are more ambiguous and contested, they serve clients instead of seeking to make a profit, their technologies are unclear and problematic, and professionals dominate the work force and decision-making process. Thus colleges and universities are not standard bureaucracies, but can best be described as "organized anarchies" (see Cohen and March, 1947).

What decision and governance processes are to be found in an organized anarchy? Does the decision process resemble a bureaucratic system, with rational problem solving and standard operating procedures? Does it resemble a collegial system in which the professional faculty participate as members of a "community of scholars"? Or does it appear to be a political process with various interest groups struggling for influence over organizational policy? Each image is valid in some sense; each image helps

TABLE 3
Images of Leadership and Management Under Three Models of Governance

	Bureaucratic	Collegial	Political
Basic leadership image	Hero	"First among equals"	Statesman
Leadership skills	Technical problem-solving skills	Interpersonal dynamics	Political strategy, interpersonal dynamics, coalition management
Management Expectation	"Scientific management" Very high: People believe the hero-leader can solve problems and he tries to play the role	Management by consensus Modest: leader is developer of consensus among professionals	Strategic decision making Modest: leader marshals political action, but is constrained by the counter efforts of other groups

complete the picture. Finally, we question the standard image of leadership and management. Classic leadership theory, based on a bureaucratic model, suggests the image of the organizational leader as a hero who uses principles of scientific management as the basis for his decisions. We have suggested that the leader's image should be that of the academic statesman, and that management should be considered a process of strategic decision making.

The research reported in this paper was supported by the Stanford Center for Research and Development in Teaching, by funds from the National Institute of Education (contract no. NE-C-00-3-0062).

Note

1. Our list of characteristics of an organized anarchy extends Cohen and March's, which contains (1) and (3), plus a characteristic called "fluid participation."

References

Allison, Graham T. *Essence of Decision.* Boston: Little, Brown, 1971.

Baldridge, J. Victor. *Power and Conflict in the University.* New York: John Wiley, 1971.

Clark, Burton R. "Faculty Organization and Authority." *The Study of Academic Administration* edited by Terry Lunsford. Boulder, Colo.: Western Interstate Commission for Higher Education, 1963. Reprinted as chapter 4 in this volume.

Cohen, Michael D., and March, James G. *Leadership and Ambiguity: The American College President.* New York: McGraw-Hill, 1974.

Dahl, Robert. *Who Governs?* New Haven, Conn.: Yale University Press, 1961.

Goodman, Paul. *The Community of Scholars.* New York: Random House, 1962.

Gross, Edward, and Grambsch, Paul V. *Changes in University Organization, 1964–1971.* New York: McGraw-Hill, 1974.

Gross, Edward. *University Goals and Academic Power.* Washington, D.C.: Office of Education, 1968.

Millett, John. *The Academic Community.* New York: McGraw-Hill, 1962.

Parsons, Talcott. "Introduction." *The Theory of Social and Economic Organization*, by Max Weber. New York: Free Press, 1947.

Stroup, Herbert. *Bureaucracy in Higher Education.* New York: Free Press, 1966.

Weber, Max. *The Theory of Social and Economic Organization.* New York: Free Press, 1947.

Higher Education and Leadership Theory

ESTELLA M. BENSIMON, ANNA NEUMANN, AND ROBERT BIRNBAUM

This section examines works on leadership in the literature of higher education from the perspective of theories discussed in the previous section, suggesting implications of these studies for effective leadership in higher education.

Although studies of leadership in higher education have traditionally been atheoretical, a resurgence of theoretical research has occurred in recent years, and several works have attempted to integrate findings in the higher education literature with more general theories of leadership. A review of the strengths and weaknesses of several conceptual approaches to studying leadership in the context of academic organizations, for example, provides a clear and concise summary of the major theories of leadership along with a comprehensive annotated bibliography of works on leadership, corporate management, and higher education administration keyed to each theory (Dill and Fullagar 1987). Another essay emphasizes the role of leaders in organizational improvement and gives considerable attention to characteristics and behaviors of leaders as developed through the Ohio State leadership studies (Fincher 1987), not only recognizing the contingent nature of leadership but also including a critical analysis of several works on the presidency.

Trait Theories

Trait theory continues to be influential in images of effective leadership in higher education, even though it is no longer a major

approach to research among organizational theorists. Works concerned primarily with describing successful presidents, with identifying the characteristics to look for in selecting individuals for positions of leadership, or with comparing the characteristics of effective and ineffective leaders are the most likely to reflect a trait approach. Even though trait theory may not necessarily be the authors' primary orientation, the tendency to associate leaders with specific traits is so common that many works on leadership refer to traits or individual qualities (see, e.g., Kerr 1984; Kerr and Gade 1986; Vaughan 1986; Walker 1979).

Successful academic leaders have been described in terms of personal attributes, interpersonal abilities, and technical management skills (Kaplowitz 1986). Personal attributes include humor, courage, judgment, integrity, intelligence, persistence, hard work, vision, and being opportunity conscious; interpersonal abilities include being open, building teams, and being compassionate. Technical management skills include producing results, resolving conflicts, analyzing and evaluating problems, being able to shape the work environment, and being goal oriented (Gilley, Fulmer, and Reithlingshoefer 1986; Vaughan 1986).

A portrait of the effective president suggests the following personal traits:

> . . . a strong drive for responsibility, vigor, persistence, willingness to take chances, originality, ability to delegate, humor, initiative in social situations, fairness, self-

"Higher Education and Leadership Theory," by Estella Bensimon, Anna Neumann, and Robert L. Birnbaum, reprinted from *Making Sense of Administrative Leadership*, ASHE-ERIC Research Report, No. 1, 1989, Association for the Study of Higher Education.

confidence, decisiveness, sense of identity, personal style, capacity to organize, willingness to act or boldness . . . (Fisher 1984, p. 24).

A belief persists that in selecting candidates for positions of leadership, one should look for individuals who appear to have such characteristics. Most often cited are confidence, courage, fairness, respect for the opinions of others, and sensitivity. Undesirable characteristics include being soft-spoken, insecure, vain, concerned with administrative pomp, and graveness (Eble 1978). The trouble, of course, is that judgments on the presence or absence of these characteristics are highly subjective. No research has shown, for example, that a college president who speaks in an assertive and strong voice will be more effective than a soft-spoken president. One study of presidential effectiveness compares the traits and behaviors of 412 presidents identified as highly effective by their peers with a group of 412 "representative" presidents (Fisher, Tack, and Wheeler 1988). The prototypical effective president was self-described as a "strong risk-taking loner with a dream" who was less likely to form close collegial relationships than typical presidents, worked longer hours, made decisions easily, and confided less frequently in other presidents. Closer examination of the data reveals, however, that effective and representative presidents were probably more alike than different. In four of five leadership factors derived from a factor analysis of survey items (managing style, human relations, image, and social reference), no significant differences were found between the two groups of presidents. Significant differences were found only for the confidence factor, which consisted of items that assessed the extent to which presidents believed they can make a difference in their institutions.

While this study suggests that effective leaders are "loners" who maintain social distance, the findings of another study suggest that successful colleges are headed by presidents who are "people-oriented—caring, supportive, and nurturing" (Gilley, Fulmer, and Reithlingshoefer 1986, p. 115). Similarly, while the former study maintains that effective leaders are risk takers, the other says that successful presidents "work feverishly to minimize

risk at every step of the way" (p. 65). These studies' conflicting findings suggest the problems of analyzing the effectiveness of leadership from a trait perspective. Few people exhibit consistent traits under all circumstances, so that both "distance" and "nurturing" may accurately represent effective leadership as manifested in different situations. If this in fact is the case, these studies provide a strong argument for the need to define the effectiveness of leadership in dynamic rather than static terms.

Power and Influence Theories

Power and influence theories fall into two types, those that consider leadership in terms of the influence or effects that leaders may have on their followers (social power theory and transformational leadership theory) and those that consider leadership in terms of mutual influence and reciprocal relationships between leaders and followers (social exchange theory and transactional leadership theory).

Social Power Theory

From this perspective, effective leaders are those who can use their power to influence the activities of others. Concepts of social power appeared to be an important influence in shaping presidents' implicit theories of leadership in one study (Birnbaum 1989a). When asked to explain what leadership meant to them, most of the presidents participating in an extensive study of institutional leadership provided definitions describing leadership as a one-way process, with the leader's function depicted as getting others to follow or accept their directives. For a small minority, the role of the leader was not to direct the group but to facilitate the emergence of leadership latent within it. Definitions that included elements of other conceptual orientations (trait theories, contingency theories, and symbolic theories) were mentioned infrequently.

The most likely sources of power for academic leaders are expert and referent power rather than legitimate, coercive, or reward powers (see the discussion of power and influence theories in the previous section): it has been proposed that college presidents can exert influence over their campuses through charismatic power, which has been questionably identified as analogous to referent power (Fisher 1984). This particular perspective maintains that academic leaders can cultivate charismatic power by remaining distant or remote from constituents, by attending to their personal appearance and style, and by exhibiting self-confidence. To establish distance and remoteness, presidents are counseled not to establish close relationships with faculty, not to be overly visible, and to emphasize the importance of the trappings of the office as symbols of its elevated state. Style consists of presidential comportment, attitude, speech, dress, mannerisms, appearance, and personal habits. Self-confidence relates to cultivating a style of speaking and walking that conveys a sense of self-assuredness. The concept of charismatic power that has been proposed here appears to be much different from referent power, which traditionally has been defined as the willingness of followers to accept influence by a leader they like and with whom they identify.

Practitioners and scholars tend to question the importance given to charismatic traits as well as whether leaders stand to gain by creating distance between themselves and their constituents. It has been suggested (Keohane 1985) that a leader who is concerned with creating an image of mystery and separateness cannot be effective at building coalitions, a critical part of leadership. High levels of campus discontent have been attributed to leaders who were considered to be too distant from their internal and external constituencies and who tended to take constituents' support for granted or to feel it was not needed (Whetten 1984). Reacting to the current preoccupation with charismatic leadership, a recent commentary published in *The Wall Street Journal says* "leadership is more doing than dash."

> It has little to do with "leadership qualities" and even less to do with "charisma . . . Charisma becomes the undoing of leaders. It makes them inflexible, convinced of their own infallibility, unable to change. This is what happened to Stalin, Hitler, and Mao, and it is a commonplace in the study of ancient history that only Alexander the Great's early death saved him from becoming an ineffectual failure" (Drucker 1988).

Social Exchange Theory/ Transactional Theory

College and university presidents can accumulate and exert power by controlling access to information, controlling the budgetary process, allocating resources to preferred projects, and assessing major faculty and administrative appointments (Corson 1960). On college campuses, however, the presence of other sources of power—the trustees' power to make policy and the faculty's professional authority—seriously limits the president's discretionary control of organizational activities. For this reason, social exchange theory is particularly useful for examining the principles of shared governance and consultation and the image of the president as first among equals, which undergirds much of the normative values of academic organizations.

Transactional theory can be particularly useful for understanding the interactions between leaders and followers. The idiosyncrasy credit (IC) model (Hollander 1987), a major transactional approach to leadership, is of particular relevance to the understanding of leaders' influence in academic organizations. This model suggests that followers will accept change and tolerate a leader's behavior that deviates from their expectations more readily if leaders first engage in actions that will demonstrate their expertise and conformity to the group's norms. The IC model, for example, explains why new presidents initially may find it beneficial to concentrate on getting to know their institutions' history, culture, and key players before proclaiming changes they plan to introduce. A study of new presidents suggests that first time presidents, not wanting to appear indecisive, may overlook the potential benefits of "getting to know" and "becoming known" by the institution. In contrast, experienced presidents, in assuming office at a new institution, recognized the importance of spending time learning about the expectations of followers (Bensimon 1987, 1989a).

Two works relate presidential failure and success in accomplishing change to presidents' initial actions. These studies show the relevance of concepts underlying the IC model. For example, a member of a new university administration attributed the failure to implement radical changes and reforms to the inability of the new president and his academic administrators to build loyalty—and to gain credits— among respected members of the faculty.

> We succeeded in infusing new blood... but we failed to recirculate the old blood. We lost an opportunity to build loyalty among respected members of the veteran faculty. If veteran faculty members had been made to feel that they, too had a future in the transformed university, they might have embraced the academic reorganization plan with some enthusiasm. Instead the veteran faculty members were hurt, indignant, and—finally—angry (Bennis 1972, p. 116).

In contrast, another study illustrates that time spent accumulating credits (e.g., fulfilling the expectations of constituents) can lead to positive outcomes (Gilley, Fulmer, and Reithlingshoefer 1986). The authors observed that presidential success was related to gaining acceptance and respect from key constituents through low-key, pleasant, and noncontroversial actions early in the presidential term. In their judgment, change and departure from established patterns were tolerated because "of the safety zone of good will they ha[d] created" (p. 66).

The influence of social exchange theory can also be detected in works that downplay the charismatic and directive role of leaders. These studies portray leaders as coordinators of ongoing activities rather than as architects of bold initiatives. This view of leadership is related to the anarchical (Cohen and March 1974), democratic-political (Walker 1979), atomistic (Kerr and Gade 1986), and cybernetic (Birnbaum 1988) models of university leadership that will be discussed in the next section.

Transformational Theory

This perspective suggests that effective leaders create and promote desirable "visions" or images of the institution. Unlike goals, tasks, and agendas, which refer to concrete and instrumental ends to be achieved, vision refers to altered perceptions, attitudes, and commitments. The transforming leader must encourage the college community to accept a vision

created by his or her symbolic actions (Green 1988b; Hesburgh 1979).

Transformation implies a "metamorphosis or a substitution of one state or system for another, so that a qualitatively different condition is present" (Cameron and Ulrich 1986, p. 1). Fear that higher education is suffering a crisis in leadership has made calls for transformational leadership a recurrent theme in recent studies. Some suggest it is an "illusion, an omnipotent fantasy" (Bennis 1972, p. 115) for a change-oriented administrator to expect that academic organizations would be receptive to this kind of leadership. In higher education, transformational leadership more appropriately may refer to the inspirational role of the leader. For example, the description of leadership as the "poetic part of the presidency" that "sweeps listeners and participants up into the nobility of intellectual and artistic adventures and the urgency of thinking well and feeling deeply about the critical issues of our time" (Keller 1983, p. 25) is unmistakably transformational in tone, as is the following eloquent and inspiring call:

> ... in the years ahead, higher education will be sorely tested. If we believe that our institutions have value, we must articulate that value and achieve adequate understanding and support. We must find leaders who are dedicated enough to the purpose of higher education that they will expend themselves, if necessary, for that purpose. . . . The qualities of transforming leadership are those that restore in organizations or society a sense of meaning and purpose and release the powerful capacity humankind has for renewal (Kauffman 1980, pp. 114–15).

A modern example of the transformational leader may be found in Theodore Hesburgh, who has been described as "brilliant, forceful, and charismatic . . . a legend on campus, where stories of students scampering up the fire escape outside his office for a glimpse of the great man are a part of the Notre Dame lore, like winning one for the Gipper" (Ward 1988, pp. 32–33). Images like this one, along with the popular belief that transformational leaders are concerned with "doing the right things" while managers are concerned with "doing things right" (Bennis and Nanus 1985; Cameron and

Ulrich 1986), make transformational leadership irresistible to leaders and nonleaders alike.

A five-step agenda derived from an analysis of the qualities possessed by great leaders like Ghandi, Martin Luther King, Jr., and Winston Churchill attempts to put transformational leadership into practical terms (Cameron and Ulrich 1986). The list includes the following steps: (1) create readiness for change by focusing attention on the unsatisfactory aspects of the organization; (2) overcome resistance by using non-threatening approaches to introduce change; (3) articulate a vision by combining rational reasoning and symbolic imagery; (4) generate commitment; and (5) institutionalize commitment. Suggested approaches on how to implement each step came mostly from examples drawn from industry and tested in case studies of two colleges in crisis whose presidents took actions that corresponded to the agenda prescribed for transformational leadership. Of course, while following these steps might result in changes that make the campus more adaptable to the demands of the environment, it might not result in changes in the perceptions, beliefs, and values of campus constituents that are at the core of transformational leadership as initially proposed (Burns 1978).

The nature of colleges and universities appears to make the exercise of transformational leadership extremely difficult except under certain conditions. Three such conditions have been suggested—institutional crisis, institutional size, and institutional quality (Birnbaum 1988). Institutional crisis is likely to encourage transformational leadership because campus members and the external community expect leaders to take strong action. Portrayals of presidents exercising transformational leadership can be found in case-study reports of institutions suffering adversity (see, e.g., Cameron and Ulrich 1986; Chaffee 1984; Clark 1970; Riesman and Fuller 1985). Transformational leadership is also more likely to emerge in small institutions where leaders can exert a great deal of personal influence through their daily interactions with the campus. Leaders in 10 small private liberal arts colleges identified as having high faculty morale displayed characteristics of the transformational orientation (Rice and Austin 1988). These leaders were seen by others as powerful influences in the life of their colleges and were credited with single-

handedly turning their institutions around. Institutions that need to be upgraded to achieve comparability with their peers also provide an opportunity for transformational leadership. Such presidents have been described as "path-breaking leaders" (Kerr and Gade 1986).

Although with few exceptions (see Bass 1985) leaders tend to be considered as being either transactional or transformational, a recent study comparing the initial activities of new presidents in institutions in crisis suggests that leaders who use transactional means (e.g., conforming to organizational culture) may be more successful in attaining transformational effects (e.g., improving the organizational culture) than leaders whose behavior reflects the pure form (one-way approach) of transformational leadership (Bensimon 1989c). Even in institutions in distress, a leadership approach that conforms to the group's norms while also seeking to improve them may be of greater benefit than heroic attempts at redesigning an institution.

Behavioral Theories

Behavior of the Leader

These theories examine whether the leader is task (initiating structure) or people (consideration) oriented or both. Blake and Mouton (1964) adapted their managerial grid into an academic grid and applied it to higher education. Their model suggests five styles of academic administration (Blake, Mouton, and Williams 1981): caretaker, authority-obedience, comfortable-pleasant, constituency-centered, and team. The optimum style is identified as team administration, which is characteristic of leaders who scored high on both concern for institutional performance and concern for people on their grid.

Some limited empirical tests of this theory have been performed. A study of department chairs found that those judged as effective by the faculty scored high both in initiating structure (task) and consideration of people (Knight and Holen 1985). On the other hand, a case study of a single institution reports that departments with high faculty morale had chairs who scored high on measures of consideration of people and participative leadership style but not in initiating structure (Madron, Craig, and

Mendel 1976). The academic grid appears to have found its greatest use as a tool for self assessment. For example, the grid was adapted into a questionnaire to assist department chairs in determining their personal styles of leadership (Tucker 1981).

Presidents' perceptions of the similarity of their role to other leadership roles were used to describe two types of presidents—mediative and authoritative, which are roughly comparable to emphasizing consideration of people and initiating structure (task), respectively (Cohen and March 1974). Mediative presidents tended to define their roles in terms of constituencies, while authoritative presidents appeared to be more directive. Additionally, mediative presidents were more likely to measure their success on the basis of faculty respect, while authoritative presidents were more likely to base it on the quality of educational programs.

Administrative styles based on the self-reported behaviors of presidents were found to be related to faculty and student outcomes in 49 small private liberal arts colleges (Astin and Scherrei 1980). These findings, however, may be influenced by the size of the institutions.

Managerial Roles

A comprehensive essay (Dill 1984) reviews the literature on administrative behavior in higher education, employing the behavioral framework developed by Mintzberg (1973). The findings (p. 91) suggest that like managers in other settings, senior administrators in higher education:

- Perform a great variety of work at a continuous pace;
- Carry out activities characterized by variety, fragmentation, and brevity;
- Prefer issues that are current, specific, and ad hoc;
- Demonstrate preference for verbal media (telephone calls, meetings, brief discussions); and
- Develop informal information systems.

Although academic leaders are likely to learn from their actions, almost no attention has been given to what leaders learn on the job. A qualitative study based on interviews with 32 presidents reports that what presidents learn from their actions varies, depending on whether they feel the action they took was wrong (substantive error) or whether they feel the action was justified but the process used (process error) was inappropriate (Neumann 1988). New presidents who made substantive errors learned how to sense situational differences that called for diverse (and new) responses, they began to identify new behaviors that were more appropriate to their new settings, and they gave up the behaviors that worked in their old settings but appeared to be dysfunctional in their new ones. From process errors, presidents tended to learn the degree of influence organizational members have on what presidents can accomplish. Some presidents also made action errors, which consisted of taking action when none should have been taken. From these errors, presidents gained respect for personal and organizational limitations.

Contingency Theories

From this perspective, effective leadership requires adapting one's style of leadership to situational factors. Applying four contingency theories to higher education, Vroom (1983) found that if used to determine the kind of leader best suited to chair academic departments, each would prescribe a different type of leader. Situational variables in Fiedler's contingency model and in House's path-goal theory prescribe a task-oriented leader who would do whatever is necessary to drive the group to complete a job. In contrast, Hersey and Blanchard's life-cycle theory and the Vroom-Yetton decision process theory identify individuals with a delegating and participative style of leadership. The contradictory prescriptions may be the result of their development in organizational settings with clearly delineated superior and subordinate roles. Thus, they may have limited applicability to the study of leadership in higher education. The Vroom-Yetton model appears to be better suited to higher education organizations, because it uses multiple criteria to determine participative or autocratic decision making (Floyd 1985).

Although the observation that "a president may be egalitarian one day and authoritarian the next" (Gilley, Fulmer, and Reithlingshoefer 1986, p. 66) is commonplace, little systematic application of contingency theory has occurred to determine under what conditions alternative forms of leadership should be displayed. Generally, contingency theories have found their greatest applicability in the study of leadership in academic departments, probably because decision making at this level is less equivocal than at higher levels of the academic organization. An application of the Vroom-Yetton model to the study of decision making among department chairs concludes that they frequently chose autocratic styles of decision making in situations where a consultative style would have increased the likelihood of the faculty's acceptance of the decision (Taylor 1982). Hersey and Blanchard's theory was used to develop a questionnaire that would help department chairs determine departmental level of maturity and select a corresponding style of leadership (Tucker 1981). An analysis of studies on the behavior of leaders (Dill 1984) suggests that "when given a choice of leader roles, faculty members consistently preferred the leader as a . . . 'facilitator' or one who smoothed out problems and sought to provide the resources necessary for the research activities of faculty members" (p. 79).

Kerr and Jermier's theory of substitutes for hierarchical leadership may be highly relevant for academic organizations. Despite being one of the few contingency theories in which leadership is not seen as residing solely with the official leader, it has received little attention in the study of academic leadership. If leadership in higher education were to be viewed from this perspective, one could conclude that directive leadership may not be effective because characteristics of academic organizations (such as faculty autonomy and a reward structure that is academic discipline and peer-based) substitute for or neutralize the influence of leaders (Birnbaum 1989a). Similarly, a consideration of the influence of administrators on the faculty's motivation asks, "What are university administrators to do in the face of so many 'substitutes' for their leadership?" (Staw 1983, p. 312). Because alternatives such as stressing local (e.g., primary identification is with the institution) rather than professional orientation (e.g., primary identification is with the academic discipline) or reducing self-

governance and self-motivation are not in the best interests of the university, it may be more fruitful for administrators to assume the role of facilitator than controller.

Cultural and Symbolic Theories

Occasionally effective leaders give symbolic meaning to events that others may see as perplexing, senseless, or chaotic. They do so by focusing attention on aspects of college life that are both familiar and meaningful to the college community. Cultural and symbolic approaches to studying leadership appear in works on organizations as cultural systems (Chaffee and Tierney 1988; Kuh and Whitt 1988). Understanding colleges and universities as cultures was originally introduced in a now-classic case study of Reed, Swarthmore, and Antioch (Clark 1970, 1972). This study suggests that leaders may play an important role in creating and maintaining institutional sagas. The role of academic leaders in the preservation of academic culture may be even more critical today than in the past, because increased specification, professionalization, and complexity have weakened the values and beliefs that provided institutions with a common sense of purpose, commitment, and order (Dill 1982). Although leaders may not be able to change culture through management, their attention to social integration and symbolic events may enable them to sustain and strengthen the culture that already exists (Dill 1982).

Cultural and symbolic perspectives on leadership have figured prominently in a small handful of recent works that examine the actions of leaders and their effects on campus during times of financial decline. A recent study suggests that college presidents who are sensitive to the faculty's interpretation of financial stress are more likely to elicit the faculty's support for their own leadership (Neumann 1989a). One of the most important contributions to the understanding of leadership from a cultural perspective is the work on the role of substantive and symbolic actions in successful turn-around situations (Chaffee 1984, 1985a, 1985b). The examination of managerial techniques of presidents in institutions suffering financial decline discloses three alternative strategic approaches—linear, adaptive, and interpretive. Linear strategists were concerned with achieving goals. Adaptive strategists were concerned with aligning the organization with the environment, for example, by changing the organizational orientation to meet current demands and thus to ensure the continued flow of resources. Interpretive strategists reflected the cultural/symbolic perspective in that they were concerned with how people saw, understood, and felt about their lives. Interpretive leaders believed that effective action involves shaping the values, symbols, and emotions that influence the behaviors of individuals. The use of interpretive strategy in combination with adaptive strategy was considerably more effective in turning institutions around than the use of adaptive strategy alone (Chaffee 1984). Presidents who employed interpretive strategies were careful to protect the essential character of their institutions and to refrain from actions and environments that compromise or disrupt the institution's self-identity and sense of integrity by only introducing new programs that were outgrowths of the old ones. For example, they reaffirmed the existing institutional mission and did not attempt to pursue programmatic thrusts that were outside the expertise of the faculty.

Strategies of change that make sense to institutional members and that therefore are likely to elicit acceptance and support may depend upon leaders' understanding an organization from cultural perspectives. To do so, leaders may be required to act as anthropologists uncovering the organizational culture by seeking to identify metaphors embedded in the language of the college community (Corbally 1984; Deshler 1985; Peck 1983; Tierney 1988). Frameworks for organizational cultures suggest that leaders can begin to understand their institutional cultures by identifying internal contradictions or incongruities between values and structure, by developing a comparative awareness, by clarifying the identity of the institution, by communicating so as "to say the right things and to say things right," and by acting on multiple and changing fronts (Chaffee and Tierney 1988, pp. 185–91).

Leaders should pose organizational questions to help them identify characteristics of the organizational environment, the influence of institutional mission on decision making, processes of socialization, the uses of information, the approaches used to make decisions, and constituents' expectations of leaders (Tierney 1988). Researchers also can gain insights into leadership by examining the symbols embedded in the language of leaders. A study of 32 presidents reveals that they used six categories of symbols—metaphorical, physical, communicative, structural, personification, and ideational—when they talked about their leadership role. Understanding the use of symbolism can help academic leaders to become more consistent by sensitizing them to contradictions between the symbols they use and the behaviors they exhibit on their campuses. Leaders may become more effective by using symbols that are consistent with the institution's culture (Tierney 1989).

The "techniques of managing meaning and social integration are the undiscussed skills of academic management" (Dill 1982, p. 304). For example, it has been suggested that leaders in community colleges have consistently failed to interpret and articulate their missions and to create positive images among their publics (Vaughan 1986). While it is clear that cultural and symbolic leadership skills are becoming increasingly important to presidents, scholars still have much to learn about the characteristics of these skills and effective ways of teaching them to present and aspiring leaders (Green 1988b). A recent examination of colleges and universities from a cultural perspective provides administrators with the following insights: Senior faculty or other core groups of institutional leaders provide continuity and maintain a cohesive institutional culture; institutional policies and practices are driven and bound by culture; culture-driven policies and practices may denigrate the integrity and worth of certain groups; institutional culture is difficult to modify intentionally; and organizational size and complexity work against distinctive patterns of values and assumptions (Kuh and Whitt 1988, p. vi).

Cognitive Theories

Cognitive theories have important implications for perceptions of leaders' effectiveness. In many situations, presidential leadership may not have measurable outcomes other than social attribution—or the tendency of campus constituents to assign to a president the credit or blame for unusual institutional outcomes. From this perspective, leaders are individuals believed by followers to have caused events (Birnbaum 1989b). Leaders themselves, in the absence of clear indicators, are subject to cognitive bias that can lead them to make predictable errors of judgment (Birnbaum 1987) and to over-estimate their effectiveness in campus improvements (Birnbaum 1986).

Summary

Trait theories and power and influence theories appear to be particularly influential in works on leadership in higher education. Several of the works reviewed tend to relate effectiveness of leaders to individual characteristics, although not necessarily the same ones. For example, while some consider "being distant" as a desirable characteristic, others propose that "being nurturing" is more important.

Even though exchange theories are more relevant to the understanding of leadership in academic organizations, works that consider leadership from the perspective of power and influence theories tend to emphasize one-way, leader-initiated and leader-directed approaches. Transformational theory, in particular, has received considerable attention, while transactional theory has for the most part been ignored.

Behavioral and contingency theories may have limited application in higher education because these theories focus their attention on the relationship between superior and subordinate roles. Within the category of behavioral theories, the most promising approach may be in the study of administrative behavior, particularly as a way of understanding how leaders learn from their actions and mistakes. Examining how leaders learn from a behavioral perspective may provide new directions and ideas for the design of training programs for academic leaders.

Within the category of contingency theories, Kerr and Jermier's theory of substitutes for hierarchical leadership may be of greatest use, even though it has been almost totally overlooked by scholars of academic leadership.

Although cultural and symbolic perspectives on leadership were first suggested in the early 1970s in Burton Clark's case study of Reed, Swarthmore, and Antioch, only recently has this view of leadership attracted serious attention. Cultural and symbolic perspectives have been shown to be especially useful for understanding the internal dynamics of institutions in financial crisis, particularly in differentiating the strategies leaders use to cope with financial stress and to communicate with constituents. Cognitive theories offer a promising new way of studying leadership, but their use in higher education to date has been limited.

Understanding the Competitive Environment of the Postsecondary Knowledge Industry

MARVIN W. PETERSON AND DAVID D. DILL

"Drift." "Reluctant accommodation." And "belated recognition that while no one was looking, change had in fact taken place." Using these words, Frederick Rudolph concluded his scholarly, insightful, and entertaining history of American higher education prior to 1950 (Rudolph, 1962). But the history of change in higher or postsecondary education in the past four decades has been decidedly more guided. Federal, state, and institutional initiatives have all directed attempts to expand, guide, and even control our systems and our institutions. Planning at the state and institutional levels has received particular attention as attempts to devise plans and develop planning structures, processes, and approaches have become commonplace.

While our definitions of, perspectives on, and approaches to planning have been varied, the primary focus of planning has been to examine environmental change and to develop institutional strategies for *responding* or *adapting*. Our traditional approaches to long-range and strategic planning assume that we compete in a system or industry consisting of other higher and postsecondary institutions. From this perspective, institutional planning involves understanding these broader environmental changes and how to compete more effectively with other post-secondary institutions.

As we approach the twenty-first century, this chapter argues that the nature of our postsecondary system itself is changing, that major forces in the larger societal environment are reshaping the nature of postsecondary education, changing it to a "postsecondary knowledge system" or industry that cuts across many of our traditional notions of system boundaries. These forces portend the growth of a postsecondary knowledge industry that delivers knowledge, information, and the capacity to teach and learn in a vast and flexible knowledge network. It also involves the active participation of many different types of institutions in the development and even educational use of this network. Postsecondary institutions are challenged not only to understand the nature of this new industry but to reconsider their institutional role and mission, their academic and administrative structure, and their academic processes.

This shift from a system of postsecondary institutions to one of a postsecondary knowledge system or industry suggests the need for a new paradigm in our thinking about the external and internal context of our institutions. Externally, it suggests competing and/or collaborating with non-postsecondary institutions and firms. Internally, it suggests potentially radical changes in the academic structure, the educational process, the conduct of research, and even the meaning of academic work in our institutions—the core of our institutional culture. A new approach to planning, *contextual planning*, is suggested (and elaborated in Chapter Seven). Chapter One provides a perspective on our changing postsecondary system. We examine the challenges reshaping postsecondary education, the nature of the

"Understanding the Competitive Environment of the Postsecondary Knowledge Industry," by Marvin W. Peterson and David D. Dill, reprinted from *Planning and Management for a Changing Environment: A Handbook on Redesigning Postsecondary Institutions*, edited by Marvin W. Peterson, David D. Dill, Lisa A. Mets, and Associates, 1997, Jossey-Bass Publishers, Inc.

emerging postsecondary knowledge network or industry, its internal and external institutional implications for planning, and a new set of planning questions that suggest the need for a new approach to planning: contextual planning.

An Expanded Planning Perspective: Society, Industry, and Institution

The literature on higher and postsecondary governance, management, and planning has long recognized our institutions as complex organizations functioning as open systems and subjected to many external societal forces and conditions. Planning is often seen as the attempt to deal with issues of the fit between institution and environment. Similarly, as a country we have prided ourself on our diverse and decentralized higher and postsecondary system; we have often viewed it as a comprehensive, loosely defined national system made up of subsets or segments of differing institutional types with somewhat more formally organized state-level governance or coordinating systems. However, we seldom focus on the nature of our higher or postsecondary education system as an industry—and the implications for institutional planning. Yet industry, as a concept that clusters similar organizations in society and differentiates them from those in other industries, is an appropriate focus—especially when the structure of the industry within which one exists is changing rapidly. Such is the case, this chapter argues, in postsecondary education today. The concept of an *industry* provides a useful tool for examining the changing, nature of competition among colleges, universities, and other organizations.

The industry concept is implicitly understood and seldom discussed, yet of critical importance to postsecondary education. An industry is often defined as a set of competing organizations that utilize similar resources or attract similar clients, and that produce similar products and services. There are two critical features to the notion of an industry. First, it helps us define our competitive market or segment of it. Second, it is often the focus of attempts at governmental control or regulation. Clearly, we can recognize our higher or post-

secondary education system as a major industry in our society.

Changing Perspectives

In understanding our current and future contexts, it is important to note that our system or industry has not been stable. This is suggested in Figure 1.

Traditional Higher Education. Prior to 1950, the higher education system or industry was viewed primarily as the public and private degree-granting, four-year, comprehensive, and university institutions in the country. Two-year institutions were still few in number and not considered core competitors. Planning was not a major institutional function or activity.

Mass Higher Education. The release of the Truman Commission Report in 1948, which recommended higher education for everyone who graduated from high school (a population whose numbers were increasing rapidly), spawned the rapid expansion of community colleges from the 1950s through the mid-1970s, as well as increasing enrollments in most other types of institutions. The industry was expanded by including a broader array of students (clients) who were absorbed in the growth of existing institutions, in the rapid expansion of two-year institutions, and in the addition of many new public four-year and university institutions. Institutional planning became a focal concern as plans were developed for new institutions, and forecasting growth and resource needs gave rise to long-range planning efforts.

Postsecondary Education. The higher education amendments of 1972 redefined the system or industry in two important ways. First, they transferred federal student aid from institutions to students who could demonstrate financial need. Second, they broadened the definition of which institutions were eligible to receive students with federal aid by including nondegree-granting postsecondary institutions and proprietary institutions. The shift in government student aid policy from institutions to students and the expanded definition of which institutions could compete for students or clients who received federal funds redefined

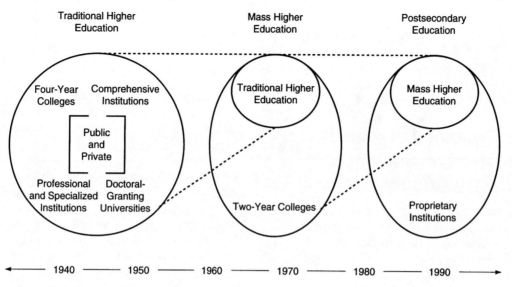

Figure 1: Redefining Our Industry

the competitive relationship and nature of the industry. The increasingly competitive market-oriented environment of the 1970s and the constrained resources of the 1980s reinforced institutional interest in planning and led to the expanded interest in strategic planning that continues into the 1990s.

These changes in the nature of our system and the structure of our industry, from traditional to mass higher education and then to postsecondary education, suggest the role of governmental action in redefining the "related organizations" in the industry and in increasing the array of "similar clients." The transitions to mass and then to postsecondary education both had the effect of expanding the industry. But it was still an industry of institutions delivering education beyond high school.

A Model of the Forces Reshaping Institutional Planning

In order to better comprehend the factors in our changing environment that will influence institutional and state-level planning in higher and postsecondary education, it is important to understand the shift from an industry composed of postsecondary educational institutions to a postsecondary knowledge system or industry. To do so it is helpful to examine both the forces that reshape an industry and the changing societal conditions that affect the industry itself (See Figure 2.) For example, the

nature of competition in the postsecondary education industry will be affected by new customer or client needs for new educational services, by possible new entrants to the industry such as telecommunications companies seeking to offer degrees over the World Wide Web, and even by improvements within the industry itself. But the structure of the industry is being reshaped by larger forces: government regulation or deregulation, and the trend toward globalization of services and products.

While the planning challenges to individual institutions are clear, it is also important to examine their impact on the industry and less-direct implications for institution planning. To clarify the nature of these impacts, it is useful to examine the specific forces that govern competition in an industry. Porter (1980) has outlined a useful model for analyzing the structure of an industry (Figure 3). This schema, slightly revised to reflect education as a service industry, helps to reveal the forces that redefine the composition of an industry and reshape the competition within it. Those basic forces are (1) the threat of entry into the industry by new organizations, (2) the bargaining power of suppliers (for example, student clientele), (3) the bargaining power of customers (for example, employers, funding sources), and (4) the threat of substitute services. We have added a fifth force to Porter's model to reflect the potentially rapid changes occurring in how teaching, research, and service are being transformed by technology: (5) technical innovation in the core processes of the industry. Each of these forces in turn affects (6) the overall degree of rivalry or competition among institutions in the industry, which changes the external environment in which institutions must plan.

The model of institutional planning that emerges thus needs to reflect how changing societal conditions impact our industry as well as our postsecondary institutions directly. The institutional impacts of the societal changes affect both the internal nature of our institutions and the character of their external relationships. Thus, the planning perspectives institutions must have as we approach the twenty-first century are shaped both by the changing industry as well as the changing societal conditions.

This model guides the remaining discussion in this chapter. The next section examines changing societal conditions or challenges that are reshaping our industry and impacting our institutions. Then the nature of an emerging postsecondary knowledge industry and its institutional implications are discussed. The chapter concludes with a new set of institu-

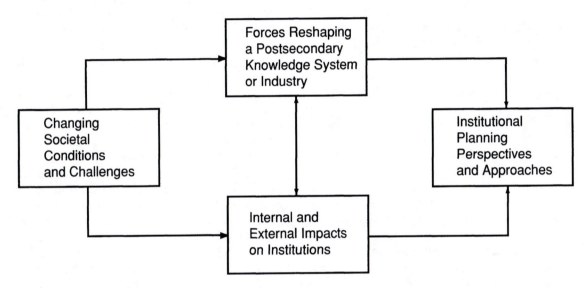

Figure 2: Influences on Institutional Planning

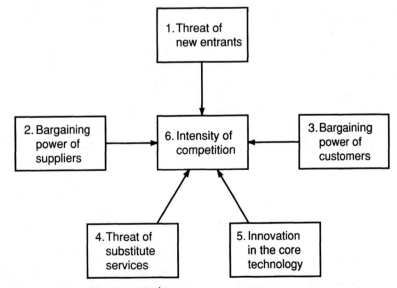

Figure 3: Forces Shaping Competition in an Industry

tional planning questions and suggests the need for a broader contextual approach to planning.

Societal Conditions and Challenges

It is beyond the scope of this chapter to deal with the infinite array of trends, issues, and possibilities that forecasters, scanners, and futurists have identified that can affect postsecondary institutions. However, many of them coalesce around a series of discrete challenges to postsecondary educational institutions. We present here six challenges that have emerged in the 1990s and that promise to continue into the new century. They are quite different in nature from the demands and challenges that reshaped our industry in its transition from traditional to higher education and then to postsecondary education. These challenges require us to revise our thinking extensively about postsecondary education, the basic nature or structure of our institutions, and the nature and meaning of academic work.

More importantly, these challenges impact postsecondary education at a time when our institutions face a common, critical condition that amounts to a seventh, overarching challenge: *constrained resources*. For example, the costs of higher education are exceeding the willingness of taxpayers, governments, parents, employers, or students to pay; there are other societal priorities for funds; and many campuses are already financially strained. Resource-constraint issues are already so well documented that they are not discussed separately as a challenge in this chapter but rather are assumed. The following is a brief description of the six other challenges, their influence on the forces reshaping our industry, and their internal and external impacts on and implications for our institutions.

Changing Patterns of Diversity

The challenge of dealing with cultural diversity and its concomitant educational and economic deprivation is widely recognized as a social reality, a public policy issue, and an institutional reality. We have had some success in the past three decades in improving access to postsecondary education for various disadvantaged groups, but our record of successful retention and graduation is still inadequate in many fields and at the graduate level (Carter and Wilson, 1993; Mintz, 1993; Musil, 1995).

There are several lessons from our experience to date. First, the operant definition of cultural diversity is constantly changing. The initial concern for African American minorities in the 1960s has expanded to include numerous other racially underrepresented groups, and even to various subdivisions within them. Issues of gender, sexual preference, and economic or educational disadvantage have further expanded and/or fragmented the definition and focus of diversity as an issue. Second, our public policy and institutional responses have shifted: from separate-but-equal to nondiscrimination, to affirmative action, to preferences, and now to attempts to dismantle affirmative action. Third, members of most minority groups have become well organized and are gaining effective political voice both on campuses and in government.

While these lessons seem clear, so are the trends. The numbers of almost all of minority groups are increasing and will continue for the foreseeable future. Their differential rate of educational attainment or improvement is leading to conflict among disadvantaged groups. The debates about affirmative action are likely to be heated and continual. But the impacts both on our industry and in our institutions are revealing.

At the *industry level* (Table 1), potential customers for postsecondary learning opportunities—both the number of individuals and the categories defined as educationally disadvantaged—continue to grow. As a client group influencing public policy, the increasing presence of minority political caucus groups at the institutional, state, and national levels makes them a more powerful force. Although there have been few new institutions of postsecondary education founded as minority institutions in recent decades (except those for American Indians), the number of institutions becoming de facto minority institutions is increasing rapidly: approximately one in five postsecondary institutions has an enrollment in which ethnic minority students exceed 50 percent. Several new minority-oriented professional associations have been founded to serve these institutions and groups and to represent their interests. Within postsecondary institutions, the increase of minority-oriented academic and support programs has often been seen as adding substitute services. Although not directly affecting the core technology of postsecondary education, the advent of minority programs, new faculty staffing patterns, new student interaction patterns, and new academic perspectives and research agendas have influenced the processes of teaching and research in significant ways. Clearly, pressure to enhance diversity has created intensive competition for scarce resources, among students seeking limited financial support and admission slots, and among institutions to attract increased numbers of more diverse students, faculty, and staff.

The *impacts on institutions* largely reflect the changes impacting the industry (Table 2). Externally, governmental and political issues reflect the growing number and influence of minority political groups that demand attention. Competition both from minority and non-minority institutions for minority students, faculty, and funds is now a reality. The lessons within our institutions are even more telling. Dealing with issues of racism, discrimination, and pluralism requires addressing not only student conduct and classroom behavior but also issues of course, program, and discipline content, of research agendas, and of faculty behavior and staffing.

Regardless of its definition, diversity is clearly a condition and challenge that will not abate soon. Indeed, the new debates about affirmative action force us to take a hard look at dealing with and responding to issues of educational disadvantage versus social, cultural, or economic disadvantage, and whether it is to be addressed as a group problem, an individual issue, or both. Diversity is an issue that is reshaping our industry and affecting its institutions. In addressing it, we need to be aware of how it is changing the nature of this postsecondary industry; the external political realities of our institutions, and the internal influences on curriculum, teaching, research, and tension over our "political ambivalence" (Smelser, 1993) about the concept itself.

The Telematics Revolution: Reinventing or Supplementing the Core Technology

Probably the most pervasive challenge to our industry and institutions is the rapid expansion and influx of interactive telecommunications networks, which link students and faculty to extensive data resources via workstations and computers capable of integrating information, sound, and video images. Whether it will lead to a sweeping reinvention of how students and faculty teach, learn, and conduct scholarship or whether it is merely a technical substitute is the source of heated debate on most campuses. There are several unique features about the current revolution: (1) its rapid development and rate of change, (2) the extent to which applications are being adopted in all areas of modern life beyond the campus, (3) its spread to national—even global—availability in a short time span, (4) its potential for use with few constraints of time and location, and (5) the increased affordability of ever more powerful technology. These features make it imperative that institutions adopt it as a tool of postsecondary education. But the capacity for use of telematics as a technology for learning (not just a teaching or communication technology) is perhaps the most critical challenge facing postsecondary institutions. The irony and difficulty is that this technology, which was spawned in universities, has taken on a life of its own. With so many societal as well as educational applications and implications, it has created its own industry as new computer hardware and software, telecommunications, and information-handling products and techniques are developed. The impacts on our postsecondary industry and our institutions will be extensive, and perhaps central, in the next decade (Green and Gilbert, 1995; Twigg, 1994; see also Chapter Twenty-Two, which provides a focused treatment of this challenge).

At the *industry level* (Table 1), this revolution has a vast potential for increasing the options for accessing electronic learning opportunities, for reaching a significant array of new customers (students or scholars), and for extending an institution's teaching potential. On the other hand, it has in many instances

TABLE 1
Challenges and Forces Reshaping the Postsecondary Industry.

Changing Societal Conditions or Challenges	Forces Reshaping an Industry					
	Bargaining Power of Customers	Bargaining Power of Suppliers	Threat of New Organization Entrants	Threat of Substitute Services	Innovation in Core Technology	Intensity of Competition
Patterns of diversity	More defined groups; increasing numbers	Stronger and more numerous political groups	Minority institutions and associations	New programs and services	New academic and research perspectives	Among students and among institutions
Telematics Revolution	More access and numbers; individualized needs	Telematics firms control key educational resources	Telecommunications, computing, and information firms	Training firms and merger of entertainment and telecommunications	New interactive, individualized T/L/R potential	New cross-industry competition
Quality Reform	Increased focus on learner needs	Increased attention to client demands	—	Minor new training options	New mode of management; limited use by academics	Improvements in efficiency and effectiveness
Economic Productivity	Increased career oriented pressure	Government and industry needs	New role or interorganizational patterns	Many new groups and government agencies	May redirect teaching and research	New regional, state, or national
Postsecondary Relearning	New groups of postsecondary learners	Employer-based funding sources	Many new forms emerging	Corporate and governmental education programs	Emphasis on personalized content and delivery	Ill-defined market; potential of many sources
Globalization of Scholarship	Not clearly defined; highly specialized	Potentially, nations and institutions	Currently informal or limited arrangements	Emergent use of technology	Traditional or new technology	Yet to be determined

TABLE 2
External and Internal Institutional Impact of Changing Conditions.

Changing Conditions and Challenges	Institutional Impacts	
	Internal	External
Changing Patterns of Diversity	Pluralism, curricular content, research perspectives, faculty role	Rise of minority political power groups, institutions, and associations
Telematics Revolution: Telecommunications, Computing, and Information Resource Firms	Teaching/research, delivery modes, new faculty and student roles	Cross-industry links: educational, information, telecommunications and entertainment firms
Academic and Institutional Quality	Academic outcomes, value added and assessment; culture of academic quality improvement	Business-government collaboration; tide of TQM/CQI
Improving Societal Economic Productivity	Resource partner, or leadership role; new managerial and academic priorities	Business government, and higher education collaboration
Postsecondary Relearning markets	Client-driven modular content, external delivery, faculty role	Growing adult and professional postsecondary market; academic collaboration and new competitors
Globalization of Scholarship and Education	Interdisciplinary and transnational colleagues, problems, and research paradigms	Multidisciplinary cross-industry and and transnational research groups; Multinational institutions

reversed the client relationship of post-secondary institutions with the telematics firms. Rather than those firms being the client seeking an institution's research results or trained students, they have become both the creator and supplier of information-handling tools, which makes the postsecondary institution the client—effectively reversing roles and making postsecondary institutions increasingly dependent on their former clients. An even bigger threat is the potential for new non-postsecondary institutions to enter the postsecondary educational arena. A small number of institutions offering postsecondary education via interactive telecommunications have emerged, and others are beginning to experiment with this mode. Large companies are adopting these technologies for their own

internal postsecondary training programs. Of greater possible significance is the merger of entertainment and telecommunication firms, further enhancing the potential of the packaging and delivery of postsecondary knowledge. (Will they make education entertaining, or entertainment more educational?)

Clearly, what makes this change so revolutionary is that it constitutes an alteration of the core technology of teaching, learning, and research. Colleges and universities cannot afford *not* to utilize it. But the critical issue for faculty is whether that will be as a substitute service for some portions of their teaching and scholarly activities, or an adoption of it as a more central mode.

One of the things that make this technological revolution so critical is the extent to which it interacts with all the other societal challenges. It enhances the capacity to reach both new and current student-customers differently. It also influences the way academics work and students learn. This technology is just beginning to reshape the way postsecondary institutions compete with each other for students and compete or cooperate with firms in other industries (telematics, entertainment, training) to deliver their educational products. New patterns of competition and cooperation in delivering educational services with firms that were not part of our postsecondary industry are emerging as they and we become part of a postsecondary knowledge industry.

At the *institutional level* (Table 2), the implications are also extensive. Externally, universities will either find themselves collaborating with public and private educational corporations, telecommunications companies, and. information-based firms and even entertainment enterprises in designing educational and knowledge-delivery systems, or competing with them. Already, researchers have the capacity to collaborate with scholars around the globe; they will increasingly do so.

Within the institution, students have access to extensive content material, educational resources, and other students and faculty without constraints of time or location. Such an educational network suggests a very different teaching-learning process. In addition to their traditional role, faculty may serve as learning facilitators, network guides, or learning-resource designers. The nature of the faculty role, the student-faculty relationship, and the course or classroom may change as the campus becomes part of a teaching-learning network.

While the investment in hardware and software for wide-scale use will strain the budgets of all institutions, its influence on faculty and the processes of teaching and research constitutes a major internal challenge to redefine the nature of academic work within the academy. The major external challenge is to develop new interinstitutional ties with various telematics firms.

Academic and Institutional Quality: A Focus on Learning and Improvement

Thus far in the 1990s, the demand for educational quality has already become pervasive

(Ewell, 1991). The meaning of academic quality, however, has changed in recent decades. In the 1960s and 1970s, academic quality was associated with the level and nature of institutional resources. In the 1980s, a new meaning evolved: assessment, with a focus on assessing results (outcomes, goal achievement, value-added). In the mid-1990s, academic quality has become associated with public accountability and a focus on student learning, faculty productivity and performance, program effectiveness, and even institutional evaluation. The debate about the definition of, criteria for, and means of improving educational quality shows no signs of diminishing and will be a continuing challenge both in government policy circles and in academic and institutional discussions (Dill, 1995a).

A more recent focus on quality is the concern for Total Quality Management (TQM or Continuous Quality Improvement (CQI) (Dill, 1992). While those ideas emerged in the private sector and have had the support of political leaders, the primary emphasis and application in postsecondary education to date has been in administrative activities and functions. Unlike the more educationally focused notions of quality, this approach suggests a comprehensive emphasis on developing an institutional culture that stresses policies and practices promoting (1) an environment of continuous improvement, (2) customer-or client-centeredness, (3) a rational approach to decision making using intensive measurement and benchmarking, (4) a focus on process design, (5) collaboration and teamwork, and (6) individual empowerment. Such a comprehensive approach promises to clash with strong traditions of academic individualism when applied to academic areas. But if this perspective can be successfully adapted to academic settings, it may also lead to rethinking our teaching, learning, and research processes and how we utilize the new technology for educational purposes. The fact that the Baldrige Award was recently extended in 1995 to postsecondary education suggests that TQM/CQI will have a continued emphasis in academic as well as administrative areas. (Chapter Twenty-Five addresses the concerns of planning for quality in greater detail.)

To date, the quality challenge has not had an extensive impact on our *postsecondary industry*, but it may increase as competition within the industry increases (Table 1). The quality challenge does force an institution to refocus on defining and differentiating its stakeholders (customers with needs and clients making demands) and designing its services (academic or administrative) with them in mind rather than with disciplinary, professional, or faculty concerns being primary. This particular challenge has not yet prompted new organizations to enter postsecondary education except in the narrow area of TQM/CQI training programs. Quality or continuous-improvement approaches initially seemed to represent a new mode of management rather than a revision of core academic technology or provision of a substitute service. However, as competition requires postsecondary institutions to attend more to cost and productivity, quality approaches may become associated with reengineering (a focus on process), downsizing, and/or prioritizing of services. As such, they are more a response to resource constraint designed to enhance institutional competitiveness than a force changing the competitiveness in the industry.

At the *institutional level* (Table 2), the major external dynamics suggest that as the public image of postsecondary education continues to decline, the emphasis both on educational quality and TQM/CQI will likely increase. Internally, the varying approaches to assessment, reinforced by accreditation and political pressures, are increasingly used for collegial accountability, redesign, or improvement (Romer, 1995). The advent of the Baldrige Award for education will no doubt also reinforce the use of TQM and CQI in administrative arenas. Whether concerns for educational quality and assessment can effectively merge with total-quality and continuous-improvement approaches will be a major management and planning challenge for the future.

Improving Economic Productivity: New Emphasis or New Function?

The contribution of postsecondary education to economic development has been the primary drive for the rapid and continuous expansion of postsecondary education (Leslie and Brinkman, 1988). Colleges and universities produced well-trained students, provided appropriate professional programs, and conducted pure

and applied research that contributed to society's well-being and improvements in the standard of living. But the decline of U.S. economic fortunes, and particularly the loss of dominance in key manufacturing industries in the global marketplace, has led to a new emphasis on enhancing economic productivity both at the national and state levels.

In the development of federal government priorities and state-level plans for economic development, it has been implicitly assumed that higher education, government, and the private business community are all key players. Postsecondary institutions have historically played, and been satisfied with playing, a "knowledge development" function, serving as primary providers of academic and professional training and of pure and applied research. In recent decades, serving as consultants and as sites for campus research parks, they have participated more directly in the "technology transfer" function. A more recent and aggressive form of this function is reflected in the growth of campus-affiliated incubator parks for new-product and new-company development. Most recently, postsecondary institutions have participated in developing "state or regional economic development strategies" (Dill, 1995b). In all of these roles, their participation can vary from resource institution to partner, or to manager of the function (Peterson, 1995). Increasingly, institutions are pressured to take on all three roles and to become a leader of the effort. The difficulty is that becoming a manager of technology transfer or economic development may involve an institution in an activity for which it is not well suited and one in which it may not be able to succeed (Feller, 1990). Yet political and economic pressures to show greater institutional accountability for and contribution to this area is likely to increase as long as our economy falters or fails to meet political expectations or promises. (See Chapter Twenty-Two for an extended examination of this challenge.)

At the *industry level* (see Table 1), this challenge has little direct effect on our primary customers (students), but it is probably reflected in their career-oriented priorities and concerns about useful programs. However, it does subject the industry to increasing demands from its primary clients (government and industry), especially in the public sector. The expansion of concern for economic productivity also introduces new entrants into postsecondary education—public and private technology development organizations—that may be better positioned than postsecondary institutions themselves are to compete for public applied research and development funds, and better staffed to carry out such activities. It may also require institutions to subsidize risky economic development activities with other funds traditionally used for academic functions (Feller, 1990). In effect, a new-mode of organization is created (the economic development agency or the technology transfer partnership) to provide a new service. In order to compete in this emerging service activity, institutions may be pressed to redirect effort away from some of the traditional postsecondary emphasis on teaching and research to supply the knowledge and trained students for economic development to active organizers of economic development activity. In most instances, this pressure for economic development involves postsecondary education directly in a new realm of competition: interregional, interstate, or even international, an arena in which it was previously only indirectly engaged.

At the *institutional level* (see Table 2), the press for economic development involves the institution in potentially different types of partnerships that cut across industry boundaries in order to engage in complex public-private corporate arrangements and to develop a new or previously peripheral function. These may be collaborative arrangements, or they may subject the institutions to new governmental controls and regulations. Internally, extensive involvement in economic development activity may require new managerial roles and approaches to engage in more entrepreneurial (for example, technology transfer) or political development activity. It may also realign faculty effort or require hiring of faculty more skilled in these less scholarly or academic realms (Fairweather, 1996).

Postsecondary Relearning: New Markets, Modes, and Models of Continuing Education

In recent decades, expanded educational services have been directed toward increasing traditional student enrollments and increasing service to underrepresented groups: minorities, women, older students. Modifications in schedules (evenings, weekends) or locale (off campus) were used to deliver traditional courses or programs to the part-time, nontraditional student. Continuing education was often an ancillary function, or primarily related to professional and occupational programs. Yet in today's increasingly competitive and technologically turbulent world, products, companies, and careers can change rapidly. The need for technological retooling and postsecondary reeducation is increasing in a wide variety of professions (Reich, 1991).

The demand for postsecondary relearning by older individuals is an exploding market. It comprises three identifiable groups. One is the post-high school but pre-baccalaureate group who need further education to reenter the job market or remain viably employed. One study (Grubb, forthcoming) suggests there are 20–30 million individuals between twenty-five and fifty years of age in this category. A second is the postbaccalaureate group who have college degrees but may need further education (but less than a full graduate degree) to remain viably employed or to change fields. While not as large as the previous group, it is rapidly growing as the proportion of degree holders continues to grow. Finally, there are the graduate and professional degree holders who need more than traditional continuing education to advance or change fields. In addition to their size and growth, these three market segments have much in common. Their educational interests and/or those of their employers often focus on professional competencies, individual educational needs, learning modules, off-campus delivery, and willingness to use distance-education modes of transmission (including technology) rather than on traditional courses, degrees, or programs.

At the *industry level* (see Table 1), these numbers suggest three substantial groups of potential customers for postsecondary reeducation. While some may pay for their own education, there is a sizable set of employer organizations that may be potential clients for such educational services for their employers. This market is currently served by internal corporate educational units, specialized training and development firms, and numerous postsecondary institutions, although often in traditional courses, programs, and delivery modes. (Eurich, 1985). It is a market with significant potential for new industry entrants and in which postsecondary institutions are expanding. But this market is still somewhat amorphous, with patterns of competition that are not well defined, especially by traditional postsecondary institutions.

At the *institutional level* (see Table 2), this is a substantial market. If traditional postsecondary institutions fail to respond, they risk losing a growing, sophisticated market for postsecondary, professional, and even postgraduate reeducation (beyond traditional continuing education in this field). But responding to this market requires working closely, even collaboratively, with the client and customer (or their employees). Within the institution, organizing, delivering, and financing customer-based education is often a complex new endeavor. It requires a responsive mode of curriculum design, new or individualized content modules, willingness to provide nontraditional delivery modes, and a substantial change of faculty roles.

Globalization: Breaking Bonds and Boundaries

The challenge of international and global perspectives as we approach the twenty-first century needs little exposition; nor is it a new phenomenon. Models of international student and faculty exchange programs, attempts to emphasize and improve foreign language instruction, and introducing global perspectives into our curriculum are widespread if not completely effective. But two emergent phenomena suggest that the need for greater global emphasis could take on new boundary-spanning forms in the near future.

While knowledge and scholars have already resisted regional and national boundaries, a new form of international network may be emerging. One author (Cohen, 1994) has coined the term "international civil societies" to describe a form of network consisting of university scholars, governmental policy researchers, and private-sector experts organized around major significant social problems or issues (for example, global warming, AIDS, human rights, etc.). These civil societies are interdisciplinary, cross-national, and cross-industry groups. Their work may combine research, learning, action or policy, and formulation. They often rely on technology and have access to a wide array of information and expertise, but they often have little managerial structure. In effect, they reflect how the knowledge and technology explosion can rewrite scholarly boundaries without institutional structure.

Another form of globalization that may emerge is more similar to the multinational corporation. While loosely structured, institutional exchange programs and research alliances crossing national boundaries are common, the prospects for a multinational university are worth contemplating. Some universities now have their own campuses in other countries. Many institutions have partnerships with multinational technology firms. Some countries such as those of the European Union have supported cross-national postsecondary alliances. A move to more formalized international consortia, degree-granting federations among institutions in different countries, and even the possibility of a multinational university, while a daunting challenge, are likely in the decade ahead. (See Chapter Twenty-Seven, which provides further insights on planning for this challenge.)

At the *industry level* (see Table 1), new forms of global organization would markedly intensify competition in postsecondary education (Dill and Sporn, 1995). Clearly, scholars, researchers, and many students who now participate in the less formal arrangements are a specialized customer group who could be attracted. Some countries as clients might support limited forms of cross-national organizations, and institutions with an extensive international mission or presence could emerge. A truly multinational focus would be an intriguing new entrant to our postsecondary industry, providing an alternate form of global and international opportunity for study and scholarship, and an interesting addition to the competitive mix.

At the *institutional Level* (see Table 2), the prospect of organizing a multinational institution or participating in a multinational partnership requires development of new mechanisms for collaboration with or competition in different cultures and in dealing with multiple government bureaucracies. The problems of internal management require guiding a more entrepreneurial, multicultural network form of organization—a skill to be advanced by those who develop such enterprises.

The Emerging Postsecondary Knowledge Industry: A New Perspective

As we face the twenty-first century, the changing societal conditions discussed earlier are all likely to continue. Each promises to have a major impact on both our postsecondary institutions and our industry (Tables 1 and 2).

In the previous transitions from higher education to mass education to a postsecondary industry, only one or two societal conditions created the need for transition, and the necessary industry change was usually expansion of clientele (students) or institutions. However, the six societal conditions discussed above affect all of the forces that reshape an industry. The resulting alteration in our notion of a postsecondary industry promises to be extensive and to call for a new paradigm: the postsecondary knowledge industry. While the exact nature of this new industry is only nascent, a review of how the forces reshaping an industry are affected by societal conditions provides some glimpses into our industry's possible evolution (Table 3).

Core Technology

Perhaps the most influential force is the potential for innovation in our core technology: the development, transmission, and dissemination of knowledge in society and in turn in our postsecondary industry. Postsecondary institutions have long believed they were the preeminent knowledge industry for postsecondary teaching, learning, and research. However, the telematics revolution has introduced a powerful new interactive information-handling technology that offers potentially revolutionary changes in moving from traditional modes of teaching, learning, and research to varied, responsive, flexible, interactive, and individualized modes. More critically, the telematics revolution makes it easier to respond to most of the other societal conditions affecting the industry (diversity, quality, economic productivity, postsecondary relearning, and globalization); and the revolution enhances all the other forces acting upon the industry (new organizational entrants, the power of customers and suppliers, the threat of substitute services, and the intensity of competition).

New Organizational Entrants

While the extent of use and effectiveness of information technology is key to our core processes of postsecondary education, the threat of new organizational entrants is perhaps the most tangible way of visualizing the reconfigured industry. Figure 1 reflects the institutional changes as our industry moved from traditional to mass education and then to postsecondary concepts. However, all of these transitions have primarily added students (customers) and new types of postsecondary educational institutions. Postsecondary now includes a broad array of public, private, and proprietary educational organizations providing varied educational offerings. But all are primarily educational organizations. Focusing on the organizations that are critical to a postsecondary knowledge industry perspective suggests the addition of many types of organizations previously thought to be part of other industries: telecommunications companies; computer software and hardware firms; information resource organizations; corporate and governmental organizations engaged in education, training, and professional development; and, perhaps, even "entertainment" firms. Figure 4 portrays this new extended industry that includes all the organizations in the postsecondary knowledge network. As our previous discussion has suggested, these new organizations are often no longer either just suppliers to, or customers of, postsecondary institutions. They are now effectively part of our postsecondary knowledge development, dissemination, and education system and need to be viewed as potential collaborators or competitors.

The Power of Customers

The analysis of societal conditions also suggests a change in perspective on our potential customers for postsecondary education (stu-

TABLE 3
A New Paradigm for the Postsecondary Knowledge Industry.

Industry Forces	Postsecondary Industry	Postsecondary Knowledge Network
Innovation in core technology	Traditional teaching, learning, research modes	Interactive information technology network for T, L, & R
Threat of new organizational entrants	Traditional colleges, universities, and proprietary institutions	Telecommunications, computing hardware and software, information resource, corporate and government education and training, and entertainment firms
Bargaining power of customers (students)	Traditional and nontraditional degree students	Growing minority and postsecondary relearning markets for individual learning needs
Bargaining power of suppliers (clients)	Primarily as employers, funding sources, and purchasers of services	Providers of information resources, educational technology, and communications networks; as pressure groups, partners, or competitors
Threat of substitute services	Limited	More extensive
Intensity of competition	Among existing postsecondary institutions or segments	Cross-industry more competitive

dents). The shift is from a focus on traditional and nontraditional students seeking regular courses and degree offerings via traditional delivery modes to a broader view of the entire market for postsecondary education, which includes those potential student customers who are interested in non-degree-oriented learning and often in nontraditional modes of delivery. The key shift in the postsecondary knowledge industry perspective is to focus on students as learners with individualized educational needs rather than as potential students for courses and programs designed and delivered by postsecondary institutions.

The Power of Suppliers and the Threat of Substitute Services

The inclusion of potential new organizational entrants in the new postsecondary knowledge industry both enlarges and suggests their increased power as suppliers. They are no longer just the customers who are employers of graduates and purchasers of our knowledge products and services or sources of funding. They are often key suppliers, providers of valuable information resources, new educational technology and advances, and access to critical communication networks. Another major shift is to recognize that in the new postsecondary knowledge environment suppliers may be not merely resource providers for and purchasers of services from postsecondary institutions but also sources of substitute (educational) services. Further, they are now potential pressure groups, educational partners, or competitors—not merely suppliers. It is clear that in a postsecondary knowledge environment other knowledge-based firms do have greater power, both as suppliers of resources or as sources of substitute services, because of the ease of access to knowledge and its utilization.

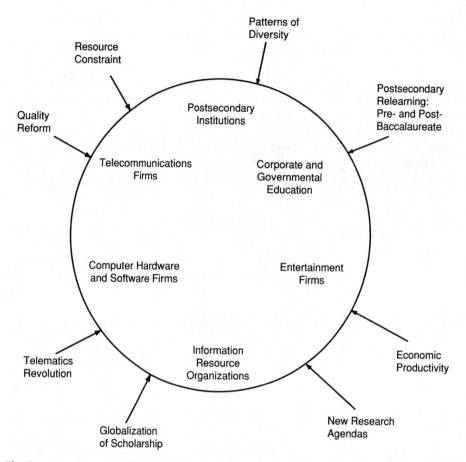

Figure 4: The Emerging Postsecondary Knowledge Industry

Competition

Finally, it is also apparent that in the postsecondary knowledge industry competition is likely to intensify. Clearly, competition among existing postsecondary institutions is intensified by the challenges to increase diversity, to improve quality, to constrain costs, and to enter the expanding postsecondary relearning markets. What is likely to be qualitatively different is competition in the knowledge industry that cuts across old industry boundaries. For instance, competing in the knowledge industry with organizations from the telecommunications, computing, or the corporate education and training world is far more entrepreneurial and fast-paced than in the traditional postsecondary world. Also, competition to engage in economic development or new global arrangements may entail both creative risks and new governmental controls or regulatory environments.

Thus, it is apparent that a postsecondary knowledge industry is substantially different from one composed only of postsecondary educational institutions. Participating in this new environment or industry requires a continued attempt to understand its evolving character and the role that traditional postsecondary institutions will play in it.

Institutional Challenges: A Contextual Planning Perspective

Discussion of changing societal conditions has implicitly identified many of the internal and external impacts on postsecondary institutions and the forces that are shaping the emerging postsecondary knowledge industry (Tables 1 and 2).

A brief review highlights the challenges for institutional leaders and planners as they provide new perspectives to their institutions in the decade ahead. First, there is the need to plan for a period of substantial external change and uncertainty in which the nature not only of our postsecondary system but of our postsecondary knowledge industry is changing. The foremost challenge is to understand the critical societal conditions and forces that are reshaping our postsecondary knowledge industry. Second, one needs to understand how interactive, technology-based information and knowledge systems will reshape our industry and our institutions. Third, there is an even more diverse array of potential educational customers needing postsecondary educational services: the growing minority and educationally disadvantaged populations, new cadres of postsecondary learners, etc. Fourth, there is an increasingly diverse and powerful set of constituent groups and organizations demanding various educational services: a more proactive business community, more varied and changing governmental interest, and a complex labyrinth of telematics and information-resource firms. Fifth, many of these external business and governmental organizations are now also potential competitors for or collaborators with existing postsecondary institutions for both the new postsecondary markets and as an alternative or substitute for our more traditional undergraduate, graduate, and professional education and research functions. Sixth, the growing diversity of customers or student clientele includes postsecondary learners interested in or willing to use interactive technology as modes of educational transmission delivered to noncampus settings and packaged in nontraditional content or competency modules rather than traditional programs or degrees. Seventh, on the educational side, there is a shift in emphasis from teaching—from faculty and instructional development—to learning, learners, learning needs, and learning development. Eighth, the nature and bounds of research are likely to be more transdisciplinary and collaborative but less limited to geographic, institutional, or even national spheres. Finally, most of these challenges call for rethinking the basic educational delivery and research processes and functions. They focus more on change in the teaching-learning process, the research process, and faculty-to-student and faculty-to-faculty relationships. They suggest extensive changes in faculty roles and behaviors—in essence, changing the academic culture of the workplace.

This set of planning challenges suggests extensive change in how we view our institutions both externally and internally. Externally it requires a planning perspective focused on the broader notion of a postsecondary knowledge industry or network rather than an industry or system of higher or postsecondary institutions. This suggests an external environment of increasing diversity and complexity, recognizing that many other types of organizations are engaged in the development, dissemination, and utilization of knowledge that is postsecondary in character. Internally, the planning perspective must recognize the potential need for extensive change in the academic structure and function and even in the nature of academic work. In essence the societal challenges to postsecondary institutions and this new paradigm of a postsecondary knowledge industry may require extensive institutional change. This suggests a need for planning which will address the following questions:

Redefinition: What is the nature of a postsecondary knowledge industry, and what is our institution's role in it?

Redirection: How should our institution's mission change to reflect these new realities, and what new external relationships should we develop?

Reorganization: How should we redesign our academic processes and structures and reorganize our management functions?

Renewal: How do we renew or re-create our academic workplace and institutional culture? Our preparation of future faculty?

In an environment of extensive and often unpredictable change that mandates rethinking the nature of our system or industry and considering the need for major institutional adaptation, current approaches to planning may be inadequate. Long-range and strategic planning typically begins with the assumption that one functions within an existing system of institutions or an industry, and that evolutionary change will allow an institution to adapt to environmental constraints and opportunities. However, in a situation in which the industry context is being reshaped and the institution may need to change drastically, a more proactive mode of planning that seeks to participate in shaping the industry and offers the possibility of more radical redesign of the institution may be called for. Contextual planning, discussed in Chapter Seven, offers an approach to addressing these broader questions of redefinition, redirection, reorganization, and renewal.

Further Reading

Those interested in exploring the changing nature of society and its implications for postsecondary education in the information age will find Peter Drucker's "The Age of Social Transformation" (1994) and *Managing for the Future* (1992) provocative and insightful. For a perspective on the changing nature of institutions as organizations, *Organizing for the Future*, by Jay Galbraith and others (1993), is an interesting generic treatment for those interested in planning postsecondary institutions. Two thought-provoking books that provide new ways of thinking about organizations in a postindustrial information age are Sally Hegelson's *The Web of Inclusion* (1995) and Margaret Wheatley's *Leadership and the New Science* (1992). Two edited volumes that focus more explicitly on our current and changing world of postsecondary education are David Dill and Barbara Sporn's *Emerging Patterns of Social Demand and University Reform: Through a Glass Darkly* (1995) and *Higher Education. in American Society* (1994, third edition, but a fourth is planned), edited by Philip Altbach, Robert Berdahl, and Patricia Gumport. These volumes feature well-prepared chapter contributions that focus on the external conditions influencing postsecondary institutions (Dill and Sporn, 1995) and on a comprehensive examination of our current postsecondary system or industry and how it is changing (Altbach, Berdahl, and Gumport, 1994). Readers are also encouraged to identify a broadly focused publication or other information source that scans and examines external forces or internal changes in postsecondary education. *On The Horizon*, edited by James Morrison

and published by Jossey-Bass, is such a useful resource focusing on education. Readers with more focused interests in the challenges to postsecondary education discussed in this chapter will want to identify a resource related to their particular interest.

References

Altbach, R. G., Berdahl, R. O., and Gumport, P. J. *Higher Education in American Society.* (3rd ed.) Amherst, N.Y: Prometheus, 1994.

Carter, D. J., and Wilson, R. *Minorities in Higher Education: American Council on Education Eleventh Annual Status Report.* Washington, D.C.: American Council on Education, 1993.

Cohen, D. W. "The Constitution of International Expertise." *Journal of the International Institute.* Ann Arbor, Mich.: University of Michigan International Institute, 1994.

Dill, D. D. "Quality by Design: Towards a Framework for Academic Quality Management." In J. Smart (ed.), *Higher Education: Handbook of Theory and Research,* Vol. VIII. New York: Agathon Press, 1992.

Dill, D. D. "Through Deming's Eyes: A Cross-National Analysis of Quality Assurance Policies in Higher Education." *Quality in Higher Education,* 1995a, *1*(2), 95–110.

Dill, D. D. "University-Industry Entrepreneurship: The Organization and Management of American University Technology Transfer Units." *Higher Education,* 1995b, *29*(4), 369–384.

Dill, D. D., and Sporn, B. "The Implications of a Postindustrial Environment for the University. An Introduction." In D. D. Dill and B. Sporn (eds.), *Emerging Patterns of Social Demand and University Reform: Through a Glass Darkly.* New York: Pergamon Press, 1995.

Drucker, P. *Managing for the Future: The 1990s and Beyond.* New York: Dutton, 1992.

Drucker, P. "The Age of Social Transformation." *Atlantic Monthly,* November 1994, pp. 53–80.

Eurich, N. F. *Corporate Classrooms, the Learning Business.* Princeton: Princeton University Press, 1985.

Ewell, P. T. "Assessment and Public Accountability: Back to the Future." *Change,* 1991, *23*(6), 12–17.

Fairweather, J. *Faculty Work and Public Trust. Restoring the Value of Teaching and Public Service in Academic Life.* Needham Heights, Mass.: Allyn & Bacon, 1996.

Feller, I. "Universities as Engines of R&D-Based Economic Growth: They Think They Can." *Research Policy,* 1990, *19*(4), 335–348.

Galbraith, J. R., Lawler, E. E., III, and Associates. *Organizing for the Future.* San Francisco: Jossey-Bass, 1993.

Green, K. C., and Gilbert, S. W "Great Expectations: Content, Communications, Productivity, and the Role of Information Technology in Higher Education." *Change,* 1995, 27(2), 8–18.

Grubb, W. N. *Working in the Middle: Strengthening the Sub-Baccalaureate Labor Force.* San Francisco: Jossey-Bass, forthcoming.

Hegelson, S. *The Web of Inclusion: A New Architecture for Building Great Organizations.* New York: Doubleday, 1995.

Leslie, L., and Brinkman, P. T. *The Economic Value of Higher Education.* New York: American Council on Education and Macmillan, 1988.

Mintz, S. D. (ed.). *Sources: Diversity Initiative in Higher Education.* Washington, D.C.: American Council on Education, 1993.

Morrison, J. L. (ed.). *On the Horizon: The Environmental Scanning Publication for Leaders in Education.* San Francisco: Jossey-Bass, 1996.

Musil, C. M. *Diversity in Higher Education: A Work in Progress.* Washington, D.C.: Association of American Colleges and Universities, 1995.

Peterson, M. W. "Images of University Structure, Governance, and Leadership: Adaptive Strategies for the New Environment." In D. Dill and B. Sporn (eds.), *Emerging Patterns of Social Demand and University Reform: Through a Glass Darkly.* New York. Pergamon Press, 1995.

Porter, M. E. *Competitive Strategy.* New York: Free Press, 1980.

Reich, R. *The Work of Nations: Preparing Ourselves for 21st Century Capitalism.* New York: Knopf, 1991.

Romer, R. *Making Quality Count in Undergraduate Education.* Denver: Education Commission of the States, 1995.

Rudolph, F. *The American College and University: A History.* New York: Random House, 1962.

Smelser, N. "The Politics of Ambivalence." *Daedalus,* 1993, 122(4), 37–54.

Twigg, C. A. "The Need for a National Learning Infrastructure." *EDUCOM Review,* 1994, 29 (5), 16–20.

Wheatley, M. J. *Leadership and the New Science: Learning About Organization from an Orderly Universe.* San Francisco: Berrett-Koehler, 1992.

CHAPTER 12

ADMINISTRATION AND MANAGEMENT

ASSOCIATE EDITOR: DAVID W. BRENEMAN

The readings in this section introduce the topics of higher education finance, legal issues, and inter-collegiate athletics, areas that occupy significant time and attention from presidents, financial vice presidents, athletic directors, legal counsel, and members of boards of trustees. The article by McPherson and Winston draws on over a decade of work accomplished at Williams College on the economics of higher education, and is a chapter from a book of essays on that topic. The article demonstrates the way that economists think about higher education finance—in this instance, through a focus on the market for college attendance. The essay explores such questions as: What determines the price charged to students as tuition, the level of subsidy provided by state governments and by private giving, and the level of expenditure per student, at the various public and private campuses in this country. Of particular significance is the authors' discussion of the limited information about college quality that is readily available to potential students, and the way in which price and other factors function as signals of quality. Purchasing a college education is not like buying laundry detergent or toothpaste, but has some similarities with markets for professional services, such as medical care or legal advice, where the purchaser typically knows less about the product or service than the provider. The article also examines the increasingly important role of student financial aid, and how it is used to produce an entering class with desired characteristics of quality and diversity. Student financial aid, including grants, loans, and work study, provided by state and federal governments and by institutions, has become a central part of the financing of higher education.

The McPherson-Winston article is written from the standpoint of institutional management, with the college viewed as an entity that must raise funds from multiple sources and allocate those revenues to advance the mission of the institution. What distinguishes U.S. higher education from systems in other countries is the absence of a central education ministry in the U.S., and a lesser reliance on government subsidy relative to the private support from tuition, endowment earnings, and philanthropy. The existence of a substantial private, non-profit, college sector is also noteworthy, enhancing the diversity of educational programs, but complicating the policy measures adopted by state and federal governments. The U.S. system of higher education is also distinguished by its high level of student access, with nearly two-thirds of recent high school graduates attending some form of postsecondary education, and older, part-time students becoming a large and growing segment of total enrollments.

The McPherson-Winston chapter does not provide financial data, but the student can obtain such information from the annual reports of the National Center of Education statistics.[1] In 1996–97, it is estimated that expenditures of colleges and universities were $225 billion, roughly three percent of gross domestic product. Data are readily available on revenues by source, on expenditures by category, on student aid, by state, and by public and private sectors.

David W. Breneman is University Professor and Dean, Curry School of Education, University of Virginia. (dwb8n@virginia.edu) The author acknowledges the assistance of Ben Boggs, of the University of Virginia, in selecting the articles for this chapter.

The article by Ruger, from the *Stetson Law Review*, provides a good survey of the nature and scope of legal issues confronting higher education. Ruger notes that university legal offices were virtually non-existent until the 1960s, when a range of issues prompted the growth of a distinct specialization in higher education law. Campus disruptions during the Vietnam War began the process, giving rise to disciplinary codes that required legal oversight. In the 1970s, growth in federal regulation spurred further need for legal services, as civil rights laws, the Family Educational Rights and Privacy Act, Title IX of the Education Amendments of 1972, and other legislation complicated the management of institutions. By 1997, the National Association of College and University Attorneys (NACUA) reported 2,762 members.

No single article could do justice to the many areas in which legal issues are involved in higher education. A specialized literature exists for each area, but the article closes with a helpful listing of the NACUA Uniform Subject-Matter Index, which organizes the field into roughly 30 categories.

Thelin and Wiseman provide in their article a good introduction to the economics of intercollegiate athletics. While the myth abounds that most NCAA Division 1-A universities make money on their sports programs overall, the reality is different. Even the high-revenue sports of football and basketball are often net revenue consumers, not net producers. This fact makes the argument that college athletics should simply be recognized as a business and run as such, with salaries paid to the athletes, awkward at best.

On the other hand, as the article makes clear, big-time college sports are often treated like a business, for a university that has opted for a given level of competition must be competitive at that level. The resulting financial treadmill is distressing to many faculty, as they witness ever-larger sums being lavished on this non-academic dimension of the institution. Unusual power often resides in the athletic director or the head football coach, and presidents struggle to maintain control over this area, as trustees and major donors often care more about athletics than academics. The authors suggest that it is time to stop thinking of intercollegiate athletics as a business, and instead view them as a subsidized activity, competing for resources with other activities within the University.

Note

1. *Digest of Educational Statistics*, Annual Editions, National Center for Education Statistics, U.S. Department of Education, Washington, D.C.

Suggested Supplementary Readings

Economics

Breneman, D. W. *Liberal Arts Colleges: Thriving, Surviving, or Endangered?*. Washington, DC: The Brookings Institution, 1994.

Breneman, D. W., Leslie, L. L., & Anderson, R. E. *ASHE Reader on Finance in Higher Education*. Needham Heights, MA: Ginn Press, 1993.

Callan, P. M., Finney, J. E., Bracco, K. R., & Doyle, W. R. (eds). *Public and Private Financing of Higher Education: Shaping Public Policy for the Future*. Phoenix: The American Council on Education, Oryx Press, 1997.

McPherson, M. S., Schapiro, M. O. *The Student Aid Game: Meeting Need and Rewarding Talent in American Higher Education*. Princeton: Princeton University Press, 1998.

McPherson, M. S., Shapiro, M. O., & Winston, G. C. *Paying the Piper: Productivity, Incentives, and Financing in U.S. Higher Education*. Ann Arbor: The University of Michigan Press, 1996.

Athletics:

Lapchick, R. E., Slaughter, J. B. *Rules of the Game: Ethics in College Sports*. New York: American Council on Education and MacMillan, 1989.

Lawrence, Paul. (1987). *Unsportsmanlike Conduct: The National Collegiate Athletic Association and the Business of College Football*. New York: Praeger Press, 1987.

Oliva, Jay. *What Trustees Should Know about Intercollegiate Athletics*. Washington, DC: Association of Governing Boards, 1989.

Padilla, A., Boucher, J. L. "On the Economics of Intercollegiate Athletic Programs," *Journal of Sport and Social Issues*, 1988,1987, *11*, 1 & 2, 61 & 73.

Sanoff, A. P., Schrof, J. M. "The Price of Victory: College Sports vs. Education" *U.S. News and World Report*, January 8, 1990, 52.

Thelin, J. R. (1996). *Games Colleges Play: Scandal and Reform in Intercollegiate Athletics*. Baltimore: The Johns Hopkins University Press, 1996.

Legal Issues:

Dahl, D. "Hot Trends at Universities," *Corporate Legal Times*, May 1994, p. 1.

Drinan, R. F. "Lawyer-Client Confidentiality in the Campus Setting," *Journal of College and University Law*, 1993, *19*, 4, 305.

Heubert, J. P. "The More We Get Together: Improving Collaboration Between Educators and Their Lawyers," *Harvard Educational Review*. 1997, *67*, 3, 531.

Kaplin, W. A. and Lee, B. *The Law of Higher Education*. 3rd Edition, 1995, 64.

Thomas, N. L. "The Attorney's Role on Campus: Options for Colleges and Universities." *Change*, May/June 1998, *30*, 3, 34–42.

The Practice and Profession
of Higher Education Law

PETER H. RUGER[*]

Writing in 1985, a leading authority on higher education law observed: "The last quarter century has witnessed an enormous expansion in the law's presence on America's campuses. Whether one is engaged in campus disputes, planning to avoid future disputes, or charting an institution's policies and priorities, law has become an indispensable component of decision-making."[1] More than a decade later, the presence of law and legal issues on the campuses of this nation has not abated. In 1985, on its twenty-fifth anniversary, the National Association of College and University Attorneys (NACUA or Association),[2] the specialty bar association for higher education lawyers, reported having approximately 2400 members.[3] Today, the membership numbers 2762.[4] With growth in numbers, and longevity of function, has come the recognition that higher education law is a distinct professional specialty, certainly different from the substantive activities of corporate lawyers in the business community.

While considerable issue overlap exists in the representation of higher education institutions and pre-college schools, major differences in the legal issues confronted exist. In particular, faculty, student, and governance issues are often quite different in the higher education arena. The extent and intensity of governmental regulation is greater for higher education than the K-12 world.[5] Charitable giving and taxation issues are infrequent in K-12 but common in higher education. The topic headings of NACUA's exchange of legal information service reflect the extensive (but by no means exclusive) range of the law of higher education

and demonstrate both the breadth and uniqueness of this area of practice.[6]

The recognition and maturation of higher education law as a distinct practice area is relatively recent. Until the early 1960s, the legal needs of colleges and universities were limited. Services were often provided, without charge, by lawyers who were prominent alumni or members of the Board of Trustees.[7] Occasionally, but rarely, the contributions of lawyers to the creation of colleges were recognized: "Judge Anson Brunson assisted the Board [of Pomona College] in the preparation of the Articles of Incorporation . . . and management of property. He was the first of a long line of lawyer members to whom the Board would be greatly indebted."[8] Zealousness to an extent exceeding propriety was attributed to one counsel: "Judge Edward H. East, as president of the Board of Trustees, did the legal work and apparently even signed a fellow judge's name to the chancery court order of August 19, 1972, that legally established Central University (the forerunner to Vanderbilt University),"[9] Generally, the contributions of clergy or politicians are recognized, to the exclusion of lawyers, in college histories.[10] Some drafting, occasional contract review, and general assurance that a course of conduct was "legal" were usually all that was required. Litigation was rare: indeed, the West Digest topic "colleges and universities" consumes only eighty-one double-columned pages in the period through the *Fourth Decennial Digest*, which covers cases from 1658 to 1936.[11] The triple-columned *Eighth Decennial Digest*, covering reported cases decided from 1966 to

"The Practice and Profession of Higher Education Law," by Peter H. Ruger, reprinted from *Stetson Law Review*, Vol. 27, No. 1, Summer 1997, Stetson University.

1976, devoted ninety-five pages to "colleges and universities";[12] that title grew to 124 pages in the *Ninth Decennial Digest*.[13] Higher education law clearly became a growth industry.

Of course, higher education needed legal services from time to time. Has anyone not heard Daniel Webster's paean to Dartmouth College—uttered in his defense of the sanctity of the college's charter in the face of antagonistic government action?[14] Even before the Dartmouth College case, the best known higher education case of the nineteenth century, a dispute arose not unlike that encountered by campus counsel today. In 1718, Ebenezer Pierpoint, a 1715 Harvard graduate, was denied his second degree by Harvard President John Leverett for "his condemning, reproaching and insulting the government of the college."[15] After a "long and impertinent" harangue, the Harvard Board upheld the denial of the degree. Pierpoint sued and, eventually, Harvard prevailed as the General Court held that Pierpoint had received a proper hearing from the College's officials.[16]

Higher education law, as a distinct professional pursuit, was born in the 1960s. The contributors to a special symposium issue of *the Journal of College and University Law* commemorating NACUA's first twenty-five years refer to events in that decade, and in the 1970s, as being the stimuli to the growth of higher education law and higher education lawyers as a distinct professional group.[17] A need for legal services to higher education was created by campus disruptions during the Vietnam era. Occasionally, court orders were sought to quell protest.[18] The *Dixon v. Alabama State Board of Education*[19] decision confirmed the existence of due process rights for students involved in disciplinary proceedings at public universities.[20] The unpopularity of the war in Southeast Asia, and the concomitant aversion to strong sanctions against anti-war demonstrators, led to the creation of disciplinary codes, at both public and private institutions, that rivaled criminal codes. The eradication of doctrines of charitable immunity exposed private colleges to tort claims for the first time.[21] A cynic might suggest that since many of the early disciplinary procedures were written by lawyers, they were created in such a way as to insure full employment. Colleges, faced with significant legal expenses for the first time, began hiring counsel, often from the firms already providing legal services to the institution.[22]

The 1970s witnessed a significant growth in the federal regulation of higher education. Civil rights laws first included higher education within their scope in the early 1970s.[23] Higher education is a labor intensive industry, often decentralized and populated with many who are accustomed to thinking and acting independently—fertile conditions for employment discrimination complaints. The Family Educational Rights and Privacy Act dates from the 1970s.[24] Tax reform in 1969 made higher education fair game for audits.[25] The complexities of the Employee Retirement Income Security Act of 1974 are mind-boggling.[26] Regulatory initiatives that were short lived, such as price controls and energy crisis measures had an impact. Title IX[27] dates from that era, as do a number of other measures having a particular impact on medical schools.[28] College and university administrations realized that, in most cases, utilization of outside counsel to develop policies and procedures would be quite expensive and, because of their lack of knowledge of the institution, marginally effective. The landmark United States Supreme Court cases of *Board of Regents v. Roth*[29] and *Perry v. Sindermann*[30] defined faculty rights in termination situations. The need to provide due process at public institutions in faculty terminations created a need for legal guidance.[31] The student enrollment boom of the 1950s and 1960s was waning, and institutions addressed issues of cutbacks and financial exigency, contentious situations that called for legal guidance.

Candid college histories document the new challenges fostering the need for campus counsel. Confronting Vanderbilt and many other colleges and universities during this period, as reported in *Gone with the Ivy*, were a variety of issues, all with legal implications: allegations of sex discrimination in a tenure decision;[32] admission of a controversial student;[33] insuring "good taste" in student publications;[34] homosexuals on campus;[35] Vietnam era protests;[36] speakers abhorrent to many in the community;[37] drug use;[38] abolition of *in loco parentis* doctrines, including student demands for autonomy in alcohol use, dorm hours, and visitation opportunities;[39] minority (African-American) unrest;[40] and merger with an adjacent college.[41] This delineation, not atypical for universities in the 1960s and 1970s, is an agenda of potential or actual conflict that required the frequent involvement of counsel. The uniqueness of the issues, and the context in which they arose, convinced many that persons with legal skills and an inclination to be strong advocates for institutional values, were needed on campus both to play an advisory role, and when necessary, to be a visible advocate for the university's position.

Another university historian described conditions on his campus, the University of Iowa, during this period that made apparent the need for counsel in higher education:

> the university was confronted with a situation in which both external and internal forces were seeking a share in its control. Federal and state legislatures, federal granting agencies, accrediting bodies, foundations and private donors all threatened its autonomy. . . . Each group emphasized its rights rather than the soundness of decisions arrived at. The university itself could be faulted for its educational conservatism, inefficiency, disorderliness, and indecisiveness.[42]

Because of the training and the inclination of the profession, the latter three traits are repugnant to lawyers. Their analytical skills had to be employed in evaluating, and often rebutting, the claims of "right" that emerged with a vigor, and lack of civility, not previously witnessed on campus.

The first campus legal office was established at the University of Alabama in 1925.[43] Before the 1960s, only about a dozen offices had been created.[44] About twenty offices were created during the 1960s, with almost sixty offices being added in the 1970s.[45] In 1983, more than one-half of all campus legal offices had been created since 1972.[46] By 1992, fifty-five percent of NACUA institutions were represented by in-house counsel compared to forty-seven percent in 1983.[47] By 1994, seventy-four percent of the NACUA institutions were represented primarily by in-house counsel.[48] Colleges and universities principally relying on outside counsel for their legal needs were primarily private institutions with annual budgets of less than $100 million. In 1994, only twelve percent of the public institutions or five percent of any institutions with a budget of at least $100 million per year

lacked in-house counsel.[49] Despite the growth of campus counsel positions, average expenditures for outside counsel increased three-fold, from $127,000 in 1983 to $350,000 in 1992.[50] Higher billing rates were paid by private institutions of higher education. Compared to rates charged to public institutions, the billing partner's rate for the private sector was nineteen percent higher, while the associates was fifteen percent greater.[51]

NACUA's 1992 survey revealed that, for the past five years, in-house counsel identified five areas that required most of their effort: preparing or reviewing documents; addressing affirmative action and non-discrimination issues; dealing with faculty personnel actions; handling student affairs matters; and providing labor relations counsel.[52] Outside counsel's division of effort was identical, except that real estate replaced labor relations.[53] For outside counsel, specialty areas in which the greatest workload increase occurred were: affirmative action and non-discrimination; employee benefits; construction matters; faculty and staff personnel actions; and preparing and reviewing documents.[54] Areas of marked growth identified by campus counsel were: affirmative action and non-discrimination; faculty and staff personnel actions; personal injury and tort defense; federal regulation; environmental law; employee benefits; and preparing and reviewing documents.[55]

The average annual campus legal office budget grew from $177,000 in 1983 to $402,000 in 1992 to $509,277 in 1994.[56] Comparing budgets for institutions with medical schools or an affiliated foundation to colleges or universities without those entities reveals a substantial gap in budgets, with the former at $951,335 in 1994, and the latter trailing at $313,314.[57] The budgets reported by private institutions were approximately twenty percent higher than the public sector.[58]

College and university counsel tend to have considerable experience in the legal profession. In 1992, about seventy percent of the campus counsel had more than ten years of legal experience.[59] Slightly more than half of campus counsel, however, had less than ten years of higher education law experience.[60] A nearly equal division of male and female members exists, with minorities comprising fifteen percent of the membership.[61]

As counsel began to appear on campus in significant numbers in the late 1960s and early 1970s, commentators sought to delineate their use and functions.[62] A "first law" for the proper use of counsel was "have one."[63] Another accurately described the essence of counsels' role:

> [T]he primary thrust of the attorneys' responsibility to the university and the primary definition of his or her role within the institution *is the providing of preventive advice* which will save the institution from formal litigation or other challenges. . . .[64]

Professor Bickel's observation has force today, but is often misunderstood, as is the impact of counsel on campus legal issues.

There are two main aspects of the salient preventive function. One is monitoring the external legal environment to insure that appropriate administrators know about new judicial decisions, legislation, and regulatory initiatives. Besides informing and educating clients of these developments, counsel should then participate in the process that examines the applicability of the new developments to the campus.[65] Counsel should also play a role in the revision of policies and practices necessitated by the external developments. This endeavor, one of "getting one's house in order," has another aspect, that of anticipating future legal issues that will confront the campus and developing a process to address them. For example, rather than rely on costly outside counsel, several campus counsels' offices in the 1980s developed a knowledge of environmental law. As regulatory efforts directed at higher education increased in the late 1980s and early 1990s, these institutions were provided with more timely and cost-effective advice than those that relied on outside counsel. Higher education clients should expect their counsel to anticipate future issues and provide guidance in preparing to address them.

The other prong of the preventive function is providing timely and competent advice to campus clients for the resolution of their legal issues. This responsibility can range from providing rather routine contract or document review to being a major participant in delicate and difficult situations, such as the termination of a faculty member, or development of a strategy to resist an attempt by graduate students to unionize. The worth of counsel is tested in dif-

ficult and stressful situations, and the most successful counsel are those who can best understand their client's needs, combining them with institutional goals and legal doctrines, to produce advice that is understandable, relevant, and useful. In this litigious age, no one, not even the most competent counsel, can prevent a lawsuit from being filed against an institution. But judicious use of competent and responsive counsel, as early in the process as possible, will greatly enhance the prospects of a successful defense of the suit.

Roderick Daane, in his seminal article about university counsel, describes six "basic roles" of university counsel: Advisor-Counselor; Educator-Mediator; Manager-Administrator; Draftsman; Litigator; and Spokesman.[66] The first four roles are most directly linked to counsel's central preventive role, with the first two (Advisor-Counselor; Educator-Mediator) the most important. Despite Daane's attempt, drawing lines between these paramount roles is difficult. The educator role is present (or should be) whenever advice is given. Unlike dealing with other organizations, it is insufficient and counterproductive to tell higher education clients to not take a particular course of action because it lacks legal justification. Higher education, with its traditions of shared governance and freedom of inquiry, is a markedly different client. Lawyers who fail to appreciate that, and who fail to educate their clients concerning the pitfalls of a proposed course of action, or who fail to delineate how the client's objectives can be met, will not thrive in higher education and are not serving their clients effectively.

A campus counsel should not be just an administrator with a law degree. Independence from organizational pressure or intrigue is essential. Counsel should report to the Board or chief executive officer and not be in some other administrator's chain of command. A counsel, in turn, must remember his or her duty as a lawyer; to provide independent advice to the client.[67] The turnover of general counsel in higher education appears to be increasing, perhaps as a result of, in part, the reluctance, or inability, of chief executives to understand that obligation. To be sure, an institution's leader faces pressures more numerous and intense than those of the 1970s and 1980s. But the appropriate response is not to figuratively follow Shakespeare's suggestion for management of counsel.[68]

The evolution of higher education law as a recognized specialty within the legal profession is paralleled, in large part, by the emergence and growth of the NACUA. NACUA was founded in 1960–61 by about a dozen lawyers representing colleges and universities. Attorneys from Northwestern University, the Universities of Alabama and Michigan, and several Ivy League institutions played major roles in NACUA's formation.[69] The first president of NACUA, in 1961–62, was Ralph A. Lesemann of the University of Illinois.[70]

NACUA differs from other bar associations by requiring that membership be institutional rather than individual.[71] Today, more than 2700 lawyers, serving 662 institutions with 1400 campuses, constitute NACUA's membership. This number includes both in-house counsel and lawyers in private practice. Approximately two-thirds of NACUA's member institutions are public and private colleges and universities with enrollments exceeding 5000 students and with budgets ranging from $50 million to more than $4 billion.[72] These institutions have a cumulative enrollment of more than seven million students. The remaining one-third of the membership are private colleges and universities with enrollments below 5000 students and annual budgets below $50 million per year.[73] Membership dues are derived from a matrix considering the institution's budget and student enrollment. Predictably, larger and more affluent institutions pay a larger share of the dues.

Member institutions are found in every state, Puerto Rico, and the District of Columbia, and range, alphabetically, from Abilene Christian University to Youngstown State University.[74] The diversity of member institutions is vast, ranging from large state systems (*e.g.,* California State University, a system with twenty-two campuses), community colleges (*e.g.,* Maricopa County Community College District, with ten campuses), technical colleges (*e.g.,* Indiana Vocational Technical College, with thirteen campuses), religious institutions (*e.g.,* Brigham Young University, Yeshiva University, Mid America Nazarene College) including seminaries (*e.g.,* Episcopal Divinity School, Jewish Theological Seminary of America), numerous small private colleges (*e.g.,* Dakota Wesleyan University, Greenville College, Williams College), and institutions with unique missions (*e.g.,* California College of Arts and Crafts, United States Coast Guard Academy, Gallaudet University, Illinois College of Optometry, Forsyth School of Dental Hygienists, The Juilliard School, Rhode Island School of Design).[75] International members are welcome, with Canadian institutions currently predominant.[76] In addition, institutional members are found in Australia, Israel, and Lebanon.[77] Lawyers serving these institutions include in-house counsel and private practitioners. At smaller institutions, an in-house counsel will often have other responsibilities, such as teaching or fund-raising.

NACUA, an educational organization exempt from income taxation, states that its "purpose is to enhance legal assistance to colleges and universities by educating attorneys and administrators about the nature of campus legal issues. It has an equally important role to play in the continuing legal education of university counsel."[78] Central to NACUA's continuing legal education activities is its annual conference. The 1997 conference held in Seattle, featured twenty-two presentation sessions and an equal number of discussion groups. Topics covered reflect the variety of legal issues confronting college counsel, such as "Aid in Dying and Medical Ethics" and "Endorsements, Athletic Apparel and Shoe Contracts."[79] In addition, NACUA's twelve specialty sections (*e.g.,* Athletics, Museums and Collections, Student Affairs) meet at the annual conference and provide an opportunity for dialogue on common issues. In recent years, at least 600 NACUA lawyers have attended the annual meeting. In addition, several one- or two-day workshops, often held in conjunction with other higher education groups, are held during the year.[80]

Another way NACUA fulfills its purpose is through publication of pertinent and timely information. A quarterly law journal, *The Journal of College and University Law,* is co-published with the University of Notre Dame Law School.[81] The *College Law Digest,* accompanying the *Education Law Reporter* thirteen times per year, provides members with timely legal information and analysis. Association matters, such as meeting announcements and job opening notices, are found in the *Digest.* Since the mid-1980s, NACUA has produced a plethora of publications ranging from compendia addressing broad legal topics to pamphlets dealing with specific issues such as bankruptcy and student records.[82] In conjunction with the Center for Constitutional Studies at Baylor University, NACUA produced a handbook for private college administrators.[83]

NACUA maintains a legal reference service that provides research assistance, sample policies, and documents and referrals to other NACUA attorneys with experience in the subject of the inquiry. The electronic age has not bypassed NACUA. A dedicated network (NACUA Net) is available to member attorneys. Many hundreds of NACUA lawyers use it now,[84] primarily to seek guidance on legal issues confronting their clients. A home page, or web site, was created in 1996.[85] It enables NACUA to store and distribute up-to-date legal and Association-related information to the membership, or anyone else visiting the site.[86] A position registry is maintained to facilitate the announcement of positions in higher education law.[87]

NACUA is governed by a Board of Directors elected annually by the membership at the annual conference. An elected officer, the President, serves a one-year term and provides general direction to the organization.[88] Traditionally, this office alternates between persons representing public institutions of higher education and, in the next year, an attorney counseling a private college or university. Five members at large are elected to the Board of Directors each year. They serve three-year terms and traditionally are not re-elected.[89] Persons elected to officer positions have served as members at large of the Board. Unlike the American Bar Association or state bar associations, NACUA members don't "run" or campaign for election to the Board or officer ranks.[90] Sections and committees perform the bulk of NACUA's educational and professional service responsibilities. The Association maintains an office in Washington, D.C., headed by an Executive Director and CEO, Sheila Trice Bell. She manages the national office staff and generally insures that the educational and service priorities determined by the Board and membership are addressed in the most appropriate manner. Along with the current year's President, the Executive Director is the spokesperson for the Association. Another important facet of the Executive Director's job is enhancing relationships with the other higher education associations.[91]

The current fiscal and programmatic strength of NACUA, and its preeminence in the field of higher education law is a result, in no small measure, of the outstanding work of its recently retired former Executive Director, Phillip M. (Mike) Grier. During his eighteen-year tenure, from 1978 to 1996, he righted a listing, bankrupt organization, and with creative leadership and gentle persuasion, quietly and effectively moved the association along an ever ascending path.

Were one to review the profession of higher education law in a dozen years, what would one observe? Gradual but limited growth in the number of in-house counsel positions will have occurred. Public colleges and universities, still under budget constraints in all but the most affluent states, will expand their in-house staffs infrequently and probably only when the degree of campus anxiety concerning certain legal issues reaches a high degree of intensity. Private colleges attempting to remain "affordable" will become leaner administratively, except in their public relations and development areas. Institutional counsel will continue to act as "triage" officers, tending to the most serious and volatile issues. Litigation and litigation-related activities (e.g., labor relations, administrative hearings, ADR) will occupy more and more of the campus counsel's time. Counsel will train other administrators in the fundamentals of transactional work, shifting to them much of the basic document preparation done by counsel. Likewise, student affairs professionals will, through attending conferences and workshops, become even more adept at avoiding legal problems. Counsel's office will become even more wedded to electronic technology, with Internet access, CD-ROMs, and dedicated services largely replacing paper libraries.

The broadly defined areas of law that occupied campus counsel in the 1990s will still be major components of their work, but the specifics will differ. Although regulatory initiatives from the federal government will not have increased, audit and compliance activities will have. The passage of the balanced budget amendment in 1999, while limiting programs and new initiatives, will trigger a dramatic increase in governmental enforcement activity, including audits and compliance reviews. Substantial fines and penalties, as well as audit charges, will be levied against many institutions. Higher education will prove to be a particularly vulnerable and lucrative target. State and local taxing authorities will challenge the tax exemptions of higher education and other charities with greater frequency.[92] Of course, given the economic impact of these issues on the college or university, counsel will be very much involved.

Student affairs professionals, and their campus counsel, will continue to address several problems encountered in the 1980s through the mid-1990s. A perennial was alcohol abuse. Concurrently, drug use became increasingly rare on campus. Sexual relationships between students and student claims of hostile environment sexual harassment against faculty and other students created difficult social/legal problems. Large-scale student demonstrations returned to campus after a thirty-year absence. Now, rather than a war in Southeast Asia, the precipitating events were the insistence by many Boards of Trustees that, for economic reasons, certain academic, social and athletic programs be cut.

Restructuring will accelerate in higher education. Related program closures and faculty and staff layoffs will keep counsel fully occupied. Collective bargaining and benefits disputes will multiply as a product of restructuring. The Supreme Court's reversal of the *NLRB v. Yeshiva University*[93] decision will lead to widespread union organizing at private colleges and universities. The uncapping of the mandatory retirement age for faculty will lead many institutions to implement post-tenure review procedures, which will in turn lead to salary reductions and termination for certain senior faculty. Salary reductions and terminations will generate claims joining age discrimination with disability allegations. Particularly troublesome will be claims by faculty members asserting a need for reasonable accommodation for perceived or actual psychiatric conditions.

Health law specialists in the university legal community will be busy, too. In addition to the faculty and staff personnel issues common to all of higher education, they will continue to deal with a plethora of managed care plans and their effects. Medical centers will be caught in the middle between assertive plan patients, empowered by pro-consumer legislation, and limitations on available treatment options and reimbursement from third-party payers. Medicare and Medicaid will not operate in the current fashion. Direct reimbursement to providers will be discontinued. In their stead, new managed care entities will be created with an accompanying increase in both the complexity and paucity of reimbursement. The PATH (Physicians at Teaching Hospitals) audit program, begun in the mid-1990s,[94] will have affected all medical schools. The extent of recoupment by the government will be the subject of congressional hearings not unlike those in the early 1990s involving indirect costs. Several medical schools, no longer economically viable, will cease operations.

While, for cost reasons, more campus counsel's offices will be handling litigation, the volume of traditional litigation will decrease, mostly as a result of the widespread use of alternative dispute resolution mechanisms. Of course, counsel will be involved in shaping that process for their clients. When confronted with additional litigation that can't be staffed internally, many campus counsel, instead of using private firms, will employ on a project basis attorneys from temporary services or from the substantial pool of unemployed or under-employed attorneys created by the glut of law school graduates produced in the 1990s and 2000s.

Campus legal offices will be forced to "do more with less."[95] NACUA will play a major role in increasing the productivity of campus offices through conferences and enhanced electronic communications. Frequent teleconferences will supplement face-to-face sessions. Facilitating the exchange of information and consultation between counsel will enhance the knowledge base of higher education law practitioners. Indeed, higher education law will become, and be recognized, as more of a specialty. An effect of this will be to generally limit entry to campus jobs to beginning positions. Campus jobs will generally not be open to novice attorneys, but instead will generally be filled by lawyers with three to four years of experience, often in employment law. Senior positions, particularly that of general counsel, will almost always be filled by persons with substantial experience in higher education law. Vacancies will attract more than 100 applicants, and competition for these positions will be intense.

Like the chancellors and presidents they serve, general counsel will change positions with greater frequency than in the 1980s and 1990s. Terms of four or five years will not be uncommon. Counsel will, of necessity, participate in decisions that will prove unpopular. Their support of the incumbent chief executive, who often hired them, can jeopardize their longevity when that person departs. NACUA will attempt, through programming with the Association of Governing Boards and the American Council on Education, to make trustees and chief executives better aware of counsel's role so as to deter premature replacement of campus counsel, often by lawyers with no higher education experience.

Relationships between outside counsel and colleges and universities will change, as well. Campus counsel will select individual attorneys from a number of firms to handle particular specialized projects.[96] While hourly billing will continue as the norm for litigation, non-litigation projects will increasingly be handled on a fixed-fee basis. A handful of law firms, often employing former general counsel, will be successful in developing national practices serving higher education. The most successful will be small (fifteen to twenty) person firms, with modest rates, that can successfully address unique and complex problems confronting higher education. Legal business directed to local firms will consist primarily of litigation. Small private and public colleges will continue to utilize private practitioners as their outside "general counsel," although a growing number will employ lawyers in dual capacities, especially as counsel and development officers. Despite their lesser utilization by campus clients, private practitioners will continue their membership in NACUA in high numbers. Indeed, the specialization of the profession will make membership essential to access the Association's resources.

As before, higher education lawyers will welcome the challenges encountered by their clients. One of the primary reasons that the practice of higher education law is so rewarding is that it is interesting! The variety and complexity of problems is virtually endless, often creating a bit of frustration among counsel because time and workload demands often prevent them from giving issues all the attention they deserve. Another source of satisfaction for higher education lawyers is that the nature of the practice is collaborative rather than combative or competitive. NACUA has done much to foster a sense of community among institutional counsel and that spirit of cooperation and mutual respect imbues most campus legal offices. Given the importance of higher education to society, one can always derive satisfaction from serving the client well. There is an ultimate purpose and benefit to what higher education lawyers do. Civility still reigns on campus to a greater extent than in other arenas. Campuses are often physically attractive and, more importantly, populated by interesting, intelligent, and decent people. Argument and persuasion, tools of the lawyer's trade, often find a receptive environment on campus. Finally, the job is more fun and entertaining than almost any other legal job. Most campus counsel regard themselves fortunate to occupy this niche in the profession.

Without doubt, higher education law will continue to be a significant professional sub-specialty. The role of campus counsel will be even more significant, particularly as institutions restructure. The anticipated contributions by lawyers to the support of the essential function of higher education will be numerous and varied. Counsel to colleges and universities will continue to be a much aspired-to, and highly rewarding, pursuit.

NACUA UNIFORM SUBJECT-MATTER INDEX

Accreditation: Judicial review of accrediting decisions, due process and antitrust considerations. Information regarding institutional regulation by accrediting agencies. Department of Education involvement in post-secondary accreditation matters.

Administrators: Sample employment contracts and procedures for the selection of administrators (Presidents/Chancellors, Deans and departmental chairpersons are considered administrators for purposes of this classification). This heading includes personal liability of administrators within the scope of their employment.

Admissions: Primarily administrative matters regarding admissions, including fraud in the admissions process. Issues concerning discrimination in admissions may be found under "Discrimination."

Athletics and Sports: Issues concerning telecasting and radio broadcasting of sporting events, NCAA regulation of collegiate athletics, and other matters involving student athletes, coaches, and others affiliated with athletic programs at institutions of higher education. This category does not include issues such as those arising under Title IX, which are indexed under "Discrimination."

Attorneys: Matters concerning the role of the college and university attorney, law office management, attorney-client privilege, and relations with outside counsel.

Auxiliary Enterprises: The operation of bookstores, child care centers, food service operations, campus museums/galleries and art collections, university presses, and other organizations directly or indirectly managed by institutions and for whose actions the institution is generally liable.

Communications: Purchase and use of telecommunication systems. The category also includes issues relating to university radio stations and new technological developments. For issues pertaining to broadcasting rights of athletic events, see "Athletics & Sports."

Computers: Matters relating to the development, ownership, use and security of computer hardware and software by faculty, staff and students.

Contracts: General contract issues as they relate to institutions of higher education. This category does not contain specific contracts. Sample contracts are filed according to subject matter. For example, employment contracts may be found within the following areas: "Administrators," "Athletics & Sports," and "Faculty." Leases and facility use agreements may be found under "Governance."

Debt Collection: Collection of financial obligations owed by students and faculty and withholding transcripts of students involved in bankruptcy proceedings. For bankruptcy of institutions, see "Financial Aspects of Institutional Management."

Discrimination: Matters of discrimination on the basis of age, race, color, religion, sex, sexual orientation, national origin, handicap, or other reason; in student relations, employment (except faculty terminations, which are discussed under "Faculty"), availability of educational opportunity/operation of state systems of higher education and in athletic programs. This category also includes information pertaining to affirmative action, sexual harassment, equal pay and comparable worth. For Race-based scholarships, see Financial Aid to Students.

Faculty: Academic freedom and First Amendment issues, sample employment contracts and appointment letters, information regarding employment benefits, sample faculty handbooks and manuals, financial exigency and retrenchment, conflict of interest and outside activities, appointment, (non)renewal, and tenure issues, and personal liability and indemnification.

Financial Aid to Students: Award criteria and federal recordkeeping requirements. Also includes Race-based scholarships. Information regarding the various sources of student financial assistance, including Title IV and scholarship sources. For matters regarding debt collections, see that topic; for athletic scholarship issues, see "Athletics & Sports."

Financial Aspects of Institutional Management: Financial obligations of institutions, charitable solicitation by institutions, fund raising, investments, and bond issues. This heading includes information on institutional bankruptcy, deferred giving, restrictive gifts involving arguably unlawful classifications, general matters of trust administration and philanthropy for the benefit of the institution, Title III funding—strengthening institutions through financial aid. The heading does not include information regarding research grant funding (see "Research") or aid to students (see "Financial Aid to Students").

Foundations: Issues regarding college-/university-related entities concerned with charitable gifts, research and alumni functions. Information regarding organizations characterized by apparent autonomy from the institution and for whose actions the institution is ostensibly not liable, including sample articles of incorporation and bylaws.

Governance: Institutional autonomy, leases, information about state action and constitutional mandates, and rules relating to regulation of public access to campus facilities. Includes issues related to campus security. Information regarding governing boards of public and private institutions. For Insurance issues, see that heading.

Health Sciences: Legal matters relating to the operation of health science programs and health service delivery programs, governance of academic health centers, relationships of health science schools to parent universities, affiliated hospitals and other institutions, methods of staff cooperation, faculty practice plans, shared resource and facility plans, governmental regulations, issues of special interest to veterinary schools, and confidentiality of medical records.

Insurance: All types of insurance and indemnification issues including sample policies.

Intellectual Property: Issues and sample policies relating to copyrights, ownership of work by the institutions, faculty, students, or other insiders; information regarding the ownership rights of research property and scientific data; information regarding ownership rights of institutions to publications and inventions created by outsiders with the assistance of institutional facilities and/or resources; issues relating to fair use and photocopying; sample institutional patent policies including royalty distribution procedures, information on disputed ownership of inventions; issues related to trademark protection for university insignia and proprietary interests therein; and other developments in intellectual property. Computer software ownership and protection issues may be found under the "Computer" heading.

Labor Law: Academic collective bargaining and all matters arising under the National Labor Relations Act and related federal labor statutes. Also includes matters relating to the employment of students.

Legislation: Primarily a referral category, for copies of pending and enacted state and federal legislation that affects the interests of institutions of higher education.

Liability: Of Institutions: agency questions, releases, and immunities. For individual liability issues, see: "Administrators," "Faculty," and "Governance." With regard to matters of insurance and indemnification, see "Insurance."

Personnel: Issues pertaining to personnel other than faculty and administrators. Includes all college and university employees other than faculty and management-level staff. For employment discrimination issues, see "Discrimination."

Real Property: Acquisition, zoning, and divestiture of realty.

Regulatory Measures: Issues of government regulation as well as aspects of particular regulatory scheme, including information relating to Open Meetings laws and requests under the Freedom of Information Act. Most regulatory issues are discussed under separate category headings. For example, matters relating to the ADA, the Rehabilitation Act, the Equal Pay Act, the ADEA, Title VII and Title IX may be found under "Discrimination."

Research: Research assistant agreements with outside entities, and government research contracts and grants. This category also includes other research-related issues such as ethics and scientific misconduct. See "Foundations" for issues regarding quasi-independent and independent research corporations set up by institutions.

Students: Matters relating to students and the student-institution relationship, including academic standards, academic and disciplinary procedures and due process, institutional regulations, issues concerning enrollment contracts, foreign students, student organizations and activities, student participation in institutional governance, criminal conduct, student publications, and student records.

Taxation: Issues such as tax-sheltered annuity programs, institutional unrelated business income, tuition remission arrangements, taxability of stipends, and issues pertaining to student income.

Tuitions and Fees: The scope of authority of governing boards to impose and expend tuition and fees, issues regarding the determination of in-state tuition status, and alternative tuition payment plans (e.g. prepaid tuition schemes).

Source: NACUA, 1996–97 Directory Of Membership Services

Footnotes

*   Peter H. Ruger is General Counsel for Southern Illinois University. From 1974 through 1992, he was General Counsel for Washington University. From 1992 through 1996, he was a partner in the Peper, Martin, Jensen, Maichel & Hetlage firm, concentrating on education and health law issues. He is an Adjunct Professor at the University of Missouri-St. Louis, and previously held similar appointments at St. Louis University School of Law and the Washington University School of Law. Mr. Ruger received his B.A. from Denison University in 1963, his graduate degree in history from Washington University in 1966, and his J.D. from Washington University School of Law in 1969. Honors include Phi Beta Kappa; Board of Editors, *Washington University Law Quarterly*; and Omicron Delta Kappa. Mr. Ruger served as the President of the National Association of College and University Attorneys in 1989–90. He was the first recipient of the Thomas Biggs Award from the Stetson University College of Law, which award recognizes contributions to the higher education legal community. He also is a member of the following professional organizations: National Health Lawyers Association; The Missouri Bar; Bar Association of Metropolitan St. Louis; and the American Bar Association. Mr. Ruger has spoken to numerous higher education and nonprofit groups and has been extensively involved in community activities in St. Louis.

1. William A. Kaplin, *Law on the Campus, 1960–1985: Years of Growth and Challenge*, 12 J.C. & U.L. 269, 269 (1985).

2. A more complete description of NACUA and its activities follows at *infra* notes 69–91 and accompanying text.

3. *See* Thomas H. Wright, Jr., *The Faculty and the Law Explosion: Assessing the Impact—A Twenty-Five-Year Perspective (1960–85) for College and University Lawyers*, 12 J.C. & U.L. 363, 365 (1985).

4. Telephone Interview with Sheila Trice Bell, Executive Director and CEO, NACUA (May 14, 1997).

5. These observations are derived from the Author's recent private practice experience, in which he represented pre-school, K-12, and higher education institutions. In addition, his observations here and elsewhere in this Article are derived from his more than 23 years as a higher education lawyer.

6. *See infra* app. A.

7. *See* Roderick K. Daane, *The Role of University Counsel*, 12 J.C. & U.L. 399, 399 (1985). The Daane article, describing the role of the higher education lawyer, with particular emphasis on the responsibilities of in-house counsel, has survived the test of time and should be read by anyone seeking appointment as a campus counsel.

8. E. Wilson Lyon, *The History of Pomona College 1887–1969*, at 8 (1977).

9. Paul K. Conkin, *Gone with ihe Ivy: A Biography of Vanderbilt University* 10 (1985).

10. *See, e.g.,* Lee J. Bennish, *Continuity and Change: Xavier University 1831–1981 (1981)*; James C. Carey, Kansas State University: *The Quest for Identity* (1977); G. Wallace Chessman, Denison: *The Story of an Ohio College* (1957); Lowell H. Harrison, Western Kentucky University (1987); Charlie Brown Hershey, Colorado College 1874–1949 (1952); Richard Kern, Findlay College: The First Hundred Years (1984).

11. *See* 6 Fourth Decennial Digest, 1926–1936 *Colleges and Universities*, at 426–37 (1937); 5 Third Decennial Edition of the American Digest, 1916–1926 *Colleges and Universities*, at 1541–51 (1928); 5 Second Decennial Edition of the American Digest, 1906–1916 *Colleges and Universities*, at 217–28 (1919); 4 Decennial Edition of the American Digest, 1897–1906 *Colleges and Universities*, at 1248–62 (1908); 10 Century Edition of the American Digest *Colleges and Universities*, at 215–50 (1899).

12. *See* 6 Eighth Decennial Digest, 1966–1976 *Colleges and Universities*, at 1056–1151 (1977).

13. *See* 7 Ninth Decennial Digest, 1981–1986 (Pt. 2) *Colleges and Universities* at 230–94 (1988); 5 Ninth Decennial Digest, 1976–1981 (Pt. 1) *Colleges and Universities*, at 1067–1127 (1982).

14. *See* Trustees of Dartmouth College v. Woodward, 17 U.S. (4 Wheat.) 518, 551–600 (1819). Chief Justice Marshall ruled that the charter of Dartmouth College, as a contract, could not be impaired without judicial proceedings. *See id.* at 650.

15. Jacob Herbst, *From Crisis to Crisis: American College Government* 1636–1819, at 26 (1982). Herbst's account contains no mention of the counsel for the college, although at a meeting with the colony's governor, President Leverett personally defended the Harvard tutor involved in the matter while the colony's Attorney General spoke on behalf of Pierpoint. The case involved political issues more important than the award of the degree. *See id.* at 27.

16. *See id.* at 26–27.

17. *See* Symposium, *Celebrating Twenty-Five Years of Law and Higher Education*, 12 J.C. & U.L. 261 (1985).

18. *See* Harrison, *supra* note 10, at 234–35.

19. 294 F.2d 150 (5th Cir. 1960).

20. *See id.* at 158.

21. *See, e.g.,* Radosevic v. Virginia Intermont College, 633 F. Supp. 1084 (W.D. Va. 1986).

22. For example, Edward "Tad" Foote became general counsel of Washington University in the early 1970s after handling several student discipline cases. Foote is now President of the University of Miami.

23. Title VII of the Civil Rights Act of 1964, 42 U.S.C. § 2000e (1994), which prohibits discrimination in employment on the basis of race, color, religion, sex or national origin, became fully applicable to higher education in 1972, *See* 42 U.S.C. § 2000e-1 note (1994). The Age Discrimination in Employment Act, 29 U.S.C. §§ 621–634, while enacted in 1967, was given effect by numerous interpretive decisions in the 1970s. The Rehabilitation Act of 1973, the precursor of the ADA, prohibited discrimination in federally funded programs against persons with handicaps. *See* 29 U.S.C. § 794 (1994).

24. *See* 20 U.S.C. § 1232g (1994) (enacted in 1974).

25. *See* Tax Reform Act of 1969, 26 U.S.C. §§ 1–7701 (1994).

26. *See* 29 U.S.C. §§ 1001–1461 (1994).

27. Title IX of the Education Amendments of 1972, 20 U.S.C. § 1681 (1994).

28. *See, e.g.,* 42 U.S.C. § 2541 (1994).

29. 408 U.S. 564 (1972).

30. 408 U.S. 593 (1972).

31. At private institutions, faculty rights are contractual and are usually expressed in a faculty handbook. To the extent that the institution follows procedures suggested by the American Association of University Professors (AAUP), private institutions provide ample "due process." The current AAUP procedures are found in its *AAUP Policy Documents and Reports* (1995) (the Redbook).

32. *See* Conkin, *supra* note 9, at 724–33.

33. *See id.* at 643.

34. *See id.* at 634–35.

35. *See id.* at 631–34.

36. *See id.* at 626–29.

37. *See id.* at 619–21.

38. *See* Conkin, *supra* note 9, at 631–32.

39. *See id.* at 638.

40. *See id.* at 641–43.

41. *See id.* at 717.

42. Stow Persons, *The University of Iowa in the Twentieth Century: An Institutional History* 208 (1990).

43. *See* NACUA, *Delivery of Legal Services to Higher Education Institutions* 5 n.1 (1984).

44. *See id.* at 5 fig. 2.

45. *See id.*

46. *See id.*

47. *See* NACUA, *Provision of Legal Services* 2 (1992).

48. *See* NACUA, Compensation and Benefits Survey Report 2 (1995) [hereinafter Compensation and Benefits]. No significant event affecting the college and university community could account for this dramatic increase. Assuming the 1994 figures are accurate, one can only assume under-reporting occurred in 1992.

49. *See id.* at 11.

50. *See* Provision of Legal Services, *supra* note 47, at 3. Administrators often assume that hiring in-house counsel will result in a dramatic reduction in outside legal fees. This is not always a correct assumption. Counsel may discover unmet needs or unresolved issues that require the attention of outside counsel. But over time, legal costs should be reduced. More transactions and advice will be handled inside. More significantly, as campus counsel fulfills preventative responsibilities, more favorable (or at least less negative) outcomes will occur.

51. *See* Compensation and Benefits, *supra* note 48, at 12.

52. *See* Provision of Legal Services, *supra* note 47, at 9.

53. *See id.* at 15.

54. *See id.* at 16.

55. *See id.* at 10.

56. *See id.* at 10; Compensation and Benefits, *supra* note 48, at 17.

57. *See* Compensation and Benefits, *supra* note 48, at 17.

58. *See id.*

59. *See* Provision of Legal Services, *supra* note 47, at 7.

60. *See id.*

61. *See id.* As a comparison, male ABA members outnumber women three-to-one. *See id.*

62. References to "early" articles can be found in footnotes 2–18 of the Daane article, *supra* note 7.

63. Daane, *supra* note 7, at 402 (quoting Norman Epstein, *The Use and Misuse of College and University Counsel*, 45 J. Higher Educ. 635, 636 (1974)).

64. Robert D. Bickel, *The Role of College or University Legal Counsel*, 3 J.L. & Educ. 73, 77 (1974) (emphasis added).

65. An example of this activity is the review by many colleges and universities of their admissions and financial aid policies for minorities in the wake of the *Hopwood v. Texas*, 78 F.3d 932 (5th Cir.), *cert. denied*, 116 S. Ct. 2581 (1996), and *Podberesky v. Kirwan*, 38 F.3d 147 (4th Cir. 1994).

66. *See* Daane, *supra* note 7, at 404–07.

67. *See* Model Code of Professional Responsibility EC 5–1 (1980).

68. "The first thing we do, let's kill all the lawyers." William Shakespeare, The Second Part of King Henry the Sixth act 4, sc. 2.

69. *See* NACUA, 1996–97 Directory Of Membership and Services 5 [hereinafter Directory].

70. *See id.* at 11. Perhaps the most unique Past President was Edmund McIlhenny of Tulane

University, the scion of the Tabasco sauce empire.

71. An associate membership category exists for individuals not eligible for full institutional membership who have professional interests common to those of NACUA's membership. Persons in this category often represent state departments of education or higher education, education associations, and enterprises principally serving higher education, such as TIAA/CREF and United Educators Insurance Risk Retention Group, Inc.

72. *See* Directory, *supra* note 69, at 5.

73. *See id.*

74. *See id.* at 61–66.

75. *See id.* at 61–66, 68–70.

76. *See id.* at 67.

77. *See id.* at 67. Australia: University of Queensland; University of Western Australia. Israel: Hebrew University of Jerusalem. Lebanon: American University of Beirut. *See id.*

78. *See* Directory, *supra* note 69, at 5.

79. *See* 1997 NACUA Annual Conference Program (copy on file with Author).

80. During the 1970s, usually one workshop per year was scheduled. This activity increased during the 1980s, with three workshops becoming the norm. During the 1990s, at least three other CLE's have been the norm. Also, other higher education associations frequently contact NACUA for the names of people to address legal topics.

81. *See* Directory, *supra* note 69, at 55.

82. *See* Diane L. McDaniel & Paul Tanaka, *The Permissibility of Withholding Transcripts Under Bankruptcy Law* (1995).

83. *Legal Deskbook for Administrators of Independent Colleges and Universities* (Kent M. Weeks & Dereck H. Davis eds., 2d ed. 1993).

84. *See* Directory, *supra* note 69, at 54–55.

85. The home page is located at <http://www.nacua.org>.

86. Some of the site's features include: on-line legal documents, cases, and sample policies for use by the Board, Committees and specialty sections, and on-line ordering and registration for NACUA publications and meetings. The site contains useful references to other legal resources on the Internet. *See id.*

87. *See id.*

88. A "ladder" system is used by the volunteer leadership of NACUA. The first rung is reached by election to the post of Second Vice-President. Other elected officers (in addition to the President and Second Vice-President) on the "ladder" are, in ascending order, First Vice-President and President-Elect. Other elected officers are the Secretary and Treasurer.

89. *See* Directory, *supra* note 69, at 41.

90. Some individuals try to campaign from time to time. They have been uniformly unsuccessful. A Nominating Committee, comprised of a cross-section of NACUA's membership, invites nominations from the entire membership for the elected posts and, after lengthy and thorough discussion, produces a slate of nominees for consideration by those attending the annual meeting. Nominations from the attendees can occur and provision exists for contested elections. A contested election occurred in the early 1980s; the challenger lost.

91. While NACUA is the principal national group serving higher education attorneys, higher education law practitioners often belong to other groups as well. Of course, many members also belong to the American Bar Association and find particular value in section activity. University health law practitioners find meetings and publications of the American Academy of Healthcare Attorneys (AAHA) and the National Health Lawyers Association (NHLA) to be rewarding. These organizations merged on July 1, 1997. The National Organization on Legal Problems of Education (NOLPE) counts among its members a number of practitioners and academicians.

92. Recent decisions rebuffing attempts by tax collectors to levy upon institutions of higher education include: *Illini Media Co. v. Illinois Department of Revenue*, 664 N.E.2d 706 (Ill. App. Ct. 1996); *University of Michigan Board of Regents v. Department of Treasury*, 553 N.W.2d 349 (Mich. Ct. App. 1996); *City of Washington v. Board of Assessment Appeals*, 666 A.2d 352 (Pa. Commw. St. 1995), *appeal granted*, 681 A.2d 1344 (Pa. 1996).

93. 444 U.S. 672 (1980). The Supreme Court held that the Yeshiva faculty were managerial employees. *See id.* at 682. The Court's definition of "managerial" is expressed at 444 U.S. 682–83. My prediction is based on the discongruity between the Supreme Court's definition and governance patterns extent on many campuses today.

94. Under the terms of the PATH program, "academic medical centers with clinic practices are permitted to self audit in lieu of a government audit." William S. Painter, *Recent Legislation, Cases and Other Developments Affecting Healthcare Providers and Integrated Delivery Systems*, SB51 ALI-ABA 114 (1997).

95. Interview with Sheila Trice Bell, *supra* note 4.

96. Private colleges and universities appeared to lag behind their public counterparts in the 1980s and 1990s in varying their choice of counsel. Frequently, one firm, often with a member on the institutions governing board, received the bulk of the legal work from the institution. A heightened sense of public accountability, and admonitions to avoid the appearance of conflict of interest, led private colleges and universities to select counsel best able to assist the institution with specific matters.

Fiscal Fitness? The Peculiar Economics of Intercollegiate Athletics

JOHN R. THELIN AND LAWRENCE L. WISEMAN

John R. Thelin is Chancellor Professor and director of the Higher Education Doctoral Program at the College of William and Mary. He is vice president and president-elect of the Faculty Assembly and a member of the Athletic Policy Advisory Committee.

Lawrence L. Wiseman is professor and chair of the Biology Department at the College of William and Mary. He served as chair of the Athletic Policy Advisory Committee and as faculty representative to the National Collegiate Athletic Association. In 1987–88 he was an American Council on Education fellow and special assistant to the president at the University of Colorado.

Scandal and shame are themes that have dominated popular press coverage of intercollegiate athletics in recent years, with exposés of altered transcripts, slush funds, and recruiting abuses. This sensationalism leads one to assume that these episodes are exceptions in an essentially healthy system; i.e., that a university can "solve" its athletic problems and restore proper balance by firing an errant coach or by expelling student-athletes who violate rules. One unintended consequence of dramatic media coverage is that it masks attention to a less-spectacular yet a more fundamental problem: intercollegiate athletic programs, especially at the Division I level of the National Collegiate Athletic Association (NCAA), show signs of precarious fiscal fitness.

Most troubling is that this eroding financial health has not been a result of "illegal" behavior, but is a product of standard practices and policies. The peculiar economics of intercollegiate athletic programs are symptomatic of weak financial controls that have only marginal connection with academic accountability and sound educational policy.

What has caused this situation? One predictable answer is the complaint that college sports have become a "business," characterized by "commercialism" and "professionalism" and indelibly linked to scandals and excesses. Our approach is different. We start with a more straightforward, less normative question: If university presidents and trustees accept that Division I college sports programs are a big business, what is the condition of these programs as measured by standards of business practice?

We rejected moral outrage as a starting point for critical analysis of the economics and finances of college sports mainly because no one denies that Division I college sports have become a large commercial enterprise. For example, in 1986 the athletic director at Florida State University commented, "I'm not afraid to say it: It's a business." During a 1975 congressional hearing the athletic director at the University of Maryland told a subcommittee that his department opposed giving equal opportunity to women's varsity sports because doing so would be "poor business and poor management." He also said the university was "in competition with professional sports and other entertainment for the consumer's money" and "did not want a lesser product to market." Similarly, a football coach at another large state university explained to reporters

"Fiscal Fitness? The Peculiar Economics of Intercollegiate Athletics," by John R. Thelin and Lawrence L. Wiseman, reprinted from *Capital Ideas: A Publication of the Forum for College Financing*, Vol. 4, No. 4, February 1990.

that a losing season and bad publicity hurt his program because, "We're in the entertainment business and are susceptible to the whims of fans who may get upset with our performance."

The Business of University Athletics:

National Survey Data

Our first concern about the business practices of major college sports programs is that they are becoming a world turned upside down. Varsity programs that are supposed to be net *revenue producers are often net revenue consumers*. A storm warning about intercollegiate athletic finances comes from a number of nationwide institutional surveys, including 1) the periodic reports Mitchell Raiborn has prepared for the NCAA since 1974, 2) a 1988 survey of intercollegiate athletic funding conducted by the State Higher Education Executive Officers, and 3) a 1986 survey by the American Association of State Colleges and Universities (AASCU) on the revenues and expenses of athletic programs. The various studies agree on one trend: as a whole and within program categories, intercollegiate athletic programs are unable to support themselves; most run deficits. To illustrate the financial condition of intercollegiate athletics, we have included two representative annual budgets: The first summarizes the $15 million budget of a typical Division 1-A. (See box on following page.) The second represents the $5 million budget of a representative Division I-AA program. (See box on the following page.)

Certainly the finding that athletic programs are usually not self-supporting is not surprising at colleges that designate their activities as a part of the educational program and make no claim that varsity sports should be self-supporting via gate receipts, or broadcast revenues. It does warrant concern for NCAA Division I institutions, at which, by NCAA definition, an "athletics program strives for regional and national excellence and prominence" and the "program serves both [the] college community and [the] general public." A university that opts for Division I standing "may award financial aid based on [a student's] athletic ability." irrespective of financial

need. Above all, the Division I institution tries "to finance its athletic programs with revenues of the program itself." Within this group of schools there are signs of severe financial strain, not to mention outright failure. For example, in 1986 the AASCU survey indicated that among 67 Division I institutions, only nine generated surplus revenue; 31 programs ran a deficit and 25 were "self-supporting" (but, as we shall discuss later, in many cases this was dependent on moneys from mandatory student fees).

One fascinating, unexpected finding from the AASCU report is that despite the Division I institutions' self-imposed emphasis on generating revenues via ticket sales, television, and donations, these sources are chronically inadequate. Ticket sales accounted for 16 percent of all program revenues; television and radio, 1 percent; and alumni and other contributions, 13 percent.

Deficit-ridden college athletic programs clash with the popular image of lucrative television contracts and sellout crowds at large stadiums. In November 1989, for example, the NCAA and CBS announced a $1 billion contract for exclusive broadcast rights to seven years of NCAA basketball games. How does one reconcile such affluence with so many institutional program deficits? On closer inspection one finds within Division I ranks a clear imbalance between big winners and big losers in what an American Council on Education report called "The Money Game." To understand the paradoxical coexistence of college sports affluence with program deficits, one needs to disaggregate nationwide survey data. An important, partial answer is the distinction between Division I-A and I-AA institutions among the allegedly self-supporting and revenue-producing intercollegiate athletics programs.

Within Division I, the NCAA distinguishes two categories of institutional programs. Division I-A represents "Mount Olympus"— such conferences as the Big Ten, the Big Eight, the Southeastern, the Pacific Ten, the Southwestern, and the Atlantic Coast, plus such prominent independent institutions as Notre Dame, Penn State, Syracuse, and Miami. Furthermore, these conferences overwhelmingly dominate the national television network broadcasts. Often overlooked is that Division I

Sample Budget for Division I-A Intercollegiate Athletics

This 1988 and 89 operating budget of $15 million is for a large flagship state university that fields national-caliber teams in football, basketball, and 16 other sports for men and women.

	Income	
Football		
Ticket sales	$5,200,000	
Season ticket surcharge	300,000	
TV bowl game rebates	800,000	
Local Broadcast Rights	310,000	
Other sources	390,000	
Total Football		**$7,000,000**
Basketball		
Ticket sales	$2,100,000	
Tournaments and preseason games	400,000	
Local broadcast rights	950,000	
Conference	250,000	
Other sources	300,000	
Total Basketball		**$4,000,000**
Other sports		110,000
Sports camps		525,000
Interest income		225,000
Gifts and grants		1,200,000
Other income		150,000
Prior year balance		1,340,000
Student activity fees		450,000
TOTAL INCOME		**$15,000,000**

	Expenses	
Football		
Grants-in-aid	$950,000	
Salaries other	4,350,000	
Total Football		**$5,300,000**
Basketball		
Grants-in-aid	150,000	
Salaries other	2,050,000	
Total Basketball		**$2,200,000**
Other sports		
Grants-in-aid	900,000	
Salaries other	1,850,000	
Total Other Sports		**$2,750,000**
Capital improvements equipment		$1,300,000
Academic program support		$1,500,000
Administrative general expenses		$1,950,000
TOTAL EXPENSES		**$15,000,000**

Sample Budget for Division I-AA Intercollegiate Athletics

This 1988 and 89 operating budget of $5 million is for a medium-size university (enrollment about 10,000) that is Division I-AA in football and I-A in basketball, and fields teams in an additional 20 sports for men and women.

	Income	
Football		**$600,000**
Basketball		200,000
Gifts and grants		850,000
TV and broadcasts		60,000
Program sales advertisements		120,000
Other sources		170,000
Student activity fees		3,000,000
TOTAL INCOME		**$5,000,000**

	Expenses	
Football		
Grants-in-aid	$600,000	
Salaries	340,000	
Other	610,000	
Total Football		**$1,550,000**
Basketball		
Grants-in-aid	$150,000	
Salaries	140,000	
Other	210,000	
Total Basketball		**$500,000**
Other sports		
Grants-in-aid	$450,000	
Salaries	380,000	
Other	420,000	
Total Other Sports		**$1,250,000**
Administrative and general expenses		**$1,700,000**
TOTAL EXPENSES		**$5,000,000**

also includes a large number of I-AA programs which subscribe to the revenue-producing ethos and are allowed to provide athletic grants-in-aid, yet do not have football stadiums with 30,000 seats or average home football attendance of 17,000.

Division I-AA Programs: Life Without Television

A closer look at Division I-AA is important for understanding the increasing strains and dilemmas for colleges and universities that wish to offer highly competitive varsity sports. The Yankee Conference provides good examples of Division I-AA teams: most are flagship state universities (e.g., the Universities of Massachusetts, Connecticut, Delaware, Main, New Hampshire, Vermont, and Rhode Island) along with two private universities (Richmond and Villanova). A good football game attendance is between 10,000 and 15,000 but attendance sometimes goes as high as 25,000.

Without television broadcast revenues and with such relatively modest crowds (compared with those attending Division I-A games), the Division I-AA teams face an increasingly difficult, almost impossible, task in trying to be self-supporting. For example, in one survey 15 prominent Division I-AA football programs reported substantial deficits in 1987 (a 16th institution did not respond to the survey). Among Virginia's state institutions, the Division I-AA football programs at James Madison University, William and Mary, and Virginia Military Institute displayed similar patterns over the 1985–87 football seasons: each program showed an annual deficit of about $700,000 and a three-year deficit of about $2 million. Such data offer two particular causes for alarm: first, since these three programs are considered quite successful and have relatively high football game attendance for Division I-AA, it is reasonable to project greater deficits for many other Division I-AA programs. Second, the deficits are for these institutions' *football programs only*, not for the so-called minor or nonrevenue varsity sports. Division I-AA football programs are hard-pressed to reduce expenses because they are committed to athletic grants-in-aid and must continually spend on marketing and publicity to promote ticket sales. At the same time, they cannot tap into the bonanza of 1980s college sports revenues because seldom, if ever, will they command broadcast television coverage by a major network or appearance in a major bowl game. To use the argot of bookmakers and loan sharks, Division I-AA programs have and will continue to have a "case of the shorts."

Trouble in Paradise: Financial Strains in Division I-A

All this might be acceptable if deficits (whether for football or for a total varsity sports program) were confined to the Division I-AA teams. Unfortunately, the same problems can be found percolating upward; i.e., within each major conference of Division I-A, one can identify "poor cousins" whose big-time varsity programs are losing money. For example, in November 1989 within the Big Ten Conference, the University of Wisconsin reported a substantial deficit ($1.9 million, according to one press report) for its intercollegiate athletic program. The anatomy of athletics budgets from selected major universities suggests how such problems evolve and persist.

Financial problems are neither new nor unexpected. Data from a decade ago for the University of Missouri at Columbia illustrate characteristic strains. Missouri's 1979–80 intercollegiate athletic budget was relatively large ($6.9 million). Although not as successful in winning or in gate receipts as, for example, the University of Oklahoma or the University of Southern California, "Mizzou" is significant because it is admittedly "big time," it belongs to the formidable Big Eight Conference, it often is among the top 10 nationally in terms of football game attendance, it has an increasingly successful basketball program, and it has the

marketing leverage of being the only Division I football team in its state. The university expected football to fund about 80 percent of the entire varsity sports program—a premise that led it to expand the stadium's seating capacity from 55,000 to 65,000. A decade ago the Missouri football program brought in $5.7 million; but operating the program cost 3.2 million, leaving a net revenue of $2.5 million. In subsequent years that surplus has dwindled because of rising costs. A cause for concern is that Missouri represents a *successful* program in terms of attendance and gate receipts; i.e., it is operating at about optimal level. Its athletic officials believe they ought not raise ticket prices much beyond annual inflation. If home football games were not selling out, the athletic department could at least plan on more aggressive marketing to increase ticket sales. The university does gain some athletic income via Big Eight Conference revenue sharing; however, since the football team usually finishes in the bottom half of the conference, it has few opportunities to be on national television or in national bowl games. The best option for raising additional income is through booster clubs and alumni donations.

How do seemingly strong athletic programs go from being merely financially stretched to being overextended? The example of the University of Maryland illustrates this problem. Since 1985 Maryland's athletic department has been struggling to maintain national-caliber play for its nonrevenue varsity men's sports along with its primary commitment to football and to men's and women's basketball. Reduction in resources and in grants-in-aid are cited as reasons for declining won-lost records in track, lacrosse, wrestling, baseball, and swimming. The most interesting data, however, are those showing that the sports which are expected to produce revenues have a long record of falling short. From 1978 to 1981 football *lost* $300,00–$400,000 each year. By 1987 the athletic department had a deficit of over $1 million; that shortfall eventually led the athletic director to fire 17 employees in the ticket office, marketing, public relations, training, and maintenance.

Why did Maryland's athletic department fail to balance its 1988 budget of $8.3 million? First, football gate receipts fell $600,000 below projections. Second, football lost an anticipated

$350,000 when the Cherry Bowl could not pay its "guaranteed" money after Maryland appeared in that 1985 postseason game. Third, men's varsity basketball showed a deficit of $150,000. Finally, the athletic department had to honor substantial salary obligations to staff who resigned or who were reassigned. An athletic director who resigned was paid $77,000 for one year as a special consultant. One former basketball coach was guaranteed $136,000 per year when he was reassigned to be assistant athletic director. Department expenses increased once again by summer 1989, when Maryland carried yet another former men's basketball coach on its payroll (at an estimated $80,000 annual salary) along with the base annual salary of $100,000 for the newly hired basketball coach. By 1989 the University of Maryland's athletic director projected an annual deficit of about $200,000 and was proposing to ask the state legislature to consider a direct subsidy to the school's intercollegiate athletics program.

The cases of the universities of Missouri and Maryland are disconcerting because both represent large public flagship universities with teams that enjoy strong support from administration and alumni, and that have the blessings of good location, affiliation with prestigious conferences, and excellent media coverage. For all these advantages, they illustrate how the alleged *revenue-producing* sports can become *revenue-consuming*. Among the 64 members of the high-powered College Football Association, one estimate is that about 40% have varsity sports programs that run a deficit.

Perhaps the most surprising news about the finances of intercollegiate athletics came in September 1988 when the University of Michigan announced projected budget deficits increasing from $2.5 million for the 1989 fiscal year to $5.2 million by 1993. Ironically, Michigan usually is cited as a model of a large, well-run program. The projections appear to be close to the mark. A summary published in the January 8, 1990, issue of *U.S. News and World Report* shows an annual budget of $21.1 million in expenses and $18.5 million in revenues. The athletic department has teams in 21 sports, a staff of 130 full-time employees (including a travel agent, mechanics, carpenters, and engineers), and several hundred part-time employees who work at sporting events. In 1987 its

facilities—12 buildings, including a stadium that seats over 100,000 spectators—were valued at over $200 million. The University of Michigan fills its stadium at home football games. In addition, Michigan appears on national television two or three times each football season, regularly goes to a major football bowl, sells out its basketball games, and enjoys substantial revenues from its NCAA championship men's basketball team. If this established program projects a deficit, the financial outlook for intercollegiate athletic programs at other universities is bleak.

Why Are College Sports Expenses So High?

In projecting a departmental deficit, the assistant athletic director at the University of Michigan noted that expenses are "likely to increase by almost 25%, while revenues are expected to increase by only 15% over the next five years." This is due partly to unavoidable increases in the costs of liability insurance, administrative compliance, data reporting, and other operating matters. Another partial explanation is that athletic departments indulge in expensive customs. Conspicuous consumption for student-athletes often is standard practice as suggested by the construction of special dormitories for them. Some precedent for current spending comes from the University of Pittsburgh, whose alumni donated over $181,000 in 1974 for refurbishing football locker rooms. The head coach commented, "Carpeting floors doesn't win ball games for you, but it sure makes things more comfortable." A younger generation of coaches has heeded his message: in November 1989 the new basketball coach at the University of Kentucky directed an intense fund-raising campaign that provided $1 million for new lockers and furnishings in the *practice* facility.

College coaches are not especially precise in their ability to select talented student-athletes. Division I-A football squads are allowed to have 95 athletes on full grant-in-aid sufficient to subsidize more than four players at each of the 22 positions in a complete starting lineup (professional teams in the National Football League, by comparison, limit squad size to 48). Reliance on a high number of scholarship players often represents a coach's hedge against several problems: high attrition due to scholastic ineligibility, failure of athletes to play to their predicted potential, and "stockpiling" athletes as a strategy to prevent opposing teams from having access to player talent. These practices are both expensive and wasteful.

Attempts at frugality are uneven. Athletic directors and football coaches have been reluctant to endorse compacts that would promote savings in athletic grants-in-aid, leading to what Chancellor Ira Heyman of the University of California, Berkeley, has called the "athletics arms race." Proposals to reduce the number of permissible grants-in-aid have been defeated at recent NCAA annual meetings. And, of course, expenses are kept high because athletic grants-in-aid are not based on a student-athlete's financial need.

Another expensive practice is that of paying high salaries for selected coaches. At several major universities the head football or basketball coaches make over $100,000 in annual base salary, sometimes more than the university president earns. (Contracts for these highly successful coaches also often include substantial income from perks, such as local television shows, that can boost total annual remuneration to the $200,000 to $700,000 range.) And, as already shown in discussing the University of Maryland budget, big-time athletic departments follow the custom of "buying up" multi-year contracts of a fired coach. The University of North Carolina at Chapel Hill, to cite another example, which is regarded as having a well-run, clean sports program, reportedly "bought up" a fired football coach's contract for over $800,000.

How Do College Sports Programs Reduce Expenses?

During a period of rising costs and inflation, athletic directors for Division I intercollegiate programs tend to favor strategies to increase revenues rather than to reduce expenses. When cost cutting does take place, it usually hits least and last in the most expensive sports, football and basketball. The reduction approach has been either to eliminate nonrevenue (minor) varsity sports or to adopt a policy of "tiering." According to the latter policy, the department targets selected sports for reduced funding, limited facilities, fewer athletic scholarships, and

local schedules. As one would expect, the usual choices for elimination or drastic reduction are fencing, riflery, and lacrosse. What has been more curious (and underreported) in the past decade is the disappearance from many major universities of traditionally established sports e.g., baseball, track, wrestling, swimming, and tennis. About a decade ago the University of Colorado eliminated varsity wrestling, baseball, and swimming. The University of Washington eliminated its nationally ranked teams in wrestling and gymnastics. Although varsity wrestling gained national stature at several institutions in the Southeastern Conference in the 1970s, the sport has been dropped. Indeed, a 1982 study indicated that the athletic directors of most Southeastern Conference institutions favored abolishing scholarships in nonrevenue sports and diverting more funds and efforts to football and basketball.

This strategy strikes us as foul play, because it tends to violate an explicit justification of big-time sports; i.e., a university endorses big-time football and, perhaps, basketball because these sports generate revenues to subsidize the minor sports. Now, even when alleged revenue-producing sports fail to provide this expected surplus (or run a deficit), the penalty of resource reduction falls on the victim (minor sports), not the offender. An additional irony is that eliminating minor sports does relatively little to reduce deficits, because nonrevenue sports often already are lean, relying on part-time coaches, local travel schedules, minuscule recruiting expenses, and few grants-in-aid.

Increasing Revenues: Philanthropy and Boosterism

The most popular solution for closing the gap between flat or saturated revenues from ticket sales and rising expenses is to increase donor solicitation. Even within many major conferences, private contributions still surpass television revenues as the pillar of athletic resources. The usual mechanism for fund-raising is through booster clubs ("athletic-educational foundations"), which are part of a semiautonomous intercollegiate athletic association. Investment in a sophisticated athletic fund-raising program often is justified by one or more of the following contentions: winning teams in football and basketball increase alumni giving to the entire institution; championship teams enhance the total reputation of a campus; and donations to intercollegiate athletics have a multiplier effect for all institutional giving. In recent years a number of economists and social scientists have attempted to systematically test these assertions. The bulk of the research literature indicates at best equivocal support for and, often, rejection of such claims. For example, political scientists Lee Sigelman and Robert Carter concluded in their classic 1979 study, "Win One for the Giver," that "there is simply no relationship between success or failure in football and basketball and increases and decreases in alumni giving." They also bring our attention to the limits of logic in university planning: despite their research findings, they doubted athletic departments would alter their practices, because so many people believe (the above-stated) relationship exists."

More problematic is how intercollegiate athletic fund-raising by a semiautonomous association or foundation meshes with total university priorities, planning, and development. Despite athletic directors' contention that their programs are integrated into institutional budgeting and decisions, intriguing data suggest athletic fund-raising can imbalance university priorities set by the *academic* leadership. For example, at the same time the University of North Carolina's Athletic Educational Foundation successfully raised $22 million in two years to build a new basketball arena, faculty salaries were frozen because of low state tax revenues and recession. The chancellor responded to faculty complaints about misplaced priorities by insisting, "The center was not a priority of the university. It was a priority of the Educational Foundation."

Policy Implications: Rethinking Concepts and Structures

Athletic-Educational Foundations

Perhaps the most critical measure is for universities (especially state institutions) to rethink their justification for creating separately incorporated "athletic associations" within their

institutional structure. In the 1940s and 1950s the original intent was to have these associations clearly separated from educational budgets; i.e., they allowed universities to create a clean, clear entity that would make varsity sports truly revenue producing and self-supporting. This distinction was made for two related yet very different reasons. First, in the wake of athletic scandals and charges of financial abuse, a number of state legislatures wanted varsity athletic programs clearly separated from the academic and educational programs by a **cordon sanitaire**, to build assurance that state appropriations and tuition moneys would not go toward intercollegiate athletics. Second, creation of the distinct athletic association was intended to provide the useful mechanism for raising money via contributions and ticket sales. Increasingly, the data suggest, athletic associations are having difficulty fulfilling either charge. Nowhere is this more evident than in the substantial, growing reliance on institutional support through mandatory student fees as a source of "revenue" for supposedly-producing and self-supporting athletic programs. The AASCU survey illustrated two dominant trends among Division I athletic programs: for one large cluster of programs, student fees accounted for 51% of revenues; for a second cluster, an average of about 38% of varsity sports revenues came from state and institutional sources. This distribution obviously is skewed among the Division I-AA institutions but the point still holds to a lesser extent in Division 1-A. For example, the University of Kentucky Athletic Association's 1988–89 projected revenues of $14.8 million included $450,000 from student activity fees.

Tracing where money comes from and where it goes in varsity sports is problematic. For example, our own earlier reference to newspaper accounts about financial strain at Division I-A institutions raises more questions than it answers. Reports of a deficit for varsity sports at the University of Wisconsin are disheartening, but not wholly surprising. In marked contrast, the University of Michigan's projected deficit in intercollegiate athletics strikes us as puzzling; i.e., at first glance it seems so troubling and unlikely that it calls for more detailed data and explanation from internal records not available to us. Are there capital projects or construction that dramatically increase the deficits? Or is the program truly operating in the red? One curious nondevelopment is that we find little evidence of follow-up investigative reporting on this significant item in the national press.

In general, data on college sports finances are uneven and often unreliable. National surveys often have low response rates. Perks and subsidies that benefit intercollegiate athletic programs tend to be understated, as they are marbled throughout the university budget in such forms as presidential discretionary funds or relatively low charges for using university facilities. Financial reports from athletic departments along with complete reports from affiliated booster clubs and athletic foundations frequently are not readily available. Given the limits of comparable nationwide data, the financial information is most useful and comprehensive when distilled to the campus level. Economists Arthur Padilla and Janice Boucher, for example, suggest that the $10 and $15 million annual operating budget of a Division I-A athletic program is comparable to the budget of a large academic unit, e.g., medium-size professional school of a university.

Subsidies Strategies

The fragility of "self-supporting" intercollegiate athletic programs is evident in the growing interest in subsidy strategies. The state of Oregon, for example, recently implemented a lottery (based on choosing winners of professional football and basketball games) to provide several millions to the intercollegiate athletic programs at the University of Oregon, Oregon State University, and Portland State University. This initiative may well represent acknowledgment at the level of public and institutional policy that ticket sales, bowl revenues, television receipts, and direct contributions are no longer adequate to support big-time intercollegiate sports.

An interesting twist in budget discussions is the shifting stance of athletic departments. Coaches and athletic administrators push the theme of college sports as a *business* to retain resources or to acquire resources to generate future funds or build winning teams. But when confronted with deficits, they depict intercollegiate athletics as an *educational* activity. This

point comes through in the recent book edited by Richard Lapchick and John Slaughter, **The Rules of the Game,** in which the football coach at Boston College and the athletic director at Southern Methodist University urge coaches and athletic directors to be and be seen as educators. This proposal would warrant more support if, for example, coaches and athletic directors had to operate under the same conditions, salaries, restraints, and budgeting processes as their fellow "educators" in modern languages, chemistry, social work, and so forth. It loses some appeal however, when one notes that most Division I programs are not connected to the educational structures of the institution and are not a defined part of the general student body experience.

A Critique of the Reform Proposal for "Professionalism"

One recurrent reform proposal deserves special attention. From time to time one hears that big-time college sports ought to be allowed to be truly "professional." The logic is that this would eliminate the hypocrisy of "shamateurism," would allow varsity athletes to receive salaries that are a fair share of the television and bowl games bonanza, and would acknowledge the true scope and character of Division I-A sports. And deregulation would enable established big-time programs to flourish.

Despite these merits, however, we think such a reform is unlikely for two related reasons: first, it would be financially disastrous for all but a handful of university athletic programs. Second, it would expose a central weakness of Division I-A college sports, self-depiction as a business. The 64 institutions that form the elite College Football Association would be the likely candidates for an intercollegiate professional football conference. But the rich-get-richer "syndrome" would accelerate, making it unlikely that the weaker members could survive. The result probably would be about 40 major football programs. Even this would be unattractive, for if all play were confined within the ranks of 40, some traditionally winning teams would by definition become losers. It would create a "devil-take-the-hindmost" situation, in which each season a growing number of teams would lose both more games and more fans support. It illustrates the attractiveness of what Paul Lawrence has called the NCAA "cartel" for propping up college sports as an "industry." Some other concerns are as follows

- Except for a relative minority of truly exceptional players, it is likely that student-athletes even in football and basketball at major universities would find a glutted market and relatively little demand for their services. To test this hypothesis, look at the low market value of football players who are cut from the National Football League rosters. So although an occasional Doug Flutie or Patrick Ewing might negotiate a great contract, players who now receive a full grant-in-aid (roughly $12,000 to $15,000 per year) and who are the 90th member of a varsity squad would command little on the open market.

- Professional teams are expensive. The World Football League went bankrupt. Last year the New England Patriots of the established National Football League had difficulty meeting their payroll. Professional team owners usually have made their fortunes elsewhere.

- A shift toward true professionalism and commercialism might force intercollegiate programs to forfeit some privileges and subsidies they receive under current structures. A Division I-A football coach is allowed 95 scholarship players; professional football squads are restricted to 48. The reform proposal shows in dramatic relief how fragile even big-time college programs are.

It is time to stop thinking of intercollegiate athletics as a **business** and to depict it instead, as a **subsidized activity**. A university may justify this subsidy on any number of grounds but the general claim that intercollegiate athletic programs are revenue producing or self-supporting is dubious. Our main recommendation is that universities at least accept that varsity sports are **revenue consuming**. Having acknowledged that fact, presidents, provosts, deans, and board members can start to ask how and why investment in athletic programs is appropriate to the vision of total university operations and mission.

Such self-study and redefinition can be useful for reforming the governance and budgeting of college sports. A college or university ought place its intercollegiate athletic program appropriately within the campus structure. For example, large universities that readily define intercollegiate athletics as a central activity in the life of the institution might consider saying so forthrightly as part of the mission statement; this could lead to creation of a vice presidency for athletics. Variations might be to place intercollegiate athletics under an appropriate existing vice presidency. Colleges that define varsity sports as an educational activity, for example, ought have the athletic director report to the vice president for academic affairs. If a campus values intercollegiate athletics as a source of institutional publicity, perhaps the athletic department could be housed under the office of the vice president for student affairs. Self-study and structural realignment have multiple benefits: first, they counter the tendency to have intercollegiate athletic programs be semiautonomous and relatively uncontrolled; second, they bring college sports into the regular budgeting process and consideration of priorities. This structural realignment and change in reporting system would bring intercollegiate athletics into line with other campus units. It would also make better use of the expertise of vice presidents, thus sparing the involvement of the university president except in the most significant policy issues regarding college sports. It is by first analyzing the budget that we can promote the proper balance of academics and athletics within the American campus.

Recommended Readings

Atwell, Robert H., Bruce Grimes, and Donna Lopiano. *The Money Game: Financing Collegiate Athletics.* Washington, D.C.: American Council on Education, 1980.

Hart-Nibbrig, Nand, and Clement Cottingham. *The Political Economy of College Sports.* Lexington, Massachusetts: Lexington Books/D.C. Heath, 1986.

Lapchik, Richard E., and John B. Slaughter. *The Rules of the Game: Ethics in College Sports.* New York: American Council on Education and Macmillan, 1989.

Lawrence, Paul. *Unsportsmanlike Conduct: The National Collegiate Athletics Association and the Business of College Football*. New York: Praeger Press, 1987.

Oliva, Jay. *What Trustees Should Know About Intercollegiate Athletics*. Washington, D.C.: Association of Governing Boards, 1989.

Padilla, Arthur, and Janice L. Boucher. "On the Economics of Intercollegiate Athletics Programs." *Journal of Sport and Social Issues* 11, nos. 1 and 2 (1987 and 88): 61 and 73.

Raiborn, Mitchell. *Revenues and Expenses of Intercollegiate Athletic Programs: Analysis of Financial Trends and Relationships, 1981 and 1985*. Mission, Kansas: National Collegiate Athletic Association, 1986.

Sanoff, Alvin, P., with Joannie M. Schrof, "The Price of Victory: College Sports vs. Education." *U.S. News and World Report* (January 8, 1990): 52.

Sigelman, Lee, and Robert Carter. "Win One For the Giver." *Social Science Quarterly* 60 (1979): 284–294.

The Economics of Cost, Price, and Quality in U.S. Higher Education

Michael S. McPherson and Gordon C. Winston

The cost-quality quandary in American higher education is, to simplify somewhat, really two problems. On one hand is the problem many states are struggling with of raising the quality of undergraduate instruction at state-run institutions. At these institutions, cost to the buyer is not a major issue because state operating subsidies keep tuition relatively low. And the major issues regarding resource costs in public higher education center more on expensive research facilities than on the cost of undergraduate teaching. On the other hand is the problem that at elite private colleges and (some) universities, where the intensity of commitment to high quality in undergraduate teaching has traditionally been highest, costs to the buyer seem to be going through the roof.

A natural link between these two problems is suggested by the role tuition revenues play in the finances of these two sets of institutions. At public institutions, tuition from students is a relatively unimportant source of revenue, and the incentive to respond to the market by teaching well is correspondingly attenuated. Unless tuition policy changes radically, the problem for states is to figure out ways to provide other incentives to public universities and colleges[1] to teach well. At private colleges and universities one source of rapid cost increases facing students is the heavy dependence of these institutions on tuition, for two reasons. First, when revenues are needed, higher tuitions are the most obvious source private institutions have to get them. Second, and more surprisingly, the great attention to student demands and preferences at private col-leges may cause them to raise tuitions faster because it pays for costly items that either provide or symbolize quality and because high tuition may itself be a signal of quality.

To make it a slogan, quality is a problem in public higher education because student demands matter too little, and cost is a problem in private higher education because student demands matter too much.

This proposition, however much it needs to be qualified and complicated, may provide a useful starting point for exploring some issues about quality and cost in higher education. The following chapter takes up these questions more from the standpoint of private than of public colleges, and especially of elite private colleges, partly because they are what we know more about and partly because the current concern about costs in higher education focuses so heavily on that small but influential group of schools. Issues about quality and cost in public higher education are certainly worthy of more attention than we have managed to give them here.

After a preliminary attempt to sort out the various meanings the terms *cost* and *quality* assume in higher education, we take up some issues about problems of cost and pricing in contexts where reliable information about quality is hard to come by. We then examine some special issues that arise from the practice in higher education of charging different prices to different customers through the vehicle of financial aid. We conclude by raising a number of issues about federal policy that are, we hope, illuminated by this analysis.

Unpacking the Notion of *Quality*

Quality and Heterogeneity

There may be some goods and services that can meaningfully and unambiguously be ranked from *best* to *worst*, but the services of higher education institutions are surely not among them. Products that can be so ranked are generally quite homogeneous and can be ranked along a single, measurable dimension, such as chemical purity or butterfat content.

But colleges and universities are too various in their missions and clienteles for any single dimensional ranking to make much sense. In fact, it is important to notice that this heterogeneity is of more than one kind.

First, most colleges and universities are multiproduct firms, aiming to provide more than one, and often many, kinds of services. The large state university, with its concerns for undergraduate, graduate, and professional teaching; for pure and applied research; for public service; for semiprofessional athletics; and so on, is the clearest example, but even simpler institutions like community colleges or liberal arts colleges have multiple objectives.

Second, even if we focus on a single broadly defined function—say the improvement of students' writing skills—institutions differ dramatically in the clienteles they serve. A team of instructors who are superbly well qualified to improve the writing performance of students who have completed four years of honors-level English in high school may be thoroughly inept at teaching basic grammar and usage to students with poor high school training, and vice versa. A high quality education for a particular group of students is one that is well adapted to their needs and capacities, thus frustrating any notion of a single scale of quality.

The closest we can get to a fully unambiguous quality ranking is to focus separately on groups of schools with similar missions and similar clienteles—or, where schools have multiple missions or clienteles, to try to compare their components separately.

Quality and Value

Another cut on the quality issue requires distinguishing these questions:

1. How well does a college do with the resources it has? versus
2. How great are this college's resources?

Back in the 1970s, we tended to think that the Volkswagen Beetle was a very high quality car in the former sense, while the Mercedes or the BMW was plainly a better car than the Volkswagen from the latter point of view. Various American car companies at the same time devoted themselves to showing that simply putting a lot of resources into a car was not enough to ensure high quality in either of these senses. Question 1 is often thought of as the question whether a product or service provides good value for the money.

It should be possible, at least in principle, to answer this "value for the money" question for schools that expend about the same amount of resources per student, provided that they have similar clienteles and missions. Similarly, if schools are at least roughly equal in cost-effectiveness (and have similar missions and clienteles) but differ substantially in the resources they make available per student, it should be possible to compare those schools in terms of question 2. Thus, one would expect the school that was deploying more resources to have smaller classes, better dormitory furniture, a more industrious or learned faculty, and the like.

It is, of course, no easy matter to compare the cost-effectiveness of schools that deploy different amounts of resources, especially since in reality there are always *some* differences in clientele and mission to deal with as well. Putting those aside, it may be meaningful to say that one school, which costs society more, is, in absolute terms, higher in quality than another less expensive school. But is the extra expenditure worth it? Does the more expensive school provide as good or better value for the money? To answer this question requires some sort of judgment about what the added quality is worth, a judgment on which different people may disagree.

Quality and the Eye of the Beholder

Still another complication in judging quality arises from the fact that, even holding constant mission, clientele, and resources per student, quality may be judged differently by different constituencies that matter to a college or university. Parents may feel differently about heavy homework assignments than students do; alumni may have a distinctive view of what good teaching is; the public at large may have a stake in educating students for citizenship that other constituencies do not feel so acutely; faculty often have a distinctive view of their institution's mission and central concerns. A full list of groups with a stake in a college's or university's conduct would surely include, among others, students, parents, alumni, faculty, staff, trustees or governing board members, legislators, and citizens. What quality is depends on how you perceive and why you care about a college.

Student Quality and Institutional Quality

A final complication in thinking about college quality is the interplay between the quality of the students and the quality of the school. In general, one of the things students care about most in choosing a school is the quality of the students. The evidence, not too surprisingly, is that the typical student wants to attend a school where his or her classmates will be somewhat, but not too much, more accomplished than he or she is (Litten 1991). Doubtless this is partly a matter of reputation—the job market prospects of a student, for example, are to some degree influenced by the average quality of his or her classmates—but there is a real educational point to this preference too. Students learn from their colleagues, and it is quite plausible that a student will typically learn most from peers who are near him or her in capacities and accomplishment, and perhaps preferably a little above.

Students function, then, both as consumers of education and as inputs to one another's education. This function considerably complicates thinking about educational quality. Thus, a school that held constant the quality and amount of all its other resources and improved the quality of its student body somewhat, say

by replacing a few of its weakest students with a few high achievers, would thereby become, in a perfectly objective sense, a better institution for most of its students. At the same time, the change would improve the reputation of the school and demand for its services, thus likely making it easier for the school to improve the quality of its other resources as well.

This institutional interest in admitting high quality students is compatible with the substantial meritocratic component in American ideas about distributing higher education, which implies that more able students should receive more expensive educations. Both the strong demand for the services of institutions that serve high ability students and this disposition to provide such students with better educational resources result in the familiar fact that, by and large, more selective institutions provide more costly educations. This fact complicates the task of disentangling the quality of the educational resources an institution provides from the quality of the clients who receive them.[2]

It would be possible to imagine a higher education system that systematically devoted more resources to less well-qualified students, perhaps out of a desire to use the educational system to compensate for social disadvantages or out of a sense that the most able students can learn pretty well on their own and from each other.[3] Contemplating such a system brings out the ambiguity inherent in notions of what constitutes a good college, since presumably in such a system the better paid and more effective teachers, the smaller classes, and the more comfortable dormitories would be found at the schools that were easiest to get into. Conceivably, such a system could produce bizarre incentive effects, as students might underperform to get into a better school.

Whatever the merits of such a system, it would clearly be quite different from the one we have now, in which a hierarchy of institutions, ranked by resources per student, subsidy per student, and academic performance of students would all (with significant exceptions) be quite similar. A bit of evidence on this point is presented in Lee 1987, which shows measures of expenditures per student and total subsidy per student in higher education according to the ability ranking of students.

Cost and Quality

We might pull together these different aspects of the notion of quality by considering some alternative interpretations of the complaint that the most expensive colleges and universities cost too much, referring here to the resource costs of the institutions rather than their price. There are at least these possible interpretations:

1. These institutions simply waste resources: they could produce exactly the quantity and quality of educational services they do now while using fewer resources.

2. These schools spend too much money on items that, while desired by some constituencies, are not genuinely educationally valuable; such frills add to the cost of education without providing comparable benefits.

3. Too much money is spent on the education of the most able students relative to what is spent on others. Society should find ways to redirect resources from this elite education to the education of lower achieving students in other higher education institutions.

4. Too much money is spent on higher education altogether. Fewer resources should be devoted to the education of both more able and less able students in higher education, and the freed resources should be devoted to other social uses that have higher priority.

Only the first of these possibilities conform unambiguously to an economist's understanding of waste. In every other case, the implied changes would reduce the cost of the most expensive colleges and universities only by reducing their quality, at least according to the values of some participants. The last three possible interpretations all raise questions about educational *priorities*, whether among the diverse educational missions and constituencies colleges serve, between institutions serving different categories of students, or between higher education and other social concerns.

Unpacking the Concept of Cost

Despite its prominence in recent debate, the notion of *the cost of a year of college education* is fraught with ambiguity. Indeed, the complications seem no less pervasive than those surrounding the idea of the quality of higher education. Some of the ambiguity about costs is due to the degree to which colleges and universities fail to follow our intuitive and usually accurate ideas about economic transactions between buyers and sellers; some ambiguity comes from our embedding in the pricing of higher education social objectives antithetical to the profit motive; and some comes from curious and arcane traditions of college and university accounting that distort their own sense of their own costs.

Whose Cost, the Buyer's or the Producer's?

The distinction between a product's price—the cost to the buyer—and its production costs—the cost to the producer—is a familiar one. But the twists and turns that distinction takes in higher education are not familiar, and intuition, schooled in ordinary commercial transactions, can be seriously misleading. In commercial transactions, there is typically not much difference between price and production costs—an oft-extolled virtue of a competitive economy. When monopolistic elements intrude, to be sure, price can exceed average production costs, and indeed, that is the rationale of the antitrust policies that are intended to eliminate such distortions.

But in higher education, in sharp contrast, prices often differ from production costs markedly, behaving quite unlike those of commercial markets. Our natural analogy fails. The price of a year of Williams education, to take a handy example, is currently $20,760 while per student production costs measured on a current services basis are on the order of $34,000. Prices in higher education are not only typically lower than production costs—the opposite of monopoly—but it is not uncommon for production cost to be one and a half to two times the price. Though our example refers to a well-endowed and expensive private college, it is not at all atypical of that influential group of colleges and universities. At public colleges and universities, it is rare for tuition revenues to cover as much as 30 percent of operating costs, and they often cover much less.

So in colleges and universities, a substantial part of the costs of production are not passed on to the consumer in the prices they pay. Instead, these institutions use endowment income, current gifts and grants, and public revenues from taxpayers—in quite different proportions depending on institution type—to reduce the price charged the student. There are, of course, quite widely shared social motives for doing this. The point here is simply that the contrast between the market institutions of higher education and the commercial markets we are more familiar with is fundamental: in higher education production costs are higher than price, and often by a very great margin.[4]

A dynamic parallel to the unique cost-price relationship of higher education derives from the fact that changes in prices need not be closely related to changes in costs. For profit-seeking enterprises, the markup between price and cost is generally set by market conditions, so that changes in price and production cost are closely linked. The intervention of gifts, public appropriations, and endowment income introduce more discretion for colleges. Particularly for private institutions that hold endowments in trust, there is a need to plan for a distant future—the obverse of the way their current fortunes depend on a distant past. One of the principal advantages of an endowment, in fact, is the capacity it gives a university to unlink expenditures and prices in the short run, helping to avoid stop-start patterns of financing that sometimes disrupt poorly endowed or public institutions. It is striking to notice that the capitalized value of the stream of revenues major state universities receive from their legislatures would be equivalent to an awesomely large endowment, but the inflexibility and uncertainty of that payment stream make it much less valuable than an equivalent endowment.

Generously endowed private universities have in principle the flexibility to gear their tuition pricing decisions to their judgment of current market conditions while tailoring their expenditure decisions to other forces like curricular need and trends in faculty labor costs. In practice, the ability of such institutions to raise substantial revenue from tuition and save the proceeds is more doubtful, given the internal pressures to spend whatever money is available.

Price and Sticker Price: The Effect of Financial Aid

Even the novel relationship between price and production costs found in higher education (and some other nonprofits) is complicated further by the injection of strong social and institutional objectives into pricing policy. For many colleges and universities, the price is only a sticker price, systematically adjusted for individual students according to their individual characteristics—traditionally, academic or athletic performance and family income. Since most institutions have at least some sources of subsidy that hold price below average production cost, the typical situation is that no student pays a price equal to the full cost of his or her education and many students—over 50 percent at some of the most expensive private institutions—do not pay even that subsidized price, paying, instead, a price lowered by scholarship grants and subsidized loans.

The motives and consequences of these discounts will come in for further discussion below. Here it is sufficient to note that colleges justify expenditure on both need and merit based aid partly on social grounds, of equity or of reward for excellence, and partly on grounds of institutional self-interest. Merit awards attract able or fleet-footed students who add to the institution's prestige, while need-based aid contributes to goals of diversity and social justice by lowering the price to those who are less able to pay—the classic strategy of a price-discriminating monopolist. Those institutions that could not fill their classes with students paying the sticker price may, like the airlines, gain more in revenue by selling some seats at a discount than by leaving them empty.

Resource Costs and Money Costs

For neither student nor college is all cost captured by money cost; even the actual money price, adjusted for financial aid, will typically not describe all the costs of going to college, while even the accounted production costs will typically not describe all the costs of producing that education. By going to college, the student sacrifices earnings that are often considerable in comparison to the price; meanwhile, the institution leaves out of its cost accounts significant parts of the resource costs of its education.

SACRIFICED STUDENT EARNINGS

Students give up potential earnings when they go to college full time, and even part-time study at night school may carry a cost in lost leisure or earning opportunity. These are the opportunity costs of economic theory that are not included in the money costs of education but are nonetheless very real and play an often crucial role in student decisions. So even the fully aided student who pays a zero price to go to school may incur significant opportunity costs if the student's absence from the workforce deprives the student or his or her family of essential earnings. Because the magnitude of these opportunity costs depends solely on what else the student would be doing if he or she weren't in school, it is, at one and the same time, important, idiosyncratic, and hard to measure.

CAPITAL COSTS AND DEPRECIATION

The institution's money costs fail to reflect real resource costs for quite different reasons, though opportunity cost again plays a central role. Capital costs plague the dubious traditions of college accounting. Colleges and universities own massive amounts of physical capital in the form of buildings, equipment, land, and facilities. Though reported values of that capital stock have their problems, a reasonable rule of thumb might be that for every dollar of operating cost, there are six to eight dollars of physical capital; so a school with a $50 million yearly operating budget may work with $300–400 million of physical capital.

But if the institution owns that capital stock, the services it yields never show up as a cost of producing the education. Two comparisons may convey the depth of that anomaly.

Some colleges own most of their capital stocks; some colleges rent theirs. (Rented capital is a fact of life especially at large urban institutions that are squeezed for on-campus space.) Yet that difference in ownership clearly cannot matter to the real resource costs of producing an education; in two otherwise identical schools, students take their classes inside heated buildings, walk on paved sidewalks, live in dry rooms, and so on. Yet the conventions of college accounting would show that the college that owns its own capital incurs much lower costs than the college that rents its capital. Rent payments include normal depreciation—wearing out—of the capital stock, and rents include as well the opportunity cost of putting those buildings to another use, reflecting their real resource value. But little of that would show up on the books of the school that owned its own capital.[5] It would, despite its being identical to the other in all real respects, appear to be more efficient, producing the same education at a lower cost.

The other useful illustration involves a slightly greater leap of imagination to a college that owned not only its buildings and grounds but its faculty and staff. In that slave system, our present college accounting conventions would happily show that the faculty and staff carried no costs except analogous to maintenance and repair, those of feeding, clothing, housing, and medical care. All else—all the productive value of their services that we now include as a central component in the cost of higher education—would be considered to be free.

The assumption of college accounting is that what the institution owns has no value and carries none other than direct costs; the opportunity costs of those resources, physical or human slave resources, are ignored.

Note that there are two distortions here in the way capital costs are accounted. One is that no costs are routinely recognized for the regular wearing out of the capital stock—colleges do not depreciate their capital. The other is that the value of capital resources in alternative uses is routinely ignored. Although there is some movement in college accounting to recognize depreciation costs, the substantially larger opportunity costs of capital are likely to continue to be ignored. Together, these two cost components represent a significant underaccounting of the real resource costs of higher education. For Williams, as one example that is amply endowed with buildings and resources, the recognition of capital costs adds almost 50 percent to total costs read straight from the operating budget; cost per student goes from $34 to roughly $49 thousand per year.

WEALTH AND DEBT

Colleges and universities are increasingly going into debt; their borrowing typically is available for and used to finance capital projects, but given the fungibility of resources, college borrowing raises broader questions than that restriction might imply. Induced by government grants of tax exempt status for their bonds, colleges and universities have run up significant debt. Although recent changes in the tax law curtail tax subsidies for such borrowing at private institutions, it is not clear that, having acquired the habit, schools will stop borrowing as a result.

Increased indebtedness is not obviously related to costs—indeed, a major incentive to borrow has been the revenues earned by interest arbitrage when institutions can take out loans at lower rates than they earn in their portfolios—but it is highly relevant to the gap between cost and price. Prudent accounting practice apparently endorses a university's issuing debt in amounts as much as one third the value of the endowment, yet such institutions traditionally issued no debt at all. Two consequences would seem to follow from such massive debt issue. An endowment illusion appears evident even at this stage—the tendency to think of endowments as if they still represented the unencumbered wealth they once were when, in fact, they are increasingly offset by outstanding debts. Institutions will think themselves quite wealthy on the basis of their gross endowments when much of that wealth is cancelled by offsetting debt. The business concept of net worth, rather than gross endowment, has become relevant, yet universities and colleges seem rarely to think in net worth terms, and indeed we have been unable to discover published data on universities' net worth despite frequent reports—lists, tables, rankings—of gross endowment. Debt service at public institutions may in a similar way represent an inadequately recognized encumbrance on future revenue streams. Along with this illusion of wealth come declining returns on gross endowment—though return on net worth may rise owing to interest arbitrage, it will be increasingly diluted by debt service.

A happy consequence of increased indebtedness is that it appears to be inducing at least a sporadic and partial recognition of the costs of capital services. So Stanford, for one, is including in its operating budget a charge for debt service on any building built with borrowed money. Though they do not yet recognize the same real resource costs for buildings built with their own gift or endowment money, what they are doing is clearly the entering wedge; it seems unlikely that they will long live with the anomaly of having two identical operations housed in identical buildings, in one of which operating costs do and in the other do not include the costs of capital. As that uncomfortable anomaly is eliminated, the recognition of capital costs may well become general. In the meantime, tax-exempt debt issue has the power significantly to alter the relationship between price and costs of higher education.

Pricing and Quality with Imperfect Information

Price, Quality, and Imperfect Information: Economists' Insights

Looked at as a product that is for sale in a market, one leading characteristic of a college education is that its quality is hard to judge. Higher education shares this characteristic with a good many other goods and services, among them medical and legal services, electronic equipment, and scholarly papers. In the last two decades, economists have examined with much more care the implications for the functioning of markets of the fact that information about the quality of products is often scarce, unreliable, and costly. Although the economic work has tended to focus on consumer goods marketed by profit-seeking firms, it is instructive to review some of the leading ideas that have emerged from the economics literature.

A good starting point is the distinction between *experience* and *inspection* goods. The quality of inspection goods can be easily observed by the buyer—some foodstuffs and many items of clothing come close to being pure inspection goods. But many consumption items can only be adequately judged by experience— books must be read, restaurant meals must be eaten, cars must be driven for years, and so on. For some such goods, the experience can be gained at low cost—unfortunately for the Coca-Cola company, it was easy enough to find out what the "New Coke" tasted like—but for others, experience takes time, and the opportunity for repeat purchases is rare. Trial and error is a risky way to select either a heart surgeon or a college education.

Both buyers and sellers have incentives to overcome the information gap that exists for experience goods; but, unfortunately, the market also generates incentives that interfere with the free flow of information. Producers of a new high quality car have incentives to advertise its exceptional performance and reliability. Unfortunately, producers of a new low quality car have incentives to make exactly the same claims. Because the enforcement of rules against misleading advertising claims is itself costly and unreliable (after all, no one knows for some years how reliable a new car will prove to be), it is very hard for a firm to make a credible advertisement of its product's special virtues. Intelligent consumers will be skeptical about all advertising claims. There is a symmetrical problem on the consumer side. A seller could say, "you try the product, and pay me what it is worth"; the buyer then has an incentive to understate the value of the product.

Both buyers and sellers look for ways to reduce buyer's uncertainty about product quality. Buyers talk with their friends and pay for the services of agencies and magazines that provide disinterested information about products. Sellers offer legally enforceable warranties. However, although these strategies can often reduce uncertainties, they cannot usually eliminate them. Products can be guaranteed against certain objectively observable defects, but a guarantee that a product will provide a consumer with a higher level of satisfaction will suffer from the problem noted above: consumers will have an incentive to report themselves unsatisfied. The generation of information from independent agencies is impeded by the fact that good information is costly to acquire and is itself hard to sell at its true value: how do you get those who value the information to pay you for it, rather than borrow a friend's copy of *Consumer Reports?* Because such information is a public good, the market will tend to produce too little of it. Government agencies may step in to add to the flow of information, as much consumer protection legislation tries to do, but government action must be limited to objective and verifiable information, while it is often more intangible or subjective aspects of a commodity that matter most to consumers. Current government interest in increased accountability in higher education, however, may well include elements of both.

When the provision of such direct information about product quality is inadequate, buyers are likely to seek, and producers will try to provide, *indirect* or *symbolic* indicators of product quality. One of the most fascinating developments in modern economics has involved the systematic exploration of the implications of such quality indicators for the performance of markets in which information is imperfect. The phenomenon is familiar: firms advertise their longevity, their prestigious customers, their size. None of these provides direct evidence about product quality, but all these items speak indirectly to the quality of the firm's performance: it has had enough satisfied customers to stay in business for eighty years or to grow large or to pass inspection from the (presumably demanding) agents of (say) the Queen of England.

Other symbolic expressions of a firm's reliability may be more subtle. Firms selling high quality products may worry inordinately about insignificant details of a product's finish or packaging. Buyers may care little about these details as such but are likely to respond to the signal such care sends about the firms' approach: if they care that much about the quality of the printing on the package, surely they must care also about the quality of the parts in the motor. More generally, most experience goods have some features that are open to inspection: the looks of a car, the leather on the chairs in a lawyer's waiting room, or the manicure of a lawn on a college campus. Firms attend to those as a signal of their willingness to attend to more substantial matters.

However, such signaling poses an obvious risk to consumers. It is easy enough to put a real turkey of a camera in a fancy box; why should consumers put any more faith in these signals than in the puffery of advertising claims? Several economists have offered an ingenious reply to this query. Suppose the signal or quality indicator is itself costly to produce. By investing in the signal, the firm is, in effect, saying, "We believe in this product. We are willing to spend money to get you to try the product once, or anyway to induce you to give it a very close inspection. If the product is a turkey, we won't get many repeat purchases or survive many close inspections. If we expected that result, it wouldn't pay us to invest in the signal." The signal, precisely because it is expensive to produce, has a kind of self-validating quality.

Philip Nelson has tellingly applied this notion to the familiar phenomenon of content-free advertising. When Pepsi pays Michael Jackson or Michael J. Fox millions of dollars to make a commercial, the only information that commercial conveys is that Pepsi believes its product is worth spending millions of dollars to advertise. If they expected the product to flop, they would not throw away money on the ads. What Veblen called "conspicuous waste" may thus serve an economic function in an information-poor environment: spending lavishly on the package really does testify to the quality of what is inside. Locating your shop in a high-rent district, running a newspaper advertisement that is mostly white space, having the waiters outnumber the customers—all these may be ways of signaling that the product is so good you can afford to invest lavishly in making it available to people.[6]

Another important signal or quality indicator is the price of the product itself. In a well-functioning market, one would expect better quality versions of a product to sell for a higher price. Given the costliness or unavailability of adequate direct information, it may be quite reasonable for buyers to judge quality by the price. The producer of a high-quality product may consciously stress its costliness as a mark of its quality. However, the preceding analysis suggests a serious problem here. Charging a high price is not an expensive signal to send. What is to prevent sellers of low-quality products from sending a misleading signal by charging a high price?

It is easiest to see the answer to this question by turning it around. What prevents a seller who has been marketing a high-quality product at a high price from dropping the qual-

ity, thereby reducing costs and adding to profit? The answer lies in the negative impact this action would have on future sales. The high price is in effect a promise of high quality; failure to keep the promise will harm the firm's reputation and hence reduce repeat purchases and produce negative word-of-mouth advertising. (A firm that knew it was going out of business would have an incentive to shortchange its customers in its closing months; the resulting customer suspicion is one reason firms tend to keep news of plans to close down quiet.)

Returning now to the original question, we can see that a low-quality producer can gain in the short run by charging a misleadingly high price only at long-run cost to its reputation. Even reverting to the former low price may not restore customer loyalty, since customers may anticipate a further quality reduction. The fly-by-night strategy of overpricing and underperforming may work if it is possible to pull up stakes easily and reestablish the business in a new location. It will not work well if there are large setup and shutdown costs in the business or if buyers are sufficiently alert to look to other reputational indicators, such as length of time in the business, in selecting the producers they deal with.

Thus a firm in a stable market that raises its price to signal an improvement in quality is going to have to make good on the signal, by investing the added revenues in providing a better product. In markets that function this way, it is rational for consumers to judge quality by price and rational for producers to set price according to quality.

These signaling mechanisms all represent imperfect responses to the problem of costly and inadequate information about product quality. Image advertising and other conspicuous waste use up resources without providing any direct benefits. Firms will devote more attention to aspects of product quality that are easily observed than they would if information on all aspects of the product were easy to get. When buyers judge quality by price, high-quality products tend to sell at a premium compared to the price that would be charged with perfect information.[7] All these strategies may be vulnerable to exploitation by opportunistic sellers who succeed in faking the relevant signals.

Yet while these market-oriented solutions are imperfect, it is not clear that any perfect solution to costly information exists. To outlaw image advertising or other conspicuous waste would, for example, deprive consumers of one more-or-less reliable source of information on product quality. To combat the phenomenon of judging quality by price through a scheme of price control that prevented charging a premium for high-quality products would eliminate the incentive for high-price producers to maintain high quality. (See note 7.) If information were perfect, of course, these problems would not arise, but wishing for perfect information is not an effective policy.

Pricing and Quality in the Higher Education Marketplace

It is our sense that these developments in the economic theory of markets with imperfect information offer useful insights about recent developments in the higher education marketplace. At the same time, they help us to recognize some important features of higher education that depart from the assumptions that lie behind the economists' models.

APPLYING THE PRICING-REPUTATION FRAMEWORK

It requires no argument to show that college education is a service whose quality is hard for the inexperienced consumer to judge. It is also apparent that both colleges and students have invested in a number of the strategies for coping with this uncertainty that we have just surveyed. The publication of guides to colleges has become a significant industry, as families turn to independent sources for information about college quality. Colleges have engaged in increasingly explicit and extensive marketing activities, intended to provide consumers with information that will influence their choices. Also increasing, we would suggest, are activities by colleges and universities intended to offer signals of high quality to prospective customers.

The signaling we have in mind involves both various forms of image advertising and an increase in various categories of expenditure that serve to signal quality indirectly to buyers who have limited access to reliable direct information about quality. Colleges have devoted increasingly substantial resources to improving the presentation of the materials they mail to prospective customers. More extensive (and quite expensive) use of full-color reproductions in catalogs and viewbooks, the development of differentiated information packets to students with different backgrounds and interests, investments in yield parties and the cultivation of alumni networks—to be sure, each of these conveys some information about the institution, but each also carries an important indirect message. That message is, we believe that if you look hard at this place, you will be impressed, and we are willing to put substantial money behind that belief.

A similar kind of signaling may be involved in the choice of on-campus investments. As noted above, some aspects of the educational enterprise are very hard to learn about except through experience, while others are more-or-less available to inspection. Investment in the latter provides some direct information about the quality of the school but also serves the purpose of signaling that the school has the confidence to put substantial resources behind those aspects of the enterprise that most attract students. These investments would not be worthwhile if other aspects of the institution proved disappointing once students were on scene.

Colleges seem to be paying substantial attention to presenting their campuses well in these respects. One would expect considerable attention to the quality and appearance of grounds and physical plant, as well as investments in architecturally striking buildings, devoted to activities whose benefits students can readily grasp. Theaters, athletic facilities, computer centers, museums, and the like would rank high on a list of such facilities, and prestigious colleges and universities have been energetic in developing such facilities in recent years.

Investment in marketing efforts and more generally in the presentation of the institution has, we believe, grown markedly in recent years, especially among the more prestigious private institutions. The economic analysis suggests some reasons why that should be so. One key point is that the mechanisms for signaling quality are all aimed principally at attracting new or poorly informed customers. For a variety of reasons, elite colleges and universities have been making strenuous efforts in the last decade to broaden their clientele. One important reason for this broadening has been a concern for diversity, to make the institution known and attractive to students of ethnic and social backgrounds that have not been well represented at thee schools. Elite institutions, like others, have also been quite concerned about the decline and significant geographical shifts in the college-age population. Strenuous marketing efforts have aimed to increase the fraction of the college-age population applying to these institutions, as a way of countering the shrinkage of the pool. Anxiety about competing effectively with high-quality public institutions has also played a role.

A second relevant factor is that colleges and universities have become more dependent on students as a source of revenue. Federal support for research and graduate education has lagged since the early 1970s, while the federal money that is available has increasingly been channeled through students as student aid. In the states, the picture is more mixed, but many states have suffered financial reverses that have reduced the relative contribution of state appropriations to public university and college revenues. At the same time, a relatively strong economy through much of the 1980s, particularly for upper-middle- and upper-income families, increased the attractions of a high-price, high-quality marketing strategy. The economic reversals of the early 1990s have certainly caused colleges to rethink that strategy.

With heightened marketing efforts across a wider range of student groups, high-cost colleges and universities have become much less cozy places than they were before World War II. In the old days, there was a much clearer understanding about what sort of people (i.e, mainly upper-class white men—or upper-class white women at the "Seven Sisters") went to the elite colleges, and in those circles, information about these institutions was relatively easily gotten, from parents and friends who had gone to these schools. In attempting to communicate with a larger and more diverse clientele, these institutions must necessarily adopt techniques that are more impersonal. Among groups where they are not well known, these institutions must also anticipate that their claims will be treated more skeptically. Simply saying the institution is good may no longer be enough; it has to demonstrate it in visible, albeit symbolic, ways to a clientele that is literally as well as figuratively from Missouri.

It is difficult to judge how much such demonstration efforts have actually contributed to cost increases. It does seem clear, though, that these efforts have contributed to an atmosphere in which quality is more closely identified with visible, and often expensive, symbols of quality.

This brings us, finally, to the notion of judging quality by price. Such an indirect quality signal is likely to be more important in a marketplace that contains more potential customers who lack other sources of reliable information on institutional quality. One good way for a college to send a strong signal that it is a high-quality place is to make sure its price is not below the price of schools that are lower in quality.

A university may in fact succeed in the short run in improving its reputation for quality simply by raising its price, but unless the university validates that signal by supplying a quality level that matches the price, it is likely to suffer in the longer run. Both word-of-mouth and repeat business (from particular families or particular high schools) will suffer if the quality claim implied by the price is not credible. A marketplace in which schools are struggling to attract an increasingly diverse student body from a declining pool of students—and in which information about quality is scarce—seems likely to exhibit both rising prices and rising quality.

The success of that strategy may rest on an environment of considerable affluence. In more stringent times, a reputation for quality can abruptly become a reputation for extravagance.

PROBLEMS WITH VIEWING EDUCATION AS A REPUTATIONAL GOOD

This economic framework helps us to understand and, in some measure, to sympathize with the efforts of schools to polish their images and pay more attention to some relatively superficial aspects of their operation which are, nonetheless, important in communicating in an information-poor environment. Yet there are also ways in which a recognition of the reputation game can make for uneasiness. Two points stand out.

First, the economic analysis here pays no attention to the variety of quality concepts that are relevant in higher education. Quality, in economic models of consumer goods markets, is simply understood as whatever dimensions of the product consumers value; it may be associated with durability or reliability or convenience, but it is ultimately understood in a purely subjective way as whatever consumers care about.

But quality in higher education includes perspectives beyond those of the student and his or her family. As noted earlier, quality may be differently defined by faculty, alumni, public officials, and other interested parties. Indeed, one of the reasons that higher education institutions are accorded not-for-profit status is precisely to recognize that there is more to the business of higher education than pleasing the paying customers. Increased attention to the marketing of the institution to potential students (and, in another context, to potential donors) means increasing the weight of that constituency in university decision making.

It is easy to see that choices faculty might wish to make, particularly regarding curriculum and program, could conflict with the institution's marketing aims. Indeed, this could be true even of choices that would in fact be in the long-run interest of students. This need not imply that students are short-sighted or Philistine: it is important to remember that they are selecting a college in the midst of a bewildering variety of choices about which, inevitably, they know relatively little. Strong, simple signals are very important.

It is worth underlining what we are *not* saying here. Schools that are responding to market pressures to supply a high-price, high-quality, high-prestige product are very likely doing exactly that. As we have argued, economic pressures will tend to make schools that charge high prices deliver the goods by providing quality commensurate with the price. In dynamic terms, if a college adds a couple of percentage points to its rate of tuition increase, that college is likely to use the added resources to develop a new program or facility or to improve an existing one. If the college simply wastes those resources, spending them on items that do not matter to students or parents, the cumulative effect of such price increases will be to make the college less competitive.

The difficulty is that this is quality as judged by the consumer—and indeed it will be especially those aspects of quality that are easiest for the consumer to observe and judge. The trouble is that these aspects of quality may not be those that other persons interested in higher education would regard as the most important.

A second point is that the quality of a higher education should be understood relative to the needs and capacities of the particular student. As noted earlier, the best school for a given student may not be the best school, simply. This principle is true only to a much more limited extent of most of the consumer goods economists have in mind with price-quality models. Although there clearly are variations with individual need and circumstance, there is a fairly clear sense in which (ability to pay aside) a BMW simply is a better car than a Chevy Nova, and almost anybody would be better off with the former car. However, there are plainly students for whom a Harvard or a Williams education is simply ill suited.

Unfortunately, this signal is quite difficult to send in a noisy and confusing marketplace. The symbols of high quality that are easy for students to grasp do not lend themselves to neat differentiation along dimensions of student need and capacity: high prices, attractive campuses, splashy athletic facilities, and the like are features that would attract almost any student. The fact that the best institutions in terms of rich physical resources also tend to attract the best students and therefore to provide the best career prospects provides further encouragement to a one-dimensional ranking of schools that makes much less sense than a similar ranking for cars or television sets.

Costs and Subsidies in Higher Education

Unlike commercial products, as we noted above, most college educations are priced below cost. This practice reflects a social judgment—or, better, the cumulative effect of a variety of judgments by social groups—that the purposes of college education are not best served by making its supply maximally dependent on the market. The effect of the subsidies provided to higher education institutions is to give those who run them more discretion about whom to admit, what to teach, and what prices to charge than they otherwise would have.[8] Much of the subsidy takes the form of contributions to operating costs, either through public appropriations or through the income generated by private gifts and grants. In addition to such generalized aid, further awards are made to individual students on the basis of their characteristics or those of their families, reducing the price for them below even the sticker price. These two kinds of aid carry several implications for costs, pricing, and quality in higher education.

Subsidies and Generalized Aid

It is possible for colleges and universities to charge a sticker price that does not cover costs because of institutional subsidies. These subsidies make the production and sale of higher education so different from conventional transactions. Public institutions are directly subsidized by current taxpayers while private subsidies are based on voluntary gifts (encouraged or discouraged by tax laws), present and past. Though subsidies to public institutions may reflect a consensus among the voters, it remains that the tax subsidies are inherently coercive transfers from the public to students. In private colleges and universities, past gifts to endowment or physical plant yield current returns in the form of income and capital services. All together, these subsidies to the institutions allow current students to pay less than the costs of their education.

The issue of coercive tax support of public higher education has been much studied with considerable emphasis on the redistributive effects of general tax support of a present and potential elite (Hansen and Weisbrod 1969). But the role of private endowments has, until quite recently, attracted much less analytical attention despite the central role endowment and gift-based subsidies have played in the production of the highest quality—at least, most costly—colleges and universities in the United States. In the past two years, however, both Henry Hansmann (1990) at Yale and William Massy (1990) at Stanford have addressed the question, why endowments? And while the issue is now firmly on the agenda, neither of their analyses has captured what seems to be the essential aspect of endowments: that they are a device by which

the elite of one generation subsidize the education of the elite of the next. And while the role of endowments is worth understanding in its own right, that understanding is given urgency by current federal threats to tax endowment income.

Our premises are two, and probably quite unexceptionable: that costly, resource-intensive education better serves to develop the talents of superior students and that those students are typically more successful than most students, with that success reflected, on the average, in higher lifetime incomes.

What appears, then, to be happening is that a very expensive high-quality education is provided at a lowered price to the superior students of one generation through an implicit loan from the preceeding generation that is to be repaid by subsequent (consequent?) increases in earnings. So a large endowment permits the sale of very high-quality education at low current prices to a highly selected (quantity-rationed) young elite whose subsequently superior performance carries with it higher average incomes, which are then voluntarily shared in repayment of that implicit loan with the next generation of elite through maintaining and expanding the endowments of these institutions. It is an intergenerational aid program among an elite leadership.[9]

This means of finance has two critical consequences for the operation of high-cost, highly selective institutions. First, were any generation to pay the full costs of its own expensive education, ability to pay would play a larger role in determining who attends, and selectivity on academic and other indices of promise would be less. Second, if the high-cost institutions had to cover their full costs from tuition, their education offerings would likely be lowered in cost and quality. Any particular student and his or her family has to view the investment in high-quality education as risky: there is considerable uncertainty about any one individual's own future success. From society's standpoint, however, that risk is effectively pooled in the admission of a highly selected student body to highly selective schools. The general subsidy to these highly selected youth, then, provides an incentive to keep the quality of education provided to the most able high school graduates high and to make ability to pay count for less and merit (as judged by the various qualities that secure admission to a selective institution) to count for more in admission to high cost schools. Among the reasons for emphasis on promoting racial and ethnic diversity in the highly selective colleges and universities is a desire to ensure that the social and professional leadership positions to which these schools provide entry are open to a wider range of the nation's populace.

An analogous argument can be (and indeed has been[10]) advanced regarding education at flagship public universities. These institutions were created with the idea in mind of broadening access to higher education, more for a technical than for a professional and social elite. Selectivity was traditionally provided more by a rigorous flunk-out policy than by selective admissions, although a number of states now follow a California model of selective admissions to the top tier of state institutions. Prices have been kept low by state operating subsidies, financed through taxes. This subsidy can be interpreted in intergenerational terms if one views the higher taxes paid by graduates of the state's institutions as providing the revenues that finance the operating subsidies. This, of course, stretches the point compared to private university subsidies, where alumni of a particular institution generally provide the bulk of the donations to that institution.

Merit, Equity, and Aid to Individual Students

Generalized aid, whether from tax revenues to public institutions or from gifts and endowment income in private institutions, is augmented by further reductions in price based on the characteristics of individual students or their families—traditionally on academic, athletic, or artistic performance or on family income. The criteria on the basis of which this individual aid is granted have become a source of contention in higher education, one that is of special importance among the high-cost and highly selective colleges and universities we have been discussing. It involves a conflict between student performance (merit) and family income (need). It is a conflict that, we will argue, is more apparent than real, though it is more dangerous for that reason.

The dominant criterion used in the past thirty years for the granting of individual aid in selective colleges has been, with few exceptions, need or ability to pay, as judged primarily by family income and wealth. This criterion is used in both public and private higher education, although the higher tuition levels in private colleges make need-based aid a much larger budget item at those schools. Combined with strict admissions standards and the fact that the more selective institutions tend to have more resources to devote to their students, the policy of need-based aid has tended to produce a meritocracy—the best education in the nation has been made available to the best students in the nation without regard to their parents' ability to pay for that education.[11]

The best of U.S. education, of course, is pricey. As noted above, it costs in the neighborhood of $50,000 to produce one year of a Williams or Harvard or Swarthmore education, and undergraduate education at the most prestigious public institutions, such as the University of California at Berkeley, is quite costly as well. But even though the student who pays the highest published sticker price pays only a fraction of that cost at many institutions, that still leaves a very large bill for the student or her family. The current disagreement centers on which characteristics should be considered in giving further discounts to individual students.

Both need and merit criteria have immediate appeal. Need-based aid satisfies our deeply ingrained desire for economic justice—that deserving young people are offered similar opportunities, regardless of their parents' financial success or lack of it. It is the essence of American equal opportunity. On the other hand, merit-based aid appeals to our deeply ingrained desire to build on the best, rewarding talent and effort and perseverance and reaping the social benefits of preparing talented people for important economic and social responsibilities.

Merit-based aid has the additional appeal, always included in pragmatic discussions of aid policy but rarely in discussions of principle, that the quality of an institution's students plays a very large role in determining the quality of the education it offers, both in the minds of the consuming public and in fact. So any institution that wants to improve (or protect) the quality of its educational product is sorely tempted to use merit-based aid to make the price of its education selectively lower for the most desirable students, to "buy" good students, if you will, in recognition of their central role in determining how good the school is and is perceived to be.

And there's the rub. The outcome of that parochial temptation is, in the language of game theory, a nearly classic Prisoners' Dilemma.[12] It is in the best interests of any individual school to use its limited financial aid resources to lure the best students away from a competing school. If it can improve its student quality, it will improve its reputation and its educational quality. To put the same thing the other way around, if its competitors are trying to bid away a school's best students, the quality of its own education will fall unless it retaliates. Those are not idle possibilities but concrete results of competitive merit-aid bidding for good students.

A strong institutional self-interest is served by merit-based aid. Against this interest is usually set the rather fragile defense of need-based aid, that it is more just. It appears that the choice is hard—merit-based aid rewards individual accomplishment and educates a deserving elite while need-based aid serves compelling interests of justice and equity.

But this appearance is wrong. Consider all the elite, high-quality colleges and universities together. They have stuck, with some wavering, to need-based aid. What has that policy produced? It has produced both equity of access to the best and most costly education and the reward, recognition, and efficiency of meritocratic selection. The best, most able students are admitted to the best institutions without regard to their financial abilities. For this set of institutions, taken as a whole, two quite different policies determine who goes and who does not: admissions policies and aid policies. Only the best students are *admitted* to these schools—that is the merit component, embedded in admissions policy—and among those good students, only the most needy are *given financial aid*—that is the equitable component, embedded in financial aid policy. Collectively, the limited aid resources have maximum impact on both quality and equity.

What is going on, of course, is that when all these schools are considered together, there are two different policies to accomplish the two different goals of equity and excellence. When one school is considered alone, aid policy has to carry the burden of both objectives. And it cannot.

To see this situation clearly, it is helpful to take the perspective of someone at one of these institutions. If we try to jockey for position using our limited financial aid resources to bid the best students away from competitors and they use their limited aid resources to counter our seductive offers, we will wind up using our aid resources, collectively limited, in a bidding war for the best students without regard to their financial need. The end result, it is easy to see, would be a set of elite schools peopled by students who either are very very good, absorbing a lot of aid dollars whether they need them or not, or can pay the sticker price in full. Those who lose out are the students who are very good but cannot afford the sticker price of these schools—students who are now heavily represented in the elite colleges but who would not be there if we had spent our aid funds on those who can well afford to pay the price.

Alternatively, it can be recognized that our very strong urge to equity is being served now along with recognition of merit. Thus a pure need-based aid program is pure need-based only from the perspective of a single institution. Among all such institutions, it is both a need- and a merit-based program.

Take a simple example. There are five rich and five poor students who want to go to Stanford and Williams. All are highly qualified, but three—two rich and one poor—are clearly the best. There are some other rich students out there, but they are not nearly as good as any of these ten. The five poor students need $5,000 each to be able to go to either school; the five rich students can pay the full $20,000 sticker price. Together, Stanford and Williams have $25,000 available for financial aid.

Under the need-based aid system, all ten wind up at Stanford or Williams—the $25,000 financial aid budget is given to the five poor students at $5,000 each, so they can go; the five rich students pay the full $20,000 sticker price, even though two of them are real hot shots. But with the bidding war inherent in a merit-based system, all $25,000 of available aid funds are spent on the three hot shots, two rich and one poor. Nothing is left for the four highly qualified poor students. So they settle for an institution that is less suited to their aptitudes while Stanford and Williams fill up their classes with the marginally qualified rich students who can afford to pay the price.

Under a need-based system, all ten of the best students can go to the best colleges; five are rich, five are poor. Under a merit-based system, nine out of ten at Stanford and Williams are rich, including four who are marginally qualified rich students, while four much better qualified poor students are denied access.

The moral of the story, of course, is that among the elite colleges, bidding against each other for merit students will not increase their number but will increase the amount of aid that goes to students who do not need it, leaving—since aid funds are inevitably limited—less for well-qualified students who do. Some individual schools may improve the quality of their students, at least for a time, but at the social cost of denying high-quality education to high-quality students who cannot afford it.

The temptations of this myopia, of institutional chauvinism, are strong, and unfortunately, they are supported by some appealingly principled-sounding arguments. The Stanford faculty, looking at its own admissions policies, is said to have taken umbrage at the fact that Stanford rewards one kind of merit handsomely, through liberal aid to quarterbacks and breaststrokers and point guards, while it still rejects academic or intellectual merit as a basis for aid. What is the sense of that in an institution dedicated to academic and intellectual values? Another apparently high road to the low road of the Prisoners' Dilemma is the argument that schools that agree on aid awards for individual students were "colluding in restraint of free, competitive trade," breaking the nation's antitrust laws.

What the first of these arguments does, of course, is simply to argue that a university should look out for its own parochial interests in increasing its own student quality without regard to what that myopia does to the broader community or society. The other antitrust argument has the same tinge of rationalizing an antisocial self-interest. It is, indeed, against U.S. law for firms to collude to fix prices. But that law exists because it is widely believed—for reasons routinely rehearsed in Economics 101—that such behavior harms society in sig-

nificant ways when profit-making firms engage in it. What is markedly different here is that colleges are not profit-making firms and that their collusive behavior protects the use of limited resources for unexceptionably valuable social purposes. Unlike profit-making firms, non-profit institutions typically charge prices that are less than production costs; unlike profit-making firms, collusion assures that we further lower our prices, in concert, to reach only the socially most deserving students. A government dedicated to society's best interests certainly should not apply the private firm concept of collusion to the universities' effort to make superior education available to students who cannot afford it.

The issues become more tangled when one considers the problem of no-need merit scholarships at institutions that are not at the top of the pecking order. Recent years have seen more intensive efforts by less selective private institutions to lure some students from the elite colleges through merit awards and increasing attempts by state systems and institutions to encourage more high-achieving students to attend home-state institutions. In each of these cases, there is obviously a Prisoners' Dilemma aspect to the situation, when one considers each such institution or system against its close competitors. Thus, regarding state systems, there is a clear irrationality if, say, New Jersey's merit awards lure students home from the University of Virginia, while Virginia's merit awards pull Virginia students home from Rutgers. And regional private institutions may similarly find themselves drawing down scarce aid funds simply to move students around among essentially similar institutions.

Things are more complicated, though, if the merit awards serve in part the purpose of moving some students from more elite to less elite institutions. The institutions offering the awards (whether public or private) presumably believe that adding some more high-achieving students to their mix will improve both the educational quality and the image of the institutions, and it is difficult to know how to judge whether the gain to students at the less elite institutions will exceed the negative educational impact at the more elite institutions resulting from the loss of one of its powerful students. The less elite institution could add an equity argument: because the generalized aid subsidy per student is typically larger at a more selective institution, if both students limit their aid awards to measured need, the student will get a larger subsidy at the more selective institution.[13] No-need awards could then be said to even the competition. One could even describe the no-need award as a payment to the student for the educational benefits that student will provide for his or her classmates.

It seems plausible that, in moderate doses, the use of no-need awards at institutions of moderate selectivity could do more good than harm from society's perspective. However, competitive forces make moderate doses of non-need-based aid hard to sustain. Institutions higher up the pecking order will find it hard to resist responding to raids from other institutions, while institutions at any particular level in the pecking order are likely to find it necessary to respond to their peers. Since more selective institutions tend to have deeper pockets, wholesale no-need competition would likely result in very little net movement of students among classes of institutions but in a sharp drop in the prices paid by high-ability students with low or no need. If the drain of resources into no-need aid comes at the expense of need-based aid, needy students of widely varying ability would find their college opportunities curtailed.

There is certainly room for debate about whether society spends too much or too little on the higher education of the highest achieving students compared to lower achievers as well as about whether the degree of stratification of college students by academic achievement is too large or too small. However, no-need awards are at best a limited and risky instrument for modifying those distributions in desirable ways.

Student Aid and Price Restraint

Has the increasing reliance of many colleges on student aid discounts contributed to the rapid price increases of the 1980s? A good deal of ink has been spilled on the notion that federal student aid has stimulated colleges and universities to raise their prices rapidly. This is a dubious argument at best, but a different kind of argument, having to do with institutions' own use of resources for student subsidy, may have more bite.

The federal aid argument is simple to state: if the federal government is willing to pay a certain fraction of college costs, colleges can capture more federal revenue by raising their prices. Because a (presumably substantial) part of the increase will be borne by federal payments rather than by families, the market provides little discouragement to this kind of activity.

There are two obvious difficulties with this argument. First, it is simply not the case that a typical college—certainly not the high-cost colleges that have borne the brunt of this attack—can get much extra federal aid by raising price. Unlike the arrangements that hold for much medical insurance (including, until recent reforms, the federal Medicare program), federal student aid programs do not commit the government to picking up a certain fraction of costs. In most cases, a student's Pell grant is determined by his or her family income and will not rise if the student attends a costlier school. The campus-based programs that pass money to schools to be spent on student aid were, in principle, designed to give more money to schools that have bigger aid budgets, and those aid budgets do tend to rise with tuition, but in fact, funding for those programs has fallen consistently below the thresholds where raising tuition could generate extra dollars. It is true that some middle-income students can qualify for bigger guaranteed student loans at more costly schools, but the amounts of subsidy involved make it very unlikely that these extra dollars are an important factor.

The second, quite simple point is that in the 1980s when costs went up fast, federal student aid did not, while in the 1970s when student aid went up fast, costs did not. In fact, it is much more plausible that the many institutions that have experienced declines in the share of their expenses covered by student aid revenue in the 1980s have raised tuition in part to finance some of those student aid expenses themselves.

There is, however, a quite different route through which the practice of discounting tuition through student aid probably does contribute to lessened price restraint in higher education. Typically, when an institution has extensive need-based student aid, aid awards to needy students automatically go up to offset tuition increases. If an institution can afford to practice full need financing, those students who lack the ability to pay are in effect held harmless from tuition increases. That makes it easier for schools to raise tuition in part because it seems—and indeed is—morally less troubling to raise tuition if you insulate those who cannot afford the increase from its effects. But it is also a straightforward matter of economics that those who are more likely to resist price increases are those who have less ability to pay, and this fact exerts a restraining influence on pricing. Thus, in many markets, the middle-class customers perform the service for more affluent customers of keeping prices lower than they would otherwise be, since, if everyone pays the same price, the price has to be geared to capture enough of the less affluent customers. If more sellers had the capacity to charge different prices to different customers, we would expect the more affluent customers to pay more than they do now and the less affluent ones to pay less.[14]

Some Policy-Oriented Questions

How do the analytical perspectives developed above bear on thinking about national policies toward higher education cost and quality, especially at the federal level? We attack this issue through posing for discussion a number of policy-oriented questions. After asking what the problems are, we consider first possible strategies for direct federal intervention to control higher education prices and costs and the indirect means the federal government might employ to influence cost, quality, and prices.

Is the Best of American Higher Education Too Good?

Few critics of American higher education would put the point this bluntly, but the question is surely worth asking. It emerges most forcefully with public reactions to high-cost, high-selectivity colleges. Can any college education really be worth $200,000—a fair estimate of the cost of the resources supplied by a college like Williams to an average undergraduate? It is worth noting that the analogous question is now being asked about medical care, an area that has also long been exempt from such queries.

It is not clear by what standard such a question can be posed for higher education. Certainly a market test, combining the willingness of families to pay with the willingness of donors to give, suggests that the purchasers and supporters of such educations see them as worth the price. They obtain a wide range of benefits from their investment in college, from improved job skills to valuable social contacts, from cultural enrichment to opportunities to participate in athletic programs. Donors presumably gain satisfaction from contributing to these activities and from being made to feel part of the college or university enterprise.

It is natural to want to duck the hard question about whether these institutions are too good by transforming it. Perhaps these colleges and universities could supply precisely the same range of services at lower costs through becoming more efficient. Or perhaps their costs should be covered differently, say by spending more out of the endowment to lower the cost to families of present education at the expense of higher prices or reduced quality for future generations. However one answers these questions, the more basic question is also worth keeping in focus: perhaps these very expensive colleges and universities really are over the top in the quality and variety of services they attempt to provide.

But if this really were the case, wouldn't the market let us know? Our earlier discussion suggests two reasons why the market here may not be a fully adequate means of settling on quality levels in elite higher education. First, the student cost of this kind of education is heavily subsidized, partly by governments but mainly by donors. If students and their families had to bear the full costs of this education, they would be likely to search harder for bargains and thereby induce cost- and quality-cutting pressures. These pressures would be further increased if need-based student aid were reduced, since that would increase the price sensitivity of an important segment of the market.

This partial insulation of higher education from the market is a product of conscious social policy; public funds and encouragement to private donations are provided because it is thought that families would underspend on higher education without such support and because it is thought that educational priorities within colleges and universities should not be too much dictated by the market. But it then becomes essentially a political and social judgment how intense or lavish this education should become; there is no magic to the levels of resource use at which we have arrived. Perhaps the only thing to be said is that those who genuinely think these colleges are too good should make some effort to say precisely what they should do less well as a way of saving money and be prepared to defend that judgment against constituencies for whom those disfavored items are a high priority.

The second weakness of the market solution stems from the signaling phenomenon discussed earlier. The poverty of information about college quality encourages institutions to invest in visible, and costly, symbols of quality, one of which is a high price. This process, it is important to stress, is not unchecked; if the symbols do not correspond to what students discover when they arrive on campus, that word will eventually spread. Still, the importance of signaling in an environment where schools are trying to broaden their client base has a dynamic that bears a certain analogy to the arms race. Each institution may wind up spending more than it wants—indeed charging more than it wants—to offset the signaling efforts of other schools.

To see the problem, imagine a university that believed it could deliver a better product, from the students' point of view, at a lower cost, through reorganizing in some ways and dispensing with some conspicuous expenditures that had little more than cosmetic value. How does this university get the message out? Surely an announcement that the institution is cutting its price, getting rid of three club sports and two interdisciplinary programs, and replacing its IBM computer facility with two minis is likely to send the wrong signal. Saying that the university is taking these steps not because it is desperate for students but because it sees ways to improve the institution's quality by refining its focus will not cut much ice, because that is precisely what an institution that *is* desperate for students would say. The competitive dynamic in an information-poor environment clearly has aspects that bias institutions toward higher costs and prices.

Has the Cost-Price Spiral Spun Itself Out?

The forces generating a cost-price spiral are not unlimited, and signs of their slowdown have become amply evident in the 1990s.

First, and quite importantly, the intense marketing efforts of elite colleges and universities are closely connected with two current developments: an urgent desire to recruit a more diverse student body and a concern to offset the demographic implications of the baby bust. The baby bust will end in a few more years, and familiarity with elite higher education among minority and disadvantaged groups is growing rapidly. Efforts to signal quality are most intense when trying to reach new clienteles (just as new brands get substantially more advertising than established brands); it is reasonable to suppose that as leading institutions become more completely known in the national market and as the echo of the baby boom approaches, these pressures for higher cost will ease.

Second, quality consciousness appears to be turning to cost consciousness among important segments of the public that higher education wants to reach. Something like this happened, albeit temporarily, in the automobile market after the oil price hike changed public views about transportation. The two kinds of conditions that have generated such a reaction in higher education appear to be, first, developments in the national economy that have made families more reluctant to pay top dollar for education and, second, a growing suspicion among students and families that the most expensive features of elite higher education are badly overrated. The political rhetoric that has nurtured this worry has not encouraged families to distinguish between extravagance and those features that are the essence of high-quality education.

Should the Federal Government Attempt to Dictate Higher Education Prices?

One policy option the federal government could consider in its worries about college costs is simply imposing price ceilings or cost ceilings on colleges and universities. Few observers have advocated anything so drastic, but it may clarify issues to pose the matter directly. Such action might also raise constitutional questions, which we are incompetent to judge, but those worries aside, is this approach at all feasible or attractive?

The idea of the federal government literally stipulating prices or expenditure levels for the more than 3,500 nonprofit and public colleges and universities is prima facie absurd. Besides posing enormous bureaucratic difficulties, such a step would fly in the face of the traditions of decentralization and pluralism in American higher education.

Two alternatives to this blunderbuss approach are not so categorically unworkable. One would be to legislate maximum rates of increases in costs or prices for all institutions. Any such action always raises complications regarding measurement: which expenditures count? are prices per credit hour or per semester? and so on. Any price control system sets up incentives for sellers to do the accounting in ways that evade the intent of the controls; although not serious in the short run, such distortions become cumulatively more distorting as time goes on.

A more serious problem is that controls that were tight enough to be binding on either price or cost would involve the federal government quite deeply in the setting of educational priorities for the nation's institutions. Either expenditure or price controls would make it very hard for individual institutions to change their missions and programs substantially, unless there were a system in place for providing approved exceptions to the limitations. But any board empowered to rule on such exceptions would in effect have the authority to determine the directions of change in program and mission for all the colleges and universities in the United States. If price controls were to extend to public higher education, the federal government would play a key role in determining the sharing of costs between state governments and students, a role few would find desirable.

A second strategy, and one that would likely be more politically popular, would simply be to regulate the costs or prices of the most expensive colleges and universities. A simple version of this regulation would be to say, for example, that no college or university whose total charges (tuition, room, and board) exceeded, say, $15,000 could raise its charges by more than, say, 1 percent per year above inflation. Imposing such regulations would compel these institutions to cut back on quality improvements, find ways to become more efficient, or draw down their endowments more rapidly or, most likely, to produce some combination of the three.

This approach is vulnerable to several strong objections. First, this approach would make the federal government the ultimate arbiter of the question whether the best of American higher education is too good. In a pluralist society, it is not at all clear that we want a univocal federal answer to that question. Second, for many high-cost institutions, undergraduate education is only one of many activities they undertake, and one that has to struggle for resources and attention with the rest. If the revenues from that activity are curtailed, while others such as graduate education, research, and consulting are not, a disproportionate withdrawal of energy and resources from the constrained activity is likely. This withdrawal might produce a sharper decline in the effectiveness of these institutions' undergraduate efforts than anyone would prefer. Finally, the approach would be a kind of sumptuary legislation with strong paternalistic overtones. If families and private donors want to sustain an educational enterprise at a rather luxurious level, why should they be prevented from doing so? It is hard to imagine federal efforts to regulate the prices of luxury cars or boats, yet even the most costly higher education seems less extravagant than those.

Should We Restrict Federal Aid to High-Cost Colleges?

This last point suggests a more limited direct federal response to high-cost education: to deny or limit federal student aid to those who elect to attend the highest cost institutions. The argument here would be, "It's fine if some family wants to spend their own money for Maserati-class education, but I'm darned if my tax dollars should support it."

This outlook plainly has a certain intuitive appeal. The appeal is partly grounded in the belief that low-income students qualify for much more federal aid by attending high-cost institutions. As we noted above, this belief is largely spurious. The fact is that it costs the federal government very little, if any, more to support a student at a high-cost, highly selective institution than at most other schools. The bulk of the aid received by needy students at high-cost institutions is in the form of institutional discounts and grants rather than federal support.

Indeed, the denial of federal support for education at high-cost institutions would likely result in more rather than less governmental expenditure on the education of the affected students. For many of these students would likely enroll instead in state-run institutions, where state appropriations cover a substantial fraction of costs.

Such a strategy of denying federal aid to high-cost places also conflicts with the unique role graduates of these institutions play (for better or worse) in our society. As we noted earlier, the need-based aid strategy has served to keep these highly selective institutions open to all students regardless of their ability to pay, and this has helped to improve access to influential social and economic positions for students from a variety of social and economic backgrounds. This process could be substantially set back by a refusal to provide federal support to students at high-cost institutions.

The hope in such a proposal might be not that these schools would become inaccessible to low-income students but rather that the schools would respond to these rules by containing their own costs. However, federal student aid support is a relatively small income item at the most expensive institutions, and its threatened loss would not be an overwhelming consideration in the policies of these institutions.

Can We Improve the Flow of Information to Students and Parents about College Quality?

If direct federal intervention to control college and university costs and prices seems unpromising, are there steps the federal government could take to create an environment in which better decisions about cost and quality would be made?

If potential consumers of higher education were perfectly informed about the characteristics and the long-run benefits of attendance at particular higher education institutions, many of the difficulties that concern us would evaporate. Judging quality by price would cease to be an issue, as would the whole range of marketing and signaling efforts colleges and universities engage in. Perfect information is, of course, a daydream, but even improved information could be an important aid.

Better direct information about what colleges had to offer would reduce the emphasis on indirect information and allow colleges to concentrate more on conveying subtler messages concerning the particular characteristics of their programs.

Both because it is difficult for schools to convey accurate information about themselves and their competitors in a credible way and because the production of information is a public good, there is plainly, in principle, a role for the federal government in certifying educational quality and disseminating information about educational alternatives. Perhaps the kind of information that would be most useful is that which would help students gauge the fit between their needs and capacities and what different schools have to offer. Such information would encourage families to make educational choices less on the grounds of overall institutional prestige and more on the basis of how well a school serves a given student.

Unfortunately, it is far from clear what practical steps can be taken to advance this goal. Markets for commercial products suffer from the same difficulty. Certain minimal characteristics of a product can be established through regulatory and certification processes: the medicine is very likely not to kill you, the car's wheels hardly ever fall off. But the kind of information that really matters in the choice between products—or between educational institutions—is extremely subtle and, in the case of higher education, varies from one individual to another. The problem is especially difficult in the current context because the concern about costs centers on the most expensive institutions. These are not schools for which the usual accrediting processes, or even suitably tuned-up versions of those, will reveal anything of interest. Neither are objective quantitative measurements, of the kind the assessment movement is attempting to popularize, likely to prove illuminating for the relatively subtle differences on which the choice among such schools depends.

Nor is it unreasonable to worry that government efforts at the dissemination of information might do more harm than good if their measures are inaccurate or if they provide information on so small a part of the overall picture—like the current call for crime statistics on campuses—that they are misleading.

It might be more useful to attempt to improve the channels of information colleges and students rely on now. Thus, efforts, such as those that the College Board has undertaken, to improve the preparation and knowledge base of high school guidance counselors, could be helpful. Perhaps ironically, another measure that might help is to search for ways to accelerate and extend the marketing efforts of the colleges themselves. To some degree, the present situation is a disequilibrium in which colleges are trying to become better known among clienteles that have traditionally been poorly informed about them. After these schools achieve more success in these efforts, it is reasonable to suppose that these intense marketing efforts will ease off, with some consequent easing in efforts to demonstrate high quality in costly ways. It is not clear what the federal role may be in stimulating such efforts. However, local, regional, and consortial efforts to sponsor college fairs and encourage other forms of information exchange may be of use in this regard.

Should We Reduce Colleges' and Universities' Dependence on the Market?

In the last decade, college and university finance has become more dependent on student payments as a revenue source. Declines in research expenditures as a share of revenues, weak economies in some states, and most recently changes in tax law that in several ways reduce the degree of tax subsidy for higher education have contributed to this trend. These trends tend to increase the weight attached to student preferences in decisions about college and university resource allocation and increase the pressure on colleges to undertake expenditures that signal high quality to students.

The argument here can be generalized. Burton Weisbrod has recently examined mod-els in which nonprofit institutions engage in some activities they find intrinsically satisfying and others they undertake to generate revenues. The larger the contributions to institutional revenues made by autonomous sources not linked to these revenue-raising activities, the more the institution concentrates its resources on the activities it most cares about. Weisbrod has argued that the relative reduction in autonomous revenue sources has increased colleges' commitment of resources to revenue producers like creative financing schemes, souvenir stores, and the like (much to the displeasure of the small business community). In the same vein, one could regard the educational services provided by colleges as including some that they ("they" might be regarded as the faculty and the administration) intrinsically value and some that they undertake essentially as revenue raisers that serve to attract paying student customers. Teaching American history might fall in the first category while conducting yield parties or recruiting high-powered student athletes might fall in the latter. A greater dependence on student tuition will tend to increase institutions' emphasis on the latter kinds of activities.

A policy response would be to provide more general purpose subsidies to institutions that are not closely linked to their performance in recruiting students. Such subsidies might be provided either directly or through increased encouragement to private donations. This would tend to increase the influence of faculty and administrators (and possibly trustees) relative to other constituencies in determining internal resource allocation.

There is an important weakness in this strategy, beyond the point that it costs money. In effect, the assumption is that the institution will care more about and have a clearer view of educational quality than students and parents do. That may be true of some institutions, but the faculty and administrators at other institutions may have objectives they rank much higher than effective undergraduate instruction. Given autonomous control over resources, they may not be at all inclined to allocate them toward undergraduates but instead use them to support, for example, research and graduate instruction.[15]

In effect, this is a fair picture of the dilemma that faces legislatures in many states, where the objectives of public institutions are very much oriented toward professional prestige and any discretionary resources go toward prestige-enhancing activities like research. It has proved very difficult to design effective incentives to encourage attention to undergraduate teaching. The fact that most private institutions strongly depend on tuition revenues provides an important incentive for effective teaching.

Should We Encourage Colleges and Universities to Collude on Price?

We noted earlier that some of the pressure for higher prices and for conspicuous expenditure at high-cost private institutions is the result of competitive pressures: a desire to provide the assurance of high quality in a market where reliable information is scarce. Such quality competition has, like the closely related competition for high-quality students through merit scholarships discussed above, an important Prisoners' Dilemma aspect. This phenomenon has been widely noted in commercial markets, where, for example, high advertising expenditures for a particular brand of cosmetics may serve mainly to offset the impact of advertising for other brands. Both producers and buyers might be better off if the producers could agree to de-escalate the conflict. But explicit agreement on pricing, product, and advertising strategies runs afoul of the antitrust laws. Most economists would probably agree that in commercial contexts the general policy of encouraging competition is justified, despite that on occasions competitive action leads to some waste of resources.

David Breneman has suggested that college pricing and the provision of new programs suffers from an excess of competition. As president of Kalamazoo College, he felt he could not afford to moderate his institution's rate of price increase unless other high-quality Midwestern institutions did the same. To cut the rate of price increase unilaterally would have risked sending a signal that Kalamazoo was in trouble; at the same time the resultant slowed growth of revenues would have impeded Kalamazoo's ability to add interesting new features to its programs while its competitors continued to do so. On the other hand, if all the Midwestern private liberal arts colleges moved in concert to keep

prices in check, none of them would suffer a relative disadvantage.

There is a delicious irony here: the suggestion is that "a conspiracy in restraint of trade" could be used as a vehicle for keeping prices down—not what our economics textbooks or our experiences with the OPEC cartel would lead us to expect. A couple considerations make this more plausible than it might seem at first glance. First, quality competition is an expensive and demanding proposition for colleges and universities. For colleges to collude in keeping prices down while keeping expenditures up would indeed fly in the face of economic logic, but the proposition is that colleges would forego some expensive building and programmatic changes at the same time they exercised more price restraint. This prospect is more reasonable for the institutions to contemplate. Second, these are not profit-seeking institutions. More collusion on price and program quality would mean, in effect, a reduction of the influence of the student market compared to that of other constituencies in determining institutional priorities. In this respect, encouraging greater collusion on price would have similar effects to providing colleges with more autonomous revenue.

The approach would have the same drawbacks as well. In the first place, the quality improvements that would be foregone through a policy of price restraint would be at least in part a genuine loss from the standpoint of buyers of higher education. Whether consumers would value their dollar savings more than the loss in the development of new wrinkles at the institutions they or their children attend is a difficult judgment to make. More seriously, the appeal of this proposal depends on the assumption that the other constituencies at the institutions in question—principally faculty and administration—in some sense have the best interests of the students at heart. But easing the pressure of the student market is likely to have quite different effects at different types of institutions. While it may be plausible that liberal arts colleges would take advantage of collusion on price and quality in ways students and parents would approve of, other sorts of institutions might substantially devalue student interests without competitive pressures.

Despite these drawbacks, it may well be that the encouragement of more agreement among groups of comparable institutions on policies toward pricing, marketing, and the development of new programs would be worthwhile. Explicit agreements on price and marketing strategies would certainly provoke nervousness in light of the current Justice Department investigation. While it might not seem reasonable to have higher education join baseball as an institution with a blanket exemption from the antitrust laws, some more limited protection to encourage agreements on price restraint and certain other kinds of coordinated action might well become an attractive public policy.

Conclusion

This paper has been offered in a spirit of exploration. Its purpose has been both to clarify and to complicate, to make distinctions involving cost and quality in higher education, but also to warn against too much precision in debate where there is in fact less. *Quality* is a word, and a goal, with many meanings; even *cost*, a term that has the ring of hard facts and bottom lines, turns out to be a much more ambiguous and multifaceted notion in higher education than may at first appear.

The tools we have used—and, more important, the perspective and framing of the issues—are those of an economist, with an economist's emphasis on imperfect information and efficiency, on pricing and equity, and also an economist's concern with public policy. Nationally, these are issues central to higher education that are yet deeply unsettled at the beginning of the 1990s; sorting them out will require a good grasp of the economist's perspective and a great deal besides. We hope our contribution to that enterprise will prove to be of some value.

Footnotes

1. Hereafter, for the sake of economy of expression, we will use the labels *college* and *university* interchangeably, except where the context otherwise makes clear.
2. For a more extended treatment of these complicated issues, see McPherson and Schapiro 1990.
3. It is not clear that society's resources are best spent on remediation at the level of higher education; there is reason to suspect that early

intervention, before primary school, is more productive.
4. For a more thorough analysis of the wealth-equivalence of such income streams, see Bradburd and Mann 1991.
5. Repair and renovation costs would typically appear, and they would be included, too, in a rental charge.
6. Plainly, this signaling function is likely to be only part of the explanation for some of these phenomena. The high-rent district is a convenient place to shop, and diners enjoy close attention from waiters.

   An important subtlety in Nelson's analysis is that neither the firms nor the customers need to be aware of the signaling function for it to work. Customers will find that buying heavily advertised products works, and firms that produce high-quality products will find that it pays to advertise, while producers of low-quality products will find it does not pay to advertise. The practices can sustain themselves even if both the firms and the consumers have quite other ideas about what is going on.
7. A firm producing a high-quality product is in effect making an investment in reputation: it maintains high quality now so that it will have strong sales in the future. If the firm did not expect a positive return—a premium—on this investment in reputation, it would not undertake it. It can be shown that the more information poor the environment in which the firm operates is, the larger the premium that must be paid to encourage firms to keep quality (Shapiro (1983).
8. Colleges and universities might encounter legal difficulties with their expenditures on student aid if they were profit-seeking institutions, for their selective discounting policies might be judged to be price discrimination. Imagine if a used car dealer required you to fill out a form detailing your income and assets before the dealer would tell you what the car would cost you.
9. At a somewhat more parochial level, and with more baggage, it is often asserted that an institution will maximize long-term income if it keeps current tuition charges lower than its students are willing to pay, thereby increasing the implicit loan to them, increasing, in turn, their sense of future obligation and hence their future contributions. While that hypothesis has not, to our knowledge, been tested (though it seems it easily could be), it has been offered as an explanation for less-than-market levels of tuition and, especially, as a warning to those who would charge a sticker price that was all its market would bear.

   A different implication of this hypothesis is that as the proportion of current costs covered by explicit loans is increased, subsequently successful students will view the repayment of those loans as fully satisfying their obligation to the institution and hence to future generations. Those effects could clearly be estimated with difficulty but with considerable value.

10. Freeman 1973.

11. Two important qualifications to this statement need to be registered. First, the best students here are those with the strongest academic credentials *when they graduate from high school.* The educational opportunities and home environments of students from different social and economic backgrounds differ enormously. Hence, the process that determines who will turn out to have strong qualifications for attendance at a highly selective college is not itself meritocratic. Second, even among selective institutions, only a handful follow a policy that combines need-blind admission with a policy of full-need financing. The rest either deny admission to some students because they would require too much aid or admit some students without offering them enough aid to make the institution affordable.

12. The district attorney has two prisoners on a misdemeanor but can convict either on a major felony if the other confesses. If one confesses and the other does not, the squealer goes free and the unfortunate partner gets ten years. If both confess, they get five years each. The misdemeanor gives them just six months each. A little thought will show that, no matter what Prisoner A does, Prisoner B is better off confessing (if Prisoner A confesses, Prisoner B cuts his term from ten years to five by also confessing; if Prisoner A stays mum, Prisoner B can walk by ratting him out). The same incentives apply to A. Selfish individualists then both confess (the district attorney is too smart to let them talk to each other and cut a deal) and go up the river for five years, whereas if they thought of the larger (i.e., their partner's) interest, they could each get out after six months.

13. A numerical example may help. Suppose the more selective school, institution A, charges $15,000 and has a resource cost per student of $30,000. Institution B, less selective and less well endowed, charges $12,000 and costs $25,000. The student and his family can pay $10,000. Then at institution A a need-based system would provide the student with $5,000 in individual aid plus a $15,000 generalized subsidy. At institution B the need-based award would be $2,000 and the generalized subsidy $13,000. Hence at A the student gets a total subsidy under a needs-based system of $20,000, and at institution B just $15,000. B could argue that a $5,000 no-need award, on top of the $2,000 need-based grant, would just even things up.

14. This does not happen more frequently partly because price discrimination is illegal. Probably at least as important as the legal prohibition is the technical difficulty of discriminating in the sale of products that can be resold. If camera stores charged affluent customers more, low-income people would be hired to buy cameras for wealthy people. Services like medicine, education, and transportation are easier to police against such resale practices, and price discrimination is more common in those industries.

15. Compare James 1978.

References

Bradburd, Ralph, and Duncan Mann. "Wealth in Higher Education Institutions." Unpublished, 1991.

Freeman, Richard B. "On Mythical Effects of Public Subsidization of Higher Education: Social Benefits and Regressive Income Redistribution." In *Does College Matter? Some Evidence on the Impacts of Higher Education,* edited by Lewis C. Solmon and Paul Taubman. New York: Academic Press, 1973.

Hansen, W. Lee, and Burton Weisbrod. *Benefits, Costs and Finance of Public Higher Education.* Chicago: Markham, 1969.

Hansmann, Henry. "Why Do Universities Have Endowments?" *Journal of Legal Studies* 19 (January 1990): 3–42.

James, Estelle. "Product Mix and Cost Disaggregation: A Reinterpretation of the Economics of Higher Education." *Journal of Human Resources* 13 (Spring 1978): 157–86.

Lee, John B. "The Equity of Higher Education Subsidies." Unpublished paper, 1987.

Litten, Larry. *Ivy Bound: High-Ability Students and College Choice.* New York: College Board Press, 1991.

Massy, William F. *Endowment: Perspectives, Policies and Management.* Washington, DC: Association of Governing Boards, 1990.

McPherson, Michael, and Morton Schapiro. *Selective Admission and the Public Interest.* New York: College Board Press, 1990.

Shapiro, Carl. "Optimal Pricing of Experience Goods." *Bell Journal of Economics* 14 (Autumn 1983): 497–507.

Weisbrod, Burton. *The Nonprofit Economy.* Cambridge, MA: Harvard University Press, 1988.

Chapter 13

Assessment and Institutional Research

Associate Editor: Trudy W. Banta

Institutional research provides information for decision-making, and assessment is an important source of this information. In 1970, information on Northeast Missouri (now Truman) State University students' performance on nationally-standardized tests and responses of Alverno College alumnae to questions about the college abilities they were using suggested directions for transforming curricula, teaching, student learning, and ultimately the regional and national images of those institutions (Ewell, 1984). Alverno and Truman State still stand almost alone as institutions transformed by the use of assessment information in decision-making. Since 1970 most colleges and universities that have collected data on student and institutional outcomes have been motivated more by external pressures like state accountability mandates and accreditation requirements than by internal calls for improvement, and the overall institutional impact has been much more modest.

In 1979 Tennessee experimented with performance funding for its public colleges and universities and for more than a decade Tennessee alone invested up to 5.45 percent of state funding for instruction to encourage institutions to test graduates in general education and major fields, survey graduates, and use assessment findings to guide improvements (Banta et al., 1996b). Currently a dozen states are considering or implementing performance funding strategies (Serban, 1998) and three-fourths of the states have instituted accountability measures for which institutional research offices have shouldered many of the reporting responsibilities.

In 1984 the Southern Association of Colleges and Schools (SACS) became the first of the six regional accrediting bodies to require institutions to assess "institutional effectiveness" (SACS, 1984); by 1990 all six had written outcomes assessment into their institutional requirements. Led by the health professions, most disciplinary accrediting agencies followed suit. Whether motivated by internal aspirations to improve programs and services or by external pressures to provide evidence of accountability, the impact of assessment is extraordinarily widespread: In 1995, the American Council on Education's annual Campus Trends survey reported that assessment initiatives were being planned or implemented on 94 percent of the nation's campuses (El Khawas, 1995). While virtually every institution has undertaken some assessment activity, the response on many campuses has been perfunctory. Where assessment has made a demonstrable difference, faculty and administrators have taken ownership of the process and used it to accomplish their own ends: more effective student services, improved approaches to general education, refreshed and consumer-responsive curricula in the major, a renewed sense of purpose and community among faculty and administrators (Farmer, 1988; Kean College, 1986; McClain & Krueger, 1985).

Throughout the 1980s most institutions used standardized tests and survey instruments to assess student achievement and satisfaction. But measurement specialists questioned the use of tests designed to assess individual differences for the new task of providing information about

Trudy Banta is Vice Chancellor for Planning and Institutional Improvement and Professor of Higher Education at Indiana University-Purdue University Indianapolis. (tbanta@iupui.edu)

group performance for use in program evaluation. Special criticism was leveled at so-called value-added testing (Baird, 1988; Hanson, 1988).

In the early 1990s the National Center for Education Statistics (NCES) proposed a national assessment of college student learning to chart progress on the national goal stated, "By the year 2000 the proportion of college graduates who can think critically, solve problems, and communicate effectively will increase substantially" (Goals 2000, 1994). NCES commissioned papers by higher education scholars to suggest the problems and possibilities associated with such an effort (e.g., Banta, 1993). The 1994 Congress withdrew funds for the testing initiative, and subsequently attention focused on the paper by Ewell and Jones (1993) suggesting use of indirect or good practice indicators (time spent studying, talking to instructors after class, working in groups) as proxy measures of hard-to-measure constructs like critical thinking and problem-solving skills. In their approaches to accountability most states have moved from a narrow focus on standardized test scores and survey responses to a much wider array of performance indicators (Borden & Banta, 1994; Gaither, Neal & Nedwick, 1995) that includes process measures (time to degree and minority enrollment figures) as well as outcomes.

Campus assessment approaches have also broadened to include many more locally-developed measures (Ewell, 1991). Mass testing of seniors using standardized tests is giving way to assessment in courses or during regularly-occurring student events such as admissions, placement testing, transition to the junior year, capstone courses, and application for graduation (Ewell, 1997). Primary trait scoring to explicate the meaning of course grades, individual and group projects, design competitions, portfolios, interviews, student self-assessments of progress, and observations of performance are among the faculty-designed assessment methods that engage students and instructors because they are integral components of teaching and learning (AAHE, 1997; Banta, 1995; Banta et al., 1996a). Disciplinary faculty collectively set learning goals and objectives and decide where they will be taught and assessed; students' work is assessed first by individual instructors for purposes of assigning a grade, then by a team of faculty looking at group achievements to see if the curriculum is helping students attain the content and skill goals faculty have set.

As a source of information for decision-making, has assessment improved teaching, enabled students to learn more, or made institutions more effective? At a handful of institutions like Alverno and Truman, where assessment has been an important tool in curriculum improvement, program review, planning, budgeting—in a comprehensive change strategy—for up to a quarter century, the answer is yes. James Rogers, who has shepherded the concept of institutional effectiveness in the southeast since it became part of the SACS accreditation criteria, says "the concept of institutional effectiveness, with its emphasis on planning, evaluation, and use of results, has made a profound difference in many, if not most, of our institutions" (Rogers, 1997, p. 2). Yet Rogers acknowledges that too few institutions recognize that assessment should be used continuously to effect needed change and improvement. And very few have undertaken the longitudinal studies necessary to demonstrate the long-term impact of assessment on teaching and learning.

Nevertheless, educators agree that the need for assessment is strengthening, not diminishing. To increase productivity and consumer satisfaction institutional research offices need assessment data to show what works best with whom in what circumstances. And these increases are essential as higher education faces ever more intense competition for public funds and even for students.

Suggested Supplementary Readings

Gardiner, L. F., C. Anderson, and B. L. Cambridge, (eds.). *Learning Through Assessment: A Resource Guide for Higher Education*. AAHE Assessment Forum. Washington, D.C.: American Association for Higher Education, 1997.

Baird, L. L. "Value Added: Using Student Gains as Yardsticks of Learning," in C. Adelman (ed.), *Performance and Judgment: Essays on Principles and Practice in the Assessment of College Student Learning*. Washington, D.C.: Government Printing Office, 1988. pp. 205–216

Banta, T. W. "Toward a Plan for Using National Assessment to Ensure Continuous Improvement of Higher Education," *Journal of General Education*, 1993, 42, 33–58.

Banta, T. W. "Using Assessment to Improve Instruction," in R. J. Menges, M. Weimer & Associates (eds.), *Teaching on Solid Ground: Using Scholarship to Improve Practice*. San Francisco: Jossey-Bass, 1995, 363–384.

Banta, T. W., Lund, J. P., Black, K. E., & Oblander, F. W. *Assessment in Practice: Putting Principles to Work on College Campuses*. San Francisco: Jossey-Bass, 1996a.

Banta, T. W., Rudolph, L. B., Van Dyke, J., & Fisher, H. S. "Performance Funding Comes of Age in Tennessee," *Journal of Higher Education*, 1996b, *67*, 23–45.

Borden, V. M. H. & Banta, T. W. (eds.). *Using Performance Indicators to Guide Strategic Decision Making*. New Directions for Institutional Research, No. 82. San Francisco: Jossey-Bass, 1994.

El Khawas, E. *Campus Trends*. Higher Education Panel Report Number 85. Washington D.C. : American Council on Education, 1995.

Ewell, P. T. *The Self-regarding Institution: Information for Excellence*. Boulder, CO: National Center for Higher Education Management Systems, 1984.

Ewell, P. T. "To Capture the Ineffable: New Forms of Assessment in Higher Education," in G. Grant (ed.), *Review of Research in Education*, No. 17. Washington, D.C.: American Educational Research Association, 1991, 75–126.

Ewell, P. T. "Strengthening Assessment for Academic Quality Improvement." In M. W. Peterson, D. D. Dill, L. A. Mets & Associates (eds.), *Planning and Management for a Changing Environment: A Handbook on Redesigning Postsecondary Institutions*. San Francisco: Jossey-Bass. 1997, 360–381.

Ewell, P. T. & Jones, D. P. "Actions Matter: The Case for Indirect Measures in Assessing Higher Education's Progress on the National Education Goals." *Journal of General Education*, 1993, *42*, 2, 123–148.

Farmer, D. W. *Enhancing Student Learning: Emphasizing Essential Student Competencies in Academic Programs*. Wilkes Barre, PA: Kings College, 1988.

Gaither, G. H., Neal, B., & Nedwick, J. *Measuring Up: The Promises and Pitfalls of Performance Indicators in Higher Education*. ASHE-ERIC Higher Education Reports. Washington, D.C.: ASHE-ERIC Clearinghouse, The George Washington University, 1995.

Goals 2000. Educate America Act. H. R. 1804, Section I, Sec. 3, Sec. 102. 103rd Congress, Second session, March 31, 1994.

Hanson, G. R. "Critical Issues in the Assessment of Value Added in Education," in T. W. Banta (ed.), *Implementing Outcomes Assessment: Promises and Perils*. New Directions for Institutional Research, No. 59. San Francisco: Jossey-Bass, 1988, 53–68.

Kean College of New Jersey. *A Proposal for Program Assessment at Kean College of New Jersey: Final Report of the Presidential Task Force on Student Learning and Development*. Union, NJ: Author, 1986.

McClain, C. J. & Krueger, D. W. "Using Outcomes Assessment: A Case Study in Institutional Change," in P. T. Ewell (ed.), *Assessing Educational Outcomes*. New Directions for Institutional Research, No. 47. San Francisco: Jossey-Bass, 1985, 33–46.

Rogers, J. T. "Assessment in Accreditation: Has It Made a Difference?" *Assessment Update*, 1997, *9*, 4, 1–2, 15.

Serban, A. "The Performance Funding Wave: Views of State Policymakers and Campus Leaders," *Assessment Update*, 1998, *10*, 2, 1–2, 10–11.

Southern Association of Colleges and Schools, Commission on Colleges. *Criteria for Accreditation*. Atlanta, GA: Author, 1984.

Using Assessment to Improve Instruction

TRUDY W. BANTA

Interest in workforce competitiveness has focused attention on higher education as a resource in the preparation of future employees. Moreover, growing interest on the part of consumers in the quality of goods and services and the scarcity of financial resources for public services are producing intense interest in accountability by enterprises such as higher education. Thus most states, all six regional higher education accrediting associations, and all disciplinary accrediting associations that are approved by the U.S. Department of Education now have policies that encourage or require colleges and universities to assess their effectiveness. A recent American Council on Education *Campus Trends* survey reveals that as a consequence, nine of ten colleges and universities in this country are either planning or are in the process of implementing a program of student-outcomes assessment (El-Khawas, 1992).

These external pressures have produced predictable campus responses: large groups of students are being tested with standardized exams in an effort to furnish evidence that participants in higher education are attaining college-level learning standards, and samples of enrolled students and graduates are being surveyed to assess their levels of satisfaction with campus programs and services. Some of this activity has a perfunctory air, as faculty and administrators do just what is needed to satisfy external requirements, giving little thought to capitalizing on the results of assessment. In fact, a follow-up survey (Johnson and others, 1992) indicated that no more than one-third of the respondents who said they were planning or implementing outcomes assess-

ment initiatives actually had a comprehensive program in place. Most were, in fact, doing a few unconnected projects in order to meet mandates.

None of this is really surprising, given the propensity of academics to find ways around external initiatives for which there is little internal support. The encouraging fact is that where thoughtful faculty and administrators have taken the process of assessment seriously and made a concerted effort to use the findings, evidence of real improvements in the design of curricula, instruction, and academic services continues to grow.

Distinguishing Features of Outcomes Assessment

Individual student assessment has been a fixture in higher education since the beginning. Professors have tested students to ascertain what they have learned and to give them formative feedback. Throughout the world, external examiners and members of licensing boards assess students' learning at the end of their academic programs for the purpose of certifying a minimally acceptable level of competence in their discipline. More recently, resulting from efforts to increase access, colleges and universities have initiated entry-level basic-skills testing for individual students. The results of this kind of assessment are currently used to advise, place, and counsel individual students.

The use of assessment in evaluating program effectiveness has a much briefer history in

"Using Assessment to Improve Instruction," by Trudy W. Banta, reprinted from *Teaching on Solid Ground*, edited by R. J. Menges, M. Weimer, and Associates, 1996, Jossey-Bass Publishers, Inc.

higher education. Alverno College and Northeast Missouri State University were pioneers in application of student assessment in the early 1970s (Ewell, 1984). In 1979, Tennessee became the first state to require its public institutions to assess student outcomes (Banta, 1988). Within five years, outcomes-assessment policies for state institutions were put into effect in New Jersey and Virginia, and a flood of states followed suit by the end of the 1980s.

Hanson (1988) and others began to argue that the theories of measurement that support individualized testing were not applicable when used to assess *groups* of students. Assessment theories and methods were needed that would enable faculty to (1) use the results of basic-skills testing to plan courses and curricula for first- and second-year college students, (2) use "rising junior" examinations to determine the effectiveness of general education programs, (3) use comprehensive exams for graduating students to assess the effectiveness of the curriculum in the major, and (4) survey enrolled students and graduates in attempts to use levels of satisfaction to direct improvements in educational programs and related student services.

This second use of assessment, as a tool in evaluating and stimulating improvements in program effectiveness, is the focus of this chapter. Hereafter, the term *assessment* will be used as shorthand for "measurement of outcomes of the student experience in higher education for the purpose of improving the programs and services which constitute that experience." Assessment thus conceptualized may be used to demonstrate accountability in institution-initiated or state-operated peer review and to obtain regional or disciplinary accreditation. The most important purpose from an institutional perspective, however, is to use outcomes assessment to suggest internal program improvements that will promote student learning.

The definition of assessment used herein is much broader than the stereotypical concept of assessment via standardized, paper-and-pencil achievement tests. It encompasses also measures of performance, perceptions, attitudes, and opinions. Its methods include essays, portfolios, surveys, interviews, and observations of behavior in naturalistic settings.

Due to the insufficiency of current instruments in furnishing reliable and valid data, no single assessment technique can provide all of the information needed to evaluate a program. The need for triangulation, or the use of multiple assessment methods, is strongly indicated. The involvement of faculty and others who are expected to use the data from assessment is essential. Those who are ultimately responsible for using the information must set the course for its collection and review the findings.

Assessment as Faculty Development

While assessment in response to a mandate can be perfunctory, it can also be a powerful force for innovation, renewal, and long-term improvement. The principal thesis of this chapter is that when faculty become fully involved in assessment, they create and become active participants in their own program of professional growth and development. Products of this effort can include stronger curricula, more effective classroom instruction, increased student-faculty interaction, and enhanced student motivation. This theme is developed here within the context of four steps in the assessment process: (1) setting objectives for student learning, (2) ensuring that these objectives are taught within the curriculum, (3) assessing student learning, and (4) using findings to improve instruction.

Step One: Setting Objectives

In establishing objectives for student learning in an academic program, constituent groups such as enrolled students, other faculty who also teach the students, student services personnel, graduates of the program, and employers of graduates, as well as faculty responsible for the academic program, should be involved. Dialogue with representatives of these groups offers faculty an opportunity to acquire new perspectives on their approaches to curriculum and instruction.

After a general discussion about goals and objectives, faculty must ask, What should students know and be able to do when they finish the set of experiences we have planned for them? Answers to this question should produce assessable goals and objectives. However, without courses in curriculum development or pedagogy, many faculty have not thought of goals and objectives in terms of behaviors students are expected to exhibit.

At the University of Tennessee, Knoxville, faculty were introduced to Bloom's Taxonomy of Educational Objectives (Bloom, 1956) and asked to write objectives that promote student development in all levels of the cognitive domain, from knowledge and comprehension, through application and analysis, to synthesis and evaluation. Learning how to write assessable objectives prepares faculty not only for outcomes assessment at the end of a program of study but also for assessment in their individual courses.

Step Two: Ensuring That Objectives Are Taught

Faculty next need to ask, What experiences within the curriculum promote student attainment of the knowledge and skills we think are important? Before outcomes assessment began to call attention to the need for this step, many curricula omitted it entirely. Programs of study were designed as series of course titles and brief descriptions. Once courses were approved for inclusion in the curriculum, no ongoing monitoring occurred to ensure that students were being exposed to the knowledge and skills specified for that course in the overall curriculum design.

An illustrative professional-development experience occurred at Samford University in Birmingham, Alabama, when the faculty charged with developing a new general education program were asked to create a content-by-skills matrix. They wrote the generic skills they wanted students to develop along the left margin of the matrix and then created columns by listing across the top the new interdisciplinary courses they hoped to develop. Then they were asked to check which of the generic competencies they thought should be covered in each of the interdisciplinary courses. The dialogue that occurred during this exercise helped the faculty agree on some fundamental issues and concepts that students should experience in each of the new core courses. This led faculty to suggest that every course instructor be evaluated periodically through review of

the course syllabus, inspection of course examinations, and even peer observations, to ensure that the core concepts continue to be taught even as the instructor continuously updates and improves the content.

Step Three: Assessing Student Learning

After constituent groups have been consulted, assessable goals and objectives have been developed, and a process is in place for ensuring that the goals and objectives are being taught, the next question can be tackled: How do we know that students are attaining the knowledge and skills we think are essential? Once again, in formulating responses to these questions, faculty become engaged in valuable professional development experiences.

Often, faculty with no formal training in pedagogy discover in their discussion of assessment that they actually know very little about the finer points of developing tests and measures. They learn that in addition to tests of cognitive skills, which utilize the familiar media of the paper-and-pencil multiple-choice exam and the inevitable short essay, a portfolio or an observation of the application of knowledge in a realistic setting might be used. Cognitive measures also can be supplemented with surveys to assess students' perceptions of how well courses and programs are serving their intended purposes. Attitudes and values should be assessed if faculty are interested in promoting student development more broadly within their courses. And finally, faculty learn that student records showing rates of self-selected participation in certain courses and programs can yield additional information about program effectiveness.

If faculty elect to use a standardized test to assess student learning, they will need to match their curriculum carefully with what the test's developers, through their choices of items, specify that a curriculum should contain. The notion of whether a given course is covering what faculty colleagues believe it should cover often emerges in this discussion.

Assessing Student Achievement in General Education. Exploratory studies at the University of Tennessee (UT), Knoxville, between 1988 and 1992 encouraged faculty groups to scrutinize four commercially developed standardized exams as tools for assessing the effectiveness of the general education curriculum (Banta and Pike, 1989). Faculty rated the congruence between the content of each of these tests and the intended content of the UT Knoxville general education curriculum; then students who took the tests provided similar ratings. Next, the psychometric properties of these exams were investigated, and their sensitivity to educational experiences was assessed. These studies led the faculty who were involved to conclude that most of the standardized exams evaluating general education programs are flawed because (1) insufficient technical work has been done on the items in these instruments, (2) norms are not true national norms but rather are based on the scores accumulated by "user" institutions, and (3) by far the most important determinant of students' scores on these exams is their prior ability and knowledge. The UT Knoxville faculty developed an appreciation for locally conceived and constructed tests because they (1) involve faculty and students in the assessment process, (2) test what the faculty intends to teach, and (3) help faculty improve their skills in designing measurement instruments and assessment activities.

In 1988, faculty at the University of Connecticut began to discuss how to assess their general education program. They organized six interdisciplinary teams—foreign language, literature and the arts, Western and non-Western civilization, philosophy and ethics, social science, and science and technology—and developed a series of assessment activities for freshmen and seniors. The dialogue about the structure of the curriculum was the most important outcome of this foray into assessment (Watt and Rodrigues, 1993).

In New Jersey, faculty from across the state engaged in substantive discussions about general education under the auspices of the College Outcomes Evaluation Program of the State Department of Higher Education (Morante and Jemmott, 1993). Faculty designed the sophomore level General Intellectual Skills Assessment, which checked levels of competence in forty-eight skills in the natural sciences, social sciences, and humanities-fine arts. Scoring of sophomores' responses created an opportunity for faculty to develop skills in evaluating essay responses: two readers were asked to evaluate each response for evidence of skill development, and two additional readers assessed the response for writing competence.

At Kean College in New Jersey, a faculty group designed a course-embedded approach to the assessment of general education. A central committee specified program outcomes for students and the types of measures that would be appropriate to assess student achievement. Then the outcomes were assigned to courses within the general education curriculum, and the related measures were embedded in course exams. Instructors then evaluated students' responses in order to determine course grades, and the central committee reviewed responses across students and across classes for the purpose of assessing program effectiveness.

Faculty across the country are developing skills in portfolio assessment (Forrest, 1990). They recognize the value of studying over time collections of students' course assignments, research papers, materials from group projects, artistic productions, self-reflective essays, correspondence, and taped presentations. Faculty at Kean College and elsewhere have found the audio- or videocassette portfolio to be particularly useful in assessing student growth in oral presentation skills, musical performances, visual artistic productions, foreign language pronunciation, interaction skills, laboratory techniques, and psychomotor skills.

Faculty experience in developing outcome assessment measures has made clear the need to use multiple measures of students' growth and development. Students' own perceptions of their growth in certain skills have been shown by Pace (1986) and others to be reasonably dependable measures. Thus more and more faculty now ask students to describe the extent to which their education has helped them learn to communicate orally and in writing, apply mathematics skills, understand literature, prepare for employment, and get along with others.

Faculty immersed in assessment also learn not to shy away from identifying goals that are difficult to measure or for which assessment tools are not readily available. They become more willing to struggle with the measurement of growth in self-esteem, capacity for ethical decision making, openness to change, capacity for self-directed learning, respect for cultural diversity, and leadership skills (Erwin, 1991).

Assessing Student Achievement in the Major. Faculty interested in assessment in some major fields have turned first to the data available from licensing and certification exams such as those developed by professional associations in nursing, accounting, engineering, law, and medicine. Some disciplinary associations also have helped assessors by developing achievement tests that can be used in evaluating program effectiveness. The Educational Testing Service has used its advanced field tests in the Graduate Record Exam series as the bases for abbreviated exams that can be applied to program evaluation in fifteen disciplines. Nevertheless, most faculties have not found the use of standardized exams alone to assess learning in a major or program satisfactory for a variety of reasons. Standardized exams are available in only a fraction of the major fields that exist in higher education. Those that are available assess only a fraction of what is taught in a given academic program. If too much emphasis is placed on students' scores on a standardized test, the content may unduly influence what is taught. Most paper-and-pencil tests assess primarily lower-order intellectual skills and may well be standardized on norm groups that do not represent the students being tested on a given campus. These tests generally provide few, if any, subscores, thus making it difficult to determine where students' strengths and weaknesses lie. And even the best standardized test does not provide information about *why* students' scores may be low.

These concerns have led faculty in almost three-fourths of the institutions responding to a recent survey (El-Khawas, 1992) to begin to develop their own assessment instruments. As in the case of the development of general education measures, the result of faculty work on tests is significant professional development for the instructors. Some faculty wanted to use a certification test to assess student exit competence but found that information insufficient; they have developed supplements for standardized measures. At UT Knoxville, faculty responsible for the French major supplemented the National Teacher Exam Specialty Area Test in French with homemade tests of reading comprehension, writing, listening comprehension, and speaking in French. In the UT Knoxville department of theatre, the faculty supplemented a traditional objective exam that they had developed with a videotaped exercise in which students criticize an excerpt from a play in terms of the directing, acting, or set design, depending on the focus of their major.

Faculty at Central Missouri State University (CMSU) evaluate senior theatre majors using a comprehensive cumulative assessment program that begins with sophomore juries, continues in the junior year with critique by faculty of a one-act play directed by each student, and culminates in faculty evaluation of a ten-minute performance or a portfolio at the senior level (Assessment in CMSU's Theatre Department, 1989). Seniors in theatre at CMSU also take a written comprehensive exam that covers all their course work, and the faculty have designed a survey for their graduates in order to round out the series of measures they feel is needed to provide a comprehensive evaluation of their program.

Faculty in the occupational therapy program at Kean College review student evaluations of instruction and students' scores on the national certification exam. But more importantly, they have developed a multiple-assessor approach to evaluating their students' experience in field work. Occupational therapy majors evaluate their own performance using an instrument developed jointly by students, faculty, graduates, and employers. Then faculty supervisors and employers who supervise field work use the same instrument in their evaluation (Knight, Lumsden, and Gallaro, 1991).

Faculty involved in assessment have developed a number of creative approaches to assessing students' abilities to apply their classroom learning in practical settings. Examples include an in-basket exercise for a hospital dietician, an advertising campaign aimed at the sponsor of a new product, identification of an unknown substance in the laboratory, and a personnel problem for the manager of a radio station.

While faculty in the humanities seem to have a particularly difficult time in agreeing upon a body of *content* that every student should master as part of their experience in the major, religious studies faculty at UT Knoxville were able to agree on a set of *skills* for their majors. They believe their majors should develop the research skills of a scholar in their field and thus be able to define a topic and write a paper that satisfies a team of faculty evaluators. These faculty developed a team-taught seminar for seniors that serves as a culminating experience for their majors. The most important seminar activity involves the development of a comprehensive paper with step-by-step faculty critique. The concept of using external examiners as reviewers of student work also has been applied here, as it has been in a consortium project developed by the Association of American Colleges (Fong, 1988). The UT Knoxville religious studies faculty enlisted colleagues at other institutions to serve as readers of their seniors' papers in exchange for the agreement by UT Knoxville faculty to read papers written by seniors on the other campuses. These reviews of students' papers and other evidence of their performance in the seminar led to curriculum redesign and a greater emphasis on the development of writing skills.

Good opportunities for faculty to review their own curricular objectives and testing strategies have taken place with the development of "cooperative tests" by Anthony Golden at Austin Peay State University. Golden has collected from faculty in political science, psychology, social work, English literature, and other fields their objectives for student learning in the major and a related set of multiple-choice test items. Any department that has contributed questions to the pool may administer a set of core items yielding a score that can be compared with that achieved by students at peer institutions, as well as subsets of items in specialty areas of the discipline that are considered strengths of the student major at that institution.

Again, as in the case of assessment in general education, faculty who have become involved in the assessment of student learning in the major have seen the need to broaden the evaluation by adding measures of student development in noncognitive as well as cognitive areas.

Step 4: Using Findings to Improve Instruction

As previously illustrated, faculty involvement in assessment sparks conversation and developmental experiences that produce improvements in curricula, instruction, and ultimately

in student learning. In addition, the findings resulting from the application of the assessment instruments and activities designed by faculty have produced other kinds of changes. Almost no research literature existed to document the effectiveness of these changes until publication of the author's 1993 book, *Making a Difference: Outcomes of a Decade of Assessment in Higher Education* (Banta, 1993). What follows is a brief overview of the findings stemming from this experience that are slowly but surely making their way into the literature.

Using Findings from Assessment in General Education. Perhaps the single most common finding in outcomes assessment studies has been that students' writing competence, even as they approach graduation from college, leaves much to be desired. Faculty have responded to this need in different ways. For instance, at Dyersburg (Tennessee) State Community College, students' responses to the Community College Student Experiences Questionnaire and feedback from employers documented the need to improve students' writing skills. Through professional development experiences, the college encouraged faculty to make more assignments requiring writing and to spend more time providing written feedback so that students would know how to improve their work. Dyersburg now has survey data that reveal an increase in employers' satisfaction with the writing skills of its graduates.

Dissatisfaction with writing skills led faculty of Lehman College of the City University of New York to develop explicit statements of student outcomes in writing and criteria for evaluating achievement of those outcomes. At UT Knoxville, a writing laboratory staffed by faculty from the department of English was expanded in response to a faculty senate policy specifying that students with writing deficiencies will be given an incomplete in the course and sent to the writing lab for remedial work. These students must reach a specified level of writing proficiency before the incomplete is removed. UT Knoxville also implemented a faculty development program in writing instruction.

At the State Technical Institute at Memphis, low scores on the Communicating subscale of the ACT College Outcome Measures Project

(COMP) exam led faculty to establish a word processing lab to help students improve their communication skills. An evaluation of lab reports before and after this facility was established documents that writing skills are improving.

Ongoing research with learning styles inventories at Virginia Military Institute (VMI) revealed that the teaching of writing is often not sensitive to variations in student learning style. Consequently, VMI faculty are encouraged to use portfolios in the assessment of writing, since this medium can foster learning for students regardless of their learning style.

Student development of mathematics skills is a second area in which many institutions have found student deficiencies. At Northeast Missouri State University, the finding that sophomores and seniors seemed to know less about math than they did when they were freshmen prompted faculty to institute an institutionwide requirement that students take and pass college algebra.

At UT Knoxville, faculty consideration of the range of cognitive levels assessed by items on the ACT COMP exam resulted in selected faculty learning to write assessable objectives for students' performance at each cognitive level and in developing the means to test for those skills. Lower-than-anticipated scores on the Problem-Solving subscale were responsible for the appointment of a universitywide committee that, after a year of study, recommended emphasis on problem solving across the curriculum accompanied by appropriate faculty development experiences.

Using Findings from Assessment in the Major. Investigation of student records by faculty has raised questions about course placement that have prompted constructive changes. At Mt. Hood Community College in Oregon, failure rates in chemistry and math courses were unacceptably high. Higher cut scores on placement tests were instituted. At Western Michigan University, faculty found that students often failed courses to which they had been admitted without presenting evidence of the proper prerequisite experiences. Careful analysis of the prerequisite system was undertaken, and those experiences found to be appropriate are now being enforced more assiduously.

At UT Knoxville, faculty in the department of geography designed a test for senior majors covering four topics: physical geography, economic geography, cultural geography, and technique. Disappointing student performance on the economic geography section of the exam led faculty to introduce a new course in that area. Dismay at the overall level of scores caused the faculty to review students' course-selection patterns; they found that students were not taking courses in all the four areas that they considered part of the core of the major. Consequently, new core-course requirements were instituted.

Evidence from a number of colleges and universities indicates that faculty involvement in the process of *test development* has resulted in the following actions aimed at improvement: assessment instrument reviewers from other campuses have made suggestions that faculty have subsequently implemented; faculty are more agreed upon specific learning outcomes for students now than they were prior to assessment; these newly developed learning outcomes are used in planning curricula as well as in assessing students; faculty approaches in core courses taught by several individuals are more consistent; and upper- and lower-division courses in the disciplines are more effectively integrated.

After faculty have administered assessment instruments to students and reviewed their work, they have been motivated to develop more stringent curriculum requirements and to place more emphasis on knowledge application in internships, field work, and research projects. The student outcome objectives that have come from the process of assessment now provide more structure for courses; students are asked to write more; assignments require more problem solving and critical thinking; and classroom tests now require the use of more complex intellectual skills.

Using Findings from Measures of Opinion. If deficient writing skill is an almost universal finding of assessment activity, student dissatisfaction with the academic service of advising is a close second. At Winthrop University in South Carolina, at Austin Peay State University in Tennessee, and at UT Knoxville, enrolled students have given some of their lowest satisfaction ratings to career advising. At UT

Knoxville, focus-group interviews uncovered the fact that although faculty thought career advising could be handled most appropriately by the Office of Career Services, leaving them to deal with academic advising, students wanted "one-stop shopping." As a consequence, Career Services is now more closely linked with academic advising through modifications in the training process for advisers. At Austin Peay, training for advisers has also been modified to include more career information. At Winthrop University, a faculty retreat focused on the need for career advising, Career Services was reorganized and expanded, and the Winthrop curriculum now includes an elective course called Career Exploration.

At Virginia Western Community College, alumni surveys suggested the need for better academic advising, and the college installed a new computerized academic advising system. When student surveys and focus groups revealed an incongruence between faculty and student perceptions of advising at Kean College, the student handbook was revised to include a broader definition of advising, and orientation sessions were held for students and faculty. Readministration of the student surveys reveals that students are more satisfied with advising, and so are faculty.

At the State Technical Institute at Memphis, students complained that faculty were not available outside class. More night office hours to accommodate working students were initiated, and the commitment of faculty to serve as staff for learning laboratories has been increased. Students now express greater satisfaction with the availability of faculty.

At Virginia Western Community College, graduates let it be known that they were experiencing difficulties in transferring to four-year institutions. This caused the college administration to undertake efforts to strengthen articulation agreements with appropriate four-year institutions.

Other outcomes of the assessment process that work to enhance the learning environment for students include increasing faculty awareness of the importance of student-faculty interaction and of the need to appropriately train and supervise graduate teaching assistants. Students at some institutions have let it be known that they were dissatisfied with the printed information available to them about

curricula in general education and in their major. A number of departments have taken steps to remedy this situation by creating new descriptive materials about their offerings, and students have responded positively to the changes.

In summary, the process of assessment can help faculty develop skills that enable them to design stronger curricula and more effective methods of instruction. In addition, assessment findings provide direction for improving academic programs and related services for students. Assessment's potential for impact on the improvement of the environment for learning is extended when it is linked with broader processes such as program review, total quality management, and faculty scholarship and research.

Assessment and Program Review

In the early 1970s, peer review of doctoral programs was inaugurated at many U.S. research universities. By the early 1980s, many institutions had extended their review process to include undergraduate and master's degree programs. However, prior to 1985, most campus peer-review processes focused almost exclusively on input and process measures such as the quality of the faculty, the ability levels of incoming students, financial resources available to the department, structure of the curriculum, quality of classroom and laboratory facilities, and extensiveness of the library collection. As early as 1983, UT Knoxville incorporated the assessment of outcomes in its review process. The guidelines for self-study at the department level were expanded to include attention to such outcomes as student achievement in general education and the major field; student perceptions of their development toward faculty-specified objectives; opinions of program quality from students, alumni, employers, and others; rates of job placement; rates of placement in graduate and professional education; and external recognition of students and graduates (Richards and Minkel, 1986).

When conscientiously implemented and linked with administrative decision making at departmental, college, and central levels, the program review can be a very powerful assessment tool. At UT Knoxville, the incorporate of student achievement data and survey responses of various constituent groups was recognized by internal and external reviewers alike as an important addition to the array of indicators of program quality and thus very helpful in the review process.

At UT Knoxville, the department of agricultural economics faculty learned from student surveys undertaken in connection with their program review that their majors were not happy with career advising, their internship experiences, or the quality of computer support in the department. The faculty responded by appointing a coordinator for internships, by expanding their contact with their own graduates to identify more placement opportunities for current students, and by introducing freshman and senior seminars with expanded opportunities for computer skill development.

Assessment data collected in connection with program reviews can help reviewers focus their questions during their visit and thus be more specific in making recommendations. Over a ten-year period of connecting outcomes assessment and program review at UT Knoxville, reviewers' recommendations have been implemented in ways that increase the sense of purpose about academic programs on the part of students as well as faculty. Faculty better focus their curricula and communicate more often with students. Linking program review with budgeting and a well-implemented follow-up process ensures that reviewers' recommendations are implemented.

Assessment and Total Quality Management

The philosophy of continuous improvement of processes and employer skills, total quality management (or TQM), relies heavily on the collection of data about processes. Much of the data of outcomes assessment can be applied to advantage within the TQM framework. The need for participatory leadership, setting assessable goals, ensuring that the goals are implemented, gathering data to serve as evidence of goal achievement, and using the results to improve the process are all TQM

principles with a familiar ring to active participants in comprehensive assessment programs.

The application of TQM in the classroom is a powerful, but virtually untapped, source of direction for improvements in teaching and learning. Students and faculty can become collaborators in a continuous process of feeding useful information back to the instructor, much like the process proposed in the Menges and Rando chapter in this volume. While the application of TQM to teaching and learning is relatively new, and few academic units have tried it, schools of business at the University of Minnesota, Rochester Institute of Technology, and the University of Chicago do report successful experiences.

Assessment as a Topic of Faculty Scholarship and Research

Program evaluation can and should be a valued part of the conduct of every academic program. Using outcomes assessment as a component of comprehensive program evaluation, faculty within a discipline can contribute to the literature of that discipline by reporting evaluation findings and creative departmental responses to them. In addition, most disciplines pay attention to the process of instruction in the field—perhaps even supporting a journal devoted to pedagogy in the discipline—and assessment used to improve teaching and learning can be the topic of scholarly articles written for such journals.

If, in fact, good teaching and good scholarly writing go together, then the involvement of faculty in assessment-related research operates as a process to improve student learning. Moreover, the incorporation of assessment-related matters in the research agenda of faculty helps to ensure that faculty will take assessment seriously and utilize its results. The rewards and recognition that accompany involvement in research and scholarly activity are often perceived as being greater than those associated with teaching and the improvement thereof. Obviously, faculty must be motivated to take part in assessment, or they will not do it.

Contributions of Outcomes Assessment to Program Improvement

This chapter has provided concrete illustrations of the benefits of assessment beyond the classroom for improving curricula and classroom instruction, and therefore student learning. First, the process initiates a dialogue among faculty about learning. This fosters faculty collaboration and teamwork that result in more coherent curriculum design, attention to the details of implementation, and systematic evaluation.

Assessment also stimulates faculty and student collaboration in setting goals and gathering data about the effectiveness of implementation. Finally, involvement in assessment promotes faculty renewal and gives faculty new reasons to be interested in their work. At most colleges and universities, the history of substantial faculty involvement in outcomes assessment is recent. Thus documented instances of increases in student learning and affective development that may be attributed to program improvements undertaken in response to assessment findings are relatively rare.

Nevertheless, institution after institution report that assessment helps faculty establish a clear sense of mission and direction and a commitment to common goals. This provides a new perspective and sense of challenge that can revitalize the higher education enterprise. Faculty who are involved experience a sense of progress and accomplishment. Management is made more efficient through the improved quality of data available for use in decision making. Positive benefits of these developments for students include a better student-institution fit, an overall improvement in the student experience, and increased student retention.

References

Assessment in CMSU's theatre department. (1989). *Assessment Update*, 1(4), 11.

Banta, T. W. (Ed.). (1988). New directions for institutional research: No. 59, *Implementing outcomes assessment: Promise and perils*. San Francisco: Jossey-Bass.

Banta, T. W., & associates (1993). *Making a difference: Outcomes of a decade of assessment in higher education*. San Francisco: Jossey-Bass.

Banta, T. W. & Pike, G. R. (1989). Methods for comparing outcomes assessment instruments. *Research in Higher Education*, 30(5), 455–470.

Bloom, B. S. (Ed.). (1956). *Taxonomy of educational objectives: Handbook I. Cognitive domain*. New York: David McKay.

El-Khawas, E. (1992). *1992 campus trends* (Higher Education Panel Report No. 78). Washington, DC: American Council on Education.

Erwin, T. D. (1991). *Assessing student learning and development in college*. San Francisco: Jossey-Bass.

Ewell, P. T. (1984). *The self-regarding institution: Information for excellence*. Boulder, CO: National Center for Higher Education Management Systems.

Fong, B. (1988). Old wineskins: The AAC external examination project. *Liberal Education*, 74(3), 12–16.

Forrest, A. (1990). *Time will tell: Portfolio-assisted assessment of general education*. Washington, DC: American Association of Higher Education.

Hanson, G. (1988). Critical issues in the assessment of value added in education. In T. W. Banta (Ed.), New directions for institutional research: No. 59. *Implementing outcomes assessment: Promise and perils* (pp. 53–68). San Francisco: Jossey-Bass.

Johnson, R., Prus J., Andersen, C., & El-Khawas, E. (1992). *Assessing assessment: An in-depth status report on the higher education assessment movement in 1990* (Higher Education Panel Report No. 79). Washington, DC: American Council on Education.

Knight, M., Lumsden, D., & Gallaro, D. (1991). *Outcomes assessment at Kean College of New Jersey: Academic programs procedures and models*. New York: University Press of America.

Morante, E., & Jemmott, N. (1993). The impact of the College Outcomes Evaluation Program (COEP) on public higher education in New Jersey. In T. W. Banta & associates, *Making a difference: Outcomes of a decade of assessment in higher education*. San Francisco: Jossey-Bass.

Pace, C. R. (1986). *Measuring the quality of the college-student experience*. Los Angeles: Higher Education Research Institute, University of California, Los Angeles.

Richards, M., & Minkel, C. W. (1986). Assessing the quality of higher education through comprehensive program review. In T. W. Banta (Ed.), *Performance funding in higher education: A critical analysis of Tennessee's experience*. Boulder, CO: National Center for Higher Education Management Systems.

Watt, J., & Rodrigues, R. (1993). Faculty-developed approaches at large universities: University of Connecticut and Colorado State. In T. W. Banta & associates, *Making a difference: Outcomes of a decade of assessment in higher education*. San Francisco: Jossey-Bass.

Strengthening Assessment for Academic Quality Improvement

PETER T. EWELL

Since its emergence as a widespread topic of national discussion in higher education some fifteen years ago, assessment has been inextricably linked with accountability. Throughout this period, explicit external demands for information about results constituted the initial reason why the majority of colleges and universities got into the assessment business. The perceived need to satisfy constituencies like state governments and accreditors also decisively colored the assessment approaches actually adopted, who got involved in assessment efforts on campuses, and the manner in which assessment results were used (Ewell, 1993a).

As is often the case, this outcome was neither what policy makers intended nor what assessment's pioneers envisioned. But the academic administrators responsible for this result were responding rationally to some real environmental conditions. On the one hand, the very existence of assessment as an external mandate meant that faculty could disengage; added to the apprehension naturally associated with any evaluation was an understandable belief that assessment was an administrative, not an academic, problem. As a result, faculty all too often felt assessment to be something that administrators should "take care of" without involving them. More significantly in this period, no real incentives for grassroots engagement were present. The 1980s, in retrospect, were a decade of relative resource abundance for higher education, and while investments in innovation occurred (and could be afforded), few real changes in academic struc-

ture and pedagogy were perceived as necessary. Like parallel "reforms" in general education, assessment became widespread but marginal: few institutions remained unaffected, but deep engagement was rare.

The fiscal and management conditions of the 1990s, in contrast, have transformed the terms of engagement. Significant fiscal shortfalls are for the first time forcing institutions to seriously examine past practices in delivering undergraduate instruction. This conversation is fueled equally by emerging technologies that promise more for less but that may also fundamentally alter the way teaching and learning occurs. At the same time, accountability has become sharper and is increasingly tied to resource allocation. In all aspects of government, "entitlements" are being replaced by contracts for specific performance—with performance defined less by the providers themselves than by client needs and expectations. This combination has decisively shaped the context for assessment. The paramount current need is to reposition assessment as a tool for academic management—effectively "recycling" methods and information designed initially to meet external demands.

A principal challenge implied by this shift is transforming the mind-set of assessment from one dominated by end-point checking on goal achievement to one that emphasizes continuous, low-level monitoring of instructional processes and their interconnections. As a consequence, a main purpose of this chapter is to explore how this fundamental and needed

"Strengthening Assessment for Academic Quality Improvement," by Peter T. Ewell, reprinted from *Planning and Management for a Changing Environment: A Handbook on Redesigning Postsecondary Institutions*, edited by Marvin W. Peterson, David D. Dill, Lisa A. Mets, and Associates, 1997, Jossey-Bass Publishers, Inc.

transformation has evolved, shaped by both external conditions and the development of assessment technology itself. A second challenge is more formidable: to find better ways to systematically embed the results of assessment into academic planning and budgeting—especially where fundamental changes are contemplated. The second section of the chapter, therefore, examines some specific ways in which assessment practices can become integral to academic decision making for the future. In both discussions, moreover, a single theme is apparent: to be useful in the new millennium, assessment practices not only most examine "value added" but must themselves add value. And only the approaches that meet this condition can and should be maintained.

An Evolving Environment for Assessment

Three factors have influenced assessment's development over the past decade and, for better or worse, decisively shaped the tools and techniques now available. Accountability requirements—chiefly on the part of state governments, but increasingly including accrediting bodies as well—created an initial "market" for assessment and strongly affected the kinds of instruments and techniques that institutions developed and deployed. Changing fiscal conditions have also had a significant part to play, reflected both in the affordability of complex assessment approaches and the fiscal parameters governing institutional responses to assessment findings. Finally, considerable technical evolution occurred as institutions gained experience with designing and implementing new methods. Because the interactions among these forces are complex, a full understanding of each is important to recognize assessment's emerging potential.

The Demand for Assessment: The Accountability Dimension

Campus assessment practice has always reflected shifting alignments between internal and external demands. The roots of the movement were both campus-centered and radical: its early proponents advanced assessment not just as a means to gather information but as a

point of entry for engaging the far broader topics of curricular reform and learner-centered pedagogy that also became prominent in the eighties.

As a result, original calls for assessment were always embedded in a wider change agenda (for example, Association of American Colleges, 1985; National Institute of Education, 1984). More importantly, recognizing the way change actually happens on college and university campuses, these approaches strongly emphasized visible faculty engagement and the development of diverse, campus-centered efforts. External interest, in contrast, resulted initially from an earlier political engagement with K-12 education. Here, "assessment" referenced a far different paradigm of change, one founded upon the visible establishment and maintenance of clear (and often centralized) standards for common student achievement (National Governors' Association, 1986).

The first interaction of these potentially conflicting agendas was benign (Ewell, 1994). Higher education leaders in most states were able to convince public officials that decentralized assessment approaches—consistent with the internal reform agenda just emerging—were both internally feasible and could simultaneously serve public purposes. Partly this was because, differently from K-12, few specific complaints about the performance of colleges and universities had arisen; higher education's "accountability problem" was therefore one of establishing public confidence in its own regulatory processes more than attaining particular standards. In part it was also because more basic goals were aligned. Many states in the mid-eighties were investing heavily in the "quality" of their public higher education systems—often in the form of addition-to-base incentive grant programs—and the assessment-for-improvement agenda of internal reform appeared highly compatible with these initiatives. Indeed, dollars provided to institutions through such mechanisms were often invested deliberately in upgrading campus-level assessment capacity in this period, usually in conjunction with other pedagogical or curricular changes.

Consistent with these developments, by 1990 over two-thirds of the states had resolved the question of assessment policy by adopting a campus-centered approach, allowing each institution to develop its own statements of expected outcomes and its own means to gather evidence of their achievement (Ewell, Finney, and Lenth, 1990). Stimulated in part by new Department of Education regulations, all six regional accreditation organizations implemented similar policies, requiring the development of local assessment programs by private as well as public institutions. The result was a pattern of institutional response demonstrated markedly in national surveys. The proportion of institutions reporting engagement in assessment rose significantly in the period 1988–1995 from 55 percent to 94 percent, while the percentage of those indicating that assessment had a real programmatic or curricular impact almost doubled from 40 percent to 76 percent; at the same time, almost half of those responding to the same survey in 1995 indicated that attention to assessment had for the most part "resulted in new reporting requirements," and two-thirds remained skeptical about misuse of results by external agencies (El-Khawas, 1995). External initiatives promoting campus-centered assessment had clearly been successful in heightening institutional attention and capacity. But simple engagement in "assessment activities" provided insufficient impetus for serious self-reflection and renewal.

Beginning about 1990, however, the accountability agenda began to change. On the one hand, significant economic downturns in many states strongly stimulated traditional concerns about academic efficiency in much the same manner as they had two decades earlier (McGuinness, 1994). With "outcomes" now a legitimate topic of discussion, however, policy makers could comfortably raise issues of performance along with cost, and they began to do so with considerable regularity. At the same time, doubts began growing about the ability of decentralized, noncomparable data-gathering approaches to effectively discharge public accountability functions (Ewell, 1991a). The result for many states was increasing separation of the "improvement" and "accountability" components of assessment policy. Few abandoned the campus-centered assessment mandates established earlier, but fifteen states had by 1995 implemented additional "performance indicator" systems using common measures (Ruppert, 1994). In stark contrast to the institution-centered approaches emphasized

throughout the eighties, the explicit intent of such systems was to compare institutional performances—often for purposes of funding as well as public reporting (Ewell, 1994).

Accompanying this trend was an important additional change in perspective. Institution-centered assessment not only allowed a diversity of evidence-gathering approaches but it also emphasized the achievement of internally established academic goals. More and more, as the nineties progressed, state governments began emphasizing higher education's role in addressing larger societal or client-driven goals (Ewell and Jones, 1993; McGuinness, 1994). As a result, emerging state indicator systems often went beyond institution-posed outcomes to include measures of employer and student satisfaction. An equally prominent theme in state policy discussions of quality were issues of protecting consumers, and of providing higher education's clients with adequate information on the basis of which to make informed customers choices (Education Commission of the States, 1995). In the period 1992–1995, moreover, a major new champion of consumer-based accountability emerged in the form of the federal government. Reacting specifically to charges of fraud and abuse with respect to federal financial aid funds, the 1992 Reauthorization of the Higher Education Act incorporated highly prescriptive new regulations governing state and accrediting-body review, several of which addressed institutional outcomes. Though substantially rolled back by Congress in 1995, these regulations did succeed in highlighting consumer issues as a continuing part of the accountability equation, whether discharged by states or by accrediting bodies.

Taken together, these changes in the accountability context have a number of implications. First, institutional capacity to engage in assessment has become a major condition of doing business. Not only is outcomes information routinely required for public reporting by many external authorities, but the prudent institution will also want the ability to reanalyze, interpret, or refute claims about its performance that will increasingly be used to make high-stakes decisions. Second, as this implies, the basic character of public funding is shifting markedly from a mode based on "subsidizing operations" to one founded on "paying for performance" (Ewell, 1991a). In this context, information about outcomes, whatever its character, increasingly drives resource allocation. Consistent with the implied "market mechanism" of performance-based allocation, moreover, institutions need to become far more responsive to concerns about performance on the part of individual clients. Partly this is because of market pressures and increasing dependence on tuition revenues. At least as prominently, it results form growing public pressures for better consumer information.

The Demand for Assessment: The Productivity Dimension

Changing accountability and market conditions such as these mean that assessment information has an increasingly direct bearing on critical institutional revenue streams. Perhaps more significant, however, is assessment's emerging relevance in helping institutions cut costs and improve instructional productivity. When assessment first emerged, this was less a concern. Both accountability and improvement rested far more visibly on a rhetoric of quality than on one of efficiency. By the early nineties, however, higher education's fiscal environment had changed decisively. Most states experienced significant economic downturns, which together with growing taxpayer resistance meant significant cutbacks in public allocation.

For public higher education, these effects were amplified by a structural condition of state budgeting: allocations to colleges and universities in most states represented virtually the only discretionary dollars available to balance state budgets after taking into account mandated (or politically untouchable) expenditures in such areas as health care, corrections, or K-12 education. Faced with these conditions, public higher education experienced an unprecedented two-year downturn in real expenditures in 1990–1992, with some states suffering cumulative cuts of over 20 percent (Hines, 1994). While tuition increases could make up some lost ground, it was clear to all but a few institutions by the mid-1990s that attention to expenditures would be required.

Significant pressures on institutional budgets, moreover, generally arose in a context where simple cutbacks were precluded. On the one hand, a now-prominent accountability agenda meant that quality could not be simply "traded-off" against cost; externally, it was clear that explicit assessment would remain in place and that institutions would be held responsible for continuing to attain quality objectives. And it was equally clear that student access could not be denied; indeed, many states expected substantial increases in the numbers of students their postsecondary systems would be required to serve. The resulting pressure on institutions to hold down expenditures while maintaining quality and increasing output yielded multiple responses.

An initial manifestation (certainly the most visible) of this new set of conditions was a wave of institutional attempts to implement Total Quality Management (TQM), a family of approaches drawn from business and industry (for example, Seymour, 1991; Sherr and Teeter, 1991). Applied first to administrative functions, colleges and universities did occasionally succeed in duplicating industry's claim to simultaneously improve productivity and cut costs. But efforts to extend this application to academic functions often encountered precisely the same kinds of intellectual objections based on the alien language and inappropriate conceptualization earlier experienced by the more "psychometric" approaches to assessment (Ewell, 1993b). As a result, initial attempts to "restructure" academic functions tended to follow a different logic. Virtually every aspect of this response, however, had a potentially significant link to assessment.

A first level of response involved cutting "nonproductive" programs. Like parallel efforts in the late 1970s, the principal criteria used here were low enrollment and degree productivity. But newly available assessment results also had a part to play in many cases, especially if these were already incorporated into established program review procedures (Miller, forthcoming). Somewhat deeper "academic restructuring" efforts often involved a more critical examination of curricular requirements (Zemsky, Massy, and Oedel, 1993). At the most basic level, this commonly resulted in reducing the number of credits needed to complete a degree, or finding ways to accelerate student progress by means of advanced placement or continuous attendance (McGuinness and Ewell, 1994). More sophisticated curricular restructuring efforts entailed delving more deeply into course sequences and requirements in order to identify instances where greater coherence could be achieved. In both kinds of restructuring, assessment has become increasingly relevant, both to identify those students who can in fact be "accelerated" and to determine the effects of such changes on eventual outcomes.

Probably the most visible restructuring efforts, however, have emphasized the application of new technology to instructional delivery, a process seen by both academic administrators and state officials as the principal "magic bullet" needed to slay the productivity dragon (Resmer, Mingle, and Oblinger, 1995). Embodied in such mechanisms as interactive video for distance delivery and computer-assisted, self-paced hypertext modules intended to be embedded in regular coursework, the application of such technologies raises fundamental questions of pedagogical impact that at some point beg to be evaluated. At the same time, the very structure of such mechanisms—especially where they require independent student demonstration of mastery at their own pace—requires that the assessment of competency be built into curricular designs from the outset (Stanford Forum on Higher Education Futures, 1995).

The Changing Face of Assessment Practice

As these many contextual shifts took place, the technical practice of assessment was changing as well. By the mid-1990s, based on a decade of experience, institutional administrators had many approaches from which to choose and had accumulated considerable experience in how to deploy them. While this technical evolution unfolded in relative isolation from trends in the higher education environment, its direction yielded instruments and approaches that were far more suited to meeting the challenges posed by environmental change than the techniques available when assessment first emerged.

A first path of development saw assessment approaches becoming increasingly comprehensive. While assessment was visibly labeled an "outcomes" movement, its advocates argued from the beginning that information on inputs and educational environments would be

required in equal measure if assessment results were to be of any real utility (Astin, 1991). Most institutions that actually engaged in assessment throughout the eighties learned this lesson empirically. A common pattern was to begin with end-point measures—often using standardized tests alone—followed by an interest in collecting data about student experiences, perceptions, and course-taking patterns after finding end-point results essentially uninterpretable (Ewell, 1991b). In what quickly became best practice, other institutions adopted a longitudinal approach from the outset by identifying a cohort of entering students and collecting data on outcomes and experiences systematically as they progressed (Katchadourian and Boli, 1985; Kellams, 1989). While few colleges and universities were ready to make the heavy investments needed to underwrite large-scale longitudinal studies, most institutional assessment programs had by the mid-nineties abandoned the exclusive use of isolated, one-shot investigations of outcomes.

Growing comprehensiveness also implied paying greater attention to examining curricular and environmental interconnections. As institutions began seriously investigating learning outcomes, they also began discovering that the curriculum as actually delivered, or as behaviorally experienced by students, often varied significantly from its original design. Such discoveries were frequently the real payoff of increasingly popular "portfolio" assessment designs, because examining samples of actual student work often revealed more about what students were taught and assigned than about the amount of learning taking place (Ewell, 1996). Other institutions began specifically using assessment techniques to examine the functioning of particular course sequences, and the ways in which individual courses acted in concert to reinforce identified core skills (Farmer, 1988; Harris and Baggett, 1992). A final theme centered on the student's own contribution to the learning process. Here, assessments of student goals (and how they change), use of time, involvement (Astin, 1992), and "quality of effort" in using available academic resources (Pace, 1984) became paramount.

A second significant evolution was toward a more "naturalistic" approach to assessment. Following classic principles of program evaluation, early assessment practice was deliberately set apart from instructional settings. The use of specially constructed evidence-gathering techniques (prominently including standardized tests) was consciously fostered, both to increase external credibility and because such approaches were thought to increase measurement precision (Ewell, 1989). As a practical matter, however, the use of obtrusive, purpose-built assessments encountered numerous difficulties. Students rarely saw participation as directly beneficial to their studies, and participation rates and levels of motivation remained a problem. At the same time, despite their methodological rigor, faculty often found the results of such exercises to be difficult to apply to their own instructional settings and circumstances. These escalating implementation difficulties, coupled with a growing impetus to render assessment methods more authentic in order to overcome institutional resistance, helped move many institutions toward less obtrusive approaches (Banta, 1988).

A first opportunity, many institutions discovered, was to take better advantage of existing points of contact with students. After systematically inventorying how they collected data from students, colleges and universities often found that many points of contact already existed but that these opportunities were organizationally dispersed and often duplicative in content (Ewell and Lisensky, 1988). This discovery in itself often led to short-term savings in data-collection costs. But at the same time, institutions often learned that existing instruments and opportunities could be more fully exploited. Prominent examples of the application of this logic were entering-student orientation and testing programs that could be expanded to gather additional information about student academic goals or perceived strengths and weaknesses, end-of-course instructor evaluation questionnaires that might contain additional items on student effort and behaviors, and upper-level student writing assessments that could be reoriented to examine disciplinary content in general education.

The ultimate existing point of contact, of course, was the classroom itself. As a result, assessment practitioners began experimenting with ways in which valid, generalizable information about student performance could be gathered using intact curricular and classroom

settings (Warren, 1988). Probably the most straightforward such methods involved resurrecting "old" curricular practices, including such devices as upper-level writing exercises, capstone courses, or senior comprehensive examinations. In addition to being individually scored, the results of such exercises could be aggregated to yield information about how particular groups of students were performing. In applied fields such as health, business, engineering, or the fine and performing arts, such constructions were often natural because complex multitrait performance ratings were already being used to grade individual students; all that remained was to examine patterns of strength and weakness across students to convert them into assessments.

Conceptually similar but more sophisticated were "course-embedded" assessment approaches, in which selected examination questions were carefully constructed to yield data on both the mastery of course content and the development of more general skills such as critical thinking and the ability to make appropriate connections among different disciplines. Using "secondary reading" techniques guided by explicit scoring rubrics, such approaches allowed faculty to use naturally occurring examination settings to collectively examine selected areas of common interest without compromising student motivation or their own instructional goals (Erwin, 1991; Ewell, 1991b). Approaches such as these were often especially suited for investigating more intractable curricular domains such as general education.

Even more attractive to many institutions were approaches based on existing student products. At the most basic level, previously graded samples of individual student work could be aggregated and their common strengths and weaknesses determined. Such approaches were often especially useful in examining course sequences, where an analysis of the specific errors students make in later work can be used directly in the improvement of prerequisite course delivery. More compellingly, portfolios of student work could be compiled, either over time for individual students to document growth or cross-sectionally across different student types to examine patterns of variation (Black, 1993). Assessment approaches based on work samples had many advantages. Because students completed the work for other purposes, there were no obvious motivational problems, and faculty could not quarrel with the authenticity of the data on which assessment conclusions were based. But unless clear guidelines on size and purpose were established, institutions also found the use of portfolios awkward and time-consuming. In many cases, as noted earlier, their utility was as much to document the kinds of assignments students were given as assessing how much learning had taken place.

Whether purposely constructed or based on a secondary reading of existing student products, naturalistic assessment techniques of this kind represented attempts to address the fact that conventional grading approaches yielded little usable data about collective performance. A final and more radical step in this path of evolutionary development, therefore, involved changing grading and classroom pedagogical procedures directly. For many professional or occupational programs, this step was already partially accomplished. The assessment of individual students against clear, observable, criterion-based competency levels was common, and using such measures to assign grades as well as to determine patterns of aggregate performance was natural. In other fields, however, changes of this kind required a major shift of culture. Nevertheless, experiments with alternative grading methods based on primary trait scoring, core scoring, or other mastery-based approaches steadily grew as it became clear that the ends of assessment and pedagogy could be served simultaneously (Walvoord and others, 1995). Coupled with both of these developments was a growing "classroom assessment" movement (Angelo and Cross, 1993) that allowed faculty to gain immediately useful feedback about classroom-level perceptions and behaviors. Though deliberately intended for use "in private" by individual instructors, widespread familiarity with such techniques had by the mid-nineties done much to legitimize assessment for line faculty.

In colleges and universities with relatively long histories of assessment, changes in context and practice gradually changed the role of the process within the institution. On the one hand, they began dropping assessment approaches that simply cost money without informing internal curricular development; seen from the outset as a "tax on the enterprise," such initia-tives were maintained only so long as they were explicitly required for accountability by external bodies. As assessment techniques became increasingly authentic and instructionally embedded, moreover, faculty began more and more to rediscover their original merits as elements of curricular design. Capstone courses, senior seminars, and major-field comprehensive examinations—once a central feature of undergraduate curricula but largely abandoned in the late 1960s and early 1970s—began reemerging in large numbers not just as vehicles for assessment but because they made good pedagogical sense. At the same time, faculty experience with constructing formal assessment devices made them better test-builders in their own classes. Developments such as these had little directly to do with assessment's role as an information system grafted onto delivery; instead they occurred because at such institutions assessment had gradually become an indistinguishable part of curricular and faculty development.

Connecting Assessment Information to Instructional Redirection and Renewal

The argument of the preceding section is clear. On the one hand, the conditions that originally gave rise to a formal assessment movement in higher education some fifteen years ago have changed decisively. The demands now placed on higher education by its environments are not just political but also economic. Cost containment requires restructured approaches to instructional delivery that need information about relative performance in a measure at least equal to that associated exclusively with accountability. At the same time, assessment technique has evolved to the point that it is potentially optimized to provide precisely the kinds of information needed to respond to these conditions. Ironically, to fulfill this new potential, assessment as a distinct and visible activity needs to be increasingly deemphasized. Instead, its principal focus must be placed on making information about academic effectiveness—drawn from whatever source—an integral part of academic planning and pedagogical design.

For the practicing academic administrator, three implications are apparent. First, information drawn from assessment is crucial to designing and operating the kinds of restructured forms of instructional delivery that will be increasingly present in the new millennium; making effective use of them, however, demands new ways of thinking about how evaluative information should be collected and deployed. Second, at the programmatic and institutional levels, assessment activities are becoming increasingly integral to academic planning, both to set priorities among programs and to ensure that program delivery is appropriately aligned with the needs of increasingly salient and vocal external clients. Finally, how assessment as an institutional activity is organized and administered has to change, and some particular implementation syndromes avoided. Only with these conditions met can assessment information and procedure be effectively "recycled" to meet emerging institutional challenges.

Assessment in a Restructured Curriculum

As noted, both new economic realities and the growing possibilities of effective technology-based instructional delivery systems are driving an unprecedented level of curricular experiment. While many of the alternatives posed are simple, others involve a significant deconstruction of the traditional instructional paradigm. Among the most prominent are time-shortened course sequences that place a premium on interconnection, self-paced (and often technology-intensive) courses in which students can proceed at their own pace or test out of requirements if they can demonstrate previously acquired mastery, and asynchronous or hypertext modes of delivery in which students can choose their own paths through complex bodies of material (Twigg, 1995). Within this environment, assessment is increasingly assuming two roles. First, it is needed summatively to help determine the degree to which such alternative delivery formats—presumably less costly—can in fact deliver learning gains equivalent to those associated with more traditional forms. More importantly, because alternative forms are increasingly competency-based, effective as-

sessment mechanisms are needed for them to operate at all.

A first manifestation of assessment's role in this new instructional environment is relatively traditional: helping to clarify goals and to actively guide the development of new curricular designs. The creation of alternative delivery mechanisms, especially those based on technology, by its very nature requires faculty to return to first principles. In an environment in which real-time, sequential coverage of equivalent blocks of content cannot be assumed as a building block, the primary foundation available for guiding curriculum or course design is intended outcomes. Often, however, the intended outcomes for the courses that alternative formats are intended to replace are not clear. Still murkier are those particular elements of current practice that are most effective and therefore ought to be preserved. And completely unknown are the possible adverse and unanticipated consequences for both learning and implementation that the widespread adoption of restructured curricula may entail. In all three areas, assessment techniques can play a relatively traditional evaluative role: helping to determine far more precisely which aspects of current delivery should remain unaltered and which might be effectively supplemented or replaced by more efficient alternatives.

A second major area of application is assessment's potential role in assuring greater connectivity. Consistent with key tenets of general education reform of the mid-eighties, curricular restructuring often rests heavily on the assurance that discrete instructional experiences, whether they be course-based or nontraditional, fit together effectively to yield a coherent whole (Gaff, 1983). At the macro level, this implies the need to examine student learning outcomes that are the joint products of many discrete experiences—not all of which may have contributed equally (or at all) to the final result. Assessment can play a familiar evaluation role in this environment, especially if it is built into naturally occurring capstone experiences that require comprehensive demonstrations of mastery. But it must also transcend this role in being able to further demonstrate the relative contributions of different factors to the joint product in question. Here it may be particularly important to couple comprehensive assessment results with detailed data on student background, experiences, and investments in order to determine which paths and patterns appear to work best. Especially useful in this latter task may be measures of student involvement and commitment (Pace, 1984) and of detailed course-taking behavior (Ratcliff, 1987). Related are overall measures of curricular structure and the incidence of instructional "good practice" that can be used in concert with outcomes measures to help monitor the actual alignment of instructional delivery with intended outcomes and established curricular designs (Ewell, 1996; Ewell and Jones, 1996).

A more direct implication of connectivity is more consistent with emerging quality management themes. Here the principal focus of concern is course sequences and, more particularly, the degree to which students are obtaining required prerequisite skills and are able to deploy these skills effectively in subsequent courses after what may be substantial lapses of time or significant changes in context. Assessment's role in this environment is far more focused, resting primarily on the development of embedded measures of essential prerequisite skills for use as pretests in subsequent courses that require such skills (Farmer, 1988), and/or analyzing the specific types of errors of fact or application that students make in subsequent coursework (Harris and Baggett, 1992). A reciprocal role is designing in-course exercises in basic courses that contextually anchor required skills in the specific kinds of applications that students face later—or, indeed, may already be facing in the courses that they are taking simultaneously. Important areas of contextual application here are written communication and quantitative analysis (most prominently, calculus and statistics). An important caveat in all such cases is that embedded assessments be constructed as much to detect patterns of strength and weakness as to provide feedback to individual students. This implies not only careful attention to design but also the development of active dissemination networks for sharing results among the faculty of associated courses and across disciplines (Baugher, 1992).

A third and final major area of application is more basic: to actively certify or credential student mastery. So long as the predominant paradigm of instructional delivery was the term-based course in which all students progressed simultaneously through a given body of material, the award of credit based primarily on "seat time" remained reasonable. As self-paced or multipath progressional alternatives continue to emerge, however, there is substantial pressure on keeping the traditional time- and content-based Carnegie unit as the principal unit of academic accounting.

Not surprisingly under these circumstances, the leading candidate for its replacement is assessed competence in some form. A simple illustration is the growing salience of advanced placement and credit-by-examination mechanisms in time-shortened degree programs, allowing students to place out of coursework whose basic curricular intention they have already attained (Miller, forthcoming). More sophisticated examples can be seen in technology-intensive self-paced course modules in such prerequisite fields as math and statistics or the introductory sciences, and in professional fields such as health care. Here the application of technology allows complex assessments of mastery to be built directly into the delivery of instruction at multiple points. This means first of all that individual students can be certified as they arrive independently at particular levels of proficiency, providing the asynchronous equivalent of traditional midterm and final examinations. Second of all, this means that all interactions and student responses can be recorded in a computer-based medium of instruction; however, it also means that revealing analyses can be undertaken of the different paths students choose and the specific difficulties that they encounter.

This emerging role of assessment in directly credentialing student achievement is also apparent in interinstitutional settings. Among networks of colleges and universities, assessed competency first provides an efficient potential alternative to increasingly cumbersome course-by-course articulation arrangements in determining the academic standing of entering transfer students. In parallel, the growing use of authentic assessment approaches to certify achievement in secondary schools has led several states to experiment with proficiency-based standards for collegiate admission (Rodriguez 1995).

All three of these implications, if realized, have assessment at the center of instructional design. Rather than being applied to instruction as a periodic means of checking on its effectiveness, assessment technology is engineered directly into the fabric of teaching and learning, to help perform standard academic functions of managing placement and awarding credit. But because the needed assessments can be designed to generate group results as well, the resulting architecture can also provide information useful for continuously monitoring instructional delivery and guiding improvement. Arguably, however, it is no longer assessment, but a regular form of academic management information.

Assessment and Academic Planning

Assessment's role in planning and administration in this emerging environment is tending toward a similar path. Increasingly, information about performance is not separate from other forms but is becoming incorporated into regularly established channels and procedures. One aspect of this development is internal, visible in such familiar processes as curricular oversight and academic program review. A second is external, manifested in the mechanisms institutions use to demonstrate their effectiveness to external clients and publics.

Within the first realm, assessment's role is largely to help inform increasingly salient decisions about program priorities. One term of this equation is, of course, determining which programs to cut or deemphasize. Traditionally, such decisions have been made largely on the grounds of efficiency, reflected in such measures as enrollments, degrees produced, and credits generated. Increasingly, however, this existing array of program performance indicators is being supplemented with available outcomes data that include graduation rates, occupational placement rates, or rates of passage in established licensure or certification procedures. This is in part simply because such data are more plentiful, having been stimulated largely by external reporting requirements. Partly, however, it reflects an emerging consensus that results as well as costs must be counted in determining overall productivity. Internal academic program review mechanisms show similar trends. Like accreditation self-studies, most institutional program review guidelines have always included questions about quality, but these were generally ad-

dressed in terms of resources rather than results. Again as a result of a decade of external mandates (both from states and from professional accreditation bodies), more and more institutions are including formal assessment requirements in such processes (Barak, 1991).

The increasing use of performance indicators as an integral part of priority setting begs a number of important questions, however. First, outcomes measures are by nature less precise than those reflecting resources and investments. This means that major abuses can occur if observed differences in program performances are not substantial. Following TQM principles of statistical quality control, this problem has led a number of institutions to establish clear statistical benchmarks to flag aberrant outcomes. Similarly, most institutions using such procedures rely on trend data of at least three years to help control for unusual circumstances or for naturally occurring statistical variation. More significantly, determining that the performance of a given program is low on an assessment measure of any kind does not in itself determine an investment decision. As with more traditional measures of efficiency, a prior determination must also be made about the relevance of the program to the institution's overall mission and goals to determine if the proper response to underperformance is additional investment, disinvestment, or phaseout (Keller, 1983).

Assessment also has a growing role to play in future program planning as new instructional delivery modes are contemplated and as institutions attempt to respond to changing client needs. Many, for example, are facing significant decisions about the acquisition of new technology with little real information about the instructional payoffs that might result from what are often significant up-front investments. As noted earlier, systematic information about the relative performance of different modes of instructional delivery for different kinds of students can be invaluable in making such decisions. At the same time, the specific needs of such key clientele groups as employers are both increasingly salient and shifting rapidly. As a result, program-level assessments that regularly monitor the performance of former students in the workplace and, where appropriate, that involve employers and professionals directly in the institution's own assessment procedures are particularly relevant.

Turning to assessment's role in external communication, several additional dimensions are apparent. Greater reporting on performance, of course, is now integral to accountability for both public and private institutions. At the same time, this function now encompasses more than just accountability because it may directly influence institutional revenue through tuition and service. In turn, the particular messages sent need to reflect internal academic planning, as new market conditions require institutions to actually follow through on promises made. In this environment, two metaphors for external communication are relevant and depend heavily on the deployment of information drawn from assessment. One, directed specifically at potential funders, is "return on investment," which highlights specific ways in which the institution's resources are deployed in order to gain particular valued returns. Its model is a corporate stockholder's report, containing on the one hand a "balance sheet" that presents the condition of the institution's core assets (faculty, resources, facilities, programs, etc.) as well as any investments made to renew and develop these critical resources, and on the other hand a "profit and loss statement" that notes the specific expenditures made and the kinds of aggregate outcomes resulting from these expenditures. Documents prepared on these lines are far more focused on results than are traditional institutional annual reports; they have already been promulgated effectively by several types of institutions.

A second relevant metaphor for guiding external communication is based explicitly on "customer service." Here the intended audience is individual students and their parents, who increasingly face an explicit and difficult set of choices. Modeled specifically on popular consumer-rating guides, reports of this kind seek to answer two quite different student-centered questions. One, an outcomes question, concerns the specific types of skills, jobs, and results that can be reliably associated with attendance. The second is an experience question, addressing the particular kinds of services and educational encounters, such as contact with faculty, small classes, appropriate advising, and responsive administrative procedures, that students can reliably expect to receive. Both types of reporting, moreover, require not only aggregate reporting but also the ability to break down assessment results for different kinds of potential students (Education Commission of the States, 1995).

In short, emerging market conditions for most colleges and universities are rapidly erasing boundaries between internal and external concerns. Academic planning requires that institutions know far more about what specific constituencies want in terms of educational products and experiences. At the same time, it requires that programs be internally aligned to actually deliver these outcomes and services once they are advertised as available. Information about results drawn from regularly established sources is increasingly requisite for discharging both functions.

Administering Assessment: Some Syndromes to Avoid

A final area of concern in this new operating environment is assessment's organization and administration. Accountability-centered assessment required clear central direction but often remained marginal to decision making. Assessment in a restructured environment, in contrast, must be integral to (and in many ways indistinguishable from) regular processes of communication and review. In particular, academic administrators should avoid a number of identifiable implementation syndromes that have repeatedly plagued institutions in the past.

The first syndrome is administrative isolation, which tends to occur particularly when professional assessment offices are created without explicit roles beyond external reporting. On the one hand, this means that those responsible for gathering and interpreting such information need to be deliberately included in discussions about academic direction setting and investment, much as budget directors and institutional researchers also should be. On the other hand, it means ensuring that the assessment function is built into the institution's regular academic planning process through appropriate committees or review bodies with an ongoing assignment. All too often, for example, the faculty-staff committees responsible for assessment see their job only as establishing a program, not developing and communicating its implications on an ongoing basis.

A second common syndrome is attempting to do too much assessment—a situation ironically caused in part by the compliance mentality associated with external mandates. If assessment is seen principally as a set of requirements to be met rather than findings to be used, it is natural to assume that all such responses are equivalent. Assessment in a restructured environment, in contrast, demands that major investments be made only in assessing areas of ongoing central importance or where specific information is needed to inform a particular decision. Consistent with this need, the best practice is increasingly to operate assessment on two levels (investing some resources in the development of a consistent base of information intended for overall monitoring of program delivery, usually in the form of indicators) and reserving remaining resources for periodic investigations in depth that are related to specific investment decisions.

A third difficulty is excessive methodological purity: attempting to impose on decision-related information the kinds of measurement criteria generally reserved for publishable research. Because assessment practitioners are often trained professionally as social scientists, standards based on statistical significance or standard tests of validity and reliability are automatically imposed in the absence of other criteria. But to be useful in a decision context, different benchmarks are required. Specifically needed instead are criteria drawn from the decision sciences that test the sensitivity of decisions to variations in obtained results (Ackoff, 1962). If sufficiently robust, in such contexts, even imprecise results can be of use.

A related fourth difficulty is excessive rigidity in planning and carrying out assessment activities. Again, this is partly a carryover of excessive research orientation. The classic evaluation methodologies upon which early assessment approaches were based emphasized established principles of scientific research, including clear hypotheses and carefully specified quasi-experimental designs. By their very nature, these required isolation from the mainstream of academic activity. Current good practice, in contrast, requires embedding multiple assessment opportunities in existing delivery and constantly reformulating goals

and hypotheses based on the emerging data. Rather than summative testing of effectiveness against fixed objectives, the appropriate metaphor is one of continuously monitoring and adjusting both targets and delivery.

A final common problem is missed opportunities for discussing assessment results. Few institutions currently possess ready-made opportunities to collectively interpret what is happening in their curricula. Rather than one-way reporting, assessment is at its best when its results provide a basis for collective discussions of this kind, and such opportunities must be deliberately created. Retreats or workshops centered on specific, collectively recognized problems of importance to the community (such as first-year retention of minority students, for example) or sessions that regularly examine the institution's progress in attaining collectively agreed-upon plans can be of particular value in this regard.

Into the Future

Future developments in assessment are likely to continue the many trends noted in this chapter. The political context for higher education and its constrained fiscal consequences promise to continue indefinitely. Accountability based on performance—both to funding authorities and to paying customers who will likely bear an increasing share of the financial burden of attendance—is well established and shows no signs of abatement. Partly because of these forces, and partly because of expanding technological possibilities, restructuring will also continue to accelerate whether institutions choose to engage in it as a conscious activity or not. Where they do, assessment continues to be a key factor in determining the most fruitful paths to take. Where they do not, assessment becomes increasingly salient anyway, as a vital and unavoidable building block for establishing and operating alternative modes of instructional delivery.

Meanwhile, assessment practice continues to evolve toward greater authenticity, further erasing remaining boundaries between outcomes data and other forms of academic management information. At the same time, assessment techniques themselves increasingly reflect the impact of new technologies. Computer-based and computer-adaptive testing approaches that allow both shortened testing time and dispersed, time-independent assessment administration eliminate many of the drawbacks associated with large-scale summative examinations. More importantly, new instructional media increasingly allow designed assessments to be engineered directly into instructional material that can provide both individual feedback and group-level results. And as these trends continue, distinctions between assessment and grading continue to erode.

For academic administrators, these developments promise both better information about effectiveness and increased demands to manage complexity. Thankfully, if past trends continue, these two will occur in equal measure.

Further Reading

Readers interested in obtaining a more in-depth treatment of assessment policy and the continuing development of performance indicators at the state level are referred especially to Ruppert (1994), Ewell and Jones (1993, 1994), Ewell (1993a), and Gaither (1995). Comprehensive discussions of the use of performance indicators at the institutional and state levels are in Gaither, Nedwick, and Neal (1995) and Ewell and Jones (1996). For an excellent example of the development and impact of assessment programs on a wide variety of college campuses, see Banta and Associates (1993), as well as Banta, Lund, Black, and Oblander (1996). After almost five years, the most comprehensive current reviews of assessment practice at the collegiate level remain Erwin (1991) and Ewell (1991b). Finally, a good ongoing source of information is the bimonthly newsletter *Assessment Update*, published by Jossey-Bass.

References

Ackoff, R. L. (with Gupta, S. K., and Minas, J. S.). *Scientific Method: Optimizing Applied Research Decisions.* New York: Wiley, 1962.

Angelo, T. A., and Cross, K. P. *Classroom Assessment Techniques: A Handbook for College Teachers.* San Francisco: Jossey-Bass, 1993.

Association of American Colleges. *Integrity in the College Curriculum: A Report to the Academic Community.* Washington, D.C.: Association of American Colleges, 1985.

Astin, A. W. *Assessment for Excellence: The Philosophy and Practice of Assessment and Evaluation in Higher Education.* New York: ACE/Macmillan, 1991.

Astin, A. W. *What Matters in College?: Four Critical Years Revisited.* San Francisco: Jossey-Bass, 1992.

Banta, T. W. (ed.). *Implementing Outcomes Assessment: Promise and Perils.* New Directions for Institutional Research, no. 59. San Francisco: Jossey-Bass, 1988.

Banta, T. W., Lund, J. P., Black, K. E., and Oblander, F. W. *Assessment in Practice: Putting Principles to Work on College Campuses.* San Francisco: Jossey-Bass, 1996.

Banta, T. W., and Associates. *Making a Difference: Outcomes of a Decade of Assessment in Higher Education.* San Francisco: Jossey-Bass, 1993.

Barak, R. J. "Assessment: A Train on Its Own Track or a Major Element of a Supertrain?" In *Assessment Update*, 1991, 3(4), 7–8.

Baugher, K. *Learn: Student Quality Team Manual.* Birmingham, Ala.: Samford University, 1992.

Black, L. C. "Portfolio Assessment." In T. W. Banta (ed.), *Making a Difference: Outcomes of a Decade of Assessment in Higher Education.* San Francisco: Jossey-Bass, 1993.

Education Commissions of the States. *Making Quality Count in Undergraduate Education.* Denver: Education Commission of the States, 1995.

El-Khawas, E. *Campus Trends 1995.* Washington, D.C.: American Council on Education, 1995.

Erwin, T. D. *Assessing Student Learning and Development.* San Francisco: Jossey-Bass, 1991.

Ewell, P. T. "Hearts and Minds: Some Reflections on the Ideologies of Assessment." In *Three Presentations from the Fourth National Conference on Assessment in Higher Education.* Washington, D.C.: American Association of Higher Education, 1989.

Ewell, P. T. "Assessment and Public Accountability: Back to the Future." *Change*, 1991a, 23(6), 12–17.

Ewell, P. T. "To Capture the Ineffable: New Forms of Assessment in Higher Education." In G. Grant (ed.), *Review of Research in Education*, 17. Washington, D.C.: American Educational Research Association, 1991b.

Ewell, P. T. "The Role of States and Accreditors in Shaping Assessment Practice." In T. W. Banta and Associates, *Making a Difference: Outcomes of a Decade of Assessment in Higher Education.* San Francisco: Jossey-Bass, 1993a.

Ewell, P. T. "Total Quality and Academic Practice: The Idea We've Been Waiting for?" *Change*, 1993b, 25(3), 49–55.

Ewell, P. T. "Developing Statewide Performance Indicators for Higher Education: Policy Themes and Variations." In S. Ruppert (ed.), *Charting Higher Education Accountability: A Sourcebook on State-Level Performance Indicators.* Denver: Education Commission of the States, 1994.

Ewell, P. T. "Indicators of Curricular Quality Within and Across Institutions." In J. W. Gaff and J. I.

Ratcliff (eds.), *Handbook of the Undergraduate Curriculum.* San Francisco: Jossey-Bass, 1996.

Ewell, P. T., Finney, J. T., and Lenth, C. "Filling in the Mosaic: The Emerging Pattern of State-Based Assessment." *AAHE Bulletin,* 1990, 1, 3–5.

Ewell, P. T., and Jones, D. P. *The Effect of State Policy on Undergraduate Education.* Denver: Education Commission of the States, 1993.

Ewell, P. T., and Jones, D. P. "Pointing the Way: Indicators as Policy Tools in Higher Education." In S. Ruppert (ed.), *Charting Higher Education Accountability: A Sourcebook on State-Level Performance Indicators.* Denver: Education Commission of the States, 1994.

Ewell, P. T., and Jones, D. P. *Indicators of "Good Practice" in Undergraduate Education: A Handbook for Development and Implementation.* Boulder, Colo.: National Center for Higher Education Management Systems (NCHEMS), 1996.

Ewell, P. T., and Lisensky, R. P. *Assessing Institutional Effectiveness: Redirecting the Self-Study Process.* Washington, D.C.: Consortium for the Advancement of Private Higher Education, 1988.

Farmer, D. W. *Enhancing Student Learning: Emphasizing Essential Competencies in Academic Programs.* Wilkes-Barre, Pa.: Kings College, 1988.

Gaff, J. *General Education Today: A Critical Analysis of Controversies, Practices, and Reforms.* San Francisco: Jossey-Bass, 1983.

Gaither, G. H. (ed.). *Assessing Performance in an Age of Accountability: Case Studies.* New Directions for Higher Education, no. 91. San Francisco: Jossey-Bass, 1995.

Gaither, G. H., Nedwick, B., and Neal, J. *Measuring Up: The Promises and Pitfalls of Performance Indicators in Higher Education.* ASHE-ERIC Higher Education Reports. Washington, D.C.: ASHE-ERIC Clearinghouse/the George Washington University, 1995.

Harris, J. W., and Baggett, J. M. (eds.). *Quality Quest in the Academic Process.* Birmingham, Ala.: Samford University, 1992.

Hines, F. R. *State Higher Education Appropriations 1993–94.* Denver: State Higher Education Executive Officers (SHEEO), 1994.

Katchadourian, H. A., and Boli, J. *Careerism and Intellectualism Among College Students.* San Francisco: Jossey-Bass, 1985.

Kellams, S. A. *University of Virginia Longitudinal Study of Undergraduate Education.* Charlottesville, Va.: Office of the Provost, University of Virginia, 1989.

Keller, G. *Academic Strategy: The Management Revolution in American Higher Education.* Baltimore, Md.: Johns Hopkins University Press, 1983.

McGuinness, A. C., Jr. *A Framework for Evaluating State Policy Roles in Improving Undergraduate Education.* Denver: Education Commission of the States, 1994.

McGuinness, A. C., Jr., and Ewell, P. T. "Improving Productivity and Quality in Higher Education." *AGB Priorities,* 1994, 2.

Miller, M. A. (ed.). *Restructuring Higher Education:*

Lessons from a State. New York: ACE Macmillan, forthcoming.

National Governors' Association. *Time for Results: The Governors' 1991 Report on Education.* Washington, D.C.: National Governors' Association, 1986.

National Institute of Education. *Involvement in Learning: Realizing the Potential of American Higher Education.* Report of the Study Group on the Conditions of Excellence in American Higher Education. Washington, D.C.: GPO, 1984.

Pace, C. R. *Measuring the Quality of Student Experiences: An Account of the Development and Use of the College Student Experiences Questionnaire.* Los Angeles: Higher Education Research Institute, University of California, Los Angeles, 1984.

Ratcliff, J. L. *The Effect of Differential Coursework Patterns on General Learned Abilities of College Students: Application of the Model to an Historical Database of Student Transcripts. (Task 3 Report).* U.S. Department of Education, Office of Institutional Research and Improvement, Contract No. OERI-R-86-0016. Ames: Iowa State University, College of Education, 1987.

Resmer, M., Mingle, J. R., and Oblinger, D. G. *Computers for All Students: A Strategy for Universal Access to Informational Resources.* Denver: State Higher Education Executive Officers (SHEEO), 1995.

Rodriguez, E. M. *College Admission Requirements: A New Role for States.* Denver: State Higher Education Executive Officers (SHEEO), 1995.

Ruppert, S. S. *Charting Higher Education Accountability: A Sourcebook on State-Level Performance Indicators.* Denver: Education Commission of the States, 1994.

Seymour, D. T. *On Q: Causing Quality in Higher Education.* New York: ACE/Macmillan, 1991.

Sherr, L. A., and Teeter, D. J. (eds.). *Total Quality Management in Higher Education.* New Directions for Institutional Research, no. 71. San Francisco: Jossey-Bass, 1991.

Stanford Forum on Higher Education Futures. *Leveraged Learning: Technology's Role in Restructuring Higher Education.* Proceedings of the Technology and Restructuring Roundtable. Stanford, Calif.: Stanford Forum on Higher Education Futures, 1995.

Twigg, C. A. *The Need for a National Learning Infrastructure.* Boulder, Colo.: EDUCOM, 1995.

Walvoord, B. E., Anderson, V. J., Breihan, J. R., McCarthy, L. P., Robison, S. M., and Sherman, A. K. "Making Graded Tests and Assignments Serve Contemporary Needs for Assessment." In T. W. Banta, J. P. Lund, K. E. Black, and F. W. Oberlander (eds.), *Assessment in Practice.* San Francisco: Jossey-Bass, 1995.

Warren, J. "Cognitive Measures in Assessing Learning." In T. W. Banta (ed.), *Implementing Outcomes Assessment: Promise and Perils.* New Directions for Institutional Research, no. 59. San Francisco: Jossey-Bass, 1988.

Zemsky, R., Massy, W. F., and Oedel, P. "On Reversing the Ratchet." *Change,* 1993, 25(3), 56–62.

Assessment in Accreditation:
Has It Made a Difference?

James T. Rogers

It was December 10, 1984, when the struggle and controversy finally ended. Little did the room full of presidents and deans at the Marriott Hotel in New Orleans realize that their decision that day would fundamentally change the way our commission evaluates and accredits institutions. After months of discussion, hundred of hours of committee meetings, rejection by the membership, and many concessions on all sides, the Commission on Colleges of the Southern Association of Colleges and Schools had finally approved a standard on assessment. So controversial and even intimidating was the "A word" that new terminology had to be found to give a broader and more acceptable definition to the concept. That new term was *institutional effectiveness*. And today, more than a decade later, that term seems to have found its way into the general lexicon of assessment terminology as well as into the standards and verbiage of many of our accreditation colleagues.

The decision made that December day by our commission was truly a leap of faith into a new era in accreditation—a leap that would extend the concept of quality beyond the traditional resource-and-process expectations into a new and more logical realm. What our membership accomplished by approving a new requirement for institutional effectiveness was to raise the benchmark of acceptable performance. Our institutions agreed to move beyond the traditional resource-and-process method of determining quality to a new dimension by asking a heretofore unasked and thus unanswered question: "How effectively are you using your institutional resources and processes, and how can this determination of effectiveness result in positive change and improvement in the institution?"

After a decade of applying this new concept to the review of our institutions, has it made a difference, and what have we learned about its impact on quality improvement? Someone once said that there's nothing more difficult to bring to fruition than a new idea. I would be less than candid if I implied that those first few years resulted in unquestioned support for this new concept. But as institutions began to realize that the new requirement was a natural extension of the old resource-and-process requirement and would actually result in activities that could fundamentally change and improve their operations, the acceptance level began to increase.

A decade of experience with our emphasis on institutional effectiveness has not eliminated all skeptics, but the number of believers increases steadily each year. Not only has a decade of experience brought our institutions to new level of appreciation for this concept, but it has done so during a period when the public's demand for more accountability has been increasing exponentially.

Without question, the concept of institutional effectiveness, with its emphasis on planning, evaluation, and use of results, has made a profound difference in many, if not most, of our institutions. There continue to be problem areas. In my opinion, the three most troublesome areas that continue to present challenges are the following:

"Assessment in Accreditation: Has It Made a Difference?" by James T. Rogers, reprinted from *Assessment Update: Progress, Trends, and Practices in Higher Education*, Vol. 9, No. 4, July/August 1997, Jossey-Bass Publishers, Inc.

First, there is the need for institutions to "close the loop." Too many of our institutions fail to realize that change and improvement are the ultimate objectives of assessment. Results of evaluations need to be applied in ways that improve student learning, institutional efficiency, and services and operations. Our review committees have increased their expectations of institutions in this regard, but closing the loop continues to present problems for some of our institutions.

Second, there is the need for institutions to view this process as ongoing. Our expectation is that all institutions will undergo reaffirmation of accreditation every ten years. Instead of viewing evaluation and improvement as continuing on a monthly or annual basis throughout this ten-year period, some institutions engage in the process solely to satisfy the accreditation team, only to drift back into the old mode of operation once the institution has been reaffirmed. As the Baldrige Award stresses, improvement is a continuing process, but some of our institutions have yet to learn this.

Third, there is the need for institutions to engage in evaluation in all areas of their operations. When the assessment movement began in our region, there was a mistaken notion that the concept applied only to academic areas. In order to correct this perception, our commission revised the criteria in 1995 to clarify our position on this matter and underscore that assessment applies equally to administrative and academic areas. Evaluation, regardless of the area, is fundamental to the process of institutional improvement.

Has our process of evaluating institutional effectiveness made a difference? Without question. Has it made our institutions more aware of the need for continuous review and improvement? Without question. Has it prepared our institutions to respond to increased demands from the public for greater accountability? Without question. Can our institutions do a better job of evaluating and planning? Without question. As we reflect on the years since 1984, our commission can take pride in its commitment to institutional improvement through accreditation and its emphasis on institutional effectiveness. In the future, increased demands on declining resources will only heighten the public's demand for greater efficiency and accountability. I believe that through our emphasis on institutional effectiveness our institutions will be prepared for the challenge.

James T. Rogers is executive director of the Commission on Colleges of the Southern Association of Colleges and Schools, Decatur, Georgia.

CHAPTER 14

FEDERAL, STATE AND COMMUNITY RELATIONS

ASSOCIATE EDITORS: HARLAND G. BLOLAND
AND CAROLYN GRISWOLD

Although much of the study of higher education concentrates on the internal aspects of higher education organizations, work in the past several decades has increasingly emphasized the importance of the external environment on the life of institutions. In organizational analysis, for example, theoretical frameworks such as resource dependence, population ecology, and institutionalism have had considerable influence on the way we think about decision making, organizational purpose, and change.

A topic of ongoing significance is the relationship between higher education institutions and government, particularly at the federal and state levels. Historically, governments have been major regulators of and resource providers for higher education. The higher education enterprise has responded by seeking to reduce regulations and increase resources through the development of lobbying activities designed to maintain continuing influence on Federal and state decisions. However, only in the past four decades have higher education scholars directed their attention to the subject of the relationship of government to higher education.

Michael Parsons discusses the policy process at the federal level with a focus on the Higher Education Act of 1965 and its subsequent modifications. He presents a clear and lucid review of the various schemes that higher education scholars have used to define policy arenas and finds them static and deficient. He turns to the political science interest group literature to introduce a more dynamic definition of the higher education policy arena in terms of four characteristics with criteria that can be used to place subgovernments along a continuum from impermeable "iron triangles" to open issue networks. The criterion characteristics are internal complexity, functional autonomy, unity within type of participant, and cooperation and conflict. His aim is to provide a description that allows for change and flexibility without losing the structure and focus of his definition.

His definition is a prelude to his use of the concept, "community" as the foundation for discussing the relationships involved in the higher education policy arena. He provides a coherent description of the policy arena, and in the process, captures the indeterminacy, dynamism and activity of the higher education community at the federal level. His notion of community is a reflection of John Dewey's ideas concerning the collective action generated communication community. Parsons sees the higher education policy arena as a community developed out of collective action.

Aims C. McGuinness, Jr. concentrates on government-higher education relations at the state level, with comments on federal-higher education relations. He provides a capsule history of the rise of state dominance in higher education policy in the 1980s and describes the character of that relationship with its increased prominence of governors, emphasis upon reform in undergraduate education, and economic development. McGuinness also describes the changes that took place at the beginning of the nineties with the onset of widespread fiscal problems at the state level, the

Harland G. Bloland is Professor Emeritus, University of Miami. Carolyn Griswold teaches in the School of Education at New York University. (cg3@is4.nyu.edu)

increased focus on elementary and secondary schools, and the growing perception among government officials and the public that higher education was not deeply involved in helping to solve such major social problems as quality improvement and reduction of crime and violence.

McGuinness introduces seven trends that he views as crucial in influencing the nature of higher education relations in the last part of the 1990s. 1. The need for student access to higher education will be greater than the resources needed to satisfy the demand. 2. Commitment to universal access will recede with a movement of resources from traditional undergraduate education to technical and training education. 3. The 1980s issue of quality improvement continues into the 1990a, but with more aggressive demands from the states and federal government for demonstrated improvement. Just what quality means remains a question. 4. Government funding will be reduced and government regulation will increase. 5. Public research universities will become more globalized as they increase their funding from such non-state sources such as multinational corporations and the federal government. Increased demands for more university effort to respond to the economic and social needs of the state will occur even as institutions of higher education are modeling themselves on the research university model which impels faculty toward research, publication, and graduate education, and away from undergraduate education. 6. Technology and distance education are transforming higher education and placing great stress on governance and accountability standards. 7. Multi-campus state systems are becoming obsolete, as the higher education environment rapidly changes. McGuinness calls for informed public debate on the issues raised by these trends, but he fears that they will not attract sufficient attention from the public and government officials.

Our attention is directed by Howard Ray Rowland to an important but currently neglected aspect of higher education and community, the connection of colleges and universities to their local communities. The "Town-Gown,' relationship is historically one of both friendly, fruitful cooperation and rancor and conflict. Rowland describes just how important community relations are to institutions of higher education and how many areas there are that do cause friction—from student misbehavior and noise, to threatening real estate values, to increased traffic congestion, to not paying enough local taxes or buying enough supplies locally, or providing enough local employment, to bringing to bear too much influence in too many areas of town life. At the same time, the local community takes pride in having a university or college which is viewed as a clean, stable industry which does provide employment and is a major customer for town businesses. The economic impact of institutions of higher education is recognized. Rowland points out that there is considerable room for misunderstanding, and the two parties quite often have incompatible expectations.

Colleges and universities can reduce the inevitable strains by thoughtfully participating in community life, providing services where they can be useful. Community colleges and urban universities have led the way in offering aid in dealing with economic and technological problems in cities. However, this is not an easy task, since cities and universities have different goals, and there are limits to what can be offered. Nevertheless, it is clear that colleges and universities need to work to improve the quality of life of their local environments, while not neglecting their own purposes and responsibilities to students, parents, faculty, and trustees.

For further reading (for bibliographic details see the Suggested Supplementary Readings below) on government-higher education relations at the federal level, Constance Cook provides an excellent, detailed examination of policy making during a specific period of time in the 1990s. Harland G. Bloland looks at the higher education policy area in the 1970s and 1980s. A useful overview of the influence of the federal government on higher education is provided by Gladieux, Hauptman, and Knapp. In their monograph, Lawrence Gladieux and Jacqueline King offer valuable perspectives for campus practitioners who must react to changes in federal policies. An historical look at early federal influence is reviewed in Clark Kerr's "Expanding Access and Changing Missions: The Federal Role in U.S. Higher Education." An insider's look at political decision-making affecting the federal role in education is vividly drawn in Terrell Bell's work.

Changing state-higher education relations are illuminated in the shifts in governance patterns at the state level. A concise history of restructuring and a survey of the determinants of restructuring is to be found in the work of Lawrence R. Marcus , while Edward R. Hines has written a useful survey of state-higher education relations.

A number of excellent articles in Leonard Goodall's *When Colleges Lobby States: The Higher Education/State Government Connection* provide a broad look at the political side of state college relationships. In Steven Gold's work, important lessons about the interplay of state fiscal conditions and higher education finances are discussed. And the importance of the financial role of governments to institutions and students is highlighted in the work of Michael McPherson and Morton Schapiro.

The challenges of college and university relations with local communities require that institutions reach out to their local constituents. Bernadine Dorich indicates some of the ways that colleges can serve their communities in "Extending the Campus." Of special concern are the relations between universities and colleges and the city. In three case studies, Michela Reichman reports on urban universities and their neighborhoods. Two books of readings (see the collections of Murphy and of Mitchell) on higher education-city relations cover a wide variety of issues and topics, including valuable historical studies, informative case histories, and strategies for reducing conflict.

Suggested Supplementary Readings

Bell, Terrell, *The Thirteenth Man: A Reagan Cabinet Memoir.* New York: The Free Press, 1988.

Bloland, Harland G., *Associations in Action*, ASHE-ERIC Higher Education Report No. 2. Washington, D.C.: ASHE, 1985.

Cook, Constance E., *Lobbying for Higher Education.* Nashville: Vanderbilt University Press, 1998.

Dewey, John, *Democracy and Education.* New York: Macmillan, 1916.

Dorich, Bernadine, "Extending the Campus," in H. R. Rowland (ed.), *Effective Community Relations: New Directions for Institutional Advancement.* No. 10. San Francisco: Jossey-Bass, 1980, 45–60.

Durkheim, Emile, *The Division of Labor in Society.* Glencoe, Ill.: Free Press, (1893), 1960.

Etzioni, Amitai, *The Spirit of Community.* New York: Crown Publishers, 1993.

Gill, Judit I. & Laura Saunders (eds.), *Developing Effective Policy Analysis in Higher Education.* San Francisco: Jossey-Bass, 1992.

Gladieux, Lawrence E., Arthur M. Hauptman, and Laura Greene Knapp, "The Federal Government and Higher Education," in Philip G. Altbach, Robert O. Berdahl, and Patricia J. Gumport, eds. *Higher Education in American Society.* Third Edition. Amherst, NY: Prometheus Books, 1994.

Gladieux, Lawrence and Jacqueline King, *Challenge and Change in the Federal Role, New Directions for Institutional Research,* #85, 1995, 21–31.

Gold, Steven, *The Fiscal Crisis of the States: Lessons for the Future.* Washington, DC: The Georgetown University Press, 1995.

Goodall, Leonard E. (ed.), *When Colleges Lobby States: The Higher Education/State Government Connection.* Washington, DC: American Association of State Colleges and Universities, 1987.

Hines, Edward R., *Higher Education and State Governments.* ASHE-ERIC Higher Education Report No. 5. Washington, D.C.: ASHE, 1988.

Kerr, Clark, "Expanding Access and Changing Missions: The Federal Role in U.S. Higher Education," *Educational Record,* 1994, 75, 4, 27–31.

Lawrence R. Marcus, "Restructuring State Higher Education Governance Patterns," in *The Review of Higher Education,* Summer, 1997, 20, #4 (399–418).

McPherson, Michael and Morton Schapiro, *Keeping College Affordable: Government and Educational Opportunity.* Washington, DC: The Brookings Institution, 1991.

Mitchell, H. E. (ed.), *The University in the Urban Crisis.* New York: Behavioral Publications, 1974.

Murphy, Thomas P. (ed.), *Universities in the Urban Crisis.* New York: Dunellen, 1975.

Reichman, Michela, "Resolving Campus-Community Conflicts," in H. R. Rowland (ed.) *Effective Community Relations: New Directions for Institutional Advancement,* No. 10. San Francisco: Jossey-Bass, 1980, 79–92.

Tierney, William G. and Estela M. Bensimon, *Promotion and Tenure.* Albany: State University of New York Press, 1996, 1–20.

The Higher Education Policy Arena

MICHAEL D. PARSONS

Political scientists, sociologists, and other students of power have traditionally sought to make explicit the implicit aspects of policy arenas to give the arenas some tangible form or shape with clearly defined boundaries forming the parameters for research. It is this approach that introduced the use of geometric shapes to describe and define policy arenas with the "iron triangle" being perhaps the most famous. While this is a popular approach, the results are less than satisfying. The geometric shapes used to define policy arenas are abstract, static forms that lose meaning as policy arena characteristics shift and change. The authentic, contingent relationships that exist between policy actors are lost when the rich, contextual nature of policy making is compressed into a flat, objective shape.

Some higher education policy analysts have sought to escape the problems associated with the use of geometric shapes by taking an approach that can be described as mapping. Mapping consists of identifying the main policy actors, their views, and their relationship to one another with the final result being a map or description of the policy arena at a given point in time. This offers some advantage over geometric shapes in that a greater sense of dynamism is captured, but one is still left with a static description that is unresponsive to change. Not only is the description static, but the addition or departure of key policy actors renders it inaccurate as a map of the policy arena. Finally, the approach offers no framework for analysis that can be used to explain changes in the policy arena or to explain policy decisions.

The purpose of this chapter is to construct a new approach to defining and describing the social relations that are policy arenas. The intent is to create an approach that captures the dynamic, contingent nature of the higher education policy arena while maintaining the flexibility to adjust to changes in the arena. In addition, the approach will serve as a framework for analysis and explanation. The approach is a definition that relies not on geometric shapes or static maps but on the use of subgovernment characteristics and the concept of community. The concept of community, first introduced in chapter 1, will be developed here and supported by the next two chapters.

The focus of this chapter is the higher education policy arena that has formed around HEA. There are other important higher education policy arenas (e.g., see), but none of the other arenas involve such a large number and diversity of policy actors, nor do other arenas compare in size, range of purpose, or economic and social impact. HEA authorized student aid programs "reached six million students (almost half of all postsecondary students), virtually every postsecondary institution in the country, agencies of every state, and thousands of lenders" (White, 1993, p. 73). Altogether, HEA contains twelve titles authorizing more than seventy programs (Manin, 1993). One program, the GSL, has created a multibillion dollar industry where none had existed. The "approximately $21.5 billion in loans, grants, and work opportunities to students" (Wolanin, 1993, p. 90) provided by HEA make this policy arena the most important higher education policy arena and a significant federal domestic policy arena.

"The Higher Education Policy Arena," by Michael D. Parsons, reprinted from *Power and Politics: Federal Higher Education Policymaking in the 1990s*, 1997, State University of New York Press.

The first part of the chapter reviews some early definitions of the higher education policy arena. These are important because of their continuing influence on contemporary scholars and as a background to the approach offered in this chapter. The next section draws on concepts from the subgovernment literature to describe the higher education policy arena in terms of criterion characteristics. While any description is open to criticism for being static, the claim made for this description is that it can be easily adjusted without abandoning or destroying the descriptive framework. The framework is not only responsive to change but can be used to explain change. The last section calls on the concept of community to define the social relations of the higher education policy arena. This may cause some problem for those who like their policy arenas defined with greater mathematical precision but it is community, not geometry, that best defines the social relations that form the higher education policy arena.

Early Definitions

The first attempt to comprehensively define the higher education policy arena might well be Wolanin and Gladieux's (1975) "The Political Culture of a Policy Arena: Higher Education." The authors define the higher education policy arena as being "characterized by substantive coherence, charter legislation, executive, congressional, and lobbying institutions, and a political culture" (p. 179). The substance of the arena is provided by the Higher Education Act (HEA). While the substance is clear, the substantive coherence is not. This may be attributable to the fact that federal programs and decision-making centers are decentralized. HEA is the charter legislation for the policy arena. Finally, the political culture rests on the assumptions of "the primacy of the states, the instrumental view of higher education, the nondiscrimination between public and private higher education, the fragmentation of federal higher education policy, and the relatively low visibility of higher education in federal policy" (Wolanin & Gladieux, 1975, p. 205). For the most part, Wolanin and Gladieux are concerned with defining the higher education policy arena so that it can serve as the background

for their larger discussion of political culture. Their definition and description of the political culture covers the contested principles identified in chapter 2 but they present the principles as a unified culture that defines the policy arena. This tends to gloss over the dynamic tensions and conflicts that exist within the arena and that are always available for renewed contest.

While Wolanin and Gladieux may have been the first to offer a description of the higher education policy arena, their work was soon joined by King (1975), Murray (1976), and Finn (1980). The work of these three authors has had a profound effect on subsequent descriptions of the higher education policy arena and continues to influence scholars today. Lauriston R. King's (1975) classification of higher education associations is still used by some scholars as a framework for organizing research on the higher education policy arena. Michael A. Murray's (1976) work builds on King's classification scheme and is cited by some authors as a successful effort to bring the policy arena into sharper focus and detail. Finally, Chester E. Finn's (1980) critique of the education policy arena provides an alternative view that is used even by scholars who disagree with and dislike Finn's analysis.

King (1975) was the first researcher to classify and describe the structure of the Washington higher education associations. He sorted the associations into three categories: major associations, special interest or satellite associations, and a catchall category of individual offices and small associations. The major associations consisted of the Association of American Colleges (AAC), American Association of Community and Junior Colleges (AACJC), American Council on Education (ACE), American Association of State Colleges and Universities (AASCU), Association of American Universities (AAU), and National Association of State and University Land-Grant Colleges (NASULGC). These later came to be called the "Big Six" (Bloland, 1985). The major associations were defined not by size, but by level of activity, namely, that they took "part most regularly and on the widest range of political concerns of all of the Washington-based higher education associations" (King, 1975, p. 19).

The special interest or satellite associations included the Council of Graduate Schools in the United States (CGSUS) and the Council for the Advancement of Small Colleges (CASC). These associations focused not on broad policy issues, but limited their concern to policy issues that effected their highly specialized constituency. According to King (1975) the defining characteristic of the special interest associations is that "except on issues of specific interest to their members, they are generally willing to let the major associations speak for them" (p. 24).

King placed the special interest associations into orbits around the major associations. Orbiting the AAU and NASULGC were associations with research and graduate studies interests such as the Association of American Medical Colleges, CGSUS, and the National Council of University Research Administrators. Orbiting the AAC and were associations that represented "colleges with religious affiliations, and those colleges of marginal status and financial condition" (King, 1975, p. 29) such as the College and University Department of the National Catholic Educational Association and CASC.

The last part of the structure is what King (1975) termed an emerging pattern of "offices representing state systems, small associations of fairly homogeneous institutions, individual colleges and universities, and schools enlisting the services of private entrepreneurs" (p. 31). Some examples of this emerging pattern include the State University of New York (SUNY) office, the Associated Colleges of the Midwest, and Harvard University.

While King's mapping of the higher education policy arena was accurate in 1975, the arena has changed remarkably since his work first appeared. The AAC, one of the two centers, is no longer a major organization having been replaced by National Association of Independent Colleges and Universities (NAICU). The Career College Association (CCA) could probably be added as a major organization, but its representation of proprietary schools certainly differentiates it from the other major associations. The Consumer Bankers Association (CBA), the National Council of Higher Education Loan Programs (NCHELP), Sallie Mae and other groups have also emerged as major policy actors. The

dependence of CBA, NCHELP and Sallie Mae on the guaranteed loan program makes it difficult to categorize them and similar associations under King's scheme.

King's classification scheme, while accurate in 1975, has decayed as the higher education associations and the policy arena in which they operated changed. If only the names and number of associations had changed over the years, then it might have been possible to maintain King's classification scheme. What makes it impossible is that changes in the policy arena and the development of contiguous policy arenas have blurred the distinctions between classifications. The fragmentation of policy making has meant that major associations have had to become increasingly specialized to be able to respond to the information needs of Congress and executive agencies. At the same time, special interest associations, especially research and graduate studies, have had to increasingly take part in the policy process because their concerns are impacted by multiple committees, subcommittees and agencies. Because of these changes, the use of King's classification scheme is of limited value in describing the current relationships and roles of higher education associations.

Bloland (1985) and others argue that Murray's (1976) work is an improvement and refinement of King's classification scheme. However, a close examination of Murray's classification system reveals that he changes only the names of the categories first identified by King. Murray replaces King's implied hierarchy of associations with a cluster of associations revolving around core associations. Murray's core groups consists of the same six associations that comprised King's major association group. The satellite lobbies that orbit around Murray's core are unchanged from King's. Finally, King's emerging pattern group is renamed the periphery by Murray.

The use of the core concept might be useful as an analytical device, but Murray (1976) cautions that the "core concept is helpful as a way of describing lobbies but it is somewhat misleading as an analytical device since it masks the deep cleavages which split the lobbies" (p. 82). This warning seems to negate the one advantage gained from dressing King's categories in new conceptual clothing. Aside from the internal weakness noted by Murray, his classification scheme suffers from the same shortcomings as King's and is of limited use in describing the current relationship and roles of the higher education associations.

Unlike King and Murray, Finn (1980) attempts to take a more analytical view of the higher education policy arena using the idea of a "liberal consensus" as his organizing scheme. The idea of a liberal consensus is apparently borrowed from Bailey (1975) who "referred to a 'lib-lab' lobby—a loose association of liberal and labor organizations that shared common values" (p. 23). Finn expands on Bailey's idea in two important ways. First he claims that a liberal consensus not only exists but that it shaped national education policy from 1965 until the election of Ronald Reagan. Second, Finn (1980) expands the definition of the liberal consensus well beyond Bailey's definition of the lib-lab lobby as can be seen in the following answer to his own question:

> What is the "liberal consensus," and how can it be characterized? In terms of its major sources and prominent members the consensus has included the Ford and Carnegie Foundations and four or five smaller ones; the elite graduate schools of education such as those at Stanford, Harvard, Chicago, and Columbia; the major national organizations of teachers and educational institutions such as the National Education Association, the American Association of School Administrators, the National School Boards Association, and the American Council on Education; the various groups represented in the Leadership Conference on Civil Rights; the big labor unions; the political appointees in the education related agencies of the federal executive branch (including, with a few exceptions, those of both Republican and Democratic presidents); half a dozen key Congressmen and perhaps two dozen Congressional staff members; a variety of "think tanks," notably including The Brookings Institution and the Aspen Institute; and the writers of education editorials of the major metropolitan newspapers including *The New York Times* and *The Washington Post*. Actively involved at various times during the last decade and a half of the ascendancy of the liberal consensus and emblematic of its best ideas and greatest achievements have been such able and distinguished individuals as Clark Keff,

"Doc" Howe, Ernest Boyer, Stephen Bailey, and Samuel Halperin. (p. 25)

According to Finn (1980), the liberal consensus served educational interests well for a time, but then it began "to grow greedy, smug, extreme and, at the same time, defensive" (p. 26). In support of his claim, Finn (1980) cites ten elements that demonstrate a pattern of change away from a broad social interest and toward a narrow self-interest:

> First, the liberal consensus today reveals a preoccupation with questions of educational equity and equality and a pronounced lack of interest in the issues of quality. (p. 26)
>
> Second, the liberal consensus today has a generalized abhorrence of tests and other measures of educational achievement. (p. 26)
>
> Third, while the liberal consensus regularly espouses the principle of "accountability," in practice it seems to resent the notion that those who supply resources to educational institutions have a legitimate interest in what is done with those resources. (p. 26)
>
> Fourth, the liberal consensus today is fixated on the concept of "need" and apathetic if not actually hostile to the concept of ability (p. 27)
>
> Fifth, there is today in the liberal consensus about education a predisposition towards statism and monopoly rather than pluralism and diversity. (p. 27)
>
> Sixth, the liberal consensus in American education is all but helpless in the presence of unreasonableness, which leaves it, the programs it created, and the government that runs them easy prey to victimization. (p. 27)
>
> Seventh, its reliance on government to solve educational problems and regulate educational practices, combined with its proclivity to appease those with extreme or unreasonable demands, means that the liberal consensus finds itself welcoming an ever-larger federal role in education and accepting the associated increase in federal control. (p. 28)
>
> Eight, the liberal consensus keeps finding itself on the side of formal and informal quota systems and of "reverse of discrimination." (p. 29)
>
> Ninth, the liberal consensus today displays a measure of greed, or at least a high

degree of tolerance toward others' greed. (p. 29)

Finally, the liberal consensus in education today embodies an unresolved paradox about the role of educators themselves (p. 29).

Finn's work is different from both King and Murray in that he does not seek to describe the higher education policy arena in terms of institutional relationships, but rather seeks to articulate the values and beliefs that define and guide the arena. In his effort to make the case that the liberal consensus that guided education policy for so long and so well has lost its bearings, Finn makes a number of errors that undermine his claims and limit the usefulness of his approach to defining the policy arena. Finn has lumped together policy arenas that are separate both conceptually and in practice. Higher education, vocational education, job training, and elementary and secondary education are separate policy arenas, but Finn combines these and other education policy arenas into one education policy arena without concern for the differences that distinguish the different arenas. As a result, the National Education Association, which is concerned with primary and secondary education, is grouped with the ACE, which is concerned with higher education. At the same time, NASULGC and other major higher education associations are not even mentioned. The "big labor unions" that Finn lists in his definition of the liberal consensus were never that big and have been steadily declining as a political force since the mid-1970s. Labor has not had a significant legislative victory at the federal level in more than two decades. Finally, the claim that higher education would or does welcome an increase in federal control is at odds with the entire history of higher education in the United States. As shown in chapter 2, higher education has been resistant to federal involvement.

None of the above definitions is adequate to the task of defining the current higher education policy arena. Rather than attempting to refurbish one of the above definitions, a new approach is needed that avoids the shortcomings of earlier definitions and accounts for changes that have taken place in the policy arena in the years since those definitions were first presented. The next section moves toward

such a definition by defining the higher education policy arena in terms of its characteristics.

Characteristics of the Higher Education Policy Arena

In contrast to the above definitions of the higher education policy arena, political scientists have developed the concept of a subgovernment to describe and explain policy formation in arenas "insulated from majority influence" (Bond, 1979, p. 651). McCool (1989) defines a subgovernment as a policy arena

controlled by a closed, three-sided alliance composed of the relevant congressional committees and subcommittees, interest groups, and government agencies. Policy making is usually characterized by autonomy, stability, and low visibility. Conflict is kept to a minimum through bargaining and logrolling and by excluding or coopting potential opponents. . . . These alliances are most likely to form around distributive policy issues . . . which are characterized by a combination of concentrated benefits and diffused costs. (p. 264)

The concept of subgovernments is introduced here for two reasons. One is that the two terms, policy arena and subgovernment, can be used interchangeably While the two terms convey the same basic concept and meaning, policy arena tends to denote a more active, contested state of affairs while subgovernment denotes a more mechanical system. The other reason is the existence of an extensive body of literature on subgovernments, that extends back over several decades. The knowledge and analytical approaches from this literature are useful in exploring and developing the higher education policy arena.

The term subgovernment probably evokes images of an iron triangle in which Congress, the White House, and interest groups produce policy, isolated from the majority, designed to assist the chosen few at the expense of the masses. This may in fact describe some subgovernments, but it appears to be more a caricature of the concept than the reality of a subgovernment in operation. A more productive way to think of subgovernments is as a continuum ranging from closed iron triangles at one end to open issue networks at the other end

(Hamm, 1986). Criterion characteristics can be used to judge where particular subgovernments fit along the continuum. The characteristics used to describe and define policy arenas are: (1) internal complexity, (2) functional autonomy, (3) unity within type of participant, and, (4) cooperation or conflict among different participants (Hamm, 1983). While these characteristics are used in an effort to give definition and focus to the higher education policy arena, the arena will not be treated as part of the traditional continuum. As discussed above, the case will be made that the higher education policy arena is better described as a community.

Internal Complexity

Internal complexity is used to refer "to the number and variety of participants in the subsystem" (Hamm, 1983, p. 381). By this definition, the higher education policy arena is a low to moderately complex policy arena. The number of key participants is small enough that most, if not all, of the participants know one another personally. Also, the variety of participants, as will be shown, is of a limited range. Finally, the number of committees involved in reauthorization consists of one in the House and one in the Senate.

CONGRESSIONAL COMMITTEES

The congressional committees and subcommittees are the central participants in the policy arena and the focus of attention for most of the other participants. They must reauthorize HEA and can hold oversight hearings on HEA programs or any related higher education concerns. The committees, and more importantly the subcommittees, are obligatory passage points for all major policy decisions within the arena. In the House, the key committee is the Education and Labor Committee while in the Senate it is the Labor and Human Resources Committee. The respective subcommittees are Postsecondary Education and Education, Arts and Humanities. The subcommittee members for the 102nd Congress are shown in tables 1 and 2.

While all of the committee and subcommittee members are well positioned to influence the reauthorization process, three members and their staffs were generally regarded as the

TABLE 1
House Subcommittee on Postsecondary Education, 102nd Congress

Democrats	Republicans
William D. Ford (Mich.) *Chairman*	E. Thomas Coleman (Mo.) *Ranking Member*
Pat Williams (Mont.)	William R Goodling (Pa.)
Charles A. Hayes (Ill.)	Marge Roukema (N.J.)
Joseph M. Gaydos (Pa.)	Steve Gunderson (Wis.)
George Miller (Calif.)	Paul B. Henry (Mich.)
Nita M. Lowey (N.Y.)	Susan Molinari (N.Y.)
Thomas C. Sawyer (Ohio)	Scott Klug (Wis.)
Donald M. Payne (N.J.)	Thomas E. Petrie (Wis.)
Jolene Unsoeld (Wash.)	Richard Armey (Tex.)
Craig Washington (Tex.)	Bill Barret (Neb.)
Jose Serrano (N.Y.)	
Patsy Mink (Hawaii)	
Robert E. Andrews (N.J.)	
William Jefferson (La.)	
John R Reed (R.I.)	
Tim Roemer (Ind.)	
Dale E. Kildee (Mich.)	

TABLE 2
Senate Subcommittee on Education, Arts and Humanities, 102nd Congress

Democrats	Republicans
Claiborne Pell (R.I.) *Chairman*	Nancy Kassebaum (Kan.) *Ranking Member*
Howard Metzenbaum (Ohio)	Orrin Hatch (Utah)
Christopher Dodd (Conn.)	Thad Cochran (Miss.)
Paul Simon (Ill.)	James Jeffords (Vt.)
Barbara Mikulski (Md.)	Strom Thurmond (S.C.)
Jeff Bingaman (N. Mex.)	Dan Coats (Ind.)
Paul Wellstone (Minn.)	David Durenberger (Minn.)
Edward Kennedy (Mass.)	
Brock Adams (Wash.)	

key policy actors for the 1992 reauthorization. The key policy actor on the House subcommittee is William D. Ford. In part, this is due to his dual role as chair of the full committee and the subcommittee, but it also comes from his more than twenty-five years of involvement and experience with education issues in the House. As noted in the last chapter, Ford was a sponsor of MISAA and has long favored expanding student aid to more middle-income families. During the 1980s, he was one of the Democrats who successfully lead the fight against Reagan administration proposals for deep cuts in student aid programs. For the 1992 reauthorization, Ford called for a major redesign of the HEA loan and grant programs (Cooper, 1992).

Among the ideas put forward by Ford were front-loading Pell Grants, eliminating Perkins loans, increasing the size of SEOG awards, increasing aid to middle-income students, and support for direct lending.

The staff director for the subcommittee is Thomas R. Wolanin, who also held the position from 1985 to 1987. Wolanin is known in Congress for his detailed knowledge of HEA and is known in academia for his writing on higher education policy issues. The recipient of a doctorate in government from Harvard University, Wolanin was at one time a professor at the University of Wisconsin but left the academy so that he could make policy rather than merely study policy. Wolanin's introduction to HEA came when he was on leave from Wisconsin working for Congressman Frank Thompson Jr. during the 1972 reauthorization.

Without question, the key policy actor on the Senate subcommittee is the chair, Claiborne Pell. As either the chair or ranking member, Pell has helped shape every HEA reauthorization since 1972. A fixture in the Senate since 1960, Pell has consistently championed equal educational opportunity, nondiscrimination between different types of postsecondary education, and aid to students rather than institutions. Coming into the 1992 reauthorization Pell continued to address his traditional concerns as well as expressing an interest in stricter licensing and accreditation standards for postsecondary institutions as a means of quality control for federal student aid expenditures, expanding aid to middle-class students, and early intervention.

The staff director of the subcommittee is David V. Evans, who has worked for Pell since 1978. During the 1986 reauthorization, Evans was the minority staff director. When the Democrats regained control of the Senate in 1987, he became the subcommittee staff director. Given the broad jurisdiction of Senate committees, Evans has shared the workload on higher education with Sarah A. Flanagan who has been with the subcommittee since 1987. Flanagan is responsible for most of the contacts and interactions with higher education lobbyists.

The third key policy actor is Senator Edward M. Kennedy a member of the subcommittee and Chair of the Committee on Labor and Human Resources. A longtime advocate of education, Kennedy's involvement with HEA dates from its creation in 1965. Kennedy outlined much of his agenda in a *Roll Call* article in early 1991. The issues that Kennedy (1991) saw as important challenges for reauthorization were "the loan-grant imbalance, the integrity of the student loan program, and the excessive complexity of the student aid process" (p. 13). In addition, he expressed an interest in early intervention programs and Pell Grant entitlement.

Terry W. Hartle is the education staff director for the Committee on Labor and Human Resources and a key aide to Senator Kennedy on higher education issues. Hartle, a former policy analyst with the American Enterprise Institute, has also written on federal student aid programs. In some of his published work, Hartle has been critical of the complexity of the system, the role and growth of the guaranteed student loan (GSL) program, and the efforts of higher education associations to promote reform of the system (e.g., Doyle & Hartle, 1985).

While these are the key policy actors, other members of the subcommittees had policy concerns that they communicated and publicized within the higher education policy arena. A number of these issues were reported to the higher education associations through *Educational Record*. In the summer of 1990, Andra Armstrong (1990) reported the views of various House and Senate members in "How the Hill sees Higher Education." Members also used *Roll Call*, public interviews, press releases, and speeches to communicate their reauthorization agendas.

THE EXECUTIVE

While the key policy actors in the executive branch should be as easy to identify as those in the Congress, the Bush administration's policies and personnel were marked by flux and turmoil. In the fall of 1990, Education Secretary Lauro F. Cavazos ruled out separate student aid programs for colleges and trade schools while announcing plans to link aid to academic achievement and student retention rates (DeLoughry, 1990, October 3). In December, Cavazos resigned as education secretary reportedly because White House Chief of Staff John H. Sununu told him it was time to leave (DeLoughry, 1990, December 19).

In January 1991, Bush nominated Lamar Alexander to become the next education secretary. Alexander had served as governor of Tennessee from 1979 through 1987 and had been president of the University of Tennessee system since 1988 (DeLoughry, 1991, January 9). Alexander brought a proven track record on education to an administration that was desperate to make good on Bush's claim of being the Education President, but the conventional wisdom was that he was not appointed on the basis of his education record and experience. One of the reasons some believed he was appointed was his close friendship with Sununu. Another was his reputation as a determined, savvy, political operative who could guide legislation through the Congress. Regardless of the exact reason for his appointment, Alexander had built a solid record as an educational reformer during his years as governor and his appointment was greeted with approval by the education community.

To give Alexander the opportunity to select his own leadership team, the White House asked for the resignations of most of the top Education Department officials (DeLoughry, 1991, April 3). Among those asked to resign was Leonard L. Haynes III, assistant secretary for postsecondary education. While Haynes left immediately, his position was not immediately filled. Instead, Michael J. Farrell, whom Alexander had selected to be assistant secretary for student financial assistance, was asked to fill the postsecondary education slot on an interim basis (DeLoughry, 1991, December 4). In November, Farrell resigned from both positions, but gave no public reason for his departure (DeLoughry, 1991, December 11).

In September, Bush announced the nomination of Carolynn Reid-Wallace to fill the position of assistant secretary of postsecondary education (DeLoughry, 1991, September 18). The announcement of her nomination to the post was favorably received by the higher education community. Reid-Wallace brought a broad range of experiences to the position including a tenure as vice chancellor for academic affairs for the City University of New York System, as assistant director of education for the National Endowment for the Humanities, as dean at Bowie State University, and as an administrator with the National Association for Equal Opportunity in Higher

Education. Farrell's resignation announcement came on the same day the Senate confirmed Reid-Wallace's nomination.

The Education Department's instability was symptomatic of the Bush administration's inability to find its footing on education issues and policy. The administration not only had trouble fashioning its leadership team for education but also never seemed to be in sync with other members of the education community. For example, in an effort to give substance and clarity to his claim of being the Education President, Bush announced "America 2000" in a speech at the White House on April 18, 1991. The "America 2000" speech presented the President's strategy to "restructure and revitalize Americas education system by the year 2000" ("America 2000," 1991, p. 1). The president did not seem to realize that the congressional subcommittees that would have to deal with the legislative proposals on "America 2000" were already busy holding hearings on HEA. Without considering the merits of the proposals, the message was off-cycle and unresponsive to the needs of the subcommittees who needed to hear what the administration had to say about higher education. The proposals for K through 12 would have to wait a year before the subcommittees were scheduled to reauthorize the legislation for secondary and elementary schools.

In summary, while the White House is the final passage point for HEA in the reauthorization process, the executive branch was in a state of confusion and flux from the very beginning of the process. No one in Congress, Democrat or Republican, seemed to know what the White House wanted from reauthorization or who was in charge. This may be because no one in the White House knew. The best example of this uncertainty is Bush's position on direct loans and Pell Grant entitlement. After initially supporting both, Bush threatened to veto legislation that contained either. The increased level of uncertainty served to increase the internal complexity of the policy arena.

THE ASSOCIATIONS

The third group of participants in the policy arena are the higher education associations that attempt to lobby the Congress and the executive branch. While they certainly lobby by any conventional definition of the term, most associations claim not to be lobbyists because of their inordinate fear of violating Section 501 (c) (3) of the Internal Revenue Code, thereby losing their tax-exempt status (Bloland, 1985). The number and diversity of higher education associations gives some credence to the lament that "no other segment of American society has so many organizations and is yet so unorganized as higher education" (Babbidge & Rosenzweig, 1962, p. 92). While there are a large number of associations, only a few are recognized as active policy actors, thus it is relatively easy to identify and discuss this segment of the policy arena.

The major higher education associations are housed in the National Center for Higher Education at One Dupont Circle in Washington, D.C., and the address has become a short-hand way to refer to higher education associations. Of the twenty plus associations that reside at One Dupont, only the American Association of Community and Junior Colleges (AACJC), the American Association of State Colleges and Universities (AASCU), the American Council on Education (ACE), the Association of American Universities (AAU), and the National Association of State Universities and Land-Grant Colleges (NASULGC) have been consistently active policy actors in the higher education policy arena. ACE, an umbrella organization, has often attempted to forge consensus positions on policy issues getting as many associations as possible to speak with one voice on the issue before attempting to influence the Congress or the executive branch. The other five associations, all of which are institutional associations, have then provided the expertise on the issues that most impact their member institutions.

ACE has long claimed to speak for all of higher education, but for many years its voice was seldom heard in Washington and its organizational structure all but prevented decision making when Congress did ask for an opinion (Babbidge & Rosenzweig, 1962). By the time ACE cleared policy positions with its member associations and institutions, Congress had either acted on the policy question or else was no longer interested in ACE's views on the matter. It was only after the burst of education legislation in the 1960s, the defeat of institu-

tional aid in 1972, and sharp public criticism from the White House and members of Congress that ACE began to undertake an internal reevaluation and reorganization aimed at improving its governmental relations function. Much of that work, directed by then President Roger Heyns and Vice President Stephen K. Bailey, took place in the mid-1970s.

One of the changes brought by Heyns and Bailey was hiring Charles B. Saunders as the new director of the Division of Governmental Relations (King, 1975). Saunders, now vice president of governmental relations, brought a wealth of experience to the task having previously served as a Senate staff member, deputy assistant secretary of education, and acting assistant secretary of education (Bloland, 1985; Graham, 1984). One of Saunders' initial acts was to organize an informal weekly meeting between members of the major education associations at One Dupont Circle, the National Association of University Business Officers (NACUBO), and the National Association of Independent Colleges and Universities (NAICU) (Bloland, 1985). Saunders later initiated a second weekly meeting with a larger group of higher education representatives. These informal meetings served different purposes. The smaller group represented an opportunity for the major associations to exchange information, identify positions, and move toward consensus. The larger group acted as a monitor of events and an information exchange for the participants. The two groups continued to meet into the 1990s and served much the same purpose for the 1992 reauthorization.

Consistent with its self-image as the lead association "to coordinate the formation of policy on the national issues and problems of higher education" (Bloland, 1985, p. 17), ACE worked to forge a broad consensus on reauthorization issues through the formation of six task forces. Established in the spring of 1989, the task forces were organized around the issues of need analysis and the student aid delivery system, low-income students, middle-income students, graduate and professional education, program development, and institutional resources. The task force reports were integrated into a comprehensive set of recommendations for reauthorization that were submitted to both the House and Senate subcommittees. Joining ACE in signing the reauthorization recommendations were the American Association of Community and Junior Colleges (AACJC), American Association of State Colleges and Universities (AASCU), Association of American Universities (AAU), Association of Catholic Colleges and Universities (ACCU), Association of Urban Universities (AUU), National Association for Equal Opportunity in Higher Education (NAFEOHE), National Association of College and University Business Officers (NACUBO), National Association of Independent Colleges and Universities (NAICU), National Association of Schools and Colleges of the United Methodist Church (NASCUMC), and the National Association of State Universities and Land-Grant Colleges (NASULGC).

ACE's coordinating role and the shared One Dupont Circle address means that the associations are often lumped together and treated as one. The terms ACE and One Dupont Circle are often used by congressional staff, observers, and scholars to refer to all of the associations housed in the National Center for Higher Education without any acknowledgment of the differences that define the individual associations. In practice, each association tends to stress what is most important to its institutional members and, at times, to take positions not covered by the consensus agreements that rule One Dupont Circle. AASCU, founded in 1961, might be the best example of an association that has been willing to step out from the One Dupont Circle group and take positions on issues not covered by consensus agreements. AASCU has a consistent record of speaking out for lower tuition and equal opportunity in higher education. As was noted in the last chapter, AASCU's position on tuition has at times put it at odds with other associations. Edward M. Elmendorf, AASCU's vice president for governmental relations and a former assistant secretary of education for postsecondary education in the Reagan administration, has been a visible and effective spokesman.

NASULGC, like AASCU, has a strong record of supporting low tuition and equal educational opportunity. Because so many of its member institutions have graduate schools, NASULGC also speaks out on graduate education, research, and international studies. Jerold

Roschwald, NASULGC director of federal relations-higher education worked closely with AASCU and AAU in preparing for the 1992 reauthorization. In addition, Thomas A. Butts, associate vice president for governmental relations at the University of Michigan, worked with NASULGC to develop and lobby for a direct loan program.

AAU was founded in 1900 by fourteen American universities offering the Ph.D. Today, AAU consists of some fifty-six American and two Canadian universities, but its focus remains research and graduate education. Given that AAU's interests often overlap with NASULGCs and with CGSUS, John C. Vaughn, AAU director of federal relations, frequently coordinates with these associations to maximize their potential impact on federal policy issues. Vaughn also led the ACE task force on graduate and professional education.

AACJC was established in 1920 to represent the interests of junior colleges. AACJC claims to have a community or junior college in every congressional district, but the nature of this higher education sector is such that many of its issues are state rather than federal issues. This may explain why Frank Mensel, AACJC vice president of federal relations, can also serve as director of federal relations for the Association of Community College Trustees.

While One Dupont Circle is home to the National Center for Higher Education, important higher education groups are also located elsewhere in Washington, D.C. One of the more important of these is the National Association of Student Financial Aid Administrators (NASFAA). NASFAA is often cited for its technical knowledge and expertise. Founded in the mid-1960s, NASFAA now speaks for some 3,200 campuses and 9,000 financial aid officers nationwide (DeWitt, 1991). Traditionally, NASFAA has been noted not only for its technical expertise but also for being the surrogate voice of college students and their parents. In 1992, under the leadership of Dallas Martin, NASFAA sought to expand its traditional role and become an actor on larger policy issues. As part of this effort, NASFAA organized its own reauthorization task force to prepare a full range of HEA proposals for the authorizing committees. In addition, Martin chaired the ACE task force on needs analysis and student aid delivery, but NASFAA did not sign the ACE consensus recommendations. Instead, it presented a separate set of policy proposals developed by the NAS-FAA reauthorization task force.

Another key association is the National Council of Educational Opportunity Associations (NCEOA). This ten-year-old association represents Upward Bound, Talent Search, Student Support Services, and other so-called TRIO programs directed toward low-income and minority students. Under the leadership of Arnold Mitchem, NCEOA has consistently convinced Congress to increase TRIO funding.

A third association outside One Dupont Circle that must be mentioned in any list of key higher education policy actors is the National Association of Independent Colleges and Universities (NAICU). Just as ACE acts as an umbrella association for higher education, NAICU acts as the umbrella association for higher education's private sector. In preparing for the 1992 reauthorization, NAICU worked with the ACE consensus group and signed the recommendations that came out of the process. Julianne S. Thrift, then NAICU executive vice president, chaired the ACE task force on middle-income students.

Finally, the Career College Association (CCA) speaks for a segment of the higher education community not represented by One Dupont Circle. CCA is the product of a merger between the National Association of Trade and Technical Schools (NATTS) and the Association of Independent Colleges and Schools (AICS). Tainted by egregious student aid abuse scandals, NATTS hired Stephen J. Blair as president in 1985 and gave him the task of cleaning up the organization. Blair, formerly director of policy and program development in the Education Department's Office of Student Financial Assistance, succeeded to the point that AICS, formerly the lead association for the sector, merged with NATTS, largely as a matter of survival. Today, CCA has six full time lobbyists and a political action committee that donates to Congressional campaigns.

Bolstering the lobbying staff was designed to overcome the political damage caused by the student aid abuse scandals. When possible, Blair hired former congressional staff members to lobby their old committees (DeParle, 1992). The hiring of Patty Sullivan, who had worked for Representative Pat Williams, is the premier

example of this tactic. Blair also hired consultants such as Bob Beckel, a member of the Mondale presidential campaign, and Haley Barbour, a member of the Reagan White House, to help CCA prepare for reauthorization.

In chapter 2, the increasing scope and size of the GSL program was mentioned several times. One result of this growth has been the increasing role of lenders and guarantors as policy actors in the higher education policy arena. While bankers may not be educators, the Consumer Bankers Association (CBA) has stressed the role its members play in helping students pay for a college education that might otherwise be denied them due to the unavailability of funds. The CBA plays down the more than $1 billion in profits that commercial banks generate from their student loan portfolios each year, a profit that is virtually 100 percent guaranteed by the federal government (Bluestone & Comcowich, 1992). Instead, it stresses the efficiency with which it delivers loans to students compared to alternatives such as direct loan programs. While CBA speaks for bankers involved in the guaranteed student loan program, the law firm of Colhan and Dean speaks for the CBA. Several members of Colhan and Dean are former congressional staff members with connections to the education committees. John E. Dean, for example, was formerly minority counsel for the House Postsecondary Education Subcommittee (Lee, 1983).

The National Council of Higher Education Loan Programs (NCHELP) is a creation of the GSL programs growth and expansion. NCHELP is a nonprofit association of guarantors, lenders, secondary markets, servicing organizations, private collection companies, and other organizations involved in the GSL program. Jean S. Frohlicker, NCHELP executive director, was involved with the original HEA in 1965 and with every reauthorization since. Like CBA, NCHELP stresses the role it plays in helping students who might otherwise have found college beyond their means. Also like CBA, NCHELP emphasizes it efficiency and the fact that for every federal dollar spent through the GSL program, private markets leverage three to four dollars more for student loans, thus giving the government a bargain while giving students a chance for higher education that might otherwise have been denied.

Sallie Mae, the Student Loan Marketing Association, was created by Congress as part of the 1972 reauthorization. The reason for Sallie Mae's creation was to improve the GSL program by creating a clearinghouse for student loans. Sallie Mae does this by buying student loans from lenders and providing services to lenders and educational institutions involved with the GSL program. By the end of 1990, Sallie Mae owned nearly 30 percent of all outstanding guaranteed student loans (Hyatt, 1991).

Sallie Mae, like CBA and NCIHELP, emphasizes the service it provides to students rather than the profits it makes from the service. Lawrence A. Hough, Sallie Mae's president and chief executive officer, likes to emphasize not only the service and efficiency of his organization, but also the way in which it acts to assist middle income students. While Hough speaks publicly for Sallie Mae, much of its day-to-day interaction with the Congress is handled by the Washington law firm of Williams and Jensen.

While other associations and organizations are active, the above are the most active higher education associations in the policy arena. The addition of other, less active organizations would not significantly alter the level of internal complexity of the higher education policy arena. At the beginning of this section, the arena was described as being of low to moderate complexity. Visually, the complexity of relationships and number of participants can be viewed in Table 3.

TABLE 3
Participants in the Higher Education Policy Arena

Executive
President
Education Secretary
Senior Ed Officials
OMB

Associations	Congress
One Dupont Circle Associations	House Education and Labor Committee
CCA	Subcommittee on Postsecondary Education
NAICU	
NASFAA	
NCEOA	Senate Labor and Human Resources Committee
Lender Associations	Subcommittee on Education, Arts, and Humanities

Functional Autonomy

Functional autonomy is "the extent to which policies are formulated and implemented within the subsystem" (Hamm, 1983, p. 381). By this definition, the higher education policy arena enjoys a high level of functional autonomy. This is not to suggest that the arena has been immune from attacks on its functional autonomy. The 1968 student conduct debates and the 1972 busing debates are primary examples of other policy arenas seeking to infringe upon the autonomy of the higher education policy arena. Another example is the Reagan administration's use of the budget to implement policy changes that it could not gain through the higher education policy arena. In each of these examples, the higher education policy arena was able to resist and to maintain its autonomy.

A threat to the arena's functional autonomy arose at the beginning of the 1992 reauthorization in the form of an investigation of the federal student loan program by the Senate Permanent Subcommittee on Investigations. Chaired by Senator Sam Nunn, a Georgia Democrat, the subcommittee held a series of hearings as part of an investigation that resulted in the report *Abuses in Federal Student Aid Programs* (1991). The findings were embraced by members of the education committees and subcommittees, who translated the findings into their own policy proposals. The net result was to diffuse the threat to the arena's autonomy without coming into conflict with other legislative policy arenas.

Finally, while there are no instruments for measuring functional autonomy, Hall and Evans (1990) do address the issue of functional autonomy indirectly in their study of the power of congressional subcommittees. Looking at three committees in the Ninety-seventh Congress, one of which was the House Committee on Education and Labor, the authors found that the education and labor subcommittees drafted 88 percent of the committee legislation, dominated the amending of legislation at the committee level, and that the reporting subcommittee lost not a single roll-call vote during the entire Congress. While this is but one study, it provides additional support for the claim that the higher education policy arena enjoys a high level of functional autonomy.

Unity within Type of Participant

Unity within type of participant is simply a way of referring to "the unity among individuals in each sector—agencies, interest groups, and committees" (Hamm, 1983, p. 382). This brief definition of unity conceals the complexity of the meaning of unity when used in discussions of subgovernments. Unity refers to unity between individuals as well as between organizations. An example would be the level of unity between associations on a key policy question. Unity also refers to agreement across sectors. For example, unity on the role of Pell Grants would be rather high across sectors. While it is widely used in describing policy arenas, the concept of unity is not well defined in the literature. Instead of working from an operational definition, researchers use examples from the subgovernment system being studied to support claims of unity or disunity in the system.

The level of unity within the higher education policy arena is rather high. One way in which this can be seen is in the language used by the policy actors. The language used to describe policy issues carries with it an acceptance and understanding of the values that guide the higher education policy arena. For example, "needs analysis" means that students need help attending college, it is the federal government's role to provide that help, and it is necessary to determine how much, if any, help should be forthcoming in a fair and consistent manner. "Equal educational opportunity" means that the federal government should play an active role in removing race, religion, sex, poverty, and other barriers that might prevent children of ability from attending college. "Access" means giving aid to students who are blocked from higher education by financial barriers. The common language and understood values help provide a coherence, unity, and logic to the policy arena.

Since almost no one in the higher education policy arena questions the basic philosophical underpinning of problems and issues, conflicts tend to arise over specific solutions. For example, the issue of whether loans should be given via direct lending or through loan vendors is not an issue of loans, but one of how to deliver loans. The same is true of the loan-grant imbalance. The issue is not student loans, but the proper balance between loans and forms of grant aid. The guiding assumptions and beliefs remain unchallenged with only the solutions open to question and conflict.

Last, unity, particularly between Congress and the associations, has evolved from a long history of cooperative activities aimed at producing workable and popular legislation. The extensive quotations from policy actors in chapter 2 demonstrates that the history has also involved angry disputes, but the policy actors have always overcome these differences to focus on the common goal of aiding students. The resolution of these disputes and the long, shared history of the policy actors has fostered emotional and intellectual bonds that unite the participants.

Cooperation or Conflict

The characteristic of cooperation or conflict among different participants is a function of the communality of interests enjoyed in the policy arena (Hamm, 1983). Communality of interests rests on a number of factors, but interest overrepresentation and circulation of personnel are key concerns in gauging the level of cooperation or conflict within a policy arena. Overrepresentation refers to a greater concentration of interested legislators on a committee or subcommittee than could be accounted for by the normal distribution of legislators. For example, the claim was often made that the oil depletion allowance in the U.S. tax code was a result of oil state overrepresentation on the tax committees (Bonds, 1979). Circulation of personnel is the extent to which "interest groups, agency positions, committee staffs, and personal staffs" (Hamm, 1983, p. 386) move between jobs and sectors within the policy arena.

What one sees in looking at the two education subcommittees is that higher education is well represented by members who have higher education as a major economic interest in their district or state and by members who have a long history of commitment to higher education policy issues. For example, House subcommittee chair Ford has a number of institutions in his district and has a long history of interest and involvement in education issues. Higher education is not a major economic interest in Montana, but Pat Williams has long held an interest in education issues. Tim Roemer is from a district in Indiana that includes an Indiana University campus, the University of Notre Dame, a Purdue University campus, and several small colleges; thus he must be concerned with higher education issues in order to represent his district. Senate subcommittee chair Pell has made his political name with education issues. Edward M. Kennedy has a well-known interest in education and higher education is a major economic interest in Massachusetts. James Jeffords is similar to Kennedy in that he holds a personal interest in higher education and it is a major economic factor in Vermont. While this brief summary does not offer the numerical output of a multiple regression analysis, it is more than enough to establish that higher education interests are well represented and probably overrepresented on the subcommittees.

The circulation of personnel within the policy arena was addressed in the discussion of internal complexity, but additional examples are provided here to reinforce the understanding of the extensive flow of personnel within the policy arena. One example is Beth B. Buehlmann, who was an education policy fellow at the National Institute of Education before she joined the minority staff of the House Committee on Education in 1979, where she remained for some twelve years before becoming the Washington representative for the California state colleges. Another is Lawrence S. Zaglaniczny, currently assistant to the president of NASFAA, who formerly worked for ACE, as a lobbyist for a student higher education group, and as a congressional staffer. Last, William A. Blakey worked in the Education Department during the Carter administration, was later the staff director of the House Subcommittee on Postsecondary Education, and now represents the United Negro College Fund as a member of the law firm of Colhan and Dean. One higher education representative summarized the circulation of personnel by noting that "we are an incestuous lot."

Finally, unity and cooperation or conflict tend to overlap. The common language, shared values, and shared history help create unity and reduce conflict within the policy arena. The exchanges, in articles, papers, and speeches, between the policy actors helps identify and work out disputes as well as helping develop the language of the arena. The circulation of personnel is a major factor in promoting cooperation and encouraging unity by giving participants shared multiple perspectives of the policy arena.

Defining the Arena

As discussed at the beginning of this chapter, the concept of community is being used to describe and define the higher education policy arena because the concept captures the dynamic, contingent social relations of the policy arena in a way that is not possible with more static approaches such as shapes and mapping. Community is also the metaphor that higher education policy arena participants use "to define and associate the different elements by which they build and explain their world" (Callon, 1986, p. 201). Many policy actors define the community in terms of a constructive partnership that benefits all members of the community.

Higher education partnership is also used by policy actors to describe the social relations in the policy arena. The exact nature of the partnership varies depending on which policy actor defines the meaning of higher education partnership. For example, one higher education association representative viewed the relationship as a partnership because of the low level of conflict the arena exhibited compared to other policy arenas she had worked in prior to entering the higher education policy arena. In addition, the opportunity for discussion, input, and participation seemed to distinguish the arena as a partnership.

A higher education lobbyist also viewed the social relationship between participants in the policy arena as a partnership, but one that had deteriorated due to neglect by the Reagan and Bush administrations. The condition of the partnership today is one in which "there's a strong relationship between Congress and the lobby," but the executive has "been pretty ineffective" (Personal interview, February 27, 1992). NASULGC's Jerold Roschwalb echoed this view of the higher education partnership suggesting that perhaps "it characterizes it too neatly in some respects. . . . [T]here's a more solid relationship . . . between the associations and the Hill . . . [T]he Department . . . just hasn't been there for awhile" (Personal interview, February 27, 1992). Thomas Wolanin summarized it more succinctly stating "a higher education partnership does exist, but the White House role is that of veto agent" (Personal interview, May 7, 1992).

The policy actors' self-definition of the policy arena as a community or partnership matches well with definitions and descriptions of community in the literature. For example, Bellah and colleagues (1985) define a community as:

> a group of people who are socially interdependent, who participate together in discussion and decision making, and who share certain *practices* (which see) that both define the community and are nurtured by it. Such a community is not quickly formed. It almost always has a history and so is also a *community of memory*, defined in part by its past and its memory of its past. (p. 333)

Suggesting that higher education policy actors are socially interdependent would be stretching the reality of the arena to fit the definition, but other elements of Bellah's definition fit quite comfortably. The policy actors do participate together in discussion and decision making. The community does not operate by consensus but participants are allowed extensive input into the bill writing process. The community also shares common practices that define and maintain the community. The subcommittee hearings, position papers, and bidirectional lobbying are examples of practices that define and maintain the community. Finally, a community memory is maintained by long-term members of the arena such as Representative Ford and Senators Pell and Kennedy and is renewed with each new reauthorization as the old members of the community educate the new members about HEA, its past, its purpose, and its future.

David A. Hollinger (1985), in an essay on intellectual history, offers a definition of community that is centered on participation in a discourse. In some ways this is a loose definition of community because it means that anyone who joins the discourse is part of the community. In other ways it is a strong definition because

participants in any given discourse are bound to share certain values, beliefs, perceptions, and concepts—"ideas," as these potentially distinctive mental elements are called for short—but the most concrete and functional elements shared, surely, are questions. . . . Questions are the points of contact between minds, where agreements are consolidated and where differences are acknowledged and dealt with; questions are the dynamisms whereby membership in a community of discourse is established, renewed, and sometimes terminated. (Hollinger, 1985, p. 132)

The higher education policy arena reflects many of the characteristics of Hollinger's community of discourse. The contested principles in chapter 2 demonstrate a community concerned with questions from the earliest stages of its development through to the present. Equal educational opportunity was the value and belief that guided the Johnson administration's original vision of HEA and continues to play a key role in decision making today. Access, equal educational opportunity, and needs analysis are part of the common language and shared values that help guide discourse and provide coherence, unity, and logic.

Describing the higher education policy arena as a community and matching its characteristics with definitions of community from the literature gives some focus to the concept of community but begs the question of what type of community is being discussed. It is important to establish the exact type of community because this will become the context for the discussion of the meaning of power in chapter 5. The basis for defining the nature of the community that is the higher education policy arena are the criterion characteristics from the subgovernment literature. From the description generated by the application of this descriptive framework, the exact nature of the higher education policy community can be interpreted.

The interpretation that follows has its roots in John Dewey's (1927/1988) communication community concept. Dewey's communication community is used because the history of the policy arena suggests a community bonded by communication. The communication community forms the basis of collective action in the higher education policy arena. Through the experience of collective action policy actors have developed a common language as well as widely understood signs and symbols that convey shared meanings in the arena. From the experience of collective action, emotional, intellectual, and moral bonds have evolved to link and bind the members of the policy arena. These different aspects of a communication community are developed below in greater detail.

Before discussing these aspects, it is necessary to develop Dewey's concept of a communication community in greater detail. A more complete development is required because Dewey himself did not fully develop the concept after suggesting it in *The Public and Its Problem* (1927/1988). Dewey's theory of a communication community starts with, rather than ends in, the process of collective action. The product of collective action, regardless of how well it is conceived and planned, produces unintended or unanticipated consequences for the public. As these problems become apparent, the institutions responsible for implementing the public will and the public interact to produce a new decision. Of paramount importance in this process is communication between individuals and institutions who are either affected by a decision or are concerned with the consequences of any new decision. Communication is what bonds the community together. The public, a true democratic public, emerges from the communication required by group problem solving. The same is true of democratic governments that exist as a function of the collective action process. Communication for problem solving, not force of arms, becomes the mechanism for social order in the communication community.

As sketched by Dewey, the communication community is a lively, free-wheeling society, but one that also places a heavy moral and political responsibility on its citizens. Individuals must be aware of community issues, the consequences of collective actions, the needs of society, and must make decisions based on the needs of the community without the possibility of passing the burden for decision making on to some higher authority or outside agent. In the communication community, power as domination is replaced by power as problem solving, thus the public must take responsibility for solving its prob-

lems. If the public fails to take responsibility, there is no external system of social control, and the internal system of social order begins to unravel.

Dewey (1927/1988) claimed that the communication community would "have its consummation when free social inquiry is indissolubly wedded to the art of full and moving communication" (p. 184), but recognized that certain prerequisites were necessary before this consummation could be achieved. One of the prerequisites was a common language that could be used and understood by all of the community. Language by itself was not enough to foster fully understood communications. The public also needed widely understood signs and symbols to convey shared meanings. In addition, groups needed to interact in cooperative activities because "the pulls and responses of different groups reinforce one another and their values accord" (Dewey, 1988, p. 148). The shared activities also produce emotional, intellectual, and moral bonds that help bind the community. As these prerequisites are met, then a community evolves that is capable of transforming the power of domination into the power of problem solving.

Returning to the history of the higher education policy arena, one discovers a community born from collective action. Its early roots can be traced to the debates over the Northwest Ordinance of 1787, the national university, and the Morrill-Land Grant Act of 1862. The Association of American Agricultural Colleges in 1887 and the National Association of State Universities in 1895 were formed in response to the federal role in higher education and in an effort to better communicate the problems and needs of higher education to the federal government. While these are the early roots of the community, its growth was slow because there was limited federal action, little need for collective action, and almost no reason for communication.

The community did not begin to take its present form until well into the 1960s. Some associations formed in direct response to federal policy decisions, while others formed to fill the needs of their members for communication between similar institutions. Whatever the reason for their original formation, the associations reached the inescapable conclusion that some level of involvement with the federal government was required given the increasing size and scope of the federal interest in higher education. Federal decisions were impacting colleges and universities more directly than ever before as government programs ranging from national defense to social equality were created with institutions of higher education serving as the instrument of implementation. While institutions might have followed a path of resistance, the only effective way to influence federal action was to enter into a dialogue with federal policymakers. In particular, with the congressional leaders responsible for federal higher education policy formation and the executive agencies charged with implementing policy.

The federal government experienced a similar need to enter into a dialogue with the associations representing colleges and universities in order to implement its own policy agenda. The first HEA focused on providing equal educational opportunity for low income and lower-middle-income students with aid programs administered primarily though campus officials. Subsequent reauthorizations expanded this focus to include more middle-income students and created various loans under the GSL program to facilitate the delivery of aid to these students. In addition, Congress expanded the definition of higher education to include a broader range of post-secondary education, thus expanding the number and type of potential aid recipients. To accomplish their policy goals, federal higher education policymakers had to enter into a dialogue with the associations. Policy actors in the federal government could not have successfully imposed programs on colleges and universities just as those institutions could not have successfully resisted the implementation of federal programs. The parties had a mutual need to communication and cooperate.

Communication did develop, but not quickly or easily. When higher education policy emerged as a distinct part of federal policy making with the passage of the 1965 HEA, the Johnson administration did not include associations in the development of the legislation and limited congressional involvement. The associations were more involved in 1972, but not as active participants in a discussion over how to refine and expand the federal student aid program. The associations, dependent on

Representative Green, lacked the ability, knowledge, and skills to participate in the debate. It was after this failure that the associations began to reorganize, and in some cases to organize for the first time, for participation in the discussions that formed and shaped federal higher education policy.

At least three factors contributed to the development and maturation of the communication community. One, already suggested, was the need of the various policy actors to discuss programs to insure that student aid programs were well conceived, planned, and implemented. Once implemented, programs usually hit snags, produce unintended or unanticipated consequences, and otherwise encounter problems that create the need for new communication, consultation, or planning. This process of interacting to resolve unanticipated problems produced a pattern of communication for problem solving that became the norm for the community. This is not to suggest that all efforts to influence policy actors through communication was altruistic, because it was not and is not. Instead, what is suggested is that ideas, discussions, suggestions, and recommendations were held to the test of helping students achieve equal educational opportunity.

A second factor is the longevity of key policy actors and the history of shared activities that comes from that longevity. Representative Ford and Senators Kennedy and Pell were part of the first HEA and remained as key policy actors in 1992. Others, such as Representative Green and Senator Stafford played key roles for a long number of years before retiring from the community. Some House and Senate staffers such as Thomas R. Wolanin have remained active in the community for a significant number of years helping develop an institutional memory that anchors the community and helps carry it into the future. Wolanin and Lawrence E. Gladieux (1976) helped define the higher education policy arena as a community with their book *Congress and the Colleges*. Finally, some policy actors have remained active for an extended duration, but have moved within the community. Beth B. Buehlmann, William A. Blakey, John Dean, Jean S. Frohlicker, and Lawrence S. Zaglaniczny were cited above as examples of the extensive circulation and flow of personnel within the policy arena. This movement has contributed to the maturation of the communication community as policy actors have shared experiences as well as gaining multiple perspectives.

The third factor is the need and demand for communication between policy actors. The 1972 reauthorization strongly underscored the need for higher education associations to participate in a dialogue with federal policymakers. Honey (1972) strongly emphasized this point when he charged that "the failure of the Washington-based spokesmen for higher education to contribute significantly to the shaping of those amendments verges on the scandalous" (p. 1234). The need to participate in a conversation over higher education policy was a mutually expressed need that was expressed and even demanded by federal policymakers. In 1970, Daniel P. Moynihan's sharply worded criticism of the federal higher education associations revolved around their failure to engage in a debate over President Nixon's higher education proposals. Senator Pell was equally critical of the higher education associations in 1972 for their failure to take "the trouble to reflect on and study our ideas which we think can help solve the problem" (quoted in Gladieux & Wolanin, 1976, p. 95).

Following the 1972 reauthorization, the higher education associations moved to increase their ability to communicate with their members, with each other, and with federal higher education policy makers. In some cases, this meant hiring new personnel and creating new offices to handle government relations. The structures for communication ranged from closed, elitists groups to open, egalitarian gatherings. One of the older, more elite, structures for communications is the Secretariat, which was formed in 1962 by the Big Six and five other associations. While the Secretariat was viewed as a powerful, exclusive group, growth in its membership limited the organization's ability to function as a decision-making body. While it continues, the heads of the Big Six formed the Brethren to exchange information and coordinate action. The government relations officers of the Big Six dubbed themselves the Sons of the Brethren and also met to exchange information, ideas, and intelligence. Finally, the Monday and Friday groups, discussed above, brought together higher education representatives to exchange information.

To a considerable degree, communication is the reason for the community's existence. As noted above, the community evolved from the need to respond to the growing federal role in higher education, to communicate the needs of higher education to the federal government, and to communicate between institutions. The reauthorization process reinforces the need for communication. Programs created or continued under previous reauthorizations have to be reviewed and considered before any new decisions can be made. Before new programs can be considered, information to support the need for a new action has to be collected and disseminated. In order to meet the needs of students and institutions, federal policymakers have to hear those needs. Always short on time and information, policymakers look to program constituent to provide information, collect additional information, and build support for programs and program ideas.

The structure of the reauthorization process demands communication. The Education Department and the education subcommittees all request written submissions from interested parties as part of their preparation for reauthorization. Federal policymakers and policy actors constantly lobby one another as written submissions in the form of position papers and recommendations are prepared. Bidirectional lobbying keeps policy proposals within the realm of the possible and keeps policy actors and policymakers in touch with one another. The mutually shaped and tested position papers and policy recommendations are the most practical example of the communication community.

The subcommittee hearings are the most visible example of communication created and demanded by the reauthorization process. The information gained through the hearings could easily and more efficiently be communicated through written submissions. The hearings are a public ritual symbolizing the communication community and its commitment to problem solving. Subcommittee members listen as problems and solutions are identified and discussed. The witnesses pledge their support to solving problems and removing barriers to participation in higher education. The members respond in kind, pledging their support to solving the identified problems and implementing the suggested solutions.

Finally, in making the case that the higher education policy arena is a communication community, no claims are being made about the meaning of power. Dewey claimed that power in a communication community would be replaced by problem solving, but to accept that definition of power at this point would mean forcing the communication community definition of power on the data instead of letting the meaning of power emerge from the data. Before the meaning of power can emerge, the current social context of policy making must be examined. In doing this, the definition of the community based on its historical context may shift and change suggesting a different type of community.

Conclusions

One of the difficulties in approaching the higher education policy arena as an area of study has been the absence of a definition and description that captures the arena's dynamic social interactions and relationships. Among the first to offer a definition of the arena were Wolanin and Gladieux (1975), but they were primarily concerned with providing a background for their larger discussion of political culture. Today, that definition is skeletal, dated, and of limited value in defining a policy arena that has changed substantially in the more than two decades since the definition was first offered.

King (1975), Murray (1976), and Finn (1980) have also offered definitions of the higher education policy arena. King's is perhaps the best of the three, but it has decayed over time. This is because King was presenting a description and definition of the policy arena as it was rather than a framework that could be used to study the arena as it evolved. Murray basically repeated King's earlier work, but dressed it in new conceptual clothing. Finn's effort is seriously flawed and probably continues to enjoy some mention on the basis of his reputation rather than on the merits of his work.

While any definition of the arena will be time- and context-bound, it is possible to use the subgovernment literature to create a framework for describing and defining the higher education policy arena in a way that allows for some adjustment and flexibility to account for changes in the characteristics of the policy arena. The criterion characteristics of internal complexity, functional autonomy, unity within type of participant, and cooperation or conflict are helpful in bringing the policy arena into focus and for adjusting that focus as the policy arena changes. Using these characteristics as a descriptive framework, researchers can discuss shifts and changes in the arena without discarding the framework. Also, changes in the arena can be explained by relating them to the criterion characteristics. The flexibility of this approach represents a significant improvement over earlier descriptions of the policy arena.

The description that comes from the application of this descriptive framework suggests a communication community. Dewey's concept of a communication community starts with the process of collective action. Through the experience of collective action policy actors have developed a common language as well as widely understood signs and symbols that convey shared meanings in the arena. From the experience of collective action, emotional, intellectual, and moral bonds evolve to link and bind members of the policy arena. At the core of this community is a continuing, mutual need to communicate and cooperate.

While Dewey's communication community concept helps define the type of community, it is too soon to extend the concept to include Dewey's definition of power. The meaning of power must emerge from the historical and social context of the community. The next chapter addresses the social context of policy making and continues to test the concept of community. The question of the meaning of power is reserved until chapter 5.

The Changing Relationships Between the States and Universities in the United States

AIMS C. MCGUINNESS, JR.

The relationship between government and higher education in the United States is in transition. After a period in which the states were the dominant force in government policy, the federal government is reemerging as a major player. What is developing is a more complex set of interactions between the federal government and the states. This presentation reviews the developments in the state role in the 1980s and how this role changed in the major recession period of 1989–1992. It then reviews seven major issues that will affect government-higher education relationships in the next decade. It comments on the relevance of trends in US government-higher education relationships to similar developments in other countries.

The Decade of the 1980s*

Clark Kerr, speaking at a Wingspread Conference on the "Governors and Higher Education" in 1985, described what he saw as a return to what had been the historic pattern of state dominance in higher education policy in the United States (Kerr, 1991). Beyond its limited constitutional role, the federal government has played a pivotal role at certain points in the evolution of the nation's colleges and universities. This was most notable in the Land-Grant Acts of the late 1800s, the support of research and graduate education in the post World War II period, and the federal government's support of equal educational opportunity through student grants and loans since the mid-1960s. Individual state higher education systems

evolved after the nation's constitutional and federal structure were well established. They therefore reflected that federal structure.

Kerr described the 1980s as the "Decade of the States". Governors would increasingly dominate policy leadership. Higher education could expect a far more aggressive state agenda aimed at connecting it to the states' social and economic priorities. He predicted that the trade-off might be improved state funding. He also suggested that it would be a period of major private initiative.

The late 1980s confirmed Kerr's prescience about these conditions. Stimulated by a series of national reports, virtually every state enacted policies aimed at spurring greater attention to undergraduate education, economic development and other state priorities. At least initially, higher education funding benefited from the strength of state economies. At work was a fundamental change. Before the 1980s, states focused primarily on questions of institutional accountability for efficient and equitable use of public resources. In the 1980s, they increasingly asked questions about the system's performance in terms of undergraduate teaching and learning and other public priorities. As costs escalated, the question, "For what?" soon shaped the public agenda. (Ewell, 1990; McGuinness *et al.*, 1994).

By the end of the decade, two-thirds of the states had in place mandates that colleges and universities assess student learning (Ewell, Finney and Lenth, 1990). More than 30 states had enacted special incentive funding mecha-

"The Changing Relationships Between the States and Universities in the United States," by Aims C. McGuinness, Jr., reprinted from *Higher Education Management*, Vol. 7, No. 3, November 1995, Organization for Economic Cooperation and Development.

nisms, several of which were designed to focus attention on undergraduate education (Berdahl and Studds, 1989). Still other state initiatives involved changes in college and university missions to emphasize undergraduate teaching, increasing admissions requirements, or establishing special faculty development centers to improve teaching and learning.

An important caveat is that many states and institutions implemented these new requirements as "add-ons" to existing responsibilities and programs. Institutions, for example, established special offices and task forces to carry out the mandates. They did not, however, make changes in the core policies and practices related to teaching and learning or faculty roles and responsibilities. Similarly, states established special assessment programs but often did not integrate these with other functions such as budgeting and program review. As indicated below, this left them vulnerable as economic conditions worsened.

In its most developed form, a new concept of the appropriate role of government-initiated reform emerged, reflected in places as far removed as the state of New Jersey and Western Europe (Ewell, 1990; Neave and van Vught, 1991):

- a broadening of the definition of "accountability" from a primary emphasis on equitable access and efficient use of resources, to an emphasis on performance/results;

- decentralization and de-regulation, with the trade-off being attention to the new accountability for performance;

- a shift from detailed expenditure controls to use of new funding schemes—special competitive, performance or incentive funding programs—designed to stimulate internal realignment of priorities and resources;

- more emphasis on public reporting of results to inform the "market" as opposed to the traditional internal bureaucratic means of accountability.

Transition To A New Decade

The situation changed dramatically in 1989–1990. State dominance continued, but as the economic crisis intensified, new questions about the state/higher education relationship were raised. The state fiscal crisis that had begun in the Northeast soon spread to virtually every state. Several key supporters of the higher education initiatives of the 1980s, such as Governor Thomas Kean of New Jersey, left office. Accelerating political turn-over meant that many of those who had sponsored earlier changes were no longer in office. The education reform movement, focused primarily on public elementary and secondary education, intensified, spurred by the Education Summit of the President and Governors in 1989. Concerns deepened among both policy-makers and the general public about the perceived lack of connection between higher education and the major issues facing society (*e.g.*, the quality of the public schools, crime and youth violence). Policy-makers' impatience with the slow pace and lack of consistency of institutionally based reform intensified. Lack of public evidence that these changes were making a difference—improving performance—led to demands for more aggressive state actions.

Both states and institutions changed the direction or put on hold initiatives enacted just a few years before. States postponed implementation of state assessment programs, although most states retained the initiatives in statute and in state agency responsibilities. Neither institutions nor state agencies that had implemented the programs as "add-ons" could afford to keep them in place. In some cases, as in New Jersey, states eliminated funding as well as the state staff responsible for the assessment initiatives. They did so in part at the urging of institutional leaders who had objected to the initiatives from the beginning or were concerned about the state's approach to implementation.

States suspended most special funding programs. They retained only those, such as the long-standing Tennessee performance funding program, that were integral to the state's approach to budgeting and resource allocation.

Despite these changes, the core concerns about performance and return-on-investment remained. A new generation of policies, some with origins in the earlier initiatives began to emerge. But now state policies reflected a new and more penetrating questioning about the underlying purposes and effectiveness of colleges and universities. Questions about faculty workload and faculty commitment to undergraduate teaching began to dominate legislative agendas (Russell, 1992).

Context for Late 1990s and Beyond

The election of President Clinton and an improving economy led to cautious optimism in the American higher education community in 1993. Yet behind this optimism, many higher education leaders recognized that severe financial constraints would be the reality for much of the coming decade (El-Khawas, 1994). In addition, the political environment in which these changes would take place was highly uncertain. Thirty-six of the fifty state governorships will be contested this Fall. Potentially more than half of these elections will result in new governors being elected. Legislative turnover is accelerating in the face of the pressures of holding public office and term limitations. Legislators who originally ran for office hoping to make a long-term difference in the quality of their state's education system are increasingly caught between federal mandates for large sections of the state's tax resources and the growing needs of the state's population. These state forces directly affect the quality of appointments to state boards, and consequently, the effectiveness of statewide coordination and governance. In general, these will contribute to an instability and lack of continuity in government policy. It will be more difficult to gain political leaders' support for long-term system reform initiatives.

Seven Issues

Besides changes in the broader context, seven points are likely to shape the relationships between higher education and government in the remaining years of the 1990s—especially at the state level.

Increasing demand will out-pace available resource

Demand is escalating across all dimensions of higher education mission: education, research and service. Student demand for access will continue to increase. This will result from increases in the number of secondary school graduates and public perceptions that a postsecondary credential is essential for access to good jobs. The education mission will continue to become more challenging as both standards and the diversity and complexity of the student population increase.

Higher educating funding can expect to benefit from economic recovery but it is unlikely that this will keep pace with increased demand. California is not typical of the nation as a whole, but it illustrates the dilemma that will confront many states:

- California institutions will have to make room for a 50 per cent growth in the number of full-time equivalent students by the year 2006, an increase from 915 000 in 1991–92 to 1.4 million.

- Based on the 1991–92 budget, state support will have to increase 52 per cent to accommodate this enrollment growth. From the more depressed 1992–93 budget, state funding of higher education will have to grow 85 per cent to accommodate these students.

- Only in the most optimistic scenario, a sustained 7 per cent annual growth in the state's economy over the decade at a time when state officials are projecting deficits throughout the 1990s, would be adequate to meet these needs (California Higher Education Policy Center, 1994).

The size of the federal deficit and the demands of other priorities for limited discretionary funding will constrain federal funding. The post-Cold War reductions in defense-related research will be especially important. State budgets are improving but the proportion of these budgets appropriated for higher education is likely to continue to decline. Prisons, health care and elementary and secondary education will be the first priorities for new funding. Tuition and fees will increase but strong public reaction to price increases will limit the extent to which they can keep pace with cost increases. Competition among public and private institutions for limited private philanthropic and corporate support will make this source problematic for most colleges and universities.

The result of the inability of public colleges and universities to obtain revenues to accommodate demand will be a steady decline in the funding per student over the next decade.

How this clash between demand and available resources is resolved will have profound effects on American higher education. The enterprise will be strikingly different ten years from now but the dimensions of the change are exceptionally difficult to predict.

The nation may move back from its commitment to universal access to higher education

The changes leading to less of a commitment to access are the result of separate reactions of many different stakeholders (*e.g.*, institutions, students and states) to fiscal constraints. The cumulative effect of these reactions underscores the potential for conflict between two values or perspectives:

- The commitment to access for all citizens as a public good and a basic right in a democracy. This is the legacy of the 1960s and is deeply ingrained in American society—especially in the middle class.

- The perspective that access to higher education is primarily a private good and that the public commitment should serve explicit public purposes (*e.g.*, ensure an adequately prepared work force or equitable participation of a diverse population in the work force and economy). From this viewpoint, enrollment should be managed to ensure that purposes are met within the constraints of available resources. This emphasis on higher education as a "strategic investment" has shaped much of state policy since the mid-1980s.

States and the federal government are retreating from public support for access to undergraduate education at the baccalaureate level, and shifting public resources to technical-level education and training equivalent to grade levels 10 through 14. This change is resulting not from deliberate policy choice but from the interplay of a number of trends and forces. Signs of this shift are already evident:

- The arena for policy making is now broadened to "post-secondary" education to encompass a wide range of occupational programs at the certificate or associate degree level. With limited resources, a priority for non-collegiate level programs will likely draw public resources from traditional collegiate-level institutions and programs. Unless deliberate financial and programmatic bridges are established throughout the system, access to "post-secondary education" for many students will not mean access to non-collegiate programs and not to colleges and universities.

- Pressures are increasing at the state level to shift funding from the university sector to community colleges to reflect the reality of enrollment shifts.

- The recently-enacted federal "School-to-Work" legislation signals the Clinton Administration's priority for programs that will reach the 50 per cent of high school graduates who do not pursue a baccalaureate degree. A growing number of corporate leaders back this priority because they believe that a high school diploma is no longer an adequate indicator that students have gained the necessary knowledge and skills for full participation in the work force. They also believe that nation needs not more students with university degrees but for more and better programs to raise the knowledge and skills of the work force at the less-than-baccalaureate level.

- Public university officials, when confronted with fiscal constraints, are choosing to limit enrollments through increased admissions requirements and other restrictive policies, and to increase tuition, in an effort to maintain quality. This is what occurred in California, where despite increased demand, enrollments dropped by 200 000 as the result of fee increases and deliberate policies to restrict enrollments (California Higher Education Policy Center, 1994).

- Many independent colleges and universities are reaching the limits of their capacity to match tuition increases with offers of student financial aid—especially to all but the students with the lowest incomes. Opportunities for students from middle income families to choose a private liberal arts college may be fast disappearing.

- The decade-long trend toward student financing through loans is accelerating. When the federal government recently liberalized the requirements for access to federal student loans, the annual dollar value of loans doubled in a single year. Students from low and middle-income families must increasingly rely on loans to finance their college education. The available federal grant aid is increasingly going to students at the lower-division and non-collegiate levels.

Without deliberate policy choices to counter these trends, the United States will move backward toward a more elite system. Baccalaureate-level education will be accessible primarily to those with exceptional academic credentials and to those who can pay or are willing to incur substantial long-term debt. Access for others may mean access to non-collegiate programs. It remains to be seen whether there will be adequate programmatic and financial "bridges" for these students to transfer to collegiate-level programs if they subsequently wish to do so. The social and educational implications of this shift for the nation's growing minority populations are serious and could have profound political consequences at the state and national levels.

Political leaders at both the state and federal level are poised to take more aggressive action on issues of quality but the meaning of "quality" is unclear

In some respects, the debate about the state role in quality improvement is a continuation of the late 1980s debate. But it is taking on a different tone. In the 1980s, state governments accepted the idea that, if prompted to do so, colleges and universities would assume responsibility for self-regulation. Most states designed initiatives, such as assessment mandates and incentive funding, to stimulate institutions to undertake their own quality improvement efforts. They did not require institutions to report the **results** of student assessment but asked them to report whether they were undertaking an assessment **process**.

But, as suggested earlier, the attitude of public officials began to change in the early 1990s. Impatient with the pace of institutional change and faced with competing priorities for limited resources, states began to take bolder steps to require institutions to demonstrate to the government and the public not only how they had quality improvement processes but that these were leading to improved student performance and institutional productivity. By 1993, 18 states had performance indicator requirements in place (Ewell, 1994). Four states had enacted new funding systems that explicitly link funding to performance and by mid-1994 more than half the states were considering such measures (Folger and Jones, 1993).

Faced with the dilemma of escalating demands far beyond available resources, several states have established aggressive initiatives to force fundamental restructuring. The Priorities, Quality and Productivity (PQP) initiative of the Illinois Board of Higher Education uses the Board's information system to identify academic programs for possible elimination and prompts institutions either to accept the Board's recommendations or demonstrate other program changes to achieve quality and productivity improvements (Illinois Board of Higher Education, 1993). Virginia is requiring public colleges and universities to submit restructuring plans "to effect long-term changes in the deployment of faculty, to ensure the effectiveness of academic offerings, to minimise administrative and instructional costs, to prepare for the demands of enrollment increases, and to address funding priorities as approved by the General Assembly" (Virginia, 1994).

The new federal requirement (Part H) that states designate agencies to monitor the quality of certain institutions identified as potential problems for the federal student assistance programs may also expand the state's regulatory role, especially with respect to independent private non-profit and proprietary institutions. It is too early to say what this impact will be on state policy (see below).

Behind the new concerns about quality is a growing gap between higher education and key stakeholders on basic questions such as what is quality, who should define quality, to whom should the academy be accountable, who should be responsible for quality assurance, and to what extent the colleges and universities must change. At issue are significantly different views of "quality". In many respects, the public debate is not about "quality" in terms understood within the academy (*e.g.*, curriculum, faculty or undergraduate teaching and learning). It is one of priorities—a sense that higher education is focused on internal priorities disconnected from the broader public interest. In other words, the issue is whether higher education "is doing the right things," not whether it is "doing things right". Corporate leaders and public officials also seem to differ on the meaning of "quality" and "quality improvement". Corporate leaders are heavily influenced by their experience with "total quality" or "continuous quality improvement". Their conceptions differ sharply from the top-down, fixed-standard approach to quality reflected in many of the new state initiatives.

Ironically, this would happen despite evidence that colleges and universities are engaged in more fundamental restructuring than any time in the past quarter century (El-Khawas, 1994; McGuinness and Ewell, 1994; Pew, 1993, 1994). It also comes at a time that national higher education leaders are acknowledging the need for reform in voluntary accreditation. Unfortunately, these actions may be coming too late to forestall more aggressive governmental involvement.

Despite this more aggressive tone in state policy, however, the reality is that, comparatively speaking, higher education problems are **not** high on state agendas. Other areas such as health, criminal justice and reform of the elementary and secondary system dominate the agenda. The danger is that state leaders, frustrated with the perceived lack of response from institutions but overwhelmed by other priorities, will cut higher education's funding or try to push the problems away by privatizing the system.

Federal policy and the consequences of federal fiscal constraints are coming to have a significant impact on the enterprise

In the past, federal policy affected higher education primarily through a combination of increased funding and the incentives imbedded in that funding. Examples include the GI bill in the late 1940s, federal research funding through the National Science Foundation and subsequent mission-oriented funding related to defense, health and other priorities, and federal student grants and loans. Now the impact is being felt not in increased funding but in the priorities implied by shifts and cuts in funding, and by the regulations that accompany funding:

- Cuts in funding for research and graduate education through the Department of Defense are unlikely to be replaced by funding in other areas and will intensify competition for limited funding available through the National Science Foundation. This is likely to put extraordinary pressures on the major public research universities which will be unable to recover lost federal funding with state funding. Efforts to shift the costs to undergraduates through tuition increases will enflame existing controversies about the costs and institutional priorities.

- Student demand, aided by the Clinton Administration's priorities, will shift federal student subsidy more toward those at the less-than-baccalaureate level. This will exacerbate the already complicated issues of quality control and cost containment, especially related to the vast proprietary trade and technical school sector.

- The federal requirements related to accreditation and state approval enacted in the 1992 amendments to the Higher Education Act (Part H) are already placing the federal government at the center of debates about quality in American higher education. Enacted primarily to address problems of fraud and abuse in the federal student loan programs, problems that were most severe in the proprietary sector, these new requirements are changing the nature of both voluntary accreditation and state oversight. The most hotly debated federal requirement is for the designation of State Postsecondary Review Entities (SPRE's). The state agencies designated as the "SPRE" are required to gather data from certain institutions "triggered" by the US Secretary of Education because of high loan defaults or other criteria. The designated agency will then have to make a determination, based on analysis of the information and an independent review, whether the institutions should be eligible to continue participating in the federal student assistance programs. The SPRE responsibilities are likely to significantly impact the roles and responsibilities of many of the nation's state coordinating and governing boards, most of which have been assigned this responsibility.

- The federal Direct Loan Program, enacted in 1993 at the urging of the Clinton Administration, will phase in over several years a new program of income-contingent loans backed by federal capital. This is intended to replace the current major program which is financed and operated through with private capital through banks and a network of state guarantee agencies. At the same time, Congress liberalized the eligibility requirements for the current program with the result that loan volume has increased 50 per cent in two years. These changes coupled with the new Direct Loan program greatly increase incentives for students to assume more responsibility for paying for their own education. Public policy is encouraging parents and students to shift the cost of higher education to the next generation. The trend toward an even greater emphasis on a privatized higher education system in the United States will accelerate.

Each of these changes in federal policy will direct and constrain actions by the states and institutions. The "intergovernmental" dimension of policy-making are becoming more complicated.

Tensions are mounting between major public research universities and their state constituents and while mission drift of other institutions toward the university model continue

At work is a basic conflict between what Kerr calls two "laws of motion":

> "1) the further internationalization of learning, and 2) the intensification of the interest of independent nation-states in the conscious use of these institutions for their own selective purposes." (Kerr, 1990).

In the United States, this conflict is most pronounced in the relationship between the major public research universities and state governments. It is these institutions (*e.g.*, the University of California, the University of Wisconsin at Madison, the University of North Carolina at Chapel Hill or Ohio State University) that usually set the tone of the relationship between higher education and state government. Being admitted to these institutions is the aspiration of the brightest students in the state. For many—especially middle-income families—attending the state university at a fairly low tuition is as much a right as a privilege. The state university's admissions requirements often are the dominant influence on secondary school standards. State political and business leaders look to the state university as a source of prestige, applied research and service for the state's economic and social well-being.

Despite these state and regional expectations, public research universities are increasingly functioning as national, if not global, institutions. Their faculty and students (especially graduate students) come from throughout the world. They define their expectations in terms of peer institutions (or competitors) on a global basis. Their funding is exceptionally diverse with only 17 to 25 per cent from state appropriations. Most obtain substantial federal research funding and are depending more and more on research support from multi-national corporations. Pressures from non-state funding sources, international networks of scholars, and the competitive forces within the professions and disciplines, tend to draw these universities and their faculties away from the concerns and priorities of the state and the immediate population.

The clash between these pressures—some state and regional and others national and international—is fueling the frustration of some political leaders who feel that state universities are either unable or unwilling to respond to major state priorities. Widespread legislative initiatives on faculty workload and faculty attention to undergraduate teaching reflect a sense that universities are driven by the internal faculty and disciplinary priorities and not by a commitment of service to students and society. The fiscal realities are leading universities to make decisions which only exacerbate the tensions. Enrollment caps deny students their "right" to attend the public university. Larger class sizes fuel concerns that students are paying more but getting less. Even though the universities' funding may come largely from non-state sources, state leaders see them as "belonging to" the state.

Two negative scenarios could result from this clash. Some states may attempt to gain even greater control of state university leadership and priorities through increased regulatory and accountability measures. Others may move the opposite direction and give the state universities greater independence as "state-assisted" private corporations. The risk under either scenario will be that states draw back from their commitment to funding.

These developments focused on the major public research universities have profound effects or other public institutions. The result is an enterprise increasingly unable to respond to state and regional demands for access and services. Pressures both in and out of the academy continue to push institutions toward the research university model. With the exception of community colleges, most state colleges and universities (the institutions that serve most students at the baccalaureate level in the United States) have converged toward a "middle" position of the comprehensive state university. This means that over the past two decades they reduced faculty teaching loads, placed more emphasis in faculty reward systems on publications in refereed journals, and established more graduate and professional degree programs, and changed their names to "university". The name change was seen as important to reflect the expanded missions and to enhance the institutions' image for prospective students, faculty and funding sources.

At a time, then, that state and regional constituencies are seeking responsiveness to their needs, more and more of the public university sector is keying its future to models, priorities and constituencies far removed from these local concerns.

Technology, distance learning and global networks of scholars and students are transforming teaching and learning and delivery of educational services in ways that may make the current structure of institutions and state government policies obsolete

Because these trends are more discussed than implemented it is difficult to anticipate their impact on the current relationships between government and higher education. Some are skeptical—especially about whether these developments will improve the capacity of the enterprise to accommodate demand or reduce costs. Others, such as James R. Mingle, executive director of the State Higher Education Executive Officers, the national association of state higher education officials, believe that technology will be the single greatest force for change in the future. It will affect the "virtual" nature of the campuses but also the relationships among students, professors, and institutional leaders. It will change governance and accountability structures from the past emphasis on satisfying public officials to a new emphasis on customers. Telecommunications will increase capacity and thereby increase the power of competition as a new force for change (SHEEO, 1994). Current policies and structures must change if they are not to be significant barriers to change. Examples include financing policies that do not provide incentives for faculty to employ new technologies in teaching and learning, and state quality assurance mechanisms that are unable to accommodate new educational delivery systems, distance learning or the increasing inter-state mobility of students and scholars.

State structures may be barriers to the capacity of institutions to respond to changing conditions

In the face of the previous six issues, the structures responsible for coordinating the relationship between higher education and the state are under increasing pressure. In some cases, they are ill-equipped to handle these relationships in the coming decade. From an international comparative perspective, US higher education is highly decentralized. But throughout the 20th century, the enterprise has undergone a steady process of consolidation and centralization (Kerr and Gade, 1989; McGuinness *et al.*, 1994). Much of this resulted from efforts of states to limit the drift of institutions to the research university model and to curb proliferation and duplication of high-cost graduate and professional programs.

Today, multi-campus or consolidated systems, systems that are governed by a single policy board, encompass seventy per cent of enrollment in public higher education. In other words, comparatively few campuses have their own governing boards. Most campus chief executive reports are appointed by and report to a system chief executive. In all but three states, one or more boards oversees all of higher education. In about half the states, this is a statewide governing board with broad policy and implementation authority for the whole system. In the other half of the states, statewide planning and coordinating boards (with responsibilities not unlike education ministries in Europe) provide policy leadership for the system while governance is relatively decentralized under boards for the state universities and college systems or community colleges.

Recent studies by the Education Commission of the States (ECS) and the National Center for Higher Education Management Systems (NCHEMS) raise serious questions about the capacity of this increasingly consolidated enterprise to respond to the rapidly changing external environment. (McGuinness, 1994*b*). In terms of multi-campus systems, a few are responding to new conditions by:

- Balancing decentralization with redefined, and more lightly staffed central leadership. Developing campuses with distinctive missions and unique cultures is important but so also are the ties of each unit with the larger whole. The system role becomes more that of educational leadership than of bureaucratic control.

- Undertaking system initiatives to promote resource-sharing and collaboration among campuses.

- Developing system-wide services through use of "lead campuses" rather than expanding the system offices.

- Greatly expanded use of technology for both educational and administrative purposes.

But many other multi-campus systems are plagued by serious problems. A number are struggling with the constraints of sheer size and the inertia that comes with the accumulation of policies and procedures over the decades. Despite the bright spots just mentioned, this is a more common pattern:

- An inwardly driven agenda defined in terms of resource needs and constraints and disconnected from the broader economic and social forces affecting the states in which they are located.

- Failure to reinforce mission-differentiation among the system campuses with differentiated policies on faculty promotion and tenure and incentives for undergraduate teaching.

- A tendency toward "one-size-fits-all"—which inevitably impose the values of research and disciplinary focus on campuses where undergraduate teaching is ostensibly the primary mission.

- The lack of clear definition of the roles that a system can play in reinforcing campus initiatives on priorities important to the public such as undergraduate education, applied research and public service.

Only a few state coordinating boards are rethinking their traditional roles and responsibilities. Many are severely limited by:

- Statutory obligations to carry out often out-dated regulations or programs accumulated over the years through actions of successive governors and legislatures.

- A lack of means—or perhaps even a recognized role—to raise questions for public debate about the long-term consequences of short-term solutions.

- A tendency to emphasize "preventing bad things from happening" rather than deliberately stimulating positive responses.

- A loss of credibility in bridging political and education perspectives—especially on an issue such as undergraduate education.

- Policies implemented without an obvious underlying concept of how institutional change takes place.

- Limited efforts to achieve policy coherence. Links between strategic planning and budgeting and the agency's substantive agenda related to undergraduate education are rare.

- Policies and procedures of state general government (*e.g.*, civil service requirements, procurement policies, budget and reporting requirements inconsistent with the unique characteristics of colleges and universities) severely hamper the capacity of institutions to respond to new realities.

Except for a few bright spots, the overall picture of state coordination and governance across the United States is one of uncertainty and stagnation. Few states have in place structures that will provide the policy leadership necessary to confront the major challenges of the decade; and few of these structures are adequate to ensure a constructive relationship between the academy and government in this period of extraordinary change.

In this uncertain climate, no clearly defined new paradigm is emerging. States appear to be grasping for alternatives:

- Some states are consolidating their systems. Minnesota, for example, is implementing a merger of all public institutions (state universities, technical institutions and community colleges) under a new consolidated governing board. The state will have two major

systems: the newly created system and the University of Minnesota.

- New Jersey recently eliminated the State Board and Department of Higher Education and decentralized its system by giving the governing boards of each public institution more authority and responsibility. It established a new, smaller and more policy-oriented (as opposed to regulatory) Commission on Higher Education to plan and coordinate the system.

- Some states are considering further "privatization" of their public systems. Oregon, for example, will be considering a proposal to make the Oregon Higher Education System (the system with all the senior colleges and universities) a "private corporation for public purposes". The system would be exempted from many state procedural controls but would continue to receive state support and be accountable to the state for performance.

Lurking behind this ambivalence are growing pressures for radical changes in state structures as fundamental as is proposed for colleges and universities. In fact, the sense is that campus change cannot and will not change unless state structures and policies change. As one observer expressed it, "A number of legislators would just like to 'blow the system apart'". The recent changes in New Jersey show that this can happen. Breaking up multicampus systems, creating new market-driven systems or even privatizing the whole enterprise are ideas that are just beginning to be debated seriously.

The Relevance of the American Experience to Other Nations

In international forums, the US is often held out as a model for government-higher education relationships. Often overlooked are the striking similarities in the underlying issues and trends between the United States and other nations. As others have observed, there is a world-wide convergence in issues and government policies (Kerr, 1987; Neave and van Vught, 1991; Goedegebuure *et al.*, 1993). The United States may be a better source of examples of what **does not work** than it is of models that should be copied and imposed on other nations and cultures.

In a broad sense, many nations are confronting these issues:

- How in a democratic society to balance the obligation to provide higher education to the nation's citizens as a basic right, with the conception of higher education as service to the state and society.

- How to accommodate escalating demand in the face of higher expectations for quality, severe fiscal constraints and the inflexibility of existing institutional structures and policies.

- How to foster and sustain diverse institutions and programs, from highly specialized technical training to major research universities, in the face of inexorable pressures for convergence toward a single model of the research university.

- How to develop higher education systems that will respond to societal expectations with respect to the quality of graduates and the application of research and technology to major social and economic problems.

- How to design and implement public policies that will stimulate and support systemic and institutional change and diversify the sources of revenue available to meet rising demands.

As illustrated by the seven issues, certain aspects of the US higher education enterprise that historically have addressed these issues are under serious strain:

- At a time when other nations are moving toward greater access and opportunity for broader segments of society, the United States may be on the verge of abandoning its commitment to access as a public commitment.

- The US traditions of institutional self-regulation and voluntary accreditation have lost their credibility as means to ensure the public of the quality and

integrity of individual colleges and university or the enterprise as a whole.

- Institutional diversity in the public sector is narrowing, as pressures continue for colleges to become universities, for faculty reward systems to converge toward the research university's expectations, and for separately governed universities to be merged into larger systems.

- The distinction between public and private is becoming blurred. Private colleges and universities are becoming more dependent on state and federal funding, and public institutions, especially the major research universities, receive only a fraction of their support from states and are aggressively seeking private funding.

- Widely acclaimed policies, such as the California Master Plan, are in serious disrepair and are inadequate as frameworks to guide policy for the next decade (California Higher Education Policy Center).

- In some respects, the relatively uncoordinated, highly decentralized, market-driven nature of the enterprise may be as much of a liability as a strength. There is little evidence that the interests of society and the state will necessarily be served by unguided entrepreneurial pursuits of universities and their faculties. But the hodgepodge of inconsistent, constantly changing federal and state policies does not represent a coherent expression of public interest.

What is lacking both at the state and federal levels is an informed public debate about the consequences of current trends and the choices that must be made if these trends are to be reversed. With the press of other priorities, it remains to be seen whether these issues will gain the attention of public officials and the general public to the extent necessary to prompt change. But even if the debate is joined, the issues will remain: What public policies are most likely to change to meet major public priorities? How can these be designed and implemented to have a long-term, constructive impact on the enterprise? The United States can learn as much from other countries as from its own experience in its effort to find answers to these questions.

References

Berdahl, R. O. and Studds, S. M. (1989), *The Tension of Excellence and Equity*, College Park National Center for Postsecondary Governance and Finance.

California Higher Education Policy Center (1994), *Time for Decision: California's Legacy and the Future of Higher Education. A Report and Recommendations*, draft, March.

Education Commission of the States (1994), *Charting Higher Education Accountability: A Sourcebook on State-Level Performance Indicators*, S. Ruppert (ed.), Denver: ECS.

El-Khawas, E. (1990), *Campus Trends 1990*, Washington, D.C.: American Council on Education.

El-Khawas, E. (1994), *Campus Trends 1994: A Time for Redirection*, Washington, D.C. American Council on Education.

Ewell, P. T. (1990). *Assessment and the "New Accountability": Challenge for Higher Education's Leadership*, Denver: Education Commission of the States, ECS.

Ewell, P. T., J. Finney and C. Lenth (1990). "Filling in the Mosaic: The Emerging Pattern of State-Based Assessment," *AAHE Bulletin*, Vol. 42, No. 8, pp. 3–5.

Ewell, P. T. (1992). "Defining the Quality-Driven Institution," *Assessment Update*, Vol. 4, No. 5. September-October 1992.

Ewell, P. T. (1993). "Total Quality and Academic Practice: The Idea We've Been Waiting For?" *Change*, Vol. 25, No. 3, May/June, pp. 49–55.

Ewell, P. T. (1994). "Developing Statewide Performance Indicators for Higher Education: Policy Themes and Variations," *Charting Higher Education Accountability*, Denver: ECS.

Folger, J. K. and D. P. Jones (1993). *The Use of Financing Policy to Achieve State Objectives*, Denver: National Center for Higher Education Management Systems and Education Commission of the States.

Goedegebuure *et al.* (eds.) (1993). *Higher Education Policy: An International Comparative Perspective*, Oxford: Pergamon Press.

Illinois Board of Higher Education (1993). "Priorities, Quality and Productivity of Illinois Higher Education: Summary and Assessment for 1992–93 and Recommendations for 1993–94," Springfield, Illinois. November 9, 1993.

Johnstone, D. B. (1993). *Learning Productivity: A New Imperative for American Higher Education*, Studies in Public Higher Education, No. 3, Albany: State University of New York.

Kerr, C. (1987). "Critical Age in the University World: Accumulated Heritage Versus Modern Imperatives," *European Journal of Education*, 22, 2.

Kerr, C. (1990), "The Internationalization of Learning and the Nationalization of the Purposes of Higher Education: Two 'Laws of Motion' in Conflict," *European Journal of Education*, 25, No. 1.

Kerr, C. (1991), "The States and Higher Education: Changes Ahead," *The Great Transformation in Higher Education, 1960–1980*, Albany: SUNY Press.

Kerr, C. and M. L. Gade (1989), *The Guardians: Boards of Trustees of American Colleges and Universities*, Washington, D.C.: Association of Governing Boards of Universities and Colleges.

McGuinness, A. C., Jr. (1992), "Lessons from European Integration for US Higher Education," paper presented at the Eleventh General Conference of IMHE Member Institutions, OECD, Paris, France, September 1992.

McGuinness, A. C., Jr., R. Martin, E. and S. Arredondo (1994), *State Postsecondary Education Structures Handbook 1994*, Denver: ECS.

McGuinness, A. C., Jr. (1994a), "State Policy and Faculty Workload: Trends across the United States," *Higher Education Policy*, Vol. 7, No. 2

McGuinness, A. C., Jr. (1994b), *A Framework for Evaluating State Policy Roles in Improving Undergraduate Education: Stimulating Long-Term Systemic Change*, Denver: ECS.

McGuinness, A. C., Jr, and P. T. Ewell (1994), "Improving Productivity and Quality in Higher Education," *AGB Priorities*, No. 2, Fall 1994.

Mingle, J. R. (1992), *State Policy and Productivity in Higher Education*, Denver, Co.: State Higher Education Executive Officers.

Neave, G. and F. A. van Vught (eds.) (1991), *Prometheus Bound, the changing relationship between government and higher education*, Pergamon Press, Oxford, 1991.

Pew Higher Education Research Program (1990), "The Lattice and the Ratchet," *Policy Perspectives*, Vol. 2, No. 4, June 1990.

Pew Higher Education Research Program (1993), "A Call to Meeting," *Policy Perspectives*, Vol. 4, No. 4 February 1993.

Pew Higher Education Research Program (1994), "To Dance with Change," *Policy Perspectives*, Vol. 5, No. 3, April 1994.

Russell, A. B. (1992), *Faculty Workload: State and System Perspectives*, Denver: State Higher Education Executive Officers and Education Commission of the States.

State Higher Education Executive Officers (1990), *The Dynamics of Academic Productivity*, Denver, Co.: State Higher Education Executive Officers.

State Higher Education Executive Officers (1994), *Redesign: Higher Education Delivery Systems for the Twenty-First Century*, Vol. 1, No. 1.

van Vught, F. A. (1994), *Higher Education in Europe: A Policy Analysis Perspective*, Enschede: Center for Higher Education Policy Studies, University of Twente.

Virginia Council of Higher Education (1994), *Council Notes: Virginia Higher Education*, Richmond, Virginia, June 14, 1994.

Footnote

* This review draws on a recent report by Aims C. McGuinness, Jr., *A Framework for Evaluating State Policy Roles in Improving Undergraduate Education: Stimulating Long-Term Systemic Change* (Denver: ECS, 1994).

The Rewards of Neighborliness

HOWARD RAY ROWLAND

Howard Ray Rowland is director of information services at St. Cloud State University, where he holds the academic rank of professor. He has taught courses in mass communications and public relations in the university's study program in Denmark. He is a former district chairperson and national secretary of the Council for Advancement and Support of Education.

Colleges and universities today are engaged in a wide range of community relations activities. Consider these cases: When the University of Minnesota needed to use an abandoned mine in northern Minnesota to conduct a research project, opposition from the local community was anticipated. To counter objections, the university hosted a dinner meeting with the community's opinion leaders, followed by a public meeting in the local school. University representatives assured residents that the project posed no danger to the community and some economic benefits would be realized. A potentially explosive situation was defused.

After a long history of antagonism, the city of New Haven and Yale University have come to terms. As allies, the city and university lobbied successfully to win state approval for a program providing state funds to cities with large amounts of tax-exempt property. Yale has made its first major financial investments off campus in a downtown redevelopment project and has revived a scholarship program for local students. Observed Yale President A. Bartlett Giamatti: "We will go forward together, or neither of us will go forward" (Powell, 1979, p. 72).

Retired business executives spend at least one day a week making fund-raising for Rockhurst College. "It's more than the contributions they collect, although that's certainly important," commented Tom Reardon, director of community relations. "They're also our personal ambassadors. They pass on news of college programs and what Rockhurst stands for to persons who otherwise might not hear" (Bartocci, 1978, p. 23).

As part of its continuing efforts to bridge the "town-gown" gap, the office of community affairs at Johns Hopkins University instituted an environmental education program using the campus and adjoining park, with their 230 acres of flora and fauna, as a classroom for area elementary school children and members of the community (Ingalls, 1978, p. 19).

Joliet Junior College benefited from a successful bond election in 1977 when 72.5 percent of those voting supported the issue. "This was not the result of a short campaign," said President Harold D. McAninch. "It was built on the positive image of the college in the community, an image we planned and developed for six years. We invited service clubs to meet on campus. We set up special programs for senior citizens. Civic groups used campus facilities at no cost. We positively related the college to as many constituencies in the district as possible" (McAninch, 1978, p. 28).

A weekly round table established by Syracuse University has launched broadly based community development projects in the Syracuse area. Participants come from government, business, education, and civic organizations. In addition, the university sponsors semi-annual retreats to which civic leaders are

"The Rewards of Neighborliness," by Howard Ray Rowland, reprinted from *Effective Community Relations: New Directions for Institutional Advancement*, No. 10, edited by Howard Ray Rowland, 1980, Jossey-Bass Publishers, Inc.

invited for intensive study of community problems (Spear, 1975, p. 98).

A Common Concern

What do these diverse activities have in common? They all suggest that institutions of higher education—regardless of size, location, or mission—recognize the importance of cultivating good relationships with their communities. Although only a small percentage of colleges and universities have identified community relations as the primary concern of an office or an individual, there is widespread acknowledgment that considerable attention must be devoted to their communities if institutional goals and objectives are to be achieved.

The consequences of neglecting community relations are usually severe and long-lasting. By their very nature, institutions of higher education can cause friction if not outright hostility wherever they are located. "The occasional tumultuous behavior of students wears thin the patience of our host communities," warns Patrick Aikman (1978, p. 46). "The sudden purchase of extensive real estate, intrusions into well-established community patterns, or other such activities may not endear us to our communities." Aikman also points out that the average income of upper-level college employees may be—or seem to be—substantially higher than that of the general population. "This along with fringe benefits not ordinarily available to the average citizens— twelve months pay for nine months work,' lengthy vacations, and sabbatical leaves—complicate the 'town-gown' relationship." Aikman notes that "the community does not fully grasp the idea that a college is an industry where productivity is not measured in metric tons, bushels per acre, or units per hour. Its results can seldom be quantified. The search for truth can be rough and tumble. Outsiders neither understand nor appreciate that debate and controversy are generally healthy and constructive."

Throughout history, colleges and universities have had some difficulties with their neighboring communities. In the Middle Ages riots between students and townspeople were frequent, observes Donald Winkler (1978, p. 8). In 1775, when Columbia University was still

King's College of Wall Street, a mob of local townspeople marched on the campus seeking the college president, Miles Cooper, a Tory sympathizer. While undergraduate Alexander Hamilton kept the angry crowd at bay, Cooper scurried out a window and down the Hudson River. The next day he boarded a ship for England, never to return. "Columbia and its presidents have had problems with the city ever since," comments Robert Price in a report prepared for the Carnegie Commission on Higher Education (Nash, 1973, p. 95).

In recent years many institutions, particularly urban universities, have taken a new look at the importance of their community relationships. A number of circumstances arose simultaneously to focus attention on the interdependence of the college or university and its community. The most important single factor was the unprecedented enrollment increases of the 1960s and 1970s, necessitating major expansions of facilities. Another was the channeling of billions of dollars of federal and state funds into higher education institutions to help solve societal problems. Student militancy associated with the Vietnam conflict and the deterioration of the inner city also contributed to "town-gown" interaction.

"The university located in an urban setting is not only an educational institution that happens to be in a city," notes the Carnegie Commission on Higher Education (*Digest of Reports . . .*, 1974, p. 146). It's a physical entity and a corporate force that has diverse and major impacts on the life and environment of the city. It is in the context of the growing urban crises, however, that these impacts have taken on new significance requiring more conscious efforts on the part of the institution to maximize positive aspects and control potentially negative effects."

Causes of Ill Will

The Carnegie Commission identifies some reasons why institutions generate ill will in their urban environments: "Uncertain expansion plans of a university can adversely affect maintenance standards of neighboring areas as well as real estate values; requirement for parking facilities and increased traffic in the vicinities of the campus may place an excessive burden on the city; and student housing patterns, from the viewpoint of some inhabitants of the neighborhood, may have undesirable effects on otherwise attractive residential areas" (*Digest of Reports . . .*, 1974, p. 146).

Gordon Seyffert points out that a college or university may antagonize townspeople by its inability to control student behavior. "Whether or not to call in local police during campus riots was a particularly vexing question. Many urban institutions felt a strong loyalty to the traditions of academic independence in disciplinary matters, while at the same time recognizing the validity of community fears of unleashed campus violence that could spread into surrounding private property" (1975, p. 146).

"Blight, obsolescence, deterioration, overcrowding, and traffic congestion are common in the areas surrounding many urban institutions," observes J. Martin Klotsche, former chancellor of the University of Wisconsin-Milwaukee (1966, p. 62). "These have a stultifying effect on institutional growth and are a deterrent to those wanting to live in the immediate vicinity of the institution. Often the university itself has contributed to these conditions. The need for inexpensive rooms and cheap food and personal services for students has often resulted in the inflow of low-cost facilities and services to meet these needs. High population density has led to the conversion of large single-family dwellings into rooming houses, "efficiency" apartments, and multiple residences. Zoning violations and substandard living conditions have occurred. Traditional street patterns, unable to handle peak load traffic and transportation problems, have impeded the efficient flow of traffic. The absence of adequate off-street parking facilities has aggravated congestion and contributed to hazardous driving conditions. High-density land coverages and indiscriminate intermingling of residential and commercial use properties have resulted in incompatible land uses."

Most colleges and universities do not pay local real estate taxes, another bone of contention. Although some institutions, such as Harvard, have voluntarily contributed to local tax revenues, there is strong sentiment in many communities that the resident college or university is not paying its fair share for city services, such as fire and police protection, street

maintenance, and parks and playgrounds. Other friction points include students voting in city elections, students competing with residents for jobs, and institutional purchasing policies (not buying from local suppliers).

Seyffert warns university administrators, who think of themselves as professionals concerned for the future of the neighborhoods they serve, that they are viewed much differently by residents, especially low-income persons living in decaying housing. "It is commonplace for residents to express fear and suspicion of the purposes of university expansion projects," he reports. "Some fear of losing their homes. Residents are frequently afraid of losing their neighborhood. Physical changes often beget social changes which long-time residents deem undesirable. Congestion, overcrowding, and noise are already evident by the time most urban universities feel the need to originate community-oriented services or physical expansion of the campus. Thus the resident feels imposed upon when the university—the source of the discomfort—presents itself as the proper midwife for the birth of community-centered planning and service programs. Aside from whatever powers of eminent domain the university may be privileged to enjoy (and this power is certainly a stumbling block to community trust), many neighborhoods view universities as elements of the community power structure" (1975, pp. 139–140).

"Company Town" Image

Another kind of problem is evident in smaller communities where the college or university is one of the largest institutions and its students and employees comprise a substantial portion of the population. As Lawrence Nolte observes: "Whenever any organization seems to have a conspicuous hand in every activity, whenever it seems to be running everything in the community, there is an adverse reaction. The old 'company town' image is a bad image even when the organization's activities are highly beneficial and unselfish. To avoid paternalism, the organization must be ready and willing to help with both manpower and money, but it must strive for an image of helpfulness rather than dominance. When an organization defies community opinion and does what it chooses without regard for the wishes of others, it can quickly develop a large group of active enemies" (1979, p. 228).

Most colleges and universities have become acutely aware of the numerous ways they can alienate their communities, whether they are sprawling urban institutions or small town campuses. They should recall that institutions of higher education also have many positive features that can be emphasized to offset the negative factors.

The college or university is generally recognized as a highly beneficial, relatively stable institution, an asset no community wants to lose. It provides a good working environment, generally noncompetitive with other institutions. It offers a wide variety of educational, cultural, and recreational programs. It requires a highly educated and talented work force and attracts students who contribute to the diversity of the community. It brings in business and visitors. On balance, the economic impact is favorable. Its production does not pollute the environment. It generally enhances the community's quality of life.

John Marston (1979) maintains that both the community and the institution have expectations which must be met if they are to be compatible. The community expects the institution to be an economic asset, not a liability; to improve the environment, not harm it; to participate in civic activities, not neglect them; to provide stability, not anxiety; and to be a source of community pride, not embarrassment. From its community the institution expects adequate services, fair treatment, good living conditions for its employees, a reliable source of labor, and support for its programs and services.

An institution cannot be regarded as a good neighbor unless it demonstrates a concern for self-improvement and community action, according to Nolte. "Self-improvement may include constructive actions such as designing buildings to be beautiful as well as functional; concealing unsightly equipment; avoiding pollution of air and water; preserving natural beauty; protection of open space; use of art, decoration, and landscaping; and minimizing the inconvenience and obstruction caused by construction," he suggests. "Community action includes all contributions that indicate

an awareness of social responsibility" (1979, pp. 237–239).

"Communities are bound together by group consensus, which is simply the development and mutual acceptance of a common set of values, goals and objectives," Charles Steinberg explains. "The institution cannot function successfully without community support, and community support implies the need for those constructive deeds in the public interest that comprise successful public relations. No institution can function effectively and remain remote from the life of the community in which it operates. Participation is inevitable, if not by design, then by force of circumstances" (1975, pp. 123, 125).

Community colleges and urban universities have taken the lead in responding to the pressing needs of their communities, sometimes by design but often by force of circumstances. Charles Stanton points out that the two-year college has incorporated a pervasive value of American education—social relevance. According to Stanton, the uniqueness of the two-year college lies in its ability to meet directly the educational and training needs of its constituent community (Stanton, 1975).

Community Services

Gundar Myran (1974, pp. 2–10) identifies community services as one of five functions of the community college. "Nearly all community colleges now have a community services administrator or a more extensive staff," he reports. "Programs offered by community colleges have increased in scope, sophistication, and impact on the community." He defines community-based education as a curriculum that includes experiences in the community as well as in the classroom. It is expected that many programs of the college will benefit the community as well as the student. The college analyzes community problems and students serve as consultants or interns to local community agencies and groups. The college draws upon the expertise of practitioners in various fields who live in the region; their on-the-job skills complement the more theoretical orientation of the professors.

Myran (1974) identifies specific responses that community colleges can make to community service challenges, mostly in urban areas.

To help a community address its economic and technological problems, for example, the community college can offer career counseling, job placement, consulting services, manpower training programs, new career programs, vocational retraining and refresher courses, small business management training, and workshops and seminars for business and industry. To provide more accessibility to educational services, the community college can encourage community use of its facilities, offer television courses, teach evening and weekend classes, establish neighborhood learning centers, operate a speakers bureau, and furnish library, museum, and gallery services.

The dominant American practice of establishing private and public colleges outside the big cities resulted in a deficit of higher education facilities in some metropolitan centers and a lack of campus experience in dealing with city problems until recent years. But American society is now irretrievably an urban civilization, and some of the nation's most urgent problems involve the quality of life in the city (*Digest of Reports . . .*, 1974).

Widespread urban involvement is a recent response by higher education to obvious needs. A survey of more than 500 colleges and universities in 1973 indicated that most of the institutions considered urban involvement to be a major function of higher education, a function which was receiving increasing attention on their campuses (Jenkins and Ross, 1975).

Until the 1960s, however, most urban universities rarely accepted any direct responsibility for solving problems in their surrounding communities. Some divisions, such as medical school hospitals, provided service to the community, but usually the teaching and research needs of the institution dominated other considerations, sometimes to the detriment of community service. A combination of social legislation, funding from major foundations, and concern of students and faculty in the issues of poverty, racism, and civil rights brought about a level of university involvement in community affairs that far exceeded previous participation. Most campuses established new relationships between academic departments and community agencies; added new service centers, frequently designated as urban affairs offices; and recruited minority students and faculty by providing supporting

services and facilities (Corbett and Levine, 1974).

Programs for Problems

Beginning in the mid-1960s, institutions of higher education developed urban courses, programs, and majors, in most cases as a reaction to the growing awareness of urban problems. Student demands for programs that were more relevant to the needs of an urban society also spurred internal changes. The creation of urban research centers helped focus university attention on urban studies as a legitimate area of scholarly activity.

Also during the 1960s the federal government helped universities establish and expand cooperative programs with local governments. Two of the programs—Title I of the Higher Education Act (1975) and the Urban Observatory Program—generated continuing relationships. Other programs, such as Professors of the City and consortium arrangements, have strengthened university-city cooperation in specific situations. Proposals for urban grant universities suggested ways of creating continuous linkages between higher education institutions and cities.

A lesson learned from all this activity, however, is that universities and cities, although mutually supportive, have different goals. As a result they employ different strategies, interact with different agencies, and respond to different challenges. Universities and local governments have institutional strengths that can be used to foster stronger relationships. However, they have similar weaknesses: rigid departmentalization, dysfunctional reward systems, and research demands versus performance requirements. These weaknesses have precluded the development of a strong, well-conceived, and continuous relationship between local governments and universities (Ross, 1973).

Universities also have learned that maintaining productive community relationships is extremely difficult in an era when urban areas are threatened by the decay of the inner city, torn by discord between races, blighted by air and water pollution, strangled by traffic congestion and mass transit breakdowns, paralyzed by massive labor disputes and strikes, endangered by crime, staggered by inflation and recession, and menaced by a scarcity of energy (Cutlip and Center, 1971).

"Most urban universities have no choice but to make the best of their location, acquiring additional land in adjacent areas, often at great expense and effort, encouraging high density use of existing properties, and participating in a variety of ways in the revitalization, rehabilitation and conservation of their area," according to Klotsche (1966, p. 17).

Klotsche argues that the urban university's central task should be to understand the city, to analyze its problems, to research and comment about them, to commit university resources, and to draw upon community resources so that the quality of urban life can be improved. Then he adds a warning: "The urban university must not, however, become so committed to the affairs of the city that the purposes for which it exists will be compromised. It would be fatal to its historic mission were problem solving and local politics to become its primary goals" (Klotsche, 1966, p. 29).

To what extent urban colleges and universities should become involved in providing services and solving problems is a controversial question. But George Nash maintains there is no debate about whether institutions of higher education should be involved in the urban crisis. "The debate revolves around the manner and style of involvement and the criteria for deciding whether a given university should attempt a given project," he declares (1973, pp. 143–144). He does not subscribe to the argument that institutions of higher education have too many major problems of their own to permit them to deal effectively with the problems of cities. Those problems, he implies are so interwoven that they cannot be separated, although there are obvious limits to the urban services that colleges and universities can provide.

In recent years John Gardner has been highly critical of institutions of higher education for not responding to the urban crisis. "They have been notably laggard," he charges. "Much of what they are doing today can only be described as 'dabbling.'" As early as 1968, he suggested that universities form urban task forces including both campus and community representatives (Nash, 1973, p. 144).

Urban Grant Universities

Perhaps the main reason why urban universities have not done more to help solve urban problems is lack of funding. Congress has never appropriated the huge sums needed to implement Clark Kerr's 1967 proposal for urban grant universities in cities with populations of 250,000 or more. These universities would focus on the cities in the same fashion that the land grant universities focused on rural and agricultural problems, Kerr suggested. He admitted that involvement of urban grant universities in their cities would inevitably lead to differences and disputes: "When you deal with urban problems, you deal with urban controversies and with urban politics. And so, for this university to work effectively, there will have to be a considerable amount of public understanding—especially understanding of the distinction between services based on application of knowledge and positions taken because of partisan politics" (Nash, 1973, pp. 146–147.

It was Kerr's Carnegie Commission on Higher Education that recommended a response by colleges and universities to the problems of the city "not only through formal education programs and research activities, but also through renewed emphasis on public service" (*Digest of Reports . . .*, 1974, p. 144). The Commission advocated that student involvement in community programs be treated as a learning experience by the college or university. It also urged institutions to consider rewarding faculty members for public service as they are rewarded for teaching, research, and publishing.

"The decision to provide a particular service seems to be much less a deliberate decision that the service is consistent with both the goals and resources in the institution than it is a result of the interests of some within the institution or a reaction to specific pressures and demands on the institution," the Commission observed. "We recommend that quasi-university agencies be established through which faculty members and/or students could provide services, even on controversial matters, without directly involving the university or college in its corporate capacity" (*Digest of Reports . . .*, 1974, p. 145). Although it offers a practical alternative to direct involvement in municipal affairs, this recommendation has not been adopted by urban institutions.

State and local officials may still see some university community activities as subversive because they often undermine authority to "get things done." Volunteer advocacy planners supplied by universities have led the fight against community-slashing highways and university legal aid has helped community groups oppose poorly planned renewal projects.

"Helping citizens fight city hall on certain issues should in no way deter universities from the positive role of helping city hall on other issues," Samuel Jackson maintains. The Urban Observatory Program, established in 1968 and sponsored by the Office of Housing and Urban Development, exemplified this role. "The program was designed to establish a practical working relationship between the university, with all of its training, technical assistance, and research resources, and the city, with all of its problems and needs for study and analysis," according to Jackson (1975, p. 9). The first ten urban observatories were located in Albuquerque, Atlanta, Baltimore, Boston, Cleveland, Denver, Kansas City, Milwaukee, Nashville, and San Diego. Some functioned better than others, but within a few years their budgets ran dry.

In 1969 the Urban Institute identified nearly 200 urban research centers at universities. The number is deceiving, however, since most received little financial support and were probably established under duress. An exception was the Human Resources Center, started in 1964 by the administration of the University of Pennsylvania as a result of student protest regarding discriminatory hiring practices (Mitchell, 1974, pp. 39–40, 48–49). The Center's programs, characterized as "action-research," included a Community Involvement Council, providing volunteer activities for some 800 undergraduates annually, and such projects as a Career Development Institute, Community Leadership Seminar, Recreation Workshop, Philadelphia Demographic Study, a study of police-community urban conflict, and a program to help suburban housewives become change agents in their communities (Mitchell, 1974).

Neighborhood Crises

Although some urban universities still have not accepted the challenge of urban service programs, most are becoming "directly involved in the mini-urban crises on their doorsteps," Jackson observes. "The university no longer ignores its surroundings, nor does it try to swallow them. Many universities are making their staffs and students available as technical advisers to community groups. Some colleges have become sponsors, even owners, of housing for low-income and moderate-income families" (1975, pp. xviii, 8).

Klotsche agrees that whatever stance the urban university takes regarding the extent and nature of its involvement in the city at large, it must devote constant attention to its immediate neighborhood. "The university and the neighborhood must plan about their common problems together so that conflicts can be minimized and varying interests reconciled," he points out (1966, pp. 78–79).

This concern for neighborhood development was in the minds of those who, in 1962, organized the University Hill Corporation in Syracuse, New York. Representing Syracuse University, the State University of New York, and merchants and property owners in the area, the corporation listed these purposes in its bylaws: to encourage long-term planning, to provide a vehicle for consultation with the city as it develops its community renewal program, and to provide a mechanism for reconciling all interests of the neighborhood.

One of the first efforts to coordinate the needs of a cluster of institutions occurred in Cleveland. Prompted by common concerns, nine institutions in 1957 created the University Circle Development Foundation. Within a few years it had twenty-nine members, including institutions of higher learning, hospitals, museums, and a symphony orchestra. Nearing completion of its twenty-five year master plan, University Circle is a 500-acre model development which has attracted the attention of cities around the world (Klotsche, 1966, p. 79).

Some newer universities have been able to capitalize on the advantages of a fresh start in a new location. In 1960 the University of South Florida opened nine miles northeast of downtown Tampa with a campus of more than 1,200 acres at its disposal. "With an industrial park south of the campus and a limited-access highway system only a short distance away, this new urban university has solved its space problems, even though located in one of America's rapidly expanding metropolitan areas," Klotsche reports. "Most institutions, however, cannot move. For these it is a fortuitous circumstance that the general flight out of the city shows signs of being reversed. Efforts to come to grips with aging urban centers are infusing new life into the mainstream of the central city. Some blighted and slum areas are in the process of being converted into livable space. Residential and commercial areas, once choice but now suffering from the impact of metropolitanization, are being revitalized" (1966, pp. 63–64).

Trouble at Temple

Temple University, which surprised Philadelphia by purchasing an eighty-acre suburban site, later reversed its decision and remained in the city, embarking on a multimillion dollar expansion program. "To retreat from the city would be to contradict our tradition, our growth, and our potential as a university in an urban setting," declared President Millard Gladfelter at Temple's seventy-fifth anniversary celebration. Temple's sister institution, the University of Pennsylvania, also considered moving to a 250-acre tract it owned in Valley Forge because of the serious deterioration of its neighborhood. But it, too, decided to remain (Klotsche, 1966, p. 64).

The period from 1967 to 1970 was especially difficult at Temple, located in the center of Philadelphia's largest black community. Although the administration attempted to develop a new dimension of neighborliness, accommodations were made in an atmosphere of crisis. Increasing pressures from the black community led to major adjustments in the campus development process, resulting in a commitment to return to the community twelve acres slated for university expansion. These compromises were embodied in the Community-Temple Agreement of 1970, signed not only by community leaders and Temple officials, but also by the governor of Pennsylvania, the mayor of Philadelphia, and other public officials. The agreement states that

Temple will inform appropriate community groups about future projects for capital improvements within its institutional development district. Moreover, community groups are to participate in the planning process preceding capital improvement decisions (Niebuhr, 1974).

Prior to reaching the agreement, Temple's community relations efforts were floundering. Although the university had been established to serve the poor, it was pictured as the "have" institution by its "have-not" neighbors. From another perspective, the success of the university in obtaining ample funds for expansion of its own buildings contrasted sharply with the essential failure of low-income housing programs. The discrepancy was clearly visible (Niebuhr, 1974).

One of the earliest and most dramatic efforts to cope with the corroding effect of metropolitan growth occurred in the University of Chicago Hyde Park-Kenwood area. As Klotsche notes, an irrevocable decision had been made early in the university's history that it should remain an urban institution. He explains: "By 1951 its campus comprised 100 acres and represented an investment of more than $200 million. As a result of a heavy influx of low income [families], a steady deterioration occurred that alarmed not only university officials but other citizens of the area. The Southeast Chicago Commission was created in 1952 to solidify university and neighborhood opinion. State legislation made it possible for neighborhood corporations to organize and, by acquiring 60 percent of the property in any given area, obtain eminent domain rights over the remaining 40 percent. Subsequently, with the support of the city, state, and federal governments a project of major significance emerged. As a result, 'major surgery' has been performed in the Hyde Park-Kenwood renewal area, comprising about 900 acres and involving an expenditure of (about) $200 million in university, local, and federal funds" (1966, pp. 71–72).

The university's long-range planning in the 1950s enabled it to undertake three major innovative involvements in urban health in the 1960s: in pediatric health care, community mental health, and drug abuse treatment. Although its Woodlawn Child Health Center has encountered many of the problems that any community-based facility must deal with, the center has emerged as a clear-cut success, according to Nash. The university has learned that the neighborhood must be included in all stages of every development if there is to be cooperation rather than confrontation. Nash believes other urban institutions should model their community relations on the Chicago experience. "The university has become involved in a number of programs in the Woodlawn area, and each has been reshaped to meet the specific needs of the people of Woodlawn," he explains. "Initial hostility between the University of Chicago and The Woodlawn Organization has been replaced by a working relationship in which the organization calls the shots and the university supplies the expertise and sometimes the resources. The university's rationale for becoming involved in these projects was not simply to provide services, but rather to learn about new methods of delivering services" (1973, pp. 15, 26).

Johns Hopkins University used Title I federal funds to establish the Greater Homewood project in its northern Baltimore neighborhood. The conditions that needed attention were typically urban: racial tensions, crowded schools, unsystematic zoning, inadequate traffic control, rising crime, deteriorating business and residential areas, and inadequate health services for the poor. For two years, starting in 1967, the faculty assisted in developing local leadership, identifying area problems, cataloguing possible resources, and establishing local mechanisms for developing and implementing community action programs. As a result of this effort, a citizen-controlled nonprofit organization was incorporated in 1969 to deal with the major problems of local concern. Activities included working toward better enforcement of housing, zoning, and health codes; alleviating traffic problems; improving schools; encouraging appropriate businesses and needed social services; and establishing a master plan for community development (Spear, 1975).

Conflict at Columbia

Even when urban universities move to escape the problems of the central city they may discover that they have exchanged one set of difficult circumstances for another. Columbia University's retreat from downtown New York City began as far back as 1857 when the institution abandoned its buildings on the grounds of Trinity Episcopal Church and moved north to the site of what is now Rockefeller Center. The city soon caught up with the institution, prompting another move uptown in 1897. The site chosen was a plateau in uptown Manhattan known as Morningside Heights. This escape seemed to guarantee the university an "academic" atmosphere. But Robert Price describes what happened: "The residential neighborhood underwent a rapid process of urban evolution and decay. Other institutions began to move into the area. By 1947 the fourteen institutions in the Heights found it necessary to form an organization to 'promote the improvement of Morningside Heights as an attractive residential, educational, and cultural area.' It employed a uniformed street patrol, largely financed by Columbia, and ran some small community service programs. The corporation also sponsored the construction of Morningside Gardens, a 1,000-unit middle-income housing development, and Grant Houses, a 2,000-unit low-income project, removing two blighted areas to the north of the Heights. The needs of a large university and the deterioration of the community led to conflict. Columbia proclaimed its intent to rid the neighborhood of a source of crime and restore it to its previous condition" (Price, 1973, pp. 95–97). But the tactics it used evoked neighborhood resentment and rancor.

In the 1960s Northeastern University took the lead among Boston institutions of higher education in providing services to the community, although the urban involvement policies of President Asa Knowles were not popular with many faculty members (Waldorf, 1973).

Urban universities in western states also are concerned about their role in community betterment. In 1973, the University of Utah decided to make its campus a model for environmental improvement and control, reports Donald Winkler. "In cooperation with industrial and civic leaders, faculty research teams developed a way to recycle city waste. Parts of the campus were set aside as a 'natural land and water preserve system' for nature enjoyment and research. The university started an Urban Survival Program to help city people learn how to live in the city and like it" (Winkler, 1978, p. 10).

Like many other cities in America, Detroit has experienced a mass exodus of its affluent, white citizens from the central city to the suburbs. Those left behind are, in large part, poor blacks, many of whom recently migrated from the South. The black migration has brought an increase in the demand for services, while the white exodus has caused a decline in taxes and revenues that has curtailed many services previously provided by the city. The result, explains Dan Waldorf (1973, p. 125), has been a myriad of social problems:

> Health problems have increased, as doctors have moved to suburban areas; the number of housing units has declined because of clearing for freeways and urban renewal, and more and better housing is needed; crime rates have increased; and persons long denied the opportunity for education are increasingly discontented with the extent and quality of education now available.

> The city of Detroit has not been able to deal with these problems. It is possible, however, that some of Detroit's problems will eventually be solved and that a new urban atmosphere may evolve. If there is hope for a solution, part of it emanates from the efforts being made by the administration, faculty, and students of Wayne State University to attack social problems. Few universities have seen and met the challenges presented by urban problems as Wayne State has.

Some of the specific programs sponsored by the university are drug addiction prevention and treatment, consumer education, community extension centers, special student services, cooperative work-study educational programs, and a Center for Urban Studies. One continuing problem is that community service does not figure in the university's reward system for faculty members (Waldorf, 1973, p. 141).

Total Involvement

Thomas Murphy also has praised Wayne State as one of the few urban universities that recognizes the impossibility of separating its urban involvement from the rest of its educational program. "Each department there relates its basic discipline to urban problems in virtually all curricula," he reports (1975, p. 302).

Recognizing that nearly three fourths of its 91,545 alumni live "within forty-five freeway minutes" from the campus, the university has established eleven metro alumni chapters in the greater Detroit area. Various incentives are used to encourage alumni to visit the campus to stay informed about the university's programs and services. "Members get generous discounts at our university bookstore, at our two theatres, and on all purchases through the Wayne State Press," reports Alumni Director Paul Andrews. "Members may borrow books from all four university libraries. They may also use our pool, gymnasia, and squash, tennis, and handball courts for a token charge per visit" (1978, pp. 32–33).

Wayne State University exemplifies the institution of higher education that understands its relationship to the community and acts accordingly. Because it is located in a troubled inner city, the university's projects are related more closely to poverty than to wealth, a reversal from earlier times for most urban institutions. As Winkler (1978) has cautioned, too many colleges and universities have tried to isolate themselves from the problems and needs of their communities or have tried to serve them in ways the communities did not desire. Also, some community groups try to use the college or university in ways it must not be used. For instance, they may try to pressure the institution to use campus resources to support a campaign for or against political issues.

The Answer Is Action

To avoid confusion and disappointment about its community relations, the institution must know what it wants to achieve through a clearly defined mission statement or a set of goals and objectives. More than ever before, colleges and universities need to recognize that little can be accomplished unless they are involved in their communities and take a major responsibility for organizing the best possible response to community needs. Nearly all institutions, large and small, can contribute resources to help solve community problems. They can involve community people in the formulation of institutional policies. They can offer a variety of community services.

"The common call to all campuses is to treat the community with respect and to keep the community informed," Winkler maintains. Community support, he suggests, comes not from football championships or Nobel prizes. It comes from "belief and confidence in what the college or university is doing to improve lives—preferably local ones" (Winkler, 1978, p. 9).

Thus, the institution's well-being is firmly linked to the well-being of its encompassing community. By serving each other, both benefit.

References

Aikman, P. "Is Your Path to Good Will an Obstacle Course?" *CASE Currents*, May 1978, p. 46.

Andrews, P. "Bring Nearby Alumni Nearer." *CASE Currents*, May 1978, pp. 32–33.

Bartocci, B. "Retired—But Not Tired." *CASE Currents*, May 1978, p. 23.

Corbett, F. J. and Levine, M. "University Involvement in the Community." In H. E. Mitchell (Ed.), *The University and the Urban Crisis*. New York: Behavioral Publications, 1974.

Cutlip, S. M., and Center, A. H. *Effective Public Relations*. (4th ed.) Englewood Cliffs, N.J.: Prentice-Hall, 1971.

Digest of Reports of the Carnegie Commission on Higher Education. New York: McGraw-Hill, 1974.

Ingalls, Z. "Ideas." *Chronicle of Higher Education*, Sept. 11, 1978, p. 19.

Jackson, S. C. "Is the University Superfluous in the Urban Crises?" In T. P. Murphy (Ed.), *Universities in the Urban Crisis*. New York: Dunellen, 1975.

Jenkins, M. D., and Ross, B. H. "The Urban Involvement of Higher Education." *Journal of Higher Education*, July-August 1975, pp. 399–407.

Klotsche, J. M. *The Urban University: And the Future of Our Cities*. New York: Harper & Row, 1966.

McAninch, H. D. "A District Says 'Yes' to Bonds." *CASE Currents*, May 1978, pp. 28–30.

Marston, J. E. *Modern Public Relations*. New York: McGraw-Hill, 1979.

Mitchell, H. E. (Ed.). *The University and the Urban Crisis*. New York: Behavioral Publications, 1974.

Murphy, T. P. (ed.). *Universities in the Urban Crisis*. New York: Dunellen, 1975.

Myran, G. A. *Community Services in the Community College*. Washington, D.C.: American Association of Community and Junior Colleges, 1974.

Nash, G. *The University and the City*. New York: McGraw-Hill, 1973.

Niebuhr, H. "Temple University and the Community Development Evolution." In H. E. Mitchell (Ed.), *The University and the Urban Crisis*. New York: Behavioral Publications, 1974.

Nolte, L. W. *Fundamentals of Public Relations*. (2nd ed.) New York: Pergamon Press, 1979.

Powell, S. "New Haven and Yale: The 'Odd Couple.'" *U.S. News & World Report*, Oct. 22, 1979, pp. 72, 75.

Price, R. E. "Columbia: Turning the University Around." In G. Nash, *The University and the City*. New York: McGraw-Hill, 1973.

Ross, B. H. *University-City Relations: From Coexistence to Cooperation*. Washington, D.C.: American Association for Higher Education, 1973.

Seyffert, M. G. "The University as an Urban Neighbor." In T. P. Murphy (Ed.), *Universities in the Urban Crisis*. New York: Dunellen, 1975.

Spear, G. E. "The University Public Service Mission." In T. P. Murphy (Ed.), *Universities in the Urban Crisis*. New York: Dunellen, 1975.

Stanton, C. M. "Community College General Education Enrichment Through Community Action." *Improving College and University Teaching*, Summer 1975, pp. 177–179.

Steinberg, C. S. *The Creation of Consent: Public Relations in Practice*. New York: Hastings House, 1975.

Waldorf, D. "Northeastern University: A Private University Serving the Urban Proletariat." In G. Nash, *The University and the City*. New York: McGraw-Hill, 1973.

Winkler, H. D. "Cultivate Your Backyard." *CASE Currents*, May 1978, pp. 8–11.

CHAPTER 15

POLICY ANALYSIS AND PLANNING

ASSOCIATE EDITOR: CAROLYN GRISWOLD

The last decade of this century has seen increasing interest in policy and policy research among higher education policy makers, researchers, and professionals. This focus can be seen in addresses to national conferences, in the formation of policy taskforces and workgroups in both the Association for the Study of Higher Education (ASHE) and the American Educational Research Association (AERA), and in the new ASHE reader focused on policy and policy issues and research.

Why so much interest in policy making and policy research? To some extent, this interest has been growing as governments have had a more active role in the lives and activities of colleges and their constituents. These roles are reviewed in the chapter in this volume discussing governments and higher education. Certainly, state and federal financing policies are central to the health and growth of both public and private institutions and systems, but they are also centers of intense debate over what their goals should be and what their effects have been.

In addition to the policies themselves, interest in policy making and policy research has been stirred by controversies that have emerged in the last few decades. One such dispute focuses on federal student financial aid programming. Who should be served? To what end? Should our financing policies ensure that poor students have access to postsecondary education, or should they ensure that the choices of middle-class students are not restricted by their families budgets? Can we do both—and should we try to? Most particularly, should we deliver aid to students as grants or loans? If loans, what are the consequences to families and society?

Another issue gaining even greater public attention is that of affirmative action and other efforts to ensure equal access and attainment. As systems and institutions have struggled to respond to policy changes that sometimes happened overnight, many policy researchers have become concerned about the lack of influence of their research in these national debates. Indeed, the current context for colleges demands that those who can inform national discussions about these and other issues find ways to do so. This poses a dilemma for social scientists, who must balance the often conflicting demands of policy-makers and their peers in the academic world. Pressures from each of these groups may affect what is researched, the way in which it is researched, and how results are understood and disseminated.

How policy researchers participate in national debates about policy depends on the policy in question and the unit with the power to effect changes. As the author of the first article in this chapter, van Vught, proposes, it is important, when considering how a policy might be effected, to consider models of policy making and the vehicles used to implement policies. Van Vught reviews these in the context of higher education systems in a number of countries, particularly in relation to their power to encourage innovation, which is frequently seen as a way of addressing governments goals and concerns. This chapter provides an interesting overview of ways in which governments may view their policy relationship with higher education institutions. Van Vught proposes that governmental policy-making may either be based on rational planning and control or self-regulation.

Carolyn Griswold teaches in the School of Education at New York University. (cg3@is4.nyu.edu)

In the first, control is held centrally over planning, policy-making, and policy implementation. It is assumed that decisions will be made rationally and that the system that it regulates is holistic, and thus, that each part of the system may be best regulated by clear rules applied at the center. Van Vught contrasts this model with that of self-regulation, in which each unit in the system is viewed as highly individualistic, best allowed to seek out its own response to challenges. In this model, governments assume that for the most part, their role is to monitor and give feedback, while focusing their policy efforts on a relatively narrow range of issues.

Van Vught proposes that each of these models interacts with the policy instruments available to governments. Such instruments may either mandate (through laws or rules) or induce (through rewards, such as subsidies, or through public discourse), and they may focus on providing information, finances, authority, or direct action. Van Vught argues that, in the case of higher education, central control based on a rational model of decision making does not lend itself to allowing units in systems to innovatively respond to challenges. Moreover, this model tends to be antithetical to the basic values and beliefs of those in higher education institutions. When institutions are, for the most part, allowed to self-regulate, their innovations better fit their values and goals, and thus have a better chance for success.

One issue that has demanded innovative planning and policy making is how to craft policies that can increase access and attainment, in the face of challenges to affirmative action. These challenges have come from lawmakers, from the courts, and from the top levels of systems themselves. The article by Rawlings and Ards describes the part these groups played in the development of policies intended to address historic inequality in Maryland, to better ensure both access and attainment. The range of responses included careful monitoring of student access and success, especially of non-white students, scholarships targeting these students, and efforts to increase the diversity of faculty members in Maryland's public colleges.

While the authors point to some indicators of success, a legal challenge to the scholarship program, yet to be resolved, did lead to a change in requirements associated with fewer minority recipients. The system and state leaders turned to new strategies, including attention to the K-12 educational experiences of the state's children. These long-term strategies may eventually lead to success, but it seems likely that in the short term, campuses will face difficult struggles in their efforts to maintain diverse student bodies.

Policies intended to promote access are not the only policies stirring public discourse. Financial aid policies at the federal and state levels have been the center of frequently contentious debate during the last few decades. Two of the articles in this section focus on what is for some one of the most worrisome trends in federal student aid programs—the shift in emphasis from grants to loans. Hearn provides an analysis of the history of this development, tracing the beginning of loan programming in the National Defense Student Loan program. The NDSL program, created by the National Defense Education Act of 1958, was a relatively small program that nonetheless led to the development of needs analyses and creation of the field of student aid professionals.

However, as the author points out, it was the 1960s that saw what Hearn calls the emergence of federal student aid policy, with the Higher Education Act of 1965, and the establishment of the Guaranteed Student Loan program. A period of refinement followed. In 1972, a number of changes were made to the original program, including the creation of the Student Loan Marketing Association (Sallie Mae) to stimulate lender interest, and the initiation of needs analyses rather than use of simple income levels. Pressure to address the perceived needs of middle-class students led to the Middle Income Student Assistance Act in 1978, which opened GSL to all students.

This change led to the beginning of what Hearn calls the destabilization period. In the late 1970s and early 1980s, use of the loan programs swelled; the problem was addressed in the 1980 reauthorization of the Higher Education Act, but a more divisive debate emerged over the appropriate goals of federal student aid. While some applauded the attempt to help middle-class students through loan programs, others worried that these programs would shift the focus of federal aid policies away from grant aid intended to help less-affluent students attain access to postsecondary education. This controversy continued into the policy drift period, which has lasted from 1981 until today. These decades were marked by increasing concern over default rates and on the influence that loan programs may have on rapidly increasing tuition rates.

This debate is discussed in depth in Michael Mumper's chapter, "The Costs and Consequences of the Transformation in Federal Student Aid Policy." The author gives an excellent overview of how federal loan guarantee programs work, including a review of the most recent program, the Federal Direct Loan program. In the excerpt from the chapter, the author makes an eloquent case that the enormous emphasis on loans has had important negative unintended consequences, affecting students, institutions, and federal student aid policy-making. Of particular concern are the influences on low-income students, who may be disheartened as they consider the debt burden they must take on to attend college. This problem is particularly intense for these students, since they and their families probably will lack the resources to repay the loan should the student have to drop or stop out. Mumper points out that, in fact, loan programs do not reduce the cost of college, since they must be paid back with interest. As college costs increase, and students are driven to take on more debt, federal policies are actually exacerbating the problem.

Thus we return to the beginning of this introduction. The issues surrounding loan policies will certainly continue to instigate controversy. The work of a number of policy researchers has and is addressing this issue. The question left for us to consider is: Will our work contribute to the understanding of policy makers and the public? Can it influence the development and improvement of policy? How may either of these be done? The issues at the center of the debates discussed by these authors are crucial to those for whom higher education is offered as the pathway to a new life.

Suggested Supplementary Bibliography

Breneman, David, *Higher Education: On a Collision Course with New Realities*. Boston: American Student Assistance, 1993.

Callan, Patrick M. and Joni E. Finney (eds.), *Public and Private Financing of Higher Education: Shaping Public Policy for the Future*. Washington, D.C.: Oryx Press, 1997.

Fossey, Richard and Mark Bateman (eds.), *Condemning Students to Debt: College Loans and Public Policy*. New York: Teachers College Press, 1998.

State and National Higher Education Agencies and Commissions, *Recommendations for Reauthorization of the Higher Education Act*. Washington, D.C.: American Council on Education, March 19, 1997.

St. John, Edward and R. Elliot, "Reframing Policy Research: A Critical Examination of Research on Federal Student Aid Programs," in J. Smart (ed.), *Higher Education: Handbook of Theory and Research*, Volume 10. New York: Agathon Press, 1994, 126-181.

Ten Public Policy Issues for Higher Education in 1995. AGB Public Policy Series NO 95-1 Washington, D.C.: Association of Governing Boards of Universities and Colleges, 1995.

International Policy

Sadlak, Jan and Phillip G. Altbach (eds.), *Higher Education Research at the Turn of the New Century: Structures, Issues, and Trends. Garland Studies in Higher Education*. Vol. 10, Paris, France: United Nations Educational, Scientific, and Cultural Organization, 1997.

Slaughter, Sheila and Larry L. Leslie, *Academic Capitalism: Politics, Policies, and the Entrepreneurial University*. Baltimore, MD: Johns Hopkins Press, 1997.

Policy Research

St. John, Edward and R. Elliot, "Reframing Policy Research: A Critical Examination of Research on Federal Student Aid Programs," in J. Smart (ed.), *Higher Education: Handbook of Theory and Research*, Vol. X, New York: Agathon Press, 1994, pp. 126–181.

Wildavsky, A. *Speaking Truth to Power: The Art and Craft of Policy Analysis*. Little, Brown, and Co.: Boston, 1979.

Shapiro, J. Z. "Evaluation Research and Educational Decision-Making: A Review of the Literature." In J. Smart (ed.), *Higher Education: Handbook of Theory and Research*, Vol. II. New York: Agathon Press, 1986, pp. 163–206.

Nisbet, J. and Broadfoot, P. *The Impact of Research on Policy and Practice in Education*. Aberdeen, Great Britain: Aberdeen University Press, 1980.

Heineman, R. A., Bluhm, W. T., Peterson, S. A., and Kearny, E. N. *The World of the Policy Analyst: Rationality, Values, and Politics*. Chatham, NJ: Chatham House Publishers, 1990.

Developing New Strategies for Enhancing Access to College in Maryland

Howard P. Rawlings and Sheila Ards

Equal access or equal outcomes? This question is at the heart of current debates over affirmative action in higher education. Too often this question is posed in either/or terms, as if these are alternatives, rather than related points along an education continuum. In Maryland, high school graduation rates and scores on college entrance examinations are seen as essential steps in enhancing access to college. They are, along with other performance indicators, also significant benchmarks that more equal education outcomes are in fact being achieved. Policies to enhance equal access to college and equal outcomes in education must be viewed together as two interrelated aspects of equity in education.

This chapter summarizes Maryland's extensive efforts to develop effective strategies to enhance college access as a way to achieve more equitable outcomes. In analysing these efforts, the chapter first looks at the context for college access in Maryland and highlights steps taken over the past two decades as well as progress to date.

Subsequent sections provide overviews of policies and strategies used to promote access to postsecondary education as well as improve the preparation of high school students for college-level work. Strategies at both levels encountered legal challenges, resource constraints and other barriers, yet progress continues to be made. The commitment among Maryland legislators and other policymakers remains strong as more effective strategies continue to evolve.

The Maryland Context

Until 1954, Maryland's segregated public higher education system included four historically black colleges: Bowie State, Morgan State, Coppin State and the University of Maryland Eastern Shore. Following the U.S. Supreme Court decision in *Brown v. Board of Education*, the University of Maryland Board of Regents opened all campuses to all students regardless of race. While this ended officially sanctioned segregation, it did not end racial discrimination on campuses or achieve fully integrated institutions. In 1974, Maryland was cited for failing to eliminate vestiges of the former dual system in public higher education, after an earlier plan was rejected as "ineffectual."

Not until 1985 and as a result of extensive negotiation with the U.S. Department of Education Office for Civil Rights (OCR) did Maryland leaders develop an approved five-year desegregation plan to address racial discrimination in higher education. Pressure from the NAACP Legal Defense Fund and African-American state legislators prompted this agreement.

Since 1985, Maryland has undertaken a concerted effort to promote equal access to higher education through statewide policies to improve the recruitment, retention and graduation of students, particularly minorities, and recruit, promote and retain minorities in faculty and professional staff positions. Policy and programmatic changes contributed to African-American undergraduate students' enrollment,

"Developing New Strategies for Enhancing Access to College in Maryland," by Howard P. Rawlings and Sheila Ards, reprinted from *State Strategies to Address Diversity and Enhance Equity in Higher Education*, 1997, State Higher Education Executive Officers and the Education Commission of the States.

retention and graduation rates reaching all time highs.

In addition, the number of African-American full-time faculty has increased significantly since 1990, and the percentage of African Americans entering graduate and professional schools also continues to increase. Today Maryland is viewed as a national leader on this issue, due to improvements in access, equity and performance across a number of areas of higher education. These areas include:

- Between 1990 and 1994, the number of African-American first-time, full-time freshmen entering Maryland's colleges and universities increased from 4,672 to 5,724, an increase of 23% (see Figure 1). Bowie State University experienced a 7.4% increase in full-time undergraduate attendance, Coppin State University experienced 4.7% growth, and Morgan State University grew 4.6%. These increases occurred during a period when overall attendance at Morgan's public four-year institutions increased by only 1.3%.

- As a percentage of undergraduate enrollment, African Americans have achieved rates similar to the percentage of African-American students graduating from Maryland high schools—24% of total undergraduate enrollment in 1994 compared to approximately 25% of graduating high school students in the state.

- Student retention into the second year of higher education is being monitored closely. As indicated in Figure 2, average second-year retention rates for African-American students fluctuated between 74 and 76%, compared to 80–83% for white students statewide. Significant differences in retention rates appear across institutions, but are less divergent within a single institution. For example, at the University of Maryland College Park (UMCP), second-year retention is 84% for African-American students compared to 86% for the total first-year class.

- College graduation rates prior to the sixth year of enrollment have increased steadily for African-American students, rising from 30% for students who began college in 1984 to 40% for those who began in 1988. Additional efforts continue such improvements.

- The number of African Americans in full-time faculty positions increased from 690 in 1990 to more than 800 in 1994. At UMCP, even though the total number of faculty declined between 1990 and 1994, the number of African-American faculty rose by 4.4%.

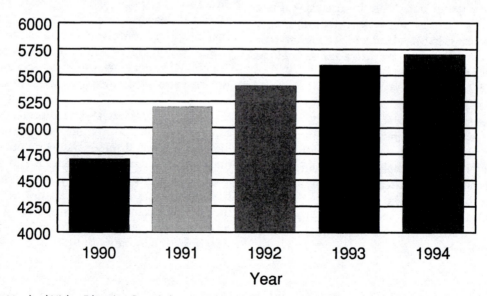

Source: Maryland Higher Education Commission

Figure 1: First-Time Full-Time African-American Enrollment 1990–1994

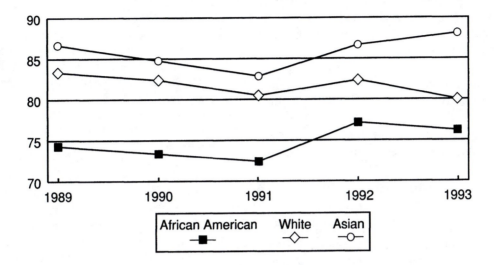

Source: Maryland Higher Education Commission

Figure 2: Second Year Retention Rates by Race. Maryland Public Four-Year Institutions 1989–1993 Cohorts

- The percent of African Americans in graduate and professional schools increased significantly. By 1995, African Americans increased to 12.6% of all students in graduate schools and 16. 1 % of all students in professional schools, up from 6.6% and 11.9%, respectively in 1987. Although many disciplines achieved gains, the largest increases occurred in law, social work and pharmacy.

- At UMCP, the number of applications from minority students increased as well as the number of acceptances. Minority applications rose from 1,324 in 1990 to more than 1,900 in 1994. African Americans had the largest growth in actual numbers of applications, although Native Americans had the highest percentage growth.

Over the past decade, Maryland improved both African-American student access to higher education and African-American faculty representation. These improvements were the result of new strategies undertaken to broaden access to Maryland's public institutions. The following sections review these strategies.

Policies and Strategies to Promote Access

When Maryland committed to OCR's 1985 desegregation plan, state policymakers recognized the need for a new administrative infrastructure to help implement the plan. As a result, in 1988 state leaders reorganized the coordinating and governing structures for public higher education. The prior state structure consisted of a coordinating board with very limited authority and two separate higher education administrative entities, one with oversight over the state college system and the other over the state university system.

Under the new structure, one major education system, the University of Maryland System, was formed with oversight over all but two of the state's public colleges and universities. Morgan State University and St. Mary's College retained their independent governing boards. This reorganization also created a much stronger coordinating entity—the Maryland Higher Education Commission—with substantial oversight over all the state's public and private higher education institutions.

Maryland and OCR officials agreed on several goals to measure continuing progress in integrating the historically white colleges and universities and enhancing the historically black institutions. A recent paper for the higher education commission succinctly stated that the State of Maryland sought to improve equal educational opportunities by achieving three overarching principles:

- Adopt a comprehensive, deliberate and systemwide approach to eliminating racial disparity and cultivating equal educational opportunity.

- Organize, shape and attune to the needs and interests of students in K-16 education.

- Be accountable educationally and fiscally to various constituency needs.

Several initiatives illustrate Maryland's serious commitment to hold education leaders accountable to constituent needs. For example, as part of a larger strategy to promote diversity, remedy past discrimination and provide financial support to students, two scholarship programs were initiated to increase minority undergraduate enrollments in Maryland's colleges and universities.

The Benjamin Banneker Scholarship Program, developed at UMCP, was part of Maryland's effort to remedy vestiges of its formerly segregated system. When established in 1978, the program offered full scholarships for up to 30 black students with 3.0 or higher grade-point averages and SAT scores of 900 or above. The scholarship covered tuition, room, board and mandatory fees for four years. Because of recent court challenges and changes to this program, funding will be provided only until 1998 and only for students currently in the program.

In 1990, Daniel Podberesky, a Hispanic student, challenged the Banneker Program in U.S. district court (*Podberesky v. Kirwan*). Podberesky applied for a Francis Scott Key Scholarship—a merit-based, race-neutral, four-year, full-financial scholarship program from the university. He was not awarded a Key Scholarship, nor was he considered for a Banneker Scholarship because he was not African American. In 1991, the district court ruled in favor of the university, saying the Banneker Program served a compelling public interest. This opinion was based in part on OCR's earlier finding that the state and university were not complying with Title VI of the 1964 Civil Rights Act.

In 1992, the U.S. Court of Appeals ruled that the lower court had failed to make a specific finding on the present effects of past discrimination and remanded the case back to the district court. In effect, the appeals court found the Banneker Program unconstitutional because only African-American students were eligible for it. The university appealed the case to the U.S. Supreme Court, which, to date, refuses to hear arguments in the case.

In response to the court decision, UMCP merged the Banneker Program with the Key Scholarship Program. Today, the sole criterion for a Banneker-Key scholarship is academic merit. Students must have at least a 3.0 grade-point average and score 1,000 on the SAT to be considered. Additionally, leadership skills, extracurricular activities, community involvement and the university's goals for maintaining a diverse student body are taken into account when awarding scholarships.

While the state-funded scholarship program survived in this modified form, the court cases and rulings negatively affected minority students. In its first year of implementation, 19 of the 72 Banneker-Key scholarship recipients were African-American students, compared to 36 who received Banneker scholarships the previous year. In response to the immediate impact of the federal court ruling on African-American student scholarships, the UMCP president made a commitment to African-American legislators that the university would find ways to support additional minority student scholarships from institutional resources.

Scholarship programs at other University of Maryland campuses also were affected. The Meyerhoff Scholarship, established at the University of Maryland Baltimore County, originally was designed as a merit-based program to promote the education of African Americans in science and engineering. The average SAT score for Meyerhoff scholars is 1,220, and most have a high school GPA of at least 3.85. Scholarship recipients also must be committed to pursuing graduate education in the sciences or mathematics. Beginning with the 1996 entering class, the scholarship program no longer is exclusively for African-American students, however. Meyerhoff scholarships now are open to all high-achieving students, based on new selection criteria that include a commitment to work with inner-city students on improving their reading and math skills and a desire to contribute to disadvantaged communities in their chosen careers.

In some ways the Banneker decision contributed to a reaffirmation of programs to ensure greater access for underserved minorities in Maryland. University and college officials are examining ways to increase the minority presence in higher education while adhering to requirements of the Banneker decision. At the state level, new grant programs and other strategies are being proposed. For example, Maryland is in the process of designing and implementing a Diversity Grant program. This program will provide funding to help colleges and universities enrich their academic environment by increasing financial aid to needy students from culturally diverse and traditionally underrepresented populations.

Another part of Maryland's strategy is to reach students at the beginning of their secondary schooling. Toward this end, the state began providing Guaranteed Access Grants in 1996. These grants provide 100% of an applicants financial need, up to the cost of full-time tuition at UMCP. These awards target the state's neediest students, who are identified in 9th grade for early intervention and college preparation. To qualify for the grant, a student must be a Maryland resident in his or her senior year at a Maryland high school, complete a college-preparatory program or an articulated tech-prep program, have a cumulative 2.5 grade-point average for grades 9–12 in high school and have a family annual income that qualifies for the federal Free Lunch Program. In 1995–96, 541 grants were awarded.

K-12 Education Strategies

Maryland policymakers understand that improvements must begin earlier in students' academic careers in order to prepare them for the challenge of college. In addition to financial support for minority students, the state began an initiative to hold schools more accountable for poor academic performance. This initiative resulted in the state-level takeover of several schools and additional state intervention in many others. The Maryland State Department of Education has proposed high school testing requirements prior to graduation to ensure students are minimally prepared for a college curriculum.

For many urban school districts, however, minority achievement revolves around funding. The current method of financing public education in many urban areas challenges the neediest district—those with a large proportion of low-income families and a dwindling tax base. Lack of resources also creates a greater need for management reform to help districts use scarce resources efficiently. In Baltimore, the state and legislature work with the Baltimore School district to promote reforms to increase student performance. Several different school finance and governance models are being explored.

Maryland officials recognized that the state would have to play a bigger role at the primary and secondary levels if change was to occur for minority students. As a result, in 1990 policymakers instituted the Maryland School Performance Program for grades K-12. Through cooperation with parents, educators and citizens, the program sets public school targets for the year 2000. Each year, schools present a "report card" to the public and other interested groups as evidence of progress toward achieving the targets. The targets help school, district and state leaders examine critical aspects of instructional programs to ensure all students receive quality instruction, hold educators accountable for quality instruction and guide efforts toward school improvement. If and when a school does not meet benchmarks toward achieving these targets, state officials work with local school improvement teams to improve the schools' academic performance, with the possibility of a state takeover as a final option.

Maryland has come a long way in providing equal access to quality education, but more work is needed before equal outcomes are obtained. Maryland leaders understand where the state is on this continuum of equal access to equal outcomes and how far it needs to go, and they have designed a system for the public, educators and others to share responsibly in obtaining equal education outcomes for all citizens.

References

Maryland Community Colleges, University of Maryland System, Morgan State University, St. Mary's College of Maryland, Maryland Higher Education Commission. *Minority Achievement Reports.* November 1994.

Maryland Higher Education Commission. *A Concept Paper Regarding Minority Education in the State of Maryland.* January 1996.

Maryland Higher Education Commission. *Maryland Diversity Grant Guidelines.* Draft, February 13, 1996.

Maryland Higher Education Commission. *1995 Minority Achievement Reports: Data Highlights.* December 1995.

Maryland Higher Education Commission. *1995 Opening Fall Enrollments.* November 1995.

Maryland Higher Education Commission. *Performance and Characteristics of Maryland Students Who Have Taken the SAT.* December 1995.

Maryland Higher Education Commission, State Scholarship Administration. *Guaranteed Access Grant.* 1996–97 Academic Year.

Maryland State Department of Education, Division of Planning, Results, and Information Management. *Maryland School Performance Report, 1995: State and School Systems.* 1995.

University of Maryland at College Park. *Minority Achievement Plan.* June 30, 1995.

Policy Models and Policy Instruments in Higher Education: The Effects of Governmental Policy-Making on the Innovative Behavior of Higher Education Institutions

FRANS A. VAN VUGHT

Introduction

Government regulation has become an increasingly important issue. Much of the attention to government regulation has been focused on private sector regulation. Economists have widely analyzed the effects of government regulation on the affected market sector (for instance: Kahn, 1971; Stigler, 1975).

The effects of public sector regulation have also attracted some attention. In disciplines like public administration and policy analysis, public sector regulation has fruitfully been studied as an issue of compliance or noncompliance. The literature on implementation processes in particular has offered some interesting results with respect to the identification of factors explaining why specific government policies have or have not succeeded (Pressman and Wildavsky, 1973; Dunsire, 1978; Rein and Rabinovitz, 1978; Bardach, 1979; Barrett and Fudge, 1981; Mazmanian and Sabatier 1981; O'Toole, 1986). With respect to the implementation of higher education policies the study by Cerych and Sabatier (1986) should be mentioned.

Generally speaking, regulation has to do with the influencing of behavior, i.e., with trying to steer the decisions and actions of others according to certain objectives and by using certain instruments. Mitnick has defined "regulation" as "the intentional restriction of a subject's choice of activity, by an entity not directly part to or involved in that activity" (Mitnick, 1980, p. 5). Government regulation can be

described as the efforts of government to steer the decisions and actions of specific societal actors according to the objectives the government has set and by using instruments government has at its disposal. There are three basic categories of rationale for government regulation: efficiency (usually pertaining to correcting market failures), distribution, and stimulating or protecting social and cultural objectives (Skolnik, 1987, p. 60).

Government regulation can be interpreted as a "framework of rules within which other decision units can make decisions without the high transaction costs of maintaining private force for the purpose of protecting their belongings or of maintaining threats to enforce the carrying out of agreed upon contracts. As a framework, the government simply delineates the boundaries within which other units determine substantive choices, the government making its own forces available to defend the established boundaries" (Sowell, 1980, p. 145).

In this chapter I will focus on these frameworks used by government in the policy field of higher education (Van Vught, 1991). I will especially discuss the general orientations that appear to guide the sets of rules that together form the frameworks of government regulation.

When designing and implementing specific policies, governments are guided by general assumptions and points of view. For these assumptions and points of view I will use the term "policy models." "Policy models" are the sets of general postures, assumptions and

"Policy Models and Policy Instruments in Higher Education: The Effects of Governmental Policy-Making on the Innovative Behavior of Higher Education Institutions," by Frans A. van Vught, reprinted from *Higher Education: A Handbook of Theory and Research*, Vol. X, 1994, Agathon Press.

guidelines that appear to be followed when governments formulate their framework of regulation. "Policy models" are what Dror has called "megapolicies: a kind of master policies, clearly distinct from detailed discrete policies" (Dror, 1971, p. 63).

In the following sections first two general policy models will be explored: the **model of rational planning and control**, and the **model of self-regulation**. These two models will then be specified in the policy context of higher education. Next, an overview will be presented of the policy instruments that can be used by governments with respect to public sector regulation. It will be argued that specific categories of policy instruments show a better fit with a specific policy model.

In the second part of this chapter the policy models and policy instruments will be evaluated from the perspective of their capacity to stimulate innovations in the field of higher education.

Policy Models

Premfors (1992) has indicated that, when we accept the point of view that in policy analysis we should at least aim at a certain level of rationality, policy models like the "garbage can model" (March and Olsen, 1976) should not be considered to be part of policy analysis. Nevertheless, says Premfors, there is "a wealth of [what he calls] models of policy processes to choose from" (Premfors, 1992, p. 1908). He mentions models like "bounded rationality" (Simon, 1957), "mixed scanning" (Etzioni, 1968) and "the normative optimum model" (Dror, 1968). Other models in the literature are the "incremental model" (Braybrooke and Lindblom, 1963), the "systems model" (Jantsch, 1972), the "communicative model" (Van Gunsteren, 1976) and the "transactive model" (Friedmann, 1973) (see Maassen and Van Vught, 1992 for an overview).

I argue that when the basic assumptions of the various models that are presented in the literature are studied, only two clearly different models appear to remain. The other models that are found in the literature can all be seen as specific (and often quite interesting) variations or combinations of these two more or less fundamental Models.

The Policy Model of Rational Planning and Control

An extreme case of a governmental approach to public sector regulation is one in which the knowledge of the object of regulation is assumed to be firm, the control over the object of regulation is presumed to be complete, and the self-image of the regulating subject is holistic. I will name this conception the policy model of rational planning and control.

A fundamental assumption of this model is that it should be performed as the normative ideal of the rationalist perspective on decision-making suggests: by comprehensively evaluating all conceivable consequences of all conceivable alternatives.

The authors who can claim to have stated this strategy first in the literature are probably Meyerson and Banfield (Meyerson and Banfield, 1955). However, from their publications it also can be concluded that they want to see the model of rational decision-making as basically a normative ideal which is worthwhile to pursue but which cannot completely be realized in reality (Banfield, 1959; Meyerson, 1956):

> . . . no choice can ever be perfectly rational, for there are usually a great—perhaps an infinite—number of possible actions open to the actor and the consequences of any one of them would ramify ad infinitum. No decision-maker could have the knowledge (or the time!) to evaluate even a small fraction of the actions open to him. It is possible, however, to be more or less systematic in the canvass of alternatives and consequences, so that the conception is not an entirely useless one. For practical purposes, a rational decision is one in which alternatives and consequences are considered as fully as the decision-maker, given the time and other resources available to him, can afford to consider them. (Banfield, 1959, p. 364)

Lindblom especially has strongly criticized this model, variously called by him the rational-deductive or the synoptic ideal (Lindblom, 1959; Lindblom, 1965; Braybrooke and Lindblom, 1970). Lindblom argues against the rational decision-making ideal from the assertion that it cannot be followed in actual practice and that attempts to do so distract decision-makers from a more feasible strategy (called by him the strategy of "disjointed incrementalism"). He argues that the "synoptic ideal" is not adapted to man's limited intellectual capacities, nor to his inadequacy of information or the costliness of analysis.

> In actual fact, therefore, no one can practice the rational-comprehensive method for really complex problems, and every administrator faced with a sufficiently complex problem must find ways drastically to simplify. (Lindblom, 1959)

Perhaps the most crucial aspect of Lindblom's criticism is his conviction that, given the limited knowledge a (governmental) policymaker can acquire, comprehensive control of an object of regulation should not be strived after. A complete or nearly complete control cannot avoid harming the object of regulation and will eventually result in imposing decisions and commanding their implementation. Rather, according to Lindblom, decisions should be taken by a large number of decision-making units, each of them free to pursue its own interests. It is this conviction that leads Lindblom to speak of "disjointed" incrementalism.

> Analysis and evaluation are disjointed in the sense that various aspects of public policy and even various aspects of any one problem or problem area are analyzed in various points, with no apparent co-ordination and without the articulation of parts that ideally characterizes subdivision of topic in synoptic problem solving.... Disjointedness has its advantages ... chief among them the advantage of preserving a rich variety of impressions and insights that are liable to be "co-ordinated" out of sight by hasty and inappropriate demands for a common plan of attack. (Braybrooke and Lindblom, 1963, pp. 105, 106)

It may be concluded for Lindblom's criticism that the policy model of rational planning and control not only is based on the assumption of the rationalist perspective on decision-making, but also implies the centralization of the decision-making process and a large amount of control both over the actual choice to be made and over the implementation of the chosen policy. The model of rational planning and control takes its point of departure in the ideal of rational decision-making, but con-

fronted with the limitations of this ideal in actual practice, it takes refuge in confidence in centralization and control.

The model of rational planning and control is an approach to governmental regulation in which much confidence is put in the capabilities of governmental actors and agencies to acquire comprehensive and true knowledge and to take the best decisions. Also, it is an approach in which these governmental actors try to steer an object of regulation by using stringent rules and extensive control mechanisms. When government designs and implements operational policies using the general policy model of rational planning and control, it sees itself as an omniscient and omnipotent actor that thinks itself able to rightfully steer a part of society according to its own objectives.

The Policy Model of Self-Regulation

The policy model of self-regulation is basically the opposite of the model of rational planning and control. Instead of the assumption that the knowledge of the object of regulation can be firm, comes the recognition that such knowledge is highly uncertain. Instead of the wish to control the object of regulation as completely as possible, comes the conviction that such control should to a large extent be avoided. Instead of a holistic self-image of the regulating subject, comes the assertion that an atomistic self-image offers important advantages.

The policy model of self-regulation is not so much based on the ideal of rational decision-making. It rather incorporates the logic and the assumptions of the cybernetic perspective on decision-making (Ashby, 1956). It puts emphasis on the principles of monitoring feedback variables. It accepts the idea that a decision-maker should only pay attention to a small set of "critical variables" which he should try to keep within tolerable ranges. And perhaps most importantly, it underlines the assumption that the fragmentation of complex decision-making processes offers the benefits of a high level of robustness, a high level of flexibility, a high level of innovativeness, and a low level of information, transaction, and administration costs (Steinbrunner, 1974).

From the field of management sciences Beer has indicated that a choice for the cybernetic perspective on decision-making is a choice for the strategy of self-regulation.

> Every manager, whether he runs the family business or a small department in a firm, whether he runs the firm itself or a major department of government, whether he runs the country or an aspect of international affairs, faces an identical problem. He faces, that is, the need to maintain a viable system far more complicated than he personally can understand. And the beginning of wisdom for management at any level is the realization that viable systems are, in large measure, self-regulating and even self-organizing. (Beer, 1975, pp. 105, 106).

Beer makes it clear that the cybernetic perspective on decision-making implies the idea of self-regulation. A cybernetic decision-making unit is able to regulate itself. When the feedback loops are working and when a repertory of operations is available, a decision-making unit hardly needs regulation from outside. Moreover, a complex system with many interrelated decision-making units, is able to realize a high level of stability. Such a system has a capacity of "homeostasis," i.e., the capacity to hold the critical variables at the level of the overall system within acceptable ranges. Confronted with such a system, the task for an external (governmental) regulator is only to monitor these critical variables making sure that they do not exceed the tolerable ranges, and to evaluate the criteria by which the critical variables and the tolerable ranges are chosen.

In the policy model of self-regulation, the role of an external regulating agency or actor is a role at another, higher level: ". . . the role . . . is to remain above the homeostatic fray, and to consider what is happening in terms of a higher level understanding" (Beer, 1975, p. 112). Beer explains this higher level role with the following illustration from the world of games.

> Suppose that as a higher manager you have the responsibility to ensure that team A wins in a game which is already being played between team A and team B, where the scoring is already even. You could dress yourself in the appropriate regalia and charge onto the field of play. The players would recognise you. Your own side might defer to your tactics . . . while the other side would do their level best to put you out of action. This is not the way to behave at

> all . . . the clever action would be to change the rules of the game so that your side must win it. (Beer, 1975, p. 112).

In the model of self-regulation emphasis is put on the self-regulatory capacities of decentralized decision-making units. The complex interrelations between these units are respected. The external regulating activities are limited to monitoring the performance of the overall system of the interrelated self-regulating decision-making units and to evaluating (and if judged necessary, changing) the rules which to a large extent define this performance.

Compared with the model of rational planning and control, the model of self-regulation is far more modest. It acknowledges the limitations of acquiring knowledge and exercising control over an object of regulation which, in itself, already consists of a complex set of mechanisms of decision-making. It tries rather to incorporate the benefits of this complex set of mechanisms by limiting itself to setting broad frameworks and by providing facilities for the behavior of decentralized units.

When government uses the policy model of self-regulation, it sees itself mainly as an arbiter. In this model government is the actor who watches the rules of a game played by relatively autonomous players and who changes these rules when the game is no longer able to lead to satisfactory results.

Policy Models in Higher Education

Looking at the characteristics of the various higher education systems in the world the two general policy models that have just been distinguished can clearly be recognized. Generally speaking, from the perspective of governmental policy-making with respect to higher education two models can be distinguished that are clearly related to the two general policy models presented before. I will call these policy models in higher education: the state control model and the state supervising model (Van Vught, 1988; Van Vught, 1992).

The State Control Model

The state control model is traditionally found in the higher education systems of the

European continent. The so-called "continental model"—to use Clark's label—(Clark, 1983a), is a combination of the authority of state bureaucracy and faculty guilds.

The higher education systems of the European continent traditionally have been "relatively pure state systems" (Van de Graaff and Furth, 1978). These systems are created by the state and almost completely financed by it. The state very often also is the overarching and highly powerful regulator of the system. A clear example is the French higher education system which is characterized by a centralized bureaucratic control exercised by the national ministry of education. In such systems the state controls, at least formally, nearly all aspects of the dynamics of the higher education system. The national ministry of education regulates the access conditions, the curriculum, the degree requirements, the examination systems, the appointment of academic staff, etc. An important objective of this detailed government regulation is the standardization of national degrees, which are often awarded by the state rather than by the higher education institutions. In federal systems (like the Federal Republic of Germany and the United States) state control is usually exercised at the subnational level.

In the continental model the overwhelming power of the state is combined with a strong authority at the level of the senior chaired professors, who hold considerable power at the lower level of the system. As has become most visible in the nineteenth century German higher education system, the chair holders are able to exercise strong collegial control within the faculties and the institutions.

The result of the combination of authority of state bureaucracy and faculty guilds is a power structure which expresses the interests of two groups: state officials and senior professors (Clark, 1983a, p. 126). The level of institutional administration is rather weak and in effect often bypassed when systemwide decisions are taken (Glenny, 1979). The power distribution of the continental model is characterized by a strong top (the state), a weak middle level (the institutional administration), and a strong bottom (the senior chair holders) (Clark, 1983a, p. 127).

The continental higher education model offers the clearest example of the state control

model. Especially when the state controls the appointments of the chair holders, it is obvious that the state exercises a major influence on the system. In these cases the state often uses the higher education system for its professional manpower needs. Both the manpower needs of the governmental bureaucracy itself and the assessed needs at the nation's labor market are expected to be fulfilled by the higher education system. The state then finds its legitimization for the detailed control of the higher education system in the self-proclaimed task to steer the nation's economy.

The State Supervising Model

The state supervising model has its roots both in the U.S. higher education system and in the traditional British higher education system. The "American and British models"—to use again Clark's labels (Clark, 1983a)—show far less governmental influence on higher education than the continental model. In the British and certainly in the American model the state plays only a minor role. Although things have changed rather drastically during the last decade in British higher education (see, for instance, Walford, 1991), the traditional British model can still serve as a conceptual tool to describe a limited state influence. The traditional British model of higher education is a combination of the authority of faculty guilds and a modest amount of influence of trustees and administrators (vice-chancellors) at the institutional level. In this traditional model, British universities are chartered corporations, responsible for their own management. Each individual university and college is allowed to decide upon its admission, its curricula, and the hiring of its faculty. In the traditional British model there is no formally organized system of national governmental control. And although during the development of British higher education the funding became largely a governmental task, the budget allocation remained (until the policy changes of the Thatcher government) in the hands of the senior professors (in the University Grants Committee).

During the last decade, things have changed dramatically in British higher education. The higher education budget has been severely cut, a businesslike management style has been introduced, an approach of quality monitoring by means of performance indicators has been developed and the University Grants Committee has been abolished. British government apparently wants to "privatize" higher education. A hierarchical businesslike organizational structure has been introduced and the influence of industry on higher education has been increased (Scott, 1988; Walford, 1991). It could be argued that the traditional British state supervising model has recently changed into a "non-British" state control model.

The U.S. higher education model shows a rather limited government regulation. The U.S. model is a combination of the authority of faculty guilds and institutional trusteeship and administration. But compared with the traditional British model, the influence of the institutional trustees (or regents) and administrators is stronger (Van de Graaff et al., ch. 7). Like the British universities, the American institutions are established as chartered corporations. But the boards of trustees and the institutional administrators (presidents) play a more important role than their British colleagues. The trustees generally appoint the university president who to a large extent has authority over the strategic and financial policies of the institution. In the U.S. the professors do not have the power of the chair holders, but the authority of the faculty is nevertheless substantial (especially in the academically stronger institutions).

The influence of government is rather limited. There is hardly any power at the federal level. The authority at the state level has been growing during the last few decades (Newman, 1987), but this increase of state authority is moving toward "adaptations of market control mechanisms" like outcomes assessment legislation and performance funding (Dill, 1992, pp. 53, 54). Compared with the level of state influence in the continental model, the U.S. state authority in higher education is still rather weak. The U.S. state level regulation largely concerns the mechanisms for the organization of quality assessment and the regulation of the right to award degrees (Berdahl and Millett, 1991).

The traditional British and the U.S. models offer examples of what has been called here the state supervising model. In this policy model the influence exercised by the state is weak.

The state sees its task of supervising the higher education system only in terms of assuring academic quality and maintaining a certain level of accountability. Government does not intrude into the higher education system by means of detailed regulation and strict control. Rather, it respects the autonomy of the higher education institutions and it stimulates the self-regulating capabilities of these institutions. The state sees itself as a supervisor, steering from a distance and using broad terms of regulation.

It may be clear from the presentation of the two models of state influence on higher education (the state control and the state supervising model), that each of these two models is related to one of the two general policy models of public sector regulation that were introduced before. The state control model is largely based on the general governmental strategy of rational planning and control. The state supervising model is a specialization of the policy model of self-regulation. Further on I will explore the effects of each of the two models on the innovative behavior of higher education institutions. But first, let us see what categories of policy instruments governments can use in each of the two general policy models (the model of rational planning and control and the model of self-regulation).

Policy Instruments

In principle every government has a number of instruments at its disposal to perform the tasks that have been assigned to it. If government wants to "produce" certain outcomes, it employs certain tools. Without such tools governmental policies would be no more than abstract ideals or fantasies.

In the policy sciences literature the concept of policy instruments recently has attracted renewed interest. Important theoretical concepts have already been developed in the classical publications of Dahl and Lindblom (1953) and Etzioni (1968). Dahl and Lindblom distinguished four sociopolitical processes which, in their opinion, should be used by "any society intelligently bent on using its resources efficiently" (Dahl and Lindblom, 1976, p. 172). These four processes are: the price system (control of and by leaders), hierarchy (control by leaders), polyarchy (control of leaders), and bargaining (control among leaders). Etzioni makes a distinction between three types of social relationships: coercive, utilitarian, and normative relationships. According to Etzioni, in any concrete case there is a mixture of these three forms, leading to different kinds of social interaction (Etzioni, 1978).

Mitnick (1980) takes Dahl and Lindblom's analysis as a starting point to develop a categorization of the instruments of government. A crucial distinction in his work is the one between "regulation by directives" and "regulation by incentives." Regulation by directives is defined as "the interferences that occur by circumscribing or directing choice in some area—i.e., making rules for behavior that may be transmitted as instruction." Regulation by incentives is described as "the interferences that occur by changing the perception of the nature of the alternatives for action subject to choice—i.e., changing the relative attractiveness of alternatives" (Mitnick, 1980, pp. 342, 343). Mitnich develops an overview of "some common regulatory means" which he classifies in his two broad instrumental categories. Figure 1 contains this overview.

Regulation by directives   public enterprise (extreme case)
common law
administrative rules or standards

Regulation by incentives   tax incentives
effluent/user charges
subsidies
promotion campaign
laissez faire (extreme case)

Figure 1: Mitnick's categorization of governmental instruments. (Source: Mitnick, 1980, p. 346.)

It seems that Mitnick's presentation of governmental instruments is based on the criterion of the level of restriction by government of the behavior of societal actors. Directives are more restrictive than incentives, and strong incentives are more restrictive than weak incentives.

Several other authors have pointed at the importance of policy instruments for policy analysis. Several studies of policy implementation emphasize the need to further analyze the effects of the various categories of instruments (Ingram and Mann, 1980; Mazmanian and Sabatier, 1981). Bardach (1979) points to the importance of the behavioral characteristics of policy instruments. Salamon (1981) asks for a

reorientation in the implementation literature toward the comparative effectiveness of policy instruments.

The literature also shows various alternative categorizations of policy instruments. Bardach (1979) proposes to distinguish four categories of instruments: prescription, enabling, positive incentives, and deterrence. Elmore (1987) and McDonnell (1988) indicate that they favor a categorization in: mandates (providing constraining rules), inducements (providing financial resources to encourage certain activities), capacity (providing financial resources to enable actors to take certain actions), and instruments of system change (that alter the arrangement of agencies in a policy network). Schneider and Ingram (1990) distinguish authority tools, incentive tools, capacity tools, symbolic and hortatory tools, and learning tools. "Authority tools are simply statements backed by the legitimate authority of government that grant permissions, prohibit, or require action under designed circumstances." Incentive tools are instruments "that rely on tangible payoffs, positive or negative, to induce compliance or encourage utilization.... Capacity tools provide information, training, education, and resources to enable individuals, groups, or agencies to make decisions or carry out activities." Symbolic and hortatory tools

> seek to change perceptions about policy-preferred behavior through appeals to intangible values ... or through the use of images, symbols and labels. ... Policy tools that promote learning provide for wide discretion by lower-level agents or even the target groups themselves, who are then able to experiment with different policy approaches. Agents are required to draw lessons from experience through formal evaluations, hearings and institutional arrangements that promote interaction among targets and agencies. (Schneider and Ingram, 1990, pp. 514–522)

For an overview of policy instruments I will follow Hood's *The Tools of Government* (1983). Hood distinguishes four categories of governmental instruments. The categories vary depending on the "basic resources" used by government in trying to reach the objectives set. For each category of "basic resources" a specific set of instruments can be indicated. For the sake of understanding the broad scale of policy instruments, a slightly modified interpretation of Hood's categorization is presented here (see Figure 2).

The first category of instruments concerns the provision of *information*. From its specific position in society, government has the advantage of being "a store of information." Compared with other institutions, governmental agencies often have extra possibilities to develop rather broad, panoramic overviews of societal conditions. Hence, government can use the information it has at its disposal to try to reach its policy objectives.

There are various ways government can "send out" information. It can provide informed responses tailored to questions from outside; it can direct standard messages without being asked to specific groups ("targeting information"); it can send out general messages to the broad public. What type of information outlet government uses depends on various factors such as the size of the informed population, the degree of attention manifested by the informed population, and, of course, the content of the message. A crucial factor is the political and legal framework government operates in.

In general, it can be said that the providing and propagating of information offers government a set of instruments with rather low or even nonexisting "authority costs." When information-oriented instruments can be used, government does not have to lay its authority on the line. It can send out the information judged to be necessary or significant, and it can wait and see if the information is accepted.

Instruments of information	responses
	messages
Instruments of treasure	contracts
	bounties
	transfers
	bearer-directed
	payments
Instruments of authority	certificates
	approvals
	conditionals
	enablements
	constraints
Instruments of action	operational activities

Figure 2: An overview of the instruments of government. (Modified from Hood, 1983).

A second category of policy instruments concerns "the power of *treasure*." Treasure is what enables government to buy favors, to court popularity, to hire mercenaries, etc.; the power of treasure is the power of signing checks. Hood therefore speaks of the instruments of "checkbook government."

Government can use its treasure in two main ways. It can "exchange" it for some good or service. Or it can "give it away"; that is, it can transfer payments without requiring any "quid pro quo."

According to Hood, the two main instruments of the exchange of treasure are "contracts" and "bounties." Contracts are governmental payments made to specific individuals or organizations, under the condition that the recipient supplies a specified product or service. Contracts are payments "with strings attached." A governmental contract payment is only made when the recipient of such a payment accepts the conditions which government requires. Like contracts, bounties also are payments made in exchange for some quid pro quo, but in the case of bounties the individual or organization which is to provide that "quid pro quo" is not specified. A bounty is awarded to anyone who produces the product or service asked for. Bounties are assumed to be especially useful to encourage or discourage specific types of societal behavior.

The two main governmental instruments of the other method of using the power of treasure (the "give it away" option) are "transfers" and "bearer-directed payments." Transfers are exchanges of treasure without a requirement of a quid pro quo; transfers are "gifts," made to specific individuals or organizations for specific purposes or reasons. Bearer-directed payments also do not involve a clear quid pro quo. But, unlike transfers, bearer-directed payments are made to all those who, by some token, are eligible for them.

The instruments of "checkbook government" can be used directly by government or indirectly through intermediaries. Intermediary organizations are an often used alternative for direct governmental allocation of resources, especially when government wants to avoid getting too closely involved in highly specialized budget decisions.

In general, the instruments of "checkbook government" are costly, in the sense that financial resources can only be spent once and the renewal of treasure implies the use of the mechanism of taxation. On the other hand, as has been argued many times before, treasure is an elegant category of instruments, often capable of achieving the kind of societal behavior government sets out to create.

The third category of policy instruments is formed by the instruments of *authority*. The instruments of authority are intended to command and to forbid, to commend and to permit.

Instruments of authority vary depending on the degree of restriction they seek to introduce into the behavior of the targeted subjects. Least constraining in this sense are "certificates" and "approvals." Certificates are authoritative declarations by government about the properties of a specific individual or object. Approvals are authoritative declarations in a general sense; approvals apply to the world at large or to whomever it may concern. Both certificates and approvals are instruments requiring no compulsive action at all from government.

A subcategory requiring more (but still not extreme) compulsive action is formed by the instruments called "conditionals" and "enablements." Conditionals are the promises by government to act in a certain way when certain conditions arise. A well-known example is the government guarantee that is provided as a kind of safety net for certain circumstances. Enablements are the tokens that permit certain activities. Modern governments use a large variety of enablements. Licenses, quotas, warrants, coupons, vouchers, and permits are all types of enablements. They all allow (but do not compel) the undertaking of certain activities.

The instrument of authority that asks for compulsive action is the instrument called "constraint." Constraints, in contrast to certificates, approvals, conditionals, and enablements, demand or prohibit certain activities. Constraints can be positive (commanding) and negative (forbidding). In both cases, they imply a compulsory restriction by government of societal behavior.

Generally speaking, the instruments of authority depend on the willingness of the public to accept them. A low level of respect for and acceptance of government can make these instruments rather ineffective. As history has shown, governments sometimes in these cases take refuge in the authority instruments with the highest level of constraint. On the other hand, when government is widely respected and accepted, the low-constraint instruments of authority may be very effective in producing the outcomes government thinks to be relevant.

Hood's fourth and final category of policy instruments is the category of (direct) *action*. Within this category fall all kinds of operational activities by government that directly influence the citizens, their property, or their environment. Government can use "its own" individuals, buildings, equipments, and stocks of lands to directly produce certain outcomes or to perform certain tasks. It can for instance act as a national banker; it usually operates a system of involuntary detention; it sometimes holds a monopoly on the production of a certain good; and it of course often takes care of defending the country, controlling crime, treating sewage, controlling traffic, lighting streets, controlling floods, etc.

The instruments of action to a large extent are related to the traditional monopoly on the use of violence and the enforcement of law. As such these instruments tend to be restricted to some specific areas of governmental control. Next to these areas the instruments of action are often used for providing "collective goods" (like defense and dikes).

In general, it should be noted that the governmental instruments of direct action are rather expensive. They should be reserved for the governmental monopoly on the use of violence, for emergencies, and for activities that might otherwise not be performed.

It may be concluded that, as is the case in several other categorizations, Hood's presentation of policy instruments is to a large extent based on the criterion of the level of restraint the instruments try to produce with respect to the behavior of societal actors.

The instruments of information are hardly at all restrictive. They are used without the explicit goal to directly limit the range of behavioral options of other actors. The objective of the use of information instruments is to try to influence the behavior of others by providing them with significant information.

The instruments of treasure are more restrictive. In particular when government acts as the most important funding agent of the activities of other actors, these actors may be strongly influenced to adapt their behavior to the ideas and wishes of government. "Checkbook government" in this sense can be very restrictive, although the restraining potential is often used in an indirect way. The power of treasure offers governmental agencies the opportunity to design and implement financial incentives and disincentives, strongly urging actors to behave according to government's wishes.

The instruments of authority range from mildly restrictive to completely restraining. The "certificates" and "approvals" are only mildly restrictive. These specific instruments provide governmental agencies with the ability to approve or disapprove. As such they can limit the behavioral options of other actors. Especially when the approval of government is sought after (e.g., because such an approval offers the right to acquire financial resources), these mildly restrictive instruments may become very effective in influencing the behavior of nongovernmental actors. The instruments called "conditionals" and "enablements" have a higher level of restrictive potential. They allow or do not allow actors to behave in a certain way, usually by providing or denying financial resources or licenses. The instruments called "constraints" are extremely restrictive. These are the instruments a government can use to command and forbid and by using them government can compel other actors to behave completely according to its wishes.

The instruments of direct (governmental) action are also, generally speaking, rather restrictive. Because these instruments are based either on the governmental monopoly on the use of violence, or on the political decision that government should provide a certain collective good, these instruments tend to strongly influence the other actors' behavior.

However, Hood's presentation seems to imply more than one criterion for the categorization of policy instruments (the level of restraint). A second criterion concerns the distinction between the particular and the general use of instruments. "Particular applications are those that are directed at specific and named individuals, organizations or items. . . . General applications are those that are beamed at the

world at large and thus apply to whomever it may concern" (Hood, 1983, p. 17). Other criteria that seem to be important in Hood's categorization are the question whether societal actors should or should not themselves try to obtain the benefits of a certain instrument, the question whether societal actors have or have not to provide a quid pro quo and the level of permanence of an instrument (for instance the instruments of authority are more durable than the instruments of treasure).

The presentation of the instruments of government has made it clear that these instruments vary according to the level of restraint they try to produce with respect to the behavior of societal actors. This variation in the level of restraint allows us to relate some specific categories of instruments to the two general policy models that were distinguished before. Generally speaking, it may be expected that the instruments that are highly restrictive are more easily applied in the policy model of rational planning and control, while the less restrictive instruments are more appropriate in the policy model of self-regulation.

In the model of rational planning and control a government sees it as its task and its capability to influence other societal actors according to its own objectives. In this model government judges it to be its prerogative to restrain the behavioral options of other actors in order to reach the goals that are thought to be relevant. In such an approach, highly restrictive instruments will be assumed to be the most effective. The highly restraining instruments of authority ("constraints') or the indirect but nevertheless often rather restrictive instruments of treasure will be applied to give concrete form to the confidence in centralized control.

In the policy model of self-regulation government puts its confidence in the self-regulatory capacities of decentralized decision-making units. Governmental activities are limited to gathering information so as to be able to watch the overall system of activities and to providing and, if judged necessary, changing the broad frameworks that enable and stimulate such a system. The instruments that may be expected to be relevant in this policy model are the instruments of information (responses and messages) and the mildly restrictive instruments of authority (certificates and approvals). A special set of instruments may be formed by the indirect instruments of treasure that may be applied at the systems level to install mechanisms that may influence actors to change their behavioral patterns without reducing their self-regulatory capacities.

It should be stressed that policy instruments are seldom used in isolation. The categories of instruments that have been presented above can only be distinguished analytically. In reality governmental instruments are used in combination and through all kinds of linkages. An example is the combination of "enablement" (a specific instrument of authority) and "bearer-directed payment" (a specific instrument of treasure): the license for a certain activity may immediately make a person eligible for a certain transfer of payment without a quid pro quo.

Nevertheless, every specific combination of instruments has its own characteristics, which will influence its effectiveness and efficiency. Also, every specific combination of instruments may lead to different results, depending on the context in which it is used.

One of the most crucial questions in present-day public sector regulation is how governmental policy models and instruments can be matched to the circumstances in which they are applied. In the second part of this chapter I will address this question by exploring the appropriateness of the policy models and policy instruments that were presented before for producing innovations in higher education systems and institutions.

The Study of Innovation

Innovation is a concept that has attracted much attention in the social sciences. In the 1950s and the 1960s there was a strong belief that the construction of a comprehensive theory and methodology of innovation would only be a matter of time. There existed a certain optimism and enthusiasm about the possibilities and the usefulness of such a theory and methodology. The general social theory of innovation would soon enable planners and policy-makers to design and implement successful changes and to create a happier society.

Since then doubt and disappointment have grown. The comprehensive theory and methodology did not arise. The growing number of empirical studies offered a picture of extreme variance among its findings. The conceptual frameworks remained vague. As Downs and Mohr concluded in 1976:

> . . . the record in the field of innovation is beyond interpretation. In spite of the large amount of energy expended, the results have not been cumulative. This is not to say that the body of existing research is useless. . . . Perhaps the most straightforward way of accounting for this empirical instability and theoretical confusion is to reject the notion that a unitary theory of innovation exists. (Downs and Mohr, 1976, p. 701).

The literature on innovation is very extensive and covers several disciplines. In the field of organizational behavior, research is underway to try to identify some important variables which are related to the tendency in organizations to adopt innovations. Variables like "degree of decentralization," "degree of formalization," "degree of specialization," and "complexity" are frequently mentioned (Hage and Aiken, 1967). In the field of social psychology several variables are suggested, which are assumed to be related to the development of an innovation process. These variables include the level of motivation of the innovator, the degree of compatibility with existing values and practices, and the level of organizational support (Davis et al., 1982).

In the literature on higher education the concept of innovation has also received some attention. Several rather creative and elegant analyses have been performed from which some interesting insights about innovation processes and outcomes in higher education systems can be deduced (e.g., Levine, 1980; Cerych and Sabatier, 1986). I will use these studies to formulate some insights about the relationships between policy models and policy instruments used by governments, and the innovations that take place in higher education systems and institutions.

The conceptual approaches to innovations and innovation processes are numerous. Besides, it is not always clear how these various conceptual approaches can be related in order to try to gain some increasing understanding of the state of the art in the literature on innovation.

Dill and Friedman (1979) have tried to identify the major theoretical frameworks in the conceptual approaches to innovations and innovation processes, with a special focus on the study of higher education. Reviewing these frameworks, they come to the conclusion that the theoretical and methodological problems related to the study of innovation processes are still quite large. The theoretical frameworks appear to be both too complex and insufficiently specified to enable researchers to undertake clear analyses. Measuring the many variables mentioned in the frameworks and paying attention to their validity and reliability is an enormous task. Dill and Friedman suggest focusing attention on the developments of less comprehensive theories.

In the remainder of this chapter I will follow this suggestion. I will limit myself to an exploration of the relationships between governmental policy models and policy instruments directed towards creating and stimulating innovations in higher education systems and institutions, and the processes and outcomes of these innovations. To be able to do this, I will first discuss some of the fundamental characteristics of higher education institutions.

Fundamental Characteristics of Higher Education Institutions

Kerr has pointed out that, looked at from without and comparatively, higher education institutions (especially research universities) have hardly changed at all during the past centuries:

> About eighty-five institutions in the Western world established by 1520 still exist in recognizable forms, with similar functions and with unbroken histories, including the Catholic church, the Parliaments of the Isle of Man, of Iceland and of Great Britain, several Swiss cantons, and seventy universities. Kings that rule, feudal lords with vassals, and guilds with monopolies are all gone. These seventy universities, however, are still in the same locations with some of the same buildings, with professors and students doing much the same things, and with governance carried on in much the same ways. (Kerr, 1982, p. 152).

This striking permanence of higher education institutions has to do with some of the most fundamental characteristics of higher education. As in the first medieval universities of Bologna, Paris, and Oxford, higher education can still be seen as a social system in which the handling of knowledge is the most crucial activity. In higher education systems knowledge is discovered, conserved, refined, transmitted, and applied (Clark, 1983a, p. 12). If there is anything fundamental to systems of higher education, it is this handling of knowledge.

The primacy of the handling of knowledge is related to some other fundamental characteristics, which can be found within higher education institutions.

A primary characteristic concerns the authority of the academic professional experts. In higher education institutions many decisions can be made only by these professional experts. These are the decisions regarding the detailed knowledge-oriented academic activities of research and teaching. In all those specialized knowledge fields, which are held together in a higher education institution, decisions on what and how to investigate, and on what and how to teach come, to a large extent, under the direct supervision of the academic experts. Only they are able to oversee their specialized fields. Only they are able to stimulate the enthusiasm of students for specific objects of study. This is why professional autonomy is so important in higher education institutions and this is why these institutions are called "professional bureaucracies" (Mintzberg, 1979).

Clark makes it clear how the professionals in higher education organization work with and upon knowledge:

> The factory floor in higher education is cluttered with bundles of knowledge that are attended by professionals. The professionals push and pull on their respective bundles. If they are doing research, they are trying to increase the size of the bundle and even to reconstitute it. If engaged in scholarship other than research, they are conserving, criticising, and reworking it. If teaching, they are trying to pass some of it on to the flow-through clientele we call students, encouraging them to think about its nature, how it may be used, and perhaps take up a career devoted to it. If engaged

outside the "plant" as advisors, consultants, or lecturers, academics further disseminate knowledge to try to draw out its implications for practical use. (Clark, 1983b, p. 20).

Of course, not all decisions in higher education institutions are taken by professionals. There is a category of purely "administrative" decisions (for example, regarding financial administration and support services) which to a large extent is beyond the professional influence. There is also a category of decisions that are mainly taken by "clients" (students, research contractors). And there is an important category of decisions mainly taken by "outsiders" (government, funding agencies, evaluating committees). Nevertheless, the influence of the professional experts on the decision-making processes in higher education institutions is extensive. In many decisions taken at these institutions professionals play an important role.

A second important characteristic is the organizational principle that in higher education institutions the knowledge areas form the basic foci of attention. The knowledge areas are the "building blocks" of a higher education organization and without some institutionalization of these knowledge areas a higher education organization cannot exist. This principle leads to the typical organizational structure of higher education institutions. Fragmentation is abundant in these organizations. Throughout the organization specialized cells exist that are only loosely coupled. Higher education institutions are "loosely coupled systems" (Weick, 1976). The crucial knowledge-oriented activities take place within the rather autonomous cells. Specialists in specific knowledge fields group together to teach and undertake research. To a large extent insulated from the rest of the organization, these specialists use their autonomy and expertise to perform the basic activities of the higher education institution.

> . . . specialized professionals have little need to relate to one another within the local shop. . . . They can produce on their own. . . . Producing separately for the most part, the many groups become an extreme case of loosely-linked production. The university is a gathering place for professionalised crafts, evermore a confederation, a conglomerate, of knowledge-bearing groups that require little operational linkage. (Clark, 1983b, p. 21)

According to Clark it is this organizational fragmentation that explains the miraculous adaptability of higher education institutions. This adaptability consists of "the capacity to add and subtract fields of knowledge and related units without disturbing all the others." Clark argues that "it is the peculiar internal constitution of universities that allow them . . . to bend and adapt themselves to a whole variety of circumstances and environments, thus producing diversity among universities . . . and, at the same time, to maintain an appearance of similarity that allows us to recognise them in all the guises which they take." (Clark, 1983a, pp. 186, 187)

A further fundamental characteristic of higher education institutions is the extreme diffusion of the decision-making power. In an organization where the production processes are knowledge-intensive, there is a need to decentralize. When besides that, such an organization is also heavily fragmented, the decision-making power will be spread over a large number of units and actors. A higher education institution therefore becomes a federal system; "semi-autonomous departments and schools, chairs and faculties act like small sovereign states as they pursue distinctive self-interests and stand over against the authority of the whole." (Clark, 1983a, pp. 266, 267)

A final characteristic, which is typical for higher education institutions based on the continental or the traditional British model, is the way authority is distributed within these institutions. Traditionally in these models, this authority has been (and in many occasions still is) located at the lower levels of the organization; that is, with the academic professionals (see before). At the level of the institutional administration authority is rather weak. Institutional administrators only have a very limited capacity to steer "their" organization.

Reviewing the fundamental characteristics of higher education institutions just mentioned, it may be concluded that the context of higher education confronts government with some specific problems when it wants to develop and implement a policy directed toward influencing higher education institutions. The extreme professional autonomy within these institutions and the rather limited administrative authority, as well as the organizational fragmentation and the diffusion of the decision-making power, make it very difficult to completely control these institutions from an external position. Higher education institutions appear to be very complex associations of largely autonomous cells. Besides, in higher education institutions the traditional guild culture, rooted in the Middle Ages, is still very much alive. Higher education institutions cherish the traditional norms and values of the "republic of science" (Polanyi, 1962), which enable them to perform their highly professional tasks.

The fundamental characteristics of higher education institutions suggest that these institutions can be controlled from outside only when the organizational variety is greatly reduced and when the professional autonomy is largely restrained. However, it should be realized that when such an external control is imposed, the professional tasks these institutions perform may be severely damaged. Confronted with detailed regulation and with an extreme restriction of their behavior, the scientists and teachers within the higher education institutions may feel the disillusionment of not being able to explore the paths their professional consciousness stimulates them to go. They may become uninterested in new developments, get bored by the routine activities they have to perform, and lose their interest in innovations.

Innovations in Higher Education

Having explored the processes of innovation in general and more specifically in the context of higher education, I will now try to develop some theoretical insights about the relationships between governmental policy models and policy instruments (directed towards the creation of innovations) on the one hand, and innovation processes in higher education systems and institutions on the other hand.

To present the theoretical insights I will classify the rather extensive literature on innovation processes in two broad categories. These categories can be described as "the organizational variables assumed to be related to success or failure of innovations" and "the

characteristics of successful innovations." I will discuss the present state of the art in the higher education literature regarding both these categories.

Organizational Variables Related to Success of Innovations

In their impressive research overview of the principal organizational variables that have appeared to influence the success or failure of innovation processes in organizations, Hage and Aiken (1970) offer seven factors that are related to the rate of change in an organization. These factors can be described as follows:

- the greater the formalization (i.e., the greater the degree of codification of jobs, the greater the number of rules specifying what is to be done, and the more strictly these rules are enforced), the lower the rate of organizational change;

- the higher the centralization (i.e., the smaller the proportion of jobs and occupations that participate in decision-making and the fewer the decision-making areas in which they are involved), the lower the rate of organizational change;

- the greater the stratification (i.e., the greater the disparity in rewards such as salaries and prestige between the top and bottom ranks of an organization), the lower the rate of organizational change;

- the greater the complexity (i.e., the greater the number of occupations/specialties of an organization and the greater the degree of professionalism of each), the greater the rate of organizational change;

- the higher the volume of production (i.e., emphasis on quantity versus quality in organizational outputs), the lower the rate of organizational change;

- the greater the emphasis on efficiency (i.e., concern with cost or resource reduction), the lower the rate of organizational change;

- the higher the job satisfaction, the greater the rate of organizational change.

Hage and Aiken's factors are discussed by Levine (1980) in the context of innovations in higher education. Levine suggests that higher education organizations are low in formalization, low in centralization, low in stratification, high in complexity, high in the emphasis on quality of outputs, low on efficiency, and high on job satisfaction. The author therefore comes to the conclusion that "institutions of higher education might be classified as low in innovation resistance relative to organizations in general." (Levine, 1980, p. 173)

The discussion of the fundamental characteristics of higher education institutions (see before) seems on the one hand to lead to the same conclusion. The high autonomy of the professionals within these organizations, the organizational fragmentation, the diffusion of the decision-making power, and the limited administrative authority indicate that higher education organizations are *not* very formalized, centralized, stratified and directed towards efficiency, but *are* very complex and by their specific nature offer possibilities for a strong emphasis on quality of production and a high level of job satisfaction.

However, as has been indicated by Kerr and many others, it should also be remembered that higher education institutions by nature are conservative and that in these organizations innovations are not likely to occur. According to Hefferlin (1969), for instance, innovations will occur in higher education institutions only when the level of instability in these institutions is high, i.e., when conditions arise like changing faculties because of expansion or turnover, low rates of tenure, rotating department chairpersons, etc.

It seems that we are confronted with two contradicting theoretical observations. Let us look at this subject from another perspective.

Clark (1983a) has argued that change is far more crucial in higher education institutions than conventional wisdom would suggest.

> Despite the belief of many observers that academic systems change significantly only when pressured by external forces, such systems increasingly exhibit innovation and adaptation among their bottom lines. Invention and diffusion are institutionalized in the work of the departments and counterpart units that embody the disci-

plines and professions.... Such change is widely overlooked.... It occurs in segments of the operating level.... In a bottom-heavy knowledge institution, grassroots innovation is a crucial form of change. (Clark, 1983a, pp. 234, 235)

Clark points once more at the characteristics of higher education institutions. Innovations take place through the professional activities in the various semiautonomous units in the organization.

Kerr (1982) seems to agree with this point of view. According to him a distinction should be made between a perspective from within and a perspective from without. "Looked at from within, universities have changed enormously in the emphases on their several functions and in their guiding spirits, but looked at from without and comparatively, they are among the least changed of institutions" (Kerr, 1982, pp. 152, 153).

Bok (1986) makes clear how the two theoretical observations, which seem to be contradictory, can be combined. He underlines Levine's conclusion that, because of their fundamental characteristics, higher education institutions in principle are low in innovation resistance. However, he also points out that these very factors make it difficult to keep innovations alive.

> Universities are large, decentralized, informal organizations with little hierarchical authority over teaching and research. These characteristics favor innovation by making it easy for any of a large number of faculty members to experiment in search of better ways of educating students. Unfortunately, the very factors that aid experimentation make it harder for successful initiatives to spread throughout the institution or from one institution to another. (Bok, 1986, p. 176)

Innovations are created easily within higher education organizations and (as Clark indicates) they may even spread among their bottom levels. But this diffusion of innovations only takes place by virtue of the professional belief that certain innovations are worthwhile. Faculty members will only adopt innovations when they judge them to be worthwhile for their own activities. As Bok observes, "... the most promising innovations can languish unless some effective force causes them to be emulated widely" (Bok, 1986, p. 176). And the most effective force is probably the conviction of professional colleagues that an innovation is an effective solution to a common problem.

This point of view leads to an important conclusion: innovations in higher education institutions may arise easily and often, but their diffusion will be difficult and will mainly take place through communication between colleagues.

Clark points at another aspect of the processes of change within higher education institutions. He indicates that innovations in higher education institutions are mainly incremental adjustments, building up to larger flows of change. Major, sudden and comprehensive changes are rare in higher education institutions. Exactly because of the fragmentation of tasks and the diffusion of power such changes are extremely difficult to effect.

It should be realized that the ideology of the academic profession incorporates a basic resistance to comprehensive changes, especially when these are launched "from above." The organizational fragmentation and the diffusion of the decision-making power demand that a relatively large number of people and groups with a wide variation in values and opinions tend to discuss a launched comprehensive reform, the result of which will often be that the reform strands in debates and political fights. Becher and Kogan (1980) argue that, because of the fundamental characteristics of higher education systems, innovation processes are localized and specific.

> . . . we are not dealing with a hierarchical system, where change can be decreed from above, but rather with a negotiative one, in which individuals, basic units and institutions each regard themselves as having the right to decide what is best for them. It follows that any innovative proposal has to be finally sanctioned by those who are in a position to put it into effect. (Becher and Kogan, 1980, p. 121)

This argument has brought many authors to the conclusion that, generally speaking, government-initiated reforms in higher education systems must fail. Referring to the study of Cerych and Sabatier (1986) (see below), Kerr (1987), for instance, comes to the conclusion that "intentional changes" have sometimes perhaps been partially successful, but most often have been a failure. Curricular reforms and changes of governance, generally speaking cannot be called a success (Kerr, 1987, p. 185).

A possible explanation for this observation can again be found in the fundamental characteristics of higher education institutions. Kerr (1982) stresses that most decisions concerning the dynamics of a higher education system are taken outside the formal system of governance.

> Most decisions about teaching, about curriculum, about research topics and methods, about amount and form of public service are made by individual faculty members. Most decisions made about majors selected, courses taken and time spent on study are made by individual students. (Kerr, 1982, p. 178)

Besides, Kerr indicates, when intense competition exists among higher education institutions (as in the U.S.), specific arrangements of governance have only minor implications.

Also, Bok points out that educational reforms in higher education institutions are seldom the result of external influences (including governmental policies). According to him, external pressures can only be successful when they link up with initiatives or opinions inside a higher education institution.

> . . . no external influence offers a reliable way of initiating constructive change or eliciting new ideas to improve the quality of education. The vital task ultimately rests within the university itself. (Bok, 1986, p. 183)

Becher and Kogan (1980) have presented an elegant analysis of innovation processes in higher education systems by differentiating between four levels of these systems: the system as a whole, the institution, the basic unit (within the institution), and the individual. According to these authors innovative attempts often fail because they are unable to accommodate to existing structural constraints.

> Academic structures and regulations for the most part evolve to protect the legitimate interests of researchers and teachers. They help to define, and also defend, the main areas of professional concern within an institution. But once established, they can prove surprisingly intractable. Even when an innovative idea is generally

accepted on intellectual grounds, it may face severe difficulty if it appears to conflict with conventional practice, or to cut across some existing organizational arrangement, (Becher and Kogan, 1980, pp. 146, 147)

Becher and Kogan therefore also put a heavy emphasis on the specific organizational characteristics of higher education institutions as important barriers to innovation. They argue that the often mentioned conservatism of higher education institutions "mainly stems from contextual, rather than from personal factors" (Becher and Kogan, 1980, p. 147).

Others have tried to take up the challenge of the "policy failure theme" in higher education. Referring to his analysis of the Swedish higher education policy which led to the reforms of 1975–1977, Lane (1985) has argued that policy-driven changes in a higher education system are possible. But, like the authors just mentioned, he also points out that, to be able to be successful, reform policies should pay attention to the basic characteristics of higher education institutions.

> Indeed organizational transformation of higher education work and higher education institutions is feasible, as long as basic features of the differentiation of work and the structure of authority inherent in the conduct of higher education activities are not threatened. Whereas public policy may effect institution-building and redefinition, it cannot do away with the bottom-dominated nature of the organization of higher education life. (Lane, 1984, p. 107)

Premfors (1984) disputes Lane's "optimism," but he does not conclude that the Swedish higher education reform policy was a complete failure.

> . . . Swedish higher education policy is a mixed bag of success and failure when judged in terms of the initial intentions of central policy-makers. . . . To an important extent . . . these outcomes have been predicated on basic features of higher education organization in Sweden. (Premfors, 1984, pp. 47, 48)

The same kind of conclusion (in a broader perspective) is drawn by Cerych and Sabatier (1986), who studied a number of policy-driven reforms in higher education systems in Europe.

Cerych and Sabatier examined the levels of success and failure of nine rather comprehensive reforms which were all largely initiated and developed by government and implemented in a higher education system through the interaction between governmental organizations and higher education institutions. In their comparative analysis Cerych and Sabatier present a general picture from which it can be concluded that both successes and failures can be distinguished.

This differentiated picture appears to underline Premfors' conclusion about the Swedish higher education reforms. Apparently reforms initiated and developed by government can be judged as "mixed bags of success and failure." An important question of course concerns the factors that might influence the levels of success and failure of these reforms.

Characteristics of Successful Innovations

In a study that has become widely known in the field, Rogers and Shoemaker (1971) have analyzed more than 1500 studies regarding the characteristics that determine an innovation's success or failure. The authors present five critical characteristics:

- the compatibility of a new idea (i.e., the degree to which an innovation is perceived as consistent with the existing values, past experiences and needs of the receiver) is positively related to its rate of adoption;
- the relative advantage of a new idea (i.e., the degree to which an innovation is perceived as being better than the idea it supersedes) is positively related to its rate of adoption;
- the complexity of an innovation (i.e., the degree to which an innovation is perceived as relatively difficult to understand and use) is *not* related to its rate of adoption;
- the triability of an innovation (i.e., the degree to which an innovation may be experimented with on a limited basis) is positively related to its rate of adoption;
- the observability of an innovation (i.e., the degree to which the results of an

innovation are visible to others) is positively related to its rate of adoption. (Rogers and Shoemaker, 1971, pp. 350–352)

In Levine's analysis (1980) (see before) some important observations can be found concerning the importance of these general characteristics in the context of higher education. This study especially focused on the "institutionalization or termination stage" of innovation processes. This stage is supposed to follow the stages of "recognition of the need for change," "planning an innovation" and "implementing the innovation." In the institutionalization or termination stage attention is concentrated on "the ways in which innovations prosper, persist, decline and fail after they have been adopted" (Levine, 1980, p. 10).

Levine has developed a theoretical model of the ways innovations can be handled in an organization. He suggests that in principle two mechanisms can be used. The first mechanism is called *boundary expansion*: ". . . an acceptance by the host [organization] of some or all of the innovation's differences." This mechanism essentially indicates a process of acceptance (which may be more or less comprehensive). Levine indicates that this acceptance can involve diffusing the innovation through the organization or establishing it as an enclave. "Diffusion is the process whereby innovation characteristics are allowed to spread through the host organization, and enclaving is the process whereby the innovation assumes an isolated position within the organization."

The other mechanism of handling an innovation in an organization is called *boundary contraction*: ". . . a constriction of organizational boundaries in such a manner as to exclude innovation differences." This mechanism labels an innovation as illegitimate or deviant. Again, two forms can be distinguished. "Resocialization occurs when the innovative unit is made to renounce its past deviance and institute the acceptable norms, values and goals. . . . Termination occurs when the innovation is eliminated" (Levine, 1980, pp. 14, 15).

Which of the four possible outcomes of the institutionalization/termination stage of innovation processes (diffusion, enclaving, resocialization, termination) will occur depends, in Levine's theoretical model, on two variables:

compatibility and profitability. Like Rogers and Shoemaker, Levine sees compatibility as the degree to which the norms, values, and goals of an innovation are congruent with those of an organization which has to adopt the innovation. Profitability is a subjective concept, rather similar to Rogers and Shoemaker's "relative advantage." It indicates the degree to which an innovation satisfies the adopter's needs or satisfies him better than the existing mechanisms.

Levine's conclusions are that compatibility and profitability are both crucial variables for explaining the success or failure of the adoption of an innovation. An innovation appears to fail (i.e., is resocialized or terminated) when the levels of compatibility and profitability of the innovation decline. Profitability is an especially important variable. When the profitability of an innovation is not disputed, an innovation can still get accepted, even when the compatibility of such an innovation is low. However, when the profitability is seriously questioned, an innovation will fail, even when the compatibility is high.

The argument that the compatibility of an innovative idea is positively related to the rate of adoption of an innovation is frequently found in the literature. We already noticed that for instance Bok (1986) stresses this point. Becher and Kogan (1980) argue that structural reforms of a system as a whole can only succeed when they relate to the fundamental values in higher education (Becher and Kogan, 1980, p. 125).

Concerning the relationship between compatibility and rate of the adoption of an innovation Cerych and Sabatier (1986) introduce an interesting amendment. Cerych and Sabatier propose a three-dimensional framework for the conceptualization of the "scope of change."

> *Depth of change* indicates the degree to which a new policy goal implies a departure from existing values and practices of higher education. . . . *Functional breadth of change* refers to the number of functional areas in which a given policy is expected to introduce more or less profound modifications: admission, teacher qualifications, internal structures, curriculum, and so forth. . . . *Level of change* indicates the target of the reform: the system as a whole; a particular sector or segment of the system

(group of institutions); a single institution or an institutional sub-unit.

Reviewing the various comprehensive reforms that were the object of their analysis, Cerych and Sabatier draw several conclusions. Regarding the interconnection between depth of change and functional breadth of change they claim that reforms that postulate a radical departure of existing rules and values, can nevertheless be successfully implemented when they are limited to a few functional areas (of the higher education institution or of the higher education system as a whole) and if at the same time most other prevailing traditions and standards are rigorously accepted. With respect to the level of change, the authors conclude that, generally speaking, a reform succeeds more easily if it affects an institutional or sub-institutional process, rather than a system as a whole (Cerych and Sabatier, 1986, pp. 244–247).

It appears that Cerych and Sabatier, although they agree with the general conclusion of Rogers and Shoemaker that the more a reform is consistent with existing values the more likely it will be implemented, also notice that a low level of compatibility does not necessarily mean that an innovation cannot be successfully implemented. An important question then is what other factors may stimulate or hamper innovations.

We already noticed that Levine has suggested that the concept of profitability is of crucial importance for the explanation of the acceptance of innovations in higher education institutions. The concept of profitability is also often mentioned in the literature as an important variable positively related to the rate of adoption of an innovation. Becher and Kogan underline their view that externally initiated innovations can be successful in higher education, provided that they are acceptable in terms of intellectual substance (compatibility) and that they establish their merits (e.g., in terms of student recruitment) (profitability) (Becher and Kogan, 1980, p. 132). With regard to the analysis of the outcomes of innovation processes, Clark uses the metaphor of a seesaw, "a long board on which reform-supporting and reform-opposing groups sit at different points in relation to the center of balance." According

to this author, a decision as to whether an innovation will or will not be accepted is the result of the distribution of power among the groups involved in the decision-making process. And the behavior of each group and individual in the decision-making process is guided by the subjective interpretation of self-interest.

> Innovations typically "fail" because the innovators cannot acquire enough power fully to protect their new ways. They are allowed to start, even to acquire a clientele, but unless they attach the interests of various groups to their own interests and persuade potential opponents at least to be moderate in their resistance, they can be tightly bounded—resocialized or terminated—as others raise their own level of concern, clarify their own self-interest with respect to the reform, and increase the bearing of their own weight. (Clark, 1983a, pp. 226, 227)

Clearly, like Levine, both Becher and Kogan and Clark combine the concepts of compatibility and profitability. In both their analytical interpretations of the potential success of an innovation the two concepts are interrelated.

The concepts of compatibility and profitability offer us the possibility of formulating some further insights about the appropriateness of governmental policy models with respect to higher education. If we follow the conclusions of the studies just discussed and if we take into account that the higher education context is characterized by a large professional autonomy, a large organizational fragmentation, a diffusion of the decision-making power, and a limited administrative authority, we may expect that governmental reform policies that pay attention to compatibility and profitability will be more effective in creating innovations than policies in which these concepts are not taken into account.

The discussion of innovation characteristics that are supposed to determine the success or failure of an innovation has so far concentrated on two of the five characteristics presented in the survey of Rogers and Shoemaker: compatibility and profitability (relative advantage). However the authors mentioned three other factors: complexity, triability, and observability.

Concerning the complexity of innovation, Rogers and Shoemaker themselves suggest that no relationship exists with the rate of adoption. According to them the degree to which an innovation is perceived to be difficult to understand or use does not really influence the process of acceptance or refusal of an innovation.

However, in the field of higher education another conclusion appears to be drawn. Cerych and Sabatier argue that a reform that is both "deep and broad" will tend to fail (Cerych and Sabatier, 1986, p. 145). When complexity is defined as the combination of the degree to which an innovation is a departure from existing values and practices with the number of functional areas aimed at by innovation, the level of complexity of an innovation process in higher education may be expected to be negatively related to the rate of adoption of the innovation. The more complex an innovation, the less successful that innovation will be in getting adopted.

The observability of an innovation is another factor presented by Rogers and Shoemaker as having a positive relationship with the rate of adoption: the more the goals and results of the innovation are visible and clear, the more likely it is that the innovation will be accepted.

In the field of higher education research Becher and Kogan (1980) come to the conclusion that the observability of an innovation is indeed of some influence. Taking the same position as Cerych and Sabatier (1986) with respect to depth and breadth of innovations (see before), they argue that

> innovations which manage ... to challenge certain accepted ideas while reinforcing others have a fair chance of success, provided that they also meet two other prerequisites: that their merits are reasonably visible and that they do not appear seriously to undermine the existing patterns of freedom and control. (Becher and Kogan, 1980, p. 146)

Becher and Kogan's second prerequisite can be translated in terms of profitability. It may be interpreted as the inclination to guard the self-perceived interests of academic groups, often expressed as the conservation of the academic definitions of legitimate activities. The first prerequisite has to do with observability: to be able to be successful the merits of innovations have to be visible.

Cerych and Sabatier also suggest that in theory a high level of clarity and consistency of the objectives of an innovation facilitates the implementation of innovations. However, from their case studies they also conclude that in practice vagueness and ambiguity of objectives appear to prevail, especially because otherwise a consensus on the proposed innovation would not have occurred (Cerych and Sabatier, 1986, pp. 13, 14, 243).

Taking the arguments by Becher and Kogan and by Cerych and Sabatier into account, it can be argued that observability as such can hardly be called an important factor for the success or failure of an innovation. At most the level of observability of the objectives and expected results of an innovation is a strategic element in presenting an innovation as compatible with existing values or as profitable for certain groups and interests. Following Levine (1980) it could be concluded that when the objective is to guarantee that others have an accurate or positive picture of an innovation, this factor has more to do with compatibility and profitability than with observability per se. Guaranteeing an accurate or positive picture implies preventing the innovation from appearing incompatible and/or unprofitable (Levine, 1980, p. 187).

This leaves us with triability as a last innovation characteristic which is supposed to be positively related to the rate of adoption. Triability concerns an organization's ability to try an innovation within a limited period and on a limited scale. Moreover, it has to do with the condition that if, after trying an innovation, the conclusion is that the results are disappointing, the situation is reversible without severe damage.

Cerych and Sabatier have found that the assumptions on which reforms are based often are erroneous. This should not surprise us. As is the case with every process of policy design, so too the process of the design of innovations in higher education has to face the basic human impotence in accurately foretelling the future. Our knowledge can only be incomplete and things may change while a policy is designed and implemented (Van Vught, 1987).

Triability is a prudent strategy for those who do not want to overrate the level of knowledge incorporated in the assumptions which form the basis of a certain reform policy or innovation. This is especially the case in higher education because it may be expected that scientists and scholars are particularly skeptical about these kinds of assumptions. It is because of this that Bok (1986) pleads for implementing innovations in higher education institutions by means of experiments. Referring to an example of the Harvard Medical School he argues:

> this tactic has obvious advantages. It relies entirely on volunteers and hence makes few, if any demands on unwilling faculty members. It costs less than an institution-wide reform. It minimizes the risks of failure by leaving traditional programs intact. These virtues are often decisive in holding open the chance of making a substantial change. (Bok, 1986, pp. 187, 188)

The major problem with the experimental strategy is of course the spreading of a successful experiment through the entire institution. As was noticed before, the diffusion of an innovation will only take place by virtue of the professional belief that an innovation is worthwhile. Regarding this issue the concepts of compatibility and profitability have provided us with some insights. Nevertheless, a strategy of experimenting with innovations must be judged to be especially suited to higher education. Therefore, governmental policies that pay attention to triability may be expected to be more successful in creating innovations in higher education institutions than policies in which the idea of triability is absent.

Reviewing the points of view and analyses of the various authors mentioned above an important conclusion should be that government-initiated innovations in higher education institutions and systems can be successful only when certain conditions are met. These conditions have to do with the specific characteristics of higher education institutions. Innovations in higher education institutions can only be brought about by governmental policies, when attention is paid in these policies to the basic values and mechanisms of academic life.

It also can be concluded that an innovative policy can be expected to be more successful when in such a strategy attention is paid to the compatibility and the profitability of the innovation. The compatibility of an innovation (i.e., the degree to which the innovation is perceived to be consistent with existent values and practices) is, generally speaking, positively related to the rate of adoption of the innovation. However, a reform that implies a radical departure from existing values and practices can nevertheless be successful when the "functional breadth of change" is limited; that is, when the reform is limited to a few functional areas while at the same time some other prevailing values and practices are rigorously accepted.

The profitability of an innovation is also positively related to the rate of adoption of the innovation. The relative advantage of the innovation (compared with the idea or practice it supersedes) should be clear to those who are supposed to accept it. The behavior of each group and individual confronted with an innovation is guided by the subjective interpretation of self-interest. The outcome of an innovation process to a large extent depends on the distribution of power among the self-interested actors involved in the decision-making process regarding the innovation.

The complexity of an innovation was found to be negatively related to the rate of adoption of the innovation. When complexity is defined as the combination of the degree to which an innovation is a departure from existing values and practices with the number of functional areas aimed at by the innovation, it may be concluded that the higher the level of complexity of an innovation, the less likely it is that the innovation will be accepted.

With respect to the observability of an innovation (i.e., the degree to which the objectives and expected results are clear) it was argued that this factor should be interpreted as a strategic element in presenting an innovation in terms of compatibility or profitability.

The triability of an innovation (i.e., the degree to which an innovation may be experimented with) was judged to be of great importance in higher education. Experimenting with innovations is a prudent strategy, especially because the professionals in higher education institutions will be particularly skeptical about the policy assumption on which these innovations are based.

Conclusion

In the beginning of this chapter it was argued that the policy model of rational planning and control on the one hand and the policy model of self-regulation on the other vary in a rather fundamental way with regard to the assumptions they are based on. The model of rational planning and control is founded on the basic assumption of the rationalist perspective on decision-making. In every practical decision-making situation it strives after the objective of trying to select the best alternative from a set that should be as complete as possible. But confronted with the limitations of this ideal, in practice the strategy of rational planning and control takes its refuge in confidence in a strong centralization of decision-making processes and a large amount of control over these decision-making processes as well as over the implementation of the chosen policy.

The policy model of self-regulation is based on the cybernetic perspective on decision-making. It tries to make use of the self-regulatory capacities of decentralized decision-making units. It limits the role of government to the monitoring of a set of "critical variables" and to the analysis and, if judged necessary, the influencing of the framework of rules guiding the behavior of decentralized actors.

With respect to governmental policies in the field of higher education two models were introduced: the state control and the state supervising model. The state control model is largely based on the policy model of rational planning and control. The state supervising model reflects the policy model of self-regulation.

In the first part of this chapter also an overview was presented of the various policy instruments governments may use when they set themselves the task to influence activities and processes in the public sector.

The questions which I will try to answer in this concluding section are: Which of the two higher education policy models (state control and state supervision) is best suited to stimulate innovations in higher education systems and institutions? And, What policy instruments may be expected to be successful in that context?

It may be hypothesized from the analysis presented above that when the basic objective is to stimulate the innovativeness of the higher education institutions, the model of state control, generally speaking, is less successful than the model of state supervision. The model of state control appears to be based on assumptions that are at odds with some of the fundamental characteristics of higher education institutions. The model of state control ignores the fundamental features of higher education institutions that are found in characteristics like the high level of professional autonomy, the large organizational fragmentation and the large diffusion of the decision-making power.

The state supervising model appears to be better suited to the context of higher education. It acknowledges the fundamental characteristics of higher education institutions and it tries to make use of some of these characteristics to stimulate the innovativeness of the whole system of higher education. By limiting itself to only global forms of steering and by putting its confidence in the self-regulatory capacities of the professionals and the basic units of the higher education institutions, this model has the potential to become an effective paradigm for successful operational policies with respect to higher education in many countries (Neave and Van Vught, 1991).

Along the same lines it may be expected that a combination of mildly restrictive policy instruments will be more successful in stimulating innovations in higher education than a combination of extreme compulsive instruments. Compulsive instruments will overrestrict the behavior of the professional scholars in higher education institutions and, by doing so, create disillusion and apathy, rather than enthusiasm and innovativeness. It may be assumed that the fundamental characteristics of higher education institutions add up to a context in which government cannot execute compulsive actions without also bringing about some negative side-effects of these actions. Using Hood's categorization of policy instruments, it may be concluded that the instruments of information (responses and messages), the mildly restrictive instruments of authority (certificates and approvals) and the "give it away" instruments of treasure (transfer and bearer-directed payments) may be expected to be the most effective in the context of higher education.

With respect to higher education Clark (1983b) especially has asked the question of "governance fit":

> What governance arrangements are "naturally" generated? What structures of governance help this or that function to operate well? What governance "fits"? (Clark, 1983b, p. 27)

Clark comes to the conclusion that

> fit is a matter of balance among alternative forms for effecting national governance. Too much emphasis in any one direction, for example on state command, produces an imbalance that leads to a "fit" in a different meaning of the term!—a sudden and violent attack of a disorder, a convulsion, an exacerbation of troubles perhaps leading to prolonged sickness. (Clark, 1983b, 27)

In this chapter an issue has been explored which is very much related to Clark's question of governance fit. My conclusion was that the state supervising model appears to fit better than the state control model and that mildly restrictive instruments fit better than compulsive instruments.

Clark argues that differentiation should be the name of the governance game in higher education. He indicates (among other things) that diverse structures accommodate the conflicting tasks of higher education better than simple structures, that diverse structures allow status differentiation and sector diversification and that diverse structures stimulate flexibility and innovation (Clark, 1983b, pp. 31–37). Along the same lines I have tried to show that the state supervising model (because of its foundation in the cybernetic perspective on decision-making) offers the advantages of flexibility and innovation, of experimenting and robustness, of self-determination and responsibility. At the same time this model is relatively low in the costs of information, transaction, and administration.

The problems with which the model of state control is confronted in higher education can to a large extent be carried back to the basic differences between this model and the funda-

mental characteristics of the higher education context. The adherents of the state control model tend to see higher education more as an object than as a complex set of subjects (Trow, 1980; Neave, 1985). Besides, they see a higher education system as an object which can be controlled from outside and which can be moulded to the wishes of government.

The state control model puts its confidence in centralization and a large amount of control. But by doing so, it alienates itself from a societal sector like higher education, which above all else is characterized by a large amount of autonomy and differentiation. Speaking of the "unitary approach" Clark (1983b) formulates the same conclusion:

> Surely what we fear most about the unitary approach is the way it cramps a multiplicity of approaches and increases the likelihood of the arbitrary dictate and the large error. Nearly every time we plan centrally we eliminate some options of the operators. In each reform we add structures that constrain future choices. If we do not want things to escape our eyes, we systemize some more, generating a rule book that clogs formal channels and in turn stimulates underground activity for getting things done. (Clark 1983b, p. 38)

It should not be surprising that the model of state control cannot be called a good fit for an innovation-oriented higher education system. The state control model overlooks the crucial issue of the costs of acquiring knowledge for the sake of creating innovations. It forgets that in a multilevel system general knowledge is usually more economically acquired by higher level decision-making units, while specific knowledge is more easily and more cheaply acquired by lower level units. And it forgets that, by introducing rigid and detailed procedures of hierarchical control, it cuts itself off from the possible knowledge advantages of the lower level decision-making units and thereby loses a large innovative potential.

> ... the effectiveness of hierarchical subordination varies with the extent to which the subordinate unit has knowledge advantages over the higher unit. In those cases where the subordinate unit has better information, then in terms of the whole decision-making process the knowledge is one place and the power is another; the quality

of decisions suffers as a result. Moreover, subordination itself becomes illusory to the extent that the lower level unit can use its knowledge to evade, counteract, or redirect the thrust of orders from its nominal superiors. (Sowell, 1980, pp. 13, 14)

Compared with the model of state control, the state supervising model seems to offer a better fit. This model seems to be better equipped to be used as a general incitement toward innovations in a higher education system. It addresses these systems while taking the fundamental characteristics of higher education institutions seriously. It leaves sufficient room for the (semi-)autonomous professionals and basic units and it does not try to coordinate the large variety of a higher education system in a limited set of rules.

By enlarging the autonomy of the higher education institutions and by limiting itself to monitoring some "critical" system variables and to (not often and not too drastically) adapting some general "rules of the game," government may find in this model an important approach which may both stimulate the innovativeness of a higher education system and secure its basic values and practices.

References

Ashby, W. R. (1956). *An Introduction to Cybernetics.* London: Chapman and Hall.

Banfield, E. C. (1959). Ends and means in planning. *International Social Science Journal* 11(3): 361–368.

Bardach, E. (1979). *The Implementation Game.* Cambridge Mass.: MIT Press.

Barret, S. C., and Fudge, C. (eds.) (1981). *Policy and Action: Essays on the Implementation of Public Policy.* London: Methuen.

Becher, T., and Kogan, M. (1980). *Process and Structure in Higher Education.* London: Heinemann.

Beer, St. (1975). *Platform for Change.* New York: John Wiley.

Berdahl, R., and Millett, J. (1991). Autonomy and accountability in U. S. higher education. In G. Neave and F. A. van Vught (eds.), *Prometheus Bound.* London: Pergamon.

Bok, D. (1986). *Higher Learning.* Cambridge: Harvard University Press.

Braybrooke, D., and Lindblom, Ch. E. (1963). *A Strategy of Decision: Policy Evaluation as a Social Process.* New York: Free Press.

Cerych, L., and Sabatier, P. (1986). *Great Expectations and Mixed Performance: the Implementation of Higher Education Reforms in Europe.* Trentham: Trentham Books.

Clark, B. R. (1983a). *The Higher Education System.* Berkeley: University of California Press.

Clark, B. R. (1983b). Governing the higher education system. In M. Chattock (ed.). *The Structure and Governance of Higher Education.* Guildford: Society for Research into Higher Education.

Dahl, R. A., and Lindblom, Ch. E. (1976, orig. 1953). *Politics, Economics and Welfare.* Chicago: University of Chicago Press.

Davis, R. H., Strand, R., Alexander, L. T., and Hussain, N. M. (1982). The impact of organizational and innovation variables on instructional innovation in higher education. *Journal of Higher Education* 53 (5): 568–586.

Dill, D. D. (1992). Quality by design: toward a framework for academic quality management. In J. Smart (ed.). *Higher Education: Handbook of Theory and Research* Vol. VIII. New York: Agathon Press.

Dill, D. D., and Friedman, Ch. P. (1979). An analysis of frameworks for research on innovation and change in higher education. *Review of Educational Research* 49(3): 411–435.

Downs, G. W., and Mohr, L. B. (1976). Conceptual issues in the study of innovation, *Administrative Science Quarterly* 21: 700–714.

Dror, Y. (1968). *Public Policymaking Re-examined.* San Francisco: Chandler.

Dror, Y. (1971). *Design for Policy Sciences.* New York: Elsevier.

Dunsire, A. (1978). *Implementation in a Bureaucracy.* Oxford: Martin Robinson.

Elmore, R. F. (1987). Instruments and strategy in public policy. *Policy Studies Review* 7(1): 174–186.

Etzioni, A. (1968). *The Active Society.* New York: Free Press.

Friedmann, J. (1973). *Retracking America: A Theory of Transactive Planning.* New York: Garden City.

Glenny, L. A. (ed.). *Funding Higher Education: A Six-Nation Analysis.* New York: Praeger.

Hage, J., and Aiken, M. (1967). Program change and organizational properties: a comparative analysis. *American Journal of Sociology* 72(5): 503–519.

Hage, J., and Aiken, M. (1970). *Social Change in Complex Organizations.* New York: Random House.

Hefferlin, J. B. (1969). *Dynamics of Academic Reform.* San Francisco: Jossey-Bass.

Hood, Chr. C. (1983). *The Tools of Government.* London: Macmillan.

Ingram, H., and Mann, D. (1980). *Why Policies Succeed or Fail.* Beverly Hills: Sage.

Jantsch, E. (1972). *Technological Planning and Social Futures.* London: Cassel/Associated Business Programmes.

Kahn, A. E. (1971). *The Economics of Regulation: Principles and Institutions* (2 vols). New York: John Wiley.

Kerr, C. (1982). *The Uses of the University* (third ed.). Cambridge: Harvard University Press.

Kerr, C. (1987). A critical age in the university world: accumulated heritage versus modern imperatives. *European Journal of Education* 22(2): 183–193.

Lane, J. E. (1984). Possibility and desirability of higher education reform. In R. Premfors (ed.). *Higher Education Organisation.* Stockholm: Almqvist and Wiksell.

Levine, A. (1980). *Why Innovation Fails: The Institutionalization and Termination of Innovation in Higher Education*. Albany: State University of New York Press.

Lindblom, Ch. E. (1959). The science of muddling through. *Public Administration Review* 19(2): 79–99.

Lindblom, Ch. E. (1965). *Intelligence of Democracy*. New York: Free Press.

Maassen, P. A. M., and Van Vught, F. A. (1992). Strategic planning. In B. R. Clark and G. Neave (eds.). *The Encyclopedia of Higher Education*. Vol 2: 1483–1494. London: Pergamon.

March, J. G., and Olsen, J. P. (1976). *Ambiguity and Choice in Organisations*. Bergen: Universitetsforlaget.

Mazmanian, D. A., and Sabatier, P. A. (1981). *Effective Policy Implementation*. Toronto: Lexington Books.

McDonnell, L. (1988). Policy design as instrument design. Paper presented at the 1988 annual meeting of the American Political Science Association. Washington D.C.

Meyerson, M. (1956). Building the middle-range bridge for comprehensive planning. *Journal of the American Institute of Planners* 22(2): 58–64.

Meyerson, M., and Banfield, E. C. (1955). *Politics, Planning and the Public Interest*. Glencoe: Free Press.

Mintzberg, H. (1979). *The Structuring of Organizations*. Englewood Cliffs: Prentice-Hall.

Mitnick, B. M. (1980). *The Political Economy of Regulation: Creating, Designing and Removing Regulatory Reforms*. New York: Columbia University Press.

Neave, G. (1985). Higher education in a period of consolidation: 1975–1985. *European Journal of Education* 20(2): 109–124.

Neave, G., and Van Vught, F. A. (eds.) (1991). *Prometheus Bound: The Changing Relationship Between Government and Higher Education in Western Europe*. London: Pergamon.

Newman, F. (1987). *Choosing Quality: Reducing Conflict Between the State and the University*. Denver: Education Commission of the States.

O'Toole, L. (1986). Policy recommendations for multi-actor implementation: an assessment of the field. *Journal of Public Policy* 6(1): 21–48.

Polanyi, M. (1962). The republic of science: its political and economic theory. *Minerva* 1: 54–73.

Premfors, R. (1984). *Higher Education Organisation*. Stockholm: Almqvist and Wiksell.

Premfors, R. (1992). Policy analysis. In B. R. Clark and G. Neave (eds.). *The Encyclopedia of Higher Education*. Vol. 3. 1907–1916. London: Pergamon.

Pressman, J. L., and Wildavsky, A. B. (1973). *Implementation*. Berkeley: University of California Press.

Rein, M., and Rabinovitz, F. (1978). Implementation: a theoretical perspective. In Burnham, W. D., and Weinberg, W. W. (eds.) *American Politics and Public Policy*. Cambridge Mass.: MIT Press.

Rogers, E. M., and Shoemaker, F. F. (1971). *Communication of Innovations*. New York: Free Press.

Salamon, L. M. (1981). Rethinking public management: third party government and the changing forms of government action. *Public Policy* 29(3): 255–275.

Schneider, A., and Ingram H. (1990). Behavioral assumptions of policy tools. *Journal of Politics* 52 (2): 510–530.

Scott, P. (1988). *The British Universities' Response to Institutional Diversification*. Paris: OECD/IMHE.

Simon, H. A. (1957). *Administrative Behavior*. 2nd ed. New York: Macmillan.

Skolnik, M. L. (1987). State control of degree granting: the establishment of a public monopoly in Canada. In C. Watson (ed.). *Governments and Higher Education: The Legitimacy of Intervention*. Toronto: Higher Education Group, The Ontario Institute for Studies in Education.

Sowell, T. (1980). *Knowledge and Decisions*. New York: Basic Books.

Steinbrunner, J. D. (1974). *The Cybernetic Theory of Decision: New Dimensions of Political Analysis*. Princeton: Princeton University Press.

Stigler, G. J. (1975). *The Citizen and the State: Essays on Regulation*. Chicago: University of Chicago Press.

Trow, M. (1980). *Dilemmas of Higher Education in the 1980's and 1990's*. Montreal: Conference of Learned Societies.

Van de Graaf, J. H., Clark, B. R., Furth, D., Goldschmidt, D., and Wheeler, D. F. (1978). *Academic Power: Patterns of Authority in Seven National Systems of Higher Education*. New York: Praeger.

Van Gunsteren, H. R. (1976). *The Quest for Control: A Critique of the Rational-Central Rule Approach in Public Affairs*. New York: Wiley.

Van Vught, F. A. (1987). Pitfalls of forecasting: fundamental problems for the methodology of forecasting from the philosophy of science. *Futures, the Journal of Forecasting and Planning* 19(2): 184–197.

Van Vught, F. A. (1988). A new autonomy in European higher education? An exploration and analysis of the strategy of self-regulation in higher education governance. *International Journal of Institutional Management in Higher Education* 12(1): 16–27.

Van Vught, F. A. (1991). Public administration. In B. R. Clark and G. Neave (eds.). *The Encyclopedia of Higher Education*. Vol. 3, 1932–1943. London: Pergamon.

Van Vught, F. A. (1992). Autonomy and accountability in government-university relationships. Paper presented at the World Bank Worldwide Senior Policy Seminar on Improvement and Innovation of Higher Education in Developing Countries. Kuala Lumpur: June 30–July 4, 1992.

Walford, G. (1991). The changing relationship between government and higher education in Britain. In G. Neave and F. van Vught (eds.). *Prometheus Bound*. London: Pergamon.

Weick, K. F. (1979). Educational organizations as loosely coupled systems. *Administrative Science Quarterly* 21(1): 1–19.

The Costs and Consequences of the Transformation in Federal Student-Aid Policy

Michael Mumper

The transformation in the federal student-aid effort over the past three decades has many dimensions. But without question, the fundamental difference between the student aid programs created in the 1960s and early 1970s and those of the 1990s, is the dramatic increase in the volume, and relative importance, of the various student loan programs. The first federally guaranteed loan program was designed to provide a convenient source of aid to middle-income students at a very low cost to the federal government. However, by the mid-1990s, after numerous modifications, revisions, and amendments, the now multiple federal student loan programs have grown dramatically in both their size and scope.

This expansion translated into important changes in the resources available to lower-income students to pay for college. As far back as 1988, Senator Claiborne Pell lamented that the typical student aid package was intended to be three-quarters grant and one-quarter loan, but now "it is precisely the opposite." This sent a clear message to lower-income students: If you can't afford to pay for college, borrow the money.

Today, almost no one is happy with the balance between grants and loans in federal student-aid policy. Potential students, former students, colleges, and the federal government all have their own concerns over the growing levels of student borrowing. Yet, in spite of these concerns, and repeated efforts at reform, an ever larger number of students borrow through these programs each year while the

cost of these programs to the federal government has continued to grow.

In this chapter, I examine the costs and consequences which have resulted from the expansion in the role of student loans in the federal effort to remove college price barriers. After reviewing how the various loan programs work, I look at why the costs of operating them have increased so rapidly since 1980. I then turn to the unintended consequences which have followed the expansion of student borrowing. In particular, I examine concerns that the prospect of substantial post-collegiate debt discourages disadvantaged students from entering college, that it distorts the career choices of those who do attend, and that they saddle borrowers with unreasonably large debts when they leave school. Finally, I explain how the growth of loans has distorted federal policy by shifting subsidies towards middle and upper-income families and away from lower-income students.

Understanding Federal Loan Guarantees

In order to understand how and why the various loan programs have grown so rapidly, it is useful to examine their operation in detail. The principle of these is the large and complex set of federally guaranteed student loan programs which are now referred to under the umbrella title "Federal Family Education Loan (FFEL) program." Unlike Pell grants and the campus-

"The Costs and Consequences of the Transformation in Federal Student-Aid Policy," by Michael Mumper, reprinted from *Removing College Price Barriers: What Government Has Done and Why It Hasn't Worked*, 1996, State University of New York Press.

based student-aid programs, the FFEL programs are not direct student aid programs at all. They are complex structures designed to encourage private lenders to make loans that they would not otherwise make. As such, most of the federal expenditures resulting from the program do not go to students at all but rather to banks and financial institutions. While this system has succeeded in making large sums of private monies available to students, it has done so at a very high price to the federal treasury and to many lower-income students.

The Logic of Loan Guarantees

In order to insure that all students have access to the capital they need to attend college, policy-makers face two problems. Potential lenders find student loans too risky and too expensive to offer, and potential borrowers find the loans too risky and too expensive to take. From the lender's perspective, student loans can be prohibitively. expensive. They are for a small amount, there is no marketable asset that can provide collateral, and the highly mobile borrowers often have no credit history. As a consequence, prior to 1965 "private education loans were virtually unavailable" unless they were based on the income and financial positions of the student's family.

Potential borrowers also face risks and costs which can make college loans unattractive, even if they can find a willing lender. While the average return for an investment in higher education is high, it is subject to a wide variance. In any individual case the future return from an investment in education can be quite risky. The student-borrower must be willing to assume that risk. Moreover, the high interest rate that a lender would charge to make such an uncollateralized loan made college loans even less attractive to potential student-borrowers.

Government loan guarantees thus serve to increase the supply of, and demand for, private student loans by lowering the costs and the risks to both lenders and borrowers. In addition to the guarantee of full repayment, the federal government pays lenders a variety of subsidies to encourage them to make loans. By holding down interest rates, and by making loans available to all students without collateral or credit checks, the federal government insures that lower-income students are both willing and able to borrow for college.

The Operation of Loan Guarantees

As first enacted in 1965, undergraduates could borrow up to $1,000 a year at a 6 percent interest rate through the GSLP. The federal government guaranteed repayment of all loans and paid the interest on loans to families with incomes of less than $15,000. While these were attractive terms, the price to the federal government remained small. In 1970, about one million students borrowed about $3.5 billion through the program.

From this relatively modest beginning, the FFEL grew at an astounding rate. In 1992, more than $4 billion in guaranteed loans were made to about four million student-borrowers. There are now five separate FFEL programs, more than 8,000 eligible education institutions, 13,000 participating lenders, 35 secondary markets, and 46 state or non-profit guarantee agencies. The costs of the programs to the federal government have also grown. In 1992, the cost to the federal government of the various loan guarantee programs was $6.3 billion.

Figure 1 shows the complex flow of funds which occurs whenever an FFEL is made. FFELs are generally provided by the private financial sector, primarily commercial banks, savings and loan institutions, and credit unions. Most students seeking a student loan never need to visit a lending institution. The application process is handled by the financial aid office at the school the student attends. To receive a guaranteed student loan, a student must first complete the Free Application for Federal Student Aid and return it to the Department of Education. Based on the information provided by the student, the federal government calculates the student's Expected Family Contribution (EFC). This is the amount the student's family is judged to be able to afford to cover college costs. Then, the school's financial aid office takes the cost of education at that school and subtracts the EFC to determine the student's financial need. If the price of the school is greater than the amount the family is judged able to contribute, the difference is considered to be the student's need. That need is the amount that the student is eligible to receive in federal financial aid.

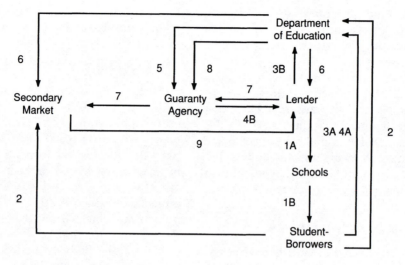

1A 1B	Loan Principle
2	Principal Plus Interest (repayment)
3A 3B	Origination Fee (5 Percent of Loan)
4A 4B	Insurance Fee (0 to 3 percent of loan)
5	Administrative Cost Allowance (1 percent of loan)
6	In school Interest Subsidy Plus Special Allowance (91 T-bill plus 3.25 percent)
7	Insurance
8	Reinsurance
9	Loan Purchase by Secondary Market (in some cases)

Source: Adapted from General Accounting Office, *Direct Loans Could Save Money and Simplify Program Administration,* September 1992, p. 17.

Figure 1: The Flow of Funds under the Federal Family Education Loan Programs

Based on the student's need, the financial aid office at the school then puts together a package of Pell grants, campus-based aid, state grants, and institutional aid tailored to the student's individual circumstances. If that aid package does not cover the full cost of the student's education, the student can then borrow the remaining amount, up to the loan limits. Once the financial aid office has determined the student's loan eligibility, that information is then forwarded to the lender. After the student has signed a promissory note agreeing to repay the loan, and has enrolled in a qualified institution of higher education, the loan disbursement check is sent by the lender directly to the school to cover tuition, fees, and room and board (if the student is living in campus housing). Anything that is left over is passed on to the student-borrower to cover living expenses. The loan becomes due following a grace period after the student leaves school unless the student applies for a deferment, and it must be repaid over a ten-year period and the minimum monthly repayment is $50.

For each loan made, the federal government provides a subsidy payment to the lender as compensation for the lower interest rate charged to the student. This payment is intended to make the return on these student loans competitive with alternative lending opportunities. The federal government also commits to pay full interest on the loan while the student remains in college. In return, an "origination fee" is deducted from the loan principle and paid to the federal government to cover their administrative costs. That fee, which is now between 5 percent and 6.5 percent of the loan, is deducted from each loan disbursement. The lender may also collect an insurance premium of up to 3 percent of the loan principle. This premium is also deducted from each disbursement.

The lender is responsible for the collection of all loans. If the student fails to repay the loan because of death, disability, bankruptcy, or default, the lender must make "due diligence" efforts, such as phone calls and letters to the defaulter, to collect the loan. After 180 days, if collection attempts have failed, the lender passes along the defaulted loan to the state's guarantee agency and receives full reimbursement.

A guaranty agency, which is established in each state, must then try to collect the loan. If they successfully collect the defaulted loan, the guaranty agency can retain 30 percent of the amount collected to reimburse its costs. But if they cannot collect, the agency can apply to the Department of Education for federal reimbursement 270 days after the loan went into default. The state guaranty agency must assume part of the responsibility for defaulted loans. Agencies with 5 percent or fewer of their loans in default are fully reimbursed. Those with higher default rates receive only partial reimbursement.

Many lenders prefer not to be involved in the collection of relatively small loans from very mobile student-borrowers. Such lenders may still participate in the origination of student loans and then sell them in one of the secondary student loan markets before they come due. These secondary markets provide liquidity for participating lenders by purchasing student loans which should, in turn, allow the originating lenders to expand their FFEL portfolios. Secondary markets also encourage the development of organizations which specialize in the collection of outstanding student loans. The largest of these secondary markets is the Student Loan Marketing Association (Sallie Mae) which is a federally chartered stock holder-owned corporation established in 1972 to provide a national secondary market for loans made under the FFEL. In 1991, Sallie Mae's outstanding loan purchases of $15.6 billion constituted approximately one-third of all dollars outstanding in the FFEL.

While Sallie Mae is the largest of the secondary student loan markets, several states have created their own secondary markets to make participation in the FFEL more attractive to local lenders. Today, the New England Educational Loan Marketing Corporation, the Nebraska Higher Education Loan program, and the California Student Loan Financing Corporation are all among the top ten holders of outstanding student loans.

The Proliferation of Loan Guarantee Programs

As the demand for student loans has grown since 1980, the federal government has responded by expanding and subdividing the FFEL to better serve the diverse types of students seeking loans. Today there are five different loan guarantee programs. Each operates by different rules and serves a different constituency. The differences between these loans are described in Table 1.

Stafford Loans. By far the largest of the FFELs is the Stafford loan program. In 1991, Stafford loans accounted for about 80 percent of all FFELs made and 78 percent of the dollar volume of all FFELs. There are two types of Stafford loans. Those students from families with demonstrated financial need may receive a federally subsidized Stafford loan to cover that documented need. Under these loans the federal government pays the interest charges on the loan while the student is in school, during the grace period, and during authorized deferments.

Students whose families do not demonstrate financial need, and therefore do not qualify for a subsidized Stafford loan, may borrow through the unsubsidized Stafford loan program. In this program the rules for borrowing are the same except that the interest rate is higher and the student, not the government, must pay the interest which accrues on the loan while the student is in school or has deferred payment.

The interest rate charged on both types of Stafford loans is variable. The rate is adjusted each year and is capped at 9 percent for subsidized and 10 percent for unsubsidized loans. Qualified students may borrow up to $4,000 during their first and second years in college. They can borrow up to $5,000 during their third through fifth year. Undergraduates can borrow no more than $23,000 under the Stafford program. However, if they subsequently go on to graduate or professional school, their loan limit is increased to $73,000.

PLUS Loans. The Education Amendments of 1980 established the Parent Loan for

TABLE 1
Characteristics of Federal Loan Guarantee Programs

Program	Need-Based Loan?	Yearly & Aggregate Loan Maximums	Interest Rates
Subsidized Stafford	Yes	Year 1–2 = $4,000 Year 3–5 = $5,000 Maximum = $23,000 for undergraduates	3.1% above the 91 day T-bill rate Capped at 9%
Unsubsidized Stafford	No	Cost of education minus financial aid No aggregate maximum	3.1 % above the 91 day T-bill rate Capped at 9%
Parent Loan for Undergraduate Students (PLUS)	No	Cost of education minus financial aid No aggregate maximum	3.1 % above the 91 day T-bill rate Capped at 10%
Supplemental Loans for Students (SLS)	No	Cost of education minus financial aid No aggregate maximum	3.1% above the 91 day T-bill rate Capped at 11%

Undergraduate Students (PLUS). This program provides additional funds for parents of dependent undergraduate students. PLUS allows families to borrow more than they can under the Stafford program. In fact, students can borrow the entire cost of their education minus any financial aid they receive. In return for these higher loan limits, the borrower must pay a higher interest rate (variable up to 10 percent) and have no grace period or deferment options. No needs test is required for the PLUS loan. In 1991, PLUS loans accounted for about 8 percent of the total volume of FFEL loans awarded.

SLS Loans. The Higher Education Amendments of 1986 created the Supplemental Loans to Students (SLS) program. It is similar to the PLUS loan except that it is available only to independent students. An independent student must apply for a subsidized Stafford loan first, then for an unsubsidized Stafford, and only then can they apply for an SLS. Like the PLUS, the SLS provides loans which cover the entire cost of the education minus any other financial aid received. The interest rate is variable and capped at 11 percent. SLS loans also allow no grace period or deferred payment options. In 1991, SLS loans accounted for about 14 percent of all FFELs.

Consolidated Loans. The Higher Education Amendments of 1986 also authorized lenders to make consolidation loans. These loans allow students to consolidate multiple Stafford, PLUS, SLS, and even Perkins loans into a single loan. This can only be done when all of the loans are in repayment or grace periods. The interest rate on consolidated loans is the weighted average of the underlying loans or 9 percent, which ever is the greatest. In 1991, consolidated loans accounted for 6 percent of the total volume of federally guaranteed loans.

The Success of Loan Guarantees

This complex system of incentives, subsidies, and guarantees was designed to insure that every student who is enrolled in an approved institution, and who is willing to take the risks inherent in borrowing to pay for a higher education, will have access to the necessary funds. The structure of the programs also guarantees that the lending institution will make a profit on each loan while incurring almost no risk. Given the structure of the program, it is easy to see why so many students are willing to take out these loans and why so many lenders are willing to make them.

Indeed, if the federal student loan programs are to be judged by their original purpose alone, they are nothing short of an overwhelming success. They have made billions of dollars of loans available to an ever larger percentage of students and have induced the creation of a large financial industry which lends huge amounts of private funds to students based on federal loan guarantees. In 1991, more than 13,000 banks, credit unions, and non-profit lenders participated in the origination of FFELs. While some of these lenders made only a few student loans, many others have made student loans a large part of their portfolios. Twenty-two different lenders each originated more than $100 million in FFELs, and another seventeen originated between $50 and $100 million of new student loans. The impressive size, and scope of the FFEL leaves little doubt that the student loans programs have firmly established themselves in the financial community.

The Creation of Direct Lending

In 1993, a system of direct lending was enacted as an alternative to the FFEL. The first direct loans will be made in the 1994–95 academic year and as much as 60 percent of all student loans will be made through direct lending by 1998. Under this plan, schools will have the option of participating in the direct lending programs. Those schools which did not wish to operate their own program would continue to participate in the loan guarantee programs.

Figure 2 shows how much simpler the flow of funds is under direct lending than it is under the FFEL. Direct lending streamlines the lending process by eliminating private lenders, guarantee agencies, and secondary loan markets. The U.S. Treasury will sell securities to meet the capital requirements of direct lending. Institutions will apply annually to the Department of Education for funding based on the estimated financial needs of their students. On behalf of the government, institutions will determine student eligibility, prepare promissory notes, and distribute loan funds to students following procedures similar to those used in the Perkins loan program.

The Department of Education will operate the servicing aspects of the direct lending program through competitive private contracts. This will relieve the schools of the burden of loan collection and eliminate the need for a secondary market. Direct loans will carry interest rates similar to those charged on Stafford loans. The origination fee and the insurance premiums would be substantially reduced. The result, it is argued, will be lower costs to the schools, to students, and to the federal government.

Disadvantages of Direct Lending

While direct lending has some obvious merit, it also presents some substantial drawbacks. It is not clear that all, or even most, institutions have the capacity, or the desire, to succeed as lending agents. Moreover, if the administrative costs of operating such a program on each campus are large, they could eat up most of the savings resulting from the by-passing of traditional lending agencies.

There is also substantial disagreement over the potential savings which will result from the switch to direct lending. A 1992 study conducted by the GAO estimated that "the federal government could save from $120 million to $1.5 billion annually by using direct rather than guaranteed loans to provide loan assistance to postsecondary students." This estimate was widely cited in the congressional debate over loan reform and may well have been responsible for its eventual enactment.

But a 1993 Congressional Research Service (CRS) study reached a starkly different conclusion. It found that the direct lending reform was likely to produce only small savings to the federal government. This savings would be achieved by reducing needlessly high subsidies to private lenders. The CRS noted, however, that substantial savings could be achieved within the existing framework simply by reducing the subsidies currently paid to banks in the FFEL.

Critics of direct lending also argue that it will not serve students and their families as well as the FFEL. Many wonder why we should expect schools, with no experience in lending, to perform this task better than banks, who are highly skilled at making loans. Further, they wonder why anyone should expect the Department of Education, with little experience in servicing and collecting loans from millions of borrowers, to perform that task better than lenders, Sallie Mae, and the

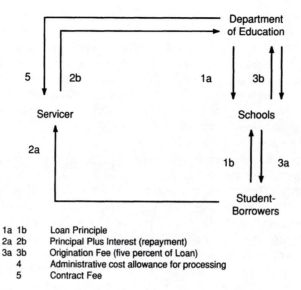

1a	1b	Loan Principle
2a	2b	Principal Plus Interest (repayment)
3a	3b	Origination Fee (five percent of Loan)
	4	Administrative cost allowance for processing
	5	Contract Fee

Source: Adapted from General Accounting Office, *Direct Loans Could Save Money and Simplify Program Administration,* September 1992, p. 17.

Figure 2: The Flow of Funds under the Direct Loan Program

other agencies who have been doing this for years. Indeed, if schools are unable to efficiently originate loans, and/or if the federal government is unable to effectively service and collect loans, direct lending could result in a deterioration in the quality of loan services.

The change to a mixed system of direct and guaranteed loans promises some cost savings to the federal government. It will reduce the large subsidies now paid to financial intermediaries and reduce default rates. But it will have virtually no impact on the college price barriers facing lower-income students. It will not change the amount they must borrow, only the source of their loan. Indeed, even if the entire system of loan guarantees was replaced with direct loans, and nothing else changed, disadvantaged students would face the same discouraging combination of large post-collegiate loans, and the high monthly payments they require. Direct loans streamline the system of student loans, and may reduce the costs of such loans to the government, but it leaves untouched the fundamental problem of more students needing to borrow more money to attend college.

Over the next decade, the number of FFELs should decline steadily and the number of direct loans should increase proportionately. Both systems will operate side by side during

the 1990s. In effect, this will constitute an experiment in which the two programs can be compared to each other. Unless Congress chooses to step in to alter the balance, the last half of the 1990s should provide a clear picture of whether direct lending can produce the cost savings and improved service promised by its supporters.

The High Cost of Loan Guarantees: Subsidies, Allowances, and Defaults

As student loans have become an essential resource for families to pay for college, and as they have become an essential element in the portfolios of many financial institutions, they have become more costly to the federal government. For each FFEL made, the federal government incurs several costs. Each of these costs has increased substantially since the late 1970s. Today, the various federally guaranteed student loan programs cost the federal government substantially more than anyone anticipated when they were created. And in spite of determined efforts since 1980 to control the costs of these programs, they have continued to grow, consuming an ever larger percentage of overall federal student aid spending.

Cost #1: Increased Loan Volume

A large part of the increased costs of the loan guarantee programs in the late 1970s and early 1980s was simply due to the fact that a great many more loans were being made. The combination of more students entering college, the loosened loan eligibility requirements, and very attractive interest rates, produced a substantial increase in the volume of student loans.

The fact that the number of loans more than doubled in the 1970s, should not be a surprise since the number of students attending college was growing and the eligibility for the loan programs was expanding rapidly. But the number of loans nearly doubled again in the 1980s when the number of college students was stable and the eligibility for the programs was being reduced. During those two decades, the dollar volume of student loans increased even more rapidly than did the number of student loans. FFEL volume increased an astonishing 200 percent in the 1970s. It then increased another 60 percent in the 1980s. Today, the $15.0 billion awarded in FFEL loans dwarfs the $6.1 billion awarded in Pell grants.

Cost #2: Increased Subsidies and Allowances

There was much more involved in the increases in the costs of the loan guarantee programs than simply an increase in the number of loans being made. Policy changes and economic conditions were making the FFEL more expensive for the federal government at all levels of lending. These factors caused the operating costs of the FFEL to increase even more rapidly than did the volume of student loans.

Each time a student loan is made, the federal government incurs a three-part financial obligation. First, if the loan is a subsidized Stafford loan, it makes payments to the lender on behalf of the borrower for interest that accrues during the in-school, grace, and authorized deferment periods. For unsubsidized Stafford, PLUS, and SLS loans, no interest subsidies are paid. Second, it pays lenders a "special allowance" based on the outstanding principle of all Stafford, PLUS, SLS, and Consolidated loans. This allowance, along with the borrowers interest payment, assures lenders an equitable yield on their loan. The special allowance was developed to insure that banks would be willing to participate in the program. Third, the federal government guarantees lenders that they will be repaid for all losses incurred as a result of borrower death, bankruptcy, or default. While both the lender and the state guarantee agency must make a serious effort to collect defaulted loans, today virtually all default claims by lenders are eventually reimbursed by the Department of Education.

Table 2 shows how the total cost of the FFEL has grown since 1980. Even after accounting for inflation, federal expenditures on these programs increased by a troubling 156 percent between 1980 and 1990. In the first half of the decade, each of the major program costs increased significantly. High interest rates forced the government to pay lenders substantially more in both interest subsidies and special allowances. The increased loan volume also translated into higher default costs. As a consequence, constant-dollar federal expenditures on student loan guarantees increased by 127 percent is just five years.

These cost increases have slowed since 1985, but only slightly. As interest rates began to drop in the late 1980s and early 1990s, the costs to the federal government for interest subsidies and special allowances also dropped. By 1990, these costs were more than $600 million less than they had been in 1985. But the

TABLE 2
Federal Expenditures for Student Loan Programs: 1980–1990 (in millions of 1994 dollars)

Federal Expenditure Type	1980	1985	1990
Interest Benefits	$693	$2,093	$1,709
Special Allowances	1,247	1,988	1,610
Reinsurance Default Claims	449	1,352	2,826
Other Expenditures	102	220	238
Total Federal Expenditures	2,491	5,652	6,381

Source: U.S. Department of Education, *FY 1992 Guaranteed Student Loan Data Book,* 1992.

late 1980s also produced a dramatic increase in the costs of loan defaults which more than overshadowed the savings in other areas. The net result was that the overall costs of the FFEL continued to rise, even as lower interest rates were producing substantial reductions in some of the principle costs of the programs.

Cost #3: Increased Default Rates

By the early 1990s, loan defaults constituted the principle cost of the federal loan-guarantee programs. This is not a new problem. As far back as 1975, Congress was holding hearings on what should be done to stem the rapidly rising costs of loan defaults. But while concerns over defaults are long standing, Table 3 provides an indication of how much worse that problem became since 1980. Even as measured in constant dollars, federal default costs increased 700 percent in the 1980s.

TABLE 3
Federal Expenditures Paid to Lenders to Cover Defaults in the Student Loan Programs: 1970–1990 (in constant 1994 dollars)

Year	Total Default Expenditures (in millions)
1970	$ 25
1975	369
1980	430
1985	1,415
1990	3,028

Source: U.S. Department of Education, *FY 1992 Guaranteed Student Loan Data Book,* 1992.

In the first years of the. program, default costs were relatively small. It was in the early 1980s that the default costs of the FFEL began to increase to alarming levels. Their $1.2 billion cost in 1985 made defaults a major topic of congressional debate during the reauthorization of the Higher Education Act in 1986. That act tightened requirements for both students and institutions to participate in the program and toughened enforcement regulations. But in spite of these efforts, these costs have continued to mount in the 1990s. In 1992, although the rates of loan defaults dropped slightly, the annual costs of defaulted loans was still $3.0 billion.

Why Defaults Increased So Rapidly

There are three principle reasons that default costs have increased so rapidly since 1980. The most obvious is that the number of loan defaults increases as the volume of student loans increases. With the number of students borrowing through the FFEL increasing from 2.3 million in 1980 to 4.5 million in 1990, the number of loan defaults also increased. The Department of Education explains that, although it may take a few years to run its full course:

> Invariably, a close relationship exists between annual loan volume and annual default costs. A sudden and sharp increase in loan volume will trigger a substantial increase in dollars entering repayment a few years later and eventually lead to increases in default costs.

Indeed, that is exactly what happened after 1980. As the number of students who had borrowed under the loosened MISAA rules in the late 1970s had their loan become due in the early 1980s, the number of defaults began to increase accordingly.

The second reason that FFEL defaults have increased since 1980 was a change in the character of the students who were borrowing under the FFEL. As net college prices rose after 1980, more lower-income and disadvantaged students began to borrow for college. In a 1990 study, *The Black Undergraduate,* Alexander Astin compared changes in the frequency of borrowing between black and white freshmen between 1978 and 1989. He found that before 1984, white students were more likely to take out a student loan. But since 1984, black students have been more likely to take such loans. Astin goes on to conclude that:

> Changes in the federal financial aid policies during the past decade have had a substantial impact on the black freshmen's financial aid package: Fewer black freshmen have access to federal grants and more must now rely on federal loans.

Using a similar approach, Thomas Mortenson examined the link between family income and borrowing for college. He found that during the 1980s, "While loans have become more widely used by all freshmen to finance their higher education, not all income groups have shared in this expanded use of loans." He concluded the use of loans increased the most rapidly among freshmen with family incomes between 100 and 200 percent of the poverty line, followed by those students whose family income was below the poverty line. The portion of students with family incomes more than 200 percent of the poverty line reporting loan use declined. The fact that more lower-income and disadvantaged students were borrowing created more costs to the federal government because these students were the most likely to default on their student loans. Students who failed to pay back their loans were disproportionately from disadvantaged backgrounds, program drop-outs or graduates of programs offering narrow vocational training, and were unemployed or earning a low wage when the loan became due. In short, defaulters were usually not wealthy deadbeats using their loans to buy new cars or stereos. Instead, the typical defaulters were, in the words of a task force of experts convened by Congress in 1988 to recommend changes in the FFEL, "individuals with very limited resources and academic preparation . . . [who] are taking out loans, enrolling in an educational program, failing to complete that program, and subsequently finding themselves unemployed." As a result, the task force concluded that "a significant portion" of the default costs are simply "uncontrollable." They are just the costs inherent in making college loans to high-risk students.

TABLE 4
Default Rates Among Stafford Loan Borrowers by Institutional Type

Type of Institution	Default Rates
4-Year Public	14%
4-Year Private	15
2-Year Public	29
2-Year Private	20
Proprietary	50
Total All Borrowers	29

Source: Data for 1987 undergraduate students drawn from the *Student Aid and the Cost of Postsecondary Education*, Washington D.C.: Congressional Budget Office, 1991.

But the fact that providing loans to disadvantaged students brings high risks, and hence high costs, is not to imply that the government should reduce lending to disadvantaged students in order to save money. Indeed, it is precisely these students who have the most difficult time securing a loan without the guarantee and who gain the most from participation in higher education. As the net price of college rises, these students have no choice but to borrow if they are to go to college.

The final cause of the increasing rates of student loan defaults is a change in the types of schools that borrowers are attending. Table 4 shows the default rates for students at various types of institutions. It makes clear that while less than 15 percent of all borrowers who attend four-year colleges eventually default on their loans, nearly half of the students from proprietary schools default.

Cost #4: The Rise of Proprietary Schools

The alarmingly high default rates among students attending proprietary schools is exacerbated by another important shift in the character of the federal loan-guarantee programs. The portion of guaranteed loans which go to students attending proprietary or for profit educational institutions, has increased dramatically since 1980.

In 1970, nearly 90 percent of all guaranteed loans went to students attending four-year colleges. Less than 6 percent of loans went to students at proprietary schools. During the 1970s, that distribution shifted only slightly. But the distribution of student loans among the various types of institutions changed fundamentally after 1980. The percent of loans recipients going to four-year colleges dropped to only 62 percent while the percent at proprietary schools jumped to 27 percent. Throughout the 1980s, more than one-in-four of all FFELs went to students at proprietary schools.

This was all part of the long chain of events which led to higher costs of the FFEL for the federal government. More loans were being made to students attending proprietary schools, and students at proprietary schools have higher default rates. This drove the default rate up for the entire FFEL. As the default rate increased, so too did the government's costs.

Difficulty of Controlling FFEL Growth

The logic of loan guarantees is that they can be used by the federal government to leverage large amounts of lending from private institutions at a very low cost to the federal government. But today when the interest subsidies, special allowances, default reimbursements and administrative costs are combined, the total cost of these programs are substantial. In 1991, for example, total federal expenditures on the FFEL was $6.1 billion. The program generated $1.3 billion in revenues from origination fees and other reimbursements, but this still left the federal treasury with a price-tag of $5.6 billion for student loan guarantees.

Looked at in one way, this price-tag looks like a bargain. The $5.6 billion of FFEL spending in 1991 generated $14.2 billion in privately originated loans. As such, each $1.00 of federal spending on the FFEL produced about $2.50 in new loans to students. This value notwithstanding, the FFEL presents some significant concerns beyond the rising price of subsidies and defaults. The structure of the program makes it difficult for policy-makers to control the growth of the dollar volume of student loans. The rapid expansion of the FFEL since 1980 did not follow an explicit policy decision to spend more on student loans. Indeed, it happened in spite of efforts by policy-makers to control and limit spending.

The federal loan-guarantee programs are funded as an entitlement. Francis Keppel, U.S. Commissioner of Education between 1962 and 1965, explains that "[t]he budget process required that costs of loan eligibility be joined with annual appropriations for the Title IV program in calculating the total appropriation for student aid." As such, Congress is obligated to appropriate all funds necessary to cover the costs of the programs each year. This type of spending is often described as "uncontrollable" because Congress does not directly determine how much will be spent on these programs. The federal appropriation is determined by the volume of loans, the rate of default, money market conditions, borrower death, and many other factors beyond the direct control of the federal government.

Of course, the Congress can always limit eligibility for the programs or reduce the size of available awards in order to reduce the programs costs. For Pell grants, and most other programs, such a reduction in eligibility or award size translates into cost savings in the next year's budget. Because fewer students will be eligible, and/or the awards will be smaller, a smaller appropriations is necessary to operate the program. However, reducing eligibility for the loan-guarantee programs, or reducing the size of loans, produces very little immediate budgetary savings. Because of its funding structure, the costs of loan guarantees are largely fixed in the short term. This is because most of the costs to the federal government for loan guarantees go to pay for obligations incurred by loans made many years before. Each year interest subsidies, special allowances, and defaults must still be paid on all outstanding student loans. Accordingly, even if the FFEL was eliminated entirely, it would still incur costs to the federal treasury, albeit at a declining rate, for at least the next decade.

The Danger of Rapid Cost Increases

Unlike the other student aid programs, the costs of the loan guarantee programs can change suddenly even when there are no changes in the program's structures or rules. This is because both the interest payments and the special allowance payments are linked to 91-day Treasury bill rates, which are extremely sensitive to changes in the economy, particularly to concerns over inflation. If short-term Treasury rates move rapidly upward, the costs of the FFEL follow directly and immediately. Robert Reischauer estimates that every one-percent increase in the T-bill interest rate equates to at least a $500 million increase in federal payments to lenders.

When interest rates are low, as they were in the early 1990s, the costs of the FFEL should also be fairly low. But because default rates increased so rapidly in the late 1980s and early 1990s, aggregate FFEL costs continued to rise even when interest rates were at record lows. When interest rates began to rise in 1994, federal government experienced an increase in the costs of the programs with no increase in the number of loans available or in the dollar volume of those loans. These increased costs are then likely to ripple through the federal budget for years to come, further reducing the funds available for other student aid programs.

The Unintended Consequences of the Transformation in Federal Student-Aid Policy

Quite apart from the increased costs of student loans in the past decade, the growth has had a number of negative consequences for students and their families. As the volume of loans continued to grow, these unintended consequences threatened to undermine its earlier successes.

Chief among these negative consequences is that the increased reliance on loans by disadvantaged families may discourage potential students from low-income families from continuing their educations, and that increased borrowing may cause students to leave college with a large debt which distorts their career- and life-choices. The growth of the loan programs also distorted overall federal student-aid effort in ways which made it less useful to lower-income and disadvantaged students.

Discouraging Disadvantaged Students

Table 5 provides an estimate of how much some typical subsidized Stafford loan borrowers would need to pay back at the point the loan comes due. These amounts are estimates based on a 9 percent interest rate (the maximum allowed) and a ten-year repayment period (the maximum allowed). It is important to remember that the total amount repaid will be lower if the interest rate is less or the loan is repaid early.

TABLE 5
Typical Repayment Schedule for Different Levels of Subsidized Stafford Loans Based on 9 Percent Interest Rates and 10 Year Repayment Period

Total Loan Amount	Monthly Payment	Total Amount Repaid
$4,000	$ 50.67	$ 6,080.44
$10,000	$126.68	$15,201.09
$18,000	$228.02	$27,361.97

This amount makes clear that both the size of the monthly payment and/or the total amount of post-collegiate debt, might dissuade a student from a disadvantaged background from borrowing for money necessary to attend college. Take the case of the first-year student who borrows $4,000 to attend college but drops out of school late in the year or chooses not to return to school the next year. This is a common circumstance among students who begin college without the skills or the maturity necessary to succeed. Even though that student received no degree or perhaps even no academic credit, he or she would face a $50 monthly payment for the next ten years.

Even students who complete their academic programs can face daunting post-graduation debts. The student who borrows the maximum Stafford loan amount for each of his or her four years of college will have borrowed $18,000 when they graduate. Six months after they have left school, that student will begin monthly payments of $228 which will continue for ten years. When the loan is finally paid off, he or she will have repaid more than $27,000.

There is widespread concern that the prospect of such debts, and the monthly payments that follow, has discouraged disadvantaged students from participating in higher education. When viewed from the perspective of a lower-income student, it is easy to see how this could happen. The pre-college family income of college students is strongly correlated with the eventual success of students in college. As a consequence, low-income students are much less likely to finish college and those who finish are less likely to do well. This higher risk of failure serves to discourage disadvantaged students from borrowing the large sums necessary to enroll in higher education.

But the differential impact goes beyond its chilling effect on the propensity of potential students to enroll in school. Students from traditionally disadvantaged groups may be just as willing to borrow as other students, but they may subsequently become more dependent upon loans because they are likely to have lower post-graduation earnings. This is because of the vast disparities in income between white males on the one hand and women and minorities on the other, even after adjusting for differences in education and work experience. These differences mean that borrowers from disadvantaged backgrounds are likely to find themselves making larger monthly payments out of a lower income than advantaged students with similar educations working in similar jobs.

Another differential impact that loans have on low-income students is that, unlike grants, loans must be repaid with interest. The student that borrows $18,000 in subsidized Stafford loans will pay more than $9,000 in interest charges. This does not include the 5 percent origination fee and the 3 percent insurance premium, a total of $1,440, which are deducted from the loan disbursement.

For a low-income student, the prospect of such large debt reinserts the cost barriers to higher education which the federal financial aid programs were designed to remove. A disadvantaged student, or a student from a lower-income family, might reasonably decide that the risks associated with such large debts are too great to take a chance on borrowing for college. But as the price of college rises, and the value of Pell grants declines, the choice not to borrow may also be the choice not to go to college at all.

The Dependence of Disadvantaged Students on Loans

While the prospect of large debts may discourage many lower-income or disadvantaged students from going to college, more of those who do enroll are taking out loans. As a consequence, even as concerns are emerging that loans were holding down the enrollments of disadvantaged students, a separate concern emerged that such students were becoming dependent on federal loans.

Table 6 shows the differences in the sources of college funds used by white and African-American freshmen. African-Americans rely much more on various types of government support while whites rely more on private family resources in order to meet college costs. This difference is especially evident in Pell grants, where African-Americans are twice as likely as whites to receive an award. But African-Americans are also more likely than whites to take out a student loan.

The fact that African-Americans are more likely to receive government aid is no surprise. Since most aid is need-based, it is awarded disproportionately to disadvantaged students.

TABLE 6
Sources of College Funds Used by African-American and White Freshman College Students: Fall 1989

Source of College Funds	Percent of Freshmen		
	African-Americans	Whites	Difference
Pell Grant	41%	20%	+21
Stafford Loan	28	23	+5
State Scholarship	17	15	+2
Personal Savings	19	32	−13
Parents or Family	71	83	−12

Source: A. Astin *The Black Undergraduate* (Los Angeles: Higher Education Research Institute, University of California, Los Angeles, 1990), p. 10.

But this distribution has important implications for future federal student-aid policy. Reductions or alterations in any of the major federal aid programs are likely to have a differential impact on African-American students.

If the continued growth in the loan guarantee programs forces policy-makers to reduce further limit the size of the maximum Pell grant, the impact will be felt disproportionately by African-American students. It is perhaps ironic that as these programs make progress toward the goal of assisting disadvantaged students in paying for college, they raise concerns that these students would be unable to get by without continued government assistance.

The Specter of Post-Collegiate Debt

Rapidly rising college costs, coupled with the increase in student borrowing, have raised concerns that federal policy was creating what Senator Pell has called "a new class of indentured servants" whose career choices and personal lives are distorted by the significant debt they have acquired to get an education. It is easy to imagine how the prospect of such debt could affect a student's career choice. Allan Ostar, worries that large postcollegiate debt, and the resulting financial squeeze, may well constrict a former student's occupational decisions. He argues that because of this debt:

> low salary professional positions such as teaching or journalism, for example, will prove far less appealing than the higher salaried positions in business or engineering to someone who graduates from college owing $10,000 or more.

John Heileman puts the problem in more blunt terms:

> Having taken the money to pay for a degree, students are frequently forced to make a bitter compromise: They must, after college, give up doing socially useful but ill-paid work, like teaching or public interest law, and settle for more uninspiring jobs that bring in enough to cover hefty monthly loan payments. For others (usually the less well-off) the fear of Student Loan Prison has them thinking twice about going to college at all.

Robert Reischauer expresses the slightly different concern that students who depend heavily on loans to finance their education may begin to view college as narrow vocational training. As such, the broader liberal arts education which can be so valuable to students in the long run may be sacrificed as students choose courses based on the degree to which they increase future job prospects rather than the intellectual value of the subject matter.

There is little systematic evidence to link the impact of post-collegiate debt to the career or life choices of students. But the concerns listed above, coupled with a large amount of anecdotal evidence from students, parents, and college financial aid officers, strongly suggests that such a link may exist. If it does, the growth of student borrowing may alter the behavior and limit the opportunities of students in ways that were unintended and even unrecognized by the program's creators.

Distorting Federal Policy

At the other end of the economic spectrum, the growth of the federal loan programs raises concerns that more and more student-aid funds are going to families that have the least need for federal support. This is because the broad availability of federally guaranteed loans may encourage upper- and middle-income students to substitute those loans for parental support and student savings.

If the federal government is going to insure that below-market-rate loans are widely available, many upper-income families will find these loans attractive. In order to insure that subsidized loans go only to the most needy students, eligibility for a subsidized Stafford loan is determined by a needs test. That test examines the financial status of the student's family each year that a loan is requested and relates that status to the cost of attending college.

But even with a needs test, many families with higher incomes qualify for subsidized loans. Students attending public colleges can qualify for a Stafford loan if their family income is less than $33,000. The income limit for a student attending a private college is about $50,000. But a cutoff of well over $100,000 is possible if a student attends a high-priced college, has few family assets, or has another child in college.

This current method of determining loan eligibility also allows, even encourages, upper-income students to participate in the program. The cost of each loan to the government is based largely on how much each student chooses to borrow and how long he or she remains in school. Among eligible students, those who attend more expensive colleges tend to borrow more money and stay in college longer. Therefore, they receive the greatest benefits from the FFEL. But, as Robert Reischauer points out, "students at higher priced schools also tend to come from families with the greatest resources and to be the borrowers who are most likely to have the highest lifetime earnings."

There is a similar concern that the growth of the loan programs is being funded largely at the expense of the grant programs. In a zero-sum spending environment, every dollar awarded to middle-income students in the form of loans is a dollar which cannot go to need-based grants.

The federal government now spends more than $13 billion on the major student aid programs. That amount has grown steadily throughout the 1970s. Aggregate federal spending on student aid continued to increase during the 1980s and into the 1990s. But student aid spending as a percent of total federal outlays reached a peak in 1980 and had held steady at about 0.8 percent. The efforts of the Reagan and Bush administrations thus stopped the overall growth of federal student-aid spending, but they were unable to make progress towards their goal of reducing it.

Table 7 shows how the balance between grant and loan aid has changed since 1970. It is here that the dramatic growth of the student loan programs is most visible. In 1980, grant aid constituted half of all federal student aid and loans less than one-third. Since that time, MISAA and the subsequent efforts to control federal spending on student aid has caused a larger portion of federal outlays to shift to loans.

TABLE 7
Types of Student Aid Awarded as a Percentage of Generally Available Federal Student Aid Selected Years, 1970–1990

Year	Grants[a]	Loans[b]	Other
1970	8%	78%	14%
1975	36	54	10
1980	26	66	8
1985	28	68	4
1990	27	69	4
1992	29	68	3

[a]Grants = Pell + SEOG
[b]Guaranteed Loans = All FFELs + Perkins Loans

The increasing concentration of federal student-aid spending in the loan-guarantee programs tends to skew federal subsidies away from the most disadvantaged students and toward middle and upper-income students. This shift erodes the traditional federal emphasis on equity and equal opportunity. As more of the federal money goes to the FFEL, if a large portion of the money is going to upper-income students, the clear losers are the disadvantaged and lower-income students whom the programs were intended to help.

Conclusion: Costs and Consequences of Increased Student Borrowing

Since 1980, the federal government has helped to make more than $100 billion in new loans available to college students. But that growth has also produced a larger than anticipated price-tag, the danger of rapidly rising future costs, and a variety of negative consequences for lower-income and disadvantaged students. As federal spending on student loans increased, it has commanded a much larger portion of overall federal student-aid spending. This, in turn, has constrained the growth of the other federal student-aid programs and distorted the national effort to improve college

affordability. The result is that federal policymakers now find that they are spending more each year on student aid, but having less to spend on those programs which aid disadvantaged students.

These developments also have had important consequences for lower income and disadvantaged students. Rising net college prices have forced increasing numbers of students to either borrow for college or not to go at all. But loans carry special risks and costs for disadvantaged students. Because they are often less prepared for college, are less likely to complete their academic program, and those who do graduate are likely to earn less, disadvantaged students are more hesitant to borrow. Those who do borrow, may have their career- or life-choices altered by the large debt they have incurred.

As federal student-aid spending shifted from grants to loans, it brought about a corresponding shift in the types of students who could receive federal aid. No longer was it just lower-income students who were receiving financial aid, but now middle- and even upper-income students were now eligible. This further reduced the value of federal aid to the lower-income and disadvantaged students as they were left to divide a smaller share of the limited amount of federal subsidies.

Perhaps most fundamental, increased borrowing for college is antithetical to the goal of removing college price barriers. Loans do not reduce college prices at all. They simply postpone their payment. When fees are deducted and interest payments added, the price that a disadvantaged student-borrower must pay to go to college is far greater than the amount paid by the student who has substantial family resources. This higher cost is further exacerbated by the fact that their post-collegiate income is likely to be much lower. The result is that even as federal student-aid spending is increasing, disadvantaged students are finding that federal aid is less and less helpful in paying the rapidly rising college prices. The growth of student loans thus has not served to open the door to college for disadvantaged students but has reinserted, and even extended, the price barriers that the federal student-aid programs were designed to eliminate.

The Growing Loan Orientation in Federal Financial Aid Policy
A Historical Perspective

James C. Hearn

In the past two decades, the federal government has dramatically changed the ways in which it aids the financing of postsecondary students' attendance. From a roughly equal emphasis on student loans and grants, the government has moved toward an approach dominated by loans. Increasingly, federally supported student aid is loan aid, not grant or work-study aid. Largely as a result of this emerging federal emphasis, loans have grown to well over half of all the student financial aid awarded in this country.

The increased use of loans as the primary instruments of federal student aid policy has created new financial challenges in students' and graduates' lives. The effects of students' rising debt levels, in particular, have been much discussed in the popular press, in the chambers of Congress, and among those closely involved in student aid issues. Often, the language used has been that of crisis. For example, a senator closely associated with the rise of federal student aid grants has worried publicly that rising debt levels might be creating "a new class of indentured servants" (Senator Claiborne Pell, cited in Kosterlitz, 1989, p. 921). In a similar vein, College Board president Donald Stewart said recently that we are facing "a deeply mortgaged future. It may be individuals who pay off the educational debts, but we as a society are co-signing the mortgage—and paying a high social cost as well" (College Board, 1995a, p. 11).

The actual short- and long-term implications of the recent loan explosion have been lit-tle studied empirically before now, and the severity of the problem is unclear (Baum, 1996). What *is* clear, however, is that the financial aspects of attending college have changed remarkably since the mid-1970s. To aid understanding of that transition, in this chapter I trace the history of student loans in federal financial aid policy. The emergence of the current federal emphasis on loans is best understood by looking back further than the past two decades and by examining more than the federal loan programs alone. Investigating the programs' development since their inception and in broad political, economic, and social context illuminates why particular paths were taken and how the legacy of taking those paths shapes contemporary policies.

The chapter is organized in three parts. The initial section provides a brief overview of the history of federal loans and other forms of federal student financial aid, focusing particularly on trends in dollar outlays and student participants. The following section profiles in more detail the often colorful policy history of the federal loan programs.[1] In the concluding section, I discuss the federal loan programs' evolving role in the financing of higher education.

An Overview of Federal Involvement in Student Loans

Prior to the passage of the Higher Education Act of 1965, the federal government supplied only one form of aid generally available to all

"The Growing Loan Orientation in Federal Financial Aid Policy: A Historical Perspective," by James C. Hearn, reprinted from *Condemning Students to Debt: College Loans and Public Policy*, edited by Richard Fossey and Mark Bateman, 1998, Teachers College Press.

college students: National Defense Student Loans. Originated in 1958, these loans were later renamed National Direct Student Loans, then renamed again, as Perkins Loans. Other federal aid prior to 1965 was specially directed to particular groups, such as that offered through the Servicemen's Readjustment Act of 1944 (the "GI Bill"). As noted in Table 1, all federal student aid totaled a little over one billion dollars in 1963–64 (in 1994 dollars).

Activist national education initiatives in the 1960s expanded the total of direct federal student aid outlays. By providing matching and cost-support funds, the federal government also spurred dramatic growth in other forms of aid in that period. By 1970–71, the total of these two kinds of federally *supported* student aid was $12.5 billion in 1994 dollars.[2] A decade later, the total was nearly twice that amount. Thus, total federally supported aid grew over 20-fold between 1963–64 and 1980–81. After relative stability in the 1980s, the number began to grow dramatically again, reaching an estimated total of over $34 billion dollars in 1994–95.

Most of the growth in federal student aid has been in programs providing aid generally available to the American public, rather than in aid targeted for special groups such as veterans. As Table 1 reveals, the generally available aid programs were over 32 times larger in 1980–81 than in 1963–64. That growth slowed in the mid-1980s but surged again in the later years of the decade. Then, between 1990–91 and 1994–95, generally available aid awards rose a remarkable 48%. At mid-decade, the programs were 59 times larger than in 1963–64.

The bulk of this recent growth came in the federally supported loan programs, and those programs now compose the great majority of the generally available federal aid. For reinforcement of that point, consider the other generally available federal programs, for grants and work-study support respectively. Federal grant programs include the massive Pell Grants program and the smaller Supplemental Educational Opportunity Grants (SEOG) and State Student Incentive Grants (SSIG) programs. After adjusting for inflation, federal grant aid has grown little for the past decade, totaling $6.2 billion in 1994–95. The other federal nonloan program, the College Work Study (CWS) program, has actually shrunk since the

1970s, and totaled only $749 million in 1994–95. The combined 1994–95 total of under $7 billion dollars in the Pell, SEOG, SSIG, and CWS programs contrasts dramatically with the over $25 billion committed under the loan programs in that year.

As suggested in the table, the federal government has initiated many loan programs over the years. A brief introduction to those programs will be provided here, with more details to come later in the chapter. Perkins loans, as noted earlier, began in 1958. These are administered by campus aid officials, and funds are supplied directly by the federal government. Income-contingent loans, which allowed students to repay at a set percentage of income, were a separate program for a period in the 1990s, but this program has been discontinued and income-contingent repayment is now provided as an option within other federal loan programs. The Federal Family Education Loan Program (FFELP) includes all the programs based in funds supplied by private lenders, mainly banks and state-licensed or controlled financing organizations. What is now the subsidized Stafford Loan program under the FFELP was once known as the Guaranteed Student Loan (GLS) program. The unsubsidized Stafford Loan program under FFELP is a newer effort to provide loan funds for students not qualifying for federal subsidies on interest while they are in school. A growing share of federal student loans (one third in 1994–95) is now unsubsidized. The Supplemental Loans for Students program was the predecessor of the unsubsidized Stafford Loan program, and has now been phased out of existence. The final FFELP program is the Parent Loans program, known as the PLUS program, which provides unsubsidized loans to the parents of students who do not qualify for sufficient subsidized loan aid to meet educational costs. Recently, three non-FFELP versions of the Stafford and PLUS programs have been funded on a trial basis: Under the new Ford Direct Student Loan Program (FDSLP), funds for loans are provided by the federal government to college aid offices, which in turn directly allocate the loans to students.

These varied loan programs will be discussed in more detail later in this chapter. For now, it is instructive to examine them as a block. Figure 4.1 traces generally available

TABLE 1
Total Aid Awards for Postsecondary Students in the United States (Selected Years, in Millions of U.S. Constant Dollars)

	1963–1964	1970–1971	1975–1976	1980–1981	1985–1986	1990–1991	Est. 1994–1995
Federally Supported Aid:							
Generally Available Federal Aid:							
Pell Grants (formerly Basic Grants)	0	0	2505	4088	4866	5436	5570
Supplementary Educational Opportunity Grants (SEOG)	0	499	538	630	559	5014	546
State Student Incentive Grants (SSIG)	0	0	53	124	103	65	72
College Work Study (CWS)	0	849	789	1131	895	806	749
Loan Programs:							
Perkins Loans	547	898	1231	1188	959	964	958
Income-Contingent Loans	0	0	0	0	0	0	0
Family Education Loans (Non-Direct):							
Subsidized Stafford Loans	0	3791	3389	10,623	11,360	11,075	13,906
Unsubsidized Stafford Loans	0	0	0	0	0	0	7039
Supplemental Loans for Students (SLS)	0	0	0	0	367	1894	32
Parent Loans (PLUS)	0	0	0	0	330	1059	1637
Direct Student Loans (Ford Program):							
Subsidized Stafford Loans	0	0	0	0	0	0	1073
Unsubsidized Stafford Loans	0	0	0	0	0	0	471
Parent Loans (PLUS)	0	0	0	0	0	0	168
Total Generally Available Federal Aid	547	6038	8505	17,784	19,439	21,806	32,221
Specially Directed Federal Aid	565	6508	14,654	6820	2245	1672	2388
Total Federally Supported Aid	1112	12,546	23,159	24,604	21,684	23,479	34,610
State Grant Aid	269	882	1311	1372	1788	2059	2628
Institutional and Other Grant Aid	1297	3125	3126	2782	4040	6379	8929
Total Federal, State, and Institutional Aid	2679	16553	25,857	28,758	27,511	31,917	46,167

Note: These data are adapted from data supplied by the Gillespie and Carlson (1983) and the College Board (1995). See text for details on the data.

federally loan support as a percentage of aid awards, using the data of Table 1. The solid line, for federally supported loans as a percentage of all generally available federal aid, suggests that the federal government's percentage in loans drifted down from a total orientation to NDSL loans in the year immediately preceding the Higher Education Act of 1965 to just under half in 1976–77. Then, the percentage began a quick climb upward to a range between 65 and 70%, where it stayed until 1992–93. In 1993–94, it rose to 76%. In 1994–95, it rose to 78%. The broad-dashed line, for loans as a percentage of all federal aid, tells a similar story. The distance between this line and the solid line above it narrows because of the decline in specially targeted federal aid. Virtually all targeted aid has been in the form of grants, so the gradual disappearance of those forms of aid spelled substantial declines for grant aid as a percentage of all federal aid.

There has also been notable growth in federally supported loans as a percentage of all federal, state, and institutional aid combined, denoted in the figure by the short-dashed line. Over the years since 1980–81, state grant aid has doubled, and institutional and other grant aid has tripled (see Table 1). Still, most of the absolute growth in aid totals has come from the growth of the dollar volume of federal loans. The figure reveals that student financial aid in the United States is increasingly composed of federally supported loan aid. That aid moved from around 20% of all aid in 1963–64 to a low of 17% in 1975–76, then rose to a high of 55% in 1994–95. The fact that federally supported loans are now over half of all aid is especially startling in light of the relatively small role that loans played in overall aid outlays as recently as 20 years ago.

Two elements in the loan data merit further attention: the growth in programs other than the Perkins program, and the increasing use of programs other than the traditional subsidized, nondirect guaranteed student loan program. The increasing dominance of the FFELP and the FDSLP over the Perkins program is clear from the raw data of Table 1: Between 1975–76 and 1994–95, the dollar investment in loan programs other than Perkins grew from $3.4 billion to over $24 billion. In the same years, the number of loans other than Perkins loans increased from 922,000 to 7 million (Gillespie &

Carlson, 1983; College Board, 1995b). Meanwhile, funding for Perkins loans has grown relatively little in real terms over the years since their inception, and they are not central elements in the recent "loan explosion."

Regarding the second important element in the historical data, policy makers and students have recently made increasing use of programs other than traditional guaranteed student loans. It is instructive to trace the history of the average nondirect subsidized Stafford loan from its inception under the original GSL program to the present. In constant-dollar terms, loans of this kind have actually decreased in size since 1970–71, according to data from the College Board (1995a). Thus, the rising spending for subsidized Stafford Loans has gone largely into additional loans for additional students, not into more generous loans to individual students. The increase in the number of students served by the subsidized Stafford program seems to be related more to increasing college costs and to the increasing number of financially independent (and, therefore, usually more needy) college students rather than to major expansion of program eligibility standards. Indeed, financial eligibility requirements for federal aid programs tightened in real terms over the 1980s, and award sizes stagnated. In response, more students and their families have qualified for modest Stafford loans and also have made more extensive use of other sources of aid, including the growing array of alternative federal loan programs.

Two good cases regarding the latter point are the PLUS program and the unsubsidized Stafford program. Both nondirect and direct PLUS loans averaged over $5,000 in 1994–95, and together those programs served an estimated 351,000 students that year. Similarly, both nondirect and direct unsubsidized Stafford loans averaged over $3,500 that year and together provided an estimated 2.1 million students with loans. In both cases, individual loan amounts were substantially larger than those in the longstanding, nondirect, subsidized Stafford loan program. Together, the number of students served by these alternative programs was far from insignificant. While 4.3 million students received the traditional, nondirect, subsidized Stafford loans in 1994–95, 2.7 million received a nondirect,

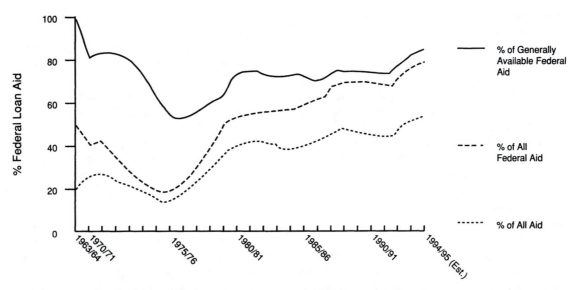

Figure 1: Generally Available Federal Loans as a Percentage of Aid Awards, 1963–1994

unsubsidized Stafford loan, a direct, subsidized Stafford loan, a direct, unsubsidized Stafford loan, a nondirect PLUS loan, a direct PLUS loan, or a combination of these (College Board, 1995b).

In sum, federal student aid policy progressed from the relatively small NDSL program of the early 1960s to a substantially greater effort with a roughly equal focus on grants and loans in the 1970s, then in the years since has moved to an even more substantial effort with a renewed emphasis on loans. Although the original NDSL (Perkins) program has grown only modestly over the years since the 1960s, other student loan programs have grown dramatically in dollar terms, in variety, and in coverage of the student population. Behind this striking growth is a colorful political history.

The Policy History of Federal Student Loans

Federally supported loans for facilitating postsecondary attendance are a relatively new aspect of the finance of higher education in the United States (Kramer, 1991). Some limited, highly targeted federal loans were made in World War II and, shortly after the war, the Truman Commission, a presidentially appointed panel, argued vigorously for federal

student loans (Presidents Commission, 1947; Woodhall, 1988). Nevertheless, federal financial aid up to the late 1950s consisted almost entirely of specially directed grant aid. At that time, however, federal leaders troubled by the nation's military, technological, and scientific status relative to the Soviet Union came to view investment in education as a productive countermeasure. Overcoming long-standing reservations regarding federal activities in education (see Morse, 1977), they implemented the National Defense Education Act of 1958. The National Defense Student Loan (NDSL) program was a prominent feature of the act. Thus, federal loan programs emerged largely out of noneducational concerns, a typical pattern in federal higher education policy making (see Brademas, 1983; Moynihan, 1975; Schuster 1982).

The NDSL program was the first federal loan program, and indeed the first federal aid program, not targeted toward particular categories of college students. Former NDSL director John Morse (1977) has noted that "it was the national panic (not too strong a word) over Russia's success in launching the first satellite that gave federal aid proponents the opening they needed" to overcome federal leaders' historic reluctance to become involved in higher education (p. 3).

NDSL funds were to be awarded to campuses, which in turn would provide loans to full-time students on the basis of need, as determined by institutions. Preference was to be given to students in the sciences, teaching, mathematics, and modern foreign languages. Forgiveness of loan debts was to be granted to students in certain careers, such as teaching. The loans were to be repaid over long terms at a low interest rate (3%). The government contributed $9 to a school's loan fund for every dollar provided by the institution. All repayments were to be reinvested by institutions in further student loans. In 1958–59, 27,600 students received these new loans, which totaled $9.5 million.

In its first few years, the NDSL program's preferences for students in certain fields were removed. Interestingly, the government consistently underestimated the interest from both students and institutions in participation in these loans, and the roster of institutional and student participants grew substantially. The total NDSL funds requested by institutional applicants regularly exceeded appropriations by a factor of 20 or more in the early years of the program, and the government found itself in the novel and awkward position of judging the relative worthiness of different institutions (Morse, 1977).

The NDSL program was the first federal effort to require testing of students' financial need, and the first to involve a contract between the federal government and institutions (Moore, 1983). For our purposes, however, the historically most notable aspect of the NDSL program is its pioneering of the notion of generally available federally supported loans for college students. Before the late 1950s, loans for college students were largely privately or institutionally originated and based on the income and financial positions of the student's parents (Bosworth, Carron, & Rhyne, 1987; Gillespie & Carlson, 1983). Some states (prominently including New York and Massachusetts) and some across-state associations initiated guaranty funds in the 1950s to support commercial lending to students, but interest on these loans was generally not publicly subsidized (see Barger & Barger, 1981). Although some of these efforts served as models for the development of later federal loan programs (Marmaduke, 1983), there was no significant federal support for commercial,

institutional, or state lending to students before the NDSL program.

The development of the NDSL program can be viewed as the initiation of the modern era of federal student aid. The consequences of this program and the federal efforts that followed it were profound for those involved in student-aid work at the campus level. Before the late 1950s, student aid administration was not developed as a professional field and student aid offices were far less complex and systematized than today. Analysis of a student's aid eligibility was rather primitive by current standards, often involving simple income cutoffs. The initiation of the NDSL program brought growing demand for institutions to measure accurately their students' actual financial needs. Seeing that their need analysis efforts could benefit from collective wisdom as well as from economies of scale in formula development and processing expenses, institutions increasingly turned to the College Scholarship Service (CSS), a service organization begun by the College Board in 1954. Integrating generalized need analysis routines with the unique need and award standards of each institution, the CSS was a harbinger of aggressive modernizing efforts in student aid in the 1960s and beyond.

Despite the stirrings brought on by the NDSL program, however, the student aid arena remained quite small at the federal level for several years. This was all to change remarkably in 1964–65. A new Social Security benefit for recipients with dependents in college and a new aid program for students in health-related fields were initiated at that time, but these developments were soon overshadowed by the passage of the watershed U.S. Higher Education Act of 1965.

Emergence of Assertive Federal Policy in Student Aid—1965 to 1972

The bywords of higher education in 1965 were *prosperity* and *growth*. Nationally, unemployment and inflation were low, and productivity was rising. In addition, the many children born in the years after World War II were enrolling in college at high rates. Postsecondary enrollments grew steadily, along with the nation's supply of institutions, especially in the community college sector, where new institutions were emerging at the rate of one every week and a half. Dramatic demographic changes in student bodies were in the future, however: Students of this era were more likely than today's students to be full-time, residential, male, and White (Breneman, 1991). Out of this context arose the U.S. Higher Education Act of 1965.

The act was a product of a wide-ranging educational initiative on the part of Congress and President Lyndon Johnson. All told, the 89th Congress passed more than two dozen acts aimed directly at American schools and colleges. Most of those were closely connected to the Democrats' War on Poverty and Great Society efforts, as well as to the Civil Rights Act of 1964. President Johnson and congressional leaders saw action in education as an effective, politically feasible policy mechanism for achieving their broader goals of eliminating poverty and discrimination in the nation. In the president's view, "The answer for all our national problems, the answer for all the problems of the world, comes down . . . to one single word—education" (cited in Gladieux & Wolanin, 1976, p. 17).

Higher education was to reap especially significant rewards from the president's linkage of educational improvement to emerging national priorities. The Higher Education Act encompassed two approaches to federal support: aid to states and institutions and aid to needy students (Gladieux & Wolanin, 1976; Leslie, 1977; Fenske, 1983). College student aid was covered mainly under Title IV of the act. For student aid, the passage of Title IV represented both a philosophical and a fiscal shift. Philosophically, it expanded the purposes of federal student aid in the equity-oriented direction suggested years earlier by the Truman Commission. Fiscally, the act laid the groundwork for massive growth in the dollars and recipients of federal aid to levels unimagined even in the 1950s.

Under Title IV, the existing NDSL program was renewed, the College Work Study (CWS) program established a year earlier was finalized, and the Guaranteed Student Loan (GSL) and the Educational Opportunity Grants (EOG) programs were inaugurated. The CWS and EOG programs, like the earlier NDSL program, were to be delivered through campus

offices (as "campus-based" aid, in the federal terminology). The GSL program was also to be administered out of campus aid offices, although private funds were to be loaned. Thus, the student aid elements of the 1965 act were to be delivered largely through existing institutional aid offices.

The new Guaranteed Student Loan program was a particular interest of President Johnson. Johnson had made his way through college with the help of loans from family friends, a bank, a local newspaper publisher, and his college (Caro, 1983; Hansen, 1987). As a consequence, he strongly supported expanding students' opportunities to borrow. As a senator from Texas in the 1950s, Johnson had introduced loan legislation, which failed to pass (Morse, 1977). The GSL program offered more than simple philosophical appeal for Johnson, however: It was designed in good part as a tactical diversion to head off legislation establishing tax credits for higher education attendance (Morse, 1977; Kramer & Van Dusen, 1986). Thus, the GSL program was not aimed primarily at socioeconomically disadvantaged students. Instead, it was initiated as a small, supplementary program operating at low federal cost and serving those not quite needy enough to qualify for the other new, more need-based aid programs (Kramer & Van Dusen, 1986; Hauptman, 1987). Specifically, the program's main intent was to address middle-income families' liquidity problems by facilitating access to funds from private lenders.

Although it was originally conceived as providing no subsidies at all, the GSL program as legislated provided interest subsidies for students while in school as well as funds to assure that states and private nonprofit agencies would work with the federal government to guarantee student loans made by commercial lenders. The initial federal interest rate subsidy was set at 6% a year while the student was in school and 3% during the repayment period, which began 9 months after graduation. The borrower was to pay the other 3%. Only those with family incomes under $15,000 could receive the subsidy, although unsubsidized GSL's were available to others. Students were given 10 years to repay loans over $2,000, and less time to repay smaller loans.

Banks, savings and loan associations, credit unions, and other financial institutions were invited to participate in the program. The guarantees on loans were to be assured through a federally supported guaranty fund in each state, equal to 10% of the face value of the loans, to protect lenders against loss through default, death, or disability of the borrower. The federal government provided states with deposits to be used to build their own guaranty funds, although most states opted to participate instead in the broader Federally Insured Student Loan (FISL) program.

These initial terms met with some concern from lenders, states, institutions, and students. Money was to be tied up in student loans for many years without payback (causing liquidity problems for lenders), the interest rates set by the government were not sufficiently high for lenders, institutions were frustrated by reporting and regulatory control mechanisms, and states were unenthusiastic about beginning their own guaranty agencies under existing guidelines (Morse, 1977; Breneman, 1991).

Having rejected such alternatives as the development of a national student loan bank (see Panel on Educational Innovation, 1967), the federal government moved to refine the GSL program into a more accepted loan policy vehicle. In 1968, it raised the statutory interest rate from to 7% and introduced "reinsurance," which merged existing state guaranty funds with federal insurance support. Nonprofit and state agencies were to provide guarantees, funded by a small administrative allowance, retention of a percentage of collections on defaulted loans, and an insurance premium paid by borrowers. The federal government assured states that it would cover 80% of a state's total losses from student default, death, or disability. This alleviated some of the pressures on state guaranty funds while creating incentives for states to monitor more closely lenders' efforts to collect loan payments.

In 1969, the federal government introduced the "special allowance," which paid all eligible lenders a supplementary amount above the statutory interest rate. The allowance, which was revised every 3 months by a committee of government officials, fluctuated between 1 and 2.5% over the next few years (Moore, 1983). Loan volume grew somewhat as a result, and by 1970, over one million borrowers received just over one billion dollars under the GSL program (Gillespie & Carlson, 1983.

The coming of the early 1970s marked the end of the initial "policy emergence" phase of federal student aid under the Higher Education Act of 1965. Through the combination of new or expanded student aid programs, federal support for spending for generally available student aid grew approximately tenfold between 1963–64 and 1972–73, in constant-dollar terms. Although new grant and work-study programs were a prominent feature of that growth, generally available federal loan programs grew at nearly the same rate.

Years of Policy Refinement and Expansion—1972 to 1978

The academic year 1972–73 marked the beginning of a second phase in the Title IV aid programs history, a phase of policy refinement and expansion. As the 1972 debates on reauthorizing the Higher Education Act approached, policy makers generally agreed that a new, expanded program of aid for college attendance was desirable, but conflict emerged among institutions, policy analysts, interest groups, and politicians over several issues (Gladieux & Wolanin, 1976; Brademas, 1987). After lengthy, detailed, and exhaustive deliberations, rough consensus was reached over the directions of expansion in the aid programs: toward channeling aid to students rather than to institutions, toward greater emphasis on facilitating student choice among institutions and persistence to the desired degree, toward an expanded pool of eligible applicants for aid, and toward a distinct, foundational role for the federal government in efforts to build equality of opportunity through student aid (Gladieux & Wolanin, 1976).

The newly created Basic Educational Opportunity Grants (BEOG) program was central to each of these directions, in that it allowed needy students to take their aid eligibility to the institutions of their choice, rather than relying on the grant funds available at one institution. Informed choices by students among competing institutions were therefore favored, under the assumption that grant portability would make institutions more sensitive to market forces favoring efficiency and quality. The BEOG program was the federal government's first major, direct, need-based grants program. It was to provide a foundation for students' aid packages, onto which other forms of federal, state, and institutional aid would be added. The 1972 reauthorization also brought expansion of the SEOG program, as well as CWS and NDSL (the latter of which was renamed the National Direct Student Loan program). Also that year, Congress initiated the State Student Incentive Grant (SSIG) program, which provided grant aid jointly with states.

In the context of all these new and expanded commitments, policy makers did not expect major growth in the loan programs (Mumper, 1996). That was to prove an accurate forecast: Federally supported loan volumes remained relatively stable throughout the early and mid-1970s, and loans diminished as a factor in federal aid, accounting during this period for only about one half of all generally available federal student aid, one fourth of all federal student aid, and about one fifth of all student aid (see Figure 1).

The primary implication of the 1972 amendments for the loan programs involved their relative priority. Loans were thenceforth to be viewed as supplemental aid for facilitating students' choice and persistence, rather than as a core "access" element in aid packages. Whether someone attended college or not was to be addressed mainly through the BEOG program, with loans and other aid programs providing supplemental support for one's attending a preferred school and attaining one's degree.

A second implication of the 1972 reauthorization for the loan programs was especially portentous. The eligible pool of institutions for federal student aid programs was expanded to include proprietary and vocational institutions. This expansion marked a transformation of the target of federal aid policy from "higher education" into "postsecondary education" (Schuster, 1982). Although the significance of this change was little noted at the time, the newly included proprietary and vocational institutions would come to dominate later reports of fraud and high default rates in loan programs.

Analyses of the 1972 reauthorization sometimes paint the results in glowing terms, but, in truth, the debate was a "debacle" of disunity and frustrated hopes for the interest groups representing higher education institutions (Hansen, 1977, p. 242). Most important, those groups favored maintaining campus officials as the dominant forces in student aid, and therefore strongly opposed the development of the portable, "voucher" concept in the basic grants program. After 1972, however, elements of consensus began to arise among interest groups. A "student aid partnership" emerged, consisting of postsecondary institutions and their associations, state government officials involved in aid policy, federal aid officials in the U.S. Department of Health, Education, and Welfare, and private organizations processing aid applications under contract (Fenske, 1983). In the mid-1970s, the partnership began to voice rather uniform views in keeping with a consensually supported focus on equal opportunity (Hansen, 1977). Policy disputes were rare in those years, and the partnership mainly worked together toward incremental operational and bureaucratic improvements in the programs (Hansen, 1977; Fenske, 1983). Federally supported aid grew 60% in real terms between 1972–73 and 1977–78, largely in the grants programs.

The period may be viewed, therefore, as a time of refinement and expansion of loan policy. A major example of refinement is the creation in 1972 of the Student Loan Marketing Association (Sallie Mae). A government-sponsored private corporation that was begun to provide liquidity and facilitate the secondary market in the GSL program, Sallie Mae sought to encourage banks' continuing participation in the program by buying loans and allowing pledges of existing student loans as collateral for new loans.

Other 1972 refinements included the introduction of need analysis to the GSL program, to replace the simple income cutoffs used in earlier years. Later in this period, to combat the influences of inflation on GSL program participation, the income level for student eligibility was raised to $25,000. In addition, the government raised overhead payments to state agencies, allowed states to keep up to 30% of their recoveries on defaulted loans to cover administrative costs, and offered 100% federal reinsurance to those states with low default rates. Also, the "special allowance" for lenders was pegged to an adjustable gross yield of 3.5% above the 90-day treasury bill rate.

Partly as a result of these reforms, the number of state loan agencies and participating financial organizations grew in the mid-1970s. Thus, although some other refinements of the time were restrictive on students and institutions, the general tone of the GSL changes in this period was expansive and the program grew notably after years of relative stability.

In the NDSL program, concern over mounting program costs led to the withdrawal of loan forgiveness for students entering military service or teaching careers. This period also brought regular rises in the administrative allowance for reimbursing institutions' NDSL costs. Overall, NDSL funding was rather stable in the mid-1970s.

Despite the seemingly calm surface surrounding the aid programs, however, this was a period of increasing demographic, economic, and political tensions in higher education (Stampen, 1987). In the late 1970s, those tensions erupted. Congress became concerned over the financial needs of middle-class parents of college-bound students, relative to lower and upper-class students (Brademas, 1987), and controversy arose over how to address the perceived problem. Congress debated between expanding the Title IV aid programs to cover more middle-income students and introducing a new program of federal tuition tax credits for college attendance. On this question, the professional and political allies of the aid partnership found themselves uncomfortably split. Longtime direct student aid proponents such as Senators Moynihan and Kennedy joined a coalition of liberal and conservative senators favoring tax credits. President Jimmy Carter and his allies countered that tax credits were wasteful in that they would go to many families who did not need aid to finance attendance, they were hard to control budgetarily, and they came too late in the academic year to influence attendance in the direction of expanded equality of opportunity.

In the end, the congressional proponents of the traditional student aid approach triumphed. The Middle Income Student Assistance Act (MISAA) was passed as the Higher Education Amendments of 1978. As a response to the perceived "middle-income squeeze," MISAA loosened the definition of need to include more middle-income families in the basic grants program and removed the $25,000 income ceiling on eligibility for GSLs. After passage of the act, any student could receive the GSL interest subsidy during enrollment, as well as the program's attractive 7% repayment rate. MISAA thus defined any student facing college expenses as needy enough to warrant federal support (Brademas, 1987).

The Policy Destabilization of 1978 to 1980–81

The passage of the expansive MISAA legislation initiated a period of destabilization of the federal aid policy agenda. Between 1977–78 and 1980–81, total federally supported aid grew a stunning 59% in constant dollars. Growth in the loan programs was especially strong. The removal of the family income ceiling on GSL eligibility in the context of dramatically rising interest rates in the general economy created substantial incentives for middle and upper-income families with discretionary resources to participate in the program.

In 1979, the government acted to assure more aggressive loan marketing to those very families. Responding to complaints by banks and other lenders that general interest rates had risen enough to make unattractive the full GSL interest rate for lenders (i.e., the statutory loan rate plus the special allowance rate), the government implemented a more liberal, variable special allowance. Soon the full interest rate rose as high as 19.5%.

Presented with an opportunity for inflation-proof, government-guaranteed returns, financial institutions quickly intensified their marketing of GSLs to the public. As families increasingly noticed this easily accessible, non-need-based, program, the number of student borrowers in the GSL program grew to 2.9 million in 1980 (College Board, 1993), and yearly program disbursements began regularly exceeding budgeted appropriations by large margins. Underestimates of demand became characteristic of the years immediately following MISAA.

The period was further troubled by growing controversy over the ultimate directions of the loan programs. Although MISAA was traditional in its use of aid awards rather than tax credits, it was a striking departure from the aid coalition's consensus favoring need-based, grants-oriented aid for the disadvantaged students. An "era of good feeling" in federal aid policy had come to an end, replaced by uncontrolled growth and philosophical uncertainty, especially regarding the appropriate clientele for the GSL program. Most participants and analysts attribute the removal of income caps on GSL eligibility to the combination of middle-class pressure for relief from college costs and heavy lobbying efforts by financing-industry officials (e.g., see McPherson, 1989). Stampen (1987) suggests that resistance to the costs of government oversight was also a factor:

> Senator Jacob Javits of New York argued, to a room charged with certainty about the excess of government regulation, that the ceiling on Guaranteed Student Loans should be eliminated so that middle- and upper-income students could become eligible. He reasoned that it was costing the government more to enforce the regulations excluding them than to remove the ceiling. The government's fiscal note, which turned out to be wildly inaccurate, estimated a cost of $9 million. Senator Javits concluded by saying he was not worried that a Rockefeller or two might receive a loan because they would repay many times through higher taxes after graduation. (p. 10)

MISAA's magnanimous terms stimulated a shift to loans in the overall balance of program allocations under Title IV, after several years of increasing emphasis on grants (see Table 1 and Figure 1). Viewed in retrospect, the middle years of the 1970s may be seen as a grants-oriented anomaly in the history of federal aid policies. The ratio of loans to other generally available federally supported aid in 1980–81 was similar to that of the mid-1960s and to that of the rest of the 1980s (see Figure 1). What is more, the ratio actually grew in the 1990s, leaving the grants orientation of the mid-1970s an ever more distant memory.

Of course, the loans emphasis in the late 1970s involved much more money than was present in the 1960s. It also involved much more controversy. The arrival of painful financial pressures on the government at that time led some critics to worry that Congress and the president had promised aid for all needy students while not reserving the funds necessary to achieve those goals (Gladieux, 1980). Although federal officials sought to step up their formal control and oversight of student aid award processes, many analysts argued that the government was not attending closely enough to program efficiency (e.g., appropriate ways to control fraud, abuse, and waste) and fairness

(e.g., the acceptability of the use of the GSL program for investment purposes by upper-income families). Some observers decried the blurring of the original purposes of the Title IV programs as aided populations expanded. What is more, the interests of public and private institutions, of higher-cost and lower-cost institutions, of selective and open-admissions institutions, and of proprietary and traditional institutions began to diverge significantly (Gladieux, 1983; Mumper, 1996; Schuster, 1982).

With controversy and fiscal restraint as a backdrop, the 1980 reauthorization of the Higher Education Act focused on redesigning the student aid programs and managing their growth. Congress created the new Parental Loans for Student program (PLUS). This program of loans for parents of dependent undergraduates was similar to the GSL program, but was open to all regardless of need, provided no interest rate subsidy, allowed larger loans, and featured higher interest rates.

That reauthorization also addressed problems with the MISAA legislation and the difficulties posed by continuing high rates of inflation and interest. Official interest rates on NDSL and GSL loans were raised, but the special allowance for GSL lenders was restricted and the growing GSL-based profits of state lending agencies were curtailed through limiting those agencies' use of tax-exempt bonds to finance student loans.

Although Congress proclaimed as a priority the control of waste, it also imposed ceilings on spending by the Department of Education and thereby reduced the department's audit and program-review capabilities. By the time Ronald Reagan entered office in early 1981, some of the major dislocations of MISAA had been addressed, and the turbulent third phase in the federal aid programs' political history was drawing to an end. The following years would bring a return to some predictability in student aid, but would not bring a return to consensus.

The Policy Drift of 1981 to the Present

The lengthy and ongoing fourth phase in the life of the Higher Education Act may be termed a period of policy drift. The overall size of the federal aid commitment has increased, and loans have continued to grow both in absolute terms and relative to grants. Yet the period has brought no real consensus to the arena regarding growth, loan emphasis, or other policy features.

In the early 1980s, Congress blocked implementation of some aspects of the 1980–81 reauthorization and provided some support for conservatives' efforts to cut federal student aid. College benefits to Social Security survivors were removed and the terms of the new PLUS loan program were toughened. Congress also enacted several measures to slow GSL program growth: Student borrowing was limited by actual need, students with family incomes over $30,000 became subject to need analysis tests for loan eligibility for the first time since 1978, and banks were allowed to charge students a loan origination fee. Loan growth slowed much less than Congress initially expected and hoped, however, and the first year of the Reagan administration was the high-water mark for supporters of retrenching federal student aid.

In the following years, the political rhetoric concerning the aid programs became more heated than ever. In the early 1980s, political conflict over student aid was based not in the details of aid programs themselves, but in the proper funding levels of those programs relative to other social and educational programs. The central parties to the conflict were not so much opposing members of Congress as distinct branches of government. There was an ongoing, almost ritualized battle of wills between the Reagan administration, which favored substantial cutbacks, and the Congress, which tended to oppose such retrenchment. The conflict continued over the years of the Reagan presidency.

Although the relative proportion of total student aid paid by states and institutions, as opposed to the federal government, increased in the 1980s after a long downward trend (see Table 1), the overall size of that shift was not nearly so dramatic as one might have expected on the basis of the Reagan administration's rhetoric. It was in this period that Education Secretary William Bennett uttered perhaps the single most famous (or infamous) quotation even in this arena, arguing for changes in student aid that would require aid-enriched students to pursue "a divestiture of certain sorts: stereo divestiture, automobile divestiture,

three-weeks-at-the-beach divestiture" (Fiske, 1985, p. A1).

In the end, the opposing forces reached something of a balance, or an inescapable impasse (Hartle, 1991). The generally available aid programs grew slightly in constant-dollar terms (College Board, 1995b) and by the end of the decade most postsecondary students were receiving at least one kind of federal aid (McPherson & Schapiro, 1991).

Despite the ongoing hostilities between Congress and the Reagan administration, they did share a concern over college students' expanding debt levels, and in this concern they were joined by the popular media (e.g., Fiske, 1986; "The Student Loan Scandal," 1987) and policy analysts (e.g., Hansen, 1987). As participation in loan programs continued to grow in the 1980s, Lawrence Gladieux (1983) of the College Board noted wryly that

> in an age of Visa, MasterCard, massive consumer credit, and "creative financing," it is perhaps not surprising that loans have been the primary focus of efforts and plans to fill the gap for students and parents. . . . Increasingly, postsecondary education has come to be looked on as another consumer item to be "financed"—stretched out and paid for from the student's and/or parent's future earnings. (pp. 422–423)

Analysts, policy makers, and media observers also shared a concern over a related problem of the period, the increased incidence of loan defaults in both the GSL and the NDSL programs. Default expenses grew sevenfold in the 1980s in constant-dollar terms (U.S. Department of Education [USDOE], 1992). Although analysts noted that students tend to be young and have few assets, the popular media and congressional critics frequently compared their default rates unfavorably with rates for standard consumer and home loans.

Unfortunately, in both the NDSL and GSL programs, the incentives and resources for preventing loan defaults were limited in this period. In the NDSL program, institutions were constrained by costs from becoming debt collectors. In the GSL program, lenders were entirely insured against default losses by the provisions of the program, and USDOE oversight was limited by budget constraints and program structure. In addition, critics argued that as participation by educational institutions and students in the proprietary sector increased dramatically in the 1980s, accrediting bodies in that sector may have failed to effectively police their member institutions' aid practices. Finally, there was a willingness of some lenders to lend to students regardless of their institution's default rates and stability, a willingness of guaranty agencies to guarantee such loans, and a willingness of secondary loan markets to provide ongoing financing (Dean, 1994). In the mid-1980s, Congress imposed more stringent "due diligence" requirements on institutions to reduce defaults, limit multiple disbursement of loans to first-year students, and limit interest billings.

In the 1986 reauthorization of the Higher Education Act, NDSLs were renamed Perkins Loans, borrowers were given the option of consolidating their student loans from various federal programs into a single loan under a single, weighted interest rate, and the Supplemental Loans to Students (SLS) program for independent students was initiated. The SLS program was analogous to the PLUS program for dependent students: it provided a way for students to finance the great majority of their college costs through unsubsidized loans.

Although Congress in this reauthorization also toughened need analysis for loan eligibility, placed a limitation on student borrowing to the assessed amount of need, and allowed lenders to charge borrowers a new premium for insurance, GSI program growth continued, no doubt greatly aided by Congress's raising of the allowable loan size and by declines in loan servicing costs, which attracted more and more financial institutions into the program (USDOE, 1992).

Two of the most notable continuing problems of the 1980s in the federal loan programs were problematic loan administration and the ever increasing complexity of the programs. Widely publicized cases of noncompliance in loan servicing lessened public and congressional confidence in the integrity of the loan programs and the quality of their management (Dean, 1994). At the same time, frequent articles catalogued complaints about complexity from policy analysts, aid officers, and students (e.g., see Flint, 1991; "17 Changes in 4 Years," 1990; Wilson, 1988). One of these articles even lampooned in full-page cartoon form the detailed, lengthy process of loan generation

and disbursement (Wilson, 1987, p. 25). Kramer and Van Dusen (1986), portrayed the guaranteed student loan program as a Rube Goldberg contraption: "a long series of devices accomplishing by extravagant means something terribly simple, like opening a tin can or putting out the cat" (p. 18). Ironically, the Education Department found that its efforts to meet public demands for greater fiscal integrity in the programs often meant earning the ire of aid officers and others frustrated by program complexity. Sometimes, the department made such sudden regulatory changes that institutions found themselves formally out of compliance without having known of the original, newly instituted regulations (Dean, 1994).

Tuition, fees, and other expenses of college-going rose at unprecedented rates in the 1980s, and the loan programs picked up the majority of the federal contribution to meeting those expenses. Between 1980 and 1990, the number of student borrowers in the GSL program grew from 2.9 million to 3.7 million (College Board, 1993, 1995b). As a result of this rapid, largely unplanned growth in the student loan programs, growth in grant programs was restricted. An increasing share of a limited pool of federal dollars was going to support the expanding volume of the federal loan programs. The federal government's expenses in supporting lenders and guaranteeing loans more than doubled between 1980 and 1985, then grew another 12% between 1985 and 1990 (USDOE, 1992).

Mumper (1996) has termed the late 1980s and early 1990s a period of "continuing deterioration" in the loan programs (p. 100). The U.S. General Accounting Office issued a scathing report in 1992, and congressional attention to loan problems also rose noticeably as the new decade began. Senator Sam Nunn brought his Permanent Senate Subcommittee on Investigations into the loan arena, focusing on abuses among proprietary schools and among private participants in the student loan industry. That committee (Nunn, 1990) found "overwhelming evidence that federal student loan programs and, particularly, those involving trade and proprietary schools, are riddled with fraud, waste, abuse, and pervasive patterns of mismanagement.... [W]e did not hear of even a single part of the guaranteed student loan program that is working efficiently and effectively

(p. 1)." Senator Nunn concluded that "nothing less than a comprehensive, sustained, and intensive reform effort is needed" (cited in Mumper, 1996, p. 100). Senator Edward Kennedy, noting that "student loan programs may be just one step ahead of disaster" (cited in Mumper, p. 100), endorsed reform as well, and Congress in the early years of the decade enacted legislation aimed at cutting off institutions with especially high student loan defaults.

As the 1992 reauthorization of the Higher Education Act arrived, a number of problems in the loan programs demanded federal attention. Program costs continued to rise, management questions continued to plague program leaders, lower-income students continued to receive more loans and less grant aid than many thought advisable, debt obligations among all kinds of students continued to grow, and rapidly rising college costs convinced many to argue for expanded loan eligibility for middle-income students.

The 1992 presidential campaign figured prominently in debates on these problems. Bill Clinton proposed a national service program to replace existing student loan programs (Clinton, 1992). Clinton linked national service initiatives with student loan reform by stressing that loan programs make repaying the loan a priority, which in turn encourages students to take high-paying jobs offering few returns to society, rather than low-paying jobs that benefit society (Mumper, 1996). After winning a campaign in which this and other student aid issues were frequently discussed, Clinton as president began to pursue formal adoption of his ideas.

His proposals have met with mixed success. Congress passed a scaled-back version of the national service idea, with each award limited to $4,750 a year and the number of participants limited to no more than 100,000 people. Another goal of the administration, alternative GSL repayment periods for students, was implemented. The small federal Income Contingent Loans program was replaced by the offering of income-contingent repayment as an option in other federal loan programs. Congress in 1992–93 also expanded eligibility for the GSL and NDSL programs, raised the limit on yearly undergraduate borrowing, placed eligibility analysis for all Title IV pro-

grams under the rather liberal "Federal Methodology," and reduced Pell eligibility for single independent students and dependent students with earnings. Each of these moves increased the demand for loans further (Zook, 1994). Finally, Guaranteed Student Loans were renamed Stafford Loans, and those loans and the PLUS and SLS loans were folded into the Federal Family Education Loan Program (FFELP).

These last changes were closely connected to the most dramatic policy option considered in the reauthorization of the Clinton years: instituting a "direct lending" program to replace the traditional guaranteed student loan approach. Under this new program proposed by Clinton, institutions would lend federal funds directly to students, without the use of private funds or the involvement of private financial institutions. Direct student loans were broached as an approach to lowering institutions' administrative costs by eliminating the need to deal with multiple private lenders and guaranty agencies participating in the Stafford Loan program. In concert with this change, it was argued, the complexity of the loan programs would be reduced and management in federal student loans improved. Coloring the direct lending debate were proponents' concerns over indications that the student-loan business was making many people in the financing industry extraordinarily wealthy (see Regional Financial Associates & Jenkins, 1991; Zook, 1993). On the negative side, many institutions expressed concerns over new administrative burdens potentially associated with the direct lending efforts. Their opposition was reinforced by analyses by Sallie Mae and the Congressional Research Service (Dean, 1994).

In the end, Congress, in August 1993, adopted a compromise, trial version of the direct lending program, under which direct lending could be instituted voluntarily at institutions while the traditional nondirect guaranteed loan program would also continue. Volunteer institutions could disburse subsidized Stafford loans, unsubsidized Stafford loans, and PLUS loans directly to students. Both sides expressed confidence that time would tell that theirs was the superior alternative (Zuckman, 1993).

Under the terms of the compromise, the volume of direct loans could grow as a proportion of all lending to as much as 60% of all federal loans by 1998. Private capital is replaced as a source of loan funds by federal treasury funds, secured by the issuance of treasury bonds or the use of tax receipts. Institutions perform the administrative functions formerly performed by private and state lenders. Loan servicing is performed by federally supported contractors. Schools are required to process adjustments in loan amounts, notify servicing contractors of changes in student status, and maintain records of funds receipt and disbursement. The Ford Direct Student Loan Program was adopted as an option by many institutions around the country and began disbursing funds in 1994–95. Intriguingly, Congress left many of the specifics of the program open for interpretation and refinement.

Between the early and mid-1990s, the landscape of student loans changed notably. Contrary to the expectations of many and the hopes of some, growth in the loan programs accelerated rather than slowed. Between 1990–91 and 1994–95, the number of student borrowers in the Stafford program grew from 3.7 million to 6.2 million (College Board, 1995b). Stafford loans came to be provided in traditional and direct form and in subsidized and unsubsidized form. Those with need received the subsidized loan for which the government paid interest during the years in school. Those without measurable need received the new unsubsidized Stafford loan, for which the interest rate was higher, and the student paid the interest accrued during attendance. Unsubsidized Stafford loans grew dramatically after their inception, mainly because of the discontinuation of the unsubsidized SLS program, which served similar purposes and was phased out in 1994–95 (College Board, 1995b).

Interestingly, the 1990s have brought noteworthy decreases in the loan participation rates of students and institutions in the proprietary sector. Stafford loans and other federal loans are now far less tilted to the for-profit sector than they were in the 1980s. Specifically, students in the proprietary sector received only ten% of the subsidized Stafford loans in 1993, down from a high of 35% in the mid-1980s (College Board, 1995b). At the institutional level, most of the more than 500 institutions that dropped out of the federal loan programs

between 1992 and 1995 were from the proprietary sector (Zook, 1995). It is in that sector that many of the worst abuses of federal aid programs have occurred, and in that sector that default rates have tended to be highest (Hansen, 1987; Mortenson, 1990). These declines in loans in the for-profit sector suggest indirectly that recent actions to address high default rates in the federal loan programs have been successful on at least some grounds.

Conclusion: Federal Loan Expansion in Broader Context

It is impossible to examine the dramatic increase in federal loan support without considering other developments taking place at roughly the same time. While federal loan efforts have been evolving since their great expansion in the late 1970s, total enrollments have risen (rather than falling, as anticipated by many analysts), the demographic characteristics of students have become more diverse, and delayed entry and part-time enrollment have increased (Hearn, 1992). At the institutional level, student aid has increasingly been viewed as an integral element in a wide variety of concerns, including admissions, fund raising, student services, and public relations (Brademas, 1983). At the same time, because of its close connections to concerns regarding cost patterns, tuition levels, grant support, program duplication, and educational quality, student aid has become a more prominent vehicle for states' initiatives in postsecondary education. Each of these trends is tightly related to the changes in federal loans.

It is especially important to examine simultaneously financing trends at the federal, state, and institutional levels. As Table 1 suggests, the federal retreat from grants and movement into loans since the 1970s has been met by some expansion in grant aid for students at the state and institutional levels. States' abilities to respond effectively to changes in federal aid have been hampered, however, by their own economic and political difficulties. Most notably, state efforts have been constrained by uncertainty over the financial feasibility of both the traditional "low-tuition-low-aid" approach to student support and the alternative "high-tuition-high-aid" approach to financing public institutions (Fischer, 1990; Hearn, Griswold, & Marine, 1996). That uncertainty over appropriate tuition and aid levels has also troubled private institutions. Under pressure, some states and some private institutions have been forced to adopt what is in essence the worst of both approaches, a "high tuition-low aid" approach (Griswold & Marine, 1996). That is, tuitions have been allowed to rise without parallel increases in student aid. A somewhat less regrettable state and institutional response, but still troubling and quite central to the concerns in this chapter, are efforts to use loans rather than grants as the dominant form of student aid in high-tuition-high aid approaches (see St. John, Andrieu, Oescher, & Starkey, 1994).

Clearly, the dramatic rises in public and private institutions' tuition levels since 1980 are closely linked to the parallel expansion of student loans. As colleges' costs for salaries and other items have risen, the burden of meeting those costs has increasingly been placed on students and their families. In some ways, these new demands on them have been immediately felt. For example, need analysis and eligibility analysis formulas for determining students' aid levels have been tightened, bringing more stringent expectations for parental contributions to college expenses, student savings, and summer work earnings, as well as tougher requirements for students wishing to be certified as financially independent of their parents. But much of the increased financial burden on students and their families has been deferred in impact, via demands that students finance more of their college attendance through loans. Postsecondary institutions, financial institutions, and governments are increasingly providing aid to be repaid later, after students are presumably more established in their adult careers. In essence, unable to slow the growth in college costs, unable or unwilling to demand more short-term contributions from students and their families, policy makers have placed much more of the burden of financing attendance on students' future lives. As the imagery and language of "downsizing" and "cost control" have come in the past decade to dominate policy arenas at the local, state, and national levels, many postsecondary leaders are reluctantly accepting students' high debt levels as ongoing facts of life.

It can be argued that appreciably higher student loan levels represent almost as significant a historical development in federal aid policy as the GI Bill or the original Higher Education Act of 1965. Yet, in contrast to those earlier events, the loan explosion has taken place incrementally over a period of years. Some years are more significant than others, of course, but there is no single watershed year in federal loan policy. Mark Twain's old parable of the hot-water frog seems appropos: Dropped in boiling water, a frog will promptly jump out, but dropped in cool water which is being slowly heated to boiling, a frog might well end up being boiled to death. Of course, the consequences of loan expansion are not nearly so dire for students or policy makers. Still, as Twain warns us, intense scrutiny of one's emerging environment is always warranted.

Acknowledgments

This chapter benefited substantially from the helpful comments of two veteran analysts of federal student loan policy: John Lee, President of JBL Associates of Bethesda, Maryland and Keith Jepsen, Director of Financial Aid at New York University. My research assistant James Eck also deserves thanks, as do Sharon Wilford and Sammy Parker, who assisted me in earlier work on the political history of federal student aid efforts.

Notes

1. Reference to the work of a number of authors is essential to understanding the policy history of federal student loans. Primary sources for the present work were Gladieux and Wolanin (1976), Morse (1977), Moore (1983), Gillespie and Carlson (1983), Gladieux (1983), Fenske (1983), Hartle (1991), Dean (1994), St. John (1994), College Board (1995b), and Mumper (1996). A political history of all the federal aid programs (including grants and work study as well as loans) is presented in Hearn (1993). Each of these sources may be consulted for further details and perspective on the historical analysis presented here.
2. Several points should be made about the data of Table 1 (for details, see College Board, 1995b). First, federally supported aid totals include some funds supplied by institutional, private, and state sources. Importantly, totals for Family Education Loans are for the amounts for the loans themselves, not for the amount supplied by the federal government for subsidies and repayments on those loans.

The actual funds supplied by the federal government are substantially smaller than the totals for these loans themselves. Second, the amounts in the table include aid for undergraduate, graduate, and professional students. Third, total loan amounts are underestimated because private loans by individuals, corporations, and schools are not included in figures, and are essentially incalculable (College Board, 1995b). Finally, reported loan values in Table 1 are for loan commitments, not the final loan amount, but the two totals are virtually identical.

References

Barger, H., & Barger, G. (1981). *College on credit: A history of United student aid funds, 1960–1980*. Indianapolis, IN: Hackett.

Baum, S. (1996, Winter). Is the student loan burden really too heavy? *Educational Record*, 77(1), 30–36.

Bosworth, B., Carron, A., & Rhyne, E. (1987). *The economics of federal credit programs*. Washington, DC: Brookings Institution.

Brademas, J. (1983). Foreword. In R. H. Fenske, R. P. Hugg, & Associates (Eds.), *Handbook of student financial aid* (pp. ix–xiii). San Francisco: Jossey-Bass.

Brademas, J. (1987). *The politics of education: Conflict and consensus on capitol hill*. Norman, OK: University of Oklahoma Press.

Breneman, D. W. (1991). Guaranteed student loans: Great success or dismal failure? In D. W. Breneman, L. L. Leslie, & R. E. Anderson (Eds.), *ASHE reader on finance in higher education* (pp. 377–387). Needham Heights, MA: Ginn Press.

Caro, R. A. (1983). *The years of Lyndon Johnson: The path to power*. New York: Vintage Books.

Clinton, W. (1992). *Putting people first*. New York: Times Books.

College Board. (1993). *Trends in student aid: 1983 to 1993*. Washington, DC: Author.

College Board. (1995a, December). College costs and student loans up. *College Board News*, 24(2), 1, 11.

College Board. (1995b). *Trends in student aid: 1985 to 1995*. Washington, DC: Author.

Dean, J. (1994). Enactment of the federal Direct Student Loan Program as a reflection of the education policy making process. In J. Jennings (Ed.), *National issues in education: Community service and student loans* (pp. 157–178). Bloomington, IN: Phi Delta Kappa International.

Fenske, R. H. (1983). Student aid past and present. In R. H. Fenske, R. P. Huff, & Associates (Eds.), *Handbook of student financial aid* (pp. 5–26). San Francisco: Jossey-Bass.

Fischer, F. J. (1990). State financing of higher education: A new look at an old problem. *Change*, 22(1), 42–56.

Fiske, E. (1985, February 12). New secretary sees many "ripped off" in higher education. *The New York Times*, pp. A1, B24.

Fiske, E. (1986, August 3). Student debt reshaping. *The New York Times*, pp. 34–38, 40–41.

Flint, T. A. (1991). Historical notes on regulation in the federal student assistance programs. *Journal of Student Financial Aid*, 21(1), 33–47.

Gillespie, D. A., & Carlson, N. (1983). *Trends in student aid: 1963 to 1983*. Washington, DC: College Board.

Gladieux, L. E. (1980, October). What has Congress wrought? *Change*, 26–27.

Gladieux, L. E. (1983). Future directions of student aid. In R. H. Fenske, R. P. Huff, & Associates (Eds.), *Handbook of student financial aid* (pp. 399–433). San Francisco: Jossey-Bass.

Gladieux, L. E., & Wolanin, T. R. (1976). *Congress and the colleges: The national politics of higher education*. Lexington, MA: Lexington (Heath).

Griswold, C. P., & Marine, G. M. (1996). Political influences on state policy: Higher-tuition, higher-aid, and the real world. *Review of Higher Education*, 19(4), 361–389.

Hansen, J. S. (1977). *The politics of federal scholarships: A case study of the development of general grant assistance for undergraduates*. Unpublished doctoral dissertation, The Woodrow Wilson School, Princeton University.

Hansen, J. S. (1987). *Student loans: Are they overburdening a generation?* New York: College Board.

Hartle, T. W. (1991). The evolution and prospects of financing alternatives for higher education. In A. M. Hauptman & R. H. Koff (Eds.), *New ways of paying for college* (pp. 33–50). New York: ACE-Macmillan.

Hauptman, A. M. (1987). The national student loan bank: Adapting an old idea for future needs. In L. E. Gladieux (Ed.), *Radical reform or incremental change?: Student loan policy alternatives for the federal government* (pp. 75–89). Washington, DC: College Board.

Hearn, J. C. (1992). Emerging variations in postsecondary attendance patterns: An investigation of part-time, delayed, and non-degree enrollment. *Research in Higher Education*, 33, 657–687.

Hearn, J. C. (1993). The paradox of growth in federal aid for college students: 1965–1990. In J. C. Smart (Ed.), *Higher education: Handbook of theory and research (Vol. 9).* (pp. 94–153). New York: Agathon.

Hearn, J. C., Griswold, C. P., & Marine, G. M. (1996). Region, resources, and reason: A contextual analysis of state tuition and student-aid policies. *Research in Higher Education*, 37(3), 241–278.

Kosterlitz, J. (1989, April 15). Losers by default. *National Journal*, 47, 924–925.

Kramer, M. (1991). Stresses in the student financial aid system. In A. M. Hauptman & R. H. Koff

(Eds.), *New ways of paying for college* (pp. 21–32). New York: ACE-Macmillan.

Kramer, M., & Van Dusen, W. D. (1986, May/June). Living on credit. *Change*, 18(3), 10–19.

Leslie, L. L. (1977). *Higher education opportunity: A decade of progress.* (ERIC/AAHE Higher Education Research Report No. 3). Washington, DC: American Association for Higher Education.

Marmaduke, A. S. (1983). State student aid programs. In R. H. Fenske, R. P. Huff, & Associates (Eds.), *Handbook of student financial aid* (pp. 55–76). San Francisco: Jossey-Bass.

McPherson, M. S. (1989). Appearance and reality in the Guaranteed Student Loan Program. In L. E. Gladieux (Ed.), *Radical reform or incremental change?: Student loan policy alternatives for the federal government.* Washington, DC: College Board.

McPherson, M. S., & Schapiro, M. O. (1991). *Keeping college affordable: Government and educational opportunity.* Washington, DC: Brookings Institution.

Moore, J. W. (1983). Student aid past and present. In R. H. Fenske, R. P. Huff, & Associates (Eds.), *Handbook of student financial aid* (pp. 5–26). San Francisco: Jossey-Bass.

Morse, J. (1977). How we got here from there: A personal reminiscence of the early days. In L. Rice (Ed.), *Student loans: Problems and policy alternatives* (pp. 3–15). New York: College Board.

Mortenson, T. G. (1990). *The impact of increased loan utilization among low family income students.* Iowa City, IA: American College Testing Program.

Moynihan, D. P. (1975). The politics of higher education. *Daedalus*, 104, 128–147.

Mumper, M. (1996). *Removing college price barriers: What government has done and why it hasn't worked.* Albany, NY: SUNY Press.

Nunn, S. (1990, October 10). Opening statement to the Permanent Subcommittee on Investigations (Hearings on Abuses in Federal Student Aid Programs). Washington, DC: United States Senate.

Panel on Educational Innovation (1967). *Educational Opportunity Bank—A report of the Panel on Educational Innovation to the U.S. Commissioner of Education, the Director of the National Science Foundation, and the Special Assistant to the President for Science and Technology.* Washington, DC: GPO.

President's Commission on Higher Education. (1947). *Higher education for American democracy.* Washington, DC: GPO.

Regional Financial Associates, & Jenkins, S. (1991). *Lender profitability in the student loan program.* Report prepared for the U.S. Department of Education. West Chester, PA: Regional Financial Associates.

St. John, E. P. (1994). *Prices, productivity and investment: Assessing financial strategies in higher education.*

(ASHE-ERIC Higher Education Report No. 3). Washington, DC: School of Education and Human Development, George Washington University.

St. John, E. P., Andrieu, S. C., Oescher, J., & Starkey, J. B. (1994). The influence of student aid on within-year persistence by traditional college-age students in four-year colleges. *Research in Higher Education*, 35(4), 455–80.

Schuster, J. H. (1982, May). Out of the frying pan: The politics of education in a new era. *Phi Delta Kappan* 63(9), 583–591.

Seventeen changes in four years: Johns Hopkins grapples with new loan rules. (1990, December 5). *Chronicle of Higher Education*, 37(14), p. A24.

Stampen, J. O. (1987). Historical perspective on federal and state financial aid. In California Postsecondary Education Commission (Ed.), *Conversations about financial aid.* Sacramento, CA: Author.

Student Loan Scandal, The. (1987, October 8). *The New York Times*, p. 26Y.

U.S. Department of Education. (1992). *Guaranteed Student Loans Program data book, FY91.* Washington, DC: Author.

U.S. General Accounting Office. (1992). *Transition series: Education issues* (Report No. GAO/OCG-93-18TR). Washington, DC: U.S. General Accounting Office.

Wilson, R. (1987, April 15). Critics blast Guaranteed Student Loan Program, charging it is too complex and is poorly policed. *Chronicle of Higher Education*, 33(31), pp. 1, 24–26.

Wilson, R. (1988, March 16). Student-aid analysts blast loan program, urge big overhaul. *Chronicle of Higher Education*, 34(27), pp. 1, 24.

Woodhall, M. (1988). Designing a student loan program for a developing country: The relevance of international experience. *Economics of Education Review*, 7(1), 153–161.

Zook, J. (1993, June 9). For Sallie Mae's top executives, 1992 was a very good year. *Chronicle of Higher Education*, 37, p. A23.

Zook, J. (1994, April 27). Record-setting debt: Changes in federal law have brought huge increases in student borrowing. *Chronicle of Higher Education*, 39, p. A21.

Zook, J. (1995, July 21). Congressional panel warned of growing Pell Grant fraud. *Chronicle of Higher Education*, 41(45), p. A26.

Zuckman, J. (1993, August 14). Both sides hope to be No. 1 in dual loan system test. *Congressional Quarterly Weekly Report*, 51, pp. 2230–2231.